JAN
782.12
SUL   Sullivan, Arthur,
                Sir

             The complete an-
             notated Gilbert

DUE DATE

THE COMPLETE ANNOTATED
GILBERT AND SULLIVAN

The Complete Annotated

GILBERT
AND
SULLIVAN

Introduced and Edited by
IAN BRADLEY

OXFORD UNIVERSITY PRESS
1996

Oxford University Press, Walton Street, Oxford OX2 6DP

Oxford New York
Athens Auckland Bangkok Bombay
Calcutta Cape Town Dar es Salaam Delhi
Florence Hong Kong Istanbul Karachi
Kuala Lumpur Madras Madrid Melbourne
Mexico City Nairobi Paris Singapore
Taipei Tokyo Toronto

and associated companies in
Berlin Ibadan

Oxford is a trade mark of Oxford University Press

Published in the United States
by Oxford University Press Inc., New York

British Library Cataloguing in Publication Data
Data available

Library of Congress Cataloging in Publication Data
Sullivan, Arthur, Sir, 1842–1900.
[Operas. Librettos. Selections]
The complete annotated Gilbert and Sullivan / introduced and
edited by Ian Bradley.
p.   cm.
Includes bibliographical references.
1. Operas—Librettos.   I. Gilbert, W. S. (William Schwenck),
1836–1911.   II. Bradley, Ian C.   III. Title.
ML49.S9A1   1996 <Case>   782.1'2026'8—dc20   95-51813
ISBN 0-19-816503-X

1 3 5 7 9 10 8 6 4 2

Typeset by Pure Tech India Limited, Pondicherry
Printed in Great Britain
on acid-free paper by
The Bath Press
Bath

CONTENTS

Introduction   vii

Suggestions for further reading   xiv

TRIAL BY JURY   1

THE SORCERER   41

H. M. S. PINAFORE   113

THE PIRATES OF PENZANCE   187

PATIENCE   265

IOLANTHE   355

PRINCESS IDA   449

THE MIKADO   551

RUDDIGORE   653

THE YEOMEN OF THE GUARD   753

THE GONDOLIERS   859

UTOPIA LIMITED   969

THE GRAND DUKE   1081

INTRODUCTION

On the morning after the opening night of *The Gondoliers* in December 1889 W. S. Gilbert wrote to Sir Arthur Sullivan thanking him for all the work that he had put into the piece. He added with rare magnanimity: 'It gives one the chance of shining right through the twentieth century with a reflected light.'

The works of Gilbert and Sullivan have, indeed, continued to shine right through the twentieth century. In fact, they are almost certainly more widely known and enjoyed as it draws to a close than they were in its early years. This is in large part due to modern technology which has made them available on records and compact discs, audio and video tapes, television, film and radio as well as through the more traditional medium of stage performances by both amateur and professional companies.

What are the reasons for the enduring popularity of the Savoy Operas? Undoubtedly the nostalgia factor is an important one. At a time of shifting values and rapid change, roots and tradition have come to assume considerable importance. The burgeoning heritage industry, which seems to be turning just about every other derelict industrial site into a working museum or theme park, testifies to the appeal of the past, and especially of the Victorian era which seems to stand for so much that we have lost in the way of reassuring solidity and self-confidence. The operas of Gilbert and Sullivan undoubtedly appeal to many people today because they are a genuine piece of Victoriana, as authentic as William Morris wallpaper, the Albert Memorial or a Penny Black stamp.

Half the charm of the Savoy Operas is that they are so dated. They seem to breathe the innocence, the naïvety and the fun of a long-vanished age. Even when they were written, of course, they had a strong element of pure escapism with their fantastic topsy-turvy settings and plots. Now, a hundred years on, their mannered dialogue and topical references to themes and personalities that have long passed into the realms of history give them an added quaintness as period pieces.

There are those who feel that our strong attachment to the works of Gilbert and Sullivan is part of the British disease of always looking backwards and never looking forwards. In a letter to *The Times* in December 1990 Sir Graham Hills, Principal of the University of Strathclyde and member of the Board of Governors of the BBC, proposed, apparently in all seriousness, a moratorium for at least five years on performances of the Savoy Operas. He wrote:

They engender in the British (and especially in the English) nostalgic fondness for Britain's imperial past which is a serious obstacle to change and reform. Everything associated with that past, from lord chancellors and the like in fancy dress to light-hearted, bone-headed military men in scarlet, gives credence to the idea that great wealth flows effortlessly and unceasingly from such cultivated minds. The facts are that our wealth-creating apparatus, in the form of business and industry, continues to decline almost monotonically, and has done so since those operas were first performed.

There is clearly room for someone to do a doctoral thesis (perhaps under Sir Graham's supervision?) on the relationship between Gilbert and Sullivan and Britain's economic decline. Perhaps he does have a point, although he would have to explain how the Savoy Operas have remained very popular in the United States in a culture which is much more foward-looking and enterprise-friendly. His call for a moratorium, I am relieved to say, has not been taken up and as far as I am aware, no operatic group, either amateur or professional, has forsaken the works of Gilbert and Sullivan as their contribution to helping Britain's economic recovery.

It is certainly true that for a long time the way in which the Savoy Operas were performed increased their period feel and was self-consciously traditionalist and nostalgic. The original D'Oyly Carte Opera Company, which managed somehow to survive until 1982, was an extraordinary anachronism in its latter years, refusing to compromise its Victorian principles of frugality, thrift, propriety and paternalism. Its productions were highly traditional, with movements, inflections and bits of stage business still often based on what Gilbert himself had laid down in the 1890s and 1900s. Presided over by Dame Bridget D'Oyly Carte from her suite of rooms in the Savoy Hotel, male members of the company were almost invariably referred to by their surnames and the females were regarded very much as 'ladies of the D'Oyly Carte' rather than 'girls of the chorus'. Indeed, when the company travelled on tour by specially chartered train there were separate carriages for male and female chorus members and for men and women principals. Chorus members received 20 per cent less than the Equity minimum rates and costumes were kept in service for thirty years or more.

For many of us who were its devoted fans, this stubborn attachment to Victorian values was one of the great charms of the old company. It was not, however, the way to ensure survival in an increasingly tough world and when it finally closed, it was perhaps as much a victim of its own endearing old-fashionedness as of the snobbery of the artistic establishment which refused any public funding for the enormously costly touring operation which took it on the road for forty-two weeks a year.

But the nostalgia factor is not the only reason for the continuing popularity of the Savoy Operas. Gilbert perhaps put his finger on another in his generous comments to Sullivan about *The Gondoliers*. Gilbert's words may have dated and his humour may creak a little at times, although it is still remarkably topical in many respects. Sullivan's melodies, on the other hand, have a timeless quality. Of course they belong to a recognizably nineteenth-century operetta style along with the work of Strauss and Offenbach and of English contemporaries like Edward German. Yet Sullivan seems to be less tied to a particular time or place than these other composers. His music is somehow more universal, more accessible, more varied and more robust. More than a hundred years after it was written it still has a remarkable freshness and vitality. I suspect that Gilbert may have been right in his prediction and that to some extent at least it is true that his words have shone through the twentieth century with a reflected light and because of the tunes to which they have been set.

The last decade or so has seen the gradual rehabilitation of Sullivan's reputation as a serious composer in his own right. For this the tireless advocacy of the Sullivan Society has been in large part instrumental. Sullivan displayed his talents over a very wide range of musical forms, including symphonic and orchestral works, chamber music, grand opera and oratorio, hymns and part songs. Yet good though many of his lesser known works undoubtedly were, their more frequent performance in recent years surely confirms that it was in the Savoy Operas, however much he felt that they were beneath his dignity, that his genius really shone and he achieved his best work.

It is ironic that while Sullivan's music is in some ways becoming a more highbrow taste, Gilbert's words and plots have been receiving ever more popular styles of treatment. This has in part been in an effort to avoid their datedness and make them more in tune with the expectations of modern audiences. It has also been a response to the video age, which has made all opera producers more visually aware and has put a premium on fast-moving visual action and excitement on stage.

For years the works of Gilbert and Sullivan formed the basis of a distinct middle-class subculture. Their songs were handed down from generation to generation in a bourgeois version of the oral folk tradition. There were subtle gradations and distinctions of rank within this subculture. Some have seen the archetypal G. & S. fan, rather like Sir Joseph Porter saw Captain Corcoran in *H. M. S. Pinafore*, as occupying a station in the lower middle class. This has been the traditional recruiting ground of amateur operatic societies, strong in Home Counties suburbia and in the industrial North and Midlands where they were often linked to Nonconformist chapels. There was also a more upper-middle-class following, found among those who had been through the independent education system and progressed from playing a sister, cousin or aunt at prep school to taking on the more manly roles of pirate, policeman or peer at public school. There has always been a substantial body of Gilbert and Sullivan fans in the professions, led, not surprisingly in view of the number of legal characters and in-jokes in the operas, by lawyers. Along with railways, Gilbert and Sullivan also seems to have a particular appeal to clergy – maybe it is the hymn- or anthem-like quality of so many of Sullivan's tunes.

In the last fifteen years or so, however, things have changed. Public schools and amateur operatic societies are now as likely to perform *Grease*, *Godspell* or

Guys and Dolls as *The Pirates of Penzance* or *H. M. S. Pinafore*. No longer do the middle classes grow up learning songs from the Savoy Operas. At the same time professional performances of Gilbert and Sullivan have increasingly been pitched 'downmarket'. A key influence in this respect was Joseph Papp's production of *The Pirates of Penzance* which opened in New York's Central Park in 1980 and went on to take both Broadway and the West End by storm. Gone was the understated, demure style of the D'Oyly Carte productions. Here rather was a raunchy, full-blooded spectacle full of swashbuckling and bravado, with synthesizers in the orchestra pit, rock stars on stage and a couple of songs imported from other operas. Audiences loved it and even traditionalists like me had to concede that it made very good entertainment and in a strange way preserved the spirit of the original. The collective genius of Gilbert and Sullivan was strong enough not just to withstand this kind of treatment but even in some respects to benefit from it. Not the least of the merits of Papp's *Pirates* was to show that the Savoy Operas were not just stuffy, creaking relics of the Victorian age but had a vitality and originality that lent themselves to more contemporary production techniques.

The launch in 1982 of lavish video productions of all the operas except *Utopia Limited* and *The Grand Duke* was another important milestone in the popularization of Gilbert and Sullivan. The man behind this $15 million venture, George Walker, former boxing promoter and casino proprietor, had no interest in the old D'Oyly Carte tradition or the nostalgia factor. When he discovered that Gilbert and Sullivan's works were performed more often than those of anyone else except the Beatles, he sensed that they would make an ideal product for the rapidly expanding home entertainment market and for screening on the public service broadcasting network in the United States. For him they were the forerunners of the big Hollywood musicals and ought to be given the same kind of treatment. He brought in transatlantic television and film stars like Frankie Howerd, Keith Michell and Vincent Price for the main comic parts while at the same time taking considerable care with the music and the final productions were often of a very high quality.

The new D'Oyly Carte Opera Company, which rose from the ashes of the old in 1988, has also tried to update the style and staging of Gilbert and Sullivan performances. Most of its productions have been noticeably successful in blending a modern stress on action and strong visual imagery with high musical standards and careful attention to diction in the tradition of the old company and only once, in its disastrous *Gondoliers*, which was greeted by boos when it opened the 1991 season, has it overdone the vulgarity and gimmickry.

The dangers of jettisoning the traditional approach completely were revealed all too clearly in Ken Russell's production of *Princess Ida* for English National Opera for the winter 1992/3 season. This was a total fiasco and was rightly panned by the critics for destroying the logic and theme of the original work and overlaying it with a wholly different and inappropriate plot. The almost unanimously adverse reaction which this production provoked should at least ensure that we will see no more like it and that the trend to popularize and modernize the Savoy Operas will be kept within sensible bounds.

Will Gilbert and Sullivan continue to shine in each other's reflected light for another hundred years? I see no reason why not. In terms of the number of both amateur and professional performances they are well ahead of more recent musical partnerships like Rogers and Hammerstein or Rice and Lloyd Webber. The extent of their future popularity depends to some extent on whether their work can find its way back into schools. The D'Oyly Carte Opera Company is making an important and highly commendable effort in this area, particularly in its home patch in and around Birmingham. In the United States my impression is that Gilbert and Sullivan is still sung a good deal in schools and colleges. On both sides of the Atlantic, the future depends more than anything on amateur groups and societies. Everything suggests that they are in good heart and good voice. There are few evenings in the winter months when the sound of singing policemen or pirates isn't wafting out of some church room or village hall. Long may amateur tenors continue to exhibit their vocal villainies and may Savoyards young and old display what Mad Margaret identified as the ultimate sign of madness – singing choruses in public.

In the introduction to the earlier Penguin edition of this book, I wrote that the works of Gilbert and Sullivan exist to be sung, hummed, whistled, performed and enjoyed, not to be annotated. I still stand by that statement, and this volume is offered primarily as a source of innocent merriment. I would not dissent from the verdict of the anonymous reviewer of my first Penguin *Annotated Gilbert and Sullivan* who said that it was 'unlikely to be surpassed as a record of that kind of Savoyard enthusiasm that borders on lunacy'. All I can say is that in the ten years or so since that book came out, I have had the great pleasure of encountering many G. & S. aficionados who are even more enthusiastic and considerably more knowledgeable about the Savoy operas than I am and who have tracked down references which had escaped me completely. It has been a delight to correspond with and meet scholars and enthusiasts on both sides of the Atlantic who have pointed out errors and omissions in previous editions. As far as possible, I have incorporated their corrections and suggestions into the pages of this new Oxford University Press edition, which for the first time includes the annotated texts of *Utopia Limited* and *The Grand Duke* and also has new introductions to each opera.

One rather striking feature of the letters I have received since the first Penguin volume appeared in 1982 is, I think, worth recording as it supports very strongly a hunch which I have long had about the appeal of Gilbert and Sullivan. Out of more than thirty letters, only one came from a woman. In my own experience, Gilbert and Sullivan is very much a male taste. The reasons for this would make the subject of another good Ph.D. thesis. Gilbert's rather gross caricaturing of middle-aged women and the absence of really strong, sympathetic and believable female roles must surely be one of the main factors. Maybe too there is something in Sullivan's music with its echoes of the parade ground and the school chapel which appeals more to the male than the female ear.

A note of caution is needed about the texts that follow. There is, alas, no such thing as a definitive version of the Savoy Operas. In the case of every work, what was performed on the first night varied from what was printed in the original libretto sent to the Lord Chamberlain for licensing and further, often substantial, alterations were made subsequently. Vocal scores often differ in wording from libretti, both in manuscript and printed editions, and there are occasional discrepancies between British and American editions of the same work. 'Gags', both authorized and unauthorized, introduced by members of the D'Oyly Carte Company during performances, creep in and out of successive editions of the libretti. Mrs Helen D'Oyly Carte, who ran the company from 1901 to 1913, often asked Gilbert to authorize a correct version of the operas, but he never did so.

The texts printed in this volume are as accurate as I can make them. They broadly follow the versions contained in the current set of libretti published by Chappell, which are used by virtually all amateur and professional companies performing the operas, and the two-volume edition of the Savoy Operas which was prepared by Dame Bridget D'Oyly Carte and Mr Colin Prestige and published by Oxford University Press in 1962–3. Some differences will be found where I have tried to bring the text into line with current practices in performance. Essentially, the version of the operas printed in this book is that in which they are generally performed now. All the thirteen operas which are still performed are included, but not *Thespis*, for which the music has been lost.

I must thank Mr Colin Prestige and the directors of the Royal Theatrical Fund for permission to reproduce material from W. S. Gilbert's unpublished papers, of which they own the copyright.

I am also very grateful for financial support towards the publication of this volume from J. Martin Haldane's Charitable Trust.

I have received much help in the preparation of this book. My initial research was greatly facilitated and encouraged by the late Dame Bridget D'Oyly Carte, Frederic Lloyd, and Peter Riley. Since then I have received support and encouragement from Sir Michael Bishop, Ray Brown, Pat Jones, Michael Jefferson, Ian Martin, Bill Clancy and Nicholas Stockton of the D'Oyly Carte Opera Company. Jonathan, Catharine, Thomas and Elinor Davies have made me welcome in Birmingham when I have been there for D'Oyly Carte opening nights. I have also derived considerable benefit from conversations and correspondence with fellow G. & S. enthusiasts, notably Robin Wilson, Selwyn Tillett, Stephen Turnbull, David Eden, Martin Yates and Arthur Jacobs.

Among those who wrote to me pointing out errors and omissions in earlier editions of this book, I am especially grateful to Geoffrey Wilson, Michael Walters, Tony Joseph, George Low, Phil Gane, Trevor Hearl, Keith Peterson, Ralph MacPhail jnr., Alice Willoughby, Jerome Sehulster and Joseph Adam

Cherepon. I trust that they and others will be indulgent over such errors that remain and for which I alone am responsible. To them I can only plead, as Wilfred Shadbolt did to Sir Richard Cholmondeley, 'My lord, 'twas I – to rashly judge forbear!'

I.B.

SUGGESTIONS FOR FURTHER READING

Reginald Allen, *The First Night Gilbert and Sullivan* (Chappell & Co., London, 1958).

Leslie Ayre, *The Gilbert and Sullivan Companion* (Pan Books, London, 1974).

Leslie Baily, *The Gilbert and Sullivan Book* (Cassell, London, 1952).

—— *Gilbert and Sullivan and their World* (Thames & Hudson, London, 1973).

Harry Benford, *The Gilbert and Sullivan Lexicon* (Richards Rosen Press, New York, 1978).

W. A. Darlington, *The World of Gilbert and Sullivan* (Thomas Crowell, New York, 1950).

Geoffrey Dixon, *The Gilbert and Sullivan Concordance* (Garland Publishing, London, 1990).

G. E. Dunn, *A Gilbert and Sullivan Dictionary* (Da Capo Press, New York, 1971).

David Eden, *Gilbert and Sullivan: The Creative Conflict* (Associated University Presses, London, 1986).

James Ellis (ed.), *The Bab Ballads by W. S. Gilbert* (Harvard University Press, Cambridge, Mass., 1970).

Darlene Geis, *The Gilbert and Sullivan Operas* (Harry Abrams, New York, 1983).

Michael Hardwick, *The Osprey Guide to Gilbert and Sullivan* (Osprey, London, 1972).

Charles Hayter, *Gilbert and Sullivan* (Macmillan, London, 1987).

Arthur Jacobs, *Arthur Sullivan: A Victorian Musician* (2nd edn., Scolar Press, Aldershot, 1992).

Alan Jefferson, *The Complete Gilbert and Sullivan Opera Guide* (Webb and Bower, London, 1984).

Frederic Lloyd and Robin Wilson, *Gilbert and Sullivan: The D'Oyly Carte Years* (Weidenfeld & Nicolson, London, 1984).

Frank Ledlie Moore, *The Handbook of Gilbert and Sullivan* (Arthur Barker, London, 1962).

Hesketh Pearson, *Gilbert and Sullivan* (Penguin, Harmondsworth, 1950).

Geoffrey Smith, *The Savoy Operas* (Hale, London, 1983).

Jane Stedman, *W. S. Gilbert* (Oxford University Press, Oxford, 1996).

TRIAL BY JURY

DRAMATIS PERSONÆ

The Learned Judge
The Plaintiff
The Defendant
Counsel for the Plaintiff
Usher
Foreman of the Jury
Associate
First Bridesmaid

TRIAL BY JURY

Trial by Jury is the earliest work by Gilbert and Sullivan which is still performed today. It was not, however, their first joint enterprise. They had collaborated in 1871 on an opera called *Thespis, or the Gods Grown Old*, which had been commissioned by John Hollingshead, the owner and manager of the Gaiety Theatre in the Strand.

Thespis is set on Mount Olympus and tells the story of a theatrical company whose members take over the roles of the Greek gods. In many ways it is highly reminiscent of Jacques Offenbach's operetta, *Orpheus in the Underworld*, which had received its English première in 1865. *Thespis* was generally well received by the critics but it was under-rehearsed and ran for only sixty-four performances. No vocal score was ever published and the manuscript score has long been lost. Although the music for one ballad ('Little Maid of Arcadee') and one chorus ('Climbing over Rocky Mountain' – later incorporated into *The Pirates of Penzance*) survives, and some brilliant detective work by Roderick Spencer and Selwyn Tillett of the Sullivan Society has unearthed much of the ballet music, it has proved impossible to reconstruct the original work.

Following *Thespis*, librettist and composer had gone their separate ways – Gilbert to write plays and Sullivan to compose church music, songs and ballads. That their remarkable talents were brought together again four years later was due partly to accident and partly to the vision and imagination of Richard D'Oyly Carte, theatrical manager and impresario.

In 1875 Carte put on Jacques Offenbach's comic opera *La Périchole* at the Royalty Theatre in Dean Street, Soho, where he was manager. It seems that he originally hoped that the French work would be accompanied by a two-act opera by Sullivan. However, this was not ready in time for the opening night on 30 January and Carte hastily substituted a domestic comedy. Meanwhile, he looked around for another short musical piece which would complete the bill and provide a popular evening's entertainment.

One story has it that Gilbert happened to walk into Carte's office one day in January, another that the two men met in the street. However it came about, their meeting was fruitful. Gilbert already had a one-act operetta up his sleeve, the libretto of which he had shown to Carte the previous summer. It was to prove the ideal companion to *La Périchole*.

Gilbert had first sketched out the bare bones of *Trial by Jury* in the 11 April 1868 issue of *Fun*, a magazine to which he regularly contributed humorous verse. In 1873 he extended it into a full-scale libretto at the suggestion of Carl Rosa, the opera impresario, who wanted to set it to music and stage it with his wife, Euphrosyne Parepa-Rosa, appearing in the leading role as the plaintiff. However, the project was abandoned when Madame Rosa suddenly died in January 1874.

When he talked to Gilbert in January 1875, Carte suggested that Sullivan would be the ideal person to set *Trial by Jury* to music. So Gilbert went round to the composer's rooms in Albert Mansions, Battersea. Over a blazing fire, Sullivan recalled, 'he read it through to me in a perturbed sort of way with a gradual crescendo of indignation, in the manner of a man considerably disappointed with what he had written. As soon as he had come to the last word he closed the manuscript up violently, apparently unconscious of the fact that he had achieved his purpose so far as I was concerned, inasmuch as I was screaming with laughter the whole time.' Sullivan immediately agreed to set the piece to music, and this he did in less than three weeks.

Trial by Jury opened at the Royalty Theatre on 25 March 1875 in a triple bill with *La Périchole* and the bewilderingly named farce, *Cryptoconchoid Syphonosto-mata*. The 'dramatic cantata', as it was described in the programme, was an immediate success, winning rapturous acclaim from audiences and critics alike. It continued at the Royalty until 18 December, and then in January 1876 it transferred to the Opéra Comique Theatre just off the Strand, with a further season at the Royal Strand Theatre in the spring of 1877. Altogether, it was performed about 300 times in its first two years.

Although it is much shorter than Gilbert and Sullivan's later works, lasting only about forty-five minutes, and differs from the rest in having only one act and lacking any spoken dialogue, *Trial by Jury* otherwise has all the distinctive features of the Savoy Operas which were to follow it. There is the gentle mockery of British institutions – in this case, the legal system – the central role for the chorus and the juxtaposition of rollicking patter song and tender romantic aria. There is also the extraordinary creative rapport between librettist and composer. As *The Times* critic observed in his review of the first night, 'It seems, as in the great Wagnerian operas, as though poem and music had proceeded simultaneously from one and the same brain.'

For Gilbert the legal world was an obvious subject to burlesque. He himself had practised as a barrister, though not very successfully, before turning to full-time writing, and therefore had plenty of opportunity to observe the quaint customs of English legal procedure. On at least two occasions, at benefit matinées for Nellie Farren in 1898 and for Ellen Terry in 1906, he played the part of the Associate, the legal official who sits at a desk below the Judge's bench throughout the entire performance and never utters a word.

Sullivan also found that the pomp and ritual of the law afforded him splendid scope for musical jokes, as in his elaborate parody of Handel for the entry of the Judge and the entrancing quartet 'A Nice Dilemma', which parodies the 'dilemma' ensembles of Italian opera and specifically, perhaps, 'D'un pensiero' from the finale of Act I of Bellini's *La sonnambula*. The absence of spoken dialogue also allowed Sullivan's prodigious talents as a dramatic composer full rein and enabled him to build up the atmosphere musically without interruption.

The old D'Oyly Carte Opera Company regularly performed *Trial by Jury* in a double bill with either *H.M.S. Pinafore* or *The Pirates of Penzance* until it was dropped from the repertoire in 1976. The new company staged it in a double bill with *H.M.S. Pinafore* in its third season which opened in the Pavilion Theatre, Bournemouth, in April 1990. The production featured a very obviously pregnant Angelina and a Judge who seemed more concerned with placing bets than listening to the proceedings in court. The Brent Walker video of the opera, released in 1982 and shown several times since on television in both Britain and the United States, also had considerable fun with the part of the Judge, who was played by Frankie Howerd.

Some recent amateur productions of *Trial by Jury* have taken considerable liberties with the original. Birmingham Savoyards played it on deck as the third act of *H.M.S. Pinafore*, with Ralph jilting Josephine, Captain Corcoran donning a wig to preside at the hearing, and Sir Joseph eventually interrupting the proceedings to declare 'I will marry her myself!' Leicester G. & S. Operatic Society expanded the opera into a full-length work entitled *Trial by Jury 2: The Whole Truth and Nothing Like the Truth*. New words were set to existing Sullivan tunes and given to additional characters such as Major General and Mrs. Hope Waning, the bride's parents, and Lucy La Sticke, the defendant's girlfriend. The show also featured a traffic warden called Rita Bucket (pronounced Bouquet in the manner of the popular BBC television series *Keeping Up Appearances*) singing the number from *Patience*, 'When I first put this uniform on'.

In May 1993 the opera was performed in Bow Street Magistrates' Court as part of the Covent Garden Festival. As Richard Morrison, the *Times* critic, observed, it would be good to see other Gilbert and Sullivan operas performed in similarly authentic locations: *Iolanthe* outside the Houses of Parliament, for example, or *H.M.S. Pinafore* on board H.M.S. *Victory*. I have always cherished the idea of a production of *Princess Ida* in an all-women's college, but they are sadly becoming rarer and rarer.

1–2 *Scene*: The D'Oyly Carte prompt-book for the 1884 revival of *Trial by Jury*, which Gilbert supervised, amplifies the rather bare description of the scene given in the libretto: 'The Bench faces the audience and extends along the back of the Court. The Judge's desk centre, with canopy overhead, Jury-box right, Counsel's seats left'. In a real courtroom, counsel would normally sit facing the judge, as it were in the orchestra pit. It is said that Gilbert modelled his courtroom on the old Clerkenwell Sessions House in which he had himself appeared during his career as a barrister.

     A printed note at the beginning of the libretto used for the 1884 revival also has some useful advice on costumes: 'Modern dresses, without any extravagance or caricature. The defendant is dressed in bridal dress. The plaintiff as a bride. The bridesmaids as bridesmaids. The Judge, Counsel and Usher etc. should be as like their prototypes at Westminster as possible.'

3–10 *Hark, the hour of ten is sounding*

     This opening chorus appeared in Gilbert's original short sketch of *Trial by Jury* in *Fun* in April 1868, the only difference from the present version being that there the second line ran 'Hearts with anxious hopes are bounding'.

  8 *subpœna*: A writ commanding a person's attendance in a court of justice. The Latin words *sub poena* ('under penalty') are the first words of the writ.

  9 *Edwin, sued by Angelina*: These names were first linked in a poem, 'The Hermit, or Edwin and Angelina', written in 1764 by Oliver Goldsmith, and included in *The Vicar of Wakefield*. The names were also used for a newly married couple, Edwin and Angelina Brown, in a series entitled 'Letters from a Young Married Lady' which appeared in the magazine *Fun* in the 1860s.

11 *Enter Usher*: An usher is a court official who shows people to their seats and leads judges into court. In *Iolanthe*, Strephon speaks of being led by a servile usher into Chancery Lane after an audience with the Lord Chancellor (Act I, line 147).

SCENE. – *A Court of Justice. Barristers, Attorneys, Jurymen and Public discovered.*

CHORUS.

Hark, the hour of ten is sounding;
Hearts with anxious fears are bounding,
Hall of Justice crowds surrounding,
    Breathing hope and fear –   5
For to-day in this arena,
Summoned by a stern subpœna,
Edwin, sued by Angelina,
    Shortly will appear.   10

(*Enter* USHER.)

SOLO – USHER.

Now, Jurymen, hear my advice –
All kinds of vulgar prejudice
    I pray you set aside:
With stern judicial frame of mind   15
From bias free of every kind,
    This trial must be tried.

CHORUS.

From bias free of every kind,
This trial must be tried.

(*During Choruses,* USHER *sings fortissimo, 'Silence in Court!'*)   20

21 *the plaintiff*: The complainant, one who brings a suit into a court of law.

29 *The . . . defendant*: A person sued in a court of law who defends the charge brought against him or her.

35 *Enter Defendant*: In the first edition of the libretto this stage direction read: '*Enter* DEFENDANT *with guitar*'. In early performances the Defendant accompanied himself on the guitar in his song 'When first my old, old love I knew'.

36 *Court of the Exchequer*: The Court of Exchequer was a common-law court which traced its origins back to the reign of Edward I and which dealt with revenue cases. It no longer existed in 1875, having been merged with two other medieval courts under the terms of the 1873 Judicature Act to form the Queen's Bench Division of the High Court. It would never in any case have dealt with actions for breach of promise. The defendant's anachronistic and legal lapses can perhaps be pardoned, however – there aren't many courts which rhyme with 'pecker'.

38 *Be firm . . . my pecker*: 'Pecker' means mouth, so this expression could be taken to mean either 'preserve a stiff upper lip' or 'keep your chin up'. It probably implies a combination of both. The phrase 'keep your pecker up' means don't get low and down-hearted. In the first edition of the libretto this line was 'Be firm, my moral pecker', recalling a phrase from one of Gilbert's *Bab Ballads*, 'The Haughty Actor':

> Dispirited became our friend –
> Depressed his moral pecker –

USHER.

Oh, listen to the plaintiff's case:
Observe the features of her face –
    The broken-hearted bride.
Condole with her distress of mind:
From bias free of every kind,   25
    This trial must be tried!

CHORUS.

From bias free, etc.

USHER.

And when amid the plaintiff's shrieks,
The ruffianly defendant speaks –
    Upon the other side;   30
What *he* may say you needn't mind –
From bias free of every kind!
    This trial must be tried!

CHORUS.

From bias free, etc. –

(*Enter* DEFENDANT.)   35

RECITATIVE – DEFENDANT.

Is this the Court of the Exchequer?

ALL.

It is!

DEFENDANT (*aside*).

Be firm, be firm, my pecker,
Your evil star's in the ascendant!

ALL.

Who are you?   40

DEFENDANT.

I'm the Defendant!

49 *You're at present in the dark*: In the early copy of the libretto sent to the Lord Chamberlain
    for licensing, the jurymen's chorus 'Oh, I was like that when a lad!' (lines 75–87) follows
    directly after this line, without the intervening chorus, 'That's a very true remark', and
    the Defendant's song, which occur in all published editions of the libretto.

57–74 *When first my old, old love I knew*
    A note by Rupert D'Oyly Carte in a 1935 copy of the libretto records that in early produc-
    tions, the Defendant tuned his guitar at the beginning of this song, with appropriate
    noises being made by the strings in the orchestra. This bit of business was later dropped.

58 *My bosom welled with joy*: The first edition of the vocal score has 'swelled with joy', but the
    libretto has always had 'welled'.

61 *No terms seemed too extravagant*: Another discrepancy between libretto and vocal score.
    The first edition of the former has 'No terms seemed extravagant', but the latter has
    from the first had the additional 'too', which scans better and is now found in all editions
    of the libretto.

65 *Tink-a-Tank*: This strange expression is supposed to be the nearest vocal approximation
    to the noise made by the plucking of guitar strings. The 1884 prompt-book mentioned
    above indicates that 'At "Tink-a-Tank" the Jury affect to be playing a guitar – the right
    hand and foot going together – the man at the right corner affects the tamborine and
    the one on the left the bones'. Thus the gentlemen of the jury transform themselves
    into a troupe of nigger minstrels.

CHORUS OF JURYMEN (*shaking their fists*).

Monster, dread our damages.
      We're the jury,
      Dread our fury!

DEFENDANT.

Hear me, hear me, if you please,   45
      These are very strange proceedings –
For permit me to remark
      On the merits of my pleadings,
You're at present in the dark.

(DEFENDANT *beckons to* JURYMEN *– they leave the box*   50
and gather round him as they sing the following):

      That's a very true remark –
            On the merits of his pleadings
      We're entirely in the dark!
      Ha! ha! Ho! ho!   55
      Ha! ha! Ho! ho!

SONG – DEFENDANT.

When first my old, old love I knew,
      My bosom welled with joy;
My riches at her feet I threw –
      I was a love-sick boy!   60
No terms seemed too extravagant
      Upon her to employ –
I used to mope, and sigh, and pant,
      Just like a love-sick boy!
            Tink-a-Tank – Tink-a-Tank.   65

But joy incessant palls the sense;
      And love, unchanged, will cloy,
And she became a bore intense
      Unto her love-sick boy!
With fitful glimmer burnt my flame,   70
      And I grew cold and coy,
At last, one morning, I became
      Another's love-sick boy.
            Tink-a-Tank – Tink-a-Tank.

85 *Singing so merrily – Trial-la-law*: This refrain appeared in Gilbert's original sketch of
    Trial by Jury in *Fun*, although in that version it was given to attorneys and barristers
    rather than jurymen. The following choruses for the two branches of the legal profes-
    sion came straight after the opening chorus in the *Fun* version:

CHORUS OF ATTORNEYS.

Attorneys are we
And we pocket our fee,
Singing so merrily, 'Trial la law!'
With our merry *ca. sa.*,
And our jolly *fi. fa.*,
Worshipping verily Trial la law!
Trial la law!
Trial la law!
Worshipping verily Trial la Law!

CHORUS OF BARRISTERS.

Barristers we
With demur and plea,
Singing so merrily, 'Trial la law!'
Be-wigged and be-gowned
We rejoice at the sound
Of the several syllables 'Trial by law!'
Trial la law!
Trial la law!
Singing so merrily, 'Trial la law!'

89 *Silence in Court*: This brief recitative for the Usher was also in the original *Fun* sketch,
    following on from the barristers' chorus above. After it, however, there was no chorus or
    song for the Judge, and Gilbert went straight on to the recitative and aria for the Coun-
    sel for the Plaintiff (lines 235–65).

93–102 *All hail, great Judge*
    In this chorus, and in the passage for the Judge and chorus which precedes 'When I,
    good friends, was called to the bar', Sullivan deliberately imitated the florid fugal style
    of Handel. There is another splendid parody of Handelian style in the song 'This hel-
    met, I suppose' in Act III of *Princess Ida*.

101 *Reversed in banc*: 'In banc' is a legal phrase meaning on the bench and is applied to sit-
    tings of a superior court of common law. So this phrase means 'reversed by a full bench
    of judges in a higher court'.

104 *Breach of Promise*: Until 1970 women could, and did, take men to court for breaking off
    engagements. A contract to marry was as binding in law as any other contract, and there-
    fore the party who broke it was liable for damages. The most famous action for breach
    of promise in Victorian literature was, of course, that brought by Mrs Bardell against
    Mr Pickwick in Charles Dickens's *The Pickwick Papers*. In that case, judgment was given
    for the plaintiff, and Mr Pickwick had to pay damages of £750.

CHORUS OF JURYMEN (*advancing stealthily*).

> Oh, I was like that when a lad! 75
>> A shocking young scamp of a rover,
> I behaved like a regular cad;
>> But that sort of thing is all over.
> I am now a respectable chap
>> And shine with a virtue resplendent, 80
> And, therefore, I haven't a scrap
>> Of sympathy with the defendant!
>>> He shall treat us with awe,
>>> If there isn't a flaw,
> Singing so merrily – Trial-la-law! 85
> Trial-la-law – Trial-la-law!
> Singing so merrily – Trial-la-law!

> (*They enter the Jury-box.*)

RECITATIVE – USHER (*on Bench*).

> Silence in Court!
> Silence in Court, and all attention lend. 90
> Behold your Judge! In due submission bend!

> (*Enter* JUDGE *on Bench.*)

CHORUS.

> All hail, great Judge!
>> To your bright rays
> We never grudge 95
>> Ecstatic praise.
>>> All hail!
> May each decree
>> As statute rank
> And never be 100
>> Reversed in banc.
>>> All hail!

RECITATIVE – JUDGE.

> For these kind words accept my thanks, I pray.
> A Breach of Promise we've to try to-day.
> But firstly, if the time you'll not begrudge, 105
> I'll tell you how I came to be a Judge.

ALL.

> He'll tell us how he came to be a Judge!

111–54 *When I, good friends, was called to the bar*
This is the first of Gilbert and Sullivan's inimitable patter songs (not counting three
early examples of the genre in *Thespis*, of which the music has not survived), and it introduces the first in a long line of comic figures which was to include a sorcerer, a First
Lord of the Admiralty, a modern Major-General and a Lord High Executioner. It was
not surprising that Gilbert should begin with a judge. As a former barrister himself, he
had been able to examine that particular species at close quarters. He was, of course, to
create another comic role from the legal world in *Iolanthe*. Indeed, the Lord Chancellor's
song 'When I went to the Bar as a very young man' has very close similarities with this
song (see the notes to lines 465–96 of *Iolanthe*, Act I).

The part of the Judge in *Trial by Jury* was created by Fred Sullivan, the composer's
brother. He was a great success in the role, which he played throughout the opening season at the Royalty Theatre and for part of the 1876 season at the Opéra Comique. However, he became seriously ill and died at the age of thirty-six in January 1877. During
Fred's last illness Arthur sat by his bedside reading verses by Adelaide Anne Procter.
One of these verses, 'The Lost Chord', he later set to music, and it became perhaps the
most popular of all Victorian drawing-room ballads.

115 *a swallow-tail coat*: A coat with a forked tail like that of a swallow.
116 *A brief*: A summary of the relevant facts and points of law in a case drawn up for a barrister, usually by a solicitor.
a booby: A dull, stupid fellow, especially one who allows himself to be imposed upon. The
word is also used for the boy who comes bottom of the class and for a species of gannet
thought to be particularly stupid.
120 *Westminster Hall*: Before the present Law Courts in the Strand came into use in 1882, the
Common Law Courts were housed in Westminster Hall adjoining the Houses of Parliament.

132 *the Bailey and Middlesex Sessions*: The Bailey, referred to in line 141 as 'Ancient Bailey', is,
of course, the Old Bailey, built in 1539 on Cheapside in the City of London, and established in 1834 as the Central Criminal Court in England and Wales. It is mentioned as
such near the end of Act II of *The Pirates of Penzance* (see the note to line 564). Sessions
were courts held four times a year in a county or other administrative area and having
limited civil and criminal jurisdiction. They are now called Crown Courts. The Middlesex Sessions, where Gilbert himself had practised and which he made the subject of an
early poem in *Fun* magazine, were held in a building in Parliament Square, London, opposite the Houses of Parliament.

JUDGE.

Let me speak!

ALL.

Let him speak, etc.
Hush! hush! He speaks.

SONG – JUDGE.

When I, good friends, was called to the bar,
    I'd an appetite fresh and hearty,
But I was, as many young barristers are,
    An impecunious party.
I'd a swallow-tail coat of a beautiful blue –
    A brief which I bought of a booby –
A couple of shirts and a collar or two,
    And a ring that looked like a ruby!

115

CHORUS.

He'd a couple of shirts, etc.

JUDGE.

In Westminster Hall I danced a dance,
    Like a semi-despondent fury;
For I thought I should never hit on a chance
    Of addressing a British Jury –
But I soon got tired of third-class journeys,
    And dinners of bread and water;
So I fell in love with a rich attorney's
    Elderly, ugly daughter.

120

125

CHORUS.

So he fell in love, etc.

JUDGE.

The rich attorney, he jumped with joy,
    And replied to my fond professions:
'You shall reap the reward of your pluck, my boy,
    At the Bailey and Middlesex Sessions.
You'll soon get used to her looks,' said he,
'And a very nice girl you will find her!

130

135 *She may very well pass for forty-three*: Gilbert had a thing about women in their forties. Poor Ruth in *The Pirates of Penzance* is mocked by Frederic for being forty-seven (see the note to Act I, line 172), while Marco is warned by Gianetta in *The Gondoliers* not to address any lady less than forty-five (see the note to Act I, line 934).

147 *the Gurneys*: A well-known Quaker banking family which hailed originally from Norwich. The London branch of the bank, Overend, Gurney and Co., failed in 1866, but the Norwich branch prospered and was taken over by Barclays in 1896.

148 *An incubus*: Defined by the *Oxford English Dictionary* as a person or thing that weighs upon and oppresses like a nightmare. It sounds a more appropriate image for the Lord Chancellor in *Iolanthe* to use in his nocturnal wanderings.

She may very well pass for forty-three 135
   In the dusk, with a light behind her!'

CHORUS.

She may very well, etc.

JUDGE.

The rich attorney was good as his word;
   The briefs came trooping gaily,
And every day my voice was heard 140
   At the Sessions or Ancient Bailey.
All thieves who could my fees afford
   Relied on my orations,
And many a burglar I've restored
   To his friends and his relations. 145

CHORUS.

And many a burglar, etc.

JUDGE.

At length I became as rich as the Gurneys –
   An incubus then I thought her,
So I threw over that rich attorney's
   Elderly, ugly daughter. 150
The rich attorney my character high
   Tried vainly to disparage –
And now, if you please, I'm ready to try
   This Breach of Promise of Marriage!

CHORUS.

And now if you please, etc. 155

JUDGE.

For now I'm a Judge!

ALL.

And a good Judge too!

JUDGE.

Yes, now I'm a Judge!

160 *Though all my law be fudge*: In the first edition of the libretto this line went: 'Though all my law is fudge'. That version is still retained in the Macmillan edition of the Savoy Operas, first published in 1926 and reprinted on numerous occasions over the next 60 years.

164 *a job*: A colloquial expression for a transaction in which duty or the public interest is sacrificed for the sake of private advantage.

169 *a nob*: An important personage. It probably derives from the oriental word 'nabob'.

172 *Enter Counsel*: Counsel is the name given to a barrister or barristers when engaged in the direction or conduct of a case in court.

175 *Kneel, Jurymen, oh, kneel*: A favourite joke among the members of the old D'Oyly Carte chorus was to ask 'Who's playing Juryman O'Neill tonight?'

ALL.

And a good Judge too!

JUDGE.

Though all my law be fudge,   160
Yet I'll never, never budge,
But I'll live and die a Judge!

ALL.

And a good Judge too!

JUDGE (*pianissimo*).

It was managed by a job –

ALL.

And a good job too!   165

JUDGE.

It was managed by a job!

ALL.

And a good job too!

JUDGE.

It is patent to the mob,
That my being made a nob
Was effected by a job.   170

ALL.

And a good job too!

(*Enter* COUNSEL *for* PLAINTIFF. *He takes his place in
front row of Counsel's seats.*)

RECITATIVE – COUNSEL.

Swear thou the Jury!

USHER.

Kneel, Jurymen, oh, kneel!   175

185 *That we will well and truly try*: The first edition of the libretto has a longer stage direction
     at this point: '*All rise with the last note, both hands in air*'. The libretto goes on with a two–
     line recitative for the Usher:

> This blind devotion is indeed a crusher –
> Pardon the tear-drop of a simple usher:

These two lines did not appear in the edition of the libretto issued for the 1884 revival. A
note by Rupert D'Oyly Carte in 1935 indicates that they were never, in fact, set to music
by Sullivan and had never been sung.

In the licence copy sent to the Lord Chamberlain the Usher's recitative is followed by
this ballad for the Foreman of the Jury, which was cut out before the first performance:

> Oh, do not blush to shed a tear
> This is your foreman's prayer.
> For if you really feel it *here* (pointing to his heart)
> Why not express it *there* (pointing to his eye)
> The tears that to your eyelid start
> Do not attempt to dry
> Your eye is but your outer heart
> Your heart is all your eye!

The Counsel's recitative 'Where is the Plaintiff?' then followed as now.

189 *Oh, Angelina*: The summoning of Angelina is accomplished with much echoing of voices
     around and outside the courtroom. A note in the prompt-book for the 1884 revival di-
     rects: 'The Usher trips à la fairy to right and calls "Angelina" and listens for echo and
     then trips across stage to left and calls "Angelina" again and listens for echo. Then trips
     to centre of stage and strikes attitude of welcome as bridesmaids enter.' In D'Oyly Carte
     productions, the 'echo' was performed by the Defendant singing with his back to the
     audience.

191 *Enter the Bridesmaids*: The original stage direction for this entrance in the first-edition
     libretto read: '*Enter the* BRIDESMAIDS, *each bearing two palm branches, their arms crossed
     on their bosoms, and rose-wreaths in their arms*'.

196 *Take, oh take these posies*: In some editions, this line appears as 'Take, oh maid these
     posies'.

(*All the* JURY *kneel in the Jury-box, and so are hidden from audience.*)

USHER.

Oh, will you swear by yonder skies,
Whatever question may arise,
'Twixt rich and poor, 'twixt low and high,   180
That you will well and truly try?

JURY (*raising their hands, which alone are visible*).

To all of this we make reply,
To all of this we make reply,
By the dull slate of yonder sky:
That we will well and truly try.   185
  (*All rise with the last note.*)

RECITATIVE – COUNSEL.

Where is the Plaintiff?
Let her now be brought.

RECITATIVE – USHER.

Oh, Angelina! Come thou into Court!
Angelina! Angelina!!   190

(*Enter the* BRIDESMAIDS.)

CHORUS OF BRIDESMAIDS.

Comes the broken flower –
 Comes the cheated maid –
Though the tempest lower,
 Rain and cloud will fade!   195
Take, oh take these posies:
 Though thy beauty rare
Shame the blushing roses,
 They are passing fair!
  Wear the flowers till they fade;
  Happy be thy life, oh maid!   200

(*The* JUDGE, *having taken a great fancy to* FIRST BRIDESMAID, *sends her a note by* USHER, *which she reads, kisses rapturously, and places in her bosom. Enter* PLAINTIFF.)

205   *the season vernal*: Spring. 'Vernal' comes from the Latin *vernalis* ('of the spring').

209, 211   *Time may do his duty . . . Winter hath a beauty*: This is the first of no fewer than fifteen occasions, exclusive of repetitions, when the words 'duty' and 'beauty' are rhymed in the
Savoy Operas. This is the only such rhyming in *Trial by Jury*. *H.M.S. Pinafore* holds the
record with four separate songs in which the words are rhymed (see the note to Act I,
lines 247–58).

218   *Wear the flowers*: The first-edition libretto had the following stage direction at this point:
'*During chorus* ANGELINA *collects wreaths of roses from* BRIDESMAIDS *and gives them to
the* JURY, *who put them on and wear them during the rest of the piece.*'

221   *Ah, sly dog*: Gilbert used this refrain in his original sketch for an operetta in *Fun* in 1868
(see the note to line 385 below).

SOLO – PLAINTIFF.

O'er the season vernal, 205
   Time may cast a shade;
Sunshine, if eternal,
   Makes the roses fade!
Time may do his duty;
   Let the thief alone – 210
Winter hath a beauty,
   That is all his own.
      Fairest days are sun and shade:
      I am no unhappy maid!

(*The* JUDGE *having by this time transferred his admiration to* PLAINTIFF, 215
directs USHER *to take the note from* FIRST BRIDESMAID *and hand it to*
PLAINTIFF, *who reads it, kisses it rapturously, and places it in her bosom.*)

CHORUS OF BRIDESMAIDS.

Wear the flowers, etc.

JUDGE.

Oh, never, never, never, since I joined the human race,
Saw I so exquisitely fair a face. 220

THE JURY (*shaking their forefingers at him*).
Ah, sly dog! Ah, sly dog!

JUDGE (*to* JURY).

How say you? Is she not designed for capture?

FOREMAN (*after consulting with the* JURY).

We've but one word, my lord, and that is – Rapture!

PLAINTIFF (*curtseying*).

Your kindness, gentlemen, quite overpowers!

JURY.

We love you fondly and would make you ours! 225

THE BRIDESMAIDS (*shaking their forefingers at* JURY).
Ah, sly dogs! Ah, sly dogs!

228–33 *Monster! Monster! dread our fury!*
The first edition of the libretto did not contain this chorus, which was certainly sung in the 1884 revival, if not before.

235 *May it please you, my lud*: The Counsel's recitative and aria appeared in almost exactly their present form in Gilbert's early *Fun* sketch, where they followed straight on from the entrance of the Judge into court.

243 *He deceived a girl*: In the licence copy this is printed as 'Or deceive a girl'. The *Fun* version, however, is as now.

JURY.

We love you fondly, and would make you ours!

(*Shaking their fists at the* DEFENDANT.)

Monster! Monster! dread our fury!
There's the Judge and we're the Jury,
Come, substantial damages!   230
Substantial damages!
Damages!
Dam—

USHER.

Silence in Court!

RECITATIVE – COUNSEL *for* PLAINTIFF.

May it please you, my lud!   235
 Gentlemen of the jury!

ARIA.

With a sense of deep emotion,
 I approach this painful case;
For I never had a notion
 That a man could be so base,   240
Or deceive a girl confiding,
Vows, *etcetera*, deriding.

ALL.

He deceived a girl confiding,
Vows, *etcetera*, deriding.

(PLAINTIFF *falls sobbing on* COUNSEL'S *breast and remains there.*) 245

COUNSEL.

See my interesting client,
 Victim of a heartless wile!
See the traitor all defiant
 Wear a supercilious smile!
Sweetly smiled my client on him,   250
Coyly woo'd and gently won him.

255 *Camberwell*: A rather undistinguished lower-middle-class suburb of London which grew up in the mid-Victorian period.

256 *Peckham*: Camberwell's neighbour to the south, further away from the centre of the capital, even less distinguished and decidedly working-class. Both Camberwell and Peckham, it should in fairness be pointed out, are now becoming 'gentrified' and, if not quite Arcadian, then certainly Bohemian.

   an Arcadian Vale: Arcadia, a mountainous area in central Peloponnesus, was regarded by the ancient Greeks as the ideal region of rural contentment and pastoral simplicity. Act I of *Iolanthe* is set in an Arcadian landscape.

257 *otto*: A scent known as 'attar of roses', distilled from rose petals and obtained from the Balkan states.

258 *Watteau*: Antoine Watteau (1684–1721) was a French painter who specialized in idyllic pastoral scenes.

259 *Breathing concentrated otto*: The *Fun* sketch, the licence copy, the first edition of the libretto and the current Macmillan edition of the Savoy Operas all render this line: 'Bless us, concentrated otto!'

260 *Picture, then, my client naming*: The 1884 prompt-book directs that at this point 'Plaintiff coquets with jury'. On the word '*trousseau*', she shows a pair of pink stockings, and at the Counsel's 'Cheer up, my pretty', she staggers into his arms.

265 *trousseau*: A bride's outfit of clothes, household linen etc. From the French word *trousse*, meaning a bundle.

272 *Is plain to see*: In the first edition of the libretto and in most Chappell editions, this line reads 'Is plain to me'. It appears in that form also in the 1962–3 Oxford University Press World's Classics edition.

274 *Recline on me*: In the licence copy, and in some editions of the libretto, though not the first one, this line appeared as 'Lean on me'.

ALL.

Sweetly smiled, etc.

COUNSEL.

Swiftly fled each honeyed hour
   Spent with this unmanly male!
Camberwell became a bower,   255
   Peckham an Arcadian Vale,
Breathing concentrated otto! –
An existence *à la* Watteau.

ALL.

Breathing concentrated otto! etc.

COUNSEL.

Picture, then, my client naming,   260
   And insisting on the day:
Picture him excuses framing –
   Going from her far away:
Doubly criminal to do so,
For the maid had bought her *trousseau*!   265

ALL.

Doubly criminal, etc.

COUNSEL (*to* PLAINTIFF, *who weeps*).

Cheer up, my pretty – oh, cheer up!

JURY.

Cheer up, cheer up, we love you!

(COUNSEL *leads* PLAINTIFF *fondly into Witness-box; he takes a tender*
leave of her, and resumes his place in Court. PLAINTIFF *reels as if about to faint.*)   270

JUDGE.

That she is reeling
   Is plain to see!

FOREMAN.

If faint you're feeling
   Recline on me!

278 *Oh, perjured lover*: Although this phrase appeared in the licence copy, it was not in the
     first published edition of the libretto, and when it did first appear in print, it was in the
     form 'Oh, perjured monster'.

286 *From far Cologne*: *Eau de Cologne* is a perfumed spirit which was invented by Johann Maria
     Farina, an Italian chemist who settled in Cologne in 1709. The recipe prescribes twelve
     drops of each of the essential oils (bergamot, citron, neroli, orange and rosemary) with
     one drum of Malabar cardamoms and a gallon of rectified spirits, all of which are dis-
     tilled together. Guaranteed to restore fainting plaintiffs to their senses.

294–318 *Oh, gentlemen, listen, I pray*
     The Defendant's song was apparently written at the last minute. It does not appear in
     the copy of the libretto sent to the Lord Chamberlain for licensing a week or so before
     the first performance. Instead there is a gap with the word 'Song' above it.
         The prompt-book for the 1884 revival has the following stage direction at the begin-
     ning of this song: '*As Defendant begins to sing the Jury turn their backs and read newspapers*'.

(*She falls sobbing on to the* FOREMAN'S *breast.*) 275

PLAINTIFF (*feebly*).

I shall recover
If left alone.

ALL (*shaking their fists at* DEFENDANT).

Oh, perjured lover,
Atone! atone!

FOREMAN.

Just like a father 280
I wish to be. (*Kissing her.*)

JUDGE (*approaching her*).

Or, if you'd rather,
Recline on me!

(*She jumps on to Bench, sits down by the* JUDGE, *and falls sobbing on his breast.*)

COUNSEL.

Oh! fetch some water 285
From far Cologne!

ALL.

For this sad slaughter
Atone! atone!

JURY (*shaking fists at* DEFENDANT).

Monster, dread our fury –
There's the Judge, and we're the Jury! 290
Monster, monster,
Dread our fury.

USHER.

Silence in Court!

SONG – DEFENDANT.

Oh, gentlemen, listen, I pray,
Though I own that my heart has been ranging, 295

306 *Consider the moral*: The 1884 stage direction as the bridesmaids rush forward at this point is: '*Jury turn and show the greatest affection – but repeat the business with papers as Defendant sings*'.

310 *To turn his attention to dinner*: The first edition of the libretto and the Macmillan edition render this line as 'To turn your attention to dinner'.

312 *To look upon him as a glutton*: In the first-edition libretto and the Macmillan edition, this line is: 'That you could hold him as a glutton'.

315 *But this I am willing to say*: The first-edition libretto has 'But this I am ready to say'. In this case, the Macmillan edition has been brought up to date.

316 *If it will appease her sorrow*: In the first-edition libretto, 'If it will appease their sorrow'.

319 *But this he is willing to say*: The stage direction in the 1884 prompt-book at this point was: 'Defendant again remonstrates with the Judge who dips his pen in ink and throws ink in Defendant's eye'.

In the first edition of the libretto, and, therefore, possibly in early performances of the opera, there were no refrains for the chorus in this song. The second verse ended with the line 'Determines to tackle the mutton', after which the Defendant repeated 'Consider the moral, I pray'. He then had a third verse, cut out by the time of the 1884 revival, which went as follows:

> Oh, beware a dilemma so strange,
> > It will soon play the deuce with your dollars,
> It will soon be illegal to change
> > Your money, your mind, or your collars;
> A singer must sing the same song
> > From the time of his youth to his latter days;
> 'Twill be eight o'clock all the day long,
> > And the week will be nothing but Saturdays!
> > > But this I am ready to say,
> > > > If it will appease their sorrow,
> > > I'll marry one lady to-day,
> > > > And I'll marry the other to-morrow!

323 *Burglaree*: It would be more accurate, and would provide just as good a rhyme, for the Defendant to have said 'Bigamee' at this point.

The 1884 prompt-book has a further stage direction here: 'The Judge now requests the Plaintiff to go down – she refuses but he insists – she then goes reluctantly a couple of paces and then rushes back and sticks pen in Judge's wig – she then comes down and flirts with the Jury and the Usher'.

325 *the reign of James the Second*: Men of learning, like the Judge, will need no prompting on this, but others may care to be reminded that James II ruled from 1685 to 1689, when he was supplanted by William of Orange in the Glorious Revolution.

Of nature the laws I obey,
    For nature is constantly changing.
The moon in her phases is found,
    The time and the wind and the weather,
The months in succession come round,   300
    And you don't find two Mondays together.
      Ah! Consider the moral, I pray,
        Nor bring a young fellow to sorrow,
      Who loves this young lady to-day,
        And loves that young lady to-morrow.   305

BRIDESMAIDS (*rushing forward, and kneeling to* JURY).

    Consider the moral, etc.

You cannot eat breakfast all day,
    Nor is it the act of a sinner,
When breakfast is taken away,
    To turn his attention to dinner;   310
And it's not in the range of belief,
    To look upon him as a glutton,
Who, when he is tired of beef,
    Determines to tackle the mutton.
      But this I am willing to say,   315
        If it will appease her sorrow,
      I'll marry this lady to-day,
        And I'll marry the other to-morrow!

BRIDESMAIDS (*rushing forward as before*).

    But this he is willing to say, etc.

RECITATIVE – JUDGE.

That seems a reasonable proposition,   320
To which, I think, your client may agree.

COUNSEL.

But, I submit, m'lud, with all submission,
To marry two at once is Burglaree!

(*Referring to law book*)

In the reign of James the Second,   325
It was generally reckoned

330 *Oh, man of learning*: At this point the licence copy continues with the following passages for the Judge, Usher and chorus, none of which was ever performed or probably even set to music:

RECITATIVE – JUDGE.

> We do not deal with artificial crime,
> Nor do we wish barbaric law to borrow.
> Besides, he does not say two at one time –
> He says, 'One wife today – one wife tomorrow'.

ALL.   Oh, Judge discerning!

SOLO – USHER.

> His lordship's always quits
>   In points like this contesting.
> This keen exchange of wits
>   Is always interesting.
> These epigrams so bright,
>   Like stars in autumn falling,
> Relieve with points of light
>   The Usher's gloomy calling.

CHORUS.   His Lordship's always right, etc.

(During this USHER *cries* 'Silence in Court').

JUDGE.   If you're quite finished will you kindly state
               There is another verse, but that can wait.

The licence copy then continues with the quartet 'A nice dilemma', as now.

340 *A nice dilemma*: At this point the 1884 prompt-book directs: 'Each of the principals singles out an imaginary person in the stalls and sings to them – but not offensively'.

As a rather serious crime
To marry two wives at one time.

(*Hands book up to* JUDGE, *who reads it.*)

ALL.

Oh, man of learning! 330

QUARTET.

JUDGE.

A nice dilemma we have here,
    That calls for all our wit,
    For all our wit:

COUNSEL.

And at this stage, it don't appear
    That we can settle it. 335

DEFENDANT (*in Witness-box*).

If I to wed the girl am loth
    A breach 'twill surely be –

PLAINTIFF.

And if he goes and marries both,
    It counts as Burglaree!

ALL.

A nice dilemma, etc. 340

DUET – PLAINTIFF *and* DEFENDANT.

PLAINTIFF (*embracing him rapturously*).

I love him – I love him – with fervour unceasing,
    I worship and madly adore;
My blind adoration is always increasing,
    My loss I shall ever deplore.
Oh, see what a blessing, what love and caressing 345
    I've lost, and remember it, pray,
When you I'm addressing, are busy assessing
    The damages Edwin must pay!
    Yes, he must pay!

350 *I smoke like a furnace*: Here the 1884 direction is: 'As Defendant begins to sing the Jury suddenly disappear. The Ladies and Barristers get up to see where they have gone'. The jurymen then rise again at the end of the song.

358 *Yes, he must pay*: This line was not in either the licence copy or the first published edition of the libretto. In the former, the Defendant continues his song as follows:

> Oh, let this Jury know
> What ought they for to do!

This leads straight into the Judge's *recitative*, 'The question, gentlemen – is one of liquor'. The first edition has the jury's 'We would be fairly acting,/But this is most distracting' but does not have their next two lines, nor the public's 'She loves him and madly adores him'. These were added after the first night. These are also missing from the Macmillan edition.

368 *He says, when tipsy, he would thrash and kick her*: In the first-edition libretto this line was 'If he, when tipsy, would assault and kick her'.

DEFENDANT (*repelling her furiously*).

I smoke like a furnace – I'm always in liquor,   350
    A ruffian – a bully – a sot;
I'm sure I should thrash her, perhaps I should kick her,
    I am such a very bad lot!
I'm not prepossessing, as you may be guessing,
    She couldn't endure me a day;   355
Recall my professing, when you are assessing
    The damages Edwin must pay!

PLAINTIFF.

Yes, he must pay!

(*She clings to him passionately; after a struggle, he
throws her off into arms of* COUNSEL.)   360

JURY.

We would be fairly acting,
But this is most distracting!
If, when in liquor, he would kick her,
That is an abatement.

PUBLIC.

She loves him and madly adores him, etc.   365

RECITATIVE – JUDGE.

The question, gentlemen – is one of liquor;
    You ask for guidance – this is my reply:
He says, when tipsy, he would thrash and kick her,
    Let's make him tipsy, gentlemen, and try!

COUNSEL.

    With all respect   370
    I do object!

PLAINTIFF.

I do object!

DEFENDANT.

I don't object!

378 *I can't sit up here all day*: In the first edition, 'I can't stop up here all day'. The licence copy, however, has the present version.

379 *I must shortly get away*: Here, the first edition has 'I must shortly go away', although once again the licence copy is as now.

382 *Gentle, simple-minded Usher*: This and the next line were not in the first-edition libretto although they were in the licence copy.

385 *I will marry her myself*: The last two lines of the Judge's song occur in Gilbert's original *Fun* sketch, the final passage of which is as follows:

SOLO – JUDGE.

In the course of my career
As a judex sitting here,
Never, never, I declare,
Have I seen a maid so fair!

ALL.   Ah! Sly dog!

See her sinking on her knees
In the Court of Common Pleas –
Place your briefs upon the shelf
I will marry her myself!
(*He throws himself into her arms.*)

ALL.   Ah! Sly dog!

RECITATIVE – JUDGE.

Come all of you – the breakfast I'll prepare –
Five hundred and eleven, Eaton Square.

FINAL CHORUS.

Trial la law! Trial la law!
Singing so merrily, Trial la law!

The licence copy continues in a rather different vein after the line 'I will marry her myself':

PLAINTIFF. Oh, rapture!
DEFENDANT.   Oh rapture!
BOTH.   Oh, joy unalloyed!
JUDGE. With this rapture,
PLAINTIFF.   This capture,
BOTH.   I am overjoyed!

ALL.   Oh, joy unbounded, etc.

388–420 *FINALE*
The finale of *Trial by Jury* has undergone a number of important changes since Gilbert first conceived it, not least in the introduction of a Grand Transformation Scene in the best pantomime tradition.

In the licence copy, lines 413–20 are rendered as follows:

JUDGE.   Though defendant is a snob,
ALL.   And a great snob too.
JUDGE.   A wretched little snob,
ALL.   And a great snob too.
JUDGE.   Though defendant is a snob,
                                       I'll reward him from my fob,
                                       Then I'll go and do the job.
ALL.   And a good job too!

ALL.

> With all respect
> We do object!   375

JUDGE (*tossing his books and papers about*).

> All the legal furies seize you!
> No proposal seems to please you,
> I can't sit up here all day,
> I must shortly get away.
> Barristers, and you, attorneys,   380
> Set out on your homeward journeys:
> Gentle, simple-minded Usher,
> Get you, if you like, to Russ*her*;
> Put your briefs upon the shelf,
> I will marry her myself!   385

(*He comes down from Bench to floor of Court.*
He embraces ANGELINA.)

FINALE.

PLAINTIFF.

> Oh, joy unbounded,
> With wealth surrounded,
> The knell is sounded   390
>   Of grief and woe.

COUNSEL.

> With love devoted
> On you he's doated.
> To castle moated
>   Away they go.   395

DEFENDANT.

> I wonder whether
> They'll live together
> In marriage tether
>   In manner true?

USHER.

> It seems to me, sir,   400
> Of such as she, sir,
> A judge is he, sir,
>   And a good judge too.

The first-edition libretto ends at line 412, as does the Macmillan edition of the Savoy Operas, although the earliest vocal score has lines 413–20 as they are now sung, except that lines 417 and 418 are given to the Judge (the latter being 'I'll reward him from my fob') rather than to the chorus.

The first-edition libretto ends with the stage direction 'JUDGE *and* PLAINTIFF *dance back, hornpipe step, and get on to the Bench – the* BRIDESMAIDS *take the eight garlands of roses from behind the Judge's desk and draw them across floor of Court, so that they radiate from the desk. Two plaster Cupids in bar wigs descend from flies. Red fire.*'

A much more elaborate transformation scene was introduced into the finale for the 1884 revival. Indeed, two surviving prompt-books from that year in the D'Oyly Carte archives have different versions of this scene. One directs that it begins at line 405: 'At "Yes, I am a Judge" the Bridesmaids clap their hands à la Minstrels, Judge and Plaintiff dance hornpipe steps. For final picture Plaintiff gets on the Judge's back à la fairy – the two Bridesmaids with counsel and Defendant fall right and left – while the remaining Bridesmaids kneel with their arms over their heads. Cupids lowered a little before curtain.'

The other prompt-book has the following even more elaborate directions for what it calls the 'Trick Change':

> At the last 'And a good Judge too!' [line 412], the gong is struck for the trick change to fairyland. The canopy revolves. The fan pieces behind judge fall. Two revolving pieces on either side of Judge come round. The Rise comes up and covers Bench front. The Judge and associate's desks open. The Chamber flats are broken and taken away and wings pushed on. Cloth in front of benches and Jury box are let down and masking for same pushed on. The Jurymen, Counsel and Ladies have blue bells which they hold over Bridesmaids for final picture. At 'Yes, I am a Judge' the Bridesmaids clap their hands à la Minstrels. For final picture the Plaintiff gets on the Judge's back, the two Bridesmaids with Counsel and Defendant fall right and left while the remaining Bridesmaids kneel with their arms over their heads. Red fire.

The transformation scene was apparently abandoned in the 1920s because of the damage sustained by the plaster cupids while the Company was on tour.

ALL.

Oh, joy unbounded, etc.

JUDGE.

Yes, I am a Judge.   405

ALL.

And a good Judge too!

JUDGE.

Yes, I am a Judge.

ALL.

And a good Judge too!

JUDGE.

Though homeward as you trudge,
You declare my law is fudge,   410
Yet of beauty I'm a judge.

ALL.

And a good Judge too!

JUDGE.

Though defendant is a snob.

ALL.

And a great snob too!

JUDGE.

Though defendant is a snob.   415

ALL.

And a great snob too!
Though defendant is a snob,
He'll reward him with his fob.
So we've settled with the job,
And a good job too!   420

CURTAIN

THE SORCERER

DRAMATIS PERSONÆ

SIR MARMADUKE POINTDEXTRE (*an Elderly Baronet*)
ALEXIS (*of the Grenadier Guards – his Son*)
DR DALY (*Vicar of Ploverleigh*)
NOTARY
JOHN WELLINGTON WELLS (*of J. W. Wells & Co., Family Sorcerers*)
LADY SANGAZURE (*a Lady of Ancient Lineage*)
ALINE (*her Daughter – betrothed to Alexis*)
MRS PARTLET (*a Pew-opener*)
CONSTANCE (*her Daughter*)

Chorus of Villagers.

ACT I. – Exterior of Sir Marmaduke's Mansion. Mid-day.
(*Twelve hours are supposed to elapse between Acts I and II*)
ACT II. – Exterior of Sir Marmaduke's Mansion. Midnight.

THE SORCERER

Following the success of *Trial by Jury* Richard D'Oyly Carte was determined to keep Gilbert and Sullivan together to establish an English school of light opera to rival the French *opéra comique* style of Offenbach. This was to take some time, however. His librettist and composer initially went their separate ways, Gilbert to write more plays and contemplate a collaboration with Carl Rosa, and Sullivan to take up first the directorship of the Glasgow Orpheus Choir and then the principalship of the National Training School of Music (now the Royal College of Music).

D'Oyly Carte persisted in his scheme. Having been informed by Gilbert that there would need to be payment in advance before any new operas were written, he recruited four backers for a new Comedy Opera Company. They were Frank Chappell and George Metzler, both music publishers, Collard Augustus Drake, an associate of Metzler's, and Edward Hodgson Bayley, who was known as 'Water cart Bayley' because he owned the vehicles which sprinkled water over the dusty streets of London. With these four men as co-directors, the Comedy Opera Company was set up in 1876.

Carte now had the money to tempt Gilbert and Sullivan into further collaborations. For their first joint full-length work Gilbert resurrected the basic plot from a story which he had written for the *Graphic*. 'An Elixir of Love', as it was called, was about the effects of a magic love potion sold by a London firm of magicians to a country curate for distribution among his parishioners. Changing the professions of the central characters around slightly, Gilbert expanded this story into a libretto for a two-act operetta entitled *The Sorcerer*.

The comic and dramatic possibilities of a plot based on the use of a love potion had an extraordinary appeal to Gilbert. The theme is found in one of his *Bab Ballads*, 'The Cunning Woman', and in his first play, *Dulcamara*, which was a burlesque of Donizetti's famous opera *L'Elisir d'amore*. In later years he was constantly trying to interest Sullivan in another collaboration based on a story about a magic lozenge. The composer would have none of it, however, and when eventually, in 1892, Gilbert did produce another opera on this theme, *The Mountebanks*, it was with music by Alfred Cellier.

Love potions and their often unexpected effects have, of course, been a favourite theme of operatic librettists and composers. They figure prominently
in Auber's *Le Philtre* and Wagner's *Tristan und Isolde* as well as in Donizetti's
well-known work mentioned above. *The Sorcerer* provided Sullivan with some
splendid opportunities to parody the operatic tradition, particularly in the incantation scene towards the end of Act I.

Richard D'Oyly Carte gave Gilbert a free hand in casting the new opera. In
picking those who were to be the first principals of the new company, he deliberately avoided well-known names and instead chose those whom he could
mould to fit his own conception of the characters. For the sorcerer he picked a
little-known piano entertainer and former police court reporter called George
Grossmith.

Grossmith, who had no pretensions to being an opera singer, was amazed
when he was offered the role. 'I should have thought you would have required a
fine man with a fine voice,' he observed to Gilbert. 'No, that is just what we
don't want' was the emphatic reply.

For the stately Lady Sangazure, Gilbert chose Mrs Howard Paul, who ran a
touring troupe of actors and singers. Mrs Paul, who helped to persuade Grossmith to join the new company, also insisted that Gilbert should take on one of
her young protégés, Rutland Barrington. Like Grossmith, he was no opera
singer, but his personality and style fitted the bill exactly: 'He's a staid, stolid
swine, and that's what I want,' said Gilbert. Grossmith and Barrington were
both, of course, to go on to become stalwarts of the D'Oyly Carte Company,
creating nearly all of the great comic baritone and bass-baritone roles in the
Savoy Operas.

The Sorcerer opened on 17 November 1877 at the Opéra Comique Theatre just
off the Strand, which Carte had leased as the temporary first home for his new
company. It ran for 178 performances until 24 May 1878. When first performed,
it had no overture: Sullivan simply used the dance movement from his incidental music to Shakespeare's *King Henry VIII*. A proper overture was written for
the opera's revival in 1884, when substantial changes were also made to the
opening of the Second Act.

The Sorcerer remained in the D'Oyly Carte repertoire until June 1939. During
the Second World War the scenery and costumes for the production were destroyed in an air-raid, and the opera was not performed again until 29 March
1971, when a new production by Michael Heyland, designed by Sir Osbert Lancaster, opened at the Palace Theatre, Manchester. It remained intermittently
in the repertoire until the company closed in 1982. Unlike most of the other
lesser-known Savoy Operas, *The Sorcerer* has never received a professional production other than by the D'Oyly Carte, and one hopes that it will be revived
by the new company.

It will certainly be a great pity if it gradually fades away. *The Sorcerer* contains
two of W. S. Gilbert's best-drawn characters, the soulful Dr Daly, who is, incidentally, the only clergyman in the Savoy Operas, and the flashy but ultimately

tragic figure of John Wellington Wells. Sir Arthur Sullivan's music is delightful and guaranteed to weave a magic spell over all those who hear it, if not actually to make them fall instantly in love with their next-door neighbours.

1   *Scene*: The first edition of the libretto gave a rather fuller description of the scene for Act
    I: '*Garden of Sir Marmaduke's Elizabethan Mansion. The end of a large marquee, open, and show-
    ing portion of a table covered with white cloth, on which are joints of meat, tea pots, cups, bread and
    butter, jam, etc. A park in the background, with spire of church seen above the trees.*' Sir Osbert
    Lancaster followed these directions in designing his set for the 1971 D'Oyly Carte
    revival. He also put a few deer into Sir Marmaduke's park.
        The first edition of the libretto also gives the date of the action of *The Sorcerer* as 'the
    present day' and describes the chorus as 'peasantry' rather than 'villagers'.

10 *Pointdextre*: Gilbert deliberately used a heraldic term for the surname of his aristocratic
    heroine. The dexter point is the top right-hand corner of a coat of arms as carried by its
    bearer, i.e. the top left-hand corner as seen by a spectator.
11 *Sangazure*: Another carefully chosen surname – literally translated from the French, *san-
    gazure* means 'blue blood', which, as we know from *Iolanthe* (see the note to Act I, line
    394), is an indication of high or noble birth. Gilbert had used the name before in a short
    story called 'Diamonds' which appeared in *Routledge's Christmas Annual* for 1867. The cen-
    tral figure of the story was the Earl of Sangazure, K.G., the Lord Lieutenant of the
    county of Turniptopshire and honorary colonel of the local yeomanry.
16 *Mrs Partlet*: Yet another name designed to fit the character who bears it. Partlet was
    frequently used as the name for a hen, as in Chaucer's *Nun's Priest's Tale*, and it cannot be
    denied that Mrs Partlet has a certain slightly clucking quality about her.
        A word is needed about her strange-sounding occupation as given in the list of
    Dramatis personæ: a pew-opener went up and down the aisles of churches opening the
    private boxed pews which were rented by wealthy members of the congregation.

ACT I

SCENE. – *Exterior of Sir Marmaduke's Elizabethan Mansion.*

CHORUS OF VILLAGERS.

Ring forth, ye bells,
　　With clarion sound –
Forget your knells,
　　For joys abound.   5
Forget your notes
　　Of mournful lay,
And from your throats
　　Pour joy to-day.

For to-day young Alexis – young Alexis Pointdextre   10
　　Is betrothed to Aline – to Aline Sangazure,
And that pride of his sex is – of his sex is to be next her,
　　At the feast on the green – on the green, oh, be sure!
　　　　Ring forth, ye bells, etc.

                                     (*Exeunt the men.*)   15

(*Enter* MRS PARTLET *with* CONSTANCE, *her daughter.*)

RECITATIVE.

MRS P.   Constance, my daughter, why this strange depression?
　　The village rings with seasonable joy,
　　Because the young and amiable Alexis,
　　Heir to the great Sir Marmaduke Pointdextre,   20
　　Is plighted to Aline, the only daughter
　　Of Annabella, Lady Sangazure.
　　You, you alone are sad and out of spirits;
　　What is the reason? Speak, my daughter, speak!

31 *must ne'er be known*: At this point the first-edition libretto has a continuation of the recitative for Mrs Partlet and her daughter:

> MRS P.   My child, be candid – think not to deceive
>   The eagle-eyed pew opener – You love!
> CON. (*aside*).   How guessed she that, my heart's most cherished secret?
>   (*aloud*).   I *do* love – fondly – madly – hopelessly!

Constance's aria 'When he is here' then follows.

34–49 *When he is here*
Although it was cut from libretti in the 1920s, a second verse to this aria still appears in the current edition of the vocal score and was sung in the last D'Oyly Carte recording of *The Sorcerer* in 1966:

> When I rejoice,
>   He shows no pleasure.
> When I am sad,
>   It grieves him not.
> His solemn voice
>   Has tones I treasure –
> My heart they glad,
>   They solace my unhappy lot!
> When I despond,
>   My woe they chasten –
> When I take heart,
>   My hope they cheer;
> With folly fond
>   To him I hasten –
> From him apart,
>   My life is very sad and drear!

In early productions, the women did not leave the stage until after the end of Constance's aria.

53 *He is here*: In the original libretto, Dr Daly makes his entrance at this point.

CON. Oh, mother, do not ask! If my complexion 25
From red to white should change in quick succession,
And then from white to red, oh, take no notice!
If my poor limbs should tremble with emotion,
Pay no attention, mother – it is nothing!
If long and deep-drawn sighs I chance to utter, 30
Oh, heed them not, their cause must ne'er be known!

(MRS PARTLET *motions to* CHORUS *to leave her with* CONSTANCE.
Exeunt Ladies of CHORUS.)

ARIA – CONSTANCE.

When he is here,
I sigh with pleasure –
When he is gone, 35
I sigh with grief.
My hopeless fear
No soul can measure –
His love alone 40
Can give my aching heart relief!
When he is cold,
I weep for sorrow –
When he is kind,
I weep for joy. 45
My grief untold
Knows no to-morrow –
My woe can find
No hope, no solace, no alloy!

MRS P. Come, tell me all about it! Do not fear – 50
I, too, have loved; but that was long ago!
Who is the object of your young affections?
CON. Hush, mother! He is here! (*Looking off.*)
MRS P. (*amazed*).   Our reverend vicar!
CON. Oh, pity me, my heart is almost broken! 55
MRS P. My child, be comforted. To such an union
I shall not offer any opposition.
Take him – he's yours! May you and he be happy!
CON. But, mother dear, he is not yours to give!
MRS P. That's true indeed! 60
CON.   He might object!
MRS P.   He might.
But come – take heart – I'll probe him on the subject.
Be comforted – leave this affair to me. (*They withdraw.*)

65 *Enter Dr Daly*: Dr Daly is the only clergyman to appear in the Savoy Operas, unless one
counts the ghost bishop in *Ruddigore* or Pooh-Bah, who, among his many other sine-
cures, holds the position of Archbishop of Titipu. There was originally to have been two
rival curates in *Patience*, but Gilbert decided to make them aesthetes instead. Dr Daly is
a saintly figure, and perhaps the most endearing of all the characters in the G. & S. repertoire. The role was created by Rutland Barrington, whose father was a clergyman. A
first-night review commented: 'Mr Barrington is wonderful. He always manages to sing
one-sixteenth of a tone flat; it's so like a vicar'. The last D'Oyly Carte principal to play
Dr Daly was Kenneth Sandford. For many Savoyards, including the present author, it
was undoubtedly his greatest role.

In Michael Heyland's production, Dr Daly made his entrance on an old lady's bicycle.
The idea for this came during rehearsals for the new production in Stratford-on-Avon
in the autumn of 1970. The landlady with whom Jimmy Marsland, then the D'Oyly Carte
staff producer, was staying, Mrs Buckingham, had an ancient bicycle in her shed which
she had been trying to get rid of for some time. Marsland and Peter Riley, then the company's stage manager, took a look at it and decided it would make the perfect 'prop' to accompany Kenneth Sandford's entrance. Mrs Buckingham was more than pleased with
the bunch of flowers she received in return. Her bicycle appeared on stage for more
than ten years and also served as a convenient form of transport for stage-hands sent
out to buy last-minute props. It is now stored, with the rest of the D'Oyly Carte costumes and props, in a warehouse in Camberwell.

After dismounting, Kenneth Sandford would walk over to the veranda in front of Sir
Marmaduke's mansion and pick a flower, which he then smelled soulfully, the scent reminding him of love long ago. At an early performance of the new 1971 production
Dame Bridget D'Oyly Carte was horrified to see that the flower he picked was a clema-
tis – a variety that has no smell. In subsequent performances the dreamy parson always
picked a rose.

75 *Forsaking even military men*: Shades of *Patience*, where the rapturous maidens forsake the
officers of the 35th Dragoon Guards for the subtler attractions of Reginald Bunthorne
and Archibald Grosvenor. The situation described in this song – of the idolization of
young clergymen by their female parishioners – was at one stage to have been the basis
of *Patience* before it was turned into a satire on the aesthetic movement.

84 *gilded dukes and belted earls*: The House of Lords was known as the Gilded Chamber, so
'gilded' is an appropriate adjective to use to denote nobility. In *H.M.S. Pinafore* (Act I,
line 214) Captain Corcoran asks Josephine if her heart is given to 'some gilded lordling'.
The phrase 'belted earl' refers to the belt and spurs with which knights and others were
invested when raised to their titles. In American usage a belted earl is a person who
claims noble birth.

92 *she is nearly eighteen*: At seventeen Constance shares with Elsie Maynard in *The Yeomen of
the Guard* and Rose Maybud in *Ruddigore* the distinction of being the youngest character
in the Savoy Operas whose age is actually mentioned. Patience is eighteen, and Phyllis
in *Iolanthe* nineteen. There is strong evidence for suggesting that Yum-Yum is even
younger, at sixteen (see *The Mikado*, Act I, line 333).

(*Enter* DR DALY. *He is pensive and does not see them.*)   65

RECITATIVE – DR DALY.

The air is charged with amatory numbers –
  Soft madrigals, and dreamy lovers' lays.
Peace, peace, old heart! Why waken from its slumbers
  The aching memory of the old, old days?

BALLAD.

Time was when Love and I were well acquainted.   70
  Time was when we walked ever hand in hand.
A saintly youth, with worldly thought untainted,
  None better-loved than I in all the land!
Time was, when maidens of the noblest station,
  Forsaking even military men,   75
Would gaze upon me, rapt in adoration –
  Ah me, I was a fair young curate then!

Had I a headache? sighed the maids assembled;
  Had I a cold? welled forth the silent tear;
Did I look pale? then half a parish trembled;   80
  And when I coughed all thought the end was near!
I had no care – no jealous doubts hung o'er me –
  For I was loved beyond all other men.
Fled gilded dukes and belted earls before me –
  Ah me, I was a pale young curate then!   85

(*At the conclusion of the ballad,* MRS PARTLET *comes
forward with* CONSTANCE.)

MRS P. Good day, reverend sir.
DR D. Ah, good Mrs Partlet, I am glad to see you. And your little
daughter, Constance! Why, she is quite a little woman, I declare!   90
CON. (*aside*). Oh, mother, I cannot speak to him!
MRS P. Yes, reverend sir, she is nearly eighteen, and as good a girl as
ever stepped. (*Aside to* DR D) Ah, sir, I'm afraid I shall soon lose her!
DR D. (*aside to* MRS P.). Dear me, you pain me very much. Is she
delicate?   95
MRS P. Oh no, sir – I don't mean that – but young girls look to get
married.
DR D. Oh, I take you. To be sure. But there's plenty of time for that. Four
or five years hence, Mrs Partlet, four or five years hence. But when the time
does come, I shall have much pleasure in marrying her myself –   100

123 *puling*: Whining, crying in a querulous or plaintive tone.

125 *Enter Sir Marmaduke and Alexis*: In early productions of *The Sorcerer* Alexis appeared in
the uniform of a Grenadier Guards officer in the First Act, and in regimental mess dress
in the Second. Sir Osbert Lancaster decided, however, that as there was no mention of
Alexis' military career in the opera (the only reference being in the list of *Dramatis personæ*), and as he was not with friends or colleagues from the regiment, he should be given
ordinary civilian clothing. In the 1971 D'Oyly Carte production, Alexis and Sir Marmaduke made their entrance with croquet mallets as though they were in the middle of a
game on the mansion lawns.

135 *May fortune bless you*: The exchange between Dr Daly and Sir Marmaduke, which is carried on to the accompaniment of a stately minuet, is, of course, a skit on the excessively
polite and formal style of conversation associated with the late eighteenth- and early
nineteenth-century aristocracy.

CON. (*aside*). Oh, mother!

DR D. To some strapping young fellow in her own rank of life.

CON. (*in tears*). He does *not* love me!

MRS P. I have often wondered, reverend sir (if you'll excuse the liberty), that *you* have never married.

DR D. (*aside*). Be still, my fluttering heart!

MRS P. A clergyman's wife does so much good in a village. Besides that, you are not as young as you were, and before very long you will want somebody to nurse you, and look after your little comforts.

DR D. Mrs Partlet, there is much truth in what you say. I am indeed getting on in years, and a helpmate would cheer my declining days. Time was when it might have been; but I have left it too long – I am an old fogy, now, am I not, my dear? (*to* CONSTANCE) – a very old fogy, indeed. Ha! ha! No, Mrs Partlet, my mind is quite made up. I shall live and die a solitary old bachelor.

CON. Oh, mother, mother! (*Sobs on* MRS PARTLET's *bosom.*)

MRS P. Come, come, dear one, don't fret. At a more fitting time we will try again – we will try again.

(*Exeunt* MRS PARTLET *and* CONSTANCE.)

DR D. (*looking after them*). Poor little girl! I'm afraid she has something on her mind. She is rather comely. Time was when this old heart would have throbbed in double-time at the sight of such a fairy form! But tush! I am puling! Here comes the young Alexis with his proud and happy father. Let me dry this tell-tale tear!

(*Enter* SIR MARMADUKE *and* ALEXIS.)

RECITATIVE.

DR D.   Sir Marmaduke – my dear young friend, Alexis –
    On this most happy, most auspicious plighting –
    Permit me, as a true old friend, to tender
    My best, my very best congratulations!

SIR M.   Sir, you are most obleeging!

ALEXIS.   Dr Daly,
    My dear old tutor, and my valued pastor,
    I thank you from the bottom of my heart!

(*Spoken through music.*)

DR D.   May fortune bless you! may the middle distance
    Of your young life be pleasant as the foreground –

152   *a reverie*: A fit of abstracted musing, a day-dream.

158   *Helen of Troy*: In Greek legend, the daughter of Zeus and Leda, and wife of Menelaus,
      king of Sparta, whose elopement with Paris brought about the siege and destruction of
      Troy. The exploits of Helen had been made the subject of a comic opera by Jacques Of-
      fenbach, *La Belle Hélène*, first performed in 1865.

163   *the lucid lake of liquid love*: A splendid piece of Gilbertian alliteration to rank with 'To sit
      in solemn silence in a dull, dark dock' in *The Mikado* and 'jerry-jailing, or jailing in joke'
      in *The Yeomen of the Guard*.

The joyous foreground! and, when you have reached it,
May that which now is the far-off horizon
(But which will then become the middle distance),
In fruitful promise be exceeded only   140
By that which will have opened, in the meantime,
Into a new and glorious horizon!

SIR M.   Dear Sir, that is an excellent example
Of an old school of stately compliment
To which I have, through life, been much addicted.   145
Will you obleege me with a copy of it,
In clerkly manuscript, that I myself
May use it on appropriate occasions?

DR D.   Sir, you shall have a fairly-written copy
Ere Sol has sunk into his western slumbers!   150

(*Exit* DR DALY.)

SIR M. (*to* ALEXIS, *who is in a reverie*). Come, come, my son – your *fiancée*
will be here in five minutes. Rouse yourself to receive her.

ALEXIS. Oh, rapture!

SIR M. Yes, you are a fortunate young fellow, and I will not disguise   155
from you that this union with the House of Sangazure realizes my fondest
wishes. Aline is rich, and she comes of a sufficiently old family, for she is the
seven thousand and thirty-seventh in direct descent from Helen of Troy.
True, there was a blot on the escutcheon of that lady – that affair with Paris
– but where is the family, other than my own, in which there is no flaw? You   160
are a lucky fellow, sir – a very lucky fellow!

ALEXIS. Father, I am welling over with limpid joy! No sicklying taint of
sorrow overlies the lucid lake of liquid love, upon which, hand in hand,
Aline and I are to float into eternity!

SIR M. Alexis, I desire that of your love for this young lady you do not   165
speak so openly. You are always singing ballads in praise of her beauty, and
you expect the very menials who wait behind your chair, to chorus your
ecstasies. It is not delicate.

ALEXIS. Father, a man who loves as I love –

SIR M. Pooh pooh, sir! fifty years ago I madly loved your future   170
mother-in-law, the Lady Sangazure, and I have reason to believe that she
returned my love. But were we guilty of the indelicacy of publicly rushing
into each other's arms, exclaiming –

'Oh, my adored one!' 'Beloved boy!'
'Ecstatic rapture!' 'Unmingled joy!'   175

which seems to be the modern fashion of love-making? No! it was 'Madam, I
trust you are in the enjoyment of good health' – 'Sir, you are vastly polite, I
protest I am mighty well' – and so forth. Much more delicate – much more

196–215 *Oh, happy young heart*

This was one of four songs to be encored on the first night of *The Sorcerer*. The others were Sir Marmaduke and Lady Sangazure's duet 'Welcome joy, adieu to sadness', John Wellington Wells's introductory patter song, and the Act II quintet 'I rejoice that it's decided'.

respectful. But see – Aline approaches – let us retire, that she may compose
herself for the interesting ceremony in which she is to play so important a part. 180

(*Exeunt* SIR MARMADUKE *and* ALEXIS.)

(*Enter* ALINE, *on terrace, preceded by Chorus of Women.*)

CHORUS OF WOMEN.

With heart and with voice
   Let us welcome this mating:
To the youth of her choice, 185
   With a heart palpitating,
     Comes the lovely Aline!

May their love never cloy!
   May their bliss be unbounded!
With a halo of joy 190
   May their lives be surrounded!
     Heaven bless our Aline!

RECITATIVE – ALINE.

My kindly friends, I thank you for this greeting,
And as you wish me every earthly joy,
I trust your wishes may have quick fulfilment! 195

ARIA – ALINE.

Oh, happy young heart!
   Comes thy young lord a-wooing
With joy in his eyes,
   And pride in his breast –
Make much of thy prize, 200
   For he is the best
That ever came a-suing.
   Yet – yet we must part,
        Young heart!
   Yet – yet we must part! 205

Oh, merry young heart,
   Bright are the days of thy wooing!
But happier far
   The days untried –
No sorrow can mar, 210
   When Love has tied

216 *Enter Lady Sangazure*: Lady Sangazure, it may interest readers to know, is the only principal part in the Savoy Operas (other than *Trial by Jury*, where there is, of course, no dialogue) which has no spoken words at all.

217–20 *My child, I join in these congratulations*
As originally conceived by Gilbert, there was a duet for Aline and her mother and then a
full-scale aria for the latter between this recitative and the chorus of men which now follows it. The licence copy sent to the Lord Chamberlain prints this duet as following immediately after the recitative:

DUET – ALINE AND LADY S.

ALINE.   Oh, why art thou sad, my mother?
                       All nature is smiling now.
                  In this village there's not another
                       As solemn and glum as thou!
                  It is idle attempt to smother
                       Sad thoughts that wring thy brow!
                  How can I console my mother?
                       Oh answer me quickly – how?
CHORUS.   How can she console her mother?
                       Oh answer her quickly – how?
LADY S.   My daughter, be blithe and merry
                       Nor think of your sad mamma;
                  My grief I will strive to bury
                       And join in the gay ha! ha!
                  My sorrows are selfish very
                       And clash with the loud huzzah!
                  They sadden the hey down derry
                       And temper the tra! la! la!
CHORUS.   Her grief it is certain very
                       Does temper the tra! la! la!

The above duet, which is similar in metre and rhythm to a song, 'Come, bumpers –
aye, ever so many', written for Act II of *The Grand Duke* but also cut, was never performed. However, the solo for Lady Sangazure which followed it in the licence copy was
also printed in the first published edition of the libretto and was probably sung at early
performances. Here it is:

BALLAD – LADY SANGAZURE.

In days gone by, these eyes were bright,
    This bosom fair, these cheeks were rosy,
This faded brow was snowy white,
    These lips were fresh as new-plucked posy;
My girlish love he never guessed,
    Until the day when we were parted;
I treasured it within my heart,
    And lived alone and broken-hearted.

These cheeks are wan with age and care,
    These weary eyes have done their duty,
As white as falling snow my hair,
    And faded all my girlish beauty.
I see my every charm depart;
    But Memory's chain I cannot sever,
For ah, within my poor old heart
    The fire of love burns bright as ever!

235–86 *Welcome joy, adieu to sadness*
The *Observer* review of the first night of *The Sorcerer* commented: 'The duet sung by Sir
Marmaduke and Lady Sangazure in Act I is a masterpiece of construction. The Baronet

The knot there's no undoing.
  Then, never to part,
      Young heart!
  Then, never to part!   215

(*Enter* LADY SANGAZURE.)

RECITATIVE – LADY S.

My child, I join in these congratulations:
Heed not the tear that dims this aged eye!
Old memories crowd around me. Though I sorrow,
'Tis for myself, Aline, and not for thee!   220

(*Enter* ALEXIS, *preceded by Chorus of Men.*)

CHORUS OF MEN.

With heart and with voice
  Let us welcome this mating;
To the maid of his choice,
  With a heart palpitating,   225
    Comes Alexis the brave!

(SIR MARMADUKE *enters.* LADY SANGAZURE *and he exhibit signs of strong emotion at the sight of each other, which they endeavour to repress.* ALEXIS *and* ALINE *rush into each other's arms.*)

RECITATIVE.

ALEXIS.	Oh, my adored one!	230
ALINE.	Beloved boy!	
ALEXIS.	Ecstatic rapture!	
ALINE.	Unmingled joy!	(*They retire up.*)

DUET – SIR MARMADUKE *and* LADY SANGAZURE.

SIR M. (*with stately courtesy*).
    Welcome joy, adieu to sadness!   235
      As Aurora gilds the day,
    So those eyes, twin orbs of gladness,
      Chase the clouds of care away.
    Irresistible incentive
      Bids me humbly kiss your hand;   240

sings to the accompaniment of a gavotte, and suddenly bursts forth into a rapid semi-quaver passage, expressive of his admiration of the lady. She follows his example, and while one sings a slow movement the other sings the *presto* movement alternately.'

236   *Aurora*: The rising light of morning, or dawn. The Roman goddess Aurora set out with her rosy fingers before the sun to proclaim the coming of each new day.

251   *apostrophe like this*: An apostrophe is an exclamatory address in the course of a public speech or a poem to a particular person or object. In *The Mikado* (Act I, line 543) Ko-Ko accuses Pish-Tush of interrupting an apostrophe to matrimony.

263   *more truly knightly*: The first-edition libretto has 'true and knightly' here, as does the Macmillan edition of the Savoy Operas. The licence copy, however, has 'truly knightly', as does the vocal score and other current editions of the libretto.

I'm your servant most attentive –
Most attentive to command!

(*Aside with frantic vehemence*)

Wild with adoration!
Mad with fascination!
To indulge my lamentation   245
    No occasion do I miss!
Goaded to distraction
By maddening inaction,
I find some satisfaction   250
    In apostrophe like this:
    'Sangazure immortal,
        Sangazure divine,
    Welcome to my portal,
        Angel, oh, be mine!'   255

(*Aloud with much ceremony*)

Irresistible incentive
    Bids me humbly kiss your hand;
I'm your servant most attentive –
    Most attentive to command!   260

LADY S.   Sir, I thank you most politely
                    For your graceful courtesee;
                 Compliment more truly knightly
                    Never yet was paid to me!
                 Chivalry is an ingredient   265
                    Sadly lacking in our land –
                 Sir, I am your most obedient,
                    Most obedient to command!

(*Aside with great vehemence*)

Wild with adoration!   270
Mad with fascination!
To indulge my lamentation
    No occasion do I miss!
Goaded to distraction
By maddening inaction,
I find some satisfaction   275
    In apostrophe like this:
    'Marmaduke immortal,
        Marmaduke divine,

287 *the Notary has entered*: The notary is an ancient legal office whose chief function is to draw up, attest and certify deeds and documents. A great many of these functions are now performed by solicitors, and it is likely that the notary employed to draw up the marriage contract between Alexis and Aline came from this branch of the legal profession. In the first-edition libretto, however, the Notary is at this point referred to as the Counsel, and in the licence copy as an equity draftsman, which would suggest that he is a barrister. The business of the signing of the marriage contract is a take-off of similar scenes in grand opera, as for example in the Second Act of Rossini's *The Barber of Seville*, where a notary presides over the marriage of Rosina and Count Almaviva.

296 *I deliver it*: In early editions of the libretto, and still in the Macmillan edition, the chorus 'See they sign, without a quiver, it' precedes the solo lines for Alexis and Aline.

Take me to thy portal,   280
Loved one, oh, be mine!'

(*Aloud with much ceremony*)

Chivalry is an ingredient
Sadly lacking in our land;
Sir, I am your most obedient,   285
Most obedient to command!

(*During this the* NOTARY *has entered, with marriage contract.*)

RECITATIVE – NOTARY.

All is prepared for sealing and for signing,
The contract has been drafted as agreed;
CHORUS.   All is prepared, etc.   290

Approach the table, oh, ye lovers pining,
With hand and seal now execute the deed!
CHORUS.   Approach the table, etc.

(ALEXIS *and* ALINE *advance and sign,* ALEXIS *supported by*
SIR MARMADUKE, ALINE *by her Mother.*)   295

ALEXIS.   I deliver it – I deliver it
As my Act and Deed!

ALINE.   I deliver it – I deliver it
As my Act and Deed!

CHORUS.

See they sign, without a quiver, it –   300
Then to seal proceed.
They deliver it – they deliver it
As their Act and Deed!

With heart and with voice
Let us welcome this mating;   305
Leave them here to rejoice,
With true love palpitating,
Alexis the brave,
And the lovely Aline!

(*Exeunt all but* ALEXIS *and* ALINE.)   310

311 *At last we are alone*: The passage of dialogue which begins here has very close similarities
with Gilbert's earlier story, 'An Elixir of Love', on which *The Sorcerer* was based. The central character in the story, it may be recalled, was the curate of Ploverleigh, the Revd
Stanley Gay, who was engaged to Jessie Lightly, the only daughter of Sir Caractacus
Lightly, a wealthy baronet who had a large house near the village.

> Mr Gay was an aesthetic Leveller. He held that as Love is the great bond of union be-
> tween man and woman, no arbitrary outside obstacle should be allowed to interfere with its
> progress. He did not desire to abolish Rank, but he *did* desire that a mere difference in rank
> should not be an obstacle in the way of making two young people happy...
>
> Stanley Gay and Jessie had for many months given themselves up to the conviction that
> it was their duty to do all in their power to bring their fellow men and women together
> in holy matrimony, without regard to distinctions of age or rank. Stanley gave lectures
> on the subject at mechanics' institutes, and the mechanics were unanimous in their
> approval of his views. He preached his doctrine in workhouses, in beer-shops, and in
> lunatic asylums, and his listeners supported him with enthusiasm. He addressed navvies
> at the roadside on the humanizing advantages that would accrue to them if they married
> refined and wealthy ladies of rank, and not a navvy dissented. In short, he felt more and
> more convinced every day that he had at last discovered the true secret of human happiness.
> Still he had a formidable battle to fight with class prejudice, and he and Jessie pondered
> gravely on the difficulties that were before them, and on the best means of overcoming
> them.
>
> 'It's no use disguising the fact, Jessie,' said Mr Gay, 'that the Countesses won't like it.' And
> little Jessie gave a sigh, and owned that she expected some difficulty with the Countesses.
> 'We must look these things in the face, Jessie, it won't do to ignore them. We have convinced
> the humble mechanics and artisans, but the aristocracy hold aloof.'
>
> 'The working man is the true Intelligence after all,' said Jessie.
>
> 'He is a noble creature when he is quite sober,' said Gay. 'God bless him.'

340–55 *Love feeds on many kinds of food, I know*
Alexis' ballad was written at the last moment. It is not included in the licence copy sent
to the Lord Chamberlain shortly before the first night. There Alexis goes straight from
'He is a noble creature when he is quite sober' (line 336) to 'But I am going to take a desperate step' (line 357).

341, 343 *some for duty... youth and beauty*: One of two instances in *The Sorcerer* of Gilbert's favourite rhyming combination (see the note to *Trial by Jury*, lines 209, 211). The other is in Sir
Marmaduke's verse in the Act II quintet:

> No high-born exacting beauty,
> Blazing like a jewelled sun –
> But a wife who'll do her duty,
> As that duty should be done!

ALEXIS. At last we are alone! My darling, you are now irrevocably betrothed to me. Are you not very, very happy?

ALINE. Oh, Alexis, can you doubt it? Do I not love you beyond all on earth, and am I not beloved in return? Is not true love, faithfully given and faithfully returned, the source of every earthly joy? 315

ALEXIS. Of that there can be no doubt. Oh, that the world could be persuaded of the truth of that maxim! Oh, that the world would break down the artificial barriers of rank, wealth, education, age, beauty, habits, taste, and temper, and recognize the glorious principle, that in marriage alone is to be found the panacea for every ill! 320

ALINE. Continue to preach that sweet doctrine, and you will succeed, oh, evangel of true happiness!

ALEXIS. I hope so, but as yet the cause progresses but slowly. Still I have made some converts to the principle, that men and women should be coupled in matrimony without distinction of rank. I have lectured on the 325 subject at Mechanics' Institutes, and the mechanics were unanimous in favour of my views. I have preached in workhouses, beershops, and Lunatic Asylums, and I have been received with enthusiasm. I have addressed navvies on the advantages that would accrue to them if they married wealthy ladies of rank, and not a navvy dissented! 330

ALINE. Noble fellows! And yet there are those who hold that the uneducated classes are not open to argument! And what do the countesses say?

ALEXIS. Why, at present, it can't be denied, the aristocracy hold aloof.

ALINE. Ah, the working man is the true Intelligence after all! 335

ALEXIS. He is a noble creature when he is quite sober. Yes, Aline, true happiness comes of true love, and true love should be independent of external influences. It should live upon itself and by itself – in itself love should live for love alone!

BALLAD – ALEXIS.

Love feeds on many kinds of food, I know, 340
    Some love for rank, and some for duty:
Some give their hearts away for empty show,
    And others love for youth and beauty.
To love for money all the world is prone:
    Some love themselves, and live all lonely: 345
Give me the love that loves for love alone –
    I love that love – I love it only!

What man for any other joy can thirst,
    Whose loving wife adores him duly?
Want, misery, and care may do their worst, 350
    If loving woman loves you truly.

359 *St Mary Axe*: The street, which is pronounced, as it is later spelt in John Wellington Wells's patter song, 'Simmery Axe', runs between Leadenhall Street and Houndsditch in the City of London. In 'An Elixir of Love' Stanley Gay and Jessie Lightly got their magic potion from the firm of Baylis and Culpepper, magicians, in St Martin's Lane.

362–3 *within twelve hours*: Gilbert originally decided that Wells's love philtre should take effect within half an hour. In early editions of the libretto, and in early productions, the time supposed to elapse between Acts I and II was just half an hour. It was later changed to twelve hours.

366 *useful thing in a house*: The licence copy and first edition at this point have the additional line for Aline: 'Quite indispensable in the present state of Thames water'. Evidently the river had been cleaned up by the time of the opera's 1884 revival, as the phrase was dropped then.

369–70 *I said a philtre*: This exchange, which anticipates the famous 'orphan'/'often' misunderstanding in *The Pirates of Penzance* (Act I, lines 526–46), was originally longer. After Alexis' line 'I said a philtre', Aline continued: 'So did I, dear. *I* said a filter.' Alexis then responded: 'No dear, you said a filter. I don't mean a filter – I mean a philtre, – ph, you know.' Aline then came in with her line 'You don't mean a love potion?'

381 *Hercules*: In Greek mythology Hercules is, of course, the hero of superhuman strength who was rewarded by Zeus for his twelve great labours with the post of porter in heaven. He is always represented as brawny, muscular and of huge proportions. His namesake in *The Sorcerer* is tiny and weedy. The part is normally played by a small boy. Sir Henry Lytton, who was later to become principal comedian in the D'Oyly Carte Company, made his Gilbert and Sullivan debut in the part in a provincial company in the 1880s.

382 *Enter a Page from tent*: An undated D'Oyly Carte Company prompt-book has the following stage direction at this point: 'Enter Page with a pot of jam which he is trying to conceal by holding it to his left side. There is jam on his mouth and as he goes off he helps himself to more in view of the audience.'

A lover's thoughts are ever with his own –
None truly loved is ever lonely:
Give me the love that loves for love alone –
I love that love – I love it only!   355

ALINE. Oh, Alexis, those are noble principles!

ALEXIS. Yes, Aline, and I am going to take a desperate step in support of them. Have you ever heard of the firm of J. W. Wells & Co., the old-established Family Sorcerers in St Mary Axe?

ALINE. I have seen their advertisement.   360

ALEXIS. They have invented a philtre, which, if report may be believed, is simply infallible. I intend to distribute it through the village, and within twelve hours of my doing so there will not be an adult in the place who will not have learnt the secret of pure and lasting happiness. What do you say to that?   365

ALINE. Well, dear, of course a filter is a very useful thing in a house; but still I don't quite see that it is the sort of thing that places its possessor on the very pinnacle of earthly joy.

ALEXIS. Aline, you misunderstand me. I didn't say a filter – I said a philtre.   370

ALINE (*alarmed*). You don't mean a love-potion?

ALEXIS. On the contrary – I *do* mean a love-potion.

ALINE. Oh, Alexis! I don't think it would be right. I don't indeed. And then – a real magician! Oh, it would be downright wicked.

ALEXIS. Aline, is it, or is it not, a laudable object to steep the whole   375
village up to its lips in love, and to couple them in matrimony without distinction of age, rank, or fortune?

ALINE. Unquestionably, but –

ALEXIS. Then unpleasant as it must be to have recourse to supernatural aid, I must nevertheless pocket my aversion, in deference to the great and   380
good end I have in view. (*Calling*) Hercules.

(Enter a Page from tent.)

PAGE. Yes, sir.

ALEXIS. Is Mr Wells there?

PAGE. He's in the tent, sir – refreshing.   385

ALEXIS. Ask him to be so good as to step this way.

PAGE. Yes, sir.   (*Exit Page.*)

ALINE. Oh, but, Alexis! A real Sorcerer! Oh, I shall be frightened to death!

ALEXIS. I trust my Aline will not yield to fear while the strong right   390
arm of her Alexis is here to protect her.

ALINE. It's nonsense, dear, to talk of your protecting me with your strong

398 *Enter Mr Wells*: The D'Oyly Carte stage direction at this point reads: 'Wells affects to be finishing a meal and cannot speak until he empties his mouth. Business of taking off his gloves and blowing them out.'

John Wellington Wells is one of the great comic roles in the Savoy Operas and can be played in a number of different ways. George Grossmith appeared in frock coat and top hat. In Michael Heyland's D'Oyly Carte production, however, Wells was played as a sharp East End 'spiv' dressed in frock coat and stylish grey bowler hat.

401 *Yes, sir, we practise Necromancy in all its branches*: For this passage of dialogue Gilbert borrowed from his earlier story. In 'An Elixir of Love' he had written:

> The firm of Baylis and Culpepper stood at the very head of the London family magicians …They had a special reputation for a class of serviceable family nativity… the establishment at St Martin's Lane was also a 'Noted House for Amulets,' and if you wanted a neat, well-finished divining-rod, I don't know any place to which I would sooner recommend you. Their curses at a shilling per dozen were the cheapest things in the trade, and they sold thousands of them in the course of the year. Their blessings – also very cheap indeed, and quite effective – were not much asked for. 'We always keep a few on hand as curiosities and for completeness, but we don't sell two in the twelvemonth,' said Mr Baylis. 'A gentleman bought one last week to send to his mother-in-law, but it turned out that he was afflicted in the head, and the persons who had charge of him declined to pay for it, and it's been returned to us. But the sale of penny curses, especially on Saturday nights, is tremendous. We can't turn 'em out fast enough.'

403 *cast… a nativity*: Draw up a horoscope based on the subject's date and time of birth.

404 *Abudah chests*: Abudah was a merchant in Baghdad, haunted every night by an old hag who appeared from a little box in his chamber and told him to seek out the talisman or Oromanes. The story of Abudah was included in *Tales of the Genii*, a collection of pseudo-Persian fairy tales by James Ridley.

408 *a rise in Unified*: A rise in the value of Government stock. In the first-night version Wells spoke of 'a rise in Turkish stock', a topical reference at a time when Turkey was borrowing heavily from Western Europe.

415-93 *My name is John Wellington Wells*

This is perhaps the greatest tongue-twister in the entire patter-song repertoire. John Reed, the D'Oyly Carte principal comedian from 1959 to 1979, described it in an interview with the *Washington Post* in 1978 as 'a killer. Just a list of words. Now that is difficult. Nothing leads you to the next one. You could put them in any shape or form if you lost the rhythm.'

When Sullivan was auditioning George Grossmith, he sang through this number and then turned to the potential new recruit. 'You can do that?' he asked him. Grossmith nodded and replied, 'Yes, I think I can do that'. 'Very well,' said Sullivan, 'if you can do that, you can do the rest'.

421 *melt a rich uncle in wax*: This is, of course, a reference to the old superstition that by melting down a wax model, you could hasten someone's death.

423 *Djinn*: In Arabian mythology a spirit of supernatural powers. The word is more commonly found as 'genie'.

424 *Number seventy, Simmery Axe*: A long correspondence filled the pages of the Gilbert and Sullivan Society's journal some years ago as to whether such an address did, in fact, exist. It seems that there was a 70 St Mary Axe, but the building which had that number was demolished.

425 *a first-rate assortment*: In the first edition of the libretto, in the Macmillan edition, and in the Oxford University Press World's Classics edition of the Savoy Operas, this phrase appears as 'a first-class assortment'. 'First-rate', however, appears in the licence copy, the vocal score and other recent editions of the libretto and was sung in D'Oyly Carte performances.

right arm, in face of the fact that this Family Sorcerer could change me into a guinea-pig before you could turn round.

ALEXIS. He *could* change you into a guinea-pig, no doubt, but it is most unlikely that he would take such a liberty. It's a most respectable firm, and I am sure he would never be guilty of so untradesmanlike an act.

(*Enter* MR WELLS *from tent.*)

MR W. Good day, sir. (ALINE *much terrified.*)

ALEXIS. Good day – I believe you are a Sorcerer.

MR W. Yes, sir, we practise Necromancy in all its branches. We've a choice assortment of wishing-caps, divining-rods, amulets, charms, and counter-charms. We can cast you a nativity at a low figure, and we have a horoscope at three-and-six that we can guarantee. Our Abudah chests, each containing a patent Hag who comes out and prophesies disasters, with spring complete, are strongly recommended. Our Aladdin lamps are very chaste, and our Prophetic Tablets, foretelling everything – from a change of Ministry down to a rise in Unified – are much enquired for. Our penny Curse – one of the cheapest things in the trade – is considered infallible. We have some very superior Blessings, too, but they're very little asked for. We've only sold one since Christmas – to a gentleman who bought it to send to his mother-in-law – but it turned out that he was afflicted in the head, and it's been returned on our hands. But our sale of penny Curses, especially on Saturday nights, is tremendous. We can't turn 'em out fast enough.

SONG – MR WELLS.

My name is John Wellington Wells,
I'm a dealer in magic and spells,
    In blessings and curses
    And ever-filled purses,
In prophecies, witches, and knells.

If you want a proud foe to 'make tracks' –
If you'd melt a rich uncle in wax –
    You've but to look in
    On our resident Djinn,
Number seventy, Simmery Axe!

We've a first-rate assortment of magic;
    And for raising a posthumous shade
With effects that are comic or tragic,
    There's no cheaper house in the trade.
Love-philtre – we've quantities of it;
    And for knowledge if any one burns,

395

400

405

410

415

420

425

430

431 *We're keeping a very small prophet*: In early editions this line began 'We keep an extremely small prophet'.

441 *He has answers oracular*: In early editions of the libretto, and in the current Macmillan version, lines 441–4 appear in the following order:

> Mirrors so magical,
> Tetrapods tragical,
> Bogies spectacular,
> Answers oracular,

Both the Macmillan and World's Classics editions print the word 'With' before 'mirrors so magical'. No doubt these lines were rearranged to make them easier to sing – it makes no difference to the sense in which order they come.

443 *Tetrapods*: Verses of four metrical feet, commonly used by Greek tragedians.

455–6 *hosts/Of ghosts*: Shades (pardon the pun) of *Ruddigore*! There, of course, we get plenty of gaunt and grisly spectres, though Gilbert resists the temptation to repeat the rhymes he has used in this song. In Sir Roderic Murgatroyd's song 'When the night wind howls', 'shrouds' are rhymed with 'clouds', not 'crowds' as here, and 'ghost' with 'toast' rather than 'host'.

We're keeping a very small prophet, a prophet
Who brings us unbounded returns:

    For he can prophesy
    With a wink *of* his eye,
    Peep with security   435
    Into futurity,
    Sum up your history,
    Clear up a mystery,
    Humour proclivity
    For a nativity – for a nativity;   440
    He has answers oracular,
    Bogies spectacular,
    Tetrapods tragical,
    Mirrors so magical,
    Facts astronomical,   445
    Solemn or comical,
    And, if you want it, he
    Makes a reduction on taking a quantity!

          Oh!
If any one anything lacks,   450
He'll find it all ready in stacks,
    If he'll only look in
    On the resident Djinn,
Number seventy, Simmery Axe!

    He can raise you hosts   455
          Of ghosts,
And that without reflectors;
    And creepy things
          With wings,
And gaunt and grisly spectres.   460
    He can fill you crowds
          Of shrouds,
And horrify you vastly;
    He can rack your brains
          With chains,   465
And gibberings grim and ghastly!

    Then, if you plan it, he
    Changes organity,
    With an urbanity,
    Full of Satanity,   470

477 *'Lectro-biology*: Electro-biology was an original branch of the study of electricity which dealt with electrical phenomena in living organisms. By the middle of the nineteenth century the phrase had come to be used for a form of hypnosis practised by popular entertainers and based on the so-called principles of animal magnetism.

478 *nosology*: The study of the classification of diseases. An even more extensive list of -ologies, which includes both ' 'lectro-biology' and nosology, appears in Gilbert's Bab Ballad 'The Student':

$$
\left.\begin{array}{l}
\text{I ask an ap-} \\
\text{Is it zo-} \\
\text{Is it conch-} \\
\text{Is it ge-} \\
\text{'Lectro-bi-} \\
\text{Meteor-} \\
\text{Is it nos-} \\
\text{Or etym-} \\
\text{P'raps it's myth-} \\
\text{Is it the-} \\
\text{Palaeont-} \\
\text{Or archae-}
\end{array}\right\} \text{ology?}
$$

495 *a Patent Oxy-Hydrogen Love-at-first-sight Philtre*: This was also the leading article of Messrs Baylis and Culpepper in 'An Elixir of Love'. They sold it at 1s. 1½d. and 2s. 3d., and demand for it was strong enough to keep the firm going, had all its other products ceased selling.

507 *In buying a quantity*: This passage was taken almost word for word from Gilbert's earlier story, where Mr Culpepper tells Stanley Gay and Jessie Lightly: 'In purchasing a large quantity, sir, we would strongly advise you taking it in the wood, and drawing it off as you happen to want it. We have it in four-and-a-half and nine-gallon casks, and we deduct ten per cent for cash payments.'

Vexes humanity
With an inanity
Fatal to vanity –
Driving your foes to the verge of insanity!

Barring tautology,   475
In demonology,
'Lectro-biology,
Mystic nosology,
Spirit philology,
High-class astrology,   480
Such is his knowledge, he
Isn't the man to require an apology!

Oh!
My name is John Wellington Wells,
I'm a dealer in magic and spells,   485
    In blessings and curses
    And ever-filled purses,
In prophecies, witches, and knells.

And if any one anything lacks,
He'll find it all ready in stacks,   490
    If he'll only look in
    On the resident Djinn,
Number seventy, Simmery Axe!

ALEXIS. I have sent for you to consult you on a very important matter. I
believe you advertise a Patent Oxy-Hydrogen Love-at-first-sight Philtre?   495
MR W. Sir, it is our leading article. (*Producing a phial.*)
ALEXIS. Now I want to know if you can confidently guarantee it as
possessing all the qualities you claim for it in your advertisement?
MR W. Sir, we are not in the habit of puffing our goods. Ours is an old-
established house with a large family connection, and every assurance held   500
out in the advertisement is fully realized. (*Hurt.*)
ALINE (*aside*). Oh, Alexis, don't offend him! He'll change us into
something dreadful – I know he will!
ALEXIS. I am anxious from purely philanthropical motives to distribute
this philtre, secretly, among the inhabitants of this village. I shall of course 505
require a quantity. How do you sell it?
MR W. In buying a quantity, sir, we should strongly advise your taking
it in the wood, and drawing it off as you happen to want it. We have it in
four-and-a-half and nine gallon casks – also in pipes and hogsheads for
laying down, and we deduct 10 per cent for prompt cash.   510

511–12   *the Army and Navy Stores*: A leading London department store, situated in Victoria Street
between Westminster Abbey and Victoria Station. Lines 511–13 were not in the first edition of the libretto and were added by Gilbert at the time of the 1884 revival, possibly in
response to an ad-lib 'gag' by one of the company. In the original libretto, after 'prompt
cash' Aline had the line 'Oh, Alexis, surely you don't want to lay any down!'

514–15   *Go and fetch the tea-pot*: In 'An Elixir of Love' Stanley Gay used a rather more potent medium than tea in which to mix his love potion and distribute it to his 140 parishioners.
He invented a somewhat implausible story that a widowed aunt who lived in Montilla
had been compelled to take a large quantity of sherry from a bankrupt wine merchant
in payment for a year's rent of her second-floor flat. Gay claimed that he had undertaken
to sell the sherry in Ploverleigh and so he announced that he was distributing sample
bottles (into which, of course, he had poured the potion) to all the villagers.

537–93   *Sprites of earth and air*
The incantation scene in *The Sorcerer* is a satire on the scene in Weber's opera *Der
Freischütz* in which Max, a young huntsman, meets Caspar, the servant of the Devil, in
the Wolf's Glen at midnight to witness the forging of seven magic bullets by Zamiel, a
demon.

ALEXIS. I should mention that I am a Member of the Army and Navy Stores.

MR W. In that case we deduct 25 per cent.

ALEXIS. Aline, the villagers will assemble to carouse in a few minutes. Go and fetch the tea-pot.   515

ALINE. But, Alexis –

ALEXIS. My dear, you must obey me, if you please. Go and fetch the tea-pot.

ALINE (*going*). I'm sure Dr Daly would disapprove of it!

                                                        (*Exit* ALINE.)   520

ALEXIS. And how soon does it take effect?

MR W. In twelve hours. Whoever drinks of it loses consciousness for that period, and on waking falls in love, as a matter of course, with the first lady he meets who has also tasted it, and his affection is at once returned. One trial will prove the fact.   525

(*Enter* ALINE *with large tea-pot.*)

ALEXIS. Good: then, Mr Wells, I shall feel obliged if you will at once pour as much philtre into this tea-pot as will suffice to affect the whole village.

ALINE. But bless me, Alexis, many of the villagers are married people!   530

MR W. Madam, this philtre is compounded on the strictest principles. On married people it has no effect whatever. But are you quite sure that you have nerve enough to carry you through the fearful ordeal?

ALEXIS. In the good cause I fear nothing.

MR W. Very good, then, we will proceed at once to the Incantation.   535

(*The stage grows dark.*)

INCANTATION.

MR W.	Sprites of earth and air –
	Fiends of flame and fire –
	Demon souls,
	Come here in shoals,
	This dreadful deed inspire!
	Appear, appear, appear.
MALE VOICES.	Good master, we are here!
MR W.	Noisome hags of night –
	Imps of deadly shade –
	Pallid ghosts,
	Arise in hosts,

540

545

And lend me all your aid.
    Appear, appear, appear!
FEMALE VOICES.   Good master, we are here! 550

ALEXIS (*aside*).   Hark, hark, they assemble,
    These fiends of the night!

ALINE (*aside*).   Oh, Alexis, I tremble,
    Seek safety in flight!

ARIA – ALINE.

Let us fly to a far-off land, 555
    Where peace and plenty dwell –
Where the sigh of the silver strand
    Is echoed in every shell.
To the joy that land will give,
    On the wings of Love we'll fly; 560
In innocence there to live –
    In innocence there to die!

CHORUS OF SPIRITS.

Too late – too late,
    It may not be!
That happy fate
    Is not for thee! 565

ALEXIS, ALINE, *and* MR WELLS.

Too late – too late,
    That may not be!
That happy fate
    Is not for { me!
                 { thee! 570

MR WELLS.

Now, shrivelled hags, with poison bags,
    Discharge your loathsome loads!
Spit flame and fire, unholy choir!
    Belch forth your venom, toads!
Ye demons fell, with yelp and yell, 575
    Shed curses far afield –
Ye fiends of night, your filthy blight
    In noisome plenty yield!

579   *pouring phial into tea-pot – flash*: This is the only real bit of pyrotechnics in the Savoy Operas and is something of a stage manager's nightmare. For Michael Heyland's D'Oyly
Carte production a special tea-pot was constructed with a false bottom concealing batteries and a fuse which triggered off a charge of flash powder. Wells operated the device
by flicking a switch on the tea-pot handle. He wore a witch's pointed hat which was also
wired up with a charge. Peter Riley can only recall one near-disaster in all his time as
stage manager when the hat caught fire and had to be speedily removed by a stage-hand
from the head of the oblivious J. W. Wells.

On the first night, Grossmith delighted the Opéra Comique audience during this
scene by shuffling round the stage clutching his tea-pot and imitating the hissing funnel
of a steam train. This 'locomotive gag', or 'tea-pot dance', as it came to be known, had
never been rehearsed and was one of the very few unauthorized bits of business which
Grossmith introduced into his stage performances in the Savoy Operas. Gilbert readily
approved it.

594   *Mr Wells beckons villagers*: The original stage direction in the first libretto continued at
this point: '*Enter villagers and all the* dramatis personæ, *dancing joyously*. SIR
MARMADUKE *enters with* LADY SANGAZURE. VICAR *enters, absorbed in thought. He is
followed by* CONSTANCE. COUNSEL *enters, followed by* MRS PARTLET. MRS PART-
LET & MR WELLS *distribute tea cups.*'

604   *Sally Lunn*: A plain, light tea-cake, which was usually split, toasted and served with jam.
It was named after an eighteenth-century street vendor in Bath. The Sally Lunn makes
two appearances in Gilbert's *Bab Ballads*. In 'Pantomimic Presentiments' it is referred to
as 'the fine old crusted Sally', while the hero of 'Jester James' breakfasts off 'rolls and
Sally Lunns'.

608   *Be happy all*: In the licence copy this is 'Be seated all'.

MR WELLS (*pouring phial into tea-pot – flash*).
>Number One!
CHORUS.   It is done!
MR W. (*same business*).   Number Two! (*flash*).   580
CHORUS.   One too few!
MR W. (*same business*).   Number Three! (*flash*).
CHORUS.   Set us free!

> Set us free – our work is done.
>   Ha! ha! ha!   585
> Set us free – our course is run!
>   Ha! ha! ha!

ALINE *and* ALEXIS (*aside*).

> Let us fly to a far-off land,
>   Where peace and plenty dwell –
> Where the sigh of the silver strand   590
>   Is echoed in every shell.

CHORUS OF FIENDS.

> Ha! ha! ha! ha! ha! ha! ha! ha! ha! ha!

(*Stage grows light.* MR WELLS *beckons villagers. Enter villagers and all the dramatis personæ, dancing joyously.* MRS PARTLET *and* MR WELLS *then*   595 *distribute tea-cups.*)

CHORUS.

> Now to the banquet we press;
>   Now for the eggs and the ham;
> Now for the mustard and cress,
>   Now for the strawberry jam!   600
> Now for the tea of our host,
>   Now for the rollicking bun,
> Now for the muffin and toast,
>   And now for the gay Sally Lunn!

WOMEN.   The eggs and the ham, and the strawberry jam!   605
MEN.   The rollicking bun, and the gay Sally Lunn!
> The rollicking, rollicking bun!

RECITATIVE – SIR MARMADUKE.

> Be happy all – the feast is spread before ye;
>   Fear nothing, but enjoy yourselves, I pray!

612–45   *TEA-CUP BRINDISI*

Brindisi is an Italian word for a toast, or health, drunk at some special occasion. It is used in this context to mean a drinking song, of the kind almost invariably found in Italian grand operas. The special feature of this particular toast, of course, is that it is entirely non-alcoholic. In calling it the 'Tea-Cup Brindisi', Gilbert may well have been having a quiet dig at the Victorian temperance movement with its rousing choruses extolling the virtues of tea and water. There is a brindisi of a more conventional kind in the original version of Act II of *The Grand Duke*, where the drink is champagne to celebrate the wedding of the Baroness von Krakenfeldt and the comedian Ludwig:

> So bumpers – aye, ever so many –
> And then, if you will, many more!
> This wine doesn't cost us a penny.
> Though it's Pommery, seventy-four!

621   *a jorum of tea*: Like *brindisi*, jorums are more usually associated with alcoholic liquor. They are large bowls of the kind used for serving punch or fruit cups. The name is thought to derive from King Joram who is described in the Bible (2 Samuel 8.10) as bringing 'vessels of silver, and vessels of gold, and vessels of brass'.

623   *A pretty stiff jorum of tea*: The first-edition libretto has the following stage direction at this point: 'DR DALY *places tea pot on tray held by* CONSTANCE. *He covers it with the cosy. She takes tray into the house.*'

Eat, aye, and drink – be merry, I implore ye,   610
   For once let thoughtless Folly rule the day.

TEA-CUP BRINDISI, 1st Verse – SIR M.

Eat, drink, and be gay,
   Banish all worry and sorrow,
Laugh gaily to-day,
   Weep, if you're sorry, to-morrow!   615
Come, pass the cup round –
   I will go bail for the liquor;
It's strong, I'll be bound,
   For it was brewed by the vicar!

CHORUS.

None so knowing as he   620
At brewing a jorum of tea,
   Ha! ha!
A pretty stiff jorum of tea.

TRIO – MR WELLS, ALINE, *and* ALEXIS (*aside*).

See – see – they drink –
   All thought unheeding,   625
The tea-cups clink,
   They are exceeding!
Their hearts will melt
   In half-an-hour –
Then will be felt   630
   The potion's power!

(*During this verse* CONSTANCE *has brought a small tea-pot, kettle, caddy, and
cosy to* DR DALY. *He makes tea scientifically.*)

BRINDISI, 2nd Verse – DR DALY (*with the tea-pot*).

Pain, trouble, and care,
   Misery, heart-ache, and worry,   635
Quick, out of your lair!
   Get you all gone in a hurry!
Toil, sorrow, and plot,
   Fly away quicker and quicker –
Three spoons to the pot –   640
   That is the brew of your vicar!

663 *The company will draw*: In early editions this line was 'Society will draw'.

664 *Those who have partaken of the philtre*: In the first edition of the libretto this stage direction
     read: '*Those who have partaken of the philtre struggle against its effects, and resume the Brindisi
     with a violent effort.*' There then followed a reprise of the first verse of the Tea-Cup Brin-
     disi. This was sung during the initial run at the Opéra Comique but cut for the 1884
     revival at the Savoy, when the present ending to Act I, with the company falling insensi-
     ble on the stage, was substituted.

CHORUS.

None so cunning as he
At brewing a jorum of tea,
   Ha! ha!
A pretty stiff jorum of tea! 645

ENSEMBLE – ALEXIS *and* ALINE (*aside*).

Oh love, true love – unworldly, abiding!
   Source of all pleasure – true fountain of joy, –
Oh love, true love – divinely confiding,
   Exquisite treasure that knows no alloy!
Oh love, true love, rich harvest of gladness, 650
   Peace-bearing tillage – great garner of bliss, –
Oh love, true love, look down on our sadness –
   Dwell in this village – oh, hear us in this!

(*It becomes evident by the strange conduct of the characters that the charm is working.
All rub their eyes, and stagger about the stage as if under the influence of a narcotic.*) 655

TUTTI (*aside*).	ALEXIS, MR WELLS, *and* ALINE (*aside*).
Oh, marvellous illusion!	A marvellous illusion!
Oh, terrible surprise!	A terrible surprise
What is this strange confusion	Excites a strange confusion
That veils my aching eyes?	Within their aching eyes –
I must regain my senses,	They must regain their senses, 660
Restoring Reason's law,	Restoring Reason's law,
Or fearful inferences	Or fearful inferences
The company will draw!	The company will draw!

(*Those who have partaken of the philtre struggle in vain against its effects, and, at
the end of the chorus, fall insensible on the stage.*) 665

END OF ACT I

1–4 *Scene*: As originally conceived and performed, Act II of *The Sorcerer* was set in the village
of Ploverleigh, with the action taking place half an hour after Act I, and with the villagers
entering to sing an opening chorus. The licence copy and first published libretto had
the following description of the scene: '*Market Place in the village. In centre a market cross or
drinking fountain. Enter* PEASANTS *dancing, coupled two and two: an old man with a young
girl, then an old woman with a young man, then other ill-assorted couples.*'

4 *a dark lantern*: A lantern with a sliding shutter of a kind often used by burglars. It is one of
the implements which Samuel distributes to his fellow pirates before their attack on Tremorden Castle in Act II of *The Pirates of Penzance*.

5–30 *'Tis twelve, I think*
In the first version of *The Sorcerer*, performed in 1877–8, there was no trio for Alexis,
Aline and Mr Wells at the beginning of Act II. Nor did the villagers have their chorus
'Why, where be oi, and what be oi a doin''. Instead there was this much shorter opening
chorus, which led straight on to Constance's aria 'Dear friends, take pity on my lot':

OPENING CHORUS.

> Happy are we in our loving frivolity,
> Happy and jolly as people of quality;
> Love is the source of all joy to humanity,
> Money, position, and rank are a vanity;
> Year after year we've been waiting and tarrying,
> Without ever dreaming of loving and marrying.
> Though we've been hitherto deaf, dumb, and blind to it,
> It's pleasant enough when you've made up your mind to it.

When the opera was revived in 1884, this chorus was cut and the trio and chorus
which now form lines 5–58 were added.

17 *A Baronet and K.C.B.*: Baronets, in whose ranks according to the list of *Dramatis personæ*
we should number Sir Marmaduke Pointdextre, are members of the lowest hereditary
titled order, which was instituted by James I in the early seventeenth century. The Murgatroyds in *Ruddigore* are baronets, and bad baronets at that. Indeed, in the opinion
of Rose Maybud, 'All baronets are bad'. Obtaining baronetcies for M.P.s is one of
the many tasks that the Duke and Duchess of Plaza-Toro will happily perform for the
appropriate fee (*The Gondoliers*, Act II, line 610).
  K.C.B. stands for Knight Commander of the Bath. This is the second class of the
Order of the Bath, the first being Grand Cross of the Bath (G.C.B.) and the third Companion of the Bath (C.B.). There are two other K.C.B.s in the Savoy Operas: Sir Joseph
Porter in *H.M.S. Pinafore* and Captain Sir Edward Corcoran in *Utopia Limited*. Neither of
them is a baronet, however. As both a baronet and a K.C.B., Sir Marmaduke has the
right to be called 'Sir' twice over, as it were.

18 *A Doctor of Divinity*: The holder of an advanced degree in theology. It would be comparatively rare for an ordinary country parson to be a doctor of divinity, but Gilbert's village
priests are obviously a scholarly lot. According to the pirates of Penzance (*Pirates*, Act I,
line 432), another such well-qualified divine lives in the vicinity of their remote seaside
lair.

19 *that respectable Q.C.*: As we have already noted (Act I, line 287), a notary is nearly always a
solicitor, and it is highly unlikely that a barrister would officiate at the signing of a marriage contract. A solicitor, however, cannot be a QC. The initials stand for Queen's
Counsel and apply to those senior barristers appointed by the Crown on the nomination
of the Lord Chancellor and often known as 'silks' because of their gowns. In the first edition of the libretto, it may be remembered, the Notary was referred to in Act I as the
Counsel and could therefore be a QC.

ACT II

SCENE. – *Exterior of* SIR MARMADUKE'S *mansion by moonlight. All the peasantry are discovered asleep on the ground, as at the end of Act I. Enter* MR WELLS, *on tiptoe, followed by* ALEXIS *and* ALINE. MR WELLS *carries a dark lantern.*

TRIO – ALEXIS, ALINE, *and* MR WELLS.

'Tis twelve, I think,   5
   And at this mystic hour
The magic drink
   Should manifest its power.
Oh, slumbering forms,
   How little have ye guessed   10
The fire that warms
   Each apathetic breast!

ALEXIS. But stay, my father is not here!

ALINE. And pray where is my mother dear?

MR WELLS. I did not think it meet to see   15
A dame of lengthy pedigree,
A Baronet and K.C.B.,
A Doctor of Divinity,
And that respectable Q.C.,
All fast asleep, al-fresco-ly,   20
And so I had them carried home
And put to bed respectably!
I trust my conduct earns your approbation.

ALEXIS. Sir, you have acted with discrimination,
And shown more delicate appreciation   25
Than we expect in persons of your station.

49   *Eh, but oi du loike you*: This rough approximation of a West Country accent is the only hint
we are given by Gilbert as to the part of the country in which *The Sorcerer* is set. In his
original story 'An Elixir of Love', however, he tells us that Ploverleigh is 'a picturesque
little village in Dorsetshire, ten miles from anywhere'. We may reasonably surmise then
that we are in Thomas Hardy country, and judging by the thickness of the accents in
this chorus, not far from the Devon border.

MR WELLS.   But soft – they waken, one by one –
     The spell has worked – the deed is done!
     I would suggest that we retire
     While Love, the Housemaid, lights her kitchen fire!   30

   (*Exeunt* MR WELLS, ALEXIS, *and* ALINE, *on tiptoe, as the villagers
     stretch their arms, yawn, rub their eyes, and sit up.*)

MEN.   Why, where be oi, and what be oi a doin',
     A sleepin' out, just when the dews du rise?
GIRLS. Why, that's the very way your health to ruin,   35
     And don't seem quite respectable likewise!
MEN (*staring at girls*). Eh, that's you!
      Only think o' that now!
GIRLS (*coyly*). What may you be at, now?
      Tell me, du!
MEN (*admiringly*). Eh, what a nose,   40
     And eh, what eyes, miss!
     Lips like a rose,
     And cheeks likewise, miss!
GIRLS (*coyly*). Oi tell you true,
     Which I've never done, sir,   45
     Oi like you
     As I never loiked none, sir!
ALL.   Eh, but oi du loike you!

MEN.   If you'll marry me, I'll dig for you and
     rake for you!
GIRLS. If you'll marry me, I'll scrub for you and   50
     bake for you!
MEN.   If you'll marry me, all others I'll forsake
     for you!
ALL.   All this will I du, if you'll marry me!

GIRLS. If you'll marry me, I'll cook for you and
     brew for you!
MEN.   If you'll marry me, I've guineas not a few
     for you!
GIRLS. If you'll marry me, I'll take you in and du   55
     for you!
ALL.   All this will I du, if you'll marry me!
     Eh, but oi du loike you!

64 *reverend rector*: Dr Daly has already informed us (Act I, line 641) that he is Vicar of Plover-
    leigh, and that is, indeed, how he appears in the list of *Dramatis personæ*. Now Constance
    tells us that he is a rector. There is a technical difference between these two clerical ti-
    tles: rectors were originally those who received the tithes in a parish and vicars those
    who did the duty of a parish for the owner or owners of the tithes. Strictly speaking, a
    parish priest is generally either a vicar or a rector, not both.

77 *You very plain old man*: In early performances, the chorus's lines preceded the Notary's
    and took the form:

> You very, very plain old man,
> She loves, she loves you madly!

The Macmillan edition of the Savoy Operas has this original version.

84 *sixty-seven nearly*: At sixty-six, the Notary shares with Scaphio in *Utopia Limited* the dis-
    tinction of having the oldest declared age in the Savoy Operas. Iolanthe, who boasts a
    couple of centuries or so, is, of course, much older, but then she is a fairy.

95 *You very plain old man*: Here again, in early libretti and in the Macmillan version, the
    chorus preceded the Notary with these lines:

> You're still everything that girls detest,
> But still she loves you dearly!

COUNTRY DANCE.

(At end of dance, enter CONSTANCE *in tears, leading*
NOTARY, *who carries an ear-trumpet.)* 60

ARIA – CONSTANCE.

Dear friends, take pity on my lot,
  My cup is not of nectar!
I long have loved – as who would not? –
  Our kind and reverend rector.
Long years ago my love began 65
  So sweetly – yet so sadly –
But when I saw this plain old man,
Away my old affection ran –
  I found I loved him madly.
    Oh! 70

(To NOTARY.)   You very, very plain old man,
  I love, I love you madly!
You very plain old man,
  I love you madly!

NOTARY.   I am a very deaf old man, 75
  And hear you very badly!

CHORUS.   You very plain old man,
  She loves you madly!

CONSTANCE.   I know not why I love him so;
  It is enchantment, surely! 80
He's dry and snuffy, deaf and slow,
  Ill-tempered, weak, and poorly!
He's ugly, and absurdly dressed,
  And sixty-seven nearly,
He's everything that I detest, 85
But if the truth must be confessed,
  I love him very dearly!
    Oh!

(To NOTARY.)   You're everything that I detest,
  But still I love you dearly!
You're all that I detest, 90
  I love you dearly!

NOTARY.   I caught that line, but for the rest
  I did not hear it clearly!

CHORUS.   You very plain old man, 95
  She loves you dearly!

111 *An anxious care*: Early editions of the libretto, the licence copy, the Oxford University
      Press World's Classics edition and the Macmillan edition all have 'A sorrow rare' instead
      of 'An anxious care', which is found in the vocal score and modern libretti and is gener-
      ally sung.

(*During this verse* ALINE *and* ALEXIS *have entered at back unobserved.*)

ALINE *and* ALEXIS.

ALEXIS.   Oh joy! oh joy!
         The charm works well,
           And all are now united.
ALINE.   The blind young boy
         Obeys the spell,
           Their troth they all have plighted!

100

ENSEMBLE.

ALINE *and* ALEXIS.	CONSTANCE.	NOTARY.
Oh joy! oh joy!	Oh, bitter joy!	Oh joy! oh joy!
The charm works well,	No words can tell	No words can tell
And all are now	How my poor heart	My state of mind
united!	is blighted!	delighted.
The blind young boy	They'll soon employ	They'll soon employ
Obeys the spell,	A marriage bell,	A marriage bell,
Their troth they all	To say that we're	To say that we're
have plighted.	united.	united.
True happiness	I do confess	True happiness
Reigns everywhere,	An anxious care	Reigns everywhere,
And dwells with both	My humbled spirit	And dwells with both
the sexes,	vexes,	the sexes,
And all will bless	And none will bless	And all will bless
The thoughtful care	Example rare	Example rare
Of their beloved	Of their beloved	Of their beloved
Alexis!	Alexis!	Alexis.

105

110

115

(*All, except* ALEXIS *and* ALINE, *exeunt lovingly.*)

ALINE. How joyful they all seem in their new-found happiness! The whole village has paired off in the happiest manner. And yet not a match has been made that the hollow world would not consider ill-advised!

ALEXIS. But we are wiser – far wiser – than the world. Observe the good that will become of these ill-assorted unions. The miserly wife will check the reckless expenditure of her too frivolous consort, the wealthy husband will shower innumerable bonnets on his penniless bride, and the young and lively spouse will cheer the declining days of her aged partner with comic songs unceasing!

ALINE. What a delightful prospect for him!

ALEXIS. But one thing remains to be done, that my happiness may be complete. We must drink the philtre ourselves, that I may be assured of your love for ever and ever.

ALINE. Oh, Alexis, do you doubt me? Is it necessary that such love as ours should be secured by artificial means? Oh, no, no, no!

120

125

130

135 *never, never change*: In Gilbert's original version of *The Sorcerer* this line was the cue for a
     ballad in which Aline swore her love for Alexis and asked him to have faith in her. The
     song, which appeared in the licence copy, went as follows:

BALLAD – ALINE.

Have faith in me – thou art my day –
  I turn to thee for love and light –
Take that life-giving love away
  And leave me in eternal night!
Thou art the hill – and I the dale –
  Thou art the sea and I the shell –
Thou art the wind and I the sail –
  Thou art the spring and I the well!
Without that spring no well would be,
  Have faith in me – have faith in me!

Have faith in me – the ripening corn
  Is faithful to the autumn sun!
Thou art the god of my young morn,
  My harvest god – oh doubting one!
Thou art the day and I the hour –
  Thou art the idol – I the throng –
Thou art the tree and I the flower –
  Thou art the singer – I the song.
Oh let the song be sung by thee –
  Have faith in me – have faith in me!

(At the end of the ballad, ALEXIS *rises and embraces* ALINE. *Enter* DR DALY.)

Before the first night and the publication of the libretto, Gilbert cut out this song and
substituted Alexis' ballad 'Thou hast the power thy vaunted love'. He later reused many
of the images from the abandoned song in the duet 'None shall part us' in *Iolanthe* (Act
I, lines 229–44).

ALEXIS. My dear Aline, time works terrible changes, and I want to place
our love beyond the chance of change.

ALINE. Alexis, it is already far beyond that chance. Have faith in me, for
my love can never, never change!   135

ALEXIS. Then you absolutely refuse?

ALINE. I do. If you cannot trust me, you have no right to love me – no
right to be loved *by* me.

ALEXIS. Enough, Aline, I shall know how to interpret this refusal.

BALLAD – ALEXIS.

Thou hast the power thy vaunted love   140
To sanctify, all doubt above,
    Despite the gathering shade:
To make that love of thine so sure
That, come what may, it must endure
    Till time itself shall fade.   145
      Thy love is but a flower
      That fades within the hour!
      If such thy love, oh, shame!
      Call it by other name –
        It is not love!   150

Thine is the power and thine alone,
To place me on so proud a throne
    That kings might envy me!
A priceless throne of love untold,
More rare than orient pearl and gold.   155
    But no! No, thou wouldst be free!
      Such love is like the ray
      That dies within the day:
      If such thy love, oh, shame!
      Call it by other name –   160
        It is not love!

(*Enter* DR DALY.)

DR D. (*musing*). It is singular – it is very singular. It has overthrown all my
calculations. It is distinctly opposed to the doctrine of averages. I cannot
understand it.   165

ALINE. Dear Dr Daly, what has puzzled you?

DR D. My dear, this village has not hitherto been addicted to marrying
and giving in marriage. Hitherto the youths of this village have not been
enterprising, and the maidens have been distinctly coy. Judge then of my

188–9 *you will, I am sure, be pleased to hear*: The passage of dialogue which begins here has very close similarities with a conversation in 'An Elixir of Love' between Jessie and her father, who has been given some of Mr Gay's sherry by Zorah Clarke, the curate's old housekeeper and cook. Sir Caractacus speaks first:

'You will, I trust, be pleased to hear that my declining years are not unlikely to be solaced by the companionship of a good, virtuous, and companionable woman.'

'My dear papa,' said Jessie, 'do you really mean that – that you are likely to be married?'

'Indeed, Jessie, I think it is more than probable! You know you are going to leave me very soon, and my dear little nurse must be replaced, or what will become of me?'

Jessie's eyes filled with tears – but they were tears of joy.

'I cannot tell you, papa – dear, dear, papa – how happy you have made me.'

'And you will, I am sure, accept your new mamma with every feeling of respect and affection.'

'Any wife of yours is a mamma of mine,' said Jessie.

'My darling! Yes, Jessie, before very long I hope to lead to the altar a bride who will love and honour me as I deserve. She is no light and giddy girl, Jessie. She is a woman of sober age and staid demeanour, yet easy and comfortable in her ways. I am going to marry Mr Gay's cook, Zorah.'

'Zorah,' cried Jessie, 'dear, dear old Zorah! Oh, indeed, I am very, very glad and happy!'

'Bless you, my child,' said the Baronet. 'I knew my pet would not blame her poor old father for acting on the impulse of a heart that has never misled him. Yes, I think – nay, I am sure – that I have taken a wise and prudent step. Zorah is not what the world calls beautiful.'

'Zorah is very good, and very clean and honest, and quite, quite sober in her habits,' said Jessie warmly, 'and that is worth more – far more than beauty, dear papa. Beauty will fade and perish, but personal cleanliness is practically undying. It can be renewed whenever it discovers symptoms of decay. Oh, I am sure you will be happy!' And Jessie hurried off to tell Stanley Gay how nobly the potion had done its work.

surprise when I tell you that the whole village came to me in a body just   170
now, and implored me to join them in matrimony with as little delay as
possible. Even your excellent father has hinted to me that before very long
it is not unlikely that he also may change his condition.

ALINE. Oh, Alexis – do you hear that? Are you not delighted?

ALEXIS. Yes. I confess that a union between your mother and my   175
father would be a happy circumstance indeed. (*Crossing to* DR DALY.) My
dear sir – the news that you bring us is very gratifying.

DR D. Yes – still, in my eyes, it has its melancholy side. This universal
marrying recalls the happy days – now, alas, gone for ever – when I myself
might have – but tush! I am puling. I am too old to marry – and yet, within   180
the last half-hour, I have greatly yearned for companionship. I never
remarked it before, but the young maidens of this village are very comely. So
likewise are the middle-aged. Also the elderly. All are comely – and (*with a
deep sigh*) all are engaged!

ALINE. Here comes your father.   185

(*Enter* SIR MARMADUKE *with* MRS PARTLET, *arm-in-arm.*)

ALINE *and* ALEXIS (*aside*). Mrs Partlet!

SIR M. Dr Daly, give me joy. Alexis, my dear boy, you will, I am sure, be
pleased to hear that my declining days are not unlikely to be solaced by the
companionship of this good, virtuous, and amiable woman.   190

ALEXIS (*rather taken aback*). My dear father, this is not altogether what I
expected. I am certainly taken somewhat by surprise. Still it can hardly be
necessary to assure you that any wife of yours is a mother of mine. (*Aside to*
ALINE.) It is not quite what I could have wished.

MRS P. (*crossing to* ALEXIS). Oh, sir, I entreat your forgiveness. I am   195
aware that socially I am not heverythink that could be desired, nor am I
blessed with an abundance of worldly goods, but I can at least confer on your
estimable father the great and priceless dowry of a true, tender, and lovin'
'art!

ALEXIS (*coldly*). I do not question it. After all, a faithful love is the true 200
source of every earthly joy.

SIR M. I knew that my boy would not blame his poor father for acting on
the impulse of a heart that has never yet misled him. Zorah is not perhaps
what the world calls beautiful –

DR D. Still she is comely – distinctly comely. (*Sighs.*)   205

ALINE. Zorah is very good, and very clean, and honest, and quite, quite
sober in her habits: and that is worth far more than beauty, dear Sir
Marmaduke.

DR D. Yes; beauty will fade and perish, but personal cleanliness is
practically undying, for it can be renewed whenever it discovers symptoms   210
of decay. My dear Sir Marmaduke, I heartily congratulate you. (*Sighs.*)

212–38 *I rejoice that it's decided*
> The first-night critics were unanimous in their praise of this number. The *Era* described
> it as 'the gem of the opera. It is written with delightful fluency and grace, is admirably
> harmonized, and the melody is fresh as the May dew.' The *Observer* commented: 'It is
> simply delicious and will be hailed with delight wherever piquant melody and exquisite
> counterpoint are appreciated.'

236 *No one's left to marry me*: In 'An Elixir of Love' the only person who finds himself unbe-
> trothed in Ploverleigh is the Bishop who happens unexpectedly to visit the village:

>> The good old Bishop had drunk freely of the philtre, but there was no one left to love him.
>> It was pitiable to see the poor love-lorn prelate as he wandered disconsolately through the
>> smiling meadows of Ploverleigh, pouring out the accents of his love to an incorporeal
>> abstraction.

> The Bishop, like Dr Daly, is destined not to remain single for long, however. Jessie
> cannot resist the temptation of trying the elixir, and he is the first person whom she
> meets after drinking it. The Bishop makes amends to the Revd Stanley Gay for taking
> his sweetheart by giving him the living of the neighbouring parish of Crawleigh, 'worth
> £1,800 per annum – the duty is extremely light, and the local society is unexceptional'.
> Gay is left as the only bachelor in Ploverleigh, and he marries off everyone else before
> taking up his new incumbency. The Bishop and Jessie live happily ever after at the Palace.

QUINTET.

Alexis, Aline, Sir Marmaduke, Zorah, *and* Dr Daly.

Alexis.

I rejoice that it's decided,
  Happy now will be his life,
For my father is provided
  With a true and tender wife.   215

Ensemble.

She will tend him, nurse him, mend him,
  Air his linen, dry his tears;
Bless the thoughtful fates that send him
  Such a wife to soothe his years!

Aline.

No young giddy thoughtless maiden,   220
  Full of graces, airs, and jeers –
But a sober widow, laden
  With the weight of fifty years!

Sir M.

No high-born exacting beauty,
  Blazing like a jewelled sun –   225
But a wife who'll do her duty,
  As that duty should be done!

Ensemble.   She will tend him, etc.

Mrs P.

I'm no saucy minx and giddy –
  Hussies such as them abound –   230
But a clean and tidy widdy
  Well be-known for miles around!

Dr D.

All the village now have mated,
  All are happy as can be –
I to live alone am fated: 235
  No one's left to marry me!

241 *Enter Mr Wells*: In early productions, when this act was set in the market place of Plover-leigh, this stage direction was: 'M R W E L L S *who has overheard part of the quintet, and who has remained concealed behind the market cross, comes down as they go off.'*

259 *Why do you gaze at me*: Early editions of the libretto and both the World's Classics and Macmillan versions have 'Why do you glare at one' here. 'Gaze at me' occurs in the vocal score and modern libretti and is usually sung now.

ENSEMBLE. No one's left to marry him!
She will tend him, etc.

(*Exeunt* SIR MARMADUKE, MRS PARTLET, *and* ALINE, *with* ALEXIS. DR DALY *looks after them sentimentally, then exits with a sigh.*)   240

(*Enter* MR WELLS.)

RECITATIVE – MR WELLS.

Oh, I have wrought much evil with my spells!
And ill I can't undo!
This is too bad of you, J. W. Wells –
What wrong have they done you?   245

And see – another love-lorn lady comes –
Alas, poor stricken dame!
A gentle pensiveness her life benumbs –
And mine, alone, the blame!

(LADY SANGAZURE *enters. She is very melancholy.*)   250

LADY S.   Alas! ah me! and well-a-day!
I sigh for love, and well I may,
For I am very old and grey.
But stay!

(*Sees* MR WELLS, *and becomes fascinated by him.*)   255

RECITATIVE.

LADY S.   What is this fairy form I see before me?
MR W.   Oh, horrible! – she's going to adore me!
This last catastrophe is overpowering!
LADY S.   Why do you gaze at me with visage lowering?
For pity's sake recoil not thus from me!   260
MR W.   My lady, leave me – this can never be!

DUET – LADY SANGAZURE *and* MR WELLS.

MR W.   Hate me! I drop my H's – have through life!
LADY S.   Love me! I'll drop them too!
MR W.   Hate me! I always eat peas with a knife!
LADY S.   Love me! I'll eat like you!   265

266 *One Tree Hill*: Harry Benford's *Gilbert and Sullivan Lexicon* lists no fewer than seven possible contenders for this reference. Perhaps the most likely, although it was closed down five years before *The Sorcerer* opened, was an amusement at Greenwich Fair. There were also One Tree Hills in the London suburbs of Blackheath, Hornsey, Honor Oak and New Cross and further out in the Langdon Hills in Essex and near Sevenoaks in Kent.

268 *Rosherville*: A pleasure garden, with a zoo, amusements and theatrical entertainments, which was established in the late 1830s in disused chalk quarries near Gravesend in Kent. It was particularly popular with working-class Londoners. In early libretti, and in the Macmillan edition, lines 266 and 268 are transposed.

270 *my prejudices I'll for ever drop*: In early editions of the libretto this phrase was 'My prejudices I will drop'.

Gilbert originally intended Wells's duet with Lady Sangazure to be followed by a second incantation scene, in which Wells appeals to his demonic master Ahrimanes to be released from his sorcerer's vows. This lengthy scene, which is similar to the prologue of Heinrich Marschner's opera *The Vampire*, occurs in the licence copy, where it follows after Lady Sangazure's exit (line 303). The first recitative survived, in a rewritten form, into the first production but was cut in the 1884 revival. The rest was never performed and was probably never set to music by Sullivan.

RECITATIVE – Mr Wells.

Oh hideous doom – to scatter desolation,
And cause unhappiness on every hand!
To foster misalliance through the nation
And breed unequal matches in the land!
By nature I am mild, humane and tender,
It racks my soul such fearful sights to see!
I can no longer bear it! I will render
My fearful gift to him who gave it me!

INCANTATION.

Spirits short and spirits long –
Spirits weak and spirits strong –
Spirits slow and spirits fleet –
Spirits mixed and spirits neat –
Spirits dark and spirits fair –
Listen to my heart-felt prayer.

(The stage has grown dark – a gauze descends – imps appear.)

Chorus of Spirits.	We hear the spells
	    J. W. Wells!
	What terrors trouble you,
	    J. W. W.?
	Ha! ha! Ha! ha!
	Some terrors trouble him
	    J. W. Double him!
	Ha! ha! Ha! ha!

(The market cross opens and Ahrimanes is seen through transparency.)

Ahr.	Presumptuous wretch – what favours do you seek? You called me – I am here! What would you? Speak!
Mr W.	Ahrimanes – mighty master – Hear me – hear me now!
Chorus.	Hear him – hear him now!
Mr W.	Avert this terrible disaster – Free me from my vow!

MR W.	Hate me! I often roll down One Tree Hill!
LADY S.	Love me! I'll meet you there!
MR W.	Hate me! I spend the day at Rosherville!
LADY S.	Love me! that joy I'll share!

LADY S.	Love me! my prejudices I'll for ever drop!	270
MR W.	Hate me! that's not enough!	
LADY S.	Love me! I'll come and help you in the shop!	
MR W.	Hate me! the life is rough!	
LADY S.	Love me! my grammar I will all forswear!	
MR W.	Hate me! abjure my lot!	275
LADY S.	Love me! I'll stick sunflowers in my hair!	
MR W.	Hate me! they'll suit you not!	

RECITATIVE – MR WELLS.

At what I am going to say be not enraged –
I may not love you – for I am engaged!

LADY S. (*horrified*).	Engaged!	280
MR W.	Engaged!	

To a maiden fair,
With bright brown hair,
And a sweet and simple smile.
Who waits for me 285
By the sounding sea,
On a South Pacific isle.

MR W. (*aside*).	A lie! No maiden waits me there!	
LADY S. (*mournfully*).	She has bright brown hair;	
MR W. (*aside*).	A lie! No maiden smiles on me!	290
LADY S. (*mournfully*).	By the sounding sea!	
ENSEMBLE.	The sounding sea.	

ENSEMBLE.

LADY SANGAZURE	MR WELLS.	
Oh, agony, rage, despair!	Oh, agony, rage, despair!	
The maiden has bright brown hair,	Oh, where will this end – oh, where?	
And mine is as white as snow!	I should like very much to know!	295
False man, it will be your fault,	It will certainly be my fault,	
If I go to my family vault,	If she goes to her family vault,	
And bury my life-long woe!	To bury her life-long woe!	

BOTH.

The family vault – the family vault.

It will certainly be $\left\{ \begin{array}{c} \text{your} \\ \text{my} \end{array} \right\}$ fault, 300

If $\left\{ \begin{array}{c} \text{I go} \\ \text{she goes} \end{array} \right\}$ to $\left\{ \begin{array}{c} \text{my} \\ \text{her} \end{array} \right\}$ family vault,

To bury $\left\{ \begin{array}{c} \text{my} \\ \text{her} \end{array} \right\}$ life-long woe!

CHORUS.   Free him from his vow!
            Hear him, hear him now!
            Ha! ha! Ha! ha! Ha! ha! Ha! ha!

SOLO – AHRIMANES.

If thou, audacious elf, will yield
    Alexis to my grasp
And let his doom be signed and sealed
    In Death's unpleasant clasp –
Or if thou wilt consent, thyself,
    To come below with me,
I'll grant thy wish, presumptuous elf!
    I want, or him, or thee!

CHORUS.   Be dutiful, and obey.
            Give us – give us our prey!
AHR.   Or thou – or he
            Which shall it be?
CHORUS.   Or thou – or he
            Which shall it be?
MR W.   Or I – or he –
            Which shall it be?
CHORUS.   Ha! ha! Ha! ha! Ha! ha! Ha! ha!
MR W.   Oh master, pity show!
CHORUS.   No! No!
MR W.   To meet your views I'll try –
            If one of us must go below –
CHORUS.   Ho! Ho!
MR W.   I'd rather he than I!
AHR.   Much rather?
MR W.   Much rather!
AHR.   Greatly prefer it?
MR W.   Greatly prefer it!
CHORUS.   Ha! ha! Ha! ha! Ha! ha! Ha! ha!
AHR.   Good – be it so.
            When he will go
            With me below,
            Just let me know.
            Ring out his knell
            And I will quell
            The fatal spell
            Till then – farewell!   (*He disappears.*)
CHORUS.   Farewell! Farewell! Farewell!
            Ha! ha! Ha! ha! Ha! ha! Ha! ha!

(*The stage gains light as* MR WELLS *makes off horror-stricken. Enter* ALINE.)

304 *Enter Aline*: In the licence copy and the first edition of the libretto, Aline has the follow-
     ing passage of dialogue after her entrance:

        This was to have been the happiest day of my life – but I am very far from happy! Alexis
        insists that I shall taste the philtre and when I try to persuade him that to do so would be an
        insult to my pure and lasting love, he tells me that I object because I do not desire that my
        love for him shall be eternal. Well (*sighing and producing a phial*), I can at least prove to him
        that, in that, he is unjust.

     The first-edition libretto then continues with the recitative 'Alexis! Doubt me not, my
     loved one'. However, the licence copy goes straight into Aline's ballad, which is given an
     additional verse before the one now sung ('The fearful deed is done'):

(*Exit* LADY SANGAZURE, *in great anguish, accompanied by* MR WELLS.)

(*Enter* ALINE.)

RECITATIVE – ALINE.

Alexis! Doubt me not, my loved one! See,   305
Thine uttered will is sovereign law to me!
All fear – all thought of ill I cast away!
It is my darling's will, and I obey!

(*She drinks the philtre.*)

The fearful deed is done,   310
My love is near!
I go to meet my own
In trembling fear!
If o'er us aught of ill
Should cast a shade,   315
It was my darling's will,
And I obeyed!

(*As* ALINE *is going off, she meets* DR DALY, *entering pensively. He is playing on
a flageolet. Under the influence of the spell she at once becomes strangely fascinated
by him, and exhibits every symptom of being hopelessly in love with him.*)   320

SONG – DR DALY.

Oh, my voice is sad and low
And with timid step I go –
For with load of love o'erladen
I enquire of every maiden,
'Will you wed me, little lady?   325
Will you share my cottage shady?'
    Little lady answers 'No! No! No!
    Thank you for your kindly proffer –
    Good your heart, and full your coffer;
    Yet I must decline your offer –   330
        I'm engaged to So-and-so!' (*flageolet solo*)
        So-and-so! So-and-so!   „   „
        So-and-so! So-and-so!   „   „
        'I'm engaged to So-and-so!'
    What a rogue young hearts to pillage;   335
    What a worker on Love's tillage!
    Every maiden in the village

No need, no need, my own,
    This spell to try.
My love is thine alone –
    For aye – for aye!
But every thought of ill
    I cast away –
It is my darling's will,
    And I obey!   (*She drinks.*)

331 *flageolet solo*: Dr Daly is not the only character in the Savoy Operas to accompany himself on the flageolet. Strephon and Phyllis are also supposed to play the small flute-like instrument at their entrances in Act I of *Iolanthe*. For the initial run of *The Sorcerer* Rutland Barrington learned how to play the flageolet and actually accompanied himself in this song. By the time of the 1884 revival, however, he had lost the knack and since then the accompaniment has generally been played from the orchestra pit. James Walker, musical director of the D'Oyly Carte Opera Company from 1968 to 1971, tried vainly to persuade Kenneth Sandford to emulate Barrington's early achievement.

354 *Rejoice with me*: In the first run of *The Sorcerer* Dr Daly and Aline ended their ensemble by singing these lines together instead of the present 'Rejoice with me':

Ye birds, and brooks, and fruitful trees,
With choral joy delight the breeze –
Rejoice, rejoice with me!

363 *Alexis, don't do that – you must not*: This line recalls the conversation in 'An Elixir of Love' between Stanley Gay and Jessie Lightly after the latter has taken the elixir and fallen in love with the Bishop:

'Why, Jessie – my own little love,' exclaimed Stanley. 'What in the world is the matter?' And he put his arms fondly round her waist, and endeavoured to raise her face to his.
'Oh, no – no – Stanley – don't – you mustn't – indeed, indeed, you musn't.'
'Why, my pet, what can you mean?'
'Oh, Stanley, Stanley – you will never, never forgive me.'
'Nonsense, child,' said he. 'My dear little Jessie is incapable of an act which is beyond the pale of forgiveness.' And he gently kissed her forehead.
'Stanley, you musn't do it – indeed you musn't.'

Is engaged to So-and-so! (*flageolet solo*)
 So-and-so! So-and-so! ,,   ,,
  So-and-so! So-and-so! ,,   ,,   340
All engaged to So-and-so!

(At the end of the song DR DALY *sees* ALINE, *and, under the influence of the potion, falls in love with her.)*

ENSEMBLE – ALINE *and* DR DALY.

Oh, joyous boon! oh, mad delight;
Oh, sun and moon! oh, day and night!
 Rejoice, rejoice with me!   345
Proclaim our joy, ye birds above –
Ye brooklets, murmur forth our love,
 In choral ecstasy:

DR D.	Oh, joyous boon!	350
ALINE.	Oh, mad delight!	
DR D.	Oh, sun and moon!	
ALINE.	Oh, day and night!	
BOTH.	Rejoice with me,	
	Rejoice with me,	355
	Rejoice, rejoice with me!	

(Enter ALEXIS.)

ALEXIS (*with rapture*). Aline, my only love, my happiness!
 The philtre – you have tasted it?
ALINE (*with confusion*). Yes! Yes!   360
ALEXIS. Oh, joy, mine, mine for ever, and for aye!

              (Embraces her.)

ALINE. Alexis, don't do that – you must not!
   (DR DALY *interposes between them.*)
ALEXIS (*amazed*). Why?   365

DUET – ALINE *and* DR DALY.

ALINE.   Alas! that lovers thus should meet:
       Oh, pity, pity me!
     Oh, charge me not with cold deceit;
       Oh, pity, pity me!
     You bade me drink – with trembling awe   370
     I drank, and, by the potion's law,

I loved the very first I saw!
  Oh, pity, pity me!

DR D. My dear young friend, consolèd be –
  We pity, pity you.   375
In this I'm not an agent free –
  We pity, pity you.
Some most extraordinary spell
O'er us has cast its magic fell –
The consequence I need not tell.   380
  We pity, pity you.

ENSEMBLE.

ALEXIS (*alone*). Some most extraordinary spell

ALL. O'er $\left\{\begin{array}{c} us \\ them \end{array}\right\}$ has cast its magic fell –

ALEXIS (*furiously*). False one, begone – I spurn thee,
  To thy new lover turn thee!   385
Thy perfidy all men shall know.
ALINE (*wildly*). I could not help it!
ALEXIS (*calling off*). Come one, come all!
DR D. We could not help it!
ALEXIS (*calling off*). Obey my call!   390
ALINE (*wildly*). I could not help it!
ALEXIS (*calling off*). Come hither, run!
DR D. We could not help it!
ALEXIS (*calling off*). Come, every one!

(*Enter all the characters except* LADY SANGAZURE *and* MR WELLS.) 395

CHORUS.

Oh, what is the matter, and what is the clatter?
  He's glowering at her, and threatens a blow!
Oh, why does he batter the girl he did flatter?
  And why does the latter recoil from him so?

RECITATIVE – ALEXIS.

Prepare for sad surprises –   400
My love Aline despises!
No thought of sorrow shames her –
Another lover claims her!
Be his, false girl, for better or for worse –
But, ere you leave me, may a lover's curse –   405

410–11 *Colonial Bishopric*: Colonial bishops figure in three of Gilbert's *Bab Ballads*. The Bishop
of the balmy isle of Rum-Ti-Foo, who is the subject of two ballads, is a good example of
the species:

> His people – twenty-three in sum –
> They played the eloquent tum-tum,
> And lived on scalps served up in rum –
>   The only sauce they knew.
>
>   .   .   .
>
> He only, of the reverend pack
> Who minister to Christians black,
> Brought any useful knowledge back
>   To his Colonial fold.
>
>   .   .   .
>
> He carried Art, he often said,
> To places where that timid maid
> (Save by Colonial Bishops' aid)
>   Could never hope to roam.

418 *Ahrimanes*: In Zoroastrian (Persian) theology, the personification of evil. He is the same
figure as Oromanes mentioned in the story of Abudah's chest (see the note to Act I, line
404). This reference would, of course, be very much clearer if Gilbert had retained the
Second Act incantation scene in which Ahrimanes actually appeared and demanded
either Wells's or Alexis' death as the price of lifting the spell.

433 *Die thou*: This and the next line were originally given to Lady Sangazure rather than Dr
Daly.

437 *popular opinion*: At some stage this phrase was changed to 'public execration'. Both the
licence copy and first-edition libretto have 'popular opinion' as now, but the Macmillan
edition has 'public execration'. A libretto dated 1923 in the D'Oyly Carte archives has
'public execration' printed, with 'opinion' written in. It is generally sung now in its original form.

DR D. (*coming forward*). Hold! Be just. This poor child drank the philtre at your instance. She hurried off to meet you – but, most unhappily, she met me instead. As you had administered the potion to both of us, the result was inevitable. But fear nothing from me – I will be no man's rival. I shall quit the country at once – and bury my sorrow in the congenial gloom of a Colonial Bishopric.   410

ALEXIS. My excellent old friend! (*Taking his hand – then turning to* MR WELLS, *who has entered with* LADY SANGAZURE.) Oh, Mr Wells, what, what is to be done?

MR W. I do not know – and yet – there is one means by which this   415
spell may be removed.

ALEXIS. Name it – oh, name it!

MR W. Or you or I must yield up his life to Ahrimanes. I would rather it were you. I should have no hesitation in sacrificing my own life to spare yours, but we take stock next week, and it would not be fair on the Co.   420

ALEXIS. True. Well, I am ready!

ALINE. No, no – Alexis – it must not be! Mr Wells, if he must die that all may be restored to their old loves, what is to become of me? I should be left out in the cold, with no love to be restored to!

MR W. True – I did not think of that. (*To the others.*) My friends, I   425
appeal to you, and I will leave the decision in your hands.

FINALE.

MR W.	Or I or he
	Must die!
	Which shall it be?
	Reply! 430
SIR M.	Die thou!
	Thou art the cause of all offending!
DR D.	Die thou!
	Yield thou to this decree unbending!
ALL.	Die thou! Die thou! Die thou! 435
MR W.	So be it! I submit! My fate is sealed.
	To popular opinion thus I yield!
	(*Falls on trap.*)
	Be happy all – leave me to my despair –
	I go – it matters not with whom – or where! 440
	(*Gong.*)

(*All quit their present partners, and rejoin their old lovers.* SIR MARMADUKE *leaves* MRS PARTLET, *and goes to* LADY SANGAZURE. ALINE *leaves* DR DALY, *and goes to* ALEXIS. DR DALY *leaves* ALINE, *and goes to* CONSTANCE. NOTARY *leaves* CONSTANCE, *and goes to* MRS   445
PARTLET. *All the* CHORUS *make a corresponding change.*)

465–6 *Mr Wells sinks through trap*: *The Sorcerer* is the only one of the Savoy Operas which requires
a trap-door for its proper production. The Second Act of *Ruddigore* originally required
one for the reappearance of Sir Roderic Murgatroyd, but that particular scene was cut
out immediately after the first night. A trap-door is sometimes used for Iolanthe's as-
cent from the stream in Act I of *Iolanthe*, but the scene does not demand one.

Not all modern theatres have trap-doors in the stage, and for their 1971 production
the D'Oyly Carte Company found it necessary to build the trap into their scenery. A
sliding door was put into the veranda of Sir Marmaduke's mansion. As this was only
three feet off the level of the stage, John Wellington Wells had to roll over quickly after
making his jump into the underworld. A stage-hand crouched by the trap ready to
trigger the flash mechanism in the tea-pot (see the note to Act I, line 579) to produce
the desired effect after his descent.

As George Grossmith sank slowly through the trap in the first run of *The Sorcerer* he
carefully wound his watch, buttoned his gloves and brushed his hat. Michael Heyland
continued this business in his production and also had Wells throwing his hat and a
shower of business cards into the air at the re-ascent of the final curtain.

In his autobiography, *The Secrets of a Savoyard*, Sir Henry Lytton tells of an embarrassing incident which once occurred when he was playing Wells and making his final
descent: 'One night the trap, having dropped a foot or so, refused to move any further,
and there was I, enveloped in smoke and brimstone, poised between earth and elsewhere. So all I could do was to jump back on to the boards, make a grimace at the
refractory trapdoor, and go off by the ordinary exit. "Hell's full!" shouted an irreverent
voice from the gods.'

ALL.

GENTLEMEN.	Oh, my adored one!
LADIES.	Beloved boy!
GENTLEMEN.	Ecstatic rapture!
LADIES.	Unmingled joy!

450

(*They embrace.*)

SIR M.   Come to my mansion, all of you! At least
We'll crown our rapture with another feast!

ENSEMBLE.

SIR MARMADUKE, LADY SANGAZURE, ALEXIS, *and* ALINE.

Now to the banquet we press –
Now for the eggs and the ham –
Now for the mustard and cress –
Now for the strawberry jam!

455

DR DALY, CONSTANCE, NOTARY, *and* MRS PARTLET.

Now for the tea of our host –
Now for the rollicking bun –
Now for the muffin and toast –
And now for the gay Sally Lunn!
Now for the muffin and toast –
And now for the gay Sally Lunn!

460

CHORUS.   The eggs and the ham, etc.

(*General Dance. During the symphony* MR WELLS *sinks
through trap amid red fire.*)

465

CURTAIN

H.M.S. PINAFORE

or

The Lass that Loved a Sailor

DRAMATIS PERSONÆ

THE RT. HON. SIR JOSEPH PORTER, K.C.B. (*First Lord of the Admiralty*)
CAPTAIN CORCORAN (*Commanding H.M.S. Pinafore*)
TOM TUCKER (*Midshipmite*)
RALPH RACKSTRAW (*Able Seaman*)
DICK DEADEYE (*Able Seaman*)
BILL BOBSTAY (*Boatswain*)
BOB BECKET (*Boatswain's Mate – Carpenter*)
JOSEPHINE (*the Captain's Daughter*)
HEBE (*Sir Joseph's First Cousin*)
MRS CRIPPS (LITTLE BUTTERCUP) (*a Portsmouth Bumboat Woman*)
First Lord's Sisters, his Cousins, his Aunts, Sailors, Marines, etc.

SCENE. – Quarter-deck of H.M.S. *Pinafore*, off Portsmouth.
ACT I. – Noon.   ACT II. – Night.

H.M.S. PINAFORE

H.M.S. Pinafore was Gilbert and Sullivan's first major success. First performed at the Opéra Comique just off the Strand on 25 May 1878, it ran for a total of 571 performances. This equalled the record for an initial West End run, which was held by a farce called *Our Boys*. Gilbert and Sullivan had found the magic touch which they were to apply to another eight operas over the next eleven years.

The nautical theme of the opera appealed strongly to Gilbert, who had seafaring blood in his veins. His father had been a naval surgeon and Gilbert liked to claim (without much justification) that a more distant ancestor was Sir Humphrey Gilbert, the Elizabethan navigator who landed at Newfoundland in 1583 and established the first British colony in North America. Jokes about the Navy had figured prominently in the *Bab Ballads*, which Gilbert had written for the humorous magazine *Fun* in the 1860s. Indeed, the ballads supplied several of the ideas and characters on which the plot was based.

Gilbert may also have drawn on real life for at least two of his characters. The possibility that W. H. Smith, founder of the newsagents' chain and First Lord of the Admiralty in Disraeli's Government, may have been the model for Sir Joseph Porter, is well known and is discussed in the notes that follow. Less well known is the fact that there may also have been a model for Little Buttercup. An obituary notice in the *Observer* of 1 February 1925, to which my attention has been drawn by Mr K. M. Jeckells of Great Yarmouth, suggests that Gilbert based the character on Mary Jane Daniell, the last survivor of the 'bumboat women' who plied their trade on the naval vessels stationed at Portsmouth. Mrs Daniell, who was born in 1839, was involved not just in selling provisions to sailors, like Little Buttercup, but also in recruiting naval ratings. As a young woman she knew many officers and men who had served with Nelson and she was said to possess 'a wonderful store of reminiscences covering our First Line of Defence in its greatest period of transition'.

H.M.S. Pinafore also provided the perfect vehicle for Sullivan to display his gifts for melody and for evocative mood music. Amazingly, he struggled to compose the opera while wracked with pain as the result of a stone in his kidneys. He wrote later: 'It is, perhaps, rather a strange fact that the music of *Pinafore*, which was thought to be so merry and spontaneous, was written while I was suffering agonies from a cruel illness. I would compose a few bars, and then be almost insensible from pain. When the paroxysm was passed, I would write a little more, until the pain overwhelmed me again.'

Early on, it looked as though *H.M.S. Pinafore* might prove to be a flop. Partly because of a fierce June heatwave, the Opéra Comique was far from full, and by July nightly takings were down to less than £40. The cast took a voluntary cut of a third in their salaries, and there were constant threats that the show would have to close. However, Sullivan gave it a boost by conducting a selection of music from the opera at the summer promenade concerts at the Royal Opera House, Covent Garden. By the end of August the weather was cooler and the theatre was full. The music had caught on, and shops in London were inundated with requests for the piano score.

H.M.S. Pinafore had no such difficulties in establishing itself on the other side of the Atlantic. In the absence of international copyright agreements, the opera was first performed in the United States by a 'pirate' company in Boston on 25 November 1878. Within a few months *Pinafore* mania was sweeping the States and more than fifty unauthorized companies were playing the piece across the country. In New York alone the opera was at one stage being performed simultaneously in eight separate theatres within five blocks of each other. There were all-negro and all-Catholic productions and performances on canal boats and Mississippi paddle steamers. One enterprising pilot in Newport, Rhode Island, learning that *H.M.S. Pinafore* was shortly to arrive there, even rowed several miles out to sea so as to be sure of getting the job of piloting her into the harbour.

Clearly, Gilbert, Sullivan and D'Oyly Carte could not let the pirates have a monopoly of performing, and reaping the profits from their own work. In the autumn of 1879 the three men sailed across the Atlantic with a cast drawn from the Comedy Opera Company. The first authorized performance of *H.M.S. Pinafore* in the United States opened at the Fifth Avenue Theater, New York, on 1 December 1879. Unbeknown to the audience, among the sailors disporting themselves on deck as the curtain went up was the librettist himself, complete with false beard, making a rare appearance in one of his own works.

H.M.S. Pinafore has had a particularly illustrious set of fans. Crown Prince William of Prussia, later Kaiser William II, greeted Sullivan on a visit to Kiel in 1881 with a rendering of 'He polished up the handle of the big front door'. Like many leading figures in the Navy, Admiral Lord Fisher, First Sea Lord at the beginning of the 1914–18 war, loved the opera and was frequently in the audience of D'Oyly Carte Company performances. Lord Wilson of Rievaulx, British Prime Minister from 1964 to 1970 and 1974 to 1976, first developed his life-long love of Gilbert and Sullivan when he played the part of a midshipman when a boy. On 16 June 1977 the D'Oyly Carte Opera Company performed *H.M.S. Pinafore* before the Queen, the Duke of Edinburgh and other members of the Royal Family at Windsor Castle. It was the first Royal Command performance of a Gilbert and Sullivan opera there since *The Gondoliers* had been performed for Queen Victoria in 1891.

In June 1984 the relatively short-lived but innovative New Sadler's Wells Opera Company staged a popular new production of the opera with Nickolas Grace as Sir Joseph Porter. This was brought back the following year. The new D'Oyly Carte Opera Company performed *H.M.S. Pinafore* in its third season, opening at the Pavilion Theatre, Bournemouth, in April 1990. The production broke with tradition in a number of ways – the opera began with the sailors asleep below decks, Captain Corcoran came on in a dressing-gown and took breakfast during his introductory song and Little Buttercup made her entrance accompanied by two charladies.

H.M.S. Pinafore has remained a particular favourite among schools and amateur operatic societies on both sides of the Atlantic. Appropriately, it was the first Gilbert and Sullivan opera to be performed by amateurs when the Harmonists' Choral Society staged it at the Kingston upon Thames Drill Hall on 30 April 1879. Since then there can have been few evenings when the 'airs from that infernal nonsense *Pinafore*' could not have been heard wafting from some school hall or church rooms.

1–2 *Scene:* The stage set for *H.M.S. Pinafore* was based on the quarter-deck of Lord Nelson's famous flagship H.M.S. *Victory,* which is still preserved in dry dock at Portsmouth. Gilbert visited Portsmouth with Sullivan six weeks before *Pinafore* was due to open and made a careful inspection of the *Victory* and other ships there. From the many sketches he made he designed the set for the opera.

In the copy of the libretto sent to the Lord Chamberlain for licensing purposes in May 1878, Gilbert specified that the set should show 'an old-fashioned three decker' with a raised poop, the deck on stage right and the mainmast on stage left. He also dated the action of the opera as 1840.

Gilbert took great care to ensure that every detail of the set was correct. It was a source of great pride to him when he was complimented by senior naval officers who came to see *Pinafore* on the accuracy of the ship's furnishings. He even had the sailors' costumes made by official Navy tailors in Portsmouth to ensure their authenticity.

3–12 *We sail the ocean blue*
This rollicking opening chorus establishes the location of H.M.S. *Pinafore*, riding at anchor outside Portsmouth. In his original note on the set for Act I, Gilbert had written 'View of Portsmouth in distance'. This town in Hampshire on the south coast of England was the site of the first ever naval dockyard in Britain, built by King Henry VIII in 1540, and has been one of the country's major naval bases ever since.

12 *plenty of time for play:* The phrase appears in this form in the original manuscript score of the opera and in the first published edition of the libretto. It appears in some editions of the libretto as 'plenty of time to play', but this seems to have been a printing error which got perpetuated.

18–33 *I'm called Little Buttercup*
The famous waltz song in which Little Buttercup (real name, as we learn from the list of *Dramatis personæ,* Mrs Cripps) introduces herself to the crew of H.M.S. *Pinafore* originally began 'For I'm called Little Buttercup' and is used again in the entr'acte played as the curtain rises on Act II. Sullivan had a pet parrot, Polly, to whom he taught the tune. 'It might not be quite a perfect rendering of the music', the composer remarked, 'but it was certainly quite as good as Gilbert's attempts.'

Little Buttercup herself was an importation from one of the *Bab Ballads* which Gilbert wrote during the 1860s. Under a different name, she is the central character in a ballad entitled 'The Bumboat Woman's Story', which anticipates one of the sub-plots in *H.M.S. Pinafore* in telling of the love between Poll Pineapple and a naval officer, Lieutenant Belaye.

ACT I

SCENE. – *Quarter-deck of H.M.S. Pinafore. Sailors, led by* BOATSWAIN, *discovered cleaning brasswork, splicing rope, etc.*

CHORUS.

We sail the ocean blue,
And our saucy ship's a beauty;
We're sober men and true,
And attentive to our duty.   5
When the balls whistle free
O'er the bright blue sea,
We stand to our guns all day;
When at anchor we ride
On the Portsmouth tide,   10
We've plenty of time for play.

(*Enter* LITTLE BUTTERCUP, *with large basket on her arm.*)

RECITATIVE.

Hail, men-o'-war's men – safeguards of your nation,
Here is an end, at last, of all privation;
You've got your pay – spare all you can afford   15
To welcome Little Buttercup on board.

ARIA.

I'm called Little Buttercup – dear Little Buttercup,
    Though I could never tell why,
But still I'm called Buttercup – poor little Buttercup,   20
    Sweet Little Buttercup I!

22 *jacky*: Twists of tobacco soaked in rum and sold to sailors for chewing. In another of Gilbert's *Bab Ballads*, the King of Canoodle-Dum orders that 'every lady and every lady's lord should masticate jacky (a kind of tobaccy) and scatter its juice abroad'.

26 *I've tea and I've coffee*: In the original libretto this was 'and excellent coffee'.
27 *Soft tommy*: Soft bread, usually in the form of fresh rolls.
28 *conies*: Wild rabbits.
    polonies: Cold smoked pork sausages named after the town of Bologna, in Italy, where they were first made.

33 *Come, of your Buttercup buy*: At the end of her song Buttercup distributes the wares from her basket to the sailors, traditionally saving until last a large stick of peppermint rock which she gives to the midshipman to whom she says 'And that's for you, my little man.' Although this line is not printed in any libretto, it has regularly occurred in D'Oyly Carte productions.

34 *Boatswain*: The crew member who first greets Buttercup, and who has been supervising the work of the sailors on deck, is the boatswain (pronounced 'bosun'). He is the warrant officer in charge of sails, rigging, anchors and cables and with direct responsibility for all work carried out on deck. It is, in fact, slightly unclear whether Bill Bobstay of H.M.S. *Pinafore* is a full-fledged boatswain or merely a boatswain's mate. He appears in both guises in different editions of the libretto and even in different places in the same edition. We may as well give him the benefit of the doubt, particularly as Gilbert refers to him as boatswain both in his letters about producing the opera and in the early libretto sent to the Lord Chamberlain to be licensed.

35 *Spithead*: The stretch of water lying off Portsmouth in the east Solent. A traditional assembly point for British war fleets, it was the scene of a famous naval mutiny in 1797 when the British Channel fleet refused to go to sea during the war against Revolutionary France.

41 *Dick Deadeye*: The odious and mis-shapen Deadeye is perhaps the nearest that Gilbert comes in the Savoy Operas to creating the archetypal stage villain of Victorian melodrama, whom the audience would be expected to hiss whenever he came on stage. Sir Despard Murgatroyd in *Ruddigore* is a more self-conscious example of the species.
    For Dick's name, Gilbert deliberately chose a nautical term. A deadeye is a wooden block with three holes, used for tightening or extending the shrouds of a sailing ship. Two other members of the *Pinafore* crew were also given names with nautical connotations, although they appear only in the list of *Dramatis personæ* and are never heard on stage. Bill Bobstay, the boatswain, takes his name from the rope used to draw down the bowsprit of a ship and keep it steady, counteracting the upward force of the foremast stays. Bob Becket, the boatswain's mate, is called after the ring or loop of rope used for holding spars.

I've snuff and tobaccy, and excellent jacky,
 I've scissors, and watches, and knives;
I've ribbons and laces to set off the faces
 Of pretty young sweethearts and wives.

I've treacle and toffee, I've tea and I've coffee,
 Soft tommy and succulent chops;
I've chickens and conies, and pretty polonies,
 And excellent peppermint drops.

Then buy of your Buttercup – dear Little Buttercup,
 Sailors should never be shy;
So, buy of your Buttercup – poor Little Buttercup;
 Come, of your Buttercup buy!

BOAT. Aye, Little Buttercup – and well called – for you're the rosiest, the roundest, and the reddest beauty in all Spithead.

BUT. Red, am I? and round – and rosy! May be, for I have dissembled well! But hark ye, my merry friend – hast ever thought that beneath a gay and frivolous exterior there may lurk a canker-worm which is slowly but surely eating its way into one's very heart?

BOAT. No, my lass, I can't say I've ever thought that.

(*Enter* DICK DEADEYE. *He pushes through sailors, and comes down.*)

DICK. *I* have thought it often. (*All recoil from him.*)

BUT. Yes, you look like it! What's the matter with the man? Isn't he well?

BOAT. Don't take no heed of *him*; that's only poor Dick Deadeye.

DICK. I say – it's a beast of a name, ain't it – Dick Deadeye?

BUT. It's not a nice name.

DICK. I'm ugly too, ain't I?

BUT. You are certainly plain.

DICK. And I'm three-cornered too, ain't I?

BUT. You are rather triangular.

DICK. Ha! ha! That's it. I'm ugly, and they hate me for it; for you all hate me, don't you?

ALL. We do!

DICK. There!

BOAT. Well, Dick, we wouldn't go for to hurt any fellow-creature's feelings, but you can't expect a chap with such a name as Dick Deadeye to be a popular character – now can you?

DICK. No.

BOAT. It's asking too much, ain't it?

DICK. It is. From such a face and form as mine the noblest sentiments

66 *Ralph Rackstraw*: It has been suggested that this name was also drawn from a seafaring term. A rack is sailors' slang for a berth on board ship, so the *Pinafore* hero's name could be interpreted as bedding straw. This seems to me a far-fetched suggestion. What is beyond doubt, however, is that his first name should be pronounced 'Rafe'. It has to rhyme with 'waif' in Little Buttercup's song 'A many years ago' (Act II, lines 461 and 463).

69–80 *The Nightingale/Sighed for the moon's bright ray*
The original version of this haunting song, as printed in the first edition libretto, began 'The nightingale/Loved the pale moon's bright ray' but was otherwise identical to the present version.

Several American audiences had the dubious pleasure of hearing this and Ralph's other songs sung by a soprano. Early productions of *Pinafore* in the United States followed the burlesque tradition of casting females in the romantic male leads. Thus the first Ralph Rackstraw in Boston was one Rose Temple, and the first on the west coast was Alice Oates.

81 *I know the value of a kindly chorus*: An appropriate line for a Gilbert and Sullivan principal to sing, since the Savoy Operas broke new ground in musical theatre in using the chorus to represent real people with a meaningful role in the action rather than just as a passive vehicle for setting a scene or telling a story. This elevation of the role of the chorus is something for which countless members of amateur operatic societies have cause to thank Gilbert, even if they may occasionally feel inclined to agree with Mad Margaret's definition of madness in *Ruddigore* as the singing of choruses in public.

83 *pain and sorrow*: In early libretti, though not in the first vocal score, this phrase appears as 'pain and trouble'.

85 *loves a lass*: The first of three rather excruciating puns which Gilbert inflicts on the *Pinafore* audience. The others are the play on 'birth' and 'berth' (lines 429–30) and Captain Corcoran's remark to Josephine that a photograph of Sir Joseph Porter may put her in a better frame of mind (line 237).

88–108 *A maiden fair to see*
As originally written by Gilbert, the second verse of this song had slightly different words:

> A suitor, lowly born,
> With hopeless passion torn,
>   And poor beyond concealing,
> Has dared for her to pine,
> At whose exalted shrine
>   A world of wealth is kneeling!

The plight of Ralph Rackstraw is foreshadowed in Gilbert's Bab Ballad 'Joe Golightly', which tells of a poor sailor, born in a workhouse, who is in love with the First Lord of the Admiralty's daughter, Lady Jane:

> Whene'er he sailed afar
> Upon a Channel cruise, he
> Unpacked his light guitar
> And sang this ballad (Boosey):

> The moon is on the sea, willow!
> The wind blows towards the lee, willow!
> But though I sigh and sob and cry,
> No Lady Jane for me, willow!

> She says, ' 'Twere folly quite, willow!
> For me to wed a wight, willow!
> Whose lot is cast before the mast',
> And possibly she's right, willow!

sound like the black utterances of a depraved imagination. It is human
nature – I am resigned.

RECITATIVE.

BUT.   But, tell me – who's the youth whose faltering feet
                 With difficulty bear him on his course?
BOAT.   That is the smartest lad in all the fleet –   65
                 Ralph Rackstraw!
BUT.   Ralph! That name! Remorse! Remorse!

(*Enter* RALPH.)

MADRIGAL – RALPH.

              The Nightingale
         Sighed for the moon's bright ray,   70
             And told his tale
       In his own melodious way!
            He sang 'Ah, well-a-day!'

ALL.   He sang 'Ah, well-a-day!'

              The lowly vale   75
       For the mountain vainly sighed,
             To his humble wail
       The echoing hills replied.
            They sang 'Ah, well-a-day!'

ALL.   They sang 'Ah, well-a-day!'   80

RECITATIVE.

       I know the value of a kindly chorus,
          But choruses yield little consolation
     When we have pain and sorrow too before us!
          I love – and love, alas, above my station!

BUT. (*aside*).   He loves – and loves a lass above his station!   85
ALL. (*aside*).   Yes, yes, the lass is much above his station!

(*Exit* LITTLE BUTTERCUP.)

BALLAD – RALPH.

              A maiden fair to see,
           The pearl of minstrelsy,
             A bud of blushing beauty;   90

112   *foremast hands*: Gilbert originally wrote 'foremast jacks', later substituted 'blue jackets' and finally produced 'foremast hands' for the 1908 revival of *Pinafore*. The term refers to those members of a ship's company who serve 'before the mast', i.e. all below the rank of officer.

117   *quarter-deck*: The stretch of deck to the aft of the mainmast where the officers and midshipmen had their quarters. Only commissioned officers could linger on the quarterdeck.

117–18   *fore-yard arm*: The ends of the large wooden spar which crossed the mast and from which sails were set. Flag signals were generally hoisted on the yard arms, and in the days when the code of punishments aboard included death by hanging they were also used for that purpose.

118–19   *main-truck*: A circular wooden cap fitted on the highest point of the mainmast.

119   *slacks*: A traditional nautical term for trousers.

126   *Captain Corcoran*: Once again, Gilbert borrowed from his earlier works to create the character of Captain Corcoran. He bears a close resemblance, for example, to the hero of the Bab Ballad 'Captain Reece':

> Of all the ships upon the blue
> No ship contained a better crew
> Than that of worthy CAPTAIN REECE,
> Commanding of *The Mantelpiece*.
>
> He was adored by all his men,
> For worthy CAPTAIN REECE, R.N.,
> Did all that lay within him to
> Promote the comfort of his crew.

There is more than a hint of Corcoran too in Captain Bang, a pirate chief in *Our Island Home*, a musical entertainment for which Gilbert wrote the words in 1870, who boasts:

> I'm a hardy sailor, too;
> I've a vessel and a crew,
> When it doesn't blow a gale
> I can reef a little sail.
> I never go below
> And I generally know
> The weather from the 'lee',
> And I'm never sick at sea.

> For whom proud nobles sigh,
>   And with each other vie
>   To do her menial's duty.

ALL.   To do her menial's duty.

> A suitor, lowly born,   95
>   With hopeless passion torn,
>   And poor beyond denying,
>   Has dared for her to pine
>   At whose exalted shrine
>   A world of wealth is sighing.   100

ALL.   A world of wealth is sighing!

> Unlearned he in aught
>   Save that which love has taught
>   (For love had been his tutor);
>   Oh, pity, pity me –   105
>   Our captain's daughter she,
>   And I that lowly suitor!

ALL.   And he that lowly suitor!

BOAT. Ah, my poor lad, you've climbed too high; our worthy captain's child won't have nothin' to say to a poor chap like you. Will she, lads?   110
ALL. No, no!
DICK. No, no, captains' daughters don't marry foremast hands.
ALL (*recoiling from him*). Shame! Shame!
BOAT. Dick Deadeye, them sentiments o' yourn are a disgrace to our common natur'.   115
RALPH. But it's a strange anomaly, that the daughter of a man who hails from the quarter-deck may not love another who lays out on the fore-yard arm. For a man is but a man, whether he hoists his flag at the main-truck or his slacks on the main-deck.
DICK. Ah, it's a queer world!   120
RALPH. Dick Deadeye, I have no desire to press hardly on you, but such a revolutionary sentiment is enough to make an honest sailor shudder.
BOAT. My lads, our gallant captain has come on deck; let us greet him as so brave an officer and so gallant a seaman deserves.   125

(*Enter* CAPTAIN CORCORAN.)

143 *I can hand, reef, and steer*: This same line is given to Lieutenant Belaye in the Bab Ballad 'The Bumboat Woman's Story'. He also makes the additional boast, not made by Captain Corcoran, that he can 'fire my big gun too'. To hand is to take in and furl a sail; to reef is to reduce the area of a sail exposed to the wind by partially furling it.

144 *ship a selvagee*: A selvagee is a strop of spun yarn either plaited into a stout rope or tied together into parallel lengths. It was used as a strap to fasten round a shroud or stay or for making a sling to lift heavy weights. One of the *Bab Ballads*, 'The Mystic Selvagee', tells of Sir Blennerhasset Portico, a Captain in the Royal Navy, who believes in removing selvagees from the maintop-stays of ships.

150–51 *What, never?/Well, hardly ever*: This became a popular catch-phrase in Britain and even more in the United States as *Pinafore* mania swept both sides of the Atlantic in the winter of 1878–9. One American newspaper editor is said to have called all his reporters into his office and complained that the phrase had occurred twenty times in the previous day's paper. 'Never let me see it again,' he ordered. 'What, never?' came the inevitable reply. 'Well, hardly ever,' he found himself responding.

RECITATIVE.

CAPT.   My gallant crew, good morning.
ALL (*saluting*).   Sir, good morning!
CAPT.   I hope you're all quite well.
ALL (*as before*).   Quite well; and you, sir?
CAPT.   I am in reasonable health, and happy   130
          To meet you all once more.
ALL (*as before*).   You do us proud, sir!

SONG – CAPTAIN.

CAPT.   I am the Captain of the *Pinafore*;
ALL.   And a right good captain, too!
CAPT.   You're very, very good,   135
             And be it understood,
         I command a right good crew.
ALL.   We're very, very good,
             And be it understood,
         He commands a right good crew.   140
CAPT.   Though related to a peer,
         I can hand, reef, and steer,
            And ship a selvagee;
         I am never known to quail   145
         At the fury of a gale,
            And I'm never, never sick at sea!
ALL.   What, never?
CAPT.   No, never!
ALL.   What, *never*?   150
CAPT.   Well, hardly ever!
ALL.   He's hardly ever sick at sea!
         Then give three cheers, and one cheer more,
         For the hardy Captain of the *Pinafore*!

CAPT.   I do my best to satisfy you all –   155
ALL.   And with you we're quite content.
CAPT.   You're exceedingly polite,
            And I think it only right
         To return the compliment.
ALL.   We're exceedingly polite,   160
            And he thinks it's only right
         To return the compliment.
CAPT.   Bad language or abuse,
            I never, never use,

168 *I never use a big, big D*: The idea of a sailor who didn't swear was evidently something
which Gilbert found particularly amusing. In 'The Bumboat Woman's Story' he alluded
to the 'gentle, well-bred crew' of the gunboat *Hot Cross Bun*:

> When Jack Tars growl, I believe they growl with a big, big D —
> But the strongest oath of *The Hot Cross Buns* was a mild 'Dear me!'

The same subject also features in another Bab Ballad, 'The Bishop of Rum-ti-Foo':

> Some sailors whom he did not know
> Had landed there not long ago,
> And taught them 'Bother', also 'Blow',
> (Of wickedness the germs).
> No need to use a casuist's pen
> To prove that they were merchantmen;
> No sailor of the Royal N.
> Would use such awful terms.

175 *Captain of the Pinafore*: In an interview in *The World* in 1880 Gilbert admitted that the
name *Pinafore* 'was suggested entirely by rhyme . . . something had to rhyme with "three
cheers more" '. He had originally christened his operatic vessel H.M.S. *Semaphore*, but
it was changed to *Pinafore* at Sullivan's suggestion.

184 *ancestral timber*: A suitably nautical if rather highfalutin expression for the family tree.

194–205 *Sorry her lot who loves too well*
The ballad which introduces Josephine may sound familiar to those who have never
heard *H.M.S. Pinafore* but have seen the Joseph Papp production of *The Pirates of Penzance*. For some reason, Papp gave Mabel Josephine's ballad to croon immediately after
her long duet with Frederic in Act II.

Whatever the emergency;   165
Though 'Bother it' I may
Occasionally say,
I never use a big, big D –

ALL.   What, never?
CAPT.   No, never!   170
ALL.   What, *never*?
CAPT.   Well, hardly ever!
ALL.   Hardly ever swears a big, big D –

Then give three cheers, and one cheer more,
For the well-bred Captain of the *Pinafore*!   175

(After song exeunt all but CAPTAIN.*)*

(Enter LITTLE BUTTERCUP.*)*

RECITATIVE.

BUT.   Sir, you are sad! The silent eloquence
                Of yonder tear that trembles on your eyelash
                Proclaims a sorrow far more deep than common;   180
                Confide in me – fear not – I am a mother!

CAPT.   Yes, Little Buttercup, I'm sad and sorry –
                My daughter, Josephine, the fairest flower
                That ever blossomed on ancestral timber,
                Is sought in marriage by Sir Joseph Porter,   185
                Our Admiralty's First Lord, but for some reason
                She does not seem to tackle kindly to it.

BUT. *(with emotion)*. Ah, poor Sir Joseph! Ah, I know too well
                The anguish of a heart that loves but vainly!
                But see, here comes your most attractive daughter.   190
                I go – Farewell!   *(Exit.)*

CAPT. *(looking after her)*. A plump and pleasing person!   *(Exit.)*

(Enter JOSEPHINE, *twining some flowers which she carries in a small basket.)*

BALLAD – JOSEPHINE.

Sorry her lot who loves too well,
    Heavy the heart that hopes but vainly,   195
Sad are the sighs that own the spell,
    Uttered by eyes that speak too plainly;

208 *Sir Joseph Porter, K.C.B.*: Snob that he is, Captain Corcoran cannot resist making the
     most of Sir Joseph Porter's knighthood. K.C.B. stands for Knight Commander of the
     Bath. This is the second class of the Order of the Bath, the first being Grand Cross of
     the Bath (G.C.B.) and the third Companion of the Bath (C.B.). There are two other
     K.C.B.s in the Savoy Operas: Sir Marmaduke Pointdextre in *The Sorcerer* and our old
     friend Captain Corcoran, who reappears as Captain Sir Edward Corcoran in *Utopia Lim-
     ited* (see the note to Act II, line 538).

227–8 *solecisms that society would never pardon*: After this line, Gilbert originally intended Cap-
     tain Corcoran to have a ballad highlighting the English obsession with the outward
     marks of class and status rather than the inner qualities of character and creativity. The
     song occurs in the copy of the intended libretto sent to the Lord Chamberlain but was
     jettisoned before the first performance. Here it is:

BALLAD – CAPTAIN.

Reflect my child, he may be brave
As any in the Royal navy
And daily fill a watery grave
The locker of poor Davy.
But ah! What gallant act
Could counteract
The fearful social ban
That falls on man
Who with his knife's sharp blade devours his prey!

ENSEMBLE.   In truth I fear
                The sneer
                That would disgrace
                Each face
                When he with blade of knife devoured his prey.

                He may a second Shakespeare be,
                Endowed with faulty* creative
                But what avail such gifts, if he
                Confounds accusative with dative,
                In what far nook of earth
                Would mortal worth,
                Or strength of lung or limb,
                Atone for him
                Whose verbs don't tally with the nominative.

ENSEMBLE.   Oh, I can tell
                Too well
                How people frown
                Him down
                Whose verbs don't tally with the nominative.

* This should surely be 'faculty' and must be a misprint in the licence copy.

> Heavy the sorrow that bows the head
> When love is alive and hope is dead!

> Sad is the hour when sets the sun –   200
>   Dark is the night to earth's poor daughters,
> When to the ark the wearied one
>   Flies from the empty waste of waters!
>   Heavy the sorrow that bows the head
>   When love is alive and hope is dead!   205

(*Enter* CAPTAIN.)

CAPT. My child, I grieve to see that you are a prey to melancholy. You should look your best to-day, for Sir Joseph Porter, K.C.B., will be here this afternoon to claim your promised hand.

JOS. Ah, father, your words cut me to the quick. I can esteem –   210
reverence – venerate Sir Joseph, for he is a great and good man; but oh, I cannot love him! My heart is already given.

CAPT. (*aside*). It is then as I feared. (*Aloud*.) Given? And to whom? Not to some gilded lordling?

JOS. No, father – the object of my love is no lordling. Oh, pity me, for   215
he is but a humble sailor on board your own ship!

CAPT. Impossible!

JOS. Yes, it is true – too true.

CAPT. A common sailor? Oh fie!

JOS. I blush for the weakness that allows me to cherish such a passion.   220
I hate myself when I think of the depth to which I have stooped in permitting myself to think tenderly of one so ignobly born, but I love him! I love him! I love him! (*Weeps*.)

CAPT. Come, my child, let us talk this over. In a matter of the heart I would not coerce my daughter – I attach but little value to rank or wealth, but   225
the line must be drawn somewhere. A man in that station may be brave and worthy, but at every step he would commit solecisms that society would never pardon.

JOS. Oh, I have thought of this night and day. But fear not, father, I have a heart, and therefore I love; but I am your daughter, and therefore I am   230
proud. Though I carry my love with me to the tomb, he shall never, never know it.

CAPT. You *are* my daughter after all. But see, Sir Joseph's barge approaches, manned by twelve trusty oarsmen and accompanied by the admiring crowd of sisters, cousins, and aunts that attend him wherever he   235
goes. Retire, my daughter, to your cabin – take this, his photograph, with you – it may help to bring you to a more reasonable frame of mind.

JOS. My own thoughtful father!

243 *the loud nine-pounders*: These were the smallest long cannons carried on Royal Navy ships in the first half of the nineteenth century. Large warships like the *Pinafore* would have them mounted on the fo'c'sle and quarter-decks, with bigger eighteen- and thirty-two-pounders providing the main armament on lower decks.

247–58 *Sir Joseph's barge is seen*
In early editions of the libretto, the first four lines of this chorus take the form of a repeat of the first four lines of the sailors' opening chorus.

Although the last words of the second and fourth lines are printed as 'beauties' and 'duties' in some modern editions of the libretto, they appear as 'beauty' and 'duty' in the vocal score and are often sung in that form.

The rhyming of 'beauty' and 'duty' occurs in fifteen separate songs in the Savoy Operas. Four of them are in *H.M.S. Pinafore* (the opening chorus and its reprise here, Ralph's ballad 'A maiden fair to see', Josephine and Ralph's duet 'Refrain, audacious tar', and Josephine's song 'A simple sailor, lowly born').

261–70 *Gaily tripping*
Like so much else in *Pinafore*, the chorus of female relatives who make their entrance to this infectiously gay tune have their origins in the *Bab Ballads*. The worthy Captain Reece, whom we have already come across as the prototype of Captain Corcoran, has ten female cousins, a niece, six sisters, an aunt or two and a widowed mother whom he philanthropically unites to unmarried members of his crew. For *Pinafore* Gilbert transfers the relatives to the First Lord of the Admiralty, just as he changes Joe Golightly's love for the First Lord's daughter into Ralph Rackstraw's passion for his captain's daughter.

(*Exit* JOSEPHINE. CAPTAIN *remains and ascends the poop-deck.*)

BARCAROLLE (*invisible*).

Over the bright blue sea   240
Comes Sir Joseph Porter, K.C.B.,
Wherever he may go
Bang-bang the loud nine-pounders go!
Shout o'er the bright blue sea
For Sir Joseph Porter, K.C.B.   245

(*During this the Crew have entered on tiptoe, listening attentively to the song.*)

CHORUS OF SAILORS.

Sir Joseph's barge is seen,
And its crowd of blushing beauties,
We hope he'll find us clean,
And attentive to our duties.   250
We sail, we sail the ocean blue,
And our saucy ship's a beauty.
We're sober, sober men and true
And attentive to our duty.
We're smart and sober men,   255
And quite devoid of fe-ar,
In all the Royal N.
None are so smart as we are.

(*Enter* SIR JOSEPH'S FEMALE RELATIVES.
They dance round stage.)   260

REL.	Gaily tripping,
	Lightly skipping,
	Flock the maidens to the shipping.
SAILORS.	Flags and guns and pennants dipping!
	All the ladies love the shipping.
REL.	Sailors sprightly
	Always rightly
	Welcome ladies so politely.
SAILORS.	Ladies who can smile so brightly,
	Sailors welcome most politely.
CAPT. (*from poop*).	Now give three cheers, I'll lead the way.
	Hurrah! hurrah!
ALL.	Hurray! hurray! hurray!

265

270

(*Enter* SIR JOSEPH *with* COUSIN HEBE.)

275–92 *I am the monarch of the sea*

Sir Joseph Porter's entrance is normally accompanied by a Royal Marine guard, consisting of a sergeant and two privates who present arms as the First Lord of the Admiralty steps on to the quarter-deck of the *Pinafore*.

When George Grossmith, the principal comic baritone with D'Oyly Carte's Comedy Opera Company, who created so many of what might be termed the 'patter song roles', first made his entrance on the opening night of *H.M.S. Pinafore*, he was made up to look like Lord Nelson. However, as the opera progressed there was little doubt in the audience's mind about the identity of the real model for Sir Joseph Porter. In background, character and attitudes he was strikingly similar to William Henry Smith, founder of the newsagent's business which still bears his name, who had been appointed First Lord of the Admiralty the previous year.

Until the post was abolished in 1964 with the incorporation of the Admiralty into the Ministry of Defence, the First Lord of the Admiralty was the Government minister in charge of the Navy. Although the office was a political one, carrying a seat in the Cabinet, it was often held in the nineteenth century by someone with personal experience in the Navy and nearly always by someone of aristocratic, or at the very least upper-middle-class, background. Smith had never been to sea and had risen from the humble origins of selling newspapers at railway-station bookstalls. Sir Joseph Porter was in a very similar position, as his next song was to make clear.

293–340 *When I was a lad I served a term*

It was this song which firmly established W. H. Smith as the model for Sir Joseph Porter in the eyes of the British public. Gilbert himself had rather mischievously denied the suggestion in a letter he wrote to Sullivan late in 1877 when he was still working out the songs of the proposed new opera:

> Among other things there is a song for the First Lord – tracing his career as office boy in cotton broker's office, clerk, traveller, junior partner, and First Lord of Britain's Navy. I think a splendid song can be made of this. Of course there will be no personality in this – the fact that the First Lord in the opera is a Radical of the most pronounced type will do away with any suspicion that W. H. Smith is intended.

Of course, Gilbert knew perfectly well that everyone would think of W. H. Smith when they heard Sir Joseph Porter chronicling his rise from office boy to ruler of the Navy and urging those who would emulate him to stick close to their desks and never go to sea. Following the success of the opera, Smith, who remained as First Lord until the fall of Disraeli's Government in 1880, became universally known as 'Pinafore Smith'. 'When I was a lad' was even played by a Royal Marine band when he went down to launch a ship at Devonport, although strict orders had gone out from the Port Admiral that music from *Pinafore* should on no account be performed.

In fact, as he indicated, Gilbert's satire was directed much more against the system which put in charge of Government depatments those who were wholly ignorant of their affairs than against W. H. Smith as an individual. In a summary of *H.M.S. Pinafore* which he later wrote for children, Gilbert explained his creation of Sir Joseph Porter: 'You would naturally think that a person who commanded the entire British Navy would be the most accomplished sailor who could be found, but that is not the way in which such things are managed in England'.

294 *an Attorney's firm*: Until 1873 those lawyers (other than barristers) who practised in the courts of equity were called solicitors and those in common law courts attorneys. The Judicature Act of that year brought the two groups together under the common title of solicitors of the Supreme Court.

296 *I polished up the handle of the big front door*: In the winter of 1881 Sullivan accompanied the Duke of Edinburgh on a Baltic cruise on board H.M.S. *Hercules*. At Kiel they were greeted by Prince William of Prussia, who bowed to the composer and sang 'He polished

SONG – Sir Joseph.

I am the monarch of the sea, 275
The ruler of the Queen's Navee,
Whose praise Great Britain loudly chants.

COUSIN HEBE. And we are his sisters, and his cousins, and his aunts!
REL. And we are his sisters, and his cousins, and his aunts!
SIR JOSEPH. When at anchor here I ride, 280
My bosom swells with pride,
And I snap my fingers at a foeman's taunts;
COUSIN HEBE. And so do his sisters, and his cousins, and his aunts!
ALL. And so do his sisters, and his cousins, and his aunts!
SIR JOSEPH. But when the breezes blow, 285
I generally go below,
And seek the seclusion that a cabin grants!
COUSIN HEBE. And so do his sisters, and his cousins, and his aunts!
ALL. And so do his sisters, and his cousins, and his aunts!
His sisters and his cousins,
Whom he reckons up by dozens, 290
And his aunts!

SONG – Sir Joseph.

When I was a lad I served a term
As office boy to an Attorney's firm.
I cleaned the windows and I swept the floor,
And I polished up the handle of the big front door. 295
    CHORUS. – He polished, etc.
I polished up that handle so carefullee
That now I am the Ruler of the Queen's Navee!
    CHORUS. – He polished, etc. 300

As office boy I made such a mark
That they gave me the post of a junior clerk.
I served the writs with a smile so bland,
And I copied all the letters in a big round hand –
    CHORUS. – He copied, etc. 305
I copied all the letters in a hand so free,
That now I am the Ruler of the Queen's Navee!
    CHORUS. – He copied, etc.

In serving writs I made such a name
That an articled clerk I soon became; 310
I wore clean collars and a brand-new suit
For the pass examination at the Institute.

up the handle of the big front door'. Sullivan noted 'I burst out laughing and so did everyone. It was too funny.' Seven years later William was the Kaiser.

303   *I served the writs:* To serve a writ is to deliver a legal document, often summoning a person to appear in court.

310   *an articled clerk:* One undergoing a form of apprenticeship before becoming a fully qualified solicitor.

312   *the Institute:* The Law Society, the governing body for solicitors, which organizes qualifying examinations for entry into the profession, was also known as the Law Institute.

326   *a pocket borough:* A parliamentary seat in the gift of a single individual, normally a wealthy landowner. Pocket boroughs, which contained at the most only a handful of electors and in some cases had none at all, were effectively abolished in the Great Reform Act of 1832. The Fairy Queen in *Iolanthe* has 'a borough or two' at her disposal and puts Strephon into the House of Commons by this means.

343   *a very small midshipman:* Midshipman is a non-commissioned rank in the Royal Navy just below the officer level. Traditionally young men destined to become officers serve first for a three-year period as midshipmen before becoming sub-lieutenants.

   In some editions of the *Pinafore* libretto the midshipman (or midshipmite, as he is sometimes called) appears in the list of *Dramatis personæ* and is given the name Tom Tucker. It is, however, a very minor part, with no lines to say and no notes to sing, and it is traditionally played by a small boy. The former British Prime Minister Lord Wilson of Rievaulx began his life-long love affair with Gilbert and Sullivan when he played the part in a production of *Pinafore* by the Milnsbridge Baptist Amateur Operatic Society near his home town of Huddersfield, Yorkshire, in 1926.

CHORUS. – For the pass examination, etc.
That pass examination did so well for me,
That now I am the Ruler of the Queen's Navee!
       CHORUS. – That pass examination, etc.

Of legal knowledge I acquired such a grip
That they took me into the partnership.
And that junior partnership, I ween,
Was the only ship that I ever had seen.
       CHORUS. – Was the only ship that he, etc.
       But that kind of ship so suited me,
       That now I am the Ruler of the Queen's Navee!
       CHORUS. – But that kind, etc.

I grew so rich that I was sent
By a pocket borough into Parliament.
I always voted at my party's call,
And I never thought of thinking for myself at all.
       CHORUS. – He never thought, etc.
       I thought so little, they rewarded me
       By making me the Ruler of the Queen's Navee!
       CHORUS. – He thought so little, etc.

Now, landsmen all, whoever you may be,
If you want to rise to the top of the tree,
If your soul isn't fettered to an office stool,
Be careful to be guided by this golden rule –
       CHORUS. – Be careful, etc.
       Stick close to your desks and never go to sea,
       And you all may be Rulers of the Queen's Navee!
       CHORUS. – Stick close, etc.

SIR JOSEPH. You've a remarkably fine crew, Captain Corcoran.
CAPT. It *is* a fine crew, Sir Joseph.
SIR JOSEPH (*examining a very small midshipman*). A British sailor is a splendid fellow, Captain Corcoran.
CAPT. A splendid fellow indeed, Sir Joseph.
SIR JOSEPH. I hope you treat your crew kindly, Captain Corcoran.
CAPT. Indeed I hope so, Sir Joseph.
SIR JOSEPH. Never forget that they are the bulwarks of England's greatness, Captain Corcoran.
CAPT. So I have always considered them, Sir Joseph.
SIR JOSEPH. No bullying, I trust – no strong language of any kind, eh?
CAPT. Oh, never, Sir Joseph.

364 *Dick comes forward*: Dick Deadeye's step forward in response to Sir Joseph's request did not feature in the earliest productions of *H.M.S. Pinafore*. Like several of Dick's lines, this particular bit of stage business was added, quite possibly on the suggestion of Richard Temple, the singer who created the role of Deadeye. It was approved by Gilbert in the libretto prepared for the 1908 revival of the opera at the Savoy Theatre.

366 *Ralph Rackstraw, three paces to the front – march*: This order was also added with Gilbert's approval for the 1908 revival, the original line being simply 'Ralph Rackstraw, come here'. It is the cue for a typical piece of D'Oyly Carte business, described by Martyn Green in his *Treasury of Gilbert and Sullivan*. As Ralph steps forward, he salutes Sir Joseph and stamps his right foot. Sir Joseph, a little taken aback by this, inspects him and indicates that he wants him to turn round. Ralph does so and again stamps his foot. His response to Sir Joseph's first comment, 'You're a remarkably fine fellow', is to stamp his foot yet again. Not to be outdone, Sir Joseph stamps his right foot too, only to bring it down hard on his left toes.

374 *topman*: A seaman stationed at the top of a mast, either to attend to the sails, or as a marksman during an engagement.

379 *all sailors should dance hornpipes*: The hornpipe was originally a wind instrument, which gave its name to the vigorous solo dance associated particularly with sailors from the eighteenth century onwards. It is said that the hornpipe was danced at sea in order to keep the blood circulating and to ward off scurvy. Sullivan wrote a hornpipe to be danced by the *Pinafore* crew after their first singing of 'A British tar is a soaring soul', but it was cut out after the first night. The one danced by Richard Dauntless in Act I of *Ruddigore* has, however, been allowed to remain and is a splendid example of the genre.

387 *I can hum a little, your honour*: Traditionally Ralph, in keeping with his common origins, drops the 'h' in 'hum', and Sir Joseph, temporarily forgetting his rapid rise from a similarly lowly station, does the same in the next line before he quickly corrects himself.

SIR JOSEPH. What, *never?*

CAPT. Well, hardly ever, Sir Joseph. They are an excellent crew, and do their work thoroughly without it. 355

SIR JOSEPH. Don't patronize them, sir – pray, don't patronize them.

CAPT. Certainly not, Sir Joseph.

SIR JOSEPH. That you are their captain is an accident of birth. I cannot permit these noble fellows to be patronized because an accident of birth has placed you above them and them below you. 360

CAPT. I am the last person to insult a British sailor, Sir Joseph.

SIR JOSEPH. You are the last person who did, Captain Corcoran. Desire that splendid seaman to step forward.

(DICK *comes forward.*)

SIR JOSEPH. No, no, the other splendid seaman. 365

CAPT. Ralph Rackstraw, three paces to the front – march!

SIR JOSEPH (*sternly*). If what?

CAPT. I beg your pardon – I don't think I understand you.

SIR JOSEPH. If you *please.*

CAPT. Oh, yes, of course. If you please. (RALPH *steps forward.*) 370

SIR JOSEPH. You're a remarkably fine fellow.

RALPH. Yes, your honour.

SIR JOSEPH. And a first-rate seaman, I'll be bound.

RALPH. There's not a smarter topman in the Navy, your honour, though I say it who shouldn't. 375

SIR JOSEPH. Not at all. Proper self-respect, nothing more. Can you dance a hornpipe?

RALPH. No, your honour.

SIR JOSEPH. That's a pity: all sailors should dance hornpipes. I will teach you one this evening, after dinner. Now tell me – don't be afraid – how 380 does your captain treat you, eh?

RALPH. A better captain don't walk the deck, your honour.

ALL. Aye! Aye!

SIR JOSEPH. Good. I like to hear you speak well of your commanding officer; I daresay he don't deserve it, but still it does you credit. Can you 385 sing?

RALPH. I can hum a little, your honour.

SIR JOSEPH. Then hum this at your leisure. (*Giving him MS. music.*) It is a song that I have composed for the use of the Royal Navy. It is designed to encourage independence of thought and action in the lower branches of 390 the service, and to teach the principle that a British sailor is any man's equal, excepting mine. Now, Captain Corcoran, a word with you in your cabin, on a tender and sentimental subject.

CAPT. Aye, aye, Sir Joseph. (*Crossing.*) Boatswain, in commemoration of

395 *grog*: In 1740 Admiral Vernon introduced a daily issue of rum diluted with water to all men serving in the Royal Navy. His intention was to mitigate the evil effects of the raw spirit which most sailors had previously taken in copious quantities. The name given to the diluted rum derived from the Admiral's nickname, 'Old Grog', a reference to the grogram trousers he habitually wore. The Navy abolished the daily issue of grog in 1970.

396 *seven bells*: The twenty-four-hour day on board ship is divided into six watches, each four hours long. The ship's bell is rung every half hour, so there are eight bells in each watch. Seven bells therefore marks the last half hour of the watch.

404 *The expression, 'if you please'*: In making Sir Joseph Porter such a stickler for good manners and good language, Gilbert may have been having another little dig at W. H. Smith, who was known to have strong views on both matters. Brought up by strict Methodist parents, and himself an evangelical Anglican, Smith deplored coarseness and lewdness of any kind.

423 *Messmates*: In Army and Navy parlance, the mess is the place where meals are served and eaten. The word mess originally meant a small portion of food and so came to be used for a group of people who sat together for meals and were served from the same dishes.

435 *What is to be done with this here hopeless chap*: In answer to this question, in D'Oyly Carte productions the crew have traditionally indicated by making a splashing sound that Dick should be thrown overboard.

this joyous occasion, see that extra grog is served out to the ship's company 395
at seven bells.

BOAT. Beg pardon. If what, your honour?

CAPT. If what? I don't think I understand you.

BOAT. If you *please*, your honour.

CAPT. What! 400

SIR JOSEPH. The gentleman is quite right. If you *please*.

CAPT. (*stamping his foot impatiently*). If you *please*! (*Exit.*)

SIR JOSEPH.   For I hold that on the seas
                 The expression, 'if you please',
                   A particularly gentlemanly tone implants. 405

COUSIN HEBE. And so do his sisters, and his cousins, and his aunts!

ALL.   And so do his sisters, and his cousins, and his aunts!
                  (*Exeunt* SIR JOSEPH *and* RELATIVES.)

BOAT. Ah! Sir Joseph's a true gentleman; courteous and considerate to
the very humblest. 410

RALPH. True, Boatswain, but we are not the very humblest. Sir Joseph
has explained our true position to us. As he says, a British seaman is any
man's equal excepting his, and if Sir Joseph says that, is it not our duty to
believe him?

ALL. Well spoke! well spoke! 415

DICK. You're on a wrong tack, and so is he. He means well, but he
don't know. When people have to obey other people's orders, equality's out
of the question.

ALL (*recoiling*). Horrible! horrible!

BOAT. Dick Deadeye, if you go for to infuriate this here ship's company 420
too far, I won't answer for being able to hold 'em in. I'm shocked! that's what
I am – shocked!

RALPH. Messmates, my mind's made up. I'll speak to the captain's
daughter, and tell her, like an honest man, of the honest love I have for her.

ALL. Aye, aye! 425

RALPH. Is not my love as good as another's? Is not my heart as true as
another's? Have I not hands and eyes and ears and limbs like another?

ALL. Aye, aye!

RALPH. True, I lack birth –

BOAT. You've a berth on board this very ship. 430

RALPH. Well said – I had forgotten that. Messmates – what do you say?
Do you approve my determination?

ALL. We do.

DICK. *I* don't.

BOAT. What is to be done with this here hopeless chap? Let us sing 435

438–55 *A British tar is a soaring soul*
This stirring three-part glee, in its tune slightly reminiscent of the popular sea shanty 'Tom Bowling', is the first of Gilbert's two great patriotic songs in *H.M.S. Pinafore*. The second is, of course, 'He is an Englishman'. In producing such flag-waving stuff Gilbert was reflecting the general mood of the country at the time *Pinafore* was written. Disraeli's decision to send the British fleet to Constantinople in February 1878 to defend it from possible Russian attack produced a wave of patriotism and military adventurism throughout Britain, which lasted for more than two months and was only just beginning to subside as *Pinafore* took to the stage. It was during this period, indeed, that the word jingoism was added to the English language as a result of the popular music-hall song written by G. W. Hunt at the same time that Gilbert was writing *Pinafore*:

> We don't want to fight, but by Jingo if we do,
> We've got the ships, we've got the men, and got the money too.
> We've fought the Bear before, and while we're Britons true,
> The Russians shall not have Constantinople.

447 *His eyes should flash*: Some of the striking anatomical postures demanded in this song were anticipated in the *Bab Ballads*. In 'Peter the Wag', a London policeman finds that the citizens of the capital are less than helpful when he asks them directions:

> Their eyes would flash – their teeth would grind –
> Their lips would tightly curl –
> They'd say, 'Thy way thyself must find,
> Thou misdirecting churl!'

The curling lip also finds its way into another Bab Ballad, 'The Scornful Colonel':

> At sight of snobs his lip would curl –
> His lips would quiver, twist, and twirl
> In an astonishing degree –
> He often curled his lip at me.

465 *How my heart beats*: In early editions of the libretto this line read 'How my head beats!' This was almost certainly a misprint.

470–71 *the Cimmerian darkness*: In the *Odyssey*, Homer says that the Cimmerians dwell in a land beyond the ocean where the sun never shines.

471 *a living ganglion*: The *Oxford English Dictionary* variously defines a ganglion as a tumour or swelling of a tendon, enlargement or knot of a nerve, collection of grey matter in the central nervous system, and (as here) a centre of force, activity or interest, a point from which many lines diverge.

him the song that Sir Joseph has kindly composed for us. Perhaps it will
bring this here miserable creetur to a proper state of mind.   (*Exit* DICK.)

GLEE – RALPH, BOATSWAIN, BOATSWAIN'S MATE, *and* CHORUS.

> A British tar is a soaring soul,
>   As free as a mountain bird,
> His energetic fist should be ready to resist
>   A dictatorial word.
> His nose should pant and his lip should curl,
> His cheeks should flame and his brow should furl,
> His bosom should heave and his heart should glow,
> And his fist be ever ready for a knock-down blow.
>   CHORUS. – His nose should pant, etc.

> His eyes should flash with an inborn fire,
>   His brow with scorn be wrung;
> He never should bow down to a domineering frown,
>   Or the tang of a tyrant tongue.
> His foot should stamp and his throat should growl,
> His hair should twirl and his face should scowl;
> His eyes should flash and his breast protrude,
> And this should be his customary attitude – (*pose*).
>   CHORUS. – His foot should stamp, etc.

(*All dance off excepting* RALPH, *who remains, leaning
pensively against bulwark.*)

(*Enter* JOSEPHINE *from cabin.*)

JOS. It is useless – Sir Joseph's attentions nauseate me. I know that he is
a truly great and good man, for he told me so himself, but to me he seems
tedious, fretful, and dictatorial. Yet his must be a mind of no common order,
or he would not dare to teach my dear father to dance a hornpipe on the
cabin table. (*Sees* RALPH.) Ralph Rackstraw! (*Overcome by emotion.*)
RALPH. Aye, lady – no other than poor Ralph Rackstraw!
JOS. (*aside*). How my heart beats! (*Aloud.*) And why poor, Ralph?
RALPH. I am poor in the essence of happiness, lady – rich only in never-
ending unrest. In me there meet a combination of antithetical elements
which are at eternal war with one another. Driven hither by objective
influences – thither by subjective emotions – wafted one moment into
blazing day, by mocking hope – plunged the next into the Cimmerian
darkness of tangible despair, I am but a living ganglion of irreconcilable
antagonisms. I hope I make myself clear, lady?

478 *Jove's armoury*: The armour of Jove, alias Jupiter, alias Zeus, the king of the gods in classical mythology, was thunder and lightning. He takes a prominent role in two of the operettas of Gilbert and Sullivan's French contemporary Jacques Offenbach (*Orpheus in the Underworld* and *La Belle Hélène*), and appears in *Thespis*.

Ralph's anything but simple eloquence is, of course, designed to show Josephine that he is not lacking in the accomplishments which come with gentlemanly birth and breeding. Inevitably it has precisely the opposite effect.

484 *Oh, my heart, my beating heart*: The word 'beating' was added by Gilbert for the 1908 revival, as was the subsequent phrase, 'Common! oh, the irony of the word!'

496–515 *Refrain, audacious tar*

In early editions of the libretto, instead of being obliged to repeat the first four lines of this song as she is now, Josephine had another four:

> Proud lords to seek my hand
> In throngs assemble,
> The loftiest in the land,
> Bow down and tremble!

Those lines make Josephine sound even more like Lady Jane, the First Lord of the Admiralty's daughter whom, it may be remembered, Joe Golightly unsuccessfully wooed in the Bab Ballad:

> The First Lord's daughter, proud,
> Snubbed Earls and Viscounts nightly,
> She sneered at Barts, aloud,
> And spurned poor Joe Golightly.

509 *That sails the water*: In early editions of the vocal score the word 'ploughs' occurs instead of 'sails', as it still does in Josephine's line in 'Never mind the why and wherefore'. The libretto, however, has always had 'sails' in this song.

Jos. Perfectly. (*Aside.*) His simple eloquence goes to my heart. Oh, if I dared – but no, the thought is madness! (*Aloud.*) Dismiss these foolish fancies, they torture you but needlessly. Come, make one effort. 475

RALPH (*aside*). I will – one. (*Aloud.*) Josephine!

Jos. (*indignantly*). Sir!

RALPH. Aye, even though Jove's armoury were launched at the head of the audacious mortal whose lips, unhallowed by relationship, dared to breathe that precious word, yet would I breathe it once, and then perchance 480 be silent evermore. Josephine, in one brief breath I will concentrate the hopes, the doubts, the anxious fears of six weary months. Josephine, I am a British sailor, and I love you!

Jos. Sir, this audacity! (*Aside.*) Oh, my heart, my beating heart! (*Aloud.*) This unwarrantable presumption on the part of a common sailor! (*Aside.*) 485 Common! oh, the irony of the word! (*Crossing, aloud.*) Oh, sir, you forget the disparity in our ranks.

RALPH. I forget nothing, haughty lady. I love you desperately, my life is in your hand – I lay it at your feet! Give me hope, and what I lack in education and polite accomplishments, that I will endeavour to acquire. 490 Drive me to despair, and in death alone I shall look for consolation. I am proud and cannot stop to implore. I have spoken and I wait your word.

Jos. You shall not wait long. Your proffered love I haughtily reject. Go, sir, and learn to cast your eyes on some village maiden in your own poor rank – they should be lowered before your captain's daughter! 495

DUET – JOSEPHINE *and* RALPH.

JOS.	Refrain, audacious tar,
	Your suit from pressing,
	Remember what you are,
	And whom addressing!
(*Aside.*)	I'd laugh my rank to scorn 500
	In union holy,
	Were he more highly born
	Or I more lowly!
RALPH.	Proud lady, have your way,
	Unfeeling beauty! 505
	You speak and I obey,
	It is my duty!
	I am the lowliest tar
	That sails the water,
	And you, proud maiden, are 510
	My captain's daughter!
(*Aside.*)	My heart with anguish torn
	Bows down before her,

532   *Rejects my humble gift, my lady*: Until 1908 the *Pinafore* libretto had the word 'love' where
the vocal score had 'gift'. The latter is much more appropriate, as it rhymes with 'adrift'
two lines down.

It is interesting that Ralph here addresses his remarks to Cousin Hebe, a figure who so
far has not assumed any great importance in the opera. In fact, Gilbert originally conceived Hebe's to be a more substantial speaking part and wrote several dialogue exchanges between her and Sir Joseph, with whom she was supposed to be infatuated.
However, the actress who was due to play Hebe, Mrs Howard Paul, left the company
shortly before the first night of *Pinafore*. The untried girl brought in hastily to replace
her, Jessie Bond (who was destined to become one of the first great stars of the D'Oyly
Carte Opera Company), protested that she was a singer rather than an actress, and so
Gilbert cut out most of the lines he had given to Hebe.

537   *I told you so*: After Dick's verse, the copy of *H.M.S. Pinafore* sent to the Lord Chamberlain
for licensing purposes has the following exchange between the First Relative (a figure
who appears only in the licence copy, where she has the singing lines later given to
Hebe) and Ralph:

FIRST RELATIVE.   Reject a British tar! The cream
                            Of all the virtues highly rated.

RALPH.   Impossible as it may seem,
                            The fact's precisely as I've stated.

She laughs my love to scorn,
Yet I adore her! 515

(Repeat refrain, ensemble, then exit JOSEPHINE *into cabin.)*

RALPH *(Recitative).* Can I survive this overbearing
Or live a life of mad despairing,
My proffered love despised, rejected?
No, no, it's not to be expected! 520
(Calling off.)
Messmates, ahoy!
Come here! Come here!

(Enter SAILORS, HEBE, RELATIVES, *and* BUTTERCUP.*)*

ALL. Aye, aye, my boy, 525
What cheer, what cheer?
Now tell us, pray,
Without delay,
What does she say –
What cheer, what cheer? 530

RALPH *(to* COUSIN HEBE*).*
The maiden treats my suit with scorn,
Rejects my humble gift, my lady;
She says I am ignobly born,
And cuts my hopes adrift, my lady.
ALL. Oh, cruel one.
DICK. She spurns your suit? Oho! Oho! 535
I told you so, I told you so.
SAILORS *and* RELATIVES.
Shall $\left\{\begin{matrix}\text{we}\\\text{they}\end{matrix}\right\}$ submit? Are $\left\{\begin{matrix}\text{we}\\\text{they}\end{matrix}\right\}$ but slaves?
Love comes alike to high and low –
Britannia's sailors rule the waves,
And shall they stoop to insult? No! No! 540
DICK. You must submit, you are but slaves;
A lady she! Oho! Oho!
You lowly toilers of the waves,
She spurns you all – I told you so!
RALPH. My friends, my leave of life I'm taking, 545
For oh, my heart, my heart is breaking.
When I am gone, oh, prithee tell
The maid that, as I died, I loved her well!

558 *For Josephine I fall*: Threats to commit suicide occur in two of the Savoy Operas, and there is an actual suicide in another: the unfortunate John Wellington Wells takes his own life at the end of *The Sorcerer* as it is the only way of removing the magic spell which has wrought such havoc to the happily married folks of Ploverleigh.

    Of those who threaten to take their own lives because of unrequited love, Ralph comes nearest to executing the deed. Nanki-Poo, discovered by Ko-Ko in the act of preparing a rope with which to hang himself in Act II of *The Mikado*, must be counted a pretty close runner-up. Ko-Ko's own threat to Katisha later in the same opera that he will kill himself unless she immediately consents to marry him must surely be taken rather less seriously.

561 *Ah! stay your hand! I love you*: Gilbert loves the dramatic device of the last-minute intervention by the leading lady just as the hero is resigning himself to utter despair. It occurs again in *The Pirates of Penzance* when Mabel rushes on to assure Frederic that there is one maiden who loves him.

ALL (*turning away, weeping*).

> Of life, alas! his leave he's taking, 550
> For ah! his faithful heart is breaking;
> When he is gone we'll surely tell
> The maid that, as he died, he loved her well.

> (*During Chorus* BOATSWAIN *has loaded pistol, which
> he hands to* RALPH.) 555

RALPH.

> Be warned, my messmates all
> Who love in rank above you –
> For Josephine I fall!

> (*Puts pistol to his head. All the sailors stop their ears.*)

> (*Enter* JOSEPHINE.) 560

JOS.   Ah! stay your hand! I love you!
ALL.   Ah! stay your hand – she loves you!
RALPH (*incredulously*). Loves me?
JOS.   Loves you!
ALL.   Yes, yes – ah, yes, – she loves you! 565

ENSEMBLE.

JOSEPHINE, HEBE *and* RALPH.

> Oh joy, oh rapture unforeseen,
> For now the sky is all serene;
> The god of day – the orb of love –
> Has hung his ensign high above,
>   The sky is all ablaze. 570

> With wooing words and loving song,
> We'll chase the lagging hours along,
> And if $\left\{\begin{array}{l}\text{I find}\\ \text{we find}\end{array}\right\}$ the maiden coy,
> $\left.\begin{array}{l}\text{I'll}\\ \text{we'll}\end{array}\right\}$ murmur forth decorous joy
>   In dreamy roundelays! 575

DICK DEADEYE.

> He thinks he's won his Josephine,
> But though the sky is now serene,
> A frowning thunderbolt above

589–601 *This very night*
This complicated number with its numerous quick parts constitutes a modern producer's (and conductor's) nightmare. Gilbert, however, tackled it with meticulous planning
and painstaking drilling of his cast, as he did every single song in the Savoy Operas. He
planned all the staging and movements initially on a model set, with coloured wooden
blocks representing each principal and member of the chorus. Once he had got his ideas
straight he translated them to his prompt-book and to the company, who were taken
through every movement and piece of business as though they were part of a military
operation.

612–15 *Let's give three cheers for the sailor's bride*
This happy, foot-tapping tune starts off the overture to *H.M.S. Pinafore*, the broad
themes of which were sketched out by Sullivan, with the details filled in probably by
Alfred Cellier, a fellow composer who conducted the Savoy Operas for five years. The
other numbers which feature in the overture are the section beginning 'I'd laugh my
rank to scorn' from 'Refrain, audacious tar', 'Never mind the why and wherefore', and 'A
British tar is a soaring soul', which, as here in Act I, provides a rousing finale.

615 *For the honest love of a sailor true*: In the libretto sent to the Lord Chamberlain these lines,
sung by the entire company, follow at this point and precede 'For a British tar':

> Though a lad in the fore
> He's the pride of the fleet;
> He can pull at an oar,
> He can tug at a sheet.
> When danger is near
> He's the pick of the crew –
> Then give him a cheer
> And his true love too.

May end their ill-assorted love
Which now is all ablaze.   580

Our captain, ere the day is gone,
Will be extremely down upon
The wicked men who art employ
To make his Josephine less coy
In many various ways.   585

JOSEPHINE, HEBE *and* RALPH.

	Oh joy, oh rapture unforeseen, etc.	
DICK.	Our captain soon, unless I'm wrong,	
	Will be extremely down upon, etc.	(*Exit* DICK.)

JOS.	This very night,	
HEBE.	With bated breath	590
RALPH.	And muffled oar –	
JOS.	Without a light,	
HEBE.	As still as death,	
RALPH.	We'll steal ashore.	
JOS.	A clergyman	
RALPH.	Shall make us one	595
BOAT.	At half-past ten,	
JOS.	And then we can	
RALPH.	Return, for none	
BOAT.	Can part them then!	600
ALL.	This very night, etc.	

(DICK *enters.*)

DICK.	Forbear, nor carry out the scheme you've planned;	
	She is a lady – you a foremast hand!	
	Remember, she's your gallant captain's daughter,	605
	And you the meanest slave that crawls the water!	

ALL.	Back, vermin, back,	
	Nor mock us!	
	Back, vermin, back,	
	You shock us!	610

(*Exit* DICK.)

Let's give three cheers for the sailor's bride
Who casts all thought of rank aside –
Who gives up home and fortune too
For the honest love of a sailor true!   615

JOSEPHINE, HEBE *and* RELATIVES.

For a British tar is a soaring soul
As free as a mountain bird!
His energetic fist should be ready to resist
A dictatorial word!
His eyes should flash with an inborn fire, 620
His brow with scorn be wrung;
He never should bow down to a domineering frown,
Or the tang of a tyrant tongue.

SAILORS.

His nose should pant and his lips should curl,
His cheeks should flame and his brow should furl, 625
His bosom should heave and his heart should glow,
And his fist be ever ready for a knock-down blow.

ENSEMBLE.

His foot should stamp and his throat should growl,
His hair should twirl and his face should scowl,
His eyes should flash and his breast protrude, 630
And this should be his customary attitude – (*pose*).

GENERAL DANCE.

END OF ACT I

1   *Captain discovered singing*: For Act II of *Pinafore* Captain Corcoran is traditionally kitted
    out in full naval mess dress, i.e. tails, black tie, white waistcoat and gold striped trousers.
    Some versions of the libretto have him accompanying himself on the guitar, others, as
    here, on the mandolin.
        There is a celebrated D'Oyly Carte Company story attached to this scene. At an early
    rehearsal of the first ever production of *Pinafore*, Gilbert told Rutland Barrington, the
    company's principal bass baritone, who was playing the part of Corcoran, to 'walk slowly
    toward the left stage, then sit on the skylight pensively.' When Barrington, who weighed
    over thirteen stone, followed the latter part of the direction, both the skylight and the
    surrounding woodwork collapsed under him. 'No,' said. Gilbert, 'that's expensively.'

4–19   *Fair moon, to thee I sing*
        This song has echoes of the Bab Ballad 'Joe Golightly'. Joe, it may be recalled, was infa-
    tuated with the First Lord of the Admiralty's daughter, and was constantly singing
    ballads to the moon to the accompaniment of his light guitar. This so annoyed his
    captain that he was given the terrible punishment of twelve years' solitary confinement
    with 500,000 lashes twice a day.
        The day after the first night of *H.M.S. Pinafore*, after reading the reviews together,
    Gilbert and Sullivan decided to cut 'Fair moon'. Rutland Barrington was unhappy with
    the ballad which he felt was too operatic for his voice and asked for a topical patter song
    instead. In the event, however, the decision to cut 'Fair moon' was rescinded, for reasons
    that are not entirely clear, and it remained in the libretto.

ACT II

Same Scene. Night. Awning removed. Moonlight. CAPTAIN *discovered singing on poop-deck, and accompanying himself on a mandolin.* LITTLE BUTTERCUP *seated on quarter-deck, gazing sentimentally at him.*

SONG – CAPTAIN.

Fair moon, to thee I sing,
　　Bright regent of the heavens,   5
Say, why is everything
　　Either at sixes or at sevens?
I have lived hitherto
　　Free from the breath of slander,
Beloved by all my crew –   10
　　A really popular commander.
But now my kindly crew rebel,
　　My daughter to a tar is partial,
Sir Joseph storms, and, sad to tell,
　　He threatens a court martial!   15
　　　Fair moon, to thee I sing,
　　　　Bright regent of the heavens,
　　　Say, why is everything
　　　　Either at sixes or at sevens?

BUT. How sweetly he carols forth his melody to the unconscious moon!   20
Of whom is he thinking? Of some high-born beauty? It may be! Who is poor
Little Buttercup that she should expect his glance to fall on one so lowly! And
yet if he knew – if he only knew!

CAPT. (*coming down*). Ah! Little Buttercup, still on board? That is not
quite right, little one. It would have been more respectable to have gone on   25
shore at dusk.

BUT. True, dear Captain – but the recollection of your sad pale face
seemed to chain me to the ship. I would fain see you smile before I go.

35 *such a one as this*: Printed as 'such an one as this' in some editions of the libretto, this
phrase recurs in *The Pirates of Penzance* in Frederic's song 'Oh, is there not one maiden
breast', with its lines 'To rescue such an one as I' and 'To such an one, if such there be'.

40 *The poor bumboat woman*: Bumboats were vessels used for conveying provisions to ships
lying off ports.

46–94 *Things are seldom what they seem*
This is one of two songs in the Savoy Operas (the other being the 'If you go in' trio in
Iolanthe) which are made up almost entirely of adaptations of traditional proverbs and
sayings. I have tried to unravel the originals and explain their meanings in the following
notes.

48 *Highlows*: Laced ankle boots of the kind typically worn by Victorian women and very different from patent leather shoes.

49 *Jackdaws strut in peacock's feathers*: This is taken from Aesop's fable about the jackdaw which
decked itself out in peacock's feathers to impress other birds and in fact only became a
general laughing-stock.

52 *Black sheep dwell in every fold*: A familiar English saying, meaning that there are bad individuals in every group, which is first found, according to the *Oxford Dictionary of English
Proverbs*, in Sir Walter Scott's *Old Mortality* (1816).

53 *All that glitters is not gold*: Adapted from the line 'All that glisters is not gold' in Shakespeare's *The Merchant of Venice*, Act II, Scene 7.

54 *Storks turn out to be but logs*: This is taken from another of Aesop's fables, 'King Log and
King Stork', which tells of a group of frogs who appealed to Jupiter for a king, and, being
dissatisfied with the log given to them, found him replaced by a stork. The normal saying is 'Neither a log nor a stork'.

55 *Bulls are but inflated frogs*: In Aesop's fable 'The Frog and the Ox', the mother frog wanted
to impress her children by making herself as big as an ox which was grazing nearby. She
puffed herself up and burst.

58 *Drops the wind and stops the mill*: The nearest proverb I can find to this is 'No weather ill, if
wind be still'.

59 *Turbot is ambitious brill*: Both turbot and brill are large flat fish, often weighing up to forty
pounds, but whereas the former is regarded as a considerable delicacy, the latter is not.

60 *Gild the farthing if you will*: I can find no original for this phrase, but its meaning is clear
enough. Until its withdrawal from circulation in 1961, the farthing, worth a quarter of a
penny, was the coin of lowest value in Britain.

CAPT. Ah! Little Buttercup, I fear it will be long before I recover my
accustomed cheerfulness, for misfortunes crowd upon me, and all my old 30
friends seem to have turned against me!

BUT. Oh no – do not say 'all', dear Captain. That were unjust to one, at
least.

CAPT. True, for you are staunch to me. (*Aside.*) If ever I gave my heart
again, methinks it would be to such a one as this! (*Aloud.*) I am touched to 35
the heart by your innocent regard for me, and were we differently situated,
I think I could have returned it. But as it is, I fear I can never be more to you
than a friend.

BUT. I understand! You hold aloof from me because you are rich and
lofty – and I poor and lowly. But take care! The poor bumboat woman has 40
gipsy blood in her veins, and she can read destinies.

CAPT. Destinies?

BUT. There is a change in store for you!

CAPT. A change?

BUT. Aye – be prepared! 45

DUET – LITTLE BUTTERCUP *and* CAPTAIN.

BUT.   Things are seldom what they seem,
                 Skim milk masquerades as cream;
                 Highlows pass as patent leathers;
                 Jackdaws strut in peacock's feathers.

CAPT. (*puzzled*).   Very true, 50
                 So they do.

BUT.   Black sheep dwell in every fold;
                 All that glitters is not gold;
                 Storks turn out to be but logs;
                 Bulls are but inflated frogs.

CAPT. (*puzzled*).   So they be, 55
                 Frequentlee.

BUT.   Drops the wind and stops the mill;
                 Turbot is ambitious brill;
                 Gild the farthing if you will, 60
                 Yet it is a farthing still.

CAPT. (*puzzled*).   Yes, I know,
                 That is so.
                 Though to catch your drift I'm striving,
                 It is shady – it is shady; 65
                 I don't see at what you're driving,
                 Mystic lady – mystic lady.

BOTH.   Stern conviction's o'er $\left\{ \begin{matrix} \text{me} \\ \text{him} \end{matrix} \right\}$ stealing,

75 *Once a cat was killed by care*: The saying 'Care killed the cat', which dates at least from the
    sixteenth century, means that you can worry yourself to death.
76 *Only brave deserve the fair*: The phrase 'None but the brave deserve the fair' occurs in John
    Dryden's ode for St Cecilia's Day, *Alexander's Feast* (1697). It is also used, in that latter
    form, in the 'If you go in' trio in *Iolanthe*.
79 *Wink is often good as nod*: The traditional saying is the other way round: 'A nod is as good
    as a wink' (first recorded use in Dorothy Wordsworth's journal in 1802).
80 *Spoils the child who spares the rod*: The phrase 'Spare the rod and spoil the child' derives
    from a biblical saying (Proverbs 23.13).
81 *Thirsty lambs run foxy dangers*: This comes from another of Aesop's fables, which tells how
    a lamb was devoured by a wolf while it was off-guard drinking from a stream.
82 *Dogs are found in many mangers*: A 'dog in a manger' is a mean-spirited individual who will
    not allow another to use something even though he does not want it himself. The phrase
    derives from yet another of Aesop's fables, in this case about a dog that fixed his place in
    a manger and would not allow an ox to come near the hay, even though he did not want
    it himself.
85 *Paw of cat the chestnut snatches*: The expression 'Take the chestnuts out of the fire with the
    cat's paw' means to use somebody else to do your dirty work. It is said to derive from a
    monkey belonging to Pope Julius II (1443–1513) which made a cat pull its chestnuts out
    of the fire.
86 *Worn-out garments show new patches*: A paraphrase of another biblical quotation, 'No man
    seweth a piece of cloth into an old garment' (Mark 2.21).
87 *Only count the chick that hatches*: 'Don't count your chickens before they are hatched' is a fa-
    vourite English saying which is first recorded back in 1575.
88 *Men are grown-up catchy-catchies*: I cannot offer an entirely satisfactory explanation for
    this phrase. The most likely one seems to be that 'catchy-catchy' was either a term of en-
    dearment given to babies when throwing them up in the air and catching them, or a
    phrase used in children's games like 'he' and 'touch'.

103 *Time alone can tell*: For the 1908 revival of *H.M.S. Pinafore* at the Savoy Theatre, Gilbert
     agreed to an additional few lines for Captain Corcoran at this point. The lines, which
     had been introduced by Rutland Barrington into his performance, went: 'Ah! Here
     comes the First Lord of the Admiralty. I will talk with him on the subject! Happily we
     are still on speaking terms.' They were cut in 1914.

	That the mystic lady's dealing	
	In oracular revealing.	70
CAPT.	Yes, I know –	
BUT.	That is so!	
CAPT.	Though I'm anything but clever,	
	I could talk like that for ever:	
	Once a cat was killed by care;	75
	Only brave deserve the fair.	
BUT.	Very true,	
	So they do.	
CAPT.	Wink is often good as nod;	
	Spoils the child who spares the rod;	80
	Thirsty lambs run foxy dangers;	
	Dogs are found in many mangers.	
BUT.	Frequentlee,	
	I agree.	
CAPT.	Paw of cat the chestnut snatches;	85
	Worn-out garments show new patches;	
	Only count the chick that hatches;	
	Men are grown-up catchy-catchies.	
BUT.	Yes, I know,	
	That is so.	90
(*Aside.*)	Though to catch my drift he's striving,	
	I'll dissemble – I'll dissemble;	
	When he sees at what I'm driving,	
	Let him tremble – let him tremble!	

ENSEMBLE.

Though a mystic tone $\left\{ \begin{array}{c} I \\ you \end{array} \right\}$ borrow, 95

$\left. \begin{array}{l} You\ will \\ I\ shall \end{array} \right\}$ learn the truth with sorrow,

Here to-day and gone to-morrow;
  Yes, I know –
  That is so!
  (*At the end exit* LITTLE BUTTERCUP *melodramatically.*) 100

 CAPT. Incomprehensible as her utterances are, I nevertheless feel that they are dictated by a sincere regard for me. But to what new misery is she referring? Time alone can tell!

(*Enter* SIR JOSEPH.)

105–6 *Captain Corcoran, I am much disappointed with your daughter*: In the licence copy of the libretto sent to the Lord Chamberlain, when it was still planned that Cousin Hebe's would be a bigger speaking part, she accompanies Sir Joseph in this entrance and repeats most of his remarks to the Captain, greatly to the First Lord's annoyance. This version was, of course, never performed.

127–44 *The hours creep on apace*
In this long passage of dramatic and heavily orchestrated recitative, Sullivan consciously imitates the florid style and exaggerated intensity of Italian opera.

136 *Rare 'blue and white'*: Blue-and-white oriental ceramics were much in vogue in the late 1870s and early 1880s, particularly among followers of the aesthetic movement. In *Patience*, Reginald Bunthorne, the fleshly poet, proclaims himself 'Such a judge of blue-and-white and other kinds of pottery' in Act I and 'A blue-and-white young man' in Act II.

138 *Gillow's*: A famous firm of house furnishers in London's Oxford Street which later amalgamated to become Waring and Gillow, now situated in the Brompton Road.

SIR JOSEPH. Captain Corcoran, I am much disappointed with your 105
daughter. In fact, I don't think she will do.

CAPT. She won't do, Sir Joseph!

SIR JOSEPH. I'm afraid not. The fact is, that although I have urged my
suit with as much eloquence as is consistent with an official utterance, I have
done so hitherto without success. How do you account for this? 110

CAPT. Really, Sir Joseph, I hardly know. Josephine is of course sensible
of your condescension.

SIR JOSEPH. She naturally would be.

CAPT. But perhaps your exalted rank dazzles her.

SIR JOSEPH. You think it does? 115

CAPT. I can hardly say; but she is a modest girl, and her social position
is far below your own. It may be that she feels she is not worthy of you.

SIR JOSEPH. That is really a very sensible suggestion, and displays
more knowledge of human nature than I had given you credit for.

CAPT. See, she comes. If your lordship would kindly reason with her 120
and assure her officially that it is a standing rule at the Admiralty that love
levels all ranks, her respect for an official utterance might induce her to look
upon your offer in its proper light.

SIR JOSEPH. It is not unlikely. I will adopt your suggestion. But soft,
she is here. Let us withdraw, and watch our opportunity. 125

(*Enter* JOSEPHINE *from cabin.* SIR JOSEPH *and* CAPTAIN *retire.*)

SCENA – JOSEPHINE.

The hours creep on apace,
My guilty heart is quaking!
Oh, that I might retrace
The step that I am taking! 130
Its folly it were easy to be showing,
What I am giving up and whither going.
On the one hand, papa's luxurious home,
Hung with ancestral armour and old brasses,
Carved oak and tapestry from distant Rome, 135
Rare 'blue and white', Venetian finger-glasses,
Rich oriental rugs, luxurious sofa pillows,
And everything that isn't old, from Gillow's.
And on the other, a dark and dingy room,
In some back street with stuffy children crying, 140
Where organs yell, and clacking housewives fume,
And clothes are hanging out all day a-drying.
With one cracked looking-glass to see your face in,
And dinner served up in a pudding basin!

145 *A simple sailor, lowly born*: The licence copy of *Pinafore* sent to the Lord Chamberlain
     omits lines 145 to 156 (from 'A simple sailor' to 'solemn duty') and has instead the follow-
     ing extension of Josephine's recitative:

> And then his relations,
> Their mean and sordid lives,
> Their vulgar explanations and their oaths,
> His father's a mechanic, I dare say,
> His soapy mother washing all the day,
> I do not mean herself, but dirty clothes.
> His sisters, what a theme for lover's sonnets!
> I think I see them in their Sunday bonnets,
> Oh dear, those bonnets,
> Oh dear, *dear*, dear, those bonnets.
> Oh no, no, no,
> I could not stand those bonnets.
> And yet he is so fair – so gentle, too,
> So young – so tender-hearted and so true,
> And so judicious in his observation,
> And then
> 'Tis he whom I would wed – not his relations!
> Yes, yes,
> 'Tis he, 'tis he – not his relations.

164 *your lordship*: Josephine's mode of addressing Sir Joseph is, in fact, wrong. 'Your lordship'
     would only be correct if he were a peer of the realm; the fact of being First Lord of the
     Admiralty is not sufficient to justify the title. Captain Corcoran makes the same mistake
     in line 120, and all three repeat it in the trio 'Never mind the why and wherefore'. Per-
     haps Gilbert deliberately caused the Captain and his daughter, arch-snobs that they
     are, to commit precisely the kind of social solecism that they would have found un-
     pardonable in others. More likely, however, he needed something to rhyme with 'on
     board-ship'.

173–228 *Never mind the why and wherefore*
     Always the most encored song in *Pinafore*, and one of the most popular in all the Savoy
     Operas, 'Never mind the why and wherefore' was described in the *Standard* review of the
     first night as 'a movement in E so vivacious and tuneful that even the First Lord has to
     retire at intervals behind the wardroom skylight and relieve his feelings by a dance, in
     which his dignified playfulness is delightful to behold'.

177 *Though your tastes are mean and flighty*: One of several instances where the words in the
     vocal score are different from those in the libretto. The former has 'her tastes' and in
     line 178 'her fortune', the latter, as here, 'your tastes' and 'your fortune'.

A simple sailor, lowly born, 145
  Unlettered and unknown,
Who toils for bread from early morn
  Till half the night has flown!
No golden rank can he impart –
  No wealth of house or land – 150
No fortune save his trusty heart
  And honest brown right hand!
And yet he is so wondrous fair
That love for one so passing rare,
So peerless in his manly beauty, 155
Were little else than solemn duty!
Oh, god of love, and god of reason, say,
Which of you twain shall my poor heart obey!

(SIR JOSEPH *and* CAPTAIN *enter.*)

SIR JOSEPH. Madam, it has been represented to me that you are 160
appalled by my exalted rank. I desire to convey to you officially my
assurance, that if your hesitation is attributable to that circumstance, it is
uncalled for.

JOS. Oh! then your lordship is of opinion that married happiness is *not*
inconsistent with discrepancy in rank? 165

SIR JOSEPH. I am officially of that opinion.

JOS. That the high and the lowly may be truly happy together, provided
that they truly love one another?

SIR JOSEPH. Madam, I desire to convey to you officially my opinion
that love is a platform upon which all ranks meet. 170

JOS. I thank you, Sir Joseph. I *did* hesitate, but I will hesitate no longer.
(*Aside.*) He little thinks how eloquently he has pleaded his rival's cause!

TRIO.

SIR JOSEPH, CAPTAIN, *and* JOSEPHINE.

CAPT.   Never mind the why and wherefore,
           Love can level ranks, and therefore,
           Though his lordship's station's mighty, 175
             Though stupendous be his brain,
           Though your tastes are mean and flighty
             And your fortune poor and plain,
CAPT. *and*   Ring the merry bells on board-ship,
SIR JOSEPH.   Rend the air with warbling wild, 180

For the union of $\left\{ \begin{array}{c} \text{his} \\ \text{my} \end{array} \right\}$ lordship

196 *In the lower middle class*: It hardly behoves Sir Joseph Porter, who started life as an office
boy polishing the handle of the big front door, to speak so disdainfully of the lower middle class. But, of course, he has risen so far and he is such a snob, for all his egalitarian
pronouncements, that he feels he can. The chorus of peers in *Iolanthe* have even more
contempt for this particular segment of society, whom they bracket with tradesmen and
the masses in the general command to bow down before them.

206 *Rend with songs the air above*: In early editions of the libretto this line was printed as 'Fill
with songs the air above'. This was almost certainly a misprint.

215 *Ring the merry bells on board-ship*: This line has traditionally been the cue for some typical
D'Oyly Carte business, particularly in encores. Among the imaginary bells that the First
Lord has pretended to play have been a front-door bell, carillon, hurdy-gurdy, triangle,
hand bells, telephone and a church bell, the 'rope' of which he inevitably loses control of
so that he is carried up into the air.
      There are other standard bits of business which D'Oyly Carte First Lords have prac-
tised during encores of this song. John Reed, who joined the company in 1951, took over
the principal comic roles in 1959 and retired, to everyone's great sadness, in 1979, leaned
on the ship's wheel and sent it spinning round, signalled in semaphore for help and
finally jumped overboard.

	With a humble captain's child!	
CAPT.	For a humble captain's daughter –	
JOS.	For a gallant captain's daughter –	
SIR JOSEPH.	And a lord who rules the water –	185
JOS. (*aside*).	And a *tar* who ploughs the water!	
ALL.	Let the air with joy be laden,	

                             Rend with songs the air above,

                        For the union of a maiden

                             With the man who owns her love!   190

| SIR JOSEPH. | Never mind the why and wherefore, | |

                             Love can level ranks, and therefore,

Though your nautical relation (*alluding to* CAPT.)

                             In my set could scarcely pass –

Though you occupy a station   195

                             In the lower middle class –

| CAPT. *and* | Ring the merry bells on board-ship, | |
| SIR JOSEPH. | Rend the air with warbling wild, | |

For the union of { my / his } lordship

                           With a humble captain's child!   200

CAPT.	For a humble captain's daughter –	
JOS.	For a gallant captain's daughter –	
SIR JOSEPH.	And a lord who rules the water –	
JOS. (*aside*).	And a *tar* who ploughs the water!	
ALL.	Let the air with joy be laden,	205

                             Rend with songs the air above,

For the union of a maiden

                             With the man who owns her love!

| JOS. | Never mind the why and wherefore, | |

                             Love can level ranks, and therefore   210

I admit the jurisdiction;

                             Ably have you played your part;

You have carried firm conviction

                             To my hesitating heart.

| CAPT. *and* | Ring the merry bells on board-ship, | 215 |
| SIR JOSEPH. | Rend the air with warbling wild, | |

For the union of { my / his } lordship

                           With a humble captain's child!

CAPT.	For a humble captain's daughter –	
JOS.	For a gallant captain's daughter –	220
SIR JOSEPH.	And a lord who rules the water –	
JOS. (*aside*).	And a *tar* who ploughs the water!	
(*Aloud*.)	Let the air with joy be laden.	

233 *this glorious country*: Originally the phrase was 'this happy country of ours'. It was altered
     to its present version, with Gilbert's authorization, for the 1908 revival of *Pinafore* at the
     Savoy Theatre.

236 *Elysian*: The Elysian fields were the abode of the blessed in Greek mythology.

247 *the kind commander that you are*: In the original vocal score this is 'the gallant captain that
     you are'.

252 *the mystic sailor that you are*: The original vocal score has this as 'the silly sailor that you
     are'.

257 *the simple captain that you are*: Once again, the original vocal score has 'the gallant captain
     that you are'.

CAPT. *and* SIR JOSEPH. Ring the merry bells on board-ship –
JOS.   For the union of a maiden –   225
CAPT. *and* SIR JOSEPH.   For her union with his lordship.
ALL.   Rend with songs the air above
                                                        For the man who owns her love!

(*Exit* JOSEPHINE.)

CAPT. Sir Joseph, I cannot express to you my delight at the happy   230
result of your eloquence. Your argument was unanswerable.

SIR JOSEPH. Captain Corcoran, it is one of the happiest characteristics
of this glorious country that official utterances are invariably regarded as
unanswerable.   (*Exit* SIR JOSEPH.)

CAPT. At last my fond hopes are to be crowned. My only daughter is to   235
be the bride of a Cabinet Minister. The prospect is Elysian. (*During this speech*
DICK DEADEYE *has entered.*)

DICK. Captain.

CAPT. Deadeye! You here? Don't! (*Recoiling from him.*)

DICK. Ah, don't shrink from me, Captain. I'm unpleasant to look at,   240
and my name's agin me, but I ain't as bad as I seem.

CAPT. What would you with me?

DICK (*mysteriously*). I'm come to give you warning.

CAPT. Indeed! do you propose to leave the Navy then?

DICK. No, no, you misunderstand me; listen!   245

DUET.

CAPTAIN *and* DICK DEADEYE.

DICK.   Kind Captain, I've important information,
                        Sing hey, the kind commander that you are,
                About a certain intimate relation,
                        Sing hey, the merry maiden and the tar.
BOTH.   The merry maiden and the tar.   250

CAPT.   Good fellow, in conundrums you are speaking,
                        Sing hey, the mystic sailor that you are;
                The answer to them vainly I am seeking;
                        Sing hey, the merry maiden and the tar.
BOTH.   The merry maiden and the tar.   255

DICK.   Kind Captain, your young lady is a-sighing,
                        Sing hey, the simple captain that you are,
                This very night with Rackstraw to be flying;
                        Sing hey, the merry maiden and the tar.

260 *The merry maiden and the tar*: In this particular refrain the Captain sings 'The much too
     merry maiden', while Deadeye sings the usual 'The merry, merry maiden'.

264 *the cat-o'-nine-tails*: A whip with nine lashes, used in both the Army and the Navy for
     punishing offenders. Its use in the Army was formally abolished in 1881. In the Navy an
     Act of 1866 limited any punishment to a maximum of forty-eight lashes. Use of the cat,
     which was traditionally administered by the boatswain's mate, was subsequently sus-
     pended, first in peace-time and then in wartime, but it has never formally been
     abolished in the senior service. The difficulty of wielding the cat-o'-nine-tails in the
     cramped confines of a ship gave rise to the expression 'There's not even room to swing
     a cat'.

286 *Hymen*: The Greek god of marriage, who crops up again in the version of *The Pirates of
     Penzance* sung at the first night in New York, and printed in the licence copy sent to the
     Lord Chamberlain, when in the finale of Act II Mabel sings:

>   Tomorrow morning early we will quickly be parsonified –
>   Hymeneally coupled, conjugally matrimonified.

Hymen also gets a mention in Gilbert and Sullivan's first collaboration, *Thespis*, when
Mercury laments in a song about the muddled state of the gods: 'But alas that determined young bachelor Hymen refuses to wed anybody at all'.

BOTH. The merry maiden and the tar. 260

CAPT. Good fellow, you have given timely warning,
Sing hey, the thoughtful sailor that you are,
I'll talk to Master Rackstraw in the morning:
Sing hey, the cat-o'-nine-tails and the tar.
(Producing a 'cat'.) 265
BOTH. The merry cat-o'-nine-tails and the tar!

CAPT. Dick Deadeye – I thank you for your timely warning – I will at
once take means to arrest their flight. This boat cloak will afford me ample
disguise – So! (*Envelops himself in a mysterious cloak, holding it before his face.*)
DICK. Ha, ha! They are foiled – foiled – foiled! 270

(*Enter Crew on tiptoe, with* RALPH *and* BOATSWAIN *meeting*
JOSEPHINE, *who enters from cabin on tiptoe, with bundle of necessaries, and ac-*
companied by LITTLE BUTTERCUP.)

ENSEMBLE.

Carefully on tiptoe stealing,
Breathing gently as we may, 275
Every step with caution feeling,
We will softly steal away.
(CAPTAIN *stamps. – Chord.*)
ALL (*much alarmed*). Goodness me –
Why, what was that? 280
DICK. Silent be,
It was the cat!
ALL (*reassured*). It was – it was the cat!
CAPT. (*producing cat-o'-nine-tails*). They're right, it was the cat!
ALL. Pull ashore, in fashion steady, 285
Hymen will defray the fare,
For a clergyman is ready
To unite the happy pair!
(*Stamp as before, and Chord.*)
ALL. Goodness me, 290
Why, what was that?

315 *the port division*: The crews of men-o'-war were traditionally divided into port and star-board watches, one of which was always on duty while the other rested. The practice is still continued on submarines. Ralph here proclaims himself one of the most junior members of the port watch.

316 *epauletted scorn*: A splendidly Gilbertian term for naval snobbery. Epaulettes, heavy and ornate shoulder badges fringed with cord, were worn by both Navy and Army officers until 1855, when the Army gave them up, leaving this particular piece of decorative adornment to the senior service.

323–35 *He is an Englishman*

The second great patriotic number in *H.M.S. Pinafore*. 'He is an Englishman' belongs to a clutch of fervently nationalistic songs in the Savoy Operas which also includes 'A British tar is a soaring soul', 'When Britain really ruled the waves' from *Iolanthe*, 'The Darned Mounseer' from *Ruddigore*, and the stirring finale from *Utopia Limited*, 'There's a little group of isles beyond the wave'. Apart from 'The Darned Mounseer', which offended several Frenchmen with its anti-Gallic sentiments, 'He is an Englishman' is the only one to contain somewhat disparaging references to other countries. In that respect it has distinct similarities with Michael Flanders and Donald Swann's famous 'Song of Patriotic Prejudice' from *At the Drop of a Hat*, 'The English, the English, the English are best'.

A correspondent to *The Times* in 1955 suggested that 'He is an Englishman' was based on a patriotic song popular in the 1870s which ran:

> 'Tis a glorious charter – deny it who can –
> That lives in the words 'I'm an Englishman'.

However, I doubt whether Gilbert needed any such direct inspiration in the generally patriotic atmosphere which prevailed in Britain during the period in which *Pinafore* was written.

When Gilbert and Sullivan went to the United States in the winter of 1879 to present the authorized version of *H.M.S. Pinafore*, one impresario suggested that they should americanize the opera, changing its name to *U.S.S. Pinafore*, hoisting the Stars and Stripes instead of the White Ensign, and anchoring the ship off Jersey Beach. Gilbert, who was appalled by the idea, humoured the man (and himself) by suggesting a new version of the boatswain's song:

> He is American!
> Though he himself has said it,
> 'Tis not much to his credit,
> That he is American.
> For he might have been a Dutchman,
> An Irish, Scotch or such man,
> Or perhaps an Englishman!
> But in spite of hanky-panky,
> He remains a true-born Yankee,
> A cute American.

Needless to say, that version was never performed.

DICK.	Silent be,
	Again the cat!
ALL.	It was again that cat!
CAPT. (*aside*).	They're right, it was the cat! 295

CAPT. (*throwing off cloak*).   Hold! (*All start.*)

    Pretty daughter of mine,
      I insist upon knowing
      Where you may be going
    With these sons of the brine,   300
      For my excellent crew,
    Though foes they could thump any,
    Are scarcely fit company,
      My daughter, for you.

CREW.   Now, hark at that, do!   305
    Though foes we could thump any,
    We are scarcely fit company
    For a lady like you!

RALPH.   Proud officer, that haughty lip uncurl!
    Vain man, suppress that supercilious sneer,   310
For I have dared to love your matchless girl,
  A fact well known to all my messmates here!

CAPT.   Oh, horror!

RALPH *and* JOS.   { I, / He, } humble, poor, and lowly born,

    The meanest in the port division –   315
    The butt of epauletted scorn –
    The mark of quarter-deck derision –
    Have } dared to raise { my } wormy eyes
    Has   his
    Above the dust to which you'd mould { me / him
    In manhood's glorious pride to rise,   320
    I am } an Englishman – behold { me! / him!
    He is

ALL.   He is an Englishman!

BOAT.   He is an Englishman!
    For he himself has said it,
    And it's greatly to his credit,   325
  That he is an Englishman!

ALL.   That he is an Englishman!

BOAT.   For he might have been a Roosian,
    A French, or Turk, or Proosian,
    Or perhaps Itali-an!   330

343   *damme*: This is the only swear word to occur in full in the text of the Savoy Operas. Major-General Stanley's 'But *damme*, you don't go' said in exasperation to the policemen in Act II of *The Pirates*, although found in nearly every production, is not actually printed in the libretto. In *Utopia Limited*, King Paramount is twice given the aside 'Da—!' but the word is never finished.

The utterance of 'damme' by the young actor playing Captain Corcoran in the special series of matinées of *Pinafore* which Richard D'Oyly Carte put on at the Opéra Comique in the winter of 1879–80, with a cast composed entirely of children, caused great distress to Lewis Carroll, the author of *Alice in Wonderland*. Carroll, who had some years earlier written to Sullivan suggesting that he might compose the music for a dramatic version of *Alice*, commented after seeing the children's version of *Pinafore*:

> One passage was to me sad beyond words. It occurs when the captain utters the oath 'Damn me!' I cannot find words to convey to the reader the pain I felt in seeing dear children taught to utter such words to amuse ears grown callous to their ghastly meaning. Put the two ideas side by side: Hell (no matter whether you believe in it or not; millions do), and those pure young lips thus sporting with its horrors – and then find what fun in it you can! How Mr Gilbert could have stooped to write, and Sir Arthur Sullivan could have prostituted his noble art to set to music, such vile trash, it passes my skill to understand.

357   *My amazement – my surprise*: George Grossmith, playing the part of Sir Joseph in the opening run of *Pinafore*, found himself moved to utter these words towards the end of a performance on the evening of 31 July 1879 when the stage of the Opéra Comique was suddenly invaded by a gang of roughs. They had been hired by three former co-directors of the Comedy Opera Company who, having been bought out by Richard D'Oyly Carte, and seeing the great popularity of *Pinafore*, decided to claim the scenery and costumes as theirs and to mount a rival production of the opera in a nearby theatre.

The invaders raised the cry of 'Fire!' to divert the audience's attention while they tried to grab what they could off the stage. However, led by Buttercup, the crew of the *Pinafore* successfully repelled the boarders and they were forced off the stage at bayonet point by the marines who were about to escort Ralph off to his dungeon cell. Carte's former co-directors were later made to pay damages in court, and in August 1879 he rechristened his own company Mr D'Oyly Carte's Opera Company, so that there could be no possible confusion about its identity or its boss.

368   *To your cabin with celerity*: In his *Treasury of Gilbert and Sullivan*, Martyn Green, principal comic singer with the D'Oyly Carte Opera Company from 1934 to 1939 and from 1946 to 1951, says that a traditional joke in the company when *Pinafore* was being performed was 'Who's playing Celerity tonight?'

ALL.   Or perhaps Itali-an!
BOAT.   But in spite of all temptations
                To belong to other nations,
                He remains an Englishman!
ALL.   For in spite of all temptations, etc.   335
CAPT. (*trying to repress his anger*).
                In uttering a reprobation
                To any British tar,
                I try to speak with moderation,
                But you have gone too far.
                I'm very sorry to disparage   340
                A humble foremast lad,
                But to seek your captain's child in marriage,
                Why, damme, it's too bad!

(*During this,* COUSIN HEBE *and* FEMALE RELATIVES *have entered.*)

ALL (*shocked*).   Oh!   345
CAPT.   Yes, damme, it's too bad!
ALL.   Oh!
CAPT. *and* DICK DEADEYE.   Yes, damme, it's too bad.

(*During this,* SIR JOSEPH *has appeared on poop-deck. He is
                horrified at the bad language.*)   350

HEBE.   Did you hear him – did you hear him?
                Oh, the monster overbearing!
                Don't go near him – don't go near him –
                He is swearing – he is swearing!
SIR JOSEPH.   My pain and my distress,   355
                I find it is not easy to express;
                My amazement – my surprise –
                You may learn from the expression of my eyes!
CAPT.   My lord – one word – the facts are not before you;
                The word was injudicious, I allow –   360
                But hear my explanation, I implore you,
                And you will be indignant too, I vow!
SIR JOSEPH.   I will hear of no defence,
                Attempt none if you're sensible.
                That word of evil sense   365
                Is wholly indefensible.
                Go, ribald, get you hence
                To your cabin with celerity.

375   *To refrain from language strong*: Sir Joseph Porter's strong reaction to Captain Corcoran's bad language may well have been intended as a further dig at the puritanical W. H. Smith.

388   *the fo'c'sle*: The forecastle, or forward part of the ship, was so called because it was raised and protected like a castle so that it could command the enemy's deck during an engagement. Decked over, the fo'c'sle normally housed the ship's bell, galley chimney and ladder to the bowsprit. It was customary for the crew's quarters to be in the fo'c'sle and those of the officers aft on the quarter-deck: hence the significance of Ralph's remarks.

392   *Darling*: This line was added for the revival of *Pinafore* in 1908. Gilbert sanctioned it, no doubt reflecting that the Edwardian audience could take what might have seemed a little too strong for the sensibilities of the Victorians. Traditionally, Sir Joseph faints into the ever-ready arms of Cousin Hebe on hearing the girl whom he had presumed was soon to become his thus addressing a common sailor.

400   *Pray, don't*: This phrase was substituted for the original 'Away with him' in the 1908 revival. Dick Deadeye's line 'They have!' was also added at the same time.

	This is the consequence	
	Of ill-advised asperity!	370
	(*Exit* CAPTAIN, *disgraced, followed by* JOSEPHINE.)	
ALL.	This is the consequence	
	Of ill-advised asperity!	
SIR JOSEPH.	For I'll teach you all, ere long,	
	To refrain from language strong,	375
	For I haven't any sympathy for ill-bred taunts!	
HEBE.	No more have his sisters, nor his cousins, nor his aunts.	
ALL.	For he is an Englishman, etc.	

(*Enter* JOSEPHINE.)

SIR JOSEPH. Now, tell me, my fine fellow – for you *are* a fine fellow —   380
RALPH. Yes, your honour.
SIR JOSEPH. How came your captain so far to forget himself? I am quite sure you had given him no cause for annoyance.
RALPH. Please your honour, it was thus-wise. You see I'm only a topman – a mere foremast hand —
SIR JOSEPH. Don't be ashamed of that. Your position as a topman is a   385
very exalted one.
RALPH. Well, your honour, love burns as brightly in the fo'c'sle as it does on the quarter-deck, and Josephine is the fairest bud that ever blossomed upon the tree of a poor fellow's wildest hopes.   390

(JOSEPHINE *rushes to* RALPH'S *arms*.)

JOS. Darling! (SIR JOSEPH *horrified*.)
RALPH. She is the figurehead of my ship of life – the bright beacon that guides me into my port of happiness – the rarest, the purest gem that ever sparkled on a poor but worthy fellow's trusting brow!
ALL. Very pretty, very pretty!   395
SIR JOSEPH. Insolent sailor, you shall repent this outrage. Seize him! (*Two Marines seize him and handcuff him*.)
JOS. Oh, Sir Joseph, spare him, for I love him tenderly.
SIR JOSEPH. Pray, don't. I will teach this presumptuous mariner to   400
discipline his affections. Have you such a thing as a dungeon on board?
ALL. We have!
DICK. They have!
SIR JOSEPH. Then load him with chains and take him there at once!

405–26 *Farewell, my own*
This is the only octet in the Savoy Operas. There is one sestet ('I hear the soft note of the echoing voice' in *Patience*) and another song ('When Britain sounds the trump of war' from *Utopia Limited*) where there are six solo singers, but for the most part individual songs are for five or fewer voices.

419 *No telephone*: This was a very up-to-date reference in 1878. Alexander Graham Bell had been granted a patent for his new invention only two years earlier. The world's first clearly audible telephone message had been transmitted by Bell to a friend on another floor of his house in Boston on 10 March 1876, and the first telephone exchange was opened at New Haven, Connecticut, in January 1878. London had its first telephone company in June 1878, the month after *Pinafore* opened, and its first exchange a year later.

Gilbert had a telephone installed in his home in 1882, and he also ordered one for the prompt desk at the Savoy Theatre so that he could monitor performances and rehearsals in his study. He also persuaded Sullivan to install a telephone at his home, and it was there, on 13 May 1883, at a party to mark the composer's forty-first birthday, that a distinguished group of guests, headed by the Prince of Wales (later Edward VII), heard a direct relay of parts of *Iolanthe* from the Savoy stage. This was probably the first ever live 'broadcast' of an opera.

428 *My pain and my distress*: Sir Joseph's next four lines, and Buttercup's four-line recitative which follows them, were not in the original *Pinafore* libretto. The licence copy sent to the Lord Chamberlain has this passage of dialogue instead:

> SIR JOSEPH. Josephine, I cannot tell you the distress I feel at this most painful revelation. I desire to express to you, officially, that I am hurt.
> HEBE. If you have five and twenty minutes to spare I will explain how it has effected [*sic*] me.
> SIR JOSEPH. Do *not* interfere.
> HEBE. Crushed.
> SIR JOSEPH. You, whom I honoured by seeking in marriage, you but the daughter of a captain in the Royal Navy.
> BUTTERCUP. Hold! I have something to say to that.
> HEBE. You had better be quiet.
> SIR JOSEPH. On the contrary, she had better proceed.
> HEBE. Of course, anybody but me. Go on, vulgar old woman.

Although Hebe's part was written out before the first performance, Sir Joseph's dialogue, without her interruptions, was kept in early productions. So was Buttercup's 'Hold! I have something to say to that', after which Sir Joseph said 'You?' Buttercup replied 'Yes, I!' before launching into her song 'A many years ago'.

OCTET.

RALPH.
  Farewell, my own,   405
   Light of my life, farewell!
  For crime unknown
   I go to a dungeon cell.

JOS.
  I will atone.
   In the meantime farewell!   410
  And all alone
   Rejoice in your dungeon cell!

SIR JOSEPH.
  A bone, a bone
   I'll pick with this sailor fell;
  Let him be shown
   At once to his dungeon cell.   415

BOATSWAIN, BOATSWAIN'S MATE, DICK DEADEYE, *and* COUSIN
HEBE.
  He'll hear no tone
   Of the maiden he loves so well!
  No telephone
   Communicates with his cell!   420

BUT. (*mysteriously*).
   But when is known
   The secret I have to tell,
  Wide will be thrown
   The door of his dungeon cell.

ALL.
  For crime unknown   425
   He goes to a dungeon cell!

         (RALPH *is led off in custody.*)

SIR JOSEPH.
  My pain and my distress
  Again it is not easy to express.
  My amazement, my surprise,   430
  Again you may discover from my eyes.

ALL. How terrible the aspect of his eyes!
BUT. Hold! Ere upon your loss
   You lay much stress,
  A long-concealèd crime
   I would confess.   435

455 *I mixed those children up*: Gilbert made much of the dramatic possibilities of people being mixed up when they were babies. It is the central feature of the plot of *The Gondoliers*, where there is first confusion about whether it was Marco or Giuseppe Palmieri who was the heir to the throne of Barataria taken away as a baby to be reared by a gondolier, and then there is the added twist provided at the end by the prince's foster-mother, Inez, when she reveals that in fact it was neither of them, but rather Luiz.

    The swapping of identities at birth also forms the basis of two of the *Bab Ballads*. 'The Baby's Vengeance' tells the story of how Paley Vollaire had crept into the cradle of his foster-brother and so inherited an enormous fortune, leaving the rightful heir, Frederick West, poor and forced to earn a living as a dustman. 'General John' describes a situation even closer to that in *Pinafore*. Private James of the Sixty-seventy-first Regiment gets the idea that he and his commanding officer, General John, 'were cruelly changed at birth'. The general generously accepts his story and swops places with the private.

472 *That is the idea I intended to convey, officially*: This, and Sir Joseph's next line, were both formally incorporated in the *Pinafore* libretto with Gilbert's approval for the 1908 revival. They were probably originally introduced, like many of the added lines, as 'ad-libs' by the D'Oyly Carte principals. Buttercup's line 'Aye! aye! yer 'onour' was added in 1914.

SONG – Buttercup.

A many years ago,
When I was young and charming,
As some of you may know,
I practised baby-farming.   440
ALL.   Now this is most alarming!
When she was young and charming,
She practised baby-farming,
A many years ago.
BUT.   Two tender babes I nussed: 445
One was of low condition,
The other, upper crust,
A regular patrician.
ALL (*explaining to each other*).
Now, this is the position:
One was of low condition,   450
The other a patrician,
A many years ago.
BUT.   Oh, bitter is my cup!
However could I do it?
I mixed those children up,   455
And not a creature knew it!
ALL.   However could you do it?
Some day, no doubt, you'll rue it,
Although no creature knew it,
So many years ago.   460
BUT.   In time each little waif
Forsook his foster-mother,
The well-born babe was Ralph –
Your captain was the other!!!
ALL.   They left their foster-mother,   465
The one was Ralph, our brother,
Our captain was the other,
A many years ago.

SIR JOSEPH. Then I am to understand that Captain Corcoran and
Ralph were exchanged in childhood's happy hour – that Ralph is really the   470
Captain, and the Captain is Ralph?
    BUT. That is the idea I intended to convey, officially!
    SIR JOSEPH. And very well you have conveyed it, Miss Buttercup.
    BUT. Aye! aye! yer 'onour.
    SIR JOSEPH. Dear me! Let them appear before me, at once!   475

476–7 *Ralph enters as Captain; Captain as a common sailor*: This rapid transformation, calling for a speedy change of costume by the two principals involved, directly recalls the last verse of the Bab Ballad 'General John':

> So GENERAL JOHN as PRIVATE JAMES
> Fell in, parade upon;
> And PRIVATE JAMES, by change of names,
> Was MAJOR-GENERAL JOHN.

Traditionally the former Captain Corcoran shows his fall in station by adopting a common Cockney accent from now on and dropping his 'h's. Archibald Grosvenor undergoes a similar transformation of accent when he appears at the end of *Patience* having shed his aestheticism and become an ordinary, matter-of-fact young man.

501 *Sad my lot and sorry*: In early productions the lines from 'Sad my lot and sorry' to the beginning of the quartet were sung as recitative, with the chorus repeating Sir Joseph's line 'What shall I do? I cannot live alone!' They were subsequently changed to spoken dialogue.

(RALPH *enters as* CAPTAIN; CAPTAIN *as a common*
sailor. JOSEPHINE *rushes to his arms.*)

JOS. My father – a common sailor!

CAPT. It is hard, is it not, my dear?

SIR JOSEPH. This is a very singular occurrence; I congratulate you   480
both. (*To* RALPH.) Captain Rackstraw, desire that remarkably fine seaman
to step forward.

RALPH. Corcoran. Three paces to the front – march!

CAPT. If what?

RALPH. If what? I don't think I understand you.   485

CAPT. If you please.

SIR JOSEPH. The gentleman is quite right. If you *please*.

RALPH. Oh! If you *please*. (CAPTAIN *steps forward*.)

SIR JOSEPH (*to* CAPTAIN). You are an extremely fine fellow.

CAPT. Yes, your honour.   490

SIR JOSEPH. So it seems that you were Ralph, and Ralph was you.

CAPT. So it seems, your honour.

SIR JOSEPH. Well, I need not tell you that after this change in your
condition, a marriage with your daughter will be out of the question.

CAPT. Don't say that, your honour – love levels all ranks.   495

SIR JOSEPH. It does to a considerable extent, but it does not level them
as much as that. (*Handing* JOSEPHINE *to* RALPH.) Here – take her, sir, and
mind you treat her kindly.

RALPH *and* JOS. Oh bliss, oh rapture!

CAPT. *and* BUT. Oh rapture, oh bliss!   500

SIR JOSEPH.   Sad my lot and sorry,
          What shall I do? I cannot live alone!

HEBE.   Fear nothing – while I live I'll not desert you.
          I'll soothe and comfort your declining days.

SIR JOSEPH. No, don't do that.   505

HEBE.   Yes, but indeed I'd rather –

SIR JOSEPH (*resigned*). Oh, very well then.
          To-morrow morn our vows shall all be plighted,
          Three loving pairs on the same day united!

QUARTET.

JOSEPHINE, HEBE, RALPH, *and* DEADEYE.

          Oh joy, oh rapture unforeseen,   510
          The clouded sky is now serene,
          The god of day – the orb of love,
          Has hung his ensign high above,
               The sky is all ablaze.

519 *In dreamy roundelay*: The licence copy sent to the Lord Chamberlain has the following additional lines after the end of the quartet for Josephine, Hebe, Ralph and Deadeye:

ALL.   Tomorrow night,
                                          With loving spouse,
                                          He'll go ashore,
                                          And then he'll plight
                                          His marriage vows
                                          For evermore.
                                          A clergyman, etc.

The song presumably continued as a reprise of the chorus towards the end of Act I.

538 *For the former Captain of the Pinafore*: In early productions this line was sung as: 'For the faithful seamen of the *Pinafore*'. That was, in fact, a more appropriate refrain, because in *Utopia Limited* (1893) Captain Corcoran reappears, surprisingly but impressively transformed into Captain Sir Edward Corcoran, K.C.B., and sings the following song:

                    I'm Captain Corcoran, K.C.B.,
                    I'll teach you how we rule the sea,
                    And terrify the simple Gauls;
                    And how the Saxon and the Celt
                    Their Europe-shaking blows have dealt
                    With Maxim gun and Nordenfeldt
                    (Or will, when the occasion calls).
                    If sailor-like you'd play your cards,
                    Unbend your sails and lower your yards,
                    Unstep your masts – you'll never want 'em more.
                    Though we're no longer hearts of oak,
                    Yet we can steer and we can stoke,
                    And, thanks to coal, and thanks to coke,
                    We never run a ship ashore!

Well, hardly ever run a ship ashore, he is forced to admit under familiar questioning from the chorus. So Corcoran evidently manages to rise again through the ranks to his former position. Of Captain Rackstraw, however, we hear no more.

540 *Though I could never tell why*: In early productions Buttercup sang 'I'm sure I shall never know why' here.

545 *And when I've married thee*: It is just as well that Hebe is Sir Joseph's cousin, and not a sister or an aunt, since marriage with either of those relations would be prohibited according to the rules of kindred and affinity in the Prayer Book.

With wooing words and loving song,   515
We'll chase the lagging hours along,
And if $\left\{\begin{array}{l}\text{he finds}\\\text{I find}\end{array}\right\}$ the maiden coy,
We'll murmur forth decorous joy,
   In dreamy roundelay.

CAPT.   For he's the Captain of the *Pinafore*.   520
ALL.   And a right good captain too!
CAPT.   And though before my fall
          I was captain of you all,
      I'm a member of the crew.
ALL.   Although before his fall, etc.   525

CAPT.   I shall marry with a wife,
      In my humble rank of life! (*turning to* BUT.)
        And you, my own, are she –
      I must wander to and fro,
      But wherever I may go,   530
        I shall never be untrue to thee!
ALL.   What, never?
CAPT.   No, never!
ALL.   What, *never*?
CAPT.   Well, hardly ever!   535
ALL.   Hardly ever be untrue to thee.
      Then give three cheers, and one cheer more
      For the former Captain of the *Pinafore*.

BUT.   For he loves Little Buttercup, dear Little Buttercup,
        Though I could never tell why;   540
      But still he loves Buttercup, poor Little Buttercup,
        Sweet Little Buttercup, aye!
ALL.   For he loves, etc.

SIR JOSEPH. I'm the monarch of the sea,
        And when I've married thee (*to* HEBE),   545
      I'll be true to the devotion that my love implants.
HEBE.   Then good-bye to your sisters, and your cousins, and your
          aunts,
      Especially your cousins,
      Whom you reckon up by dozens,
      Your sisters, and your cousins, and your aunts!   550

555   *That he is an Englishman*: For several years during the ultra-patriotic and jingoistic Ed-
      wardian period, performances of *H.M.S. Pinafore* did not end with this line but with a
      rendering of 'Rule, Britannia'. It can be heard on the 1908 D'Oyly Carte recording. A
      master copy of the *Pinafore* libretto dating from 1923 and now in the D'Oyly Carte ar-
      chives has 'Rule, Britannia' printed after the end of 'He is an Englishman' and before
      the curtain. Against it there is a handwritten note by Rupert D'Oyly Carte which reads:
      'Rule Britannia was not originally sung and is not sung by my company now (1924).' It is
      not in the 1923 D'Oyly Carte recording.

ALL.   Then good-bye, etc.
                   For he is an Englishman,
                       And he himself hath said it,
                       And it's greatly to his credit
                   That he is an Englishman!   555

                        CURTAIN

THE PIRATES OF PENZANCE

or

The Slave of Duty

DRAMATIS PERSONÆ

MAJOR-GENERAL STANLEY
THE PIRATE KING
SAMUEL (*his Lieutenant*)
FREDERIC (*the Pirate Apprentice*)
SERGEANT OF POLICE
MABEL
EDITH
KATE   } (*General Stanley's Daughters*)
ISABEL
RUTH (*a Pirate Maid of all Work*)
Chorus of Pirates, Police, and General Stanley's Daughters.

ACT I. – A Rocky Sea-shore on the Coast of Cornwall.
ACT II. – A Ruined Chapel by Moonlight.

THE PIRATES OF PENZANCE

The Pirates of Penzance has the unique distinction among Gilbert and Sullivan's operas of having received its première in the United States of America. It opened at the Fifth Avenue Theater, New York, on 31 December 1879, with the composer himself conducting.

Gilbert and Sullivan had travelled to the United States with Richard D'Oyly Carte and his company to present the authorized version of *H.M.S. Pinafore*. When they set out from Britain in October 1879 they had already made substantial progress on the next opera for the company to perform, which they intended should be premièred in the States. Gilbert had completed the libretto and Sullivan had sketched out most of the songs for the first act and made a start on the second.

When their ship docked in New York and Sullivan unpacked his bags, he made a terrible discovery. As he wrote to his mother: 'I fear I have left all the sketches of the first act at home, as I have searched everywhere for them. I would have telegraphed for them but they would not have arrived in time. It is a great nuisance as I have to rewrite it all now, and can't recollect every number I did.'

Working partly from memory, and partly from scratch in the periods when he was not either rehearsing or conducting *Pinafore*, the composer set about reconstructing the lost songs from Act I as well as completing Act II. To this day, a plaque set in the wall of No. 45, East 20th Street, New York, where his hotel stood, records that 'On this site Sir Arthur Sullivan composed *The Pirates of Penzance* during 1879.'

Sullivan worked furiously to complete the opera in time for the scheduled first performance on the last day of the year. He slaved away right through Christmas Day and finally finished the full score at 7 a.m. on 28 December, the day before the dress rehearsal and two days before the opening night. In these last forty-eight hours he also had to face the added headache of a threatened strike by the members of the orchestra, who claimed that the new work was an opera rather than an operetta and they should therefore be paid on a higher scale.

Sullivan countered the threat by announcing that he would bring over the orchestra of the Royal Opera House, Covent Garden, which, he said, had nothing much to do until the start of the opera season in the spring and would gladly come to New York for not much more than expenses. In the meantime, the piece would be played with accompaniment from himself on the piano and his friend and associate Alfred Cellier on the harmonium. In the face of this display of British *sang-froid* the American musicians backed down, much to the relief of Sullivan, who later admitted: 'the idea of getting the Covent Garden band over was hardly less absurd than the ludicrous idea of using the pianoforte and harmonium in a big theatre'.

The day of the opening performance was an ordeal for the composer. He finally finished the overture at 5 a.m. and spent the morning rehearsing the orchestra at the theatre. After breakfasting at his hotel at 1.45 he went to bed but was unable to sleep. In the evening he had twelve oysters and a glass of champagne at the New York Club before taking his position in the orchestra pit. 'Went into the orchestra more dead than alive,' his diary records, 'but got better when I took the stick in my hand. Fine reception. Piece went marvellously well. Grand success.' After the triumphant première, there was a grand party to see in the New Year and Sullivan did not finally get to his bed until 3.30 the following morning.

In order to protect the British copyright, a performance of *The Pirates of Penzance* had, in fact, already been given in the Bijou Theatre, Paignton, Devon, the day before the New York opening. The reason for this remote venue was not its proximity to the location of the opera but rather the fact that the members of the D'Oyly Carte touring company were in nearby Torquay performing *H.M.S. Pinafore*. For their single performance of the new opera, the cast read from handwritten sheets of music newly arrived from America, and wore their *Pinafore* costumes with only minimal changes, like scarves round the heads of those playing pirates. The music for a number of the songs had still not reached Paignton when the performance took place, and the modern major-general was one of several characters who had to introduce himself in verse rather than song.

The London première of *The Pirates* took place on 3 April 1880 at the Opéra Comique. The opera ran for almost exactly a year, closing on 2 April 1881 after 363 performances. Meanwhile, it was by now so successful in the United States that it was being performed by four separate companies established by D'Oyly Carte. The original Fifth Avenue company went on to Boston; a second company played in Philadelphia; a third opened at Newark, New Jersey, and went on to tour Pennsylvania, Ohio, Indiana, Michigan, Missouri, Kansas, Nebraska, Iowa, Minnesota and Wisconsin; and a fourth, launched in Buffalo, went from Chicago and St Louis to New Orleans, Memphis, Nashville and Louisville.

Both the plot and the music of *The Pirates of Penzance* have continued to delight audiences on both sides of the Atlantic ever since. Surprisingly, Gilbert had not originally intended the opera to be about pirates at all. Its first provisional title was *The Robbers* and it was to be about the relations between a group of burglars and a group of policemen. While in the United States he decided to recast the burglars as pirates, who had already figured in one of his previous plays, *Our Island Home* (1870). The policemen, luckily, remained as an object for

Gilbert's gentle satire along with the Army, the House of Lords and, of course, the overpowering sense of duty which is the opera's main theme and which provides its sub-title.

Sullivan found that the songs, and particularly the duets, with which he was provided by Gilbert in *The Pirates* gave him full scope to show his potential as an operatic composer. Indeed one has some sympathy with the striking musicians of the Fifth Avenue Theater. *The Pirates* comes closer to grand opera than any other of the works of Gilbert and Sullivan, with the possible exception of *The Yeomen of the Guard*. The composer himself wrote to his mother: 'The music is infinitely superior in every way to the *Pinafore* – tunier, and more developed – of a higher class altogether'. Nor, at a less lofty level, did he neglect the comic possibilities of a chorus of British bobbies, for whom he provided two of the most popular tunes in the entire Savoy Operas.

The closing decades of the twentieth century have given *The Pirates of Penzance* a new lease of life. A lively modern production by Joseph Papp, which cast rock singers in the roles of Frederic and Mabel and put electric guitars and synthesizers in the orchestra pit, opened in New York's Central Park on 15 July 1980 and went on to take both Broadway and London's West End by storm. Papp's production was also turned into a film which was released in 1982 and starred Kevin Kline, Angela Lansbury, and Linda Ronstadt.

Whatever purists may have made of Papp's production, which involved transporting to Penzance the 'matter' trio from *Ruddigore* and Josephine's first act ballad from *H.M.S. Pinafore*, there can be no doubting its vivacity, its popularity and its influence on subsequent professional productions of the operetta. Its most notable feature, perhaps, was in making the pirates much more swashbuckling and athletic, inclined to leap off rocks and shin down rigging at the slightest provocation and much given to daring sword play. This theme was also very much to the fore in the Brent Walker video, where the Pirate King was played by Peter Allen and the Major General by Keith Michell.

The revived D'Oyly Carte Opera Company chose *The Pirates of Penzance* to launch its second season, which opened at the New Theatre, Hull, in March 1989. Keith Warner's production was notable for its colourful set, which resembled a Victorian toy theatre and made much use of opening doors and windows. It also featured an appearance by Queen Victoria in the Act II finale. For its 1993 season the company brought to Britain a production by Stuart Maunder previously seen in Australia. It made good use of a huge ship at the back of the stage from which the pirates descended for their opening chorus and on which Frederic and Mabel embarked for their honeymoon voyage at the end. Major-General Stanley was played by Aberdonian Alan Watt in a kilt and pith helmet, complete with shooting stick. Indeed, it is becoming something of a rarity now to find a Major-General, outside amateur performances, in full Victorian dress uniform.

1–5 *Scene: The Pirates of Penzance* is not the only Savoy Opera to be set in Cornwall. The action of *Ruddigore* takes place in the fictitious fishing village of Rederring in the same county. There is, of course, nothing fictitious about Penzance, which is an important fishing, market and tourist centre on the south coast of Cornwall, the terminus of the main West Country railway line from London and the most westerly town in England.

Gilbert originally conceived a very different opening to the opera from the present one. The description of the scene in the copy sent to the Lord Chamberlain for licensing reads 'A cavern by the sea-shore. Pirates discovered carousing. Thomas, the Pirate King, waiting on them, busying himself with wiping glasses etc. and generally acting as a servant while the others are enjoying themselves.'

6 *Pour, oh, pour the private sherry*: In the licence copy, and in early vocal scores, in keeping with Gilbert's original intention to portray the Pirate King as the servant of his band, this chorus begins:

> Pour, oh King, the pirate sherry;
> Fill, oh King, the pirate glass, etc.

9 *bumper*: A well-filled glass or mug.

10 *For to-day our pirate 'prentice*: In the licence copy, and presumably in the original Paignton performance of the opera, while this first verse was given to Samuel, the next (beginning 'Two-and-twenty now he's rising') was given to another pirate, James. ' 'Prentice' is, of course, short for 'apprentice'. Indentures are sealed agreements binding an apprentice to his master for a particular period of time.

ACT I

S C E N E. – *A rocky sea-shore on the coast of Cornwall. In the distance is a calm sea, on which a schooner is lying at anchor. As the curtain rises groups of pirates are discovered – some drinking, some playing cards.* S A M U E L, *the Pirate Lieutenant, is going from one group to another, filling the cups from a flask.* F R E D E R I C *is seated in a despondent attitude at the back of the scene.*   5

OPENING CHORUS.

Pour, oh, pour the pirate sherry;
   Fill, oh, fill the pirate glass;
And, to make us more than merry,
   Let the pirate bumper pass.

S A M.   For to-day our pirate 'prentice   10
                     Rises from indenture freed;
           Strong his arm and keen his scent is,
                     He's a pirate now indeed!

A L L.   Here's good luck to Frederic's ventures!
           Frederic's out of his indentures.   15

S A M.   Two-and-twenty now he's rising,
                     And alone he's fit to fly,
           Which we're bent on signalizing
                     With unusual revelry.

A L L.   Here's good luck to Frederic's ventures!   20
           Frederic's out of his indentures.
           Pour, oh, pour the pirate sherry, etc.

(F R E D E R I C *rises and comes forward with* P I R A T E K I N G, *who enters.*)

32–3 *scuttling a Cunarder*: To scuttle is to sink. The Cunard line was founded by Samuel Cunard (1787–1865), who in 1839 established the British and North American Royal Mail
Steam Packet Company to run regular mail and passenger services between Liverpool
and the East Coast of North America. In 1878 it was re-formed as a public company
with the title The Cunard Steam-Ship Company. It was a Cunard liner, the *Aurania*,
which took Richard D'Oyly Carte and his company secretly to the United States in the
summer of 1885 to perform *The Mikado* (see p. 555). Cunard still runs passenger services
across the Atlantic in its flag-ship, the *QE2*.

33 *cutting out a P. & O.*: To cut out is to capture or destroy one ship in a fleet by separating it
from the rest. The Peninsular and Oriental Steam Navigation Company, better known
as the P. & O., began in 1835 as the Peninsular Steam Navigation Company, with a regular
steamer service to the Iberian peninsula, including the carrying of mail to Gibraltar. It
acquired its present name in 1840, having started a service on the Gibraltar–Alexandria
route, and later extended its operations through the Suez Canal to India, Ceylon and
the Far East.

In early productions of *The Pirates* in the United States, including the première, the
Pirate King did not refer to the P. & O. but to the White Star Line, which was presumably
better-known across the Atlantic. Founded as the Oceanic Steam Navigation Company
in 1869 by Thomas Henry Ismay, the line operated services on both the North Atlantic
and the Australian routes. Its liner *Oceanic*, launched in 1870 for the Liverpool to New
York run, was the world's first express luxury liner. In 1934 the line was merged with
Cunard to form Cunard White Star Ltd.

never shipped a handspike: A handspike is a lever, generally made of wood, fitted into a
windlass or capstan to heave up an anchor or heavy chain.

43–60 *When Frederic was a little lad*
Gilbert's original intention, as revealed in the licence copy of *The Pirates* sent to the Lord
Chamberlain, was to have no dialogue at all until the end of this number, which was conceived as a duet for Frederic and Ruth rather than a solo as now. The opening chorus
was to be followed immediately by a song for the Pirate King, after which there was to
be a recitative for Frederic covering much the same points as those now contained in
the dialogue in lines 24 to 42. Then came the duet for Frederic and Ruth. I reproduce
the entire sequence below, as it appears in the licence copy (i.e. with a serious lack
of punctuation; unlike all the other Savoy Opera libretti sent to the Lord Chamberlain
before their first performance, that for *The Pirates* is not printed but written out in an
evidently hurried long-hand, a further sign of the pressures under which the opera
was completed).

This sequence is interesting both in its own right, in showing, for example, a very different character for the Pirate King from the one later adopted, and also because it
seems to have been the version which was performed at Paignton on 30 December 1879.
It follows straight on from the opening chorus:

KING.   Yes I am a Pirate King!
ALL.   You are!
             Hurrah for our Pirate King!
KING.   And it is, it is a glorious thing
             To be a Pirate King!
ALL.   Hurrah,
             Hurrah for our Pirate King.
KING.   It's true I have to work all day
             Like a genial help in a humble way
ALL (*significantly*).   You should!
             You should if you'd be our king!

KING. Yes, Frederic, from to-day you rank as a full-blown member of
our band.   25

ALL. Hurrah!

FRED. My friends, I thank you all, from my heart, for your kindly
wishes. Would that I could repay them as they deserve!

KING. What do you mean?

FRED. To-day I am out of my indentures, and to-day I leave you for   30
ever.

KING. But this is quite unaccountable; a keener hand at scuttling a
Cunarder or cutting out a P. & O. never shipped a handspike.

FRED. Yes, I have done my best for you. And why? It was my duty
under my indentures, and I am the slave of duty. As a child I was regularly 35
apprenticed to your band. It was through an error – no matter, the mistake
was ours, not yours, and I was in honour bound by it.

SAM. An error? What error?

FRED. I may not tell you; it would reflect upon my well-loved Ruth.

(RUTH *rises and comes forward*.)   40

RUTH. Nay, dear master, my mind has long been gnawed by the
cankering tooth of mystery. Better have it out at once.

SONG – RUTH.

When Frederic was a little lad he proved so brave and daring,
His father thought he'd 'prentice him to some career sea-faring.
I was, alas! his nurserymaid, and so it fell to *my* lot   45
To take and bind the promising boy apprentice to a *pilot* –
A life not bad for a hardy lad, though surely not a high lot,
Though I'm a nurse, you might do worse than make your boy a pilot.

I was a stupid nurserymaid, on breakers always steering,
And I did not catch the word aright, through being hard of hearing;   50
Mistaking my instructions, which within my brain did gyrate,
I took and bound this promising boy apprentice to a *pirate*.
A sad mistake it was to make and doom him to a vile lot.
I bound him to a pirate – you – instead of to a pilot.

I soon found out, beyond all doubt, the scope of this disaster,   55
But I hadn't the face to return to my place, and break it to my master.
A nurserymaid is not afraid of what you people *call* work,
So I made up my mind to go as a kind of piratical maid-of-all-work.
And that is how you find me now, a member of your shy lot,
Which you wouldn't have found, had he been bound apprentice to a pilot.   60

KING. But to cook your meals I don't refuse
And I black piratical boots and shoes
I clean your knives, I bake your bread
I light your fires – I make your beds
I answer all the bells that ring
Cling! cling! cling! cling! cling! cling!
For if I said I'd rather not
(I know you! I know you!)
You would depose me like a shot!
ALL. We would!
Hurrah for our Pirate King!
KING. Well many a king on a first class throne
If he wants to call his crown his own
Must manage somehow to get through
More dirty work than ever I do
Though I wash and boil
And scrub and toil
And answer bells that ring cling! cling!
ALL. Cling! cling! cling! cling! cling! cling!
KING. But menial duties carry no sting
When one reflects what a glorious thing
It is to be a king
ALL. Hurrah!
Hurrah for our Pirate King!
So pour, oh King, the pirate sherry etc.

RECITATIVE.

FRED. My generous friends, with all my heart I thank you
Although as brethren I no longer rank you!
ALL. Oh, oh?
How so?
Although with all his heart he thanks us
As brethren he no longer ranks us!
Oh, oh!
How so? How so? How so? How so?
FRED. Bear with me pray
Although I bring you tidings that will grieve you
This very day
I'm out of my indentures and I leave you.
ALL. You leave us?
FRED. I leave you!
Don't estimate me at too high appraisement
ALL. Wonder, surprise, confusion and amazement.
FRED. I've always loathed your pillaging and branding
But for a most absurd misunderstanding
Upon the part of one who little knew you
I never should have been apprenticed to you.
Once more – don't estimate me at too high appraisement
ALL. Once more surprise, confusion and amazement.

DUET AND CHORUS.

FRED. When I was but a child of three
I proved so brave and daring
My father thought he'd prentice me
To some career seafaring
A servant girl in his employ
He sent in charge of my lot

RUTH. Oh, pardon! Frederic, pardon! (*Kneels.*)

FRED. Rise, sweet one, I have long pardoned you.

RUTH (*rises*). The two words were so much alike!

FRED. They were. They still are, though years have rolled over their heads. But this afternoon my obligation ceases. Individually, I love you all   65
with affection unspeakable, but, collectively, I look upon you with a disgust that amounts to absolute detestation. Oh! pity me, my beloved friends, for such is my sense of duty that, once out of my indentures, I shall feel myself bound to devote myself heart and soul to your extermination!

ALL. Poor lad – poor lad! (*All weep.*)   70

KING. Well, Frederic, if you conscientiously feel that it is your duty to destroy us, we cannot blame you for acting on that conviction. Always act in accordance with the dictates of your conscience, my boy, and chance the consequences.

SAM. Besides, we can offer you but little temptation to remain with us.   75
We don't seem to make piracy pay. I'm sure I don't know why, but we don't.

FRED. *I* know why, but, alas! I mustn't tell you; it wouldn't be right.

KING. Why not, my boy? It's only half-past eleven, and you are one of us until the clock strikes twelve.

SAM. True, and until then you are bound to protect our interests.   80

ALL. Hear, hear!

FRED. Well, then, it is my duty, as a pirate, to tell you that you are too tender-hearted. For instance, you make a point of never attacking a weaker party than yourselves, and when you attack a stronger party you invariably get thrashed.   85

KING. There is some truth in that.

FRED. Then, again, you make a point of never molesting an orphan!

SAM. Of course: we are orphans ourselves, and know what it is.

FRED. Yes, but it has got about, and what is the consequence? Every one we capture says he's an orphan. The last three ships we took proved to   90
be manned entirely by orphans, and so we had to let them go. One would think that Great Britain's mercantile navy was recruited solely from her orphan asylums – which we know is not the case.

SAM. But, hang it all! you wouldn't have us absolutely merciless?

FRED. There's my difficulty; until twelve o'clock I would, after twelve I   95
wouldn't. Was ever a man placed in so delicate a situation?

RUTH. And Ruth, your own Ruth, whom you love so well, and who has won her middle-aged way into your boyish heart, what is to become of *her*?

KING. Oh, he will take you with him.

(*Hands* RUTH *to* FREDERIC.)   100

FRED. Well, Ruth, I feel some little difficulty about you. It is true that I admire you very much, but I have been constantly at sea since I was eight

	Instructing her to bind his boy
	Apprentice to a pilot –
KING, SAMUEL & JAMES.	A pilot?
FRED.	A pilot.
	A very respectable line of life, though certainly not a high lot.
KING, SAMUEL & JAMES.	An odd mistake
	You surely make
	You mean of course a Pirate
FRED.	No, no, no, no.
	A *pi*lot, *pi*lot, a *pi*lot, a *pi*lot.
	A highly respectable line of life though certainly not a high lot –
	I hope I'm clear
KING.	Yes, yes, we hear
	Now pray do not get irate
	You said 'a respectable line of life' we thought you meant a pirate
ALL.	He said 'a respectable line of life' we thought you meant a pirate
RUTH (*coming forward*).	
	Ah me, I was that nurserymaid
	Forgive my interfering
	My strict commands I disobeyed
	Through being hard of hearing
	His father's words were spoken that wild
	That in my brain did gyrate
	And I understood he wished his son
	Apprenticed to a pirate
KING, JAMES & SAMUEL.	A pirate?
RUTH.	A pirate.
	A very contemptible line of life, with a premium at a high rate.
KING, SAMUEL & JAMES.	An odd mistake
	You surely make
	You mean of course a pilot.
RUTH (*irritated*).	No, no, no, no
	A pirate, a pirate, a pirate, a pirate.
	A very contemptible line of life, you stupid triumvirate,
	I hope I'm clear?
KING.	Yes, yes, we hear
	Though ours is not a vile lot
	You said 'a contemptible line of life', we thought you meant a pilot.
ALL.	She said 'a contemptible line of life', we thought she meant a pilot.

The licence copy then continues with this dialogue line:

> FRED. Yes my friends, my being apprenticed to you was entirely due to my excellent nurse's mistake.
> RUTH. Oh pardon, pardon, pardon.

126 *Well, it's the top of the tide*: The original version, found in the licence copy and performed at Paignton, contained another piece of recitative at this point instead of the dialogue which begins 'Well, it's the top of the tide':

SAMUEL.	Your Majesty, we must get underway
	To lose the tide we should be worse than crazy
KING.	Is it essential we put out today?
	To tell the truth I feel a little lazy –
	How would it be if I remained behind?
	On this hot day the cavern is delicious
JAMES.	We rather think your majesty would find
	That course of action highly injudicious

years old, and yours is the only woman's face I have seen during that time.
I think it is a sweet face.

RUTH. It is – oh, it is!

FRED. I say I *think* it is; that is my impression. But as I have never had
an opportunity of comparing you with other women, it is just possible I may
be mistaken.

KING. True.

FRED. What a terrible thing it would be if I were to marry this innocent
person, and then find out that she is, on the whole, plain!

KING. Oh, Ruth is very well, very well indeed.

SAM. Yes, there are the remains of a fine woman about Ruth.

FRED. Do you really think so?

SAM. I do.

FRED. Then I will not be so selfish as to take her from you. In justice to her,
and in consideration for you, I will leave her behind. (*Hands* RUTH *to* KING.)

KING. No, Frederic, this must not be. We are rough men who lead a
rough life, but we are not so utterly heartless as to deprive thee of thy love.
I think I am right in saying that there is not one here who would
rob thee of this inestimable treasure for all the world holds dear.

ALL (*loudly*). Not one!

KING. No, I thought there wasn't. Keep thy love, Frederic, keep thy
love. (*Hands her back to* FREDERIC.)

FRED. You're very good, I'm sure.

(*Exit* RUTH.)

KING. Well, it's the top of the tide, and we must be off. Farewell,
Frederic. When your process of extermination begins, let our deaths be as
swift and painless as you can conveniently make them.

FRED. I will! By the love I have for you, I swear it! Would that you
could render this extermination unnecessary by accompanying me back to
civilization!

KING. No, Frederic, it cannot be. I don't think much of our profession,
but, contrasted with respectability, it is comparatively honest. No, Frederic,
I shall live and die a Pirate King.

SONG – PIRATE KING.

Oh, better far to live and die
Under the brave black flag I fly,
Than play a sanctimonious part,
With a pirate head and a pirate heart.
Away to the cheating world go you,
Where pirates all are well-to-do;
But I'll be true to the song I sing,

ALL (*drawing knives*).   We rather think, etc.

SAMUEL.   Who would there be to knot and reef and splice
                 Or take in canvas when the storm is lowering

KING (*sighing*).   True, true – I thank you for your very good advice.
                 (*loading himself with kegs etc.*)
                 The cares of government are overpowering.
                 For I am a Pirate King etc.

After repeating the final refrain of the Pirate King's song, the pirates depart, leaving
Ruth and Frederic alone, and the dialogue continues as now (line 168).

144   *For I am a Pirate King*: The Pirate King, played by Prince Charles when he was a boy at
Gordonstoun School in 1967 and turned into an Errol-Flynn-type swashbuckling mati-
née idol by Joseph Papp, is one of the most likeable villains in the Savoy Operas. In an
earlier musical play, *Our Island Home*, written in 1870 in collaboration with the composer
Thomas German Reed, Gilbert had created a character who is in many ways the prototype of the Pirate King in *The Pirates of Penzance*. Captain Bang introduces himself in a
similar if rather more threatening way:

> Oh tremble! I'm a Pirate Chief;
> Who comes upon me comes to grief,
> For I'm a murderer and a thief;
> A Pirate Captain, I.
> I spare nor age nor sex nor rank.
> For every one my fetters clank,
> Until they're made to walk the plank,
> A Pirate Captain, I.

The story of Captain Bang in *Our Island Home* also anticipates the plight of Frederic in
The Pirates. He is the only son of an indulgent father and mother who had asked him,
when he was seven, what he wanted to be. He replied that he had a hankering for a seafaring life, but didn't want to be away from home for long, so he told them that he wanted
to be a pilot. 'My kind papa consented and sent me with my nurse to the nearest sea-
front, telling her to apprentice me to a pilot. The girl – a very good girl, but stupid, –
mistaking her instructions, apprenticed me to a pirate of her acquaintance and bound
me over to serve him diligently and faithfully until I reached the age of 21.'

172   *You will find me a wife of a thousand*: This same joke occurs in the Bab Ballad 'Haunted', in
which a man reflects on the social ghosts which haunt him:

> I pass to critical seventeen:
> The ghost of that terrible wedding scene,
> When an elderly colonel stole my queen,
> And woke my dream of heaven:
> No school-girl decked in her nursery curls
> Was my gushing innocent queen of pearls;
> If she wasn't a girl of a thousand girls,
> She was one of forty-seven!

Gilbert, who was himself forty-six when he wrote *The Pirates*, seems to have found women
in their forties a source of particular amusement. In the judge's song in *Trial by Jury* we
are told that the rich attorney says of the daughter whom he is hoping to marry off:

> She may very well pass for forty-three
> In the dusk, with a light behind her!

	And live and die a Pirate King.	
	For I am a Pirate King.	
ALL.	You are!	145
	Hurrah for the Pirate King!	
KING.	And it is, it is a glorious thing	
	To be a Pirate King.	
ALL.	It is!	
	Hurrah for our Pirate King!	150
KING.	When I sally forth to seek my prey	

KING. When I sally forth to seek my prey
I help myself in a royal way:
I sink a few more ships, it's true,
Than a well-bred monarch ought to do;
But many a king on a first-class throne,   155
If he wants to call his crown his own,
Must manage somehow to get through
More dirty work than ever *I* do,
For I am a Pirate King.
ALL.   You are!   160
Hurrah for the Pirate King!
KING. And it is, it is a glorious thing
To be a Pirate King!
ALL.   It is!
Hurrah for our Pirate King!   165

(*Exeunt all except* FREDERIC.)

(*Enter* RUTH.)

RUTH. Oh, take me with you! I cannot live if I am left behind.

FRED. Ruth, I will be quite candid with you. You are very dear to me,
as you know, but I must be circumspect. You see, you are considerably older   170
than I. A lad of twenty-one usually looks for a wife of seventeen.

RUTH. A wife of seventeen! You will find me a wife of a thousand!

FRED. No, but I shall find you a wife of forty-seven, and that is quite
enough. Ruth, tell me candidly, and without reserve: compared with other
women – how are *you*?   175

RUTH. I will answer you truthfully, master – I have a slight cold, but
otherwise I am quite well.

FRED. I am sorry for your cold, but I was referring rather to your
personal appearance. Compared with other women, are you beautiful?

RUTH (*bashfully*). I have been told so, dear master.   180

FRED. Ah, but lately?

RUTH. Oh, no, years and years ago.

FRED. What do you think of yourself?

191 *Can it be Custom House*: For the most part, the Joseph Papp production of *The Pirates*
sticks faithfully to Gilbert's original dialogue. At this point, however, Papp makes a
small concession to his American audience by substituting 'the Coastguard' for 'Custom
House' in Frederic's speech. 'Custom House' anyway seems a strange phrase to use to
describe the officers of Her Majesty's Department of Customs and Excise. 'The reven-
uemen' would be more usual.

203–20 *You told me you were fair as gold*
This duet is the first of several songs in *The Pirates* in which Sullivan's music comes
nearer to being in the category of grand opera than operetta. He was, of course, a serious
composer, with several operas, oratorios, a symphony and numerous hymn tunes and
songs to his credit, and it was in those areas that he believed his true talents lay and that
he was happiest working. Yet, although his serious music was played and recognized, it
never brought him the same fame and popularity as the Savoy Operas.
     Several critics shared Sullivan's view that the comic opera collaborations with Gilbert
were really beneath his talents. One wrote of *The Pirates*: 'Certain passages in the first
duet between Frederic and Ruth and elsewhere, where the composer becomes serious
in spite of himself, make one regret what might have been, or, perhaps, might still be if
Mr Sullivan would attempt a genuine dramatic effort'.
     In fact, Sullivan went on to write at least one major dramatic grand opera. *Ivanhoe*,
based on the story by Sir Walter Scott, opened in January 1891 at the new Royal English
Opera House (now the Palace Theatre), which Richard D'Oyly Carte had built to be the
home of English grand opera. Although it ran for 155 consecutive performances, a record
for grand opera, it has hardly ever been heard since, and Carte was forced to abandon
his plans to do for English grand opera what he had so successfully done for English comic opera.

RUTH. It is a delicate question to answer, but I think I am a fine woman.
FRED. That is your candid opinion?   185
RUTH. Yes, I should be deceiving you if I told you otherwise.
FRED. Thank you, Ruth, I believe you, for I am sure you would not
practise on my inexperience; I wish to do the right thing, and if – I say *if* –
you are really a fine woman, your age shall be no obstacle to our union!
(*Chorus of Girls heard in the distance.*) Hark! Surely I hear voices! Who has   190
ventured to approach our all but inaccessible lair? Can it be Custom House?
No, it does not sound like Custom House.
RUTH (*aside*). Confusion! it is the voices of young girls! If he should see
them I am lost.
FRED. (*looking off*). By all that's marvellous, a bevy of beautiful maidens!   195
RUTH (*aside*). Lost! lost! lost!
FRED. How lovely! how surpassingly lovely is the plainest of them!
What grace – what delicacy – what refinement! And Ruth – Ruth told me she
was beautiful!

RECITATIVE.

FRED.	Oh, false one, you have deceived me!	200
RUTH.	I have deceived you?	
FRED.	Yes, deceived me!	(*Denouncing her.*)

DUET – FREDERIC *and* RUTH.

FRED.   You told me you were fair as gold!
RUTH (*wildly*). And, master, am I not so?
FRED.   And now I see you're plain and old.   205
RUTH.   I am sure I am not a jot so.
FRED.   Upon my innocence you play.
RUTH.   I'm not the one to plot so.
FRED.   Your face is lined, your hair is grey.
RUTH.   It's gradually got so.   210
FRED.   Faithless woman, to deceive me,
        I who trusted so!
RUTH.   Master, master, do not leave me!
        Hear me, ere you go!
        My love without reflecting,   215
        Oh, do not be rejecting.
    Take a maiden tender – her affection raw and green,
        At very highest rating,
        Has been accumulating
    Summers seventeen – summers seventeen.   220

230   *in this alarming costume*: This phrase originally went 'in this detested costume'. The word
      'detested' was almost certainly dropped because it proved difficult to sing. The same rea-
      son probably explains the subsitution of 'innocence' for the original 'ignorance' in line
      207. 'Detested costume' appears in all editions of the vocal score, so it was probably in-
      troduced before the first performance.

234–62   *Climbing over rocky mountain*
         This song was substantially 'lifted' from Gilbert and Sullivan's first joint work, *Thespis*.
         There it was sung by a troupe of actors who had come to Mount Olympus for a picnic.
         In adapting it for the new opera, Gilbert made only minimal changes to the last two
         lines of the chorus, which had originally run 'Climb the hardy lads and lasses, / Till the
         mountain top they gain'. In its slightly modified form, the song strikes an incongruous
         note in its new setting. Gaining access to a Cornish beach hardly requires 'Climbing
         over rocky mountain' or 'Scaling rough and rugged passes' in the way that ascending
         Mount Olympus no doubt would.
             The verses sung by Edith and Kate are also taken from the same song in *Thespis*,
         although here Gilbert was careful to make more alterations to suit the different circum-
         stances of *The Pirates*. The lines now given to Kate, for example, were rather different
         when sung by the Thespians climbing Mount Olympus:

> Far away from grief and care,
> High up in the mountain air,
> Let us live and reign alone
> In a world that's all our own.
> Here enthroned in the sky,
> Far away from mortal eye,
> We'll be gods and make decrees,
> Those may honour them who please.

         'Climbing over rocky mountain' is, in fact, one of only two songs in *Thespis* of which
         the music still survives. The other is the ballad 'Little Maid of Arcadee'.
             The licence copy of *The Pirates* has an eight-line introductory chorus for General
         Stanley's daughters before they embark on 'Climbing over rocky mountain'. This was
         presumably sung at the Paignton performance:

> With timid step and watchful eye
> And pleasing palpitation

ENSEMBLE.

RUTH.	FREDERIC.
Don't, beloved master,	Yes, your former master
Crush me with disaster.	Saves you from disaster.
What is such a dower to the dower	Your love would be uncomfortably
I have here?	fervid, it is clear,
My love unabating	If, as you are stating,
Has been accumulating	It's been accumulating
Forty-seven year – forty-seven year!	Forty-seven year – forty-seven year!

225

(At the end he renounces her, and she goes off in despair.)

RECITATIVE – FREDERIC.

What shall I do? Before these gentle maidens
I dare not show in this alarming costume.
No, no, I must remain in close concealment
Until I can appear in decent clothing!

230

(Hides in cave as they enter climbing over the rocks.)

GIRLS.   Climbing over rocky mountain,
Skipping rivulet and fountain,
Passing where the willows quiver
By the ever-rolling river,
   Swollen with the summer rain;
Threading long and leafy mazes
Dotted with unnumbered daisies;
Scaling rough and rugged passes,
Climb the hardy little lasses,
   Till the bright sea-shore they gain!

235

240

EDITH.   Let us gaily tread the measure,
Make the most of fleeting leisure;
Hail it as a true ally,
Though it perish by and by.

245

ALL.   Hail it as a true ally,
Though it perish by and by.

EDITH.   Every moment brings a treasure
Of its own especial pleasure,
Though the moments quickly die,
Greet them gaily as they fly.

250

> We will continue bye and bye
> Our work of explanation
> This cavern will afford us rest
> Within its shade romantic
> While we inhale, with grateful zest,
> The breath of the Atlantic

'Explanation' at the end of the fourth line should surely be 'exploration' and must have been a mistake made by the hasty transcriber of the licence copy.

271 *Who are only human beings down to the waist*: This idea is employed again in *Iolanthe*, where Strephon is a fairy down to the waist and a mortal below it.

291 *Ladies, do not shun me*: The line originally written by Gilbert was 'Ladies, do not shudder!' Once again, it was probably changed because it proved difficult to sing. 'Shun me' is in all editions of the vocal score. In the following line, 'wild profession' was substituted for the original 'vile profession', which still appears in some editions of the libretto and is often sung.

KATE.

Far away from toil and care,
Revelling in fresh sea air,
Here we live and reign alone
In a world that's all our own.
Here in this our rocky den,
Far away from mortal men,
We'll be queens, and make decrees –
They may honour them who please.

255

260

ALL.

Let us gaily tread the measure, etc.

KATE. What a picturesque spot! I wonder where we are!

EDITH. And I wonder where papa is. We have left him ever so far behind.

ISABEL. Oh, he will be here presently! Remember poor papa is not as
young as we are, and we have come over a rather difficult country.

265

KATE. But how thoroughly delightful it is to be so entirely alone! Why,
in all probability we are the first human beings who ever set foot on this
enchanting spot.

ISABEL. Except the mermaids – it's the very place for mermaids.

270

KATE. Who are only human beings down to the waist!

EDITH. And who can't be said strictly to set *foot* anywhere. Tails they
may, but feet they *cannot*.

KATE. But what shall we do until papa and the servants arrive with the
luncheon?

275

EDITH. We are quite alone, and the sea is as smooth as glass. Suppose
we take off our shoes and stockings and paddle?

ALL. Yes, yes! The very thing! (*They prepare to carry out the suggestion. They
have all taken off one shoe, when* FREDERIC *comes forward from cave.*)

FRED. (*recitative*). Stop, ladies, pray!

ALL (*hopping on one foot*).   A man!

280

FRED.

                                                        I had intended
Not to intrude myself upon your notice
In this effective but alarming costume,
But under these peculiar circumstances
It is my bounden duty to inform you
That your proceedings will not be unwitnessed!

285

EDITH.   But who are you, sir? Speak!   (*All hopping.*)

FRED.   I am a pirate!

ALL (*recoiling, hopping*).   A pirate! Horror!

290

FRED.   Ladies, do not shun me!
This evening I renounce my wild profession;
And to that end, oh, pure and peerless maidens!
Oh, blushing buds of ever-blooming beauty!

299–322 *Oh, is there not one maiden breast*
The rhyming of 'beauty' and 'duty', which we noted in four songs in *H.M.S. Pinafore*, occurs in only three in *The Pirates*, despite the opera's sub-title and theme. In addition to
this song, they are the girls' recitative 'The question is, had he not been/A thing of
beauty' and Mabel's solo 'Did ever maiden wake/From dream of homely duty'.

This song shows very clearly how far Sullivan's music can, at times, transcend Gilbert's words to give a wholly different effect from that achieved by reading the lyrics in
print. The beginning of the second verse, and particularly the line 'Whose homely face
and bad complexion', reads like a comic dig from the *Bab Ballads*. Yet when sung to Sullivan's powerful, swelling melody it strikes a note of extreme pathos.

Gilbert's original version of this song would have been even less suitable for setting to
Sullivan's soul-stirring tune:

FREDERIC.   Oh do not spurn the pirate's tear,
                  Nor deem his grief unreal and frothy,
                  He longs to doff his pirate gear
                  And turn tall-hatty and broad-clothy.
                  He hates his life upon the wave,
                  And longs 'on change' to try his luck, oh –
                  He loathes his rude and draughty cave,
                  And sighs for brick relieved with stucco.

ALL.   We do not spurn the pirate's tear,
                  Nor deem his grief unreal and frothy.
                  He's right to drop his pirate gear
                  And turn tall-hatty and broad-clothy.

330 *Yes, 'tis Mabel*: In the licence copy, and likewise in the original Paignton performance,
there was no recitative or solo song for Mabel after she had so dramatically responded
to Frederic's plea. Instead, there was the following ensemble, sung, it would seem, to the
same tune as Frederic's earlier solo:

FREDERIC.   Oh joy, of all the maidens here
                  The fairest with the best complexion
                  So sweet a face and eyes so clear
                  Might chain an anchorite's affection!

MABEL.   Although indifferent I fear
                  My face and form and my complexion
                  These blemishes will disappear
                  Before the ardour of affection!

EDITH.   Yes, yes, it is extremely clear
                  Her homely face and bad complexion
                  Have caused all hope to disappear
                  Of ever winning man's affection

ALL.   Yes, yes, it is extremely clear etc.

295

	I, sore at heart, implore your kind assistance.
EDITH.	How pitiful his tale!
KATE.	How rare his beauty!
ALL.	How pitiful his tale! How rare his beauty!

SONG – FREDERIC.

Oh, is there not one maiden breast
　　Which does not feel the moral beauty   300
Of making worldly interest
　　Subordinate to sense of duty?
Who would not give up willingly
　　All matrimonial ambition,
To rescue such an one as I   305
　　From his unfortunate position?

ALL.　　Alas! there's not one maiden breast
　　　　Which seems to feel the moral beauty
　　Of making worldly interest
　　　　Subordinate to sense of duty!   310

FRED.　Oh, is there not one maiden here
　　　　Whose homely face and bad complexion
　　Have caused all hopes to disappear
　　　　Of ever winning man's affection?
　　To such an one, if such there be,   315
　　　　I swear by Heaven's arch above you,
　　If you will cast your eyes on me –
　　　　However plain you be – I'll love you!

ALL.　　Alas! there's not one maiden here
　　　　Whose homely face and bad complexion
　　Have caused all hope to disappear   320
　　　　Of ever winning man's affection!

FRED. (*in despair*). Not one?
ALL.　　　　　　　　No, no – not one!
FRED. Not one?   325
ALL.　　No, no!

(MABEL *enters.*)

MABEL.　　　　　Yes, one!
ALL.　　'Tis Mabel!
MABEL.　Yes, 'tis Mabel!
330

343–56 *Poor wandering one*

This seductive waltz song, with its dazzling coloratura trills and cadences – the 'farm-yard effects', as Sullivan called them – was at least in part a deliberate skit on the 'oper-acrobatics' which Gounod and other French and Italian opera composers had made fashionable. Whether parody or not, however, it stands as a perfect and delightful example of the genre.

As already noted above, 'Poor wandering one' was composed at the last minute for the American production of *The Pirates* and did not figure in the licence copy or the Paignton performance. The last line of the first section, following 'Thy steps retrace', was originally 'Be not afraid'. It was probably altered to 'Poor wandering one!' by Sullivan as being easier to set in that form.

360–75 *What ought we to do*: In the licence copy Edith and Kate's verses are replaced by a passage for Edith and the chorus:

EDITH.	Now stern propriety we know Bids us remain in solemn tether
ALL.	Yes, yes. Yes, yes.
EDITH.	While delicacy bids us go And leave the plighted pair together
ALL.	Yes, yes, yes, yes.
EDITH.	Suppose we make a compromise For oh, our hearts are not of leather.
ALL.	Yes, yes, yes, yes.
EDITH.	Suppose we stop and shut our eyes And talk discreetly of the weather?
ALL.	Yes, yes, yes, yes, We'll talk discreetly of the weather.

RECITATIVE – MABEL.

Oh, sisters, deaf to pity's name,
    For shame!
It's true that he has gone astray,
    But pray
Is that a reason good and true   335
    Why you
Should all be deaf to pity's name?

ALL (*aside*).   The question is, had he not been
    A thing of beauty,
Would she be swayed by quite as keen   340
    A sense of duty?

MABEL.   For shame, for shame, for shame!

SONG – MABEL.

Poor wandering one!
Though thou hast surely strayed,
    Take heart of grace,
    Thy steps retrace,   345
Poor wandering one!
Poor wandering one!
If such poor love as mine
    Can help thee find
    True peace of mind –   350
Why, take it, it is thine!
    Take heart, fair days will shine;
    Take any heart – take mine!

ALL.   Take heart; no danger lowers;   355
Take any heart – but ours!

(*Exeunt* MABEL *and* FREDERIC.)

(EDITH *beckons her sisters, who form in a semicircle
around her.*)

EDITH.

What ought we to do,   360
    Gentle sisters, say?
Propriety, we know,
    Says we ought to stay;

377–84 *How beautifully blue the sky*
The simultaneous singing of two tunes with completely different speeds and moods, which occurs here with dramatic effect, is a trick which Sullivan used several times in the Savoy Operas. It happens again in Act II of *The Pirates*, when Mabel and Edith's 'Go, ye heroes, go to glory' is sung over the policemen's 'When the foeman bears his steel'. Perhaps the most sophisticated example is the lead-in to the trio 'To sit in solemn silence' in *The Mikado*, where Nanki-Poo, Pooh-Bah and Pish-Tush each have their own tune to express their particular mood.

While sympathy exclaims,
   'Free them from your tether –
Play at other games –
   Leave them here together.'

365

KATE.

Her case may, any day,
   Be yours, my dear, or mine.
Let her make her hay
   While the sun doth shine.
Let us compromise,
   (Our hearts are not of leather.)
Let us shut our eyes,
   And talk about the weather.

370

375

GIRLS.   Yes, yes, let's talk about the weather.

CHATTERING CHORUS.

How beautifully blue the sky,
The glass is rising very high,
Continue fine I hope it may,
And yet it rained but yesterday.
To-morrow it may pour again
(I hear the country wants some rain),
Yet people say, I know not why,
That we shall have a warm July.

380

(*Enter* MABEL *and* FREDERIC.)

385

(*During* MABEL'S *solo the Girls continue chatter pianissimo,
but listening eagerly all the time.*)

SOLO – MABEL.

Did ever maiden wake
   From dream of homely duty,
To find her daylight break
   With such exceeding beauty?
Did ever maiden close
   Her eyes on waking sadness,
To dream of such exceeding gladness?

390

FRED.   Oh, yes! ah, yes! this is exceeding gladness.

395

GIRLS.   How beautifully blue the sky, etc.

399–402 *Did ever pirate roll*
In editions of the libretto up to 1914, Frederic's solo balanced Mabel's and had these extra lines, together with a final response from Mabel, which followed 'With peace and virtue beaming?':

> Did ever pirate loathed
> Forsake his hideous mission,
> To find himself betrothed
> To a lady of position?

MABEL.   Ah yes, ah, yes, I am a lady of position.

In fact the lines beginning 'Did ever pirate loathed' are now generally sung by Frederic in the ensemble which follows his solo.

415 *Nice companions for young ladies*: The original libretto had 'nice associates for young ladies'. The word was almost certainly changed before the opening night, no doubt because it was difficult to sing. 'Companions' appears in the earliest vocal score.

416 *Let us disappear*: This line should really read: 'Let us disap- (*shriek*)' for so it is always sung: the pirates appear before the ladies can finish the word.

In the licence copy and the first Paignton performance the entrance of the pirates was slightly postponed, allowing the ladies to finish their chorus and giving Edith a chance to change her mind and ask Frederic whether there might not be another pirate for her to help along the path of virtue:

EDITH.   Stay, before we terminate this most romantic of adventures
              Tell me, are there any others nearly out of their indentures
              And prentice who desirous to give up his dreadful trade is
              If so we will gladly help him

FRED.   No there isn't one, young ladies
              All confirmed desperadoes they would certainly be termed.

EDITH (*disappointed*). I'm sorry they are desperadoes but I'm glad they've been confirmed.

ALL.   We're sorry that they are desperadoes, but we're glad they've been confirmed.

              Come, we must not lose our senses, etc.

SOLO – FREDERIC.

(During this, Girls continue their chatter pianissimo as before, but listening intently all the time.)

Did ever pirate roll
  His soul in guilty dreaming,   400
And wake to find that soul
  With peace and virtue beaming?

ENSEMBLE.

MABEL.	FREDERIC.	GIRLS.
Did ever maiden wake, etc.	Did ever pirate loathed, etc.	How beautifully blue the sky, etc.

RECITATIVE – FREDERIC.

Stay, we must not lose our senses;
  Men who stick at no offences   405
    Will anon be here.
Piracy their dreadful trade is;
  Pray you, get you hence, young ladies,
    While the coast is clear.

(FREDERIC *and* MABEL *retire.*)   410

GIRLS.   No, we must not lose our senses,
              If they stick at no offences
                We should not be here.
            Piracy their dreadful trade is –
              Nice companions for young ladies!   415
                Let us disappear.

(During this chorus the Pirates have entered stealthily, and formed in a semicircle behind the Girls. As the Girls move to go off each Pirate seizes a girl. KING *seizes* EDITH *and* ISABEL, SAMUEL *seizes* KATE.*)*

ALL.   Too late!   420
PIRATES.   Ha! Ha!
ALL.   Too late!
PIRATES.   Ho! Ho!
  Ha! ha! ha! ha! Ho! ho! ho! ho!

438 *your pirate caravanserai*: 'Caravanserai' is a curious word to use in connection with Cornish pirates, being more usually associated with travellers in the Middle East. The word, which is of Persian origin, actually means a building for sheltering caravans with a large inner court for camels and mules, surrounded by rooms for the travellers to rest and store their goods. But I suppose some licence is permissible when you are trying to find something to rhyme with 'Wards in Chancery'.

440 *we are Wards in Chancery*: Even granted Gilbert's special fondness for Wards in Chancery (he makes Phyllis one in *Iolanthe*) it is a little difficult to see why Major-General Stanley's daughters should have been put into this category. Minors are normally put under the care and guardianship of the Court of Chancery if they are orphans or to protect them from their parents. Neither of those reasons would seem applicable here. The most likely explanation is that, faced with so many daughters to clothe and educate, Stanley himself had them made wards so that he could release money which they were due to inherit. Those due to inherit property when they come of age become wards of court if any legal question arises about the property.

441 *Major-General*: The most junior rank of general in the British Army; a major-general commands a division or district or holds a senior staff appointment. Above him comes a lieutenant-general, who commands a corps, and a full general, who commands an army in the field or holds a staff appointment of great importance.

452–96 *I am the very model of a modern Major-General*
Major-General Stanley introduces himself in one of the fastest and most famous of all the Gilbert and Sullivan patter songs. It must also be one of the most parodied. The American comedian Tom Lehrer set the entire table of chemical elements to the tune, beginning 'There's antimony, arsenic, aluminum, selenium'.

In its original version the song began 'I am the very pattern of a modern Major-General'. Its distinctive rhythm, with sixteen syllables to the line, is found in the Grand Duke Rudolph's song 'A pattern to professors of monarchical autonomy' in *The Grand Duke*, which contains the major-general-like line 'I weigh out tea and sugar with precision mathematical'.

ENSEMBLE.

(Pirates pass in front of Girls.)	*(Girls pass in front of Pirates.)*	425
PIRATES.	GIRLS.	

Here's a first-rate opportunity	We have missed our opportunity
To get married with impunity,	Of escaping with impunity;
And indulge in the felicity	So farewell to the felicity
Of unbounded domesticity.	Of our maiden domesticity!
You shall quickly be parsonified,	We shall quickly be parsonified,
Conjugally matrimonified,	Conjugally matrimonified,
By a doctor of divinity,	By a doctor of divinity,
Who resides in this vicinity.	Who resides in this vicinity.

430

ALL.

By a doctor of divinity,
Who resides in this vicinity,   435
By a doctor, a doctor, a doctor,
Of divinity, of divinity.

MABEL (*coming forward*).

RECITATIVE.

Hold, monsters! Ere your pirate caravanserai
Proceed, against our will, to wed us all,
Just bear in mind that we are Wards in Chancery,   440
And father is a Major-General!

SAM. (*cowed*).   We'd better pause, or danger may befall,
Their father is a Major-General.

GIRLS. Yes, yes; he is a Major-General!

(*The* MAJOR-GENERAL *has entered unnoticed, on rock.*)   445

GEN.   Yes, I am a Major-General!
SAM.   For he is a Major-General!
ALL.   He is! Hurrah for the Major-General!
GEN.   And it is – it is a glorious thing
    To be a Major-General!   450
ALL.   It is! Hurrah for the Major-General!

SONG – MAJOR-GENERAL.

I am the very model of a modern Major-General,
I've information vegetable, animal, and mineral,

455   *From Marathon to Waterloo*: The battle of Marathon was fought between the Greeks and
      the Persians in 490 B.C. A messenger ran the twenty-two miles from the battle site to
      Athens to convey the news of the Greek victory and dropped down dead on arrival.
      Marathon races take their name from this incident. The battle of Waterloo was fought
      between the English and the French in 1815 ten miles south of Brussels but won, accord-
      ing to the Duke of Wellington, on the playing fields of Eton.

458   *binomial theorem*: The law of the formation of any power of a binomial, i.e. an expression
      of two terms connected by the signs plus or minus, which was first expounded by Sir
      Isaac Newton. And if you can understand that, you are a cleverer man than I. There is
      an echo of the Major-General's mathematical ability in Gilbert's Bab Ballad 'My Dream',
      where the writer dreams that he is living in a land of highly numerate babies:

> For, as their nurses dandle them,
> They crow binomial theorem,
> With views (it seems absurd to us)
> On differential calculus.

461   *integral and differential calculus*: Differential calculus is the branch of mathematics dealing
      with the calculation of the rate of change of variable quantities. Integral calculus deals
      with the calculation of variable quantities from their rate of change and also with the
      calculation of areas and volumes. Together, these two branches are sometimes known as
      'infinitesimal calculus', so the Major-General was doubtless very good at that too.

462   *beings animalculous*: An animalcule is a microscopic animal.

467   *King Arthur's and Sir Caradoc's*: The historical evidence for King Arthur, who is said to
      have been a British king who led the natives' fight against the advancing Saxons in the
      sixth century A.D., is scanty but there is an abundance of myth and legend about him
      and his knights of the Round Table. Sir Caradoc was one of those knights. An old ballad
      tells how the chastity of the ladies at King Arthur's court was tested by a boy using his
      mantle, a boar's head and a golden horn. Sir Caradoc's wife alone underwent the ordeal
      and proved her fidelity.

468   *hard acrostics*: Acrostics was a popular Victorian parlour game, rather like charades, in
      which players had to guess at one-word answers to a series of clues. The first letters of
      these answers spelt out the overall answer.

469   *elegiacs*: The classical verse form of alternating hexameters and pentameters in which
      elegies were written.
      Heliogabalus: Perhaps the most dissolute of all Roman emperors. He ruled from A.D. 218
      to 222 under the name Marcus Aurelius Antonius and was murdered by the pretorian
      guards. He is also mentioned in *Utopia Limited* when Tarara, the Public Exploder, says
      that the King of Utopia is 'one of the most Heliogabalian profligates that ever disgraced
      an autocratic throne'.

470   *conics*: The geometric properties of a cone when cut by imaginary planes.
      parabolous: Pertaining to parabolas. The usual adjective is 'parabolic', but try rhyming
      that with 'Heliogabalus'.

471   *undoubted Raphaels*: The Italian artist Raffaello Sanzio (1483–1520), better-known as Ra-
      phael, was one of the creators of the movement in art known as the Renaissance. In the
      mid-nineteenth century a group of artists calling themselves the Pre-Raphaelites
      sought to re-create the pre-Renaissance style of painting. It was the affectations of this
      latter group, and the aesthetic movement which they helped to create, which Gilbert
      satirized in *Patience*.
      Gerard Dows: Gerard Dou (1613–75), a Dutch portrait painter and pupil of Rembrandt.
      Zoffanies: Johann Zoffany (1725–1810), a portrait painter who was born in Germany but
      settled in England, becoming a founder member of the Royal Academy.

472   *the Frogs of Aristophanes*: *The Frogs*, with its croaking chorus 'Berkekekex, koax, koax', is

I know the kings of England, and I quote the fights historical,
From Marathon to Waterloo, in order categorical;   455
I'm very well acquainted too with matters mathematical,
I understand equations, both the simple and quadratical,
About binomial theorem I'm teeming with a lot o' news –
With many cheerful facts about the square of the hypotenuse.

ALL.   With many cheerful facts, etc.   460

GEN.   I'm very good at integral and differential calculus,
       I know the scientific names of beings animalculous;
       In short, in matters vegetable, animal, and mineral,
       I am the very model of a modern Major-General.

ALL.   In short, in matters vegetable, animal, and mineral,
       He is the very model of a modern Major-General.   465

GEN.   I know our mythic history, King Arthur's and Sir Caradoc's,
       I answer hard acrostics, I've a pretty taste for paradox,
       I quote in elegiacs all the crimes of Heliogabalus,
       In conics I can floor peculiarities parabolous.   470
       I can tell undoubted Raphaels from Gerard Dows and Zoffanies,
       I know the croaking chorus from the *Frogs* of Aristophanes,
       Then I can hum a fugue of which I've heard the music's din afore,
       And whistle all the airs from that infernal nonsense *Pinafore*.

ALL.   And whistle all the airs, etc.   475

GEN.   Then I can write a washing bill in Babylonic cuneiform,
       And tell you every detail of Caractacus's uniform;
       In short, in matters vegetable, animal, and mineral,
       I am the very model of a modern Major-General.

ALL.   In short, in matters vegetable, animal, and mineral,   480
       He is the very model of a modern Major-General.

GEN.   In fact, when I know what is meant by 'mamelon' and 'ravelin',
       When I can tell at sight a Mauser rifle from a javelin,
       When such affairs as sorties and surprises I'm more wary at,
       And when I know precisely what is meant by 'commissariat',   485
       When I have learnt what progress has been made in modern
              gunnery,
       When I know more of tactics than a novice in a nunnery;
       In short, when I've a smattering of elemental strategy,
       You'll say a better Major-Gener*al* has never *sat* a gee –

perhaps the best-known of the plays of the Greek dramatist Aristophanes (*c.* 445–385 B.C.).

473 *fugue*: A musical composition based on a short theme which is contrapuntally harmo-nized and reintroduced from time to time. Among the Mikado's punishments designed to fit the crime is compulsory attendance by the music-hall singer at 'a series of masses and fugues and "ops" by Bach'.

474 *that infernal nonsense Pinafore*: This is one of two occasions when one Savoy Opera is mentioned in another. The Mikado of Japan is mentioned in *Utopia Limited*. Captain Corcoran of *H.M.S. Pinafore* makes a re-appearance in the same opera, but the name of his ship is not mentioned.

476 *Babylonic cuneiform*: A system of writing used extensively in the Near East from around the end of the fourth millennium B.C. to the end of the first century B.C. The charac-ters were pressed into soft clay tablets with the slanted edge of a stylus and thus had a wedge-shaped appearance. The Latin word *cuneus* means wedge.

477 *Caractacus's uniform*: Caractacus was the Roman name for the British chief Caradoc (not to be confused with the much later Sir Caradoc), who maintained a fierce resistance to the Romans after they landed in Britain in A.D. 43. He usually went into battle clad only in body paint, so his uniform was not as difficult to describe as Major-General Stanley's boast suggests.

482 *'mamelon' and 'ravelin'*: Major-General Stanley need make no apology for being ignorant of these words, which are both archaic terms relating to earthworks and hardly necessary to the vocabulary of a modern major-general. A mamelon was a rounded hillock or mound suitable for use in an ambush or sniping attack; a ravelin was a detached outwork outside the main ditch of a fort.

483 *Mauser rifle*: Gilbert originally wrote 'Chassepôt rifle' here, and the line still appears in that form in certain editions of the libretto, including the Macmillan paperback. A Chas-sepôt rifle, named after its inventor, was used by the French in the Franco-Prussian War of 1870. Towards the end of his life, certainly after the 1907 revival of *The Pirates*, when 'Chassepôt' was still sung, Gilbert changed the phrase to 'Mauser rifle'. The Mauser rifle, better-known than the Chassepôt, was developed for the Prussian army in the early 1870s.

485 *commissariat*: The food and stores department of an army.

489 *sat a gee*: Sat on a horse ('gee-gee'). At this point in many productions of *The Pirates* the Major-General gallops around the stage on an imaginary horse. In the D'Oyly Carte en-cores of this verse, the Major-General surprised and confused the chorus by coming out with the line 'You'll say a better Major-General has never rode a horse'.

493 *But still in matters vegetable*: In early versions, the word 'learning' occurs instead of 'mat-ters' in the Major-General's last verse and in the final chorus. The order of the phrase is, of course, normally 'animal, vegetable and mineral', as it was in the popular quiz ser-ies 'Twenty Questions' which ran through the 1950s and 1960s on BBC radio.

497 *now that I've introduced myself*: Like Sir Joseph Porter in *H.M.S. Pinafore*, Major-General Stanley was at least partly modelled by Gilbert on a well-known contemporary figure. George Grossmith, who created the role in London, was given the elegantly twirled moustache and the slightly imperious manner of Sir Garnet Wolseley, one of the most dashing commanders in the British Army, who had led the British forces in the Ashanti Wars of 1873 and who was to be sent out to Khartoum in 1885 to relieve General Gordon.

At the time when *The Pirates of Penzance* was being written, Lieutenant-General Wolseley (he had been promoted from Major-General the previous year) was leading a successful expedition to capture the rebellious Zulu king, Cetewayo. He returned to the War Office as quartermaster-general with specific responsibility for reforming the structure of the Army.

Unlike Major-General Stanley, Sir Garnet Wolseley was the very model of a modern military commander. In 1869 he had published *The Soldier's Pocket Book*, a manual of military organization and tactics which was the forerunner of the modern field service

ALL. You'll say a better, etc.   490

GEN. For my military knowledge, though I'm plucky and adventury,
      Has only been brought down to the beginning of the century;
      But still in matters vegetable, animal, and mineral,
      I am the very model of a modern Major-General.

ALL. But still in matters vegetable, animal, and mineral,   495
      He is the very model of a modern Major-General.

GEN. And now that I've introduced myself I should like to have some
idea of what's going on.
      KATE. Oh, papa – we —
      SAM. Permit me, I'll explain in two words: we propose to marry your   500
daughters.
      GEN. Dear me!
      GIRLS. Against our wills, papa – against our wills!
      GEN. Oh, but you mustn't do that! May I ask – this is a picturesque
uniform, but I'm not familiar with it – What are you?   505
      KING. We are all single gentlemen.
      GEN. Yes, I gathered that – anything else?
      KING. No, nothing else.
      EDITH. Papa, don't believe them; they are pirates – the famous Pirates
of Penzance!   510
      GEN. The Pirates of Penzance! I have often heard of them.
      MABEL. All except this gentleman – (*indicating* FREDERIC) – who was
a pirate once, but who is out of his indentures to-day, and who means to
lead a blameless life evermore.
      GEN. But wait a bit. I object to pirates as sons-in-law.   515
      KING. We object to Major-Generals as fathers-in-law. But we waive
that point. We do not press it. We look over it.
      GEN. (*aside.*) Hah! an idea! (*Aloud.*) And do you mean to say that you
would deliberately rob me of these, the sole remaining props of my old age,
and leave me to go through the remainder of my life unfriended,   520
unprotected, and alone?
      KING. Well, yes, that's the idea.
      GEN. Tell me, have you ever known what it is to be an orphan?
      PIRATES (*disgusted*). Oh, dash it all!
      KING. Here we are again!   525
      GEN. I ask you, have you ever known what it is to be an orphan?
      KING. Often!
      GEN. Yes, orphan. Have you ever known what it is to be one?
      KING. I say, often.
      ALL (*disgusted*). Often, often, often. (*Turning away.*)   530

regulations. His considerable skills of organization and management gave rise to the saying 'All Sir Garnet', meaning all's well, while his military adventuring was commended in another of the Savoy Operas when Colonel Calverley in *Patience* sang of the 'Skill of Sir Garnet in thrashing a cannibal'.

Wolseley, who revelled in publicity, was delighted to be taken as the model for the modern Major-General and enjoyed singing the patter song to his friends and family at home.

Wolseley may not have been the only contemporary figure that Gilbert had in mind when he created the character of Major-General Stanley. Trevor Hearl, a historian of Victorian military education, believes that Sir Edward Hamley, commandant of the Staff College at Camberley from 1870 to 1877, may also have been a model for the modern Major-General. Hamley believed that military history was more valuable to soldiers than military science – a sentiment which would certainly have found favour with Major-General Stanley.

531 *I don't think we quite understand one another*: Feeling that the 'orphan'/'often' joke went on for too long and became rather laboured, the D'Oyly Carte Opera Company generally cut all the dialogue from this point until the Major-General's remark: 'When you said "orphan", did you mean "orphan" – a person who has lost his parents, or "often" – frequently?' Joseph Papp, however, retained the full exchange between the Major-General and the King.

It is interesting to note that Sir Garnet Wolseley was himself orphaned, or at least half-orphaned, at the age of seven, when his father died, leaving his mother to bring up four sons and three daughters, although it seems unlikely that this was the source of Gilbert's idea.

553 *How sad – an orphan boy*: At this point, and before the Major-General's solo, the licence copy, and presumably also the Paignton performance, had an ensemble which anticipates the later 'I'm telling a terrible story':

ENSEMBLE

GENERAL (*aside*)
Oh what a story I am telling
My parents close to us are dwelling
These simple pirates I am selling
Oh what a story I am telling

GIRLS (*aside*)
Oh what a fib papa is telling
His parents close to us are dwelling
These simple privates* he is selling
Oh what a fib papa is telling

PIRATES (*in tears*)

Oh sad indeed the tale he's telling
And pity from our bosoms welling
All ferocity is quelling
Sad indeed the tale he's telling

* This should presumably be 'pirates'.

GEN. I don't think we quite understand one another. I ask you, have you ever known what it is to be an orphan, and you say 'orphan'. As I understand you, you are merely repeating the word 'orphan' to show that you understand me.

KING. I didn't repeat the word often.   535

GEN. Pardon me, you did indeed.

KING. I only repeated it once.

GEN. True, but you repeated it.

KING. But not often.

GEN. Stop: I think I see where we are getting confused. When you said   540
'orphan', did you mean 'orphan' – a person who has lost his parents, or 'often' – frequently?

KING. Ah! I beg pardon – I see what you mean – frequently.

GEN. Ah! you said often – frequently.

KING. No, only once.   545

GEN. (*irritated*). Exactly – you said often, frequently, only once.

RECITATIVE – GENERAL.

Oh, men of dark and dismal fate,
 Forgo your cruel employ,
Have pity on my lonely state,
 I am an orphan boy!   550

KING *and* SAM.   An orphan boy?

GEN.   An orphan boy!

PIRATES. How sad – an orphan boy.

SOLO – GENERAL.

These children whom you see
 Are all that I can call my own!   555

PIRATES.   Poor fellow!

GEN. Take them away from me
  And I shall be indeed alone.

PIRATES.   Poor fellow!

GEN. If pity you can feel,   560
  Leave me my sole remaining joy –
 See, at your feet they kneel;
 Your hearts you cannot steel
Against the sad, sad tale of the lonely orphan boy!

PIRATES (*sobbing*).   Poor fellow!   565
  See at our feet they kneel;
  Our hearts we cannot steel
Against the sad, sad tale of the lonely orphan boy!

588–91 *Hail, Poetry, thou heaven-born maid*

Listening to this remarkable hymn to poetry, which is sung unaccompanied, it is not difficult to see why Sullivan was regarded as one of the leading composers of sacred music in Victorian Britain. He produced numerous anthems and sacred part-songs as well as forty-one hymn tunes. Among the hymns which are still sung to his tunes are 'Onward, Christian soldiers', 'Lead, kindly Light', 'Love Divine, all loves excelling', 'God moves in a mysterious way' and 'Rock of ages'.

Possibly because of Sullivan's difficulty in setting this hymn, Gilbert's original manuscript shows that the line 'Thou gildest e'en the pirate's trade' was rewritten four times, twice being changed to 'That gild'st the Pirates' trade' before it was finally restored to the original version.

SAM. The orphan boy!

SAM *and* KING. The orphan boy!
See at our feet they kneel, etc.

ENSEMBLE.

GENERAL (*aside*).
I'm telling a terrible story,
But it doesn't diminish my glory;
For they would have taken my daughters
Over the billowy waters,
If I hadn't, in elegant diction,
Indulged in an innocent fiction;
Which is not the same categ*ory*
As a regular terrible story.

GIRLS (*aside*).
He's telling a terrible story,
Which will tend to diminish his glory;
Though they would have taken his daughters
Over the billowy waters.
It's easy, in elegant diction,
To call it an innocent fiction,
But it comes in the same categ*ory*
As a regular terrible story.

PIRATES (*aside*).
If he's telling a terrible story,
He shall die by a death that is gory,
One of the cruellest slaughters
That ever were known in these waters;
And we'll finish his moral affliction
By a very complete male-diction,
As a compliment valedict*ory*,
If he's telling a terrible story.

KING. Although our dark career
Sometimes involves the crime of stealing,
We rather think that we're
Not altogether void of feeling.
Although we live by strife,
We're always sorry to begin it,
For what, we ask, is life
Without a touch of Poetry in it?

ALL (*kneeling*). Hail, Poetry, thou heaven-born maid!
Thou gildest e'en the pirate's trade:
Hail, flowing fount of sentiment!
All hail, Divine Emollient! (*All rise.*)

KING. You may go, for you're at liberty, our pirate rules protect you,
And honorary members of our band we do elect you!

SAM. For he is an orphan boy.

CHORUS. He is! Hurrah for the orphan boy.

GEN. And it sometimes is a useful thing
To be an orphan boy.

CHORUS. It is! Hurrah for the orphan boy!

616–23 *Pray observe the magnanimity*
The licence copy and the original Paignton production had a different finale to Act I from that performed at the New York première and ever since. Instead of the final ensemble it has the following song for the Pirate King and chorus:

KING.   Comrades, let us join in plighting
             These, our honorary members
             May the fire of friendship's lightning
             Never sink to dust and embers

CHORUS.   May the fire, etc.

KING.   Oh remember – Major-General
             And remember – Wards in Chancery
             You are welcome – nine or ten – or all
             To our Pirate Caravanserai

ALL.   We ⎫
             They ⎭ are welcome nine or ten or all.

             To ⎰ their ⎱ pirate caravanserai
                ⎱ our ⎰

KING.   For we all are orphan boys

ALL.   We are!
             Hurrah for the orphan boys

KING.   And it is, it is a Kindly Thing
             To spare all orphan boys

ALL.   It is! Hurrah for the orphan boys.

617 *dimity*: Cotton cloth with raised thread patterns, traditionally used for bedroom hangings.

ENSEMBLE.

Oh, happy day, with joyous glee
We ⎱
They ⎰ will away and married be;   600
Should it befall auspiciously,
My ⎱
Her ⎰ sisters all will bridesmaids be!

(RUTH *enters and comes down to* FREDERIC.)

RUTH. Oh, master, hear one word, I do implore you!
   Remember Ruth, your Ruth, who kneels before you! 605
PIRATES. Yes, yes, remember Ruth, who kneels before you!
FRED. Away, you did deceive me! (*Pirates threaten* RUTH.)
PIRATES. Away, you did deceive him!

RUTH. Oh, do not leave me!
PIRATES. Oh, do not leave her!   610

FRED. Away, you grieve me!
PIRATES. Away, you grieve him!

FRED. I wish you'd leave me!
       (FREDERIC *casts* RUTH *from him. Exit* RUTH.)
PIRATES. We wish you'd leave him!   615

ENSEMBLE.

Pray observe the magnanimity
We ⎱
They ⎰ display to lace and dimity!
Never was such opportunity
To get married with impunity,
But ⎰ we ⎱ give up the felicity   620
  ⎱ they ⎰
Of unbounded domesticity,
Though a doctor of divinity
Resides in this vicinity.

(*Girls and* GENERAL *go up rocks, while Pirates indulge in a wild dance of delight
on stage. The* GENERAL *produces a British flag, and the* PIRATE KING 625
produces a black flag with skull and cross-bones. Enter* RUTH, *who makes a final
appeal to* FREDERIC, *who casts her from him.*)

END OF ACT I

4 *That dews that martial cheek*: The same imagery occurs towards the end of Act I of *Patience* in the Duke of Dunstable's line 'A tear-drop dews each martial eye'.

16 *heaven has lit her lamp*: This phrase is reminiscent of the first line of the much-loved Victorian parlour ballad 'The moon has raised her lamp above' from Benedict's operetta *The Lily of Killarney*.

17 *The twilight hour is past*: Gilbert wrote this line as 'The midnight hour is past', and so it still appears in the Macmillan edition. Yet a little later on, at lines 49–51, he has Frederic announcing that 'At eleven, and before midnight I hope to have atoned for my involuntary association with the pestilent scourges by sweeping them from the face of the earth'. A note by Rupert D'Oyly Carte in his copy of the libretto reads: 'This seems to be Gilbert nodding or Frederic's watch is wrong'. Since 1930 the D'Oyly Carte Company has substituted 'twilight' for 'midnight' in Mabel's song to make chronological sense of this apparent paradox.

ACT II

S CENE. – *A ruined chapel by moonlight. Ruined Gothic windows at back.*
GENERAL STANLEY *discovered seated pensively, surrounded by his daughters.*

CHORUS.

Oh, dry the glistening tear
   That dews that martial cheek;
Thy loving children hear,   5
   In them thy comfort seek.
With sympathetic care
   Their arms around thee creep,
For oh, they cannot bear
   To see their father weep!   10

(*Enter* MABEL.)

SOLO – MABEL.

Dear father, why leave your bed
   At this untimely hour,
When happy daylight is dead,
   And darksome dangers lower?   15
See, heaven has lit her lamp,
   The twilight hour is past,
The chilly night air is damp,
   And the dews are falling fast!
Dear father, why leave your bed   20
When happy daylight is dead?

CHORUS.   Oh, dry the glistening tear, etc.

(FREDERIC *enters*.)

34   *the stucco in your baronial hall*: This was originally 'the stucco on your baronial castle'.
      'Stucco' is a word of Italian origin for a smooth plaster made of lime and sand, used to
      face walls. The original phrase is still found in American editions of the libretto and
      was used in Joseph Papp's production on both sides of the Atlantic.

35–6 *With the estate, I bought the chapel and its contents*: Gilbert's sharp social comment on the
      attitudes of the *nouveaux riches* in this and the next few lines is sometimes taken as
      a further dig at Sir Garnet Wolseley, who bought land as a way of establishing himself
      as a man of position and escaping from his relatively humble origins. I am doubtful,
      however, if Gilbert had this in mind when writing these lines. It was not a conspicuous
      part of Wolseley's make-up and he certainly never boasted about his newly acquired
      ancestors as Stanley does. He didn't need to: his own family were a junior branch of the
      well-established Staffordshire Wolseleys and had held land in County Carlow, Ireland,
      under William III.

43–4 *I assure you, Frederic*: The passage beginning 'I assure you' and ending 'most disastrous to
      myself' was added for the 1908 revival of *The Pirates* with Gilbert's apparent approval. It
      is also found in an expanded form, in the licence copy.

59–119 *When the foeman bares his steel*
      The entrance of the Sergeant of Police (in the original New York production of *The
      Pirates* given the name Edward) and his trusty if rather nervous constables is one of the
      funniest moments in all the Savoy Operas. It almost invariably involves some business
      on stage. In D'Oyly Carte productions the sergeant trips up on some imaginary object
      on stage, which he ever afterwards steps gingerly over although no one else is troubled
      by it.

MABEL. Oh, Frederic, cannot you, in the calm excellence of your wisdom, reconcile it with your conscience to say something that will relieve my father's sorrow? 25

FRED. I will try, dear Mabel. But why does he sit, night after night, in this draughty old ruin?

GEN. Why do I sit here? To escape from the pirates' clutches, I described myself as an orphan, and, heaven help me, I am no orphan! I come 30 here to humble myself before the tombs of my ancestors, and to implore their pardon for having brought dishonour on the family escutcheon.

FRED. But you forget, sir, you only bought the property a year ago, and the stucco in your baronial hall is scarcely dry.

GEN. Frederic, in this chapel are ancestors: you cannot deny that. With 35 the estate, I bought the chapel and its contents. I don't know whose ancestors they *were*, but I know whose ancestors they *are*, and I shudder to think that their descendant by purchase (if I may so describe myself) should have brought disgrace upon what, I have no doubt, was an unstained escutcheon.

FRED. Be comforted. Had you not acted as you did, these reckless men 40 would assuredly have called in the nearest clergyman, and have married your large family on the spot.

GEN. I thank you for your proffered solace, but it is unavailing. I assure you, Frederic, that such is the anguish and remorse I feel at the abominable falsehood by which I escaped these easily deluded pirates, that I would go 45 to their simple-minded chief this very night and confess all, did I not fear that the consequences would be most disastrous to myself. At what time does your expedition march against these scoundrels?

FRED. At eleven, and before midnight I hope to have atoned for my involuntary association with the pestilent scourges by sweeping them from 50 the face of the earth – and then, dear Mabel, you will be mine!

GEN. Are your devoted followers at hand?

FRED. They are, they only wait my orders.

RECITATIVE – GENERAL.

Then, Frederic, let your escort lion-hearted
Be summoned to receive a General's blessing, 55
Ere they depart upon their dread adventure.

FRED. Dear sir, they come.

(*Enter Police, marching in single file. They form in line facing audience.*)

SONG – SERGEANT, *with* POLICE.

When the foeman bares his steel,
    Tarantara! tarantara!
60

Sullivan had a particular reason for responding to Gilbert's idea of a chorus of singing policemen. As organist at St Michael's, Chester Square, a fashionable West End church, in the late 1860s, he had made its choir one of the best in London. 'We were well off for soprani and contralti', he wrote later, 'but at first I was at my wit's end for tenors and basses. However, close by St Michael's Church was Cottage Row Police Station, and here I completed my choir. The Chief Superintendant threw himself heartily into my scheme, and from the police I gathered six tenors and six basses, with a small reserve. And capital fellows they were. However tired they might be when they came off duty, they never missed a practice. I used to think of them sometimes when I was composing the music for *The Pirates of Penzance*.'

67   *emeutes*: A French word for brawls. One can see why Gilbert could not use the English word – the obvious rhyme in the next line would have severely shocked a Victorian audience. To rhyme with 'emeutes' the word 'boots' has to be pronounced in a rather strange way. The late Owen Brannigan, who played the Sergeant in many concert and stage versions of *The Pirates*, and whose performance is preserved on the HMV recording under Sir Malcolm Sargent, developed a particularly resonant rendition which can only (but poorly) be reproduced in print as 'bewts'.

The 'tarantara' refrain which figures so prominently in this song was originally conceived as having something of the same function and significance as a Wagnerian leitmotif. In a letter to Sullivan in August 1879, when he was still thinking in terms of robbers rather than pirates, Gilbert wrote:

> By the way, I've made great use of the 'Tarantara' business in Act II. The police always sing 'Tarantara' when they desire to work their courage to sticking-point. They are naturally timid, but through the agency of this talisman they are enabled to acquit themselves well when concealed. In Act II, when the robbers approach, their courage begins to fail them, but recourse to 'Tarantara' (pianissimo) has the desired effect. I mention this that you may bear it in mind in setting the General's 'Tarantara' song.

The phrase 'Tarantara, tarantara' was used as the title of a play about Gilbert and Sullivan by Ian Taylor, which was first performed at the Bristol Old Vic in May 1975.

We uncomfortable feel,
                    Tarantara!
And we find the wisest thing,
                    Tarantara! tarantara!
Is to slap our chests and sing   65
                    Tarantara!
For when threatened with emeutes,
                    Tarantara! tarantara!
And your heart is in your boots,
                    Tarantara!   70
There is nothing brings it round,
                    Tarantara! tarantara!
Like the trumpet's martial sound,
                    Tarantara! tarantara!
Tarantara-ra-ra-ra-ra!   75

ALL.   Tarantara-ra-ra-ra-ra!

MABEL.   Go, ye heroes, go to glory,
            Though you die in combat gory,
            Ye shall live in song and story.
                    Go to immortality!   80
            Go to death, and go to slaughter;
            Die, and every Cornish daughter
            With her tears your grave shall water.
                    Go, ye heroes, go and die!

ALL.   Go, ye heroes, go and die!   85

            SERGEANT *with* POLICE.

            Though to us it's evident,
                    Tarantara! tarantara!
            These attentions are well meant,
                    Tarantara!
            Such expressions don't appear,   90
                    Tarantara! tarantara!
            Calculated men to cheer,
                    Tarantara!
            Who are going to meet their fate
            In a highly nervous state,   95
                    Tarantara! tarantara! tarantara!
            Still to us it's evident
            These attentions are well meant.
                    Tarantara! tarantara! tarantara!

129   *Yes, but you don't go*: Although it is not in any of the printed editions of the libretto, the
      Major-General in exasperation finally utters the words 'But *damme*, you don't go' to the
      reluctant policemen. I have not been able to discover when this swear word was first in-
      troduced. It is not used on early recordings. But whenever it came in, it does not seem
      to have provoked the same outcry as Captain Corcoran's use of 'damme' in *H.M.S. Pina-
      fore*. This whole passage is, of course, a skit on those scenes in grand opera where people
      spend a lot of time singing about something that they are just going to do but never
      seem to get round to doing it.

EDITH.	Go and do your best endeavour, And before all links we sever, We will say farewell for ever. Go to glory and the grave!	100
GIRLS.	Go to glory and the grave! For your foes are fierce and ruthless, False, unmerciful, and truthless. Young and tender, old and toothless, All in vain their mercy crave.	105
SERG.	We observe too great a stress, On the risks that on us press, And of reference a lack To our chance of coming back. Still, perhaps it would be wise Not to carp or criticize, For it's very evident These attentions are well meant.	110 115
POLICE.	Yes, it's very evident These attentions are well meant, etc.	

ENSEMBLE.

Chorus of all but Police.	*Chorus of Police.*
Go, ye heroes, etc.	When the foeman, etc.

GEN.	Away, away!	120
POLICE (*without moving*).	Yes, yes, we go.	
GEN.	These pirates slay.	
POLICE.	Tarantara!	
GEN.	Then do not stay.	
POLICE.	Tarantara!	
GEN.	Then why this delay?	125
POLICE.	All right – we go. Yes, forward on the foe!	
GEN.	Yes, but you *don't* go!	
POLICE.	We go, we go! Yes, forward on the foe!	130
GEN.	Yes, but you *don't* go!	
ALL.	At last they really go.	

(*Exeunt Police.* MABEL *tears herself from* FREDERIC *and exit, followed by her sisters, consoling her. The* GENERAL *and others follow.* FREDERIC *remains.*) 135

156–84 *When you had left our pirate fold*
As first performed, the second line of the paradox trio (as this song is generally called) had the word 'cheer' instead of 'raise'.

The licence copy has the following additional verses for Ruth and Frederic after the King's verse (which ends, in this version, with the line 'To tell it to our Prentice Boy'):

RUTH.

This is the jest and when unfurled
The truth of what we say 'twill show
You came into this wicked world
Just one and twenty years ago
But though since you by me were nursed
Years twenty one have passed away
You have not seen the twenty first
Recurrence of your natal day

FRED.

'Twill be our death that paradox.

(*Puzzled*)

Now let me see how can that be
I'm twenty one that's very clear
Moreover it is plain to me
Man has birthday once a year
To solve the quip I see no way
All common sense the statement mocks
I beg of you without delay
Explain this startling paradox.

At this point the King begins his chant, as in the present version.

RECITATIVE – FREDERIC.

Now for the pirates' lair! Oh, joy unbounded!
Oh, sweet relief! Oh, rapture unexampled!
At last I may atone, in some slight measure,
For the repeated acts of theft and pillage 140
Which, at a sense of duty's stern dictation,
I, circumstance's victim, have been guilty.

(KING *and* RUTH *appear armed.*)

KING.   Young Frederic! (*Covering him with pistol.*)
FRED.   Who calls?
KING.   Your late commander! 145
RUTH.   And I, your little Ruth! (*Covering him with pistol.*)
FRED.   Oh, mad intruders,
How dare ye face me? Know ye not, oh rash ones,
That I have doomed you to extermination? 150

(KING *and* RUTH *hold a pistol to each ear.*)

KING.   Have mercy on us, hear us, ere you slaughter.
FRED.   I do not think I ought to listen to you.
Yet, mercy should alloy our stern resentment,
And so I will be merciful – say on! 155

TRIO – RUTH, KING, *and* FREDERIC.

RUTH.   When you had left our pirate fold
              We tried to raise our spirits faint,
          According to our custom old,
              With quip and quibble quaint.
          But all in vain the quips we heard, 160
              We lay and sobbed upon the rocks,
          Until to somebody occurred
              A startling paradox.
FRED.   A paradox?
RUTH.   A paradox! 165
          A most ingenious paradox!
          We've quips and quibbles heard in flocks,
          But none to beat this paradox!
ALL.   A paradox, a paradox, etc.
          Ha, ha, ha, this paradox! 170
KING.   We knew your taste for curious quips,
              For cranks and contradictions queer,

186 *the Astronomer Royal*: A title used between 1675 and 1972 for the director of the Observatory at Greenwich. As the name implies, it was a royal appointment. The Astronomer Royal is now an honorary title bestowed on an outstanding British astronomer.

190 *leap-year*: The time taken for the earth to complete its orbit round the sun is 365.2421988 days (or 365 days, 5 hours, 48 minutes and 46 seconds). To make up the odd quarter day which is 'lost' every year by having only 365 days, an extra calendar day is added every four years at the end of February. A year is a leap year if its last two digits can be divided by four.
    having been born in . . . February: Gilbert takes a certain amount of dramatic licence here. From this passage it is clear that *The Pirates of Penzance* is set at the end of February with Frederic about to celebrate his twenty-first, or more accurately his fifth and a quarter, birthday. Yet the atmosphere of the First Act, which we know to be set only a few hours before the Second, suggests the middle of summer. Surely the Major-General's daughters would not be taking off their shoes to paddle and singing 'How beautifully blue the sky' in what is traditionally one of the coldest months of the English winter. A paradox indeed!

And with the laughter on our lips,
    We wished you there to hear.
We said, 'If we could tell it him,
    How Frederic would the joke enjoy!'   175
And so we've risked both life and limb
    To tell it to our boy.

FRED. (*interested*).   That paradox?
KING (*laughing*).   That paradox. That most ingenious paradox!   180
                We've quips and quibbles heard in flocks
                But none to beat that paradox!
ALL.   A paradox, a paradox, etc.
                Ha, ha, ha, that paradox!

CHANT – KING.

For some ridiculous reason, to which, however, I've no desire to be disloyal,   185
Some person in authority, I don't know who, very likely the Astronomer
    Royal,
Has decided that, although for such a beastly month as February, twenty-
    eight days as a rule are plenty,
One year in every four his days shall be reckoned as nine-and-twenty.
Through some singular coincidence – I shouldn't be surprised if it were
    owing to the agency of an ill-natured fairy –
You are the victim of this clumsy arrangement, having been born in leap-
    year, on the twenty-ninth of February,   190
And so, by a simple arithmetical process, you'll easily discover,
That though you've lived twenty-one years, yet, if we go by birthdays,
    you're only five and a little bit over!
RUTH *and*   Ha! ha! ha! ha!
KING.   Ho! ho! ho! ho!
FRED.   Dear me!
                Let's see! (*counting on fingers*).   195
                Yes, yes; with yours my fingers do agree!
ALL.   Ha! ha! ha! ha! Ha! ha! ha! ha!
                (FREDERIC *more amused than any.*)
FRED.   How quaint the ways of Paradox!   200
                At common sense she gaily mocks!
                Though counting in the usual way,
                    Years twenty-one I've been alive,
                Yet, reckoning by my natal day,
                    I am a little boy of five!   205
KING *and* RUTH. He is a little boy of five! Ha! ha! ha!
ALL.   A paradox, a paradox,

217–18 *I'm afraid you don't appreciate the delicacy of your position*: The position in which Frederic now
finds himself is somewhat similar to the predicament of Captain Bang, the Pirate Chief
in Gilbert's earlier musical play *Our Island Home*. Like Frederic (or, rather, like Frederic
thinks he is), Bang is on the verge of celebrating his twenty-first birthday and so ending
his association with the pirate band to which he was apprenticed by his stupid nurse.
However, just before the time when his articles are due to expire he has the misfortune
to capture his own parents, whom, by pirate law, he is obliged to slaughter instantly. Re-
sourcefully, he manages to avoid this gruesome duty by working out that as he was born
at Greenwich, and is now at a longitude fifty degrees east of Greenwich, allowing for
the time difference he technically came of age twenty minutes before capturing his parents. So he is able to spare them and start his post-piratical existence untroubled.

243 *General Stanley*: This is the first mention of the Major-General's name in the course of
the opera. It would have had two strong contemporary associations for British audiences
at early performances. The Secretary of State for War from April 1878 to April 1880 was
Sir Frederick Stanley, later the 16th Earl of Derby. In the Cabinet, Stanley was, of course,
closely associated with W. H. Smith, the First Lord of the Admiralty and the model for
Sir Joseph Porter in *H.M.S. Pinafore*. However, there is nothing to suggest that the War
Secretary was in any way a model for the modern Major-General. The other well-
known Stanley whose name might well have been rather more on Gilbert's mind when
he cast around for a surname for his military adventurer was Henry Morton Stanley,
the explorer and journalist, well-known in both the United States and Britain as the
man who had 'discovered' David Livingstone in darkest Africa in 1871. At the time *The
Pirates* was being written Stanley had just gone out to the Congo, where he was to spend
five years colonizing and administering that territory.

A most ingenious paradox!
    Ha! ha! ha! ha! Ha! ha! ha! ha! (RUTH *and* KING *throw
    themselves back on seats, exhausted with laughter.*)

FRED. Upon my word, this is most curious – most absurdly whimsical.
Five-and-a-quarter! No one would think it to look at me!

RUTH. You are glad now, I'll be bound, that you spared us. You would
never have forgiven yourself when you discovered that you had killed *two of
your comrades*:

FRED. My comrades?

KING (*rises*). I'm afraid you don't appreciate the delicacy of your
position. You were apprenticed to us —

FRED. Until I reached my twenty-first year.

KING. No, until you reached your twenty-first *birthday* (*producing
document*), and, going by birthdays, you are as yet only five-and-a-quarter.

FRED. You don't mean to say you are going to hold me to that?

KING. No, we merely remind you of the fact, and leave the rest to your
sense of duty.

RUTH. Your sense of duty!

FRED. (*wildly*). Don't put it on that footing! As I was merciful to you
just now, be merciful to me! I implore you not to insist on the letter of your
bond just as the cup of happiness is at my lips!

RUTH. We insist on nothing; we content ourselves with pointing out to
you *your duty.*

KING. Your duty!

FRED. (*after a pause*). Well, you have appealed to my sense of duty, and
my duty is only too clear. I abhor your infamous calling; I shudder at the
thought that I have ever been mixed up with it; but duty is before all – at any
price I will do my duty.

KING. Bravely spoken! Come, you are one of us once more.

FRED. Lead on, I follow. (*Suddenly.*) Oh, horror!

KING. ⎱
RUTH. ⎰ What is the matter?

FRED. Ought I to tell you? No, no, I cannot do it; and yet, as one of
your band —

KING. Speak out, I charge you by that sense of conscientiousness to
which we have never yet appealed in vain.

FRED. General Stanley, the father of my Mabel —

KING. ⎱
RUTH. ⎰ Yes, yes!

FRED. He escaped from you on the plea that he was an orphan!

KING. He did!

FRED. It breaks my heart to betray the honoured father of the girl I
adore, but as your apprentice I have no alternative. It is my duty to tell you
that General Stanley is no orphan!

255　*Tremorden Castle*: This is a fictitious location, but a perfectly plausible name for a place in Cornwall. The Cornish word *tre* means hamlet or homestead and is found at the beginning of many place names in the county. There is a village of Tremore, for example, four miles west of Bodmin.

260　*This very night*: Gilbert originally wrote 'this very day', once again forgetting the lines he had given Frederic only a few pages earlier which suggested it was not yet eleven in the evening. It was changed to 'night' for the same reason that Mabel's phrase 'The midnight hour' was changed to 'The twilight hour' (line 17).

KING. ⎫
RUTH. ⎭ What!　　　　　　　　　　　　　　　　　　　　　　250

FRED. More than that, he never was one!

KING. Am I to understand that, to save his contemptible life, he dared to practise on our credulous simplicity? (FREDERIC *nods as he weeps*.) Our revenge shall be swift and terrible. We will go and collect our band and attack Tremorden Castle this very night.　　　　　　　　　255

FRED. But – stay —

KING. Not a word! He is doomed!

TRIO.

KING *and* RUTH.	FREDERIC.
Away, away! my heart's on fire,	Away, away! ere I expire –
I burn this base deception to repay,	I find my duty hard to do to-day!
This very night my vengeance dire	My heart is filled with anguish dire, 260
Shall glut itself in gore. Away, away!	It strikes me to the core. Away, away!

KING.

With falsehood foul
He tricked us of our brides.
　　Let vengeance howl;
The Pirate so decides.
　　Our nature stern
He softened with his lies,
　　And, in return,
To-night the traitor dies.　　　　　　　　　265

ALL.　　　　Yes, yes! to-night the traitor dies.　　　　270

RUTH.　　　　　To-night he dies!
KING.　　　Yes, or early to-morrow.
FRED.　　　　His girls likewise?
RUTH.　　They will welter in sorrow.
KING.　　　　The one soft spot　　　　　　　275
FRED.　　In their natures they cherish –
RUTH.　　　　And all who plot
KING.　　To abuse it shall perish!
ALL.　　　　To-night he dies, etc.

　　　　　　　　　(*Exeunt* KING *and* RUTH.)　　280

　　　　(*Enter* MABEL.)

292 *till 1940*: Another paradox, of which Gilbert may or may not have been aware. Frederic has a birthday every four years. Therefore he will not reach his twenty-first birthday until he is, in fact, eighty-four. On the face of it, if he is to reach the age of eighty-four in 1940, he must have been born on 29 February 1856, and *The Pirates of Penzance* must therefore be set in 1877 (two years before its first performance), when Frederic reaches his twenty-first year.

However, the Astronomer Royal has another trick up his sleeve. We have already noted that it is not exactly a full quarter day which needs to be added to each year to bring it in line with the time taken for the earth to revolve round the sun, but rather a fraction below that amount – 0.242 days, to be exact, rather than 0.25. The addition of one full day to the calendar every leap year, therefore, makes up more 'lost' time than it should (four times 0.25 days rather than four times 0.242 days, i.e. 24 hours rather than 23 hours, 4 minutes and 36 seconds). To compensate for this inaccuracy, leap days are only taken in century years which are exactly divisible by four. Thus while 1600 was a leap year, and 2000 will be one, 1700, 1800 and, most important for our present calculations, 1900 were not. Frederic therefore faces one eight-year gap between birthdays (from 1896 to 1904). This means that to be twenty-one in 1940 he must, in fact, have been born four years earlier than we first supposed, in 1852. In that case the action of *The Pirates* takes place in 1873, six years before the opera was written and first performed. Alternatively, if the play is set in 1877, and Frederic was born in 1856, he will not reach his twenty-first birthday until 1944. All this may seem of purely academic interest, but it is on such points as these that Gilbert and Sullivan fans love to speculate, and, after all, it cannot have been entirely of academic interest to Mabel to know whether she had to wait until her lover was a ripe old eighty-eight or whether he would be hers at the tender age of eighty-four.

RECITATIVE – MABEL.

	All is prepared, your gallant crew await you.	
	My Frederic in tears? It cannot be	
	That lion-heart quails at the coming conflict?	
FRED.	No, Mabel, no. A terrible disclosure	285
	Has just been made! Mabel, my dearly-loved one,	
	I bound myself to serve the pirate captain	
	Until I reached my one-and-twentieth birthday –	
MABEL.	But you *are* twenty-one?	
FRED.	I've just discovered	290
	That I was born in leap-year, and that birthday	
	Will not be reached by me till 1940.	
MABEL.	Oh, horrible! catastrophe appalling!	
FRED.	And so, farewell!	
MABEL.	No, no! Ah, Frederic, hear me.	295

DUET – MABEL *and* FREDERIC.

MABEL.	Stay, Frederic, stay!	
	They have no legal claim,	
	No shadow of a shame	
	Will fall upon thy name.	
	Stay, Frederic, stay!	300
FRED.	Nay, Mabel, nay!	
	To-night I quit these walls,	
	The thought my soul appals,	
	But when stern Duty calls,	
	I must obey.	305
MABEL.	Stay, Frederic, stay!	
FRED.	Nay, Mabel, nay!	
MABEL.	They have no claim –	
FRED.	But Duty's name!	
	The thought my soul appals,	
	But when stern Duty calls,	310
	I must obey.	

DUET – MABEL *and* FREDERIC.

MABEL.	Ah, leave me not to pine	
	Alone and desolate;	
	No fate seemed fair as mine,	
	No happiness so great!	315

337–40 *Oh, here is love, and here is truth*

In early performances of *The Pirates*, including the Paignton and New York first nights, there was a second verse to this ensemble and an added recitative for Mabel:

What joy to know that though $\left\{\begin{array}{c}\text{he}\\\text{I}\end{array}\right\}$ must

Embrace piratical adventures,

$\left.\begin{array}{c}\text{He}\\\text{She}\end{array}\right\}$ will be faithful to $\left\{\begin{array}{c}\text{his}\\\text{her}\end{array}\right\}$ trust

Till $\left\{\begin{array}{c}\text{he is}\\\text{I am}\end{array}\right\}$ out of $\left\{\begin{array}{c}\text{his}\\\text{my}\end{array}\right\}$ indentures!

FRED.   Farewell! Adieu!

MABEL.   The same to you!

BOTH.   Farewell! Adieu!

(FREDERIC *rushes to window and leaps out.*)

MABEL.   Distraction! Frederic! loved me! oh return! With love I burn
(*recollecting*) Stay! I'm a Stanley! Even to the grave I will be brave.
                His conscience bids him give up love and all at duty's call;
                Mine teaches me that though I love him so,
                He is my foe.

In the Paignton performance, Mabel then had a full-scale aria about her family descent. This stirring number was not sung at either the New York or London premières:

When conquering William's legions came
To spoil our island dear
More likely someone of our name
Accompanied him here
But if with that great conqueror
That somebody arrived
Great Shade, if thou hadst being then
Such was thy modesty
Thy name the dread of Saxon men
Historians have passed by
But though to Norman blood my claim
Rests on hypothesis
Yet if with him the Stanleys came
I'm very sure of this
Although he loved his mistress much
He loved his duty more
And I will not discredit such
A glorious ancestor
Ancestral hero deathless shade
(If such a shade there be)
With strength inspire a simple maid
Great Possibility

Mabel's recitative about her family descent then followed (lines 341–4). In early productions this began 'Yes, I am brave' instead of the later form, 'No, I'll be brave'.

And nature, day by day,
   Has sung, in accents clear,
This joyous roundelay,
   'He loves thee – he is here.   320
      Fa-la, la, la, Fal-la, la, la.'

FRED.

Ah, must I leave thee here
   In endless night to dream,
Where joy is dark and drear,
   And sorrow all supreme!   325
Where nature, day by day,
   Will sing, in altered tone,
This weary roundelay,
   'He loves thee – he is gone.
      Fa-la, la, la, Fal-la, la, la.'   330

FRED.   In 1940 I of age shall be,
        I'll then return, and claim you – I declare it.
MABEL.   It seems so long!
FRED.   Swear that, till then, you will be true to me.
MABEL.   Yes, I'll be strong!   335
        By all the Stanleys dead and gone, I swear it.

ENSEMBLE.

Oh, here is love, and here is truth,
   And here is food for joyous laughter.
He ⎱
She ⎰ will be faithful to ⎰ his ⎱ sooth
                  ⎱ her ⎰
Till we are wed, and even after.   (*Exit* FREDERIC.)   340

MABEL (*almost fainting*). No, I'll be brave! Oh, family descent,
    How great thy charm, thy sway how excellent!
    Come, one and all, undaunted men in blue,
    A crisis, now, affairs are coming to!

(*Enter Police, marching in single file.*)   345

SERGEANT *with* POLICE.

Though in body and in mind,
       Tarantara, tarantara!
We are timidly inclined,
       Tarantara!
And anything but blind,   350
       Tarantara, tarantara!

363   *That is not a pleasant way of putting it*: This, and the policemen's subsequent lines, are traditionally sung in plainsong as though they are the verses of a psalm. Shades of Sullivan's
policemen's church choir again.

371   *endeared him to me tenfold*: In early performances of *The Pirates* Mabel had an extra sentence at this point: 'But if it is his duty to constitute himself my foe, it is likewise my
duty to regard him in that light.' She continued 'He has done his duty' etc. as now.

374   *Right oh*: Gilbert originally wrote 'Very well' here but altered it for the 1900 revival of *The
Pirates*, possibly at the request of Walter Passmore, who took over the role of the Sergeant, originally played in London by Rutland Barrington. Certainly 'Right oh' fits
better into the rhythm of the policemen's chanting of their responses.

387-424 *When a felon's not engaged in his employment*
One of the most popular of all Gilbert and Sullivan's songs and the favourite party piece
of many a beery bass in the public bar near closing time. It is almost invariably encored.
Rutland Barrington was even moved to ask Gilbert to give him an extra verse to use
when the audience shouted for more. 'Encore means sing it again' was the librettist's
brusque reply.

The policemen's song has been parodied many times. Sydney Dark and Rowland
Gray's book *W. S. Gilbert: His Life and Letters* (Methuen, 1923) even quotes a Latin ver-
sion, the first verse by Dr Arthur Chilton, then prebendary of St Paul's Cathedral, and
later rector of Colne Engaine, Essex, and the second by the then suffragan bishop of
Southampton.
It begins:

> *Ubi fraudibus fraudator abrogatis*
> > *Abrogatis*
> *Secum mediatur nil nefarii*
> > *'arii*
> *Innocentis erit capax voluptatis*
> > *Voluptatis*
> *Sicut ego, sicut tu et ceteri*
> > *Ceteri.*

387   *felon*: One who has committed a felony, i.e. an offence, such as murder or burglary, which
is in a graver category than mere misdemeanours. In early English law a felony was punishable by loss of life or limb or forfeiture of goods and chattels.

To the danger that's behind,
       Tarantara!
Yet, when the danger's near,
       Tarantara, tarantara!   355
We manage to appear,
       Tarantara!
As insensible to fear
As anybody here.
       Tarantara, tarantara-ra-ra-ra-ra!   360

MABEL. Sergeant, approach! Young Frederic was to have led you to death and glory.

ALL. That is not a pleasant way of putting it.

MABEL. No matter; he will not so lead you, for he has allied himself once more with his old associates.   365

ALL. He has acted shamefully!

MABEL. You speak falsely. You know nothing about it. He has acted nobly.

ALL. He has acted nobly!

MABEL. Dearly as I loved him before, his heroic sacrific to his sense of duty has endeared him to me tenfold. He has done his duty. I will do mine. Go ye and do yours.   370

                                   (*Exit* MABEL.)

ALL. Right oh!

SERG. This is perplexing.

ALL. We cannot understand it at all.   375

SERG. Still, as he is actuated by a sense of duty —

ALL. That makes a difference, of course. At the same time we repeat, we cannot understand it at all.

SERG. No matter; our course is clear. We must do our best to capture these pirates alone. It is most distressing to us to be the agents whereby our erring fellow-creatures are deprived of that liberty which is so dear to all — but we should have thought of that before we joined the Force.   380

ALL. We should!

SERG. It is too late now!

ALL. It is!   385

SONG – SERGEANT.

SERG.	When a felon's not engaged in his employment –
ALL.	His employment,
SERG.	Or maturing his felonious little plans –
ALL.	Little plans, 390

414 *coster*: A shortened form of 'costermonger', i.e. a street salesman selling fruit, vegetables or fish from a barrow. Costermongers had a reputation for rough behaviour.

430 *the manor*: In earlier editions, I suggested that Gilbert was here using the slang word for a police district. I am now persuaded that the phrase means no more than the precincts of General Stanley's estate.

SERG.	His capacity for innocent enjoyment –
ALL.	'Cent enjoyment
SERG.	Is just as great as any honest man's –
ALL.	Honest man's.
SERG.	Our feelings we with difficulty smother –
ALL.	'Culty smother
SERG.	When constabulary duty's to be done –
ALL.	To be done.
SERG.	Ah, take one consideration with another –
ALL.	With another,
SERG.	A policeman's lot is not a happy one.
ALL.	Ah! When constabulary duty's to be done –
	To be done,
	The policeman's lot is not a happy one –
	Happy one.
SERG.	When the enterprising burglar's not a-burgling –
ALL.	Not a-burgling,
SERG.	When the cut-throat isn't occupied in crime –
ALL.	'Pied in crime,
SERG.	He loves to hear the little brook a-gurgling –
ALL.	Brook a-gurgling,
SERG.	And listen to the merry village chime –
ALL.	Village chime.
SERG.	When the coster's finished jumping on his mother –
ALL.	On his mother,
SERG.	He loves to lie a-basking in the sun –
ALL.	In the sun.
SERG.	Ah, take one consideration with another –
ALL.	With another,
SERG.	The policeman's lot is not a happy one.
ALL.	When constabulary duty's to be done –
	To be done,
	The policeman's lot is not a happy one –
	Happy one.

395

400

405

410

415

420

(Chorus of Pirates without, in the distance.)   425

A rollicking band of pirates we,
Who, tired of tossing on the sea,
Are trying their hand at a burglaree,
With weapons grim and gory.

SERG.	Hush, hush! I hear them on the manor poaching,
	With stealthy step the pirates are approaching.

430

443   *They come in force*: The original version of these lines, sung at early performances, was:

> They come in force,
> The bold, burglarious elves;
> Our obvious course
> Is to conceal ourselves

459–63   *Come, friends, who plough the sea*
This number was not sung in the original Paignton performance and did not appear in the British libretto until 1914. It was, however, heard at the New York opening night. Its tune was subsequently taken up by Americans for the chant:

> Hail! Hail! The Gang's all here.
> What the hell do we care?
> What the hell do we care?

   The first known printing of this transatlantic version of the pirate's chorus dates from 1908. It was sung at a Democratic Party Convention in Saratoga early this century, and the words of the American version were copyrighted in 1917. Since then it has been sung thousands of times at gatherings of clubs, college alumni and servicemen's reunions.

465   *crowbar*: Bar made of iron, with one end bent and edged, used for levering open doors, windows and lids. An essential part of a burglar's tool kit.
   centrebit: A drill which turns on a projecting centre point and is used for making cylindrical holes in wood or metal. A burglar would use it to cut into doors so as to open locks from the inside.

466   *life-preserver*: A stick or bludgeon loaded with lead and intended for self-defence. No wonder the unarmed policemen were rather nervous about going off to do battle with their pirate foes.

(*Chorus of Pirates, resumed nearer.*)

> We are not coming for plate or gold –
> A story General Stanley's told –
> We seek a penalty fifty-fold,
> For General Stanley's story.

435

POLICE.   They seek a penalty –
PIRATES (*without*).   Fifty-fold,
          We seek a penalty –
POLICE.   Fifty-fold,
ALL.   We ⎱ seek a penalty fifty-fold,

440

          They ⎰
          For General Stanley's story.
SERG.   They come in force, with stealthy stride,
          Our obvious course is now – to hide.

(*Police conceal themselves. As they do so, the Pirates are seen appearing at ruined
windows. They enter cautiously, and come down stage.* SAMUEL *is laden with
burglarious tools and pistols, etc.*)

445

CHORUS – PIRATES (*very loud*).

> With cat-like tread,
> Upon our prey we steal,
> In silence dread
> Our cautious way we feel.
> No sound at all,
> We never speak a word,
> A fly's foot-fall
> Would be distinctly heard –

450

POLICE (*pianissimo*).   Tarantara, tarantara!
PIRATES.   So stealthily the pirate creeps,
          While all the household soundly sleeps.
          Come, friends, who plough the sea,
> Truce to navigation,
> Take another station;
          Let's vary piracee
          With a little burglaree!

455

460

POLICE (*pianissimo*).   Tarantara, tarantara!
SAM. (*distributing implements to various members of the gang*).
          Here's your crowbar and your centrebit,
          Your life-preserver – you may want to hit;

465

467   *silent matches*: Early matches were made by coating wooden sticks with sulphur and tip-
      ping them with chlorate of potash. The matches were ignited not, as now, by being
      struck against an abrasive surface, but by being dipped into a bottle of asbestos and
      sulphuric acid – a process which was at least silent if rather cumbersome.

468   *skeletonic keys*: Light keys with almost the whole substance of the bit (the part which en-
      gages with the levers of a lock) filed away. As a result, skeleton keys can fit many different
      locks and are therefore another popular item in the burglar's equipment.

      In the original version of *The Pirates* performed at Paignton, and contained in the
      licence copy, the distribution of the burglarious tools was made by the Pirate King,
      who also handed out a revolver and a wedge while he sang that:

> It is my kingly privilege
> According to our pirate rules
> To carry these burglarious tools

      before launching into yet another reprise of 'For I am a Pirate King'.

488   *No, all is still*: This line of General Stanley's following the *fortissimo* interruption by
      the chorus is reminiscent of the Countess Almaviva's remark 'I heard nothing' to her
      jealous husband just after her young admirer Cherubino has made a resounding thump
      off-stage in Act II of Mozart's *The Marriage of Figaro*.

      That the latter half of the Second Act of *The Pirates* is a deliberate parody of Italian op-
      era is confirmed in an interview which Sullivan gave to the London correspondent of
      The New York Times about his new work before leaving Britain in 1879:

> The notion chiefly develops a burlesque of Italian opera. It is a mere incident. An old
> gentleman returns home in the evening with his six daughters from a party. Nice bit of soft
> music takes them off for the night. Then a big orchestral crash, which introduces six bur-
> glars. They commence their knavish operations in a mysterious chorus, lights down. Pre-
> sently, the old gentleman thinks he hears someone stirring; comes on; of course, sees
> nobody though the burglars are actively at work. The only noise is the sighing of the wind,
> or gentle evening breeze. The old gentleman and the burglars perform a bit of concerted
> music, and in due course the six ladies enter. The six burglars are struck by their beauty, for-
> get their villainous purposes and make love . . . then there is a rescue by policemen and
> other numerous conceits of Gilbert's.

494–523   *Sighing softly to the river*
      With the possible exception of Jack Point's 'I have a song to sing, O!' in *The Yeomen of the
      Guard*, this is the most moving and melodious song given to the comic lead in any of
      the Savoy Operas. It is said in some quarters that it was originally introduced in a rather
      malicious spirit for the fun that could be had out of George Grossmith, who created the
      role of the Major-General in London and who had a poor singing voice, trying to get
      his tongue round a serious ballad. Whatever the reason for its inclusion, however, it is
      a delightful number, for which Sullivan provided a particularly charming undulating
      accompaniment that imitates the rippling of the brook and the waving of the poplars.

      As originally written, the song began:

> Softly sighing to the river
> Comes the lonely breeze

Your silent matches, your dark lantern seize,
Take your file and your skeletonic keys.

(*Enter* KING, FREDERIC, *and* RUTH.)

PIRATES (*fortissimo*). With cat-like tread, etc.
POLICE (*pianissimo*). Tarantara, tarantara!   470

RECITATIVE.

FRED.   Hush, hush, not a word! I see a light inside!
                     The Major-General comes, so quickly hide!
PIRATES.   Yes, yes, the Major-General comes!

(PIRATES *conceal themselves. Exeunt* KING, FREDERIC,   475
                              SAMUEL, *and* RUTH.)

POLICE.   Yes, yes, the Major-General comes!
GEN. (*entering in dressing-gown, carrying a light*).
                     Yes, yes, the Major-General comes!

SOLO – GENERAL.

Tormented with the anguish dread
    Of falsehood unatoned,
I lay upon my sleepless bed,   480
    And tossed and turned and groaned.
The man who finds his conscience ache
    No peace at all enjoys,
And as I lay in bed awake   485
    I thought I heard a noise.
PIRATES *and* POLICE. He thought he heard a noise – ha! ha!
GEN.   No, all is still
                    In dale, on hill;
                    My mind is set at ease.   490
                    So still the scene –
                    It must have been
                    The sighing of the breeze.

BALLAD – GENERAL.

Sighing softly to the river
    Comes the loving breeze,
Setting nature all a-quiver,   495
    Rustling through the trees –

505   *River, river*: The D'Oyly Carte Opera Company sometimes cut the lines from 'River, river, little river' to 'Nobody can woo so well' (line 519).

524   *peignoirs*: A French word for women's dressing gowns.

ALL.	Through the trees.
GEN.	And the brook, in rippling measure,
	Laughs for very love,
	While the poplars, in their pleasure, 500
	Wave their arms above.

POLICE
and
PIRATES.
  Yes, the trees, for very love,
  Wave their leafy arms above,
   River, river, little river,
  May thy loving prosper ever. 505
  Heaven speed thee, poplar tree,
  May thy wooing happy be.

GEN. Yet, the breeze is but a rover;
   When he wings away,
  Brook and poplar mourn a lover! 510
   Sighing well-a-day!

ALL.   Well-a-day!

GEN. Ah! the doing and undoing,
   That the rogue could tell!
  When the breeze is out a-wooing, 515
   Who can woo so well?

POLICE
and
PIRATES.
  Shocking tales the rogue could tell,
  Nobody can woo so well.
   Pretty brook, thy dream is over,
  For thy love is but a rover! 520
  Sad the lot of poplar trees,
  Courted by a fickle breeze!

(*Enter the* GENERAL'S *daughters led by Mabel, all in white peignoirs and
night-caps, and carrying lighted candles.*) 525

GIRLS. Now what is this, and what is that, and why
   does father leave his rest
  At such a time of night as this, so very
   incompletely dressed?
  Dear father is, and always was, the most
   methodical of men!
  It's his invariable rule to go to bed at half-past
   ten.
  What strange occurrence can it be that calls
   dear father from his rest 530
  At such a time of night as this, so very
   incompletely dressed?

533 *seize that General there*: In the New York first-night production, the Pirate King at this
      point had the additional line 'His life is over'. After the pirates' line 'Yes, we're the
      pirates, so despair!' they seized the Major-General, and the King went straight into
      his song 'With base deceit'. Then Frederic came forward with the echoing line 'Alas!
      alas! unhappy General Stanley', whereupon the General went on, as now, 'Frederic
      here? Oh joy! oh rapture!'

541 *I would if I could, but I am not able*: During one rehearsal for *The Pirates* in London, the te-
      nor playing Frederic was temporarily absent from the stage at the time this section was
      being sung. After Mabel had delivered her line 'Frederic, save us!' Gilbert's voice was
      heard from the stalls, 'Beautiful Mabel, I'd sing if I could, but I am not able'.

551 *unshriven*: Without having made confession and received absolution of his sins.
      unannealed: Without having received extreme unction. The word should be spelt
      'unaneled'; it comes from the verb to anele, meaning to anoint. Extreme unction is a
      sacrament of the Roman Catholic Church in which the dying are anointed by a priest.
      In Shakespeare's *Hamlet*, Act I, Scene 5, the Ghost speaks of dying 'Unhouseled,
      disappointed, unaneled'.

564 *the Central Criminal Court*: The Old Bailey, built in 1539 on Cheapside in the City of Lon-
      don, was used for many celebrated criminal trials. In 1834 the Central Criminal Court
      Act officially recognized it as the major criminal court in the land. The present court
      building, which is still known as the Old Bailey, was built between 1902 and 1907 on the
      site of the old Newgate Prison. The Old Bailey is also mentioned in the Judge's song in
      Trial by Jury ('And every day my voice was heard/At the Sessions or Ancient Bailey').

(*Enter* KING, SAMUEL, *and* FREDERIC.)

KING.   Forward, my men, and seize that General there!

(*They seize the* GENERAL.)

GIRLS.   The pirates! the pirates! Oh, despair!
PIRATES (*springing up*).   Yes, we're the pirates, so despair!   535
GEN.   Frederic here! Oh, joy! Oh, rapture!
        Summon your men and effect their capture!
MABEL.   Frederic, save us!
FRED.   Beautiful Mabel,
        I would if I could, but I am not able.   540
PIRATES.   He's telling the truth, he is not able.
KING.   With base deceit
            You worked upon our feelings!
        Revenge is sweet,
            And flavours all our dealings!   545
        With courage rare
            And resolution manly,
        For death prepare,
            Unhappy General Stanley.   550

MABEL (*wildly*).   Is he to die, unshriven – unannealed?
GIRLS.   Oh, spare him!
MABEL.   Will no one in his cause a weapon wield?
GIRLS.   Oh, spare him!
POLICE (*springing up*).   Yes, we are here, though
                hitherto concealed!
GIRLS.   Oh, rapture!   555
POLICE.   So to Constabulary, pirates, yield!
GIRLS.   Oh, rapture!

(*A struggle ensues between Pirates and Police. Eventually the Police are overcome,
    and fall prostrate, the Pirates standing over them with drawn swords.*)   560

CHORUS OF POLICE AND PIRATES.

You ⎱
We ⎰ triumph now, for well we trow
        Our mortal career's cut short,
    No pirate band will take its stand
        At the Central Criminal Court.
SERG.   To gain a brief advantage you've contrived,   565

569　*in Queen Victoria's name*: For the 1908 revival of *The Pirates* Gilbert changed this line to 'We charge you yield, in good King Edward's name!' and the Pirate King's reply became:

> We yield at once, without a sting,
> Because with all our faults, we love our King.

In subsequent productions, the lines reverted to their original form.

Both the British and American first-night performances of *The Pirates* had finales very different from the present one. In the Paignton production the policeman's line 'We charge you yield, in Queen Victoria's name' was followed by:

RUTH.　　　　　　　Alas, alas, we don't resist the claim
　　　　　　　　　　All Britons bow to Queen Victoria's name.

KING.　　　　　　　It is enough you've deftly played your cards
　　　　　　　　　　That is a spell no Briton disregards.

(Pirates kneel – Police stand over them triumphantly)

QUARTET – MABEL, KING, FREDERIC & RUTH *kneeling.*

> To Queen Victoria's name we bow
> As true born Britons should
> We can resist no longer now
> And would not if we could
> The man who dares to disregard
> A summons in that name
> We look on as a wretch ill-starred
> And lost to sense of shame.

ALL.　　　　　　　We look on as a wretch, etc.

KING.　　　　　　We yield at once, with humble mien, etc.

The action then continued as it does now, with the pirates yielding and Ruth making her announcement that they are, in fact, all noblemen who have gone wrong. Then, after the girls' repetition of the line 'They are all noblemen who have gone wrong', both the Paignton and the New York first-night productions continued *Pinafore*-like as follows:

GENERAL.　　　　What all noblemen?

KING.　　　　　　Yes, all noblemen.

GENERAL.　　　　What, all?

KING.　　　　　　Well, nearly all.

ALL.　　　　　　　They are nearly all noblemen who have gone wrong.
　　　　　　　　　　Then give three cheers both loud and long
　　　　　　　　　　For the twenty noblemen who have gone wrong,
　　　　　　　　　　Then give three cheers both loud and long,
　　　　　　　　　　For the noblemen who have gone wrong.

GENERAL.　　　　No Englishman unmoved that statement hears,
　　　　　　　　　　Because, with all our faults, we love our House of Peers.

At this point, the two first-night versions diverged again. The Paignton production finished with the following 'Hymn to the Nobility':

GENERAL.　　　　Let foreigners look down with scorn
　　　　　　　　　　On legislators heaven-born;
　　　　　　　　　　We know what limpid wisdom runs

	But your proud triumph will not be long-lived.	
KING.	Don't say you are orphans, for we know that game.	
SERG.	On your allegiance we've a stronger claim –	
	We charge you yield, in Queen Victoria's name!	

KING (*baffled*). You do!

570

POLICE.   We do!

We charge you yield, in Queen Victoria's name!

(*Pirates kneel, Police stand over them triumphantly.*)

KING.   We yield at once, with humbled mien,
            Because, with all our faults, we love our Queen.   575

POLICE.   Yes, yes, with all their faults, they love their Queen.
GIRLS.   Yes, yes, with all, etc.

(*Police, holding Pirates by the collar, take out handkerchiefs and weep.*)

GEN.   Away with them, and place them at the bar!

(*Enter* RUTH.)   580

RUTH.   One moment! let me tell you who they are.
            They are no members of the common throng;
            They are all noblemen who have gone wrong!

GEN.   No Englishman unmoved that statement hears,
            Because, with all our faults, we love our House of Peers.   585

RECITATIVE – GENERAL.

I pray you, pardon me, ex-Pirate King,
Peers will be peers, and youth will have its fling.
Resume your ranks and legislative duties,
And take my daughters, all of whom are beauties.

FINALE.

MABEL.   Poor wandering ones!   590
                      Though ye have surely strayed,
                      Take heart of grace,
                      Your steps retrace,
                    Poor wandering ones!
                    Poor wandering ones!
                      If such poor love as ours   595

> From Peers and all their eldest sons.
> Enrapt the true-born Briton hears
> The wisdom of his House of Peers

SERGEANT.

> And if a noble lord should die
> And leave no nearer progeny,
> His twentieth cousin takes his place
> And legislates with equal grace.

RUTH.

> But should a son and heir survive,
> Or other nearer relative,
> Then twentieth cousins get you hence –
> You're persons of no consequence.
> When issue male their chances bar,
> How paltry twentieth cousins are!

MABEL.

> How doubly blest that glorious land
> Where rank and brains go hand in hand,
> Where wisdom pure and virtue hale
> Obey the law of strict entail,
> No harm can touch a country when
> It's ruled by British noblemen.

CURTAIN

The American first-night production had a much shorter hymn to the nobility, sung by the entire company, following the General's line 'Because, with all our faults, we love our House of Peers':

> Hail, ever hail, O House of Peers!
> To wisdom that mankind reveres
> We listen with respectful ears,
> For oh! we love our House of Peers!

The General then had his recitative 'I pray you, pardon me, ex-Pirate King', as now. (During the 1908 revival of *The Pirates* at the Savoy Theatre, incidentally, Gilbert showed his low opinion of the female chorus, which for once he had played no part in selecting, by altering the last line in this recitative to 'And take my daughters, some of whom are beauties'.)

For the finale, the New York first-night production did not use the reprise of 'Poor wandering one' that is now sung but instead had the following variation on the Major-General's song. This is also used by Joseph Papp in the finale of his production:

RUTH.   At length we are provided, with unusual facility,
               To change piratic crime for dignified respectability.

KING.   Combined, I needn't say, with the unparalleled felicity
               Of what we have been longing for – unbounded domesticity.

MABEL.   Tomorrow morning early we will quickly be parsonified –
               Hymeneally coupled, conjugally matrimonified.

SERGEANT.   And this shall be accomplished by that doctor of divinity
               Who happily resides in the immediate vicinity.

CHORUS.   Who happily resides in the immediate vicinity, etc.

GENERAL.   My military knowledge, though I'm plucky and adventury,
               Has only been brought down to the beginning of the century.
               But still, in getting off my daughters – eight or nine or ten in all,
               I've shown myself a model of a modern Major-General.

Can help you find
True peace of mind,
Why, take it, it is yours!

ALL.   Poor wandering ones! etc.   600

CURTAIN

CHORUS.   His military knowledge etc.

DANCE

CURTAIN

PATIENCE

or

Bunthorne's Bride

DRAMATIS PERSONÆ

COLONEL CALVERLEY
MAJOR MURGATROYD
LIEUT. THE DUKE OF DUNSTABLE } (*Officers of Dragoon Guards*)

REGINALD BUNTHORNE (*a Fleshly Poet*)
ARCHIBALD GROSVENOR (*an Idyllic Poet*)
MR BUNTHORNE'S SOLICITOR
THE LADY ANGELA
THE LADY SAPHIR
THE LADY ELLA } (*Rapturous Maidens*)
THE LADY JANE
PATIENCE (*a Dairy Maid*)

Chorus of Rapturous Maidens and Officers of Dragoon Guards.

ACT I. – Exterior of Castle Bunthorne.
ACT II. – A Glade.

PATIENCE

There is more direct contemporary satire in *Patience* than in any other Savoy
Opera. Its target was the aesthetic movement, which flourished in Britain between 1870 and the mid-1880s and introduced the new religion of beauty as a
reaction against the ugliness of the Victorian age.

In some ways this strictly contemporary theme makes *Patience* the most dated
of all Gilbert and Sullivan's works. Yet modern audiences have little trouble in
either enjoying or understanding it. This is no doubt partly because most of us
have some impression of the style and mannerisms of the leading figures of the
aesthetic movement. Few people nowadays may read Algernon Swinburne's
poems or gaze on James Whistler's paintings, but most are at least aware of Oscar Wilde and the Pre-Raphaelites. But there is also another reason why *Patience*
is not as dated as it might seem. It is essentially a satire on the affectation and
excesses which can accompany artistic movements and cultural fads and of
which we have certainly not been free in the latter part of the twentieth century.

Certainly the aesthetic movement was more affected than most and lent itself naturally to ridicule and satire. In 1877 the art world had been torn asunder
by a libel action brought by Whistler, the high priest of the aesthetic style in
painting, against the critic John Ruskin, who had described one of his paintings, exhibited at the newly opened Grosvenor Gallery, as 'flinging a pot of
paint in the public's face'. The subsequent court case, which was finally resolved with Whistler being awarded damages of a penny, produced a string of
witnesses arguing the merits of primary colours, Japanese art, and harmony of
form before a bemused British judge and jury. It may also have given Gilbert
the initial idea for a work based on the intense rivalry and jealousy which evidently existed among those who worshipped purity and beauty.

The following year London had its first sight of the figure who was to person-
ify more than anyone else the excesses of aestheticism. Oscar Wilde arrived
from Oxford clutching his sacred lily, enthusing about blue and white china
and the paintings of the Pre-Raphaelites and describing Henry Irving's legs as
'distinctly precious'.

It was not long before the satirists got to work on this rich material. In 1878
George du Maurier, the leading *Punch* cartoonist, started caricaturing the Pre-
Raphaelites and their followers. Four West End plays produced between December 1877 and February 1881 burlesqued the aesthetic movement. The most
successful was *The Colonel* by F. C. Burnand (who was, incidentally, Sullivan's

librettist for *Cox and Box*), which opened just two months before *Patience*. To make clear that no plagiarism was involved, Richard D'Oyly Carte printed a note in the programme of Gilbert and Sullivan's new opera indicating that it had been completed before Burnand's work was performed.

Gilbert had, in fact, taken rather longer than usual over the libretto of *Patience*, because he had twice changed its basic subject matter. He started out intending to make it a satire on the aesthetic movement but then decided that he could have more fun by poking fun at the prevailing Anglo-Catholic or Tractarian movement in the Church of England, which, with its stress on rituals, vestments, and 'bells and smells', was not altogether dissimilar from the style and attitudes of the Pre-Raphaelites.

Gilbert set to work on this new clerical version in the summer of 1880, basing his plot on one of his *Bab Ballads*, 'The Rival Curates', which told of how two clergymen vied with each other in mildness and insipidity until one of them was persuaded to dance, smoke, play croquet, and generally adopt a more jocular approach to life. For the opera, he planned to follow the same theme, adding a female chorus of devoted parishioners of the Revd Lawn Tennison, and a male chorus of soldiers whose no-nonsense manliness would contrast with the rather effete ways of the two central characters.

In a letter to Sullivan in November 1880, however, Gilbert announced that he had changed his mind: 'I mistrust the clerical element. I feel hampered by the restrictions which the nature of the subject places upon my freedom of action, and I want to revert to my old idea.' So the rival curates became rival aesthetes once again and the ladies their devoted admirers. The soldiers remained to play much the same role as before.

Patience opened at the Opéra Comique on 23 April 1881 and was an instant success. No fewer than eight of the numbers received an encore on the first night, including Sullivan's haunting madrigal 'I hear the soft note' and the tender duet 'Prithee, pretty maiden'. Altogether, the music for *Patience* shows a greater maturity and originality than that of the earlier Gilbert and Sullivan operas. There are fewer recitatives and solo arias imitative of the grand opera tradition and more duets, trios, and other concerted pieces.

On 10 October *Patience* transferred to the brand-new Savoy Theatre which Richard D'Oyly Carte had just built on the south side of the Strand. The theatre was the first in Britain to be lit by electric light. Shortly before the curtain went up for the first time Carte appeared on stage to assure a slightly apprehensive audience that there was no danger in this novel method of illumination. To prove its safety, indeed, he broke an electric lamp without causing a fire. 'A few minutes after Mr Carte had disappeared', the *Orchestra and the Choir* magazine reported, 'the 38 incandescent lamps placed around the dress circle, upper circle and gallery were set in action, the gas was at once extinguished, and a blaze of illumination proclaimed "the light of the future".'

Patience originally ran for 578 performances, one of the longest first runs of all the Savoy Operas. It is, I think, fair to say that it has not been quite so popular with modern audiences. It is, perhaps, something of an acquired taste. Dame Bridget D'Oyly Carte told me that it never went down very well in places like Sunderland or Blackpool, although it was always popular in Oxford. A new production designed by Peter Goffin in 1957 was in the D'Oyly Carte repertoire until the 1978–9 season.

In 1969 *Patience* became the third Gilbert and Sullivan opera to be performed by the Sadler's Wells Opera Company, later the English National Opera, at the London Coliseum. John Cox, the producer, was at first tempted to update it by satirizing the 1960s cult of 'flower power' and turning Bunthorne and Grosvenor into hippies, but he resisted the idea, deciding that the theme of 'the military against the beautiful people' was still essentially relevant. The production went to Vienna in 1975 and was revived in London in 1979.

Although originally intended as a piece of ridicule, *Patience* in fact had the overall effect of greatly publicizing and even enhancing the reputation of the aesthetic movement. Several of its leading members delighted in the new fame which the opera gave them. When George Grossmith wrote to James Whistler for permission to reproduce the artist's distinctive lock of white hair in his make-up for Bunthorne, back came the reply: 'Je te savois – mais je ne te savois pas plus brave que moy' – which is roughly translated: 'I knew you, but I did not know you were better than me.'

Oscar Wilde also found new fame as a result of the success of *Patience*. Shortly after the opera had opened in the United States, he was sent across the Atlantic by D'Oyly Carte on a lecture tour, to be, in the words of Max Beerbohm, 'a sandwich board for *Patience*'. Wilde was carefully scheduled to appear in each city just as the opera was about to open there. In Omaha, the local paper reported, 'He wore the suit of black velvet with knee breeches which has been his usual dress in this country. His hair fell about his shoulders in heavy masses, his dreamy, poetic face grew animated, and his large dark eyes lighted up as he entered upon his subject.' A most intense young man, indeed. The Midwesterners must have wondered just who was imitating whom between the fleshly poet Bunthorne and the fleshly poet Wilde.

1–4 *Scene*: Early libretti included the direction that the entrance to Castle Bunthorne was by a draw-bridge over a moat. A note appended to an early edition of the libretto pointed out that 'the aesthetic dresses are designed by the author'. At one stage Gilbert had toyed with the idea of getting Du Maurier, the *Punch* cartoonist, to design them.

It was originally intended that Lady Jane should be on stage as the curtain rose on Act I. The licence copy contains the following direction: 'JANE, *a gaunt, formidable, portentous, black-haired, heavy-browed aesthete, sits gloomily apart with her back to audience, wrapt in grief.*'

It is interesting to compare the present scene for Act I with the scene Gilbert envisaged when he was intending the opera to be about two rival clergymen (henceforth this will be referred to as the clerical version). The notes for this earlier version survive in the British Library and contain the following description of the opening scene: 'Exterior of country vicarage. Ladies discovered seated on lawn in despairing attitudes, headed by Angela, Ella and Saphir. They are waiting to congratulate the Revd Lawn Tennison on his birthday, and to give him slippers, comforters, braces etc. which they are working upon.'

5–10 *Twenty love-sick maidens we*
The opening phrase of this song is identical with that of 'Hark, those chimes so sweetly sounding', one of the numbers in William Vincent Wallace's opera *Maritana*, written in 1845 and very popular with the Victorians.

Frederic Lloyd, general manager of the D'Oyly Carte Opera Company from 1951 to 1980, was once threatened with prosecution under the Trades Descriptions Act for not fielding a twenty-strong ladies' chorus in performances of *Patience*. He replied that there was nothing in their song to say that all twenty of the love-sick maidens had to be on stage at the same time.

11 *Love feeds on hope*: This line was originally sung as 'Love feeds on love'.

ACT I

SCENE. – *Exterior of Castle Bunthorne. Young maidens dressed in æsthetic draperies are grouped about the stage. They play on lutes, mandolins, etc., as they sing, and all are in the last stage of despair.* ANGELA, ELLA, *and* SAPHIR *lead them.*

CHORUS.

Twenty love-sick maidens we,
   Love-sick all against our will.   5
Twenty years hence we shall be
   Twenty love-sick maidens still.
Twenty love-sick maidens we,
And we die for love of thee.   10

SOLO – ANGELA.

Love feeds on hope, they say, or love will die –
ALL.   Ah, miserie!
Yet my love lives, although no hope have I!
ALL.   Ah, miserie!
Alas, poor heart, go hide thyself away –
To weeping concords tune thy roundelay!   15
        Ah, miserie!

CHORUS.

All our love is all for one,
   Yet that love he heedeth not,
He is coy and cares for none,
   Sad and sorry is our lot!   20
        Ah, miserie!

23-30 *Go, breaking heart*
Lady Ella's solo is one of the few songs which survived unchanged Gilbert's transition from a clerical to an aesthetic theme. In the former version, it followed a slightly different opening chorus:

> Twenty love-sick maidens we,
> Sitting by a running rill.
> Twenty years hence we shall be
> Twenty love-sick maidens still.
> Ah, miserie!

> All our love is love for one,
> Yet that love he prizes not,
> He is coy and cares for none,
> Sad and sorry is our lot!
> Ah, miserie!

37 *cynosure*: A centre of attraction. The word comes originally from a Greek phrase meaning dog's tail which was applied to the constellation Ursa Minor, better known as the Pole Star, used by mariners for guiding their ships and a focal point in the heavens.

43 *Happy receipts*: This phrase does not occur in the first edition of the libretto and was introduced by Gilbert for the 1900 revival, probably incorporating an ad-lib made by the cast of the original production.

44 *Fools*: In his manuscript notes on the Savoy Operas J. M. Gordon, who joined the D'Oyly Carte Company in 1883 to play the role of the Colonel in *Patience* and finally retired in 1939 after twenty-nine years as stage manager, made the following observations about the character of Lady Jane and the way that this and her next line should be delivered:

> Lady Jane, an elderly lady who is nearly 'left on the shelf', is a really pathetic figure, not a burlesque of womanhood, but one who begins to see 'her beauty disappear' and hope of marriage fading away. Her first entrance, and first words 'Fools! Fools and blind!' should not be shouted like a bully. She has just made a discovery that may affect them all!

49 *Patience, the village milkmaid*: In Gilbert's earlier clerical version of the opera, Patience was cast as the village schoolmistress, who alone of all the maidens in the parish remained insensible to the charms of the Revd Lawn Tennison.

55 *'twill quickly wear away*: In early libretti, and in the Macmillan edition of the Savoy Operas, this appears as ' 'twill quickly pass away'.

59 *Patience appears*: The costume worn by Miss Leonora Braham, who created the role of Patience, would have been instantly recognizable to the first-night audience at the Opéra Comique. It was a copy of the dress worn by the milkmaid in Sir Luke Fildes's painting *'Where are you going to, my pretty maid?'*, reproductions of which hung on many Victorian parlour walls.

SOLO – ELLA.

Go, breaking heart,
  Go, dream of love requited;
Go, foolish heart,
  Go, dream of lovers plighted;   25
Go, madcap heart,
  Go, dream of never waking;
And in thy dream
  Forget that thou art breaking!   30

CHORUS.   Ah, miserie!
ELLA.   Forget that thou art breaking!
CHORUS.   Twenty love-sick maidens, etc.

ANG. There is a strange magic in this love of ours! Rivals as we all are in the affections of our Reginald, the very hopelessness of our love is a bond that binds us to one another!   35

SAPH. Jealousy is merged in misery. While he, the very cynosure of our eyes and hearts, remains icy insensible – what have we to strive for?

ELLA. The love of maidens is, to him, as interesting as the taxes!

SAPH. Would that it were! He pays his taxes.   40

ANG. And cherishes the receipts!

(*Enter* LADY JANE.)

SAPH. Happy receipts!

JANE (*suddenly*). Fools!

ANG. I beg your pardon?

JANE. Fools and blind! The man loves – wildly loves!   45

ANG. But whom? None of us!

JANE. No, none of us. His weird fancy has lighted, for the nonce, on Patience, the village milkmaid!

SAPH. On Patience? Oh, it cannot be!   50

JANE. Bah! But yesterday I caught him in her dairy, eating fresh butter with a tablespoon. To-day he is not well!

SAPH. But Patience boasts that she has never loved – that love is, to her, a sealed book! Oh, he cannot be serious!

JANE. 'Tis but a fleeting fancy – 'twill quickly wear away. (*Aside.*) Oh,   55
Reginald, if you but knew what a wealth of golden love is waiting for you, stored up in this rugged old bosom of mine, the milkmaid's triumph would be short indeed!

(PATIENCE *appears on an eminence. She looks down
with pity on the despondent Maidens.*)   60

61–4 *Still brooding on their mad infatuation*

In the clerical version of *Patience*, this recitative was replaced by the following passage:

RECITATIVE.

ANG.	See – hither comes the village schoolmistress,
	Poor Patience – who alone of all womankind
	Remains insensate to his calm attractions!
SAPH.	Unhappy girl – her heart has ne'er known love –
ELLA.	Benighted creature!
ANG.	Miserable maid!

(PATIENCE *appears*.)

PA.	Your pardon, ladies. I intrude upon you. (*Going*.)
ANG.	Come hither, Patience – tell us, is it true
	That you have never loved?
PA.	Most true indeed.
SOPRANOS.	Most marvellous!
CONTRALTOS.	And most deplorable!

Patience's song, 'I cannot tell what this love may be', then followed, as now, after which the Revd Lawn Tennison entered, preceded by a sexton and a beadle whose duties were to keep off the ladies, and followed by 'two grim and portentous middle-aged females dressed in heavy black – Sister Jane and Sister Ann'.

RECITATIVE – P̲ᴀᴛɪᴇɴᴄᴇ.

Still brooding on their mad infatuation!
   I thank thee, Love, thou comest not to me!
Far happier I, free from thy ministration,
   Than dukes or duchesses who love can be!

Sᴀᴘʜ. (*looking up*). 'Tis Patience – happy girl! Loved by a Poet!   65
Pᴀ.   Your pardon, ladies. I intrude upon you. (*Going.*)
Aɴɢ.   Nay, pretty child, come hither. Is it true
              That you have never loved?
Pᴀ.   Most true indeed.
Sᴏᴘʀᴀɴᴏs.   Most marvellous!
                                    70
Cᴏɴᴛʀᴀʟᴛᴏs.   And most deplorable!

SONG – P̲ᴀᴛɪᴇɴᴄᴇ.

I cannot tell what this love may be
That cometh to all, but not to me.
It cannot be kind as they'd imply,
Or why do these ladies sigh?
It cannot be joy and rapture deep,   75
Or why do these gentle ladies weep?
It cannot be blissful as 'tis said,
Or why are their eyes so wonderous red?
   Though everywhere true love I see   80
   A-coming to all, but not to me,
   I cannot tell what this love may be!
      For I am blithe and I am gay,
      While they sit sighing night and day.
      Think of the gulf 'twixt them and me,   85
      'Fal la la la!' – and 'Miserie!'

Cʜᴏʀᴜs.   Yes, she is blithe, etc.

Pᴀ.   If love is a thorn, they show no wit
          Who foolishly hug and foster it.
          If love is a weed, how simple they
          Who gather it, day by day!   90
          If love is a nettle that makes you smart,
          Then why do you wear it next your heart?
          And if it be none of these, say I,
          Ah, why do you sit and sob and sigh?
             Though everywhere, etc.   95

Cʜᴏʀᴜs.   For she is blithe, etc.

106 *The 35th Dragoon Guards*: Military characters appear in nine of the thirteen Savoy
Operas. In addition to the Dragoon Guards in *Patience*, there are the marines in *H.M.S.
Pinafore*, the First Life Guards in *Utopia Limited*, the chorus of bucks and blades in *Ruddi-
gore*, who were originally dressed as officers of the twenty leading cavalry and infantry
regiments of the British Army, the soldiers in *Princess Ida*, and, of course, the Yeomen of
the Guard. Then there is Alexis, the Grenadier Guards officer, in *The Sorcerer*, Major-
General Stanley in *The Pirates of Penzance* and Private Willis, also of the Grenadier
Guards, in *Iolanthe*.

Gilbert himself had a fondness for the Army (see the note to lines 338–69) and he was
writing at a time of great militarism and jingoism in Britain. The Afghan and Zulu wars
were just over when *Patience* was first performed, and British occupation of Egypt was
about to begin.

In his earlier clerical version of *Patience* Gilbert had made his soldiers the 21st Hussars. It is not clear why, other than to rhyme them with 'tunes', he changed them for the
aesthetic version to Dragoons. These were mounted infantrymen who took their name
from their weapons, carbines called dragons because they spouted fire like the fabulous
beasts. As opposed to light cavalry regiments, dragoons were traditionally 'heavies', i.e.
burly men who carried fairly heavy weapons.

121–8 *The soldiers of our Queen*
Listening to this splendidly catchy oom-pah-pah tune, it is not difficult to detect the influence on Sullivan of his upbringing in a household where military music must often
have been heard. His father was bandmaster at the Royal Military College, Sandhurst,
and later a professor at the Army's School of Music at Kneller Hall.

The clerical version contained a two-verse chorus in which the 21st Hussars introduced themselves:

> The twenty-first hussars,
>   Are linked in friendly tether;
> Upon the field of Mars
>   They fight the foe together.
> There every mother's son
>   Prepared to fight and fall is;
> The enemy of one
>   The enemy of all is!
>
> United as a clan
>   We have arranged between us
> To introduce this plan
>   Within the courts of Venus:
> With one emotion stirred
>   Beneath our belts of leather,
> The Colonel gives the word
>   And all propose together!

130–73 *If you want a receipt for that popular mystery*
A song which probably requires more annotation than any other in the entire Gilbert
and Sullivan repertoire. Here goes, but first this is how it began when Gilbert was thinking in terms of Hussars rather than Dragoons:

> If you want a receipt of that popular mystery,
>   Known to the world as a British Hussar,
> Take all the remarkable people in history,
>   Choose the best points from each eminent star.

ANG. Ah, Patience, if you have never loved, you have never known true happiness! (*All sigh.*)

PA. But the truly happy always seem to have so much on their minds. The truly happy never seem quite well.

JANE. There is a transcendentality of delirium – an acute accentuation of supremest ecstasy – which the earthy might easily mistake for indigestion. But it is *not* indigestion – it is æsthetic transfiguration! (*To the others.*) Enough of babble. Come!

PA. But stay, I have some news for you. The 35th Dragoon Guards have halted in the village, and are even now on their way to this very spot.

ANG. The 35th Dragoon Guards!

SAPH. They are fleshly men, of full habit!

ELLA. We care nothing for Dragoon Guards!

PA. But, bless me, you were all engaged to them a year ago!

SAPH. A year ago!

ANG. My poor child, you don't understand these things. A year ago they were very well in our eyes, but since then our tastes have been etherealized, our perceptions exalted. (*To others.*) Come, it is time to lift up our voices in morning carol to our Reginald. Let us to his door.

(*The Maidens go off, two and two, into the Castle, singing refrain of 'Twenty love-sick maidens we', and accompanying themselves on harps and mandolins.* PATIENCE *watches them in surprise, as she climbs the rock by which she entered.*)

(*March, Enter Officers of Dragoon Guards, led by* MAJOR.)

CHORUS OF DRAGOONS.

The soldiers of our Queen
    Are linked in friendly tether;
Upon the battle scene
    They fight the foe together.
There every mother's son
    Prepared to fight and fall is;
The enemy of one
    The enemy of all is!

(*Enter* COLONEL.)

SONG – COLONEL.

If you want a receipt for that popular mystery,
    Known to the world as a Heavy Dragoon,
Take all the remarkable people in history,
    Rattle them off to a popular tune.

134 *Victory*: Nelson's flagship at the battle of Trafalgar, which provided the model for H.M.S.
     Pinafore.

135 *Bismarck*: The German Chancellor from 1871 to 1890.

136 *Fielding*: Opinions differ as to which Fielding Gilbert has in mind here, but it is probably
     either Henry, the author of *Tom Jones*, or his half-brother, Sir John, a magistrate who
     tried to ban performances of *The Beggar's Opera*.

137 *Paget*: Sir Joseph Paget (1814–99), an eminent surgeon and pathologist. Trepanning is a
     surgical operation on the skull.

138 *Jullien*: Louis Antoine Jullien (1812–60), a French-born conductor who organized con-
     certs and operatic performances at the Drury Lane Theatre in London. In his *Songs of a
     Savoyard* Gilbert rewrote this line: 'The grace of Mozart, that unparalleled musico'.

139 *Macaulay*: Thomas Babington Macaulay (1800–1859), the Whig historian and politician.

140 *Boucicault*: Dion Boucicault (1822–90), an Irish actor and playwright.

141 *Bishop of Sodor and Man*: The diocese of Sodor and Man is one of the oldest in Britain,
     having been founded in 447. It now covers only the Isle of Man but it originally also in-
     cluded the Western Isles off Scotland.

142 *D'Orsay*: Count Alfred D'Orsay was an early nineteenth-century Parisian dandy.

144 *Victor Emmanuel*: Victor Emmanuel II (1820–78), King of Italy from 1861 to his death.
     Peveril: Sir Geoffrey Peveril, an old Cavalier who lived in the Peak District of Derbyshire,
     is the hero of Sir Walter Scott's novel *Peveril of the Peak*.

145 *Thomas Aquinas*: Italian theologian and philosopher (1227–74), was canonized in 1323.
     Doctor Sacheverell: Ecclesiastic and politician (1672–1724), impeached before the House
     of Lords for preaching against the principles of the 1688 Revolution.

146 *Tupper*: Martin Tupper (1810–89), a popular Victorian author whose most famous work
     was *Proverbial Philosophy*.

147 *Anthony Trollope*: I know that Trollope, along with Dickens, Thackeray, Tennyson and
     Defoe, does not need to be explained to a literate and cultured readership, but I cannot
     resist drawing your attention to the curious coincidence that he died on the last night
     of the original run of *Patience*, 22 November 1882.
     Mr Guizot: François Guizot (1787–1874), French politician and historian.

158 *Lord Waterford*: Henry Beresford, 3rd Marquis of Waterford (1811–59), a well-known
     practical joker who was killed while hunting.

159 *Roderick*: There are two contenders for this reference: Roderick Dhu, a Scottish outlaw
     leader defeated by the Saxons who figures in Scott's narrative poem *The Lady of the
     Lake*, and Roderick, the last Gothic king of Spain, whose overthrow by the Moors is the
     subject of Scott's poem *The Vision of Don Roderick* and of Southey's *Roderick, the last of the
     Goths*. Either character would seem to fit.

160 *Paddington Pollaky*: Ignatius Paul Pollaky, a well-known Victorian detective who was based
     at Paddington Police Station.

161 *Odalisque*: a female member of a harem.

163 *Sir Garnet*: Sir Garnet Wolseley (1833–1913), the Victorian swashbuckling military com-
     mander and imperial adventurer who was the model for the modern Major-General in
     The Pirates of Penzance. For the 1900 revival of *Patience* Gilbert altered this line to 'Skill of
     Lord Roberts', a topical tribute to one of the heroes of the Boer War, and in 1907 he
     changed it to 'Skill of Lord Wolseley'.

164 *the Stranger*: A tragedy by Benjamin Thompson based on a German story about a Count
     who leaves his wife and roams the world known only as 'The Stranger'. It was first per-
     formed in London in 1798 and often revived.

165 *Manfred*: Once again there are two possibilities here, either the hero of Byron's play
     Manfred, who sells himself to the Devil and lives in solitude in the Alps, or the King of
     Naples and Sicily who died at the battle of Benevento in 1266.

166 *Beadle of Burlington*: This is almost certainly a reference to the world's smallest police
     force, the three beadles who patrol the Burlington Arcade just off Piccadilly in the heart

The pluck of Lord Nelson on board of the *Victory* –
Genius of Bismarck devising a plan –
The humour of Fielding (which sounds contradictory) – 135
Coolness of Paget about to trepan –
The science of Jullien, the eminent musico –
Wit of Macaulay, who wrote of Queen Anne –
The pathos of Paddy, as rendered by Boucicault –
Style of the Bishop of Sodor and Man – 140
The dash of a D'Orsay, divested of quackery –
Narrative powers of Dickens and Thackeray –
Victor Emmanuel – peak-haunting Peveril –
Thomas Aquinas, and Doctor Sacheverell – 145
Tupper and Tennyson – Daniel Defoe –
Anthony Trollope and Mr Guizot! Ah!
Take of these elements all that is fusible,
Melt them all down in a pipkin or crucible,
Set them to simmer and take off the scum,
And a Heavy Dragoon is the residuum! 150

CHORUS.   Yes! yes! yes! yes!
A Heavy Dragoon is the residuum!

COL.   If you want a receipt for this soldier-like paragon,
Get at the wealth of the Czar (if you can) –
The family pride of a Spaniard from Aragon – 155
Force of Mephisto pronouncing a ban –
A smack of Lord Waterford, reckless and rollicky –
Swagger of Roderick, heading his clan –
The keen penetration of Paddington Pollaky – 160
Grace of an Odalisque on a divan –
The genius strategic of Cæsar or Hannibal –
Skill of Sir Garnet in thrashing a cannibal –
Flavour of Hamlet – the Stranger, a touch of him –
Little of Manfred (but not very much of him) – 165
Beadle of Burlington – Richardson's show –
Mr Micawber and Madame Tussaud! Ah!
Take of these elements all that is fusible,
Melt them all down in a pipkin or crucible,
Set them to simmer and take off the scum,
And a Heavy Dragoon is the residuum! 170

CHORUS.   Yes! yes! yes! yes!
A Heavy Dragoon is the residuum!

of London. They were set up in 1819 to make sure that no one whistled, hummed or otherwise disturbed the decorum of the fashionable shopping precinct. A year or two ago the beadles managed to stave off a move to replace their £380 top-hats with economy models costing only £170. American Savoyards have an alternative explanation that this line refers to Erasmus F. Beadle of Burlington, New Jersey, the inventor of the 'dime novel'.

Richardson's show: A travelling show which included melodrama, pantomime, comic songs and incidental music and was a major attraction at Victorian fairs. John Richardson, the founder, died in a workhouse in 1837 at the age of seventy.

167   *Mr Micawber*: Wilkins Micawber is one of the main characters in Dickens's *David Copperfield*.

Madame Tussaud: The waxwork modeller who came to England from France in 1802 also gets a mention in the Mikado's list of punishments that fit the crime (*The Mikado*, Act II, line 354).

I cannot conclude the notes on this song without remarking that Dr Cyril Alington, headmaster of Eton from 1917 to 1933, produced a fine parody which began 'If you want a receipt to construct Aristophanes'. Sadly lack of space prevents me from reproducing it in full.

182   *are you fond of toffee*: In the first American edition of *Patience*, published in 1881 by J. M. Stoddart & Co. and apparently authorized by Gilbert and Sullivan, the word 'candy' is substituted for 'toffee' throughout this exchange.

204   *here I am*: At this point Gilbert originally intended the Duke to have a solo. It is printed in the licence copy, and is bound in at the back of the autograph score, having been torn out of its original position. The song was given its première in a production at Banbury Grammar School in 1967 and subsequently performed by Colin Wright at a D'Oyly Carte last night, although the tune had to be guessed, as the melodic line had disappeared and only the accompaniment was extant. The song goes as follows:

DUKE.	Though men of rank may useless seem,
	    They do good in their generation,
	They make the wealthy upstart teem
	    With Christian love and self-negation;
	The bitterest tongue that ever lashed
	    Man's folly, drops with milk and honey,
	While Scandal hides her head abashed,
	    Brought face to face with Rank and Money!

DRAGOONS.	Yes, Scandal hides her head, etc.
DUKE.	Society forgets her laws, And Prudery her affectation, While Mrs Grundy pleads our cause, And talks 'wild oats' and toleration: Archbishops wink at what they'd think A downright crime is common shoddy, Although Archbishops shouldn't wink At anything – or anybody!
DRAGOONS.	A good Archbishop shouldn't wink At anything – or anybody!

COL. Well, here we are once more on the scene of our former triumphs. But where's the Duke? 175

(*Enter* DUKE, *listlessly, and in low spirits.*)

DUKE. Here I am! (*Sighs.*)

COL. Come, cheer up, don't give way!

DUKE. Oh, for that, I'm as cheerful as a poor devil can be expected to be who has the misfortune to be a duke, with a thousand a day! 180

MAJ. Humph! Most men would envy you!

DUKE. Envy *me*? Tell me, Major, are you fond of toffee?

MAJ. Very!

COL. We are all fond of toffee.

ALL. We are!

DUKE. Yes, and toffee in moderation is a capital thing. But to *live* on 185 toffee – toffee for breakfast, toffee for dinner, toffee for tea – to have it supposed that you care for nothing *but* toffee, and that you would consider yourself insulted if anything but toffee were offered to you – how would you like *that*? 190

COL. I can quite believe that, under those circumstances, even toffee would become monotonous.

DUKE. For 'toffee' read flattery, adulation, and abject deference, carried to such a pitch that I began, at last, to think that man was born bent at an angle of forty-five degrees! Great Heavens, what is there to adulate in me! 195 Am I particularly intelligent, or remarkably studious, or excruciatingly witty, or unusually accomplished, or exceptionally virtuous?

COL. You're about as commonplace a young man as ever I saw.

ALL. You are!

DUKE. Exactly! That's it exactly! That describes me to a T! Thank you 200 all very much! Well, I couldn't stand it any longer, so I joined this second-class cavalry regiment. In the Army, thought I, I shall be occasionally snubbed, perhaps even bullied, who knows? The thought was rapture, and here I am.

COL. (*looking off*). Yes, and here are the ladies! 205

DUKE. But who is the gentleman with the long hair?

COL. I don't know.

DUKE. He seems popular!

COL. He *does* seem popular!

(BUNTHORNE *enters, followed by Maidens, two and two, singing and playing* 210 *on harps as before. He is composing a poem, and quite absorbed. He sees no one, but walks across the stage, followed by Maidens. They take no notice of Dragoons – to the surprise and indignation of those Officers.*)

214–19 *In a doleful train*
As originally written, this song began:

> In a melancholy train
> Two and two we walk all day –
> Pity those who love in vain!
> None so sorrowful as they . . .

220–30 *Now is not this ridiculous*
The manuscript of Gilbert's clerical version of *Patience* contains the following numbers
at this point:

CHORUS OF SOLDIERS.

> Now is not this ridiculous and is not this preposterous
> And is it not to suicide enough to urge a man?
> Instead of rushing eagerly to cherish us and foster us
> They all prefer this excellent but very prosy clergyman.
> Instead of slyly peering at us,
> Casting looks endearing at us,
> Flushing at us – blushing at us – flirting with a fan;
> They're actually sneering at us – fleering at us – jeering at us!
> Pretty sort of treatment for a military man!
> They're actually sneering at us – fleering at us – jeering at us!
> Pretty sort of treatment for a military man!

CHORUS OF MAIDENS.

> In a melancholy train
> Two and two we walk all day –
> Pity those who love in vain!
> None so sorrowful as they,
> Who can only sigh and say
> Woe is me: alack-a-day!

1ST LADY.	Gentle vicar, hear our prayer –
	Twenty love-sick maidens we,
	Young and pretty, dark and fair,
	[*The next four lines are illegible*]
MR L. TENNISON	Though my book I seem to scan
	Like a serious clergyman
	Who despises female clay,
	I hear plainly all they say,
	Twenty love-sick maidens they!
BEADLE *and* SEXTON.	He hears plainly all they say,
(*to Officers*)	Twenty love-sick maidens they!
OFFICERS (*to each other*).	He hears plainly, etc.
2ND LADY.	Though so excellently wise
	For a moment mortal be,
	Deign to raise thy gentle eyes
	From thy dry theology –
	Twenty love-sick maidens see –
	Each is kneeling on her knee!
CHORUS OF MAIDENS.	Twenty love-sick maidens see,
	Each is kneeling on her knee!
OFFICERS.	Twenty love-sick maidens, etc.

CHORUS OF LADIES.

In a doleful train
  Two and two we walk all day –
For we love in vain!
  None so sorrowful as they
    Who can only sigh and say,
    Woe is me, alackaday!

215

CHORUS OF DRAGOONS.

Now is not this ridiculous – and is not this preposterous?
  A thorough-paced absurdity – explain it if you can.
Instead of rushing eagerly to cherish us and foster us,
  They all prefer this melancholy literary man.
    Instead of slyly peering at us,
    Casting looks endearing at us,
Blushing at us, flushing at us – flirting with a fan;
They're actually sneering at us, fleering at us, jeering at us!
  Pretty sort of treatment for a military man!
They're actually sneering at us, fleering at us, jeering at us!
  Pretty sort of treatment for a military man!

220

225

230

ANG.   Mystic poet, hear our prayer,
               Twenty love-sick maidens we –
          Young and wealthy, dark and fair –
          All of county family.
              And we die for love of thee –
              Twenty love-sick maidens we!

235

CHORUS OF LADIES.   Yes, we die for love of thee –
              Twenty love-sick maidens we!

BUN. (*aside – slyly*).   Though my book I seem to scan
           In a rapt ecstatic way,
       Like a literary man
          Who despises female clay,
     I hear plainly all they say,
     Twenty love-sick maidens they!

240

OFFICERS (*to each other*).   He hears plainly, etc.

245

SAPH.   Though so excellently wise,
            For a moment mortal be,

MR L. TENNISON.   Though as I remarked before
                              Anyone convinced would be,
                          That a work of musty lore
                              Is monopolizing me,
                          Round the corner I can see
                              Each is down upon her knee.

BEADLE *and* SEXTON.   Round the corner he can see, etc.

OFFICERS.   Round the corner he can see, etc.

260 *Now is not this ridiculous*: This ensemble provides a striking example of a musical effect
     which Sullivan claimed to have invented, the setting of two apparently incompatible
     choruses in counterpoint to each other. A similar effect is produced in *The Pirates of Pen-
     zance*, Act II, line 119.

268 *Good old Bunthorne*: In early editions of the libretto this line was 'Bravo, Bunthorne'.
269 *I droop despairingly*: In an early edition this was 'I despair droopingly'.

Deign to raise thy purple eyes
From thy heart-drawn poesy.
Twenty love-sick maidens see –
Each is kneeling on her knee!   (*All kneel.*)   250

CHORUS OF LADIES.   Twenty love-sick, etc.

BUN. (*aside*).   Though, as I remarked before,
                Any one convinced would be
             That some transcendental lore   255
                Is monopolizing me,
             Round the corner I can see
             Each is kneeling on her knee!

OFFICERS (*to each other*).   Round the corner, etc.

ENSEMBLE.

OFFICERS.   LADIES.
Now is not this ridiculous, etc.   In a doleful train, etc.   260

COL. Angela! what is the meaning of this?
ANG. Oh, sir, leave us; our minds are but ill-tuned to light love-talk.
MAJ. But what in the world has come over you all?
JANE. Bunthorne! *He* has come over us. He has come among us, and he
has idealized us.
                                                                           265
DUKE. Has he succeeded in idealizing *you*?
JANE. He has!
DUKE. Good old Bunthorne!
JANE. My eyes are open; I droop despairingly; I am soulfully intense; I am
limp and I cling!
                                                                           270

(*During this* BUNTHORNE *is seen in all the agonies of composition. The
Maidens are watching him intently as he writhes. At last he hits on the word he
wants and writes it down. A general sense of relief.*)

BUN. Finished! At last! Finished!

(*He staggers, overcome with the mental strain, into arms of* COLONEL.)   275

COL. Are you better now?
BUN. Yes – oh, it's you – I am better now. The poem is finished, and my
soul had gone out into it. That was all. It was nothing worth mentioning,
it occurs three times a day. (*Sees* PATIENCE, *who has entered during this
scene.*) Ah, Patience! Dear Patience! (*Holds her hand; she seems frightened.*)   280

287 *a . . . fleshly thing*: Something carnal or sensual. In describing Bunthorne as a fleshly poet, Gilbert was not just referring to his size but was establishing him as a true member of the Pre-Raphaelite Brotherhood. In 1871 the poet Robert Buchanan created a sensation in the literary world by publishing a violent attack on the works of Algernon Swinburne, William Morris, Dante Gabriel Rossetti and their followers under the title 'The Fleshly School of Poetry'. The Pre-Raphaelites were furious and vigorously counter- attacked.

292 *think of faint lilies*: Bunthorne has a thing about lilies – he mentions them twice in his patter song ('A languid love for lilies does *not* blight me' and 'If you walk down Piccadilly with a poppy or a lily in your mediæval hand'). They were very much associated with the Pre-Raphaelites, for whom they were a symbol of both purity and beauty. They figure as such in Dante Gabriel Rossetti's painting *The Blessed Damozel*. Oscar Wilde had a particular passion for the flower, and in Max Beerbohm's famous cartoon, *Rossetti's name is heard in America*, he is depicted clasping an enormous and distinctly faint lily in his left hand.

297 *amaranthine asphodel*: More lilies. 'Amaranthine' means everlasting and was applied by the ancient Greeks particularly to flowers that never fade. The asphodel is a member of the lily family, associated with death and the underworld in Greek mythology. The word daffodil is a corruption of 'asphodel'. So this expression could be rendered into plain, modern English as 'fadeless daffodil'. Like the allusion above to faint lilies, this reference provides important ammunition for those who maintain that Bunthorne is based on Oscar Wilde. The reporter from the *Sporting Times* described Wilde's presence at the first night of *Patience* in these words: 'There with the sacred daffodil . . . stood the exponent of uncut hair'.

300 *calomel*: Mercurous chloride, used medicinally as a laxative.

302 *colocynth*: Another strong purgative, derived from the pulp of a bitter apple or gourd-like fruit.

303 *aloe*: I cannot do better than quote the *Oxford English Dictionary*'s definition: 'A nauseous bitter purgative, procured from the inspissated juice of the plant.' The aloe plant itself is a shrub found mostly in South Africa. The purgative drug is extracted from its leaves.

ANG. Will it please you read it to us, sir?
SAPH. This we supplicate. (*All kneel.*)
BUN. Shall I?
ALL THE DRAGOONS. No!
BUN. (*annoyed – to* PATIENCE). I will read it if *you* bid me!   285
PA. (*much frightened*). You can if you like!
BUN. It is a wild, weird, fleshly thing; yet very tender, very yearning, very precious. It is called, 'Oh, Hollow! Hollow! Hollow!'
PA. Is it a hunting song?
BUN. A hunting song? No, it is *not* a hunting song. It is the wail of the   290
poet's heart on discovering that everything is commonplace. To understand it, cling passionately to one another and think of faint lilies. (*They do so as he recites*) –

'OH, HOLLOW! HOLLOW! HOLLOW!'

What time the poet hath hymned
The writhing maid, lithe-limbed,   295
  Quivering on amaranthine asphodel,
How can he paint her woes,
Knowing, as well he knows,
  That all can be set right with calomel?   300

When from the poet's plinth
The amorous colocynth
  Yearns for the aloe, faint with rapturous thrills,
How can he hymn their throes
Knowing, as well he knows,   305
  That they are only uncompounded pills?

Is it, and can it be,
Nature hath this decree,
  Nothing poetic in the world shall dwell?
Or that in all her works
Something poetic lurks,   310
  Even in colocynth and calomel?
            I cannot tell.

(*Exit* BUNTHORNE.)

ANG. How purely fragrant!
SAPH. How earnestly precious!   315
PA. Well, it seems to me to be nonsense.
SAPH. Nonsense, yes, perhaps – but oh, what precious nonsense!
COL. This is all very well, but you seem to forget that you are engaged to us.
      320

321 *Empyrean*: Celestial, pertaining to the highest heaven or the abode of God and the angels. At the beginning of Act II of *Princess Ida* the girl graduates sing that they have already taken several easy flights

> Towards the empyrean heights
> Of every kind of lore.

Della Cruscan: The Accademia della Crusca was an institute founded in Florence in the sixteenth century and dedicated to purifying the Italian language. The name was adopted in the late eighteenth century by a group of English poets who were noted for their affected sentimentality.

322 *Early English*: The style of architecture which succeeded the Norman, characterized by pointed arches and lancet windows. It was much favoured by Victorian medievalists and Pre-Raphaelites.

324 *Primary colours*: In general, the Pre-Raphaelites scorned bold, primary colours and preferred to paint in more sombre or pastel shades like the cobwebby grey velvet, with the bloom like cold gravy, so beloved by Lady Jane.

324–5 *Oh, South Kensington*: South Kensington, with its famous School of Design and its recently established museums, was one of the cultural centres of London in the 1880s and a fashionable haunt of artists and Bohemians. Gilbert himself lived in the area, although he would hardly have counted himself among the aesthetic brotherhood.

331 *something Japanese*: A reminder of that penchant for Japanese *objets d'art* among the English upper classes in the 1880s which was to be one of the inspirations for *The Mikado*.

336 *A uniform*: In his earlier clerical version, where Gilbert had already used the phrase about 'the field of Mars' and 'the courts of Venus' in his opening chorus for the soldiers, he rendered this line: 'A uniform that is accustomed to carry everything before it'.

338–69 *When I first put this uniform on*
Gilbert wrote this song from the heart. He himself could not resist the lure of the uniform. As a young man he wanted very much to go into the Royal Artillery. However, the ending of the Crimean War in 1856 when he was just twenty meant that no more officers were required in the regular Army. He consoled himself by joining the militia and was for twenty years an officer in the Royal Aberdeenshire Highlanders, later the 3rd Battalion of the Gordon Highlanders. He retired with the honorary rank of major in 1883. Sixteen years later, at the age of sixty-three, he volunteered for service in the South African War against the Boers.

346 *Hessians*: High boots with tassels, originally worn by the cavalry in the German state of Hesse and later copied by other European armies.

348 *A fact that I counted upon*: In the earlier clerical version this line was 'Like Elkington's window I shone'. Elkington's was a Birmingham firm which in 1840 patented the technique of electroplating silver and was famous for its fine displays of silver-plate.

352 *occurred to me*: Early editions of the libretto and the Macmillan edition add an extra syllable to this line by ending it 'occurred to me, too'.

SAPH. It can never be. You are not Empyrean. You are not Della Cruscan. You are not even Early English. Oh, be Early English ere it is too late!
(*Officers look at each other in astonishment.*)

JANE (*looking at uniform*). Red and Yellow! Primary colours! Oh, South Kensington!

DUKE. We didn't design our uniforms, but we don't see how they could be improved.

JANE. No, you wouldn't. Still, there *is* a cobwebby grey velvet, with a tender bloom like cold gravy, which, made Florentine fourteenth-century, trimmed with Venetian leather and Spanish altar lace, and surmounted with something Japanese – it matters not what – would at least be Early English! Come, maidens.

(*Exeunt Maidens, two and two, singing refrain of 'Twenty love-sick maidens we'. The Officers watch them off in astonishment.*)

DUKE. Gentlemen, this is an insult to the British uniform —

COL. A uniform that has been as successful in the courts of Venus as on the field of Mars!

SONG – COLONEL.

When I first put this uniform on,
  I said, as I looked in the glass,
    'It's one to a million
    That any civilian
My figure and form will surpass.
  Gold lace has a charm for the fair,
  And I've plenty of that, and to spare,
    While a lover's professions,
    When uttered in Hessians,
Are eloquent everywhere!'
    A fact that I counted upon,
    When I first put this uniform on!

CHORUS OF DRAGOONS.

By a simple coincidence, few
    Could ever have counted upon,
  The same thing occurred to me,
    When I first put this uniform on!

COL.
    I said, when I first put it on,
    'It is plain to the veriest dunce

361 *But the peripatetics*: 'Peripatetics' is the term given to the philosophy of Aristotle, who
     used to walk about as he taught his followers. In the clerical version this and the next
     line had an ecclesiastical flavour:

>   The glitter ecstatic
>   Of cope and dalmatic . . .

370 *The Dragoons go off angrily*: In the licence copy, the maidens remain on stage for the sing-
     ing of 'When I first put this uniform on', and this stage direction reads: '*Dragoons go off
     angrily, left. The ladies go off two and two, right, looking back from time to time sorrowfully at
     Bunthorne. They sing refrain of "In a melancholy train"*. PATIENCE *goes with them.*'

373–96 *Am I alone*
     With Bunthorne on the verge of his famous confessional patter song, this is, perhaps, a
     good point at which to consider the nature of his character.
        J. M. Gordon, who in his fifty-six years with the D'Oyly Carte Company had more
     time than most to reflect on the characters in the operas, summed up Bunthorne thus:
     'He is not a young man, but middle-aged, and can be classed as one of the "New Rich",
     a definite humbug! His aestheticism is to get admiration.'
        Several different candidates have been put forward over the years as the most likely
     model for Bunthorne. The first-night reviewer for *The Times* was convinced that the
     fleshly poet was based on Algernon Swinburne, the distinctly affected and languid poet
     who had led the Pre-Raphaelites' counter-attack against Robert Buchanan's criticism of
     their work in 'The Fleshly School of Poetry'. In support of this thesis, an American
     scholar, John Bush Jones, has pointed out (in an essay in *W. S. Gilbert: A Century of Scho-
     larship and Commentary*, New York, 1970) that the metres of Bunthorne's two poems,
     'Oh, Hollow! Hollow! Hollow!' and 'Heart Foam', are similar to those used by Swin-
     burne, as are the structure and use of words.
        Sir Henry Lytton, who played the part many times between 1895 and 1934, was, how-
     ever, equally emphatic that Bunthorne was modelled on the artist James Whistler, whose
     libel action against Ruskin almost certainly helped to inspire Gilbert's parody of the jea-
     lousy of the artistic world. Many others have seen Bunthorne as essentially a caricature
     of Oscar Wilde, famous for his worship of lilies, blue-and-white china and things Japa-
     nese. It was, indeed, Wilde whom D'Oyly Carte sent to the U.S.A. to publicize *Patience*,
     but against his claim to be regarded as the main model for Bunthorne must be set the
     fact that, unlike both Swinburne and Whistler, he was still very little known in 1881. His
     first volume of poems, for example, did not appear until three months after the opera
     was first performed.
        The truth is almost certainly that Gilbert had no single model for the part but drew
     on the distinctive characteristics and mannerisms of several of the leading aesthetes of
     the time. When George Grossmith first appeared on stage in the role of Bunthorne he
     had the white lock of hair and eyeglass which were Whistler's hallmarks, a velvet coat of
     the kind worn by Walter Crane, the designer and engraver, and the velvet breeches asso-
     ciated with Wilde. Audrey Williamson has also spotted traces of Edward Burne-Jones
     and Dante Gabriel Rossetti in Bunthorne's make-up. Perhaps we should simply con-
     clude that he is a kind of all-purpose super-aesthetical Pre-Raphaelite figure.

That every beauty
Will feel it her duty
To yield to its glamour at once.
They will see that I'm freely gold-laced
In a uniform handsome and chaste' –   360
But the peripatetics
Of long-haired æsthetics
Are very much more to their taste –
Which I never counted upon,
When I first put this uniform on!   365

CHORUS.   By a simple coincidence, few
Could ever have reckoned upon,
I didn't anticipate that,
When I first put this uniform on!

(*The Dragoons go off angrily.*)   370

(*Enter* BUNTHORNE, *who changes his manner and
becomes intensely melodramatic.*)

RECITATIVE AND SONG – BUNTHORNE.

Am I alone,
And unobserved? I am!
Then let me own
I'm an æsthetic sham!   375
This air severe
Is but a mere
Veneer!
This cynic smile
Is but a wile   380
Of guile!
This costume chaste
Is but good taste
Misplaced!   385
Let me confess!
A languid love for lilies does *not* blight me!
Lank limbs and haggard cheeks do *not* delight me!
I do *not* care for dirty greens
By any means.   390

I do *not* long for all one sees
That's Japanese.
I am *not* fond of uttering platitudes
In stained-glass attitudes.

397 *If you're anxious for to shine*: In an early prompt-book in the D'Oyly Carte archives, almost
     certainly prepared for the 1907 revival of *Patience*, the word 'anxious' has been altered in
     Gilbert's handwriting to 'eager'. The song appears to have been sung in this latter form
     in early D'Oyly Carte productions, but 'eager' does not appear in any printed copies of
     the libretto.

406 *the reign of good Queen Anne*: 1702–14, in case you like to know these things.

408 *the Empress Josephine*: Marie Josèphe Rose Tascher de la Pagerie, to give her her full name,
     was born in 1763 and married Napoleon Bonaparte in 1796. During her husband's con-
     sulate and empire, she held a brilliant court and helped to confirm the reputation of
     Paris as the artistic capital of the world.

414 *à la Plato*: Platonic love is a condition of friendship and affection in which sexuality plays
     no part. The Greek philosopher originally applied the concept to Socrates' love for
     young men, which, he maintained, was entirely pure, though not quite as pure, perhaps,
     as an attachment to a potato or French bean.

416 *with a poppy or a lily in your mediæval hand*: A very Wildean touch (see the note to line 292
     above). The poppy was another flower much favoured by the Pre-Raphaelites. It appears
     prominently in Rossetti's famous painting *Beata Beatrix*.

In short, my mediævalism's affectation,   395
Born of a morbid love of admiration!

SONG.

If you're anxious for to shine in the high æsthetic line as a man of culture
    rare,
You must get up all the germs of the transcendental terms, and plant
    them everywhere.
You must lie upon the daisies and discourse in novel phrases of your
    complicated state of mind,
The meaning doesn't matter if it's only idle chatter of a transcendental
    kind.
              And every one will say,   400
              As you walk your mystic way,
'If this young man expresses himself in terms too deep for *me*,
Why, what a very singularly deep young man this deep young man
    must be!'
Be eloquent in praise of the very dull old days which have long since
    passed away,
And convince 'em, if you can, that the reign of good Queen Anne was   405
    Culture's palmiest day.
Of course you will pooh-pooh whatever's fresh and new, and declare it's
    crude and mean,
For Art stopped short in the cultivated court of the Empress Josephine.
              And every one will say,
              As you walk your mystic way,   410
'If that's not good enough for him which is good enough for *me*,
Why, what a very cultivated kind of youth this kind of youth must be!'
Then a sentimental passion of a vegetable fashion must excite your languid
    spleen,
An attachment *à la* Plato for a bashful young potato, or a not-too-French
    French bean!
Though the Philistines may jostle, you will rank as an apostle in the high
    æsthetic band,   415
If you walk down Piccadilly with a poppy or a lily in your mediæval hand.
              And every one will say,
              As you walk your flowery way,
'If he's content with a vegetable love which would certainly not suit *me*,
Why, what a most particularly pure young man this pure young man
    must be!'
                              420

    (*At the end of his song* PATIENCE *enters. He sees her.*)

BUN. Ah! Patience, come hither. I am pleased with thee. The bitter-

425 *No, thanks, I have dined*: This line does not occur in the first-edition libretto and was probably an ad-lib made in early performances and later incorporated into the libretto.

443 *Elysian Fields*: The abode of the blessed in Greek mythology, and therefore the happy land. They turn up again in *Ruddigore* (Act I, line 706).

450–51 *If you are fond of touch-and-go jocularity*: Another probable ad-lib which was not in the first-edition libretto.

463 *Aceldama*: A field of blood, or scene of great slaughter. Aceldama was originally the potter's field near Jerusalem which was purchased with the money Judas had taken for betraying Christ (Matthew 27. 7–8). A correspondent to the *Gilbert and Sullivan Journal* in 1926 suggested that this line might provide the sole example in the Savoy Operas of a metrical error on the part of Gilbert. The name Aceldama should properly be pronounced 'Akel'dama' (with the accent on the 'kel'), but this would not scan properly and the word is always incorrectly pronounced with a soft 'c' and the accent on '*dama*'.

hearted one, who finds all else hollow, is pleased with thee. For you are not hollow. *Are* you?

PA. No, thanks, I have dined; but – I beg your pardon – I interrupt you. 425

BUN. Life is made up of interruptions. The tortured soul, yearning for solitude, writhes under them. Oh, but my heart is a-weary! Oh, I am a cursed thing! Don't go.

PA. Really, I'm very sorry —

BUN. Tell me, girl, do you ever yearn? 430

PA. (*misunderstanding him*). I earn my living.

BUN. (*impatiently*). No, no! Do you know what it is to be heart-hungry? Do you know what it is to yearn for the Indefinable, and yet to be brought face to face, daily, with the Multiplication Table? Do you know what it is to seek oceans and to find puddles? – to long for whirlwinds and yet to have to 435 do the best you can with the bellows? That's my case. Oh, I am a cursed thing! Don't go.

PA. If you please, I don't understand you – you frighten me!

BUN. Don't be frightened – it's only poetry.

PA. Well, if that's poetry, I don't like poetry. 440

BUN. (*eagerly*). Don't you? (*Aside.*) Can I trust her? (*Aloud.*) Patience, you don't like poetry – well, between you and me, *I* don't like poetry. It's hollow, unsubstantial – unsatisfactory. What's the use of yearning for Elysian Fields when you know you can't get 'em, and would only let 'em out on building leases if you had 'em? 445

PA. Sir, I —

BUN. Patience, I have long loved you. Let me tell you a secret. I am not as bilious as I look. If you like, I will cut my hair. There is more innocent fun within me than a casual spectator would imagine. You have never seen me frolicsome. Be a good girl – a very good girl – and one day you shall. If you 450 are fond of touch-and-go jocularity – this is the shop for it.

PA. Sir, I will speak plainly. In the matter of love I am untaught. I have never loved but my great-aunt. But I am quite certain that, under any circumstances, I couldn't possibly love *you*.

BUN. Oh, you think not? 455

PA. I'm quite sure of it. Quite sure. Quite.

BUN. Very good. Life is henceforth a blank. I don't care what becomes of me. I have only to ask that you will not abuse my confidence; though *you* despise me, I am extremely popular with the other young ladies.

PA. I only ask that you will leave me and never renew the subject. 460

BUN. Certainly. Broken-hearted and desolate, I go. (*Recites.*)

> 'Oh, to be wafted away
>   From this black Aceldama of sorrow,
> Where the dust of an earthy to-day
>   Is the earth of a dusty to-morrow!' 465

477–8 *the abstraction of refinement*: In the first-night libretto, the dialogue continued at this point:

> ANG. [*continuing*] . . . the idealization of utter unselfishness.
> PA. Love is?
> ANG. Yes.
> PA. Dear me. Go on.
> ANG. True love refines, purifies, elevates, exalts, and chastens. It is the one romantic feature in this chaos of materialism; it is the one unselfish emotion in this whirlpool of grasping greed!

497–519 *Long years ago*
There was originally a second verse to this song, cut soon after the opening night:

> PA.   Time fled, and one unhappy day –
>   The first I'd ever known –
>   They took my little friend away,
>   And left me weeping all alone!
>   Ah, how I sobbed, and how I cried,
>   Then I fell ill and nearly died,
>   And even now I weep apace
>   When I recall that baby face!
>   We had one hope – one heart – one will –
>   One life, in one employ;
>   And though it's not material, still
>   He was a little *boy*!
>
> ANG.   Ah, old, old tale of Cupid's touch, etc.
>
> PA.   Pray don't misconstrue what I say, etc.
>
> ANG.   No doubt, yet spite of all your pains, etc.
>
> PA.   Ah, yes, in spite of all my pains, etc.

It is a little thing of my own. I call it 'Heart Foam'. I shall not publish it.
Farewell! Patience, Patience, farewell!

(*Exit* BUNTHORNE.)

PA. What on earth does it all mean? Why does he love me? Why does he
expect me to love him? He's not a relation! It frightens me! 470

(*Enter* ANGELA.)

ANG. Why, Patience, what is the matter?

PA. Lady Angela, tell me two things. Firstly, what on earth is this love
that upsets everybody; and, secondly, how is it to be distinguished from
insanity?

ANG. Poor blind child! Oh, forgive her, Eros! Why, love is of all passions 475
the most essential! It is the embodiment of purity, the abstraction of
refinement! It is the one unselfish emotion in this whirlpool of grasping
greed!

PA. Oh, dear, oh! (*Beginning to cry.*)

ANG. Why are you crying? 480

PA. To think that I have lived all these years without having experienced
this ennobling and unselfish passion! Why, what a wicked girl I must be! For
it *is* unselfish, isn't it?

ANG. Absolutely! Love that is tainted with selfishness is no love. Oh, 485
try, try to love! It really isn't difficult if you give your whole mind to it.

PA. I'll set about it at once. I won't go to bed until I'm head over ears in
love with somebody.

ANG. Noble girl! But is it possible that you have never loved anybody?

PA. Yes, one. 490

ANG. Ah! Whom?

PA. My great-aunt—

ANG. Great-aunts don't count.

PA. Then there's nobody. At least – no, nobody. Not since I was a baby.
But *that* doesn't count, I suppose. 495

ANG. I don't know. Tell me about it.

DUET – PATIENCE *and* ANGELA.

Long years ago – fourteen, maybe –
  When but a tiny babe of four,
Another baby played with me,
  My elder by a year or more;
A little child of beauty rare, 500
With marvellous eyes and wondrous hair,

520   *It's perfectly dreadful*: This line originally began: 'It's perfectly appalling to think of the
      dreadful state'.

523   *Enter Grosvenor*: The character of the idyllic poet and arch-rival to Bunthorne is well
      summed-up by J. M. Gordon: 'Grosvenor is quite sincere and although undoubtedly
      vain and conceited, he embraced aestheticism because he thought he had a mission to
      keep beautiful'. Many Gilbert and Sullivan scholars have seen Oscar Wilde as the main
      model for Grosvenor, but in his essay 'In Search of Archibald Grosvenor: A New Look
      at Gilbert's *Patience*', John Bush Jones convincingly advances the claims of William Mor-
      ris, the poet, designer and pioneer socialist, and Coventry Patmore, the Pre-Raphaelite
      Roman Catholic poet (see the notes to line 575 and Act II, lines 60–61).

524–51 *Prithee, pretty maiden*
      This delightful duet was sung by Derek Oldham and Sylvia Cecil at a party in the White
      House, Washington, before the presidential inauguration of Franklin D. Roosevelt, a
      keen Gilbert and Sullivan enthusiast.

           Who, in my child-eyes, seemed to me
           All that a little child should be!
              Ah, how we loved, that child and I!   505
                How pure our baby joy!
           How true our love – and, by the by,
              He was a little boy!

ANG.   Ah, old, old tale of Cupid's touch!
           I thought as much – I thought as much!   510
              He *was* a little boy!
PA. (*shocked*).   Pray don't misconstrue what I say –
           Remember, pray – remember, pray,
              He was a *little* boy!

ANG.   No doubt! Yet, spite of all your pains,   515
           The interesting fact remains –
              He was a little *boy*!

ENSEMBLE.   { Ah, yes, in } spite of all { my   } pains, etc.
            { No doubt! Yet, }   { your }

                          (*Exit* ANGELA.)

    PA. It's perfectly dreadful to think of the appalling state I must be in! I 520
had no idea that love was a duty. No wonder they all look so unhappy! Upon
my word, I hardly like to associate with myself. I don't think I'm respectable.
I'll go at once and fall in love with — (*Enter* GROSVENOR.) A stranger!

          DUET – PATIENCE *and* GROSVENOR.

GROS.   Prithee, pretty maiden – prithee, tell me true,
            (Hey, but I'm doleful, willow willow waly!) 525
          Have you e'er a lover a-dangling after you?
              Hey willow waly O!
                I would fain discover
                If you have a lover?
              Hey willow waly O!   530

PA.   Gentle sir, my heart is frolicsome and free –
            (Hey, but he's doleful, willow willow waly!)
          Nobody I care for comes a-courting me –
              Hey willow waly O!
                Nobody I care for
                Comes a-courting – therefore,   535
              Hey willow waly O!

540 *I'm a man of propertee*: This admission and the subsequent comment 'Money, I despise it'
are cited by John Bush Jones in support of his thesis that Grosvenor is at least partly
based on William Morris. Without his own comfortable middle-class upbringing, and
the £900 annual income which he inherited at the age of twenty-one, it is doubtful if
Morris could ever have embarked on the 'holy warfare' against the forces of capitalism
which occupied most of his life.

556 *your Archibald*: Gilbert at first gave Grosvenor the Christian name Algernon, but changed it to Archibald when it was pointed out that a member of the Duke of Westminster's
family had the name Algernon Grosvenor. 'Algernon' appears throughout in the licence
copy, and it survived in one or two places in the first edition (see the note to line 608).

557 *Chronos*: The Greek word for time, which has given us such terms as chronicle and
chronological.

561 *I am much taller and much stouter*: Gilbert originally wrote this line: 'I am much taller and a
little stouter than I was'. He apparently altered it to suit the dimensions of the artist
playing Grosvenor at a revival.

569–70 *to be madly loved at first sight*: As performed on the first night, the dialogue continued at
this point:

> GROS. [*continuing*] . . . by every woman who sets eyes on me!
> PA. Horrible indeed!
> GROS. Ah, Patience, you may thank your stars that you are not cursed with the fatal gift
> of beauty. It has been my bane through life!
> PA. But why do you make yourself so picturesque, etc.

572 *to escape this persecution*: At this point in an early proof copy is added in red ink: 'A paste-
board nose would do it'.

575 *I am a trustee for Beauty*: John Bush Jones cites this line and Grosvenor's subsequent remark 'I am the Apostle of Simplicity' as further evidence that he is based on William
Morris, who was well known for his strong views that objects should be both beautiful
and simple.

579 *for I am infallible*: The use of the word 'infallible', which does not appear in the licence
copy, may possibly be a survival from Gilbert's earlier clerical version of *Patience*. The
phrase 'Apostle of Simplicity' is, perhaps, also more appropriate to a clergyman than a
poet.

GROS.	Prithee, pretty maiden, will you marry me?
	(Hey, but I'm hopeful, willow willow waly!)
	I may say, at once, I'm a man of propertee – 540
	Hey willow waly O!
	Money, I despise it;
	Many people prize it,
	Hey willow waly O!
PA.	Gentle sir, although to marry I design – 545
	(Hey, but he's hopeful, willow willow waly!)
	As yet I do not know you, and so I must decline.
	Hey willow waly O!
	To other maidens go you –
	As yet I do not know you,
BOTH.	Hey willow waly O! 550

GROS. Patience! Can it be that you don't recognize me?

PA. Recognize you? No, indeed I don't!

GROS. Have fifteen years so greatly changed me?

PA. Fifteen years? What do you mean?   555

GROS. Have you forgotten the friend of your youth, your Archibald? – your little playfellow? Oh, Chronos, Chronos, this is too bad of you!

PA. Archibald! Is it possible? Why, let me look! It is! It is! It must be! Oh, how happy I am! I thought we should never meet again! And how you've grown!   560

GROS. Yes, Patience, I am much taller and much stouter than I was.

PA. And how you've improved!

GROS. Yes, Patience, I am very beautiful! (*Sighs.*)

PA. But surely *that* doesn't make you unhappy?

GROS. Yes, Patience. Gifted as I am with a beauty which probably has   565 not its rival on earth, I am, nevertheless, utterly and completely miserable.

PA. Oh – but why?

GROS. My child-love for you has never faded. Conceive, then, the horror of my situation when I tell you that it is my hideous destiny to be madly loved at first sight by every woman I come across!   570

PA. But why do you make yourself so picturesque? Why not disguise yourself, disfigure yourself, anything to escape this persecution?

GROS. No, Patience, that may not be. These gifts – irksome as they are – were given to me for the enjoyment and delectation of my fellow-creatures. I am a trustee for Beauty, and it is my duty to see that the conditions of my   575 trust are faithfully discharged.

PA. And you, too, are a Poet?

GROS. Yes, I am the Apostle of Simplicity. I am called 'Archibald the All-Right' – for I am infallible!

587 *We will never, never part*: In the first edition, Patience had a longer line at this point: 'The purifying gift – the ennobling influence has descended upon me, and I am inconceivably happy! We will never, never part!'

598 *To monopolize those features*: Another line which was originally longer. As first performed, it ran: 'To monopolize those features on which all women love to linger; to keep to myself those attributes which were designed for the enjoyment and delectation of my fellow creatures? It would be unpardonable!'

608 *Farewell, Archibald*: This line was not changed from 'Farewell, Algernon' until the fifth edition of the libretto was published in the early 1910s.

616–22 *Though to marry you would very selfish be*
The licence copy has a new duet for Patience and Grosvenor here instead of the reprise of 'Prithee, pretty maiden' which they now sing:

PA.   Love me with a love enduring –
                           You have my complete permission –
                       Think of everything alluring
                           In my girlish disposition.
                       I shall sneer, but you must flatter –
                       I shall scoff, but that don't matter –
                           Let no slight your passion tame –
                           Go on loving just the same!

ENSEMBLE.   Ah, true love, celestial vision,
                           How unselfish is your aim –
                       Though { I treat him / she treats him } with derision,
                       He will / I shall } love { me / her } just the same!

GROS.   Though I burn with hopeless passion,
                           Don't surrender, I implore you –
                       Though I perish, Romeo fashion,
                           Keep your duty well before you!
                       Act the cold imperious beauty –
                       Keep me off – it is your duty –
                       Cover me with scorn and shame –
                           I shall love you just the same!

ENSEMBLE.   Ah, true love, celestial vision, etc.

The above number was cut out before rehearsals began. At rehearsal, however, Gilbert and Sullivan realized that at the end of their passage of dialogue Patience and Grosvenor were left on stage with no reason to get off and make way for the finale. The coda of 'Prithee, pretty maiden' was introduced so that they could sing themselves off the stage. It does not appear in early American libretti nor in the 1881 or 1900 editions of the vocal score.

PA. And is it possible that you condescend to love such a girl as I? 580

GROS. Yes, Patience, is it not strange? I have loved you with a Florentine fourteenth-century frenzy for full fifteen years!

PA. Oh, marvellous! I have hitherto been deaf to the voice of love. I seem now to know what love is! It has been revealed to me – it is Archibald Grosvenor!

GROS. Yes, Patience, it is! 585

PA. (*as in a trance*). We will never, never part!

GROS. We will live and die together!

PA. I swear it!

GROS. We both swear it!

PA. (*recoiling from him*). But – oh, horror! 590

GROS. What's the matter?

PA. Why, you are perfection! A source of endless ecstasy to all who know you!

GROS. I know I am. Well?

PA. Then, bless my heart, there can be nothing unselfish in loving *you*! 595

GROS. Merciful powers! I never thought of that!

PA. To monopolize those features on which all women love to linger! It would be unpardonable!

GROS. Why, so it would! Oh, fatal perfection, again you interpose 600 between me and my happiness!

PA. Oh, if you were but a thought less beautiful than you are!

GROS. Would that I were; but candour compels me to admit that I'm not!

PA. Our duty is clear; we must part, and for ever! 605

GROS. Oh, misery! And yet I cannot question the propriety of your decision. Farewell, Patience!

PA. Farewell, Archibald! But stay!

GROS. Yes, Patience?

PA. Although I may not love *you* – for you are perfection – there is 610 nothing to prevent your loving *me*. I am plain, homely, unattractive!

GROS. Why, that's true!

PA. The love of such a man as you for such a girl as I must be unselfish!

GROS. Unselfishness itself! 615

DUET – PATIENCE *and* GROSVENOR.

PA.	Though to marry you would very selfish be –
GROS.	Hey, but I'm doleful – willow willow waly!
PA.	You may, all the same, continue loving me –
GROS.	Hey willow waly O!
BOTH.	All the world ignoring, 620

630 *Pandæan pleasure*: Pan, the Greek god who presided over shepherds and their flocks, de-
     lighted in rural music and was often portrayed playing his row of pipes. The word Pan-
     daean was used in the nineteenth century to describe those who played the pipes of Pan.
631 *Daphnephoric*: In Greek mythology Daphne, the daughter of a river-god, was turned into
     a bay tree to avoid the amorous advances of Apollo.

You'll } go on adoring –
I'll }

Hey willow waly O!

(*At the end, exeunt despairingly, in opposite directions.*)

FINALE – ACT I.

(*Enter* BUNTHORNE, *crowned with roses and hung about with garlands, and looking very miserable. He is led by* ANGELA *and* SAPHIR (*each of whom holds an end of the rose-garland by which he is bound*), *and accompanied by procession of Maidens. They are dancing classically, and playing on cymbals, double pipes, and other archaic instruments.*)

625

CHORUS.

Let the merry cymbals sound,
　Gaily pipe Pandæan pleasure,
With a Daphnephoric bound
　Tread a gay but classic measure,
　Tread a gay but classic measure.
Every heart with hope is beating,
For at this exciting meeting
　Fickle Fortune will decide
　Who shall be our Bunthorne's bride!

630

635

(*Enter Dragoons, led by* COLONEL, MAJOR, *and* DUKE.
They are surprised at proceedings.)

CHORUS OF DRAGOONS.

　Now tell us, we pray you,
　Why thus they array you –
　Oh, poet, how say you –
　　What is it you've done?

640

DUKE.

　Of rite sacrificial,
　By sentence judicial,
　This seems the initial,
　　Then why don't you run?

645

COL.

　They cannot have led you
　To hang or behead you,
　Nor may they *all* wed you,
　　Unfortunate one!

650

658   *my solicitor*: Mr Bunthorne's solicitor must surely have the doubtful distinction of
      appearing for the shortest time on stage of any principal in the Savoy Operas. The Mid-
      shipman in *H.M.S. Pinafore* is another non-speaking role listed in the *Dramatis personæ*,
      but he is on stage for much of the First Act. Hercules, the page who appears in Act I of
      The Sorcerer, has an even briefer moment of glory, but his name does not appear in the
      Dramatis personæ and so, strictly speaking, he is not a principal as the Solicitor is.

659   *a deserving charity*: Bunthorne's raffling of himself in aid of a deserving charity has cer-
      tain similarities with another famous scene in operetta, when Danilo, the hero of Franz
      Lehár's *The Merry Widow* (1905), offers his dance with Anna Glawari to any of her many
      admirers for 10,000 francs, the proceeds to be devoted to missions overseas.

677–90 *Your maiden hearts, ah, do not steel*
      This splendid number, in which the soldiers show their emotions in perfect unison at
      the Duke's command, recalls two earlier verses with a similar theme, one by Gilbert
      and another by the mid-Victorian humorous dramatist James Robinson Planché.

      Planché's play *The Fair One with the Golden Locks* (1843) has the following scene, on
      which Gilbert may perhaps, either consciously or unconsciously, have drawn:

GRAND CHAMBERLAIN.
                    Yes, noble friends, the news is sad as may be,
                    Our mighty king is crying like a baby.
                    His nerves have had the cruellest of shocks –
                    Rejected by the Fair with Golden Locks,
                    He comes: prepare to show your loyal griefs,
                    If not by tears, at least by handkerchiefs,
                    Let every soldier draw out his bandanna
                    And bear't before him in a decent manner.

CAPTAIN OF THE GUARD.
                    Draw kerchiefs! (*Soldiers do so.*)
                    Present kerchiefs! (*They hold them to their eyes.*)
                    Steady there!
                    Eyes wet, long faces! Smile men, if you dare.
                    (*Enter King and ministers.*)
                    Recover kerchiefs!
                    (*Soldiers return handkerchiefs to their pockets.*)

      In his own Bab Ballad 'The Scornful Colonel', Gilbert portrayed an officer who gave
      his men six hours a day of sneering drill:

                    Now by your right, prepare to 'Whish'!
                    Come, all at once and smartly, 'Pish'!
                    Prepare to 'Bah'! By sections, 'Phew'!
                    Good, at three hundred yards, 'Pooh-Pooh'!

CHORUS OF DRAGOONS.

Then tell us, we pray you,
Why thus they array you –
Oh, poet, how say you –
    What is it you've done?

655

(*Enter* SOLICITOR.)

RECITATIVE – BUNTHORNE.

Heart-broken at my Patience's barbarity,
  By the advice of my solicitor (*introducing his Solicitor*),
In aid – in aid of a deserving charity,
  I've put myself up to be raffled for!

660

MAIDENS.   By the advice of his solicitor
             He's put himself up to be raffled for!

DRAGOONS.   Oh, horror! urged by his solicitor,
             He's put himself up to be raffled for!

MAIDENS.   Oh, heaven's blessing on his solicitor!

665

DRAGOONS.   A hideous curse on his solicitor!

(*The* SOLICITOR, *horrified at the Dragoons' curse, rushes off.*)

COL.   Stay, we implore you,
        Before our hopes are blighted;
     You see before you
        The men to whom you're plighted!

670

CHORUS OF DRAGOONS.

Stay, we implore you,
For we adore you;
To us you're plighted
To be united –
    Stay, we implore you!

675

SOLO – DUKE.

Your maiden hearts, ah, do not steel
To pity's eloquent appeal,
Such conduct British soldiers feel.

689   *A tear-drop dews each martial eye*: The same imagery occurs in the opening chorus to Act II
      of *The Pirates of Penzance* when General Stanley's daughters call on him to dry the tear
      'That dews that martial cheek'.

700   *blue-and-white . . . pottery*: Blue-and-white oriental ceramics were much in vogue in the
      late 1870s and early 1880s, particularly among followers of the aesthetic cult. Bunthorne
      later describes himself as 'A blue-and-white young man' (Act II, line 497). In her Act II
      aria in *H.M.S. Pinafore* Josephine sings of the 'Rare "blue and white"' in her father's lux-
      urious home.

709   *There's fish in the sea*: This line is based on the old English saying 'There's as good fish in
      the sea as ever came out of it', meaning that you shouldn't be disheartened if you have
      lost the chance of something good, because you'll soon get another. The saying is also
      paraphrased in the finales to Acts I and II of *The Mikado* in the line: 'There's lots of
      good fish in the sea'.

(*Aside to Dragoons.*)   Sigh, sigh, all sigh!   680
                                                    (*They all sigh.*)

                        To foeman's steel we rarely see
                        A British soldier bend the knee,
                        Yet, one and all, they kneel to ye –
(*Aside to Dragoons.*)   Kneel, kneel, all kneel!   685
                                                    (*They all kneel.*)

                        Our soldiers very seldom cry,
                        And yet – I need not tell you why –
                        A tear-drop dews each martial eye!
(*Aside to Dragoons.*)   Weep, weep, all weep!   690
                                                    (*They all weep.*)

                        ENSEMBLE.

                Our soldiers very seldom cry,
                And yet $\left\{ \begin{array}{c} \text{they} \\ \text{we} \end{array} \right\}$ need not tell $\left\{ \begin{array}{c} \text{us} \\ \text{you} \end{array} \right\}$ why –
                A tear-drop dews each martial eye!
                        Weep, weep, all weep!   695

                BUNTHORNE (*who has been impatient during this appeal*).

Come, walk up, and purchase with avidity,
Overcome your diffidence and natural timidity,
Tickets for the raffle should be purchased with rapidity,
        Put in half a guinea and a husband you may gain –
Such a judge of blue-and-white and other kinds of pottery –   700
From early Oriental down to modern terra-cotta-ry –
Put in half a guinea – you may draw him in a lottery –
        Such an opportunity may not occur again.

CHORUS.   Such a judge of blue-and-white, etc.

        (*Maidens crowd up to purchase tickets; during this Dragoons dance   705
            in single file round stage, to express their indifference.*)

DRAGOONS.   We've been thrown over, we're aware
                        But we don't care – but we don't care!
                        There's fish in the sea, no doubt of it,

719 *Maidens blindfold themselves*: This is not the only occasion in the Savoy Operas when characters are blindfolded on stage. In Act I of *The Gondoliers* Marco and Giuseppe Palmieri
have handkerchiefs tied over their eyes before selecting the girls they will marry.

727 *Jane puts hand in bag*: The first-edition libretto has a slightly different stage direction at
this point: 'JANE *draws a paper, and is about to open it, when* PATIENCE *enters.* PATIENCE
snatches paper from JANE *and tears it up.*'

739 *If you, with one so lowly, still*: In the licence copy the Dragoons and Bunthorne are given
this and the next three lines to repeat before all sing 'Oh, shameless one!'

As good as ever came out of it,
And some day we shall get our share,
So we don't care – so we don't care!

710

(During this the Maidens have been buying tickets. At last JANE *presents herself.* BUNTHORNE *looks at her with aversion.)*

RECITATIVE.

BUN.   And are *you* going a ticket for to buy?
JANE (*surprised*). Most certainly I am; why shouldn't I?   715
BUN. (*aside*).   Oh, Fortune, this is hard! (*Aloud.*) Blindfold your eyes;
       Two minutes will decide who wins the prize!
        (Maidens blindfold themselves.)

CHORUS OF MAIDENS.

Oh, Fortune, to my aching heart be kind!
Like us, thou art blindfolded, but not blind! (*Each uncovers one eye.*) 720
Just raise your bandage, thus, that you may see,
And give the prize, and give the prize to me! (*They cover their eyes again.*)
BUN. Come, Lady Jane, I pray you draw the first!
JANE (*joyfully*). He loves me best!
BUN. (*aside*).   I want to know the worst!   725

*(*JANE *puts hand in bag to draw ticket.* PATIENCE *enters and prevents her doing so.)*

PA. Hold! Stay your hand!
ALL (*uncovering their eyes*). What means this interference?
  Of this bold girl I pray you make a clearance!   730
JANE. Away with you, away with you, and to your milk-pails go!
BUN. (*suddenly*). She wants a ticket! Take a dozen!
PA.   No!

SOLO – PATIENCE (*kneeling to* BUNTHORNE).

Ah! If there be pardon in your breast
  For this poor penitent,   735
Who, with remorseful thought opprest,
  Sincerely doth repent;
If you, with one so lowly, still
  Desire to be allied,
Then you may take me, if you will,   740
  For I will be your bride!

770 *Exactly so*: In the licence copy this last 'Exactly so!' is given to the Dragoons, who then
continue:

> It's very clear the maiden who
> Devotes herself to loving you
> Is prompted by no selfish view –

BUN. (*meekly*).   Exactly so!

The Dragoons now dance round the stage and then repeat their chorus 'We've been
thrown over, we're aware'. After this, the licence copy has a solo for the Colonel, sung as
an aside to the audience:

> Oh, do not suppose that a Heavy Dragoon
>   Can throw off a blighted affection so soon!
> Don't judge by our actions or words, we beseech,
>   For our hearts are as soft as an over-ripe peach,
> And though we assume an indifferent air,
>   'Tis but to conceal our enduring despair;
> If you knew what we suffer, you wouldn't impugn
>   That pink of perfection – a Heavy Dragoon!

SAPH.   Are you resolved, etc.

777–84 *I hear the soft note*
François Cellier, who conducted the first run of *Patience*, wrote that this was easily the
best number in the opera:

> Here the composer gives a remarkable exhibition of his genius for adapting music to the
> occasion. Moreover, it is a striking instance of Gilbert's appreciation of his colleague's
> music. In order to give the best effect to the sestette, it was sung by principals and chorus
> without the slightest movement or action on the stage. In other words, precisely as it might
> be rendered on a concert platform, except that Gilbert took special pains as regards the
> picturesque and most effective grouping of the company.

Although described as a sestet, 'I hear the soft note' can equally be described as a madrigal (see the note to *Ruddigore*, Act I, lines 870–903).

ALL.   Oh, shameless one!
                           Oh, bold-faced thing!
                        Away you run,   745
                           Go, take you wing,
                        You shameless one!
                           You bold-faced thing!

BUN.   How strong is love! For many and many a week
                        She's loved me fondly and has feared to speak,   750
                        But Nature, for restraint too mighty far,
                        Has burst the bonds of Art – and here we are!

PA.   No, Mr Bunthorne, no – you're wrong again;
                        Permit me – I'll endeavour to explain!

SONG – PATIENCE.

PA.   True love must single-hearted be –
BUN.   Exactly so!   755
PA.   From every selfish fancy free –
BUN.   Exactly so!
PA.   No idle thought of gain or joy
          A maiden's fancy should employ –
          True love must be without alloy.   760
ALL.   Exactly so!
PA.   Imposture to contempt must lead –
COL.   Exactly so!
PA.   Blind vanity's dissension's seed –
MAJ.   Exactly so!   765
PA.   It follows, then, a maiden who
          Devotes herself to loving you (*indicating* BUNTHORNE)
          Is prompted by no selfish view –
ALL.   Exactly so!   770

SAPH.   Are you resolved to wed this shameless one?
ANG.   Is there no chance for any other?
BUN. (*decisively*).   None! (*Embraces* PATIENCE.)
                        (*Exeunt* PATIENCE *and* BUNTHORNE.)

(ANGELA, SAPHIR, *and* ELLA *take* COLONEL, DUKE, *and* MAJOR   775
    down, while Maidens gaze fondly at other Officers.)

SESTET.

I hear the soft note of the echoing voice
Of an old, old love, long dead –

783–4 *And never, oh never . . . old, old love again*: The tune to which these lines are sung bears a striking resemblance to the last four bars of the Victorian hymn tune *Pilgrims*, composed by Henry Smart for R. W. Faber's hymn 'Hark! hark, my soul! angelic songs are swelling'.

807–15 *ENSEMBLE*
As printed in the first edition of the libretto, each of the verses in the ensemble which ends Act I has another four lines. The original full version is as follows:

MAIDENS.	GROSVENOR.
Oh, list while we a love confess	Again my cursed comeliness
That words imperfectly express.	Spreads hopeless anguish and distress;
Those shell-like ears, ah, do not close	Thine ears, oh, Fortune, do not close
To blighted love's distracting woes!	To my intolerable woes.
Nor be distressed, nor scandalized	Let me be hideous, undersized,
If what we do is ill-advised,	Contemned, degraded, loathed, despised,
Or we shall seek within the tomb	Or bid me seek within the tomb
Relief from our appalling doom!	Relief from my detested doom!

It whispers my sorrowing heart 'rejoice' –
    For the last sad tear is shed –
The pain that is all but a pleasure will change 780
    For the pleasure that's all but pain,
And never, oh never, our hearts will range
    From that old, old love again!
              (*Maidens embrace Officers.*) 785

CHORUS.   Yes, the pain that is all, etc. (*Embrace.*)

(*Enter* PATIENCE *and* BUNTHORNE.)

(*As the Dragoons and Maidens are embracing, enter* GROSVENOR, *reading. He takes no notice of them, but comes slowly down, still reading. The Maidens are all strangely fascinated by him, and gradually withdraw from Dragoons.*) 790

ANG.   But who is this, whose god-like grace
                  Proclaims he comes of noble race?
                  And who is this, whose manly face
                  Bears sorrow's interesting trace?

ENSEMBLE – TUTTI.

                  Yes, who is this, etc. 795

GROS.   I am a broken-hearted troubadour,
                  Whose mind's æsthetic and whose tastes are pure!
ANG.   Æsthetic! He is æsthetic!
GROS.   Yes, yes – I am æsthetic
                        And poetic! 800
ALL THE LADIES.   Then, we love you!

(*The Maidens leave Dragoons and group, kneeling, around* GROSVENOR.
Fury of BUNTHORNE, *who recognizes a rival.*)

DRAGOONS.   They love him! Horror!
BUN. *and* PA.   They love him! Horror!
GROS.   They love me! Horror! Horror! Horror! 805

ENSEMBLE – TUTTI.

MAIDENS.	GROSVENOR.
Oh, list while we a love confess	Again my cursed comeliness
That words imperfectly express.	Spreads hopeless anguish and
Those shell-like ears, ah, do not	distress!
close	Thine ears, oh Fortune, do not
To blighted love's distracting	close
woes!	To my intolerable woes.

810

PATIENCE.	BUNTHORNE.
List, Reginald, while I confess	My jealousy I can't express,
A love that's all unselfishness;	Their love they openly confess,
That it's unselfish, goodness knows,	His shell-like ear he does not close
You won't dispute it, I suppose.	To their recital of their woes –
For you are hideous – undersized,	I'm more than angry and surprised,
And everything that I've despised,	I'm pained, and shocked, and scandalized,
And I shall love you, I presume,	But he shall meet a hideous doom
Until I sink into the tomb!	Prepared for him by – I know whom!

In his *First Night Gilbert and Sullivan*, Reginald Allen states that the last four lines of these verses were sung on the first night and were not, in fact, deleted from the libretto until the fifth edition. However, a note by Rupert D'Oyly Carte in the D'Oyly Carte archives says that the additional lines were never set to music by Sullivan and presumably, therefore, never sung.

PATIENCE.
List, Reginald, while I confess
A love that's all unselfishness;
That it's unselfish, goodness knows,
You won't dispute it, I suppose?

BUNTHORNE.
My jealousy I can't express,
Their love they openly confess;
His shell-like ears he does not close
To their recital of their woes.

DRAGOONS.
Now is not this ridiculous, etc.

8I5

END OF ACT I

1–3 *Scene*: The direction in the first-night libretto for the Act II stage setting read: '*A glade. In the centre a small sheet of water*'. The licence copy further stipulated that there should be both a tree stump and a rock on stage. At the first performances at the Opéra Comique, there was a lake, but this proved impossible to construct on the stage of the Savoy Theatre, with the result that when *Patience* moved there, a significant alteration had to be made to one of the scenes in the Second Act (see the first note to line 409).

Both the licence copy and the first American libretto have Lady Jane leaning on a double bass rather than a cello, but the latter instrument was specified in the first British edition and has generally been used in productions here. In the 1969 Sadler's Wells Opera Company production Heather Begg played a real double-bass herself, but when Gillian Knight took over the part she did not do so. The D'Oyly Carte Company latterly used a 'prop' cello painted entirely white, on which Lady Jane vigorously scraped away while the real music came from the orchestra pit. This scene may well have been intended as a skit on the common custom in early Italian opera for contraltos to be accompanied by the cello or double bass.

8 *they are decaying*: A note by Rupert D'Oyly Carte on a libretto, probably made in the 1930s, states: 'Instead of "decaying", "deteriorating" has been used, decaying being thought too strong.'

16 *lip-salve*: Ointment for the lips.

pearly grey: Face powder. In Gilbert's Bab Ballad 'King Borria Bungalee Boo', the African warriors endeavoured to make themselves fair by applying 'a crimson and pearly-white dye'.

18–33 *Silvered is the raven hair*

Gilbert intended this to be a humorous song, poking fun in a rather ungallant way at the waning attractions of ageing women, very much in the spirit of 'There is beauty in the bellow of the blast' (*The Mikado*, Act II, lines 759–806). However, Sullivan provided a particularly soulful and haunting tune which gives a much sadder and more pathetic flavour to the words than the librettist probably originally intended.

Seeing the suitability of Sullivan's tune for a poignant parlour ballad, the music publishers Chappells commissioned the poet Hugh Conway to provide new lyrics. In this revised form, the song was a popular Victorian fireside favourite:

> In the twilight of our love,
>   In the darkness falling fast;
> Broken by no gleam above;
>   What must be our thoughts the last,
> Silent ere we say farewell,
>   Pausing ere we turn to part,
> Whilst one wish we dare not tell,
>   Echoes yet from heart to heart
> Saddest of all sad regret,
>   'Would we two had never met'.

ACT II

SCENE. – *A glade.* JANE *is discovered leaning on a violoncello, upon which she presently accompanies herself. Chorus of Maidens are heard singing in the distance.*

JANE. The fickle crew have deserted Reginald and sworn allegiance to his rival, and all, forsooth, because he has glanced with passing favour on a puling milkmaid! Fools! of that fancy he will soon weary – and then I, who alone am faithful to him, shall reap my reward. But do not dally too long, Reginald, for my charms are ripe, Reginald, and already they are decaying. Better secure me ere I have gone too far!

5

RECITATIVE – JANE.

Sad is that woman's lot who, year by year,
Sees, one by one, her beauties disappear,
When Time, grown weary of her heart-drawn sighs,
Impatiently begins to 'dim her eyes'!
Compelled, at last, in life's uncertain gloamings,
To wreathe her wrinkled brow with well-saved 'combings',
Reduced, with rouge, lip-salve, and pearly grey,
To 'make up' for lost time as best she may!

10

15

SONG – JANE.

Silvered is the raven hair,
  Spreading is the parting straight,
Mottled the complexion fair,
  Halting is the youthful gait,
Hollow is the laughter free,
  Spectacled the limpid eye –
Little will be left of me
  In the coming by and by!

20

25

28 *severely laced*: This phrase was originally written and sung as 'securely laced'.

60–61 *a decalet – a pure and simple thing*: A decalet is a poetic stanza of ten lines. In his essay mentioned earlier (see the notes to Act I, lines 373–96 and 523), John Bush Jones cites Grosvenor's two poems as evidence that Gilbert based his character on Coventry Patmore, whose early poems were about simple domestic subjects. It might be added that the *Cautionary Tales* which Hilaire Belloc published in 1907 also bear more than a passing resemblance to Grosvenor's poems.

Fading is the taper waist,
   Shapeless grows the shapely limb,
And although severely laced,
   Spreading is the figure trim!
Stouter than I used to be,   30
   Still more corpulent grow I –
There will be too much of me
   In the coming by and by!

(*Exit* JANE.)

(*Enter* GROSVENOR, *followed by Maidens, two and two, each playing on an ar-* 35
chaic instrument, as in Act I. He is reading abstractedly, as BUNTHORNE *did in*
Act I, and pays no attention to them.)

CHORUS OF MAIDENS.

Turn, oh, turn in this direction,
   Shed, oh, shed a gentle smile,
With a glance of sad perfection   40
   Our poor fainting hearts beguile!
On such eyes as maidens cherish
   Let thy fond adorers gaze,
Or incontinently perish
   In their all-consuming rays!   45

(*He sits – they group around him.*)

GROS. (*aside*). The old, old tale. How rapturously these maidens love me,
and how hopelessly! Oh, Patience, Patience, with the love of thee in
my heart, what have I for these poor mad maidens but an unvalued pity?
Alas, they will die of hopeless love for me, as I shall die of hopeless love for 50
thee!
  ANG. Sir, will it please you read to us?
  GROS. (*sighing*). Yes, child, if you will. What shall I read?
  ANG. One of your own poems.
  GROS. One of my own poems? Better not, my child. *They* will not cure 55
thee of thy love.
  ELLA. Mr Bunthorne used to read us a poem of his own every day.
  SAPH. And, to do him justice, he read them extremely well.
  GROS. Oh, did he so? Well, who am I that I should take upon myself
to withhold my gifts from you? What am I but a trustee? Here is a decalet – 60
a pure and simple thing, a very daisy – a babe might understand it. To
appreciate it, it is not necessary to think of anything at all.
  ANG. Let us think of nothing at all!

64–73, *Gentle Jane . . . Teasing Tom*: Gilbert wrote both these poems for his earlier clerical

79–88 version of *Patience*, where they were given to the Revd Lawn Tennison to declaim. In that
version, each of the poems had a refrain for the chorus at the end:

> Oh may we all endeavour to gain
> The happy rewards of Gentle Jane!

and

> Oh may we all take warning from
> The wicked career of Teasing Tom!

'Teasing Tom' has echoes of one of Gilbert's *Bab Ballads*, 'Gentle Archibald', which
tells of a little boy prone to equally unpleasant acts:

> He boiled his little sister JANE;
> He painted blue his aged mother;
> Sat down upon his little brother;
> Tripped up his cousins with his hoop;
> Put pussy in his father's soup;
> Placed beetles in his uncle's shoe;
> Cut a policeman right in two;
> Spread devastation round, and, ah,
> He red-hot-pokered his papa!

In early performances, Saphir had the following line after Grosvenor had finished his
poems and before Angela came in with 'Marked you how grandly . . .': 'How simple,
how earnest – how true'.

92 *Oh, sir, you are indeed a true poet*: In the first edition of the libretto Ella did not say anything
at this point but had a longer version of the later line now given to Saphir: 'Oh, sir, do
not send us from you, for our love leaps to our lips, and our hearts go out to you.'

94 *Ladies, I am sorry*: As originally performed, Grosvenor's lines at this point went: 'Ladies,
I am sorry to distress you, but you have been following me about ever since Monday,
and this is Saturday. I should like the usual half-holiday, and if you will kindly allow me
to close early today, I shall take it as a personal favour'. By the late 1870s the Saturday
half-holiday, which had originally been a privilege largely restricted to those working in
the textile trade, had become general for most working people.

GROSVENOR *recites.*

> Gentle Jane was as good as gold,
> She always did as she was told;
> She never spoke when her mouth was full,
> Or caught bluebottles their legs to pull,
> Or spilt plum jam on her nice new frock,
> Or put white mice in the eight-day clock,
> Or vivisected her last new doll,
> Or fostered a passion for alcohol.
> And when she grew up she was given in marriage
> To a first-class earl who keeps his carriage!

GROS. I believe I am right in saying that there is not one word in that decalet which is calculated to bring the blush of shame to the cheek of modesty.

ANG. Not one; it is purity itself.

GROS. Here's another.

> Teasing Tom was a very bad boy,
> A great big squirt was his favourite toy;
> He put live shrimps in his father's boots,
> And sewed up the sleeves of his Sunday suits;
> He punched his poor little sisters' heads,
> And cayenne-peppered their four-post beds,
> He plastered their hair with cobbler's wax,
> And dropped hot halfpennies down their backs.
>   The consequence was he was lost to*tally*,
>   And married a girl in the *corps de bally*!

ANG. Marked you how grandly – how relentlessly – the damning catalogue of crime strode on, till Retribution, like a poisèd hawk, came swooping down upon the Wrong-Doer? Oh, it was terrible!

ELLA. Oh, sir, you are indeed a true poet, for you touch our hearts, and they go out to you!

GROS. (*aside*). This is simply cloying. (*Aloud.*) Ladies, I am sorry to appear ungallant, but this is Saturday, and you have been following me about ever since Monday. I should like the usual half-holiday. I shall take it as a personal favour if you will kindly allow me to close early to-day.

SAPH. Oh, sir, do not send us from you!

GROS. Poor, poor girls! It is best to speak plainly. I know that I am loved by you, but I never can love you in return, for my heart is fixed elsewhere! Remember the fable of the Magnet and the Churn!

65

70

75

80

85

90

95

100

105–38 *A magnet hung in a hardware shop*
This song is associated with an embarrassing incident which occurred on the first night of *Patience* at the Savoy Theatre. Rutland Barrington, who created the part of Archibald Grosvenor, recalls in his memoirs:

> When I took my seat on a rustic tree-tunk preparatory to singing 'The Magnet and the Churn', I heard an ominous kind of r-r-r-i-p-p and immediately felt conscious of a horrible draught on my right leg. My beautiful knee breeches had gone crack. It was an awful moment. Had they but been made of red velvet it would not have mattered so much, for I felt I was blushing all over and it might have escaped notice, though some of the aesthetic maidens were already choking with laughter.

'The Magnet and the Churn' was parodied in *The Poet and the Puppets*, a burlesque about Oscar Wilde by Charles Brookfield which was first produced in London in 1892, just after Wilde's first play, *Lady Windermere's Fan*, had opened in the West End:

> A poet lived in a handsome style,
>   His books had sold and he'd made his pile.
> His articles, stories and lectures too
>   Had brought success, as ev'rbody knew.
> But the poet was tired of writing tales
>   Of curious women and singular males,
> So, soon as he'd finished his Dorian Gray,
>   He set to work on a four-act play.
> A four-act play, a four-act play.
> A most aesthetic, very magnetic fancy, let us say.
> He filled his purse by writing verse,
>   So why not a four-act play?

ANG. (*wildly*). But we don't know the fable of the Magnet and the
Churn.
GROS. Don't you? Then I will sing it to you.

SONG – GROSVENOR.

> A magnet hung in a hardware shop,   105
> And all around was a loving crop
> Of scissors and needles, nails and knives,
> Offering love for all their lives;
> But for iron the magnet felt no whim,
> Though he charmed iron, it charmed not him;   110
> From needles and nails and knives he'd turn,
> For he'd set his love on a Silver Churn!

ALL.   A Silver Churn?
GROS.   A Silver Churn!

> His most æsthetic,   115
> Very magnetic
> Fancy took this turn –
> 'If I can wheedle
> A knife or a needle,
> Why not a Silver Churn?'   120

CHORUS.   His most æsthetic, etc.

GROS.   And Iron and Steel expressed surprise,
> The needles opened their well-drilled eyes,
> The penknives felt 'shut up', no doubt,
> The scissors declared themselves 'cut out',   125
> The kettles they boiled with rage, 'tis said,
> While every nail went off its head,
> And hither and thither began to roam,
> Till a hammer came up – and drove them home.

ALL.   It drove them home?
GROS.   It drove them home!   130

> While this magnetic,
> Peripatetic
> Lover he lived to learn,
> By no endeavour   135
> Can magnet ever
> Attract a Silver Churn!

139 *They go off in low spirits*: The stage direction in the licence copy at this point reads: '*They go off as in Act I singing "In a melancholy train", and gazing back at him from time to time*'.

152 *Madly, hopelessly, despairingly*: Grosvenor's words foreshadow the response of Rose May-bud to Sir Ruthven's question whether she loves him: 'Madly, passionately' (*Ruddigore*, Act II, lines 589, 592 and 595).

ALL.   While this magnetic, etc.

(*They go off in low spirits, gazing back at him from time to time.*)

GROS. At last they are gone! What is this mysterious fascination that I   140
seem to exercise over all I come across? A curse on my fatal beauty, for I am
sick of conquests!

(PATIENCE *appears.*)

PA. Archibald!
GROS. (*turns and sees her*). Patience!   145
PA. I have escaped with difficulty from my Reginald. I wanted to see you
so much that I might ask you if you still love me as fondly as ever?
GROS. Love you? If the devotion of a lifetime — (*Seizes her hand.*)
PA. (*indignantly*). Hold! Unhand me, or I scream! (*He releases her.*) If you
are a gentleman, pray remember that I am another's! (*Very tenderly.*) But you   150
do love me, don't you?
GROS. Madly, hopelessly, despairingly!
PA. That's right! I never can be yours; but that's right!
GROS. And you love this Bunthorne?
PA. With a heart-whole ecstasy that withers, and scorches, and burns,   155
and stings! (*Sadly.*) It is my duty.
GROS. Admirable girl! But you are not happy with him?
PA. Happy? I am miserable beyond description!
GROS. That's right! I never can be yours; but that's right!
PA. But go now. I see dear Reginald approaching. Farewell, dear   160
Archibald; I cannot tell you how happy it has made me to know that you still
love me.
GROS. Ah, if I only dared — (*Advances towards her.*)
PA. Sir! this language to one who is promised to another! (*Tenderly.*) Oh,
Archibald, think of me sometimes, for my heart is breaking! He is so   165
unkind to me, and you would be so loving!
GROS. Loving! (*Advances towards her.*)
PA. Advance one step, and as I am a good and pure woman, I scream!
(*Tenderly.*) Farewell, Archibald! (*Sternly.*) Stop there! (*Tenderly.*) Think of me
sometimes! (*Angrily.*) Advance at your peril! Once more, adieu!   170

(GROSVENOR *sighs, gazes sorrowfully at her, sighs deeply, and exits. She*
bursts into tears.)

(*Enter* BUNTHORNE, *followed by* JANE. *He is moody and preoccupied.*)

185 *Don't you interfere*: Echoes of yet another Savoy Opera here, this time the exchange
between Cousin Hebe and Sir Joseph Porter originally intended for Act II of *H.M.S.
Pinafore* but cut out before the first performance (see the note to *H.M.S. Pinafore*, Act II,
line 428).

204 *Oh, can't you, though*: This and the next line for Bunthorne were not in the first-edition
libretto and were inserted in an early prompt copy, apparently to incorporate an ad-lib
gag which Gilbert approved.

JANE *sings.*

In a doleful train,
   One and one I walk all day;
For I love in vain –   175
    None so sorrowful as they
    Who can only sigh and say,
    Woe is me, alackaday!
    Woe is me, alackaday, and woe!   180

BUN. (*seeing* PATIENCE). Crying, eh? What are you crying about?
PA. I've only been thinking how dearly I love you!
BUN. Love me! Bah!
JANE. Love him! Bah!
BUN. (*to* JANE). Don't you interfere.   185
JANE. He always crushes me!
PA. (*going to him*). What is the matter, dear Reginald? If you have any
sorrow, tell it to me, that I may share it with you. (*Sighing.*) It is my duty!
BUN. (*snappishly*). Whom were you talking with just now?
PA. With dear Archibald.
BUN. (*furiously*). With dear Archibald! Upon my honour, this is too   190
much!
JANE. A great deal too much!
BUN. (*angrily to* JANE). Do be quiet!
JANE. Crushed again!
PA. I think he is the noblest, purest, and most perfect being I have ever   195
met. But I don't love him. It is true that he is devotedly attached to me, but
indeed I don't love *him.* Whenever he grows affectionate, I scream. It is my
duty! (*Sighing.*)
BUN. I dare say!
JANE. So do I! *I* dare say!   200
PA. Why, how could I love him and love you too? You can't love two
people at once!
BUN. Oh, can't you, though!
PA. No, you can't; I only wish you could.
BUN. I don't believe you know what love is!   205
PA. (*sighing*). Yes, I do. There was a happy time when I didn't, but a bitter
experience has taught me.

(Exeunt BUNTHORNE and JANE.)

BALLAD – PATIENCE.

Love is a plaintive song,   210
   Sung by a suffering maid,

236 *smug-faced idiot*: Originally this was 'idyllic idiot'.

238 *Too mild*: This is another of the lines cited by John Bush Jones in his argument that Gilbert had Coventry Patmore at least partially in mind when he created the character of
Grosvenor. Patmore was frequently criticized for his excessive mildness and 'insipid
amiability'. But this line could also be a hangover from the clerical version of *Patience*,
where the two clergymen vie with each other in their mildness in the manner of the rival
curates in Gilbert's earlier Bab Ballad.

Telling a tale of wrong,
   Telling of hope betrayed;
Tuned to each changing note,
   Sorry when *he* is sad,   215
Blind to his every mote,
   Merry when he is glad!
     Love that no wrong can cure,
       Love that is always new,
     That is the love that's pure,   220
       That is the love that's true!

Rendering good for ill,
   Smiling at every frown,
Yielding your own self-will,
   Laughing your tear-drops down;   225
Never a selfish whim,
   Trouble, or pain to stir;
Everything for him,
   Nothing at all for her!
     Love that will aye endure,   230
       Though the rewards be few,
     That is the love that's pure,
       That is the love that's true!

(*At the end of ballad exit* PATIENCE, *weeping.*)

(*Enter* BUNTHORNE *and* JANE.)   235

BUN. Everything has gone wrong with me since that smug-faced idiot came here. Before that I was admired – I may say, loved.

JANE. Too mild – adored!

BUN. Do let a poet soliloquize! The damozels used to follow me wherever I went; now they all follow him!   240

JANE. Not all! *I* am still faithful to you.

BUN. Yes, and a pretty damozel *you* are!

JANE. No, not pretty. Massive. Cheer up! I will never leave you, I swear it!

BUN. Oh, thank you! I know what it is; it's his confounded mildness. They find me too highly spiced, if you please! And no doubt I *am* highly spiced.   245

JANE. Not for my taste!

BUN. (*savagely*). No, but I am for theirs. But I will show the world I can be as mild as he. If they want insipidity, they shall have it. I'll meet this fellow on his own ground and beat him on it.   250

254–89 *So go to him and say to him, with compliment ironical*
The *Illustrated London News* reported that on the opening night this number had the unique distinction of receiving a triple encore. It has been a particular favourite with audiences ever since.

258 *Your style is much too sanctified*: This line looks distinctly as though it has been left over from the clerical version, being much more appropriate to clergymen than aesthetic poets. However, there is no trace of it in the manuscript of Gilbert's earlier version which survives in the British Library.

280 *quiddity*: The *Oxford English Dictionary* defines a quiddity as 'a captious nicety in argument, a quirk or quibble'. The word derives from the Latin word *quid* and originally meant the real nature of things. It is all very philosophical – better, surely, to be like Ruth and the Pirate King in *The Pirates of Penzance* and just concentrate on quips and quibbles.

JANE. You shall. And I will help you.

BUN. You will? Jane, there's a good deal of good in you, after all!

DUET – BUNTHORNE *and* JANE.

JANE.
BUN.
> So go to him and say to him, with compliment ironical –
> Sing 'Hey to you –
> Good day to you' –
> And that's what I shall say! 255

JANE.
BUN.
> 'Your style is much too sanctified – your cut is too canonical' –
> Sing 'Bah to you –
> Ha! ha! to you' –
> And that's what I shall say! 260

JANE.
> 'I was the beau ideal of the morbid young æsthetical –
> To doubt my inspiration was regarded as heretical –
> Until you cut me out with your placidity emetical.' –

BUN.
> Sing 'Booh to you –
> Pooh, pooh to you' –
> And that's what I shall say! 265

BOTH.
> Sing 'Hey to you – good day to you' –
> Sing 'Bah to you – ha! ha! to you' –
> Sing 'Booh to you – pooh, pooh to you' – 270
> And that's what $\left\{ \begin{array}{l} \text{you should} \\ \text{I shall} \end{array} \right\}$ say!

BUN.
JANE.
> I'll tell him that unless he will consent to be more jocular –
> Sing 'Booh to you –
> Pooh, pooh to you' –
> And that's what you should say! 275

BUN.
JANE.
> To cut his curly hair, and stick an eyeglass in his ocular –
> Sing 'Bah to you –
> Ha! ha! to you' –
> And that's what you should say!

BUN.
> To stuff his conversation full of quibble and of quiddity – 280
> To dine on chops and roly-poly pudding with avidity –
> He'd better clear away with all convenient rapidity.

JANE.
> Sing 'Hey to you –
> Good day to you' –
> And that's what you should say! 285

290 *Exeunt Jane and Bunthorne together*: For a long time in D'Oyly Carte productions Lady Jane at this point picked up Bunthorne in her arms and carried him off the stage. In his autobiography, *The Secrets of a Savoyard*, Sir Henry Lytton recalls being dropped with a terrible crash by Miss Bertha Lewis, the company's leading contralto for twenty years until her untimely death following a car accident in 1931. Lytton writes: 'In the shelter of the wings I remonstrated with her, pointing out that this was a distinct departure from what Gilbert intended. All the sympathy I got was, "Well, I've dropped you only twice in eight years".'

296–315 *It's clear that mediæval art alone retains its zest*

The transformation of the soldiers into aesthetes was always conceived by Gilbert as one of the show-stopping scenes in *Patience*. In the letter he sent to Sullivan announcing that he had decided to abandon the idea of basing the plot around clergymen and to return instead to his original idea of a skit on the Pre-Raphaelites, he wrote: 'The Hussars will become aesthetic young men (abandoning their profession for the purpose) – in this latter capacity they will carry lilies in their hands, wear long hair, and stand in stained glass attitudes'.

There is a celebrated photograph taken in 1881 of the original Duke, Colonel and Major (Durward Lely, Richard Temple and Frank Thornton) with droopy moustaches, striking stained glass attitudes and clad in velvet floppy hats and suits. I have reproduced it in my book *William Morris and His World* (1978). The *Daily News* first-night reviewer commented that the three officers appeared 'looking like figures cut out of a Pre-Raphaelite picture and vivified. The constrained attitudes, distorted positions, and grotesque gestures of the three, and the quaint music which they sing, produced a richly humorous effect.'

In the licence copy, this song had only one verse, going straight from 'angular and flat' (line 302) to 'To cultivate the trim' (line 313). The American scholar Jane Steadman has pointed out in her essay 'The Genesis of *Patience*' (in *W.S. Gilbert: A Century of Scholarship and Commentary*, New York, 1970) that in its original form the song could apply equally well to the Victorian High Church movement as to the Pre-Raphaelites. It is true that a predilection for medievalism and Early English architecture was common to both these groups. However, this song does not appear in Gilbert's manuscript for the clerical version of the opera, and there is no particular reason to think that he originally conceived it as a number in which the soldiers would assume the somewhat affected manners and attitudes of the Tractarians in the Church of England.

BOTH.　　Sing 'Booh to you – pooh, pooh to you' –
　　　　　Sing 'Bah to you – ha! ha! to you' –
　　　　　Sing 'Hey to you – good day to you' –
　　　　　And that's what $\left\{ \begin{array}{c} \text{you should} \\ \text{I shall} \end{array} \right\}$ say!

　　　　　　　　　　　(*Exeunt* JANE *and* BUNTHORNE *together.*)　290

(*Enter* DUKE, COLONEL, *and* MAJOR. *They have abandoned their uni-forms, and are dressed and made up in imitation of Æsthetics. They have long hair, and other outward signs of attachment to the brotherhood. As they sing they walk in stiff, constrained, and angular attitudes – a grotesque exaggeration of the attitudes adopted by* BUNTHORNE *and the Maidens in Act I.*)　295

TRIO – DUKE, COLONEL, *and* MAJOR.

It's clear that mediæval art alone retains its zest,
To charm and please its devotees we've done our little best.
We're not quite sure if all we do has the Early English ring;
But, as far as we can judge, it's something like this sort of thing:
　　　　You hold yourself like this (*attitude*),　　　　　　　300
　　　　You hold yourself like that (*attitude*),
By hook and crook you try to look both angular and flat (*attitude*).
　　　　We venture to expect
　　　　That what we recollect,
Though but a part of true High Art, will have its due effect.　305

If this is not exactly right, we hope you won't upbraid;
You can't get high Æsthetic tastes, like trousers, ready made.
True views on Mediævalism Time alone will bring,
But, as far as we can judge, it's something like this sort of thing:
　　　　You hold yourself like this (*attitude*),　　　　　　　310
　　　　You hold yourself like that (*attitude*),
By hook and crook you try to look both angular and flat (*attitude*).
　　　　To cultivate the trim
　　　　Rigidity of limb,
You ought to get a Marionette, and form your style on him (*attitude*).　315

COL. (*attitude*). Yes, it's quite clear that our only chance of making a lasting impression on these young ladies is to become as æsthetic as they are.

MAJ. (*attitude*). No doubt. The only question is how far we've succeeded in doing so. I don't know why, but I've an idea that this is not quite right.　320

DUKE. (*attitude*). *I* don't like it. I never did. I don't see what it means. I do it, but I don't like it.

333 *the Inner Brotherhood*: This phrase removes any possible doubt about who it is that the soldiers are trying to imitate; it was the term which the Pre-Raphaelites applied to themselves. The Pre-Raphaelite Brotherhood was set up in 1848 by William Holman Hunt, John Everett Millais, Dante Gabriel Rossetti and four friends. They chose the word 'Brotherhood' because of its medieval associations and its aura of secrecy.

336 *How Botticellian! How Fra Angelican*: The guiding principle which gave the Pre-Raphaelites their name was, of course, their desire to return to the pure principles of medieval art before they had begun to be corrupted by the academic and classical approach of Renaissance artists like Raphael (1483–1520). Fra Angelico (1400–1455) and Botticelli (1445–1510) were early Renaissance Florentine artists whose work was admired by the Pre-Raphaelites.

341 *jolly utter*: The aesthetic movement developed its own rather over-blown vocabulary in which such words as 'supreme', 'utter', 'consummate', 'precious' and 'intense' figured prominently. In this line Gilbert creates a splendidly discordant effect by pairing the ultra-philistine 'jolly' with the super-aesthetic 'utter'.

356 *By sections of threes – Rapture*: This echoes the command of the Scornful Colonel in Gilbert's Bab Ballad of that name: 'By sections, "Phew"!' (see the note to lines 677–90 in Act I).

363 *hooking you*: In several editions of the libretto the Colonel's speech is followed by a further passage of essentially superfluous dialogue before the singing of the quintet:

> DUKE. Won't it be rather awkward?
> COL. Awkward, not at all. Observe, suppose you choose Angela, I take Saphir, Major takes nobody. Suppose you choose Saphir, Major takes Angela, I take nobody. Suppose you choose neither, I take Angela, Major takes Saphir. Clear as day!
> ANG. Capital!
> SAPH. The very thing!

COL. My good friend, the question is not whether we like it, but whether they do. They understand these things – we don't. Now I shouldn't be surprised if this is effective enough – at a distance.   325

MAJ. I can't help thinking we're a little stiff at it. It would be extremely awkward if we were to be 'struck' so!

COL. I don't think we shall be struck so. Perhaps we're a little awkward at first – but everything must have a beginning. Oh, here they come! 'Tention!   330

(*They strike fresh attitudes, as* ANGELA *and* SAPHIR *enter.*)

ANG. (*seeing them*). Oh, Saphir – see – see! The immortal fire has descended on them, and they are of the Inner Brotherhood – perceptively intense and consummately utter. (*The Officers have some difficulty in maintaining their constrained attitudes.*)   335

SAPH. (*in admiration*). How Botticellian! How Fra Angelican! Oh, Art, we thank thee for this boon!

COL. (*apologetically*). I'm afraid we're not quite right.

ANG. Not supremely, perhaps, but oh, so all-but! (*To* SAPHIR.) Oh, Saphir, are they not quite too all-but?   340

SAPH. They are indeed jolly utter!

MAJ. (*in agony*). I wonder what the Inner Brotherhood usually recommend for cramp?

COL. Ladies, we will not deceive you. We are doing this at some personal inconvenience with a view of expressing the extremity of our devotion to   345
you. We trust that it is not without its effect.

ANG. We will not deny that we are much moved by this proof of your attachment.

SAPH. Yes, your conversion to the principles of Æsthetic Art in its highest development has touched us deeply.   350

ANG. And if Mr Grosvenor should remain obdurate –

SAPH. Which we have every reason to believe he will –

MAJ. (*aside, in agony*). I wish they'd make haste.

ANG. We are not prepared to say that our yearning hearts will not go out to you.   355

COL. (*as giving a word of command*). By sections of threes – Rapture! (*All strike a fresh attitude, expressive of æsthetic rapture.*)

SAPH. Oh, it's extremely good – for beginners it's admirable.

MAJ. The only question is, who will take who?

COL. Oh, the Duke chooses first, as a matter of course.   360

DUKE. Oh, I couldn't think of it – you are really too good!

COL. Nothing of the kind. You are a great matrimonial fish, and it's only fair that each of these ladies should have a chance of hooking you.

QUINTET.

DUKE, COLONEL, MAJOR, ANGELA, *and* SAPHIR.

DUKE (*taking* SAPHIR).

If Saphir I choose to marry,
    I shall be fixed up for life;
Then the Colonel need not tarry,
    Angela can be his wife.

365

(*Handing* ANGELA *to* COLONEL.)

(DUKE *dances with* SAPHIR, COLONEL *with* ANGELA,
    MAJOR *dances alone*.)

370

MAJOR (*dancing alone*).

In that case unprecedented,
    Single I shall live and die –
I shall have to be contented
    With their heartfelt sympathy!

ALL (*dancing as before*).

He will have to be contented
    With our heartfelt sympathy!

375

DUKE (*taking* ANGELA).

If on Angy I determine,
    At my wedding she'll appear
Decked in diamond and ermine,
    Major then can take Saphir!

380

(*Handing* SAPHIR *to* MAJOR.)

(DUKE *dances with* ANGELA, MAJOR *with* SAPHIR,
    COLONEL *dances alone*.)

COLONEL (*dancing*).

In that case unprecedented,
    Single I shall live and die –
I shall have to be contented
    With their heartfelt sympathy!

385

409   *Looking at his reflection in hand-mirror*: As originally performed at the Opéra Comique,
       Bunthorne at this point gazed into a lake on the stage. The stage direction in the first-
       edition libretto reads: '*Reclining on bank of lake, and looking at his reflection in the water*'. It
       was not practicable to re-create the lake on the stage of the new Savoy Theatre and
       when the opera moved there, the business with the hand-mirror was substituted. It has
       continued ever since.
       Narcissus: One with excessive self-admiration. In Greek mythology Narcissus was a
       beautiful youth who saw his reflection in a fountain and thought that it must be the pre-
       siding nymph of the place. He jumped in to reach it and drowned.

410   *Enter Bunthorne, moodily*: The direction in the licence copy for this entrance gives the ad-
       ditional information that '*His hair now resembles Grosvenor's – that is to say it is lank instead
       of being bushy; and he has shaved his moustache*'.

413   *Ah, Bunthorne*: As originally performed, this exchange went as follows:

> GROS. Ah, Bunthorne! come here – look! Is it not beautiful?
> (BUN. *also reclines behind lake, so that the actions of both are reflected in the water.*)
> BUN. (*looking in lake*). Which?
> GROS. Mine.
> BUN. Bah! I am in no mood for trifling.

ALL (*dancing as before*).

He will have to be contented
With our heartfelt sympathy!

DUKE (*taking both* ANGELA *and* SAPHIR).

After some debate internal,   390
   If on neither I decide,
Saphir then can take the Colonel,
         (*Handing* SAPHIR *to* COLONEL.)
   Angy be the Major's bride!
         (*Handing* ANGELA *to* MAJOR.)   395

(COLONEL *dances with* SAPHIR, MAJOR *with* ANGELA,
DUKE *dances alone.*)

DUKE (*dancing*).

In that case unprecedented,
   Single I must live and die –
I shall have to be contented   400
   With their heartfelt sympathy!

ALL (*dancing as before*).

He will have to be contented
With our heartfelt sympathy.

(*At the end,* DUKE, COLONEL, *and* MAJOR, *and two girls dance off arm-
in-arm.*)   405

(*Enter* GROSVENOR.)

GROS. It is very pleasant to be alone. It is pleasant to be able to gaze at leisure upon those features which all others may gaze upon at their good will! (*Looking at his reflection in hand-mirror.*) Ah, I am a very Narcissus!

(*Enter* BUNTHORNE, *moodily.*)   410

BUN. It's no use; I can't live without admiration. Since Grosvenor came here, insipidity has been at a premium. Ah, he is there!
GROS. Ah, Bunthorne! come here – look! Very graceful, isn't it!
BUN. (*taking hand-mirror*). Allow me; I haven't seen it. Yes, it is graceful.

434–5   *have a back parting*: This is not in the original libretto and was almost certainly an ad-lib incorporated with Gilbert's approval into later editions. The whole idea of a back parting would have struck the Pre-Raphaelites as appallingly philistine and prosaic. If they parted their hair at all, it was generally in the middle. On the D'Oyly Carte recording of *Patience*, produced by Decca in 1961, Grosvenor interjects 'Beg pardon' at the words 'back parting' and Bunthorne repeats them.

439   *I am a man with a mission*: Originally Grosvenor had a longer speech at this point: 'I am a man with a mission. I am here to preach, in my own person, the Principles of Perfection. I am, as it were, a Banquet of Beauty upon which all who will may feast. It is most unpleasant to be a Banquet, but I must not shirk my responsibilities.'

GROS. (*re-taking hand-mirror*). Oh, good gracious! not that – this —

BUN. You don't mean that! Bah! I am in no mood for trifling.

GROS. And what is amiss?

BUN. Ever since you came here, you have entirely monopolized the attentions of the young ladies. I don't like it, sir!

GROS. My dear sir, how can I help it? They are the plague of my life. My dear Mr Bunthorne, with your personal disadvantages, you can have no idea of the inconvenience of being madly loved, at first sight, by every woman you meet.

BUN. Sir, until you came here I was adored!

GROS. Exactly – until I came here. That's my grievance. I cut everybody out! I assure you, if you could only suggest some means whereby, consistently with my duty to society, I could escape these inconvenient attentions, you would earn my everlasting gratitude.

BUN. I will do so at once. However popular it may be with the world at large, your personal appearance is highly objectionable to *me*.

GROS. It is? (*Shaking his hand.*) Oh, thank you! thank you! How can I express my gratitude?

BUN. By making a complete change at once. Your conversation must henceforth be perfectly matter-of-fact. You must cut your hair, and have a back parting. In appearance and costume you must be absolutely commonplace.

GROS. (*decidedly*). No. Pardon me, that's impossible.

BUN. Take care! When I am thwarted I am very terrible.

GROS. I can't help that. I am a man with a mission. And that mission must be fulfilled.

BUN. I don't think you quite appreciate the consequences of thwarting me.

GROS. I don't care what they are.

BUN. Suppose – I won't go so far as to say that I will do it – but suppose for one moment I were to curse you? (GROSVENOR *quails*.) Ah! Very well. Take care.

GROS. But surely you would never do that? (*In great alarm.*)

BUN. I don't know. It would be an extreme measure, no doubt. Still —

GROS. (*wildly*). But you would not do it – I am sure you would not. (*Throwing himself at* BUNTHORNE'S *knees, and clinging to him.*) Oh, reflect, reflect! You had a mother once.

BUN. Never!

GROS. Then you had an aunt! (BUNTHORNE *affected.*) Ah! I see you had! By the memory of that aunt, I implore you to pause ere you resort to this last fearful expedient. Oh, Mr Bunthorne, reflect, reflect! (*Weeping.*)

BUN. (*aside, after a struggle with himself*). I must not allow myself to be unmanned! (*Aloud.*) It is useless. Consent at once, or may a nephew's curse —

415

420

425

430

435

440

445

450

455

478 *A most intense young man*: In early libretti, Bunthorne sang lines 478–81 as a solo before they were repeated by both men singing together. Similarly, Grosvenor first sang lines 492–5 on his own.

486 *black-and-tan*: A breed of small terrier dog.

488 *Monday Pops*: Forerunners of the modern Promenade Concerts, the Monday Pops were weekly concerts of classical music organized by the music publishers Chappells. They began in 1859 in the St James's Hall and in 1901 transferred to the Queen's Hall. They are mentioned by the Mikado as a suitable punishment for the music-hall singer (*The Mikado*, Act II, line 376).

494 *jolly Bank-holiday*: A highly topical reference when *Patience* was written. Two measures successfully piloted through Parliament in 1871 and 1875 by the Liberal M.P. Sir John Lubbock had established Boxing Day, Easter Monday, Whit Monday and the first Monday in August as bank (i.e. public) holidays.

GROS. Hold! Are you absolutely resolved?
BUN. Absolutely.
GROS. Will nothing shake you?   460
BUN. Nothing. I am adamant.
GROS. Very good. (*Rising*.) Then I yield.
BUN. Ha! You swear it?
GROS. I do, cheerfully. I have long wished for a reasonable pretext for   465
such a change as you suggest. It has come at last. I do it on compulsion!
BUN. Victory! I triumph!

DUET – BUNTHORNE *and* GROSVENOR.

BUN.   When I go out of door,
            Of damozels a score
                (All sighing and burning,
                And clinging and yearning)   470
            Will follow me as before.
            I shall, with cultured taste,
            Distinguish gems from paste,
                And 'High diddle diddle'
                Will rank as an idyll,   475
            If I pronounce it chaste!

BOTH.   A most intense young man,
                A soulful-eyed young man,
            An ultra-poetical, super-æsthetical,   480
                Out-of-the-way young man!

GROS.   Conceive me, if you can,
            An every-day young man:
                A commonplace type,
                With a stick and a pipe,   485
            And a half-bred black-and-tan;
                Who thinks suburban 'hops'
                More fun than 'Monday Pops',
            Who's fond of his dinner,
            And doesn't get thinner   490
                On bottled beer and chops.

BOTH.   A commonplace young man,
                A matter-of-fact young man,
            A steady and stolid-y, jolly Bank-holiday
                Every-day young man!
                                                                 495

497   *A blue-and-white young man*: See the note to line 700 in Act I.

498   *Francesca di Rimini*: Francesca da Rimini was the daughter of a thirteenth-century Lord of Ravenna who was killed by her husband for being the secret lover of his brother. The story was immortalized in Dante's *Inferno*.

500   *Chancery Lane*: The street which goes through the heart of legal London, joining Gray's Inn to the north with Fleet Street (the Law Courts and the Middle and Inner Temples) to the south and Lincoln's Inn halfway down. Strephon speaks in Act I of *Iolanthe* of being led there, singing, by a servile usher.

501   *Somerset House*: A large and imposing building constructed in 1776 on the site of Protector Somerset's town house between the Strand and the Thames. In its time, it has housed many Government departments, including the Navy Office, the Board of Inland Revenue and the Registrar of Births, Marriages and Deaths.

503   *Threepenny-bus*: The first buses to run in London charged fares of sixpence to a shilling depending on the distance. However, competition between rival companies was so intense that the fares came down to a uniform threepence. For the 1900 revival of *Patience*, Gilbert changed the phrase to 'twopenny tube'. The Central London Underground Railway, which had opened that year, charged a uniform fare of twopence on its journeys between Shepherd's Bush and Bank stations. Since the turn of the century there has been no attempt to up-date this line to match rising prices – which is, perhaps, just as well.

506   *greenery-yallery*: Green and yellow were much favoured by the Pre-Raphaelite painters. The rhythm and sound of this line bear a striking resemblance to a refrain from one of Gilbert's *Bab Ballads*, 'Down to the Derby':

> Palery alery, smokery, jokery, rambling,
>   scrambling, crash along, dash along –
> Down to the Derby as all of us go.

Grosvenor Gallery: Founded by Sir Coutts Lindsay in New Bond Street in 1877, the Grosvenor Gallery was much patronized by the Pre-Raphaelites and came to rival the Royal Academy as the leading arbiter of artistic taste in Britain. Whistler's painting *Nocturne in Black and Gold*, which provoked Ruskin's damning comment mentioned in the introduction, was one of the gallery's first exhibits.

508   *Sewell & Cross*: A high-class drapers and costumiers in Soho. It also gets a mention in *Princess Ida* (Act II, line 132).

509   *Howell & James*: Another fashionable Victorian drapery store in Regent Street.

510   *What's the next article*: This derives from the favourite phrase of the eager young salesman behind the counter: 'What's the next article I can show you?'

511   *Waterloo House*: Waterloo House was a large and imposing Regency building which formerly stood in Cockspur Street, just off Trafalgar Square, and which was for some time occupied by yet another leading drapery firm, Halling, Pearce and Stone. The firm later merged with the department store Swan and Edgar.

521   *Reginald! Dancing*: In the first-edition libretto this line continued: 'And – what in the world have you done to yourself?'

BUN.	A Japanese young man,
	A blue-and-white young man,
	Francesca di Rimini, miminy, piminy,
	Je-ne-sais-quoi young man!

GROS.	A Chancery Lane young man,	500
	A Somerset House young man,	
	A very delectable, highly respectable,	
	Threepenny-bus young man!	

BUN.	A pallid and thin young man,	
	A haggard and lank young man,	505
	A greenery-yallery, Grosvenor Gallery,	
	Foot-in-the-grave young man!	

GROS.	A Sewell & Cross young man,	
	A Howell & James young man,	
	A pushing young particle – 'What's the next article?' –	510
	Waterloo House young man!	

ENSEMBLE.

BUN.	GROS.	
Conceive me, if you can,	Conceive me, if you can,	
A crotchety, cracked young man,	A matter-of-fact young man,	
An ultra-poetical, super-æsthetical,	An alphabetical, arithmetical,	
Out-of-the-way young man!	Every-day young man!	515

(*At the end,* GROSVENOR *dances off.* BUNTHORNE *remains.*)

BUN. It is all right! I have committed my last act of ill-nature, and henceforth I'm a changed character. (*Dances about stage, humming refrain of last air.*)

(*Enter* PATIENCE. *She gazes in astonishment at him.*) 520

PA. Reginald! Dancing! And – what in the world is the matter with you?

BUN. Patience, I'm a changed man. Hitherto I've been gloomy, moody, fitful – uncertain in temper and selfish in disposition –

PA. You have, indeed! (*Sighing.*) 525

BUN. All that is changed. I have reformed. I have modelled myself upon Mr Grosvenor. Henceforth I am mildly cheerful. My conversation will blend amusement with instruction. I shall still be æsthetic; but my æstheticism will be of the most pastoral kind.

547 *But, stop a bit*: As originally performed, there was a longer passage of dialogue at this point than now survives:

BUN. But –
PA. It is useless, Reginald. When you were objectionable I could love you conscientiously, but now that you are endowed with every quality that can make a woman happy, it would be the height of selfishness even to think of such a thing.
BUN. But stop a bit, I don't want to reform – I'll relapse – I'll be as I was.
PA. No; love should purify – it should never debase. Farewell, Reginald – think of me sometimes as one who did her duty to you at all cost – at all sacrifice.
BUN. But I assure you, I – interrupted.

550 *suit of dittoes*: A suit made of the same material throughout, so that the jacket, waistcoat and trousers all match. In D'Oyly Carte productions the new-look Grosvenor appeared in a suit of extremely loud checks.

551 *a pot hat*: A small round hat not unlike a bowler.

557 *Swears & Wells*: A famous firm of furriers and costumiers which originally traded from Regent Street and later moved to Oxford Street. Its shop there has since been taken over by Cheap Jacks, selling jeans.

558 *Madame Louise*: A fashionable Regent Street milliners.

This chorus was originally written to be sung in the following way:

GROS. I'm a Waterloo House young man,
GIRLS. We're Swears and Wells young girls,
GROS. I'm a Sewell & Cross young man,
GIRLS. We're Madame Louise young girls

ENSEMBLE.

GROS.	GIRLS.
A steady and stolid-y, jolly Bank-holiday	We're prettily pattering, cheerily chattering,
Every-day young man!	Every-day young girls!

PA. Oh, Reginald! Is all this true? 530

BUN. Quite true. Observe how amiable I am. (*Assuming a fixed smile.*)

PA. But, Reginald, how long will this last?

BUN. With occasional intervals for rest and refreshment, as long as I do.

PA. Oh, Reginald, I'm so happy! (*In his arms.*) Oh, dear, dear Reginald, I cannot express the joy I feel at this change. It will no longer be a duty to love 535 you, but a pleasure – a rapture – an ecstasy!

BUN. My darling!

PA. But – oh, horror! (*Recoiling from him.*)

BUN. What's the matter?

PA. Is it quite certain that you have absolutely reformed – that you are 540 henceforth a perfect being – utterly free from defect of any kind?

BUN. It is quite certain. I have sworn it.

PA. Then I never can be yours!

BUN. Why not?

PA. Love, to be pure, must be absolutely unselfish, and there can be 545 nothing unselfish in loving so perfect a being as you have now become!

BUN. But, stop a bit! I don't want to change – I'll relapse – I'll be as I was – interrupted!

(*Enter* GROSVENOR, *followed by all the 'every-day young girls', who are followed by Chorus of Dragoons. He has had his hair cut, and is dressed in an* 550 *ordinary suit of dittoes and a pot hat. They all dance cheerfully round the stage in marked contrast to their former languor.*)

CHORUS – GROSVENOR *and* GIRLS.

GROSVENOR.

I'm a Waterloo House young man,
A Sewell & Cross young man,
A steady and stolid-y, jolly Bank-holiday, 555
Every-day young man!

GIRLS.

We're Swears & Wells young girls,
We're Madame Louise young girls,
We're prettily pattering, cheerily chattering,
Every-day young girls! 560

BUN. Angela – Ella – Saphir – what – what does this mean?

ANG. It means that Archibald the All-Right cannot be all-wrong; and if the All-Right chooses to discard æstheticism, it proves that æstheticism ought to be discarded.

566 *I can't help it*: In delivering this and his subsequent lines, Grosvenor exchanges his
affected aesthetic tones for a strong Cockney accent. Captain Corcoran undergoes a
similar vocal metamorphosis at the end of Act II of *H.M.S. Pinafore*.

567 *never set eyes on you again*: In the 1961 D'Oyly Carte recording Grosvenor interjects here
'Oh, I say'.

578 *Crushed again*: This line is not in the licence copy. Instead Bunthorne says 'Oh mercy! I'm
lost! lost! lost!'

587 *Ladies, the Duke has at length determined to select a bride*: Gilbert originally intended both the
Colonel and the Duke to express their sentiments in song before the finale. The li-
cence-copy version, which was probably never set to music, of this passage, following
the flourish and the entrance of the three officers, is as follows:

RECITATIVE – D U K E.

Ladies, I've great and glorious news for you,
His grace the Duke, whose social position
Is rivalled only by his wealth stupendous,
To choose a bride from you has just decided!

A L L.   Oh rapture!

SOLO – D U K E.

I have a goodly prize to give away,
Which I must do without more hesitation;
You are all beautiful as a summer's day,
For all I feel an equal admiration;
I'd share it with you all right willingly,
If that could be arranged with due propriety,
But that, I need not say, can scarcely be,
Until we have recognized society.
I have resolved – for men of high degree
Should show the way in self-denying actions –
To give it to that maid who seems to be
Most wanting in material attractions!
Jane!

J A N E (*leaving* B U N T H O R N E ' S *arms*). Duke! (J A N E *and* D U K E *embrace*. B U N. *is utterly
miserable*).
(J A N E *pairs off with* D U K E, A N G. *with* C O L., S A P H. *with* M A J O R, E L L A *with* C A P T.
Each girl takes a Dragoon. P A T I E N C E *of course, has paired with* G R O S V E N O R.)

There is a blank after the title 'FINALE' in the licence copy.

PA. Oh, Archibald! Archibald! I'm shocked – surprised – horrified! 565
GROS. I can't help it. I'm not a free agent. I do it on compulsion.
PA. This is terrible. Go! I shall never set eyes on you again. But – oh, joy!
GROS. What is the matter?
PA. Is it quite, quite certain that you will always be a commonplace 570
young man?
GROS. Always – I've sworn it.
PA. Why, then, there's nothing to prevent my loving you with all the fervour at my command!
GROS. Why, that's true.
PA. My Archibald! 575
GROS. My Patience! (*They embrace.*)
BUN. Crushed again!

(*Enter* JANE.)

JANE. (*who is still æsthetic*). Cheer up! I am still here. I have never left you, 580
and I never will!
BUN. Thank you, Jane. After all, there is no denying it, you're a fine figure of a woman!
JANE. My Reginald!
BUN. My Jane!
585

(*Flourish. Enter* COLONEL, DUKE, *and* MAJOR.)

COL. Ladies, the Duke has at length determined to select a bride! (*General excitement.*)
DUKE. I have a great gift to bestow. Approach, such of you as are truly lovely. (*All come forward, bashfully, except* JANE *and* PATIENCE.) In personal 590
appearance you have all that is necessary to make a woman happy. In common fairness, I think I ought to choose the only one among you who has the misfortune to be distinctly plain. (*Girls retire disappointed.*) Jane!
JANE (*leaving* BUNTHORNE'S *arms*). Duke! (JANE *and* DUKE *embrace.*
BUNTHORNE *is utterly disgusted.*)
BUN. Crushed again! 595

FINALE.

DUKE.   After much debate internal,
                      I on Lady Jane decide,
                 Saphir now may take the Colonel,
                     Angy be the Major's bride!
600

(SAPHIR *pairs off with* COLONEL, ANGELA *with* MAJOR,
ELLA *with* SOLICITOR.)

BUN.

   In that case unprecedented,
    Single I must live and die –
   I shall have to be contented
    With a tulip or li*ly*!   605

(Takes a lily from button-hole and gazes affectionately at it.)

ALL.

   He will have to be contented
    With a tulip or li*ly*!

   Greatly pleased with one another,   610
    To get married we decide.
   Each of us will wed the other,
    Nobody be Bunthorne's Bride!

     DANCE.

     CURTAIN

IOLANTHE

or

The Peer and the Peri

DRAMATIS PERSONÆ

THE LORD CHANCELLOR
EARL OF MOUNTARARAT
EARL TOLLOLLER
PRIVATE WILLIS (*of the Grenadier Guards*)
STREPHON (*an Arcadian Shepherd*)
QUEEN OF THE FAIRIES
IOLANTHE (*a Fairy, Strephon's Mother*)
CELIA ⎫
LEILA ⎬ Fairies
FLETA ⎭
PHYLLIS (*an Arcadian Shepherdess and Ward in Chancery*)
Chorus of Dukes, Marquises, Earls, Viscounts, Barons, and Fairies

ACT I. – An Arcadian Landscape.
ACT II. – Palace Yard, Westminster.

IOLANTHE

Iolanthe made theatrical history on 25 November 1882 when it became the first play ever to open in Britain and the United States on the same night. New Yorkers filing into the Standard Theater already knew of the show's success in London from a cable sent from the Savoy Theatre, where the first performance had ended barely an hour earlier.

As originally conceived by Gilbert, *Iolanthe* had a rather different plot from the one with which we are now familiar. He had first explored the comic possibilities of a marriage between a fairy and a mortal in his Bab Ballad 'The Fairy Curate'. In his preliminary notes for an opera based on the same theme, he first proposed that the fairy heroine should marry a prosaic solicitor aged forty-five. This was later changed to the rather grander idea that the entire female chorus of fairies should marry barristers of the Northern Circuit, with the action being set in a court of law, just like the first of Gilbert and Sullivan's collaborations for Richard D'Oyly Carte, *Trial by Jury.*

As he worked on the plot of the new opera Gilbert realized that he could have much more fun by switching from a legal to a political setting. He decided that the Fairy Queen should marry the Prime Minister (this was later changed to the Foreign Secretary), with the other principal fairies pairing off with the Home Secretary, the Attorney General, and other ministers of state. The scene was to be the House of Commons.

Finally Gilbert hit on a formula which satisfied him and which enabled him to produce a comic masterpiece. The setting of the opera would be the House of Lords, in its own way as romantic and as far removed from the real world as fairyland; the Fairy Queen would be set against the Lord Chancellor; and the chorus of fairies would fall in love with a chorus of peers. With the introduction of an Arcadian shepherdess and her shepherd lover to give a rustic and romantic note the plot was broadly complete.

The British House of Lords is an obvious subject for satirists and humorists. The idea of birth being the qualification for membership of the upper house of Parliament strongly appealed to Gilbert's sense of the ridiculous. He had poked fun at it in *The Pirates of Penzance*, particularly in the finales of the original British and American versions, and was to do so again in *Utopia Limited*. *Iolanthe* gave him the opportunity to devote an entire opera to the gentle mockery of an institution for which, like most Englishmen, he, in fact, had a deep affection.

The power of the House of Lords was a highly topical issue in 1882. Resistance in the upper house to much of the reforming legislation of Gladstone's Liberal Government, which had been elected in 1880, led to a growing call for reform of the Lords and an end to their veto. Gilbert knew that his digs at the peerage would win ready applause from a contemporary audience, just as he could be sure of a cheer when he lampooned that other bogey of the British political tradition, the two-party system.

There have been some elaborate explanations of the contemporary political satire contained in *Iolanthe*. One of the most ingenious was made in an article in the *Daily Telegraph* on 23 January 1978 by Kenneth Baker, Conservative M.P. and later Minister in Mrs Thatcher's governments and chairman of the Conservative Party. He suggested that Gilbert clearly meant the Fairy Queen to be Queen Victoria, with Private Willis representing her faithful and manly ghillie John Brown. The Lord Chancellor, with his bad relations with the Queen and his nocturnal wanderings and eye for pretty young girls, was clearly Mr Gladstone, while Strephon was Lord Randolph Churchill, the quixotic exponent of Tory democracy whose so-called 'Fourth Party' of maverick Conservatives had already made the leaders of the established parties shake in their shoes. An alternative model for Strephon was proposed by the historian Owen Dudley Edwards writing in the programme for Scottish Opera's production of *Iolanthe* in 1986. He suggested that Gilbert might have had in mind the figure of Charles Stewart Parnell, leader of the Irish party, whose obstructionist tactics had forced many late-night sittings on weary M.P.s and peers.

These are attractive theories and there may be some truth in them, although I doubt if Gilbert set out quite so deliberately to caricature the leading figures of the day. Certainly the satire in *Iolanthe* was sharp – too sharp, indeed, for contemporary tastes; two songs were cut from the opera because their biting social comment and angry political message were condemned by reviewers as being out of keeping with the gentle and humorous quality of the rest of the work.

The fact is that, like all the Savoy Operas, *Iolanthe* should not be taken too seriously. It is as much the vehicle for splendid pageantry – the entrance of the peers – and for parody of Wagnerian opera – the summoning of Iolanthe from the depths of the stream – as it is for political satire. After all, it is a fairy-tale opera, and that is the magic that weaves its spell over the audience. One of the girls who played a fairy in the original London run even won the heart of a real peer, who came night after night to see her tripping hither and thither around the stage.

Sullivan produced some of his most memorable melodies for *Iolanthe*, ranging from the triumphal march of the peers to the delicate 'None shall part us' duet for Strephon and Phyllis. In the music for Iolanthe herself there is also a haunting sadness which goes deeper than almost anything else in the Savoy Operas. The composer began work on the opera just a few days after his beloved mother died, and this almost certainly influenced the character of some of the music.

Iolanthe was the first of Gilbert and Sullivan's operas to open at the Savoy Theatre, which Richard D'Oyly Carte had built just off the Strand as the home for his company. It is, therefore, strictly speaking the first of the Savoy Operas. The theatre had opened in October 1881 with the transfer of *Patience* from the Opéra Comique. It was the first theatre in Britain to be lit by electricity. During the initial run of *Iolanthe* Carte made another innovation by introducing for the first time in Britain the French system of queuing for people waiting outside the theatre for unreserved seats. He was much commended for turning what had hitherto been an uncontrolled scramble into something 'dignified and stately'.

Iolanthe ran initially at the Savoy for 398 performances, more than *The Pirates of Penzance*, although not as many as its immediate predecessor, *Patience*. It has continued to be very popular ever since, particularly in Britain. The premiership of Margaret Thatcher between 1979 and 1991 gave a new significance to the line 'This comes of women interfering in politics', while frequently canvassed proposals by the Labour Party to abolish or at least modify the House of Lords have kept the subject of hereditary peerages and the Upper Chamber firmly on the political agenda.

On 24 January 1962 *Iolanthe* became the first Gilbert and Sullivan opera to receive a professional production out of copyright when it was performed by Sadler's Wells Opera Company. In July 1977 the D'Oyly Carte Opera Company mounted a new production with a dramatic set designed by Bruno Santini which featured a silvery cobweb which disappeared at the entry of the peers to reveal an Arcadian landscape. In their efforts to draw attention to their financial plight in 1981, members of the company toured London in an open topped bus, the men dressed as peers from *Iolanthe* and the women as sisters, cousins and aunts from *H.M.S. Pinafore*. They were joined at the House of Lords by a former Prime Minister, Lord Wilson of Rievaulx, and a former Lord Chancellor, Lord Elwyn Jones.

In 1986 Scottish Opera brought *Iolanthe* into its repertoire and it was one of the two works (the other being *The Yeomen of the Guard*) which launched the birth of the new D'Oyly Carte Opera Company in April 1988. Opening at the Empire Theatre, Sunderland, it moved in July to the Cambridge Theatre for the new company's first London season, which was ushered in by the Band of the Grenadier Guards playing outside the theatre before the first performance and in the boxes on either side of the auditorium during it. The company returned to *Iolanthe* for their 1991 tour, launched in Birmingham, this time with a new production by Andrew Wickes full of delightful touches such as a cricket match between Liberal and Conservative peers during 'Loudly let the trumpet bray' and an ingenious model of the Houses of Parliament with a drinks cupboard in the tower of Big Ben and a bunk bed for the Lord Chancellor in the roof.

1   *Scene*: In an early D'Oyly Carte prompt copy of *Iolanthe* the date of the action is given as
    between 1700 and 1882.
    An Arcadian Landscape: Arcadia, a mountainous area of small valleys and villages in cen-
    tral Peloponnesus, was regarded by the ancient Greeks as the ideal region of rural con-
    tentment and pastoral simplicity. Sullivan composed the music for the First Act of
    Iolanthe while he was himself in the somewhat Arcadian landscape of Cornwall. He was
    staying at Pencarrow House, near Bodmin, the home of Sir William Molesworth.
2–3   *Leila, Celia, and Fleta*: Gilbert had originally intended calling his principal fairies Lola,
    Astarte and Lettie.

7   *our fairy ring*: This is, of course, also the term used to describe the rings in lawns or
    grassland formed by various species of mushroom.

8–15   *We are dainty little fairies*
    Some of the critics who attended the London opening of *Iolanthe* felt that the fairies were
    not as dainty as they might be, musically speaking at least. *The Times* ventured the opi-
    nion that

> In the first scene of the play Mr Sullivan has somewhat neglected what was, perhaps, his
> best opportunity for musical development. His fairy revels are of the tamest. There is here
> nothing of the brightness and lightness which Weber and Mendelssohn would have given
> to such a scene. But then, it should be remembered that Mr Gilbert's fairies are very differ-
> ent from those of *Oberon* and *A Midsummer Night's Dream*. Here, as in so many occasions in
> these operettas, the chances of the musician have been sacrificed to the humour of the poet.

ACT I

SCENE. – *An Arcadian Landscape. A river runs around the back of the stage. A rustic bridge crosses the river. Enter Fairies, led by* LEILA, CELIA, *and* FLETA. *They trip around the stage, singing as they dance.*

CHORUS.

Tripping hither, tripping thither,
Nobody knows why or whither;
We must dance and we must sing   5
Round about our fairy ring!

SOLO – CELIA.

We are dainty little fairies,
   Ever singing, ever dancing;
We indulge in our vagaries   10
   In a fashion most entrancing.
If you ask the special function
   Of our never-ceasing motion,
We reply, without compunction,
   That we haven't any notion!   15

CHORUS.

No, we haven't any notion!
   Tripping hither, etc.

SOLO – LEILA.

If you ask us how we live,
Lovers all essentials give –
   We can ride on lovers' sighs,   20
   Warm ourselves in lovers' eyes,
   Bathe ourselves in lovers' tears,

39　*Something awful*: Gilbert originally intended that Leila should have a song at this point. It is printed in the copy of the libretto sent to the Lord Chamberlain for licensing purposes and follows Fleta's question, 'What could she have done to have deserved such a terrible punishment?' Leila responds: 'Something too shocking – too terrible – too dreadful to be told. I'll tell it to you':

Song–Leila.

Five and twenty years ago
She, a fairy,
All unwary,
To a man of mortal clay
Gave her foolish heart away.
They were wed for weal or woe
Five and twenty years ago!

By a law that fairies prize
(Arbitrary
　　For a fairy)
She who marries mortal, dies –
Heedless of her heart-drawn cries
We prepared the fatal blow
Five and twenty years ago!

But our Queen, whose heart was rent
By her wailing
Unavailing,
Changed her doom to banishment,
With a merciful intent
And politely told her so
Five and twenty years ago!

44　*Enter Fairy Queen*: The Fairy Queen is one of the great contralto roles in the Savoy Operas, 'great' being used in all senses of the word. In early performances the Queen, whom Gilbert had originally intended should have the name Varine, was dressed to look like Brünnhilde, the formidable chief of the Valkyries and favourite daughter of Wotan in Wagner's *Ring* cycle of operas. Alice Barnett, who created the role, wore a winged helmet and silver mail armour. As we will see, there are other touches of Wagner in both the First and Second Acts of *Iolanthe*.

48–9　*on her head*: 'On your head' was a familiar Victorian catch-phrase meaning 'with ease'. It is still used in the form 'You can do it standing on your head'. Gilbert's use of it here seems rather unnecessary.

Clothe ourselves with lovers' fears,
Arm ourselves with lovers' darts,
Hide ourselves in lovers' hearts. 25
When you know us, you'll discover
That we almost live on lover!

CHORUS.

Yes, we live on lover!
Tripping hither, etc.

(*At the end of Chorus, all sigh wearily.*) 30

CELIA. Ah, it's all very well, but since our Queen banished Iolanthe, fairy revels have not been what they were!

LEILA. Iolanthe was the life and soul of Fairyland. Why, she wrote all our songs and arranged all our dances! We sing her songs and we trip her measures, but we don't enjoy ourselves! 35

FLETA. To think that five-and-twenty years have elapsed since she was banished! What could she have done to have deserved so terrible a punishment?

LEILA. Something awful! She married a mortal!

FLETA. Oh! Is it injudicious to marry a mortal? 40

LEILA. Injudicious? It strikes at the root of the whole fairy system! By our laws, the fairy who marries a mortal dies!

CELIA. But Iolanthe didn't die!

(*Enter* FAIRY QUEEN.)

QUEEN. No, because your Queen, who loved her with a surpassing 45
love, commuted her sentence to penal servitude for life, on condition that she left her husband and never communicated with him again!

LEILA. That sentence of penal servitude she is now working out, on her head, at the bottom of that stream!

QUEEN. Yes, but when I banished her, I gave her all the pleasant 50
places of the earth to dwell in. I'm sure I never intended that she should go and live at the bottom of a stream! It makes me perfectly wretched to think of the discomfort she must have undergone!

LEILA. Think of the damp! And her chest was always delicate.

QUEEN. And the frogs! Ugh! I never shall enjoy any peace of mind 55
until I know why Iolanthe went to live among the frogs!

FLETA. Then why not summon her and ask her?

QUEEN. Why? Because if I set eyes on her I should forgive her at once!

CELIA. Then why not forgive her? Twenty-five years – it's a long time!

LEILA. Think how we loved her! 60

62 *Who taught me to curl myself inside a buttercup*: This is one of the prettiest passages which Gilbert ever wrote and shows that inside the satirist's skin there was a delicate lyric poet trying to get out. It has faint echoes of Ariel's song in Shakespeare's *The Tempest*, Act V, Scene 1:

> Where the bee sucks, there suck I.
> In a cowslip's bell I lie;
> There I couch when owls do cry.

73–94 *Invocation – Queen*
This scene, in which Iolanthe rises from the depths of the stream in response to the Queen's command, has a distinctly Wagnerian atmosphere. It has obvious similarities with Scene I of *Das Rheingold*, the first opera in the *Ring* cycle, which is set at the bottom of the River Rhine. The music played while Iolanthe rises from her watery prison bears a close resemblance to the theme 'Die alte Weise' from the Third Act of Wagner's opera *Tristan und Isolde*, which was itself partially set in Cornwall.

81 *Iolanthe*: During rehearsals both the opera and the character now known as *Iolanthe* were called *Perola*. At the final run-through at the Savoy, Sullivan told the company: 'You have been rehearsing *Perola*, but when the curtain goes up the opera will be called *Iolanthe*. Will you please change the name Perola to Iolanthe throughout.'

In fact, Gilbert and Sullivan had always intended to call their new work *Iolanthe*, but this title had leaked out, and to confuse would-be competitors and pirates they had changed the name to *Perola* for the duration of rehearsals.

There may also have been some concern about possible copyright complications in using the name *Iolanthe*. It was already the title of a lyrical drama by the Danish playwright Henrik Hertz based on an old story about a blind princess called Yolande. In 1880 an English translation of Hertz's play by W. G. Wills opened in London with the same title and with Ellen Terry and Henry Irving in the leading roles. In a letter written on 13 October 1882, just six weeks before the opera was due to open, Gilbert asked D'Oyly Carte to request permission to use the name from Irving, to whom Wills had sold the rights.

QUEEN. Loved her? What was your love to mine? Why, she was invaluable to me! Who taught me to curl myself inside a buttercup? Iolanthe! Who taught me to swing upon a cobweb? Iolanthe! Who taught me to dive into a dewdrop – to nestle in a nutshell – to gambol upon gossamer? Iolanthe!

LEILA. She certainly did surprising things!

FLETA. Oh, give her back to us, great Queen, for your sake if not for ours! (*All kneel in supplication.*)

QUEEN (*irresolute*). Oh, I should be strong, but I am weak! I should be marble, but I am clay! Her punishment has been heavier than I intended. I did not mean that she should live among the frogs – and – well, well, it shall be as you wish – it shall be as you wish!

INVOCATION – QUEEN.

                Iolanthe!
    From thy dark exile thou art summoned!
            Come to our call –
          Come, come, Iolanthe!
CELIA.   Iolanthe!
LEILA.   Iolanthe!
ALL.   Come to our call, Iolanthe!
            Iolanthe, come!

(IOLANTHE *rises from the water. She is clad in water-weeds. She approaches the* QUEEN *with head bent and arms crossed.*)

IOLANTHE.   With humbled breast
            And every hope laid low,
          To thy behest,
          Offended Queen, I bow!

QUEEN.   For a dark sin against our fairy laws
          We sent thee into life-long banishment;
          But mercy holds her sway within our hearts –
          Rise – thou art pardoned!
IOL.   Pardoned!
ALL.   Pardoned!

(*Her weeds fall from her, and she appears clothed as a fairy. The* QUEEN *places a diamond coronet on her head, and embraces her. The others also embrace her.*)

CHORUS.

          Welcome to our hearts again,
            Iolanthe! Iolanthe!

65

70

75

80

85

90

95

105 *my son, Strephon*: The character of Strephon, half fairy and half mortal, is based on an idea originally developed by Gilbert in his Bab Ballad 'The Fairy Curate', which begins, rather like the song originally intended for Leila in *Iolanthe*:

> Once a fairy
> Light and airy
> Married with a mortal.

The ballad goes on to describe the circumstances of the marriage, with the fairy flying down to Ealing, where she meets and later weds an attorney. Their son, Georgie, becomes a curate in the Church of England but falls prey to High Church practices and ritualism to an extent which alarms his mother. She flies down to Ealing again to have words with him, only to be confronted by his Bishop, who refuses to believe she is his mother (see the note to line 558). The ballad ends with poor Georgie changing religion and becoming a Mormon.

118–19 *a Ward in Chancery* (also referred to as 'Ward of Chancery' and 'Ward of Court'): A minor whose guardianship is vested in the Court of Chancery for various legal reasons, often in cases of broken or difficult homes or where a dispute has arisen over property or inheritance. It is contempt of court to marry a Ward of Chancery without the court's consent. Major-General Stanley's daughters in *The Pirates of Penzance* are all wards of Chancery.

In the copy of the libretto sent to the Lord Chamberlain this line read 'and he loves Phyllis, a Ward in Chancery, who owns this farm'.

121 *a fairy down to the waist*: This same imagery is used about mermaids in Act I of *The Pirates of Penzance* when Kate says that they 'are only human beings down to the waist'.

127 *Enter Strephon . . . playing on a flageolet*: Gilbert had originally intended to call his shepherd hero Corydon. This name, used by the classical authors Virgil (in his *Eclogues*) and Theocritus (in his *Idylls*), became conventional in pastoral poetry. Corydon's name was traditionally linked with that of Phyllis, the ideal shepherdess. In John Milton's poem *L'Allegro* (1632), for example, Phyllis is described as giving dinner to Corydon and his fellow shepherd Thyrsis. However, Gilbert later decided to break with the convention and call his hero Strephon, a name he had already used in an earlier play (see the note to lines 229–44).

The flageolet, on which Strephon accompanies himself (as does Phyllis, at her entrance a little later in this act), is a small wind instrument similar to a flute, with a mouthpiece at one end, six principal holes and sometimes keys as well. Strephon and Phyllis are not the only characters in the Savoy Operas to come on stage playing a flageolet. Dr Daly, the vicar of Ploverleigh, does so in the Second Act of *The Sorcerer* before singing his haunting song 'Oh, my voice is sad and low'. Like Strephon's 'Good morrow, good mother!' that song has the most beautiful flageolet accompaniment, played, of course, from the orchestra pit rather than the stage.

> We have shared thy bitter pain,
>> Iolanthe! Iolanthe!
> Every heart and every hand
> In our loving little band   100
> Welcomes thee to Fairyland,
>> Iolanthe!

QUEEN. And now, tell me, with all the world to choose from, why on earth did you decide to live at the bottom of that stream?

IOL. To be near my son, Strephon.   105

QUEEN. Bless my heart, I didn't know you had a son.

IOL. He was born soon after I left my husband by your royal command – but he does not even know of his father's existence.

FLETA. How old is he?

IOL. Twenty-four.   110

LEILA. Twenty-four! No one, to look at you, would think you had a son of twenty-four! But that's one of the advantages of being immortal. We never grow old! Is he pretty?

IOL. He's extremely pretty, but he's inclined to be stout.

ALL (*disappointed*). Oh!   115

QUEEN. I see no objection to stoutness, in moderation.

CELIA. And what is he?

IOL. He's an Arcadian shepherd – and he loves Phyllis, a Ward in Chancery.

CELIA. A mere shepherd! and he half a fairy!   120

IOL. He's a fairy down to the waist – but his legs are mortal.

ALL. Dear me!

QUEEN. I have no reason to suppose that I am more curious than other people, but I confess I should like to see a person who is a fairy down to the waist, but whose legs are mortal.   125

IOL. Nothing easier, for here he comes!

(*Enter* STREPHON, *singing and dancing and playing on a flageolet. He does not see the Fairies, who retire up stage as he enters.*)

SONG – STREPHON.

> Good morrow, good mother!
>> Good mother, good morrow!   130
> By some means or other,
>> Pray banish your sorrow!
> With joy beyond telling
> My bosom is swelling,
> So join in a measure   135
> Expressive of pleasure,

141 *the Lord Chancellor*: The highest judicial functionary in England, the Lord Chancellor ranks in order of precedence above all peers, except princes of the blood (i.e. the Royal Family) and the Archbishop of Canterbury. He acts as Speaker of the House of Lords and presides over the Chancery Division of the Supreme Court of Judicature.

146 *the Bar*: A collective noun for the whole profession of barristers. The word is derived from the barrier or partition which used to separate the seats of benchers and readers (i.e. senior and fully established members) of one of the Inns of Court from those of the students who sat in the rest of the hall. When fully qualified, the students were called to this barrier to take part in the 'mootings' and business of the Inn – hence the expression still used to describe qualification as a barrister, 'called to the Bar'.

147 *A servile usher*: The usher is the officer who acts as doorkeeper in a court of law, showing persons to their seats and leading those of rank, like judges, into the court. In *Trial by Jury* the usher is given a solo part, although any pretensions above his station which this elevation might give him are dispelled when the judge contemptuously yells:

> Gentle, simple-minded Usher,
> Get you, if you like, to Russher!

crumpled bands: Bands are the strips of white cloth, normally cotton, which are worn hanging from the neck by clergymen and lawyers. An usher would not normally wear bands.

148 *rusty bombazine*: Bombazine is the black material from which legal and clerical gowns are made.

Chancery Lane: The street which goes through the heart of legal London, joining Gray's Inn to the north with Fleet Street (the Law Courts and the Middle and Inner Temples) to the south. Before the present Law Courts came into use – they were opened just a month after *Iolanthe* was first performed – Chancery cases were sometimes heard in the hall of Lincoln's Inn or in the Old Rolls Court of the now demolished Clifford's Inn, both of which were off Chancery Lane. The street also makes an appearance in Act II of *Patience* when Archibald Grosvenor, newly transformed from aesthete into matter-of-fact young man, proclaims himself 'A Chancery Lane young man'.

159 *My dear aunt*: This line was introduced by Gilbert for the 1907 revival of *Iolanthe* at the Savoy Theatre. The fairies' line 'Poor fellow!' (line 167) was also added at the same time.

169–70 *I've a borough or two at my disposal*: In early-nineteenth-century Britain, up to 200 parliamentary seats were in the private patronage of wealthy and influential individuals. These were the so-called pocket boroughs, where there was often only a handful of electors, and where the local landowner could get his own nominee into the House of Commons without any difficulty. Although most pocket boroughs were abolished by the Great Reform Act of 1832, there were still about sixty M.P.s who were nominated by individuals, mostly peers. Sir Joseph Porter in *H.M.S. Pinafore*, it may be remembered, was returned to Parliament for a pocket borough.

174 *confounded Radicals*: In the 1880s the word 'Radicals' was associated with advanced and left-wing members of the Liberal Party who stressed the need for social and economic reform. In 1885 Joseph Chamberlain, the acknowledged leader of this group, issued the *Radical Programme* (also known as the Unauthorized Programme), which called for much greater government intervention in social and economic matters and seemed to more traditional Liberals to come dangerously near to advocating socialism.

For the 1901 revival of *Iolanthe*, at the height of the war between Britain and the South African Boers, Gilbert changed this line to 'my legs are a couple of confounded Radicals, but this one is a pro-Boer'. The Liberal Party, and left-wing opinion in general, was split in its attitude to the war.

175 *the wrong lobby*: When a bell sounds indicating a division in the House of Commons, members have a few minutes in which to take their seats in the Chamber. Then the doors are locked and they file into one of two lobbies which run parallel to the Chamber. The

> For I'm to be married to-day – to-day –
> Yes, I'm to be married to-day!

CHORUS (*aside*).   Yes, he's to be married to-day – to-day –
Yes, he's to be married to-day!   140

IOL. Then the Lord Chancellor has at last given his consent to your marriage with his beautiful ward, Phyllis?

STREPH. Not he, indeed. To all my tearful prayers he answers me, 'A shepherd lad is no fit helpmate for a Ward of Chancery.' I stood in court, and there I sang him songs of Arcadee, with flageolet accompaniment – in vain.   145 At first he seemed amused, so did the Bar; but quickly wearying of my song and pipe, bade me get out. A servile usher then, in crumpled bands and rusty bombazine, led me, still singing, into Chancery Lane! I'll go no more; I'll marry her to-day, and brave the upshot, be it what it may! (*Sees Fairies.*) But who are these?   150

IOL. Oh, Strephon! rejoice with me, my Queen has pardoned me!

STREPH. Pardoned you, mother? This is good news indeed.

IOL. And these ladies are my beloved sisters.

STREPH. Your sisters! Then they are – my aunts!

QUEEN. A pleasant piece of news for your bride on her wedding day!   155

STREPH. Hush! My bride knows nothing of my fairyhood. I dare not tell her, lest it frighten her. She thinks me mortal, and prefers me so.

LEILA. Your fairyhood doesn't seem to have done you much good.

STREPH. Much good! My dear aunt! it's the curse of my existence! What's the use of being half a fairy? My body can creep through a keyhole,   160 but what's the good of that when my legs are left kicking behind? I can make myself invisible down to the waist, but that's of no use when my legs remain exposed to view! My brain is a fairy brain, but from the waist downwards I'm a gibbering idiot. My upper half is immortal, but my lower half grows older every day, and some day or other must die of old age. What's to become of   165 my upper half when I've buried my lower half I really don't know!

FAIRIES. Poor fellow!

QUEEN. I see your difficulty, but with a fairy brain you should seek an intellectual sphere of action. Let me see. I've a borough or two at my disposal. Would you like to go into Parliament?   170

IOL. A fairy Member! That would be delightful!

STREPH. I'm afraid I should do no good there – you see, down to the waist, I'm a Tory of the most determined description, but my legs are a couple of confounded Radicals, and, on a division, they'd be sure to take me into the wrong lobby. You see, they're two to one, which is a strong working   175 majority.

QUEEN. Don't let that distress you; you shall be returned as a Liberal-Conservative, and your legs shall be our peculiar care.

'Aye' lobby (for those in favour of the motion beng put to the vote) is entered to the right of the Speaker's chair, the 'No' lobby (for those against) to the left. Once in the lobbies members give their names to clerks and as they leave they are counted by tellers. Members wishing to abstain on the division remain seated in the Chamber.

177–8 *a Liberal-Conservative*: This phrase was also the object of alteration for topical purposes, being changed for a period to 'Liberal-Unionist'. The Liberal Unionists, led by Joseph Chamberlain and Lord Hartington, broke away from the Liberal Party in 1886 because they could not stomach its policy of Home Rule for Ireland. They remained as a separate political grouping until 1912, when they amalgamated with the Conservative Party, which has since then had the full title 'Conservative and Unionist Party'.

The change of 'Liberal-Conservative' to 'Liberal-Unionist' in the Fairy Queen's line presumably took place some time between 1886 and 1912, although it does not appear in print until the fifth edition of the *Iolanthe* libretto, which was published around 1920, some years after the Liberal Unionists had ceased to exist. It still appears in the Macmillan edition of the Savoy Operas, but both the Chappell edition of the libretto and the Oxford University Press World's Classics edition of the operas have reverted to the original 'Liberal-Conservative', which is now normally sung. Perhaps 'Liberal Democrat' would be more appropriate today.

194 *Good morrow, good lover*: After Phyllis's introductory song, Gilbert originally planned a passage of dialogue in which she would tell us more about herself, including why she is a ward of Chancery. It is printed in the licence copy of the libretto sent to the Lord Chamberlain but was cut before the opera's first performance. Here it is:

> STREPHON. Is everything prepared?
>
> PHYLLIS. Yes, and papa has arrived from Wellington barracks – on pass!
>
> STREPHON. O, nice and sober?
>
> PHYL. Quite sober, bless him. His regiment says it thinks it can manage without him for a whole day.
>
> STREPH. Won't it cripple their movements?
>
> PHYL. No – I think not. But oh, Strephon, I tremble at the step I'm taking! I believe it's penal servitude for life to marry a Ward in Chancery without the Lord Chancellor's permission!
>
> STREPH. And what right has he to refuse it? Because I'm only a shepherd. I'm a *decorative* shepherd.
>
> PHYL. Anyway you're as good as I am. Papa's only a private soldier, and that's why they made me a Ward in Chancery – they said he wasn't fit to look after my money. And I shan't be of age for two years.
>
> STREPH. Two years? I can't wait two years while half the House of Lords is sighing at your feet.
>
> PHYL. The House of Lords is certainly extremely attentive.

The dialogue then continues as now (line 224).

213 *Have you ever looked in the glass*: This line, and Phyllis's 'No, never', were added for the 1907 revival. It is somewhat reminiscent of the scene in the Second Act of *Patience* where Archibald Grosvenor enters gazing at his reflection in a hand-mirror. He later hands it to Reginald Bunthorne, who becomes equally obsessed with his own reflection.

STREPH. (*bowing*). I see your Majesty does not do things by halves.

QUEEN. No, we are fairies down to the feet. 180

ENSEMBLE.

QUEEN.	Fare thee well, attractive stranger.
FAIRIES.	Fare thee well, attractive stranger.
QUEEN.	Shouldst thou be in doubt or danger,
	Peril or perplexitee,
	Call us, and we'll come to thee! 185
FAIRIES.	Aye! Call us, and we'll come to thee!
	Tripping hither, tripping thither,
	Nobody knows why or whither;
	We must now be taking wing
	To another fairy ring! 190

(*Fairies and* QUEEN *trip off,* IOLANTHE, *who takes an affectionate farewell of her son, going off last.*)

(*Enter* PHYLLIS, *singing and dancing, and accompanying herself on a flageolet.*)

SONG – PHYLLIS.

Good morrow, good lover!
   Good lover, good morrow! 195
I prithee discover,
   Steal, purchase, or borrow
     Some means of concealing
     The care you are feeling,
     And join in a measure 200
     Expressive of pleasure,
For we're to be married to-day – to-day!
   Yes, we're to be married to-day!

BOTH.   Yes, we're to be married, etc.

STREPH. (*embracing her*). My Phyllis! And to-day we are to be made 205
happy for ever.

PHYL. Well, we're to be married.

STREPH. It's the same thing.

PHYL. I suppose it is. But oh, Strephon, I tremble at the step I'm taking!
I believe it's penal servitude for life to marry a Ward of Court without the 210
Lord Chancellor's consent! I shall be of age in two years. Don't you think you
could wait two years?

STREPH. Two years. Have you ever looked in the glass?

225 *grass-plot*: A piece of ground covered with turf, and sometimes also with ornamental flower-beds, generally found around large country houses. Possession of such land seems to place Phyllis in a rather higher social station than that of a mere army private's daughter, or indeed an Arcadian shepherdess.

228 *delays are dangerous*: In the licence copy the duet 'If we're weak enough to tarry', now sung in Act II, follows at this point. This line of dialogue makes a much more natural introduction to that song that it does to 'None shall part us', which was hastily written and slotted in here shortly before the first performance.

229–44 *None shall part us from each other*
This delightful duet, with its charming metaphors drawn from rural life, firmly establishes Phyllis and Strephon as the perfect fairy-tale shepherd and shepherdess. For many years in D'Oyly Carte Company productions they were made to look like eighteenth-century Dresden figurines with powdered wigs, faces made up to give the impression of porcelain, and shiny satin clothes patterned with flowers.

Ten years before writing *Iolanthe* Gilbert had caricatured the idyllic pastoral couple whom he was to re-create for the opera. His play *Happy Arcadia* (1872), set to music by Fred Clay, has among its cast of characters Strephon, 'a happy Arcadian betrothed to Chloe', and Chloe, 'a happy Arcadian betrothed to Strephon'. He is fed up with the pipes he has to play every day, and she is equally bored with the little lamb she is forced to go around with. In *Iolanthe* he drops his cynicism and pokes only the most gentle fun at the conventions of pastoral poetry.

247–61 *Loudly let the trumpet bray*
The entrance of the peers in *Iolanthe* is undoubtedly the most spectacular scene in any of the Savoy Operas. Indeed it must rank alongside the triumphal march in Verdi's *Aïda* and the procession of apprentices and masters in the last act of Wagner's *Die Meistersinger* as one of the greatest processional scenes in the entire world of opera.

In several D'Oyly Carte productions, including the first night at the Savoy, the peers were led on to the stage by a section of the band of the Grenadier Guards. Gilbert's stage direction reads: 'Band cross bridge in double rank from left to right. Enter peers on bridge marching with great state in single rank and somewhat swaggering gesture, as fancying themselves, basses leading and tenors last.' At the phrases 'ye lower middle classes' and 'ye tradesmen' and 'ye masses', he notes that the peers should 'point imperiously to the ground'.

No expense was spared in dressing the peers. Their robes were specially made by Messrs Ede and Sons, robemakers to Queen Victoria's Court, and they wore the full insignia of Britain's highest orders of chivalry. Richard D'Oyly Carte was worried that this might cause offence in high circles. He wrote to his secretary 'If it gets over to the Lord Chamberlain's office that the sacred orders of the Garter, Thistle, Patrick and Bath are going on the stage the office may come down bang and forbid it being done'. However, although Queen Victoria is reported not to have been amused in general by *Iolanthe*, no royal complaint was received on that particular point.

Gilbert had a rather different concern about the possible reaction to the gorgeous spectacle that he was putting on stage. He remarked on the eve of the first night 'Some of our American friends who will be seeing *Iolanthe* in New York tomorrow will probably imagine that British lords are to be seen walking about our streets garbed in this fashion.' Certainly it is reported that the opera's New York run led to a greatly increased demand among American heiresses for eligible members of the British aristocracy.

Gilbert also decided that for added effect the peers should be completely shaven, except for a single tuft under their chins and mutton-chop whiskers. Under their coronets their heads were to be completely bald. 'Let your coronets remain off longer, gentlemen,' he said at one rehearsal. 'There is £12's worth of bald heads on the stage and we must make the most of them.'

PHYL. No, never.

STREPH. Here, look at that (*showing her a pocket mirror*), and tell me if 215
you think it rational to expect me to wait two years?

PHYL. (*looking at herself*). No. You're quite right – it's asking too much.
One must be reasonable.

STREPH. Besides, who knows what will happen in two years? Why,
you might fall in love with the Lord Chancellor himself by that time! 220

PHYL. Yes. He's a clean old gentleman.

STREPH. As it is, half the House of Lords are sighing at your feet.

PHYL. The House of Lords are certainly extremely attentive.

STREPH. Attentive? I should think they were! Why did five-and-twenty
Liberal Peers come down to shoot over your grass-plot last autumn? It 225
couldn't have been the sparrows. Why did five-and-twenty Conservative
Peers come down to fish your pond? Don't tell me it was the gold-fish! No,
no – delays are dangerous, and if we are to marry, the sooner the better.

DUET – STREPHON *and* PHYLLIS.

PHYLLIS.	None shall part us from each other,
	One in life and death are we: 230
	All in all to one another –
	I to thee and thou to me!
BOTH.	Thou the tree and I the flower –
	Thou the idol; I the throng –
	Thou the day and I the hour – 235
	Thou the singer; I the song!
STREPH.	All in all since that fond meeting
	When, in joy, I woke to find
	Mine the heart within thee beating,
	Mine the love that heart enshrined! 240
BOTH.	Thou the stream and I the willow –
	Thou the sculptor; I the clay –
	Thou the ocean; I the billow –
	Thou the sunrise; I the day!

(*Exeunt* STREPHON *and* PHYLLIS *together.*) 245

(*March. Enter Procession of Peers.*)

CHORUS.

Loudly let the trumpet bray!
Tantantara!
Proudly bang the sounding brasses!
Tzing! Boom! 250

263-95 *The Law is the true embodiment*
This is the one song in the Savoy Operas where Sullivan's indication of speed has traditionally been ignored in D'Oyly Carte Opera Company performances. In the vocal score it is marked *Allegro vivace*, but it is generally sung at the slightly slower speed of *Allegro non troppo*. In his book *W. S. Gilbert, Stage Director* (1977) William Cox-Ife, chorus director of the D'Oyly Carte Company from 1950 to 1968, says that Sullivan's *Allegro vivace* was almost certainly a slip of the pen, understandable in view of the short time in which he completed the *Iolanthe* score.

Cox-Ife also maintains that 'there is incontrovertible proof that the speed at which this song is sung in the D'Oyly Carte performances is the one agreed upon by both Gilbert and Sullivan'. He points out that Martyn Green, whom he first heard singing it, took the song at the same speed as his predecessor in the comic roles, Sir Henry Lytton. Lytton, who first played the part of the Lord Chancellor in 1891 in one of the D'Oyly Carte touring companies, was personally directed by Gilbert. However, in an early D'Oyly Carte recording C. H. Workman sings the number *Allegro vivace*, as marked, so it is just possible that Cox-Ife was wrong.

When George Grossmith appeared on stage to sing this song on the first night of *Iolanthe* at the Savoy Theatre, there was naturally much speculation in the audience as to which well-known contemporary figure Gilbert had chosen as the model for his latest comic lead. There did not seem to be any close similarities between the stage Lord Chancellor and his real-life contemporary counterpart, Lord Selborne, who held the office in Gladstone's 1880–85 Government. Indeed the general view was that this time Gilbert had gone back into history and had loosely based his Lord Chancellor on Lord Lyndhurst (1772–1863), one of the most distinguished holders of the office in the nineteenth century. Lyndhurst, a Boston American by birth, was Lord Chancellor from 1827 to 1830 and was known for the mastery of his judicial summings-up and his ability to digest a mass of evidence.

As upon its lordly way
    This unique procession passes,
      Tantantara! Tzing! Boom!
Bow, bow, ye lower middle classes!
Bow, bow, ye tradesmen, bow, ye masses!   255
Blow the trumpets, bang the brasses!
      Tantantara! Tzing! Boom!
We are peers of highest station,
Paragons of legislation,
Pillars of the British nation!   260
      Tantantara! Tzing! Boom!

(*Enter the* LORD CHANCELLOR, *followed by his train-bearer.*)

SONG – LORD CHANCELLOR.

The Law is the true embodiment
Of everything that's excellent.
It has no kind of fault or flaw,   265
And I, my Lords, embody the Law.
The constitutional guardian I
Of pretty young Wards in Chancery,
All very agreeable girls – and none
Are over the age of twenty-one.   270
    A pleasant occupation for
    A rather susceptible Chancellor!

ALL.   A pleasant, etc.

But though the compliment implied
Inflates me with legitimate pride,   275
It nevertheless can't be denied
That it has its inconvenient side.
For I'm not so old, and not so plain,
And I'm quite prepared to marry again,
But there'd be the deuce to pay in the Lords   280
If I fell in love with one of my Wards!
    Which rather tries my temper, for
    I'm *such* a susceptible Chancellor!

ALL.   Which rather, etc.

And every one who'd marry a Ward   285
Must come to me for my accord,
And in my court I sit all day,

301 *her cottage*: Gilbert seems to be a trifle uncertain about Phyllis's exact station in life. First, in his original version of the *Iolanthe* libretto, we are told that she owns the farm on which Act I is set (see the note to lines 118–19). That information is later cut out, as is the subsequent and rather conflicting intelligence that she is the daughter of a private stationed at the Wellington barracks. Next, Strephon informs us that she has both a grass-plot and a fish-pond, yet here we are told that she lives in a cottage. It is all rather confusing.

317–18 *contempt of . . . Court*: Action of any kind which interferes with the proper administration of justice. It includes any disobedience to the rules, orders or process of a court and any gross display of disrespect to the judge or officials.

318 *counsel*: The name given to a barrister or barristers when engaged in the direction or conduct of a case in court.

320 *woolsack*: A square couch said to have been originally placed in the House of Lords in the reign of Edward III and stuffed with wool clippings as a reminder of England's staple trade. It is now filled with a blend of wool from Britain and the Commonwealth. When the House of Lords is sitting, the woolsack is the seat of the Lord Chancellor. However, it is technically outside the precincts of the House, so when he wishes to address his fellow peers he has to stand aside from the woolsack and so 'enter' the chamber.

323–4 *the Bar of this House*: This is a completely different Bar from that referred to in line 146 above. In both the House of Commons and the House of Lords, a barrier separates from the main chamber a space near the door to which non-members may be admitted for business purposes. In the House of Lords the Bar consists of two rods which can be drawn across the end of the rows of benches. Offenders appealing to the Lords appear before the Bar, where they must traditionally kneel, and it is also the point to which the Speaker and members of the House of Commons come when they attend the monarch's opening of Parliament.

Giving agreeable girls away,
With one for him – and one for he –
And one for you – and one for ye –
And one for thou – and one for thee –
But never, oh, never a one for me!
   Which is exasperating for
   A highly susceptible Chancellor!

290

ALL.   Which is, etc.

295

(*Enter* LORD TOLLOLLER.)

LORD TOLL. And now, my Lords, to the business of the day.
  LORD CH. By all means. Phyllis, who is a Ward of Court, has so
powerfully affected your Lordships, that you have appealed to me in a body
to give her to whichever one of you she may think proper to select, and a
noble Lord has just gone to her cottage to request her immediate attendance.
It would be idle to deny that I, myself, have the misfortune to be singularly
attracted by this young person. My regard for her is rapidly undermining my
constitution. Three months ago I was a stout man. I need say no more. If I
could reconcile it with my duty, I should unhesitatingly award her to myself,
for I can conscientiously say that I know no man who is so well fitted to
render her exceptionally happy. (PEERS: Hear, hear!) But such an award
would be open to misconstruction, and therefore, at whatever personal
inconvenience, I waive my claim.
  LORD TOLL. My Lord, I desire, on the part of this House, to express
its sincere sympathy with your Lordship's most painful position.
  LORD CH. I thank your Lordships. The feelings of a Lord Chancellor
who is in love with a Ward of Court are not to be envied. What is his
position? Can he give his own consent to his own marriage with his own
Ward? Can he marry his own Ward without his own consent? And if he
marries his own Ward without his own consent, can he commit himself for
contempt of his own Court? And if he commit himself for contempt of his
own Court, can he appear by counsel before himself, to move for arrest of his
own judgement? Ah, my Lords, it is indeed painful to have to sit upon a
woolsack which is stuffed with such thorns as these!

300

305

310

315

320

(*Enter* LORD MOUNTARARAT.)

LORD MOUNT. My Lord, I have much pleasure in announcing that I
have succeeded in inducing the young person to present herself at the Bar
of this House.

(*Enter* PHYLLIS.)

325

330–49 *Of all the young ladies I know*
The predicament of Phyllis, pursued by two peers of the realm as well as by the humble
Strephon, is anticipated in Gilbert's Bab Ballad 'The Periwinkle Girl'. This tells the
story of Mary, a winkle seller, who is eagerly sought after by two dukes, Duke Bailey and
Duke Humphy, as well as by an earl, a less exalted member of the peerage. As these concluding verses show, Mary was initially attracted by the ducal overtures, but they were
to prove less appealing on closer examination:

> 'Two Dukes would Mary make a bride,
> And from her foes defend her' –
> 'Well, not exactly that,' they cried,
> 'We offer guilty splendour.
>
> 'We do not promise marriage rite,
> So please dismiss the notion!'
> 'Oh dear,' said she, 'that alters quite
> The state of my emotion.'
>
> The Earl he ups and says, says he,
> 'Dismiss them to their orgies,
> For I am game to marry thee
> Quite reg'lar at St George's.'
>
> He'd had, it happily befell,
> A decent education,
> His views would have befitted well
> A far superior station.
>
> His sterling worth had worked a cure,
> She never heard him grumble;
> She saw his soul was good and pure,
> Although his rank was humble.
>
> Her views of earldoms and their lot,
> All underwent expansion –
> Come, Virtue in an earldom's cot!
> Go, Vice in ducal mansion.

351 *tabors*: Small drums.

RECITATIVE – PHYLLIS.

My well-loved Lord and Guardian dear,
You summoned me, and I am here!

CHORUS OF PEERS.

Oh, rapture, how beautiful!
How gentle – how dutiful!

SOLO – LORD TOLLOLLER.

Of all the young ladies I know
    This pretty young lady's the fairest;   330
Her lips have the rosiest show,
    Her eyes are the richest and rarest.
Her origin's lowly, it's true,
    But of birth and position I've plenty;   335
I've grammar and spelling for two,
    And blood and behaviour for twenty!
    Her origin's lowly, it's true,
    I've grammar and spelling for two;

CHORUS.   Of birth and position he's plenty,   340
    With blood and behaviour for twenty!

SOLO – LORD MOUNTARARAT.

Though the views of the House have diverged
    On every conceivable motion,
All questions of Party are merged
    In a frenzy of love and devotion;   345
If you ask us distinctly to say
    What Party we claim to belong to,
We reply, without doubt or delay,
    The Party we're singing this song to!

SOLO – PHYLLIS.

I'm very much pained to refuse,   350
    But I'll stick to my pipes and my tabors;
I can spell all the words that I use,
    And my grammar's as good as my neighbours'.
As for birth – I was born like the rest,
    My behaviour is rustic but hearty,
And I know where to turn for the best,   355
    When I want a particular Party!

362 *Nay, tempt me not*: In the original version of *Perola* there was a lengthy series of couplets and a longer recitative for Phyllis between the end of the repetition of the last part of her song (line 361) and the beginning of Lord Tolloller's ballad (line 368). They are printed in the licence copy:

LORD CH.	Nay, do not recklessly refuse their proffer.
	Attend to the advantages they offer.

COUPLETS.

LORD CH.	On you they'd set
	A coronet.
PHYL.	Oh, a coronet.
LORD CH.	What joy to be a noble's pet,
	And walk about in a coronet!
CHORUS.	What joy, etc.
LORD TOLL.	You'll breathe the air of Grosvenor Square.
PHYL.	Oh Grosvenor, Grosvenor Square.
LORD TOLL.	What joy to breathe the balmy air
	Of Grosvenor Square, of Grosvenor Square.
ALL.	What joy, etc.
LORD MOUNT.	On every lip
	'Your ladyship!'
PHYL.	Oh lady – ladyship!
LORD MOUNT.	What joy to hear on every lip
	'Your ladyship', 'Your ladyship!'
ALL.	What joy, etc.
LORD CH.	There'll be no dearth
	Of clothes from Worth!
PHYL. (*aside*).	Oh, tasty tempting Worth!
LORD CH.	Oh, is there purer joy on earth
	Than to be dressed by Mister Worth!
ALL.	Oh, is there, etc.
LORD MOUNT.	With footmen rare
	In powdered hair!
PHYL. (*aside*).	Oh, powdered – powdered hair!
LORD MOUNT.	What joy to drive through Vanity Fair
	With footmen rare in powdered hair!
ALL.	What joy, etc.
LORD TOLL.	With a coachman big
	In a curly wig!
PHYL. (*aside*).	Oh, a curly, curly wig!
LORD TOLL.	What joy to drive about full fig,
	With a coachman big
	In a curly wig!
ALL.	What joy, etc.

PEERS.	PHYLLIS.
You'll breathe the air	I do not care
Of Grosvenor Square,	For Grosvenor Square;
There'll be no dearth	And who on earth
Of clothes from Worth,	Is Mister Worth?
With footmen rare	So bait no snare
In powdered hair,	With footmen rare,
And a coachman big	Or a coachman big
In a curly wig!	In a curly wig;
What joy to drive about full fig	Indeed, I do not care a fig
With a coachman big in a curly wig!	For a coachman big in a curly wig!

PHYLLIS, LORD TOLL., *and* LORD MOUNT.

Though $\left\{ \begin{array}{c} \text{my} \\ \text{her} \end{array} \right\}$ station is none of the best,

I suppose $\left\{ \begin{array}{c} \text{I} \\ \text{she} \end{array} \right\}$ was born like the rest;

And $\left\{ \begin{array}{c} \text{I know} \\ \text{she knows} \end{array} \right\}$ where to look for $\left\{ \begin{array}{c} \text{my} \\ \text{her} \end{array} \right\}$ hearty,   360

When $\left\{ \begin{array}{c} \text{I want} \\ \text{she wants} \end{array} \right\}$ a particular Party!

RECITATIVE – PHYLLIS.

Nay, tempt me not.
    To rank I'll not be bound;
In lowly cot
    Alone is virtue found!   365

CHORUS.   No, no; indeed high rank will never hurt you,
The Peerage is not destitute of virtue.

BALLAD – LORD TOLLOLLER.

Spurn not the nobly born
    With love affected,
Nor treat with virtuous scorn
    The well-connected.   370
High rank involves no shame –
We boast an equal claim
With him of humble name
    To be respected!   375
Blue blood! blue blood!
    When virtuous love is sought
    Thy power is naught,
Though dating from the Flood,
    Blue blood! Ah, blue blood!   380

CHORUS.   When virtuous love is sought, etc.

Spare us the bitter pain
    Of stern denials,
Nor with low-born disdain
    Augment our trials.
Hearts just as pure and fair   385

RECITATIVE – PHYLLIS.

No, no! it may not be, though I may mention,
I much appreciate your condescension,
I am a girl of lowly education,
And should disgrace your elevated station!

ALL.   No, no, despite defects of education
                    You would adorn our elevated station.

There then follows Lord Tolloller's ballad, 'Spurn not the nobly born'.

363 *To rank I'll not be bound*: In the vocal score and the Chappell edition of the libretto this is printed 'To wealth I'll not be bound'.

366 *No, no; indeed high rank will never hurt you*: In the first edition of the libretto this line was sung as 'Nay, do not shrink from us – we will not hurt you'.

387 *Belgrave Square*: One of the grandest squares in London, situated between Knightsbridge and Victoria, which gets its name from one of the titles of the ground landlord, the Duke of Westminster. The surrounding area, known as Belgravia, is a favourite location for embassies. In *Utopia Limited* the King, boasting about his successful attempt to anglicize his country, sings

> Our city we have beautified – we've done it willy-nilly –
> And all that isn't Belgrave Square is Strand and Piccadilly.

389 *Seven Dials*: A point in Monmouth Street, north of Leicester Square and south of High Holborn in the centre of London, where seven streets converge. During Charles II's reign a doric pillar was erected at the crossroads with sundials facing the seven streets. The area came to be notorious for squalor and crime, and as the headquarters of London's street ballad printers and sellers. Now, however, with the 'trendification' of nearby Covent Garden it has become positively fashionable.

394 *Blue blood*: High or noble birth. The phrase is of Spanish origin and derives from the fact that the veins of pure-blooded Spanish aristocrats, untainted by any Moorish influences, were more blue than the veins of those with mixed ancestry.

Gilbert's prompt copy of *Iolanthe* indicates that during the music following Lord Tolloller's ballad 'the peers take out handkerchiefs, wipe right eye, left eye, *nose* and throw handkerchiefs into coronets at last note, and resume coronets'.

412 *Of Arcadee*: This spelling of Arcady for the purpose of rhyming also occurs in the first line of a song in Gilbert and Sullivan's first joint work, *Thespis*, 'Little maid of Arcadee'. Reference to Arcady, or Arcadia, as it is more often called, also occurs in *Trial by Jury* in the Counsel for the Plaintiff's line 'Camberwell became a bower,/Peckham an Arcadian vale'.

May beat in Belgrave Square
As in the lowly air
Of Seven Dials!
Blue blood! blue blood!
Of what avail art thou
To serve us now?
Though dating from the Flood,
Blue blood! Ah, blue blood!

CHORUS.   Of what avail art thou, etc.

RECITATIVE – PHYLLIS.

My Lords, it may not be.
With grief my heart is riven!
You waste your time on me,
For ah! my heart is given!

ALL.   Given!
PHYL.   Yes, given!
ALL.   Oh, horror!!!

RECITATIVE – LORD CHANCELLOR.

And who has dared to brave our high displeasure,
And thus defy our definite command?

(*Enter* STREPHON.)

STREPH.   'Tis I – young Strephon! mine this priceless treasure!
          Against the world I claim my darling's hand!
               (PHYLLIS *rushes to his arms.*)
          A shepherd I –
ALL.   A shepherd he!
STREPH.   Of Arcady –
ALL.   Of Arcadee!
STREPH.   Betrothed are we!
ALL.   Betrothed are they –
STREPH.   And mean to be –
ALL.   Espoused to-day!

438–9   *Manent Lord Chancellor and Strephon*: In this stage direction Gilbert shows that, like the fairies and peers, he has had a good classical education. *Manent* is from the Latin word *maneo*, meaning 'remain'. It is a standard stage direction.

441   *Court of Chancery*: Now one of the divisions of the High Court of Justice, the Court of Chancery has traditionally dealt with cases involving equity and also with the wardship of infants.

442–61   *I go by Nature's Acts of Parliament*: In this passage, reminiscent of Ralph Rackstraw's 'simple eloquence' to Josephine in *H.M.S. Pinafore* and of some of Frederic's musings in *The Pirates of Penzance*, Strephon proves that, just like these other Gilbertian heroes, his humble origins have not prevented him from developing impressive powers of expression. In its review of the London first night of *Iolanthe*, the *Sunday Times* described the ensuing dialogue between Strephon and the Lord Chancellor as 'one of the most comical bits in the piece'.

Some other papers, however, were distinctly critical of this passage. Both the *Whitehall Review* and *Punch*, which generally took a low view of Gilbert's work, perhaps not unconnected with the fact that his Bab Ballads had appeared in the pages of its great rival *Fun*, detected more than a hint of plagiarism. They suggested that the Lord Chancellor's rejection of Strephon's eloquent testimony from nature on the grounds that it was not evidence (line 458) was borrowed directly from the passage in Charles Dickens's *The Pickwick Papers* where Sam Weller is rebuked by Mr Justice Stareleigh for spicing his evidence with the phrase 'as the soldier said'. Stareleigh retorted 'You must not tell us what the soldier, or any other man, said, sir . . . it's not evidence.'

Whether or not Gilbert did borrow from Dickens, this remains a superb piece of comic dialogue. It is important not to 'ham' it, as is clear from the following extract from *The Secrets of a Savoyard*, the memoirs of Sir Henry Lytton, the D'Oyly Carte Company's principal exponent of the comic roles from 1908 to 1934:

> Now if an actor in these operas has to be careful of one thing above everything else, it is that of avoiding forcing a point . . . The lines must be declaimed in deadly seriousness just as if the actor believes absolutely in the fanciful and extravagant thing he is saying. I can think of no better illustration of this than the scene in *Iolanthe* where Strephon rejects recourse to the Chancery Court and says his code of conduct is regulated only by 'Nature's Acts of Parliament'. The Lord Chancellor then talks about the absurdity of 'an affidavit from a thunderstorm or a few words on oath from a heavy shower'.

> What a typical Gilbertian fancy! Well, you know how the 'comic' man would say that, how he would whip up his coat collar and shiver at the suggestion of rain, and how he would do his poor best to make it sound and look 'funny'. And the result would be that he would kill the wittiness of the lines by burlesque. The Lord Chancellor says the words as if he believed an affidavit from a thunderstorm was at least a possibility, and the suggestion that he does think it possible makes the very idea, in the audience's mind, more whimsical still.

ENSEMBLE.

STREPH.	THE OTHERS.
A shepherd I	A shepherd he
Of Arcady,	Of Arcadee,
Betrothed are we,	Betrothed are they,
And mean to be	And mean to be
Espoused to-day!	Espoused to-day!

420

DUET – LORD MOUNTARAT *and* LORD TOLLOLLER
(*aside to each other*).

'Neath this blow,
    Worse than stab of dagger –
Though we mo-
    Mentarily stagger,
In each heart
    Proud are we innately –
Let's depart,
    Dignified and stately!

ALL.   Let's depart,
        Dignified and stately!

425

430

CHORUS OF PEERS.

Though our hearts she's badly bruising,
In another suitor choosing,
Let's pretend it's most amusing.
Ha! ha! ha! Tan-ta-ra!

435

(*Exeunt all the Peers, marching round stage with much dignity.*
LORD CHANCELLOR *separates* PHYLLIS *from* STREPHON
and orders her off. She follows Peers. Manent LORD
CHANCELLOR *and* STREPHON.)

LORD CH. Now, sir, what excuse have you to offer for having
disobeyed an order of the Court of Chancery?

STREPH. My Lord, I know no Courts of Chancery; I go by Nature's
Acts of Parliament. The bees – the breeze – the seas – the rooks – the brooks
– the gales – the vales – the fountains and the mountains cry, 'You love this
maiden – take her, we command you!' 'Tis writ in heaven by the bright
barbèd dart that leaps forth into lurid light from each grim thundercloud.
The very rain pours forth her sad and sodden sympathy! When chorused
Nature bids me take my love, shall I reply, 'Nay, but a certain Chancellor
forbids it'? Sir, you are England's Lord High Chancellor, but are you

440

445

458   *an affidavit from a thunderstorm*: An affidavit is a statement made in writing, and confirmed on oath, which is intended to be used in court.

465–96   *When I went to the Bar as a very young man*
This song has been sung by at least two real Lord Chancellors as well as by the stage
variety. Sir Henry Lytton in his autobiography recalls a word-perfect rendering from
memory by Lord Birkenhead, Lord Chancellor from 1919 to 1922. More recently, in December 1978, Lord Elwyn-Jones, who held the office from 1974 to 1979, performed the
song as a duet with John Reed of the D'Oyly Carte Company at a special performance of
the Bar Musical Society before the Queen Mother in the hall of the Middle Temple.

Gilbert's Lord Chancellor has, in fact, endeared himself to many of those who have
held the office in real life. Lord Sankey, Lord Chancellor from 1929 to 1935, told Lytton,
'There is no doubt about it that Lytton's Lord Chancellor has given more pleasure to
the public than mine . . . Ordinary Lord Chancellors go in and out with their governments, but you are a permanent official'. Lord Elwyn-Jones expressed similar sentiments to James Conroy-Ward, the last D'Oyly Carte principal comedian, when he met a
deputation from the company outside the House of Lords in the summer of 1981.

'When I went to the Bar' has close similarities with the judge's song in *Trial by Jury*,
'When I, good friends, was called to the Bar'. Gilbert probably put a bit of himself into
both songs. He himself was called to the Bar in 1864, having been a student at the Inner
Temple. He practised as a barrister for four years but was singularly unsuccessful,
making only £75 in that period. It was in the long waits for clients that he started writing
humorous articles and began to realize where his true talents lay.

Punch, needless to say, in reviewing *Iolanthe*, found another example of Gilbertian
plagiarism in this song. It suggested that the idea was taken from an old song, 'Says I to
myself as I walked by myself,/And myself says again to me'.

471   *attorney*: Until 1873 those lawyers, other than barristers, who dealt in equity cases were
known as solicitors and those who dealt in common law cases were called attorneys.
The Judicature Act of that year brought the two groups together under the single title
of Solicitors of the Supreme Court. Sir Joseph Porter, the First Lord of the Admiralty in
H.M.S. Pinafore, began his legal career as office boy to an attorney's firm. The term is, of
course, still used in the United States.

brief: A summary of the facts of a case, with reference to the points of law applicable to
them, drawn up by a solicitor for the instruction of counsel conducting the case in
court. The phrase 'to take a brief' means to accept the conduct of a case.

481   *throw dust in a juryman's eyes*: To throw dust in someone's eyes is to mislead him. The
phrase is said to derive from the dust thrown up into the eyes of runners in a race from
the heels of the leading runner. Mohammedans are said to have made a practice of casting dust into the air to confound their enemies.

486   *Exchequer, Queen's Bench, Common Pleas, or Divorce*: The courts of Exchequer, Common
Pleas and Queen's (or King's) Bench were separate common law courts which traced
their origins back to the reign of Edward I. The first decided revenue cases, the second
civil actions between subject and subject, and the third, which was originally presided
over by the sovereign, criminal actions. The Judicature Act of 1873 merged these three
courts together into the Queen's Bench division of the Supreme Court of Judicature, or
the High Court. It also brought together into a second division three special courts –
the High Court of Admiralty, the Court of Probate, and the Court for Divorce and Matrimonial Causes. The third division created by the Act, which was the work of Lord
Selborne, the Lord Chancellor of England at the time that *Iolanthe* was written and first
performed, was that of Chancery. The effect of the Act was to bring together England's
two legal traditions, common law and equity, into a single system.

487   *Have perjured themselves*: To perjure is to swear falsely or break one's oath.

Chancellor of birds and trees, King of the winds and Prince of   450
thunderclouds?

LORD CH. No. It's a nice point. I don't know that I ever met it before.
But my difficulty is that at present there's no evidence before the Court that
chorused Nature has interested herself in the matter.

STREPH. No evidence! You have my word for it. I tell you that she   455
bade me take my love.

LORD CH. Ah! but, my good sir, you mustn't tell us what she told you
– it's not evidence. Now an affidavit from a thunderstorm, or a few words on
oath from a heavy shower, would meet with all the attention they deserve.

STREPH. And have you the heart to apply the prosaic rules of evidence   460
to a case which bubbles over with poetical emotion?

LORD CH. Distinctly. I have always kept my duty strictly before my
eyes, and it is to that fact that I owe my advancement to my present
distinguished position.

SONG – LORD CHANCELLOR.

When I went to the Bar as a very young man,   465
   (Said I to myself – said I),
I'll work on a new and original plan,
   (Said I to myself – said I),
I'll never assume that a rogue or a thief
Is a gentleman worthy implicit belief,   470
Because his attorney has sent me a brief,
   (Said I to myself – said I!).

Ere I go into court I will read my brief through
   (Said I to myself – said I),
And I'll never take work I'm unable to do   475
   (Said I to myself – said I),
My learned profession I'll never disgrace
By taking a fee with a grin on my face,
When I haven't been there to attend to the case
   (Said I to myself – said I!).   480

I'll never throw dust in a juryman's eyes
   (Said I to myself – said I),
Or hoodwink a judge who is not over-wise
   (Said I to myself – said I),
Or assume that the witnesses summoned in force   485
In Exchequer, Queen's Bench, Common Pleas, or Divorce,
Have perjured themselves as a matter of course
   (Said I to myself – said I!).

516 *Finale*: In a interview with the magazine *Home News*, in 1889, Sullivan said 'I think *Iolanthe* contained the longest finale I ever wrote. Goodness knows how many pages of the score it covered.' In fact, the First Act finale of *Iolanthe* runs to thirty-five pages in the vocal score, beating by just one page the next longest finale in the Savoy Operas, that of Act I of *The Grand Duke*.

In other professions in which men engage
    (Said I to myself – said I),   490
The Army, the Navy, the Church, and the Stage
    (Said I to myself – said I),
Professional licence, if carried too far,
Your chance of promotion will certainly mar –
And I fancy the rule might apply to the Bar   495
    (Said I to myself – said I!).

(Exit LORD CHANCELLOR.)

(Enter IOLANTHE.)

STREPH. Oh, Phyllis, Phyllis! To be taken from you just as I was on the point of making you my own! Oh, it's too much – it's too much!   500

IOL. (*to* STREPHON, *who is in tears*). My son in tears – and on his wedding day!

STREPH. My wedding day! Oh, mother, weep with me, for the Law has interposed between us, and the Lord Chancellor has separated us for ever!   505

IOL. The Lord Chancellor! (*Aside.*) Oh, if he did but know!

STREPH. (*overhearing her*). If he did but know what?

IOL. No matter! The Lord Chancellor has no power over you. Remember you are half a fairy. You can defy him – down to the waist.

STREPH. Yes, but from the waist downwards he can commit me to   510
prison for years! Of what avail is it that my body is free, if my legs are working out seven years' penal servitude?

IOL. True. But take heart – our Queen has promised you her special protection. I'll go to her and lay your peculiar case before her.

STREPH. My beloved mother! how can I repay the debt I owe you?   515

FINALE – QUARTET.

(*As it commences, the Peers appear at the back, advancing unseen and on tiptoe.* LORD MOUNTARARAT *and* LORD TOLLOLLER *lead* PHYLLIS *between them, who listens in horror to what she hears.*)

STREPH. (*to* IOLANTHE). When darkly looms the day,
                And all is dull and grey,   520
                To chase the gloom away,
                  On thee I'll call!

PHYL. (*speaking aside to* LORD MOUNTARARAT). What was that?

LORD MOUNT. (*aside to* PHYLLIS).
                I think I heard him say,

530 *thy bark*: Nothing to do with dogs, but a word derived from the French *barque*, meaning a small sailing boat.

537 *St James's Park*: Lying behind Whitehall, between the Mall and Birdcage Walk, St James's Park is the oldest of the six Royal Parks in central London. It was originally established by Henry VIII in 1532, when he took swampy ground which had previously belonged to the Sisters of St James in the Field and built St James's Palace at its western end. The park was opened to the public in the seventeenth century, and in 1828 it was remodelled by John Nash for George III. In the nineteenth century it had something of a reputation as a haunt for prostitutes.

That on a rainy day, 525
To while the time away,
On her he'd call!

CHORUS.   We think we heard him say, etc.

(PHYLLIS *much agitated at her lover's supposed faithlessness.*)

IOL. (*to* STREPHON).   When tempests wreck thy bark, 530
And all is drear and dark,
If thou shouldst need an Ark,
I'll give thee one!

PHYL. (*speaking aside to* LORD TOLLOLLER).   What was that?

LORD TOLL. (*aside to* PHYLLIS).
I heard the minx remark,
She'd meet him after dark, 535
Inside St James's Park,
And give him one!

CHORUS.   We heard the minx remark, etc.

PHYL., IOL., LORD TOLL., STREPH.

The prospect's $\begin{Bmatrix} \text{very} \\ \text{not so} \end{Bmatrix}$ bad, 540

$\begin{rcases} \text{My} \\ \text{Thy} \end{rcases}$ heart so sore and sad
May very soon be glad
As summer's sun;

For when the sky is dark

And tempests wreck $\begin{Bmatrix} \text{his} \\ \text{thy} \\ \text{my} \end{Bmatrix}$ bark, 545

If $\begin{Bmatrix} \text{he should} \\ \text{thou shouldst} \\ \text{I should} \end{Bmatrix}$ need an Ark,

$\begin{rcases} \text{Sh'll} \\ \text{I'll} \end{rcases}$ give $\begin{Bmatrix} \text{him} \\ \text{thee} \\ \text{me} \end{Bmatrix}$ one!

PHYL. (*revealing herself*).   Ah!

558   *This lady's his what*: The peers' incredulity at the idea that Strephon, at nearly twenty-five,
      can have a mother of seventeen echoes the reaction of the Bishop in Gilbert's Bab Ballad
      'The Fairy Curate' when he is confronted with Georgie's fairy mother (see the note to
      line 105):

> 'Who is this, sir,
> Ballet miss, sir?'
> Said the Bishop coldly.
> ' 'Tis my mother
> And no other,'
> Georgie answered boldly.
> 'Go along sir!
> You are wrong, sir,
> You have years in plenty;
> While this hussy
> (Gracious mussy!)
> Isn't two and twenty!'

564   *Enter Lord Chancellor*: Gilbert's own stage direction at this point reads: 'Lord Chancellor
      enters over stile and stands on step of stile during his recitative "What means this mirth
      unseemly?" '

571   *dolce far niente*: Gilbert makes much use of the rhyming possibilities of foreign phrases,
      particularly here in the Act I finale of *Iolanthe*. *Dolce far niente* is an Italian expression
      meaning literally 'sweet doing nothing', i.e. delightful idleness. Appropriately, it is used
      again in *The Gondoliers*, where Fiametta and Vittoria bid Antonio 'enjoy your *dolce far
      niente*', and in the chorus 'Quaff the nectar' in Act I of *Utopia Limited*, when the guards,
      nobles and dancing girls 'Sing the songs of *far niente*'.

577   *festina lente*: a Latin expression meaning to make haste slowly, picked up in the English
      saying 'The more haste, the less speed'.

(IOLANTHE *and* STREPHON *much confused.*)

PHYL.	Oh, shameless one, tremble!	550
	Nay, do not endeavour	
	Thy fault to dissemble,	
	We part – and for ever!	
	I worshipped him blindly	
	He worships another –	555
STREPH.	Attend to me kindly,	
	This lady's my mother!	
TOLL.	This lady's his *what?*	
STREPH.	This lady's my mother!	
TENORS.	This lady's his *what?*	560
BASSES.	He says she's his mother!	

(*They point derisively to* IOLANTHE, *laughing heartily
at her. She goes for protection to* STREPHON.)

(*Enter* LORD CHANCELLOR. IOLANTHE *veils herself.*)

LORD CH.	What means this mirth unseemly,	565
	That shakes the listening earth?	

LORD TOLL.	The joke is good extremely,	
	And justifies our mirth.	

LORD MOUNT.	This gentleman is seen,	
	With a maid of seventeen,	
	A-taking of his *dolce far niente*;	570
	And wonders he'd achieve,	
	For he asks us to believe	
	She's his mother – and he's nearly five-and-twenty!	

LORD CH. (*sternly*).	Recollect yourself, I pray,	575
	And be careful what you say –	
	As the ancient Romans said, *festina lente*.	
	For I really do not see	
	How so young a girl could be	
	The mother of a man of five-and-twenty.	580

ALL.	Ha! ha! ha! ha! ha!

STREPH.	My Lord, of evidence I have no dearth –
	She is – has been – my mother from my birth!

584–91 *In babyhood*

Both *The Times* and the *Standard* reviewers of the first-night performance ventured the suggestion that this pretty ballad was inspired by the air *Sonst spielt ich mit Szepter und Kron* ('In childhood with crown and sceptre I played') from the opera *Zar und Zimmermann (Tsar and Carpenter)* by the German composer Gustav Lortzing (1801–51).

587 *Moistenèd my clay*: To moisten one's clay is to drink. The word clay in this context means the human body. It derives from the biblical statement that earth was the original material for the human body, an idea still preserved, of course, in the Christian burial service with its phrase 'dust to dust, ashes to ashes'. The word occurs with a slightly different connotation in the Fairy Queen's phrase 'I should be marble, but I am clay' early on in the opera (lines 69–70).

BALLAD.

> In babyhood
> Upon her lap I lay,
>> With infant food
> She moistenèd my clay;
>> Had she withheld
> The succour she supplied,
>> By hunger quelled,
> Your Strephon might have died!

585

590

LORD CH. (*much moved*).

> Had that refreshment been denied,
> Indeed our Strephon might have died!

ALL (*much affected*).

> Had that refreshment been denied,
> Indeed our Strephon might have died!

595

LORD MOUNT.

> But as she's not
> His mother, it appears,
>> Why weep these hot
> Unnecessary tears?
>> And by what laws
> Should we so joyously
>> Rejoice, because
> Our Strephon did not die?
> Oh rather let us pipe our eye
> Because our Strephon did not die!

600

605

ALL.

> That's very true – let's pipe our eye
> Because our Strephon did not die!

(*All weep.* IOLANTHE, *who has succeeded in hiding her face from* LORD CHANCELLOR, *escapes unnoticed.*)

PHYL.   Go, traitorous one – for ever we must part: 610
         To one of you, my Lords, I give my heart!
ALL.   Oh, rapture!
STREPH. Hear me, Phyllis, ere you leave me.
PHYL.   Not a word – you did deceive me.
ALL.   Not a word – you did deceive her.   615

(*Exit* STREPHON.)

620 *swain*: An archaic word, suitable for an Arcadian fairy story, for a shepherd or country-
man. In his poem *The Faerie Queene* Edmund Spenser writes of 'The gentle Shepeard
swaynes, which sat keeping their fleecie flockes'.

623–4 *A heart that's aching, quaking, breaking*: The music that accompanies these lines (and lines
632–3) is an almost direct quote from Wagner's *Tristan und Isolde*.

631 *As this couple of lords*: Once again, this song directly echoes the Bab Ballad 'The Periwinkle
Girl' (see the note to lines 330–49).

635 *To you I give my heart so rich*: In the copy of *Perola* (as it was then called) sent to the Lord
Chancellor, this song was repeated by the peers, with the tenors and basses taking alternate lines. Thus, after Phyllis's final 'I do not care', the tenors began 'To them she gives
her heart so rich', with the basses coming in 'To which?', the tenors replying 'She does
not care' and so on.

650 *'Countess' is the title*: Although there are no counts in England, there are countesses; the
term is used for the wives of earls, and, as we know from the list of *Dramatis personæ*,
that is the rank of both Lords Tolloller and Mountararat.

BALLAD – PHYLLIS.

For riches and rank I do not long –
   Their pleasures are false and vain;
I gave up the love of a lordly throng
   For the love of a simple swain.
But now that simple swain's untrue,
With sorrowful heart I turn to you –
    A heart that's aching,
    Quaking, breaking,
As sorrowful hearts are wont to do! 625

The riches and rank that you befall
   Are the only baits you use,
So the richest and rankiest of you all
   My sorrowful heart shall choose.
As none are so noble – none so rich 630
As this couple of lords, I'll find a niche
    In my heart that's aching,
    Quaking, breaking,
For one of you two – and I don't care which!

ENSEMBLE.

PHYL. (*to* LORD MOUNTARARAT *and* LORD TOLLOLLER).
   To you I give my heart so rich! 635
ALL (*puzzled*).   To which?
PHYL.   I do not care!
   To you I yield – it is my doom!
ALL.   To whom?
PHYL.   I'm not aware! 640
   I'm yours for life if you but choose.
ALL.   She's whose?
PHYL.   That's your affair!
   I'll be a countess, shall I not?
ALL.   Of what? 645
PHYL.   I do not care!
ALL.   Lucky little lady!
   Strephon's lot is shady;
   Rank, it seems, is vital,
   'Countess' is the title, 650
   But of what I'm not aware!

(*Enter* STREPHON.)

668 *young Strephon is a rogue*: This is one of the several instances where Sullivan changed a
     line of Gilbert's for musical reasons. He added the word 'young' before Strephon to
     give a more pleasing flow to the melody. 'Our' was added for the same reason in lines
     676, 691 and 700.
670 *Taradiddle, taradiddle, tol lol lay*: 'Taradiddle' is a slang word for a lie or fib. The line 'Tol
     the riddle, lol the riddle, lol lol lay' is sung by the chorus in *The Grand Duke*.

681 *And she's but seventeen*: Clearly a favourite age for Gilbert. In the First Act of *The Pirates of
     Penzance* Frederic tells Ruth that 'A lad of twenty-one usually looks for a wife of seven-
     teen'. In *Ages Ago*, a play written by Gilbert in 1869 and set to music by Fred Clay, the
     idea of paintings which come to life, later developed in *Ruddigore*, is employed to pro-
     duce a situation where Lord Carnaby Poppytop, painted in 1713 at the age of sixty-five,
     is attracted to his grandmother, Lady Maud, painted at the age of seventeen in the
     fifteenth century. This produces the rather *Iolanthe*-like verse:

               So strange a meeting ne'er was seen
               For sure as I'm alive,
               His grandmama is seventeen,
               And he is sixty-five.

686 *repente*: A word found in both Latin and Italian meaning suddenly, unexpectedly, all of a
     sudden.

STREPH.	Can I inactive see my fortune fade?
	No, no!
PEERS.	Ho, ho!	655
STREPH.	Mighty protectress, hasten to my aid!

(*Enter Fairies, tripping, headed by* CELIA, LEILA, *and*
FLETA, *and followed by* QUEEN.)

CHORUS OF FAIRIES.

Tripping hither, tripping thither.
Nobody knows why or whither;
Why you want us we don't know, 660
But you've summoned us, and so
Enter all the little fairies
To their usual tripping measure!
To oblige you all our care is – 665
Tell us, pray, what is your pleasure!

STREPH.	The lady of my love has caught me talking to another –
PEERS.	Oh, fie! young Strephon is a rogue!
STREPH.	I tell her very plainly that the lady is my mother –
PEERS.	Taradiddle, taradiddle, tol lol lay!	670
STREPH.	She won't believe my statement, and declares we must be parted,
	Because on a career of double-dealing I have started,
	Then gives her hand to one of these, and leaves me
	broken-hearted –
PEERS.	Taradiddle, taradiddle, tol lol lay!

QUEEN.	Ah, cruel ones, to separate two lovers from each other!	675
FAIRIES.	Oh, fie! our Strephon's not a rogue!
QUEEN.	You've done him an injustice, for the lady *is* his mother!
FAIRIES.	Taradiddle, taradiddle, tol lol lay!
LORD CH.	That fable perhaps may serve his turn as well as any other.
(*Aside.*)	I didn't see her face, but if they fondled one another,	680
	And she's but seventeen – I don't believe it was his mother!
	Taradiddle, taradiddle.
ALL.	Tol lol lay!

LORD TOLL.	I have often had a use
	For a thorough-bred excuse
	Of a sudden (which is English for '*repente*'),	685
	But of all I ever heard
	This is much the most absurd,
	For she's seventeen, and he is five-and-twenty!

694   *contradicente*: From the Latin word *contradico*, meaning to contradict, gainsay or deny. The phrase *nem. con.*, short for *nemine contradicente*, is used in legal and political circles to mean unanimously, without opposition.

699   *To say she is his mother*: During the singing of this line at a performance of *Iolanthe* which he was attending, Lytton Strachey, the author of *Eminent Victorians*, turned to his neighbour, Maurice Baring, and said 'That's what I call poetry'. He added that he thought the most enduring achievement of the Victorian age would be Gilbert and Sullivan and predicted that their work would be remembered long after that of Gladstone and Disraeli had been forgotten.

703   *could be reckoned as injurious*: This was originally written as 'could be construed as injurious', but 'construed' proved difficult to sing and it was changed to 'reckoned'.

707-57   *Go away, madam*

This verbal passage of arms between the Lord Chancellor and the Fairy Queen was one of the main pieces of evidence cited by Kenneth Baker to support his argument that Gilbert had based the former character on William Ewart Gladstone and the latter on Queen Victoria (see page 358). There is no doubt that relations were strained between the Queen and Gladstone, who was Prime Minister when *Iolanthe* was written and first performed. Unlike his Conservative opponent Disraeli, who often addressed her as the Fairy Queen, Gladstone did not believe in flattering his sovereign. Indeed, he became positively impatient with her for continuing her retreat from public life and official duties long after the death of her beloved husband Prince Albert. For her part, the Queen complained that the Liberal leader addressed her as though she were a public meeting. Perhaps Gilbert had this in mind when he put these lines in the mouth of his Fairy Queen:

> Oh! Chancellor unwary,
> It's highly necessary
> Your tongue to teach
> Respectful speech.

There is no direct evidence that Gilbert modelled his Lord Chancellor and Fairy Queen on the Prime Minister and monarch of the day. We know that Victoria was not greatly amused by *Iolanthe*. Gladstone rather enjoyed the piece, telling Sullivan 'Nothing, I thought, could be happier than the manner in which the comic strain of this piece was blended with its harmonies of sight and sound, so good in taste and so admirable in execution from beginning to end.' There is no indication, however, that either of them recognized themselves in the characters on stage, nor indeed that any of their contemporaries did.

In a long letter to me full of interesting comments, Keith Peterson of New York points out the close similarity between the tune to this song and a theme in Beethoven's Tempest Sonata.

ALL.   Though she is seventeen, and he is only five-and-twenty!   690
            Oh, fie! our Strephon's not a rogue!

LORD MOUNT. Now, listen, pray, to me,
            For this paradox will be
         Carried, nobody at all *contradicente*.
            Her age, upon the date   695
             Of his birth, was *minus* eight,
       If she's seventeen, and he is five-and-twenty!

PEERS *and* FAIRIES. If she is seventeen, and he is only five-and-twenty.

ALL.   To say she is his mother is an utter bit of folly!
       Oh, fie! our { Strephon is   } a rogue!   700
            { Strephon's not }
    Perhaps his brain is addled, and it's very melancholy!
       Taradiddle, taradiddle, tol lol lay!
    I wouldn't say a word that could be reckoned as injurious,
    But to find a mother younger than her son is very curious,
    And that's a kind of mother that is usually spurious.   705
       Taradiddle, taradiddle, tol lol lay!

LORD CH. Go away, madam;
         I should say, madam,
         You display, madam,
           Shocking taste.   710

         It is rude, madam,
         To intrude, madam,
         With your brood, madam,
           Brazen-faced!

         You come here, madam,   715
         Interfere, madam,
         With a peer, madam.
           (I am one.)

         You're aware, madam,
         What you dare, madam,   720
         So take care, madam,
           And begone!

FAIRIES (*to* QUEEN). Let us stay, madam;
         I should say, madam,

753   *badinage*: A French word meaning light trifling raillery or humorous banter.

They display, madam,   725
    Shocking taste.

It is rude, madam,
To allude, madam,
To your brood, madam,
    Brazen-faced!   730

We don't fear, madam,
Any peer, madam,
Though, my dear madam,
    This is one.

They will stare, madam,   735
When aware, madam,
What they dare, madam –
    What they've done!

QUEEN (*furious*).   Bearded by these puny mortals!
I will launch from fairy portals
All the most terrific thunders   740
In my armoury of wonders!

PHYL. (*aside*).   Should they launch terrific wonders,
All would then repent their blunders.
Surely these must be immortals.   745

ENSEMBLE.

PEERS.	FAIRIES.
Go away, madam, etc.	Let us stay, madam, etc.

(*Exit* PHYLLIS.)

QUEEN.   Oh! Chancellor unwary,
It's highly necessary
    Your tongue to teach   750
    Respectful speech –
Your attitude to vary!

Your badinage so airy,
Your manner arbitrary,
    Are out of place
    When face to face   755
With an influential Fairy.

761 *vagary*: Digression, rambling from the subject, frolic or prank.
762 *quandary*: State of uncertainty or perplexity.

767 *Andersen's library*: This is a reference to the well-known Danish writer of fairy-tales, Hans
     Christian Andersen, who lived from 1805 to 1875.

770 *a Ladies' Seminary*: Gilbert and Sullivan's next Savoy Opera after *Iolanthe*, *Princess Ida*, was
     to be partly set in a ladies' seminary. It tells the story of a trio of young men who dress
     up as women to gain entrance to the all-female establishment and allows Gilbert ample
     scope for digs at the idea of women's education.

780 *Take down our sentence as we speak it*: Gilbert's direction in his original prompt-book
     at this point reads: 'Peers get out notebooks and write with book on knees, for Queen's
     dictation (they turn backs to Queen as they write in stooping attitude)'. D'Oyly Carte
     performances traditionally maintained this bit of business.

ALL THE PEERS (*aside*).	We never knew We were talking to An influential Fairy!

760

LORD CH.	A plague on this vagary, I'm in a nice quandary! Of hasty tone With dames unknown I ought to be more chary; It seems that she's a fairy From Andersen's library, And I took her for The proprietor Of a Ladies' Seminary!

765

770

PEERS.	We took her for The proprietor Of a Ladies' Seminary!

QUEEN.	When next your Houses do assemble, You may tremble!

775

CELIA.	Our wrath, when gentlemen offend us, Is tremendous!

LEILA.	They meet, who underrate our calling, Doom appalling!

QUEEN.	Take down our sentence as we speak it, And *he* shall wreak it! (*Indicating* STREPHON.)

780

PEERS.	Oh, spare us!

QUEEN.	Henceforth, Strephon, cast away Crooks and pipes and ribbons so gay – Flocks and herds that bleat and low; Into Parliament you shall go!

785

ALL.	Into Parliament he shall go! Backed by our supreme authority, He'll command a large majority; Into Parliament he shall go!

790

QUEEN.	In the Parliamentary hive, Liberal or Conservative –

793 *Whig or Tory*: Both these terms had effectively been superseded by the more modern 'Liberal' and 'Conservative' by 1882, but then, as now, 'Tory' was a common nickname for Conservatives, and there were more Whigs around than there are now. A word on the origins of the party labels may be of interest here. 'Whig' is almost certainly a short-ened form of 'whiggamore', a term used for the adherents of the Presbyterian cause in Scotland who marched on Edinburgh in 1648. Later in the seventeenth century it came to be applied to those who opposed the Stuart cause, and particularly to those unhappy at the accession to the British throne in 1679 of the Roman Catholic, James, Duke of York. The 'glorious revolution' of 1685–8 which brought the Protestant William of Orange to the throne is normally seen as a triumph for the Whigs and their notion of limited constitutional monarchy. Whigs dominated politics under the Hanoverian kings of the eighteenth century, when they stood broadly for political reform and religious tol-eration. In the mid-nineteenth century they gradually gave way to the less oligarchic and more middle-class Liberal Party which took over as the main party of progress. Gladstone is generally seen as the first distinctly Liberal Prime Minister in Great Brit-ain, but his Cabinets contained several men who still regarded themselves as Whigs, and the word did not die out until the end of the nineteenth century.

The word Tory also dates from the seventeenth century and was originally applied to dispossessed Irishmen who became outlaws. It later came to be used for all Irish Catho-lics and Royalists in arms, and specifically to those who supported James, Duke of York's accession to the throne. The Tories dominated British politics in the aftermath of the Stuart restoration in 1660 and again in the late eighteenth and early nineteenth centu-ries, when they were led by the younger Pitt and Lord Liverpool. The change of the party's name to Conservative is normally dated to 1833 and is credited to the journalist and politician J. W. Croker. The Conservative leader at the time when *Iolanthe* was first performed was Lord Salisbury, who had taken over after the death of Benjamin Disraeli, Earl of Beaconsfield, in 1881.

802 *Through the grouse and salmon season*: Acts of Parliament regulate the periods during which game and fish can be caught in Britain, the so-called 'open season'. The open season for shooting grouse begins on 12 August (known as 'the glorious twelfth') and ends on 10 December. The open season for salmon fishing begins on 1 February and ends on 31 August. The grouse moors continued to be a traditional haunt of politicians, particu-larly Conservatives, well into the twentieth century.

804–5 *the cherished rights . . . on Friday nights*: When Gilbert originally wrote these lines, the cherished rights were enjoyed on Wednesday, not Friday. Between 1852 and 1902 that was the so-called short sitting day in Parliament, when the Commons sat from 12 noon until 6 p.m. instead of its usual time of from 3 p.m. until late in the evening. The Lords very seldom sat at all on Wednesdays during this period, and if they did it was only for judicial business. So for most peers Wednesday as a whole was a day of rest. One particu-lar cherished right that the Fairy Queen must surely have had on her little list for Strephon to end was the Lords' practice of never sitting on the first Wednesday in June – Derby Day. That persisted until the First World War.

In 1902 Arthur Balfour, the Conservative Prime Minister, introduced a series of re-forms in parliamentary procedure which included changing the short sitting day from Wednesday to Friday, where it has remained ever since. The *Iolanthe* libretto was altered accordingly. In 1980 the Commons' hours of sitting on Fridays were made even earlier, from 9.30 a.m. to 3 p.m., to give M.P.s plenty of time to travel to their constituencies for the weekend. Friday sittings in the Commons are generally very sparsely attended. The Lords meet very rarely on a Friday.

808 *Marriage with deceased wife's sister*: Many Liberals, including Mr Gladstone, supported the campaign to allow a man to marry his deceased wife's sister, which was led by the Mar-riage Law Reform Association after such a union had been included in the Church's list

Whig or Tory – I don't know –
But into Parliament you shall go!

ALL.   Into Parliament, etc.   795

QUEEN (*speaking through music*).

Every Bill and every measure
That may gratify his pleasure,
Though your fury it arouses,
Shall be passed by both your Houses!

PEERS.   Oh!   800

QUEEN.   You shall sit, if he sees reason,
Through the grouse and salmon season;

PEERS.   No!

QUEEN.   He shall end the cherished rights
You enjoy on Friday nights: 805

PEERS.   No!

QUEEN.   He shall prick that annual blister,
Marriage with deceased wife's sister:

PEERS.   Mercy!

QUEEN.   Titles shall ennoble, then,   810
All the Common Councilmen:

PEERS.   Spare us!

QUEEN.   Peers shall teem in Christendom,
And a Duke's exalted station
Be attainable by Com-   815
Petitive Examination!

PEERS.   FAIRIES *and* PHYLLIS.

Oh, horror!   Their horror
They can't dissemble
Nor hide the fear that makes them
tremble!

of prohibited marriages in 1835. As the Fairy Queen's remark indicates, the subject was constantly coming up in Parliament. The Liberals' enthusiasm for promoting legislation on it was mocked by Matthew Arnold, who suggested that, 'the Liberal party must supplement that Bill by two others: one enabling people to marry their brothers' and sisters' children, the other enabling a man to marry his brother's wife'. The reformers, however, contented themselves with the matter of the deceased wife's sister and finally secured victory for their cause in 1907.

In the original version of the opera, contained in the licence copy and in the first American libretto (which was published before the British one), the Fairy Queen had two additional horrors with which to frighten the peers at this point:

> He shall offer to the many
> Peerages at three a penny

and, after the lines still sung about the Common Councilmen:

> Earldoms shall be sold apart
> Daily at the auction-mart.

811   *Common Councilmen*: Representatives of the population of a municipality. The City of London was traditionally governed by a Lord Mayor, aldermen and common councilmen.

815–16   *Competitive Examination*: Gladstonian Liberals had a passion for competitive examination, which they had already introduced as the main means of recruitment into the Civil Service, and the idea that the principle should now be extended to entry into the peerage would have tickled an audience in the 1880s. Gilbert himself had obtained his first job by passing a competitive examination at the age of twenty-one in 1857. It secured him a post as assistant clerk in the education department of the Privy Council, for which he received the princely salary of £120 a year. 'It was one of the worst bargains any Government ever made', he commented later. He hated the job but held it down for four years before a legacy from an aunt enabled him to read for the Bar.

849   *canaille*: Rabble or riff-raff.

853   *plebs*: The name given to the general body of Roman citizens who did not fall into the privileged category of patricians. In the later Roman Republic the word 'plebeian' became a rather derogatory term for those in the lower social orders. It is still used in that sense today.

ENSEMBLE.

PEERS.	FAIRIES, PHYLLIS, *and* STREPHON.	
Young Strephon is the kind of lout	With Strephon for your foe, no doubt,	820
We do not care a fig about!	A fearful prospect opens out,	
We cannot say	And who shall say	
What evils may	What evils may	
Result in consequence.	Result in consequence?	

But lordly vengeance will pursue	A hideous vengeance will pursue	825
All kinds of common people who	All noblemen who venture to	
Oppose our views,	Oppose his views,	
Or boldly choose	Or boldly choose	
To offer us offence.	To offer him offence.	

FAIRIES.   'Twill plunge them into grief and shame;   830
His kind forbearance they must claim,
    If they'd escape
    In any shape
A very painful wrench.

PEERS.   Your powers we dauntlessly pooh-pooh: 835
A dire revenge will fall on you,
    If you besiege
    Our high *prestige*
FAIRIES.   (The word '*prestige*' is French).

PEERS.	FAIRIES *and* QUEEN.	
Your powers we dauntlessly pooh-pooh:	Although our threats you now pooh-pooh,	840
A dire revenge will fall on you.	A dire revenge will fall on you.	
Young Strephon is the kind of lout	With Strephon for your foe, no doubt	
We do not care a fig about!	A fearful prospect opens out,	
We cannot say	And who shall say	
What evils may	What evils may	845
Result in consequence.	Result in consequence?	

PEERS.   Our lordly style
    You shall not quench
With base *canaille*!
FAIRIES.   (That word is French.)   850
PEERS.   Distinction ebbs
    Before a herd
Of vulgar *plebs*!
FAIRIES.   (A Latin word.)
PEERS.   'Twould fill with joy,   855
    And madness stark

857   οἱ πολλοὶ: Pronounced 'hoi polloi', this phrase is the Greek equivalent of the Latin
      'plebs'. Literally meaning 'the many', it has come to be used in the same rather slighting
      sense as 'plebs' to mean the unenlightened masses.

879   *Fairies threaten Peers with their wands*: It seems that this direction was followed by the
      D'Oyly Carte fairies rather too enthusiastically on the opening night of *Iolanthe* at the
      Savoy Theatre. Gilbert had to tell the ladies of the chorus the following day: 'You must
      not bang your wands on the stage, ladies. The diamonds in the heads drop out. The
      stage was strewn with diamonds last night.'

	The *οἱ πολλοὶ!*	
FAIRIES.	(A Greek remark.)	
PEERS.	One Latin word, one Greek remark,	
	And one that's French.	860
FAIRIES.	Your lordly style	
	We'll quickly quench	
	With base *canaille!*	
PEERS.	(That word is French.)	
FAIRIES.	Distinction ebbs	865
	Before a herd	
	Of vulgar *plebs!*	
PEERS.	(A Latin word.)	
FAIRIES.	'Twill fill with joy	
	And madness stark	870
	The *οἱ πολλοὶ!*	
PEERS.	(A Greek remark.)	
FAIRIES.	One Latin word, one Greek remark,	
	And one that's French.	

PEERS.	FAIRIES.	
You needn't wait:	We will not wait:	875
Away you fly!	We go sky-high!	
Your threatened hate	Our threatened hate	
We thus defy!	You won't defy!	

(Fairies threaten Peers with their wands. Peers kneel as begging for mercy. PHYLLIS *implores* STREPHON *to relent. He casts her from him, and she falls fainting into the arms of* LORD MOUNTARARAT *and* LORD TOLLOLLER.) 880

END OF ACT I

1 *Scene*: Palace Yard is the open court-yard at the eastern (Whitehall) end of the Houses of
Parliament into which M.P.s drive on their way into the Commons. It was recently remodelled to allow the building of an underground car park and now has a fine fountain
in the centre. It is closed to the public, who gain admission to the House of Commons
further west at St Stephen's entrance.

As the stage directions indicate, Palace Yard is bounded on one side by Westminster
Hall, the only substantial part of the old medieval Palace of Westminster to survive the
disastrous fire of 1834, and on the other, at the rear, by the clock tower better known as
Big Ben. In its review of the opening night of *Iolanthe* at the Savoy, the *Morning Post* noted
two points which were inconsistent with the 'otherwise excellent realisation of the scene.
The House is supposed to be sitting, yet there is no light in the tower, and the clock
persistently pointed to a time nearly half an hour after midnight. This may have been a
satirical allusion – the want of progress in the House shown by the unmoving hands of
the dial.'

Gilbert obviously took the criticism to heart, for, at the time of the 1901 revival of the
opera, he wrote to Mrs Helen D'Oyly Carte (who had taken over the running of the company on her husband's death) suggesting that the clock should have a real mechanism
and should show the correct time throughout the performance of Act II. I have not
been able to discover whether the suggestion was taken up.

A more serious inaccuracy in the setting of Act II of *Iolanthe* was overlooked by many
reviewers. The Houses of Parliament are not guarded by soldiers, but rather by policemen. Strictly speaking, Private Willis should be replaced by one of the constabulary
from *The Pirates of Penzance*. However, he makes a more colourful figure to be set in front
of the slightly sombre background of Sir Charles Barry's great neo-Gothic building,
which was only completed five years before *Iolanthe* was written.

Willis may have been in the wrong uniform, but he certainly had the right rifle. The
first-night review in the *Echo* commented: 'At many theatres he would have been armed
with a "property" musket, with old bayonet. Mr Gilbert's sentry is correct to attention,
and he shoulders properly a Martini-Henry rifle with the long bayonet of the newest
pattern.'

15 *Is either a little Liberal*: Private Willis's well-known reflections on the rigidity of the British
two-party system have never been revised to take account of the rise of the Labour Party.
Substitution of 'a little Socialist' for 'a little Liberal' would have provided a more accurate description of the prevailing political climate for most of the twentieth century,
although in our present era of mould-breaking goodness knows what a modern Private
Willis should sing. Perhaps it is best, after all, to leave him in those happy days when
there were just Liberals and Conservatives.

The British party system comes under further scrutiny in Gilbert and Sullivan's
penultimate opera, *Utopia Limited*, and in a song from *Ruddigore*, rarely performed nowadays, in which Sir Ruthven Murgatroyd casts scorn on:

> Ye supple M.P.s who go down on your knees,
> Your precious identity sinking,
> And vote black or white as your leaders indite
> (Which saves you the trouble of thinking).

19 *cerebellum*: A Latin word used to describe the back part of the brain which is concerned
with the co-ordination of movement and the maintenance of equilibrium.

ACT II

SCENE. – *Palace Yard, Westminster. Westminster Hall,* L. *Clock tower up,* R.C. PRIVATE WILLIS *discovered on sentry,* R. *Moonlight.*

SONG – PRIVATE WILLIS.

When all night long a chap remains
    On sentry-go, to chase monotony
He exercises of his brains,
    That is, assuming that he's got any.   5
Though never nurtured in the lap
    Of luxury, yet I admonish you,
I am an intellectual chap,
    And think of things that would astonish you.   10
        I often think it's comical – Fal, lal, la!
        How Nature always does contrive – Fal, lal, la!
           That every boy and every gal
             That's born into the world alive
           Is either a little Liberal   15
             Or else a little Conservative!
             Fal, lal, la!

When in that House M.P.s divide,
    If they've a brain and cerebellum, too,
They've got to leave that brain outside,   20
    And vote just as their leaders tell 'em to.
But then the prospect of a lot
    Of dull M.P.s in close proximity,
All thinking for themselves, is what
    No man can face with equanimity.   25
        Then let's rejoice with loud Fal la – Fal lal la!
        That Nature always does contrive – Fal lal la!
           That every boy and every gal

33 *Enter . . . Celia, Leila, and Fleta*: The Act II entrance of the three principal fairies caused
    great excitement on the opening night at the Savoy Theatre as they were wearing electric
    star lights on their heads. The Fairy Queen was also kitted out with one of these lamps,
    which were made by the Swan United Electric Company and worked off a battery carried
    on the shoulder and hidden by the fairies' long flowing hair. Most of the audience were
    enchanted by the effect created by the fairy lights on the dimly lit stage. Not so the re-
    viewer from the *Figaro*, however, who wrote: 'The light dazzled the eyes and gave rise to
    an uncomfortable suspicion of possible danger. For, although the wires are doubtless
    completely insulated, yet a facture or a rub would imply instant death to the unhappy
    lady who wears the lamp.' Mercifully, no such mishaps seem to have occurred.

35–59 *Strephon's a Member of Parliament*
    Punch regarded this chorus as the best number in *Iolanthe*. Gilbert's original version,
    printed in the licence copy, differs considerably from the present one:

FAIRIES.	Strephon's a Member of Parliament!
	All his measures have our assent!
	We've been slighted –
	We'll be righted –
	Strephon's a Member of Parliament!
LEILA.	Strephon every measure carries!
	Strephon every question parries!
	All the Peers are down in the blues –
	Strephon makes them shake in their shoes!
ALL.	Shake in their shoes!
	Shake in their shoes!
	All his measures have our assent –
	Strephon's a Member of Parliament!
PEERS.	Here's a pretty kettle of fish!
	For that Member most mysterious
	Carries every Bill he may wish!
	Really it's extremely serious!
LORD MOUNT.	Tells the House to pass his Bill –
	What is more surprising still,
	They obey his tone imperious –
	Really it's extremely serious!
PEERS *and* FAIRIES.	Carries every Bill he may wish –
	Here's a pretty kettle of fish!
LORD TOLL.	Fairy Queen her threat fulfils,
	All support against their wills,
	All his measures deleterious!
	Really it's extremely serious!
CHORUS.	Carries every Bill he may wish, etc.

56 *a pretty kettle of fish*: An awkward state of affairs, a mess, or a muddle. The phrase may pos-
    sibly derive from the old Border expression 'a kettle of fish' to describe a riverside picnic
    where a newly caught salmon was boiled and eaten – a messy if otherwise pleasant sort
    of occasion.

That's born into the world alive
Is either a little Liberal   30
Or else a little Conservative!
Fal lal la!

(*Enter Fairies, with* CELIA, LEILA, *and* FLETA.
They trip round stage.)

CHORUS OF FAIRIES.

Strephon's a Member of Parliament!   35
Carries every Bill he chooses.
To his measures all assent –
   Showing that fairies have their uses.
     Whigs and Tories
     Dim their glories,   40
Giving an ear to all his stories –
Lords and Commons are both in the blues!
Strephon makes them shake in their shoes!
     Shake in their shoes!
     Shake in their shoes!   45
Strephon makes them shake in their shoes!

(*Enter Peers from Westminster Hall.*)

CHORUS OF PEERS.

Strephon's a Member of Parliament!
   Running a-muck of all abuses.
His unqualified assent   50
   Somehow nobody now refuses.
     Whigs and Tories
     Dim their glories,
Giving an ear to all his stories –
Carrying every Bill he may wish: 55
Here's a pretty kettle of fish!
     Kettle of fish!
     Kettle of fish!
Here's a pretty kettle of fish!

(*Enter* LORD MOUNTARARAT *and* LORD TOLLOLLER   60
from Westminster Hall.)

CELIA. You seem annoyed.
LORD MOUNT. Annoyed! I should think so! Why, this ridiculous

67–8   *Parliamentary Pickford*: Pickfords are a famous firm of carriers and removers. The slogan on their vans used to be 'We carry everything'. They are also mentioned in one of Gilbert's early plays, *No Cards*, when one of the characters, Mrs Penrose, says 'Bless me, if I'm run over by a Pickford's van in Fleet Street, is that any reason why you should never go east of Charing Cross?'

79–80   *a House of Peers composed exclusively of people of intellect*: Gilbert toyed with this idea again in *Utopia Limited*. King Paramount proudly sings:

> Our Peerage we've remodelled on an intellectual basis,
> Which certainly is rough on our hereditary races.

At the time *Iolanthe* was written, the House of Lords was almost entirely composed of hereditary members who sat there by virtue of belonging to noble families. The Appellate Jurisdiction Act of 1876 allowed certain eminent judges to be created lords of appeal with a seat in the House of Lords for life, and there were, of course, also bishops in the Upper House; but it was not until half-way through the twentieth century (1958) that the Crown was empowered to confer life peerages on any man or woman. As presently constituted, the House of Lords is a mixture of hereditary and life peers. Lords Mountararat and Tolloller would still be quite at home there – it is not yet composed exclusively of people of intellect.

86–109   *When Britain really ruled the waves*
One of the most popular of Gilbert's patriotic songs, this very seldom fails to secure an encore in performances of *Iolanthe*. Remarkably, Sullivan composed the music for it, as well as for three other songs originally intended for Act II ('Fold your flapping wings', 'Heigho, love is a thorn', and 'He loves'), in the space of a single night. He started work after dinner and finished at five in the morning.

91   *bays*: Wreaths for conquerors and heroes, made from the leaves of the laurel or baytree.

94   *When Wellington thrashed Bonaparte*: This was, of course, at the battle of Waterloo (1815), which also gets a mention in *The Pirates of Penzance* as one of the 'fights historical' quoted by Major-General Stanley.

100   *good King George*: The particular King George on the throne at the time of Waterloo was George III.

102–9   *And while the House of Peers withholds*: In 1909 some of the Liberals campaigning against the House of Lords' power of veto after its rejection of Lloyd George's radical budget of that year asked Gilbert for permission to quote this verse. He replied rather pepperily: 'I cannot permit the verses from *Iolanthe* to be used for electioneering purposes. They do not at all express my own view. They are supposed to be the views of the wrong-headed donkey who sings them.' With or without the help of *Iolanthe*, however, the Liberal reformers achieved their aims and in 1911 the Parliament Act was passed, curtailing the House of Lords' power to veto legislation already passed by the Commons. Since then noble statesmen have largely withheld their legislative hand and contented themselves with moving amendments to Bills sent up from the Lower House.

protégé of yours is playing the deuce with everything! To-night is the second
reading of his Bill to throw the Peerage open to Competitive Examination! 65

LORD TOLL. And he'll carry it, too!

LORD MOUNT. Carry it? Of course he will! He's a Parliamentary
Pickford – he carries everything!

LEILA. Yes. If you please, that's our fault!

LORD MOUNT. The deuce it is! 70

CELIA. Yes; we influence the members, and compel them to vote just
as he wishes them to.

LEILA. It's our system. It shortens the debates.

LORD TOLL. Well, but think what it all means. I don't so much mind
for myself, but with a House of Peers with no grandfathers worth 75
mentioning, the country must go to the dogs!

LEILA. I suppose it must!

LORD MOUNT. I don't want to say a word against brains – I've a great
respect for brains – I often wish I had some myself – but with a House of
Peers composed exclusively of people of intellect, what's to become of the 80
House of Commons?

LEILA. I never thought of that!

LORD MOUNT. This comes of women interfering in politics. It so
happens that if there is an institution in Great Britain which is not
susceptible of any improvement at all, it is the House of Peers! 85

SONG – LORD MOUNTARARAT.

> When Britain really ruled the waves –
>   (In good Queen Bess's time)
> The House of Peers made no pretence
> To intellectual eminence,
>   Or scholarship sublime; 90
> Yet Britain won her proudest bays
> In good Queen Bess's glorious days!

CHORUS.　　　　Yes, Britain won, etc.

> When Wellington thrashed Bonaparte,
>   As every child can tell, 95
> The House of Peers, throughout the war,
> Did nothing in particular,
>   And did it very well:
> Yet Britain set the world ablaze
> In good King George's glorious days! 100

CHORUS.　　　　Yes, Britain set, etc.

> And while the House of Peers withholds
>   Its legislative hand,

113 *a British Representative Peer*: Before the establishment of the Irish Free State in 1922, twenty-eight Irish peers were elected for life to sit in the House of Lords as representatives of the entire Irish peerage. Until 1963, sixteen Scottish peers were elected by their fellow peers each Parliament to serve a similar function. There are no longer any representative peers in the upper chamber.

118–49 *In vain to us you plead*

This delightful song, in which the fairies cannot conceal their infatuation with the peers, for all their angry words, won considerable praise from the reviewers when it was first performed at the Savoy. The *Advertiser* singled out for particular mention its 'charmingly fanciful and piquant accompaniment for the strings pizzicato'.

The lines of the second verse must have had a special significance for one real-life noble lord who was often to be found in the Savoy stalls during the initial run of *Iolanthe*. Lord Garmoyle, later to become the 2nd Earl Cairns, was captivated by Miss May Fortescue, who created the part of Celia. Eventually they became engaged, but he later jilted her, proving that make-believe peers are to be preferred to real ones.

And noble statesmen do not itch
To interfere with matters which 105
They do not understand,
As bright will shine Great Britain's rays
As in King George's glorious days!

CHORUS.   As bright will shine, etc.

LEILA (*who has been much attracted by the Peers during this song*). Charm- 110
ing persons, are they not?

CELIA. Distinctly. For self-contained dignity, combined with airy
condescension, give me a British Representative Peer!

LORD TOLL. Then pray stop this *protégé* of yours before it's too late.
Think of the mischief you're doing! 115

LEILA (*crying*). But we *can't* stop him now. (*Aside to* CELIA.) Aren't
they lovely! (*Aloud.*) Oh, why did you go and defy us, you great geese!

DUET – LEILA *and* CELIA.

LEILA.

In vain to us you plead –
Don't go!
Your prayers we do not heed – 120
Don't go!
It's true we sigh,
But don't suppose
A tearful eye
Forgiveness shows. 125
Oh, no!
We're very cross indeed –
Yes, very cross,
Don't go!

FAIRIES.

It's true we sigh, etc. 130

CELIA.

Your disrespectful sneers –
Don't go!
Call forth indignant tears –
Don't go!
You break our laws – 135
You are our foe:
We cry because
We hate you so!
You know!
You very wicked Peers! 140
You wicked Peers!
Don't go!

150   *Exeunt Lord Mountararat, Lord Tolloller*: During the scene just ended, and for their other appearances in the Second Act of *Iolanthe*, Mountararat and Tolloller were originally dressed in D'Oyly Carte productions in plain court dress (dark velvet jackets and breeches). In a letter to Mrs Helen D'Oyly Carte at the time of the 1901 revival, however, Gilbert suggested something more fancy:

> We were *quite wrong* in putting the two Earls, in Act II, into plain Court dress. That is the dress of men who have no rank above baronets – or at all events who are not peers and knights of orders. A GCB or KG would never appear in velvet court dress – he would be certain to hold some appointment that would give him the right to wear a uniform. I should say that it would be best to put them into Lords Lieutenants dress (red coats, silver striped trousers, general's gold belt and cocked hat). These are posts that are (with one or two exceptions) held by peers of considerable landed property and would be perfectly suitable to these two earls – who ought also to wear the *star* of the order of knighthood assigned to them in Act I. Plain Court dress would be impossible for such howling swells.

In fact, D'Oyly Carte stuck to velvet court dress for the two principal Earls and did not adopt Gilbert's gaudier and more expensive alternative. His suggestion of letting them wear the stars of their respective orders of knighthood in the Second Act was, however, accepted.

163–4   1st Grenadier Guards: The First Regiment of Foot Guards in Britain, the Grenadiers are traditionally known for their height, physique and general discipline. As their name implies, the grenadiers were originally those soldiers equipped with grenades for throwing in battle. They are commemorated in the well-known song, dating from the sixteenth century, *The British Grenadiers*.

<table>
<tr><td>FAIRIES.</td><td>LORDS MOUNT. *and* TOLL.</td></tr>
</table>

FAIRIES.	LORDS MOUNT. *and* TOLL.	
You break our laws –	Our disrespectful sneers,	
You are our foe:	Ha, ha!	
We cry because	Call forth indignant tears,	145
We hate you so!	Ha, ha!	
You know!	If that's the case, my dears –	
You very wicked Peers!	FAIRIES. Don't go!	
Don't go!	PEERS. We'll go!	

(*Exeunt* LORD MOUNTARARAT, LORD TOLLOLLER, *and*   150
Peers. Fairies gaze wistfully after them.*)

(*Enter* FAIRY QUEEN.)

QUEEN. Oh, shame – shame upon you! Is this your fidelity to the laws you are bound to obey? Know ye not that it is death to marry a mortal?

LEILA. Yes, but it's not death to *wish* to marry a mortal!   155

FLETA. If it were, you'd have to execute us all!

QUEEN. Oh, this is weakness! Subdue it!

CELIA. We know it's weakness, but the weakness is so strong!

LEILA. We are not all as tough as you are!

QUEEN. Tough! Do you suppose that I am insensible to the effect of   160 manly beauty? Look at that man! (*Referring to Sentry.*) A perfect picture! (*To Sentry.*) Who are you, sir?

WILLIS (*coming to 'attention'*). Private Willis, B Company, 1st Grenadier Guards.

QUEEN. You're a very fine fellow, sir.   165

WILLIS. I am generally admired.

QUEEN. I can quite understand it. (*To Fairies.*) Now here is a man whose physical attributes are simply godlike. That man has a most extraordinary effect upon me. If I yielded to a natural impulse, I should fall down and worship that man. But I mortify this inclination; I wrestle with it,   170 and it lies beneath my feet! That is how I treat my regard for that man!

SONG – FAIRY QUEEN.

Oh, foolish fay,
   Think you, because
His brave array
   My bosom thaws,
I'd disobey   175
   Our fairy laws?
Because I fly
   In realms above,

185 *Type of Ovidius Naso*: A reference to the Latin amatory poet Ovid (43 B.C.–A.D. 17), who was nicknamed 'Naso' because of his big nose. He likened himself to a dove, hence the Fairy Queen's allusion here. Ovid also gets a mention in *Princess Ida*, the next Savoy Opera after *Iolanthe*, when Lady Psyche tells Melissa that if she wishes to succeed in Classics she must read Ovid's *Metamorphoses*. In *Ruddigore* Robin Oakapple compares his own talents as a poet to those of Ovid, greatly to the disadvantage of the latter, in his boasting song 'If you wish in the world to advance'.

201 *A Captain Shaw*: Captain Eyre Massey Shaw was chief of the Metropolitan Fire Brigade from 1861 to 1891. During that time he transformed London's old independent fire-fighting teams, financed by insurance companies, into the country's first public fire brigade. The fire-boat *Massey Shaw*, which was named after him, is now in the collection of historic vessels in St Katharine's Dock near the Tower of London.

    Captain Shaw was sitting in the middle of the stalls at the first-night performance of *Iolanthe* at the Savoy Theatre to hear the Fairy Queen's tribute to him. A few nights later he was at the nearby Alhambra Theatre in a rather different capacity, fighting a fire which caused severe damage. A special matinée of *Iolanthe* was put on at the Savoy to benefit those who had lost their livelihood as a result of the fire.

    In a note in his collection of *Iolanthe* material in the Pierpont Morgan Library, New York, Reginald Allen suggests that the Fairy Queen's description of Captain Shaw as 'Type of true love kept under' may be a reference to a scandal details of which were going round the drawing rooms of Mayfair at the time *Iolanthe* was being written. The wife of Lord Colin Campbell, a notorious profligate and bully, apparently sought consolation by striking up close friendships with a number of other men, including Captain Shaw. In 1884 Lady Campbell won a separation from her husband, but in revenge he brought a case naming four prominent figures, including Shaw, with whom she was alleged to have had relationships. When he gave evidence in this case, Shaw is reported to have 'burned with love for the lady but never declared himself'. Shaw's descendants told Reginald Allen that they were sure the Fairy Queen's remark about 'true love kept under' referred to the circumstances which led up to this case.

210 *I can't think why I'm not in better spirits*: In the original libretto of *Perola*, as printed in the licence copy but cut before the first performance, Phyllis has a ballad after this passage of dialogue and while she is still on her own on the stage:

> My love for him is dead,
>   And yet I sigh!
> My eyes are very red:
>   I wonder why?
> Love fills my heart no more,
> I've turned it out of door –
> And yet my heart is sore!
>   I wonder why!
> His falsehood I detest:
>   From him I fly,
> And yet I know no rest –
>   I wonder why!
> Maybe in spite of ill
> The heart subdues the will –
> Maybe I love him still!
>   I wonder why!

216 *Phyllis! My darling*: In the first performances in both London and New York, Mount-ararat alone came on to the stage at this point. He had the following conversation with Phyllis before launching into another song about the peerage:

LORD MOUNT. Phyllis! My own!
PHYL. Don't! How dare you! But perhaps you are one of the noblemen I am engaged to.

	In tendency	180
	To fall in love,	
	Resemble I	
	The amorous dove?	
(*Aside.*)	Oh, amorous dove!	
	Type of Ovidius Naso!	185
	This heart of mine	
	Is soft as thine,	
	Although I dare not say so!	
CHORUS.	Oh, amorous dove, etc.	

	On fire that glows	190
	With heat intense	
	I turn the hose	
	Of common sense,	
	And out it goes	
	At small expense!	195
	We must maintain	
	Our fairy law;	
	That is the main	
	On which to draw –	
	In that we gain	200
	A Captain Shaw!	
(*Aside.*)	Oh, Captain Shaw!	
	Type of true love kept under!	
	Could thy Brigade	
	With cold cascade	205
	Quench my great love, I wonder!	
CHORUS.	Oh, Captain Shaw! etc.	

(*Exeunt Fairies and* FAIRY QUEEN, *sorrowfully.*)

(*Enter* PHYLLIS.)

PHYL. (*half crying*). I can't think why I'm not in better spirits. I'm   210
engaged to two noblemen at once. That ought to be enough to make any girl
happy. But I'm miserable! Don't suppose it's because I care for Strephon, for
I hate him! No girl *could* care for a man who goes about with a mother
considerably younger than himself!

(*Enter* LORD MOUNTARARAT *and* LORD TOLLOLLER.)   215

LORD MOUNT. Phyllis! My darling!
LORD TOLL. Phyllis! My own!

MOUNT. I am one of them.

PHYL. Oh! But how come *you* to have a peerage?

MOUNT. It's a prize for being born first.

PHYL. A kind of Derby Cup.

MOUNT. Not exactly. I'm of a very old and distinguished family.

PHYL. And you're proud of your race? Of course you are – you won it. But why are people *made* peers?

MOUNT. The principle is not easy to explain. I'll give you an example.

De Belville was regarded as the Crichton of his age:
His tragedies were reckoned much too thoughtful for the stage:
His poems held a noble rank – although it's very true
That, being very proper, they were read by very few.
He was a famous painter, too, and shone upon the Line,
And even Mister Ruskin came and worshipped at his shrine:
But, alas, the school he followed was heroically high –
The kind of Art men rave about, but very seldom buy.
                    And everybody said,
                        'How can he be repaid –
        This very great – this very good – this very gifted man?'
        But nobody could hit upon a practicable plan!

He was a great Inventor, and discovered, all alone,
A plan for making everybody's fortune but his own;
For in business an Inventor's little better than a fool,
And my highly gifted friend was no exception to the rule.
His poems – people read 'em in the sixpenny Reviews;
His pictures – they engraved 'em in the *Illustrated News*;
His inventions – they perhaps might have enriched him by degrees,
But all his little income went to Patent Office fees!
                    So everybody said
                        'How can he be repaid –
        This *very* great – this *very* good – this *very* gifted man?'
        But nobody could hit upon a practicable plan!

At last the point was given up in absolute despair,
When a distant cousin died, and he became a millionaire!
With a county seat in Parliament, a moor or two of grouse,
And a taste for making inconvenient speeches in the House:
Then, Government conferred on him the highest of rewards –
They took him from the Commons and they put him in the Lords!
And who so fit to sit in it, deny it if you can,
As this very great – this very good – this very gifted man?
                    Though I'm more than half afraid
                    That it sometimes may be said
That we never should have revelled in that source of proper pride –
However great his merits – if his cousin hadn't died!

At the London first night of *Iolanthe* the above verses were recited, rather than sung, by Rutland Barrington. He omitted the second verse entirely, much to the disappointment of the *Advertiser*, which commented that 'not a line of so good a thing should be lost'. Many critics, however, took a very different view and complained that the song held up the action and was rather too heavy in its message. Gilbert and Sullivan responded by cutting it early on in the Savoy run. In New York, however, where it was sung to a tune described by one reviewer as 'not altogether free from the influence of Mozart', it survived rather longer. Gilbert included the song in the 1897 edition of the *Bab Ballads*, giving it the title 'The Reward of Merit'. Sadly, the music does not survive.

PHYL. Don't! How dare you? Oh, but perhaps you're the two noblemen I'm engaged to?

LORD MOUNT. I am one of them.

LORD TOLL. I am the other.

PHYL. Oh, then, my darling! (*to* LORD MOUNTARARAT). My own! (*to* LORD TOLLOLLER). Well, have you settled which it's to be?

LORD TOLL. Not altogether. It's a difficult position. It would be hardly delicate to toss up. On the whole we would rather leave it to you.

PHYL. How can it possibly concern me? You are both Earls, and you are both rich, and you are both plain.

LORD MOUNT. So we are. At least I am.

LORD TOLL. So am I.

LORD MOUNT. No, no!

LORD TOLL. I am indeed. Very plain.

LORD MOUNT. Well, well – perhaps you are.

PHYL. There's really nothing to choose between you. If one of you would forgo his title, and distribute his estates among his Irish tenantry, why, then, I should then see a reason for accepting the other.

LORD MOUNT. Tolloller, are you prepared to make this sacrifice?

LORD TOLL. No!

LORD MOUNT. Not even to oblige a lady?

LORD TOLL. No! not even to oblige a lady.

LORD MOUNT. Then, the only question is, which of us shall give way to the other? Perhaps, on the whole, she would be happier with me. I don't know. I may be wrong.

LORD TOLL. No. I don't know that you are. I really believe she would. But the awkward part of the thing is that if you rob me of the girl of my heart, we must fight, and one of us must die. It's a family tradition that I have sworn to respect. It's a painful position, for I have a very strong regard for you, George.

LORD MOUNT. (*much affected*). My dear Thomas!

LORD TOLL. You are very dear to me, George. We were boys together – at least *I* was. If I were to survive you, my existence would be hopelessly embittered.

LORD MOUNT. Then, my dear Thomas, you must not do it. I say it again and again – if it will have this effect upon you, you must not do it. No, no. If one of us is to destroy the other, let it be me!

LORD TOLL. No, no!

LORD MOUNT. Ah, yes! – by our boyish friendship I implore you!

LORD TOLL. (*much moved*). Well, well, be it so. But, no – no! – I cannot consent to an act which would crush you with unavailing remorse. –

LORD MOUNT. But it would not do so. I should be very sad at first – oh, who would not be? – but it would wear off. I like you *very much* – but not, perhaps, as much as you like me.

220

225

230

235

240

245

250

255

260

After the 'De Belville' song, Lord Tolloller appeared on stage with the greeting 'Phyllis, my darling!' Phyllis then asked the two Earls whether they had settled which it was to be, and the dialogue continued very much as it does now (from line 224).

267 *it would not last a day*: Another 'lost' song occurred at this point in Gilbert's original *Perola* libretto:

> PHYL. (*coming down*). Oh dear, I'm a very wretched girl, to be the cause of so much misery! Why can't people fall in love with people that want to be fallen in love with? There are plenty of them about. I'm sure I don't want either of you!

TRIO. PHYLLIS, LORD MOUNTARARAT *and* LORD TOLLOLLER.

PHYL.	I dislike you both extremely!
(*Crying*.)	Boo, hoo! boo, hoo! boo, hoo, hoo!
	To distinguish were unseemly –
(*Crying*.)	Boo, hoo! boo, hoo! boo, hoo, hoo!
	I regret my explanation
	Ends in sad ejaculation,
	But in such a situation
	It would be sheer affectation
	To sing tra, la, la, la, la! (*wild dance*)
	To sing tra, la, la, la, etc.
	(*After dance, all burst out crying*.)
TOLL.	Though our lives we dearly cherish –
(*Crying*.)	Boo, hoo! boo, hoo! boo, hoo, hoo!
	Clearly one of us must perish.
(*Crying*.)	Boo, hoo! boo, hoo! boo, hoo, hoo!
	Fate with mortals never fences;
	We obey her exigences
	With such dismal consequences,
	No one in his sober senses
	Would sing tra la la, etc.
	(*Dance as before, ending with Boo, hoo*.)
MOUNT.	You'll regret it, if you lose me,
(*Crying*.)	Boo, hoo! boo, hoo! boo, hoo, hoo!
	I can't help it – pray excuse me!
(*Crying*.)	Boo, hoo! boo, hoo! boo, hoo, hoo!
	If to perish you elect me,
	At post mortem they'll dissect me,
	With such horrors to deject me,
	Surely no one will expect me
	To sing tra, la, la etc.

(*Dance as before, ending with Boo, hoo, etc. At the end exeunt*
PHYLLIS, LORD MOUNTARARAT *and* LORD TOLLOLLER.)

The quartet 'Though p'r'aps I may incur your blame' was substituted for the above trio some time before the first performance of *Iolanthe*.

293–6 *Love, unrequited, robs me of my rest*
This recitative was cited by Kenneth Baker in his article suggesting that the character of the Lord Chancellor was based on W. E. Gladstone (see page 358) and the note to Act I, lines 707–57). The Liberal Prime Minister was well-known for his nocturnal ramblings through London in search of prostitutes to redeem and convert from their wicked ways. It was hardly a case of unrequited love robbing him of his rest, however.

L O R D T O L L. George, you're a noble fellow, but that tell-tale tear betrays you. No, George; you are very fond of me, and I cannot consent to give you a week's uneasiness on my account.

L O R D M O U N T. But, dear Thomas, it would not last a week! 265
Remember, you lead the House of Lords! On your demise I shall take your place! Oh, Thomas, it would not last a day!

P H Y L. (*coming down*). Now, I do hope you're not going to fight about me, because it's really not worth while.

L O R D T O L L. (*looking at her*). Well, I don't believe it is! 270

L O R D M O U N T. Nor I. The sacred ties of Friendship are paramount.

QUARTET – L O R D M O U N T A R A R A T,
L O R D T O L L O L L E R, P H Y L L I S, *and* P R I V A T E W I L L I S.

L O R D T O L L.	Though p'r'aps I may incur your blame,
	The things are few
	I would not do
	In Friendship's name! 275

L O R D M O U N T.	And I may say I think the same;
	Not even love
	Should rank above
	True Friendship's name!

P H Y L.	Then free me, pray; be mine the blame; 280
	Forget your craze
	And go your ways
	In Friendship's name!

A L L.	Oh, many a man, in Friendship's name,
	Has yielded fortune, rank, and fame! 285
	But no one yet, in the world so wide,
	Has yielded up a promised bride!

W I L L I S.	Accept, O Friendship, all the same,

A L L.	This sacrifice to thy dear name!

(*Exeunt* L O R D M O U N T A R A R A T *and* L O R D T O L L O L L E R, *lovingly, in* 290
one direction, and P H Y L L I S *in another. Exit Sentry.*)

(*Enter* L O R D C H A N C E L L O R, *very miserable.*)

297–328   *When you're lying awake with a dismal headache*

The nightmare song, as this is called, is perhaps the most brilliant of all Gilbert and Sullivan's patter songs. It is certainly the longest and fastest, and woe betide the singer who stumbles over a phrase half-way through.

Punch accused Gilbert of taking the idea for the song from a comic recitation by the dramatist James Robinson Planché (1796–1880), which began 'I'm in such a flutter, I can scarcely utter'. However, it is much more likely to have been a Gilbertian original. He had, in fact, experimented with the metre later used for the nightmare song in a poem entitled 'Sixty-Three and Sixty-Four' which appeared in *Fun* in 1864 and which began:

> Oh, you who complain that the drawing's insane, or too much for your noodles have found it,
> But listen a minute, I'll tell you what's in it – completely explain and expound it.

302   *ticking*: A case or cover containing feathers or other stuffing to form a mattress or a pillow.

307   *tossing about in a steamer from Harwich*: Strictly speaking, steamers from Harwich cross the southern part of the North Sea rather than the English Channel. The main routes from the Essex port are to the Netherlands and Denmark.

An earlier poem by Gilbert, 'The Return from My Berth', which appeared in *Punch* in October 1864, gives a more lurid account of a Channel crossing:

> The big Channel steamer is rolling,
> Frenchmen around me are bilious and fat
> And prone on the floor are behaving unheedingly,
> It's a 'sick transit', but never mind that!

In the early 1960s the American comedian and singer Danny Kaye recorded a transatlantic version of the nightmare song with new words written by his wife, Sylvia Fine. The lines about crossing the Channel became:

> For you dream that you're ill, having swallowed a pill,
> That was made out of ossified onyx
> And that doctor you've found, he is trav'ling around,
> On a subway that's bound for the Bronnyx.

308   *bathing machine*: A portable changing room, resembling a horse-drawn gipsy caravan, which could be towed out into the sea to allow modest Victorians to take to the water without anyone seeing them in their bathing apparel.

310   *Sloane Square and South Kensington Stations*: These are adjacent stations on the District Line of the London Underground, which was opened in 1868. In a letter to me Kenneth Baker suggested that this line referred to two well-known Radical politicians, Sir Charles Dilke, who lived in Sloane Street and was M.P. for Chelsea, and Joseph Chamberlain, who lived just off Exhibition Road, South Kensington. Both men were certainly something of a nightmare for Mr Gladstone.

311   *attorney*: See the note to Act I, line 471.

313   *a four-wheeler*: A four-wheeled hackney carriage. There is a celebrated story about the occasion when Gilbert was mistaken for a doorman by someone emerging from the Haymarket Theatre, who went up to him and said 'Call me a cab!' 'Very well,' Gilbert replied, 'you're a four-wheeler.' 'What on earth do you mean by that?' was the man's startled response. 'Well, sir,' said Gilbert, 'you asked me to call you a cab, and I certainly couldn't call you "Hansom".'

314   *ties pay the dealer*: In games such as pontoon and blackjack a player loses to the dealer (who holds the 'bank') if he has a lower, or even an equal, hand of cards (i.e. if he ties with the dealer).

RECITATIVE – Lord Chancellor.

Love, unrequited, robs me of my rest:
Love, hopeless love, my ardent soul encumbers:
Love, nightmare-like, lies heavy on my chest, 295
And weaves itself into my midnight slumbers!

SONG – Lord Chancellor.

When you're lying awake with a dismal headache, and repose is taboo'd by
anxiety,
I conceive you may use any language you choose to indulge in, without
impropriety;
For your brain is on fire – the bedclothes conspire of usual slumber to
plunder you:
First your counterpane goes, and uncovers your toes, and your sheet slips
demurely from under you; 300
Then the blanketing tickles – you feel like mixed pickles – so terribly sharp
is the pricking,
And you're hot, and you're cross, and you tumble and toss till there's
nothing 'twixt you and the ticking.
Then the bedclothes all creep to the ground in a heap, and you pick 'em all
up in a tangle;
Next your pillow resigns and politely declines to remain at its usual angle!
Well, you get some repose in the form of a doze, with hot eye-balls and head
ever aching. 305
But your slumbering teems with such horrible dreams that you'd very much
better be waking;
For you dream you are crossing the Channel, and tossing about in a steamer
from Harwich –
Which is something between a large bathing machine and a very small
second-class carriage –
And you're giving a treat (penny ice and cold meat) to a party of friends and
relations –
They're a ravenous horde – and they all came on board at Sloane Square and
South Kensington Stations. 310
And bound on that journey you find your attorney (who started that
morning from Devon);
He's a bit undersized, and you don't feel surprised when he tells you he's
only eleven.
Well, you're driving like mad with this singular lad (by the by, the ship's
now a four-wheeler),
And you're playing round games, and he calls you bad names when you tell
him that 'ties pay the dealer';

321   *boot-tree*: A shaped block inserted into a boot to stretch it.

324   *cherry brandy*: This may seem an odd commodity for a pastrycook to sell, but it was in fact
        served in some such establishments in Victorian times to provide a refined tipple for
        ladies, who would not venture into a public house or hotel bar.
        three-corners: Triangular Danish pastries.
        Banburys: Banbury cakes have a filling of currants and spice encased in pastry. They take
        their name from the Oxfordshire town of Banbury.
325   *Rothschild and Baring*: Two of the leading banking houses in Victorian Britain, both of
        which are still going strong today. The Rothschilds are, of course, the most famous of all
        the European banking families; at the time of *Iolanthe* the head of the firm in Britain
        was Sir Nathan Meyer Rothschild, who in 1885 became the 1st Baron Rothschild. He is
        remembered particularly for having helped Disraeli to get Britain a controlling interest
        in the Suez Canal in 1875. The name also occurs in *Utopia Limited* in a song for Mr Gold-
        bury, the company promoter.
            Barings was founded in 1770 by two brothers, John and Francis Baring, sons of a cloth
        manufacturer who had emigrated to London from Germany. The head of the firm at the
        time of *Iolanthe* was Edward Charles Baring, who, like Rothschild, was raised to the peer-
        age in 1885.
327   *needles and pins*: This uncomfortable condition is also mentioned in Gilbert's earlier
        poem 'The Return from My Berth' in the verse:

> There's pleasure in feeling so coldly and clammily
> Joy in the needles and pins in my leg;
> Pleasure in watching that foreigner's family
> Eating stick chocolate mixed with hard egg.

328   *ditto ditto my song*: At almost every performance the nightmare song is not too long for
        the audience, who invariably demand an encore from the exhausted Lord Chancellor.
        The D'Oyly Carte practice was to start the encore at 'And he and the crew are on bicycles
        too' (line 317).

But this you can't stand, so you throw up your hand, and you find you're as
    cold as an icicle, 315
In your shirt and your socks (the black silk with gold clocks), crossing
    Salisbury Plain on a bicycle:
And he and the crew are on bicycles too – which they've somehow or other
    invested in –
And he's telling the tars all the particu*lars* of a company he's interested in –
It's a scheme of devices, to get at low prices all goods from cough mixtures
    to cables
(Which tickled the sailors), by treating retailers as though they were all
    vege*ta*bles – 320
You get a good spadesman to plant a small tradesman (first take off his boots
    with a boot-tree),
And his legs will take root, and his fingers will shoot, and they'll blossom
    and bud like a fruit-tree –
From the greengrocer tree you get grapes and green pea, cauliflower,
    pineapple, and cranberries,
While the pastrycook plant cherry brandy will grant, apple puffs, and three-
    corners, and Banburys –
The shares are a penny, and ever so many are taken by Rothschild and
    Baring, 325
And just as a few are allotted to you, you awake with a shudder despairing –
You're a regular wreck, with a crick in your neck, and no wonder you snore,
    for your head's on the floor, and you've needles and pins from your
    soles to your shins, and your flesh is a-creep, for your left leg's asleep,
    and you've cramp in your toes, and a fly on your nose, and some fluff
    in your lung, and a feverish tongue, and a thirst that's intense, and a
    general sense that you haven't been sleeping in clover;
But the darkness has passed, and it's daylight at last, and the night has been
    long – ditto ditto my song – and thank goodness they're both of them
    over!

(LORD CHANCELLOR *falls exhausted on a seat*.)

(*Enter* LORDS MOUNTARARAT *and* TOLLOLLER.) 330

LORD MOUNT. I am much distressed to see your Lordship in this
condition.

LORD CH. Ah, my Lords, it is seldom that a Lord Chancellor has
reason to envy the position of another, but I am free to confess that I would
rather be two Earls engaged to Phyllis than any other half-dozen noblemen 335
upon the face of the globe.

LORD TOLL. (*without enthusiasm*). Yes. It's an enviable position when
you're the only one.

343 *in six-eight time*: Whether by accident or design, Gilbert hit on an appropriate figure
here. Six-eight is the time signature both for the nightmare song and for 'The Law is
the true embodiment'. It is indeed the most common time signature in *Iolanthe*, being
used for nine of the songs and for the overture.

362–97 *If you go in*
This exuberant trio, traditionally much encored, and finally ending in D'Oyly Carte
performances with the Lord Chancellor dancing into Private Willis's sentry box to take
refuge, ranks with 'Things are seldom what they seem' from Act II of *H.M.S. Pinafore* in
its use of old proverbs and sayings. By my calculations, the *Pinafore* duet wins, with sixteen identifiable proverbs against eleven in this song.

367 *Faint heart never won fair lady*: According to the *Oxford Dictionary of English Proverbs* the
first recorded use of this saying was in 1569, when it appeared in the form 'Faint hearts
faire ladies never win'.

370 *Every journey has an end*: This is an original Gilbertianism, if the word original can be applied to such an obvious truism.

372 *Dark the dawn when day is nigh*: The earliest recorded version of this saying, 'The darkest
hour is that before the dawn', dates from 1650.

373 *don't say die*: Curiously, the first use of this expression recorded in the *Oxford Dictionary of
English Proverbs* is as late as 1837, in Charles Dickens's *The Pickwick Papers*, where it occurs
in the form 'Never say die'.

LORD MOUNT. Oh yes, no doubt – most enviable. At the same time, seeing you thus, we naturally say to ourselves, 'This is very sad. His Lordship is constitutionally as blithe as a bird – he trills upon the bench like a thing of song and gladness. His series of judgements in F sharp minor, given *andante* in six-eight time, are among the most remarkable effects ever produced in a Court of Chancery. He is, perhaps, the only living instance of a judge whose decrees have received the honour of a double *encore*. How can we bring ourselves to do that which will deprive the Court of Chancery of one of its most attractive features?'

LORD CH. I feel the force of your remarks, but I am here in two capacities, and they clash, my Lords, they clash! I deeply grieve to say that in declining to entertain my last application to myself, I presumed to address myself in terms which render it impossible for me ever to apply to myself again. It was a most painful scene, my Lords – most painful!

LORD TOLL. This is what it is to have two capacities! Let us be thankful that we are persons of no capacity whatever.

LORD MOUNT. Come, come. Remember you are a very just and kindly old gentleman, and you need have no hesitation in approaching yourself, so that you do so respectfully and with a proper show of deference.

LORD CH. Do you really think so?

LORD MOUNT. I do.

LORD CH. Well, I will nerve myself to another effort, and, if that fails, I resign myself to my fate!

TRIO – LORD CHANCELLOR, LORDS MOUNTARARAT
and TOLLOLLER.

LORD MOUNT.
    If you go in
    You're sure to win –
Yours will be the charming maidie:
    Be your law
    The ancient saw,
'Faint heart never won fair lady!'

ALL.
Never, never, never,
Faint heart never won fair lady!

    Every journey has an end –
When at the worst affairs will mend –
Dark the dawn when day is nigh –
Hustle your horse and don't say die!

LORD TOLL.
    He who shies
    At such a prize

340

345

350

355

360

365

370

375

376 *a maravedi*: A Spanish copper coin minted in 1848, with a value of only about one thirteenth of an English penny. This saying is, I think, a Gilbertian original.

382 *While the sun shines make your hay*: The first recorded appearance in print was in 1546 in the form 'Whan the sunne shinth make hay'. It is more normally inverted: 'Make hay while the sun shines'.

383 *Where a will is, there's a way*: Usually found in the form 'Where there's a will, there's a way'. The first recorded appearance is in 1836.

384 *Beard the lion in his lair*: Originally biblical, deriving from the well-known story of Daniel in the lion's den (Daniel 6.11–23). It means to tackle the enemy in his stronghold.

385 *None but the brave deserve the fair*: The only saying which occurs in both the *Iolanthe* trio and the *Pinafore* duet. It is found in John Dryden's ode *Alexander's Feast* (1697).

394 *Nothing venture, nothing win*: First recorded use 1668.

395 *Blood is thick, but water's thin*: Normally used in the form 'Blood is thicker than water', meaning that the ties of family and kinship are stronger than any others. Its first recorded use is in Sir Walter Scott's *Guy Mannering* (1815).

396 *In for a penny, in for a pound*: First recorded use 1695.

397 *It's Love that makes the world go round*: Some commentators, including Harry Benford in his *Gilbert and Sullivan Lexicon*, have suggested that this was Gilbert's own creation, involving a paraphrase of the old saying 'It's drink that makes the world go round'. In fact, the phrase 'Love makes the world go round' was well-known in nineteenth-century England. It occurs in Charles Dickens's *Our Mutual Friend* (1865). A French version, *C'est l'amour, l'amour qui fait le monde à la ronde*, is recorded as early as 1700.

399 *Enter Strephon, in very low spirits*: In early performances of *Iolanthe* in both London and New York, Strephon entered at this point to sing the following recitative and aria:

RECITATIVE.

My Bill has now been read a second time:
His ready vote no member now refuses;
In verity I wield a power sublime,
And one that I can turn to mighty uses.
What joy to carry, in the very teeth
Of Ministry, Cross-Bench and Opposition,
Some rather urgent measures – quite beneath
The ken of patriot and politician!

SONG.

Fold your flapping wings,
    Soaring Legislature!
Stoop to little things –
    Stoop to Human Nature!
Never need to roam,
    Members patriotic,
Let's begin at home –
    Crime is no exotic!
        Bitter is your bane –
            Terrible your trials –
        Dingy Drury Lane!
            Soapless Seven Dials!

Take a tipsy lout
    Gathered from the gutter –
Hustle him about –
    Strap him to a shutter:
What am I but he,
    Washed at hours stated –

Is not worth a maravedi,
    Be so kind
    To bear in mind –
Faint heart never won fair lady!

ALL.   Never, never, never,   380
                  Faint heart never won fair lady!

While the sun shines make your hay –
Where a will is, there's a way –
Beard the lion in his lair –
None but the brave deserve the fair!   385

LORD CH.   I'll take heart
                  And make a start –
        Though I fear the prospect's shady –
                  Much I'd spend
                  To gain my end –   390
        Faint heart never won fair lady!

ALL.   Never, never, never,
                  Faint heart never won fair lady!

Nothing venture, nothing win –
Blood is thick, but water's thin –   395
In for a penny, in for a pound –
It's Love that makes the world go round!
                  (*Dance, and exeunt arm-in-arm together.*)

(*Enter* STREPHON, *in very low spirits.*)

STREPH. I suppose one ought to enjoy oneself in Parliament, when one   400
leads both Parties, as I do! But I'm miserable, poor, broken-hearted fool that
I am! Oh, Phyllis, Phyllis! –

(*Enter* PHYLLIS.)

PHYL. Yes.
STREPH. (*surprised*). Phyllis! But I suppose I should say 'My Lady'. I   405
have not yet been informed which title your ladyship has pleased to select?
PHYL. I – I haven't quite decided. You see, *I* have no *mother* to advise
me!
STREPH. No. I have.

> Fed on filigree –
>> Clothed and educated?
>>> He's a mark of scorn –
>>>> I might be another,
>>> If I had been born
>>>> Of a tipsy mother!
>
> Take a wretched thief
>> Through the city sneaking,
> Pocket handkerchief
>> Ever, ever seeking:
> What is he but I
>> Robbed of all my chances –
> Picking pockets by
>> Force of circumstances?
>>> I might be as bad –
>>>> As unlucky, rather –
>>> If I'd only had
>>>> Fagin for a father!

'Fold your flapping wings' came in for considerable criticism in some of the first-night reviews. The magazine *Truth* complained that 'to eke out the time, the clown, now a Member of Parliament, has to sing a lengthy ditty, in which he ponderously explains that he never sees a criminal without thinking that it might have been himself'. The *Theatre* reviewer commented:

> The libretto of *Iolanthe* has been utilized by its author as the vehicle for conveying to society at large a feeling protest on behalf of the indigent, and a scathing satire upon the hereditary moiety of our Legislature. Advocacy and denunciation of this sort are all very well in melodrama, where telling 'points' may always be made with the unmerited wrongs of the poor and the reprehensible uselessness of the aristocracy. But they jar upon the ear and taste alike when brought to bear upon us through the medium of a song sung by half a fairy in a professedly comic opera.

Gilbert took this criticism to heart, and 'Fold your flapping wings' was cut during the initial Savoy run. It was, however, printed in both the first and second British editions of the libretto and in the first American edition of the vocal score, from which we can discover that it had an appealing waltz-time tune.

427–8 *half a dozen I don't*: For the 1907 revival of *Iolanthe* Phyllis was given an extra line at this point, 'Half a mortal's better than no bread'. This rather corny addition to the original libretto, apparently approved by Gilbert, was cut again in 1914 and has not been used in subsequent performances. Strephon's earlier line 'Don't do that' (line 423) was also added in 1907, as were the words 'I hate that sort of thing' immediately after it. The second part of the line was cut in 1914 to leave the present version.

442–65 *If we're weak enough to tarry*
As previously mentioned (see the note to Act I, line 228), this song was originally intended for Act I. In the licence copy of the *Perola* libretto, the dialogue between Strephon and Phyllis continues straight from 'I think we shall be very happy!' (line 436) to 'But does your mother know' (line 466).

PHYL. Yes; a *young* mother.　　　　　　　　　　　　　　410
STREPH. Not very – a couple of centuries or so.
PHYL. Oh! She wears well.
STREPH. She does. She's a fairy.
PHYL. I beg your pardon – a what?
STREPH. Oh, I've no longer any reason to conceal the fact – she's a　　415
fairy.
PHYL. A fairy! Well, but – that would account for a good many things!
Then – I suppose *you're* a fairy?
STREPH. I'm half a fairy.
PHYL. Which half?　　　　　　　　　　　　　　420
STREPH. The upper half – down to the waistcoat.
PHYL. Dear me! (*Prodding him with her fingers.*) There is nothing to show it!
STREPH. Don't do that.
PHYL. But why didn't you tell me this before?
STREPH. I thought you would take a dislike to me. But as it's all off,　　425
you may as well know the truth – I'm only half a mortal!
PHYL. (*crying*). But I'd rather have half a mortal I do love, than half a
dozen I don't!
STREPH. Oh, I think not – go to your half-dozen.
PHYL. (*crying*). It's only two! and I hate 'em! Please forgive me!　　430
STREPH. I don't think I ought to. Besides, all sorts of difficulties will
arise. You know, my grandmother looks quite as young as my mother. So do
all my aunts.
PHYL. I quite understand. Whenever I see you kissing a very young
lady, I shall know it's an elderly relative.　　　　　　　　　435
STREPH. You will? Then, Phyllis, I think we shall be very happy!
(*Embracing her.*)
PHYL. We won't wait long.
STREPH. No. We might change our minds. We'll get married first.
PHYL. And change our minds afterwards?　　　　　　　　440
STREPH. That's the usual course.

DUET – STREPHON *and* PHYLLIS.

STREPH.　　　　　　　If we're weak enough to tarry
　　　　　　　　　　　Ere we marry,
　　　　　　　　　　　　　You and I,
　　　　　　　　　　Of the feeling I inspire　　　　　　　445
　　　　　　　　　　　You may tire
　　　　　　　　　　　　　By and by.
　　　　　　　　　For peers with flowing coffers
　　　　　　　　　　Press their offers –
　　　　　　　　　　　That is why　　　　　　　　450

466 *But does your mother know*: This was a well-known catch-phrase among the Victorian
working classes, particularly in the form 'Does your mother know you're out?'

477 *You know not what you ask*: After delivering this line Iolanthe/Perola has the following
song in the licence copy:

SONG – PEROLA.

> A fairy once, as well you know
> (Heigho, love is a thorn)
> She loved a mortal years ago –
> (And it's oh my beating heart!)
> They married were, this foolish pair,
> And then was born a son and heir,
> I'm sure of my facts, for I was there!
> (And it's oh for my beating heart!)

ALL.   Heigho, love is a thorn,
        And it's oh my beating heart!

> I was that fond and foolish fay
> (Heigho, etc.)
> That you were the son, I need not say.
> (And it's oh, etc.)
> The mortal – your progenitor –
> Whom I gave up my freedom for –
> He is the present Lord Chancellor!
> And it's oh my beating heart!

ALL.   Heigho, love is a thorn,
        And it's oh my beating heart!

The dialogue then continued:

STREPH. The Lord Chancellor my father! But he knows nothing of this?
PEROLA. No, by our Queen's command, I quitted him shortly after our marriage. He
believes me to be dead: and, dearly as I love him, I am bound, under penalty of death, never
to undeceive him.
STREPH. Then, Phyllis, I really don't see what is to become of us.
PEROLA. Nay, there is hope. I will disguise myself, and plead your case as best I may. He
comes! This veil will conceal my face. Oh that I could so easily veil my trembling voice!

(*Enter* LORD CHANCELLOR.)

> I am sure we should not tarry
>   Ere we marry,
>   You and I!

PHYL.
> If we're weak enough to tarry
>   Ere we marry,
>   You and I,
> With a more attractive maiden,
>   Jewel-laden,
>   You may fly.
> If by chance we should be parted,
>   Broken-hearted
>   I should die –
> So I think we will not tarry
>   Ere we marry,
>   You and I.

455

460

465

PHYL. But does your mother know you're – I mean, is she aware of our engagement?

(*Enter* IOLANTHE.)

IOL. She is; and thus she welcomes her daughter-in-law! (*Kisses her.*)
PHYL. She kisses just like other people! But the Lord Chancellor?
STREPH. I forgot him! Mother, none can resist your fairy eloquence; you will go to him and plead for us?
IOL. (*much agitated*). No, no; impossible!
STREPH. But our happiness – our very lives – depend upon our obtaining his consent!
PHYL. Oh, madam, you cannot refuse to do this!
IOL. You know not what you ask! The Lord Chancellor is – my husband!
STREPH. *and* PHYL. Your husband!
IOL. My husband and your father! (*Addressing* STREPHON, *who is much moved.*)
PHYL. Then our course is plain; on his learning that Strephon is his son, all objection to our marriage will be at once removed!
IOL. No; he must never know! He believes me to have died childless, and, dearly as I love him, I am bound, under penalty of death, not to undeceive him. But see – he comes! Quick – my veil!

470

475

480

485

(IOLANTHE *veils herself.* STREPHON *and* PHYLLIS *go off on tiptoe.*)

(*Enter* LORD CHANCELLOR.)

505–20 *He loves! If in the bygone years*

Gilbert wrote the part of Iolanthe specially for Jessie Bond, the D'Oyly Carte's leading mezzo-soprano, who had joined the company to sing the role of Hebe in the first production of *H.M.S. Pinafore*. At the time *Iolanthe* was being written, she was incapacitated by a serious accident which made any vigorous movement impossible. Gilbert told her 'You will not have to dance and hardly to move, and as you are always laughing, I have written a song to show you can be serious when you have the chance'. The song was, of course, 'He loves', which is one of the saddest and most moving in all the Savoy Operas.

In setting 'He loves' to music, Sullivan must surely have been profoundly influenced by the death of his mother, which had occurred only a few days before he started work on the *Iolanthe* score. The line 'Sad thoughts of her arise' must have had particularly poignant echoes for the composer, who was deeply distraught at the loss of one to whom he had always been very close. Perhaps indeed he even saw this song as standing in some way as a memorial to her, just as his overture *In Memoriam* (1866) was written as a memorial to his father, and his famous song *The Lost Chord* (1877) was inspired by the death of his brother.

LORD CH. Victory! Victory! Success has crowned my efforts, and I may consider myself engaged to Phyllis! At first I wouldn't hear of it – it was out of the question. But I took heart. I pointed out to myself that I was no stranger to myself; that, in point of fact, I had been personally acquainted with myself for some years. This had its effect. I admitted that I had watched my professional advancement with considerable interest, and I handsomely added that I yielded to no one in admiration for my private and professional virtues. This was a great point gained. I then endeavoured to work upon my feelings. Conceive my joy when I distinctly perceived a tear glistening in my own eye! Eventually, after a severe struggle with myself, I reluctantly – most reluctantly – consented.

490

495

(IOLANTHE *comes down veiled.*)

500

RECITATIVE – IOLANTHE (*kneeling*).

My lord, a suppliant at your feet I kneel,
Oh, listen to a mother's fond appeal!
Hear me to-night! I come in urgent need –
'Tis for my son, young Strephon, that I plead!

BALLAD – IOLANTHE.

He loves! If in the bygone years
  Thine eyes have ever shed
Tears – bitter, unavailing tears,
  For one untimely dead –
If, in the eventide of life,
  Sad thoughts of her arise,
Then let the memory of thy wife
  Plead for my boy – he dies!

505

510

He dies! If fondly laid aside
  In some old cabinet,
Memorials of thy long-dead bride
  Lie, dearly treasured yet,
Then let her hallowed bridal dress –
  Her little dainty gloves –
Her withered flowers – her faded tress –
  Plead for my boy – he loves!

515

520

(*The* LORD CHANCELLOR *is moved by this appeal. After a pause.*)

LORD CH.   It may not be – for so the fates decide!
        Learn thou that Phyllis is my promised bride.

545 *Willahalah! Willaloo*: Another Wagnerian touch; the fairies' chorus is reminiscent of the
     wailing of the Rhinedaughters in *Das Rheingold*: 'Wag-a-la-weia, Wa-la-la, Wei-la-la,
     Weia'.

561 *Equity draftsman*: An old name given to a barrister practising in the Court of Chancery
     who drafted pleadings to be heard in that court.
562 *The subtleties of the legal mind*: The legal mind receives another 'puff' in *The Grand Duke*
     when the notary says: 'It is always amusing to the legal mind to see a parcel of laymen
     bothering themselves about a matter which to a trained lawyer presents no difficulty
     whatever.'

IOL. (*in horror*).	Thy bride! No! no!
LORD CH.	It shall be so!
	Those who would separate us woe betide!
IOL.	My doom thy lips have spoken –
	I plead in vain!
CHORUS OF FAIRIES (*without*).	Forbear! forbear!
IOL.	A vow already broken
	I break again!
CHORUS OF FAIRIES (*without*).	Forbear! forbear!
IOL.	For him – for her – for thee
	I yield my life.
	Behold – it may not be!
	I am thy wife.
CHORUS OF FAIRIES (*without*).	Aiaiah! Aiaiah! Willaloo!
LORD CH. (*recognizing her*).	Iolanthe! thou livest?
IOL.	Aye!
	I live! Now let me die!

525

530

535

540

(*Enter* FAIRY QUEEN *and Fairies.* IOLANTHE *kneels to her.*)

QUEEN.	Once again thy vows are broken:
	Thou thyself thy doom hast spoken!
CHORUS OF FAIRIES.	Aiaiah! Aiaiah!
	Willahalah! Willaloo!
	Willahalah! Willaloo!
QUEEN.	Bow thy head to Destiny:
	Death thy doom, and thou shalt die!
CHORUS OF FAIRIES.	Aiaiah! Aiaiah! etc.

545

(*Peers and Sentry enter. The* QUEEN *raises her spear.*)

550

LEILA. Hold! If Iolanthe must die, so must we all; for, as she has sinned, so have we!

QUEEN. What?

CELIA. We are all fairy duchesses, marchionesses, countesses, viscountesses, and baronesses.

LORD MOUNT. It's our fault. They couldn't help themselves.

555

QUEEN. It seems they *have* helped themselves, and pretty freely, too! (*After a pause.*) You have all incurred death; but I can't slaughter the whole company! And yet (*unfolding a scroll*) the law is clear – every fairy must die who marries a mortal!

560

LORD CH. Allow me, as an old Equity draftsman, to make a suggestion. The subtleties of the legal mind are equal to the emergency. The thing is really quite simple – the insertion of a single word will do it. Let it

567   *Private Willis*: In the 1907 revival, the Fairy Queen at this point had the extra line, reminiscent of Captain Corcoran's command to Ralph Rackstraw in *H.M.S. Pinafore*, 'Three paces to the front'. It was cut again in 1914.

572   *ill-convenience*: In the manner of the Victorian lower classes, Private Willis pronounces his 'v's as 'w's. The word is, indeed, printed as 'inconwenience' in several editions of the libretto.

582   *Wings spring from shoulders of Peers*: Gilbert's note in his prompt-book reads: 'At "off we go to Fairyland", each principal pulls a string which is fastened to the pin which keeps his wings down. On release, the wings fly up. The soldier's wings have appeared on his shoulder before this – that is to say when the Fairy Queen says, "You are a fairy from this moment".'

stand that every fairy shall die who *doesn't* marry a mortal, and there you are, out of your difficulty at once!

QUEEN. We like your humour. Very well! (*Altering the MS. in pencil.*) Private Willis!

SENTRY (*coming forward*). Ma'am!

QUEEN. To save my life, it is necessary that I marry at once. How should you like to be a fairy guardsman?

SENTRY. Well, ma'am, I don't think much of the British soldier who wouldn't ill-convenience himself to save a female in distress.

QUEEN. You are a brave fellow. You're a fairy from this moment. (*Wings spring from Sentry's shoulders.*) And you, my Lords, how say you, will you join our ranks?

(*Fairies kneel to Peers and implore them to do so.*)

(PHYLLIS *and* STREPHON *enter.*)

LORD MOUNT. (*to* LORD TOLLOLLER). Well, now that the Peers are to be recruited entirely from persons of intelligence, I really don't see what use *we* are, down here, do you, Tolloller?

LORD TOLL. None whatever.

QUEEN. Good! (*Wings spring from shoulders of Peers.*) Then away we go to Fairyland.

FINALE.

PHYL.
 Soon as we may,
 Off and away!
 We'll commence our journey airy –
 Happy are we –
 As you can see,
 Every one is now a fairy!

ALL.
 Every, every, every,
 Every one is now a fairy!

IOL., QUEEN, *and* PHYL.
 Though as a general rule we know
 Two strings go to every bow,
 Make up your minds that grief 'twill bring
 If you've two beaux to every string.

ALL.
 Though as a general rule, etc.

LORD CH.
 Up in the sky,
 Ever so high,

602 *House of Peris*: Peris originally appeared in Persian mythology as a race of beautiful but
     malevolent fairy-like creatures who were descended from fallen angels and excluded
     from Paradise until they had completed their penance. They were held responsible for
     comets, eclipses of the sun and moon, and the failure of crops. Later the word came to
     be used more generally for fairies and, indeed, for any beautiful girl.

Pleasures come in endless series;
We will arrange
Happy exchange –
House of Peers for House of Peris!

600

ALL.   Peris, Peris, Peris,
House of Peers for House of Peris!

LORDS CH.,   Up in the air, sky-high, sky-high,   605
MOUNT.,   Free from Wards in Chancery,
and TOLL. $\left.\begin{matrix} \text{I} \\ \text{He} \end{matrix}\right\}$ will be surely happier, for

$\left.\begin{matrix} \text{I'm} \\ \text{He's} \end{matrix}\right\}$ such a susceptible Chancellor.

ALL.   Up in the air, etc.

CURTAIN

PRINCESS IDA
or
Castle Adamant

DRAMATIS PERSONÆ

KING HILDEBRAND
HILARION (*his Son*)
CYRIL $\Big\}$ (*Hilarion's Friends*)
FLORIAN
KING GAMA
ARAC
GURON $\Big\}$ (*his Sons*)
SCYNTHIUS
PRINCESS IDA (*Gama's Daughter*)
LADY BLANCHE (*Professor of Abstract Science*)
LADY PSYCHE (*Professor of Humanities*)
MELISSA (*Lady Blanche's Daughter*)
SACHARISSA
CHLOE $\Big\}$ (*Girl Graduates*)
ADA

Soldiers, Courtiers, 'Girl Graduates', 'Daughters of the Plough', etc.

ACT I. – Pavilion in King Hildebrand's Palace.
ACT II. – Gardens of Castle Adamant.
ACT III. – Courtyard of Castle Adamant.

PRINCESS IDA

Princess Ida is the only Savoy Opera to have three acts and to be written in blank verse. Gilbert lifted nearly all of the dialogue from his earlier play, *The Princess*, which had been performed at the Olympic Theatre in 1870. That play was itself based on Alfred, Lord Tennyson's long poem *The Princess*, which had first appeared in 1847. The new opera was accordingly billed as 'A Respectful Operatic Per-Version of Tennyson's "Princess".'

In both his play and his opera libretto, Gilbert closely followed the details of the Poet Laureate's story. It tells of a prince who had been betrothed in childhood to Princess Ida, daughter of the neighbouring King Gama. Becoming a devotee of women's rights, however, the princess has abjured men and set up an all-female university. The prince and two companions gain entrance to the university disguised as girl students, but their true identity is discovered by the two tutors, Lady Psyche and Lady Blanche, and eventually by the princess herself. A battle ensues between the forces of the prince's father and those of King Gama, led by his mighty son Arac. There is much bloodshed and the university is turned into a hospital. Womanly pity eventually leads Princess Ida to accept her betrothal to the prince, and so all ends happily.

With such an epic theme as his basis, Gilbert was not able in *Princess Ida* to create his usual mixture of mistaken identities, magic potions, and sharp satirical digs at contemporary figures. It is true that he was able to poke some gentle fun at the movement for women's education, which had gained momentum in the 1870s with the founding of Girton and Newnham colleges at Cambridge and Somerville and Lady Margaret Hall at Oxford. But, although *Princess Ida* is not devoid of patter songs and humorous moments, it is a much more serious work than any of the Savoy Operas which preceded it.

As such, it must have come as something of a relief to Sullivan, who was becoming increasingly impatient with Gilbert's topsy-turvy plots. The two men had fallen out in the summer of 1883 over the theme for their next joint work, with the composer firmly resisting the librettist's proposals for another opera based on his favourite idea of a magic lozenge. Sullivan had been knighted in May of that year and felt himself now to be above the role of mere tune-smith to his dominant partner. It was probably only because of the relative seriousness of the *Princess Ida* libretto that he agreed to participate. In the event, he produced a delightful score, which is closer to grand opera in its harmonies and ensembles than any of his earlier works.

The opera opened at the Savoy Theatre on 5 January 1884. Sullivan was only just able to conduct the first performance. A combination of fatigue, strain and a recurrence of a chronic kidney complaint had reduced him to a state of near collapse, and he was not expected to be present at the first night. Indeed, D'Oyly Carte had printed in the programme that François Cellier would conduct. However, by injecting himself with large quantities of morphine and taking copious cups of black coffee, Sullivan was able to get up from his sick bed and stagger to the theatre.

Sullivan did not take his place at the conductor's rostrum until nearly half an hour after the performance was due to start and, with unduly long intervals for scene changes between the acts, he did not finally lay down his baton until nearly midnight. He collapsed just after taking his bow with Gilbert. In his diary, however, he noted that the evening had been a 'brilliant success'.

Certainly the first-night audience seems to have enjoyed the new work. Gilbert was sitting quietly in the green room reading the paper during the last act when the Frenchman whom he had commissioned to design the silver-gilt armour for Gama's three sons burst in shouting excitedly: '*Mais savez-vous, monsieur, que vous avez là un succès solide?*' The librettist, slightly taken aback by this display of Gallic temperament, replied that it seemed to be going quite well. '*Mais vous êtes si calme!*' was the astonished Frenchman's response. 'I suppose he expected to see me kissing all the carpenters,' Gilbert later remarked.

In retrospect, Gilbert was right to be cautious. The critics were by no means as enthusiastic about *Princess Ida* as the first-night audience had been, and its initial run of 246 performances was one of the shortest of all the Savoy Operas. Three weeks after the opening, Sullivan told Gilbert that he would not work on any more comic operas, and it looked as though their collaboration was at an end.

Its length and its subject-matter, so closely tied to the work of a now largely unread poet, have meant that *Princess Ida* has not fared particularly well in the twentieth century. It was not revived in London until 1919 and was always one of the least frequently performed works in the D'Oyly Carte repertoire. A new production directed by Robert Gibson and designed by James Wade was introduced in 1954 to replace one the costumes and scenery for which had been destroyed in the war. This version, which with its fantastic Gothic designs succeeded in capturing the dream-like quality of Tennyson's original poem, received its final British performance in Nottingham on 7 March 1978 and its last-ever performance at the National Arts Centre, Ottawa, Canada, on 4 August 1978.

For more than a decade it seemed that *Princess Ida* might fade away into oblivion. In 1992, however, came the news that it was to be performed by English National Opera at the London Coliseum. The production by avant-garde film director, Ken Russell, opened in November and was universally panned by the critics. The location was changed to Buck and Yen Palace, a theme park created with the sale of Buckingham Palace to a consortium of Japanese and Americans. King Gama was turned into a Sushi-King, his sons appeared as a cross between Sumo wrestlers and Hell's Angels, while King Hildebrand was dressed in a kilt and fitted with giant ears to look like Prince Charles. The *Times* critic described it as 'desperate stuff which starts without a premise and leads nowhere', the *Financial Times* as 'a heedlessly energetic blending of the crass, the coarse and the witless', while the *Daily Telegraph*'s verdict was that 'clumsily choreographed and ineptly directed, it fails miserably on every level, whether simply as entertainment or as a send-up of amateur G & S productions'.

It is to be hoped that this disastrous production does not reduce further the chances of rehabilitation for an opera which includes some of the finest music which Sullivan ever wrote, ranging from the poignant delicacy of 'The world is but a broken toy' and the 'Expressive glances' trio to the Handelian splendour of 'This helmet I suppose'.

Whatever its ultimate fate, however, *Princess Ida* has at least had one moment of glory and earned itself a small footnote in twentieth-century British history. Before Neville Chamberlain's historic statement of 3 September 1939 announcing a state of war between the United Kingdom and Germany the BBC broadcast a recorded selection of music from the opera. It seems that the music was faded out at the end of the song 'We are warriors three' on the words 'Order comes to fight, ha! ha! Order is obeyed' (Act I, lines 200–1).

1–3 *Scene*: In the first edition of the libretto, this act was described as a prologue, the present
      Act II as Act I, and Act III as Act II.

13 *Prince Hilarion*: In Tennyson's *The Princess* neither the prince betrothed as a child to Prin-
      cess Ida nor his father is named. Gilbert gave them the names Hilarion and Hildebrand
      for his play and retained them for the opera.

16 *Ida*: Princess Ida, on the other hand, was given her name by Tennyson rather than Gil-
      bert. Ida was a mountain in Phrygia near Troy from whose summit, according to ancient
      Greek legend, the gods watched the Trojan War. There was another Mount Ida in Crete,
      where Zeus was said to have been brought up.

ACT I

SCENE. – *Pavilion attached to* KING HILDEBRAND'S *Palace. Soldiers and Courtiers discovered looking out through opera-glasses, telescopes, etc.,* FLORIAN *leading.*

CHORUS.

Search throughout the panorama
For a sign of royal Gama, 5
   Who to-day should cross the water
   With his fascinating daughter –
    Ida is her name.

Some misfortune evidently
Has detained them – consequently 10
   Search throughout the panorama
   For the daughter of King Gama,
    Prince Hilarion's flame!

SOLO.

FLOR.   Will Prince Hilarion's hopes be sadly blighted?
ALL.   Who can tell?   Who can tell? 15
FLOR.   Will Ida break the vows that she has plighted?
ALL.   Who can tell?   Who can tell?
FLOR.   Will she back out, and say she did not mean them?
ALL.   Who can tell?
FLOR.   If so, there'll be the deuce to pay between them! 20

ALL.   No, no – we'll not despair, we'll not despair,
      For Gama would not dare
      To make a deadly foe
      Of Hildebrand, and so,
        Search throughout, etc. 25

(*Enter* KING HILDEBRAND, *with* CYRIL.)

27 *See you no sign of Gama*: The blank verse in which all the dialogue of *Princess Ida* is written
is made up of heroic metres, i.e. lines of ten syllables. For the most part Gilbert lifted it
directly from his earlier play *The Princess*.

39 *As though Dame Nature*: For his new 1954 D'Oyly Carte production Robert Gibson proposed several cuts in dialogue to speed up the action of the opera. Among them were
this and the succeeding line, line 46, and lines 51–2.

46 *His 'sting' is present*: Until now, the dialogue of *Princess Ida* has exactly followed that of Gilbert's *The Princess*; this is the first line that is different. In *The Princess* Hilarion continues
after 'his sting lay in his tongue':

> His bitter insolence still rankles here
> Although a score of years have come and gone.
> His sting is present – though his tongue is past.
> His outer man, gnarled, knotted, as it was,
> Seemed to his cruel and tyrannical within
> Hyperion to a Saturday Review.

CYR.   Oh bear with him. He is an old man.
> Old men are fretful – peevish – as we know –
> A worm will sometimes turn. So will the milk
> Of human kindness, if it's kept too long.

FLOR.   But stay, my liege, o'er yonder mountain's brow, etc.

57 *en cavalier*: Like a knight.

62 *For Gama place the richest robes*: This whole passage (lines 62–70) was another cut proposed
by Robert Gibson. He no doubt felt that it was superfluous, since Hildebrand's subsequent song makes exactly the same point. However, he reckoned without the combined
forces of the D'Oyly Carte artistes and fans, who objected to what they regarded as the
mutilation of Gilbert's words. Several of the cuts which Gibson tried to introduce in
1954 were ignored, and gradually more and more of the original dialogue was restored.

HILD.　See you no sign of Gama?

FLOR.　　　　　　　　None, my liege!

HILD.　It's very odd indeed. If Gama fail
　　　　To put in an appearance at our Court　　　　　　　30
　　　　Before the sun has set in yonder west,
　　　　And fail to bring the Princess Ida here
　　　　To whom our son Hilarion was betrothed
　　　　At the extremely early age of one,
　　　　There's war between King Gama and ourselves!　　35
　　　　(*Aside to* CYRIL.) Oh, Cyril, how I dread this interview!
　　　　It's twenty years since he and I have met.
　　　　He was a twisted monster – all awry –
　　　　As though Dame Nature, angry with her work,
　　　　Had crumpled it in fitful petulance!　　　　　　40

CYR.　But, sir, a twisted and ungainly trunk
　　　　Often bears goodly fruit. Perhaps he was
　　　　A kind, well-spoken gentleman?

HILD.　　　　　　　　　　　Oh, no!
　　　　For, adder-like, his sting lay in his tongue.　　　45
　　　　(His 'sting' is present, though his 'stung' is past.)

FLOR. (*looking through glass*). But stay, my liege; o'er yonder mountain's brow
　　　　Comes a small body, bearing Gama's arms;
　　　　And now I look more closely at it, sir,
　　　　I see attached to it King Gama's legs;　　　　　50
　　　　From which I gather this corollary
　　　　That that small body must be Gama's own!

HILD.　Ha! Is the Princess with him?

FLOR.　　　　　　　　　Well, my liege,
　　　　Unless her highness is full six feet high,　　　55
　　　　And wears mustachios too – and smokes cigars –
　　　　And rides *en cavalier* in coat of steel –
　　　　I do not think she is.

HILD.　　　　　　　　One never knows.
　　　　She's a strange girl, I've heard, and does odd things!　60
　　　　Come, bustle there!
　　　　For Gama place the richest robes we own –
　　　　For Gama place the coarsest prison dress –
　　　　For Gama let our best spare bed be aired –
　　　　For Gama let our deepest dungeon yawn –　　　65
　　　　For Gama lay the costliest banquet out –
　　　　For Gama place cold water and dry bread!
　　　　For as King Gama brings the Princess here,
　　　　Or brings her not, so shall King Gama have
　　　　Much more than everything – much less than nothing!　70

94 *quarter-day*: Quarter-days are not quite as sure as this chorus makes them seem. It all depends on whether you go for the new style – in which case they fall on 25 March, 24 June, 29 September and 25 December – or the old – where they occur on 6 April, 6 July, 11 October and 6 January. In Scotland, needless to say, things are different, and the quarter-days fall on 2 February, 15 May, 1 August and 11 November.

SONG – HILDEBRAND *and* CHORUS.

HILD.   Now hearken to my strict command
        On every hand, on every hand –

CHORUS.

        To your command,
        On every hand,
        We dutifully bow!   75

HILD.   If Gama bring the Princess here,
        Give him good cheer, give him good cheer.

CHORUS.

        If she come here
        We'll give him a cheer,
        And we will show you how.   80
        Hip, hip, hurrah! hip, hip, hurrah!
        Hip, hip, hurrah! hurrah! hurrah!
        We'll shout and sing
        Long live the King,
        And his daughter, too, I trow!   85
        Then shout ha! ha! hip, hip, hurrah!
        Hip, hip, hip, hip, hurrah!
        For the fair Princess and her good papa,
        Hurrah! hurrah!

HILD.   But if he fails to keep his troth,   90
        Upon our oath, we'll trounce them both!

CHORUS.

        He'll trounce them both,
        Upon his oath,
        As sure as quarter-day!

HILD.   We'll shut him up in a dungeon cell,   95
        And toll his knell on a funeral bell.

CHORUS.

        From dungeon cell,
        His funeral knell
        Shall strike him with dismay!

115–30 *Ida was a twelvemonth old*

In making Princess Ida only one at the time of her betrothal, Gilbert departed from Tennyson's original. Here is the relevant passage from the Poet Laureate's *Princess*, in which, incidentally, the prince is the story-teller:

> Now it chanced that I had been,
> While life was yet in bud and blade, betroth'd
> To one, a neighbouring Princess: she to me
> Was proxy wedded with a bootless calf
> At eight years old; and still from time to time
> Came murmurs of her beauty from the South.

Ida and Hilarion are not the only characters in the Savoy Operas betrothed at a very early age. Luiz and Casilda in *The Gondoliers* shared the same happy experience. The situation of Patience and Archibald Grosvenor in *Patience* is, of course, similar but not identical: they were only ever childhood friends and were never engaged.

133 *King Gama is in sight*: This and the next two lines depart slightly from the text of Gilbert's earlier play, which at this point has the lines:

HILD.   My son, King Gama's host is now in sight –
                         Prepare to meet the fascinating bride
                         To whom you were betrothed so long ago.
                         Why, how you sigh!
HIL.   My liege, I'm much afraid
                         The Princess Ida has not come with him.
                         I've heard she has forsworn the world, etc.

In Tennyson's poem, it is Gama who tells the prince and his companions of his daughter's renunciation of the world of men:

> At last she begg'd a boon,
> A certain summer-palace which I have
> Hard by your father's frontier: I said no,
> Yet being an easy man, gave it: and there,
> All wild to found a University
> For maidens, on the spur she fled; and more
> We know not, – only this: they see no men.

Hip, hip, hurrah! hip, hip, hurrah!　　　　　　100
Hip, hip, hurrah! hurrah! hurrah!
　　As up we string
　　The faithless King,
　　In the old familiar way!
We'll shout ha! ha! hip, hip, hurrah!　　　　105
Hip, hip, hip, hip, hurrah!
As we make an end of her false papa,
　　Hurrah! hurrah!

　　　　　　　　　　　　　　　　　(Exeunt all.)

　　　　　(Enter HILARION.)　　　　　　110

RECITATIVE – HILARION.

To-day we meet, my baby bride and I –
　　But ah, my hopes are balanced by my fears!
What transmutations have been conjured by
　　The silent alchemy of twenty years!

BALLAD – HILARION.

Ida was a twelvemonth old,　　　　　　　115
　　Twenty years ago!
I was twice her age, I'm told,
　　Twenty years ago!
Husband twice as old as wife
Argues ill for married life,　　　　　　　120
Baleful prophecies were rife,
　　Twenty years ago!

Still, I was a tiny prince
　　Twenty years ago.
She has gained upon me, since　　　　　　125
　　Twenty years ago.
Though she's twenty-one, it's true,
I am barely twenty-two –
False and foolish prophets you,
　　Twenty years ago!　　　　　　　　　130

　　　　　(Enter HILDEBRAND.)

HIL.　　　Well, father, is there news for me at last?
HILD.　　King Gama is in sight, but much I fear
　　　　　With no Princess!

146 *I think I see her now*: Hilarion's exchange with his father recalls a passage from Shake-
     speare's *Hamlet*, Act I, Scene 2:

     HAMLET.   ...methinks I see my father.
     HORATIO.   Where, my lord?
     HAMLET.   In my mind's eye, Horatio.

150 *How exquisite she looked*: Much of this passage (lines 150–51, 153–4 and 157–9) was
     included in Robert Gibson's original list of cuts for the 1954 revival. The *Gilbert and
     Sullivan Journal*, which had led a campaign against the cuts, delightedly reported in its
     January 1955 issue, however, that all but two of the lines (153–4) had been restored.

164 *From the distant panorama*: The first American edition of the *Princess Ida* libretto has a
     longer version of this chorus, the first four lines of which, followed by 'Ida is her name',
     as in the opening chorus, are also in the licence copy and first British libretto:

                    From the distant panorama
                    Come the sons of royal Gama.
                    Who, today, should cross the water
                    With his fascinating daughter –
                    Should she not refuse.

                    They are heralds evidently,
                    And are sacred consequently,
                    Let us hail sons of Gama,
                    Who from yonder panorama
                    Come to bring us news!

169 *Enter Arac, Guron, and Scynthius*: Only Arac is mentioned by name in Tennyson's *Princess*,
     although it is revealed there that he has two brothers who are twins.
       Sullivan provided some splendid clodhopping staccato chords for the entrance of the
     three brothers. An early D'Oyly Carte prompt-book contains a detailed direction as to
     how they were to be used to best effect: 'The three enter, great swords held in right
     hand only and sloping down over right shoulder – start on last 8 bars of the 2/4, take 7
     steps to centre and front, then through symphony in 3/2 take 12 steps to front (3 steps
     to a bar), and bring swords down point to ground on 13th beat'.

HIL.	Alas, my liege, I've heard 135
	That Princess Ida has forsworn the world,
	And, with a band of women, shut herself
	Within a lonely country house, and there
	Devotes herself to stern philosophies!
HILD.	Then I should say the loss of such a wife 140
	Is one to which a reasonable man
	Would easily be reconciled.
HIL.	Oh, no!
	Or I am not a reasonable man.
	She *is* my wife – has been for twenty years! 145
	(*Holding glass*). I think I see her now.
HILD.	Ha! let me look!
HIL.	In my mind's eye, I mean – a blushing bride,
	All bib and tucker, frill and furbelow!
	How exquisite she looked as she was borne, 150
	Recumbent, in her foster-mother's arms!
	How the bride wept – nor would be comforted
	Until the hireling mother-for-the-nonce
	Administered refreshment in the vestry.
	And I remember feeling much annoyed 155
	That she should weep at marrying with me.
	But then I thought, 'These brides are all alike.
	You cry at marrying me? How much more cause
	You'd have to cry if it were broken off!'
	These were my thoughts; I kept them to myself, 160
	For at that age I had not learnt to speak.

(*Exeunt* HILDEBRAND *and* HILARION.)

(*Enter Courtiers.*)

CHORUS.

From the distant panorama
Come the sons of royal Gama. 165
  They are heralds evidently,
  And are sacred consequently,
    Sons of Gama, hail! oh, hail!

(*Enter* ARAC, GURON, *and* SCYNTHIUS.)

170–202 *We are warriors three*

This trio was much appreciated by several first-night reviewers. The *Sunday Times* commented:

> It begins with a pure bit of Handel, the deep voice or voices running in strict counterpart against the unison of the lower strings; the effect of this is exceedingly droll, and it is still more so later on when the brass come in with their soft chords, and the flutes with their delicate embroidery.

The *Saturday Review* was equally enthusiastic:

> There is a distinct drollery in the accompaniment to the song and trio for Arac and his brethren, 'We are warriors three'. Bass chords support the first verse, brass boldly aids the assertion 'On the whole we are not intelligent', and the delight of the warriors in their own trade of fighting is emphasized by rapid and elaborate passages for the flute.

201 *Order is obeyed*: These were almost certainly the last words to be heard on the B.B.C. Home Service on the morning of 3 September 1939 before Neville Chamberlain's announcement that Britain was at war with Germany (see p. 453).

SONG – ARAC.

We are warriors three,   170
   Sons of Gama, Rex.
Like most sons are we,
   Masculine in sex.

ALL THREE.   Yes, yes, yes,
              Masculine in sex.   175

ARAC.   Politics we bar,
             They are not our bent;
         On the whole we are
             Not intelligent.

ALL THREE.   No, no, no,   180
             Not intelligent.

ARAC.   But with doughty heart,
             And with trusty blade
         We can play our part –
             Fighting is our trade.   185

ALL THREE.   Yes, yes, yes,
             Fighting is our trade.

ALL THREE.   Bold, and fierce, and strong, ha! ha!
             For a war we burn,
         With its right or wrong, ha! ha!   190
             We have no concern.
         Order comes to fight, ha! ha!
             Order is obeyed,
         We are men of might, ha! ha!
             Fighting is our trade.   195
             Yes, yes, yes,
        Fighting is our trade, ha! ha!

CHORUS.

They are men of might, ha! ha!
Fighting is their trade.
Order comes to fight, ha! ha!   200
Order is obeyed,
   Fighting is their trade!

(*Enter* KING GAMA.)

204-30 *If you give me your attention, I will tell you what I am*
And if you give me yours, I will tell you something more about Gama. Gilbert based his
character fairly closely on Tennyson's original, as described in *The Princess*:

> His name was Gama; crack'd and small his voice,
> But bland the smile that like a wrinkling wind
> On glassy water drove his cheeks in lines;
> A little dry old man, without a star,
> Not like a king.

In one important respect, Gilbert added his own element to the character of Gama
built up by the Poet Laureate. Tennyson never specifically mentions that the king is a
hunchback. In the Gilbertian version he is, of course, 'a twisted monster all awry', or, as
the *Morning Post* first-night reviewer described him, 'a compound of Louis XVI, Dick
Deadeye and Richard III'.

Gama has always been played by D'Oyly Carte comedians as a particularly ugly and
grotesque figure. It took Sir Henry Lytton more than an hour to apply the make-up
needed to turn his normally cheerful countenance into something suitably 'grim and
ghastly'.

George Grossmith, who created the role of Gama, was at first slightly worried that
this introductory patter song might have been directed at himself. Gilbert assured him
that far from this being the case: 'I meant it for myself. I thought it my duty to live up to
my own reputation.'

231 *He can't think why*: This chorus was omitted from early libretti, though not from the vocal
score.

233 *So this is Castle Hildebrand*: Gama's visit to Hildebrand's court is another departure from
Tennyson's story. In the original *Princess*, Hilarion, Florian and Cyril go to Gama's court,
where they find out from him about Ida's university.

SONG – GAMA.

If you give me your attention, I will tell you what I am:
I'm a genuine philanthropist – all other kinds are sham.
Each little fault of temper and each social defect
In my erring fellow-creatures I endeavour to correct.
To all their little weaknesses I open people's eyes;
And little plans to snub the self-sufficient I devise;
I love my fellow-creatures – I do all the good I can –
Yet everybody says I'm such a disagreeable man!
    And I can't think why!

To compliments inflated I've a withering reply;
And vanity I always do my best to mortify;
A charitable action I can skilfully dissect;
And interested motives I'm delighted to detect;
I know everybody's income and what everybody earns;
And I carefully compare it with the income-tax returns;
But to benefit humanity however much I plan,
Yet everybody says I'm such a disagreeable man!
    And I can't think why!

I'm sure I'm no ascetic; I'm as pleasant as can be;
You'll always find me ready with a crushing repartee,
I've an irritating chuckle, I've a celebrated sneer,
I've an entertaining snigger, I've a fascinating leer.
To everybody's prejudice I know a thing or two;
I can tell a woman's age in half a minute – and I do.
But although I try to make myself as pleasant as I can,
Yet everybody says I am a disagreeable man!
    And I can't think why!

CHORUS.   He can't think why!

(*Enter* HILDEBRAND, HILARION, CYRIL, *and* FLORIAN.)

GAMA.   So this is Castle Hildebrand? Well, well!
           Dame Rumour whispered that the place was grand;
           She told me that your taste was exquisite,
           Superb, unparalleled!
HILD. (*gratified*).   Oh, really, King!
GAMA.   But she's a liar! Why, how old you've grown!
           Is this Hilarion? Why, you've changed too –
           You were a singularly handsome child!

205

210

215

220

225

230

235

240

255–6 *am I not the worst/Of Nature's blunders*: Gama's deliberate tactic of playing up his physical ugliness and unpleasantness recalls Dick Deadeye's remarks in Act I of *H.M.S. Pinafore*:

DICK. I'm ugly too, ain't I?
BUTTERCUP. You are certainly plain.
DICK. And I'm three-cornered too, ain't I?
BUTTERCUP. You are rather triangular.

(*To* FLOR.)	Are you a courtier? Come, then, ply your trade,
	Tell me some lies. How do you like your King?
	Vile rumour says he's all but imbecile.
	Now, that's not true?
FLOR.	My lord, we love our King.

His wise remarks are valued by his court
As precious stones.

GAMA.   And for the self-same cause,
Like precious stones, his sensible remarks
Derive their value from their scarcity!
Come now, be honest, tell the truth for once!
Tell it of me. Come, come, I'll harm you not.
This leg is crooked – this foot is ill-designed –
This shoulder wears a hump! Come, out with it!
Look, here's my face! Now, am I not the worst
Of Nature's blunders?

CYR.   Nature never errs.
To those who know the workings of your mind,
Your face and figure, sir, suggest a book
Appropriately bound.

GAMA (*enraged*).   Why, harkye, sir,
How dare you bandy words with me?

CYR.   No need
To bandy aught that appertains to you.

GAMA (*furiously*).   Do you permit this, King?

HILD.   We are in doubt
Whether to treat you as an honoured guest,
Or as a traitor knave who plights his word
And breaks it.

GAMA (*quickly*).   If the casting vote's with me,
I give it for the former!

HILD.   We shall see.
By the terms of our contract, signed and sealed,
You're bound to bring the Princess here to-day:
Why is she not with you?

GAMA.   Answer me this:
What think you of a wealthy purse-proud man,
Who, when he calls upon a starving friend,
Pulls out his gold and flourishes his notes,
And flashes diamonds in the pauper's eyes?
What name have you for such an one?

HILD.   A snob.

GAMA.   Just so. The girl has beauty, virtue, wit,
Grace, humour, wisdom, charity, and pluck.

295 *a woman's University*: In setting up her all-female college, Princess Ida was following a
distinguished group of pioneers. The first women's college in the vicinity of Cambridge
had been founded in 1869 by Miss Anne Clough. Originally sited at Hitchin, it moved
to the village of Girton, two miles north-west of Cambridge, in 1873. Two years later the
combined efforts of Mrs Josephine Butler, Professor Henry Sidgwick, John Stuart Mill
and Professor Henry Fawcett established Newnham College. Oxford followed suit in
1879 with the setting up of Somerville College and Lady Margaret Hall.

296 *a hundred girls*: In Gilbert's play *The Princess* the size of Ida's university is given as 500 girls.
Presumably the figure was scaled down for the opera so that the dozen D'Oyly Carte
chorus girls would not seem too disproportionately small a sample of the total student
body.

301 *With all my heart, if she's the prettiest*: This is the first point in *Princess Ida* where Gilbert adds
new dialogue that he had not already used in *The Princess*. Part of the passage between
lines 301 and 320 was specially written for the opera, although the remarks about Dr
Watts's hymns and the accomplished hen who crows were in the earlier play, where they
were given to Gobbo, the old porter at the university who is the only character from Gilbert's *The Princess* not to appear in *Princess Ida*.

307 *safety matches*: Gama's reference to safety matches, like his subsequent remark about Dr
Watts, is, of course, an anachronism. The manufacture of the first safety match, which
could be ignited only by being struck against a specially prepared surface on the side of
the box, took place in 1855.

309 *So you've no chance*: In Gilbert's play this line is the cue for a speech by Hilarion which anticipates some of the metaphors used in the song 'Expressive glances':

> We'll try, at all events.
> Cyril and Florian here will go with me
> And we will storm them ere the week is out!
> With sighs we'll charge our mines and countermines
> Dance steps shall be our scaling-ladders, with
> Those croquet mallets for our battering rams.
> Fair flowers shall bear the only blades we wield
> Our eyes shall be our very deadliest darts
> And bon-bon crackers our artillery!

315 *Dr Watts*: Isaac Watts (1674–1748) was a Nonconformist minister who wrote some of the
greatest hymns in the English language including 'O God Our Help in Ages Past' and
'When I survey the Wondrous Cross'.

321–38 *Perhaps if you address the lady*
This is one of only four duets in the Savoy Operas for the principal comedian and baritone characters, the George Grossmith and Rutland Barrington roles, as they have been
dubbed. The others are 'When I go out of door' for Bunthorne and Grosvenor in
Patience, 'Hereupon we're both agreed' for Jack Point and Wilfred Shadbolt in *The Yeomen
of the Guard* and 'Big bombs, small bombs, great guns and little ones' for Rudolph and
Ludwig in *The Grand Duke*.

285

Would it be kindly, think you, to parade
These brilliant qualities before *your* eyes?
Oh, no, King Hildebrand, I am no snob!

HILD. (*furiously*). Stop that tongue,
  Or you shall lose the monkey head that holds it!

GAMA. Bravo! your King deprives me of my head,
  That he and I may meet on equal terms! 290

HILD. Where is she now?

GAMA.   In Castle Adamant,
  One of my many country houses. There
  She rules a woman's University,
  With full a hundred girls, who learn of her. 295

CYR. A hundred girls! A hundred ecstasies!

GAMA. But no mere girls, my good young gentleman;
  With all the college learning that you boast,
  The youngest there will prove a match for *you*. 300

CYR. With all my heart, if she's the prettiest!
(*To* FLOR.) Fancy, a hundred matches – all alight! –
  That's if I strike them as I hope to do!

GAMA. Despair your hope; their hearts are dead to men.
  He who desires to gain their favour must 305
  Be qualified to strike their teeming brains,
  And not their hearts. They're safety matches, sir,
  And they light only on the knowledge box –
  So *you've* no chance!

FLOR. Are there no males whatever in those walls? 310

GAMA. None, gentlemen, excepting letter mails –
  And they are driven (as males often are
  In other large communities) by women.
  Why, bless my heart, she's so particular
  She'll scarcely suffer Dr Watts's hymns – 315
  And all the animals she owns are 'hers'!
  The ladies rise at cockcrow every morn –

CYR. Ah, then they have male poultry?

GAMA.   Not at all,
(*Confidentially.*) The crowing's done by an accomplished hen! 320

DUET – GAMA *and* HILDEBRAND.

GAMA. Perhaps if you address the lady
   Most politely, most politely –
  Flatter and impress the lady,
   Most politely, most politely –
  Humbly beg and humbly sue – 325

347 *Sillery*: A very high-class sparkling wine, produced in and around the village of Sillery in Champagne.

353 *triolet*: A stanza of eight lines, constructed on two rhymes, in which the first line is repeated as the fourth and seventh, and the second as the eighth. 'Expressive glances' is not, therefore, strictly speaking a triolet at all.

She may deign to look on you,
But your doing you must do
   Most politely, most politely, most politely!
CHORUS.   Humbly beg and humbly sue, etc.
HILD.   Go you, and inform the lady, 330
   Most politely, most politely,
If she don't, we'll storm the lady
   Most politely, most politely!
(*To* GAMA.)   You'll remain as hostage here;
Should Hilarion disappear, 335
We will hang you, never fear,
   Most politely, most politely, most politely!
CHORUS.   You'll remain as hostage here, etc.

(GAMA, ARAC, GURON, *and* SCYNTHIUS *are marched off in custody,*
          HILDEBRAND *following.*) 340

RECITATIVE – HILARION.

Come, Cyril, Florian, our course is plain,
   To-morrow morn fair Ida we'll engage;
But we will use no force her love to gain,
   Nature has armed us for the war we wage!

TRIO – HILARION, CYRIL, *and* FLORIAN.

HIL.   Expressive glances 345
Shall be our lances,
   And pops of Sillery
   Our light artillery.
We'll storm their bowers
With scented showers 350
Of fairest flowers
   That we can buy!

CHORUS.   Oh, dainty triolet!
Oh, fragrant violet!
Oh, gentle heigho-let 355
   (Or little sigh).
On sweet urbanity,
Though mere inanity
To touch their vanity
   We will rely! 360

383 *This seems unnecessarily severe*: The part of King Gama is smaller than most of Gilbert and
     Sullivan's comic roles. He does not appear at all in the long Second Act, and apart from
     these two lines here, his singing is confined to the two patter songs in Acts I and III and
     his Act I duet with Hildebrand. George Grossmith became extremely irritated at having
     to sit through long rehearsals, and he eventually asked Sullivan with some exasperation:
     'Could you tell me, Sir Arthur, what the words "This seems unnecessarily severe" have
     reference to?' The composer replied 'Because you are to be detained in prison, of
     course.' 'Thank you,' Grossmith responded. 'I thought they had reference to my having
     been detained here three hours a day for the past fortnight to sing them.' Sullivan took
     the hint and excused Grossmith from the remaining rehearsals.

393 *the rum-tum-tum*: This tongue-twisting chorus appears with more booms and less tum-
     tums in the first-edition libretto:

                              Boom! boom! boom! boom!
                              Rum-tummy-tummy-tum!
                              Boom! boom!

CYR.   When day is fading,
             With serenading
                And such frivolity
                We'll prove our quality.
             A sweet profusion   365
             Of soft allusion
             This bold intrusion
                Shall justify.

CHORUS.   Oh, dainty triolet, etc.

FLOR.   We'll charm their senses   370
             With verbal fences,
                With ballads amatory
                And declamatory.
             Little heeding
             Their pretty pleading,   375
             Our love exceeding
                We'll justify!

CHORUS.   Oh, dainty triolet, etc.

(*Re-enter* GAMA, ARAC, GURON, *and* SCYNTHIUS *heavily ironed,*
    followed by HILDEBRAND.)   380

RECITATIVE.

GAMA.   Must we, till then, in prison cell be thrust?
HILD.   You must!
GAMA.   This seems unnecessarily severe!
ARAC, GURON, *and* SCYNTHIUS.   Hear, hear!

TRIO – ARAC, GURON, *and* SCYNTHIUS.

             For a month to dwell   385
             In a dungeon cell;
                Growing thin and wizen
                In a solitary prison,
             Is a poor look-out
             For a soldier stout,   390
                Who is longing for the rattle
                Of a complicated battle –
             For the rum-tum-tum
             Of the military drum,
                And the guns that go boom! boom! 395

406–7 *Yes, the fascinating rattle*: This and the next line do not appear in the first-edition libretto, and are not in the Macmillan edition.

417 *Gama, Arac, Guron, and Scynthius are marched off*: In a letter which he sent to Sullivan on 22 September 1883 together with the completed manuscript of Act I Gilbert wrote:

> Don't you think the Act might end with 'Oh dainty triolet, etc'. followed by the departure of the princes, Arac, Guron and Scynthius breaking from their captors to rush after Hilarion, Cyril and Florian – to be recaptured at once, as the Act drop falls, this business to be without words, and done to symphony? It would make a good picture, I think.

This proposal was not taken up. Instead in D'Oyly Carte productions the act ended with Gama making a return entrance and shaking his fist at Hildebrand to make a picture as the curtain fell.

ALL.   The rum-tum-tum
        Of the military drum, etc.

HILD.   When Hilarion's bride
        Has at length complied
         With the just conditions
         Of our requisitions,   400
        You may go in haste
        And indulge your taste
         For the fascinating rattle
         Of a complicated battle –
         Yes, the fascinating rattle 405
         Of a complicated battle.
        For the rum-tum-tum
        Of the military drum,
         And the guns that go boom! boom! 410

ALL.   For the rum-tum-tum
        Of the military drum, etc.

ALL.   But till that time { we'll / you'll } here remain,

        And bail { they / we } will not entertain,

        Should she { his / our } mandate disobey, 415

        Our / Your } lives the penalty will pay!

   (GAMA, ARAC, GURON, *and* SCYNTHIUS *are marched off.*)

      END OF ACT I

1–3   *Scene*: In order to economize on scene changes, the same set was used for both Acts II and III in the 1954 D'Oyly Carte revival of *Princess Ida*. It depicted the garden courtyard of Castle Adamant, with a moat at the rear.

     The first-night reviewer for *The Times* commented on the frivolity of the scene at Castle Adamant compared with the stately atmosphere of Ida's university in Tennyson's poem. He singled out the gowns of the lady students for particular remark: 'They are beautifully designed and grouped together, form a perfect bouquet of harmonious colour; they will, we seriously apprehend, cause a revolution at Newnham and Girton, but they certainly do not suggest the severity of academic discipline.'

4   *empyrean heights*: The highest heaven, the abode of God and the angels. In Act I of *Patience* Saphir, besotted with aestheticism, tells Colonel Calverley scornfully 'You are not Empyrean. You are not Della Cruscan. You are not even Early English.'

14–21   *If you'd climb the Helicon*

     The authors whom Lady Psyche lists in this song are all noted for their eroticism or obscenity – a nice little Gilbertian dig at classical education and the difficulties of extending it to the fairer sex. The first-night reviewer for the *Theatre* magazine took exception to Psyche's list, not for its indelicacy but for the liberties it took with classical pronunciation. 'It is surely inelegant', he wrote, 'to coerce *Helicon* into rhyming with *Anacreon*, *Metamorphoses* with *Aristophanes*, and *horresco referens*! *Juvenal* with *all*.'

14   *Helicon*: The home of the Muses, a part of Parnassus which contained the fountains of Aganippe and Hippocrene.

15   *Anacreon*: A Greek lyric poet, born *c.* 570 B.C., who wrote chiefly in praise of women and wine.

16   *Ovid's Metamorphoses*: The *Metamorphoses*, a collection of poems which ran to fifteen books, was one of the longest works of the Latin poet Publius Ovidius Naso (43 B.C.– *c.* A.D. 18). They begin with the change of the universe from chaos to order and end with the transformation of Julius Caesar into a god. Ovid is mentioned in both *Ruddigore* (see the note to Act I, line 401) and *Iolanthe*.

17   *Aristophanes*: The great Greek comic dramatist (*c.* 450–385 B.C.) whose famous croaking chorus from *The Frogs*, you may recall, is known to Major-General Stanley in *The Pirates of Penzance*.

18   *Juvenal*: A Roman satirist (A.D. 60–140) whose work included a strong attack on women.

21   *Bowdlerized*: Cleansed of any passages which might be calculated to bring a blush of shame to a modest maiden's cheek. The term derives from Thomas Bowdler, who in 1818 brought out an edition of Shakespeare from which 'those words are omitted which cannot with propriety be read aloud in a family'.

22   *Ah! we will get them Bowdlerized*: In the licence copy a two-line chorus is printed here:

               Yes, we'll do as we're advised,
               We will get them Bowdlerized.

ACT II

SCENE. – *Gardens in Castle Adamant. A river runs across the back of the stage, crossed by a rustic bridge. Castle Adamant in the distance. Girl graduates discovered seated at the feet of* LADY PSYCHE.

CHORUS.

Towards the empyrean heights
    Of every kind of lore,
We've taken several easy flights,   5
    And mean to take some more.
In trying to achieve success
    No envy racks our heart,
And all the knowledge we possess,   10
    We mutually impart.

SONG – MELISSA.

Pray, what authors should she read
Who in Classics would succeed?

PSYCHE.

If you'd climb the Helicon,
You should read Anacreon,   15
Ovid's *Metamorphoses*,
Likewise Aristophanes,
And the works of Juvenal:
These are worth attention, all;
But, if you will be advised,   20
You will get them Bowdlerized!

CHORUS.

Ah! we will get them Bowdlerized!

45 *Enter Lady Blanche*: Gilbert retained both the names and the essential characteristics of
   the two professors in Tennyson's poem. In *The Princess* Lady Psyche was described as
   both the prettier and the better natured. Blanche is traditionally played as a formidable
   and extremely crusty battle-axe.

47 *The Princess Ida's list of punishments*: In Gilbert's earlier play *The Princess*, Ida had a rather
   long list of punishments to mete out. Sacharissa was expelled, as in the opera, for bringing a set of chessmen into the university, Chloe was gated for a week for declining 'that
   hideous verse *amo*' (to which the girl rejoined 'I really thought she wished all students to
   decline to love'). Phyllis lost three terms for a sketch of a double perambulator, and Sylvia
   was rusticated for a month because she had put three rows of lace round her graduate's
   gown.

SOLO – Sacharissa.

Pray you, tell us, if you can,
What's the thing that's known as Man?

Psyche.

Man will swear and Man will storm –   25
Man is not at all good form –
Man is of no kind of use –
Man's a donkey – Man's a goose –
Man is coarse and Man is plain –
Man is more or less insane –   30
Man's a ribald – Man's a rake,
Man is Nature's sole mistake!

Chorus.

We'll a memorandum make –
Man is Nature's sole mistake!

And thus to empyrean height   35
   Of every kind of lore,
In search of wisdom's pure delight,
   Ambitiously we soar.
In trying to achieve success
   No envy racks our heart,   40
For all we know and all we guess,
   We mutually impart!
And all the knowledge we possess
   We mutually impart!

(*Enter* Lady Blanche. *All stand up demurely.*)   45

Bla.	Attention, ladies, while I read to you
	The Princess Ida's list of punishments.
	The first is Sacharissa. She's expelled!
All.	Expelled!
Bla.	Expelled, because although she knew
	No man of any kind may pass our walls,
	She dared to bring a set of chessmen here!
Sach. (*crying*).	I meant no harm; they're only men of wood!
Bla.	They're men with whom you give each other mate,
	And that's enough! The next is Chloe.
Chloe.	Ah!

50

55

61 *Double perambulator*: This curious contraption was to figure again in Gilbert's writings. In his story 'The Fairy's Dilemma', which appeared in the Christmas 1900 number of the *Graphic*, he wrote: 'I see a nursemaid advancing with a double perambulator, and escorted by a trooper of the 2nd Life Guards.'

74 *Enter the Princess*: Here is Tennyson's description of Princess Ida as first seen by Hilarion:

> There at a board by tome and paper sat,
> With two tame leopards couch'd beside her throne,
> All beauty compass'd in a female form,
> The Princess; liker to the inhabitant
> Of some clear planet close upon the Sun
> Than our man's earth; such eyes were in her head,
> And so much grace and power, breathing down
> From over her arch'd brows, with every turn
> Lived through her to the tips of her long hands,
> And to the feet.

79 *Minerva*: A Roman goddess, identified with the Greek Athena, who was patroness of the arts and goddess of memory and warfare.

80–89 *Oh, goddess wise*
As originally sung in early productions, the order of this aria was reversed, with lines 84–7 preceding lines 80–83.

90 *Neophytes*: New converts, novices.

BLA.	Chloe will lose three terms, for yesterday,

BLA.   Chloe will lose three terms, for yesterday,
       When looking through her drawing-book, I found
       A sketch of a perambulator!
ALL (*horrified*).   Oh!   60
BLA.   *Double* perambulator, shameless girl!
       That's all at present. Now, attention, pray;
       Your Principal the Princess comes to give
       Her usual inaugural address
       To those young ladies who joined yesterday. 65

CHORUS.

    Mighty maiden with a mission,
      Paragon of common sense,
    Running fount of erudition,
      Miracle of eloquence,
      We are blind, and we would see; 70
      We are bound, and would be free;
      We are dumb, and we would talk;
      We are lame, and we would walk.

(*Enter the* PRINCESS.)

    Mighty maiden with a mission – 75
      Paragon of common sense;
    Running fount of erudition –
      Miracle of eloquence!

PRIN. (*recitative*.)   Minerva! Minerva, oh, hear me!

ARIA.

    Oh, goddess wise 80
      That lovest light,
      Endow with sight
    Their unillumined eyes.
    At this my call,
      A fervent few 85
      Have come to woo
    The rays that from thee fall.
  Let fervent words and fervent thoughts be mine,
  That I may lead them to thy sacred shrine!

  Women of Adamant, fair Neophytes – 90
  Who thirst for such instruction as we give,

92   *while I unfold a parable*: The entire passage of dialogue from here down to 'Logic?' (line 109) was among the cuts made in the 1954 D'Oyly Carte production.

114   *He'd rather pass the day*: This was originally written 'He'd rather spend the day'.

122   *Let red be worn with yellow*: Primary colours! Lady Jane would have a fit! (See *Patience*, Act I, line 324.)

131   *Let Swan secede from Edgar*: Here begins a plug for some of the most fashionable drapery and millinery establishments in late Victorian London. Swan and Edgar, the last to disappear, were first of all in Regent Street and then just off Piccadilly Circus. The first-night review in the *Sportsman* commented that the girl graduates 'were dressed with a quaint richness, suggesting Portia after a visit to Swan and Edgar's'. Gask and Gask in Leicester Square specialized in silks; Sewell and Cross, who also received a mention in *Patience* (Act II, line 508), were in Soho; and Lewis and Allenby were in St George's House, on the corner of Conduit Street and Regent Street. Mention of these largely defunct trade names led to lines 131–2 also being among the proposed cuts in 1954. A note in a D'Oyly Carte prompt copy of *c.* 1955, however, states that 'These cuts in Ida's speech are still liable to change', and it goes on to indicate that at the time of writing only these lines were out, and lines 92–109 mentioned above were in again.

Attend, while I unfold a parable.
The elephant is mightier than Man,
Yet Man subdues him. Why? The elephant
Is elephantine everywhere but here (*tapping her forehead*),   95
And Man, whose brain is to the elephant's
As Woman's brain to Man's – (that's rule of three), –
Conquers the foolish giant of the woods,
As Woman, in her turn, shall conquer Man.
In Mathematics, Woman leads the way: 100
The narrow-minded pedant still believes
That two and two make four! Why, we can prove,
We women – household drudges as we are –
That two and two make five – or three – or seven;
Or five-and-twenty, if the case demands!   105
Diplomacy? The wiliest diplomat
Is absolutely helpless in our hands,
He wheedles monarchs – woman wheedles him!
Logic? Why, tyrant Man himself admits
It's waste of time to argue with a woman!   110
Then we excel in social qualities:
Though Man professes that he holds our sex
In utter scorn, I venture to believe
He'd rather pass the day with one of you,
Than with five hundred of his fellow-men!   115
In all things we excel. Believing this,
A hundred maidens here have sworn to place
Their feet upon his neck. If we succeed,
We'll treat him better than he treated us:
But if we fail, why, then let hope fail too!   120
Let no one care a penny how she looks –
Let red be worn with yellow – blue with green –
Crimson with scarlet – violet with blue!
Let all your things misfit, and you yourselves
At inconvenient moments come undone!   125
Let hair-pins lose their virtue; let the hook
Disdain the fascination of the eye –
The bashful button modestly evade
The soft embraces of the button-hole!
Let old associations all dissolve,   130
Let Swan secede from Edgar – Gask from Gask,
Sewell from Cross – Lewis from Allenby!
In other words – let Chaos come again!
(*Coming down.*) Who lectures in the Hall of Arts to-day?

135   *Abstract Philosophy*: This subject might seem more in Lady Psyche's line. She is, after all, the Professor of Humanities. In Gilbert's earlier play, however, she was the Professor of Experimental Science, contrasting with Lady Blanche's role as Professor of Abstract Science.

147   *The Princess Ida Is our head*: Lady Blanche's feeling that she had been ousted by Lady Psyche in Princess Ida's affections is made much of in Tennyson's poem, where Melissa tells Hilarion and his friends:

> My mother, 'tis her wont from night to night
> To rail at Lady Psyche and her side.
> She says the Princess should have been the Head,
> Herself and Lady Psyche the two arms;
> And so it was agreed when first they came;
> But Lady Psyche was the right hand now,
> And she the left, or not, or seldom used...

Tennyson also explains, again through Melissa talking to Hilarion, the story of how Lady Blanche came to be supplanted:

> She had the care of Lady Ida's youth,
> And from the Queen's decease she brought her up
> But when your sister came she won the heart
> Of Ida: they were still together, grew
> (For so they said themselves) inosculated;
> Consonant chords that shiver to one note;
> One mind in all things: yet my mother still
> Affirms your Psyche thieved her theories,
> And angled with them for her pupil's love:
> She calls her plagiarist; I know not what.

164–87   *Come, mighty Must*
This burlesque of the rather over-blown Victorian drawing-room ballad was for a long time cut in D'Oyly Carte productions. A note by Rupert D'Oyly Carte in a prompt copy indicates that it was not sung in 1930, and this cut continued until the war. It was also omitted from the 1954 revival, although it was reintroduced by the company for the 1977–8 season.

BLA.   I, madam, on Abstract Philosophy.   135
            There I propose considering, at length,
            Three points – The Is, the Might Be, and the Must.
            Whether the Is, from being actual fact,
            Is more important than the vague Might Be,
            Or the Might Be, from taking wider scope,   140
            Is for that reason greater than the Is:
            And lastly, how the Is and Might Be stand
            Compared with the inevitable Must!

PRIN.   The subject's deep – how do you treat it, pray?

BLA.   Madam, I take three possibilities,   145
            And strike a balance, then, between the three:
            As thus: The Princess Ida Is our head,
            The Lady Psyche Might Be, – Lady Blanche,
            Neglected Blanche, inevitably Must.
            Given these three hypotheses – to find   150
            The actual betting against each of them!

PRIN.   Your theme's ambitious: pray you, bear in mind
            Who highest soar fall farthest. Fare you well,
            You and your pupils! Maidens, follow me.

            (*Exeunt* PRINCESS *and Maidens singing refrain of chorus, 'And thus to*   155
                    empyrean heights', *etc. Manet* LADY BLANCHE.)

BLA.   I should command here – I was born to rule,
            But do I rule? I don't. Why? I don't know.
            I shall some day. Not yet. I bide my time.
            I once was Some One – and the Was Will Be.   160
            The Present as we speak becomes the Past,
            The Past repeats itself, and so is Future!
            This sounds involved. It's not. It's right enough.

                    SONG – LADY BLANCHE.

                    Come, mighty Must!
                        Inevitable Shall!   165
                    In thee I trust.
                        Time weaves my coronal!
                    Go, mocking Is!
                        Go, disappointing Was!
                    That I am this   170
                        Ye are the cursèd cause!

189   *Enter Hilarion, Cyril, and Florian*: The stage direction at this point in an early D'Oyly Carte prompt-book reads: 'Symphony – All heads appear top of wall – then down. Hilarion comes over wall on 12th bar on to rostrum and down steps – looks off right, Cyril on 16th bar follows Hilarion, Florian on 18th bar comes down. Dust clothes with their handkerchiefs.'

191–218   *Gently, gently*
This number was adopted in the 1920s as the theme song of the Oxford University Gilbert and Sullivan Society and sung at the beginning and end of each meeting.

More recently, it was sung with particular aptness on the evening of 23 February 1977 when a bomb scare at Sadler's Wells Theatre brought the curtain down on a D'Oyly Carte production just as the three intrepid chums were about to clamber into view. The audience were forced to spend an hour outside in the street until the theatre was searched and cleared. The first words that they heard from stage when they had finally filed back in again were the moderately reassuring: 'Gently, gently,/Evidently/We are safe so far'.

Yet humble second shall be first,
   I ween;
And dead and buried be the curst
    Has Been!   175

Oh, weak Might Be!
   Oh, May, Might, Could, Would, Should!
How powerless ye
   For evil or for good!
In every sense   180
   Your moods I cheerless call,
Whate'er your tense
   Ye are Imperfect, all!
Ye have deceived the trust I've shown
   In ye!   185
Away! The Mighty Must alone
   Shall be!

               (*Exit* LADY BLANCHE.)

(*Enter* HILARION, CYRIL, *and* FLORIAN, *climbing over wall, and creeping
   cautiously among the trees and rocks at the back of the stage.*)   190

    TRIO – HILARION, CYRIL, FLORIAN.

      Gently, gently,
      Evidently
        We are safe so far,
      After scaling
      Fence and paling,   195
        Here, at last, we are!

      In this college
      Useful knowledge
        Everywhere one finds,
      And already,   200
      Growing steady,
        We've enlarged our minds.

CYR.   We've learnt that prickly cactus
         Has the power to attract us
            When we fall.   205
HIL. *and* FLOR.   When we fall!
HIL.   That nothing man unsettles
         Like a bed of stinging nettles,
            Short or tall.

211 *throttles*: The human rather than the automobile variety, of course: i.e. the throat.

227 *they'll set the Thames on fire*: Do something remarkable and exciting. Similar sayings exist in Germany and France, where the respective rivers are the Rhine and the Seine; and the ancient Romans had an expression *Tiberium accendere nequaquam potest* ('It is not at all possible to set light to the Tiber').

231 *Circe*: A sorceress in Greek mythology who lived on the island of Aeaea. When Ulysses landed there, she turned his companions into swine.

234 *trepan*: Ensnare or catch in a trap. The word occurs with a very different meaning in Colonel Calverley's recipe for a Heavy Dragoon in *Patience*, when he sings of the 'Coolness of Paget about to trepan' (Act 1, line 137).

235 *sunbeams from cucumbers*: This curious notion is taken from a passage in *Gulliver's Travels* in which Jonathan Swift recounts that his hero 'had been eight years upon a project for extracting sunbeams out of cucumbers, which were to be put into phials hermetically sealed, and let out to warm the air in raw inclement summers'.

241–4 *These are the phenomena*
In the licence copy and the first edition of the libretto the last two lines of this refrain are printed as:

> Hopes that we shall see
> At this Universitee!

The Macmillan edition has a slightly different version of these lines:

> Is hoping we shall see
> At her Universitee!

CYR. *and* FLOR.	Short or tall!	210
FLOR.	That bull-dogs feed on throttles –	
	That we don't like broken bottles	
	On a wall.	
CYR. *and* HIL.	On a wall!	
HIL.	That spring-guns breathe defiance!	215
	And that burglary's a science	
	After all!	
CYR. *and* FLOR.	After all!	

RECITATIVE – FLORIAN.

A Woman's college! maddest folly going!
What can girls learn within its walls worth knowing?   220
I'll lay a crown (the Princess shall decide it)
I'll teach them twice as much in half-an-hour outside it.

HILARION.

Hush, scoffer; ere you sound your puny thunder,
List to their aims, and bow your head in wonder!

They intend to send a wire   225
To the moon – to the moon;
And they'll set the Thames on fire
Very soon – very soon;
Then they learn to make silk purses
With their rigs – with their rigs,   230
From the ears of Lady Circe's
Piggy-wigs – piggy-wigs.
And weasels at their slumbers
They trepan – they trepan;
To get sunbeams from cu*cum*bers,   235
They've a plan – they've a plan.
They've a firmly rooted notion
They can cross the Polar Ocean,
And they'll find Perpetual Motion,
If they can – if they can.   240

ALL.
These are the phenomena
That every pretty domina
Is hoping at her Universitee
We shall see!

CYR.
As for fashion, they forswear it,   245
So they say – so they say;

251   *And they'll practise what they're preaching*: Until the war this line was sung as 'And the nig-gers they'll be bleaching'. It was changed for the 1954 revival for the same reason that the word 'nigger' was removed from *The Mikado* in 1948 (see the notes to Act I, line 251, and Act II, line 358, of *The Mikado*).

262–7   *In this college*
This refrain does not appear in the first edition.

268   *So that's the Princess Ida's castle*: For the 1954 revival, in keeping with the new stage setting for Act II, these lines were changed to:

> So this is the Princess Ida's castle! Well,
> They must be lovely girls, indeed, if it requires
> Such walls as these to keep intruders off!

278   *matriculate*: Enrol as students.
Let's try them on: A stage direction in an early D'Oyly Carte prompt copy reads: 'Florian throws Cyril's (robe) to Hilarion, who passes it on to him – then Hilarion's and retains third one. Hilarion gets into his at once. Florian also – makes muff of scarf part. Cyril has difficulty – first getting into sleeves – then buttons up robe inside his legs. Hilarion assists him.'

And the circle – they will square it
　　Some fine day – some fine day;
Then the little pigs they're teaching
　　For to fly – for to fly;   250
And they'll practise what they're preaching
　　By and by – by and by!
Each newly-joined aspirant
　　To the clan – to the clan –
Must repudiate the tyrant   255
　　Known as Man – known as Man.
They mock at him and flout him,
For they do not care about him,
And they're 'going to do without him'
　　If they can – if they can!   260

ALL.　　　　　These are the phenomena, etc.

　　　In this college
　　　Useful knowledge
　　　Ev'rywhere one finds,
　　　And already,   265
　　　Growing steady,
　　　We've enlarg'd our minds.

HIL.　　So that's the Princess Ida's castle! Well,
　　They must be lovely girls, indeed, if it requires
　　Such walls as those to keep intruders off!   270
CYR.　　To keep men off is only half their charge,
　　And that the easier half. I must suspect
　　The object of these walls is not so much
　　To keep men off as keep the maidens in!
FLOR.　　But what are these? (*Examining some Collegiate robes.*)   275
HIL. (*looking at them*). Why, Academic robes,
　　Worn by the lady undergraduates
　　When they matriculate. Let's try them on. (*They do so.*)
　　Why, see, – we're covered to the very toes.
　　Three lovely lady undergraduates   280
　　Who, weary of the world and all its wooing –
FLOR.　　And penitent for deeds there's no undoing –
CYR.　　Looked at askance by well-conducted maids –
ALL.　　Seek sanctuary in these classic shades!

TRIO – HILARION, CYRIL, FLORIAN.

HIL.　　　　I am a maiden, cold and stately,   285
　　　　Heartless I, with a face divine.

289   *Haughty, humble, coy, or free*: The same prompt-book has the direction here: 'Actions:
      "Haughty" – both hands out flat to left. "Humble" – cross hands on breast. "Coy" – left
      hand under right elbow, right finger to lips, curtsey. "Free" – throw both hands out
      open.' These actions continued to be used in D'Oyly Carte productions to the end.

310   *We are three students*: Compare Tennyson's original lines:

>   Three ladies of the Northern empire pray
>   Your Highness would enroll them with your own
>   As Lady Psyche's pupils.

What do I want with a heart, innately?
Every heart I meet is mine!

ALL. Haughty, humble, coy, or free,
Little care I what maid may be. 290
So that a maid is fair to see,
Every maid is the maid for me! (*Dance.*)

CYR. I am a maiden frank and simple,
Brimming with joyous roguery;
Merriment lurks in every dimple, 295
Nobody breaks more hearts than I!

ALL. Haughty, humble, coy, or free, etc. (*Dance.*)

FLOR. I am a maiden coyly blushing,
Timid am I as a startled hind;
Every suitor sets me flushing: 300
I am the maid that wins mankind!

ALL. Haughty, humble, coy, or free, etc.

(*Enter the* PRINCESS *reading. She does not see them.*)

FLOR. But who comes here? The Princess, as I live!
What shall we do? 305
HIL. (*aside*). Why, we must brave it out!
(*Aloud*). Madam, accept our humblest reverence.

(*They bow, then, suddenly recollecting themselves, curtsey.*)

PRIN. (*surprised*). We greet you, ladies. What would you with us?
HIL. (*aside*). What shall I say? (*Aloud.*) We are three students, ma'am, 310
Three well-born maids of liberal estate,
Who wish to join this University.

(HILARION *and* FLORIAN *curtsey again.* CYRIL *bows extravagantly, then, being recalled to himself by* FLORIAN, *curtsies.*)

PRIN. If, as you say, you wish to join our ranks, 315
And will subscribe to all our rules, 'tis well.
FLOR. To all your rules we cheerfully subscribe.
PRIN. You say you're noblewomen. Well, you'll find
No sham degrees for noblewomen here.

320 *sizars . . . servitors*: Students who received their board and lodging free in return for per-
     forming duties of the kind that would normally be done by servants. They were called
     sizars at Cambridge and Trinity College, Dublin, and servitors at Oxford. Lines 320–24
     were cut in the 1954 production.
322 *tufts*: Gold tassels worn on the caps of peers' sons at Oxford.

328 *will you swear*: In Tennyson's poem, Hilarion and his two friends were required to agree
     to a slightly different set of rules when they enrolled as students at the princess's univer-
     sity:

> Not for three years to correspond with home;
> Not for three years to cross the liberties;
> Not for three years to speak with any men.

344 *And we have never fished*: Lines 344–52 were cut in the 1954 revival.

You'll find no sizars here, or servitors, 320
Or other cruel distinctions, meant to draw
A line 'twixt rich and poor: you'll find no tufts
To mark nobility, except such tufts
As indicate nobility of brain.
As for your fellow-students, mark me well: 325
There are a hundred maids within these walls,
All good, all learned, and all beautiful:
They are prepared to love you: will you swear
To give the fullness of your love to them?

HIL. Upon our words and honours, ma'am, we will! 330
PRIN. But we go further: will you undertake
That you will never marry any man?
FLOR. Indeed we never will!
PRIN.   Consider well,
You must prefer our maids to all mankind! 335
HIL. To all mankind we much prefer your maids!
CYR. We should be dolts indeed, if we did not,
Seeing how fair —
HIL. (*aside to* CYRIL). Take care – that's rather strong!
PRIN. But have you left no lovers at your home 340
Who may pursue you here?
HIL.   No, madam, none.
We're homely ladies, as no doubt you see,
And we have never fished for lover's love.
We smile at girls who deck themselves with gems, 345
False hair, and meretricious ornament,
To chain the fleeting fancy of a man,
But do not imitate them. What we have
Of hair, is all our own. Our colour, too,
Unladylike, but not unwomanly, 350
Is Nature's handiwork, and man has learnt
To reckon Nature an impertinence.
PRIN. Well, beauty counts for naught within these walls;
If all you say is true, you'll pass with us
A happy, happy time! 355
CYR.   If, as you say,
A hundred lovely maidens wait within,
To welcome us with smiles and open arms,
I think there's very little doubt we shall!

QUARTET – PRINCESS, HILARION, CYRIL, FLORIAN.

PRIN.   The world is but a broken toy, 360

374 *Unreal its loveliest hue*: In the first-edition libretto and vocal score, and therefore possibly in early performances, Hilarion's verse was succeeded by the following ensemble:

PRINCESS.	HILARION, CYRIL *and* FLORIAN.
The world is but a broken toy,	The world is but a broken toy,
Its pleasure hollow – false its joy,	We freely give it up with joy,
Unreal its loveliest hue,	Unreal its loveliest hue,
Alas!	Alas!
Its pains alone are true,	We quite agree with you,
Alas!	Alas!
Its pains alone are true!	We quite agree with you!

Its pleasure hollow – false its joy,
Unreal its loveliest hue,
                    Alas!
Its pains alone are true,
                    Alas!   365
Its pains alone are true.

HIL.   The world is everything you say,
         The world we think has had its day.
         Its merriment is slow,
                    Alas!   370
         We've tried it, and we know,
                    Alas!
         We've tried it and we know.

ALL.   Unreal its loveliest hue,
         Its pains alone are true.   375
                    Alas!
         The world is but a broken toy,
         Its pleasure hollow – false its joy,
         Unreal its loveliest hue,
                    Alas!   380
         Its pains alone are true,
                    Alas!
         Its pains alone are true!

(*Exit* PRINCESS. *The three gentlemen watch her off.* LADY PSYCHE *enters,
                    and regards them with amazement.*)   385

HIL.   I'faith, the plunge is taken, gentlemen!
       For, willy-nilly, we are maidens now,
       And maids against our will we must remain!
                                        (*All laugh heartily.*)

PSY. (*aside*). These ladies are unseemly in their mirth.   390

              (*The gentlemen see her, and, in confusion, resume
                    their modest demeanour.*)

FLOR. (*aside*). Here's a catastrophe, Hilarion!
       This is my sister! She'll remember me,
       Though years have passed since she and I have met!   395
HIL. (*aside to* FLORIAN). Then make a virtue of necessity,
       And trust our secret to her gentle care.
FLOR. (*to* PSYCHE, *who has watched* CYRIL *in amazement*). Psyche!
       Why, don't you know me? Florian!

411 *Are you that learned little Psyche*: This passage bears a close resemblance to Tennyson's original:

> 'Are you that Psyche,' Florian added; 'she
> With whom I sang about the morning hills,
> Flung ball, flew kite, and raced the purple fly,
> And snared the squirrel of the glen? are you
> That Psyche wont to bind my throbbing brow,
> To smooth my pillow, mix the foaming draught
> Of fever, tell me pleasant tales, and read
> My sickness down to happy dreams? are you
> That brother-sister Psyche, both in one?

421 *Hipparchus*: If the Greek astronomer first determined longitude in 163 B.C., then it was at the extremely early age of minus three, as most sources agree in putting his birth at *c.* 160 B.C. Hipparchus, who worked at Rhodes, was the world's first systematic astronomer and the inventor of trigonometry.

422 *that small phenomenon*: Shades of the infant phenomenon in Charles Dickens's *Nicholas Nickleby* (1839). Lines 414–23 were also cut in the 1954 D'Oyly Carte revival.

433–66 *A Lady fair, of lineage high*
     The tune of this song, which was entitled in the first-edition libretto 'The Ape and the Lady', was thought by some critics to be distinctly derivative. The *Weekly Times* commented on its resemblance to 'The Bailiff's Daughter of Islington', while the *Saturday Review* noted ' "The Ape and the Lady" did duty in *Patience* as "The Magnet and the Churn" '.

PSY. (*amazed*). Why, Florian! 400
FLOR.   My sister! (*embraces her*).
PSY.   Oh, my dear!
    What are you doing here – and who are these?
HIL.   I am that Prince Hilarion to whom
    Your Princess is betrothed. I come to claim 405
    Her plighted love. Your brother Florian
    And Cyril come to see me safely through.
PSY.   The Prince Hilarion? Cyril too? How strange!
    My earliest playfellows!
HIL.   Why, let me look! 410
    Are you that learned little Psyche who
    At school alarmed her mates because she called
    A buttercup 'ranunculus bulbosus'?
CYR.   Are you indeed that Lady Psyche who
    At children's parties drove the conjurer wild, 415
    Explaining all his tricks before he did them?
HIL.   Are you that learned little Psyche who
    At dinner parties, brought in to dessert,
    Would tackle visitors with 'You don't know
    Who first determined longitude – I do – 420
    Hipparchus 'twas – B.C. one sixty-three!'
    Are you indeed that small phenomenon?
PSY.   That small phenomenon indeed am I!
    But, gentlemen, 'tis death to enter here:
    We have all promised to renounce mankind! 425
FLOR.   Renounce mankind? On what ground do you base
    This senseless resolution?
PSY.   Senseless? No.
    We are all taught, and, being taught, believe
    That Man, sprung from an Ape, is Ape at heart. 430
CYR.   That's rather strong.
PSY.   The truth is always strong!

SONG – LADY PSYCHE.

    A Lady fair, of lineage high,
    Was loved by an Ape, in the days gone by.
    The Maid was radiant as the sun,
    The Ape was a most unsightly one – 435
        So it would not do –
        His scheme fell through,
    For the Maid, when his love took formal shape,

458   *Darwinian Man*: A nice dig at the theory of evolution, which had been propounded by
      Charles Darwin in his book *The Origin of Species* in 1859.

464   *While a man, however well-behaved*: The licence copy and first-edition libretto have this
      version, which was sung in recent D'Oyly Carte productions. The vocal score, Oxford
      University Press World's Classics edition and Macmillan edition, however, have 'While
      Darwinian Man, though well-behaved'.

468   *Oh, Lady Psyche*: Here is how Tennyson handled this incident:

> Then Lady Psyche, 'Ah – Melissa – you!
> You heard us?' and Melissa, 'O pardon me
> I heard, I could not help it, did not wish:
> But, dearest Lady, pray you fear me not,
> Nor think I bear that heart within my breast,
> To give three gallant gentlemen to death.'

Expressed such terror　　　　　　　　　　　　440
At his monstrous error,
That he stammered an apology and made his 'scape,
The picture of a disconcerted Ape.

With a view to rise in the social scale,
He shaved his bristles, and he docked his tail,　　445
He grew moustachios, and he took his tub,
And he paid a guinea to a toilet club –
　　But it would not do,
　　The scheme fell through –
For the Maid was Beauty's fairest Queen,　　　450
　　With golden tresses,
　　Like a real princess's,
While the Ape, despite his razor keen,
Was the apiest Ape that ever was seen!

He bought white ties, and he bought dress suits,　455
He crammed his feet into bright tight boots –
And to start in life on a brand-new plan,
He christened himself Darwinian Man!
　　But it would not do,
　　The scheme fell through –　　　　　　　　460
For the Maiden fair, whom the monkey craved,
　　Was a radiant Being,
　　With a brain far-seeing –
While a man, however well-behaved,
At best is only a monkey shaved!　　　　　　465

ALL.　　　While Darwinian Man, etc.

(*During this* MELISSA *has entered unobserved; she looks on in amazement.*)

MEL. (*coming down*). Oh, Lady Psyche!
PSY. (*terrified*).　　　　　　What! you heard us then?
　　Oh, all is lost!　　　　　　　　　　　　　470
MEL.　　　　　Not so! I'll breathe no word!

　　　　　(*Advancing in astonishment to* FLORIAN.)

How marvellously strange! and are you then
Indeed young men?
FLOR.　　　　　Well, yes, just now we are –　　475
But hope by dint of study to become,
In course of time, young women.
MEL. (*eagerly*).　　　　　　　No, no, no –

491–520 *The woman of the wisest wit*

The first American edition of the libretto has a completely different version of this quintet; it is presumably the original version, which was in the British libretto when it was shipped out to the U.S.A. for rehearsal there. Gilbert subsequently changed the song but was unable to get the new version across the Atlantic in time for it to appear in the first U.S. edition:

QUINTET.

PSYCHE, MELISSA, HILARION, CYRIL, FLORIAN.

PSY.
If we discharged our duty clear
We should denounce your presence here,
    What should we do
    We plainly view
    In speculum veluti.*

HIL.
If that's the case, don't wait a bit
But trick it, cheat it, swindle it;
    'Twere pity great
    To hesitate
Distinctly 'do' your duty!

ALL.
Oh duty, when you check our ease,
Uncertain, coy, and hard to please†
When you are 'done', as you are now,
An unimportant person thou!

MEL.
But if we 'did' our duty thus
The consequence might fall on us;
    'Twould give you pain
    To see us slain
In all your youth and beauty!

CYR.
If 'doing' it distress you so,
Dismiss it, sack it, let it go;
    Don't pause a while
    Dispense with it
In fact, 'discharge' your duty!

ALL.
Oh duty, when you check our ease,
Uncertain, coy, and hard to please,
When you're discharged as you are now
An unimportant person thou!

* 'As if in a mirror'.
† This line is borrowed from Sir Walter Scott's poem *Marmion*.

Oh, don't do that! Is this indeed a man?
I've often heard of them, but, till to-day,   480
Never set eyes on one. They told me men
Were hideous, idiotic, and deformed!
They're quite as beautiful as women are!
As beautiful, they're infinitely more so!
Their cheeks have not that pulpy softness which   485
One gets so weary of in womankind:
Their features are more marked – and – oh, their chins!
How curious! (*Feeling his chin.*)

FLOR.   I fear it's rather rough.

MEL. (*eagerly*). Oh, don't apologize – I like it so!   490

QUINTET – PSYCHE, MELISSA, HILARION,
CYRIL, FLORIAN.

PSY.   The woman of the wisest wit
             May sometimes be mistaken, O!
         In Ida's views, I must admit,
             My faith is somewhat shaken, O!

CYR.   On every other point than this   495
             Her learning is untainted, O!
         But Man's a theme with which she is
             Entirely unacquainted, O!
                 – acquainted, O!
                 – acquainted, O!   500
             Entirely unacquainted, O!

ALL.   Then jump for joy and gaily bound,
         The truth is found – the truth is found!
         Set bells a-ringing through the air –
         Ring here and there and everywhere –   505
         And echo forth the joyous sound,
         The truth is found – the truth is found!

                                    (*Dance.*)

MEL.   My natural instinct teaches me
             (And instinct is important, O!)   510
         You're everything you ought to be,
             And nothing that you oughtn't, O!

HIL.   That fact was seen at once by you
             In casual conversation, O!
         Which is most creditable to   515
             Your powers of observation, O!
                 – servation, O!

536 *Two are tenors, one is a baritone*: In the first edition of the libretto this line is 'One is a tenor, two are baritones'. However, it is doubtful if this was ever said, since Hilarion, Cyril and Florian were originally played by Henry Bracy (tenor), Durward Lely (tenor) and Charles Ryley (baritone).

542 *an étui*: A needle-case. In some editions of the libretto, 'cigar case' has been substituted for '*étui*'. The reference to an *étui* containing scissors and needles is a hangover from Gilbert's earlier play. There, in the absence of any singing, Lady Blanche establishes the true sex of Hilarion and his friends when, her suspicions already aroused, she finds that they are unable to carry out a simple test in needlework which she sets them.

– servation, O!

Your powers of observation, O!

ALL.   Then jump for joy, etc.   520

(Exeunt PSYCHE, HILARION, CYRIL, *and* FLORIAN. MELISSA *going.)*
(Enter LADY BLANCHE.)

BLA.   Melissa!

MEL. *(returning)*.   Mother!

BLA.   Here – a word with you.   525

Those are the three new students?

MEL. *(confused)*.   Yes, they are.

They're charming girls.

BLA.   Particularly so.

So graceful, and so very womanly!   530

So skilled in all a girl's accomplishments!

MEL. *(confused)*.   Yes – very skilled.

BLA.   They sing so nicely too!

MEL.   They *do* sing nicely!

BLA.   Humph! It's very odd.   535

Two are tenors, one is a baritone!

MEL. *(much agitated)*.   They've all got colds!

BLA.   Colds! Bah! D'ye think I'm blind?

These 'girls' are men disguised!

MEL.   Oh no – indeed!   540

You wrong these gentlemen – I mean – why, see,

Here is an *étui* dropped by one of them (*picking up an étui*)

Containing scissors, needles, and —

BLA. *(opening it)*.   Cigars!

Why, these *are* men! And you knew this, you minx!   545

MEL.   Oh, spare them – they are gentlemen indeed.

The Prince Hilarion (married years ago

To Princess Ida) with two trusted friends!

Consider, mother, he's her husband now,

And has been, twenty years! Consider, too,   550

You're only second here – you should be first.

Assist the Prince's plan, and when he gains

The Princess Ida, why, you *will* be first.

You will design the fashions – think of that –

And always serve out all the punishments!   555

The scheme is harmless, mother – wink at it!

BLA. *(aside)*.   The prospect's tempting! Well, well, well, I'll try –

Though I've not winked at anything for years!

'Tis but one step towards my destiny –

The mighty Must! the inevitable Shall!   560

561 *Now wouldn't you like to rule the roast*: This phrase is often quoted in the form 'rule the roost' and assumed to derive from a cock keeping his hens in order. In fact this is a modern version of the original saying, which was as Gilbert has it here, and which perhaps referred to the person who supervised the roasting of the family joint of meat in the kitchen. Thomas Heywood's *History of Women* (*c.* 1630) refers to 'her that ruled the roast in the kitchen'.

577 *Plantagenet*: The name given since the seventeenth century to the British monarchs from Henry II to Richard III, i.e. the descendants of Geoffrey, Count of Anjou. It probably derives from Geoffrey's habit of wearing a sprig of broom (*planta genista*) in his cap.

DUET – MELISSA *and* LADY BLANCHE.

MEL.	Now wouldn't you like to rule the roast,
	And guide this University?
BLA.	I must agree
	'Twould pleasant be.
	(Sing hey, a Proper Pride!) 565
MEL.	And wouldn't you like to clear the coast
	Of malice and perversity?
BLA.	Without a doubt
	I'll bundle 'em out,
	Sing hey, when I preside! 570
BOTH.	Sing hey! Sing, hoity, toity! Sorry for some!

Sing, marry come up and $\left\{ \begin{array}{c} \text{my} \\ \text{her} \end{array} \right\}$ day will come!

	Sing, Proper Pride
	Is the horse to ride,
	And Happy-go-lucky, my Lady, O! 575
BLA.	For years I've writhed beneath her sneers,
	Although a born Plantagenet!
MEL.	You're much too meek,
	Or you would speak.
	(Sing hey, I'll say no more!) 580
BLA.	Her elder I, by several years,
	Although you'd ne'er imagine it.
MEL.	Sing, so I've heard
	But never a word
	Have I e'er believed before! 585
BOTH.	Sing hey! Sing, hoity, toity! Sorry for some!

Sing, marry come up and $\left\{ \begin{array}{c} \text{my} \\ \text{her} \end{array} \right\}$ day will come!

	Sing, she shall learn
	That a worm will turn.
	Sing Happy-go-lucky, my Lady, O! 590

(*Exit* LADY BLANCHE.)

MEL.	Saved for a time, at least!

(*Enter* FLORIAN, *on tiptoe.*)

FLOR. (*whispering*).	Melissa – come!
MEL.	Oh, sir! you must away from this at once – 595
	My mother guessed your sex! It was my fault –
	I blushed and stammered so that she exclaimed,
	'Can these be men?' Then, seeing this, 'Why, these ——

599–600   *'are men'/Stuck in her throat*: A take-off of the celebrated passage in Shakespeare's *Macbeth*,
Act II, Scene 2, when Macbeth is describing to his wife the murder of Duncan:

> But wherefore could not I pronounce 'Amen'?
> I had most need of blessing, and 'Amen'
> Stuck in my throat.

607   *Daughters of the Plough*: These Amazonian beings are described thus in Tennyson's poem:

> Eight daughters of the plough, stronger than men,
> Huge women blowzed with health, and wind, and rain,
> And labour. Each was like a Druid rock.

In Gilbert's play *The Princess*, Hilarion and his companions are told by Gobbo, the porter
and only male in Ida's stronghold, that the daughters of the plough were 'rescued in
time from perilous husbandry' to do manual work at the university.
bearing luncheon: The stage direction originally read *'bearing luncheon, which they spread on
the rocks'*. This is one of two scenes in which meals are taken on stage in the Savoy Operas, not counting the spaghetti consumed by the Duke of Plaza-Toro and his retinue in
the 1968 D'Oyly Carte production of *The Gondoliers* (see the note to Act I, line 572). The
other is the feast at the end of Act I of *The Sorcerer*.

Peter Riley, the last general manager of the D'Oyly Carte company, remembers this
scene as a prop master's nightmare: 'You never came off the stage with as much prop
food as you'd gone on with. The chorus girls used to delight in pulling the heads off the
pheasants and legs off the chickens. We eventually tried substituting real biscuits and
crisps but the girls ate them before they got on.'

609   *asphodel*: An echo of *Patience* and Bunthorne's 'amaranthine asphodel' (Act I, line 297).
Asphodels are lilies; in Greek mythology the everlasting flowers that carpeted the Elysian fields.

631   *to droop and pine and mope*: Just like a love-sick boy. Compare *Trial by Jury*, line 63: 'I used
to mope, and sigh, and pant'.

'*Are men*', she would have added, but '*are men*'
Stuck in her throat! She keeps your secret, sir,   600
For reasons of her own – but fly from this
And take me with you – that is – no – not that!

FLOR.   I'll go, but not without you! (*Bell.*) Why, what's that?
MEL.   The luncheon bell.
FLOR.   I'll wait for luncheon then!   605

(*Enter* HILARION *with* PRINCESS, CYRIL *with* PSYCHE, LADY
BLANCHE *and* LADIES. *Also 'Daughters of the Plough' bearing luncheon.*)

CHORUS.

Merrily ring the luncheon bell!
Here in meadow of asphodel,
Feast we body and mind as well,   610
Merrily ring the luncheon bell!

SOLO – BLANCHE.

Hunger, I beg to state,
Is highly indelicate,
This is a fact profoundly true,
So learn your appetites to subdue.   615

CHORUS.   Yes, yes,
We'll learn our appetites to subdue!

SOLO – CYRIL (*eating*).

Madam, your words so wise,
Nobody should despise,
Cursed with an appetite keen I am   620
        And I'll subdue it –
        I'll subdue it –
        I'll subdue it with cold roast lamb!

CHORUS.   Yes – yes –
We'll subdue it with cold roast lamb!   625

Merrily ring, etc.

PRIN.   You say you know the court of Hildebrand?
          There is a Prince there – I forget his name –
HIL.   Hilarion?
PRIN.   Exactly – is he well?   630
HIL.   If it be well to droop and pine and mope,

637　*booby*: Another throw-back to *Trial by Jury*, where the Judge, it may be remembered, had a brief which he bought from a booby. In this case a booby means a fool or dunce.

671–94　*Would you know the kind of maid*
　　　　Cyril's drunken kissing-song has its parallel in Tennyson's poem:

> Cyril, with whom the bell-mouth'd glass had wrought,
> Or master'd by the sense of sport, began
> To troll a careless, careless tavern-catch
> Of Moll and Meg, and strange experiences
> Unmeet for ladies. Florian nodded at him,
> I frowning; Psyche flush'd and wann'd and shook;
> The lilylike Melissa droop'd her brows;
> 'Forbear,' the Princess cried; 'Forbear, Sir' I;
> And heated thro' and thro' with wrath and love,
> I smote him on the breast; he started up;
> There rose a shriek as of a city sack'd;
> Melissa clamour'd 'Flee the death;' 'To horse'
> Said Ida; 'home! to horse' and fled.

To sigh 'Oh, Ida! Ida!' all day long,
  'Ida! my love! my life! Oh, come to me!'
  If it be well, I say, to do all this,
  Then Prince Hilarion is very well.   635
PRIN. He breathes *our* name? Well, it's a common one!
  And is the booby comely?
HIL.   Pretty well.
  I've heard it said that if I dressed myself
  In Prince Hilarion's clothes (supposing this   640
  Consisted with my maiden modesty),
  I might be taken for Hilarion's self.
  But what is this to you or me, who think
  Of all mankind with undisguised contempt?
PRIN. Contempt? Why, damsel, when I think of man, 645
  Contempt is not the word.
CYR. (*getting tipsy*).   I'm sure of that,
  Or if it is, it surely should not be!
HIL. (*aside to* CYRIL). Be quiet, idiot, or they'll find us out.
CYR. The Prince Hilarion's a goodly lad!   650
PRIN. *You* know him then?
CYR. (*tipsily*).   I rather think I do!
  We are inseparables!
PRIN.   Why, what's this?
  You love him then?   655
CYR.   We do indeed – all three!
HIL. Madam, she jests! (*Aside to* CYRIL.) Remember where you are!
CYR. Jests? Not at all! Why, bless my heart alive,
  You and Hilarion, when at the Court,
  Rode the same horse!   660
PRIN. (*horrified*)   Astride?
CYR.   Of course! Why not?
  Wore the same clothes – and once or twice, I think,
  Got tipsy in the same good company!
PRIN. Well, these are nice young ladies, on my word! 665
CYR. (*tipsy*). Don't you remember that old kissing-song
  He'd sing to blushing Mistress Lalage,
  The hostess of the Pigeons? Thus it ran:

SONG – CYRIL.

(*During symphony* HILARION *and* FLORIAN *try to stop* CYRIL. *He shakes
them off angrily.*)   670

Would you know the kind of maid

705   *Loses her balance, and falls into the stream*: The incident of Ida's fall into the moat, and her
subsequent rescue by Hilarion, which Gilbert took from Tennyson's original, was, most
unusually for a piece of D'Oyly Carte business, clumsily staged in the first production
of *Princess Ida*. The *Sporting Times* commented: 'The water is so hard and so near the platform that Miss Braham always remains in sight, and as she jumps in face foremost the
portion of her person that is not usually presented to an audience is most prominent.'
The *Sportsman* was equally unimpressed: 'The plunge and Hilarion's jump into the
water were badly managed and evoked the derisive laughter of "the gods", the simple
facts of the case being that the scene had not been studied from the theatrical Olympian
heights.'

Sets my heart aflame-a?
Eyes must be downcast and staid,
  Cheeks must flush for shame-a!
   She may neither dance nor sing, 675
   But, demure in everything,
   Hang her head in modest way,
   With pouting lips that seem to say,
  'Oh, kiss me, kiss me, kiss me, kiss me,
   Though I die of shame-a!' 680
  Please you, that's the kind of maid
  Sets my heart aflame-a!

When a maid is bold and gay
  With a tongue goes clang-a,
Flaunting it in brave array, 685
  Maiden may go hang-a!
   Sunflower gay and hollyhock
   Never shall my garden stock;
   Mine the blushing rose of May,
   With pouting lips that seem to say, 690
  'Oh, kiss me, kiss me, kiss me, kiss me,
   Though I die of shame-a!'
  Please you, that's the kind of maid
  Sets my heart aflame-a!

PRIN.   Infamous creature, get you hence away! 695

(HILARION, *who has been with difficulty restrained by* FLORIAN *during this song, breaks from him and strikes* CYRIL *furiously on the breast*.)

HIL.   Dog! there is something more to sing about!
CYR. (*sobered*).   Hilarion, are you mad?
PRIN. (*horrified*).   Hilarion? Help! 700
    Why, these are men! Lost! lost! betrayed! undone!
                         (*Running on to bridge.*)
    Girls, get you hence! Man-monsters, if you dare
    Approach one step, I — Ah!
         (*Loses her balance, and falls into the stream.*) 705
PSY.   Oh! save her, sir!
BLA.   It's useless, sir, – you'll only catch your death!
                        (HILARION *springs in.*)

715 *She's saved*: In the earliest published libretto there was a stage direction here before the finale: '*Hilarion is seen swimming with the Princess in one arm. The Princess and he are brought to land.*'

SACH.	He catches her!
MEL.	And now he lets her go!
	Again she's in his grasp —
PSY.	And now she's not.
	He seizes her back hair!
BLA. (*not looking*).	And it comes off!
PSY.	No, no! She's saved! – she's saved! – she's saved! – she's saved!

710

715

FINALE

CHORUS OF LADIES.

Oh! joy, our chief is saved,
  And by Hilarion's hand;
The torrent fierce he braved,
  And brought her safe to land!
    For his intrusion we must own
    This doughty deed may well atone!

720

PRIN.
      Stand forth ye three,
      Whoe'er ye be,
And hearken to our stern decree!

HIL., CYR., *and* FLOR.   Have mercy, O lady, – disregard your oaths!

725

PRIN.   I know not mercy, men in women's clothes!
     The man whose sacrilegious eyes
     Invade our strict seclusion, dies.
     Arrest these coarse intruding spies!

(*They are arrested by the 'Daughters of the Plough'.*)

730

FLOR., CYR., *and* LADIES. Have mercy, O lady, – disregard your oaths!
PRIN.   I know not mercy, men in women's clothes!

(CYRIL *and* FLORIAN *are bound.*)

SONG – HILARION.

Whom thou hast chained must wear his chain,
  Thou canst not set him free,
He wrestles with his bonds in vain
  Who lives by loving thee!
If heart of stone for heart of fire,
  Be all thou hast to give,
If dead to me my heart's desire,
Why should I wish to live?

735

740

742 *Have mercy, O lady*: This interpolation is not found in the first edition of the libretto.

764 *Is battered by them*: The first edition of the libretto has three additional lines for the
chorus, to be sung after the yielding of the gate and entrance of the soldiers:

ALL.   Too late – too late!
                                            The castle gate
                                            Is battered by them!

FLOR., CYR., *and* LADIES.   Have mercy, O lady!

> No word of thine – no stern command
>   Can teach my heart to rove,
> Then rather perish by thy hand,
>   Than live without thy love!   745
> A loveless life apart from thee
>   Were hopeless slavery,
> If kindly death will set me free,
>   Why should I fear to die?   750

LADIES.   Have mercy! Have mercy!

*(He is bound by two of the attendants, and the three
gentlemen are marched off.)*

(Enter MELISSA.*)*

MEL.   Madam, without the castle walls   755
     An armèd band
     Demand admittance to our halls
     For Hildebrand!

ALL.   Oh, horror!

PRIN.   Deny them!   760
     We will defy them!

ALL.   Too late – too late!
     The castle gate
     Is battered by them!

(The gate yields. SOLDIERS *rush in.* ARAC, GURON, *and* SCYNTHIUS   765
are with them, but with their hands handcuffed.)

ENSEMBLE.

GIRLS.	MEN.
Rend the air with wailing,	Walls and fences scaling,
Shed the shameful tear!	Promptly we appear;
Walls are unavailing,	Walls are unavailing,
Man has entered here!	We have entered here.
Shame and desecration	Female execration
Are his staunch allies,	Stifle if you're wise,
Let your lamentation	Stop your lamentation,
Echo to the skies!	Dry your pretty eyes!

770

777 *beard a maiden in her lair*: It is normally, of course, lions who are bearded in their lairs, as in the proverb song in *Iolanthe* (Act II, line 384). The expression means defying someone directly and face to face.

(*Enter* HILDEBRAND.)

RECITATIVE.

PRIN.   Audacious tyrant, do you dare
To beard a maiden in her lair?

HILD.   Since you inquire,
We've no desire
To beard a maiden here, or anywhere!   780

SOL.   No, no – we've no desire
To beard a maiden here, or anywhere!
No, no, no, no.

SOLO – HILDEBRAND.

Some years ago
No doubt you know   785
(And if you don't I'll tell you so)
You gave your troth
Upon your oath
To Hilarion my son.
A vow you make   790
You must not break,
(If you think you may, it's a great mistake),
For a bride's a bride
Though the knot were tied
At the early age of one!   795
And I'm a peppery kind of King,
Who's indisposed for parleying
To fit the wit of a bit of a chit,
And that's the long and the short of it!

SOL.   For he's a peppery kind of King, etc.   800

If you decide
To pocket your pride
And let Hilarion claim his bride,
Why, well and good,
It's understood   805
We'll let bygones go by –
But if you choose
To sulk in the blues

822–3 *we're taught/To shame it*: The rather fastidious reviewer of *The Theatre* took great exception to this line: 'Death, figuratively speaking, may be braved, defied, scorned, met with courage and the reverse; but it cannot be shamed.'

841 *I rather think I dare*: This line was not in the original libretto.

I'll make the whole of you shake in your shoes.

I'll storm your walls, 810
And level your halls,
In the twinkling of an eye!
For I'm a peppery Potentate,
Who's little inclined his claim to bate,
To fit the wit of a bit of a chit, 815
And that's the long and the short of it!

SOL.　　　For he's a peppery Potentate, etc.

TRIO – ARAC, GURON, *and* SCYNTHIUS.

We may remark, though nothing can
Dismay us,
That if you thwart this gentleman, 820
He'll slay us.
We don't fear death, of course – we're taught
To shame it;
But still upon the whole we thought
We'd name it. 825

(*To each other.*) Yes, yes, yes, better perhaps to name it.

Our interests we would not press
With chatter,
Three hulking brothers more or less
Don't matter; 830
If you'd pooh-pooh this monarch's plan,
Pooh-pooh it,
But when he says he'll hang a man,
He'll do it.

(*To each other.*) Yes, yes, yes, devil doubt he'll do it. 835

PRIN. (*Recitative*). Be reassured, nor fear his anger blind,
His menaces are idle as the wind.
He dares not kill you – vengeance lurks behind!

AR., GUR., SCYN. We rather think he dares, but never mind!
No, no, no, – never, never mind! 840

HILD.　　　I rather think I dare, but never, never mind!
Enough of parley – as a special boon,
We give you till to-morrow afternoon;
Release Hilarion, then, and be his bride,
Or you'll incur the guilt of fratricide! 845

ENSEMBLE.

PRINCESS.	THE OTHERS.
To yield at once to such a foe	Oh! yield at once, 'twere better so
With shame were rife;	Than risk a strife!
So quick! away with him, although	And let the Prince Hilarion go –
He saved my life!	He saved thy life!
That he is fair, and strong, and	Hilarion's fair, and strong, and
tall,	tall –
Is very evident to all,	A worse misfortune might befall –
Yet I will die before I call	It's not so dreadful, after all,
Myself his wife!	To be his wife!

850

SOLO – PRINCESS.

Though I am but a girl,
Defiance thus I hurl,
    Our banners all
    On outer wall
We fearlessly unfurl.

855

ALL.   Though she is but a girl, etc.

PRINCESS.	THE OTHERS.
To yield at once, etc.	Oh! yield at once, etc.

860

(The PRINCESS *stands, surrounded by girls kneeling.* HILDEBRAND *and soldiers stand on built rocks at back and sides of stage. Picture.)*

END OF ACT II

1–2 *Scene*: Tennyson gives a vivid description of the courtyard of the university in *The Princess*:

> a court
> Compact of lucid marbles, boss'd with lengths
> Of classic frieze, with ample awnings gay
> Betwixt the pillars, and with great urns of flowers.
> The Muses and the Graces, group'd in threes,
> Enring'd a billowing fountain in the midst;
> And here and there on lattice edges lay
> Or book or lute.

3–10 *Death to the invader*

An early D'Oyly Carte prompt-book gives the following directions for this number:

Death to the invader!	*arms up*
Strike a deadly blow,	*blow*
As an old Crusader	*arms up*
Struck his Paynim foe!	*blow*
Let our martial thunder	
Fill his soul with wonder	
Tear his ranks asunder,	*arms open*
Lay the tyrant low!	*point*

6 *Paynim*: Pagan or heathen. The word was originally applied to the Saracens who fought the Crusaders.

ACT III

SCENE. – *Outer Walls and Courtyard of Castle Adamant.* MELISSA,
SACHARISSA, *and ladies discovered, armed with battleaxes.*

CHORUS.

Death to the invader!
  Strike a deadly blow,
As an old Crusader   5
  Struck his Paynim foe!
Let our martial thunder
Fill his soul with wonder,
Tear his ranks asunder,
  Lay the tyrant low!   10

SOLO – MELISSA.

Thus our courage, all untarnished
  We're instructed to display:
But to tell the truth unvarnished,
  We are more inclined to say,
  'Please you, do not hurt us.'   15

CHORUS.	'Do not hurt us, if it please you!'
MEL.	'Please you let us be.'
CHORUS.	'Let us be – let us be!'
MEL.	'Soldiers disconcert us.'
CHORUS.	'Disconcert us, if it please you!'
MEL.	'Frightened maids are we.'
CHORUS.	'Maids are we – maids are we!'

20

MELISSA.

But 'twould be an error
To confess our terror,

27 *Death to the invader*: In early libretti, the chorus repeated all eight lines of 'Death to the invader' at this point, not just the first four as now.

38 *One moment, ma'am*: The passage from here to line 49 was among the cuts proposed for the 1954 D'Oyly Carte revival, but a *stet* is written against it in the prompt copy, and in the end it was not removed. Other proposed cuts which were implemented include the phrases 'get you hence' (line 68) and 'That in the heat and turmoil of the fight' (line 75), and the passage from 'But, happily' to 'such as soldiers love' (lines 85–8).

So, in Ida's name, 25
Boldly we exclaim:

Chorus.

Death to the invader!
  Strike a deadly blow,
As an old Crusader
  Struck his Paynim foe! 30

(*Flourish. Enter* Princess, *armed, attended by*
Blanche *and* Psyche.)

Prin.	I like your spirit, girls! We have to meet
	Stern bearded warriors in fight to-day:
	Wear naught but what is necessary to 35
	Preserve your dignity before their eyes,
	And give your limbs full play.
Bla.	One moment, ma'am,
	Here is a paradox we should not pass
	Without inquiry. We are prone to say, 40
	'This thing is Needful – that, Superfluous' –
	Yet they invariably co-exist!
	We find the Needful comprehended in
	The circle of the grand Superfluous,
	Yet the Superfluous cannot be bought 45
	Unless you're amply furnished with the Needful.
	These singular considerations are –
Prin.	Superfluous, yet not Needful – so you see
	The terms may independently exist.
(*To Ladies.*)	Women of Adamant, we have to show 50
	That Woman, educated to the task,
	Can meet Man, face to face, on his own ground,
	And beat him there. Now let us set to work:
	Where is our lady surgeon?
Sac.	Madam, here! 55
Prin.	We shall require your skill to heal the wounds
	Of those that fall.
Sac. (*alarmed*).	What, heal the wounded?
Prin.	Yes!
Sac.	And cut off real live legs and arms? 60
Prin.	Of course!
Sac.	I wouldn't do it for a thousand pounds!
Prin.	Why, how is this? Are you faint-hearted, girl?
	You've often cut them off in theory!

70 *My fusiliers, advance*: In Gilbert's earlier play, this passage was:

> My Amazons, advance!
> Where are your muskets, pray?

96 *fulminating*: Exploding, from the Latin word *fulminare*, meaning to send forth thunder or lightning.

98 *saltpetre*: A crystalline substance, with the chemical name potassium nitrate, which is the chief constituent of gunpowder.

105 *Exeunt all but Princess*: In early libretti the stage direction here read: 'Exeunt all but Princess, singing refrain of "Death to the Invader" *pianissimo*.'

For a period before the war the D'Oyly Carte company altered the order of the Third Act of *Princess Ida*. Ida's next two lines and her song 'I built upon a rock' were moved from their original position, and introduced instead just before the gates are opened to let in the soldiers (line 234). I cannot discover exactly when this change was made, although it was certainly in operation at the time of the D'Oyly Carte recordings in 1923 and 1930. The 1954 revival restored the original order.

SAC.	In theory I'll cut them off again 65
	With pleasure, and as often as you like,
	But not in practice.
PRIN.	Coward! get you hence,
	I've craft enough for that, and courage too,
	I'll do your work! My fusiliers, advance! 70
	Why, you are armed with axes! Gilded toys!
	Where are your rifles, pray?
CHLOE.	Why, please you, ma'am,
	We left them in the armoury, for fear
	That in the heat and turmoil of the fight, 75
	They might go off!
PRIN.	'They might!' Oh, craven souls!
	Go off yourselves! Thank heaven, I have a heart
	That quails not at the thought of meeting men;
	I will discharge your rifles! Off with you! 80
	Where's my bandmistress?
ADA.	Please you, ma'am, the band
	Do not feel well, and can't come out to-day!
PRIN.	Why, this is flat rebellion! I've no time
	To talk to them just now. But, happily, 85
	I can play several instruments at once,
	And I will drown the shrieks of those that fall
	With trumpet music, such as soldiers love!
	How stand we with respect to gunpowder?
	My Lady Psyche – you who superintend 90
	Our lab'ratory – are you well prepared
	To blow these bearded rascals into shreds?
PSY.	Why, madam –
PRIN.	Well?
PSY.	Let us try gentler means. 95
	We can dispense with fulminating grains
	While we have eyes with which to flash our rage!
	We can dispense with villainous saltpetre
	While we have tongues with which to blow them up!
	We can dispense, in short, with all the arts 100
	That brutalize the practical polemist!
PRIN. (*contemptuously*).	I never knew a more dispensing chemist!
	Away, away – I'll meet these men alone
	Since all my women have deserted me!

(*Exeunt all but* PRINCESS.) 105

PRIN.	So fail my cherished plans – so fails my faith –
	And with it hope, and all that comes of hope!

108–35 *I built upon a rock*

This is one of the nearest approximations to a grand-opera aria in the entire Savoy repertoire. It is also strongly suggestive of the sacred oratorio style of which Sullivan was a leading exponent. The critics were generally enthusiastic. *The Times* described it as 'the best musical lyric in the score', the *Daily Telegraph* detected the influence of Schubert, and the *Saturday Review* commented that it appeared as though in this case Sullivan was setting Tennyson rather than Gilbert. The only dissenting note was struck by *Truth*, which suggested that the song might advantageously have been cut: 'It is the right music in the wrong place.'

As originally written, Ida's song was shorter and in a different form from the present version. This is how it appears in the first edition of the libretto:

> I built upon a rock,
>> But ere Destruction's hand
>>> Dealt equal lot
>>> To Court and cot,
>> My rock had turned to sand!
>>> Ah, faithless rock,
>>> My simple faith to mock!
>
> I leant upon an oak,
>> But in the hour of need,
>>> Alack-a-day,
>>> My trusted stay
>> Was but a bruised reed!
>>> Ah, trait'rous oak,
>>> Thy worthlessness to cloak!
>
> I drew a sword of steel,
>> But when to home and hearth
>>> The battle's breath
>>> Bore fire and death,
>> My sword was but a lath!
>>> Ah, coward steel,
>>> That fear can unanneal!

126 *lath*: A thin, narrow piece of wood.

133 *unanneal*: Steel is annealed or toughened by being exposed to continuous and gradually diminishing heat. The word 'unannealed' also appears in *The Pirates of Penzance* (Act II, line 551) but is wrongly used there (see the note).

SONG – PRINCESS.

I built upon a rock,
  But ere Destruction's hand
    Dealt equal lot   110
    To Court and cot,
  My rock had turned to sand!
I leant upon an oak,
  But in the hour of need,
    Alack-a-day,   115
    My trusted stay
Was but a bruisèd reed!
    Ah, faithless rock,
    My simple faith to mock!
    Ah, trait'rous oak,   120
    Thy worthlessness to cloak.

I drew a sword of steel,
  But when to home and hearth
    The battle's breath
    Bore fire and death,
  My sword was but a lath!   125
I lit a beacon fire,
  But on a stormy day
    Of frost and rime,
    In wintertime,
  My fire had died away!   130
    Ah, coward steel,
    That fear can unanneal!
    Ah, false fire indeed,
    To fail me in my need!   135

(She sinks on a seat. Enter CHLOE *and all the ladies.)*

CHLOE.   Madam, your father and your brothers claim
An audience!
PRIN.   What do they do here?
CHLOE.   They come   140
To fight for you!
PRIN.   Admit them!
BLA.   Infamous!
One's brothers, ma'am, are men!
PRIN.   So I have heard.   145
But all my women seem to fail me when

160 *popinjays*: An old name for a parrot, figuratively applied to people to suggest vanity and empty conceit. In 'I have a song to sing, O' in Act I of *The Yeomen of the Guard*, Jack Point sings:

> It's a song of a popinjay, bravely born,
> Who turned up his noble nose with scorn...

161 *jack-a-dandy*: Smart, foppish, pert or conceited.

167–8 *I am possessed/By the pale devil of a shaking heart*: This was another of the lines to which *The Theatre* took exception (see the note to Act II, lines 822–3). It commented: 'Confusion of metaphor makes sheer nonsense of this utterance. The frightened monarch might just as plausibly claim to be possessed by the green phantom of a crawling liver.'

180–227 *Whene'er I spoke*

The tune of Gama's patter song was altered by Sullivan only a few days before the first performance, much to the dismay of George Grossmith, who found it very difficult to unlearn the old tune and substitute the new one.

The Macmillan edition of the Savoy Operas has 'Whene'er I poke' as the first line of the song. This may possibly be a hang-over from an early present-tense version of the song. The licence copy and all editions of the libretto that I have seen have 'Whene'er I spoke', which of course, fits with the past tense of 'smiled' and 'voted'.

I need them most. In this emergency,
Even one's brothers may be turned to use.

(*Enter* GAMA, *quite pale and unnerved.*)

GAMA.   My daughter!
PRIN.   Father! thou art free!   150
GAMA.   Aye, free!
Free as a tethered ass! I come to thee
With words from Hildebrand. Those duly given
I must return to blank captivity.   155
I'm free so far.
PRIN.   Your message.
GAMA.   Hildebrand
Is loth to war with women. Pit my sons,
My three brave sons, against these popinjays,   160
These tufted jack-a-dandy featherheads,
And on the issue let thy hand depend!
PRIN.   Insult on insult's head! Are we a stake
For fighting men? What fiend possesses thee,
That thou hast come with offers such as these   165
From such as he to such an one as I?
GAMA.   I am possessed
By the pale devil of a shaking heart!
My stubborn will is bent. I dare not face
That devilish monarch's black malignity!   170
He tortures me with torments worse than death,
I haven't anything to grumble at!
He finds out what particular meats I love,
And gives me them. The very choicest wines,
The costliest robes – the richest rooms are mine: 175
He suffers none to thwart my simplest plan,
And gives strict orders none should contradict me!
He's made my life a curse! (*weeps*).
PRIN.   My tortured father!

SONG – GAMA.

Whene'er I spoke   180
Sarcastic joke
          Replete with malice spiteful,
This people mild
Politely smiled,
          And voted me delightful!   185

197 *German bands*: Irritating fellow countrymen of the 'mystical Germans/Who preach from
     ten till four' who so annoyed the Mikado (*The Mikado*, Act II, lines 348–9), German mu-
     sicians were a common sight on the streets of Victorian London. They tended to wear
     uniforms and play marches and other stirring oom-pah-pah numbers. A correspondent
     to the *Gilbert and Sullivan Journal* in the 1930s recalled that they were in the habit of
     erecting music stands in the street for their performances.

207 *hurdy-gurds*: The hurdy-gurdy was originally a lute-like instrument with strings,
     sounded by turning a handle. The words later came to be applied to the barrel organs
     which were so familiar a feature of the street life of Victorian Britain.

211 *I offered gold*: The first American edition of the libretto, which almost certainly contains
     material originally in the British libretto but later altered (see the note to Act II, lines
     491–520), has a different version of this third verse:

                          Upon the stage
                          Plays, ripe with age,
                       And not too much protracted,
                          With faultless taste
                          Were always placed
                       And excellently acted;
                          Now when he sees
                          Good comedies
                       It irritates King Gama,
                          With no excuse
                          For rank abuse
                       Who can enjoy the drama?

Now when a wight
Sits up all night
   Ill-natured jokes devising,
And all his wiles
Are met with smiles,
   It's hard, there's no disguising! Ah!   190

Oh, don't the days seem lank and long
When all goes right and nothing goes wrong,
And isn't your life extremely flat
With nothing whatever to grumble at!   195

CHORUS.   Oh, isn't your life, etc.

      When German bands
      From music stands
    Played Wagner imper*fect*ly –
      I bade them go –   200
      They didn't say no,
   But off they went directly!
      The organ boys
      They stopped their noise
   With readiness surprising,   205
      And grinning herds
      Of hurdy-gurds
   Retired apologizing! Ah!

Oh, don't the days seem lank and long, etc.

CHORUS.   Oh, isn't your life, etc.   210

      I offered gold
      In sums untold
   To all who'd contradict me –
      I said I'd pay
      A pound a day   215
   To anyone who kicked me –
      I bribed with toys
      Great vulgar boys
   To utter something spiteful,
      But, bless you, no!
      They *would* be so   220
   Confoundedly politeful! Ah!

232   *Open the gates*: This and the next line were among the cuts made in 1954.

247   *molly-coddle*: A pampered creature.

In short, these aggravating lads,
They tickle my tastes, they feed my fads,
They give me this and they give me that,   225
And I've nothing whatever to grumble at!

CHORUS.   Oh, isn't your life, etc.

(*He bursts into tears, and falls sobbing on a seat.*)

PRIN.   My poor old father! How he must have suffered!
          Well, well, I yield!   230
GAMA (*hysterically*). She yields! I'm saved, I'm saved!   (*Exit.*)
PRIN.   Open the gates – admit these warriors,
          Then get you all within the castle walls.   (*Exit.*)

(*The gates are opened, and the girls mount the battlements as soldiers enter. Also*
ARAC, GURON, *and* SCYNTHIUS.)   235

CHORUS OF SOLDIERS.

When anger spreads his wing,
    And all seems dark as night for it,
    There's nothing but to fight for it,
But ere you pitch your ring,
    Select a pretty site for it,   240
    (This spot is suited quite for it),
And then you gaily sing,

'Oh, I love the jolly rattle
Of an ordeal by battle,
There's an end of tittle-tattle,   245
    When your enemy is dead.
It's an arrant molly-coddle
Fears a crack upon his noddle
And he's only fit to swaddle
    In a downy feather-bed!' –   250

ENSEMBLE.

GIRLS.	MEN.
For a fight's a kind of thing	Oh, I love the jolly rattle, etc.
That I love to look upon,	
So let us sing,	
Long live the King,	
And his son Hilarion!	

255

256–90 *This helmet, I suppose*

This splendid spoof of Handelian style was originally sung slightly later in Act III, just before the full-scale fight between the forces of Hildebrand and Gama (line 327). In the first edition of the libretto the stage direction and subsequent dialogue which now start at line 292 followed straight on from 'For a fight's a kind of thing'. The current Macmillan edition still has the original placing of 'This helmet, I suppose', although it was certainly changed to its present position before 1930.

The American first edition of the libretto has a different version of the song, with an introductory chorus:

CHORUS.

With hearts resolved and courage grave,
  The warriors now begin
May fortune's shield protect the brave,
  And may the best men win!

SOLO – ARAC.

Where'er we go
To fight the foe
We never throw a chance away,
  And at last
  We always cast
Each useless circumstance away.
  A helmet bright
  Is far from light,
Life guardsmen know how true it is.
  (*Taking off helmet*).

  A bright cuirass
  We also class
With useless superfluities (*taking off cuirass*)
  All this array
  Is in the way
It is, upon my word it is –
  For who can fight
  When locked up tight
In lobster-like absurdities?
(*By this time they have removed all their armour and wear nothing but a close-fitting shape suit.*)

  Though brasses
    And tasses
  And showy cuirasses
Are all very useful to dazzle the lasses,
  He clashes with asses
  Who cumbers with masses
    Of metal
    His fettle,
  Tra, la, la, la, la!

THE THREE.   Yes, yes, yes!
              Tra, la, la, la, la!
ALL.   Yes, yes, yes!
              Tra, la, la, la, la!

265 *cuirass*: A piece of armour reaching down to the waist and consisting of a breast-plate and back-plate fastened together. The term cuirass was sometimes also used for the breast-plate alone.

SONG – Arac.

This helmet, I suppose,
Was meant to ward off blows,
 It's very hot,
 And weighs a lot,
As many a guardsman knows,   260
So off that helmet goes.

ALL.   Yes, yes, yes,
So off that helmet goes!

         (*Giving their helmets to attendants.*)

ARAC.   This tight-fitting cuirass   265
Is but a useless mass,
  It's made of steel,
  And weighs a deal,
A man is but an ass
Who fights in a cuirass,   270
So off goes that cuirass.

ALL.   Yes, yes, yes,
So off goes that cuirass!

         (*Removing cuirasses.*)

ARAC.   These brassets, truth to tell,   275
May look uncommon well,
  But in a fight
  They're much too tight,
They're like a lobster shell!

ALL.   Yes, yes, yes,   280
They're like a lobster shell.

         (*Removing their brassets.*)

ARAC.   These things I treat the same (*indicating leg pieces*).
(I quite forget their name)
  They turn one's legs   285
  To cribbage pegs –
Their aid I thus disclaim,
Though I forget their name!

ALL.   Yes, yes, yes,
Their aid $\left\{ \begin{matrix} \text{we} \\ \text{they} \end{matrix} \right\}$ thus disclaim!   290

(*They remove their leg pieces and wear close-fitting shape suits.*)

275 *brassets*: Armour for the upper arm, more usually spelt 'brassards' or 'brassarts'.
291 *shape suits*: Tight-fitting pants and pullover tunic.

306 *virago*: A man-like or heroic woman; an Amazon.
      termagant: An impudent or quarrelsome woman, a shrew.

(HILARION, FLORIAN, *and* CYRIL *are brought out by the 'Daughters of the Plough'. They are still bound and wear the robes. Enter* GAMA.)

GAMA.	Hilarion! Cyril! Florian! dressed as women!
	Is this indeed Hilarion?
HIL.	Yes, it is!
GAMA.	Why, you look handsome in your women's clothes!
	Stick to 'em! men's attire becomes you not!

(*To* CYRIL *and* FLORIAN.) And you, young ladies, will you please to pray
King Hildebrand to set me free again?
Hang on his neck and gaze into his eyes,
He never could resist a pretty face!

HIL.	You dog, you'll find, though I wear woman's garb,
	My sword is long and sharp!
GAMA.	Hush, pretty one!

Here's a virago! Here's a termagant!
If length and sharpness go for anything,
You'll want no sword while you can wag your tongue!

CYR.	What need to waste your words on such as he?
	He's old and crippled.
GAMA.	Aye, but I've three sons,

Fine fellows, young, and muscular, and brave,
They're well worth talking to! Come, what d'ye say?

ARAC.	Aye, pretty ones, engage yourselves with us,
	If three rude warriors affright you not!
HIL.	Old as you are, I'd wring your shrivelled neck
	If you were not the Princess Ida's father.
GAMA.	If I were not the Princess Ida's father,

And so had not her brothers for my sons,
No doubt you'd wring my neck – in safety too!
Come, come, Hilarion, begin, begin!
Give them no quarter – they will give you none.
You've this advantage over warriors
Who kill their country's enemies for pay, –
You know what you are fighting for – look there!
(*Pointing to Ladies on the battlements.*)

(*Desperate fight between the three Princes and the three Knights, during which the Ladies on the battlements and the Soldiers on the stage sing the following chorus:*)

This is our duty plain towards
Our Princess all immaculate,
We ought to bless her brothers' swords
And piously ejaculate:

295

300

305

310

315

320

325

330

333   *Oh, Hungary*: This sudden suggestion that Gama and his sons are from Hungary was not well received by the *Theatre* reviewer:

> Why Hungary, I humbly ask? Up to the moment at which this astounding invocation is pronounced, with scarcely less amazing unanimity, by the rival hosts of Hildebrand and Ida, the author has not even so much as hinted to us that Castle Adamant is situate in the Realm of the Five Rivers. Barely ten minutes before the final fall of the curtain – and for no conceivable reason connected with the story of the play – he informs us that Gama and his sons are Magyars to a man. But stay: can it be that Mr Gilbert confers this nationality upon one of his two Royal Families in order to obtain a rhyme for the word 'ironmongery', which occurs later on in the above-quoted verse? It must be; but I contend that such a *pis-aller* is scarcely worthy of so facile and fertile a rhymster.

The American first edition has a second verse to the soldiers' chorus:

> But if our hearts assert their sway,
>   (And hearts are all fantastical)
> We shall be more disposed to say
>   These words enthusiastical:
>   Hilarion!
>   Hilarion!
> Oh prosper, Prince Hilarion!
>   In mode complete
>   May you defeat
> Each meddlesome Hungarian!

344   *Ladies, my brothers*: This and the next line were among the cuts made in the 1954 production. An early D'Oyly Carte prompt-book has the following stage direction after the words 'Bind up their wounds': 'Sacharissa goes to Arac, Chloe to Scynthius, and Ada to Guron. They place bandages (linen) round their heads as they lie on the ground, the three then rise and stand in places till curtain.'

365   *If you enlist*: This and the following line were cut in the 1954 revival, as was the passage from line 377 to line 382.

Oh, Hungary!
Oh, Hungary!
Oh, doughty sons of Hungary!   335
May all success
Attend and bless
Your warlike ironmongery!
Hilarion! Hilarion! Hilarion!

(*By this time,* ARAC, GURON, *and* SCYNTHIUS *are on the ground, wounded*   340
    –HILARION, CYRIL, *and* FLORIAN *stand over them.*)

PRIN. (*entering through gate and followed by Ladies,* HILDEBRAND, *and*
GAMA). Hold! stay your hands! – we yield ourselves to you!
        Ladies, my brothers all lie bleeding there!
        Bind up their wounds – but look the other way.   345
(*Coming down.*) Is this the end? (*bitterly to* LADY BLANCHE). How say
            you, Lady Blanche –
        Can I with dignity my post resign?
        And if I do, will you then take my place?
BLA.   To answer this, it's meet that we consult
        The great Potential Mysteries; I mean   350
        The five Subjunctive Possibilities –
        The May, the Might, the Would, the Could, the Should.
        Can you resign? The prince May claim you; if
        He Might, you Could – and if you Should, I Would!
PRIN.   I thought as much! Then, to my fate I yield –   355
        So ends my cherished scheme! Oh, I had hoped
        To band all women with my maiden throng,
        And make them all abjure tyrannic Man!
HILD.   A noble aim!
PRIN.   You ridicule it now;   360
        But if I carried out this glorious scheme,
        At my exalted name Posterity
        Would bow in gratitude!
HILD.   But pray reflect –
        If you enlist all women in your cause,   365
        And make them all abjure tyrannic Man,
        The obvious question then arises, 'How
        Is this Posterity to be provided?'
PRIN.   I never thought of that! My Lady Blanche,
        How do you solve the riddle?   370
BLA.   Don't ask me –
        Abstract Philosophy won't answer it.
        Take him – he is your Shall. Give in to Fate!

380–81 *Experiments, the proverb says, are made/On humble subjects*: The saying *Fiat experimentum in corpore vile* is said to derive from the experience of the French humorist Muret (1526–85), who, while in a trance, narrowly escaped dissection by experimenting surgeons.

403–6 *We will walk this world... I love thee – Come*: This is the only occasion in his 'Respectful Operatic Per-Version' where Gilbert quotes the words of the Poet Laureate. These lines come towards the end of *The Princess*. They are followed there by these concluding lines:

> Yield thyself up: my hopes and thine are one:
> Accomplish thou my manhood and thyself;
> Lay thy sweet hands in mine and trust to me.

407–31 *FINALE*

In his autobiographical notes written *c.* 1939 and reflecting on his long career with the D'Oyly Carte company, J. M. Gordon mentions some inappropriate clowning that went on in the finale of *Princess Ida*: 'Lady Blanche standing legs apart – to support Gama when he leans against her, a distinguished lady of title, and continuing to let him do so and not resenting this indignity. It is not the Savoy tradition of 1884 but vulgarity brought in years ago.'

PRIN. And you desert me. I alone am staunch!
HIL. Madam, you placed your trust in Woman – well,   375
       Woman has failed you utterly – try Man,
       Give him one chance, it's only fair – besides,
       Women are far too precious, too divine,
       To try unproven theories upon.
       Experiments, the proverb says, are made   380
       On humble subjects – try our grosser clay,
       And mould it as you will!
CYR.   Remember, too,
       Dear Madam, if at any time you feel
       A-weary of the Prince, you can return   385
       To Castle Adamant, and rule your girls
       As heretofore, you know.
PRIN.   And shall I find
       The Lady Psyche here?
PSY.   If Cyril, ma'am,   390
       Does not behave himself, I think you will.
PRIN. And you, Melissa, shall I find *you* here?
MEL. Madam, however Florian turns out,
       Unhesitatingly I answer, No!
GAMA. Consider this, my love, if your mamma   395
       Had looked on matters from your point of view
       (I wish she had), why, where would you have been?
BLA. There's an unbounded field of speculation,
       On which I could discourse for hours!
PRIN.   No doubt!   400
       We will not trouble you. Hilarion,
       I have been wrong – I see my error now.
       Take me, Hilarion – 'We will walk this world
       Yoked in all exercise of noble end!
       And so through those dark gates across the wild   405
       That no man knows! Indeed, I love thee – Come!'

                          FINALE.

PRIN.   With joy abiding,
                   Together gliding
                     Through life's variety,
                     In sweet society,   410
                   And thus enthroning
                   The love I'm owning,
                   On this atoning
                     I will rely!

432 *CURTAIN*: A stage direction in an early prompt-book reads: 'For return curtain Hildebrand and Gama are seen grasping each other's hands – the feud is ended.'

CHORUS.   It were profanity   415
                          For poor humanity
                          To treat as vanity
                              The sway of Love.
                          In no locality
                          Or principality   420
                          Is our mortality
                              Its sway above!

HILARION.   When day is fading,
                          With serenading
                              And such frivolity   425
                              Of tender quality –
                          With scented showers
                          Of fairest flowers,
                          The happy hours
                              Will gaily fly!   430

CHORUS.   It were profanity, etc.

CURTAIN

THE MIKADO

or

The Town of Titipu

DRAMATIS PERSONÆ

THE MIKADO OF JAPAN
NANKI-POO (*his Son, disguised as a wandering minstrel, and in love with* YUM-YUM)
KO-KO (*Lord High Executioner of Titipu*)
POOH-BAH (*Lord High Everything Else*)
PISH-TUSH (*a Noble Lord*)
GO-TO (*a Noble Lord*)
YUM-YUM
PITTI-SING   } *Three Sisters – Wards of* KO-KO
PEEP-BO
KATISHA (*an elderly Lady, in love with* NANKI-POO)

Chorus of School-girls, Nobles, Guards, and Coolies.

ACT I. – Courtyard of Ko-Ko's Official Residence.
ACT II. – Ko-Ko's Garden.

THE MIKADO

The Mikado has been performed more times than any other Gilbert and Sullivan opera. Its initial run at the Savoy Theatre, which began on 14 March 1885, stretched to 672 performances and lasted very nearly two years. It has continued to delight audiences ever since in many different forms. It was the first Savoy Opera to be filmed when in 1938 the D'Oyly Carte Company led by Martyn Green as Ko-Ko performed in front of the cameras at Pinewood Studios. More recently, Jonathan Miller's stylish black and white production for English National Opera set in the 1920s has been a consistent box office attraction at the London Coliseum since it opened in September 1986 and has also been seen on television. The revived D'Oyly Carte Opera Company has staged two *Mikados* – one for its second season, which opened at Hull in March 1989, and the second in 1992. This latter production, which put both John Rath as the Mikado (permanently) and Fenton Gray as Ko-Ko (temporarily) on stilts and dressed Pish-Tush as a Keystone Cop, was shown on BBC television on Boxing Day 1992. It has also been released as a video to compete with the Brent-Walker version, which stars William Conrad, best known from the television series *Cannon* in the title role. Clearly *The Mikado* still spells very good business.

Surprisingly, perhaps, *The Mikado* was written at a time when the spirits of Gilbert and Sullivan were at a low ebb and when relations between them were rather strained. By the late spring of 1884 audiences for *Princess Ida* were dropping off and Richard D'Oyly Carte was demanding a new opera to revive the flagging fortunes of his company. In fact, *Ida* was to continue until October, when it was replaced at the Savoy by a revival of *The Sorcerer* in a double bill with *Trial by Jury*.

Gilbert responded to Carte's request for a new piece by resurrecting his favourite and rather fanciful opera plot based on a magic lozenge. Sullivan rejected this idea, as he had two years earlier, and told Gilbert in no uncertain terms that he was fed up with ridiculous plots and topsy-turvy situations and wanted a more straightforward libretto where the music would not be subordinate to the words but could stand on its own.

Gilbert took this response as a personal slight and wrote back 'I cannot consent to construct another plot for the next opera.' Sullivan, equally emphatically, replied: 'The tone of your letter convinces me that your decision is final and therefore further discussion is useless.' D'Oyly Carte desperately tried to mediate between his two difficult protégés but his efforts were in vain and it began to look as though the partnership which had produced seven highly successful comic operas had now come to an end.

The situation was saved, at least according to a story which may well be apocryphal but is too good not to tell here, by a dramatic accident which could have inflicted a much more tragic and conclusive blow to the partnership. One day in May 1884, as Gilbert was pacing up and down in the library of his new house in Harrington Gardens, Kensington, a large Japanese executioner's sword fell from its mounting on the wall and crashed to the floor. This, so the story goes, inspired the dramatist with the theme for his next opera. He decided to set it in Japan and make one of the leading characters an executioner. The resulting libretto, although hardly free of topsy-turvydom, was straightforward and dramatic enough for Sullivan to feel happy with, and composer and librettist were once again reconciled.

Things Japanese were all the rage in England in the mid-1880s. Oriental prints and ceramics were on sale in the most fashionable West End stores. Liberty's was enjoying a spectacular success with its Japanese-style fabrics and dresses. There was even a Japanese village which had been set up in Knightsbridge, complete with real geisha girls serving tea in the traditional manner. So Gilbert was developing a fashionable contemporary theme in setting his new opera in the far-away Pacific islands, which were beginning to be washed by the strong currents of Western influence.

The location of *The Mikado* was to lead to a typically Gilbertian piece of official silliness early in the twentieth century. Shortly before the official visit to Britain of Crown Prince Fushimi of Japan in 1907, the Lord Chamberlain announced an indefinite ban on all performances of the opera on the grounds that it was offensive to the Japanese. Several M.P.s protested about the ban; one asked whether it applied to military bands playing excerpts from *The Mikado* (it apparently did), while another pointed out that as Shakespeare's *Hamlet* portrayed the King of Denmark as a murderer, and as Denmark was a friendly power, presumably it should be banned for the same reason. In the event the ban lasted for six weeks before it was withdrawn by the Home Secretary. Gilbert, who was honoured with a knighthood shortly afterwards, commented that before long 'we shall probably be at war with Japan about India, and they will offer me a high price to permit *The Mikado* to be played'.

It was, of course, absurd to ban *The Mikado* on the grounds that it might offend the Japanese. Despite its setting, the opera is quite clearly about Britain, and its satire is directed at domestic rather than foreign targets. There is nothing very Japanese about the pluralist Pooh-Bah, with his offices (*inter alia*) of Archbishop, Paymaster-General and Lord Chief Justice, or about a Mikado whose ideas of suitable punishments for criminals include sending them to Madame Tussaud's or making them ride on the buffers of Parliamentary trains. As G. K. Chesterton observed, 'I doubt if there is a single joke in the whole play that fits the Japanese. But all the jokes in the play fit the English.'

Certainly the music for *The Mikado* could hardly have been more English. It is true that there are one or two Japanese touches like the use of the pentatonic scale for the opening chorus and the quotation of the Imperial marching song 'Miya sama'. But the dominant musical influence is the English folk-song tradition, seen particularly in Nanki-Poo's opening number, 'A wandering minstrel I', the madrigal 'Brightly dawns our wedding day' and the delightful duet 'The flowers that bloom in the spring'. Even the entrance of the Lord High Executioner is set to a tune remarkably similar to the traditional air 'A Fine Old English Gentleman'.

More than any other of the Savoy Operas, *The Mikado* has been the subject of changes and widely different interpretations in the twentieth century. Several of the 'gags' introduced in early performances by Rutland Barrington when he was playing Pooh-Bah are still used today although they failed to secure Gilbert's approval. In 1948 two of the best-loved songs in the opera, Ko-Ko's 'I've got a little list' and the Mikado's 'My object all sublime', had to be altered when it was found that the word 'nigger' caused offence to American audiences.

The Mikado has been more widely translated than any other Gilbert and Sullivan Opera and rapidly established itself on the Continent. By 1900 it had been performed in German, Hungarian, French, Russian, Swedish, Croatian, Danish and Italian. A jazz version performed in Berlin in 1927 had Nanki-Poo doing the Charleston in Oxford bags and double-breasted blazer and Yum-Yum singing 'The sun whose rays' while sitting naked in the bath. One of the more bizarre shows at the 1987 Glasgow Mayfest was a production of *El Mikado* in Catalan by a company from Barcelona who increased the number of little maids from three to five.

In the United States *The Mikado* was a hit from the outset. Richard D'Oyly Carte tried to beat the many pirate companies which were putting on unauthorized productions by secretly assembling a company and shipping it incognito on a Cunard liner from Liverpool to New York. It opened at the Fifth Avenue Theater on 19 August 1885. The opera became so popular that on one evening in 1886 there were said to have been 170 separate performances across the United States, no doubt including at least one in the city of Mikado, Michigan, which was named in that year. Richard D'Oyly Carte had five companies touring North America, four in Britain and another touring Continental Europe.

North America has subsequently produced some zany versions of the opera. An all-black cast presented *The Swing Mikado* in Chicago in 1938, while the following year *The Hot Mikado*, another all-black show, starred the tap-dancing Bill 'Bojangles' Robinson as a bowler-hatted Mikado. *The Hot Mikado* was revived in London in 1995, opening at the Queen's Theatre, Shaftesbury Avenue, on 18 May. In 1960 a complete performance was broadcast across the United States by the Bell Telephone Company. The cast included Groucho Marx as Ko-Ko and Stanley Holloway as Pooh-Bah. Two years later a film entitled *The Cool Mikado*, featuring Frankie Howerd as Ko-Ko and Stubby Kaye as the Mikado, transferred the location of the opera to an aeroplane leaving Tokyo.

Nanki-Poo became Hank Mikado, son of the Chief Justice of Illinois, who had enlisted for military service in Japan to escape from the girl his father wanted him to marry and had fallen for Yum-Yum, a student at the Tokyo Art School whom he met in a coffee bar.

Some idea of the enormous popularity of *The Mikado* can be gauged from the number of recordings that have been made of its 'hit' tunes. The BBC record library has no less than forty-five different versions of 'A Wandering Minstrel' in its catalogue – I know because I counted them while I was compiling material for a Radio 4 programme on the centenary of the opera in 1985. The artistes range from Webster Booth with the Hallé Orchestra to John Boulter with the Black and White Minstrels. Other unexpected delights that I unearthed include 'Tit willow' rendered by the Muppets, Nelson Eddy singing 'My object all sublime' and 'Three little maids' turned into a duet by Dr Evadne Hinge and Dame Hilda Brackett!

1 *Scene*: Having decided to set his new opera in Japan, Gilbert told a reporter of the *New York Tribune* in 1885:

> the next thing was to decide upon two scenes, which should be characteristic and effective. The respective advantages of a street in Nagasaki, a Japanese market-place, a wharf with shipping, a Japanese garden, a seaside beach, and the courtyard of a Japanese palace were duly weighed; and the courtyard and the Japanese garden were finally decided upon.

3–16 *If you want to know who we are*
Considerable care was taken by both Gilbert and Sullivan to give their opening chorus an authentic Japanese atmosphere. The nobles were clad in splendid printed silk robes based on original oriental designs, and they were schooled in traditional Japanese movements and gestures. The opening vocal phrases of the chorus are confined to the pentatonic scale, a scale of five notes without semitones on which oriental music was traditionally based.

Sullivan's autograph score has a different version of the second verse:

> Polite etiquette demands,
>   That persons of either sex,
> Shall suffer cramp in the hand
>   And a crick in their outstretched necks.
>   When suffering from constraint,
>   We're always allowed to faint,
>   You're wrong if you think we mayn't, oh!

18 *obi*: A brightly coloured sash worn, like a cummerbund, round the waist, but usually by Japanese women and children rather than men. In most editions of the libretto, this stage direction has been changed to '*in his hand*'.

ACT I

SCENE. – *Courtyard of* Ko-Ko's *Palace in Titipu. Japanese nobles discovered standing and sitting in attitudes suggested by native drawings.*

CHORUS OF NOBLES.

If you want to know who we are,
    We are gentlemen of Japan:
On many a vase and jar –   5
    On many a screen and fan,
      We figure in lively paint:
      Our attitude's queer and quaint –
      You're wrong if you think it ain't, oh!

If you think we are worked by strings,   10
    Like a Japanese marionette,
You don't understand these things:
    It is simply Court etiquette.
      Perhaps you suppose this throng
      Can't keep it up all day long?   15
      If that's your idea, you're wrong, oh!

(*Enter* NANKI-POO *in great excitement. He carries a native guitar on his back and a bundle of ballads in his obi.*)

RECITATIVE – NANKI-POO.

Gentlemen, I pray you tell me
Where a gentle maiden dwelleth,   20
Named Yum-Yum, the ward of Ko-Ko?
In pity speak – oh, speak, I pray you!

A NOBLE.   Why, who are you who ask this question?

25–72   *A wandering minstrel I*
With its double change of mood from romantic ballad to rousing martial tune to rollicking sea shanty, this is one of the best-known and best-loved of all Gilbert and Sullivan's songs. Its first line was used by Sir Henry Lytton, a member of the D'Oyly Carte Opera Company for almost forty-nine years, as the title of his autobiography. It could equally well apply to the company as a whole, faithful guardian of the Savoy Opera tradition for more than a century until its sad demise at the beginning of 1982. From the very start the D'Oyly Carte was first and foremost a touring company, on the road for thirty-five weeks a year and taking the works of Gilbert and Sullivan to towns as far apart as Inverness and Torquay. It was, indeed, this wandering minstrel existence, unique in British theatrical or musical life, which ultimately led to the company's downfall. The high costs of touring proved impossible to meet from box-office revenue and, denied any public financial support in England, the D'Oyly Carte was forced to close. Oh, sorrow, sorrow!

35   *Oh, sorrow*: Gilbert originally wrote this line, and the subsequent lines 38 and 43, as 'Oh, willow'. They appear in that form in early editions of the libretto, but not in any vocal scores.

44   *if patriotic sentiment is wanted*: This phrase was used by Decca Records as the title for a long-playing record and cassette, now sadly deleted, featuring all the patriotic songs from the Savoy Operas, sung by members of the D'Oyly Carte Opera Company.

56   *a-trip*: Clear of mud and ready to be hauled aboard.
a-lee: Away from the wind. In other words, the helm has been placed to bring the rudder to leeward and to swing the ship's bow into the wind ready to make sail.

NANK.   Come gather round me, and I'll tell you.

SONG AND CHORUS – NANKI-POO.

A wandering minstrel I –   25
    A thing of shreds and patches,
    Of ballads, songs and snatches,
And dreamy lullaby!

My catalogue is long,
    Through every passion ranging,   30
    And to your humours changing
I tune my supple song!

    Are you in sentimental mood?
      I'll sigh with you,
        Oh, sorrow,   35
    On maiden's coldness do you brood?
      I'll do so, too –
        Oh, sorrow, sorrow!
    I'll charm your willing ears
    With songs of lovers' fears,
    While sympathetic tears   40
      My cheeks bedew –
        Oh, sorrow, sorrow!

But if patriotic sentiment is wanted,
    I've patriotic ballads cut and dried;
For where'er our country's banner may be planted,   45
    All other local banners are defied!
Our warriors, in serried ranks assembled,
    Never quail – or they conceal it if they do –
And I shouldn't be surprised if nations trembled   50
    Before the mighty troops of Titipu!

CHORUS.   We shouldn't be surprised, etc.

NANK.   And if you call for a song of the sea,
    We'll heave the capstan round,
With a yeo heave ho, for the wind is free,   55
Her anchor's a-trip and her helm's a-lee,
    Hurrah for the homeward bound!

CHORUS.   Yeo-ho – heave-ho –
    Hurrah for the homeward bound!

60 *lay aloft*: Climb into the rigging to raise or lower sails.

70 *rumbelow*: A meaningless combination of syllables or words, like 'yeo heave ho', used as a
    refrain by sailors when rowing or performing some other routine and rhythmical task.
    In some editions of the libretto the phrase is altered to 'a rum below'.

73 *Enter Pish-Tush*: Gilbert had first invented the names he was to give to two of his noble
    lords in *The Mikado* in his Bab Ballad 'King Borria Bungalee Boo', which first appeared
    in the magazine *Fun* in July 1886:

> There was haughty PISH-TUSH-POOH-BAH,
> There was lumbering DOODLE-DUM-DEH . . .

For the opera, of course, the name was split and Pish-Tush and Pooh-Bah are separate
characters.

78 *Ko-Ko*: Apart from the Emperor himself, Ko-Ko is the only one of the characters in *The
    Mikado* to have a real Japanese name. According to a Japanese-speaking friend of mine,
    the word Ko-Ko has no fewer than thirty-seven different meanings, depending on how
    it is pronounced. As pronounced in *The Mikado* (i.e. with the vowels long so that it
    sounds like 'cocoa'), it can mean pickles, filial piety, succeeding clause, grammar school,
    navigation, mineshaft or pithead, estuary, prince and marquess, month, trussed girder,
    bright, or so-and-so. Perhaps the first and last terms are most appropriate for the cheap
    tailor turned Lord High Executioner.

86-133 *Our great Mikado, virtuous man*
    This song, with its mockery of the Mikado of Japan and the practices of his country, was
    no doubt one which the British Government felt would cause offence to Crown Prince
    Fushimi and which led to the ban on all performances of *The Mikado* around the time of
    his state visit in 1907 (see page 554). Although most people felt that the ban was ridicu-
    lous, a small minority agreed that the opera was offensive to the Japanese. Mr Joseph
    Longford, who had been British consul in Japan for thirty-three years, wrote to *The
    Times* calling for a permanent ban on the grounds that 'the production of *The Mikado*
    was from the first an insult to the most sacred sentiments of the Japanese, galling and
    humiliating in every way'.

    Lord de Saumarez, a former secretary to the British legation in Tokyo, argued in si-
    milar terms, maintaining that 'the very name given to this play is most offensive to the
    feelings of every Japanese, whatever disclaimer any individual Japanese, actuated by the
    national somewhat exaggerated politeness, may verbally make when assailed by an inter-
    ested interviewer'. He went on to point out that in Japan the Mikado was invested with
    a religious character, and he asked what the feelings of Roman Catholics would be if a
    comic opera entitled 'The Pope of Rome' was put on the stage, 'and the sacred office of
    the Pope were made the subject of burlesque'.

To lay aloft in a howling breeze 60
  May tickle a landsman's taste,
But the happiest hour a sailor sees
  Is when he's down
  At an inland town,
With his Nancy on his knees, yeo-ho! 65
And his arm around her waist!

CHORUS.   Then man the capstan – off we go,
  As the fiddler swings us round,
With a yeo heave ho,
And a rumbelow, 70
  Hurrah for the homeward bound!

A wandering minstrel I, etc.

(*Enter* PISH-TUSH.)

PISH. And what may be your business with Yum-Yum?
NANK. I'll tell you. A year ago I was a member of the Titipu town 75
band. It was my duty to take the cap round for contributions. While
discharging this delicate office, I saw Yum-Yum. We loved each other at
once, but she was betrothed to her guardian Ko-Ko, a cheap tailor, and I saw
that my suit was hopeless. Overwhelmed with despair, I quitted the town.
Judge of my delight when I heard, a month ago, that Ko-Ko had been 80
condemned to death for flirting! I hurried back at once, in the hope of finding
Yum-Yum at liberty to listen to my protestations.
PISH. It is true that Ko-Ko was condemned to death for flirting, but he
was reprieved at the last moment, and raised to the exalted rank of Lord
High Executioner under the following remarkable circumstances: 85

SONG – PISH-TUSH *and* CHORUS.

Our great Mikado, virtuous man,
When he to rule our land began,
  Resolved to try
  A plan whereby
  Young men might best be steadied. 90
So he decreed, in words succinct,
That all who flirted, leered or winked
(Unless connubially linked),
  Should forthwith be beheaded.
And I expect you'll all agree 95

108   *non-connubial*: Not directed to a married partner, out of wedlock (from the Latin word *connubium*, meaning 'marriage').

124   *decapited*: The word is, of course, 'decapitated' but Gilbert shortened it for the purposes of scansion.

That he was right to so decree.
                And I am right,
                And you are right,
            And all is right as right can be!

CHORUS.   And you are right,   100
                           And we are right, etc.

This stern decree, you'll understand,
Caused great dismay throughout the land!
                For young and old
                And shy and bold   105
            Were equally affected.
The youth who winked a roving eye,
Or breathed a non-connubial sigh,
Was thereupon condemned to die –
                He usually objected.   110

            And you'll allow, as I expect,
            That he was right to so object.
                And I am right,
                And you are right,
            And everything is quite correct!   115

CHORUS.   And you are right,
                           And we are right, etc.

And so we straight let out on bail
A convict from the county jail,
                Whose head was next   120
                On some pretext
            Condemnëd to be mown off,
And made *him* Headsman, for we said,
'Who's next to be decapited
Cannot cut off another's head   125
            Until he's cut his own off.'

            And we are right, I think you'll say,
            To argue in this kind of way;
                And I am right,
                And you are right,   130
            And all is right – too-looral-lay!

135 *Enter Pooh-Bah*: In an article written at the time of the 1907 ban, G. K. Chesterton de-
     scribed Pooh-Bah as 'the great creation' of *The Mikado*. He went on to argue that this
     character above all others showed that the play was a satire on the English rather than
     the Japanese. Pluralism, he wrote, was not specially a vice of the East, yet

> about England Pooh-Bah is something more than a satire; he is the truth. It is true of Brit-
> ish politics (probably not of Japanese) that we meet the same man twenty times as twenty
> different officials. There is a quarrel between a landlord, Lord Jones, and a railway company
> presided over by Lord Smith. Strong comments are made on the case by a newspaper
> (owned by Lord Brown), and after infinite litigation, it is sent up to the House of Lords,
> that is, Lords Jones, Smith, and Brown. Generally the characters are more mixed. The land-
> lord cannot live by land, but does live as director of the railway. The railway lord is so rich
> that he buys up the newspaper. The general result can be expressed only in the two syllables
> (to be uttered with the utmost energy of the lungs): Pooh-Bah.

145 *of pre-Adamite ancestral descent*: As well as making Pooh-Bah the archetypal pluralist and
     corrupt official, Gilbert also uses him to poke some fun at the controversy over the the-
     ory of evolution which raged so passionately in the latter half of the nineteenth century
     following the publication of Charles Darwin's *Origin of Species*. Accepting Darwin's theo-
     ry that man did not appear fully formed on earth, as the Bible says, but rather derived
     originally from 'a protoplasmal primordial atomic globule', Gilbert turns it with charac-
     teristic wit and skill into a source of great pride to Pooh-Bah, neatly reversing the anti-
     evolutionists' cry that such a descent greatly demeaned the dignity of man.

153–6 *as First Lord of the Treasury . . .*: It has been suggested that Gilbert got the idea for Pooh-
     Bah from the Victorian humorist and dramatist James Robinson Planché, whose play
     The Sleeping Beauty (1840) included the following lines for the Lord Factotum:

> As Lord High Chamberlain, I slumber never;
> As Lord High Steward, in a stew I'm ever;
> As Lord High Constable, I watch all day;
> As Lord High Treasurer, I've the deuce to pay;
> As Great Grand Cup-bearer, I'm handled queerly,
> As Great Grand Carver, I'm cut up severely.
> In other states, the honours are divided,
> But here, they're one and all to me confided.

161 *I dance at cheap suburban parties*: Rutland Barrington, who created the role of Pooh-Bah,
     was an arch ad-libber and introduced into his performance numerous gags which Gil-
     bert had not originally intended. After delivering this line, for example, he gave a brief
     display of a dancing Pooh-Bah. A pencilled note in Helen D'Oyly Carte's copy of the
     libretto records: 'This was not objected to by the author'.

165 *Another insult, and, I think, a light one*: Another of Barrington's gags came at this point. He
     turned to Pish-Tush and asked 'Do you want it?' This one, however, was not approved
     by Gilbert.

CHORUS.   And you are right,
                    And we are right, etc.

                                        (*Exeunt* CHORUS.)

        (*Enter* POOH-BAH.)   135

NANK. Ko-Ko, the cheap tailor, Lord High Executioner of Titipu! Why, that's the highest rank a citizen can attain!

POOH. It is. Our logical Mikado, seeing no moral difference between the dignified judge who condemns a criminal to die, and the industrious mechanic who carries out the sentence, has rolled the two offices into one,   140 and every judge is now his own executioner.

NANK. But how good of you (for I see that you are a nobleman of the highest rank) to condescend to tell all this to me, a mere strolling minstrel!

POOH. Don't mention it. I am, in point of fact, a particularly haughty and exclusive person, of pre-Adamite ancestral descent. You will understand   145 this when I tell you that I can trace my ancestry back to a protoplasmal primordial atomic globule. Consequently, my family pride is something inconceivable. I can't help it. I was born sneering. But I struggle hard to overcome this defect. I mortify my pride continually. When all the great officers of State resigned in a body, because they were too proud to serve   150 under an ex-tailor, did I not unhesitatingly accept all their posts at once?

PISH. And the salaries attached to them? You did.

POOH. It is consequently my degrading duty to serve this upstart as First Lord of the Treasury, Lord Chief Justice, Commander-in-Chief, Lord High Admiral, Master of the Buckhounds, Groom of the Back Stairs,   155 Archbishop of Titipu, and Lord Mayor, both acting and elect, all rolled into one. And at a salary! A Pooh-Bah paid for his services! I a salaried minion! But I do it! It revolts me, but I do it!

NANK. And it does you credit.

POOH. But I don't stop at that. I go and dine with middle-class people   160 on reasonable terms. I dance at cheap suburban parties for a moderate fee. I accept refreshment at any hands, however lowly. I also retail State secrets at a very low figure. For instance, any further information about Yum-Yum would come under the head of a State secret. (NANKI-POO *takes the hint, and gives him money.*) (*Aside.*) Another insult, and, I think, a light one!   165

SONG – POOH-BAH *with* NANKI-POO *and* PISH-TUSH.

            Young man, despair,
                Likewise go to,
            Yum-Yum the fair
                You must not woo.
                It will not do: 170

172 *ablutioner*: Presumably one who performs the act of ablution, or washing. There is, in fact, no such word as 'ablutioner' in the dictionary, but what else – apart, of course, from 'diminutioner' – rhymes with 'executioner'?

185 *With the Lord High Executioner!*: Gilbert originally added another two lines to Poo-Bah's verse here:

> From what I say you may infer
> It's as good as a play for him and her.

They occur in the original libretto, but were apparently never used or set by Sullivan.

207 *The fact appears to be as you've recited*: This was the cue for another unauthorized gag introduced by Rutland Barrington. After 'you've recited' he added the line 'Good morning!', and at the end of the next line he turned to Nanki-Poo and asked 'Got any more money?', to which the reply from the wandering minstrel was 'No! Certainly not!'

I'm sorry for you,
You very imperfect ablutioner!
This very day
From school Yum-Yum
Will wend her way,   175
And homeward come,
With beat of drum
And a rum-tum-tum,
To wed the Lord High Executioner!
And the brass will crash,   180
And the trumpets bray,
And they'll cut a dash
On their wedding day.
She'll toddle away, as all aver,
With the Lord High Executioner!   185

NANK. *and* PISH. And the brass will crash, etc.
ALL.   She'll toddle away, etc.

It's a hopeless case,
As you may see,
And in your place   190
Away I'd flee;
But don't blame me –
I'm sorry to be
Of your pleasure a diminutioner.
They'll vow their pact   195
Extremely soon,
In point of fact
This afternoon.
Her honeymoon
With that buffoon   200
At seven commences, so *you* shun her!

NANK. *and* PISH. And the brass will crash, etc.
ALL.   She'll toddle away, etc.   (*Exit* PISH-TUSH.)

RECITATIVE – NANKI-POO *and* POOH-BAH.

NANK.   And I have journeyed for a month, or nearly,
To learn that Yum-Yum, whom I love so dearly,   205
This day to Ko-Ko is to be united!
POOH.   The fact appears to be as you've recited:
But here he comes, equipped as suits his station;
He'll give you any further information.

212–17 *Behold the Lord High Executioner*
         This chorus recalls the tune of the old English air 'A Fine Old English Gentleman'.
218 *Enter Ko-Ko attended*: When George Grossmith made his entrance as Ko-Ko on the
         opening night of *The Mikado* at the Savoy Theatre on 14 March 1885, he carried the Japa-
         nese executioner's sword which, at least according to popular legend, had fallen from
         the wall of Gilbert's study and inspired the writing of the opera. In subsequent produc-
         tions, Ko-Ko was attended by a sword-bearer. It was in that role that Sir Malcolm Sar-
         gent, the great British conductor, made his stage debut at the age of thirteen in a
         production of the Stamford Amateur Operatic Society in 1908. Sargent went on to have
         a life-long association with Gilbert and Sullivan, conducting the D'Oyly Carte Opera
         Company first in 1926 and last in 1964, three years before his death.
221 *bail*: Security given by or on behalf of an accused person, who would otherwise be kept in
         prison, that he or she will appear for trial at a particular place and time in return for
         being allowed free in the interim.
222 *recognizances*: Bond by which a person engages before a court or magistrate to observe
         some condition, such as paying a debt or keeping the peace.
234–8 *Gentlemen, I'm much touched by this reception*: In the first-night performance, Ko-Ko's 'little
         list' song came later in Act I (see the note to line 551). Ko-Ko's speech at this point did
         not contain the sentence beginning 'If I should ever be called upon' but instead went on
         to announce the imminent arrival of Yum-Yum, Pitti-Sing and Peep-Bo and then con-
         tinued with the words addressed to Pooh-Bah about the festivities in connection with
         the approaching marriage which now appear at line 276.
239–74 *As some day it may happen that a victim must be found*
         Ko-Ko's 'little list' song has almost certainly been altered more than any other number in
         the Savoy Operas. Gilbert originally wrote it to be sung much later in Act I, after the
         trio 'To sit in solemn silence', and it appears there in the licence copy sent to the Lord
         Chamberlain. For the opening performance it was moved slightly forward so that it
         came after Yum-Yum and Nanki-Poo's duet 'Were you not to Ko-Ko plighted'. However,
         after only a few performances it was moved again to its present position, with the words
         being considerably altered.
             Apart from these changes, Gilbert also made several alterations to the song during
         his lifetime, substituting various topical allusions for the phrase 'lady novelist' and add-
         ing a whole new verse in 1908. The practice of introducing up-to-date references has
         continued ever since, and in 1948 the D'Oyly Carte Opera Company felt obliged to
         make a change to the wording of the second verse for reasons of taste (see the note to
         line 251).
             As originally written, when it was conceived that Ko-Ko would sing the song after re-
         ceiving word from the Mikado that he must carry out an execution within a month, the
         first verse began:

> As it seems to be essential that a victim must be found,
>   I've got a little list – I've got a little list
> Of social offenders who might well be underground,
>   And who never would be missed – who never would be missed!

That version was sung by George Grossmith on the opening night but was changed
soon after to the present opening when the song was moved.
    The licence copy contains an early version of the rest of the first verse which also ap-
pears in the full score published in Leipzig in 1898:

> There's the Income Tax Commissioners with all their prying clerks,
> And vulgar little streetboys who are rude in their remarks,
> All persons with presentiments, a very wholesome rule,
> And next-door neighbours everywhere, and boys at home from school,
> All men who bite their nails, all people who revoke at whist.

(*Exeunt* POOH-BAH *and* NANKI-POO.) 210

(*Enter* CHORUS OF NOBLES.)

Behold the Lord High Executioner!
  A personage of noble rank and title –
A dignified and potent officer,
  Whose functions are particularly vital! 215
    Defer, defer,
  To the Lord High Executioner!

(*Enter* KO-KO *attended.*)

SOLO – KO-KO.

Taken from the county jail
  By a set of curious chances; 220
Liberated then on bail,
  On my own recognizances;
Wafted by a favouring gale
  As one sometimes is in trances,
To a height that few can scale, 225
  Save by long and weary dances;
Surely, never had a male
  Under such-like circumstances
So adventurous a tale,
  Which may rank with most romances. 230

CHORUS.   Taken from the county jail, etc.
        Defer, defer,
      To the Lord High Executioner, etc.

KO. Gentlemen, I'm much touched by this reception. I can only trust
that by strict attention to duty I shall ensure a continuance of those favours 235
which it will ever be my study to deserve. If I should ever be called upon to
act professionally, I am happy to think that there will be no difficulty in
finding plenty of people whose loss will be a distinct gain to society at large.

SONG – KO-KO *with* CHORUS OF MEN.

As some day it may happen that a victim must be found,
  I've got a little list – I've got a little list 240
Of society offenders who might well be underground,
  And who never would be missed – who never would be missed!
There's the pestilential nuisances who write for autographs –

251 *the banjo serenader*: Until 1948 the phrase always sung at this point was 'the nigger serena-
     der'. The word 'nigger' also occurred in the Mikado's song 'My object all sublime' (see
     the note to Act II, line 358). In a letter to *The Times* on 28 May of that year Rupert D'Oyly
     Carte wrote:

> We found recently in America that much objection was taken by coloured persons to a
> word used twice in *The Mikado*, a word which I will not quote but which your readers may
> easily guess. Many protests and letters were received, and we consulted the witty writer on
> whose shoulders the lyrical mantle of Gilbert may be said to have fallen. He made several
> suggestions, one of which we adopted in America, and it seems well to continue doing so in
> the British Empire. Gilbert would surely have approved, and the alteration will be heard
> during our season at Sadler's Wells.

     The witty writer mentioned by Carte was the late A. P. Herbert and it was he who
     came up with the substitute 'banjo serenader', which has been used ever since and now
     appears in all libretti and vocal scores.

252 *the piano-organist*: Piano organs were similar to barrel organs, played in the streets often
     by men accompanied by monkeys.

258 *doesn't think she dances*: This was originally written as 'doesn't think she waltzes'. As far as I
     can discover, it was changed to 'dances' in 1923, presumably on the grounds that even la-
     dies from the provinces were no longer waltzing. The Macmillan edition of the libretto
     still has 'waltzes', but both the Chappell libretto and the 1963 Oxford University Press
     edition of the operas prepared by Dame Bridget D'Oyly Carte have 'dances'.

259 *the lady novelist*: Even within Gilbert's lifetime there ceased to be anything either singular
     or anomalous about the lady novelist (if indeed there ever had been), and for Edwardian
     revivals he variously substituted 'the critic dramatist', 'the scorching bicyclist' and 'the
     scorching motorist'. Throughout the 1920s and the early 1930s Sir Henry Lytton sang of
     'that singular anomaly, the prohibitionist', while in 1942 it became 'the clothing ration-
     ist'.

263 *Nisi Prius*: A Latin term literally meaning 'unless before' and formerly used in law for
     civil actions heard in local assize courts when they should technically have been heard
     in London. Such actions were entered for hearing at the Royal Courts of Justice 'unless
     heard before'. Assize judges were known as '*nisi prius*' judges, and it is to the humorous
     qualities of these individuals that Ko-Ko is presumably referring in the next line.

264 *The Judicial humorist*: This somewhat obscure category has been replaced by rather more
     topical ones in recent D'Oyly Carte performances. In the 1950s Peter Pratt sang of 'The
     televisionist', and in 1975, when Britain's future membership of the E.E.C. was being
     decided by referendum, John Reed referred to 'the referendumist'. On the opening day
     of the 1980 Olympic Games James Conroy-Ward sang of 'The Olympic boycott-ist'.

267 *apologetic statesmen*: For the 1908 revival Gilbert changed this to 'Little England states-
     men', showing his own sympathies in the contemporary political debate between
     Imperialists and 'Little Englanders'.
     Several well-known politicians have found themselves caricatured over the years

All people who have flabby hands and irritating laughs –
All children who are up in dates, and floor you with 'em flat –   245
All persons who in shaking hands, shake hands with you like *that* –
And all third persons who on spoiling *tête-à- têtes* insist –
   They'd none of 'em be missed – they'd none of 'em be missed!

CHORUS.   He's got 'em on the list – he's got 'em on the list;
         And they'll none of 'em be missed – they'll none of 'em
           be missed.   250

There's the banjo serenader, and the others of his race,
   And the piano-organist – I've got him on the list!
And the people who eat peppermint and puff it in your face,
   They never would be missed – they never would be missed!
Then the idiot who praises, with enthusiastic tone,   255
All centuries but this, and every country but his own;
And the lady from the provinces, who dresses like a guy,
And who 'doesn't think she dances, but would rather like to try';
And that singular anomaly, the lady novelist –
   I don't think she'd be missed – I'm *sure* she'd not be missed!   260

CHORUS.   He's got her on the list – he's got her on the list;
         And I don't think she'll be missed – I'm *sure* she'll not
          be missed!

And that *Nisi Prius* nuisance, who just now is rather rife,
   The Judicial humorist – I've got *him* on the list!
All funny fellows, comic men, and clowns of private life –   265
   They'd none of 'em be missed – they'd none of 'em be missed.
And apologetic statesmen of a compromising kind,
Such as – What d'ye call him – Thing'em-bob, and likewise – Never-mind,
And 'St – 'st – 'st – and What's-his-name, and also You-know-who –
The task of filling up the blanks I'd rather leave to *you*.   270
But it really doesn't matter whom you put upon the list,
   For they'd none of 'em be missed – they'd none of 'em be missed!

CHORUS.   You may put 'em on the list – you may put 'em on the list;
         And they'll none of 'em be missed – they'll none of 'em
          be missed!   (*Exeunt* CHORUS.)

(*Enter* POOH-BAH.)   275

KO. Pooh-Bah, it seems that the festivities in connection with my
approaching marriage must last a week. I should like to do it handsomely,
and I want to consult you as to the amount I ought to spend upon them.

during the singing of this last part of Ko-Ko's song. George Grossmith helped the first-night audience in their task of filling up the blanks by successively donning the large collars always worn by Mr Gladstone, beards similar to those worn by Lord Salisbury and the Marquess of Hartington, and the monocle and floral button-hole that were the trade-mark of Joseph Chamberlain. Subsequent Ko-Kos have imitated the golf stroke of David Lloyd George, the pipe-lighting of Stanley Baldwin, and the distinctive shoulder-hunching laugh of Edward Heath.

In 1908 Gilbert wrote an extra verse of the 'little list' to be used as an encore:

> That well-intentioned lady who's too bulky for her boots,
> The lovely suffragist – I've got her on the list.
> That single-minded patriot, who doesn't bank with Coutts,
> The red hot Socialist – I don't think he'd be missed.
> All those who hold that publicans it's virtuous to fleece,
> And impose a heavy war tax in these piping times of peace,
> And preach the code that moralists like Robin Hood held true,
> That to benefit the pauper you must rob the well-to-do,
> That peculiar variety of sham philanthropist,
> I don't think he'd be missed, I'm sure he'd not be missed.

A year later Gilbert produced yet more verses for a special children's version of the opera:

> There's the nursemaid who each evening in curlpapers does your hair,
> With an aggravating twist – *she* never would be missed –
> And tells you that you mustn't cough or sneeze or yawn or stare,
> She never would be missed – I'm sure she'd not be missed.
> All those who hold that children shouldn't have too much to eat,
> And think cold suet pudding a delicious birthday treat,
> Who say that little girls to bed at seven should be sent,
> And consider pocket-money isn't given to be spent,
> And doctors who on giving you unpleasant draughts insist –
> They never would be missed – they'd none of them be missed.

> Then the teacher who for hours keeps you practising your scales,
> With an ever-aching wrist – she never would be missed.
> And children, too, who out of school are fond of telling tales,
> They never would be missed – I'm sure they'd not be missed.
> All people who maintain (in solemn earnest – not in joke)
> That quantities of sugar-plums are bad for little folk,
> And those who hold the principle, unalterably fixed,
> That instruction with amusement should most carefully be mixed;
> All these (and many others) I have placed upon the list,
> For they never would be missed – never, never would be missed.

312 *they wouldn't be sufficiently degraded*: Gilbert originally wrote this and the next line in the first person, but Rutland Barrington changed it to the third, and there it has remained ever since.

317 *No money – no grovel*: Another of Barrington's gags. Gilbert refused to authorize it, but it has nonetheless passed into general use and is to be found in both the current Chappell libretto and the 1963 Oxford University Press edition, although not in the Macmillan version. A handwritten note in Helen D'Oyly Carte's copy of the 1908 libretto suggests that the gag was originally much longer and went as follows (after Ko-Ko's 'would be esteemed a favour'):

> POOH. Grovels is an extra.
> KO. Throw in a grovel, Pooh-Bah.
> POOH. No money, no grovel.
> KO. You will be grossly insulted as usual.

POOH. Certainly. In which of my capacities? As First Lord of the Treasury,
Lord Chamberlain, Attorney-General, Chancellor of the Exchequer, Privy   280
Purse, or Private Secretary?

KO. Suppose we say as Private Secretary.

POOH. Speaking as your Private Secretary, I should say that, as the city
will have to pay for it, don't stint yourself, do it well.

KO. Exactly – as the city will have to pay for it. That is your advice.   285

POOH. As Private Secretary. Of course you will understand that, as
Chancellor of the Exchequer, I am bound to see that due economy is
observed.

KO. Oh! But you said just now 'Don't stint yourself, do it well'.

POOH. As Private Secretary.   290

KO. And now you say that due economy must be observed.

POOH. As Chancellor of the Exchequer.

KO. I see. Come over here, where the Chancellor can't hear us. (*They
cross the stage.*) Now, as my Solicitor, how do you advise me to deal with this
difficulty?   295

POOH. Oh, as your Solicitor, I should have no hesitation in saying
'Chance it —'

KO. Thank you. (*Shaking his hand.*) I will.

POOH. If it were not that, as Lord Chief Justice, I am bound to see that
the law isn't violated.   300

KO. I see. Come over here where the Chief Justice can't hear us. (*They
cross the stage.*) Now, then, as First Lord of the Treasury?

POOH. Of course, as First Lord of the Treasury, I could propose a
special vote that would cover all expenses, if it were not that, as Leader of
the Opposition, it would be my duty to resist it, tooth and nail. Or, as   305
Paymaster-General, I could so cook the accounts that, as Lord High Auditor,
I should never discover the fraud. But then, as Archbishop of Titipu, it
would be my duty to denounce my dishonesty and give myself into my own
custody as First Commissioner of Police.

KO. That's extremely awkward.   310

POOH. I don't say that all these distinguished people couldn't be squared;
but it is right to tell you that they wouldn't be sufficiently degraded in their
own estimation unless they were insulted with a very considerable bribe.

KO. The matter shall have my careful consideration. But my bride and her
sisters approach, and any little compliment on your part, such as an abject   315
grovel in a characteristic Japanese attitude, would be esteemed a favour.

POOH. No money – no grovel!

(*Exeunt together.*)

(*Enter procession of* YUM-YUM's *schoolfellows, heralding* YUM-YUM,
PEEP-BO, *and* PITTI-SING.)   320

321–36 *Comes a train of little ladies*
For the opening performance at the Savoy, the female chorus was splendidly attired in Japanese silk kimonos made specially by Liberty's, the Regent Street fashion house. There was a certain amount of consternation when it was discovered that Japanese women did not wear petticoats. In the interests of modesty, and of warmth, the D'Oyly Carte ladies wore special 'combinations' of chamois leather and thin silk.

Gilbert had taken great pains to school both the male and female chorus in the niceties of Japanese etiquette. The girls came on with short, shuffling steps and fluttered their fans with a precision that would have delighted a regimental sergeant-major. The magazine *Moonshine* commented in its review of the first night: 'Society will discover a new source of entertainment after witnessing the fan operations. There will be "fan drill" at boarding schools. Present fans! unfurl fans! flutter fans! recover fans!'

333 *eighteen and under*: In an interesting article in the January 1978 issue of *The Savoyard*, Stephen J. Baston pointed out that in the autograph vocal score this phrase appeared as 'sixteen and under' and suggested that this was Gilbert's original intention. Certainly, that would seem to square with Nanki-Poo's later comment (lines 469–70) that in Japan 'from seventeen to forty-nine are considered years of indiscretion', which seems to suggest that the school-leaving age and the age of Yum-Yum are both sixteen.

337–60 *Three little maids from school are we*
This has always been a show-stopper. Rutland Barrington noted after the first night that it 'was received with such enthusiasm and insistent encores as no musical number in my experience, or I believe anyone else's, has ever equalled'. The song achieved wide exposure in the 1981 award-winning British film *Chariots of Fire* about the 1924 Olympic gold medallist Harold Abrahams. In the film, Abrahams marries Sybil Gordon, principal soprano with the D'Oyly Carte Opera Company in the 1920s, whom he first sees when she is playing the part of Yum-Yum at the Savoy Theatre. The film has a scene in which Alice Krige, playing the part of Sybil Gordon, sings 'Three little maids' with Lorraine Daniels and Roberta Morrell of the D'Oyly Carte Company. Unfortunately, *Chariots of Fire* is inaccurate on this point – it was not Sybil Gordon whom Abrahams married in real life but rather Sybil Evers, who was a minor soprano with the D'Oyly Carte from March 1930 to September 1931 and who never played Yum-Yum, except possibly as an understudy. Still, it makes a more romantic story the way the film tells it.

'Three little maids' was one of the first of the songs in *The Mikado* which Sullivan set to music. He composed it on 21 December 1884. The bassoon 'gurgle' which follows the line 'Freed from its genius tutelary' was added much later, possibly at a rehearsal in 1895.

To coach the three little maids in their movements, Gilbert hired a geisha girl from the Japanese village in Knightsbridge. She was responsible for getting Yum-Yum, Peep-Bo and Pitti-Sing to giggle in an appropriately Japanese way and to use their fans properly. The tutor became known as 'the sixpence girl' since her only two words of English were 'sixpence, please', the price of a cup of tea at the village.

346 *a ladies' seminary*: This phrase also occurs in *Iolanthe*, when the Lord Chancellor mistakes the Fairy Queen for the proprietor of a ladies' seminary.

347 *tutelary*: Having the status of protector or guardian.

CHORUS OF GIRLS.

Comes a train of little ladies
    From scholastic trammels free,
Each a little bit afraid is,
    Wondering what the world can be!

Is it but a world of trouble –   325
    Sadness set to song?
Is its beauty but a bubble
    Bound to break ere long?

Are its palaces and pleasures
    Fantasies that fade?   330
And the glory of its treasures
    Shadow of a shade?

Schoolgirls we, eighteen and under,
    From scholastic trammels free,
And we wonder – how we wonder! –   335
    What on earth the world can be!

TRIO.

YUM-YUM, PEEP-BO, *and* PITTI-SING, *with* CHORUS OF GIRLS.

THE THREE.	Three little maids from school are we,
	Pert as a school-girl well can be
	Filled to the brim with girlish glee,
	Three little maids from school! 340
YUM-YUM.	Everything is a source of fun. (*Chuckle.*)
PEEP-BO.	Nobody's safe, for we care for none! (*Chuckle.*)
PITTI-SING.	Life is a joke that's just begun! (*Chuckle.*)
THE THREE.	Three little maids from school!
ALL (*dancing*).	Three little maids who, all unwary, 345
	Come from a ladies' seminary,
	Freed from its genius tutelary –
THE THREE (*suddenly demure*).	Three little maids from school!

YUM-YUM.	One little maid is a bride, Yum-Yum –
PEEP-BO.	Two little maids in attendance come – 350
PITTI-SING.	Three little maids is the total sum.
THE THREE.	Three little maids from school!
YUM-YUM.	From three little maids take one away.
PEEP-BO.	Two little maids remain, and they –

363 *You're not going to kiss me before all these people*: In 1907 Gilbert agreed to an ad-lib which had been introduced at this point, once again probably at the instigation of Rutland Barrington. Ko-Ko replied to Yum-Yum 'Well, I'm certainly not going to kiss you after them'. This line was dropped again in 1914.

370 *Eh, Lord Chamberlain*: For the 1908 revival, this line was changed to 'Eh, Licenser of Plays?' and Pooh-Bah's reply became 'I have known it done. I have not blue-pencilled it yet.' These additions appear in Helen D'Oyly Carte's copy of the 1908 libretto, which was approved by Gilbert, but they were dropped again in 1914.

376–84 *Oh, I'm so glad . . .*: In the licence copy submitted by Gilbert to the Lord Chamberlain before the first performance, the speeches delivered simultaneously at this point are longer than in the final version:

> YUM. Oh, I'm so glad! I haven't seen you for ever so long, and you can't imagine how often I've thought of you, and it is nice to come upon you in this unexpected way, and I'm right at the top of the school, etc.
> PEEP. And how have you been and have you got an engagement? Yum-Yum's got one, but she don't like it at all, it's to old Ko-Ko, and she's going to be married to him, and I think she'd ever so much rather it was you, and I expect I shall be married soon. I've come home for good, etc.
> PITTI. Now tell us all the news, because you go about everywhere and we've been shut up in a stupid old school, learning ridiculous lessons that will never be the least use to us afterwards, but thank goodness, etc.

393 *On the Marine Parade*: Little can Gilbert have realized when he wrote this line how apt it was to be and how many bandstands on real marine parades and coastal promenades would be echoing to the strains of *The Mikado* for a century and more to come.

PITTI-SING.	Won't have to wait very long, they say –	355
THE THREE.	Three little maids from school!	
ALL (*dancing*).	Three little maids who, all unwary,	
	Come from a ladies' seminary,	
	Freed from its genius tutelary –	
THE THREE (*suddenly demure*).	Three little maids from school!	360

(*Enter* KO-KO *and* POOH-BAH.)

KO. At last, my bride that is to be! (*About to embrace her.*)

YUM. You're not going to kiss me before all these people?

KO. Well, that was the idea.

YUM. (*aside to* PEEP-BO). It seems odd, doesn't it? 365

PEEP. It's rather peculiar.

PITTI. Oh, I expect it's all right. Must have a beginning, you know.

YUM. Well, of course I know nothing about these things; but I've no objection if it's usual.

KO. Oh, it's quite usual, I think. Eh, Lord Chamberlain? (*Appealing to* 370 POOH-BAH.)

POOH. I have known it done. (KO-KO *embraces her.*)

YUM. Thank goodness that's over! (*Sees* NANKI-POO, *and rushes to him.*) Why, that's never you? (*The Three Girls rush to him and shake his hands, all speaking at once.*) 375

⎧ YUM. Oh, I'm so glad! I haven't seen you for ever so long, and I'm right at the top of the school, and I've got three prizes, and I've come home for good, and I'm not going back any more!

PEEP. And have you got an engagement? – Yum-Yum's got one, but she doesn't like it, and she'd ever so much rather it was you! I've come 380 home for good, and I'm not going back any more!

PITTI. Now tell us all the news, because you go about everywhere, and we've been at school, but, thank goodness, that's all over now, and ⎩ we've come home for good, and we're not going back any more!

(*These three speeches are spoken together in one breath.*) 385

KO. I beg your pardon. Will you present me?

YUM. ⎧ Oh, this is the musician who used –
PEEP. ⎨ Oh, this is the gentleman who used –
PITTI. ⎩ Oh, it is only Nanki-Poo who used –

KO. One at a time, if you please. 390

YUM. Oh, if you please he's the gentleman who used to play so beautifully on the – on the —

PITTI. On the Marine Parade.

YUM. Yes, I think that was the name of the instrument.

403 *That is a Tremendous Swell*: The *Oxford English Dictionary* defines 'swell' in its colloquial sense as 'a fashionably or stylishly dressed person; hence, a person of good social position, a highly distinguished person'. It is in that latter sense that Ko-Ko applies the term to Pooh-Bah, although he is probably rather cheekily thinking also of the more usual meaning of 'swell' as 'the condition of being swollen, distended, or increased in bulk'. Pooh-Bah is always played as a large gentleman, and even some of the more well-endowed bass-baritones in the D'Oyly Carte Company have had to be padded out with cushions to produce the desired effect. The word 'swell' also occurs in Gilbert and Sullivan's last joint work, *The Grand Duke*, when Ben Hashbaz, a costumier, says 'Oh, he's a swell – he's the Duke of Riviera!'

404 *Oh, it's alive*: This line was added, with Gilbert's approval, early on in the original run. Helen D'Oyly Carte's copy of the libretto has the stage note at this point: 'Pitti-Sing prods Pooh-Bah with fan, he flicks his fan'.

422 *he can't help it*: Another line added for the 1908 revival, as was a subsequent line, later cut, for the three little maids: 'Poor fellow', which followed 'he's under treatment for it'.

NANK. Sir, I have the misfortune to love your ward, Yum-Yum – oh, I   395
know I deserve your anger!

KO. Anger! not a bit, my boy. Why, I love her myself. Charming little
girl, isn't she? Pretty eyes, nice hair. Taking little thing, altogether. Very glad
to hear my opinion backed by a competent authority. Thank you very much.
Good-bye. (*To* PISH-TUSH.) Take him away. (PISH-TUSH *removes him.*)   400

PITTI. (*who has been examining* POOH-BAH). I beg your pardon, but
what is this? Customer come to try on?

KO. That is a Tremendous Swell.

PITTI. Oh, it's alive. (*She starts back in alarm.*)

POOH. Go away, little girls. Can't talk to little girls like you. Go away,   405
there's dears.

KO. Allow me to present you, Pooh-Bah. These are my three wards.
The one in the middle is my bride elect.

POOH. What do you want me to do to them? Mind, I *will not* kiss them.

KO. No, no, you shan't kiss them; a little bow – a mere nothing – you   410
needn't mean it, you know.

POOH. It goes against the grain. They are not young ladies, they are
young persons.

KO. Come, come, make an effort, there's a good nobleman.

POOH. (*aside to* KO-KO). Well, I shan't mean it. (*With a great effort.*)   415
How de do, little girls, how de do? (*Aside.*) Oh, my protoplasmal ancestor!

KO. That's very good. (*Girls indulge in suppressed laughter.*)

POOH. I see nothing to laugh at. It is very painful to me to have to say
'How de do, little girls, how de do?' to young persons. I'm not in the habit
of saying 'How de do, little girls, how de do?' to anybody under the rank of   420
a Stockbroker.

KO. (*aside to girls*). Don't laugh at him, he can't help it – he's under
treatment for it. (*Aside to* POOH-BAH.) Never mind them, they don't
understand the delicacy of your position.

POOH. We know how delicate it is, don't we?   425

KO. I should think we did! How a nobleman of your importance can do
it at all is a thing I never can, never shall understand.

(KO-KO *retires up and goes off.*)

QUARTET AND CHORUS OF GIRLS.

YUM-YUM, PEEP-BO, PITTI-SING, *and* POOH-BAH.

YUM., PEEP. *and* PITTI.	So please you, sir, we much regret If we have failed in etiquette 430 Towards a man of rank so high – We shall know better by and by.
YUM.	But youth, of course, must have its fling,

439 *If we're inclined to dance and sing*: In the licence copy and the early vocal scores this line ran
     'If we're designed to dance and sing' and in early editions of the libretto 'If we're disposed
     to dance and sing'. Here's a pretty mess!

455 *Exeunt all but Yum-Yum*: In the first-night performance, Yum-Yum sang 'The sun, whose
     rays' at this point, having first had the following soliloquy:

> YUM. How pitiable is the condition of a young and innocent child brought from the
> gloom of a ladies' academy into the full-blown blaze of her own marriage ceremony; and
> with a man for whom I care nothing! True, he loves me, but everybody does that.
> Sometimes I sit and wonder, etc.

Her speech continued as now in Act II, lines 26–30. 'The sun, whose rays', which then
followed, was moved to its present position in Act II only a few days into the first London
run.

463 *Modified rapture*: In the original libretto this line was simply 'Rapture!' At an early rehear-
     sal Gilbert had to check Durward Lely, the tenor playing the part of Nanki-Poo, for the
     vehemence with which he spoke the word. 'Modified rapture', Gilbert called from his
     seat in the stalls. 'Modified rapture', retorted the actor from the stage, and so it has re-
     mained ever since.

471 *plays a wind instrument*: Like the reference to the piano-organist in Ko-Ko's 'little list'
     song (see the note to line 252), Sullivan might well have felt this line was a little too close
     to home. His own father had started his working life playing the clarinet in the orchestra
     at the Surrey Theatre, London, for a guinea a week. He later rose to become a professor
     at the Army's School of Music at Kneller Hall.

	So pardon us,	
	So pardon us,	435
PITTI.	And don't, in girlhood's happy spring,	
	Be hard on us,	
	Be hard on us,	
	If we're inclined to dance and sing.	
	Tra la la, etc. (*Dancing.*)	440

CHORUS OF GIRLS.   But youth, of course, etc.

POOH.   I think you ought to recollect
             You cannot show too much respect
             Towards the highly titled few;
             But nobody does, and why should you?   445
             That youth at us should have its fling,
                  Is hard on us,
                  Is hard on us;
             To our prerogative we cling –
                  So pardon us,   450
                  So pardon us,
             If we decline to dance and sing.
                  Tra la la, etc. (*Dancing.*)

CHORUS OF GIRLS.   But youth, of course, must have its fling, etc.

                                              (*Exeunt all but* YUM-YUM.)   455

                   (*Enter* NANKI-POO.)

NANK. Yum-Yum, at last we are alone! I have sought you night and
day for three weeks, in the belief that your guardian was beheaded, and I
find that you are about to be married to him this afternoon!

YUM. Alas, yes!   460

NANK. But you do not love him?

YUM. Alas, no!

NANK. Modified rapture! But why do you not refuse him?

YUM. What good would that do? He's my guardian, and he wouldn't
let me marry you!   465

NANK. But I would wait until you were of age!

YUM. You forget that in Japan girls do not arrive at years of discretion
until they are fifty.

NANK. True; from seventeen to forty-nine are considered years of
indiscretion.   470

YUM. Besides – a wandering minstrel, who plays a wind instrument
outside tea-houses, is hardly a fitting husband for the ward of a Lord High
Executioner.

NANK. But — (*Aside.*) Shall I tell her? Yes! She will not betray me!
(*Aloud.*) What if it should prove that, after all, I am no musician?   475

485 *Lucius Junius Brutus*: The first consul of Rome, who in 509 B.C. sentenced his own sons to death for their part in a conspiracy to restore the Tarquins.

487 *a Second Trombone*: It has been suggested that Gilbert was poking a little gentle fun at his collaborator here. Most theatre orchestras had only one trombone, and Sullivan was always grumbling about the effects of this restriction on his composing. He finally won a second trombone from Richard D'Oyly Carte for *The Yeomen of the Guard*.

493 *To flirt is capital*: Neither this line nor the next one appeared in the original libretto, which simply had Yum-Yum saying: 'To flirt is illegal and we must obey the law'. However, the form of words now used was obviously introduced at an early stage. A note in 1907 by Helen D'Oyly Carte against the modern version records: 'This has always been said'. Gilbert agreed to the change.

515–36 *Were you not to Ko-Ko plighted*

The licence copy, the autograph score and the first-night performance of *The Mikado* all had a different version of this song to the one now sung:

YUM.	Were I not to Ko-Ko plighted I would say in tender tone, 'Loved one, let us be united – Let us be each other's own!' I would say 'Oh gentle stranger, Press me closely to thy heart, Sharing ev'ry joy and danger, We will never, never part!'
BOTH.	We will never, never part!
YUM.	But as I'm to marry Ko-Ko, To express my love '*con fuoco*' Would distinctly be no *gioco*, And for yam I should get toco!
BOTH.	Toco, toco, toco, toco!
YUM.	So I will not say 'Oh stranger, Press me closely to thy heart, Sharing ev'ry joy and danger, We will never, never part!' Clearly understand, I pray, This is what I never say – This – oh, this – oh, this – oh, this – This is what I'll never say.
NANKI.	Were you not to Ko-Ko plighted I should thrill at words like those, Joy of joys is love requited, Love despised is woe of woes. I would merge all rank and station, Worldly sneers are nought to us, And, to mark my admiration, I would kiss you fondly thus –

YUM. There! I was certain of it, directly I heard you play!

NANK. What if it should prove that I am no other than the son of his Majesty the Mikado?

YUM. The son of the Mikado! But why is your Highness disguised? And what has your Highness done? And will your Highness promise never to do it again? 480

NANK. Some years ago I had the misfortune to captivate Katisha, an elderly lady of my father's Court. She misconstrued my customary affability into expressions of affection, and claimed me in marriage, under my father's law. My father, the Lucius Junius Brutus of his race, ordered me to marry her 485 within a week, or perish ignominiously on the scaffold. That night I fled his Court, and, assuming the disguise of a Second Trombone, I joined the band in which you found me when I had the happiness of seeing you! (*Approaching her.*)

YUM. (*retreating*). If you please, I think your Highness had better not 490 come too near. The laws against flirting are excessively severe.

NANK. But we are quite alone, and nobody can see us.

YUM. Still, that doesn't make it right. To flirt is capital.

NANK. It *is* capital!

YUM. And we must obey the law. 495

NANK. Deuce take the law!

YUM. I wish it would, but it won't!

NANK. If it were not for that, how happy we might be!

YUM. Happy indeed!

NANK. If it were not for the law, we should now be sitting side by side, 500 like that. (*Sits by her.*)

YUM. Instead of being obliged to sit half a mile off, like that. (*Crosses and sits at other side of stage.*)

NANK. We should be gazing into each other's eyes, like that. (*Gazing at her sentimentally.*) 505

YUM. Breathing sighs of unutterable love – like that. (*Sighing and gazing lovingly at him.*)

NANK. With our arms round each other's waists, like that. (*Embracing her.*)

YUM. Yes, if it wasn't for the law.

NANK. If it wasn't for the law. 510

YUM. As it is, of course we couldn't do anything of the kind.

NANK. Not for worlds!

YUM. Being engaged to Ko-Ko, you know!

NANK. Being engaged to Ko-Ko!

DUET – YUM-YUM *and* NANKI-POO.

NANK.   Were you not to Ko-Ko plighted, 515
        I would say in tender tone,

The duet then continued as it does now. The original, longer version was reduced to the present shorter one in the second edition of the libretto.

525 *con fuoco*: An Italian term meaning 'passionately' (literally, 'with fire').

526 *giuoco*: Another Italian word, meaning 'joke' or 'jest'. In many editions of the libretto and vocal score it is spelt *gioco*.

527 *And for yam I should get toko*: The yam is a sweet potato, found mostly in tropical countries. Toko (also spelt 'toco') was a Victorian schoolboys' expression, derived from Hindu, for punishment, in the form either of a beating or of a diet of bread and water. The sense of this line, therefore, appears to be 'Instead of something sweet, I would get something nasty'. In one edition of the libretto – that published by Macmillan in 1926 – I have found the line printed 'And for jam I should get toko'. Although this makes it more intelligible to the average Englishman, I fear it is a misprint.

537 *Exeunt in opposite directions*: In the licence copy, Yum-Yum and Nanki-Poo's duet is followed immediately by the entrance of the nobles and Pish-Tush:

CHORUS OF NOBLES.

Fire and thunder,
For a wonder,
We have made a serious blunder!
Chopped asunder,
Statute under,
Short'ly,
Mort'lly,
We shall be.

KO-KO (*entering*).

Will you kindly be explicit
As to this informal visit,
What the dooce (or dickens) is it?
Rude t'you –
Who do you
Wish to see?

PISH. (*reading document*).

Here's a note from our Mikado,
Which in spite of all bravado,
Comes on us like a tornado,
Rushingly,
Crushingly,
So say we!

CHORUS.

Fire and thunder, etc.

Pooh-Bah then delivers the lines now given to Ko-Ko about the Mikado being struck by the fact that no executions have taken place (lines 547–50), and the dialogue continues as now.

543 *an apostrophe*: An exclamatory address, in the course of a public speech or a poem, to a particular person or object. There is a good example in *The Sorcerer*, where both Sir Marmaduke Pointdextre and Lady Sangazure sing 'I find some satisfaction/In apostrophe like this' before enthusiastically addressing their respective loves.

551 *irretrievable ruin*: In the very earliest productions of *The Mikado* Ko-Ko's 'little list' song followed at this point, cued in by this speech:

KO. Yes – somebody will have to suffer. Send the Recorder to me. (*Exit* PISH-TUSH.) I expected something of this sort! I knew it couldn't go on! Well, they've brought it on themselves, and the only question is, who shall it be? Fortunately, there will be no difficulty in pitching upon somebody whose death will be a distinct gain to society.

The song then followed with its original opening ('As it seems to be essential that a

'Loved one, let us be united –
    Let us be each other's own!'
I would merge all rank and station,
    Worldly sneers are nought to us,   520
And, to mark my admiration,
    I would kiss you fondly thus – (*Kisses her.*)

BOTH. $\begin{Bmatrix} I \\ He \end{Bmatrix}$ would kiss $\begin{Bmatrix} you \\ me \end{Bmatrix}$ fondly thus – (*Kiss.*)

YUM. But as I'm engaged to Ko-Ko,
    To embrace you thus, *con fuoco*,   525
    Would distinctly be no *giuoco*,
    And for yam I should get toko –

BOTH.   Toko, toko, toko, toko!

NANK. So, in spite of all temptation,
    Such a theme I'll not discuss,   530
And on no consideration
    Will I kiss you fondly thus – (*Kissing her.*)
Let me make it clear to you,
This is what I'll never do!
    This, oh, this, oh, this, oh, this – (*Kissing her.*)   535

TOGETHER. This, oh, this, etc.

(*Exeunt in opposite directions.*)

(*Enter* KO-KO.)

KO. (*looking after* YUM-YUM). There she goes! To think how entirely
my future happiness is wrapped up in that little parcel! Really, it hardly   540
seems worth while! Oh, matrimony! – (*Enter* POOH-BAH *and* PISH-
TUSH.) Now then, what is it? Can't you see I'm soliloquizing? You have
interrupted an apostrophe, sir!

PISH. I am the bearer of a letter from his Majesty the Mikado.

KO. (*taking it from him reverentially*). A letter from the Mikado! What in   545
the world can he have to say to me? (*Reads letter.*) Ah, here it is at last! I
thought it would come sooner or later! The Mikado is struck by the fact that
no executions have taken place in Titipu for a year, and decrees that unless
somebody is beheaded within one month the post of Lord High Executioner
shall be abolished, and the city reduced to the rank of a village!   550

PISH. But that will involve us all in irretrievable ruin!

KO. Yes. There is no help for it, I shall have to execute somebody at
once. The only question is, who shall it be?

POOH. Well, it seems unkind to say so, but as you're already under
sentence of death for flirting, everything seems to point to *you*.   555

KO. To me? What are you talking about? I can't execute myself.

POOH. Why not?

victim must be found' – see the note to lines 239–74). The first edition of the libretto also includes the following additional refrain for Ko-Ko at the end of each verse:

> As a victim must be found,
> If you'll only look around,
> There are criminals at large
> (And enough to fill a barge),
> Whose swift decapitation
> Would be hailed with acclamation,
> If accomplished by the nation
> At a reasonable charge.

It is doubtful if this refrain was, in fact, ever sung. The 'little list' song was revised and moved to its present position earlier in the act only a few days after the opening night.

566–7   *that would be something*: This was the cue for another gag introduced in early productions. Ko-Ko responded to Pish-Tush's remark by saying 'Really! You don't say so! how awfully jolly!' Gilbert, however, vetoed this addition, and it was cut in the 1908 revival.

582–608   *My brain it teems/I am so proud/I heard one day*
On 9 December 1884 Gilbert wrote to Sullivan 'I send a trio for Ko-Ko, Pooh-Bah, and Pish-Tush. I think it ought to be quaint and effective. I have put the three verses side by side for convenience' sake, but, of course, they will be sung separately. I fancy the metre admits of each verse being set differently from the others, but I may be wrong in this.'

Sullivan did indeed set the three verses to different tunes which match the different moods of the characters singing them. Ko-Ko's 'My brain it teems' is distracted and confused, Pooh-Bah's 'I am so proud' is haughty and pompous, and Pish-Tush's 'I heard one day' is bright and carefree. Set against each other, as they are in the reprise, the verses have a striking effect comparable to that achieved in the quartet 'In a contemplative fashion' in *The Gondoliers*.

Ko. Why not? Because, in the first place, self-decapitation is an extremely difficult, not to say dangerous, thing to attempt; and, in the second it's suicide, and suicide is a capital offence. 560

Pooh. That is so, no doubt.

Pish. We might reserve that point.

Pooh. True, it could be argued six months hence, before the full Court.

Ko. Besides, I don't see how a man *can* cut off his own head.

Pooh. A man might try. 565

Pish. Even if you only succeeded in cutting it half off, that would be something.

Pooh. It would be taken as an earnest of your desire to comply with the Imperial will.

Ko. No. Pardon me, but there I am adamant. As official Headsman, my 570 reputation is at stake, and I can't consent to embark on a professional operation unless I see my way to a successful result.

Pooh. This professional conscientiousness is highly creditable to *you*, but it places us in a very awkward position.

Ko. My good sir, the awkwardness of your position is grace itself 575 compared with that of a man engaged in the act of cutting off his own head.

Pish. I am afraid that, unless you can obtain a substitute —

Ko. A substitute? Oh, certainly – nothing easier. (*To* Pooh-Bah.) Pooh-Bah, I appoint you Lord High Substitute.

Pooh. I should be delighted. Such an appointment would realize my fond- 580 est dreams. But no, at any sacrifice, I must set bounds to my insatiable ambition!

TRIO.

Ko-Ko.	Pooh-Bah.	Pish-Tush.	
My brain it teems	I am so proud,	I heard one day	
With endless schemes	If I allowed	A gentleman say	
Both good and new	My family pride	That criminals who	
For Titipu;	To be my guide,	Are cut in two	585
But if I flit,	I'd volunteer	Can hardly feel	
The benefit	To quit this sphere	The fatal steel,	
That I'd diffuse	Instead of you,	And so are slain	
The town would lose!	In a minute or two.	Without much pain.	
Now every man	But family pride	If this is true,	590
To aid his clan	Must be denied,	It's jolly for you;	
Should plot and plan	And set aside,	Your courage screw	
As best he can,	And mortified.	To bid us adieu,	
And so,	And so,	And go	
Although	Although	And show	595
I'm ready to go,	I wish to go,	Both friend and foe	
Yet recollect	And greatly pine	How much you dare.	
'Twere disrespect	To brightly shine,	I'm quite aware	
Did I neglect	And take the line	It's your affair,	
To thus effect	Of a hero fine,	Yet I declare	600
This aim direct,	With grief condign	I'd take your share,	
So I object –	I must decline –	But I don't much care –	
So I object –	I must decline –	I don't much care –	
So I object –	I must decline –	I don't much care –	

605–8   *To sit in solemn silence in a dull, dark dock*
This is the only substantial piece of alliteration to occur in a song in the Savoy Operas, although there are several alliterative passages of dialogue. Perhaps the best occurs early in Act II of *The Yeomen of the Guard*, when Jack Point, the strolling player, addresses Wilfred Shadbolt, head jailer of the Tower of London: 'Ha! friend jailer! Jailer that wast – jailer that never shalt be more! Jailer that jailed not, or that jailed, if jail he did, so unjailerly that 'twas by jerry-jailing, or jailing in joke – though no joke to him who, by unjailerlike jailing, did so jeopardize his jailership.'
Gilbert anticipated the distinctive rhythm of this song in an Indian trio which he wrote for *Princess Toto*, an early work with music by Fred Clay:

> With feathers, paint and patches and a tom, tom, tom,
> That with our colour matches, with a tom, tom, tom.

609   *Exeunt Pooh. and Pish.*: Gilbert's very first intention was to have Ko-Ko sing his 'little list' song at this point in the opera. The licence copy has the following speech for Ko-Ko as a prelude to the original version of the song:

> KO. This is exceedingly hard on me. It was distinctly stated, when I was asked to accept the post of Lord High Executioner, that the duties were purely nominal. And here I am, called upon to behead the very person of all others for whom I entertain the most affection-ate regard, unless I can find a substitute within half an hour! If someone *must* be beheaded, why not choose somebody whose death would be a distinct gain to society? There are plenty of them about!

The 'little list' song then follows in its original version.

620   *to marry the girl I adore*: In early performances the dialogue continued as follows:

> KO. And do you suppose that I am likely to stand quietly by while you deliberately take your life?
> NANK. Please yourself. You can withdraw if you prefer it.
> KO. Withdraw if I prefer it! Are you aware, sir, that I am Lord High Executioner of this city, and that in that capacity, it is my duty to prevent unnecessary bloodshed?
> NANK. I know nothing about your capacity. I only know that I die to-day.
> KO. Nonsense, sir, etc.

The dialogue continues as now from line 621.

625   *the Happy Despatch*: Japanese military and government officials who were in disgrace or whose honour had been seriously impugned traditionally committed suicide by disem-bowelling themselves. This practice was known as the Happy Despatch or, in Japanese, as *hara-kiri* (literally, 'cutting the belly'). It ceased to be obligatory in 1868.

629   *Substitute*: Although this word was said from very early on in performances, it was not actually in the original libretto. Gilbert authorized its inclusion at the time of the 1908 revival.

645   *bands*: When playing Ko-Ko, Sir Henry Lytton would at this point hold his nose and hum 'The Campbells are Coming', striking his throat with his other hand to produce the effect of bagpipes.

ALL.   To sit in solemn silence in a dull, dark dock,   605
            In a pestilential prison, with a life-long lock,
            Awaiting the sensation of a short, sharp shock,
            From a cheap and chippy chopper on a big black block!

                                    (*Exeunt* POOH. *and* PISH.)

KO. This is simply appalling! I, who allowed myself to be respited at   610
the last moment, simply in order to benefit my native town, am now
required to die within a month, and that by a man whom I have loaded
with honours! Is this public gratitude? Is this — (*Enter* NANKI-POO, *with
a rope in his hands.*) Go away, sir! How dare you? Am I never to be
permitted to soliloquize?   615

NANK. Oh, go on – don't mind me.

KO. What are you going to do with that rope?

NANK. I am about to terminate an unendurable existence.

KO. Terminate your existence? Oh, nonsense! What for?

NANK. Because you are going to marry the girl I adore.   620

KO. Nonsense, sir. I won't permit it. I am a humane man, and if you
attempt anything of the kind I shall order your instant arrest. Come, sir,
desist at once, or I summon my guard.

NANK. That's absurd. If you attempt to raise an alarm, I instantly
perform the Happy Despatch with this dagger.   625

KO. No, no, don't do that. This is horrible! (*Suddenly.*) Why, you cold-
blooded scoundrel, are you aware that, in taking your life, you are
committing a crime which – which – which is — Oh! (*Struck by an idea.*)
Substitute!

NANK. What's the matter?   630

KO. Is it *absolutely certain* that you are resolved to die?

NANK. Absolutely!

KO. Will *nothing* shake your resolution?

NANK. Nothing.

KO. Threats, entreaties, prayers – all useless?   635

NANK. All! My mind is made up.

KO. Then, if you really mean what you say, and if you are absolutely
resolved to die, and if nothing whatever will shake your determination –
don't spoil yourself by committing suicide, but be beheaded handsomely at
the hands of the Public Executioner!   640

NANK. I don't see how that would benefit me.

KO. You don't? Observe: you'll have a month to live, and you'll live like
a fighting-cock at my expense. When the day comes there'll be a grand
public ceremonial – you'll be the central figure – no one will attempt
to deprive you of that distinction. There'll be a procession – bands – dead   645
march – bells tolling – all the girls in tears – Yum-Yum distracted – then,

658   *Life without Yum-Yum*: It sounds like an advertising slogan and, indeed, was used as such
      by one enterprising American entrepreneur in the 1880s. E. M. Statler, running a not
      very successful restaurant in Buffalo, New York State, decided that he could improve
      his business by cashing in on the *Mikado* craze then sweeping the States. So he adver-
      tised and served 'Yum-Yum' ice-cream shaped in the form of a Japanese lady with a
      paper parasol. As an added incentive to his customers, he put five-dollar pieces in some
      of the figures. Sales boomed, his business took off and with the profits he founded the
      well-known Statler hotel chain.
         Characters from *The Mikado* were, in fact, used extensively in advertisements in the
      United States. Ko-Ko and Katisha appeared together on posters extolling the virtues of
      J. & P. Coats' thread, the three little maids from school advertised spool silk, dental
      cream, soap, cotton thread, Waterbury matches and corsets, while the Mikado himself
      promoted Lautz Brothers' 'Pure and Healthy Soap' and even had a kerosene stove named
      after him.

when it's all over, general rejoicings, and a display of fireworks in the evening. *You* won't see them, but they'll be there all the same.

NANK. Do you think Yum-Yum would really be distracted at my death?

KO. I am convinced of it. Bless you, she's the most tender-hearted little 650
creature alive.

NANK. I should be sorry to cause her pain. Perhaps, after all, if I were to withdraw from Japan, and travel in Europe for a couple of years, I might contrive to forget her.

KO. Oh, I don't think you could forget Yum-Yum so easily; and, after 655
all, what is more miserable than a love-blighted life?

NANK. True.

KO. Life without Yum-Yum – why, it seems absurd!

NANK. And yet there are a good many people in the world who have to endure it. 660

KO. Poor devils, yes! You are quite right not to be of their number.

NANK. (*suddenly*). I *won't* be of their number!

KO. Noble fellow!

NANK. I'll tell you how we'll manage it. Let me marry Yum-Yum to-morrow, and in a month you may behead me. 665

KO. No, no. I draw the line at Yum-Yum.

NANK. Very good. If you can draw the line, so can I. (*Preparing rope.*)

KO. Stop, stop – listen one moment – be reasonable. How can I consent to your marrying Yum-Yum if I'm going to marry her myself?

NANK. My good friend, she'll be a widow in a month, and you can 670
marry her then.

KO. That's true, of course. I quite see that. But, dear me! my position during the next month will be most unpleasant – most unpleasant.

NANK. Not half so unpleasant as my position at the end of it.

KO. But – dear me! – well – I agree – after all, it's only putting off my 675
wedding for a month. But you won't prejudice her against me, will you? You see, I've educated her to be my wife; she's been taught to regard me as a wise and good man. Now I shouldn't like her views on that point disturbed.

NANK. Trust me, she shall never learn the truth from me.

FINALE.

(*Enter* CHORUS, POOH-BAH, *and* PISH-TUSH.) 680

CHORUS.

With aspect stern
  And gloomy stride,
We come to learn
  How you decide.

705   *Take her – she's yours*: This line was the occasion for another ad-lib gag in early produc-
      tions. Taking his cue from Ko-Ko's 'Take her', Pitti-Sing came forward to grab Nanki-
      Poo. Ko-Ko rebuffed her with the words 'Not you silly'. This phrase was written into
      the 1914 D'Oyly Carte master copy of the libretto but then scratched out. As far as I can
      establish, it has never appeared in any printed edition of the libretto, although it was
      included in comparatively recent D'Oyly Carte productions.

707–22 *The threatened cloud has passed away*
      In the original libretto the first ten lines of this song (everything from 'The threatened
      cloud' to 'our brief career') were first given to Yum-Yum and Nanki-Poo, singing to-
      gether, with the chorus repeating everything from 'Then let the throng'. The lines from
      'A day, a week, a month, a year' to 'You'll live at least a honeymoon!' (lines 717–20) were
      given to Pitti-Sing as a solo, with all singing the refrain beginning 'Then let the throng'.
      This seems to have been a piece of carelessness in the drafting of the libretto and the
      musical lines written by Sullivan suggest that the ensemble was never performed in this
      way.

Don't hesitate 685
　　Your choice to name,
A dreadful fate
　　You'll suffer all the same.

POOH.　　To ask you what you mean to do we punctually appear.
KO.　　Congratulate me, gentlemen, I've found a Volunteer! 690
ALL.　　The Japanese equivalent for Hear, Hear, Hear!
KO. (*presenting him*).　　'Tis Nanki-Poo!
ALL.　　Hail, Nanki-Poo!
KO.　　I think he'll do?
ALL.　　Yes, yes, he'll do! 695

KO.　　He yields his life if I'll Yum-Yum surrender.
　　Now I adore that girl with passion tender,
　　And could not yield her with a ready will,
　　　　Or her allot,
　　　　If I did not
　　Adore myself with passion tenderer still! 700

(*Enter* YUM-YUM, PEEP-BO, *and* PITTI-SING.)

ALL.　　Ah, yes!
　　He loves himself with passion tenderer still!
KO. (*to* NANKI-POO).　　Take her — she's yours! 705

(*Exit* KO-KO.)

ENSEMBLE.

NANKI-POO.　　The threatened cloud has passed away,
YUM-YUM.　　And brightly shines the dawning day;
NANKI-POO.　　What though the night may come too soon,
YUM-YUM.　　There's yet a month of afternoon! 710

NANKI-POO, POOH-BAH, PISH-TUSH, YUM-YUM, PITTI-SING,
and PEEP-BO.

Then let the throng
Our joy advance,
With laughing song
And merry dance,

CHORUS.　　With joyous shout and ringing cheer, 715
　　Inaugurate our brief career!

723 *As in a month you've got to die*: Gilbert originally wrote 'As in three weeks you've got to die' but authorized the change to 'a month' at the time of the 1908 revival, presumably to tie in with the specific time-scale mentioned in Nanki-Poo's discussions with Ko-Ko in lines 642–79. Line 727 was also altered at the same time, but Pooh-Bah's toast was left, slightly incongruously, as 'three times three'.

730 *Long life to you*: This line is delivered by Pooh-Bah in the form of a very long and very impressive cadenza. Rutland Barrington was in the habit of breaking the cadenza up with the following gags:

> (*During cadenza* PITTI-SING, NANKI-POO *and* PISH-TUSH *laugh*.)

> POOH. I am addressing myself to you sir.
> NANK. I beg your pardon.
> POOH. I should think you did. (*Resumes cadenza.*)
> NANK. Thank you very much.
> POOH. I've not nearly finished. (POOH *finishes cadenza.*)

Gilbert approved this bit of business and it was included in the 1908 revival. However, it was cut again in 1914.

737 *Enter Katisha*: When Rosina Brandram entered as Katisha on the first night she was wearing a Japanese costume which was reputed to be 200 years old. Gilbert had also bought some antique Japanese armour for the male chorus, but it was found to be far too small and too heavy for any of the men to wear.

738–45 *Your revels cease! Assist me, all of you*
In the licence copy, Katisha is given the following lines after her entrance:

> Your revels cease – assist me, all of you,
> I come to claim my lover Nanki-Poo.
> I've sought him everywhere for nearly a year,
> And now I find him masquerading here.

Nanki-Poo then comes in with his line 'Ah!/'Tis Katisha' etc.

PITTI-SING.	A day, a week, a month, a year —
YUM.	Or far or near, or far or near,
POOH.	Life's eventime comes much too soon,
PITTI-SING.	You'll live at least a honeymoon!
ALL.	Then let the throng, etc.
CHORUS.	With joyous shout, etc.

720

SOLO – POOH-BAH.

As in a month you've got to die,
　　If Ko-Ko tells us true,
'Twere empty compliment to cry 725
　　'Long life to Nanki-Poo!'
But as one month you have to live
　　As fellow-citizen,
This toast with three times three we'll give –
　　'Long life to you – till then!' 730

(Exit POOH-BAH.*)*

CHORUS.	May all good fortune prosper you,
	May you have health and riches too,
	May you succeed in all you do!
	Long life to you – till then!

735

(Dance.)

(Enter KATISHA *melodramatically.)*

KAT.	Your revels cease! Assist me, all of you!
CHORUS.	Why, who is this whose evil eyes
	Rain blight on our festivities?
KAT.	I claim my perjured lover, Nanki-Poo!
	Oh, fool! to shun delights that never cloy!
CHORUS.	Go, leave thy deadly work undone!
KAT.	Come back, oh, shallow fool! come back to joy!
CHORUS.	Away, away! ill-favoured one!

740

745

NANK. (*aside to* YUM-YUM). Ah!
　　'Tis Katisha!
　　The maid of whom I told you. (*About to go.*)
KAT. (*detaining him*). No!
　　You shall not go, 750
　　These arms shall thus enfold you!

759   *dole*: Not, in this case, unemployment benefit, but the original meaning of the word, which is a share or portion.

769   *Heroic nerves*: This line was originally written as 'Steel-tempered nerves', but was apparently changed to 'heroic nerves' before the opening night, probably because of the difficulty of singing the original.

771   *Lore-laden years*: Years filled with teaching and instruction.

772   *smooth tongue*: This appears in early vocal scores as 'sweet tongue'.

776   *knell*: The sound made by a bell when rung slowly and solemnly, as at a funeral, and therefore a sound announcing death. In *Princess Ida* King Hildebrand sings of King Gama:

> We'll shut him up in a dungeon cell,
> And toll his knell on a funeral bell.

SONG – KATISHA.

KAT. (*addressing* NANKI-POO).

    Oh fool, that fleest
      My hallowed joys!
    Oh blind, that seest
      No equipoise!   755
    Oh rash, that judgest
      From half, the whole!
    Oh base, that grudgest
      Love's lightest dole!
        Thy heart unbind,   760
        Oh fool, oh blind!
        Give me my place,
        Oh rash, oh base!

CHORUS.
    If she's thy bride, restore her place,
    Oh fool, oh blind, oh rash, oh base!   765

KAT. (*addressing* YUM-YUM).

    Pink cheek, that rulest
      Where wisdom serves!
    Bright eye, that foolest
      Heroic nerves!
    Rose lip, that scornest   770
      Lore-laden years!
    Smooth tongue, that warnest
      Who rightly hears!
        Thy doom is nigh,
        Pink cheek, bright eye!   775
        Thy knell is rung,
        Rose lip, smooth tongue!

CHORUS.
    If true her tale, thy knell is rung,
    Pink cheek, bright eye, rose lip, smooth tongue!

PITTI-SING.
    Away, nor prosecute your quest –   780
    From our intention, well expressed,
      You cannot turn us!
    The state of your connubial views
    Towards the person you accuse
      Does not concern us!   785
    For he's going to marry Yum-Yum –

ALL.
        Yum-Yum!

799   *There's lots of good fish in the sea*: This line is based on the old English saying 'There's as
       good fish in the sea as ever came out of it', meaning don't be disheartened if you have
       lost the chance of something good, because you'll soon get another. In the finale of Act I
       of *Patience*, the dragoons sing:

> There's fish in the sea, no doubt of it,
> As good as ever came out of it.

820   *O ni! bikkuri shakkuri to*: All sorts of translations have been offered for this line. Leslie
       Ayre in *The Gilbert and Sullivan Companion* (1972) agrees with the Oxford University Press
       edition of *The Savoy Operas* (1963) that it means 'O! he was frightened to death!' The
       glossary in D'Oyly Carte programmes for *The Mikado* gives 'O, no such thing, what a sur-
       prise and shock', while Harry Benford in his *Gilbert and Sullivan Lexicon* suggests: 'Oh!
       You she devil! We are so shocked by you it makes us hiccup. Bah!' The Japanese expert
       whom I have consulted says that a literal translation of the line would be 'surprise, with
       a hiccup', which seems a suitably Gilbertian phrase.
            In early productions the line was first given to Nanki-Poo and Yum-Yum, with the
       chorus coming in for the repeats from line 823 onwards. In one early revival, instead of
       singing the Japanese words, Nanki-Poo drowned Katisha by producing his trombone
       and blowing fierce blasts into her face.
826   *gambado*: A word of Spanish origin, normally used in the plural, meaning a caper or sud-
       den action.

PITTI.	Your anger pray bury,
	For all will be merry,
	I think you had better succumb –
ALL.	Cumb – cumb!
PITTI.	And join our expressions of glee.
	On this subject I pray you be dumb –
ALL.	Dumb – dumb.
PITTI.	You'll find there are many
	Who'll wed for a penny –
	The word for your guidance is 'Mum' –
ALL.	Mum – mum!
PITTI.	There's lots of good fish in the sea!
ALL.	On this subject we pray you be dumb, etc.

790

795

800

SOLO – KATISHA.

The hour of gladness
    Is dead and gone;
In silent sadness
    I live alone!
The hope I cherished
    All lifeless lies,
And all has perished
    Save love, which never dies!
Oh, faithless one, this insult you shall rue!
In vain for mercy on your knees you'll sue.
    I'll tear the mask from your disguising!

805

810

NANK. (*aside*).	Now comes the blow!
KAT.	Prepare yourselves for news surprising!
NANK. (*aside*).	How foil my foe?
KAT.	No minstrel he, despite bravado!
YUM. (*aside, struck by an idea*).	Ha! ha! I know!
KAT.	He is the son of your —

815

(NANKI-POO, YUM-YUM, *and* CHORUS, *interrupting, sing Japanese
words, to drown her voice.*)

	O ni! bikkuri shakkuri to!
KAT.	In vain you interrupt with this tornado!
	He is the only son of your —
ALL.	O ni! bikkuri shakkuri to!
KAT.	I'll spoil —
ALL.	O ni! bikkuri shakkuri to!
KAT.	Your gay gambado!

820

825

843 *My wrongs with vengeance shall be crowned*: This line was originally written as 'And when he learns his son is found'. It was changed to its present form in the 1914 edition of the libretto, although the vocal score always had 'My wrongs with vengeance shall be crowned'.

	He is the son —	
ALL.	O ni! bikkuri shakkuri to!	
KAT.	Of your —	
ALL.	O ni! bikkuri shakkuri to!	830
KAT.	The son of your —	
ALL.	O ni! bikkuri shakkuri to! oya! oya!	

ENSEMBLE.

KATISHA.	THE OTHERS.
Ye torrents roar!	We'll hear no more,
Ye tempests howl!	Ill-omened owl,
Your wrath outpour	To joy we soar,
With angry growl!	Despite your scowl!
Do ye your worst, my vengeance call	The echoes of our festival
Shall rise triumphant over all!	Shall rise triumphant over all!
Prepare for woe,	Away you go,
Ye haughty lords,	Collect your hordes;
At once I go	Proclaim your woe
Mikado-wards,	In dismal chords;
My wrongs with vengeance shall be crowned!	We do not heed their dismal sound,
My wrongs with vengeance shall be crowned!	For joy reigns everywhere around.

835

840

(KATISHA *rushes furiously up stage, clearing the crowd away right and left, finishing on steps at the back of stage.*)

845

END OF ACT I

10 *Emphasize the grace*: There was a feeling among some critics that, graceful as they undoubtedly were, the costumes worn by the girls' chorus in *The Mikado* did not sufficiently emphasize their femininity. Reginald Allen in his *First Night Gilbert and Sullivan*
quotes one reviewer's complaint that 'they obliterate the natural distinction between
the sexes, imparting to the prettiest girl's figure the seeming of a bolster loosely wrapped
up in a dressing-gown'.

The *Daily News* reviewer, also quoted by Allen, was rather more enthusiastic:

> The Japanese gowns, with their delicate tints, their richly embroidered conceits and fan-
> tasies, and their ample sashes, lent not a little aid to the oddly pleasing effect. If the enthu-
> siasm of the ladies among the audience may afford a token, sashes rising halfway from the
> waist to the shoulders and tied in huge double bows upon the backs of the wearers, may
> find a place ere long among the fashions of the day.

14 *Sit with downcast eye*: There was nothing very downcast, or modest, about the performance of the original Pitti-Sing, Miss Jessie Bond. Determining that she should be
singled out from the other little maids, she persuaded the wardrobe mistress to give her
an obi twice as big as the others, with an enormous bow at the back. 'I made the most of
my big, big bow,' she recalled in her memoirs, 'turning my back to the audience whenever I got the chance and waggling it. The gallery was delighted, but *I* nearly got the
sack for that prank! However, I did get noticed, which was what I wanted.'

ACT II

SCENE. – Ko-Ko's *Garden.* YUM-YUM *discovered seated at her bridal toilet, surrounded by maidens, who are dressing her hair and painting her face and lips, as she judges of the effect in a mirror.*

SOLO – PITTI-SING *and* CHORUS OF GIRLS.

CHORUS.
    Braid the raven hair –
      Weave the supple tress –   5
    Deck the maiden fair
      In her loveliness –
    Paint the pretty face –
      Dye the coral lip –
    Emphasize the grace   10
      Of her ladyship!
    Art and nature, thus allied,
    Go to make a pretty bride.

SOLO – PITTI-SING.

    Sit with downcast eye –
      Let it brim with dew –   15
    Try if you can cry –
      We will do so, too.
    When you're summoned, start
      Like a frightened roe –
    Flutter, little heart,   20
      Colour, come and go!
    Modesty at marriage-tide
    Well becomes a pretty bride!

CHORUS.

    Braid the raven hair, etc.

    (*Exeunt* PITTI-SING, PEEP-BO, *and* CHORUS.)   25

31-62 *The sun, whose rays*

This song was originally designed to be sung in the First Act, following 'Three little maids from school' and the quartet 'So please you, sir, we much regret'. At a rehearsal the morning after the opening night, however, Miss Leonora Braham, who was playing Yum-Yum, told Sullivan that she had been too exhausted by the earlier two songs to do justice to her solo number. The composer agreed to move it to Act II to give her a breathing space.

A resemblance to the 'Song of the Bird' in Wagner's *Siegfried* has been detected by some critics. Whether he was influenced by Wagner or not, there is no doubt that Sullivan produced one of his loveliest tunes for this song and showed his supreme gift for melody. Dr Percy Buck, a former professor of music at London University, wrote in his book *The Scope of Music*:

> The writing of a learned eight-part fugue is within the power of any musician who cares to waste his time in learning how to do it; but if he tries to reset the words, 'The sun whose rays are all ablaze' and then compares his music to Sullivan's, he will have no doubts as to which is the more serious task.

In an early unauthorized version of *The Mikado* performed in Texas in 1888, the opening lines of this song became:

> The sun, whose rays
> Are all ablaze
>   With ever-living glory,
> Shines brightly forth
> On all Fort Worth,
>   And makes things hunki-dori!

YUM. Yes, I am indeed beautiful! Sometimes I sit and wonder, in my artless Japanese way, why it is that I am so much more attractive than anybody else in the whole world. Can this be vanity? No! Nature is lovely and rejoices in her loveliness. I am a child of Nature, and take after my mother. 30

SONG – YUM-YUM.

The sun, whose rays
Are all ablaze
　　With ever-living glory,
Does not deny
His majesty – 35
　　He scorns to tell a story!
He don't exclaim,
　　'I blush for shame,
　　So kindly be indulgent.'
But, fierce and bold, 40
In fiery gold
　　He glories all effulgent!

　　　I mean to rule the earth,
　　　　As he the sky –
　　　We really know our worth, 45
　　　　The sun and I!

Observe his flame,
That placid dame,
　　The moon's Celestial Highness;
There's not a trace 50
Upon her face
　　Of diffidence or shyness:
She borrows light
That, through the night,
　　Mankind may all acclaim her! 55
And, truth to tell,
She lights up well,
　　So I, for one, don't blame her!

　　　Ah, pray make no mistake,
　　　　We are not shy; 60
　　　We're very wide awake,
　　　　The moon and I!

(*Enter* PITTI-SING *and* PEEP-BO.)

70–71   *It does seem to take the top off it, you know*: Another ad-lib gag not found in the original libretto but authorized by Gilbert in 1907.

79   *Go-To*: Go-To is not found in the list of *Dramatis personæ* in the original libretto and vocal score of *The Mikado*, nor, indeed, is the part included in the Macmillan and Chappell editions of the libretto. It was, in fact, added during the opera's initial run at the Savoy Theatre. Frederick Bovill, who created the role of Pish-Tush, found that he was unable to reach the low bass notes of his part in the madrigal 'Brightly dawns our wedding day'. So Gilbert introduced the new character of Go-To simply to sing the bass line in the madrigal.

The D'Oyly Carte Opera Company generally thereafter kept Go-To as a separate character, giving him also the line in Act I 'Why, who are you who ask this question?' (line 23), which the libretto simply assigns to 'A Noble'. However, many amateur companies have dispensed with his services and allowed their Pish-Tushes to show their command of the lower reaches of the bass-baritone register in the madrigal.

86   *How some bridegrooms*: Several editions of the libretto misprint this phrase as 'Now, some bridegrooms'. I regret to say that my earlier Penguin edition of this work was one of them.

93–4   *four hours and three-quarters*: For the 1908 revival, with Gilbert's approval, Pitti-Sing was given the extra line 'Silly little cuckoo' at this point. It was cut again in 1914.

YUM. Yes, everything seems to smile upon me. I am to be married to-day to the man I love best, and I believe I am the very happiest girl in Japan! 65

PEEP. The happiest girl indeed, for she is indeed to be envied who has attained happiness in all but perfection.

YUM. In 'all but' perfection?

PEEP. Well, dear, it can't be denied that the fact that your husband is to be beheaded in a month is, in its way, a drawback. It does seem to take the 70 top off it, you know.

PITTI. I don't know about that. It all depends!

PEEP. At all events, *he* will find it a drawback!

PITTI. Not necessarily. Bless you, it all depends!

YUM. (*in tears*). I think it very indelicate of you to refer to such a subject 75 on such a day. If my married happiness *is* to be – to be —

PEEP. Cut short.

YUM. Well, cut short – in a month, can't you let me forget it? (*Weeping.*)

(*Enter* NANKI-POO, *followed by* GO-TO.)

NANK. Yum-Yum in tears – and on her wedding morn! 80

YUM. (*sobbing*). They've been reminding me that in a month you're to be beheaded! (*Bursts into tears.*)

PITTI. Yes, we've been reminding her that you're to be beheaded. (*Bursts into tears.*)

PEEP. It's quite true, you know, you *are* to be beheaded! (*Bursts into tears.*) 85

NANK. (*aside.*) Humph! How some bridegrooms would be depressed by this sort of thing! (*Aloud.*) A month? Well, what's a month? Bah! These divisions of time are purely arbitrary. Who says twenty-four hours make a day?

PITTI. There's a popular impression to that effect.

NANK. Then we'll efface it. We'll call each second a minute – each 90 minute an hour – each hour a day – and each day a year. At that rate we've about thirty years of married happiness before us!

PEEP. And, at that rate, this interview has already lasted four hours and three-quarters!

(*Exit* PEEP-BO.) 95

YUM. (*still sobbing*). Yes. How time flies when one is thoroughly enjoying oneself!

NANK. That's the way to look at it! Don't let's be downhearted! There's a silver lining to every cloud.

YUM. Certainly. Let's – let's be perfectly happy! (*Almost in tears.*) 100

GO. By all means. Let's – let's thoroughly enjoy ourselves.

PITTI. It's – it's absurd to cry! (*Trying to force a laugh.*)

YUM. Quite ridiculous! (*Trying to laugh.*)

105–28 *Brightly dawns our wedding day*
  Nothing could be more thoroughly English than this charming madrigal. There is only one other song formally described as a madrigal in the Savoy Operas, 'When the buds are blossoming' from Act I of *Ruddigore*. However, both 'Strange adventure' in Act II of *The Yeomen of the Guard*, which is described as a quartet, and 'I hear the soft note of the echoing voice' in Act I of *Patience*, described as a sestet, conform to the dictionary definition of madrigal as a contrapuntal and largely unaccompanied partsong for several voices.

111 *tocsin*: A word of French origin meaning an alarm signal sounded by the ringing of a bell, and later extended to mean a bell used to sound an alarm.

132 *Go on – don't mind me*: In the licence copy there is a slightly different version of the ensuing dialogue between Ko-Ko, Nanki-Poo and Yum-Yum, as follows:

  KO. Well, I hope you are getting on pretty comfortably?
  NANK. Oh yes! There's only one drawback to our happiness – the reflection that it can only be enjoyed at the expense of your peace of mind.
  KO. How good of you to think of that!
  YUM. We can't help thinking how miserable we are making you. For instance, this sort of thing (*embracing* NANKI-POO), must be perfect torture to you.
  KO. It's most unpleasant – *most* unpleasant.
  NANK. I suppose we can't even sit like this without causing you serious inconvenience.
  KO. It's particularly disagreeable to me.
  NANK. It must be! (*embracing* YUM-YUM) But come, look at its bright side. In a month she will be yours.
  YUM. My darling! (*embracing* NANKI-POO.)
  KO. Thank you, my boy, for the kind thought that prompted the suggestion; but it's no use deluding oneself with false hopes, etc.

The dialogue continues as now from line 145.

(All break into a forced and melancholy laugh.)

MADRIGAL.

YUM-YUM, PITTI-SING, NANKI-POO, *and* GO-TO.

Brightly dawns our wedding day; 105
    Joyous hour, we give thee greeting!
    Whither, whither art thou fleeting?
Fickle moment, prithee stay!
    What though mortal joys be hollow?
    Pleasures come, if sorrows follow: 110
Though the tocsin sound, ere long,
    Ding dong! Ding dong!
Yet until the shadows fall
Over one and over all,
Sing a merry madrigal – 115
Fal-la – fal-la! etc. *(Ending in tears.)*

Let us dry the ready tear,
    Though the hours are surely creeping
    Little need for woeful weeping,
Till the sad sundown is near. 120
    All must sip the cup of sorrow –
    I to-day and thou to-morrow;
This the close of every song –
    Ding dong! Ding dong!
What, though solemn shadows fall, 125
Sooner, later, over all?
Sing a merry madrigal –
Fal-la – fal-la! etc. *(Ending in tears.)*

(Exeunt PITTI-SING *and* GO-TO.*)*

*(*NANKI-POO *embraces* YUM-YUM. *Enter* KO-KO. NANKI-POO 130
releases YUM-YUM.)*

KO. Go on – don't mind me.
NANK. I'm afraid we're distressing you.
KO. Never mind, I must get used to it. Only please do it by degrees.
Begin by putting your arm round her waist. (NANKI-POO *does so.*) There; 135
let me get used to that first.
    YUM. Oh, wouldn't you like to retire? It must pain you to see us so
affectionate together!

152 *I'm so glad*: This line, and Nanki-Poo's 'Like that' above (line 141) were added, with Gilbert's approval, in the libretto used for the 1908 revival.

177 *I call it a beast of a death*: This seems to have been another ad-lib which received official sanction from Gilbert. It first appears in the 1887 libretto as 'I call it a beastly death' and in its present form in 1914.

KO. No, I must learn to bear it! Now oblige me by allowing her head to
rest on your shoulder.   140

NANK. Like that? (*He does so.* KO-KO *much affected.*)

KO. I am much obliged to you. Now – kiss her! (*He does so.* KO-KO
writhes with anguish.) Thank you – it's simple torture!

YUM. Come, come, bear up. After all, it's only for a month.

KO. No. It's no use deluding oneself with false hopes.   145

NANK. ⎫
YUM. ⎬ What do you mean?

KO. (*to* YUM-YUM). My child – my poor child! (*Aside.*) How shall I
break it to her? (*Aloud.*) My little bride that was to have been —

YUM. (*delighted*). *Was* to have been?

KO. Yes, you never can be mine!   150

NANK. ⎫ (*in ecstasy*). ⎰ What!
YUM. ⎭   ⎱ I'm so glad!

KO. I've just ascertained that, by the Mikado's law, when a married
man is beheaded his wife is buried alive.

NANK. ⎫
YUM. ⎬ Buried alive!   155

KO. Buried alive. It's a most unpleasant death.

NANK. But whom did you get that from?

KO. Oh, from Pooh-Bah. He's my Solicitor.

YUM. But he may be mistaken!

KO. So I thought; so I consulted the Attorney-General, the Lord Chief   160
Justice, the Master of the Rolls, the Judge Ordinary, and the Lord
Chancellor. They're all of the same opinion. Never knew such unanimity on
a point of law in my life!

NANK. But stop a bit! This law has never been put in force.

KO. Not yet. You see, flirting is the only crime punishable with   165
decapitation, and married men never flirt.

NANK. Of course they don't. I quite forgot that! Well, I suppose I may
take it that my dream of happiness is at an end!

YUM. Darling – I don't want to appear selfish, and I love you with all
my heart – I don't suppose I shall ever love anybody else half as much – but   170
when I agreed to marry you – my own – I had no idea – pet – that I should
have to be buried alive in a month!

NANK. Nor I! It's the very first I've heard of it!

YUM. It – makes a difference, doesn't it?

NANK. It *does* make a difference, of course.   175

YUM. You see – burial alive – it's such a stuffy death!

NANK. I call it a beast of a death.

YUM. You see my difficulty, don't you?

NANK. Yes, and I see my own. If I insist on your carrying out your promise,
I doom you to a hideous death; if I release you, you marry Ko-Ko at once!   180

181–206 *Here's a how-de-do*

One of the most encored numbers in *The Mikado*. In an article in the *Gilbert and Sullivan Journal* for January 1960, Colin Prestige calculated that Isidore Godfrey, musical director of the D'Oyly Carte Opera Company from 1929 to 1968, must have conducted it 13,000 times. Martyn Green, principal comedian with the company from 1934 to 1939 and from 1946 to 1951, used the first line of the song as the title for his memoirs, published in 1952.

The song has always offered plenty of opportunities for comic business on stage. At the final line, 'Here's a pretty how-de-do', Sir Henry Lytton snapped open a fan which promptly split in two. In encores he opened what was apparently the same fan, now miraculously intact. Martyn Green pulled out a different fan from his sleeve at every encore, each smaller than the previous one. It was also usual during encores for Ko-Ko to address a few words in 'Japanese' to a bewildered Yum-Yum.

TRIO – Yum-Yum, Nanki-Poo, *and* Ko-Ko.

YUM.

Here's a how-de-do!
If I marry you,
When your time has come to perish,
Then the maiden whom you cherish
  Must be slaughtered, too!   185
  Here's a how-de-do!

NANK.

Here's a pretty mess!
In a month, or less,
I must die without a wedding!
Let the bitter tears I'm shedding   190
  Witness my distress,
  Here's a pretty mess!

KO.

Here's a state of things!
To her life she clings!
Matrimonial devotion   195
Doesn't seem to suit her notion –
  Burial it brings!
  Here's a state of things!

ENSEMBLE.

YUM-YUM *and* NANKI-POO.	KO-KO.	
With a passion that's intense	With a passion that's intense	
I worship and adore,	You worship and adore,	200
But the laws of common sense	But the laws of common sense	
We oughtn't to ignore.	You oughtn't to ignore.	
If what he says is true,	If what I say is true,	
'Tis death to marry you!	'Tis death to marry you!	
Here's a pretty state of things!	Here's a pretty state of things!	205
Here's a pretty how-de-do!	Here's a pretty how-de-do!	

(*Exit* YUM-YUM.)

KO. (*going up to* NANKI-POO). My poor boy, I'm really very sorry for you.

NANK. Thanks, old fellow. I'm sure you are.

KO. You see I'm quite helpless.   210

NANK. I quite see that.

KO. I can't conceive anything more distressing than to have one's marriage broken off at the last moment. But you shan't be disappointed of a wedding – you shall come to mine.

NANK. It's awfully kind of you, but that's impossible.   215

KO. Why so?

NANK. To-day I die.

228 *Now then, Lord Mayor, what is it*: When Pooh-Bah was played by the twenty-stone Fred Billington, who regularly took the role in D'Oyly Carte touring productions from the 1880s until his death in 1917, Ko-Ko changed this line to 'Now, feather-weight, what is it?' In a set of notes sent to Gilbert in 1907 about unauthorized changes to the libretto, Helen D'Oyly Carte commented: 'This seems to have been said recently only – in allusion to Mr Billington's size – it seems *undesirable*'. Gilbert agreed and the interpolation was forbidden.

229–30 *and will be here in ten minutes*: In another unauthorized ad-lib this line was altered to 'and they'll do it in eleven minutes'. In the set of notes referred to above, Helen D'Oyly Carte commented: 'I have had this omitted as soon as I heard of it', to which Gilbert added 'Quite right'.

232 *carried out*: At this point Pooh-Bah was wont to interject 'Yes, and you'll be carried out too, old chap'. Gilbert did not approve this gag, but it was nonetheless included in the libretto for the 1908 revival.

237 *What, now*: the cue for yet another ad-lib by Pooh-Bah: 'Cut it off, Ko-Ko, he don't want it'. Gilbert's comment on this one was 'Not authorised. Please omit'.

240 *I don't go about . . .*: This time an occasion for some ad-libbing by Ko-Ko, who changed this line to 'I don't go about prepared to execute orders while you wait'. According to Helen D'Oyly Carte, 'This appears to have crept in without authorisation – it is said to go well – but it is of course for Mr Gilbert's decision.' Mr Gilbert was adamant: 'Omit. It is a most impertinent alteration.'

242 *Still, as Lord High Executioner*: Nearly all of these unauthorized alterations to the libretto which were the subject of scrutiny by Gilbert and Mrs D'Oyly Carte in 1907 had originally been introduced by Rutland Barrington, who was to return to play the part of Pooh-Bah in the 1908 revival. This line he had altered to 'Still you know, Ko-Ko, as Lord High Bluebottle – I mean executioner'. This was one of the few Barrington gags which Gilbert did authorize, but, curiously, it does not appear in the copy of the libretto prepared by Helen D'Oyly Carte for the 1908 revival.

Ko. What do you mean?

NANK. I can't live without Yum-Yum. This afternoon I perform the Happy Despatch. 220

Ko. No, no – pardon me – I can't allow that.

NANK. Why not?

Ko. Why, hang it all, you're under contract to die by the hand of the Public Executioner in a month's time! If you kill yourself, what's to become of me? Why, I shall have to be executed in your place! 225

NANK. It would certainly seem so!

(Enter POOH-BAH.*)*

Ko. Now then, Lord Mayor, what is it?

POOH. The Mikado and his suite are approaching the city, and will be here in ten minutes. 230

Ko. The Mikado! He's coming to see whether his orders have been carried out! *(To* NANKI-POO.*)* Now look here, you know – this is getting serious – a bargain's a bargain, and you really mustn't frustrate the ends of justice by committing suicide. As a man of honour and a gentleman, you are bound to die ignominiously by the hands of the Public Executioner. 235

NANK. Very well, then – behead me.

Ko. What, now?

NANK. Certainly; at once.

POOH. Chop it off! Chop it off!

Ko. My good sir, I don't go about prepared to execute gentlemen at a 240 moment's notice. Why, I never even killed a blue-bottle!

POOH. Still, as Lord High Executioner —

Ko. My good sir, as Lord High Executioner, I've got to behead him in a month. I'm not ready yet. I don't know how it's done. I'm going to take lessons. I mean to begin with a guinea pig, and work my way through the 245 animal kingdom till I come to a Second Trombone. Why, you don't suppose that, as a humane man, I'd have accepted the post of Lord High Executioner if I hadn't thought the duties were purely nominal? I *can't* kill you – I can't kill anything! I can't kill anybody! *(Weeps.)*

NANK. Come, my poor fellow, we all have unpleasant duties to 250 discharge at times; after all, what is it? If I don't mind, why should you? Remember, sooner or later it must be done.

Ko. *(springing up suddenly).* Must *it?* I'm not so sure about that!

NANK. What do you mean?

Ko. Why should I kill you when making an affidavit that you've been 255 executed will do just as well? Here are plenty of witnesses – the Lord Chief Justice, Lord High Admiral, Commander-in-Chief, Secretary of State for the Home Department, First Lord of the Treasury, and Chief Commissioner of Police.

271–2   *Commissionaire*: Helen D'Oyly Carte's marked copy of the 1908 libretto has 'District mes-
        senger' substituted at this point. 'Commissionaire' was restored in 1914. In 1975, at the
        last night of the D'Oyly Carte London season, always an occasion for high-jinks, Pooh-
        Bah made his entrance at line 274 wearing a Savoy Hotel commissionaire's cap. He had
        previously appeared, at line 227, with a lord mayor's top hat and chain of office, and at
        line 279 he changed to a bishop's mitre.

282–3   *Nanki-Poo will explain all*: The licence copy has the following extra lines for Ko-Ko at this
        point: 'I'll have a couple of horses ready for you at the back kitchen door, and, as soon as
        you're married, gallop away, and don't ever come back any more.'

292–6 *Miya sama, miya sama*
        This is the one genuine Japanese song in *The Mikado*. Known as 'The Tokotonyare Song'
        after its chorus, it was composed by Masujiro Omura with words by Yajiro Shinagawa in
        the early years of the Meiji era, which began in 1868. It was a war song of the Japanese Im-
        perial Army and was sung by the loyalist troops under Prince Arisugawa who put down
        a rebellion against the Mikado by the leaders of the old feudal order in 1877.
        Translated, the first verse seems to mean: 'Your majesty, your majesty, what is it that
        flutters in front of the stallion?' The second verse of the song, which is not used here,
        answers this question: 'Do you not know that it is the imperial banner of silken brocade,
        signifying our intention to defeat the enemies of the Crown'.
        There is some difficulty about translating the chorus '*Toko tonyaré tonyaré na*'. Tokoton
        is a slang word for 'the finish' in an idiom corresponding to 'a fight to the finish', but it
        also has obscene connotations. In his *The Gilbert and Sullivan Book* Leslie Baily writes:

> The legend has grown up that Sullivan did not know the meaning of these words and that
> it was only in later years that a Japanese told him it was 'the foulest song ever sung in the
> lowest tea-house in Japan'; it is a nice story, especially when one thinks of the innocent ama-
> teur societies who have chanted these 'foul words' so many thousands of times, but it isn't
> true.

        I have myself been offered an obscene translation of this line, however, which I feel
        compelled to withhold from the eyes of my gentle readers.

NANK. But where are they? 260

KO. There they are. They'll all swear to it – won't you? (*To* POOH-BAH.)

POOH. Am I to understand that all of us high Officers of State are required to perjure ourselves to ensure your safety?

KO. Why not? You'll be grossly insulted, as usual.

POOH. Will the insult be cash down, or at a date? 265

KO. It will be a ready-money transaction.

POOH. (*Aside.*) Well, it will be a useful discipline. (*Aloud.*) Very good. Choose your fiction, and I'll endorse it! (*Aside.*) Ha! ha! Family Pride, how do you like *that*, my buck?

NANK. But I tell you that life without Yum-Yum — 270

KO. Oh, Yum-Yum, Yum-Yum! Bother Yum-Yum! Here, Commission-aire (*to* POOH-BAH), go and fetch Yum-Yum. (*Exit* POOH-BAH.) Take Yum-Yum and marry Yum-Yum, only go away and never come back again. (*Enter* POOH-BAH *with* YUM-YUM.) Here she is. Yum-Yum, are you particularly busy?

YUM. Not particularly. 275

KO. You've five minutes to spare?

YUM. Yes.

KO. Then go along with his Grace the Archbishop of Titipu; he'll marry you at once. 280

YUM. But if I'm to be buried alive?

KO. Now, don't ask any questions, but do as I tell you, and Nanki-Poo will explain all.

NANK. But one moment —

KO. Not for worlds. Here comes the Mikado, no doubt to ascertain 285 whether I've obeyed his decree, and if he finds you alive I shall have the greatest difficulty in persuading him that I've beheaded you. (*Exeunt* NANKI-POO *and* YUM-YUM, *followed by* POOH-BAH.) Close thing that, for here he comes!

(*Exit* KO-KO.) 290

(*March – Enter procession, heralding* MIKADO, *with* KATISHA.)

Entrance of MIKADO *and* KATISHA.
('*March of the Mikado's troops.*')

CHORUS.   Miya sama, miya sama,
On n'm-ma no mayé ni
Pira-Pira suru no wa
Nan gia na
Toko tonyaré tonyaré na? 295

312   *In a fatherly kind of way*: This is, perhaps, an appropriate point at which to look at the situation of the real Mikado of Japan at the time the opera was written. The word 'Mikado' is, incidentally, a perfectly respectable Japanese 'elevated' expression for the Emperor – its literal meaning is 'Honourable Gate'.

In 1885 the Emperor of Japan was indeed governing his country in a fatherly kind of way. The Meiji Restoration seventeen years earlier had brought back direct imperial rule to the country after a long period where effective power had rested with the feudal lords, or *shoguns*, led by the Tokugawa family.

The Emperor Mutsuhito, whose reign from 1867 to 1912 inaugurated the Meiji era, transformed Japan from a feudal oligarchy into a Western-style constitutional monarchy. He introduced strong centralized government and in 1889 established a two-chamber legislature based on the British model.

There is, of course, still an Emperor of Japan, who is the current representative of the longest reigning imperial dynasty in the world. However, since 1946 he has had no power and has been simply a figurehead. In 1885 he was still a force to be reckoned with, even if he was a more humane, and a more Westernized Mikado than had ever existed before.

327–88   *A more humane Mikado*

Unbelievable as it may seem, the famous song in which the Mikado tries to make the punishment fit the crime was very nearly struck out of the opera and never performed. Gilbert announced his decision to cut it at the dress rehearsal, and only a last-minute deputation from the chorus led him to change his mind and keep it in.

Since its first-night performance by Richard Temple it has, of course, been one of the most popular numbers in the entire Gilbert and Sullivan repertoire. Its greatest exponent was almost certainly Darrel Fancourt, who played the role of the Mikado more than 3,000 times in D'Oyly Carte productions between 1920 and 1953, and who developed the blood-curdling laugh between verses which had been introduced by earlier performers and which has been a feature of D'Oyly Carte Mikados ever since.

Gilbert originally wrote a different version of the first verse from the one now sung. It is in the licence copy:

> All men who give indifferent dinners,
> And poison their friends and mine
> With two shilling sillery
> Stand in a pillory
> Every day at nine.
> All prosy dull society sinners
> Who chatter and bleat and bore,
> Are sent to hear sermons
> From mystical Germans
> Who preach from ten till four.
> And every big and bulky fellow,
> Of elephantine weights,
> Is made to run races
> On gravelly places
> In eighteenpenny skates.

DUET – MIKADO *and* KATISHA.

MIK.   From every kind of man
      Obedience I expect;
    I'm the Emperor of Japan –

KAT.   And I'm his daughter-in-law elect!   300
      He'll marry his son
      (He's only got one)
    To his daughter-in-law elect!

MIK.   My morals have been declared
      Particularly correct;   305

KAT.   But they're nothing at all, compared
    With those of his daughter-in-law elect!
      Bow – Bow –
    To his daughter-in-law elect!

ALL.   Bow – Bow –
    To his daughter-in-law elect.   310

MIK.   In a fatherly kind of way
      I govern each tribe and sect,
    All cheerfully own my sway –

KAT.   Except his daughter-in-law elect!
      As tough as a bone,   315
      With a will of her own,
    Is his daughter-in-law elect!

MIK.   My nature is love and light –
      My freedom from all defect –
                  320

KAT.   Is insignificant quite,
    Compared with his daughter-in-law elect!
      Bow – Bow –
    To his daughter-in-law elect!

ALL.   Bow – Bow –
    To his daughter-in-law elect!   325

SONG – MIKADO *and* CHORUS.

A more humane Mikado never
    Did in Japan exist,

348 *mystical Germans*: This is thought to be a reference to a group of zealous, and evidently rather long-winded, Lutheran evangelists, who had recently been over in England on a preaching tour.

354 *Madame Tussaud's waxwork*: Madam Tussaud came to England in the early 1800s from her native France, where she had been compelled to make wax casts of the heads of victims of the guillotine. She toured the country with her waxworks exhibition and finally established a permanent museum in Baker Street, London. Madame Tussaud's moved to its present site in the Marylebone Road in 1884. She also gets a mention in Colonel Calverley's list of 'all the remarkable people in history' in Act I of *Patience*.

358 *Is painted with vigour*: Until 1948 this line was sung 'Is blacked like a nigger' (with the next line continuing 'With permanent walnut juice'). In that year it was amended for the same reason as 'the nigger serenader' in Ko-Ko's 'little list' song (see the note to Act I, line 251). A. P. Herbert, who provided the new line, offered two other alternatives to Rupert D'Oyly Carte, which would have involved more extensive alteration of Gilbert's original and were, therefore, rejected:

> (1) The lady who dyes a chemical yellow
> Or stains her grey hair green,
> Is taken to Dover
> And painted all over
> A horrible ultramarine.

> (2) The lady who dyes a chemical yellow
> Or stains her grey hair puce,
> Is made to wear feathers
> In all the worst weathers
> And legibly labelled 'Goose'.

364 *Parliamentary trains*: An Act of 1844 had compelled railway companies to run at least one train a day on all lines which stopped at every station with a fare of one penny a mile. These came to be known as Parliamentary trains and brought the benefits of rail travel, albeit at a rather slow speed, to the working classes. In 1962 Donald Adams, principal bass with the D'Oyly Carte Company from 1953 to 1969, substituted 'slow suburban trains', although he reverted to 'Parliamentary trains' for the 1965 recording.

To nobody second,
I'm certainly reckoned
A true philanthropist.   330
It is my very humane endeavour
To make, to some extent,
Each evil liver
A running river
Of harmless merriment.   335

My object all sublime
I shall achieve in time –
To let the punishment fit the crime –
The punishment fit the crime;
And make each prisoner pent   340
Unwillingly represent
A source of innocent merriment!
Of innocent merriment!

All prosy dull society sinners,
Who chatter and bleat and bore,   345
Are sent to hear sermons
From mystical Germans
Who preach from ten till four.
The amateur tenor, whose vocal villainies
All desire to shirk,   350
Shall, during off-hours,
Exhibit his powers
To Madame Tussaud's waxwork.

The lady who dyes a chemical yellow
Or stains her grey hair puce,   355
Or pinches her figger,
Is painted with vigour
And permanent walnut juice.
The idiot who, in railway carriages,
Scribbles on window-panes,   360
We only suffer
To ride on a buffer
In Parliamentary trains.

My object all sublime, etc.   365

CHORUS.   His object all sublime, etc.

374 *By Bach*: At this point Sullivan introduced into his orchestration the first twelve notes of Bach's *Fugue in G minor*, to be played by bassoon and clarinet.

376 *Monday Pops*: Forerunners of the modern-day Promenade Concerts, the Monday Pops were weekly concerts of classical music organized by Chappells, the music publishers. They began in 1859 in the St James's Hall, on the site of the present Piccadilly Hotel, and continued there until 1901, when they were transferred to the Queen's Hall. They are also mentioned in *Patience*, when Archibald Grosvenor portrays himself as an every-day young man

> Who thinks suburban 'hops'
> More fun than 'Monday Pops'.

377 *The billiard sharp*: Gilbert was himself something of a billiard sharp. In a letter sent to Sullivan when the composer was abroad, quoted in Leslie Ayre's *Gilbert and Sullivan Companion*, he wrote: 'I send you Cook on Billiards – the study of that work has made me what I am in Billiards, and if you devote six or eight hours a day to it regularly, you may hope to play up to my form when you return'.

381 *a spot that's always barred*: 'Spot' is the word used for the marked places on a billiard table where the balls are put, and particularly for the one where the red ball is placed.

The advertising quack who wearies
With tales of countless cures,
His teeth, I've enacted,
Shall all be extracted   370
By terrified amateurs.
The music-hall singer attends a series
Of masses and fugues and 'ops'
By Bach, interwoven
With Spohr and Beethoven,   375
At classical Monday Pops.

The billiard sharp whom any one catches,
His doom's extremely hard –
He's made to dwell –
In a dungeon cell   380
On a spot that's always barred.
And there he plays extravagant matches
In fitless finger-stalls
On a cloth untrue,
With a twisted cue   385
And elliptical billiard balls!

My object all sublime, etc.

CHORUS.   His object all sublime, etc.

(*Enter* POOH-BAH, KO-KO, *and* PITTI-SING. *All kneel.*)

(POOH-BAH *hands a paper to* KO-KO.)   390

KO. I am honoured in being permitted to welcome your Majesty. I guess the object of your Majesty's visit – your wishes have been attended to. The execution has taken place.
MIK. Oh, you've had an execution, have you?
KO. Yes. The Coroner has just handed me his certificate.   395
POOH. I am the Coroner. (KO-KO *hands certificate to* MIKADO.)
MIK. And this is the certificate of his death. (*Reads.*) 'At Titipu, in the presence of the Lord Chancellor, Lord Chief Justice, Attorney-General, Secretary of State for the Home Department, Lord Mayor, and Groom of the Second Floor Front —'
POOH. They were all present, your Majesty. I counted them myself.   400
MIK. Very good house. I wish I'd been in time for the performance.
KO. A tough fellow he was, too – a man of gigantic strength. His struggles were terrific. It was really a remarkable scene.
MIK. Describe it.   405

414   *snickersnee*: A word of Dutch origin meaning a knife or dagger.

421–6   *We know him well*
       G. K. Chesterton, in an essay on Gilbert and Sullivan in *The Eighteen Eighties*, suggested
       that this chorus was written in mockery of the Victorians' absurdly exaggerated belief in
       the probity and gentlemanliness of their upper classes. A correct interpretation of these
       lines, according to this argument, would be 'This is a man belonging to a class so exqui-
       sitely well-bred that even when he tries to tell lies he cannot bring it off'. But this, as
       W. A. Darlington argued in his *The World of Gilbert and Sullivan*, is mistakenly to read
       deep social satire into what was simply a humorous chorus. Anyway, Ko-Ko could hardly
       be described as upper-class.

432   *he whistled an air*: At this point Sullivan added a suitable piccolo solo in the orchestral
       score. At first it was a snatch from the very popular 'Cotillion Waltz', but later a phrase
       from the traditional song 'The Girl I Left Behind Me' was substituted.

435   *His cervical vertebræ*: The seven bones forming the upper part of the spine, also known as
       the neck bones.

TRIO AND CHORUS.

KO-KO, PITTI-SING, POOH-BAH *and* CHORUS.

Ko.   The criminal cried, as he dropped him down,
     In a state of wild alarm –
    With a frightful, frantic, fearful frown,
     I bared my big right arm.
    I seized him by his little pig-tail,   410
     And on his knees fell he,
      As he squirmed and struggled,
      And gurgled and guggled,
     I drew my snickersnee!
      Oh, never shall I   415
      Forget the cry,
    Or the shriek that shriekèd he,
      As I gnashed my teeth,
      When from its sheath
    I drew my snickersnee!   420

CHORUS.

    We know him well,
    He cannot tell
  Untrue or groundless tales –
    He always tries
    To utter lies,   425
  And every time he fails.

PITTI.   He shivered and shook as he gave the sign
     For the stroke he didn't deserve;
    When all of a sudden his eye met mine,
     And it seemed to brace his nerve; 430
    For he nodded his head and kissed his hand,
     And he whistled an air, did he,
      As the sabre true
      Cut cleanly through
    His cervical vertebræ!   435
      When a man's afraid,
      A beautiful maid
    Is a cheering sight to see;
      And it's oh, I'm glad
      That moment sad   440
    Was soothed by sight of me!

452 *none of your impudent off-hand nods*: In another bit of Barrington-inspired business, Pitti-Sing touched Pooh-Bah during the singing of this line, and he said 'Go away'. According to Helen D'Oyly Carte, 'This was not objected to by WSG'.

456 *To a man of pedigree*: Cue for another ad-lib gag – Pooh-Bah is interrupted by Pitti-Sing while in the middle of singing the word 'pedigree' and says to her 'I'll give you such a Japanese smack in a minute'. In her notes Helen D'Oyly Carte wrote: 'This was never authorized. It seems to have sprung out of some "business" between Miss Bond and Mr Barrington, and he said something to this effect.' Gilbert's verdict was 'utterly stupid – please omit'.

CHORUS.

> Her terrible tale
> You can't assail,
> With truth it quite agrees:
> Her taste exact
> For faultless fact
> Amounts to a disease.

445

POOH.

> Now though you'd have said that head was dead
>   (For its owner dead was he),
> It stood on its neck, with a smile well-bred,
>   And bowed three times to me!
> It was none of your impudent off-hand nods,
>   But as humble as could be;
>   For it clearly knew
>   The deference due
>   To a man of pedigree!
>   And it's oh, I vow,
>   This deathly bow
>   Was a touching sight to see;
>   Though trunkless, yet
>   It couldn't forget
>   The deference due to me!

450

455

460

CHORUS.

> This haughty youth,
> He speaks the truth
> Whenever he finds it pays:
>   And in this case
>   It all took place
> Exactly as he says!   (*Exeunt* CHORUS.)

465

MIK. All this is very interesting, and I should like to have seen it. But we came about a totally different matter. A year ago my son, the heir to the throne of Japan, bolted from our Imperial Court.

470

KO. Indeed! Had he any reason to be dissatisfied with his position?

KAT. None whatever. On the contrary, I was going to marry him – yet he fled!

POOH. I am surprised that he should have fled from one so lovely!

475

KAT. That's not true.

POOH. No!

KAT. You hold that I am not beautiful because my face is plain. But you

487 *it is the largest in the world*: In early performances, Katisha had more anatomical delights to
reveal, as follows:

> K AT. Observe this ear.
> Ko. Large.
> K AT. Large? Enormous! But think of its delicate internal mechanism. It is fraught with
> beauty! As for this tooth, it almost stands alone. Many have tried to draw it, but in vain.

In the licence copy, Katisha's speech then continued:

> I took this young man in hand, and endeavoured to teach him my theory, but he was dull,
> and it took time. My theory is not learnt in a moment. It takes years to master. Just as the
> light was about to break upon this young man's darkened soul, he fled.

499 *Knightsbridge*: The reason for this apparently strange location was, of course, that it was
where the Japanese village had been erected in 1885. After the dismantling of the village,
the reference became somewhat obscure, and Gilbert took the unusual step of telling
Mrs D'Oyly Carte, at the time of the 1908 revival, 'the location in The Mikado can be
varied according to circumstances'. The D'Oyly Carte Company adopted certain standard locations when it was on tour. Thus in Liverpool performances Nanki-Poo's
address was Wigan, in Manchester it was Oldham, and in Birmingham, Small Heath.
    There were many other variations to suit topical events. A correspondent to *The Times*
in 1954 noted that in the 101 performances of *The Mikado* which he had seen since 1913,
there had been seventy different addresses for Nanki-Poo. They included Croydon at
the time of Amy Johnson's return from Australia to the airport there in 1930; Battersea
Park and the South Bank at the time of the Festival of Britain; Epsom on Derby Day;
The Oval during cricket Test matches; Putney on Boat Race day; and 'he's gone down'
in Oxford.

508 *I beg to offer an unqualified apology*: This and the next line were Barrington gags which Gilbert did not approve but which nonetheless found their way into both the 1887 libretto
and the edition authorized for the 1908 revival.

515 *thoroughly deserved all he got*: At this point Barrington was wont to remark 'He did, and he
got it'. Gilbert's comment on this gag was 'No. Please omit – it is idiotic'.

know nothing; you are still unenlightened. Learn, then, that it is not in the face alone that beauty is to be sought. My face is unattractive! 480

POOH. It is.

KAT. But I have a left shoulder-blade that is a miracle of loveliness. People come miles to see it. My right elbow has a fascination that few can resist.

POOH. Allow me! 485

KAT. It is on view Tuesdays and Fridays, on presentation of visiting card. As for my circulation, it is the largest in the world.

KO. And yet he fled!

MIK. And is now masquerading in this town, disguised as a Second Trombone. 490

KO. ⎫
POOH. ⎬ A Second Trombone!
PITTI. ⎭

MIK. Yes; would it be troubling you too much if I asked you to produce him? He goes by the name of —

KAT. Nanki-Poo.

MIK. Nanki-Poo. 495

KO. It's quite easy. That is, it's rather difficult. In point of fact, he's gone abroad!

MIK. Gone abroad! His address.

KO. Knightsbridge!

KAT. (*who is reading certificate of death*). Ha! 500

MIK. What's the matter?

KAT. See here – his name – Nanki-Poo – beheaded this morning. Oh, where shall I find another? Where shall I find another?

(KO-KO, POOH-BAH *and* PITTI-SING *fall on their knees.*)

MIK. (*looking at paper*). Dear, dear, dear! this is very tiresome. (*To* KO- 505
KO.) My poor fellow, in your anxiety to carry out my wishes you have beheaded the heir to the throne of Japan!

KO. I beg to offer an unqualified apology.

POOH. I desire to associate myself with that expression of regret.

PITTI. We really hadn't the least notion — 510

MIK. Of course you hadn't. How could you? Come, come, my good fellow, don't distress yourself – it was no fault of yours. If a man of exalted rank chooses to disguise himself as a Second Trombone, he must take the consequences. It really distresses me to see you take on so. I've no doubt he thoroughly deserved all he got. (*They rise.*) 515

KO. We are infinitely obliged to your Majesty —

PITTI. Much obliged, your Majesty.

520 *who the gentleman really was*: Yet another Barrington alteration. The original line went 'We couldn't know that he was the Heir Apparent'. This time Gilbert authorized the change.

526 *They drop down on their knees again*: It was at this point that a celebrated bit of business was first developed during the long initial run of *The Mikado*. While Pitti-Sing, Pooh-Bah and Ko-Ko were kneeling before the Mikado, Jessie Bond gave George Grossmith a push and he rolled right over. Gilbert was not amused and told Grossmith to cut out the gag. 'But I got a big laugh', the comic protested. 'So you would if you sat on a pork pie' was Gilbert's chilly reply.

Despite Gilbert's disapproval, variations on the gag continued. In 1907 Helen D'Oyly Carte noted that Pooh-Bah now rolled over Ko-Ko, with Pitti-Sing saying 'Pull him off quick'. Gilbert wrote against this note: 'No – there is too much clowning in this scene'. The business, however, continued. One night when Sir Henry Lytton was playing Ko-Ko he concealed a bladder under his costume so that when Fred Billington – all twenty stone of him – rolled over him there was a loud explosion. 'What's happened, Harry?' he whispered anxiously, 'what have I done?'

529 *either boiling oil or melted lead*: This line is said to have caused particular amusement to Queen Victoria during a special command performance of *The Mikado* which was given at Balmoral Castle in Scotland in September 1891.

556 *I don't want any lunch*: One of Barrington's more inspired additions to Gilbert's text, which the author agreed should be incorporated in the libretto. It appears in the 1887 libretto, where it is placed before the Mikado's line 'Then we'll make it after luncheon'.

POOH. Very much obliged, your Majesty.

MIK. Obliged? not a bit. Don't mention it. How *could* you tell?

POOH. No, of course we couldn't tell who the gentleman really was.   520

PITTI. It wasn't written on his forehead, you know.

KO. It might have been on his pocket-handkerchief, but Japanese don't use pocket-handkerchiefs! Ha! ha! ha!

MIK. Ha! ha! ha! (*To* KATISHA.) I forget the punishment for compassing the death of the Heir Apparent.   525

KO.
POOH. } Punishment. (*They drop down on their knees again.*)
PITTI.

MIK. Yes. Something lingering, with boiling oil in it, I fancy. Something of that sort. I think boiling oil occurs in it, but I'm not sure. I know it's something humorous, but lingering, with either boiling oil or melted lead. Come, come, don't fret – I'm not a bit angry.   530

KO. (*in abject terror*). If your Majesty will accept our assurance, we had no idea —

MIK. Of course —

PITTI. I knew nothing about it.

POOH. I wasn't there.   535

MIK. That's the pathetic part of it. Unfortunately, the fool of an Act says 'compassing the death of the Heir Apparent.' There's not a word about a mistake —

KO., PITTI., *and* POOH. No!

MIK. Or not knowing —   540

KO. No!

MIK. Or having no notion —

PITTI. No!

MIK. Or not being there —

POOH. No!   545

MIK. There should be, of course —

KO., PITTI., *and* POOH. Yes!

MIK. But there isn't.

KO., PITTI., *and* POOH. Oh!

MIK. That's the slovenly way in which these Acts are always drawn.   550
However, cheer up, it'll be all right. I'll have it altered next session. Now, let's see about your execution – will after luncheon suit you? Can you wait till then?

KO., PITTI., *and* POOH. Oh, yes – we can wait till then!

MIK. Then we'll make it after luncheon.   555

POOH. I don't want any lunch.

MIK. I'm really very sorry for you all, but it's an unjust world, and virtue is triumphant only in theatrical performances.

559–86 *See how the Fates their gifts allot*
Gilbert uses the same device of letters of the alphabet standing for individuals in the
second verse of Jack Point's song 'Oh! a private buffoon is a light-hearted loon' in Act II
of *The Yeomen of the Guard*:

> What is all right for B would quite scandalize C
>   (For C is so very particular);
> And D may be dull, and E's very thick skull
>   Is as empty of brains as a ladle;
> While F is F sharp, and will cry with a carp
>   That he's known your best joke from his cradle!

In the second verse of 'Were I a king in very truth' in Act I of *The Grand Duke* Ernest
Dummkopf manages to get as far as the letter G:

> Both A and B rehearsal slight –
> They say they'll be 'all right at night'
>   (They've both to go to school yet);
> C in each act *must* change her dress,
> D *will* attempt to 'square the press',
> E won't play Romeo unless
>   His grandmother plays Juliet;
> F claims all hoydens as her rights
>   (She's played them thirty seasons);
> And G must show herself in tights
>   For two convincing reasons –
>   Two very well-shaped reasons!

596 *But how about your big right arm*: Barrington changed this line to 'Yes, well; you can't say
much, Ko-Ko; look at that rubbish about your big right arm, look at it'. Gilbert said in
1907 that this alteration was not authorized 'but it can remain'. It was not, however,
included in the libretto for the 1908 revival.

GLEE.

PITTI-SING, KATISHA, KO-KO, POOH-BAH, *and* MIKADO.

MIK.   See how the Fates their gifts allot,
                          For A is happy – B is not.   560
                          Yet B is worthy, I dare say,
                          Of more prosperity than A!

KO., POOH., *and* PITTI.   *Is* B more worthy?
KAT.   I should say
                          He's worth a great deal more than A.   565

ENSEMBLE.   Yet A is happy!
                            Oh, so happy!
                        Laughing, Ha! ha!
                        Chaffing, Ha! ha!
                    Nectar quaffing, Ha! ha! ha!   570
                        Ever joyous, ever gay,
                        Happy, undeserving A!

KO., POOH., *and* PITTI.
                        If I were Fortune – which I'm not –
                        B should enjoy A's happy lot,
                        And A should die in miserie –   575
                        That is, assuming I am B.

MIK. *and* KAT.   But *should* A perish?
KO., POOH., *and* PITTI.   That should he
                        (Of course, assuming I am B).
                        B should be happy!   580
                          Oh, so happy!
                        Laughing, Ha! ha!
                        Chaffing, Ha! ha!
                    Nectar quaffing, Ha! ha! ha!
                    But condemned to die is he,   585
                    Wretched meritorious B!

                      (*Exeunt* MIKADO *and* KATISHA.)

KO. Well, a nice mess you've got us into, with your nodding head and the deference due to a man of pedigree!

POOH. Merely corroborative detail, intended to give artistic veri- 590
similitude to an otherwise bald and unconvincing narrative.

PITTI. Corroborative detail indeed! Corroborative fiddlestick!

KO. And you're just as bad as he is with your cock-and-a-bull stories about catching his eye and his whistling an air. But that's so like you! You must put in your oar!   595

POOH. But how about your big right arm?

600 *Enter Nanki-Poo*: Traditionally, Nanki-Poo enters with a bundle of belongings tied on a pole which he carries over his shoulder. Miss Beti Lloyd-Jones, who joined the D'Oyly Carte Company in 1956 and was still singing contralto roles when it closed in 1982, has told me that one of the favourite 'dirty tricks' occasionally played on leading tenors was to load Nanki-Poo's bundle with a 56-lb. stage weight just before he shouldered it for this entrance.

632–55 *The flowers that bloom in the spring*
Another song that never fails to get an encore. It received a triple encore at the first-night performance, as did 'Three little maids'. Sullivan composed the music for 'The flowers that bloom in the spring' one evening between tea and dinner.

In the licence copy the song is preceded by a short recitative for Nanki-Poo instead of the speech which he was later given in lines 629–31:

> Now hear my resolution – it's suggested by my wife –
> While Katisha is single I decline to come to life –
> When Katisha is married, that is quite another thing –
> Existence will be welcome as the flowers in the spring.

During the first-night performance George Grossmith, who was notoriously nervous on such occasions, slipped and fell in the middle of this song. This was greeted by so much laughter from the audience that Gilbert told him to make a regular feature of it.

Another famous bit of D'Oyly Carte business also has its origins in an accident during the singing of 'The flowers that bloom in the spring'. While dancing around between verses, Sir Henry Lytton trod on a tack that had been left on the stage and drew his foot back with the pain. His autobiography records:

> From the audience there came a tremendous roar of laughter. For a moment I could not understand it at all. Looking down, however, I was amazed to find my big toe upright, almost at right angles to the rest of the foot. With my fan I pressed it down – then raised it again. This provoked such merriment among the audience that I did it a second time, and a third. All this time the theatre was convulsed. I confess that to myself it seemed jolly funny.

PITTI. Yes, and your snickersnee!

KO. Well, well, never mind that now. There's only one thing to be done. Nanki-Poo hasn't started yet – he must come to life again at once. (*Enter* NANKI-POO *and* YUM-YUM *prepared for journey.*) Here he comes. 600
Here, Nanki-Poo, I've good news for you – you're reprieved.

NANK. Oh, but it's too late. I'm a dead man, and I'm off for my honeymoon.

KO. Nonsense! A terrible thing has just happened. It seems you're the son of the Mikado. 605

NANK. Yes, but that happened some time ago.

KO. Is this a time for airy persiflage? Your father is here, and with Katisha!

NANK. My father! And with Katisha!

KO. Yes, he wants you particularly. 610

POOH. So does she.

YUM. Oh, but he's married now.

KO. But, bless my heart! what has that to do with it?

NANK. Katisha claims me in marriage, but I can't marry her because I'm married already – consequently she will insist on my execution, and if I'm 615
executed, my wife will have to be buried alive.

YUM. You see our difficulty.

KO. Yes. I don't know what's to be done.

NANK. There's one chance for you. If you could persuade Katisha to marry you, she would have no further claim on me, and in that case I could 620
come to life without any fear of being put to death.

KO. I marry Katisha!

YUM. I really think it's the only course.

KO. But, my good girl, have you seen her? She's something appalling!

PITTI. Ah! that's only her face. She has a left elbow which people come 625
miles to see!

POOH. I am told that her right heel is much admired by connoisseurs.

KO. My good sir, I decline to pin my heart upon any lady's right heel.

NANK. It comes to this: While Katisha is single, I prefer to be a disembodied spirit. When Katisha is married, existence will be as welcome 630
as the flowers in spring.

DUET – NANKI-POO *and* KO-KO.

(*With* YUM-YUM, PITTI-SING, *and* POOH-BAH.)

NANK.   The flowers that bloom in the spring,
                    Tra la,
              Breathe promise of merry sunshine –
              As we merrily dance and we sing, 635
                    Tra la,

659–62 *Alone, and yet alive*
This recitative, and Katisha's subsequent solo, 'Hearts do not break', are sometimes cut.
663–81 *Hearts do not break*
The licence copy contains a second verse of this song, cut before the first performance:

> Hearts do not break!
> If I mistake
> Why sleep, and wake
>   To life-long gloom?
> If love betrayed
> Can kill a maid
> As poets have said,
>   Where is thy tomb?
> Oh, life-long gloom –
> Dark demon, whom
> In dread I shun
> Go, loathly one!
> Come, haven sure,
> Come, grave obscure,
> Come, relatively cheerful tomb!

We welcome the hope that they bring,
  Tra la,
Of a summer of roses and wine.
  And that's what we mean when we say that a thing 640
  Is welcome as flowers that bloom in the spring.
   Tra la la la la la, etc.

ALL.   Tra la la la, etc.

KO.   The flowers that bloom in the spring,
    Tra la,
   Having nothing to do with the case. 645
  I've got to take under my wing,
    Tra la,
  A most unattractive old thing,
    Tra la,
   With a caricature of a face, 650
    And that's what I mean when I say, or I sing,
    'Oh, bother the flowers that bloom in the spring.'
     Tra la la la la la, etc.

ALL.   Tra la la la, Tra la la la, etc. 655

(Dance and exeunt NANKI-POO, YUM-YUM, POOH-BAH, PITTI-
SING, *and* KO-KO.)

(Enter KATISHA.)

RECITATIVE AND SONG – KATISHA.

Alone, and yet alive! Oh, sepulchre!
My soul is still my body's prisoner! 660
Remote the peace that Death alone can give –
My doom, to wait! my punishment, to live!

SONG.

 Hearts do not break!
 They sting and ache
 For old love's sake,
  But do not die, 665
 Though with each breath
 They long for death
 As witnesseth
  The living I! 670

706 *Darling*: This was added to the libretto at the time of the 1908 revival, although doubtless it had been said for some time before that.

713 *You know not what you say*: An almost identical phrase, 'You know not what you ask', occurs in *Iolanthe* and was originally the cue for the song 'A fairy once, as well you know' (see the note to line 477 on page 438).

Oh, living I!
Come, tell me why,
When hope is gone,
Dost thou stay on?
Why linger here,   675
Where all is drear?
Oh, living I!
Come, tell me why,
When hope is gone,
Dost thou stay on?   680
May not a cheated maiden die?

KO. (*entering and approaching her timidly*). Katisha!
KAT. The miscreant who robbed me of my love! But vengeance pursues
– they are heating the cauldron!
KO. Katisha – behold a suppliant at your feet! Katisha – mercy!   685
KAT. Mercy? Had you mercy on him? See here, you! You have slain my
love. He did not love *me*, but he would have loved me in time. I am an
acquired taste – only the educated palate can appreciate *me*. I was educating
his palate when he left me. Well, he is dead, and where shall I find another?
It takes years to train a man to love me. Am I to go through the weary round 690
again, and, at the same time, implore mercy for you who robbed me of my
prey – I mean my pupil – just as his education was on the point of
completion? Oh, where shall I find another?
KO. (*suddenly, and with great vehemence*). Here! – Here!
KAT. What!!!   695
KO. (*with intense passion*). Katisha, for years I have loved you with a
white-hot passion that is slowly but surely consuming my very vitals! Ah,
shrink not from me! If there is aught of woman's mercy in your heart, turn
not away from a love-sick suppliant whose every fibre thrills at your tiniest
touch! True it is that, under a poor mask of disgust, I have endeavoured to   700
conceal a passion whose inner fires are broiling the soul within me! But the
fire will not be smothered – it defies all attempts at extinction, and, breaking
forth, all the more eagerly for its long restraint, it declares itself in words that
will not be weighed – that cannot be schooled – that should not be too
severely criticized. Katisha, I dare not hope for your love – but I will not live 705
without it! Darling!
KAT. You, whose hands still reek with the blood of my betrothed,
dare to address words of passion to the woman you have so foully
wronged!
KO. I do – accept my love, or I perish on the spot!   710
KAT. Go to! Who knows so well as I that no one ever yet died of a
broken heart!
KO. You know not what you say. Listen!

714–37 *On a tree by a river a little tom–tit*
In *The Gilbert and Sullivan Book* Leslie Baily points to the close similarity between Gilbert's famous lines and verses by the poet Nicholas Rowe (1674–1718):

> To the Brook and the Willow that heard him complain,
>   Ah Willow, Willow,
> Poor Colin sat weeping and told them his pain,
>   Ah, Willow, Willow; ah Willow, Willow.
> Sweet stream, he cry'd sadly, I'll teach thee to flow;
> And the waters shall rise to the brink with my woe,
>   Ah Willow, Willow.

There is, of course, an even earlier parallel to Ko-Ko's ditty in the Willow Song from Shakespeare's *Othello* for which Sullivan wrote a setting not wholly dissimilar from his tune for Tit Willow.

Students of Gilbert and Sullivan have been much exercised by what might be called the ornithological aspects of this song. A correspondent to *The Times* in May 1959 suggested that Gilbert must have been glancing through the index of a book on birds when he came across the entry 'Tit, willow' and was attracted by its rhythm. A pencilled note in the margin of the copy of G. E. Dunn's *A Gilbert and Sullivan Dictionary* in the music library on the Berkeley campus of the University of California reads 'the song is that of the American bob-white quail which Sullivan must have heard on his visit a few years earlier'. It also points out that true tits only very rarely eat worms.

There have been many parodies of the 'titwillow' song. One of the best, quoted in *The Gilbert and Sullivan Book*, appeared in a London newspaper in 1907 at the time of the ban on *The Mikado*:

> In a house by the River the stalls and the pit
>   Wanted 'Willow, tit-willow, tit-willow.'
> But were told they'd no right to hear even a bit
>   Of 'Willow, tit-willow, tit-willow.'
> 'Why this utter inanity?' every one cried,
> As they asked the Lord Chamberlain why he had shied
> At the musical play which alone can provide
>   Us with 'Willow, tit-willow, tit-willow.'
>
> Is it true that Japan doesn't like us to sing
>   'Oh, willow – tit-willow, tit-willow'?
> For we're cutting 'The Flowers that Bloom in the Spring'
>   Besides 'Willow, tit-willow, tit-willow.'
> We've lost the Mikado; the scenes we all know,
> Pooh-Bah and Yum-Yum and the schoolgirls must go,
> With Katisha and also the cheerful Ko-Ko
>   Who sang 'Willow, tit-willow, tit-willow.'
>
> Now, the light-hearted natives of distant Japan
>   Hearing 'Willow, tit-willow, tit-willow'
> Could scarcely do aught but respond, to a man,
>   And 'Willow, tit-willow, tit-willow'
> Might quickly become (I see no reason why
> Not) a joy to Japan; Japanese passers-by
> I can picture delightedly shouting 'Banzai!
>   That's Willow, tit-willow, tit-willow.'

SONG – Ko-Ko.

On a tree by a river a little tom-tit
    Sang 'Willow, titwillow, titwillow!'
And I said to him, 'Dicky-bird, why do you sit 715
    Singing "Willow, titwillow, titwillow"?'
'Is it weakness of intellect, birdie?' I cried,
'Or a rather tough worm in your little inside?'
With a shake of his poor little head, he replied, 720
    'Oh, willow, titwillow, titwillow!'

He slapped at his chest, as he sat on that bough,
    Singing 'Willow, titwillow, titwillow!'
And a cold perspiration bespangled his brow,
    Oh, willow, titwillow, titwillow!' 725
He sobbed and he sighed, and a gurgle he gave,
Then he plunged himself into the billowy wave,
And an echo arose from the suicide's grave –
    'Oh, willow, titwillow, titwillow!'

Now I feel just as sure as I'm sure that my name 730
    Isn't Willow, titwillow, titwillow,
That 'twas blighted affection that made him exclaim,
    'Oh, willow, titwillow, titwillow!'
And if you remain callous and obdurate, I
Shall perish as he did, and you will know why, 735
Though I probably shall not exclaim as I die,
    'Oh, willow, titwillow, titwillow!'

(*During this song* KATISHA *has been greatly affected,
and at the end is almost in tears.*)

KAT. (*whimpering*). Did he really die of love? 740
Ko. He really did.
KAT. All on account of a cruel little hen?
Ko. Yes.
KAT. Poor little chap!
Ko. It's an affecting tale, and quite true. I knew the bird intimately. 745
KAT. Did you? He must have been very fond of her.
Ko. His devotion was something extraordinary.
KAT. (*still whimpering*). Poor little chap! And – and if I refuse you, will you go and do the same?
Ko. At once. 750
KAT. No, no – you mustn't! Anything but that! (*Falls on his breast.*) Oh, I'm a silly little goose!

765 *the Congo or the Niger*: As a cheap tailor, Ko-Ko can, perhaps, be pardoned a serious lapse
      in his knowledge of geography and natural history here. Tigers are, of course, only found
      in Asia, while both the Congo and the Niger are in West Africa.
         The Congo was much in the news at the time *The Mikado* was written. In 1878 the ex-
      plorer H. M. Stanley had returned to Europe after establishing the source of the river,
      the longest in Africa. As a result of an agreement which he made with King Leopold II,
      Belgium acquired sovereignty over the surrounding territory. At the Berlin Conference
      in 1885 Belgium's sovereignty over the Congo was recognized by the other powers and
      Leopold II took the title of ruler of the Independent State of the Congo.
         The upper reaches of the Niger river were also being extensively explored and opened
      up during the 1880s. The French gradually consolidated their hold on the surrounding
      territory and established the Federation of French West Africa in 1895.

784 *Do you fancy you are elderly enough*: Gilbert has sometimes been taken to task by critics for
      his morbid and most ungentlemanly obsession with the ageing of women and the decay
      of their attractive features. Compared to some of the other principal contraltos in the
      Savoy Operas, Katisha in fact comes off fairly lightly in this respect. Perhaps the cruel-
      lest song of all that a Gilbertian matron has to sing is Lady Jane's 'Silvered is the raven
      hair' at the beginning of Act II of *Patience*:

> Fading is the taper waist,
>   Shapeless grows the shapely limb,
> And although severely laced,
>   Spreading is the figure trim!
> Stouter than I used to be,
>   Still more corpulent grow I –
> There will be too much of me
>   In the coming by and by!

Ko. (*making a wry face*). You are!

KAT. And you won't hate me because I'm just a little teeny weeny wee bit bloodthirsty, will you? 755

Ko. Hate you? Oh, Katisha! is there not beauty even in bloodthirstiness?

KAT. My idea exactly.

DUET – KATISHA *and* KO-KO.

KAT.
　There is beauty in the bellow of the blast,
　　There is grandeur in the growling of the gale, 760
　　　There is eloquent outpouring
　　　When the lion is a-roaring,
　　And the tiger is a-lashing of his tail!

Ko.
　　　Yes, I like to see a tiger
　　　From the Congo or the Niger, 765
　　And especially when lashing of his tail!

KAT.
　Volcanoes have a splendour that is grim,
　　And earthquakes only terrify the dolts,
　　　But to him who's scientific
　　　There is nothing that's terrific 770
　　In the falling of a flight of thunderbolts!

Ko.
　　　Yes, in spite of all my meekness,
　　　If I have a little weakness,
　　It's a passion for a flight of thunderbolts!

BOTH.
　　　If that is so, 775
　　　　Sing derry down derry!
　　　It's evident, very,
　　　　　Our tastes are one.
　　　Away we'll go,
　　　　And merrily marry, 780
　　　Nor tardily tarry
　　　　Till day is done!

Ko.
　There is beauty in extreme old age –
　　Do you fancy you are elderly enough?
　　　Information I'm requesting 785
　　　On a subject interesting:
　　Is a maiden all the better when she's tough?

KAT.
　　　Throughout this wide dominion
　　　It's the general opinion
　　That she'll last a good deal longer when she's tough. 790

Ko.
　Are you old enough to marry, do you think?
　　Won't you wait until you're eighty in the shade?

819　*Mercy even for Pooh-Bah*: This, I am sure, was another of Rutland Barrington's gags. Although it is not in the list drawn up in 1907 by Helen D'Oyly Carte to put to Gilbert for approval, it does not appear in the original libretto and is written in by hand in the master-copy of the libretto for the 1908 revival.

823　*We were married*: In another Barrington gag, Ko-Ko altered this line to 'We were married after lunch before the Registrar'. Gilbert approved this change in 1907. The 1908 libretto also changes Pooh-Bah's next line to 'I am the after luncheon Registrar'.

    There's a fascination frantic
    In a ruin that's romantic;
   Do you think you are sufficiently decayed? 795
KAT.   To the matter that you mention
    I have given some attention,
   And I think I am sufficiently decayed.
BOTH.   If that is so,
     Sing derry down derry! 800
    It's evident, very,
     Our tastes are one!
   Away we'll go,
    And merrily marry,
    Nor tardily tarry 805
    Till day is done!

        (*Exeunt together.*)

(*Flourish. Enter the* MIKADO, *attended by* PISH-TUSH *and Court.*)

MIK. Now then, we've had a capital lunch, and we're quite ready. Have
all the painful preparations been made? 810
 PISH. Your Majesty, all is prepared.
 MIK. Then produce the unfortunate gentleman and his two well-
meaning but misguided accomplices.

(*Enter* KO-KO, KATISHA, POOH-BAH, *and* PITTI-SING. *They throw
themselves at the* MIKADO'S *feet.*) 815

 KAT. Mercy! Mercy for Ko-Ko! Mercy for Pitti-Sing! Mercy even for
Pooh-Bah!
 MIK. I beg your pardon, I don't think I quite caught that remark.
 POOH. Mercy even for Pooh-Bah.
 KAT. Mercy! My husband that was to have been is dead, and I have 820
just married this miserable object.
 MIK. Oh! You've not been long about it!
 KO. We were married before the Registrar.
 POOH. *I* am the Registrar.
 MIK. I see. But my difficulty is that, as you have slain the Heir 825
Apparent —

(*Enter* NANKI-POO *and* YUM-YUM. *They kneel.*)

 NANKI. The Heir Apparent is *not* slain.
 MIK. Bless my heart, my son!

831   *seizing Ko-Ko*: As Katisha vigorously shook Ko-Ko, Rutland Barrington would call out 'Time'. Gilbert authorized this gag in 1907.

846–77 '*For he's gone and married Yum-Yum*
      In early editions of the libretto, the reprise of 'For he's gone and married Yum-Yum' was not sung and the finale simply consisted of 'The threatened cloud has passed away', arranged, as now, with Yum-Yum and Nanki-Poo singing the first four lines and everyone else singing the rest. It is very doubtful if this version was ever performed, however, as all editions of the vocal score have the present arrangement which was almost certainly produced before the opening night.
      The finale of the Texas version of *The Mikado* in 1888, mentioned above in the note to lines 31–62, went:

> For he's going to stay in Fort Worth –
> Fort Worth,
> Now pocket your malice
> And slip off to Dallas,
> Or come and partake of our mirth –
> Mirth – mirth,
> And join our expressions of glee.

YUM. And your daughter-in-law elected! 830

KAT. (*seizing* KO-KO). Traitor, you have deceived me!

MIK. Yes, you are entitled to a little explanation, but I think he will give it better whole than in pieces.

KO. Your Majesty, it's like this: It is true that I stated that I had killed Nanki-Poo — 835

MIK. Yes, with most affecting particulars.

POOH. Merely corroborative detail intended to give artistic verisimilitude to a bald and —

KO. *Will* you refrain from putting in your oar? (*To* MIKADO.) It's like this: When your Majesty says, 'Let a thing be done,' it's as good as done – 840 practically, it *is* done – because your Majesty's will is law. Your Majesty says, 'Kill a gentleman,' and a gentleman is told off to be killed. Consequently, that gentleman is as good as dead – practically, he *is* dead – and if he is dead, why not say so?

MIK. I see. Nothing could possibly be more satisfactory! 845

FINALE.

PITTI.	For he's gone and married Yum-Yum –
ALL.	Yum-Yum!
PITTI.	Your anger pray bury,
	For all will be merry,
	I think you had better succumb – 850
ALL.	Cumb – cumb.
PITTI.	And join our expressions of glee!
KO.	On this subject I pray you be dumb –
ALL.	Dumb – dumb!
KO.	Your notions, though many, 855
	Are not worth a penny,
	The word for your guidance is 'Mum' –
ALL.	Mum – mum!
KO.	You've a very good bargain in me.
ALL.	On this subject we pray you be dumb – 860
	Dumb – dumb!
	We think you had better succumb –
	Cumb – Cumb!
	You'll find there are many
	Who'll wed for a penny, 865
	There are lots of good fish in the sea.
YUM. *and* NANK.	The threatened cloud has passed away,
	And brightly shines the dawning day;
	What though the night may come too soon,
	We've years and years of afternoon! 870

ALL.   Then let the throng
                          Our joy advance,
                       With laughing song
                          And merry dance,
                       With joyous shout and ringing cheer,   875
                       Inaugurate our new career!
                          Then let the throng, etc.

                             CURTAIN

RUDDIGORE

or

The Witch's Curse

DRAMATIS PERSONÆ

MORTALS

SIR RUTHVEN MURGATROYD (*disguised as Robin Oakapple, a Young Farmer*)
RICHARD DAUNTLESS (*his Foster-Brother – a Man-o'-war's man*)
SIR DESPARD MURGATROYD, OF RUDDIGORE (*a Wicked Baronet*)
OLD ADAM GOODHEART (*Robin's Faithful Servant*)
ROSE MAYBUD (*a Village Maiden*)
MAD MARGARET
DAME HANNAH (*Rose's Aunt*)
ZORAH ⎫ (*Professional Bridesmaids*)
RUTH ⎭

GHOSTS

SIR RUPERT MURGATROYD (*the First Baronet*)
SIR JASPER MURGATROYD (*the Third Baronet*)
SIR LIONEL MURGATROYD (*the Sixth Baronet*)
SIR CONRAD MURGATROYD (*the Twelfth Baronet*)
SIR DESMOND MURGATROYD (*the Sixteenth Baronet*)
SIR GILBERT MURGATROYD (*the Eighteenth Baronet*)
SIR MERVYN MURGATROYD (*the Twentieth Baronet*)
  AND
SIR RODERIC MURGATROYD (*the Twenty-first Baronet*)

Chorus of Officers, Ancestors, Professional Bridesmaids, and Villagers.

ACT I. – The Fishing Village of Rederring, in Cornwall.
ACT II. – The Picture Gallery in Ruddigore Castle.
Time – Early in the 19th century.

RUDDIGORE

Ruddigore was the first of Gilbert and Sullivan's works to receive a less than rapturous reception from the first-night audience. Boos and hisses mingled with the applause when the curtain went down on the first performance at the Savoy Theatre on 22 January 1887.

It was, of course, extraordinarily difficult to produce a work that could match the popularity of *The Mikado*, which had been taken off at the Savoy on 19 January after a record run of 672 performances. But it was not just in comparison with their previous work that critics and public alike judged Gilbert and Sullivan's new opera to be something of a flop. There were other more specific weaknesses which they detected in the burlesque of Victorian melodrama about bad baronets and innocent maidens.

The original title of the opera, which was *Ruddygore*, caused considerable offence. It was felt to be decidedly coarse for a work intended for a respectable family audience. Gilbert at first made light of the objections. When a fellow member of his club commented that he saw no difference between *Ruddygore* and *Bloodygore*, the author responded: 'Then I suppose you'll take it that if I say "I admire your ruddy countenance," I mean "I like your bloody cheek."' He impishly suggested to another detractor that the opera should be re-titled 'Kensington Gore, or Not so good as the *Mikado*'. Within a few days, however, he had taken heed of the criticism and changed the title to the less offensive *Ruddigore*.

The construction of the opera also provoked complaint. The First Act, although long (running to eighty-eight minutes, it is, indeed, the longest first act in all the Savoy repertoire), was reasonably well received by audiences and critics alike. The Second Act, however, was thought to drag and to lack any dramatic shape. The scene in which the ghosts step down from their portraits was clumsily managed in early performances, and the later encounter between Dame Hannah and the ghost of Sir Roderic Murgatroyd was generally thought to lack conviction and by some also to lack taste. A second appearance by the ghosts at the end of the act also jarred on many. Gilbert and Sullivan responded by substantially altering the Second Act and reducing its length.

In fact, *Ruddigore* was not in the end the disaster that it threatened to be on the opening night. It ran at the Savoy for a total of 288 performances, more than the first run of *Princess Ida*. Gilbert commented: 'I could do with a few more such failures.' It was not revived until 1920, when it was performed at the

King's Theatre, Glasgow, with further substantial cuts made in both the First and Second Acts and with a new overture by Geoffrey Toye to replace Sullivan's original, which contained several tunes which were no longer heard in the opera. This production was extremely popular, and Gilbert's widow considered it much better than her husband's original. The D'Oyly Carte costumes and scenery were destroyed in the war, and in the autumn of 1948 a new production was mounted by Peter Goffin. Rehearsals for this were only just getting under way when Rupert D'Oyly Carte died, and his daughter, Bridget, was suddenly thrown into running the company and seeing the new *Ruddigore* on to the stage. This she did most successfully. It opened in Newcastle in November 1948, was seen in London the following year, and remained in the D'Oyly Carte repertoire until the company's closure.

Thankfully, the demise of the old D'Oyly Carte Company in 1982 did not mean *Ruddigore*'s disappearance from the professional repertoire. The Brent Walker video released that year gave it a star-studded cast led by Vincent Price, who put all his Hammer Films horror training into the role of Sir Despard Murgatroyd, Keith Michell as Robin Oakapple and D'Oyly Carte veteran Donald Adams as Sir Roderic Murgatroyd. In 1987 New Sadler's Wells Opera toured an excellent production by Ian Judge which was notable for its restoration of several passages of music which had long been cut. They included the ghost march in Act II which was removed after Gilbert complained that 'it was as though one inserted fifty lines of *Paradise Lost* into a farcical comedy'. It was also originally intended to include Robin's Act II patter song, 'Henceforth all the crimes that I find in *The Times*' in the New Sadler's Wells stage production but in the event the song only made it into the recording that was made on the TER label.

It is certainly to be hoped that *Ruddigore* continues to receive at least occasional professional performances. Sullivan, who set the songs in intervals from composing his oratorio *The Golden Legend*, based on a poem by Henry Longfellow, produced some memorable tunes, ranging from the delicate 'If somebody there chanced to be' and 'There grew a little flower' to the breezy 'In sailing o'er life's ocean wide' and the frighteningly eerie 'When the night wind howls'. Gilbert's take-off of the black-and-white morality and crude characterization of Victorian melodrama, while perhaps itself a little dated and heavy-handed now, still has an undeniable humour and produces in the figure of Sir Despard Murgatroyd a perfect caricature of the stage villain.

Ruddigore also has an important place in D'Oyly Carte folk history. It was as Sir Ruthven Murgatroyd, alias the poor and blameless peasant Robin Oakapple, that one of the greatest ever Savoyards made his first appearance as a principal with the company. George Grossmith had been taken seriously ill with peritonitis at the end of the first week of the opera's initial run. His understudy, who had only been in the job for a week and who had to go on at a few hours' notice, was a young man who used the stage name H. A. Henri but whose real name was Henry Lytton. He was an enormous success in the role and went on to play all the principal baritone and comic parts in the Savoy Operas. After a brief period away he returned to the company in 1908 and ten years later became the principal comedian. Lytton was knighted in 1930 and retired in 1934, fifty years after he had first joined the D'Oyly Carte Company as a member of the chorus in *Princess Ida*.

1–3　*Scene: Ruddigore* is not the only Gilbert and Sullivan opera to be set in Cornwall. So also, of course, is *The Pirates of Penzance*, although, unlike Penzance, Rederring is an entirely fictional location and not to be taken too seriously.

Gilbert sems to have had several changes of mind about the period in which the opera should be set, but eventually he opted for the beginning of the nineteenth century. *The World* noted 'The time is George III' and *The Times* that 'the opening scene represents a fishing village eighty or ninety years ago'.

The set for Act I changed very little in successive D'Oyly Carte productions. The *Sporting Life*'s description of the scene at the first performance could equally well describe the 1948 setting that was in use up to 1982: 'The main part of the village itself straggles away from Rose Maybud's cottage along the cliffs, which, with the porched cottage aforesaid, lock in a picturesque harbour. Some spreading chestnut trees occupy the side of the picture of the scene. The sea opens in the centre.'

4–11　*Fair is Rose as bright May-day*

Although successive editions of the vocal score print the words of this opening chorus as they are given opposite, and that is how it is generally sung, nearly all editions of the libretti add an extra syllable to each line by inserting a 'the' as follows:

> Fair is Rose as the bright May-day;
> Soft is Rose as the warm west-wind;
> Sweet is Rose as the new-mown hay –
> Rose is the queen of maiden-kind!

15　*Can't long remain unclaimed*: In a pre-production copy of *Ruddigore* which pre-dates the licence copy and in early published editions of the libretto this line appears as 'Won't very long remain unclaimed', and lines 18–19 appear as:

> And though she's the fairest flower that blows,
> Nobody yet has married Rose!

In his pre-production copy these lines are altered in Gilbert's handwriting to their present version.

ACT I

S CENE. – *The fishing village of Rederring (in Cornwall).* ROSE MAYBUD'S *cottage is seen* L. *Villagers and* DAME HANNAH *discovered. Enter Chorus of Bridesmaids. They range themselves in front of* ROSE'S *cottage.*

CHORUS OF BRIDESMAIDS.

Fair is Rose as bright May-day;
   Soft is Rose as warm west-wind;   5
Sweet is Rose as new-mown hay –
   Rose is queen of maiden-kind!
     Rose, all glowing
       With virgin blushes, say –
     Is anybody going   10
       To marry you to-day?

SOLO – ZORAH.

Every day, as the days roll on,
Bridesmaids' garb we gaily don,
Sure that a maid so fairly famed
Can't long remain unclaimed.   15
Hour by hour and day by day,
Several months have passed away,
Though she's the fairest flower that blows,
No one has married Rose!

CHORUS.

Rose, all glowing   20
   With virgin blushes, say –
Is anybody going
   To marry you to-day?

47–8   *one of the bad Baronets of Ruddigore*: Baronets are members of the lowest hereditary titled
order in Britain, which was instituted by James I in the early seventeenth century. They
are styled 'Sir' and the title is normally shortened to 'Bart' after their names. Apart from
Ruddigore, which is fairly stuffed with them, the only other Savoy Opera to contain a
baronet is *The Sorcerer*, with Sir Marmaduke Pointdextre as an elderly example of the
species.

Gilbert was to return to the theme of bad baronets in his story 'The Fairy's Dilemma'
which appeared in the Christmas 1900 edition of the *Graphic* magazine. It tells of an apparently wicked baronet, Sir Trevor Mauleverer, who is assisted by the Demon Alcohol
to carry off a virtuous young governess to whom he had taken a fancy. In the event, however, Sir Trevor proves to be a good baronet, as the Demon explains to the fairy who tries
to help the girl:

> I rashly assumed, as you did, that, being a Baronet, he must be a bad one. Such a name,
> too – Sir Trevor Mauleverer! There's villainy in every letter of it! But (it's just like my luck)
> when I appeared to him and offered to help him to carry off Miss Collins, he indignantly
> rebuked me and gave me this tract! (producing a leaflet headed 'Where the Devil are you
> Going?') He turns out to be a Nonconformist Baronet of the very strictest principles.

58–103 *Sir Rupert Murgatroyd*
This song evidently caused Gilbert some difficulty. The pre-production libretto referred
to above contains three crossings-out and substitutions in his hand, only one of which
was incorporated into the final libretto. The word 'ruthlessly' in line 60 is crossed out
and 'cruelly' inserted instead, the original 'And broil them at the stake' (line 66) is scored

ZORAH.   Hour by hour and day by day,
            Months have passed away.   25

CHORUS.   Fair is Rose as bright May-day, etc.

            (DAME HANNAH *comes down*.)

HANNAH. Nay, gentle maidens, you sing well but vainly, for Rose is still
heart-free, and looks but coldly upon her many suitors.

ZORAH. It's very disappointing. Every young man in the village is in   30
love with her, but they are appalled by her beauty and modesty, and won't
declare themselves; so, until she makes her own choice, there's no chance for
anybody else.

RUTH. This is, perhaps, the only village in the world that possesses an
endowed corps of professional bridesmaids who are bound to be on duty   35
every day from ten to four – and it is at least six months since our services
were required. The pious charity by which we exist is practically wasted!

ZOR. We shall be disendowed – that will be the end of it! Dame
Hannah – you're a nice old person – *you* could marry if you liked. There's old
Adam – Robin's faithful servant – he loves you with all the frenzy of a boy   40
of fourteen.

HAN. Nay – that may never be, for I am pledged!

ALL. To whom?

HAN. To an eternal maidenhood! Many years ago I was betrothed to a
god-like youth who woo'd me under an assumed name. But on the very day   45
upon which our wedding was to have been celebrated, I discovered that he
was no other than Sir Roderic Murgatroyd, one of the bad Baronets of
Ruddigore, and the uncle of the man who now bears that title. As a son of
that accursed race he was no husband for an honest girl, so, madly as I loved
him, I left him then and there. He died but ten years since, but I never saw   50
him again.

ZOR. But why should you not marry a bad Baronet of Ruddigore?

RUTH. All baronets are bad; but was he worse than other baronets?

HAN. My child, he was accursed.

ZOR. But who cursed him? Not you, I trust!   55

HAN. The curse is on all his line and has been, ever since the time of Sir
Rupert, the first Baronet. Listen, and you shall hear the legend:

LEGEND – HANNAH.

Sir Rupert Murgatroyd
    His leisure and his riches
He ruthlessly employed
    In persecuting witches.   60

out and replaced by the present version, and 'on each withered limb' (line 77) is replaced by 'on each palsied limb'.

The chorus 'This sport he much enjoyed' was dropped from the 1920 revival of *Ruddigore* but reinstated in the 1948 production. The pre-production libretto has the following additional chorus after the third verse (to be sung after line 89), which was, however, dropped before the first performance:

> This doom they can't avoid,
> These lords of Murgatroyd –
>   Both last and first,
>   You're all accurst
> Oh, House of Murgatroyd!

With fear he'd make them quake –
He'd duck them in his lake –
   He'd break their bones
   With sticks and stones,
And burn them at the stake! 65

CHORUS.   This sport he much enjoyed,
    Did Rupert Murgatroyd –
      No sense of shame
      Or pity came 70
    To Rupert Murgatroyd!

Once, on the village green,
   A palsied hag he roasted,
And what took place, I ween,
   Shook his composure boasted; 75
For, as the torture grim
Seized on each withered limb,
   The writhing dame
   'Mid fire and flame
Yelled forth this curse on him: 80

'Each lord of Ruddigore,
   Despite his best endeavour,
Shall do one crime, or more,
   Once, every day, for ever!
This doom he can't defy, 85
However he may try,
   For should he stay
   His hand, that day
In torture he shall die!'

The prophecy came true: 90
   Each heir who held the title
Had, every day, to do
   Some crime of import vital;
Until, with guilt o'erplied,
'I'll sin no more!' he cried, 95
   And on the day
   He said that say,
In agony he died!

CHORUS.   And thus, with sinning cloyed,
   Has died each Murgatroyd, 100

110 *Rowbottom*: The pre-production libretto includes a further item in Rose's list of gifts at
this point: 'a pair of spectacles for blind Timothy'. This rather tasteless joke did not
find its way into the licence copy or first edition of the libretto.

118–19 *a plated dish-cover*: A dome-shaped, silver plated cover for dishes of hot food.
119 *the workhouse door*: With this heart-tugging description of her origins Rose Maybud
establishes herself as a tragic heroine in the best tradition of Victorian melodrama.
Workhouses were, of course, institutions established for paupers and vagrants, and it
was not uncommon for desperate mothers to dump their babies on the doorstep so that
they could be looked after by the parish.
123 *the wife of a Lord Mayor*: This remark caused much amusement at the opening night of
Ruddigore. In the absence of royalty, the royal box at the Savoy was occupied by the Lord
Mayor of London, Sir Richard Hanson, and his wife, who must have been conscious of
many heads turning in her direction at this point.

133 *the manners of a Marquis*: Marquis (also spelt 'Marquess') is the second highest title of
nobility in Britain ranking immediately below that of duke and above that of earl. It was
first conferred on Richard II's favourite, Robert de Vere, who was created Marquess of
Dublin in 1385.
133–4 *the morals of a Methodist*: 'Methodist' was, of course, the term applied to John Wesley and
his followers who forsook the Church of England in the 1730s and 1740s and formed
what they regarded as a simpler and purer church. The Methodists have since been one
of the largest Nonconformist denominations in Britain and also one of the biggest
churches in the U.S.A. In *The Gondoliers* (Act I, lines 311–12) the Duke of Plaza-Toro re-
lates how the King of Barataria became a Wesleyan Methodist 'of the most bigoted and
persecuting type'.

And so shall fall,
Both one and all,
Each coming Murgatroyd!

(*Exeunt Chorus of Bridesmaids.*)

(*Enter* ROSE MAYBUD *from cottage, with small basket on her arm.*)   105

HAN. Whither away, dear Rose? On some errand of charity, as is thy
wont?

ROSE. A few gifts, dear aunt, for deserving villagers. Lo, here is some
peppermint rock for old gaffer Gadderby, a set of false teeth for pretty little
Ruth Rowbottom, and a pound of snuff for the poor orphan girl on the hill.   110

HAN. Ah, Rose, pity that so much goodness should not help to make
some gallant youth happy for life! Rose, why dost thou harden that little
heart of thine? Is there none hereaway whom thou couldst love?

ROSE. And if there were such an one, verily it would ill become me to tell
him so.   115

HAN. Nay, dear one, where true love is, there is little need of prim
formality.

ROSE. Hush, dear aunt, for thy words pain me sorely. Hung in a plated
dish-cover to the knocker of the workhouse door, with naught that I could
call mine own, save a change of baby-linen and a book of etiquette, little   120
wonder if I have always regarded that work as a voice from a parent's tomb.
This hallowed volume (*producing a book of etiquette*), composed, if I may
believe the title-page, by no less an authority than the wife of a Lord Mayor,
has been, through life, my guide and monitor. By its solemn precepts I have
learnt to test the moral worth of all who approach me. The man who bites his   125
bread, or eats peas with a knife, I look upon as a lost creature, and he who
has not acquired the proper way of entering and leaving a room is the object
of my pitying horror. There are those in this village who bite their nails, dear
aunt, and nearly all are wont to use their pocket combs in public places. In
truth I could pursue this painful theme much further, but behold, I have said   130
enough.

HAN. But is there not one among them who is faultless, in thine eyes? For
example – young Robin. He combines the manners of a Marquis with the
morals of a Methodist. Couldst thou not love *him*?

ROSE. And even if I could, how should I confess it unto him? For lo, he   135
is shy, and sayeth naught!

BALLAD – ROSE.

If somebody there chanced to be
Who loved me in a manner true,

146, 166 *Ah*: These sustained notes are the cure for a change of key from A minor to A major, which greatly enhances the haunting effect of this waltz song.

My heart would point him out to me,
  And I would point him out to you. 140
(*Referring to book.*) But here it says of those who point,
  Their manners must be out of joint –
    You *may* not point –
    You *must* not point –
  It's manners out of joint, to point! 145
Ah! Had I the love of such as he,
  Some quiet spot he'd take me to,
Then he could whisper it to me,
  And I could whisper it to you.
(*Referring to book.*) But whispering, I've somewhere met, 150
Is contrary to etiquette:
    Where can it be? (*Searching book.*)
    Now let me see – (*Finding reference.*)
    Yes, yes!
It's contrary to etiquette! 155

(*Showing it to* DAME HANNAH.)

If any well-bred youth I knew,
  Polite and gentle, neat and trim,
Then I would hint as much to you,
  And you could hint as much to him. 160
(*Referring to book.*) But here it says, in plainest print,
  'It's most unladylike to hint' –
    You *may* not hint,
    You *must* not hint –
  It says you mustn't hint, in print! 165
Ah! And if I loved him through and through –
  (True love and not a passing whim),
Then I could speak of it to you,
  And you could speak of it to him.
(*Referring to book.*) But here I find it doesn't do 170
To speak until you're spoken to.
    Where can it be? (*Searching book.*)
    Now let me see – (*Finding reference.*)
    Yes, yes!
'Don't speak until you're spoken to!' 175

(*Exit* DAME HANNAH.)

ROSE. Poor aunt! Little did the good soul think, when she breathed the hallowed name of Robin, that he would do even as well as another. But he

184 *I wished to say that*: In his biography of George Grossmith, privately published in 1982, Tony Joseph points to the similarity between this passage for Rose and Robin and the opening dialogue of Grossmith's comic piece *Cups and Saucers*, which had been written eleven years earlier than *Ruddigore*:

GENERAL.	How fine it was today.
MRS WORCESTER.	It was.
GENERAL.	It was.
MRS WORCESTER.	Yes, it was. (*Pause*).
GENERAL.	And yesterday was wet.
MRS WORCESTER.	It was.
GENERAL.	It was.
MRS WORCESTER.	Yes, it was.

After this hesitant and bashful start, the relationship between the general and Mrs Worcester blossoms, and in the end, like Robin and Rose Maybud, they marry and live happily ever after.

203–45 *I know a youth who loves a little maid*
This delightful little duet echoes the theme of one of Gilbert's *Bab Ballads*, 'The Modest Couple':

> When man and maiden meet, I like to see a drooping eye,
> I always droop my own – I am the shyest of the shy.
> I'm also fond of bashfulness, and sitting down on thorns,
> For modesty's a quality that womankind adorns.
>
> Whenever I am introduced to any pretty maid,
> My knees they knock together, just as if I were afraid;
> I flutter, and I stammer, and I turn a pleasing red,
> For to laugh, and flirt, and ogle I consider most ill-bred.

In his prompt copy, Gilbert wrote the following directions beside this song:

As each sings they regard the other and then look away sheepishly.
Between each verse both take *one* step towards each other.
For the last verse they are back to back.

resembleth all the youths in this village, in that he is unduly bashful in my
presence, and lo, it is hard to bring him to the point. But soft, he is here!   180

(ROSE *is about to go when* ROBIN *enters and calls her.*)

ROBIN. Mistress Rose!
ROSE. (*Surprised.*) Master Robin!
ROB. I wished to say that – it is fine.
ROSE. It is passing fine.   185
ROB. But we do want rain.
ROSE. Aye, sorely! Is that all?
ROB. (*Sighing.*) That is all.
ROSE. Good day, Master Robin!
ROB. Good day, Mistress Rose! (*Both going – both stop.*)   190
ROSE. ⎫ I crave pardon, I —
ROB. ⎭ I beg pardon, I —
ROSE. You were about to say? —
ROB. I would fain consult you —
ROSE. Truly?   195
ROB. It is about a friend.
ROSE. In truth I have a friend myself.
ROB. Indeed? I mean, of course —
ROSE. And I would fain consult you —
ROB. (*Anxiously.*) About him?   200
ROSE. (*Prudishly.*) About *her*.
ROB. (*Relieved.*) Let us consult one another.

DUET – ROBIN *and* ROSE.

ROB.   I know a youth who loves a little maid –
                 (Hey, but his face is a sight for to see!)
             Silent is he, for he's modest and afraid –   205
                 (Hey, but he's timid as a youth can be!)

ROSE.   I know a maid who loves a gallant youth,
                 (Hey, but she sickens as the days go by!)
             She cannot tell him all the sad, sad truth –
                 (Hey, but I think that little maid will die!)   210

ROB.   Poor little man!

ROSE.   Poor little maid!

ROB.   Poor little man!

221 *She's very thin*: In the pre-production libretto, Gilbert crossed out 'thin' and substituted 'sad'.

233 *I should fan his honest flame*: In the pre-production version, licence copy and first published edition of the libretto this line appeared as 'I would feed his honest flame'.

ROSE.	Poor little maid!	
BOTH.	Now tell me pray, and tell me true,	215

What in the world should the $\left\{\begin{array}{c}\text{young man}\\\text{maiden}\end{array}\right\}$ do?

ROB.   He cannot eat and he cannot sleep –
    (Hey, but his face is a sight for to see!)
    Daily he goes for to wail – for to weep
    (Hey, but he's wretched as a youth can be!)   220

ROSE.   She's very thin and she's very pale –
    (Hey, but she sickens as the days go by!)
    Daily she goes for to weep – for to wail –
    (Hey, but I think that little maid will die!)

ROB.	Poor little maid!	225
ROSE.	Poor little man!	
ROB.	Poor little maid!	
ROSE.	Poor little man!	
BOTH.	Now tell me pray, and tell me true,	

What in the world should the $\left\{\begin{array}{c}\text{young man}\\\text{maiden}\end{array}\right\}$ do?   230

ROSE.   If I were the youth I should offer her my name –
    (Hey, but her face is a sight for to see!)

ROB.   If I were the maid I should fan his honest flame –
    (Hey, but he's bashful as a youth can be!)

ROSE.   If I were the youth I should speak to her to-day –   235
    (Hey, but she sickens as the days go by!)

ROB.   If I were the maid I should meet the lad half way –
    (For I really do believe that timid youth will die!)

ROSE.	Poor little man!	
ROB.	Poor little maid!	240
ROSE.	Poor little man!	
ROB.	Poor little maid!	

248 *Enter Old Adam*: Old Adam Goodheart, while a caricature of all faithful retainers, is
     clearly specifically modelled on Adam, the elderly servant in Shakespeare's *As You Like
     It*, who is given to such utterances as: 'O my gentle master! O my sweet master!'

249 *Sir Ruthven Murgatroyd*: Ruthven (pronounced 'Rivven') is an old Scottish family name
     which was, indeed, hated. In 1600 the Earl of Gowrie, whose family name was Ruthven,
     kidnapped James VI of Scotland (later to be James I of England). In retribution, a law
     was passed banning the name Ruthven for all time. It was later relaxed for one branch of
     the family. Ruthven was also the name of the central character in Marschner's opera *Der
     Vampyr* (1828), a vampire held in thrall by an evil master and forced to commit murder-
     ous deeds.

254 *Oakapple*: The gall or swelling on oak leaves. Oakapple Day is celebrated in England on
     29 May, the birthday of King Charles II, who, after his defeat in the battle of Worcester
     in the English Civil War, evaded capture by hiding in an oak tree at Boscobel in Shrop-
     shire. In the original list of *Dramatis personæ* Robin appears simply as Robin Oakapple,
     with no mention of being Sir Ruthven Murgatroyd. In most editions of the libretto his
     name appears as Robin throughout, but in some it is changed in the Second Act to Sir
     Ruthven.

BOTH. I thank you, $\left\{\begin{array}{c}\text{miss,}\\\text{sir,}\end{array}\right\}$ for your counsel true;

I'll tell that $\left\{\begin{array}{c}\text{youth}\\\text{maid}\end{array}\right\}$ what $\left\{\begin{array}{c}\text{he}\\\text{she}\end{array}\right\}$ ought to do!

(*Exit* ROSE.) 245

ROB. Poor child! I sometimes think that if she wasn't quite so particular I might venture – but no, no – even then I should be unworthy of her!

(*He sits desponding. Enter* OLD ADAM.)

ADAM. My kind master is sad! Dear Sir Ruthven Murgatroyd —

ROB. Hush! As you love me, breathe not that hated name. Twenty   250
years ago, in horror at the prospect of inheriting that hideous title, and with it the ban that compels all who succeed to the baronetcy to commit at least one deadly crime per day, for life, I fled my home, and concealed myself in this innocent village under the name of Robin Oakapple. My younger brother, Despard, believing me to be dead, succeeded to the title and its   255
attendant curse. For twenty years I have been dead and buried. Don't dig me up now.

ADAM. Dear master, it shall be as you wish, for have I not sworn to obey you for ever in all things? Yet, as we are here alone, and as I belong to that particular description of good old man to whom the truth is a refreshing   260
novelty, let me call you by your own right title once more! (ROBIN *assents*.) Sir Ruthven Murgatroyd! Baronet! Of Ruddigore! Whew! It's like eight hours at the seaside!

ROB. My poor old friend! Would there were more like you!

ADAM. Would there were indeed! But I bring you good tidings. Your   265
foster-brother, Richard, has returned from sea – his ship the *Tom-Tit* rides yonder at anchor, and he himself is even now in this very village!

ROB. My beloved foster-brother? No, no – it cannot be!

ADAM. It is even so – and see, he comes this way!

(*Exeunt together.*) 270

(*Enter Chorus of Bridesmaids.*)

CHORUS.

From the briny sea
   Comes young Richard, all victorious!
Valorous is he –
   His achievements all are glorious!   275

276 *welkin*: The sky, or firmament.

285 *a Revenue sloop*: A patrol boat engaged on coastal duties to deter smuggling.

286 *Cape Finistere*: The most westerly point in Spain, Cape Finisterre (properly spelt that way and not as in the libretto) juts into the Atlantic about thirty miles west of Santiago.

285–329 *I shipped, d'ye see, in a Revenue sloop*:

This rollicking sea shanty caused considerable offence to the French, who were persuaded by the London correspondent of *Le Figaro* that it mocked them and depicted them as criminal and cowardly. *Figaro* published this translation of the second verse:

> *Notre capitaine est debout et il dit,*
>   *Nous n'avons pas à craindre ce navire,*
>   *Nous le prendrons si nous voulons,*
>   *Il ne saurait combattre,*
> *Ce n'est qu'un sale Monsieur.*
> *Mais attaquer un Français, c'est frapper une fille,*
>   *Voilà une besogne honteuse.*
> *Avec tous nos défauts, nous sommes de fiers Bretons;*
> *Eux ne sont que des misérables 'Parlez-vous'.*

The Paris correspondent of the *Daily Telegraph* reported:

> Quite a storm of indignation has been raised here owing to the fact that Mr Gilbert's funny stanzas in *Ruddygore* about the British revenue cutter steering away from the French frigate have been deplorably misunderstood. The two Savoyards, Messrs Gilbert & Sullivan, are calmly invited by one critic to come across the Channel and find out for themselves the difference between a Frenchman and a 'gal'.

The Era commented:

> We can only hope that, in the present electric state of the European atmosphere, a declaration of war between the two countries may not be the ultimate result of the misunderstanding. This would certainly be an excellent advertisement for the latest Savoy opera; but the contrast between means and end, in such a case, would be a little too much like the primitive method of obtaining roast pork in Charles Lamb's Chinamen, who burnt down their huts to cook their dinners.

In the event, war was avoided. Gallic tempers cooled, and perhaps some Frenchman studied the whole song and came to realize that far from being an attack on them it was, in fact, just as much, if not more, a send-up of the British and a satire on their patriotic fervour.

292 *up with her ports*: Open the hinged covers over the gun-ports so that the cannon could be fired.

303 *strike*: Strike her colours and pull down her flag, i.e. surrender.

Let the welkin ring
With the news we bring
Sing it – shout it –
Tell about it –
Shout it! 280
Safe and sound returneth he,
All victorious from the sea!

(*Enter* RICHARD. *The girls welcome him as he greets
old acquaintances.*)

BALLAD – RICHARD.

I shipped, d'ye see, in a Revenue sloop, 285
And, off Cape Finistere,
A merchantman we see,
A Frenchman, going free,
So we made for the bold Mounseer,
D'ye see? 290
We made for the bold Mounseer.
But she proved to be a Frigate – and she up with her ports,
And fires with a thirty-two!
It come uncommon near,
But we answered with a cheer, 295
Which paralysed the Parley-voo,
D'ye see?
Which paralysed the Parley-voo!

CHORUS. Which paralysed the Parley-voo, etc.

Then our Captain he up and he says, says he, 300
'That chap we need not fear, –
We can take her, if we like,
She is sartin for to strike,
For she's only a darned Mounseer,
D'ye see? 305
She's only a darned Mounseer!
But to fight a French fal-lal – it's like hittin' of a gal –
It's a lubberly thing for to do;
For we, with all our faults,
Why, we're sturdy British salts, 310
While she's only a Parley-voo,
D'ye see?
While she's only a poor Parley-voo!'

315 *up with our helm*: Move the tiller so that the bow of the ship is turned away from the wind.
     scuds before the breeze: Sail down wind.

329 *Hornpipe*: The idea of a hornpipe to follow Richard Dauntless's opening song was sug-
     gested at an early rehearsal by Durward Lely, who created the role. Gilbert took up the
     suggestion and asked the tenor if he could dance a hornpipe. Lely replied that he didn't
     know, as he had never tried, but went off to learn the steps from the ballet master at the
     Drury Lane Theatre. He later recalled:

> Sullivan wrote a hornpipe – really the old stereotyped sailor's hornpipe musically in-
> verted – and I set to work to learn the ten or twelve steps. It was the success of the opening
> night. The 'Parlez-voo' went well but the dance that followed brought down the house. I un-
> derstand that the tenors touring in the provinces cursed me, as they all had to go through
> the hornpipe whether they could dance or not.

340 *stow my jawin' tackle*: Stop talking.
341 *belay*: Make fast or stop.
     'vast heavin': Stop sighing.
341–2 *a-cockbill*: Out of sorts. In nautical terminology the phrase usually refers either to the
     condition of the anchor when it turns on its side and will not dig into the mud as it
     should, or to the yards when they are placed at an angle with the deck. Traditionally the
     foreyard arm was put a-cockbill, and moved from its usual horizontal position, as a sign
     of sorrow, and particularly when the ship was about to be scrapped.
345 *to'-gall'n'-m'st*: The topgallant-mast is the highest section of the mast above the topsail.
346 *fore-stay*: Rigging which holds the mast in position and prevents it from leaning back-
     wards.
     barrowknight: Slang for baronet.

CHORUS. While she's only a Parley-voo, etc.

So we up with our helm, and we scuds before the breeze 315
  As we gives a compassionating cheer;
    Froggee answers with a shout
    As he sees us go about,
  Which was grateful of the poor Mounseer,
      D'ye see? 320
  Which was grateful of the poor Mounseer!
And I'll wager in their joy they kissed each other's cheek
  (Which is what them furriners do),
    And they blessed their lucky stars
    We were hardy British tars 325
  Who had pity on a poor Parley-voo,
      D'ye see?
  Who had pity on a poor Parley-voo!

CHORUS. Who had pity on a poor Parley-voo, etc. (*Hornpipe.*)

(*Exeunt* CHORUS.) 330

(*Enter* ROBIN.)

ROB. Richard!

RICH. Robin!

ROB. My beloved foster-brother, and very dearest friend, welcome home again after ten long years at sea! It is such deeds as yours that cause 335
our flag to be loved and dreaded throughout the civilized world!

RICH. Why, lord love ye, Rob, that's but a trifle to what we *have* done in the way of sparing life! I believe I may say, without exaggeration, that the marciful little *Tom-Tit* has spared more French frigates than any craft afloat!
But 'taint for a British seaman to brag, so I'll just stow my jawin' tackle and 340
belay. (ROBIN *sighs.*) But 'vast heavin', messmate, what's brought *you* all a-cockbill?

ROB. Alas, Dick, I love Rose Maybud, and love in vain!

RICH. *You* love in vain? Come, that's too good! Why, you're a fine strapping muscular young fellow – tall and strong as a to'-gall'n'-m'st – taut 345
as a fore-stay – aye, and a barrowknight to boot, if all had their rights!

ROB. Hush, Richard – not a word about my true rank, which none here suspect. Yes, I know well enough that few men are better calculated to win a woman's heart than I. I'm a fine fellow, Dick, and worthy any woman's love – happy the girl who gets me, say I. But I'm timid, Dick; shy – nervous 350
– modest – retiring – diffident – and I cannot tell her, Dick, I cannot tell her!
Ah, you've no idea what a poor opinion I have of myself, and how little I deserve it.

360 *binnacle light*: Compass light.
    on a bowline: Close-hauled, i.e. sailing close to the wind.
365 *under my lee*: Sheltered from the wind by me.
365–6 *fish you two together*: Splice or join you.
367–8 *feeling his pulse*: An early D'Oyly Carte prompt-book has the following direction at this
    point: 'Robin takes watch from his pocket, listens to see that it is going and then looks
    at watch, holding Richard's hand'.
370 *a bos'n's mate*: The assistant to the boatswain (pronounced 'bosun'), the warrant officer in
    charge of sails, rigging, anchors and cables and responsible for all work carried out on
    deck. *H.M.S. Pinafore* has a boatswain's mate, Bob Becket, among its crew members.
373–410 *My boy, you may take it from me*
    A rather clever parody of this song appeared in the periodical *Jack and Jill* on 12 Febru-
    ary 1887, shortly after *Ruddigore* had been altered to meet the complaints of critics and
    public about the Second Act:

> Dear Ed., – You may take it from me,
>   That of all the big blunders accurst,
>   With which a play's saddled
>   And all its points addled,
>   A weak second act is the worst.
> Though as brilliant as brilliant can be,
>   Be the start of your early romance,
>   You must not be uncertain
>   About your last curtain,
>   Or your piece will not have a fair chance.
>
>   If you wish with your play to advance
>   Beyond the so-called op'ras from France,
>   You must heed it and knead it,
>   And carefully 'weed' it,
>   Or really you'd have little chance.
>
> Alas! this, at first, was the case
>   With the startlingly named *Ruddygore*,
>   Tho' in all London City
>   No writer's so witty
>   As Gilbert – he's proved it before.
> The defects of his shady Act Two
>   His denouement so ghastly,
>   Have been raised vastly,
>   And now you may reckon 'twill do.
>
>   So *Ruddygore* now will advance,
>   Yea, on to success will it prance,
>   Savoyards then stump it,
>   And blow praise's trumpet,
>   As soon as you all get a chance.

379 *A Crichton of early romance*: James Crichton was a sixteenth-century Scottish scholar and
    adventurer who earned the nickname 'the Admirable Crichton' for his accomplishments
    and adventures. In early performances of *Iolanthe* Lord Mountararat had a song, later
    cut out, which began 'De Belville was regarded as the Crichton of his age' (see the note
    to *Iolanthe*, Act II, line 216).

RICH. Robin, do you call to mind how, years ago, we swore that, come
what might, we would always act upon our hearts' dictates? 355

ROB. Aye, Dick, and I've always kept that oath. In doubt, difficulty, and
danger I've always asked my heart what I should do, and it has never failed
me.

RICH. Right! Let your heart be your compass, with a clear conscience for
your binnacle light, and you'll sail ten knots on a bowline, clear of shoals, 360
rocks, and quicksands! Well, now, what does my heart say in this here
difficult situation? Why, it says, 'Dick,' it says – (it calls me Dick acos it's
known me from a babby) – 'Dick,' it says, '*you* ain't shy – *you* ain't modest
– speak you up for him as is!' Robin, my lad, just you lay me alongside, and
when she's becalmed under my lee, I'll spin her a yarn that shall sarve to fish 365
you two together for life!

ROB. Will you do this thing for me? Can you, do you think? Yes (*feeling
his pulse*). There's no false modesty about *you*. Your – what I would call
bumptious self-assertiveness (I mean the expression in its complimentary
sense) has already made you a bos'n's mate, and it will make an admiral of 370
you in time, if you work it properly, you dear, incompetent old impostor! My
dear fellow, I'd give my right arm for one tenth of your modest assurance!

SONG – ROBIN.

My boy, you may take it from me,
   That of all the afflictions accurst
      With which a man's saddled
      And hampered and addled, 375
   A diffident nature's the worst.
Though clever as clever can be –
   A Crichton of early romance –
      You must stir it and stump it, 380
      And blow your own trumpet,
   Or, trust me, you haven't a chance!

   If you wish in the world to advance,
   Your merits you're bound to enhance,
      You must stir it and stump it, 385
      And blow your own trumpet,
   Or, trust me, you haven't a chance!

Now take, for example, *my* case:
   I've a bright intellectual brain –
      In all London city 390
      There's no one so witty –
   I've thought so again and again.

401 *Ovid and Horace*: The Latin amatory poet Ovidius Naso turns up also in the Fairy
    Queen's song 'Oh, foolish fay' in *Iolanthe* (Act II, line 185) and in the Lady Psyche's list of
    classical authors to be read by young ladies in *Princess Ida* (Act II, line 16). This is the
    only mention in the Savoy Operas, however, of Horace, the Roman lyric poet who lived
    from 65 B.C. to A.D. 8 and is remembered chiefly for his odes.

402 *Swinburne and Morris*: A decidedly anachronistic reference if *Ruddigore* is set, as early
    libretti suggest, in the reign of George III. Neither of these gentlemen was around at
    that time. Algernon Charles Swinburne, who was born in 1837 and died in 1909, was the
    languid Pre-Raphaelite poet who probably provided at least one of the models for the
    character of Bunthorne in *Patience*. William Morris (1834–96) was the shaggy, rumbus-
    tious designer, poet and revolutionary socialist who may conceivably have been in
    Gilbert's mind when he created the character of Bunthorne's great rival, Archibald
    Grosvenor. Morris gets another mention, this time for his famous wallpapers, in
    Rudolph's song 'When you find you're a broken-down critter' in Act I of *The Grand Duke*.

413 *Plead for him*: Gilbert originally intended Rose Maybud to enter at this point. A note in
    his prompt-book reads: 'Rose enters at "Plead for him". She affects to be interested
    with the shipping, and is at the top of the steps at "fit to marry Lord Nelson" .'

419–20 *took flat aback*: Stopped dead. The term is used of a square-rigged ship when a change in
    the direction of the wind causes it to stop moving forward.

426 *Parbuckle*: Raise or lower objects such as casks or guns by means of a sling slipped under
    them.

I've a highly intelligent face –
 My features cannot be denied –
  But, whatever I try, sir,
  I fail in – and why, sir?
 I'm modesty personified!

  If you wish in the world to advance, etc.

As a poet, I'm tender and quaint –
 I've passion and fervour and grace –
  From Ovid and Horace
  To Swinburne and Morris,
 They all of them take a back place.
Then I sing and I play and I paint:
 Though none are accomplished as I,
  To say so were treason:
  You ask me the reason?
 I'm diffident, modest, and shy!

  If you wish in the world to advance, etc.

BOTH. If you wish in the world to advance, etc.   (*Exit* ROBIN.)   410

RICH. (*looking after him*). Ah, it's a thousand pities he's such a poor opinion of himself, for a finer fellow don't walk! Well, I'll do my best for him. 'Plead for him as though it was for your own father' – that's what my heart's a-remarkin' to me just now. But here she comes! Steady! Steady it is! (*Enter* ROSE – *he is much struck by her.*) By the Port Admiral, but she's a tight little craft! Come, come, she's not for you, Dick, and yet – she's fit to marry Lord Nelson! By the Flag of Old England, I can't look at her unmoved.

ROSE. Sir, you are agitated —

RICH. Aye, aye, my lass, well said! I am agitated, true enough! – took flat aback, my girl; but 'tis naught – 'twill pass. (*Aside.*) This here heart of mine's a-dictatin' to me like anythink. Question is, Have I a right to disregard its promptings?

ROSE. Can I do aught to relieve thine anguish, for it seemeth to me that thou art in sore trouble? This apple – (*offering a damaged apple*).

RICH. (*looking at it and returning it*). No, my lass, 'tain't that: I'm – I'm took flat aback – I never see anything like you in all my born days. Parbuckle me, if you ain't the loveliest gal I've ever set eyes on. There – I can't say fairer than that, can I?

ROSE. No. (*Aside.*) The question is, Is it meet that an utter stranger should thus express himself? (*Refers to book.*) Yes – 'Always speak the truth.'

RICH. I'd no thoughts of sayin' this here to you on my own account, for, truth to tell, I was chartered by another; but when I see you my heart it up

435 *never sail under false colours*: The expression 'to sail under false colours', which means to use deception to attain your object, derives from the practice of pirate ships approaching their unsuspecting victims with a false flag at the mast.

447 *blue-jacket*: Sailor. The name derives from the colour of their jackets.

454–77 *The battle's roar is over*
This duet was dropped in the 1920 revival and in the 1948 production, although it was sung in the 1922 and 1962 D'Oyly Carte recordings. It was reinstated in 1977.

458 *welter*: The rolling, tossing or tumbling of waves.
459 *From war's alarms*: In his pre-production copy, Gilbert crossed out 'war's' and substituted 'waves'', but this alteration was not incorporated in the final libretto.

and it says, says it, 'This is the very lass for *you*, Dick' – 'speak up to her, Dick,' it says – (it calls me Dick acos we was at school together) – 'tell her all, Dick,' it says, 'never sail under false colours – it's mean!' *That's* what my heart tells me to say, and in my rough, common-sailor fashion, I've said it, and I'm a-waiting for your reply. I'm a-tremblin', miss. Lookye here – (*holding out his hand*). That's narvousness!

ROSE (*aside*.) Now, how should a maiden deal with such an one? (*Consults book.*) 'Keep no one in unnecessary suspense.' (*Aloud.*) Behold, I will not keep you in unnecessary suspense. (*Refers to book.*) 'In accepting an offer of marriage, do so with apparent hesitation.' (*Aloud.*) I take you, but with a certain show of reluctance. (*Refers to book.*) 'Avoid any appearance of eagerness.' (*Aloud.*) Though you will bear in mind that I am far from anxious to do so. (*Refers to book.*) 'A little show of emotion will not be misplaced!' (*Aloud.*) Pardon this tear! (*Wipes her eye.*)

RICH. Rose, you've made me the happiest blue-jacket in England! I wouldn't change places with the Admiral of the Fleet, no matter who he's a-huggin' of at this present moment! But, axin' your pardon, miss (*wiping his lips with his hand*), might I be permitted to salute the flag I'm a-goin' to sail under?

ROSE (*referring to book*). 'An engaged young lady should not permit too many familiarities.' (*Aloud.*) Once! (RICHARD *kisses her.*)

DUET – RICHARD *and* ROSE.

RICH.
> The battle's roar is over,
>   O my love!
> Embrace thy tender lover,
>   O my love!
>   From tempests' welter,
>   From war's alarms,
>   O give me shelter
>   Within those arms!
>   Thy smile alluring,
>   All heart-ache curing,
>   Gives peace enduring,
>   O my love!

ROSE.
> If heart both true and tender,
>   O my love!
> A life-love can engender,
>   O my love!
>   A truce to sighing
>   And tears of brine,
>   For joy undying
>   Shall aye be mine,

485   *Let the nuptial knot*: This and the next three lines do not appear in the first edition of the
      libretto.

BOTH.

And thou and I, love,
Shall live and die, love,
Without a sigh, love –
My own, my love!

475

(*Enter* ROBIN, *with* CHORUS OF BRIDESMAIDS.)

CHORUS.

If well his suit has sped,
Oh, may they soon be wed!
Oh, tell us, tell us, pray,
What doth the maiden say?
In singing are we justified,
  Hail the Bridegroom – hail the Bride!
Let the nuptial knot be tied:
    In fair phrases
    Hymn their praises,
  Hail the Bridegroom – hail the Bride?

480

485

ROB. Well – what news? Have you spoken to her?
RICH. Aye, my lad, I have – so to speak – spoke her.
ROB. And she refuses?
RICH. Why, no, I can't truly say she do.
ROB. Then she accepts! My darling! (*Embraces her.*)

490

BRIDESMAIDS. Hail the Bridegroom – hail the Bride! etc.

ROSE (*aside, referring to her book*). Now, what should a maiden do when she is embraced by the wrong gentleman?
RICH. Belay, my lad, belay. You don't understand.
ROSE. Oh, sir, belay, I beseech you!
RICH. You see, it's like this: she accepts – but it's *me*!
ROB. You! (RICHARD *embraces* ROSE.)

495

500

BRIDESMAIDS. Hail the Bridegroom – hail the Bride!
      When the nuptial knot is tied —

ROB. (*interrupting angrily*). Hold your tongues, will you! Now then, what does this mean?
RICH. My poor lad, my heart grieves for thee, but it's like this: the moment I see her, and just as I was a-goin' to mention your name, my heart it up and it says, says it – 'Dick, you've fell in love with her yourself,' it says. 'Be honest and sailor-like – don't skulk under false colours – speak up,' it says, 'take her, you dog, and with her my blessin'!'

505

517–18 *for behold*: The Biblical language which Rose is given further confirms the impression of
an innocent, virtuous, chaste young maiden, the archetypcal heroine of Victorian melodrama.

536 *Thankye, Rob*: At this point Gilbert's pre-production prompt copy contains the direction 'Richard dances', followed by this additional line:

ROB. (*as* RICH. *dances*). There! that's only a bit of it.

This line was used in all D'Oyly Carte productions.

546 *You are, you know you are, you dog*: Gilbert used this same form of words in one of his *Bab
Ballads*, 'Babette's Love':

He called his Bill, who pulled his curl,
He said, 'My Bill, I understand
You've captivated some young gurl
    On this here French and foreign land.
Her tender heart your beauties jog –
They do, you know they do, you dog.

547 *Lothario*: A seducer of women and debauchee. The name derives from a character in
Nicholas Rowe's play *The Fair Penitent* (1703). Rowe probably based his Lothario on an
earlier character with the same name in Sir William Davenant's play *Cruel Brother* (1630).

548 *turning-in a dead-eye*: A dead-eye is a round block of wood with three holes drilled
through it which is used as a block and tackle to apply tension to the sides of the mast.
Gilbert used the expression for the surname of the villainous and misshapen sailor in
H.M.S. Pinafore. To turn in a dead-eye is to wrap rope around it and bind it with lighter
cord.

BRIDESMAIDS. Hail the Bridegroom – hail the Bride! —   510

ROB. Will you be quiet! Go away! (CHORUS *make faces at him and exeunt.*) Vulgar girls!

RICH. What could I do? I'm bound to obey my heart's dictates.

ROB. Of course – no doubt. It's quite right – I don't mind – that is, not particularly – only it's – it *is* disappointing, you know.   515

ROSE (*to* ROBIN). Oh, but, sir, I knew not that thou didst seek me in wedlock, or in very truth I should not have hearkened unto this man, for behold, he is but a lowly mariner, and very poor withal, whereas thou art a tiller of the land, and thou hast fat oxen, and many sheep and swine, a considerable dairy farm and much corn and oil!   520

RICH. That's true, my lass, but it's done now, ain't it, Rob?

ROSE. Still it may be that I should not be happy in thy love. I am passing young and little able to judge. Moreover, as to thy character I know naught!

ROB. Nay, Rose, I'll answer for that. Dick has won thy love fairly.   525
Broken-hearted as I am, I'll stand up for Dick through thick and thin!

RICH. (*with emotion*). Thankye, messmate! that's well said. That's spoken honest. Thankye, Rob! (*Grasps his hand.*)

ROSE. Yet methinks I have heard that sailors are but worldly men, and little prone to lead serious and thoughtful lives!   530

ROB. And what then? Admit that Dick is *not* a steady character, and that when he's excited he uses language that would make your hair curl. Grant that – he does. It's the truth, and I'm not going to deny it. But look at his *good* qualities. He's as nimble as a pony, and his hornpipe is the talk of the Fleet!   535

RICH. Thankye, Rob! That's well spoken. Thankye, Rob!

ROSE. But it may be that he drinketh strong waters which do bemuse a man, and make him even as the wild beasts of the desert!

ROB. Well, suppose he does, and I don't say he don't, for rum's his bane, and ever has been. He *does* drink – I won't deny it. But what of that?   540
Look at his arms – tattooed to the shoulder! (RICH. *rolls up his sleeves.*) No, no – I won't hear a word against Dick!

ROSE. But they say that mariners are but rarely true to those whom they profess to love!

ROB. Granted – granted – and I don't say that Dick isn't as bad as any   545
of 'em. (RICH. *chuckles.*) You are, you know you are, you dog! a devil of a fellow – a regular out-and-out Lothario! But what then? You can't have everything, and a better hand at turning-in a dead-eye don't walk a deck! And what an accomplishment *that* is in a family man! No, no – not a word against Dick. I'll stick up for him through thick and thin!   550

RICH. Thankye, Rob, thankye. You're a true friend. I've acted accordin' to my heart's dictates, and such orders as them no man should disobey.

561   *If other man*: This appears erroneously in some editions as 'If other men'.

565   *My heart says, 'You've a prosperous lot'.* The original version of Robin's verse, altered by Gilbert to the present version in his pre-production prompt copy, was:

> My heart says, 'You're a prosperous man,
>   With acres wide;
> You mean to settle all you can
>   Upon your bride.'

ENSEMBLE – RICHARD, ROBIN, *and* ROSE.

> In sailing o'er life's ocean wide
> Your heart should be your only guide;
> With summer sea and favouring wind,   555
> Yourself in port you'll surely find.

SOLO – RICHARD.

> *My* heart says, 'To this maiden strike –
>   She's captured you.
> She's just the sort of girl you like –
>   You know you do.   560
> If other man her heart should gain,
>   I shall resign.'
> That's what it says to me quite plain,
>   This heart of mine.

SOLO – ROBIN.

> *My* heart says, 'You've a prosperous lot,   565
>   With acres wide;
> You mean to settle all you've got
>   Upon your bride.'
> It don't pretend to shape my acts
>   By word or sign;   570
> It merely states these simple facts,
>   This heart of mine!

SOLO – ROSE.

> Ten minutes since my heart said 'white' –
>   It now says 'black'.
> It then said 'left' – it now says 'right' –   575
>   Hearts often tack.
> It must obey its latest strain –
>   You tell me so. (*To* RICHARD.)
> But should it change its mind again,
>   I'll let you know.   580
> (*Turning from* RICHARD *to* ROBIN, *who embraces her.*)

ENSEMBLE.

> In sailing o'er life's ocean wide
> No doubt the heart should be your guide;

589–619 *Cheerily carols the lark*
Mad Margaret's opening recitative, quite unlike anything else in the Savoy Operas in its evocation of distraction and confusion, was parodied in the issue of *Jack and Jill* quoted from above (see the note to lines 373–410):

> Lo! We would make a remark
> (Hinder us not)
> Re – the latest Gilbertian 'lark'
> The Savoyards have got.
> And that lark
> We'd remark
> (Keep it dark),
> At first dragged somewhat.
>
> Humorous, mind, is each speech
> Penned by great G,
> And the songs are the same – all and each
> Bubble with glee.
> Yet each speech
> Seemed to reach
> To a 'preach'
> Near the end – d'ye see?

607 *Daft Madge*: Amateur and professional performers alike are often uncertain as to exactly how Mad Margaret should be played. Gilbert introduces her with the comment that she is 'an obvious caricature of stage madness', but does this mean she should be played in a wildly histrionic style, with exaggerated ravings and outbursts? Jessie Bond, the mezzo-soprano who created the role, which was her favourite part, emphatically rejected such an interpretation. She wrote in the December 1927 edition of the *Gilbert and Sullivan Journal*:

> Why, oh! why, must she be played like a raving lunatic whose only place should be the asylum? Margaret is not a mad girl really. She is a distraught girl – a genuine creature of pity, possibly – but a wild maniac she most certainly is not on any possible showing.
>
> > 'Tis only
> > That I'm
> > Love-lonely!
> > That's all.
>
> In these few, simple words, which are really the key to the reading of the part, she tells her own story. Love-loneliness – that is her trouble. She is just a sad, solitary figure whose head has been turned crazy, but not demented, by heart-hungry grief. Suggesting her as a wild-eyed, gabbling idiot is not only inartistic, but it shows a woeful mis-reading of the spirit of the part.

But it is awkward when you find
A heart that does not know its mind! 585

(*Exeunt* ROBIN *with* ROSE L., *and* RICHARD, *weeping*, R.)

(*Enter* MAD MARGARET. *She is wildly dressed in picturesque tatters, and is an obvious caricature of theatrical madness.*)

SCENA – MARGARET.

Cheerily carols the lark
Over the cot. 590
Merrily whistles the clerk
Scratching a blot.
But the lark
And the clerk,
I remark, 595
Comfort me not!

Over the ripening peach
Buzzes the bee.
Splash on the billowy beach
Tumbles the sea. 600
But the peach
And the beach
They are each
Nothing to me!

And why? 605
Who am I?
Daft Madge! Crazy Meg!
Mad Margaret! Poor Peg!
He! he! he! (*chuckling*).

Mad, I? 610
Yes, very!
But why?
Mystery!
Don't call!

No crime – 615
'Tis only
That I'm
Love-lonely!
That's all!

620–39   *To a garden full of posies*

This ballad was not originally written for *Ruddigore*. It first appeared in the Christmas 1881 edition of the *Illustrated Sporting and Dramatic News* and was reused by Gilbert six years later for this opera.

628   *Cytherean posies*: In Greek mythology the island of Cythera, off the Peloponnese, was the place where Aphrodite, the goddess of love and sensual beauty, and the equivalent of the Roman Venus, rose from the sea.

635   *Hope lay nestling*: The pre-production libretto has 'Love lay nestling' here.

BALLAD.

To a garden full of posies 620
  Cometh one to gather flowers,
  And he wanders through its bowers
Toying with the wanton roses,
  Who, uprising from their beds,
  Hold on high their shameless heads 625
With their pretty lips a-pouting,
Never doubting – never doubting
  That for Cytherean posies
  He would gather aught but roses!

In a nest of weeds and nettles 630
  Lay a violet, half-hidden,
  Hoping that his glance unbidden
Yet might fall upon her petals.
  Though she lived alone, apart,
  Hope lay nestling at her heart, 635
But, alas, the cruel awaking
Set her little heart a-breaking,
  For he gathered for his posies
  Only roses – only roses!

                          (*Bursts into tears.*) 640

        (*Enter* ROSE.)

ROSE. A maiden, and in tears? Can I do aught to soften thy sorrow? This apple – (*offering apple*).

MAR. (*Examines it and rejects it.*) No! (*Mysteriously.*) Tell me, are you mad? 645

ROSE. I? No! That is, I think not.

MAR. That's well! Then you don't love Sir Despard Murgatroyd? All mad girls love him. *I* love him. I'm poor Mad Margaret – Crazy Meg – Poor Peg! He! he! he! he! (*chuckling*).

ROSE. Thou lovest the bad Baronet of Ruddigore? Oh, horrible – too 650 horrible!

MAR. You pity me? Then be my mother! The squirrel had a mother, but she drank and the squirrel fled! Hush! They sing a brave song in our parts – it runs somewhat thus: (*Sings.*)

      'The cat and the dog and the little puppee 655
      Sat down in a – down in a – in a —'

666 *an Italian glance*: There is some doubt as to the origins and precise meaning of this
     phrase. In his *The Gilbert and Sullivan Operas – A Concordance* (New York, 1935) Frederick
     J. Halton suggested that the expression derived from Machiavelli and denoted cynicism
     and lack of feeling. The American scholar Jane Steadman gives a different interpreta-
     tion, however, suggesting that Gilbert had in mind the Gothic villain in Ann Radcliffe's
     novel *The Italian* (1797).
        Gilbert himself gave the following stage direction in his prompt-book for the 'busi-
     ness' of the glance: 'For the Italian glance Margaret folds arms and approaches Rose
     melodramatically – looks rudely into her face and steps back into attitude'.

680 *affidavit*: A statement made in writing, and confirmed on oath, which is intended to be
     used in court. An affidavit is normally sworn before a Commissioner for Oaths. In
     Iolanthe (Act I, line 458) the Lord Chancellor tells Strephon that 'an affidavit from a
     thunderstorm' would be acceptable as evidence in his defence that chorused Nature
     had bid him disobey an order of the Court of Chancery.

684 *They sing choruses in public*: This line never fails to raise an amused titter from audiences.
     The Savoy Operas are of course stuffed full of people singing choruses in public. They
     broke new ground in musical theatre in using the chorus to represent real people with a
     meaningful role in the action rather than just as a passive vehicle for setting the scene
     or telling a story. Mad they may occasionally feel, but countless members of choirs and
     amateur operatic societies have cause to thank Gilbert and Sullivan for giving them so
     many splendid choruses to sing.

688 *Enter Chorus of Bucks and Blades*: In the original production, and in the 1920 revival, the
     Bucks and Blades (i.e. dashing Regency dandies) made their entrance dressed in the
     uniforms worn by officers of the twenty cavalry and infantry regiments which made up
     the British Army in the period of the Napoleonic Wars. For the 1948 production the
     uniforms were dropped and the male chorus dressed instead in grey top hats and
     coloured frock coats.

696 *Hearty greeting offer we*: In the first-edition libretto, the bridesmaids had another seven
     lines, balancing the male chorus:

                         Your exceeding
                         Easy breeding
                    Just the thing our hearts to pillage –
                         Cheers us, charms us,
                         Quite disarms us:
                    Welcome, welcome to our village;
                         To our village welcome be.

I forget what they sat down in, but so the song goes! Listen – I've come to pinch her!

ROSE. Mercy, whom?

MAR. You mean 'who'. 660

ROSE. Nay! it is the accusative after the verb.

MAR. True. (*Whispers melodramatically.*) I have come to pinch Rose Maybud!

ROSE. (*Aside, alarmed.*) Rose Maybud!

MAR. Aye! I love him – he loved me once. But that's all gone, Fisht! He 665
gave me an Italian glance – thus – (*business*) – and made me his. He will give *her* an Italian glance, and make *her* his. But it shall not be, for I'll stamp on her – stamp on her – stamp on her! Did you ever kill anybody? No? Why not? Listen – I killed a fly this morning! It buzzed, and I wouldn't have it. So it died – pop! So shall she! 670

ROSE. But, behold, *I* am Rose Maybud, and I would fain not die 'pop'.

MAR. You are Rose Maybud?

ROSE. Yes, sweet Rose Maybud!

MAR. Strange! They told me she was beautiful! And *he* loves *you*! No, no! If I thought that, I would treat you as the auctioneer and land-agent 675
treated the lady-bird – I would rend you asunder!

ROSE. Nay, be pacified, for behold I am pledged to another, and lo, we are to be wedded this very day!

MAR. Swear me that! Come to a Commissioner and let me have it on affidavit! *I* once made an affidavit – but it died – it died – it died! But see, they 680
come – Sir Despard and his evil crew! Hide, hide – they are all mad – quite mad!

ROSE. What makes you think that?

MAR. Hush! They sing choruses in public. That's mad enough, I think! Go – hide away, or they will seize you! Hush! Quite softly – quite, quite 685
softly!

(*Exeunt together, on tiptoe.*)

(*Enter Chorus of Bucks and Blades, heralded by
Chorus of Bridesmaids.*)

CHORUS OF BRIDESMAIDS.

Welcome, gentry, 690
For your entry
Sets our tender hearts a-beating.
Men of station,
Admiration
Prompts this unaffected greeting. 695
Hearty greeting offer we!

706 *Elysian*: In Greek mythology, the Elysian Fields were the abode of the blessed. They also
     crop up in *Patience* (Act I, line 444).
707 *Amaryllis*: A rustic sweetheart. The name occurs in the pastoral poetry of Virgil and
     Theocritus, and John Milton's poem *Lycidas* contains the famous line: 'To sport with
     Amaryllis in the shade'.
708 *Chloe and Phyllis*: Both these names were used for shepherdesses in Greek pastoral poet-
     ry and so came to symbolize idyllic rustic maidenhood. Gilbert had used both names
     for heroines in earlier works: Chloe in *Happy Arcadia* (1872) and Phyllis in *Iolanthe* (1882).

724 *Enter Sir Despard Murgatroyd*: The supreme caricature of the stage villain in Victorian me-
     lodrama (the sort of character audiences were expected to hiss every time he came on to
     the stage), Sir Despard originally made his entrance dressed in the uniform of the Tenth
     Hussars. In the 1948 revival, however, he was given a suitably melodramatic costume of
     pillar-box red and billiard-table green, primary colours of a clashing intensity that
     would have filled Lady Jane with Pre-Raphaelite horror (see *Patience*, Act I, line 324).

CHORUS OF BUCKS AND BLADES.

When thoroughly tired
Of being admired
By ladies of gentle degree – degree,
With flattery sated,
High-flown and inflated,
Away from the city we flee – we flee!

From charms intramural
To prettiness rural
The sudden transition
Is simply Elysian,
Come, Amaryllis,
Come, Chloe and Phyllis,
Your slaves, for the moment, are we!

CHORUS OF BRIDESMAIDS.

The sons of the tillage
Who dwell in this village
Are people of lowly degree – degree.
Though honest and active,
They're most unattractive,
And awkward as awkward can be – can be.
They're clumsy clodhoppers
With axes and choppers,
And shepherds and ploughmen
And drovers and cowmen,
Hedgers and reapers
And carters and keepers,
But never a lover for me!

ENSEMBLE.

BRIDESMAIDS.	BUCKS AND BLADES.
So, welcome, gentry, etc.	When thoroughly tired, etc.

(*Enter* SIR DESPARD MURGATROYD.)

SONG AND CHORUS – SIR DESPARD.

SIR D.   Oh, why am I moody and sad?
CH.   Can't guess!
SIR D.   And why am I guiltily mad?
CH.   Confess!

700

705

710

715

720

725

732 *why am I husky and hoarse*: The first-night reviewer for *The Times* somewhat unkindly took this line to be an allusion to the vocal qualities of Rutland Barrington, who created the role of Sir Despard. Barrington, who was no opera singer, is said to have had a rather husky delivery, though he was in better voice for the opening of *Ruddigore* than for the first night of *Patience*, when he had had to struggle through the role of Grosvenor while nursing a severe sore throat.

767 *All the Girls express their horror of Sir Despard*: Gilbert's own stage direction for the first production at this point reads: 'Sir Despard offers flower to ladies right. They shrink from him as he does so – he stamps – they scream and exit. He does the same business with ladies left and again to ladies up stage right centre. He then stamps upon the flower and strikes attitude of disgust.'

769 *Poor children*: Gilbert originally intended Mad Margaret to enter in the middle of this speech by Sir Despard, and he wrote a substantial passage of dialogue and a duet for them which was cut out before the first performance. It survives in the pre-production libretto, though not in the later licence copy. This is how the scene was originally conceived:

> SIR D. Poor children, how they loathe me – me whose hands are certainly steeped in infamy, but whose heart is as the heart of a little child! Oh Ruthven, my elder brother, if you had not died mysteriously in childhood, you would have been me, I should have been you, and all would have been well!
>
> (*Enter* MARGARET.)
>
> MAR. (*wildly*). Despard. How de do? How de do? How de do?
> SIR D. Margaret Mackintosh? Why do you follow me about everywhere?
> MAR. You are here to carry off Rose Maybud! But, don't do it – don't do it! Better not – better not – he! he! he! (*chuckling*).
> SIR D. My good girl, I don't want Rose Maybud. But what is a poor baronet to do . . . [as now].

SIR D.	Because I am thoroughly bad!
CH.	Oh yes –
SIR D.	You'll see it at once in my face.
	Oh, why am I husky and hoarse?
CH.	Ah, why?
SIR D.	It's the workings of conscience, of course.
CH.	Fie, fie!
SIR D.	And huskiness stands for remorse,
CH.	Oh my!
SIR D.	At least it does so in my case!

SIR D.	When in crime one is fully employed –
CH.	Like you –
SIR D.	Your expression gets warped and destroyed:
CH.	It do.
SIR D.	It's a penalty none can avoid;
CH.	How true!
SIR D.	I once was a nice-looking youth;
	But like stone from a strong catapult –
CH. (*explaining to each other*).	A trice –
SIR D.	I rushed at my terrible cult –
CH. (*explaining to each other*).	That's vice –
SIR D.	Observe the unpleasant result!
CH.	Not nice.
SIR D.	Indeed I am telling the truth!

SIR D.	Oh, innocent, happy though poor!
CH.	That's we –
SIR D.	If I had been virtuous, I'm sure –
CH.	Like me –
SIR D.	I should be as nice-looking as you're!
CH.	May be.
SIR D.	You are very nice-looking indeed!
	Oh, innocents, listen in time –
CH.	We *doe*,
SIR D.	Avoid an existence of crime –
CH.	Just so –
SIR D.	Or you'll be as ugly as I'm –
CH. (*loudly*).	No! No!
SIR D.	And now, if you please, we'll proceed.

730

735

740

745

750

755

760

765

(*All the Girls express their horror of* SIR DESPARD. *As he approaches them they
fly from him, terror-stricken, leaving him alone on the stage.*)

SIR D. Poor children, how they loathe me – me whose hands are
certainly steeped in infamy, but whose heart is as the heart of a little child!

770

776 *and built an orphan asylum*: At this point, the original dialogue continued:

> SIR D. Yesterday I fractured a skull and founded a hospital. This morning I robbed a bank and endowed a bishopric. Tomorrow I carry off Rose –
> MAR. (*significantly*). Tomorrow – you – carry off Rose?
> SIR D. Certainly – and build a cathedral.
> MAR. (*with intensity*). If you carry off Rose Maybud, I'll bite you!
> SIR D. Really, Margaret, if a man commit an error – and atone with a cathedral.
> MAR. Not a word. I am desperate.

DUET – MARGARET, SIR DESPARD *and* CHORUS.

MAR.   If you attempt to take the girl and carry her off, away –
SIR D.   Sing hey, sing ho, and exactly so,
             (*to audience*) And it's all for the love of a lad, poor thing.
MAR.   Your doom shall be a terrible one, and fill you with dismay.
SIR D.   Sing bless my soul, with a poison bowl!
             (*to audience*) And it's all for the love of a lad, poor thing.
MAR.   A nightly course of apple-pie beds, tin-tacks upon your chair –
             And prickly things, with terrible stings, shall tickle you everywhere –
             I rather think you'll find your razors rasp you when you shave,
             And I'll hurry you, worry you, flurry you, scurry you, into an early grave!
CHORUS.   And the owl shall smile, and the snail shall sneeze,
             And the tadpole kneel on his bended knees;
             The slug shall shout, and the crow turn pale,
             Before Mad Margaret's curse shall fail!
SIR D.   (*aside*) And it's all for the love of a lad, poor thing!
MAR.   Your breakfast bread I'll daily spread with mouldy mothery jam!
SIR D.   Sing hey the dart in her wounded heart,
             (*aside*) And it's all for the love of a lad, poor thing!
MAR.   You shall eat French eggs, Australian beef, and American hardboiled ham!
SIR D.   Sing hey the lead in her poor thick head,
             (*aside*) And it's all for the love of a lad, poor thing!
MAR.   If this you do, your sheets I'll strew with Abernethy crumbs,
             I'll line your hat with cobbler's wax – your gloves shall split at the thumbs –
             With damp cigars and flat champagne I'll blight you in your bloom,
             And I'll hurry you, worry you, flurry you, scurry you into an early tomb.
CHORUS.   And the cat shall crow, and the gnat shall neigh,
             And the toad shall trot, and the bat shall bray,
             And the snake shall snore, and the worm shall wail,
             Before Mad Margaret's curse shall fail!
SIR D. (*aside*) And it's all for the love of a lad, poor thing!

Sir Despard then continued with his speech 'This is what it is to be the sport and toy of a Picture Gallery' as now.

779–80 *I will give them all to the Nation*: Following the refusal of the Arts Council to give a grant to the D'Oyly Carte Opera Company in 1980, Kenneth Sandford changed this line to 'I will give them all to the Arts Council'. Audiences roared in approval of this sentiment and turned their boos and hisses from Sir Despard to the gentlemen responsible for dispensing public money to the arts, but to no avail. Despite petitions and many entreaties in the press, the Arts Council would not change its mind and, denied any support from public funds, the company which had faithfully performed the works of Gilbert and Sullivan for more than a century was forced to break up in March 1982.

But what *is* a poor baronet to do, when a whole picture gallery of ancestors
step down from their frames and threaten him with an excruciating death if
he hesitate to commit his daily crime? But ha! ha! I am even with them!
(*Mysteriously.*) I get my crime over the first thing in the morning, and then,
ha! ha! for the rest of the day I do good – I do good – I do good! (*Melo-*   775
dramatically.) Two days since, I stole a child and built an orphan asylum.
Yesterday I robbed a bank and endowed a bishopric. To-day I carry off Rose
Maybud and atone with a cathedral! This is what it is to be the sport and toy
of a Picture Gallery! But I will be bitterly revenged upon them! I will give
them all to the Nation, and nobody shall ever look upon their faces again!   780

(*Enter* RICHARD.)

RICH. Ax your honour's pardon, but —
SIR D. Ha! observed! And by a mariner! What would you with me,
fellow?
RICH. Your honour, I'm a poor man-o'-war's man, becalmed in the   785
doldrums —
SIR D. I don't know them.
RICH. And I make bold to ax your honour's advice. Does your honour
know what it is to have a heart?
SIR D. My honour knows what it is to have a complete apparatus for   790
conducting the circulation of the blood through the veins and arteries of the
human body.
RICH. Aye, but has your honour a heart that ups and looks you in the
face, and gives you quarter-deck orders that it's life and death to disobey?
SIR D. I have not a heart of that description, but I have a Picture   795
Gallery that presumes to take that liberty.
RICH. Well, your honour, it's like this – Your honour had an elder
brother —
SIR D. It had.
RICH. Who should have inherited your title and, with it, its cuss.   800
SIR D. Aye, but he died. Oh, Ruthven! —
RICH. He didn't.
SIR D. He did *not*?
RICH. He didn't. On the contrary, he lives in this here very village,
under the name of Robin Oakapple, and he's a-going to marry Rose Maybud   805
this very day.
SIR D. Ruthven alive, and going to marry Rose Maybud! Can this be
possible?
RICH. Now the question I was going to ask your honour is – Ought I to
tell your honour this?   810
SIR D. I don't know. It's a delicate point. I think you ought. Mind, I'm
not sure, but I think so.

815 *stand off and on*: Vacillate or dither. In nautical terminology, the expression means to tack
     in and out along the shore.
817 *bring her to*: Stop her advance.

824–47 *You understand*
     This duet must be one of the most tiring of all the Savoy numbers to perform. Richard
     and Sir Despard traditionally sing it while skipping from one foot to the other and dance
     round between each verse. At the end there is further 'business', dating back to the first
     production and recorded in Gilbert's prompt-book, when each waves the other to go off
     the stage first in an elaborate and seemingly never-ending show of politeness.

RICH. That's what my heart says. It says, 'Dick,' it says (it calls me
Dick acos it's entitled to take that liberty), 'that there young gal would recoil
from him if she knowed what he really were. Ought you to stand off and on,   815
and let this young gal take this false step and never fire a shot across her
bows to bring her to? No,' it says, 'you did *not* ought.' And I won't ought,
accordin'.

SIR D. Then you really feel yourself at liberty to tell me that my elder
brother lives – that I may charge him with his cruel deceit, and transfer to his   820
shoulders the hideous thraldom under which I have laboured for so many
years! Free – free at last! Free to live a blameless life, and to die beloved and
regretted by all who knew me!

DUET – SIR DESPARD *and* RICHARD.

RICH.	You understand?
SIR D.	I think I do; 825
	With vigour unshaken
	This step shall be taken.
	It's neatly planned.
RICH.	I think so too;
	I'll readily bet it 830
	You'll never regret it!
BOTH.	For duty, duty must be done;
	The rule applies to every one,
	And painful though that duty be,
	To shirk the task were fiddle-de-dee! 835
SIR D.	The bridegroom comes –
RICH.	Likewise the bride –
	The maidens are very
	Elated and merry;
	They are her chums. 840
SIR D.	To lash their pride
	Were almost a pity,
	The pretty committee!
BOTH.	But duty, duty must be done;
	The rule applies to every one, 845
	And painful though that duty be,
	To shirk the task were fiddle-de-dee!

(*Exeunt* RICHARD *and* SIR DESPARD.)

(*Enter Chorus of Bridesmaids and Bucks.*)

866 *True and trusty*: In the first published libretto, the Bucks and Blades were given another
     five lines to sing so that their chorus was the same length as the girls':

> Happiness untold awaits them
> When the parson consecrates them;
>   People near them,
>   Loudly cheer them –
> You'll be bridegrooms some fine day.

870–903 *When the buds are blossoming*
         This song, which appeared in early libretti as 'Where the buds are blossoming', is one of
         only two numbers which are described as madrigals in the Savoy Operas. The other is
         'Brightly dawns our wedding day' in Act II of *The Mikado*. However, both 'Strange
         adventure' in Act II of *The Yeomen of the Guard*, which is described as a quartet, and 'I
         hear the soft note' in Act I of *Patience*, which is described as a sestet, broadly conform to
         the dictionary definition of a madrigal as a contrapuntal and generally unaccompanied
         part-song for several voices.

CHORUS OF BRIDESMAIDS.

Hail the bride of seventeen summers: 850
    In fair phrases
    Hymn her praises;
Lift your song on high, all comers.
    She rejoices
    In your voices. 855
Smiling summer beams upon her,
Shedding every blessing on her:
    Maidens greet her –
    Kindly treat her –
You may all be brides some day! 860

CHORUS OF BUCKS.

Hail the bridegroom who advances,
    Agitated,
    Yet elated.
He's in easy circumstances,
    Young and lusty, 865
    True and trusty.

ALL.   Smiling summer beams upon her, etc.

(*Enter* ROBIN, *attended by* RICHARD *and* OLD ADAM, *meeting* ROSE, *attended by* ZORAH *and* DAME HANNAH. ROSE *and* ROBIN *embrace*.)

MADRIGAL.

ROSE, DAME HANNAH, RICHARD, OLD ADAM *with* CHORUS.

ROSE.	When the buds are blossoming, 870
	Smiling welcome to the spring,
	Lovers choose a wedding day –
	Life is love in merry May!
GIRLS.	Spring is green –
	Summer's rose – 875
QUARTET.	It is sad when summer goes,
	Fa la, la, etc.
MEN.	Autumn's gold –
	Winter's grey –
QUARTET.	Winter still is far away – 880
	Fa la, la, etc.
CHORUS.	Leaves in autumn fade and fall,
	Winter is the end of all.

906 *my elder brother*: At this point in the original production, Robin interjected 'Ah, lost one!'

909 *O wonder*: This line was not sung in the original production. The earliest pre-production libretto has four lines for the chorus at this point which were cut out before the first night:

> What means this interfering?
> At once be disappearing,
> Or cheer with welcome hearty
> Our Rose's wedding party.

	Spring and summer teem with glee:	
	Spring and summer, then, for me!	885
	Fa la, la, etc.	

HANNAH.

In the spring-time seed is sown:
In the summer grass is mown:
In the autumn you may reap:
Winter is the time for sleep.

GIRLS.

Spring is hope –
Summer's joy –

QUARTET.

Spring and summer never cloy,
Fa la, la, etc.

MEN.

Autumn, toil –
Winter, rest –

QUARTET.

Winter, after all, is best –
Fa la, la, etc.

CHORUS.

Spring and summer pleasure you,
Autumn, aye, and winter too –
Every season has its cheer,
Life is lovely all the year!
Fa la, la, etc.

890

895

900

GAVOTTE.

(*After Gavotte, enter* SIR DESPARD.)

SIR D.

Hold, bride and bridegroom, ere you wed each other,
I claim young Robin as my elder brother!
His rightful title I have long enjoyed:
I claim him as Sir Ruthven Murgatroyd!

905

CHORUS. O wonder!

ROSE (*wildly*).

Deny the falsehood, Robin, as you should,
It is a plot!

ROB.

I would, if conscientiously I could,
But I cannot!

910

CHORUS. Ah, base one! Ah, base one!

SOLO – ROBIN.

As pure and blameless peasant,
I cannot, I regret,
Deny a truth unpleasant,
I am that Baronet!

915

926 *taradiddles*: Lies or fibs. In the finale of Act I of *Iolanthe*, the peers and fairies have considerable fun singing 'Taradiddle, taradiddle, tol loy lay!' to show what they think of each
others' stories.

| CHORUS. | He is that Baronet! |
| | |

But when completely rated 920
Bad Baronet am I,
That I am what he's stated
I'll recklessly deny!

CHORUS. He'll recklessly deny!

ROB. When I'm a bad Bart, I will tell taradiddles! 925
CHORUS. He'll tell taradiddles when he's a bad Bart.
ROB. I'll play a bad part on the falsest of fiddles.
CHORUS. On very false fiddles he'll play a bad part!
ROB. But until that takes place I must be conscientious –
CHORUS. He'll be conscientious until that takes place. 930
ROB. Then adieu with good grace to my morals sententious!
CHORUS. To morals sententious adieu with good grace!
ROB. *and* When $\left\{\begin{array}{l}\text{I'm}\\\text{he's}\end{array}\right\}$ a bad Bart $\left\{\begin{array}{l}\text{I}\\\text{he}\end{array}\right\}$ will tell taradiddles, etc.
CHORUS.

ZOR. Who is the wretch who hath betrayed thee?
Let him stand forth! 935
RICH. (*coming forward*). 'Twas I!
ALL. Die, traitor!
RICH. Hold! my conscience made me!
Withhold your wrath!

SOLO – RICHARD.

Within this breast there beats a heart 940
Whose voice can't be gainsaid.
It bade me thy true rank impart,
And I at once obeyed.
I knew 'twould blight thy budding fate –
I knew 'twould cause thee anguish great – 945
But did I therefore hesitate?
No! I at once obeyed!

ALL. Acclaim him who, when his true heart
Bade him young Robin's rank impart,
Immediately obeyed! 950

SOLO – ROSE (*addressing* ROBIN).

Farewell!
Thou hadst my heart –

962   *I am thy bride*: In the first edition of the libretto, the chorus was given a shout of 'hurray'
      at the end of Rose's solo.

985   *Hail the Bridegroom – hail the Bride*: In the first edition of the libretto this line appeared as
      'Let the nuptial knot be tied'.

'Twas quickly won!
But now we part –
  Thy face I shun!
    Farewell!   955
Go bend the knee
  At Vice's shrine,
Of life with me
  All hope resign.   960
  Farewell! Farewell! Farewell!

(*To* SIR DESPARD.)   Take me – I am thy bride!

BRIDESMAIDS.

Hail the Bridegroom – hail the Bride!
When the nuptial knot is tied;
Every day will bring some joy   965
That can never, never cloy!

(*Enter* MARGARET, *who listens.*)

SIR D.   Excuse me, I'm a virtuous person now –
ROSE.   That's why I wed you!
SIR D.   And I to Margaret must keep my vow!   970
MAR.   Have I misread you?
     Oh, joy! with newly kindled rapture warmed,
     I kneel before you! (*Kneels.*)
SIR D.   I once disliked you; now that I've reformed,
     How I adore you! (*They embrace.*)   975

BRIDESMAIDS.

Hail the Bridegroom – hail the Bride!
When the nuptial knot is tied;
Every day will bring some joy
That can never, never cloy!

ROSE.   Richard, of him I love bereft,   980
         Through thy design,
     Thou art the only one that's left,
         So I am thine! (*They embrace.*)

BRIDESMAIDS.

Hail the Bridegroom – hail the Bride!
Hail the Bridegroom – hail the Bride!   985

1008   *opossum*: A small marsupial mammal of nocturnal habits found in America and Austra-
       lia. Opossums are distinguished for their versatile big toes, which they use for grasping
       things. They do indeed live in trees but seem an unlikely species for early nineteenth-
       century Cornish folk to come across. However, if you try rhyming cats or squirrels with
       'come across 'em', you'll see exactly why Gilbert had to go abroad on this particular oc-
       casion.

DUET – ROSE *and* RICHARD.

Oh, happy the lily
    When kissed by the bee;
And, sipping tranquilly,
    Quite happy is he;
And happy the filly
    That neighs in her pride;   990
But happier than any,
A pound to a penny,
A lover is, when he
    Embraces his bride!   995

DUET – SIR DESPARD *and* MARGARET.

Oh, happy the flowers
    That blossom in June,
And happy the bowers
    That gain by the boon,
But happier by hours
    The man of descent,   1000
Who, folly regretting,
Is bent on forgetting
His bad baronetting,
    And means to repent!   1005

TRIO – HANNAH, ADAM, *and* ZORAH.

Oh, happy the blossom
    That blooms on the lea,
Likewise the opossum
    That sits on a tree,
But when you come across 'em,   1010
    They cannot compare
With those who are treading
The dance at a wedding,
While people are spreading
    The best of good fare!   1015

SOLO – ROBIN.

Oh, wretched the debtor
    Who's singing a deed!
And wretched the letter
    That no one can read!

1027 *DANCE*

In his original prompt-book Gilbert directed 'Robin joins wildly in dance (with Zorah) falling senseless at end'. The first published libretto included the printed direction at the end of Act I '*At the end of the dance* ROBIN *falls senseless on the stage. Picture*'. Although this direction is retained in the Macmillan edition, it does not appear in most modern versions of the libretto. For the 1920 revival a new direction was substituted: '*Dance is broken up as Robin comes down and all exit in confusion at nearest exits. Girls scream in terror as they rush off right and left.*' The 1948 production broadly followed this formula, with Robin appearing in the same brilliant red and green garb as Sir Despard and cracking his whip menacingly as the curtain fell.

But very much better   1020
    Their lot it must be
Than that of the person
I'm making this verse on,
Whose head there's a curse on –
    Alluding to me!   1025

ENSEMBLE with CHORUS.

Oh, happy the lily, etc.

DANCE.

END of ACT I

2 *from the time of James I*: The Murgatroyds must be representatives of one of the oldest baronetcies in England and they must also be among the shortest-lived. The order itself was instituted by James I, who reigned from 1603 to 1625. The action of *Ruddigore* is set early in the nineteenth century, and we are told in the list of *Dramatis personæ* that Sir Roderic was the twenty-first baronet. So the family has got through twenty-one senior members in about 200 years, with each Murgatroyd holding his title for an average of only $9\frac{1}{2}$ years!

4 *Sir Roderic*: In the pre-production libretto Sir Roderic was described in the directions at the beginning of Act II as being 'attired as a Lord Mayor'. In D'Oyly Carte productions he was always portrayed wearing a cloak and tricorn hat.

10 *elision*: The action of dropping a letter or syllable in pronunciation. Its use here suggests that Robin should in the next line pronounce his real name as it is written rather than as 'Rivven'.

12 *valley-de-sham*: A corruption of the French *valet de chambre*, meaning personal man-servant.

20 *valley-de-sham*: In the original libretto there were three additional verses to this song:

> ROB.   My face is the index to my mind,
>   All venom and spleen and gall – ha! ha!
>   Or, properly speaking,
>   It soon will be reeking
>   With venom and spleen and gall – ha! ha!
>
> ADAM.   My name from Adam Goodheart you'll find
>   I've changed to Gideon Crawle – ha! ha!
>   For a bad Bart's steward
>   Whose heart is much too hard,
>   Is always Gideon Crawle – ha! ha!
>
> BOTH.   How providential when you find
>   The face an index to the mind,
>   And evil men compelled to call
>   Themselves by names like Gideon Crawle!

21 *old Adam*: In keeping with the verses quoted above, throughout the first edition of the libretto Old Adam is always referred to as 'Gideon Crawle' in the Second Act. Gilbert later decided against this change of name and restored 'old Adam'. However, line 308 was overlooked and remained in successive editions of the libretto until 1959 as 'Gideon Crawle, it won't do'.

24–5 *greatest villain unhung*: Gilbert's original dialogue, as contained in the pre-production libretto, continued at this point:

> ADAM. [continuing] . . . It's a dreadful position for a good old man.
> ROB. Very likely, but don't be gratuitously offensive, Gideon Crawle.
> ADAM. Sir, I am the ready instrument of your abominable misdeeds because I have sworn to obey you in all things, but I have *not* sworn to allow deliberate and systematic villainy to pass unreproved. If you insist upon it I will swear that, too, but I have not sworn it yet.
> ROB. Come, Gideon, I haven't done anything very bad, so far.
> ADAM. No. Owing to a series of evasions which, as a blameless character, I must denounce as contemptible, you have, so far, nothing serious on your conscience. But that can't last, and the sooner you yield to your destiny the better. Now, sir, to business . . . [as now].

ACT II

SCENE. – *Picture Gallery in Ruddigore Castle. The walls are covered with full-length portraits of the Baronets of Ruddigore from the time of* JAMES I – *the first being that of* SIR RUPERT, *alluded to in the legend; the last, that of the last deceased Baronet,* SIR RODERIC. *Enter* ROBIN *and* ADAM *melodramatically. They are greatly altered in appearance,* ROBIN *wearing the haggard aspect of a guilty roué;* ADAM, *that of the wicked steward to such a man.*

5

DUET – ROBIN *and* ADAM.

ROB.   I once was as meek as a new-born lamb,
                I'm now Sir Murgatroyd – ha! ha!
                   With greater precision
                   (Without the elision),
                Sir Ruthven Murgatroyd – ha! ha!   10

ADAM.   And I, who was once his *valley-de-sham*,
                As steward I'm now employed – ha! ha!
                   The dickens may take him –
                   I'll never forsake him!
                As steward I'm now employed – ha! ha!   15

BOTH.   How dreadful when an innocent heart
                Becomes, perforce, a bad young Bart.,
                And still more hard on old Adam,
                His former faithful *valley-de-sham*!   20

ROB. This is a painful state of things, old Adam!

ADAM. Painful, indeed! Ah, my poor master, when I swore that, come what would, I would serve you in all things for ever, I little thought to what a pass it would bring me! The confidential adviser to the greatest villain unhung! Now, sir, to business. What crime do you propose to commit to-day?   25

41 *It would be simply rude*: In the pre-production libretto Adam had a longer speech at this point and the bridesmaids sang a chorus on their entrance as follows:

> ADAM. It would be simply rude – nothing more. Now if you were to seize Rose Maybud and confine her in the lowest dungeon beneath the castle moat, that would be disgraceful indeed. But soft – they come!

(ADAM *and* ROBIN *retire up as* CHORUS OF BRIDESMAIDS *enters*.)

CHORUS OF BRIDESMAIDS.

Although in fashion regular
Both Rose and Richard plighted are –
A picturesque event –
The wedding would be null and void
Unless Sir Ruthven Murgatroyd
Accorded his consent.
　　Which to refuse
　　He will not choose –
　　Of that we're confident.

And so we come in duty bound,
His views upon the point to sound
(The usual compliment).
Our landlord he – it would not do
Sir Ruthven's wishes to pooh-pooh;
　　Or he might raise our rent –
　　And that would be
　　To you and me
　　Most inconvenient!

(*Enter* RICHARD *and* ROSE.)

CHORUS.　　　　　Hail the bridegroom – hail the bride!
When the nuptial knot is tied,
Life will be one happy dream,
Joyfulness reign all supreme.

The duet 'Happily coupled are we' followed on immediately after this chorus. In the pre-production copy, all the above is crossed out in Gilbert's hand.

ROB. How should I know? As my confidential adviser, it's your duty to suggest something.

ADAM. Sir, I loathe the life you are leading, but a good old man's oath is paramount, and I obey. Richard Dauntless is here with pretty Rose   30
Maybud, to ask your consent to their marriage. Poison their beer.

ROB. No – not that – I know I'm a bad Bart., but I'm not as bad a Bart. as all that.

ADAM. Well, there you are, you see! It's no use my making suggestions if you don't adopt them.   35

ROB. (*melodramatically*). How would it be, do you think, were I to lure him here with cunning wile – bind him with good stout rope to yonder post – and then, by making hideous faces at him, curdle the heart-blood in his arteries, and freeze the very marrow in his bones? How say you, Adam, is not the scheme well planned?   40

ADAM. It would be simply rude – nothing more. But soft – they come!

(ADAM *and* ROBIN *exeunt as* RICHARD *and* ROSE *enter, preceded by*
Chorus of Bridesmaids.)

DUET – RICHARD *and* ROSE.

RICH. Happily coupled are we,
　　　　　　You see –   45
　　I am a jolly Jack Tar,
　　　　　My star,
　　And you are the fairest,
　　The richest and rarest
　　Of innocent lasses you are,   50
　　　　　By far –
　　Of innocent lasses you are!
　　Fanned by a favouring gale,
　　　　　You'll sail
　　Over life's treacherous sea   55
　　　　　With me,
　　And as for bad weather,
　　We'll brave it together,
　　And you shall creep under my lee,
　　　　　My wee!   60
　　And you shall creep under my lee!

　　For you are such a smart little craft –
　　Such a neat little, sweet little craft,
　　　Such a bright little, tight little,
　　　Slight little, light little,   65
　　Trim little, prim little craft!

68 *My hopes will be blighted, I fear*: The whole of Rose's verse was cut in the 1920 revival and has only occasionally been heard since in D'Oyly Carte productions. It was not sung on the company's last recording of *Ruddigore* in 1962.

96 *producing a Union Jack*: This is one of two occasions in the Savoy Operas when the stage directions call for a display of the British flag, the other being at the end of Act I of *The Pirates of Penzance*, where Major-General Stanley defiantly waves a Union Jack at the skull and cross-bones of the Pirate King.

Several reviewers felt that the business with the Union Jack did not really come off very well. The *Sunday Express* critic, for example, pointed to the similarity with the scene in *The Pirates* and went on: 'In itself it is not funny, it is not particularly happy as a parody as ridiculing national sentiment'. There was some suggestion, in fact, that in this scene Gilbert was not just ridiculing patriotic sentiment but also making a jibe at the Unionists who opposed Home Rule for Ireland. He himself vehemently denied that any such political satire was intended.

Gilbert's original stage direction for the business with the Union Jack was: 'Richard takes flag from Zorah. Ladies kneel, Rose with arms crossed on breast and seraphic smile. Richard waves flag with left hand through his speech.'

CHORUS.	For she is such, etc.

ROSE.

My hopes will be blighted, I fear,
    My dear;
In a month you'll be going to sea,   70
    Quite free,
And all of my wishes
  You'll throw to the fishes
As though they were never to be;
    Poor me!   75
As though they were never to be.
And I shall be left all alone
    To moan,
And weep at your cruel deceit,
    Complete;   80
While you'll be asserting
  Your freedom by flirting
With every woman you meet,
    You cheat – Ah!
With every woman you meet! Ah!   85

Though I am such a smart little craft –
Such a neat little, sweet little craft,
  Such a bright little, tight little,
  Slight little, light little,
Trim little, prim little craft!   90

CHORUS.	Though she is such, etc.

(*Enter* ROBIN.)

ROB. Soho! pretty one – in my power at last, eh? Know ye not that I have those within my call who, at my lightest bidding, would immure ye in an uncomfortable dungeon? (*Calling.*) What ho! within there!   95
    RICH. Hold – we are prepared for this (*producing a Union Jack*). Here is a flag that none dare defy (*all kneel*), and while this glorious rag floats over Rose Maybud's head, the man does not live who would dare to lay unlicensed hand upon her!
    ROB. Foiled – and by a Union Jack! But a time will come, and then —   100
    ROSE. Nay, let me plead with him. (*To* ROBIN.) Sir Ruthven, have pity. In my book of etiquette the case of a maiden about to be wedded to one who unexpectedly turns out to be a baronet with a curse on him is not considered. Time was when you loved me madly. Prove that this was no selfish love by according your consent to my marriage with one who, if he   105
be not you yourself, is the next best thing – your dearest friend!

107–14 *In bygone days I had thy love*
Rose's ballad originally had a second verse which was cut after ten performances:

> My heart that once in truth was thine,
> Another claims –
> Ah, who can laws to love assign,
> Or rule its flames?
> Our plighted heart-bond gently bless,
> The seal of thy consent impress.
> Upon our promised happiness –
> Grant thou our prayer!

135 *Oh, my forefathers*: When Henry Lytton was going through this speech after unexpectedly being called to fill in for the ill Grossmith (see the introduction), he was pulled up by Gilbert for hurrying it. In his memoirs Lytton recalls Gilbert as saying:

> That speech, 'Oh, my forefathers' is now a short speech, but originally it consisted of three pages of closely-written manuscript. I condensed and condensed. Every word I could I removed until it was of the length you find it today. Each word that is left serves some purpose – there is not one word too many. So when you know that it took me three months to perfect that one speech, I am sure you will not hurry it.

141 *The stage darkens for a moment*: Gilbert had first used the dramatic device of a picture gallery coming to life in his operetta *Ages Ago*, which had been put on at the Royal Gallery of Illustration in 1869. It was at a rehearsal of this work that Gilbert and Sullivan were introduced to each other by the composer Frederic Clay.

The scene in which the portraits become living people has always been difficult to stage effectively. It requires first of all a total blackout which can lead to difficulties for the orchestra as they try to follow an invisible conductor. In the original run this problem was overcome by giving the conductor an illuminated baton made out of a glass tube with fine platinum wires inside attached to batteries. I well remember the anguished cry of the pianist at one amateur performance of *Ruddigore* I attended when she found that her lamp was extinguished along with everything else.

The *Times* critic was singularly unimpressed by the way the scene was handled on the opening night:

> The ghost scene of the Second Act, representing the descent of the Murgatroyd ancestry from their picture frames, of which preliminary notices and the hints of the initiated had led one to expect much, was a very tame affair . . . A set of very ugly daubs, pulled up as you might a patent iron shutter to reveal a figure in the recess behind, can scarcely be called a good example of modern stage contrivance, especially when, as on Saturday night, one of these blinds or shutters comes down at an odd moment, while another refused to move.

BALLAD – Rose.

In bygone days I had thy love –
    Thou hadst my heart.
But Fate, all human vows above,
    Our lives did part!   110
By the old love thou hadst for me –
By the fond heart that beat for thee –
By joys that never now can be,
    Grant thou my prayer!

ALL (*kneeling*).	Grant thou her prayer!	115
ROB. (*recitative*).	Take her – I yield!	
ALL (*recitative*).	Oh, rapture!	(*All rising.*)

CHORUS.   Away to the parson we go –
                     Say we're solicitous very
               That he will turn two into one –   120
                     Singing hey, derry down derry!

RICH.	For she *is* such a smart little craft –	
ROSE.	Such a neat little, sweet little craft –	
RICH.	Such a bright little –	
ROSE.	Tight little –	125
RICH.	Slight little –	
ROSE.	Light little –	
BOTH.	Trim little, prim little craft!	

CHORUS.   For she *is* such a smart little craft, etc.

                              (*Exeunt all but* ROBIN.)   130

ROB. For a week I have fulfilled my accursed doom! I have duly committed a crime a day! Not a great crime, I trust, but still, in the eyes of one as strictly regulated as I used to be, a crime. But will my ghostly ancestors be satisfied with what I have done, or will they regard it as an unworthy subterfuge? (*Addressing Pictures.*) Oh, my forefathers, wallowers in   135 blood, there came at last a day when, sick of crime, you, each and every, vowed to sin no more, and so, in agony, called welcome Death to free you from your cloying guiltiness. Let the sweet psalm of that repentant hour soften your long-dead hearts, and tune your souls to mercy on your poor posterity! (*kneeling*).   140

        (*The Stage darkens for a moment. It becomes light again, and the
                Pictures are seen to have become animated.*)

143–6 *Painted emblems of a race*
The first seven notes of this chorus are the same as those of Sullivan's famous tune for the hymn 'Onward Christian Soldiers', the only difference being that 'Painted emblems' is in a minor key.

147–8 *march round the stage*: Sullivan originally wrote a thirty-two-bar march for the ghosts at this point, but it was cut during rehearsals after Gilbert complained that it was 'out of place' in a comic opera. It is as though one inserted fifty lines of *Paradise Lost* into a farcical comedy.'

153 *poltroon*: A spiritless coward, a worthless wretch.

162 *Beware! beware! beware*: Sir Roderic's ghostly admonition was originally preceded by a passage for him and the chorus. It was sung on the first night but later cut. Here it is:

SIR ROD.	By the curse upon our race –
CHORUS.	Dead and hearsèd All accursèd!
SIR ROD.	Each inheriting their place –
CHORUS.	Sorrows shake it! Devil take it!
SIR ROD.	Must perforce, or yea or nay –
CHORUS.	Yea or naying Be obeying!
SIR ROD.	Do a deadly crime each day!
CHORUS.	Fire and thunder, We knocked under – Some atrocious crime committed Daily ere the world we quitted!

171 *Alas, poor ghost*: Compare *Hamlet*, Act I, Scene 5:

HAMLET.	Alas! poor ghost.
GHOST.	Pity me not.

C HORUS OF F AMILY P ORTRAITS.

Painted emblems of a race,
　　All accurst in days of yore,
Each from his accustomed place   145
　　Steps into the world once more.

(*The Pictures step from their frames and march round the stage.*)

Baronet of Ruddigore,
　　Last of our accursèd line,   150
Down upon the oaken floor –
　　Down upon those knees of thine.

　　Coward, poltroon, shaker, squeamer,
　　Blockhead, sluggard, dullard, dreamer,
　　Shirker, shuffler, crawler, creeper,   155
　　Sniffer, snuffler, wailer, weeper,
　　Earthworm, maggot, tadpole, weevil!
　　Set upon thy course of evil,
　　Lest the King of Spectre-Land
　　Set on thee his grisly hand!   160

(*The Spectre of* S IR R ODERIC *descends from his frame.*)

SIR ROD.　　Beware! beware! beware!

ROB.　　　　　　Gaunt vision, who art thou
　　　　　That thus, with icy glare
　　　　　　　And stern relentless brow,   165
　　　　　　　Appearest, who knows how?

SIR ROD.　　I am the spectre of the late
　　　　　　　Sir Roderic Murgatroyd,
　　　　　Who comes to warn thee that thy fate
　　　　　　　Thou canst not now avoid.   170

ROB.　　　　Alas, poor ghost!
SIR ROD.　　　　　　　　The pity you
　　　　　　　Express for nothing goes:
　　　　　We spectres are a jollier crew
　　　　　　　Than you, perhaps, suppose!   175

CHORUS.　　We spectres are a jollier crew
　　　　　　　Than you, perhaps, suppose!

178–96   *When the night wind howls*
> The words of this famous song, for which Sullivan provided one of his most effective and operatic settings, recall an early poem written by Gilbert for the magazine *Fun*:

> > Fair phantom come!
> > The moon's awake.
> > The owl hoots gaily from its brake,
> > The blithesome bat's a-wing.
> > Come, soar to yonder silent clouds,
> > The other teems with peopled shrouds:
> > We'll fly the lightsome spectre crowds,
> > Thou cloudly, clammy thing!

197   *you are the picture*: In keeping with his initial intention to make Sir Roderic a Lord Mayor (see the note to line 4), Gilbert originally wrote this line as 'You are the Lord Mayor that hangs etc'. However, he changed it before the first night.

202   *as a work of art you are poor*: In the licence copy and the first edition the ghosts echo this remark as follows:

> 1st GHOST. That's true.
> 2ND GHOST. No doubt.
> 3RD GHOST. Wants tone.
> 4TH GHOST. Not mellow enough.

205   *you spoke lightly of me*: In the pre-production libretto, the following exchange followed Sir Roderic's speech at this point:

> ROB. How came you to be a Lord Mayor?
> SIR ROD. I couldn't help it. It was part of my hideous doom.
> ROB. Poor soul! And may I ask . . . [as now].

SONG – SIR RODERIC.

When the night wind howls in the chimney cowls, and the bat in the
    moonlight flies,
And inky clouds, like funeral shrouds, sail over the midnight skies –
When the footpads quail at the night-bird's wail, and black dogs bay at the
    moon,   180
Then is the spectres' holiday – then is the ghosts' high-noon!
    CHORUS.   Ha! ha!
            Then is the ghosts' high-noon!

As the sob of the breeze sweeps over the trees, and the mists lie low on the
    fen,
From grey tomb-stones are gathered the bones that once were women and
    men,   185
And away they go, with a mop and a mow, to the revel that ends too soon,
For cockcrow limits our holiday – the dead of the night's high-noon!
    CHORUS.   Ha! ha!
            The dead of the night's high-noon!

And then each ghost with his ladye-toast to their churchyard beds takes
    flight,   190
With a kiss, perhaps, on her lantern chaps, and a grisly grim 'good-night';
Till the welcome knell of the midnight bell rings forth its jolliest tune,
And ushers in our next high holiday – the dead of the night's high-noon!
    CHORUS.   Ha! ha!
            The dead of the night's high-noon!   195
            Ha! ha! ha! ha!

ROB. I recognize you now – you are the picture that hangs at the end of
the gallery.
    SIR ROD. In a bad light. I am.
    ROB. Are you considered a good likeness?   200
    SIR ROD. Pretty well. Flattering.
    ROB. Because as a work of art you are poor.
    SIR ROD. I am crude in colour, but I have only been painted ten years.
In a couple of centuries I shall be an Old Master, and then you will be sorry
you spoke lightly of me.   205
    ROB. And may I ask why you have left your frames?
    SIR ROD. It is our duty to see that our successors commit their daily
crimes in a conscientious and workmanlike fashion. It is our duty to remind
you that you are evading the conditions under which you are permitted to
exist.   210

214 *Bank Holiday*: See the note to *Patience*, Act II, line 494.

230 *Yes, it seems reasonable*: This and the next line were dropped in recent D'Oyly Carte pro-
     ductions.

244 *I forged his cheque*: Originally this line was echoed by the ghosts as follows:

     1ST GHOST. That's true.
     2ND GHOST. Yes, it seems reasonable.
     3RD GHOST. At first glance it does.
     4TH GHOST. Fallacy somewhere!

251 *can I disinherit*: Another line originally taken up by the ghosts:

     1ST GHOST. That's right enough.
     2ND GHOST. Yes, it seems reasonable.
     3RD GHOST. At first sight it does.
     4TH GHOST. Fallacy somewhere!

ROB. Really, I don't know what you'd have. I've only been a bad baronet a week, and I've committed a crime punctually every day.

SIR ROD. Let us inquire into this. Monday?

ROB. Monday was a Bank Holiday.

SIR ROD. True. Tuesday? 215

ROB. On Tuesday I made a false income-tax return.

ALL. Ha! ha!

1ST GHOST. That's nothing.

2ND GHOST. Nothing at all.

3RD GHOST. Everybody does that. 220

4TH GHOST. It's expected of you.

SIR ROD. Wednesday?

ROB. (*melodramatically*). On Wednesday I forged a will.

SIR ROD. Whose will?

ROB. My own. 225

SIR ROD. My good sir, you can't forge your own will!

ROB. Can't I, though! I like that! I *did*! Besides, if a man can't forge his own will, whose will can he forge?

1ST GHOST. There's something in that.

2ND GHOST. Yes, it seems reasonable. 230

3RD GHOST. At first sight it does.

4TH GHOST. Fallacy somewhere, I fancy!

ROB. A man can do what he likes with his own!

SIR ROD. I suppose he can.

ROB. Well, then, he can forge his own will, stoopid! On Thursday I 235
shot a fox.

1ST GHOST. Hear, hear!

SIR ROD. That's better (*addressing Ghosts*). Pass the fox, I think? (*They assent.*) Yes, pass the fox. Friday?

ROB. On Friday I forged a cheque. 240

SIR ROD. Whose cheque?

ROB. Old Adam's.

SIR ROD. But Old Adam hasn't a banker.

ROB. I didn't say I forged his banker – I said I forged his cheque. On Saturday I disinherited my only son. 245

SIR ROD. But you haven't got a son.

ROB. No – not yet. I disinherited him in advance, to save time. You see – by this arrangement – he'll be born ready disinherited.

SIR ROD. I see. But I don't think you can do that.

ROB. My good sir, if I can't disinherit my own unborn son, whose 250
unborn son can I disinherit?

SIR ROD. Humph! These arguments sound very well, but I can't help thinking that, if they were reduced to syllogistic form, they wouldn't hold water. Now quite understand us. We are foggy, but we don't permit our

281–2 *anything like that*: Gilbert originally intended to make this the cue for a duet for Robin and Sir Roderic, to be followed by a chorus:

DUET and CHORUS.

ROB.   Pray you, sir, excuse, in charity,
                           Any act of impropriety
                        To my unfamiliarity
                           With the rules of ghost society.
                        Pray withhold your animosity:
                           Though it's awkward for a gentleman
                        To embark on wild ferocity
                           Like a cut-throat Oriental man,
                        I'll forego my wild identity,
                           So, without undue tautology,
                        Pray accept from this nonentity
                           All appropriate apology!
                        Though the prospect does not fascinate,
                           Like a baronet, bad but sensible,
                        I will murder – rob – assassinate –
                           Everything that's reprehensible!

CHORUS.   Though the prospect, etc.

SIR ROD.   If you speak in all sincerity,
                           And obey with due humility,
                        Pray forgive me my asperity
                           Prompted by your imbecility.
                        Your obedience will gratify –
                           We have gained a moral victory,
                        But before the terms I ratify,
                           Hear my counsel valedictory.
                        Set to work with due rapidity,
                           Make away with all impediment –
                        Naught will serve you, quip or quiddity,
                           Pray believe that I said what I meant.
                        Poison, stab, defame and dissipate –
                           Let your deeds be indefensible,
                        You'll commit, as I anticipate,
                           Everything that's reprehensible!

CHORUS.   Poison, stab, defame, etc.

CHORUS.

                        Baronet of Ruddigore,
                           Ere we seek our penal flames,
                        Your forgiveness we implore
                           For miscalling you such names
                        As 'coward, poltroon, shaker, squeamer,
                        Blockhead, sluggard, dull-head, dreamer,
                        Shaker, shuffler, crawler, creeper,
                        Sniffler, snuffler, waiter, weeper,
                        Earthworm, maggot, tadpole, weevil',
                        All these names are most uncivil –
                           This is our apology,
                           Pardon – pardon us – or die!

ROB. (*in terror, on his knees*).   I pardon you!
ALL.   He pardons us!
                           Ha! Ha!

fogginess to be presumed upon. Unless you undertake to – well, suppose we 255
say, carry off a lady? (*Addressing Ghosts.*) Those who are in favour of his
carrying off a lady? (*All hold up their hands except a Bishop.*) Those of the
contrary opinion? (*Bishop holds up his hands.*) Oh, you're never satisfied! Yes,
unless you undertake to carry off a lady at once – I don't care what lady – any
lady – choose your lady – you perish in inconceivable agonies. 260

ROB. Carry off a lady? Certainly not, on any account. I've the greatest
respect for ladies, and I wouldn't do anything of the kind for worlds! No, no.
I'm not that kind of baronet, I assure you! If that's all you've got to say, you'd
better go back to your frames.

SIR ROD. Very good – then let the agonies commence. 265

(*Ghosts make passes.* ROBIN *begins to writhe in agony.*)

ROB. Oh! Oh! Don't do that! I can't stand it!
SIR ROD. Painful, isn't it? It gets worse by degrees.
ROB. Oh – Oh! Stop a bit! Stop it, will you? I want to speak.

(SIR RODERIC *makes signs to Ghosts, who resume* 270
their attitudes.)

SIR ROD. Better?
ROB. Yes – better now! Whew!
SIR ROD. Well, do you consent?
ROB. But it's such an ungentlemanly thing to do! 275
SIR ROD. As you please. (*To Ghosts.*) Carry on!
ROB. Stop – I can't stand it! I agree! I promise! It shall be done!
SIR ROD. To-day?
ROB. To-day!
SIR ROD. At once? 280
ROB. At once! I retract! I apologize! I had no idea it was anything like
that!

CHORUS.

He yields! He answers to our call!
We do not ask for more.
A sturdy fellow, after all, 285
This latest Ruddigore!
All perish in unheard-of woe
Who dare our wills defy;
We want your pardon, ere we go,
For having agonized you so – 290

CHORUS.   Painted emblems, etc.

All the above is crossed out in Gilbert's hand in the pre-production libretto and the chorus 'He yields' substituted instead.

313 *Fly*: Observant readers of *Ruddigore* will have noticed that this opera lacks one of the essential ingredients of the Savoy repertoire, a patter song. In fact, there was originally a patter song for Robin at this point, preceded by a brief recitative. It went as follows:

RECITATIVE AND SONG – ROBIN.

Away Remorse!
  Compunction, hence!
Go, Moral Force!
  Go, Penitence!
To Virtue's plea
  A long farewell –
Propriety,
  I ring your knell!
Come guiltiness of deadliest hue,
Come desperate deeds of derring-do!

For thirty-five years I've been sober and wary –
My favourite tipple came straight from a dairy –
I kept guinea-pigs and a Belgian canary –
  A squirrel, white mice, and a small black-and-tan.
I played on the flute, and I drank lemon squashes –
I wore chamois leather, thick boots, and macintoshes,
And things that will some day be known as galoshes,
  The type of a highly respectable man!

For the rest of my life I abandon propriety –
Visit the haunts of Bohemian society,
Wax-works, and other resorts of impiety,
  Placed by the moralist under a ban.
My ways must be those of a regular satyr,
At carryings-on I must be a first-rater –
Go night after night to a wicked theayter –
  It's hard on a highly respectable man!

Well, the man who has spent the first half of his tether,
On all the bad deeds you can bracket together,
Then goes and repents – in his cap it's a feather –
  Society pets him as much as it can.
It's a comfort to think, if I now go a cropper,
I sha'n't, on the whole, have done more that's improper
Than he who was once an abandoned tip-topper,
  But now is a highly respectable man!

On the day after the opening performance, Gilbert wrote to Sullivan: 'I can't help thinking that the 2nd Act would be greatly improved if the recitation before Grossmith's song were omitted, and the song reset to an air that would admit of his singing it desperately – almost in a passion – the torrent of which would take him off the stage at the end.'

The recitative, in fact, remained, but a new patter song was written for the third edition of the libretto, published on 2 February, only eleven days after the opening night. It was dropped in the 1920 revival and has not been sung since professionally on stage, although it was included in two B.B.C. productions where it was sung by Peter Pratt and Derek Hammond-Stroud respectively. This second version went as follows:

	So pardon us –
	So pardon us –
	So pardon us –
	Or die!

ROB.	I pardon you!	295
	I pardon you!	

ALL.	He pardons us –
	Hurrah!

(*The Ghosts return to their frames.*)

CHORUS.	Painted emblems of a race,	300
	All accurst in days of yore,	
	Each to his accustomed place	
	Steps unwillingly once more!	

(*By this time the Ghosts have changed to pictures again.*
ROBIN is overcome by emotion.)   305

(*Enter* ADAM.)

ADAM. My poor master, you are not well —
ROB. Adam, it won't do – I've seen 'em – all my ancestors – they're just
gone. They say that I must do something desperate at once, or perish in
horrible agonies. Go – go to yonder village – carry off a maiden – bring her   310
here at once – any one – I don't care which —
ADAM. But —
ROB. Not a word, but obey! Fly!

(*Exeunt* ADAM *and* ROBIN.)

(*Enter* DESPARD *and* MARGARET. *They are both dressed in sober black of*   315
formal cut, and present a strong contrast to their appearance in Act I.)

DUET.

DES.	I once was a very abandoned person –	
MAR.	Making the most of evil chances.	
DES.	Nobody could conceive a worse 'un –	
MAR.	Even in all the old romances.	320
DES.	I blush for my wild extravagances,	
	But be so kind	
	To bear in mind,	

Henceforth all the crimes that I find in theTimes,
    I've promised to perpetrate daily;
To-morrow I start, with a petrified heart,
    On a regular course of Old Bailey.
There's confidence tricking, bad coin, pocket-picking,
    And several other disgraces –
There's postage-stamp prigging, and then thimble-rigging
    The three-card delusion at races!
Oh! a baronet's rank is exceedingly nice,
    But the title's uncommonly dear at the price!

Ye well-to-do squires, who live in the shires,
    Where petty distinctions are vital,
Who found Athenaeums and local museums,
    With views to a baronet's title –
Ye butchers and bakers and candlestick makers
    Who sneer at all things that are tradey –
Whose middle-class lives are embarrassed by wives
    Who long to parade as 'My Lady,'
Oh! allow me to offer a word of advice,
    The title's uncommonly dear at the price!

Ye supple M.P.'s, who go down on your knees,
    Your precious identity sinking,
And vote black and white as your leaders indite
    (Which saves you the trouble of thinking),
For your country's good fame, her repute, or her shame,
    You don't care the snuff of a candle –
But you're paid for your game when you're told that your name
    Will be graced by a baronet's handle –
Oh! allow me to give you a word of advice –
    The title's uncommonly dear at the price!

339 *penny readings*: Entertainments consisting of songs, dramatic recitations and readings held in church or village halls and for which the admission charge was a penny. George Grossmith was a dab at penny readings, particularly for the Young Men's Christian Association.

343 *A National School*: The name given in the nineteenth century to church schools, set up under the auspices of the National Society for the Education of the Poor in the Principles of the Established Church. In the first edition of the libretto this line appeared as 'A Sunday School' but it was never apparently sung as such, as the first-night review of the *Weekly Despatch* makes clear:

> Mr Gilbert is very respectful to the susceptibilities of the religious public. When Miss Jessie Bond, attired in Methodistical garments, dances her grotesque dance with Mr Barrington, she ought to sing, according to the book: 'And now we rule a Sunday School'. But she sings 'a National School' instead. No doubt the change was made at the last moment in deference to the feelings of Sunday-school teachers who are sure to be present in great numbers at the first morning performance of *Ruddygore*.

346 *This sort of thing takes a deal of training*: Indeed it does. Sir Despard and Margaret's dance is traditionally performed with the aid of a sharpened umbrella which is stuck into the stage. Peter Riley, for many years the D'Oyly Carte stage manager, recalls one terrible moment on tour when Kenneth Sandford realized that he was on a concrete stage, with no hope of performing the usual trick with the umbrella, and another when his umbrella disintegrated in mid-dance.

351 *So calm*: Various lines in this dialogue between Sir Despard and Margaret were cut when the Second Act was shortened early on in the initial run. After 'So calm!', for example,

MAR.	We were the victims of circumstances!
	(Dance.) 325
	That is one of our blameless dances.

MAR.	I was once an exceedingly odd young lady –
DES.	Suffering much from spleen and vapours.
MAR.	Clergymen thought my conduct shady –
DES.	She didn't spend much upon linen-drapers.
MAR.	It certainly entertained the gapers.
	My ways were strange
	Beyond all range –
DES.	Paragraphs got into all the papers.
	(Dance.) 335
	We only cut respectable capers.

DES.	I've given up all my wild proceedings.
MAR.	My taste for a wandering life is waning.
DES.	Now I'm a dab at penny readings.
MAR.	They are not remarkably entertaining.
DES.	A moderate livelihood we're gaining.
MAR.	In fact we rule
	A National School.
DES.	The duties are dull, but I'm not complaining.
	(Dance.) 345
	This sort of thing takes a deal of training!

DES. We have been married a week.

MAR. One happy, happy week!

DES. Our new life –

MAR. Is delightful indeed!

DES. So calm!

MAR. So unimpassioned! (*wildly*). Master, all this I owe to you! See, I am no longer wild and untidy. My hair is combed. My face is washed. My boots fit!

DES. Margaret, don't. Pray restrain yourself. Remember, you are now a district visitor.

MAR. A gentle district visitor!

DES. You are orderly, methodical, neat; you have your emotions well under control.

MAR. I have! (*wildly*). Master, when I think of all you have done for me, I fall at your feet. I embrace your ankles. I hug your knees! (*Doing so.*)

330

340

350

355

360

Margaret originally said 'So pure!' and Despard 'So peaceful!' before Margaret's 'So un-impassioned!'

355 *Margaret, don't*: Another shortened passage. It originally went:

> D E S . Margaret, don't. Pray restrain yourself. Be demure, I beg.
> M A R . Demure it is. (*Resumes her quiet manner.*)
> D E S . Then make it so. Remember, you are now a district visitor.

371 *for a sick-room*: Despard originally continued at this point:

> Then again, as I've frequently told you, it is quite possible to take too much medicine.
> M A R . What, when you're ill?
> D E S . Certainly. These are valuable remedies but they should be administered with dis-cretion.
> M A R . How strange . . . [as now].

381 *Basingstoke*: Various explanations have been put forward as to why Gilbert chose the name of the rather undistinguished Hampshire town for the word which would bring Mad Margaret to her senses. Madge Terry in her book *An Operatic Glossary* suggests it was because there was a well-known mental hospital there but this was not, in fact, built at the time *Ruddigore* was written. A more convincing theory is perhaps that expounded by Geoffrey Wilson in the *Savoyard* for September 1978. He pointed out that the town had figured in a novel by Gilbert's father *The Doctor of Beauvoir*, and also that Gilbert's father and his sister lived at Salisbury, and so the dramatist must often have passed through Basingstoke on his way to visit them by train. It may be, in fact, that Basingstoke was not Gilbert's original choice for the 'word that teems with hidden meaning'. The magazine *Figaro* reported in December 1886 that reports from the rehearsals of the latest opera at the Savoy indicated there was a character called Mad Margaret 'with that blessed word Barnstaple'.

397 *a pure and blameless ratepayer*: The first-edition libretto continued at this point:

> R O B . That's all very well, but you seem to forget that on the day I reform I perish in excruciating torment.
> D E S . Oh, better that than pursue a course of life-long villainy. Oh, seek refuge in death, I implore you!
> M A R . Why not die? Others have died and no one has cared. You will not be mourned.
> D E S . True – you could die so well!
> R O B . You didn't seem to be of this opinion when *you* were a bad baronet.
> D E S . No, because *I* had no good brother at my elbow to check *me* when about to go wrong.
> R O B . A home-thrust indeed! (*Aloud*) But I've done no wrong yet.

DES. Hush. This is not well. This is calculated to provoke remark. Be composed, I beg!

MAR. Ah! you are angry with poor little Mad Margaret!

DES. No, not angry; but a district visitor should learn to eschew melodrama. Visit the poor, by all means, and give them tea and barley-water, but don't do it as if you were administering a bowl of deadly nightshade. It upsets them. Then when you nurse sick people, and find them not as well as could be expected, why go into hysterics?

MAR. Why not?

DES. Because it's too jumpy for a sick-room.

MAR. How strange! Oh, Master! Master! – how shall I express the all-absorbing gratitude that – (*about to throw herself at his feet*).

DES. Now! (*warningly*).

MAR. Yes, I know, dear – it shan't occur again. (*He is seated – she sits on the ground by him.*) Shall I tell you one of poor Mad Margaret's odd thoughts? Well, then, when I am lying awake at night, and the pale moonlight streams through the latticed casement, strange fancies crowd upon my poor mad brain, and I sometimes think that if we could hit upon some word for you to use whenever I am about to relapse – some word that teems with hidden meaning – like 'Basingstoke' – it might recall me to my saner self. For, after all, I am only Mad Margaret! Daft Meg! Poor Meg! He! he! he!

DES. Poor child, she wanders! But soft – some one comes – Margaret – pray recollect yourself – Basingstoke, I beg! Margaret, if you don't Basingstoke at once, I shall be seriously angry.

MAR. (*recovering herself*). Basingstoke it is!

DES. Then make it so.

(*Enter* ROBIN. *He starts on seeing them.*)

ROB. Despard! And his young wife! This visit is unexpected.

MAR. Shall I fly at him? Shall I tear him limb from limb? Shall I rend him asunder? Say but the word and —

DES. Basingstoke!

MAR. (*suddenly demure*). Basingstoke it is!

DES. (*aside*). Then make it so. (*Aloud.*) My brother – I call you brother still, despite your horrible profligacy – we have come to urge you to abandon the evil courses to which you have committed yourself, and at any cost to become a pure and blameless ratepayer.

ROB. But I've done no wrong yet.

MAR. (*wildly*). No wrong! He has done no wrong! Did you hear that!

DES. Basingstoke!

MAR. (*recovering herself*). Basingstoke it is!

DES. My brother – I still call you brother, you observe – you forget that you have been, in the eye of the law, a Bad Baronet of Ruddigore for ten

405 *your place*: The first edition continues here:

> ROB. Meaning you?
> DES. Meaning me.

407 *Wasn't he*: The cue for another line cut after the first edition:

> MAR. Desperate! Oh, you were a flirt!

413 *she trusted you*: At this point the original dialogue continued:

> ROB. Meaning *you*?
> DES. Nothing of the kind, sir. I was simply your representative.
> ROB. Well, meaning *us*, then. What a scoundrel we must have been! There, there . . . [as now].

431–63 *My eyes are fully open to my awful situation*
The 'matter trio' is one of the most difficult numbers to sing in the entire Gilbert and Sullivan repertoire. It should be taken at a breathtaking pace, and it is just as well that Gilbert made clear in the last lines that it doesn't really matter whether the words are heard or not.

The satirical magazine *Funny Folks* published a parody of the matter trio in its issue of 12 February 1887. It is entitled 'Randy in the South' and refers to the departure from English politics to the U.S.A. of Lord Randolph Churchill, father of Sir Winston:

> I am sitting 'neath a palm-tree, in an easy chair of wicker,
> In my mouth a prime Havanna, by my side a glass of 'licker',
> Something Yankeefied and coolish, in the which dissolving ice is,
> And the breeze is very balmy, and the sunshine very nice is.
> I can lounge and I can idle to day's end from its beginnin',
> In a helmet that is pithy, and a suit of snowy linen;
> Which is pleasanter than harking to the House's dreary chatter –
> To a load of doosid rubbish, which you know don't really matter.
> Which you know don't really matter, etc.

years – and you are therefore responsible – in the eye of the law – for all the misdeeds committed by the unhappy gentleman who occupied your place.

ROB. I see! Bless my heart, I never thought of that! Was I very bad?

DES. Awful. Wasn't he? (*to* MARGARET).

ROB. And I've been going on like this for how long?

DES. Ten years! Think of all the atrocities you have committed – by attorney as it were – during that period. Remember how you trifled with this poor child's affections – how you raised her hopes on high (don't cry, my love – Basingstoke, you know), only to trample them in the dust when they were at the very zenith of their fullness. Oh fie, sir, fie – she trusted you!

ROB. Did she? What a scoundrel I must have been! There, there – don't cry, my dear (*to* MARGARET, *who is sobbing on* ROBIN's *breast*), it's all right now. Birmingham, you know – Birmingham —

MAR. (*sobbing*). It's Ba – Ba – Basingstoke!

ROB. Basingstoke! of course it is – Basingstoke.

MAR. Then make it so!

ROB. There, there – it's all right – he's married you now – that is, *I've* married you (*turning to* DESPARD) – I say, which of us has married her?

DES. Oh, *I've* married her.

ROB. (*aside*). Oh, I'm glad of that. (*To* MARGARET.) Yes, *he's* married you now (*passing her over to* DESPARD), and anything more disreputable than my conduct seems to have been I've never even heard of. But my mind is made up – I *will* defy my ancestors. I *will* refuse to obey their behests, thus, by courting death, atone in some degree for the infamy of my career!

MAR. I knew it – I knew it – God bless you – (*hysterically*).

DES. Basingstoke!

MAR. Basingstoke it is! (*Recovers herself.*)

405

410

415

420

425

430

PATTER-TRIO.

ROBIN, DESPARD, *and* MARGARET.

ROB. My eyes are fully open to my awful situation –
    I shall go at once to Roderic and make him an oration.
    I shall tell him I've recovered my forgotten moral senses,
    And I don't care twopence-halfpenny for any consequences.
    Now I do not want to perish by the sword or by the dagger,
    But a martyr may indulge a little pardonable swagger,
    And a word or two of compliment my vanity would flatter,
    But I've got to die to-morrow, so it really doesn't matter!

435

DES.   So it really doesn't matter –

MAR.   So it really doesn't matter –

440

457 *My existence*: In his pre-production copy, Gilbert crossed out 'existence' and substituted 'story'. The line appears in that form in the licence copy and the current Macmillan edition, but 'existence' appears in the vocal score and is generally sung.

466 *Master – the deed is done*: In the pre-production libretto Robin had the following lines before Adam's arrival:

> Yes, my mind is made up. I don't know what crimes I may not have committed by deputy, but since I've been the worst baronet that ever lived, my life has been practically blameless. Today I will commit no crime and consequently, tonight I perish!

473 *foiled again*: The pre-production libretto had the following exchange here:

> ROB. But I am foiled again – and by a stripling!
> ADAM. Nay, I am no stripling!
> ROB. Produce her – and leave us!

ALL. So it really doesn't matter, matter, matter, matter, matter!

MAR. If I were not a little mad and generally silly
I should give you my advice upon the subject, willy-nilly;
I should show you in a moment how to grapple with the question,
And you'd really be astonished at the force of my suggestion. 445
On the subject I shall write you a most valuable letter,
Full of excellent suggestions, when I feel a little better,
But at present, I'm afraid I am as mad as any hatter,
So I'll keep 'em to myself, for my opinion doesn't matter!

DES. Her opinion doesn't matter – 450

ROB. Her opinion doesn't matter –

ALL. Her opinion doesn't matter, matter, matter, matter, matter!

DES. If I had been so lucky as to have a steady brother
Who could talk to me as we are talking now to one another –
Who could give me good advice when he discovered I was erring 455
(Which is just the very favour which on you I am conferring),
My existence would have made a rather interesting idyll,
And I might have lived and died a very decent indiwiddle.
This particularly rapid, unintelligible patter
Isn't generally heard, and if it is it doesn't matter! 460

ROB. If it is it doesn't matter –

MAR. If it is it doesn't matter –

ALL. If it is it doesn't matter, matter, matter, matter, matter!

(*Exeunt* DESPARD *and* MARGARET.)

(*Enter* ADAM.) 465

ADAM (*guiltily*). Master – the deed is done!
ROB. What deed?
ADAM. She is here – alone, unprotected —
ROB. Who?
ADAM. The maiden. I've carried her off – I had a hard task, for she 470
fought like a tiger-cat!
ROB. Great heaven, I had forgotten her! I had hoped to have died
unspotted by crime, but I am foiled again – and by a tiger-cat! Produce her
– and leave us!

481   *difficult country*: In the pre-production libretto Hannah continued at this point:

> Prompted by I know not what infernal motive, he has carried me hither unprotected, save by the atmosphere of innocence that environs a pure and spotless woman, and left me helpless and trembling at your mercy.

485-6 *what I intended*: As originally performed, Robin and Hannah had a longer exchange at this point which went as follows:

> ROB. Circumstances of a delicate nature compelled me to request your presence in this confounded castle for a brief period – but anything more correct – more deeply respectful than my intentions towards you, it would be impossible for anyone – however particular – to desire.
>
> HAN. (*wildly*). Am I a toy – a bauble – a pretty plaything – to grace your roystering banquets and amuse your ribald friends? Am I a gew-gaw to while away an idle hour withal, and then be cast aside like some old glove, when the whim quits you? Harkye, sir, do you take me for a gaw of this description?
>
> ROB. (*appalled*). Certainly not – nothing of the kind – anything more profoundly respectable –
>
> HAN. Bah, I am not to be tricked . . . [as now].

The *Sunday Express* reviewer commented of this scene: 'Hannah's mock heroics and noisy defence of her virtue were not only ineffective – they were jarring. Whether they were too earnest, whether they were not sufficiently exaggerated, I cannot say: but they certainly missed the correct tone.' It was doubtless partly in response to such criticism, as well as in an effort to shorten Act II, that Gilbert cut down the dialogue.

495   *Dame Hannah*: Rosina Brandram, who created the role of Hannah, told the following story of an occasion when she could not find the dagger with which she had to make her Act II entrance:

> I absolutely refused to go on, as without it, it was quite impossible to play the scene. Everyone urged and implored me, and Mr Barrington, seeing the stage wait, went into the property-room and brought out something which he thrust into my hand, at the same time giving me a push which caused me to appear in sight of the audience; so, *nolens volens*, I had to proceed, knowing that in my hand I carried an insignificant gas key. I did the best I could to conceal this fact, and went on with the business. I had to rush and snatch a large dagger from a figure in armour and fling my supposed poignard to Mr Grossmith . . . Imagine my consternation when I saw by the expression on Mr Grossmith's face, as he stooped to pick up the key, that he meant mischief; my heart went right into my shoes, but I did not think he was going to give me away in the manner in which he did, for, holding up the gas key to the audience, he said: 'How can I defend myself with this?' Of course there was a laugh; my feelings may be better imagined than described. If ever I contemplated murder it was at that moment. I would willingly have slain both Mr Grossmith and Mr Barrington.

503   *Sir Roderic enters*: Originally Sir Roderic appeared through a trap-door in the stage with red flames rising around him. His method of entrance was changed to its present form in the first ten days of performance.

(ADAM *introduces* DAME HANNAH, *very much excited, and exits.*) 475

ROB. Dame Hannah! This is – this is not what I expected.

HAN. Well, sir, and what would you with me? Oh, you have begun bravely – bravely indeed! Unappalled by the calm dignity of blameless womanhood, your minion has torn me from my spotless home, and dragged me, blindfold and shrieking, through hedges, over stiles, and across a very 480 difficult country, and left me, helpless and trembling, at your mercy! Yet not helpless, coward sir, for approach one step – nay, but the twentieth part of one poor inch – and this poniard (*produces a very small dagger*) shall teach ye what it is to lay unholy hands on old Stephen Trusty's daughter!

ROB. Madam, I am extremely sorry for this. It is not at all what I 485 intended – anything more correct – more deeply respectful than my intentions towards you, it would be impossible for any one – however particular – to desire.

HAN. Bah, I am not to be tricked by smooth words, hypocrite! But be warned in time, for there are, without, a hundred gallant hearts whose 490 trusty blades would hack him limb from limb who dared to lay unholy hands on old Stephen Trusty's daughter!

ROB. And this is what it is to embark upon a career of unlicensed pleasure!

(DAME HANNAH, *who has taken a formidable dagger from one of the armed* 495
figures, throws her small dagger to ROBIN.)

HAN. Harkye, miscreant, you have secured me, and I am your poor prisoner; but if you think I cannot take care of myself you are very much mistaken. Now then, it's one to one, and let the best man win! (*Making for him.*) 500

ROB. (*in an agony of terror*). Don't! don't look at me like that! I can't bear it! Roderic! Uncle! Save me!

(SIR RODERIC *enters, from his picture. He comes down*
the stage.)

ROD. What is the matter? Have you carried her off? 505

ROB. I have – she is there – look at her – she terrifies me!

ROD. (*looking at* HANNAH). Little Nannikin!

HAN. (*amazed*). Roddy-doddy!

ROD. My own old love! Why, how came *you* here?

HAN. This brute – he carried me off! Bodily! But I'll show him! (*about to* 510
rush at ROBIN).

ROD. Stop! (*To* ROB.) What do you mean by carrying off this lady? Are you aware that once upon a time she was engaged to be married to me? I'm very angry – very angry indeed.

517 *Yes, uncle*: Originally Sir Roderic (who was still below the level of the stage on his trap-door), Hannah and Robin had the following exchange at this point:

> ROD. Has he treated you with proper respect since you've been here, Nannikin?
> HAN. Pretty well, Roddy. Come quite up, dear!
> ROD. No, I don't think I shall.
> ROB. No, I don't think you should.
> ROD. Hold your tongue.
> ROB. Yes, uncle.
> ROD. I'm very much annoyed. Have you given him any encouragement?

522 *to desire*: Again, there was originally a longer exchange between Hannah, Sir Roderic and Robin here, which – like the passage above – was cut early on in the first run:

> HAN. There now – come up, dear.
> ROD. (*reluctantly*). Very well, but you don't deserve it, you know (*comes up*.)
> ROB. Before we go any further, I am anxious to assure you on my honour as a gentleman, and with all the emphasis at my command, that anything more profoundly respectful –
> ROD. You go away.

530 *You don't deserve to be*:
As originally performed, Hannah's speech began: 'You don't deserve to be, you bad, bad boy, for you behaved very shabbily to poor old Stephen Trusty's daughter. For I loved you all the while . . .'

551 *mickle*: This word properly means much, great or many, but Gilbert, following the usage of the Scottish proverb 'Many a mickle makes a muckle', gives it the opposite meaning. He uses it both here and in Phoebe's lines ' 'Tis but mickle/Sister reaps' in *The Yeomen of the Guard* (Act II, lines 567–8) to mean small or little.

ROB. Now I hope this will be a lesson to you in future not to —   515
ROD. Hold your tongue, sir.
ROB. Yes, uncle.
ROD. Have you given him any encouragement?
HAN. (*to* ROB). Have I given you any encouragement? Frankly now,
have I?   520
ROB. No. Frankly, you have not. Anything more scrupulously correct
than your conduct, it would be impossible to desire.
ROD. You go away.
ROB. Yes, uncle.   (*Exit* ROBIN.)
ROD. This is strange meeting after so many years!   525
HAN. Very. I thought you were dead.
ROD. I am. I died ten years ago.
HAN. And are you pretty comfortable?
ROD. Pretty well – that is – yes, pretty well.

HAN. You don't deserve to be, for I loved you all the while, dear; and   530
it made me dreadfully unhappy to hear of all your goings-on, you bad, bad
boy!

BALLAD – DAME HANNAH.

There grew a little flower
  'Neath a great oak tree:
When the tempest 'gan to lower   535
  Little heeded she:
No need had she to cower,
For she dreaded not its power –
She was happy in the bower
  Of her great oak tree!   540
  Sing hey,
  Lackaday!
Let the tears fall free
For the pretty little flower and the great oak tree!
BOTH. Sing hey,   545
  Lackaday! etc.

When she found that he was fickle,
  Was that great oak tree,
She was in a pretty pickle,
  As she well might be –   550
But his gallantries were mickle,
For Death followed with his sickle,
And her tears began to trickle
  For her great oak tree!

571 *Falls weeping*: In the first-night performance, 'There grew a little flower' was followed by this passage of dialogue between Sir Roderic and Hannah, which was later cut:

> ROD. Little Nannikin!
> HAN. Roddy-doddy!
> ROD. It's not too late, is it?
> HAN. Oh Roddy! (*Bashfully*).
> ROD. I'm quite respectable now, you know.
> HAN. But you're a ghost, ain't you?
> ROD. Well, yes – a kind of ghost.
> HAN. But what would be my legal *status* as a ghost's wife?
> ROD. It would be a very respectable position.
> HAN. But I should be the wife of a dead husband, Roddy!
> ROD. No doubt.
> HAN. But the wife of a dead husband is a widow, Roddy!
> ROD. I suppose she is.
> HAN. And a widow is at liberty to marry again, Roddy!
> ROD. Dear me, yes – that's awkward. I never thought of that.
> HAN. No, Roddy – I thought you hadn't.
> ROD. When you've been a ghost for a considerable time it's astonishing how foggy you become!

586 *Then I'm practically alive*: In the first-night performance Roderic said: 'We are all practically alive' and the dialogue and action thereafter continued:

> ROB. Every man jack of you!
> ROD. My brother ancestors! Down from your frames! (*The Ancestors descend.*) You believe yourselves to be dead – you may take it from me that you're not, and an application to the Supreme Court is all that is necessary to prove that you never ought to have died at all!
>
> (*The Ancestors embrace the Bridesmaids. Enter* RICHARD *and* ROSE, *also* SIR DESPARD *and* MARGARET.)
>
> ROB. Rose, when you believed . . . [as now].

The reappearance of the ancestral ghosts, which had not gone down well with the critics, was cut a few days after the opening performance and the present version, where the Bucks and Blades appear with the Bridesmaids, was substituted.

Sing hey,
Lackaday! etc.   555

BOTH.   Sing hey,
                        Lackaday! etc.

Said she, 'He loved me never,
          Did that great oak tree,   560
But I'm neither rich nor clever,
          And so why should he?
But though fate our fortunes sever,
To be constant I'll endeavour,
Aye, for ever and for ever,   565
          To my great oak tree!'
          Sing hey,
          Lackaday! etc.

BOTH.   Sing hey,
                        Lackaday! etc.   570

(*Falls weeping on* SIR RODERIC'S *bosom.*)

(*Enter* ROBIN, *excitedly, followed by all the characters
and Chorus of Bridesmaids.*)

ROB. Stop a bit – both of you.
ROD. This intrusion is unmannerly.   575
HAN. I'm surprised at you.
ROB. I can't stop to apologize – an idea has just occurred to me. A
Baronet of Ruddigore can only die through refusing to commit his daily
crime.
ROD. No doubt.   580
ROB. Therefore, to refuse to commit a daily crime is tantamount to
suicide!
ROD. It would seem so.
ROB. But suicide is, itself, a crime – and so, by your own showing, you
ought never to have died at all!   585
ROD. I see – I understand! Then I'm practically alive!
ROB. Undoubtedly! (SIR RODERIC *embraces* DAME HANNAH.) Rose,
when you believed that I was a simple farmer, I believe you loved me?
ROSE. Madly, passionately!
ROB. But when I became a bad baronet, you very properly loved   590
Richard instead?
ROSE. Passionately, madly!

598   *My darling*: The first-night version continued at this point as follows:

CHORUS.

Hail the Bridegroom – hail the Bride!

RICH. (*Interrupting them*). Will you be quiet? (*To Robin.*) Belay, my lad, belay, you don't understand!

ROSE. Oh sir, belay, it's absolutely necessary.

ROB. Belay? Certainly not. (*To Rich.*) You see, it's like this – as all my ancestors are alive, it follows, as a matter of course, that the eldest of them is the family baronet, and I revert to my former condition.

RICH. (*Going to Zorah*). Well, I think it's exceedingly unfair!

ROB. (*To 1st Ghost*). Here, great uncle, allow me to present you. (*To the others.*) Baronet of Ruddygore!

ALL. Hurrah.

1ST GHOST. Fallacy somewhere!

FINALE.

602–31   *When a man has been a naughty baronet*

In the licence copy and the Macmillan edition, the order of these verses is different, with Robin's coming first, then Rose's, then Richard's and finally Despard and Margaret's.

In the 1920 revival these verses were dropped and the finale was left consisting of the reprise of 'Oh, happy the lily'. It is printed in that version in the Oxford University Press World's Classics edition of the operas and sung thus in the 1962 D'Oyly Carte recording. The original version was, however, reinstated by Royston Nash shortly after he joined the company as musical director in 1971, and was sung right up to the last performance in 1982.

ROB. But if I should turn out *not* to be a bad baronet after all, how would you love me then?

ROSE. Madly, passionately! 595

ROB. As before?

ROSE. Why, of course!

ROB. My darling! (*They embrace.*)

RICH. Here, I say, belay!

ROSE. Oh sir, belay, if it's absolutely necessary! 600

ROB. Belay? Certainly not!

FINALE.

ROSE.
When a man has been a naughty baronet,
And expresses deep repentance and regret,
   You should help him, if you're able,
   Like the mousie in the fable, 605
That's the teaching of my Book of Etiquette.

CHORUS.
That's the teaching in her Book of Etiquette.

RICH.
If you ask me why I do not pipe my eye,
Like an honest British sailor, I reply,
   That with Zorah for my missis, 610
   There'll be bread and cheese and kisses,
Which is just the sort of ration I enjye!

CHORUS.
Which is just the sort of ration you enjye!

ROB.
Having been a wicked baronet a week,
Once again a modest livelihood I seek. 615
   Agricultural employment
   Is to me a keen enjoyment,
For I'm naturally diffident and meek!

CHORUS.
For he's naturally diffident and meek!

DES. *and* MAR.
Prompted by a keen desire to evoke 620
All the blessed calm of matrimony's yoke,
   We shall toddle off to-morrow,
   From this scene of sin and sorrow,
For to settle in the town of Basingstoke!

ALL.
Prompted by a keen desire, etc. 625
For happy the lily, the lily

When kissed by the bee;
But happier than any,
But happier than any,
A lover is, when he
Embraces his bride.

630

CURTAIN

THE YEOMEN OF THE GUARD

or

The Merryman and his Maid

DRAMATIS PERSONÆ

SIR RICHARD CHOLMONDELEY (*Lieutenant of the Tower*)
COLONEL FAIRFAX (*under sentence of death*)
SERGEANT MERYLL (*of the Yeomen of the Guard*)
LEONARD MERYLL (*his Son*)
JACK POINT (*a Strolling Jester*)
WILFRED SHADBOLT (*Head Jailer and Assistant Tormentor*)
THE HEADSMAN
FIRST YEOMAN
SECOND YEOMAN
FIRST CITIZEN
SECOND CITIZEN
ELSIE MAYNARD (*a Strolling Singer*)
PHŒBE MERYLL (*Sergeant Meryll's Daughter*)
DAME CARRUTHERS (*Housekeeper to the Tower*)
KATE (*her Niece*)

Chorus of Yeomen of the Guard, Gentlemen, Citizens, etc.

ACT I. – Tower Green.
ACT II. – The same – Moonlight.
Time – Sixteenth century.

THE YEOMEN OF THE GUARD

The Yeomen of the Guard is the nearest that Gilbert and Sullivan got to a grand opera. Both librettist and composer had a high opinion of the work. Gilbert said that he regarded it as 'the best thing we have done', and Sullivan told the *Strand Musical Magazine* that it was his favourite opera.

After the relative failure of *Ruddigore*, which ended its run at the Savoy in November 1887, the morale of Gilbert, Sullivan and D'Oyly Carte was at a low ebb. There was no new opera to put on in its place, and *H.M.S. Pinafore* had to be revived as a stop-gap. Gilbert proposed yet another version of his beloved lozenge plot, and Sullivan once again rejected it.

The situation was saved by one of those chance incidents which inspired several of the best Savoy Operas. While waiting for a train one morning at Uxbridge Station Gilbert's eye was attracted by a poster advertising the Tower Furnishing Company, which showed a beefeater against a background of the Tower of London. 'I thought the beefeater would make a good picturesque central figure for another Savoy opera,' he later wrote, 'and my intention was to give it a modern setting, with the characteristics and development of burlesque – to make it another *Sorcerer*. But then I decided to make it a romantic and dramatic piece, and to put it back into Elizabethan times.'

Gilbert's decision to set his new opera in the great days of Tudor England was no doubt partly influenced by the wave of patriotism and nostalgia which swept Britain in the wake of Queen Victoria's golden jubilee. He seems to have taken as the basis for his plot a French play, *Don César de Bazan*, which told of a knight languishing in prison and condemned to die who married a gipsy dancer and, after escaping being shot, returned disguised as a monk. The story had already formed the basis of another opera, *Maritana* by Wallace.

Writing to Sullivan about the new work, Gilbert reassuringly pointed out: 'It is quite a consistent and effective story, without anachronisms or pathos of any kind, and I hope you will like it.' He was not to be disappointed. The composer's diary for Christmas Day 1887 reads: 'Gilbert read the plot of the new piece (The Tower of London): immensely pleased with it. Pretty story, no topsy-turvydom, very human and funny also.'

The new opera went through several changes of name. As Sullivan's diary indicates, it was originally called *The Tower of London*. This was later changed to *The Tower Warder* and then to *The Beefeaters*. However, Sullivan, perhaps with memories of *Ruddygore* in his mind, thought this a rather coarse and ugly name, and at his suggestion *The Yeomen of the Guard* was finally adopted.

The opera was composed and completed in a great rush. Sullivan wrote the overture in the auditorium during a final rehearsal and threw the parts to the players in the orchestra as he completed them, the ink on the paper scarcely dry. Tempers frequently flared between composer and librettist, and only an hour or so before the curtain went up on the first performance they had a somewhat stormy meeting to iron out some major production problems.

The first night, on 3 October 1888, was, however, an unqualified success. The *Daily Telegraph* spoke for critics and audience alike when it said of Sullivan's score: 'We place the songs and choruses in *The Yeoman of the Guard* before all his previous efforts of this particular kind. Thus the music follows the book to a higher plane, and we have a genuine English opera, forerunner of many others, let us hope, and possibly a sign of an advance towards a national lyric stage.'

The American première took place at the Casino Theater, New York, on 17 October 1888, just a fortnight after the London opening. *The Yeomen of the Guard* continued there until January 1889 – a run of 100 performances. The opera made its Australian début in Melbourne on 20 April 1889. It also received two early productions in German. The first, which opened at the Carlstheater, Vienna, on 2 February 1889, had the curious title, *Capitän Wilson*. Gilbert's text had been adapted by Victor Leon, later to be librettist of *The Merry Widow*, and Carl Lindau, while Sullivan's orchestrations had been largely rewritten by Julius Stern, who also apparently added five new songs to the opera, much to the composer's annoyance. The other German production, which opened in Berlin on 25 December 1889, had the more orthodox title, *Der Königsgardist*. It also had Sullivan's approval, although it made several radical departures from the original, giving 'When our gallant Norman foes' to Sergeant Meryll and introducing the 'matter' trio from *Ruddigore* into the second act. A D'Oyly Carte touring company took *The Yeomen of the Guard* to South Africa in 1896–7 and again in 1902–3.

The original London run ended on 30 November 1889 after 423 performances. It was revived in 1897 and was subsequently seldom out of the D'Oyly Carte repertoire. Gilbert himself directed revivals at the Savoy Theatre in 1906–7 and 1909. The opera was redesigned for the 1919–20 and 1927 seasons and in 1940 it became the first Savoy Opera to have a modern set – the work of Peter Goffin. This production lasted until the demise of the old D'Oyly Carte company in 1982.

In 1962 Anthony Besch staged a highly successful outdoor production at the Tower of London itself as part of the City of London Festival. This was revived in 1964 and 1966 and the idea was taken up again in July 1978, as part of the festivities to mark the 900th anniversary of the Tower. This last production starred the rock-and-roll singer Tommy Steele as Jack Point. In the 1982 Brent Walker video of the opera Point was played by Joel Grey, almost certainly best known for his portrayal of the master of ceremonies in the film *Cabaret*, and Wilfred Shadbolt by comedian Alfred Marks.

The Yeomen of the Guard was the only one of the 'big five' Gilbert and Sullivan operas not to receive a professional performance in the period between the demise of the old D'Oyly Carte Opera Company and the appearance of its successor. It was therefore an obvious and happy choice for the new company's first season in 1988. Christopher Renshaw's production stressed the work's cruel and tragic side. A dark cavernous chamber replaced the traditional cardboard cut-out of the Tower of London and for the first act finale and the whole of the second act the stage was dominated by a huge executioner's block. Of the principals, Philip Creasy shone as a dashing and nonchalantly cavalier Colonel Fairfax and Eric Roberts made a very lively, and very Welsh, Jack Point.

In 1992 the D'Oyly Carte Company returned to *The Yeomen*, this time with a taut and spare production by Andrew Wickes which had a minimum of extraneous business or distraction and pointed up the powerfulness of Sullivan's music by making discreet references to the world of grand opera. Act I had distinct overtones of *Fidelio* with the prison motif reinforced by a set which made much use of iron grilles and bars. Point, played with great poignancy by Fenton Gray, was cast as a tragic hunchback in the mould of Rigoletto. This production was also welcome for restoring the long-dropped song 'A laughing boy but yesterday' in Act I but sadly it dropped the delightful 'Rapture, rapture' from Act II. Maybe it was felt that this introduces an inappropriate note of frivolity in what is meant to be a tragic denouement – but neither Gilbert nor Sullivan could stay solemn for too long and it is a shame, even in this their deepest and most serious collaboration, to cut the jibes and jokes that gild the philosophic pill.

More recently, *The Yeomen* has been performed by the Welsh National Opera conducted by Sir Charles Mackerras. In April 1995 this production was taken to Covent Garden, where it became the first complete Gilbert and Sullivan opera to be staged at the Royal Opera House. It has also been recorded on the Telarc label and is one of relatively few recordings of the Savoy Operas (the Mackerras/Welsh National Opera Versions of *H.M.S. Pinafore*, *The Pirates of Penzance* and *The Mikado* being the others) to gain an 'exceptional' five star rating in the valuable discography produced by the Sir Arthur Sullivan Society.

1 *Scene*: Until 1940 the D'Oyly Carte backcloth for *The Yeomen of the Guard* showed the White Tower in the middle background with the Cold Harbour (now the Guard House) and Lieutenant's house to the right of stage as seen by the audience. Peter Goffin's wartime production swept away this conventional representation in favour of a bare, angular set which showed none of the familiar features of one of London's best-known buildings. The critics were generally unhappy about this new look. The *Daily Mail* commented: 'Frankly the only adjective strong enough for this Tower of London is that which is traditionally associated with one of its towers'.

Another feature of the staging for the 1940 production which proved controversial was an interior set used to give the impression that Phœbe was sitting in a room. This set was 'flown' during the music preceding the entrance of the chorus (line 67) to reveal Tower Green. It was later abandoned.

This is not the only one of Gilbert's plays to open with a girl sitting spinning alone on the stage. His earlier work *Eyes and No Eyes*, an entertainment with music by Thomas German Reed, which was performed in 1875, began with a similar opening number in which the heroine, Clochette, sang 'As I at my wheel sit spinning'.

2–21 *When maiden loves*
The Yeomen of the Guard is the only Gilbert and Sullivan opera to begin with a solo rather than a chorus. This puts an added strain on the singer playing the role of Phœbe. Jessie Bond, who created the part, had to cope not only with her own first-night nerves but with Gilbert's anxieties as well, as she later recalled in her autobiography:

> I remember the first night of *The Yeomen* very well. Gilbert was always dreadfully overwrought on these occasions, but this time he was almost beside himself with nervousness and excitement...I am afraid he made himself a perfect nuisance behind the scenes, and did his best, poor fellow, to upset us all...It will be remembered that the curtain rises on Phœbe alone at her spinning-wheel; and Gilbert kept fussing about, 'Oh, Jessie, are you sure you're all right?' – Jessie this – Jessie that – until I was almost as demented as he was. At last I turned on him savagely. 'For Heaven's sake, Mr Gilbert, go away and leave me alone, or I shan't be able to sing a note!' He gave me a final frenzied hug, and vanished.

6 *heigho*: There is some doubt as to how this phrase should be pronounced: in early D'Oyly Carte productions it was sung 'Hi-ho' but latterly it was changed to 'Hay-ho'.

22 *Enter Wilfred*: In his book *The Secrets of a Savoyard*, Sir Henry Lytton, who played the part of Wilfred Shadbolt in the 1897 revival of *The Yeomen*, says that Gilbert based the character of the gaoler on 'a wicked, wizened little wretch who, in the sixteenth century, so legend says, haunted the Tower when an execution was due, and offered the unhappy felon a handful of dust, which was, he said "a powder that will save you from pain". For reward he claimed the victim's valuables.'

Shadbolt is not, however, usually played as a small and wizened character like King Gama, but rather as a big, stocky oaf. A note by A. F. Harris, a director of the theatrical costumiers Charles Fox Ltd., in a 1926 issue of the *Gilbert and Sullivan Journal* indicates his traditional costume: 'Wilfred Shadbolt's burly frame is attired in a dark green cloth jerkin, black ballet shirt, breeches to below the knee, puffed green stockings, heavy square-toed shoes, and large leather belt from which hangs a heavy bunch of keys. These should be made of wood to obviate the noise that might be made by metal keys rubbing together when Phœbe stealthily removes them.'

ACT I

SCENE. – *Tower Green.* PHŒBE *discovered spinning.*

SONG – PHŒBE.

When maiden loves, she sits and sighs,
    She wanders to and fro;
Unbidden tear-drops fill her eyes,
And to all questions she replies
      With a sad 'heigho!'   5
      'Tis but a little word – 'heigho!'
      So soft, 'tis scarcely heard – 'heigho!'
      An idle breath –
      Yet life and death   10
      May hang upon a maid's 'heigho!'

When maiden loves, she mopes apart,
    As owl mopes on a tree;
Although she keenly feels the smart,
She cannot tell what ails her heart,
      With its sad 'Ah me!'   15
      'Tis but a foolish sigh – 'Ah me!'
      Born but to droop and die – 'Ah me!'
      Yet all the sense
      Of eloquence   20
      Lies hidden in a maid's 'Ah me!' (*weeps*).

(*Enter* WILFRED.)

WIL. Mistress Meryll!
PHŒ. (*looking up*). Eh! Oh! it's you, is it? You may go away, if you like.
Because I don't want you, you know.   25
  WIL. Haven't you anything to say to me?

28 *the Little Ease*: a dungeon in the Tower. Guy Fawkes, the perpetrator of the Gunpowder Plot to blow up Parliament, is said to have spent fifty days imprisoned there.

36 *Colonel Fairfax*: Although Fairfax is a well-known name in English history – its most famous bearer being Thomas Fairfax, the commander of Cromwell's New Model Army – the hero of *The Yeomen of the Guard* is purely fictitious.

40 *Beauchamp Tower*: Pronounced 'Beecham', this tower derives from Thomas Beauchamp, Earl of Warwick, who was imprisoned in it by King Richard II in 1397.

43 *at half-past seven*: The time of Fairfax's execution became progressively later in Gilbert's various drafts of the libretto. In the licence copy, it was set for 1.30, in the pre-production copy for 4.30, and in an early prompt-book it was changed to 6.30.

66 *Exit Wilfred*: Gilbert originally gave Wilfred a solo to sing before his exit. It appears in a pre-production prompt copy in the D'Oyly Carte archives but is not in the licence copy sent to the Lord Chamberlain. It may well have been written for Rutland Barrington, who was expected to create the role of Shadbolt, but cut when he suddenly announced he was leaving the D'Oyly Carte company to try his hand at theatrical management. The role had to be given instead to a newcomer, W. H. Denny, for whom this solo might have been regarded as a little too much. Here it is:

> When jealous torments reach my soul
> My agonies I can't control;
> Oh, better sit on red-hot coal
>   Than love a heartless jade!
> The red-hot coal will hurt, no doubt,
> But red-hot coals in time die out –
> But jealousy you cannot rout;
>   Its fires will never fade.
>   It's much less painful on the whole
>   To go and sit on red-hot coal
>   Till you're completely flayed –
>   Or ask some kindly friend to crack,
>   Your wretched bones upon the rack,
>   Than love a heartless jade!
>
> The kerchief on your neck of snow
> I look on as a deadly foe –
> It goeth where I may not go,
>   And stops there all day long!
> The belt that holds you in its grasp
> Is to my peace of mind a rasp,
> It claspeth what I may not clasp –
>   Correct me if I'm wrong!
>   It's much less painful, etc.
>
> The bird that breakfasts on your lip;
> I would I had him in my grip –
> He suppeth where I may not sip –
>   I can't get over that.
> The cat you fondle – soft and sly,
> He lieth where I may not lie,
> We're not on terms, that cat and I –
>   I do not like that cat!
>   It's much less painful, etc.

PHŒ. Oh yes! Are the birds all caged? The wild beasts all littered down? All the locks, chains, bolts, and bars in good order? Is the Little Ease sufficiently uncomfortable? The racks, pincers, and thumbscrews all ready for work? Ugh! you brute!

WIL. These allusions to my professional duties are in doubtful taste. I didn't become a head-jailer because I like head-jailing. I didn't become an assistant-tormentor because I like assistant-tormenting. We can't *all* be sorcerers, you know. (PHŒBE *annoyed.*) Ah! you brought that upon yourself.

PHŒ. Colonel Fairfax is *not* a sorcerer. He's a man of science and an alchemist.

WIL. Well, whatever he is, he won't be one for long, for he's to be beheaded to-day for dealings with the devil. His master nearly had him last night, when the fire broke out in the Beauchamp Tower.

PHŒ. Oh! how I wish he had escaped in the confusion! But take care; there's still time for a reply to his petition for mercy.

WIL. Ah! I'm content to chance that. This evening at half-past seven – ah!

PHŒ. You're a cruel monster to speak so unfeelingly of the death of a young and handsome soldier.

WIL. Young and handsome! How do *you* know he's young and handsome?

PHŒ. Because I've seen him every day for weeks past taking his exercise on the Beauchamp Tower.

WIL. Curse him!

PHŒ. There, I believe you're jealous of *him*, now. Jealous of a man I've never spoken to! Jealous of a poor soul who's to die in an hour!

WIL. I am! I'm jealous of everybody and everything. I'm jealous of the very words I speak to you – because they reach your ears – and I mustn't go near 'em!

PHŒ. How unjust you are! Jealous of the words you speak to me! Why, you know as well as I do that I don't even like them.

WIL. You used to like 'em.

PHŒ. I used to *pretend* I liked them. It was mere politeness to comparative strangers.   (*Exit* PHŒBE, *with spinning wheel.*)
WIL. I don't believe you know what jealousy is! I don't believe you know how it eats into a man's heart – and disorders his digestion – and turns his interior into boiling lead. Oh, you are a heartless jade to trifle with the delicate organization of the human interior!

(*Exit* WILFRED.)

(*Enter Crowd of Men and Women, followed
by Yeomen of the Guard.*)

69   *Tower Warders*: The Corps of Yeoman Warders of the Tower of London, known for short
     as the Tower Warders, was set up in 1548, i.e. four years after the death of Sir Richard
     Cholmondeley and therefore after the period in which this opera is set (see the note to
     line 257). The Yeomen of the Guard were a different body of men, established by Henry
     VII at his coronation in 1485 as a personal bodyguard for the sovereign. There is no evi-
     dence that they undertook duties as custodians of the Tower; they would more likely
     have been found at the monarch's residence at Windsor Castle. So, strictly speaking,
     Gilbert may be wrong on two counts in having Tower Warders or Yeomen of the Guard
     on duty in the Tower in the first half of the sixteenth century.
        He is, however, quite right to have his chorus sing of their 'bygone days of daring'.
     Both the Yeomen of the Guard and the Tower Warders were made up of retired members
     of the Army and Royal Marines. They appear on stage in the full-dress Tudor outfit of
     red tunics reaching almost to the knees with large puffed sleeves trimmed in yellow and
     black and with the royal cypher (in this case H.R.) emblazoned on the front, with the
     Royal Crown above and the Rose of England below.

89–98   *This the autumn of our life*
        This solo was given in early performances to Sergeant Meryll, who originally entered
        with the Yeomen.

CHORUS (*as Yeomen march on*).

Tower Warders,
Under orders, 70
Gallant pikemen, valiant sworders!
Brave in bearing,
Foemen scaring,
In their bygone days of daring!
Ne'er a stranger 75
There to danger –
Each was o'er the world a ranger;
To the story
Of our glory
Each a bold contributory! 80

CHORUS OF YEOMEN.

In the autumn of our life,
Here at rest in ample clover,
We rejoice in telling over
Our impetuous May and June.
In the evening of our day, 85
With the sun of life declining,
We recall without repining
All the heat of bygone noon.

SOLO – 2ND YEOMAN.

This the autumn of our life,
This the evening of our day; 90
Weary we of battle strife,
Weary we of mortal fray.
But our year is not so spent,
And our days are not so faded,
But that we with one consent, 95
Were our lovèd land invaded,
Still would face a foreign foe,
As in days of long ago.

CHORUS.   Still would face a foreign foe,
As in days of long ago. 100

PEOPLE.	YEOMEN.
Tower Warders,	This the autumn of our life, etc.
Under orders, etc.	

(*Exeunt Crowd. Manent Yeomen.*)

105 *A good day to you*: In the pre-production prompt copy this line is 'A good day to you, cor-
poral'. In early performances, it was 'A good day to you, sergeant', and Sergeant Meryll
had the lines now given to the Second Yeoman.

111 *No. 14 in the Cold Harbour*: The Coldharbour Gate, with cells above it, was built by Henry
III adjacent to the White Tower. The Coldharbour was demolished in the 1670s. In the
licence and pre-production copies this line is 'No. 14 in the White Tower'.

124 *old Blunderbore*: The name of the giant in the fairy story *Jack the Giant Killer*, who grinds
other men's bones to make his bread.

129–62 *When our gallant Norman foes*
The musical theme which introduces this song is the nearest that Sullivan gets in the
Savoy Operas to a Wagnerian *Leitmotiv* used throughout the course of a work to suggest
a particular mood or theme. It opens the overture and is heard again at the beginning of
the finale to Act I.

137 *Though a queen to save her head should come a-suing*: Two queens of England, both wives of
Henry VIII, were executed on Tower Green during the first half of the sixteenth cen-
tury, Anne Boleyn in May 1536 and Catherine Howard in February 1542. A third queen,
Lady Jane Grey, who ruled for just nine days, was executed in the Tower in 1554.

(*Enter* DAME CARRUTHERS.)

DAME. A good day to you!   105

2ND YEOMAN. Good day, Dame Carruthers. Busy to-day?

DAME. Busy, aye! the fire in the Beauchamp last night has given me work
enough. A dozen poor prisoners – Richard Colfax, Sir Martin Byfleet,
Colonel Fairfax, Warren the preacher-poet, and half-a-score others – all
packed into one small cell, not six feet square. Poor Colonel Fairfax, who's   110
to die to-day, is to be removed to No. 14 in the Cold Harbour that he may
have his last hour alone with his confessor; and I've to see to that.

2ND YEO. Poor gentleman! He'll die bravely. I fought under him two
years since, and he valued his life as it were a feather!

PHŒ. He's the bravest, the handsomest, and the best young gentleman   115
in England! He twice saved my father's life; and it's a cruel thing, a wicked
thing, and a barbarous thing that so gallant a hero should lose his head – for
it's the handsomest head in England!

DAME. For dealing with the devil. Aye! if all were beheaded who dealt
with *him*, there'd be busy doings on Tower Green.   120

PHŒ. You know very well that Colonel Fairfax is a student of alchemy –
nothing more, and nothing less; but this wicked Tower, like a cruel giant in
a fairy-tale, must be fed with blood, and that blood must be the best and
bravest in England, or it's not good enough for the old Blunderbore. Ugh!

DAME. Silence, you silly girl; you know not what you say. I was born   125
in the old keep, and I've grown grey in it, and, please God, I shall die and
be buried in it; and there's not a stone in its walls that is not as dear to me
as my own right hand.

SONG WITH CHORUS – DAME CARRUTHERS *and* YEOMEN.

When our gallant Norman foes
   Made our merry land their own,   130
      And the Saxons from the Conqueror were flying,
At his bidding it arose,
   In its panoply of stone,
      A sentinel unliving and undying.
Insensible, I trow,   135
   As a sentinel should be,
      Though a queen to save her head should come a-suing,
There's a legend on its brow
   That is eloquent to me,
      And it tells of duty done and duty doing.   140

    'The screw may twist and the rack may turn,
    And men may bleed and men may burn,

143   *O'er London town*: This and the next line were originally written as:

> O'er London town and all its hoard
> I keep my solemn watch and ward.

154, 157   *all its beauty... of its duty*: The sole example in this opera of Gilbert's favourite rhyming combination (see the note to *H.M.S. Pinafore*, Act I, lines 247–58).

161   *I keep my silent*: In early performances this line was 'It keeps its silent watch and ward'.

166   *who, as a reward*: This line and the next down to 'hanged him' were cut from D'Oyly Carte performances in the 1970s. So also were the phrases 'brave' (line 173), 'a brave fellow, and' (line 191 – leaving just 'He's the bravest among brave fellows'), 'my brave boy' (line 195), 'Aye' (lines 197, 201 and 204), 'nay, my body' (line 202), 'the brave' (line 215), 'who saved his flag and cut his way through fifty foes who thirsted for his life' (lines 215–16), 'mind I say, I *think*' (line 221) and 'carefully' (line 226). These cuts were, however, substantially restored in Wilfred Judd's 1981 D'Oyly Carte production.

O'er London town and its golden hoard
I keep my silent watch and ward!'

CHORUS.   The screw may twist, etc.   145

Within its wall of rock
  The flower of the brave
    Have perished with a constancy unshaken.
From the dungeon to the block,
  From the scaffold to the grave,   150
    Is a journey many gallant hearts have taken.
And the wicked flames may hiss
  Round the heroes who have fought
    For conscience and for home in all its beauty,
But the grim old fortalice   155
  Takes little heed of aught
    That comes not in the measure of its duty.

'The screw may twist and the rack may turn,
And men may bleed and men may burn,
O'er London town and its golden hoard   160
I keep my silent watch and ward!'

CHORUS.   The screw may twist, etc.

(*Exeunt all but* PHŒBE. *Enter* SERGEANT MERYLL.)

PHŒ. Father! Has no reprieve arrived for the poor gentleman?
  MER. No, my lass; but there's one hope yet. Thy brother Leonard,   165
who, as a reward for his valour in saving his standard and cutting his way
through fifty foes who would have hanged him, has been appointed a
Yeoman of the Guard, will arrive to-day; and as he comes straight from
Windsor, where the Court is, it may be – it *may* be – that he will bring the
expected reprieve with him.   170
  PHŒ. Oh, that he may!
  MER. Amen to that! For the Colonel twice saved my life, and I'd give the
rest of my life to save his! And wilt thou not be glad to welcome thy brave
brother, with the fame of whose exploits all England is a-ringing?
  PHŒ. Aye, truly, if he brings the reprieve.   175
  MER. And not otherwise?
  PHŒ. Well, he's a brave fellow indeed, and I love brave men.
  MER. *All* brave men?
  PHŒ. Most of them, I verily believe! But I hope Leonard will not be too
strict with me – they say he is a very dragon of virtue and circumspection!   180
Now, my dear old father is kindness itself, and —

192 *he robbed the Lieutenant's orchard*: In the first performance this line was the cue for the following song, in which Sergeant Meryll extolled his son's virtues:

SONG – MERYLL.

A laughing boy but yesterday,
A merry urchin, blithe and gay!
Whose joyous shout
Came ringing out,
Unchecked by care or sorrow –
To-day, a warrior, all sun-brown,
Whose deeds of soliderly renown
Are all the boast of London Town:
A veteran, to-morrow!

When at my Leonard's deeds sublime
A soldier's pulse beats double time,
And brave hearts thrill,
As brave hearts will,
At tales of martial glory,
I burn with flush of pride and joy,
A pride unbittered by alloy,
To find my boy – my darling boy –
The theme of song and story!

Gilbert had not originally intended to have this song for Meryll – it does not appear in the pre-production copy and is written into the licence copy as a late insertion – and it seems that he never liked it. In a letter to Sullivan on the day of the first performance he wrote:

I desire before the production of our piece to place upon record the conviction that I have so frequently expressed to you in the course of rehearsal, that unless Meryll's introduced and wholly irrelevant song is withdrawn, the success of the first act will be most seriously imperilled. Let me recapitulate:
The Act commences with Phœbe's song – *tearful in character*. This is followed by the entrance of wardens – *serious and martial in character*. This is followed by Dame Carruthers' 'Tower' song – *grim in character*. This is followed by trio for Meryll, Phœbe and Leonard – *sentimental in character*. Thus it is that a professedly comic opera commences.

At a conference just an hour or so before the opening performance, composer and librettist agreed to cut the song but to keep it in just for the first night, largely for the benefit of Richard Temple, who was playing Meryll. It was restored for the 1962, 1964 and 1978 productions at the Tower of London but never reinstated in D'Oyly Carte stage performances.

MER. And leaves thee pretty well to thine own ways, eh? Well, I've no fears for thee; thou hast a feather-brain, but thou'rt a good lass.

PHŒ. Yes, that's all very well, but if Leonard is going to tell me that I may not do this and I may not do that, and I must not talk to this one, or walk with that one, but go through the world with my lips pursed up and my eyes cast down, like a poor nun who has renounced mankind – why, as I have *not* renounced mankind, and don't mean to renounce mankind, I won't have it – there! 185

MER. Nay, he'll not check thee more than is good for thee, Phœbe! He's a brave fellow, and bravest among brave fellows, and yet it seems but yesterday that he robbed the Lieutenant's orchard. 190

(*Enter* LEONARD MERYLL.)

LEON. Father!

MER. Leonard! my brave boy! I'm right glad to see thee, and so is Phœbe! 195

PHŒ. Aye – hast thou brought Colonel Fairfax's reprieve?

LEON. Nay, I have here a despatch for the Lieutenant, but no reprieve for the Colonel!

PHŒ. Poor gentleman! poor gentleman! 200

LEON. Aye, I would I had brought better news. I'd give my right hand – nay, my body – my life, to save his!

MER. Dost thou speak in earnest, my lad?

LEON. Aye, father – I'm no braggart. Did he not save thy life? and am I not his foster-brother? 205

MER. Then hearken to me. Thou hast come to join the Yeomen of the Guard!

LEON. Well?

MER. None has seen thee but ourselves?

LEON. And a sentry, who took but scant notice of me. 210

MER. Now to prove thy words. Give me the despatch, and get thee hence at once! Here is money, and I'll send thee more. Lie hidden for a space, and let no one know. I'll convey a suit of Yeoman's uniform to the Colonel's cell – he shall shave off his beard, so that none shall know him, and I'll own him as my son, the brave Leonard Meryll, who saved his flag and cut his way through fifty foes who thirsted for his life. He will be welcomed without question by my brother-Yeomen, I'll warrant that. Now, how to get access to the Colonel's cell? (*To* PHŒBE.) The key is with thy sour-faced admirer, Wilfred Shadbolt. 215

PHŒ. (*demurely*). I think – I say, I *think* – I can get anything I want from Wilfred. I think – mind I say, I *think* – you may leave that to me. 220

MER. Then get thee hence at once, lad – and bless thee for this sacrifice.

240   *And shall I reckon*: In early libretti this and the next three lines were sung by Leonard.

244   *And shall we reckon*: In early libretti this and the next two lines were given to all, and lines 247–8 were then sung solo by Phœbe before being repeated by everyone.

PHŒ. And take my blessing, too, dear, dear Leonard!

LEON. And thine, eh? Humph! Thy love is new-born; wrap it up 225
carefully, lest it take cold and die.

TRIO – PHŒBE, LEONARD, MERYLL.

PHŒ.   Alas! I waver to and fro!
                Dark danger hangs upon the deed!

ALL.   Dark danger hangs upon the deed!

LEON.   The scheme is rash and well may fail, 230
                But ours are not the hearts that quail,
                The hands that shrink, the cheeks that pale
                        In hours of need!

ALL.   No, ours are not the hearts that quail,
                The hands that shrink, the cheeks that pale 235
                        In hours of need!

MER.   The air I breathe to him I owe:
                My life is his – I count it naught!

PHŒ. *and* LEON.   That life is his – so count it naught!

MER.   And shall I reckon risks I run 240
                When services are to be done
                To save the life of such an one?
                        Unworthy thought!

PHŒ. *and* LEON.   And shall we reckon risks we run
                To save the life of such an one? 245

ALL.   Unworthy thought!
                We may succeed – who can foretell?
                May heaven help our hope – farewell!

(LEONARD *embraces* MERYLL *and* PHŒBE, *and then exits.* PHŒBE
                                                                weeping.) 250

MER. Nay, lass, be of good cheer, we may save him yet.

PHŒ. Oh! see, father – they bring the poor gentleman from the
Beauchamp! Oh, father! his hour is not yet come?

MER. No, no, – they lead him to the Cold Harbour Tower to await his
end in solitude. But softly – the Lieutenant approaches! He should not see 255
thee weep.

257   *The Lieutenant enters*: The Lieutenant, listed in the *Dramatis personæ* as Sir Richard Cholmondeley, is the one real historical figure to appear as a character in the Savoy Operas.
Sir Richard Cholmondeley (pronounced 'Chumley') was appointed Lieutenant of the
Tower of London in 1513 and left the post in 1524, although he did not die until 1544. He
was knighted after the battle of Flodden. In 1522 he had a tomb built for himself and his
wife in the church of St Peter ad Vincula in the Tower, but he never occupied it, being
buried at his country home in Cheshire. The action of *The Yeomen of the Guard* presumably takes place, therefore, some time during Cholmondeley's lieutenancy, i.e. between
1513 and 1524.

In his article already referred to on the costumes for *The Yeomen* (see the note to line
22), A. F. Harris comments:

> The Lieutenant of the Tower is most certainly striking in his plum velvet uniform,
> slashed blue velvet and trimmed gold, with black top boots, back and front plate, armhole
> robe and tight fitting hat with square top similar to a lancer's helmet.

276   *Thou and I*: This sentence (down to 'such goodly fashion') was cut from D'Oyly Carte
productions in the 1970s.

281–302   *Is life a boon*
Sullivan produced three different settings for this song before Gilbert was satisfied that
he had it right. He also took great trouble altering some of the notes so that they would
be comfortably within the compass of Courtice Pounds, the new D'Oyly Carte lyric tenor, who was to create the role of Fairfax. His painstaking efforts were rewarded by the
universally ecstatic reception that the song received from audience and critics alike.

When Sullivan died in 1900 Gilbert chose the first four lines of this song to be in-
scribed on his memorial, which can still be seen in the Embankment Gardens between
the Savoy Theatre and the River Thames.

(*Enter* FAIRFAX, *guarded. The* LIEUTENANT *enters,
meeting him.*)

LIEUT. Halt! Colonel Fairfax, my old friend, we meet but sadly.

FAIR. Sir, I greet you with all good-will; and I thank you for the   260
zealous care with which you have guarded me from the pestilent dangers
which threaten human life outside. In this happy little community, Death,
when he comes, doth so in punctual and businesslike fashion; and, like a
courtly gentleman, giveth due notice of his advent, that one may not be
taken unawares.
          265
LIEUT. Sir, you bear this bravely, as a brave man should.

FAIR. Why, sir, it is no light boon to die swiftly and surely at a given
hour and in a given fashion! Truth to tell, I would gladly have my life; but
if that may not be, I have the next best thing to it, which is death. Believe me,
sir, my lot is not so much amiss!
          270
PHŒ. (*aside to* MERYLL). Oh, father, father, I cannot bear it!

MER. My poor lass!

FAIR. Nay, pretty one, why weepest thou? Come, be comforted. Such a
life as mine is not worth weeping for. (*Sees* MERYLL.) Sergeant Meryll, is it not?
(*To* LIEUT.) May I greet my old friend? (*Shakes* MERYLL's *hand.*)   275
Why, man, what's all this? Thou and I have faced the grim old king a dozen
times, and never has his majesty come to me in such goodly fashion. Keep
a stout heart, good fellow – we are soldiers, and we know how to die, thou
and I. Take my word for it, it is easier to die well than to live well – for, in
sooth, I have tried both.
          280

BALLAD – FAIRFAX.

Is life a boon?
   If so, it must befall
   That Death, whene'er he call,
Must call too soon.
   Though fourscore years he give,   285
   Yet one would pray to live
Another moon!
   What kind of plaint have I,
   Who perish in July?
   I might have had to die,   290
Perchance, in June!

Is life a thorn?
   Then count it not a whit!
   Man is well done with it;
Soon as he's born   295

320 *a hundred crowns*: A crown was an old British coin worth a quarter of a pound, i.e. five
     shillings. Half-a-crown coins, worth two shillings and sixpence, were in circulation un-
     til the decimalization of the British coinage.

He should all means essay
To put the plague away;
And I, war-torn,
    Poor captured fugitive,
    My life most gladly give –   300
    I might have had to live
Another morn!

(*At the end,* PHŒBE *is led off, weeping, by* MERYLL.)

FAIR. And now, Sir Richard, I have a boon to beg. I am in this strait for
no better reason than because my kinsman, Sir Clarence Poltwhistle, one of   305
the Secretaries of State, has charged me with sorcery, in order that he may
succeed to my estate, which devolves to him provided I die unmarried.

LIEUT. As thou wilt most surely do.

FAIR. Nay, as I will most surely *not* do, by your worship's grace! I have
a mind to thwart this good cousin of mine.   310

LIEUT. How?

FAIR. By marrying forthwith, to be sure!

LIEUT. But heaven ha' mercy, whom wouldst thou marry?

FAIR. Nay, I am indifferent on that score. Coming Death hath made of
me a true and chivalrous knight, who holds all womankind in such esteem   315
that the oldest, and the meanest, and the worst-favoured of them is good
enough for him. So, my good Lieutenant, if thou wouldst serve a poor
soldier who has but an hour to live, find me the first that comes – my
confessor shall marry us, and her dower shall be my dishonoured name and
a hundred crowns to boot. No such poor dower for an hour of matrimony!   320

LIEUT. A strange request. I doubt that I should be warranted in granting
it.

FAIR. There never was a marriage fraught with so little of evil to the
contracting parties. In an hour she'll be a widow, and I – a bachelor again for
aught I know!   325

LIEUT. Well, I will see what can be done, for I hold thy kinsman in
abhorrence for the scurvy trick he has played thee.

FAIR. A thousand thanks, good sir; we meet again on this spot in an hour
or so. I shall be a bridegroom then, and your worship will wish me joy. Till
then, farewell. (*To Guard.*) I am ready, good fellows.   330

(*Exit with Guard into Cold Harbour Tower.*)

LIEUT. He is a brave fellow, and it is a pity that he should die. Now, how
to find him a bride at such short notice? Well, the task should be easy!

(*Exit.*)

335 *Enter Jack Point*: Sir Henry Lytton, who played the role of Jack Point countless times
between 1897 and 1934, had this to say in his *Secrets of a Savoyard* about the jester's first
entrance:

> From the moment he enters the audience should know the manner of man that he is, and
> he must win their sympathy immediately. He is a poor strolling player who has been
> dragged from pillar to post. Footsore and weary though he is, Jack Point is anxious to please
> the crowd who have roughly chased him and Elsie Maynard in, for if he fails them have they
> not threatened to duck him in the nearest pond?

Traditionally, in D'Oyly Carte productions, on making his entrance Jack Point hit a
citizen or two on the head with his pig's bladder. This essential item of a jester's equip-
ment was for many years supplied by the meat department of the Savoy Hotel, but when
this source of supply dried up, Peter Riley, the company's stage manager, turned to Harrods. On tour he was often forced to pump up balloons with a bicycle pump.

341 *follify*: A Gilbertian invention, although there is a word 'folliful', meaning full of foolish-
ness.

342 *vapidly*: Without animation.

(*Enter* JACK POINT *and* ELSIE MAYNARD, *pursued by a crowd of men and* 335
women. POINT *and* ELSIE *are much terrified;* POINT, *however, assuming an*
appearance of self-possession.)

CHORUS.

Here's a man of jollity,
　　Jibe, joke, jollify!
Give us of your quality, 340
　　Come, fool, follify!

If you vapour vapidly,
River runneth rapidly,
　　Into it we fling
　　Bird who doesn't sing! 345

Give us an experiment
In the art of merriment;
　　Into it we throw
　　Cock who doesn't crow!

Banish your timidity, 350
And with all rapidity
Give us quip and quiddity –
　　Willy-nilly, O!

River none can mollify; –
　　Into it we throw 355
Fool who doesn't follify,
　　Cock who doesn't crow!

Banish your timidity, etc.

POINT (*alarmed*). My masters, I pray you bear with us, and we will
satisfy you, for we are merry folk who would make all merry as ourselves. 360
For, look you, there is humour in all things, and the truest philosophy is that
which teaches us to find it and to make the most of it.

ELSIE (*struggling with one of the crowd*). Hands off, I say, unmannerly
fellow!

POINT (*to 1st Citizen*). Ha! Didst thou hear her say, 'Hands off'? 365

1ST CIT. Aye, I heard her say it, and I felt her do it! What then?

POINT. Thou dost not see the humour of that?

1ST CIT. Nay, if I do, hang me!

POINT. Thou dost not? Now observe. She said, 'Hands off!' Whose
hands? Thine. Off whom? Off *her*. Why? Because she is a woman. Now, had 370

375   *men and women marry every day*: This was originally 'men and women marry and are made one flesh', but Gilbert changed it to its present form before the first performance, perhaps because of the religious connotations of the first version.

377–8   *couplet... ballade*: Couplets are pairs of successive lines of verse rhyming with each other; triolets are stanzas of eight lines, much favoured by Hilarion and his friends in *Princess Ida*; quatrains are stanzas of four lines, usually with alternate rhymes; sonnets consist of fourteen lines; rondolets are short poems having only two rhymes throughout, and with the opening words used twice as a refrain; and ballades are poems consisting of one or more triplets of seven-lined stanzas, each ending with the same line as the refrain – and I bet Jack Point didn't know all that.

378–9   *saraband...Jumping Joan*: The saraband is a slow and stately Spanish dance in triple time; the gondolet is probably an English corruption of the Basque dance 'godalet', the carole is a dance performed by men and women grouped in a ring and singing; the Pimpernel and Jumping Joan may well have been old English dances, or they may equally well be Gilbertian inventions – I can find no mention of them in any works of reference.

383–444   *I have a song to sing, O*

This is, perhaps, the best-loved of all Gilbert and Sullivan's songs. It was the one most constantly requested by ladies approaching the composer with their autograph albums. The *Morning Advertiser* echoed the views of many when it commented in its first-night review: 'Sir Arthur Sullivan has never written anything more delicately melodious and elegant than this; in fact of its kind he has never equalled it and probably never will.' In more recent times, the first line of the song has been used by the great D'Oyly Carte comic singer John Reed as the title both for a record and for a one-man show at the Savoy Theatre.

In fact, Sullivan found this song more difficult to set than any other he was given by Gilbert. It took him a fortnight to get the right tune. The main difficulty lay in what he called 'the House that Jack built' character about the number with an additional phrase being added to each verse. Eventually Gilbert came to his aid by humming him the tune of an old sea shanty which he had had in his mind when writing the words. Gilbert's account of how he helped Sullivan to get the tune, which throws much light on their working arrangements, is worth quoting in full:

> The verse always preceded the music, or even any hint of it. Sometimes – very rarely – Sullivan would say of some song I had given him, 'My dear fellow, I can't make anything of this' – and then I would rewrite it entirely – never tinker at it. But, of course, I don't mean to say that I 'invented' all the rhythms and stanzas in the operas. Often a rhythm would be suggested by some old tune or other running in my head, and I would fit my words to it more or less exactly. When Sullivan knew I had done so, he would say, 'Don't tell me what the tune is, or I shan't be able to get it out of my head.' But once, I remember, I did tell him. There is a duet in *The Yeomen of the Guard* beginning:
>
> > I have a song to sing, O!
> > Sing me your song, O!
>
> It was suggested to me by an old chantey I used to hear the sailors on board my yacht singing in the 'dog-watch' on Saturday evenings, beginning:
>
> > Come, and I will sing to you –
> > What will you sing me?
> > I will sing you one, O!
> > What is your one, O!
>
> And so on. Well, when I gave Sullivan the words of the duet, he found the utmost difficulty in setting it. He tried hard for a fortnight, but in vain. I offered to recast it in another mould, but he expressed himself so delighted with it in its then form that he was determined to work it out to a satisfactory issue. At last, he came to me and said: 'You often have some old air in your mind which prompts the metre of your songs; if anything prompted you in this one, hum it to me – it may help me.' Only a rash man ever asks me to hum, but the situation

she *not* been a woman, thine hands had not been set upon her at all. So the
reason for the laying on of hands is the reason for the taking off of hands,
and herein is contradiction contradicted! It is the very marriage of *pro* with
con; and no such lopsided union either, as times go, for *pro* is not more unlike
con than man is unlike woman – yet men and women marry every day with
none to say, 'Oh, the pity of it!' but I and fools like me! Now wherewithal
shall we please you? We can rhyme you couplet, triolet, quatrain, sonnet,
rondolet, ballade, what you will. Or we can dance you saraband, gondolet,
carole, Pimpernel, or Jumping Joan.

ELSIE. Let us give them the singing farce of the Merryman and his
Maid – therein is song and dance too.

ALL. Aye, the Merryman and his Maid!

DUET – ELSIE *and* POINT.

POINT. I have a song to sing, O!

ELSIE. Sing me your song, O!

POINT.
It is sung to the moon
By a love-lorn loon,
Who fled from the mocking throng, O!
It's a song of a merryman, moping mum,
Whose soul was sad, and whose glance was glum,
Who sipped no sup, and who craved no crumb,
As he sighed for the love of a ladye.
Heighdy! heighdy!
Misery me, lackadaydee!
He sipped no sup, and he craved no crumb,
As he sighed for the love of a ladye.

ELSIE. I have a song to sing, O!

POINT. What is your song, O?

ELSIE.
It is sung with the ring
Of the songs maids sing
Who love with a love life-long, O!
It's the song of a merrymaid, peerly proud,
Who loved a lord, and who laughed aloud
At the moan of the merryman, moping mum,
Whose soul was sad, and whose glance was glum,
Who sipped no sup, and who craved no crumb,
As he sighed for the love of a ladye!
Heighdy! heighdy!

was desperate, and I did my best to convey to him the air of the chantey that had suggested the song to me. I was so far successful that before I had hummed a dozen bars he exclaimed: 'That will do – I've got it!' And in an hour he produced the charming air as it appears in the opera. I have sometimes thought that he exclaimed 'That will do – I've got it' because my humming was more than he could bear; but he always assured me that it had given him the necessary clue to the proper setting of the song . . .

I remember it [the chantey] as my sailors used to sing it. I found out afterwards that it was a very much corrupted form of an old Cornish carol. This was their version of it:

FIRST VOICE.	Come, and I will sing you –
ALL.	What will you sing me?
FIRST VOICE.	I will sing you one, O!
ALL.	What is your one, O!
FIRST VOICE.	One of them is all alone,
	And ever will remain so.
ALL.	One of them, etc.
SECOND VOICE.	Come, and I will sing you –
ALL.	What will you sing me?
SECOND VOICE.	I will sing you two, O!
ALL.	What is your two, O!
SECOND VOICE.	Two of them are lilywhite maids,
	Dressed all in green, O!
ALL.	One of them is all alone,
	And ever will remain so.
THIRD VOICE.	Come, and I will sing you –
ALL.	What will you sing me?
THIRD VOICE.	I will sing you three, O!
ALL.	What is your three, O!
THIRD VOICE.	Three of them are strangers.
ALL.	Two of them are lilywhite maids,
	Dressed all in green, O!
	One of them is all alone,
	And ever will remain so!

And so on until twelve is reached.

THIRD VOICE.	Come, and I will sing you –
ALL.	What will you sing me?
THIRD VOICE.	I will sing you twelve, O!
ALL.	What is your twelve, O!
THIRD VOICE.	Twelve are the twelve apostles,
ALL.	Eleven of them have gone to heaven.
	Ten are the Ten Commandments,
	Nine is the moonlight bright and clear,
	Eight are the eight archangels,
	Seven are the seven stars in the sky,
	Six are the cheerful waiters (!)
	Five are the ferrymen in the boats,
	Four are the gospel preachers,
	Three of them are strangers,
	Two of them are lilywhite maids,
	Dressed all in green, O;
	One of them is all alone,
	And ever will remain so!

399 *What is your song, O*: In the first and second editions of the libretto this line was 'Sing me your song, O!'

404 *Whose soul was sad*: In the licence copy and early editions of the libretto this line began 'Whose soul was sore'. It was changed in the third edition to conform with the other verses.

Misery me, lackadaydee!
He sipped no sup, etc.

POINT.   I have a song to sing, O!   410

ELSIE.   Sing me your song, O!

POINT.   It is sung to the knell

Of a churchyard bell,
And a doleful dirge, ding dong, O!
It's a song of a popinjay, bravely born,   415
Who turned up his noble nose with scorn
At the humble merrymaid, peerly proud,
Who loved a lord, and who laughed aloud
At the moan of the merryman, moping mum,
Whose soul was sad, and whose glance was glum,   420
Who sipped no sup, and who craved no crumb,
As he sighed for the love of a ladye!

BOTH.   Heighdy! heighdy!

Misery me, lackadaydee!
He sipped no sup, etc.   425

ELSIE.   I have a song to sing, O!

POINT.   Sing me your song, O!

ELSIE.   It is sung with a sigh

And a tear in the eye,
For it tells of a righted wrong, O!   430
It's a song of the merrymaid, once so gay,
Who turned on her heel and tripped away
From the peacock popinjay, bravely born,
Who turned up his noble nose with scorn
At the humble heart that he did not prize: 435
So she begged on her knees, with downcast eyes,
For the love of the merryman, moping mum,
Whose soul was sad, and whose glance was glum,
Who sipped no sup, and who craved no crumb,
As he sighed for the love of a ladye!   440

ALL.   Heighdy! heighdy!

Misery me, lackadaydee!
His pains were o'er, and he sighed no more,
For he lived in the love of a ladye!

436 *So she begged on her knees*: In the pre-production prompt copy, and therefore presumably as originally written by Gilbert, this and the next two lines ran:

> So she changed her tone and, with downcast eyes,
> She begged on her knees, with a heart forlorn,
> For the love of a merryman, etc.

468 *electuary*: A medicine made up with honey, syrup or some similarly sweet substance to disguise the taste.

477 *on this very spot*: In the pre-production copy this was 'on Tower Green'. It is, in fact, highly unlikely that Fairfax would have been executed within the precincts of the Tower on Tower Green. That place was reserved for the most exalted victims of the executioner's axe. Only six people were ever beheaded there: Anne Boleyn, Catherine Howard, Lady Jane Grey, the Earl of Essex, the Viscountess Rochford and the Countess of Salisbury. Commoners were executed on Tower Hill outside the Tower walls.

1ST CIT. Well sung and well danced!
2ND CIT. A kiss for that, pretty maid!   445
ALL. Aye, a kiss all round.
ELSIE (*drawing dagger*). Best beware! I am armed!
POINT. Back, sirs – back! This is going too far.
2ND CIT. Thou dost not see the humour of it, eh? Yet there is humour   450
in all things – even in this. (*Trying to kiss her.*)
ELSIE. Help! help!

(*Enter* LIEUTENANT *with Guard. Crowd falls back.*)

LIEUT. What is this pother?
ELSIE. Sir, we sang to these folk, and they would have repaid us with   455
gross courtesy, but for your honour's coming.
LIEUT. (*to Mob*). Away with ye! Clear the rabble. (*Guards push Crowd off,
and go off with them.*) Now, my girl, who are you, and what do you
here?
ELSIE. May it please you, sir, we are two strolling players, Jack Point   460
and I, Elsie Maynard, at your worship's service. We go from fair to fair,
singing, and dancing, and playing brief interludes; and so we make a poor
living.
LIEUT. You two, eh? Are ye man and wife?
POINT. No, sir; for though I'm a fool, there is a limit to my folly. Her   465
mother, old Bridget Maynard, travels with us (for Elsie is a good girl), but the
old woman is a-bed with fever, and we have come here to pick up some
silver to buy an electuary for her.
LIEUT. Hark ye, my girl! Your mother is ill?
ELSIE. Sorely ill, sir.
LIEUT. And needs good food, and many things that thou canst not   470
buy?
ELSIE. Alas! sir, it is too true.
LIEUT. Wouldst thou earn an hundred crowns?
ELSIE. An hundred crowns! They might save her life!   475
LIEUT. Then listen! A worthy but unhappy gentleman is to be
beheaded in an hour on this very spot. For sufficient reasons, he desires to
marry before he dies, and he hath asked me to find him a wife. Wilt thou be
that wife?
ELSIE. The wife of a man I have never seen!   480
POINT. Why, sir, look you, I am concerned in this; for though I am not
yet wedded to Elsie Maynard, time works wonders, and there's no knowing
what may be in store for us. Have we your worship's word for it that this
gentleman will die to-day?
LIEUT. Nothing is more certain, I grieve to say.   485

492–525 *How say you, maiden, will you wed*
The first edition of the libretto had a version of this song which was substantially different from the one substituted in the second edition and now sung. Here it is:

TRIO.

ELSIE, POINT, LIEUTENANT.

LIEUTENANT.

How say you maiden, will you wed
A man about to lose his head?
No harm to you can thence arise,
In half an hour, poor soul, he dies.
For half an hour
You'll be a wife,
And then the dower
Is yours for life.
This tempting offer why refuse?
If truth the poets tell,
Most men, before they marry, lose
Both head and heart as well!

ALL.

Temptation, oh temptation,
Were we, in truth, intended
To shun, whate'er our station,
Your fascinations splendid;
Or fall, whene'er we view you,
Head over heels into you!

ELSIE.

A strange proposal you reveal,
It almost makes my senses reel.
Alas! I'm very poor indeed,
And such a sum I sorely need.
Unfortunately,
Life and death
Have hung till lately
On a breath.
My mother, sir, is like to die;
This money life may bring.
Bear this in mind, I pray, if I
Consent to do this thing!

ALL.

Temptation, oh temptation, etc.

POINT.

Though as a general rule of life
I don't allow my promised wife,
My lovely bride that is to be,
To marry anyone but me,
The circumstances
Of this case
May set such fancies
Out of place;
So, if the fee is duly paid,
And he, in well-earned grave,
Within the hour is duly laid,
Objection I will waive!

ALL.

Temptation, oh temptation, etc.

498 *A headless bridegroom why refuse*: Keen to help Sullivan, Gilbert supplied him with two
versions of this and the next three lines with different metres. The second version, which
the composer did not choose, went as follows:

POINT. And that the maiden will be allowed to depart the very instant the ceremony is at an end?

LIEUT. The very instant. I pledge my honour that it shall be so.

POINT. An hundred crowns?

LIEUT. An hundred crowns!   490

POINT. For my part, I consent. It is for Elsie to speak.

TRIO – ELSIE, POINT, *and* LIEUTENANT.

LIEUT.

How say you, maiden, will you wed
A man about to lose his head?
  For half an hour
    You'll be a wife,   495
  And then the dower
    Is yours for life.
A headless bridegroom why refuse?
  If truth the poets tell,
Most bridegrooms, ere they marry, lose   500
  Both head and heart as well!

ELSIE.

A strange proposal you reveal,
It almost makes my senses reel.
Alas! I'm very poor indeed,
And such a sum I sorely need.   505
  My mother, sir, is like to die,
    This money life may bring.
  Bear this in mind, I pray, if I
    Consent to do this thing!

POINT.

Though as a general rule of life   510
I don't allow my promised wife,
My lovely bride that is to be,
To marry any one but me,
  Yet if the fee is promptly paid,
    And he, in well-earned grave,   515
  Within the hour is duly laid,
    Objection I will waive!
    Yes, objection I will waive!

ALL.

Temptation, oh, temptation,
  Were we, I pray, intended   520
To shun, whate'er our station,
  Your fascinations splendid;
Or fall, whene'er we view you,

What matter, though
  His head should fall?
This trifling blow
  Need not appal.
Most men who wed,
  So poets tell,
Have lost both head
  And heart as well!

541   *I've jibe and joke*: In the licence copy Jack Point's song began 'I've jest and joke'.

Head over heels into you?
Temptation, oh, temptation, etc.   525

(*During this, the* LIEUTENANT *has whispered to* WILFRED (*who has entered*). WILFRED *binds* ELSIE'S *eyes with a kerchief, and leads her into the Cold Harbour Tower.*)

LIEUT. And so, good fellow, you are a jester?
POINT. Aye, sir, and, like some of my jests, out of place.   530
LIEUT. I have a vacancy for such an one. Tell me, what are your qualifications for such a post?
POINT. Marry, sir, I have a pretty wit. I can rhyme you extempore; I can convulse you with quip and conundrum; I have the lighter philosophies at my tongue's tip; I can be merry, wise, quaint, grim, and sardonic, one by one, or all at once; I have a pretty turn for anecdote; I know all the jests – ancient and modern – past, present, and to come; I can riddle you from dawn of day to set of sun, and, if that content you not, well on to midnight and the small hours. Oh, sir, a pretty wit, I warrant you – a pretty, pretty wit!   535   540

RECITATIVE AND SONG – POINT.

I've jibe and joke
  And quip and crank
For lowly folk
  And men of rank.
I ply my craft
  And know no fear,   545
But aim my shaft
  At prince or peer.
At peer or prince – at prince or peer,
I aim my shaft and know no fear!   550

I've wisdom from the East and from the West,
  That's subject to no academic rule;
You may find it in the jeering of a jest,
  Or distil it from the folly of a fool.
I can teach you with a quip, if I've a mind;   555
  I can trick you into learning with a laugh;
Oh, winnow all my folly, and you'll find
  A grain or two of truth among the chaff!

I can set a braggart quailing with a quip,
  The upstart I can wither with a whim;   560

566 *gild the philosophic pill*: It was the custom of doctors in medieval and Tudor times to make their pills more attractive by gilding them with a thin coating of sugar. To gild the pill means to make something unattractive at least appear desirable.

576 *the dignified clergy*: Those occupying senior positions in the hierarchy of the Church of England. Parish priests and curates were known as the undignified clergy.

579 *my jests are most carefully selected*: Compare this remark about Jester James, the subject of one of Gilbert's *Bab Ballads* published in *Time* magazine in 1879:

> His antic jokes were modelled on severely classic rules,
> And all his quips passed muster at the strictest ladies' schools.

590–91 *what is underdone cannot be helped*: This joke, and the one in line 598, first appeared in an earlier play by Gilbert, *Foggerty's Fairy*, which was performed at the Savoy Theatre in December 1881.

He may wear a merry laugh upon his lip,
　　But his laughter has an echo that is grim!
When they're offered to the world in merry guise,
　　Unpleasant truths are swallowed with a will –
For he who'd make his fellow-creatures wise
　　Should always gild the philosophic pill! 565

LIEUT. And how came you to leave your last employ?

POINT. Why, sir, it was in this wise. My Lord was the Archbishop of
Canterbury, and it was considered that one of my jokes was unsuited to His
Grace's family circle. In truth, I ventured to ask a poor riddle, sir – Wherein 570
lay the difference between His Grace and poor Jack Point? His Grace was
pleased to give it up, sir. And thereupon I told him that whereas His Grace
was paid £10,000 a year for being good, poor Jack Point was good – for
nothing. 'Twas but a harmless jest, but it offended His Grace, who whipped
me and set me in the stocks for a scurril rogue, and so we parted. I had as 575
lief not take post again with the dignified clergy.
　LIEUT. But I trust you are very careful not to give offence. I have
daughters.
　POINT. Sir, my jests are most carefully selected, and anything
objectionable is expunged. If your honour pleases, I will try them first on 580
your honour's chaplain.
　LIEUT. Can you give me an example? Say that I had sat me down
hurriedly on something sharp?
　POINT. Sir, I should say that you had sat down on the spur of the
moment. 585
　LIEUT. Humph! I don't think much of that. Is that the best you can do?
　POINT. It has always been much admired, sir, but we will try again.
　LIEUT. Well, then, I am at dinner, and the joint of meat is but half
cooked.
　POINT. Why, then, sir, I should say that what is *under*done cannot be 590
helped.
　LIEUT. I see. I think that manner of thing would be somewhat
irritating.
　POINT. At first, sir, perhaps; but use is everything, and you would
come in time to like it. 595
　LIEUT. We will suppose that I caught you kissing the kitchen wench
under my very nose.
　POINT. Under *her* very nose, good sir – not under yours! *That* is where *I*
would kiss her. Do you take me? Oh, sir, a pretty wit – a pretty, pretty
wit! 600
　LIEUT. The maiden comes. Follow me, friend, and we will discuss this
matter at length in my library.

607   *my best conundrum wasted*: Sir Henry Lytton once asked Gilbert what the answer to this
      conundrum was and was told by the librettist that he would leave it in his will. Needless
      to say, when he died, it wasn't there. The truth is that Gilbert had never bothered about
      answering his own riddle. Many others have had a go at it, but no one has produced any-
      thing either plausible or even very amusing.

611–16 *'Tis done! I am a bride*
      The opening recitative which precedes Elsie's song was added at a late stage. It is miss-
      ing from both the licence copy and pre-production prompt copy.

629   *Ah me! what profit we*: In early editions of the libretto, Elsie's song lacked lines 629–32 and
      645–8. They were added in the third edition.

POINT. I am your worship's servant. That is to say, I trust I soon shall be. But, before proceeding to a more serious topic, can you tell me, sir, why a cook's brain-pan is like an overwound clock?   605

LIEUT. A truce to this fooling – follow me.

POINT. Just my luck; my best conundrum wasted!

(Exeunt.)

(Enter ELSIE *from Tower, led by* WILFRED, *who removes the bandage from her eyes, and exits.)*   610

RECITATIVE AND SONG – ELSIE.

'Tis done! I am a bride! Oh, little ring,
   That bearest in thy circlet all the gladness
That lovers hope for, and that poets sing,
   What bringest thou to me but gold and sadness?
A bridegroom all unknown, save in this wise,   615
To-day he dies! To-day, alas, he dies!

    Though tear and long-drawn sigh
       Ill fit a bride,
   No sadder wife than I
      The whole world wide!   620
       Ah me! Ah me!
       Yet maids there be
    Who would consent to lose
     The very rose of youth,
       The flower of life,   625
      To be, in honest truth,
       A wedded wife,
       No matter whose!

    Ah me! what profit we,
      O maids that sigh,   630
    Though gold should live
      If wedded love must die?
    Ere half an hour has rung,
     A widow I!

  Ah, heaven, he is too young,   635
    Too brave to die!
     Ah me! Ah me!
    Yet wives there be
   So weary worn, I trow,
     That they would scarce complain,   640
      So that they could

656 *Now what could he have wanted*: Wilfred's remark in lines 656–7 was not in the first edition
    of the libretto. A note by Rupert D'Oyly Carte in 1923 says 'Not original – probably a gag
    by W. H. Denny approved by W.S.G.'

666 *a live ass is better than a dead lion*: This seems to mix up two traditional sayings, the biblical
    saw 'A living dog is better than a dead lion' (Ecclesiastes 9.4) and the Italian proverb 'A
    live ass is better than a dead doctor'.

676 *In the nice regulation of a thumbscrew*: Wilfred's demonstration of his grisly trade to Phœbe
    recalls the behaviour of Gilbert Clay, a gentle executioner who described his craft to his
    lover Annie Protheroe in a Bab Ballad which Gilbert contributed to *Fun* in October 1868:

> And sometimes he'd explain to her, which charmed her very much,
> How famous operators vary very much in touch,
> And then, perhaps, he'd show how he himself performed the trick,
> And illustrate his meaning with a poppy and a stick.

In half an hour attain
To widowhood,
No matter how!

O weary wives 645
Who widowhood would win,
Rejoice that ye have time
To weary in.

(Exit ELSIE *as* WILFRED *re-enters.)*

WIL. *(looking after* ELSIE*).* 'Tis an odd freak, for a dying man and his 650
confessor to be closeted alone with a strange singing girl. I would fain have
espied them, but they stopped up the keyhole. *My* keyhole!

(Enter PHŒBE *with* MERYLL. MERYLL *remains in the background,*
unobserved by WILFRED.*)*

PHŒ. *(aside).* Wilfred – and alone! 655
WIL. Now what could he have wanted with her? That's what puzzles
me!
PHŒ. *(aside).* Now to get the keys from him. *(Aloud.)* Wilfred – has no
reprieve arrived?
WIL. None. Thine adored Fairfax is to die. 660
PHŒ. Nay, thou knowest that I have naught but pity for the poor
condemned gentleman.
WIL. I know that he who is about to die is more to thee than I, who am
alive and well.
PHŒ. Why, that were out of reason, dear Wilfred. Do they not say that 665
a live ass is better than a dead lion? No, I don't mean that!
WIL. Oh, they say that, do they?
PHŒ. It's unpardonably rude of them, but I believe they put it in that
way. Not that it applies to thee, who art clever beyond all telling!
WILL. Oh yes, as an assistant-tormentor. 670
PHŒ. Nay, as a wit, as a humorist, as a most philosophic commentator on
the vanity of human resolution.

(PHŒBE *slyly takes bunch of keys from* WILFRED'S *waistband and hands*
them to MERYLL, *who enters the Tower, unnoticed by* WILFRED.*)*

WIL. Truly, I have seen great resolution give way under my persuasive 675
methods *(working a small thumbscrew).* In the nice regulation of a thumbscrew
– in the hundredth part of a single revolution lieth all the difference between
stony reticence and a torrent of impulsive unbosoming that the pen can
scarcely follow. Ha! ha! I am a mad wag.

701–42　*Were I thy bride*

This delightful song, which Gilbert reportedly said that he had written to show that English could be just as tuneful a language as Italian, has echoes of the Bab Ballad 'To Phœbe':

> 'Gentle, modest, little flower,
> 　Sweet epitome of May,
> Love me but for half-an-hour,
> 　Love me, love me, little fay'.
> Sentences so fiercely flaming
> 　In your tiny shell–like ear,
> I should always be exclaiming
> 　If I loved you, Phœbe, dear.
>
> 'Smiles that thrill from any distance
> 　Shed upon me while I sing!
> Please ecstaticize existence,
> 　Love me, oh, thou fairy thing!'
> Words like these, outpouring sadly,
> 　You'd perpetually hear,
> If I loved you, fondly, madly; –
> 　But I do not, Phœbe, dear.

A good deal of unofficial and unapproved D'Oyly Carte 'business' crept into this song, as an article by Jessie Bond in the December 1927 issue of the *Gilbert and Sullivan Journal* makes clear:

> What I hate is that senseless 'business' in 'Were I thy bride'. You know what I mean – the scratching of the jailer's chin, the ruffling of his hair, the ogling of the eyes, and all those 'comic' antics which, goodness knows why, are supposed to be funny.
> 　I think it is wicked that there should be this vulgarity in one of the loveliest of all the songs in the operas. Sir William Gilbert would not have endured it for a moment. He intended that the audience should hear this most beautiful lyric – and they never hear it today.
> 　During the rehearsals I remember that Gilbert asked me how I would wheedle Wilfred Shadbolt. 'Well Mr Gilbert', I answered, 'I might just gently stroke his chin, and I might...' He stopped me. 'That will do!' he exclaimed, 'that will be splendid.' You see what he meant! He wanted the wheedling suggested, but he did not want a lot of low comedy introduced, and still less did he want the action to mar the effect of the song.

PHŒ. (*with a grimace*). Thou art a most light-hearted and delightful 680
companion, Master Wilfred. Thine anecdotes of the torture-chamber are
the prettiest hearing.

WIL. I'm a pleasant fellow an I choose. I believe I am the merriest dog that
barks. Ah, we might be passing happy together —

PHŒ. Perhaps. I do not know. 685

WIL. For thou wouldst make a most tender and loving wife.

PHŒ. Aye, to one whom I really loved. For there is a wealth of love within
this little heart – saving up for – I wonder whom? Now, of all the world of
men, I wonder whom? To think that he whom I am to wed is now
alive and somewhere! Perhaps far away, perhaps close at hand! And I know 690
him not! It seemeth that I am wasting time in not knowing him.

WIL. Now say that it is I – nay! suppose it for the nonce. Say that we
are wed – suppose it only – say that thou art my very bride, and I thy cheery,
joyous, bright, frolicsome husband – and that, the day's work being done,
and the prisoners stored away for the night, thou and I are alone together – 695
with a long, long evening before us!

PHŒ. (*with a grimace*). It is a pretty picture – but I scarcely know. It cometh
so unexpectedly – and yet – and yet – *were* I thy bride —

WIL. Aye! – wert thou my bride —?

PHŒ. Oh, how I would love thee! 700

SONG – PHŒBE.

Were I thy bride,
Then all the world beside
Were not too wide
    To hold my wealth of love –
Were I thy bride!

705

Upon thy breast
My loving head would rest,
As on her nest
    The tender turtle dove –
Were I thy bride!

710

This heart of mine
Would be one heart with thine,
And in that shrine
    Our happiness would dwell –
Were I thy bride!

715

And all day long
Our lives should be a song:

744　*No, thou'rt not*: Wilfred's speech was a late addition by Gilbert; originally he had Wilfred exiting with Phœbe. Delivered by Kenneth Sandford, the last D'Oyly Carte principal to play Shadbolt, who always repeated the last phrase 'Aye, if she die for it', the speech never failed to win a round of applause.

No grief, no wrong
    Should make my heart rebel –
Were I thy bride! 720

The silvery flute,
The melancholy lute,
    Were night-owl's hoot
        To my low-whispered coo –
Were I thy bride! 725

The skylark's trill
Were but discordance shrill
    To the soft thrill
        Of wooing as I'd woo –
Were I thy bride! 730

(MERYLL *re-enters; gives keys to* PHŒBE, *who replaces them at*
WILFRED'S *girdle, unnoticed by him. Exit* MERYLL.)

The rose's sigh
Were as a carrion's cry
    To lullaby 735
        Such as I'd sing to thee,
Were I thy bride!

A feather's press
Were leaden heaviness
    To my caress. 740
        But then, of course, you see,
I'm not thy bride!

(*Exit* PHŒBE.)

WIL. No, thou'rt not – not yet! But, Lord, how she woo'd! I should be
no mean judge of wooing, seeing that I have been more hotly woo'd than 745
most men. I have been woo'd by maid, widow, and wife. I have been woo'd
boldly, timidly, tearfully, shyly – by direct assault, by suggestion, by
implication, by inference, and by innuendo. But this wooing is not of the
common order: it is the wooing of one who must needs woo me, if she die
for it! (*Exit* WILFRED.) 750

(*Enter* MERYLL, *cautiously, from Tower.*)

MER. (*looking after them*). The deed is, so far, safely accomplished. The
slyboots, how she wheedled him! What a helpless ninny is a love-sick man!

760–61   *You make a brave Yeoman*: The earliest version of Gilbert's libretto contains no reference
at all to 'Yeoman' in the text – another word is always used instead. Thus in the pre-
production prompt copy this passage runs 'You make a brave Beefeater, sir! So – this
ruff is too high; So – and the belt should be thus. Here is your halbert, sir; carry it thus.
The warders come...'.

768–77   *Oh, Sergeant Meryll, is it true*
This chorus was not in early libretti and was only added in the third edition, which came
out after the 1907 revival.

778   *Ye Tower Warders*: As sung on the first night this recitative began 'Ye Tower Yeomen'. The
licence copy, however, has 'Warders', as now.

He is but as a lute in a woman's hands – she plays upon him whatever tune
she will. But the Colonel comes. I' faith, he's just in time, for the Yeomen   755
parade here for his execution in two minutes!

(*Enter* FAIRFAX, *without beard and moustache, and dressed in
Yeoman's uniform.*)

FAIR. My good and kind friend, thou runnest a grave risk for me!
MER. Tut, sir, no risk. I'll warrant none here will recognize you. You   760
make a brave Yeoman, sir! So – this ruff is too high; so – and the sword
should hang thus. Here is your halbert, sir; carry it thus. The Yeomen come.
Now remember, you are my brave son, Leonard Meryll.
FAIR. If I may not bear mine own name, there is none other I would
bear so readily.   765
MER. Now, sir, put a bold face on it, for they come.

FINALE – ACT I.

(*Enter Yeomen of the Guard.*)

CHORUS.

Oh, Sergeant Meryll, is it true –
    The welcome news we read in orders?
Thy son, whose deeds of derring-do   770
Are echoed all the country through,
    Has come to join the Tower Warders?
If so, we come to meet him,
That we may fitly greet him,
And welcome his arrival here   775
With shout on shout and cheer on cheer –
    Hurrah! Hurrah! Hurrah!

RECITATIVE – SERGEANT MERYLL.

Ye Tower Warders, nursed in war's alarms,
    Suckled on gunpowder, and weaned on glory,
Behold my son, whose all-subduing arms   780
    Have formed the theme of many a song and story!
    Forgive his aged father's pride; nor jeer
    His aged father's sympathetic tear!

(*Pretending to weep.*)

795   *Have been prodigiously exaggerated*: This line was originally 'Are all prodigiously exaggerated'.

800   *Standard lost in last campaign*: In an article in the January 1978 edition of *The Savoyard* Charles Low suggested that Leonard Meryll's 'last campaign' was probably the battle at Jedburgh in the Scottish Border country in September 1523 in which the Earl of Surrey defeated the claimant to the Scottish throne, the Duke of Albany. In that case, Low suggests, the action of *The Yeoman of the Guard* should be dated to July 1524, at the end of Sir Richard Cholmondeley's period as Lieutenant of the Tower.

An earlier alternative might be the battle of Flodden in 1513, when an invasion of England by James IV of Scotland was beaten back. It is also possible, Low suggests, that Leonard Meryll lost his standard in the raids against France which were made in 1522–3.

CHORUS.

Leonard Meryll!   785
Leonard Meryll!
Dauntless he in time of peril!
    Man of power,
    Knighthood's flower,
Welcome to the grim old Tower,   790
To the Tower, welcome thou!

RECITATIVE – FAIRFAX.

Forbear, my friends, and spare me this ovation,
I have small claim to such consideration;
The tales that of my prowess are narrated
Have been prodigiously exaggerated!   795

CHORUS.

    'Tis ever thus!
Wherever valour true is found,
True modesty will there abound.

COUPLETS.

1ST. YEOMAN. Didst thou not, oh, Leonard Meryll!
                Standard lost in last campaign,   800
             Rescue it at deadly peril –
                Bear it safely back again?

CHORUS.   Leonard Meryll, at his peril,
             Bore it safely back again!

2ND YEOMAN. Didst thou not, when prisoner taken,   805
                And debarred from all escape,
             Face, with gallant heart unshaken,
                Death in most appalling shape?

CHORUS.   Leonard Meryll faced his peril,
             Death in most appalling shape!   810

FAIR. (*aside*). Truly I was to be pitied,
                Having but an hour to live,
             I reluctantly submitted,
                I had no alternative!

815 *Oh! the tales that are narrated*: In early performances this line was sung: 'Oh! the facts that
have been stated', and there was an additional line between lines 818 and 819: 'Mon-
strously exaggerated'. According to Peter Riley, the whole passage from lines 815–19 and
the chorus which follows it were for many years dropped from D'Oyly Carte productions, being reinstated in the late 1960s. I have not been able to establish the exact period
of this cut.

820 *They are not exaggerated*: The first edition of the libretto had additional couplets for the
Third and Fourth Yeomen and another verse for Fairfax:

3RD YEOMAN.	You, when brought to execution,
	Like a demigod of yore,
	With heroic resolution
	Snatched a sword and killed a score!
CHORUS.	Leonard Meryll, Leonard Meryll
	Snatched a sword and killed a score!
4TH YEOMAN.	Then escaping from the foemen,
	Bolstered with the blood you shed,
	You, defiant, fearing no men,
	Saved your honour and your head!
CHORUS.	Leonard Meryll, Leonard Meryll
	Saved his honour and his head!
FAIRFAX.	True, my course with judgment shaping,
	Favoured, too, by lucky star,
	I succeeded in escaping
	Prison bolt and prison bar!
	Oh! the tales that have been stated
	Of my deeds of derring-do,
	Have been much exaggerated, etc.
CHORUS.	They are not exaggerated, etc.

Gilbert wrote to Sullivan on the morning of the first performance saying: 'The Warders' couplets in the finale are too long, and should be reduced by one half. This, you
will observe is not "cutting out your music", but cutting out a *repeat* of your music. And
may I remind you that I am proposing to cut, not only your music, but my words.' Sullivan's diary for 3 October records that he met Gilbert at the theatre shortly before the
curtain went up and 'arranged to cut down second verse of couplets in Finale'; so it
seems that they were never sung on stage.

| (*Aloud.*) | Oh! the tales that are narrated | 815 |

                  Of my deeds of derring-do
                  Have been much exaggerated,
                  Very much exaggerated,
                    Scarce a word of them is true!

CHORUS.   They are not exaggerated, etc.   820

(*Enter* PHŒBE. *She rushes to* FAIRFAX. *Enter* WILFRED.)

RECITATIVE.

PHŒ.   Leonard!
FAIR. (*puzzled*).   I beg your pardon?
PHŒ.   Don't you know me?
    I'm little Phœbe!   825
FAIR. (*still puzzled*).   Phœbe? Is this Phœbe?
    What! little Phœbe? (*Aside.*) Who the deuce may *she* be?
    It can't be Phœbe, surely?
WIL.   Yes, 'tis Phœbe —
    Your sister Phœbe! Your own little sister!   830
CHORUS.   Aye, he speaks the truth;
    'Tis Phœbe!
FAIR. (*pretending to recognize her*).   Sister Phœbe!
PHŒ.   Oh, my brother!
FAIR.   Why, how you've grown! I did not recognize you!   835
PHŒ.   So many years! Oh, brother!
FAIR.   Oh, my sister!
WIL.   Aye, hug him, girl! There are three thou mayst hug —
    Thy father and thy brother and – myself!
FAIR.   Thyself, forsooth? And who art thou thyself?   840
WIL.   Good sir, we are betrothed. (FAIRFAX *turns inquiringly to*
    PHŒBE.)
PHŒ.   Or more or less —
    But rather less than more!
WIL.   To thy fond care   845
    I do commend thy sister. Be to her
    An ever-watchful guardian – eagle-eyed!
    And when she feels (as sometimes she does feel)
    Disposed to indiscriminate caress,
    Be thou at hand to take those favours from her!   850
CHORUS. Be thou at hand to take those favours from her!
PHŒ.   Yes, yes.
    Be thou at hand to take those favours from me!

867 *From morn to afternoon*: This chorus was changed to its present version in the third edition of the libretto. Before that the chorus sang 'Oh! grant, I pray, this boon' etc. at line 867, 'So grant, I pray, this boon' etc. at line 881, and 'He freely grants that boon' at line 895.

878 *From two to eventide*: These lines were changed to their present form after the First World War. Before that they went:

> From two till day is done –
> From dim twilight to 'leven at night
> All kinds of risk I run!

TRIO – W ILFRED , F AIRFAX , *and* P H Œ BE .

W IL .
> To thy fraternal care
>> Thy sister I commend; 855
> From every lurking snare
>> Thy lovely charge defend:
> And to achieve this end,
> Oh! grant, I pray, this boon –
>> She shall not quit thy sight: 860
> From morn to afternoon –
>> From afternoon to night –
> From seven o'clock to two –
>> From two to eventide –
> From dim twilight to 'leven at night 865
>> She shall not quit thy side!

C HORUS .
> From morn to afternoon, etc.

P H Œ .
> So amiable I've grown,
>> So innocent as well,
> That if I'm left alone 870
>> The consequences fell
>> No mortal can foretell.
> So grant, I pray, this boon –
>> I shall not quit thy sight:
> From morn to afternoon – 875
>> From afternoon to night –
> From seven o'clock to two –
>> From two to eventide –
> From dim twilight to 'leven at night
>> I shall not quit thy side. 880

C HORUS .
> From morn to afternoon, etc.

F AIR .
> With brotherly readiness,
>> For my fair sister's sake,
> At once I answer 'Yes' –
>> That task I undertake – 885
>> My word I never break.
> I freely grant that boon,
>> And I'll repeat my plight.
> From morn to afternoon –   (*kiss*)
>> From afternoon to night –   (*kiss*) 890
> From seven o'clock to two –   (*kiss*)
>> From two to evening meal –   (*kiss*)

896 *The bell of St Peter's begins to toll*: The bell of the church of St Peter ad Vincula, which stands within the precincts of the Tower of London adjoining Tower Green, was always rung during an execution.

Getting the right balance and rhythm for the tolling which accompanies the chorus 'The prisoner comes to meet his doom' is a difficult matter. J. M. Gordon, stage manager of the D'Oyly Carte Company for more than thirty years in the early part of this century, noted in his reminiscences that 'the Bell chorus was a great difficulty, it being a real bell of almost two hundredweights set behind the flats, and the slightest taps overpowering the chorus, it was moved more and more away, and eventually taken up to the fly tower where the conductor could be seen and the balance of tone correct with the chorus'.

Peter Riley, a more recent stage manager, found the tolling of the bell equally difficult to manage. 'We originally did it off stage but that proved unsatisfactory because it has to be tolled on every eighth beat and so the chap doing it really has to see the conductor, so we later transferred it to the orchestra pit. On the eleventh toll the headsman comes in.'

904 *May Heaven have mercy on his soul*: Originally Dame Carruthers was given a solo verse between the chorus and Elsie's solo. It appears in the pre-production prompt copy and the licence copy:

> Thou solemn bell, whose iron tongue
> So many a brave man's knell has rung,
> Of all that thou hast tolled away,
> The bravest he who dies today!

905–8 *Oh, Mercy, thou whose smile has shone*
As sung in early performances, Elsie's solo was slightly different from the present version:

> Oh, Mercy, thou whose smile has shone
> So many a captive on;
> Of all immured within these walls,
> The very worthiest falls!

909 *Oh, Mercy, etc.*: In early performances, the chorus at this point repeated 'The prisoner comes to meet his doom' instead of the reprise of Elsie's solo which they now have.

From dim twilight to 'leven at night
That compact I will seal.   (*kiss*)

CHORUS.   From morn to afternoon, etc.   895

(*The bell of St Peter's begins to toll. The Crowd enters; the block is brought on to the stage, and the Headsman takes his place. The Yeomen of the Guard form up. The* LIEUTENANT *enters and takes his place, and tells off* FAIRFAX *and two others to bring the prisoner to execution.* WILFRED, FAIRFAX, *and two Yeomen exeunt to Tower.*)   900

CHORUS (*to tolling accompaniment*).

The prisoner comes to meet his doom:
The block, the headsman, and the tomb.
The funeral bell begins to toll –
May Heaven have mercy on his soul!

SOLO – ELSIE, *with* CHORUS.

Oh, Mercy, thou whose smile has shone   905
So many a captive heart upon;
Of all immured within these walls,
To-day the very worthiest falls!

CHORUS.   Oh, Mercy, etc.

(*Enter* FAIRFAX *and two other Yeomen from Tower in   910
great excitement.*)

FAIR.   My lord! I know not how to tell
The news I bear!
I and my comrades sought the prisoner's cell –
He is not there!   915

CHORUS.   He is not there!
They sought the prisoner's cell – he is not there!

TRIO – FAIRFAX *and two Yeomen.*

As escort for the prisoner
We sought his cell, in duty bound;
The double gratings open were,   920
No prisoner at all we found!

> We hunted high, we hunted low,
>> We hunted here, we hunted there –
> The man we sought with anxious care
>> Had vanished into empty air! 925

(Exit LIEUTENANT.*)*

GIRLS. Now, by my troth, the news is fair,
The man has vanished into air!

ALL. As escort for the prisoner
We
They } sought his cell in duty bound, etc. 930

(Enter WILFRED, *followed by* LIEUTENANT.*)*

LIEUT. Astounding news! The prisoner fled!
(To WILFRED.*)* Thy life shall forfeit be instead!

*(*WILFRED *is arrested.)*

WIL. My lord, I did not set him free, 935
I hate the man – my rival he!

*(*WILFRED *is taken away.)*

MER. The prisoner gone – I'm all agape!
Who could have helped him to escape?

PHŒ. Indeed I can't imagine who! 940
I've no idea at all – have you?

(Enter JACK POINT.*)*

DAME. Of his escape no traces lurk,
Enchantment must have been at work!

ELSIE *(aside to* POINT.*)*
What have I done! Oh, woe is me! 945
I am his wife, and he is free!

POINT. Oh, woe is *you?* Your anguish sink!
Oh, woe is *me*, I rather think!
Oh, woe is *me*, I rather think!
Yes, woe is *me*, I rather think! 950
Whate'er betide
You are his bride,

957–64 *All frenzied with despair I rave*
In early performances Elsie and Point were given the following verses to sing in this ensemble, with everyone else singing the Lieutenant's verse with altered pronouns as now:

ELSIE.	POINT.
All frenzied with despair I rave,	All frenzied with despair I rave,
My anguish rends my heart in two.	My anguish rends my heart in two.
Unloved, to him my hand I gave;	Your hand to him you freely gave;
To him, unloved, bound to be true!	It's woe to me, not woe to you!
Unloved, unknown, unseen – the brand	My laugh is dead, my heart unmanned,
Of infamy upon his head:	A jester with a soul of lead!
A bride that's husbandless, I stand	A lover loverless I stand,
To all mankind for ever dead!	To womankind for ever dead!

963 *A thousand marks*: A mark was worth two thirds of a pound, i.e. thirteen shillings and fourpence.

And I am left
Alone – bereft!
Yes, woe is *me*, I rather think!   955
Yes, woe is *me*, I rather think!

ENSEMBLE – LIEUTENANT, PRINCIPALS, *and* CHORUS.

All frenzied with despair I rave,
  The grave is cheated of its due.
Who is the misbegotten knave
  Who hath contrived this deed to do?   960
Let search be made throughout the land,

Or $\left\{ \begin{array}{c} \text{his} \\ \text{my} \end{array} \right\}$ vindictive anger dread –

A thousand marks to him $\left\{ \begin{array}{c} \text{he'll} \\ \text{I'll} \end{array} \right\}$ hand

Who brings him here, alive or dead.

(At the end, ELSIE *faints in* FAIRFAX'S *arms; all the Yeomen and populace rush off the*   965
stage in different directions, to hunt for the fugitive, leaving only the Headsman on the
stage, and ELSIE *insensible in* FAIRFAX'S *arms.)*

END OF ACT I

1–2 *Scene*: A note by Rupert D'Oyly Carte records: 'At the 1899 revival Act II was given a different setting to Act I, described as "The Tower from the Wharf". Nothing seemed to be gained by this and it was dropped later.'

3–10 *Night has spread her pall once more*
In early libretti this chorus, as now, was given to the women but with the men joining in to repeat all from 'He has shaken off his yoke' (line 7).

6 *Useless his dungeon key*: many editions have 'Useless now his dungeon key'.

22 *Pretty warders are ye*: This chorus was not sung in early performances.

ACT II

SCENE. – *The same.* – *Moonlight. Two days have elapsed. Women and Yeomen of the Guard discovered.*

CHORUS OF WOMEN.

Night has spread her pall once more,
   And the prisoner still is free:
Open is his dungeon door,   5
   Useless his dungeon key!
He has shaken off his yoke –
   How, no mortal man can tell!
Shame on loutish jailer-folk –
   Shame on sleepy sentinel!   10

(*Enter* DAME CARRUTHERS *and* KATE.)

SOLO – DAME CARRUTHERS.

Warders are ye?
   Whom do ye ward?
Bolt, bar, and key,
   Shackle and cord,   15
Fetter and chain,
   Dungeon of stone,
All are in vain –
   Prisoner's flown!
Spite of ye all, he is free – he is free!   20
Whom do ye ward? Pretty warders are ye!

CHORUS OF WOMEN. Pretty warders are ye, etc.

YEOMEN.   Up and down, and in and out,
                Here and there, and round about;

34 *reading from a huge volume*: Beti Lloyd-Jones, who was with the D'Oyly Carte Company as a contralto chorus member and soloist from September 1956 until the company folded in February 1982, acted as 'stage mother' to John Reed, the principal comedian for much of that time. She told me 'One of the little traditions we developed over those years was that before the Second Act of *Yeomen* I would always read a long screed to him from his book of jokes'.

39–40 *The councillor laughed hugely*: According to a note by Rupert D'Oyly Carte, George Thorne, who played Jack Point in D'Oyly Carte tours between 1888 and 1899, delivered this line as 'The sage was so pleased with this saw that he gave him a sausage'.

47 *Jailer that jailed not . . .* : The most alliterative passage in the Savoy Operas (see the note to *The Mikado*, Act I, lines 605–8).

Every chamber, every house,   25
Every chink that holds a mouse,
Every crevice in the keep,
Where a beetle black could creep,
Every outlet, every drain,
Have we searched, but all in vain.   30

ENSEMBLE.   Warders are $\left\{ \begin{matrix} ye \\ we \end{matrix} \right\}$,

Whom do $\left\{ \begin{matrix} ye \\ we \end{matrix} \right\}$ ward? etc.

(Exeunt all.)

(Enter JACK POINT, *in low spirits, reading from a huge volume.)*

POINT *(reads)*. 'The Merrie Jestes of Hugh Ambrose. No. 7863. The Poor   35
Wit and the Rich Councillor. A certayne poor wit, being an-hungered, did
meet a well-fed councillor. "Marry, fool," quoth the councillor, "whither
away?" "In truth," said the poor wag, "in that I have eaten naught these two
dayes, I do wither away, and that right rapidly!" The councillor laughed
hugely, and gave him a sausage.' Humph! The councillor was easier to   40
please than my new master the Lieutenant. I would like to take post under
the councillor. Ah! 'tis but melancholy mumming when poor heart-broken,
jilted Jack Point must needs turn to Hugh Ambrose for original light humour!

(Enter WILFRED, *also in low spirits.)*

WIL. *(sighing)*. Ah, Master Point!   45
POINT *(changing his manner)*. Ha! friend jailer! Jailer that wast – jailer that
never shalt be more! Jailer that jailed not, or that jailed, if jail he did, so
unjailerly that 'twas but jerry-jailing, or jailing in joke – though no joke to
him who, by unjailerlike jailing, did so jeopardize his jailership. Come, take
heart, smile, laugh, wink, twinkle, thou tormentor that tormentest none –   50
thou racker that rackest not – thou pincher out of place – come, take heart,
and be merry, as I am! – *(aside, dolefully)* – as I am!
WIL. Aye, it's well for thee to laugh. Thou has a good post, and hast
cause to be merry.
POINT *(bitterly)*. Cause? Have we not all cause? Is not the world a big butt   55
of humour, into which all who will may drive a gimlet? See, I am a salaried
wit; and is there aught in nature more ridiculous? A poor, dull, heart-broken
man, who must needs be merry, or he will be whipped; who must rejoice,
lest he starve; who must jest you, jibe you, quip you, crank you, wrack you,
riddle you, from hour to hour, from day to day, from year to year, lest he   60
dwindle, perish, starve, pine, and die! Why, when there's naught else to
laugh at, I laugh at myself till I ache for it!

73–137 *Oh! a private buffoon*

An undated prompt copy which belonged to the late Dame Bridget D'Oyly Carte has a note pencilled against the first verse of this song: 'This verse is now omitted at the Savoy'. The prompt copy in the British Library has the first verse stroked out. I have been unable to discover the dates when this verse was cut and when reinstated. In the 1910 D'Oyly Carte recording C. H. Workman sang the first verse, but not the third!

WIL. Yet I have often thought that a jester's calling would suit me to a hair.

POINT. Thee? Would suit *thee*, thou death's head and cross-bones? 65

WIL. Aye, I have a pretty wit – a light, airy, joysome wit, spiced with anecdotes of prison cells and the torture-chamber. Oh, a very delicate wit! I have tried it on many a prisoner, and there have been some who smiled. Now it is not easy to make a prisoner smile. And it should not be difficult to be a good jester, seeing that thou art one. 70

POINT. Difficult? Nothing easier. Nothing easier. Attend, and I will prove it to thee!

SONG – POINT.

Oh! a private buffoon is a light-hearted loon,
    If you listen to popular rumour;
From the morn to the night he's so joyous and bright, 75
    And he bubbles with wit and good humour!
He's so quaint and so terse, both in prose and in verse;
    Yet though people forgive his transgression,
There are one or two rules that all family fools
    Must observe, if they love their profession. 80
        There are one or two rules,
        Half a dozen, maybe,
        That all family fools,
        Of whatever degree,
    Must observe, if they love their profession. 85

If you wish to succeed as a jester, you'll need
    To consider each person's auricular:
What is all right for B would quite scandalize C
    (For C is so very particular);
And D may be dull, and E's very thick skull 90
    Is as empty of brains as a ladle;
While F is F sharp, and will cry with a carp
    That he's known your best joke from his cradle!
        When your humour they flout,
        You can't let yourself go; 95
        And it *does* put you out
        When a person says, 'Oh,
    I have known that old joke from my cradle!'

If your master is surly, from getting up early
    (And tempers are short in the morning), 100
An inopportune joke is enough to provoke
    Him to give you, at once, a month's warning.

112 *D.D.*: Doctor of Divinity. This distinguished species of clergyman also gets a mention in *The Sorcerer* (Act II, line 18) and in *The Pirates of Penzance* (Act I, line 432).

Then if you refrain, he is at you again,
  For he likes to get value for money;
He'll ask then and there, with an insolent stare,   105
  'If you know that you're paid to be funny?'
     It adds to the tasks
       Of a merryman's place,
     When your principal asks,
       With a scowl on his face,   110
  If you know that you're paid to be funny?

Comes a Bishop, maybe, or a solemn D.D. –
  Oh, beware of his anger provoking!
Better not pull his hair – don't stick pins in his chair;
  He don't understand practical joking.   115
If the jests that you crack have an orthodox smack,
  You may get a bland smile from these sages;
But should they, by chance, be imported from France,
  Half-a-crown is stopped out of your wages!
     It's a general rule,   120
       Though your zeal it may quench,
     If the family fool
       Tells a joke that's too French,
  Half-a-crown is stopped out of his wages!

Though your head it may rack with a bilious attack,   125
  And your senses with toothache you're losing,
Don't be mopy and flat – they don't fine you for that,
  If you're properly quaint and amusing!
Though your wife ran away with a soldier that day,
  And took with her your trifle of money;   130
Bless your heart, they don't mind – they're exceedingly kind –
  They don't blame you – as long as you're funny!
     It's a comfort to feel,
       If your partner should flit,
     Though *you* suffer a deal,   135
       They don't mind it a bit –
  They don't blame you – so long as you're funny!

POINT. And so thou wouldst be a jester, eh?

WIL. Aye!

POINT. Now, listen! My sweetheart, Elsie Maynard, was secretly wed to   140
this Fairfax half an hour ere he escaped.

WIL. She did well.

161–94 *Hereupon we're both agreed*
This spirited song was originally sung as an ensemble, with Point and Wilfred singing together throughout rather than, as now, dividing up some of the lines between them.

175   *a tale of cock and bull*: A 'cock and bull story' is a long, rambling and generally incredible yarn. The origins of the term seem to lie in an old fable about cocks, bulls and other animals discoursing in human language.

POINT. She did nothing of the kind, so hold thy peace and perpend.
Now, while he liveth she is dead to me and I to her, and so, my jibes and
jokes notwithstanding, I am the saddest and the sorriest dog in England!   145

WIL. Thou art a very dull dog indeed.

POINT. Now, if thou wilt swear that thou didst shoot this Fairfax while
he was trying to swim across the river – it needs but the discharge of an
arquebus on a dark night – and that he sank and was seen no more, I'll make
thee the very Archbishop of jesters, and that in two days' time! Now, what   150
sayest thou?

WIL. I am to lie?

POINT. Heartily. But thy lie must be a lie of circumstance, which I will
support with the testimony of eyes, ears, and tongue.

WIL. And thou wilt qualify me as a jester?   155

POINT. As a jester among jesters. I will teach thee all my original songs,
my self-constructed riddles, my own ingenious paradoxes; nay, more, I will
reveal to thee the source whence I get them. Now, what sayest thou?

WIL. Why, if it be but a lie thou wantest of me, I hold it cheap enough, and
I say yes, it is a bargain!   160

DUET – POINT *and* WILFRED.

BOTH.   Hereupon we're both agreed,
                            All that we two
                            Do agree to
                    We'll secure by solemn deed,
                            To prevent all   165
                            Error mental.

POINT.   You on Elsie are to call
                            With a story
                            Grim and gory;

WIL.   How this Fairfax died, and all   170
                            I declare to
                            You're to swear to.

POINT.   I to swear to!
WIL.   I declare to!

BOTH.   Tell a tale of cock and bull,   175
                    Of convincing detail full,
                            Tale tremendous,
                            Heaven defend us!
                    What a tale of cock and bull!

197   *Two days gone*: In the first edition this line began 'A day and a half gone'.

BOTH.	In return for $\left\{ \begin{array}{c} \text{your} \\ \text{my} \end{array} \right\}$ own part	180

You are
I am $\Big\}$ making
　Undertaking
To instruct $\left\{ \begin{array}{c} \text{me} \\ \text{you} \end{array} \right\}$ in the art
　(Art amazing,
　Wonder raising) 185

POINT.　Of a jester, jesting free.
　　　　　Proud position –
　　　　　High ambition!

WIL.　And a lively one I'll be,
　　　　Wag-a-wagging, 190
　　　　Never flagging!
POINT.　Wag-a-wagging!
WIL.　Never flagging!

BOTH.　Tell a tale of cock and bull, etc.

　　　　　　　　　　　　　　(*Exeunt together.*) 195

(*Enter* FAIRFAX.)

FAIR. Two days gone, and no news of poor Fairfax. The dolts! They seek him everywhere save within a dozen yards of his dungeon. So I am free! Free, but for the cursed haste with which I hurried headlong into the bonds of matrimony with – Heaven knows whom! As far as I remember, she should 200 have been young; but even had not her face been concealed by her kerchief, I doubt whether, in my then plight, I should have taken much note of her. Free? Bah! The Tower bonds were but a thread of silk compared with these conjugal fetters which I, fool that I was, placed upon mine own hands. From the one I broke readily enough – how to break the other! 205

BALLAD – FAIRFAX.

Free from his fetters grim –
　Free to depart;
Free both in life and limb –
　In all but heart!
Bound to an unknown bride 210
　For good and ill;
Ah, is not one so tied
　A prisoner still?

216 *Gyves*: Leg-irons.

218 *Although a monarch's hand*: In the licence and pre-production prompt copies this line appears as 'Although King Henry's hand', a clear indication that Gilbert envisaged the opera as being set during the reign of Henry VIII (1509–47).

Free, yet in fetters held
   Till his last hour,   215
Gyves that no smith can weld,
   No rust devour!
Although a monarch's hand
   Had set him free,
Of all the captive band   220
   The saddest he!

(*Enter* MERYLL.)

FAIR. Well, Sergeant Meryll, and how fares thy pretty charge, Elsie
Maynard?
   MER. Well enough, sir. She is quite strong again, and leaves us   225
to-night.
   FAIR. Thanks to Dame Carruthers' kind nursing, eh?
   MER. Aye, deuce take the old witch! Ah, 'twas but a sorry trick you
played me, sir, to bring the fainting girl to me. It gave the old lady an excuse
for taking up her quarters in my house, and for the last two years I've   230
shunned her like the plague. Another day of it and she would have married
me! (*Enter* DAME CARRUTHERS *and* KATE.) Good Lord, here she is again!
I'll e'en go. (*Going.*)
   DAME. Nay, Sergeant Meryll, don't go. I have something of grave import
to say to thee.   235
   MER. (*aside*). It's coming.
   FAIR. (*laughing*). I'faith, I think I'm not wanted here. (*Going.*)
   DAME. Nay, Master Leonard, I've naught to say to thy father that his son
may not hear.
   FAIR. (*aside*). True. I'm one of the family; I had forgotten!   240
   DAME. 'Tis about this Elsie Maynard. A pretty girl, Master Leonard.
   FAIR. Aye, fair as a peach blossom – what then?
   DAME. She hath a liking for thee, or I mistake not.
   FAIR. With all my heart. She's as dainty a little maid as you'll find in a
midsummer day's march.   245
   DAME. Then be warned in time, and give not thy heart to her. Oh, *I* know
what it is to give my heart to one who will have none of it!
   MER. (*aside*). Aye, *she* knows all about that. (*Aloud.*) And why is my boy
to take heed of her? She's a good girl, Dame Carruthers.
   DAME. Good enough, for aught I know. But she's no girl. She's a married   250
woman.
   MER. A married woman! Tush, old lady – she's promised to Jack Point,
the Lieutenant's new jester.
   DAME. Tush in thy teeth, old man! As my niece Kate sat by her
bedside to-day, this Elsie slept, and as she slept she moaned and groaned,   255

264   *kirtle*: A skirt or outer petticoat. In the pre-production prompt copy this phrase reads 'or I'll swallow my farthingale'.

and turned this way and that way – and, 'How shall I marry one I have never seen?' quoth she – then, 'An hundred crowns!' quoth she – then, 'Is it certain he will die in an hour?' quoth she – then, 'I love him not, and yet I am his wife,' quoth she! Is it not so, Kate?

KATE. Aye, aunt, 'tis even so.　　　260

FAIR. Art thou sure of all this?

KATE. Aye, sir, for I wrote it all down on my tablets.

DAME. Now, mark my words: it was of this Fairfax she spake, and he is her husband, or I'll swallow my kirtle!

MER. (*aside*). Is it true, sir?　　　265

FAIR. (*aside to* MERYLL). True? Why, the girl was raving! (*Aloud.*) Why should she marry a man who had but an hour to live?

DAME. Marry? There be those who would marry but for a minute, rather than die old maids.

MER. (*aside*). Aye, I know one of them!　　　270

QUARTET.

FAIRFAX, SERGEANT MERYLL, DAME CARRUTHERS, *and* KATE.

> Strange adventure! Maiden wedded
>   To a groom she's never seen –
>   Never, never, never seen!
> Groom about to be beheaded,
>   In an hour on Tower Green!　　　275
>   Tower, Tower, Tower Green!
> Groom in dreary dungeon lying,
> Groom as good as dead, or dying,
> For a pretty maiden sighing –
>   Pretty maid of seventeen!　　　280
>   Seven – seven – seventeen!
>
> Strange adventure that we're trolling:
>   Modest maid and gallant groom –
>   Gallant, gallant, gallant groom! –
> While the funeral bell is tolling,　　　285
>   Tolling, tolling, Bim-a-boom!
>   Bim-a, Bim-a, Bim-a-boom!
> Modest maiden will not tarry;
> Though but sixteen years she carry,
> She must marry, she must marry,　　　290
>   Though the altar be a tomb –
>   Tower – Tower – Tower tomb!

(*Exeunt* DAME CARRUTHERS, MERYLL, *and* KATE.)

298 *Enter Elsie*: Gilbert originally gave Elsie a recitative and song at this entrance. It is
printed in the pre-production copy and in the licence copy, where it is crossed out.

RECITATIVE – ELSIE.

Unloved, unseen, unknown, the brand
  Of infamy upon his head!
A bride all husbandless I stand,
  To all mankind for ever dead!

SONG – ELSIE.

There's many a maid
    In best arrayed
Comes tripping, tripping over the lea,
    And many, and more,
      Rare tales can tell
    Of gallants a score
      Who spoke them well,
And left them jilted – sorry, but free.
A tripping, tripping over the lea;
But never a maid that you'll espy
Can tell so sorry a tale as I!
Ah me! how merry a maid may be
A-tripping, tripping over the lea!

    Oh maidens fair,
      Who, free from care,
Come tripping, tripping over the lea,
      Pity the bride
        All husbandless,
      What sorrows betide
        No one can guess!
Oh maidens, maidens, happy are ye
A-tripping, tripping over the lea!
For though I'm a wife, the wife of none!
Than maid and widow and wife in one,
'Tis better a jilted maid to be,
A-tripping, tripping over the lea!

FAIR. So my mysterious bride is no other than this winsome Elsie! By my
hand, 'tis no such ill plunge in Fortune's lucky bag! I might have fared worse   295
with my eyes open! But she comes. Now to test her principles. 'Tis not
every husband who has a chance of wooing his own wife!

(*Enter* ELSIE.)

FAIR. Mistress Elsie!
ELSIE. Master Leonard!   300
FAIR. So thou leavest us to-night?
ELSIE. Yes, Master Leonard. I have been kindly tended, and I almost fear
I am loth to go.
FAIR. And this Fairfax. Wast thou glad when he escaped?
ELSIE. Why, truly, Master Leonard, it is a sad thing that a young and   305
gallant gentleman should die in the very fullness of his life.
FAIR. Then when thou didst faint in my arms, it was for joy at his
safety?
ELSIE. It may be so. I was highly wrought, Master Leonard, and I am but
a girl, and so, when I am highly wrought, I faint.   310
FAIR. Now, dost thou know, I am consumed with a parlous jealousy?
ELSIE. Thou? And of whom?
FAIR. Why, of this Fairfax, surely!
ELSIE. Of Colonel Fairfax?
FAIR. Aye. Shall I be frank with thee? Elsie – I love thee, ardently,   315
passionately! (ELSIE *alarmed and surprised*.) Elsie, I have loved thee these two
days – which is a long time – and I would fain join my life to thine!
ELSIE. Master Leonard! Thou art jesting!
FAIR. Jesting? May I shrivel into raisins if I jest! I love thee with a love that
is a fever – with a love that is a frenzy – with a love that eateth up my heart!   320
What sayest thou? Thou wilt not let my heart be eaten up?
ELSIE (*aside*). Oh, mercy! What am I to say?
FAIR. Dost thou love me, or hast thou been insensible these two days?
ELSIE. I love all brave men.
FAIR. Nay, there is love in excess. I thank heaven there are many brave   325
men in England; but if thou lovest them all, I withdraw my thanks.
ELSIE. I love the bravest best. But, sir, I may not listen – I am not free –
I – I am a wife!
FAIR. Thou a wife? Whose? His name? His hours are numbered – nay, his
grave is dug and his epitaph set up! Come, his name?   330
ELSIE. Oh, sir! keep my secret – it is the only barrier that Fate could set
up between us. My husband is none other than Colonel Fairfax!
FAIR. The greatest villain unhung! The most ill-favoured, ill-mannered,
ill-natured, ill-omened, ill-tempered dog in Christendom!
ELSIE. It is very like. He is naught to me – for I never saw him. I was   335

355 *arquebus*: A very up-to-date reference – the *Oxford English Dictionary* dates the first
recorded use of the word as being in 1532, eight years after Sir Richard Cholmondeley's
departure from the Tower. It goes on to define an arquebus as 'The early type of portable
gun, varying in size, and, when used in the field, supported on a tripod, trestle or other
carriage, or upon a forked rest. The name in German meant literally "hook-gun", from
the hook, cast along with it, by which it was attached to the carriage.'

blindfolded, and he was to have died within the hour; and he did not die –
and I am wedded to him, and my heart is broken!

FAIR. He was to have died, and he did *not* die? The scoundrel! The
perjured, traitorous villain! Thou shouldst have insisted on his dying first, to
make sure. 'Tis the only way with these Fairfaxes. 340

ELSIE. I now wish I had!

FAIR. (*aside*). Bloodthirsty little maiden! (*Aloud.*) A fig for this Fairfax! Be
mine – he will never know – he dares not show himself; and if he dare, what
art thou to him? Fly with me, Elsie – we will be married to-morrow, and thou
shalt be the happiest wife in England! 345

ELSIE. Master Leonard! I am amazed! Is it thus that brave soldiers speak
to poor girls? Oh! for shame, for shame! I am wed – not the less because I
love not my husband. I am a wife, sir, and I have a duty, and – oh, sir! thy
words terrify me – they are not honest – they are wicked words, and
unworthy thy great and brave heart! Oh, shame upon thee! shame upon 350
thee!

FAIR. Nay, Elsie, I did but jest. I spake but to try thee — (*Shot heard.*)

(*Enter* MERYLL *hastily.*)

MER. (*recitative*). Hark! What was that, sir?

FAIR.   Why, an arquebus – 355
         Fired from the wharf, unless I much mistake.

MER.   Strange – and at such an hour! What can it mean?

(*Enter* CHORUS.)

CHORUS.

Now what can that have been –
    A shot so late at night, 360
    Enough to cause a fright!
What can the portent mean?

Are foemen in the land?
    Is London to be wrecked?
    What are we to expect? 365
What danger is at hand?
    Let us understand
    What danger is at hand!

(LIEUTENANT *enters, also* POINT *and* WILFRED.)

393 *Colonel Fairfax and no other*: In early editions of the libretto, this and the next line were first repeated by Fairfax before the chorus took them up as follows:

> Colonel Fairfax and no other
> >Was the man to whom he clung!
> Yes – they closed with one another
> In a rough-and-tumble smother;
> Colonel Fairfax and no other
> >Was the man to whom he clung!

RECITATIVE.

LIEUT.	Who fired that shot? At once the truth declare!	370
WIL.	My lord, 'twas I – to rashly judge forbear!	
POINT.	My lord, 'twas he – to rashly judge forbear!	

DUET AND CHORUS – WILFRED *and* POINT.

WIL. Like a ghost his vigil keeping –

POINT. Or a spectre all-appalling –

WIL. I beheld a figure creeping – 375

POINT. I should rather call it crawling –

WIL. He was creeping –

POINT. He was crawling –

WIL. He was creeping, creeping –

POINT. Crawling! 380

WIL. He was creeping –

POINT. He was crawling –

WIL. He was creeping, creeping –

POINT. Crawling!

WIL. Not a moment's hesitation – 385
 I myself upon him flung,
With a hurried exclamation
 To his draperies I hung;
Then we closed with one another
In a rough-and-tumble smother; 390
Colonel Fairfax and no other
 Was the man to whom I clung!

ALL. Colonel Fairfax and no other
 Was the man to whom he clung!

WIL. After mighty tug and tussle – 395

405 *Down he dived into the river*: This line and the chorus's repeat in line 409 were originally sung: 'He plunged headlong in the river'.

417 *With an ounce or two of lead*: This line was not sung in early performances, everyone merely repeating line 416.

423 *He discharged it without winking*: This and the next three lines were not in the first edition of the libretto used for early performances.

POINT.	It resembled more a struggle –
WIL.	He, by dint of stronger muscle –
POINT.	Or by some infernal juggle –
WIL.	From my clutches quickly sliding –
POINT.	I should rather call it slipping –
WIL.	With a view, no doubt, of hiding –
POINT.	Or escaping to the shipping –
WIL.	With a gasp, and with a quiver –
POINT.	I'd describe it as a shiver –
WIL.	Down he dived into the river,
	And, alas, I cannot swim.
ALL.	It's enough to make one shiver –
	With a gasp and with a quiver,
	Down he dived into the river;
	It was very brave of him!
WIL.	Ingenuity is catching;
	With the view my king of pleasing,
	Arquebus from sentry snatching –
POINT.	I should rather call it seizing –
WIL.	With an ounce or two of lead
	He despatched him through the head!
ALL.	With an ounce or two of lead
	He despatched him through the head!
WIL.	I discharged it without winking,
	Little time I lost in thinking,
	Like a stone I saw him sinking –
POINT.	I should say a lump of lead.
ALL.	He discharged it without winking,
	Little time he lost in thinking.

400

405

410

415

420

429 *Anyhow, the man is dead*: In early performances Wilfred had this line only to himself, with
everyone then joining him to finish the song thus:

> ALL.   Whether stone or lump of lead,
>   Arquebus from sentry seizing,
>   With the view his king of pleasing,
>   Wilfred shot him through the head,
>   And he's very, very dead.
>   And it matters very little whether stone or lump of lead,
>   It is very, very certain that he's very, very dead!

The chorus then sang the refrain 'Hail the valiant fellow' (lines 448–51).

448–51 *Hail the valiant fellow*
In early libretti this chorus was sung twice: once, as noted above, before the Lieutenant's
recitative, and then again, as now, after it. On both occasions it was sung without line
452.

WIL.	Like a stone I saw him sinking –	425

POINT.   I should say a lump of lead.

WIL.   Like a stone, my boy, I said –

POINT.   Like a heavy lump of lead.

WIL.   Anyhow, the man is dead,
            Whether stone or lump of lead!   430

ALL.   Anyhow, the man is dead,
                  Whether stone or lump of lead!
            Arquebus from sentry seizing,
            With the view his king of pleasing,
                  Wilfred shot him through the head,   435
                  And he's very, very dead.
            And it matters very little whether stone or lump of lead;
            It is very, very certain that he's very, very dead!

RECITATIVE – LIEUTENANT.

The river must be dragged – no time be lost;
The body must be found, at any cost.   440
To this attend without undue delay;
So set to work with what despatch ye may!

                                          (*Exit.*)

ALL.   Yes, yes,
            We'll set to work with what despatch we may!   445

(*Four men raise* WILFRED, *and carry him off on
their shoulders.*)

CHORUS.

Hail the valiant fellow who
Did this deed of derring-do!
Honours wait on such an one;   450
By my head, 'twas bravely done!
Now, by my head, 'twas bravely done!

(*Exeunt all but* ELSIE, POINT, FAIRFAX, *and* PHŒBE.)

POINT (*to* ELSIE, *who is weeping*). Nay, sweetheart, be comforted. This
Fairfax was but a pestilent fellow, and, as he had to die, he might as well die   455
thus as any other way. 'Twas a good death.

ELSIE. Still, he was my husband, and had he not been, he was
nevertheless a living man, and now he is dead; and so, by your leave, my
tears may flow unchidden, Master Point.

FAIR. And thou didst see all this?   460

POINT. Aye, with both eyes at once – this and that. The testimony of one
eye is naught – he may lie. But when it is corroborated by the other, it is good
evidence that none may gainsay. Here are both present in court, ready to
swear to him!

PHŒ. But art thou sure it was Colonel Fairfax? Saw you his face?   465

POINT. Aye, and a plaguey ill-favoured face too. A very hang-dog face –
a felon face – a face to fright the headsman himself, and make him strike
awry. Oh, a plaguey, bad face, take my word for 't. (PHŒBE *and*
FAIRFAX *laugh*.) How they laugh! 'Tis ever thus with simple folk – an
accepted wit has but to say 'Pass the mustard,' and they roar their ribs out!   470

FAIR. (*aside*). If ever I come to life again, thou shalt pay for this, Master
Point!

POINT. Now, Elsie, thou art free to choose again, so behold me: I am
young and well-favoured. I have a pretty wit. I can jest you, jibe you, quip
you, crank you, wrack you, riddle you —   475

FAIR. Tush, man, thou knowest not how to woo. 'Tis not to be done with
time-worn jests and thread-bare sophistries; with quips, conundrums,
rhymes, and paradoxes. 'Tis an art in itself, and must be studied gravely and
conscientiously.

TRIO – ELSIE, PHŒBE, *and* FAIRFAX.

FAIR.   A man who would woo a fair maid   480
                Should 'prentice himself to the trade,
                        And study all day,
                        In methodical way,
                How to flatter, cajole, and persuade;
                He should 'prentice himself at fourteen,   485
                And practise from morning to e'en;
                        And when he's of age,
                        If he will, I'll engage,
                He may capture the heart of a queen!

ALL.   It is purely a matter of skill,   490
                Which all may attain if they will:
                        But every Jack,
                        He must study the knack
                If he wants to make sure of his Jill!

496 *His twig he'll so carefully lime*: In medieval and Tudor times people caught birds by smearing twigs with a sticky substance called bird-lime. The phrase 'to lime a twig' came to be used figuratively, as in Shakespeare's 'Madam, myself have limed a bush for her' (*Henry VI, Part 2*, Act I, Scene 3).

ELSIE.   If he's made the best use of his time,   495
                His twig he'll so carefully lime
                        That every bird
                        Will come down at his word,
                Whatever its plumage or clime.
                He must learn that the thrill of a touch   500
                May mean little, or nothing, or much:
                        It's an instrument rare,
                        To be handled with care,
                And ought to be treated as such.

ALL.   It is purely a matter of skill, etc.   505

PHŒ.   Then a glance may be timid or free,
                It will vary in mighty degree,
                        From an impudent stare
                        To a look of despair
                That no maid without pity can see!   510
                And a glance of despair is no guide –
                It may have its ridiculous side;
                        It may draw you a tear
                        Or a box on the ear;
                You can never be sure till you've tried!   515

ALL.   It is purely a matter of skill, etc.

FAIR. (*aside to* POINT). Now, listen to me – 'tis done thus – (*aloud*) –
Mistress Elsie, there is one here who, as thou knowest, loves thee right well!
    POINT (*aside*). That he does – right well!
    FAIR. He is but a man of poor estate, but he hath a loving, honest heart.   520
He will be a true and trusty husband to thee, and if thou wilt be his wife,
thou shalt lie curled up in his heart, like a little squirrel in its nest!
    POINT (*aside*). 'Tis a pretty figure. A maggot in a nut lies closer, but a
squirrel will do.
    FAIR. He knoweth that thou wast a wife – an unloved and unloving   525
wife, and his poor heart was near to breaking. But now that thine unloving
husband is dead, and thou art free, he would fain pray that thou wouldst
hearken unto him, and give him hope that thou wouldst one day be his!
    PHŒ. (*alarmed*). He presses her hands – and he whispers in her ear! Ods
bodikins, what does it mean?   530
    FAIR. Now, sweetheart, tell me – wilt thou be this poor good fellow's
wife?
    ELSIE. If the good, brave man – *is* he a brave man?
    FAIR. So men say.

535 *That's not true, but let it pass*: In early performances Point said 'That's not true, but let it pass this once'.

549–84 *When a wooer/Goes a-wooing*

François Cellier, musical director of the D'Oyly Carte Company from 1880 until 1913, disclosed in an interview with the *Westminster Gazette* the reason why this much-loved song never received an encore:

> In 'The Yeomen of the Guard' we always have a passionate demand for a repetition, which I avoid with the utmost care. All lovers of this opera will remember the quartette towards the end 'When a lover [*sic*] goes a-wooing' – a very sad number for Phœbe and Jack Point. The latter retires in distress at the loss of Elsie, and Phœbe is left on the stage to mourn the loss of Fairfax. Not only have Fairfax and Elsie to change too quickly to allow of the encore being taken, but Sir Arthur Sullivan expressly desired that a repetition should not be given, on the ground that the dramatic effect would be utterly spoiled.

567 *mickle*: The word mickle properly means much or a lot. It is used both here and by Dame Hannah in *Ruddigore* (Act II, line 551) erroneously to mean little.

That, at least, is what the *Oxford English Dictionary* would have us believe. However, in company with several correspondents who have written to me on this matter, I am inclined to the view that Gilbert was simply following the well-attested usage of the Scottish proverb 'Many a mickle makes a muckle' and was not deliberately misusing the English language.

POINT (*aside*). That's not true, but let it pass.   535
ELSIE. If the brave man will be content with a poor, penniless, untaught
maid —
POINT (*aside*). Widow — but let *that* pass.
ELSIE. I will be his true and loving wife, and that with my heart of hearts!
FAIR. My own dear love! (*Embracing her.*)   540
PHŒ. (*in great agitation*). Why, what's all this? Brother — brother — it is not
seemly!
POINT (*also alarmed, aside*). Oh, I can't let *that* pass! (*Aloud.*) Hold, enough,
Master Leonard! An advocate should have his fee, but methinks thou art
over-paying thyself!   545
FAIR. Nay, that is for Elsie to say. I promised thee I would show thee how
to woo, and herein lies the proof of the virtue of my teaching. Go thou, and
apply it elsewhere! (PHŒBE *bursts into tears.*)

QUARTET — ELSIE, PHŒBE, FAIRFAX, *and* POINT.

ELSIE.   When a wooer
                                 Goes a-wooing,   550
                          Naught is truer
                                 Than his joy.
FAIR.   Maiden hushing
                                 All his suing —
                          Boldly blushing —   555
                                 Bravely coy!

ALL.   Oh, the happy days of doing!
                          Oh, the sighing and the suing!
                          When a wooer goes a-wooing,
                                 Oh, the sweets that never cloy!   560

PHŒ. (*weeping*).   When a brother
                                 Leaves his sister
                          For another,
                                 Sister weeps.
                          Tears that trickle,   565
                                 Tears that blister —
                          'Tis but mickle
                                 Sister reaps!

ALL.   Oh, the doing and undoing,
                          Oh, the sighing and the suing,
                          When a brother goes a-wooing,   570
                          And a sobbing sister weeps!

POINT.   When a jester
                          Is outwitted,
                          Feelings fester,   575
                              Heart is lead!
                          Food for fishes
                              Only fitted,
                          Jester wishes
                              He was dead!   580

ALL.   Oh, the doing and undoing,
                          Oh, the sighing and the suing,
                          When a jester goes a-wooing,
                          And he wishes he was dead!

                          (*Exeunt all but* PHŒBE, *who remains weeping.*)   585

PHŒ. And I helped that man to escape, and I've kept his secret, and
pretended that I was his dearly loving sister, and done everything I could
think of to make folk believe I *was* his loving sister, and this is his gratitude!
Before I pretend to be sister to anybody again, I'll turn nun, and be sister to
everybody – one as much as another!   590

                          (*Enter* WILFRED.)

WIL. In tears, eh? what a plague art thou grizzling for now?
PHŒ. Why am I grizzling? Thou hast often wept for jealousy – well, 'tis
for jealousy I weep now. Aye, yellow, bilious, jaundiced jealousy. So make
the most of that, Master Wilfred.   595
WIL. But I have never given thee cause for jealousy. The Lieutenant's
cook-maid and I are but the merest gossips!
PHŒ. Jealous of thee! Bah! I'm jealous of no craven cock-on-a-hill, who
crows about what he'd do an he dared! I am jealous of another and a better
man than thou – set that down, Master Wilfred. And he is to marry Elsie   600
Maynard, the little pale fool – set that down, Master Wilfred – and my heart
is wellnigh broken! There, thou hast it all! Make the most of it!
WIL. The man thou lovest is to marry Elsie Maynard? Why, that is no
other than thy brother, Leonard Meryll!
PHŒ. (*aside*). Oh, mercy! what have I said?   605
WIL. Why, what manner of brother is this, thou lying little jade? Speak!
Who is this man whom thou hast called brother, and fondled, and coddled,
and kissed! – with my connivance, too! Oh Lord! with my connivance! Ha!
should it be this Fairfax! (PHŒBE *starts.*) It is! It is this accursed Fairfax! It's
Fairfax! Fairfax, who —   610
PHŒ. Whom thou has just shot through the head, and who lies at the
bottom of the river!

624   *Enter Leonard, hastily*: In the 1978 Tower of London production, Leonard made this entrance on a white charger, which was then left to swish its tail at the back of the orchestra
pit during the finale.

     Originally, Gilbert had intended Leonard's entrance to come later in Act II. The pre-
production prompt copy in the D'Oyly Carte archives has Meryll and Dame Carruthers
entering at this point. They then have the dialogue which now appears in lines 657–85.
After the singing of 'Rapture, rapture' Phœbe and Wilfred appear to have the following
conversation after seeing Meryll and Dame Carruthers going off together:

> PHŒ. There – see what has come of thine intermeddling! I am to have thee as a husband
> and that cackling old hen wife as a mother!
> WIL. And thou hast lost a brother, eh?
> PHŒ. Aye, a very loving brother!
> WIL. To the devil with his love! It maddens me to think of it. Why, who is this?

     At this point Leonard enters, as now, and the dialogue continues from line 625 to line
652, at which point the finale begins.

632   *Ods bobs*: Short for 'ods bodkins', a corruption of 'God's body' – a common oath from
the sixteenth to the nineteenth centuries.

637   *cockatrice*: A grotesque mythical creature with the head, wings and feet of a cock and the
tail of a dragon or serpent. The word came to be used as a term of reproach for a woman.

638   *cleave thee to the chine*: Split you to the backbone. Gilbert used the phrase in his Bab Ballad
'Sir Conrad and the Rusty One':

> Ho! stand, Sir Knight, if thou be brave,
>   And try thy might with mine,
> Unless you wish this trusty glaive
>   To cleave you to the chine!

WIL. A – I – I may have been mistaken. We are but fallible mortals, the best of us. But I'll make sure – I'll make sure. (*Going.*)

PHŒ. Stay – one word. I think it cannot be Fairfax – mind, I say I *think* 615 because thou hast just slain Fairfax. But whether he be Fairfax or no Fairfax, he is to marry Elsie – and – and – as thou hast shot him through the head, and he is dead, be content with that, and I will be thy wife!

WIL. Is that sure?

PHŒ. Aye, sure enough, for there's no help for it! Thou art a very brute 620 – but even brutes must marry, I suppose.

WIL. My beloved! (*Embraces her.*)

PHŒ. (*aside*). Ugh!

(*Enter* LEONARD, *hastily.*)

LEON. Phœbe, rejoice, for I bring glad tidings. Colonel Fairfax's 625 reprieve was signed two days since, but it was foully and maliciously kept back by Secretary Poltwhistle, who designed that it should arrive after the Colonel's death. It hath just come to hand, and it is now in the Lieutenant's possession!

PHŒ. Then the Colonel is free? Oh, kiss me, kiss me, my dear! Kiss 630 me, again, and again!

WIL. (*dancing with fury*). Ods bobs, death o' my life! Art thou mad! Am *I* mad? Are we *all* mad?

PHŒ. Oh, my dear – my dear, I'm wellnigh crazed with joy! (*Kissing* LEONARD.) 635

WIL. Come away from him, thou hussy – thou jade – thou kissing, clinging cockatrice! And as for thee, sir, devil take thee, I'll rip thee like a herring for this! I'll skin thee for it! I'll cleave thee to the chine! I'll – oh! Phœbe! Phœbe! Who is this man?

PHŒ. Peace, fool. He is my brother! 640

WIL. Another brother! Are there any more of them? Produce them all at once, and let me know the worst!

PHŒ. This is the real Leonard, dolt; the other was but his substitute. The *real* Leonard, I say – my father's own son.

WIL. How do I know this? Has he 'brother' writ large on his brow? I 645 mistrust thy brothers! Thou art but a false jade!

(*Exit* LEONARD.)

PHŒ. Now, Wilfred, be just. Truly I did deceive thee before – but it was to save a precious life – and to save it, not for me, but for another. They are to be wed this very day. Is not this enough for thee? Come – I am thy Phœbe 650 – thy very own – and we will be wed in a year – or two – or three, at the most. Is not that enough for thee?

686–718 *Rapture, rapture*

This song was added to the opera to give Elsie and Fairfax time to change into their wedding garments. It was subsequently dropped when it was found that there was, in fact, enough time for the costume change without it. Wilfred Judd reinstated it in his 1981 D'Oyly Carte production.

(*Enter* MERYLL, *excitedly, followed by* DAME CARRUTHERS, *who listens, unobserved.*)

MER. Phœbe, hast thou heard the brave news? 655
PHŒ. (*still in* WILFRED's *arms*). Aye, father.
MER. I'm nigh mad with joy! (*Seeing* WILFRED.) Why, what's all this?
PHŒ. Oh, father, he discovered our secret through my folly, and the price of his silence is —
WIL. Phœbe's heart. 660
PHŒ. Oh dear, no – Phœbe's hand.
WIL. It's the same thing!
PHŒ. *Is* it?

(*Exeunt* WILFRED *and* PHŒBE.)

MER. (*looking after them*). 'Tis pity, but the Colonel had to be saved at any 665
cost, and as thy folly revealed our secret, thy folly must e'en suffer for it!
(DAME CARRUTHERS *comes down.*) Dame Carruthers!
DAME. So this is a plot to shield this arch-fiend, and I have detected it. A word from me, and three heads besides his would roll from their shoulders! 670
MER. Nay, Colonel Fairfax is reprieved. (*Aside.*) Yet, if my complicity in his escape were known! Plague on the old meddler! There's nothing for it – (*aloud*) – Hush, pretty one! Such bloodthirsty words ill become those cherry lips! (*Aside.*) Ugh!
DAME (*bashfully*). Sergeant Meryll! 675
MER. Why, look ye, chuck – for many a month I've – I've thought to myself – 'There's snug love saving up in that middle-aged bosom for some one, and why not for thee – that's me – so take heart and tell her – that's thee – that thou – that's me – lovest her – thee – and – and – well, I'm a miserable old man, and I've done it – and that's me!' But not a word about Fairfax! The 680
price of thy silence is —
DAME. Meryll's heart?
MER. No, Meryll's *hand.*
DAME. It's the same thing!
MER. *Is* it! 685

DUET – DAME CARRUTHERS *and* SERGEANT MERYLL.

DAME. Rapture, rapture!
When love's votary,
Flushed with capture,
Seeks the notary,
Joy and jollity 690

                    Then is polity;
                    Reigns frivolity!
              Rapture, rapture!

MER.   Doleful, doleful!
                    When humanity,   695
              With its soul full
                    Of satanity,
                          Courting privity,
                          Down declivity
                          Seeks captivity!   700
              Doleful, doleful!

DAME.   Joyful, joyful!
                    When virginity
              Seeks, all coyful,
                    Man's affinity;   705
                    Fate all flowery,
                    Bright and bowery,
                    Is her dowery!
              Joyful, joyful!

MER.   Ghastly, ghastly!   710
                    When man, sorrowful,
              Firstly, lastly,
                    Of to-morrow full,
                          After tarrying,
                          Yields to harrying –   715
                          Goes a-marrying.
              Ghastly, ghastly!

BOTH.   Rapture, etc.

                              (*Exeunt* DAME *and* MERYLL.)

              FINALE.

              (*Enter Yeomen and Women.*)   720

              CHORUS OF WOMEN.
                 (ELEGIACS.)

Comes the pretty young bride, a-blushing, timidly shrinking –
    Set all thy fears aside – cheerily, pretty young bride!
Brave is the youth to whom thy lot thou art willingly linking!
    Flower of valour is he – loving as loving can be!

730 *Enter... Elsie as Bride*: In early performances, before 'Rapture, rapture' was cut, Elsie appeared before the chorus 'Comes the pretty young bride'.
Gilbert wrote to Richard D'Oyly Carte:

> Elsie should change her dress to something like a wedding dress at the end of the piece. It should not be a wedding dress of a modern type (of course), but a dress of Henry VIII time that will suggest something of a matrimonial nature to the spectator. White silk or satin, and white bars, and a wreath of white flowers would do – but kept 'bourgeoise' in cut.

731–8 *'Tis said that joy in full perfection*
In the licence copy this is given to Elsie as a solo.

739 *Yes, yes*: In early performances the chorus sang:

> Yes, yes
> This is her joy-day unalloyed!

746 *No! no!*: In early performances Elsie had a longer solo here:

> No! no! recall those words – it cannot be!
> Leonard, my Leonard, come, oh, come to me!
> Leonard, my own – my loved one – where art thou?
> I knew not how I loved thine heart till now!

747–54 *Oh, day of terror*
In early performances this ensemble was sung as follows:

ELSIE *and* PHŒBE.	CHORUS *and others.*
Oh, day of terror! day of tears!	Oh, day of terror! day of tears!
What fearful tidings greet mine ears?	What words are these that greet our ears?
Oh, Leonard, come thou to my side,	Who is the man who, in his pride,
And claim me as thy loving bride.	So boldly claims thee as his bride?

> LIEUTENANT *and* POINT.
> Come, dry these unbecoming tears,
> Most joyful tidings greet thine ears.
> The man to whom thou art allied
> Appears to claim thee as his bride.

Brightly thy summer is shining,   725
Fair as the dawn of the day;
   Take him, be true to him –
   Tender his due to him –
Honour him, love and obey!

(*Enter* DAME, PHŒBE, *and* ELSIE *as Bride*.)   730

TRIO – PHŒBE, ELSIE, *and* DAME CARRUTHERS.

'Tis said that joy in full perfection
   Comes only once to womankind –
That, other times, on close inspection,
   Some lurking bitter we shall find.
If this be so, and men say truly,   735
My day of joy has broken duly.
   With happiness $\left\{ \begin{array}{c} \text{my} \\ \text{her} \end{array} \right\}$ soul is cloyed –

   This is $\left\{ \begin{array}{c} \text{my} \\ \text{her} \end{array} \right\}$ joy-day unalloyed!

ALL.   Yes, yes, with happiness her soul is cloyed!
        This is her joy-day unalloyed!   740

(*Flourish. Enter* LIEUTENANT.)

LIEUT.   Hold, pretty one! I bring to thee
       News – good or ill, it is for thee to say.
      Thy husband lives – and he is free,
       And comes to claim his bride this very day!   745

ELSIE. No! no! recall those words – it cannot be!

ENSEMBLE.

KATE *and* CHORUS.	DAME CARRUTHERS *and* PHŒBE.
Oh, day of terror! Day of tears!	Oh, day of terror! Day of tears!
Who is the man who, in his pride,	The man to whom thou art allied
Claims thee as his bride?	Appears to claim thee as his bride.
Day of terror! Day of tears!	Day of terror! Day of tears! 750

LIEUT., MERYLL, *and* WILFRED.	ELSIE.
Come, dry these unbecoming tears,	Oh, Leonard, come thou to my side,
Most joyful tidings greet thine ears,	And claim me as thy loving bride!
The man to whom thou art allied	Day of terror! Day of tears!
Appears to claim thee as his bride.	

757 *All thought of Leonard Meryll:* The pre-production prompt copy, the licence copy, and the draft manuscript have the following lines at this point, crossed out in Gilbert's hand and changed to the present version:

FAIR. (*sternly*).	All thought of Leonard Meryll set aside.
	Thou art mine own! I claim thee as my bride.
ALL.	Thou art his own – his own!
	Alas, he claims thee as his own!

Repeat Ensemble.

ELSIE.	A suppliant at your feet I kneel,
	Thy heart will yield!
FAIR. (*sternly*).	I have a heart that cannot feel,
	It is a heart of tempered steel
	Three times annealed!
ELSIE.	My piteous cry, oh, do not mock,
	But set me free.
FAIR. (*sternly*).	Mine is a heart of massive rock,
	Unmoved by sentimental shock,
	Come thou with me!
CHORUS.	He has a heart of tempered steel,
	That cannot feel.
	He has a heart of massive rock,
	That naught can shock:
	Thy husband he!
ELSIE.	Leonard, my loved one, etc.

(*Flourish. Enter* COLONEL FAIRFAX, *handsomely dressed,* 755
and attended by other Gentlemen.)

FAIR. (*sternly*).	All thought of Leonard Meryll set aside.
	Thou art mine own! I claim thee as my bride.
CHORUS.	Thou art his own! Alas! he claims thee as his bride.
ELSIE.	A suppliant at thy feet I fall; 760
	Thine heart will yield to pity's call!
FAIR.	Mine is a heart of massive rock,
	Unmoved by sentimental shock!
CHORUS.	Thy husband he!
ELSIE (*aside*).	Leonard, my loved one – come to me. 765
	They bear me hence away!
	But though they take me far from thee,
	My heart is thine for aye!
	My bruisèd heart,
	My broken heart, 770
	Is thine, my own, for aye!

(*To* FAIRFAX.)	Sir, I obey!
	I am thy bride;
	But ere the fatal hour
	I said the say 775
	That placed me in thy power
	Would I had died!
	Sir, I obey!
	I am thy bride!

(*Looks up and recognizes* FAIRFAX.) Leonard! 780

FAIR.	My own!

ELSIE.	Ah! (*Embrace.*)

ELSIE *and*	⎰ With happiness my soul is cloyed,
FAIR.	⎱ This is our joy-day unalloyed!
CHORUS.	Yes, yes! 785
	With happiness their souls are cloyed,
	This is their joy-day unalloyed!

(*Enter* JACK POINT.)

POINT.	Oh, thoughtless crew!
	Ye know not what ye do! 790

810 *It's the song of a merrymaid*: Gilbert at first gave Elsie a much less sympathetic parting song. During the first run she sang:

> It's the song of a merrymaid, peerly proud,
> Who loved a lord and who laughed aloud
> At the moan of the merryman moping mum,
> Whose soul was sad and whose glance was glum, etc.

The words were changed by Gilbert to the present version for the first revival in 1897.

821 *Point falls insensible at their feet*: The question of whether Point is meant to die at the end of the opera, or merely to faint, is one that has long exercised Savoyards, and no doubt it always will. The fact is that different actors have interpreted Gilbert's final direction in different ways, and Gilbert himself seems to have been content to leave Jack Point's fate to the audience to decide on as they wished.

According to Sir Henry Lytton, admittedly a somewhat biased source, George Grossmith, who created the role of Point, played the final scene for laughs, falling down in a way that was 'irresistibly funny'. It was even said that when the curtain went down on the first-night performance the 'insensible' jester, lying prostrate on the stage, raised a leg and waggled it in the air. The review in *The Era* certainly commented 'The finale ...ends the opera brightly...and all ends happily'. However, another critic who saw Grossmith in the role of Point on several occasions said 'The pathos of [his] final fall struck me as being very fine indeed'.

The first artist to make Jack Point 'die' at the end of the opera was George Thorne, who played the role in the first provincial tour of *The Yeomen*, which opened in Manchester on 1 November 1888. A fortnight later Henry Lytton, playing in another D'Oyly Carte touring company, introduced a similarly tragic ending at a performance in Bath.

Lytton continued his tragic interpretation of the final scene right through until his last appearance with the D'Oyly Carte Company, appropriately playing the role of Point, in Dublin on 30 June 1934. In his book *The Secrets of a Savoyard* he maintained that Gilbert had always intended Point to die and had only toned down the ending in response to Grossmith's reputation as a great jester and his feeling that, whatever he did at the end, the audience would laugh.

Lytton says in his book that he once asked Gilbert if his tragic portrayal of Point should be modified in any way. 'No' was the dramatist's reported reply. 'Keep on like that. It is just what I want. Jack Point should die and the end of the opera should be a tragedy.'

That supposed remark, however, almost certainly gives a false impression of Gilbert's feelings about this scene. He had plenty of opportunities in successive editions of the libretto to change the word 'insensible' to 'dead' if he wanted to make absolutely clear that he meant the ending to be tragic. Yet he never did so. Nor are his early directions in the licence copy or pre-production prompt-book any stronger on this point. The only direction which appears in these early editions of the libretto, and not subsequently, is that 'As Point falls *except* Warders point towards him'.

The best guide to Gilbert's intentions in this scene is the remark which he made to J. M. Gordon, the D'Oyly Carte stage manager after Lytton had 'died' on stage: 'The fate of Jack Point is in the hands of the audience, who may please themselves whether he lives or dies'. Gordon adds in his manuscript reminiscences, *The Making of a Stage Manager and Producer*, 'This is the only direct statement from Gilbert on the subject and confirms the directions on the libretto'.

Attend to me, and shed a tear or two –
For I have a song to sing, O!

CHORUS.   Sing me your song, O!

POINT.   It is sung to the moon
                    By a love-lorn loon,   795
             Who fled from the mocking throng, O!
It's the song of a merryman, moping mum,
Whose soul was sad, and whose glance was glum,
Who sipped no sup, and who craved no crumb,
      As he sighed for the love of a ladye!   800

CHORUS.   Heighdy! heighdy!
                    Misery me, lackadaydee!
      He sipped no sup, and he craved no crumb,
      As he sighed for the love of a ladye!

ELSIE.   I have a song to sing, O!   805

CHORUS.   What is your song, O?

ELSIE.   It is sung with the ring
                    Of the songs maids sing
             Who love with a love life-long, O!
It's the song of a merrymaid, nestling near,   810
Who loved her lord – but who dropped a tear
At the moan of the merryman, moping mum,
Whose soul was sad, and whose glance was glum,
Who sipped no sup, and who craved no crumb,
      As he sighed for the love of a ladye!   815

CHORUS.   Heighdy! heighdy!
                    Misery me, lackadaydee!
      He sipped no sup, and he craved no crumb,
      As he sighed for the love of a ladye!
             Heighdy! Heighdy! Heighdy!   820

(FAIRFAX *embraces* ELSIE *as* POINT *falls insensible at their feet.*)

CURTAIN

THE GONDOLIERS

or

The King of Barataria

DRAMATIS PERSONÆ

THE DUKE OF PLAZA-TORO (*a Grandee of Spain*)
LUIZ (*his Attendant*)
DON ALHAMBRA DEL BOLERO (*the Grand Inquisitor*)
MARCO PALMIERI ⎫
GIUSEPPE PALMIERI ⎪
ANTONIO ⎪
FRANCESCO ⎬ (*Venetian Gondoliers*)
GIORGIO ⎪
ANNIBALE ⎭
THE DUCHESS OF PLAZA-TORO
CASILDA (*her Daughter*)
GIANETTA ⎫
TESSA ⎪
FIAMETTA ⎬ (*Contadine*)
VITTORIA ⎪
GIULIA ⎭
INEZ (*the King's Foster-mother*)

Chorus of Gondoliers and Contadine, Men-at-Arms, Heralds, and Pages.

ACT I. – The Piazzetta, Venice.
ACT II. – Pavilion in the Palace of Barataria.

(*An interval of three months is supposed to elapse between Acts I and II.*)

Date – 1750.

THE GONDOLIERS

The Gondoliers was not conceived in the most auspicious circumstances. Sullivan had found *The Yeomen of the Guard* a great deal more to his taste than the earlier Savoy Operas and it had quickened his resolve to turn his talents to grand opera. Gilbert, however, mindful of the relative lack of success of their latest collaboration compared to that of their lighter works, urged that they work together on another comic opera. His suggestion, put to Sullivan while the latter was on a tour of the Continent in March 1889, drew a distinctly negative response:

I have lost the liking for comic opera and entertain very great doubts about my power of doing it. You yourself have reproached me directly and indirectly with the seriousness of my music, fitted more for the cathedral than the comic opera stage, and I cannot but feel that in many cases the reproach is just. I have lost the necessary nerve for it, and it is not too much to say that it is distasteful to me. The types used over and over again (unavoidable in a company like ours), the Grossmith part, the middle-aged woman with fading charms, cannot again be clothed with music by me. Nor can I write again to any wildly improbable plot in which there is not some human interest.

You say that in a serious opera, you must more or less sacrifice yourself. I say that this is just what I have been doing in all our joint pieces, and, what is more, must continue to do in comic opera to make it successful. Business and syllabic setting assume an importance which, however much they fetter me, cannot be overlooked. I am bound, in the interests of the piece, to give way. Hence the reason of my wishing to do a work where the music is to be the first consideration – where words are to suggest music, not govern it.

Gilbert replied in even more emphatic terms:

If you are really under the astounding impression that you have been effacing yourself during the last twelve years – and if you are in earnest when you say that you wish to write an opera with me in which 'the music shall be the first consideration' (by which I understand an opera in which the libretto, and consequently the librettist, must occupy a subordinate place) there is certainly no 'modus vivendi' to be found that shall be satisfactory to both of us.

You are an adept in your profession, and I am an adept in mine. If we meet, it is to be as master and master – not master and servant.

A lively correspondence across the Channel ensued, becoming gradually less acerbic, partly because of the intervention of Richard D'Oyly Carte, who suggested that Sullivan might be able to combine working on a grand opera with

another librettist and producing another lighter work with Gilbert and also
perhaps because of the soothing effects on the composer of a particularly happy sojourn in Venice. On his return from his Continental jaunt in April, Sullivan wrote to Gilbert in much more conciliatory mood, indicating that 'there
should now be no difficulty in working harmoniously together in another piece,
as we both thoroughly understand the position, and I am quite prepared to set
to work at once upon a light or comic opera with you (provided of course that
we are thoroughly agreed upon the subject) and to think no more of our rather
sharp discussion'. The following month he offered further encouragement to
Gilbert:

I understand from Carte some time ago that you had some subject connected with Venice and Venetian life, and this seemed to me to hold out great chances of bright colour
and taking music. Can you not develop this with something we can both go into with
warmth and enthusiasm and thus give me a subject in which (like the *Mikado* or *Patience*)
we can both be interested, which will relieve all necessity for argument and discussion?

Gilbert was also happy to join in this new-found mood of conciliation. When
he sent Sullivan the first instalment of the new work on 1 July, not only was it
the Venetian piece rather than the story of a travelling theatrical company
which the librettist himself preferred, but there was a further olive branch in
the form of an opening sequence which gave the composer fifteen minutes of
music without any interruption.

Both men spent longer on *The Gondoliers* than they had on their previous
works. Gilbert took the best part of five months to write the libretto, a brilliant
satire on the emerging enthusiasm for republicanism and egalitarianism, and
Sullivan was occupied on the music for the whole of the summer of 1889, which
he spent at Weybridge, Surrey. He received the songs to be set one or two at a
time, and numerous letters passed between composer and librettist about re-
drafting or dropping particular numbers once the overall structure of the work
became clearer.

The comparatively long period of preparation did not prevent the run-up to
the opening performance being a frantic rush. Sullivan did not have his first orchestral rehearsal until five days before the London first night. After taking the
rehearsal, he dined at home and then sat down until three the following morning composing the overture. He was up again after only a few hours' sleep to
agree with Gilbert the title of the piece, which had, characteristically, been left
to the last minute. Two days later the dress rehearsal lasted for a marathon seven hours.

The Gondoliers opened at the Savoy Theatre on 7 December 1889 and ran for
559 performances until 20 June 1891. The critics were almost unanimous in
their praise, and the audience's reaction was little short of ecstatic. In the United States, however, its reception was markedly cooler. A D'Oyly Carte company sailed out from Britain in secret to beat the pirates and opened at the
Park Theater, New York, on 7 January 1890. Their lack of success at the box

office earned the opera the nickname 'The Gone Dollars', and D'Oyly Carte himself came out to revamp the production. Even in its new form, it only ran until April, by which time no fewer than seven actors had been tried in the role of the Duke of Plaza-Toro. Meanwhile a pirate company in New Jersey was having rather more success with a hammed-up version in which the Grand Inquisitor dropped a real tear, with a splash worked from the wings, and Marco and Giuseppe were discovered on stage at the beginning of Act II busily ironing their shirts.

In some ways *The Gondoliers* stands as the supreme achievement of the distinct yet united talents of Gilbert and Sullivan. The libretto manages to pack a considerable satirical punch without being either heavy-handed or overtly silly. It also enabled Sullivan to achieve his object of making his music more dominant than it had been in earlier works. Of the forty-seven pages in the original edition of the libretto, only fourteen are dialogue. *The Gondoliers* has the longest vocal score of any of the Savoy Operas, including the three-act *Princess Ida*.

Happily, the opera's success inspired from both composer and librettist rare but heartfelt tributes to the talents of the other. Gilbert wrote to Sullivan the morning after the opening night: 'I must thank you for the magnificent work you have put into the piece. It gives one the chance of shining right through the twentieth century with a reflected light.' Sullivan replied, 'Don't talk of reflected light. In such a perfect book as *The Gondoliers* you shone with an individual brilliancy which no other writer can hope to attain.' A case, for once, of a librettist and composer 'who act in perfect unity'!

The Gondoliers has not been without controversy in recent years. A bizarre and ill-conceived production by Tim Hopkins which was chosen to launch the revived D'Oyly Carte Opera Company's first season at its Birmingham base was greeted with prolonged booing by a section of the audience at its gala opening night in the city's Alexandra Theatre on 7 March 1991. What particularly offended traditionalists was a garish set which seemed to belong to the world of Pop Art rather than operetta and an unending series of vulgar and distracting gimmicks which diverted attention from both words and music, which were performed to a very high standard. In the first act the cast were forced to perform on a steeply raked block of undulating orange waves and to contend with a fascist-like red and white banner, an exclamation mark in its centre, which was pulled across the stage at every opportunity. Wholly inappropriate appearances were made by a corgi in a car and a fox resembling the television character 'Basil Brush', while a further incongruity involved the chorus in Act II gathered around a television set that had somehow found its way into the Baratarian Court. If the company's intention was to secure publicity, then it certainly succeeded – a report of the outrage that greeted the opening night appeared on the front page of *The Times* – but I am glad to say that there have been no further productions of this kind and I think we can rest assured that when the new D'Oyly Carte Company next performs *The Gondoliers* it will be with more traditional and appropriate staging and business.

1   *Scene*: The Piazzetta in Venice lies to the south-east of St Mark's Square and is one of the
main tourist attractions in that most romantic of all European cities. Gilbert's stage direction establishes that the audience is looking at the Piazzetta from the north side, i.e.
as though from St Mark's Square. On the left (stage right) is the famous Doge's Palace,
built in the fourteenth and fifteenth centuries, faced with pink and white marble arranged in a diamond pattern, and with its two arcades of delicately traceried windows.
In his book *The Stones of Venice*, published in 1853, the great Victorian art critic John
Ruskin described the palace as the perfect union of Gothic and early Renaissance styles
and 'the central building of the world'.

   To be totally faithful to the location, the backcloth for this act should show the lagoon
with the island of San Giorgio Maggiore in the distance and, in the foreground, the two
great columns which were brought from the east in the twelfth century and erected at
the top of the steps leading down to the water's edge. One is surmounted by a winged
lion, the heraldic emblem of the Venetian Republic, and the other by a statue of St
Theodore, the city's patron saint.

4–35   *List and learn, ye dainty roses*

This chorus begins a sequence of music which continues, unbroken by dialogue, for
more than eighteen minutes. It is the longest opening sequence and very nearly the
longest continuous passage of music in any of the Savoy Operas, being only marginally
shorter than the Act I finale to *Iolanthe*.

   There is some evidence that Gilbert had originally intended to have a very different
style of opening chorus which would establish the political theme of the opera. He had
apparently got the initial idea for *The Gondoliers* from a book on Venice in the fifteenth
century which made much of the city's strong republicanism. Gilbert saw that a satire
on republican ideas would have an appeal to a contemporary audience. More than fifty
Republican Clubs had been established in Britain in the 1870s, and anti-monarchical
and pro-egalitarian principles were also being vociferously championed by the various
groups which grew up in the 1880s to propagate the new creed of socialism.

   According to Leslie Baily in his *Gilbert and Sullivan Book*, Gilbert's original manuscript contained an opening chorus which introduced

>A people, dignified and polished,
>Who class-distinctions have abolished,
>And one and all with zeal combine
>To make their monarch toe the line.

I have not been able to trace this original manuscript, but it is interesting that the lines
quoted by Baily occur in the song written for Pietro at the beginning of Act II but cut
out before the first performance (see the note to Act II, lines 15–22). I wonder if, in fact,

ACT I

SCENE. – THE PIAZZETTA, VENICE. *The Ducal Palace on the right.*
FIAMETTA, GIULIA, VITTORIA, *and other Contadine discovered, each*
tying a bouquet of roses.

CHORUS OF CONTADINE.

List and learn, ye dainty roses,
  Roses white and roses red,   5
Why we bind you into posies
  Ere your morning bloom has fled.
By a law of maiden's making,
Accents of a heart that's aching,
Even though that heart be breaking,   10
  Should by maiden be unsaid:
Though they love with love exceeding,
They must seem to be unheeding –
Go ye then and do their pleading,
  Roses white and roses red!   15

FIAMETTA.

Two there are for whom, in duty,
  Every maid in Venice sighs –
Two so peerless in their beauty
  That they shame the summer skies.
We have hearts for them, in plenty,   20
  They have hearts, but all too few,
We, alas, are four-and-twenty!
  They, alas, are only two!
We, alas!

CHORUS.   Alas!   25
FIA. Are four-and-twenty,
  They, alas!

it was this number to which Leslie Baily was referring. It is, of course, quite possible that the lines were originally written for an opening chorus in Act I and later transferred to the song in Act II.

Either way, this seems to be the so-called 'growling chorus' to which Gilbert refers in a letter to Sullivan in August 1889. Sullivan did not like the chorus. If it was, indeed, written for the start of Act I one can see that he would feel that it jarred with the generally romantic and light-hearted atmosphere of the rest of the opera's opening. Gilbert, however, was unhappy about cutting it out:

> It seems to me that the piece as it stands at present wants it. The Venetians of the fifteenth century were red-hot Republicans. One of their party is made king and invites his friends to form a Court. They object because they are Republicans. He replies that he has considered that and proposed to institute a Court in which all people shall be equal, and to this they agree. In Act II the absurdity of this state of things is shown. Without the dissatisfaction expressed by the 'Growling' chorus (which can be rewritten if it won't do in its present form) the story would be unintelligible.

Sullivan had his way, however. The 'growling chorus' was cut and the republican theme overall was less emphasized than Gilbert had apparently first intended.

Gilbert's letter to Sullivan also shows that another major change was made to the overall structure of the opera during the summer months in which both composer and librettist worked on it. Gilbert apparently planned initially to set the action in the fifteenth century, when the Venetian Republic was at the height of its power and influence. However, he later shifted it to the mid-eighteenth century, by which time Venice was no longer of political importance. At the end of that century, indeed, it lost its independence, being handed over by Napoleon to the Austrians. It remained under Austrian rule for much of the nineteenth century, becoming part of the newly unified country of Italy in 1866. The reason for this shift in the dating of the opera is unclear. Apart from the Duke of Plaza-Toro's reference to Wesleyan Methodism (Act I, line 311), there is not very much in the libretto which is incompatible with a fifteenth-century setting. The Duke's status as a limited company would, of course, be somewhat anachronistic, but so it is in the present mid-eighteenth-century setting.

54 *dolce far niente*: The first of several genuine Italian expressions introduced into *The Gondoliers*. Its literal meaning is 'sweet doing nothing', i.e. delightful idleness. It also makes an appearance in Act I of *Iolanthe*, when Lord Mountararat sings of Strephon 'A-taking of his *dolce far niente*', and in Act I of *Utopia Limited*, where the guards, nobles and dancing girls 'Sing the songs of *far niente*'.

55 *contradicente*: From the Italian (and Latin) word *contradico*, meaning to contradict, gainsay or deny. It is used in Britain in the form *nemine contradicente*, usually shortened to *nem. con.*, to mean unanimously, with no dissent. The word also occurs in the Act I finale of *Iolanthe*.

CHORUS.	Alas!
FIA.	Are only two.
CHORUS.	They, alas, are only two, alas! 30
	Now ye know, ye dainty roses,
	Roses white and roses red,
	Why we bind you into posies,
	Ere your morning bloom has fled,
	Roses white and roses red! 35

(*During this chorus* ANTONIO, FRANCESCO, GIORGIO, *and other Gondoliers have entered unobserved by the Girls – at first two, then two more, then four, then half a dozen, then the remainder of the Chorus.*)

SOLI.

FRANC.	Good morrow, pretty maids; for whom prepare ye
	These floral tributes extraordinary? 40
FIA.	For Marco and Giuseppe Palmieri,
	The pink and flower of all the Gondolieri.
GIU.	They're coming here, as we have heard but lately,
	To choose two brides from us who sit sedately.
ANT.	Do all you maidens love them? 45
ALL.	Passionately!
ANT.	These gondoliers are to be envied greatly!
GIOR.	But what of us, who one and all adore you?
	Have pity on our passion, we implore you!
FIA.	These gentlemen must make their choice before you; 50
VIT.	In the meantime we tacitly ignore you.
GIU.	When they have chosen two that leaves you plenty –
	Two dozen we, and ye are four-and-twenty.
FIA. *and* VIT.	Till then, enjoy your *dolce far niente*.
ANT.	With pleasure, nobody *contradicente*! 55

SONG – ANTONIO *and* CHORUS.

For the merriest fellows are we, tra la,
That ply on the emerald sea, tra la;
     With loving and laughing,
     And quipping and quaffing,
We're happy as happy can be, tra la –   60
     With loving and laughing, etc.

With sorrow we've nothing to do, tra la,
And care is a thing to pooh-pooh, tra la;

71 *ben'venuti*: Welcome. The phrase derives from the words *bene*, meaning well, and the verb *venire*, to come.

75–95 *Buon'giorno, signorine*
The exchange in Italian between Marco and Giuseppe and the chorus of girls translates as follows:

> MAR. *and* GIU.   Good morning, young ladies!
> GIRLS.   Dearest gondoliers!
>   We are country maidens!
> MAR. *and* GIU. (*bowing*).   Your humble servants!
>   For whom are these flowers –
>   These most beautiful flowers?
> GIRLS.   For you, good gentlemen,
>   O most excellent!

> (*The Girls present their bouquets to* MARCO *and* GIUSEPPE, *who are overwhelmed with them, and carry them with difficulty.*)

> MAR. *and* GIU. (*their arms full of flowers*).   O heaven! O heaven!
> GIRLS.   Good morning, cavaliers!
> MAR. *and* GIU. (*deprecatingly*).   We are gondoliers.
>   (*To* FIA. *and* VIT.)   Young lady, I love you!
> GIRLS (*deprecatingly*).   We are country maidens.
> MAR. *and* GIU.   Young ladies!
> GIRLS (*deprecatingly*).   Country maidens!
>   (*Curtseying to* MAR. *and* GIU.)   Cavaliers!
> MAR. *and* GIU. (*deprecatingly*).   Gondoliers!
>   Poor gondoliers!
> CHORUS.   Good morning, young ladies, etc.

96–120 *We're called gondolieri*
Sullivan deliberately chose an Italian folk-song idiom for this seductively lazy and lilting song in which the two principal gondoliers introduce themselves. Its elongated cadences are, in fact, more reminiscent of the Neapolitan than the Venetian style.

The trade plied by Marco and Giuseppe is, of course, an old and distinguished one in the city of Venice with its twenty-eight miles of waterways. Gondolas have been in use there since the early Middle Ages, although it was not until the seventeenth century that they took on their present distinctive long, sleek, double-ended shape. In keeping

And Jealousy yellow,
Unfortunate fellow, 65
We drown in the shimmering blue, tra la –
And Jealousy yellow, etc.

FIA. (*looking off*). See, see, at last they come to make their choice –
    Let us acclaim them with united voice.

(MARCO *and* GIUSEPPE *appear in gondola at back*.) 70

CHORUS (*Girls*). Hail, hail! gallant gondolieri, ben' venuti! ben' venuti!
    Accept our love, our homage, and our duty.
    Ben' venuti! ben' venuti!

(MARCO *and* GIUSEPPE *jump ashore – the Girls salute them*.)

DUET – MARCO *and* GIUSEPPE, *with* CHORUS OF GIRLS.

MAR. *and* GIU.	Buon' giorno, signorine! 75
GIRLS.	Gondolieri carissimi!
	Siamo contadine!
MAR. *and* GIU. (*bowing*).	Servitori umilissimi!
	Per chi questi fiori –
	Questi fiori bellissimi? 80
GIRLS.	Per voi, bei signori,
	O eccellentissimi!

(*The Girls present their bouquets to* MARCO *and* GIUSEPPE, *who are*
overwhelmed with them, and carry them with difficulty.)

MAR. *and* GIU. (*their arms full of flowers*).	O ciel'! O ciel'! 85
GIRLS.	Buon' giorno, cavalieri!
MAR. *and* GIU. (*deprecatingly*).	Siamo gondolieri.
(*To* FIA. *and* VIT.)	Signorina, io t' amo!
GIRLS (*deprecatingly*).	Contadine siamo.
MAR. *and* GIU.	Signorine! 90
GIRLS (*deprecatingly*).	Contadine!
(*Curtseying to* MAR. *and* GIU.)	Cavalieri.
MAR. *and* GIU. (*deprecatingly*).	Gondolieri!
	Poveri gondolieri!
CHORUS.	Buon' giorno, signorine, etc. 95

DUET – MARCO *and* GIUSEPPE.

We're called *gondolieri*,
But that's a vagary,

with the Venetians' dislike of ostentation in civil dress and decoration, an ordinance of 1562 laid down that all gondolas should be painted black, and so they have remained ever since.

102 *To beauty devoted*: This line was originally 'To ladies devoted' and was changed in the third edition of the libretto. 'To beauty devoted' is, however, found in all editions of the vocal score.

126 *A bias to disclose*: Helen D'Oyly Carte's annotated copy of the libretto prepared for the 1907 revival has this line struck out and 'To pitch on these or those' substituted. The line also occurs in that form in Sullivan's autograph score and the prompt copy in the British Library. The present version was re-introduced in the libretto in 1914.

131 *Viva*: Hurrah.

It's quite honorary
    The trade that we ply.
For gallantry noted   100
Since we were short-coated,
To beauty devoted,
    Giuseppe ⎱
    Are Marco ⎰ and I;
When morning is breaking,
Our couches forsaking,   105
To greet their awaking
    With carols we come.
At summer day's nooning,
When weary lagooning,
Our mandolins tuning,   110
    We lazily thrum.
When vespers are ringing,
To hope ever clinging,
With songs of our singing
    A vigil we keep,   115
When daylight is fading,
Enwrapt in night's shading,
With soft serenading
    We sing them to sleep.
We're called *gondolieri*, etc.   120

RECITATIVE – MARCO *and* GIUSEPPE.

MAR.	And now to choose our brides!
GIU.	As all are young and fair,
	And amiable besides,
BOTH.	We really do not care
	A preference to declare. 125
MAR.	A bias to disclose
	Would be indelicate –
GIU.	And therefore we propose
	To let impartial Fate
	Select for us a mate! 130
ALL.	Viva!
GIRLS.	A bias to disclose
	Would be indelicate –
MEN.	But how do they propose
	To let impartial Fate 135
	Select for them a mate?
GIU.	These handkerchiefs upon our eyes be good enough to bind,

166–70 *My papa he keeps three horses*

Although this sounds like an old nursery rhyme, and Sullivan's tune is strongly reminiscent of a children's chant, I think the words are original to Gilbert. I can find no trace of them in either the *Oxford Dictionary of Nursery Rhymes* compiled by Iona and Peter Opie or the same authors' *Children's Games in Street and Playground*.

172 *Business of blind-man's buff*: This, by contrast, goes back long before Gilbert, of course. The Opies describe it as probably the best-known of all children's games in Britain and cite references to it dating back to the sixteenth century. They also point out that the game is known in Italian as *mosca cieca* ('blind fly'), which is, presumably, how Marco and Giuseppe would have known it.

Characteristically, Gilbert took immense trouble over this bit of business and he drilled the cast in it for three whole days before the opening performance. In a letter to Helen D'Oyly Carte in July 1898 he wrote: 'If you revive *The Gondoliers* I hope you will take care to have at least three chorus rehearsals for business. The ladies got fearfully slack towards the end of the run – in the blindfold scene they used to walk in circles instead of dancing.'

MAR.   And take good care that both of us are absolutely blind;
BOTH.   Then turn us round – and we, with all convenient despatch,
        Will undertake to marry any two of you we catch!   140
ALL.   Viva!

They undertake to marry any two of $\left\{\begin{array}{l}\text{us they catch!}\\\text{them they catch!}\end{array}\right.$

(*The Girls prepare to bind their eyes as directed.*)

FIA. (*to* MARCO).   Are you peeping?
                      Can you see me?   145
MAR.   Dark I'm keeping,
                      Dark and dreamy!   (MARCO *shyly lifts bandage*.)
VIT. (*to* GIUSEPPE). If you're blinded
                      Truly, say so.
GIU.   All right-minded   150
                      Players play so!   (*shyly lifts bandage*).
FIA. (*detecting* MARCO). Conduct shady!
                      They are cheating!
                      Surely they de-
                      Serve a beating!   (*replaces bandage*).   155
VIT. (*detecting* GIUSEPPE). This too much is;
                      Maidens mocking –
                      Conduct such is
                      Truly shocking!   (*replaces bandage*).
GIRLS.   You can spy, sir!   160
                      Shut your eye, sir!
                      You may use it by and by, sir!
ALL.   You can see, sir!
                      Don't tell me, sir!
                      That will do – now let it be, sir!   165
CHORUS OF   My papa he keeps three horses,
GIRLS.   Black, and white, and dapple grey, sir;
                      Turn three times, then take your courses,
                      Catch whichever girl you may, sir!
CHORUS OF MEN.   My papa, etc.   170

(MARCO *and* GIUSEPPE *turn round, as directed, and try to catch the girls.
Business of blind-man's buff. Eventually* MARCO *catches* GIANETTA, *and*
GIUSEPPE *catches* TESSA. *The two girls try to escape, but in vain. The two
men pass their hands over the girls' faces to discover their identity.*)

GIU.   I've at length achieved a capture!   175
(*Guessing.*) This is Tessa! (*removes bandage*). Rapture, rapture!

205–16 *Thank you, gallant gondolieri*

On the opening night the chorus of girls did not simply repeat Gianetta's opening verse as they do now, but had their own slightly different version of the song:

> To these gallant *gondolieri*,
>> In a set and formal measure,
> It is scarcely necessary
>> To express their pride and pleasure.
>> Each of us to prove a treasure,
> Conjugal and monetary,
>> Gladly will devote her leisure,
> To the other *gondolieri*!
> Tra, la, la, la, la, la, etc.

219 *A gondola arrives at the Piazzetta steps*: In his autobiography, *A Wandering Minstrel*, Sir Henry Lytton recalls an opening night in New York when the D'Oyly Carte gondola had been lost in transit from Britain and a substitute had to be constructed out of soap boxes. It fell to pieces as it was being pulled across the back of the stage and so Lytton, playing the part of the Duke of Plaza-Toro, abandoned the presumably sinking craft and pretended to rescue his wife and daughter and swim ashore. As he made his way to the front of the stage to begin 'From the sunny Spanish shore', a voice from the audience cried 'You ain't very wet, mister.'

CHORUS.	Rapture, rapture!	
MAR. (*guessing*).	To me Gianetta fate has granted!	(*removes bandage*).
	Just the very girl I wanted!	
CHORUS.	Just the very girl he wanted!	180
GIU. (*politely to* MAR.).	If you'd rather change –	
TESS.	My goodness!	
	This indeed is simple rudeness.	
MAR. (*politely to* GIU.).	I've no preference whatever –	
GIA.	Listen to him! Well, I never!	185

(*Each man kisses each girl.*)

GIA.

> Thank you, gallant *gondolieri*!
> > In a set and formal measure
> It is scarcely necessary
> > To express our pleasure.   190
> > Each of us to prove a treasure,
> Conjugal and monetary,
> > Gladly will devote our leisure,
> Gallant *gondolieri*.
> > Tra, la, la, la, la, la, etc.   195

TESS.

> Gay and gallant *gondolieri*,
> > Take us both and hold us tightly,
> You have luck extraordinary;
> > We might have been unsightly!
> > If we judge your conduct rightly,   200
> 'Twas a choice involuntary;
> > Still we thank you most politely,
> Gay and gallant *gondolieri*!
> > Tra, la, la, la, la, la, etc.

CHORUS OF GIRLS.

> Thank you, gallant *gondolieri*;   205
> > In a set and formal measure,
> It is scarcely necessary
> > To express our pleasure.
> > Each of us to prove a treasure
> > Gladly will devote our leisure,   210
> Gay and gallant *gondolieri*!
> > Tra, la, la, la, la, la, etc.

ALL.

> Fate in this has put his finger –
> > Let us bow to Fate's decree,
> Then no longer let us linger,   215
> > To the altar hurry we!

(*They all dance off two and two –* GIANETTA *with* MARCO,
TESSA *with* GIUSEPPE.)

224-43 *From the sunny Spanish shore*
The clear implication of this song is that the Duke of Plaza-Toro and his suite have made the entire journey from Spain to 'Venetia's shores' by sea, rather than taking the shorter route of sailing over to Genoa and then crossing to Venice by land. If that is indeed the case, then it is no wonder that they never want to cross the sea again.

The autograph score of *The Gondoliers* contains an earlier version of this song which began 'From the country of the Cid,/The Duke of Valladolid'. Gilbert rewrote it to produce the present version before the opening night.

234 *that Grandee from the Spanish shore*: 'Grandee' was the term used in Spain or Portugal for a nobleman of the highest rank, one of whose distinguishing privileges was that he could wear his hat in the presence of royalty. The Duke of Plaza-Toro later contradicts this exalted description of his position by telling us (line 245) that he is a hidalgo, i.e. a member of the lowest order of Spanish nobility. I suspect that the latter is a more truthful description of his status, but 'grandee' sounds good in the song.

243 *Cross the sea again*: In the licence copy sent to the Lord Chamberlain for vetting, there follows at this point a song which was cut out before the opening night and has never been performed.

SOLO – DUCHESS.

The Duke of Plaza-Tor'
　　Though poor in purse and land,
He owns a goodly store
　　Of condescension bland;
And that, when it comes from a Ducal chair,
Is a coin that's current everywhere.

ALL.　　　　　　Yes, everywhere!
　　　　　　　　Yes, everywhere!
　　　　　　　　It's a coin that's current everywhere.

DUCH.　　　　　And of all the Dukes who have coin to spare,
　　　　　　　　That haughty Duke can alone declare
　　　　　　　　That he always pays his bills of fare
　　　　　　　　With a coin that is current everywhere!

ALL.　　　　　　With a coin, etc.

DUCH.　　　　　With words of gracious praise,
　　　　　　　　　And high-flown compliment,
　　　　　　　　And condescending ways,
　　　　　　　　　And bunkum eloquent,
　　　　　　　　And bows of stately etiquette,
　　　　　　　　He every day pays every debt.

ALL.　　　　　　Pays every debt!
　　　　　　　　Pays every debt!
　　　　　　　　He every day pays every debt.

DUCH.　　　　　And of all the Dukes I have known as yet,
　　　　　　　　In our own exclusive high-born set,
　　　　　　　　He's the only Duke I've ever met
　　　　　　　　Who every day pays every debt.

ALL.　　　　　　And of all the Dukes, etc.

245 *it is here that the Grand Inquisitor resides*: It is something of a mystery why the Grand Inquisitor of Spain (for so Don Alhambra is identified in line 484) should be residing in the Doge's Palace in Venice. The abduction of the young heir to the Baratarian throne, which originally brought him there, took place many years before the action of the opera. It is

(*Flourish. A gondola arrives at the Piazzetta steps, from which enter the* DUKE OF PLAZA-TORO, *the* DUCHESS, *their daughter* CASILDA, *and their attendant* LUIZ, *who carries a drum. All are dressed in pompous but old and faded clothes.*)   220

(*Entrance of* DUKE, DUCHESS, CASILDA, *and* LUIZ.)

DUKE.	From the sunny Spanish shore,
	The Duke of Plaza-Tor' –
DUCH.	And His Grace's Duchess true –
CAS.	And His Grace's daughter, too –
LUIZ.	And His Grace's private drum
	To Venetia's shores have come:
ALL.	If ever, ever, ever
	They get back to Spain,
	They will never, never, never
	Cross the sea again –
DUKE.	Neither that Grandee from the Spanish shore,
	The noble Duke of Plaza Tor –
DUCH.	Nor His Grace's Duchess, staunch and true –
CAS.	You may add, His Grace's daughter, too –
LUIZ.	Nor His Grace's own particular drum
	To Venetia's shores will come:
ALL.	If ever, ever, ever
	They get back to Spain,
	They will never, never, never
	Cross the sea again!

225

230

235

240

DUKE. At last we have arrived at our destination. This is the Ducal Palace, and it is here that the Grand Inquisitor resides. As a Castilian hidalgo of ninety-five quarterings, I regret that I am unable to pay my state visit on a horse. As a Castilian hidalgo of that description, I should have preferred to ride through the streets of Venice; but owing, I presume, to an unusually wet season, the streets are in such a condition that equestrian exercise is impracticable. No matter. Where is our suite?   245

LUIZ (*coming forward*). Your Grace, I am here.

DUCH. Why do you not do yourself the honour to kneel when you address His Grace?

DUKE. My love, it is so small a matter! (*To* LUIZ.) Still, you may as well do it. (LUIZ *kneels.*)   255

CAS. The young man seems to entertain but an imperfect appreciation of the respect due from a menial to a Castilian hidalgo.

DUKE. My child, you are hard upon our suite.

CAS. Papa, I've no patience with the presumption of persons in his

250

true that parts of Italy were under Spanish rule in the mid-eighteenth century, and therefore, presumably, under the jurisdiction of the Spanish Inquisition (on which see the note to line 427). They did not, however, include Venice, which retained its staunch republican independence. Indeed one would have thought that a Spanish Grand Inquisitor would not be at all welcome in that city. But perhaps Don Alhambra found the Doge's instruments of torture infinitely more exciting than those back home.

246 *of ninety-five quarterings*: 'Quarterings' are the divisions on a heraldic shield, each containing a different coat of arms and indicating the number of noble families from which the owner of the shield is descended. Plaza-Toro is here maintaining that his family has, over the years, married into ninety-five other blue-blooded families. In a version of *The Gondoliers* apparently adapted by Helen D'Oyly Carte in the 1900s for performance in the United States, this line was altered to 'possessing nineteen castles, all in Spain, and nearly all ruined'.

249 *the streets are in such a condition*: This line recalls the celebrated cable which the American humorist Robert Benchley (1889–1945) sent back to New York after arriving in Venice: 'Streets full of water. Please advise'. In the American version of the libretto mentioned above, this line is changed to 'The streets are so uncomfortably damp that equestrian exercise is impracticable'.

259 *I've no patience . . .* : Decima Moore, who was brought into the D'Oyly Carte Opera Company as a totally inexperienced newcomer at the age of eighteen to create the role of Casilda, later gave the following description of Gilbert's unique method of training his actors:

> Exact diction; every word to be heard at the back of the dress circle; the rhythm of the lines to be scrupulously followed. He would read a line of dialogue out, clapping his hands between the words to emphasize their rhythm, thus: 'I've no patience (clap) with the presumption (clap) of persons (clap) in his plebeian (clap) position.'

264 *halberdiers*: Soldiers, and in particular civic guards, who carry halberds, a combination of a spear and battle-axe consisting of a sharp-edged blade mounted on a handle, often as a badge of office.

278 *cornet-à-piston*: A brass instrument, more commonly known simply as a cornet, with valves or pistons for producing notes additional to the natural harmonics.

The exchange about the cornet-à-piston, and, indeed, everything from 'Well, let us hope' in line 277 to 'our suite's feelings' in line 286, were cut from many old D'Oyly Carte productions, although they were reinstated shortly before the company's demise.

In the version of the libretto prepared for American audiences and mentioned above (in the note to line 246), this passage of dialogue was rewritten as follows:

> DUKE. Well, let us hope that the Grand Inquisitor may also prove to be a deaf gentleman. However a trumpeter to announce our approach appears essential. You do not happen to possess the accomplishment of ta-ran-ta-ra-ing like a trumpet?
> LUIZ. Alas, no, Your Grace! But my imitation of a cat is invariably received with great applause.
> DUKE. I don't see how that would help us, etc.

287-8 *the Duke of Plaza-Toro, Count Matadoro, Baron Picadoro*: All these titles are derived from the national Spanish sport of bull-fighting. Plaza-Toro means literally 'the place of the bull', i.e. the arena. The matador is the official who waves a red handkerchief in front of the bull to work up its anger, while the picador further torments the unfortunate creature by attacking it with a lance. The final assault is, of course, left to the toreador.

305 *Barataria*: Gilbert takes the name of his imaginary island 'That lies in a Southern sea' from Miguel De Cervantes' famous story *Don Quixote*. Readers of that work will recall that Barataria was the island 'surrounded by land' of which Don Quixote made his faithful companion Sancho Panza governor. The description of the latter's arrival in Barataria

plebeian position. If he does not appreciate that position, let him be whipped   260
until he does.

DUKE. Let us hope the omission was not intended as a slight. I should
be much hurt if I thought it was. So would he. (*To* LUIZ.) Where are the
halberdiers who were to have had the honour of meeting us here, that our
visit to the Grand Inquisitor might be made in becoming state?   265

LUIZ. Your Grace, the halberdiers are mercenary people who stipulated
for a trifle on account.

DUKE. How tiresome! Well, let us hope the Grand Inquisitor is a blind
gentleman. And the band who were to have had the honour of escorting us?
I see no band!   270

LUIZ. Your Grace, the band are sordid persons who required to be paid
in advance.

DUCH. That's so like a band!

DUKE (*annoyed*). Insuperable difficulties meet me at every turn!

DUCH. But surely they know His Grace?   275

LUIZ. Exactly – they know His Grace.

DUKE. Well, let us hope that the Grand Inquisitor is a deaf gentleman.
A cornet-à-piston would be something. You do not happen to possess the
accomplishment of tootling like a cornet-à- piston?

LUIZ. Alas, no, Your Grace! But I can imitate a farmyard.   280

DUKE (*doubtfully*). I don't see how that would help us. I don't see how
we could bring it in.

CAS. It would not help us in the least. We are not a parcel of graziers
come to market, dolt!

(LUIZ *rises*.)   285

DUKE. My love, our suite's feelings! (*To* LUIZ.) Be so good as to ring
the bell and inform the Grand Inquisitor that his Grace the Duke of Plaza-
Toro, Count Matadoro, Baron Picadoro –

DUCH. And suite –

DUKE. And suite – have arrived at Venice, and seek –   290

CAS. Desire –

DUCH. Demand!

DUKE. And demand an audience.

LUIZ. Your Grace has but to command.

DUKE (*much moved*). I felt sure of it – I felt sure of it! (*Exit* LUIZ *into*   295
Ducal Palace.) And now, my love – (*aside to* DUCHESS) Shall we tell her? I
think so – (*aloud to* CASILDA) And now, my love, prepare for a
magnificent surprise. It is my agreeable duty to reveal to you a secret which
should make you the happiest young lady in Venice!

CAS. A secret?   300

DUCH. A secret which, for State reasons, it has been necessary to
preserve for twenty years.

may also have influenced the passage in *The Gondoliers* in which the Duke of Plaza-Toro complains of the lack of ceremony attending his own arrival there (Act II, lines 707–23): 'As soon as he came to the gates the magistrates came out to receive him, the bells rang, and all the people gave demonstrations of joy.'

311 *a Wesleyan Methodist*: The King of Barataria must have been a remarkably early convert to Methodism. The action of *The Gondoliers* takes place in 1750. We are told here that the King became a Methodist shortly after the marriage of his infant son to the baby Casilda. That event must have taken place at least eighteen years or so before the conversation we are now witnessing, say around 1732. Yet the foundation in Oxford by John and Charles Wesley of the Holy Club, the group which is normally taken to be the precursor of the Methodists, had only taken place in 1729, and it was not until 1738 that John Wesley was converted to 'vital religion' and started to apply the term 'Methodist' to himself and his followers. The term 'Wesleyan Methodist', incidentally, used to identify those who saw themselves as belonging specifically to his church as distinct from other Methodist denominations, was of even later application, being first recorded in the United States in 1796 and in Britain not until 1858.

In the version of the opera adapted by Helen D'Oyly Carte for performance in America, the phrase 'became a Wesleyan Methodist' was changed to 'joined the Salvation Army'. In a production in Belfast at the time when the Revd Ian Paisley was beginning his rise to prominence in Northern Irish politics the Duke spoke of 'a Free Presbyterian of the most bigoted and persecuting type'.

314 *conveyed to Venice*: Venice seems a curious place for a Spanish Grand Inquisitor to take the infant son of the King of Barataria in an effort to prevent him falling victim to heresy. Although certainly free from Methodist influence, the home of red-hot republicanism was hardly the most fervent centre of Roman Catholicism in Europe. Why, one wonders, did Don Alhambra not take the baby back to Spain or at least to one of her Italian possessions?

329 *after allotment*: When a limited company is formed it issues a prospectus and invites investors to apply for shares. The company then allots the shares. In Britain the Duke of Plaza-Toro would not have been able to form himself into a limited company in 1750, but Venice may well have been more advanced in these matters (see the note to Act II, line 601). I have not, I fear, researched too deeply into Venetian company law!

For her American audience, Helen D'Oyly Carte altered this passage to read:

> DUKE. A joint stock company, under the title the Duke of Plaza-Toro, Limited, has been organized for the purpose of working me. An influential syndicate will supply the capital – and I shall supply myself.
>
> CAS. Am I to understand that the Queen of Barataria may be called upon at any time to hear her honoured sire quoted below par, or behold him in the hand of a receiver?
>
> DUCH. The speculation is not exempt from that drawback. If your father should stop, it will, of course, be necessary to wind him up.
>
> CAS. But it's so undignified – it's so degrading! A Grandee of Spain turned into a public corporation.
>
> DUKE. There is every reason to believe that I shall command a handsome premium. If I am issued as a first mortgage bond, that gratifying result is almost certain.
>
> CAS. But such a thing was never heard of!

340–93 *In enterprise of martial kind*

There is no proper patter song in *The Gondoliers*. This is the nearest equivalent, but it is

DUKE. When you were a prattling babe of six months old you were married by proxy to no less a personage than the infant son and heir of His Majesty the immeasurably wealthy King of Barataria! 305

CAS. Married to the infant son of the King of Barataria? Was I consulted? (DUKE *shakes his head.*) Then it was a most unpardonable liberty!

DUKE. Consider his extreme youth and forgive him. Shortly after the ceremony that misguided monarch abandoned the creed of his 310 forefathers, and became a Wesleyan Methodist of the most bigoted and persecuting type. The Grand Inquisitor, determined that the innovation should not be perpetuated in Barataria, caused your smiling and unconscious husband to be stolen and conveyed to Venice. A fortnight since the Methodist Monarch and all his Wesleyan Court were killed in 315 an insurrection, and we are here to ascertain the whereabouts of your husband, and to hail you, our daughter, as Her Majesty, the reigning Queen of Barataria! (*Kneels.*)

(*During this speech* LUIZ *re-enters.*)

DUCH. Your Majesty! (*Kneels.*) (*Drum roll.*) 320

DUKE. It is at such moments as these that one feels how necessary it is to travel with a full band.

CAS. I, the Queen of Barataria! But I've nothing to wear! We are practically penniless!

DUKE. That point has not escaped me. Although I am unhappily in 325 straitened circumstances at present, my social influence is something enormous; and a Company, to be called the Duke of Plaza-Toro, Limited, is in course of formation to work me. An influential directorate has been secured, and I shall myself join the Board after allotment.

CAS. Am I to understand that the Queen of Barataria may be called 330 upon at any time to witness her honoured sire in process of liquidation?

DUCH. The speculation is not exempt from that drawback. If your father should stop, it will, of course, be necessary to wind him up.

CAS. But it's so undignified – it's so degrading! A Grandee of Spain turned into a public company! Such a thing was never heard of! 335

DUKE. My child, the Duke of Plaza-Toro does not follow fashions – he leads them. He always leads everybody. When he was in the army he led his regiment. He occasionally led them into action. He invariably led them out of it.

SONG – DUKE OF PLAZA-TORO.

In enterprise of martial kind, 340
   When there was any fighting,

not really in quite the same genre as the songs given to the 'funny men' in the other Savoy Operas. The reason for this apparently strange omission may well be that for the first time since the opening of *The Sorcerer* in 1877 George Grossmith was not available to play the comic lead. He had left the D'Oyly Carte Company in the summer of 1889 to go back to his old job as a piano-entertainer. The role of the Duke of Plaza-Toro in the new opera was given to Frank Wyatt, a well-known actor in the straight theatre who had, however, no previous experience as a singer. Both Gilbert and Sullivan may well have felt that it would be very risky, and very unkind, to subject an untried newcomer to the rigours of a patter song.

He led his regiment from behind –
He found it less exciting.
But when away his regiment ran,
    His place was at the fore, O –   345
        That celebrated,
        Cultivated,
        Underrated
          Nobleman,
    The Duke of Plaza-Toro!   350

ALL.   In the first and foremost flight, ha, ha!
You always found that knight, ha, ha!
        That celebrated,
        Cultivated,
        Underrated   355
          Nobleman,
    The Duke of Plaza-Toro!

When, to evade Destruction's hand,
    To hide they all proceeded,
No soldier in that gallant band   360
    Hid half as well as he did.
He lay concealed throughout the war,
    And so preserved his gore, O!
        That unaffected,
        Undetected,   365
        Well-connected
          Warrior,
    The Duke of Plaza-Toro!

ALL.   In every doughty deed, ha, ha!
He always took the lead, ha, ha!   370
        That unaffected,
        Undetected,
        Well-connected
          Warrior,
    The Duke of Plaza-Toro!   375

When told that they would all be shot
    Unless they left the service,
That hero hesitated not,
    So marvellous his nerve is.
He sent his resignation in,   380
    The first of all his corps, O!

385   *Paladin*: Originally one of the twelve famous warriors of the Emperor Charlemagne's court, of whom the Count Palatine was the foremost. The word later came to be applied to any knightly hero or renowned champion.

397–415   *O rapture, when alone together*
In early performances, Casilda and Luiz sang both verses of this recitative as an ensemble rather than as two solos. It was then followed by a ballad for Luiz which was replaced early on in the original run by the duet 'Ah, well-beloved':

BALLAD – Luiz.

Thy wintry scorn I dearly prize,
    Thy mocking pride I bless;
Thy scorn is love in deep disguise,
    Thy pride is loneliness.
        Thy cold disdain,
        It gives no pain –
        'Tis mercy, played
        In masquerade.
        Thine angry frown
        Is but a gown
        That serves to dress
        Thy gentleness!

If angry frown and deep disdain
    Be love in masked array,
So much the bitterer their arraign,
    So much the sweeter they!
        With mocking smile
        My love beguile;
        With idle jest
        Appease my breast;
        With angry voice
        My soul rejoice;
        Beguile with scorn
        My heart forlorn!

Oh, happy he who is content to gain
Thy scorn, thine angry frown, thy deep disdain!

That very knowing,
Overflowing
Easy-going
　　Paladin,
The Duke of Plaza-Toro!　　　　　385

ALL.　　　To men of grosser clay, ha, ha!
He always showed the way, ha, ha!
That very knowing,
Overflowing,　　　　　390
Easy-going
　　Paladin,
The Duke of Plaza-Toro!

(*Exeunt* DUKE *and* DUCHESS *into Ducal Palace. As soon as
they have disappeared,* LUIZ *and* CASILDA *rush to*　　395
each other's arms.)

RECITATIVE AND DUET – CASILDA AND LUIZ.

O rapture, when alone together
　　Two loving hearts and those that bear them
May join in temporary tether,
　　Though Fate apart should rudely tear them.　　400

CAS.　　Necessity, Invention's mother,
　　Compelled me to a course of feigning –
But, left alone with one another,
　　I will atone for my disdaining!

　　Ah, well-beloved,　　　　　405
　　Mine angry frown
　　Is but a gown
　　That serves to dress
　　My gentleness!

LUIZ.　　　　Ah, well-beloved,　　　　　410
　　Thy cold disdain,
　　It gives no pain –
　　'Tis mercy, played
　　In masquerade!

BOTH.　　　　Ah, well-beloved, etc.　　　　　415

422 *Casilda*: Until shortly before the opening night, the Duke of Plaza-Toro's daughter was known as Carlotta. It is not clear why this was changed to Casilda at the last moment.

427 *the Inquisition*: The name given to the ecclesiastical courts set up in Roman Catholic countries in the Middle Ages to deal with the trial and prosecution of heretics. The Spanish Inquisition, established in 1479, was particularly brutal, and during the term of office of its first Grand Inquisitor, Torquemada, some two thousand heretics were burned alive. The Spanish Inquisition was abolished by Joseph Bonaparte in 1808, reintroduced in 1814 and finally terminated in 1834.

454 *Perhaps not*: At this point, the dialogue originally continued:

> CAS. We may recollect an embrace – I recollect many – but we must not repeat them.
> LUIZ. Then let us recollect a few!
> (*A moment's pause, as they recollect, then both heave a deep sigh.*)
> LUIZ. Ah, Casilda, you were to me as the sun is to the earth!
> CAS. A quarter of an hour ago?
> LUIZ. About that.
> CAS. And to think that, but for this miserable discovery, you would have been my own for life!
> LUIZ. Through life to death – a quarter of an hour ago!
> CAS. How greedily my thirsty ears would have drunk the golden melody of those sweet words a quarter – well it's now about twenty minutes since (*looking at her watch*).
> LUIZ. About that. In such a matter one cannot be too precise.

In its first-night review the *Daily News* commented that 'both the ballad of Luiz and the paradoxical dialogue in which the lady confesses how much she loved him "a quarter of an hour ago" somehow missed their point'. Gilbert accepted the criticism and both items were removed. They are, however, printed in several modern editions of the libretto and are performed by many amateur societies.

CAS. O Luiz, Luiz – what have you said? What have I done? What have I allowed you to do?

LUIZ. Nothing, I trust, that you will ever have reason to repent. (*Offering to embrace her.*)

CAS. (*withdrawing from him*). Nay, Luiz, it may not be. I have embraced you for the last time. 420

LUIZ (*amazed*). Casilda!

CAS. I have just learnt, to my surprise and indignation, that I was wed in babyhood to the infant son of the King of Barataria! 425

LUIZ. The son of the King of Barataria? The child who was stolen in infancy by the Inquisition?

CAS. The same. But, of course, you know his story.

LUIZ. Know his story? Why, I have often told you that my mother was the nurse to whose charge he was entrusted! 430

CAS. True. I had forgotten. Well, he has been discovered, and my father has brought me here to claim his hand.

LUIZ. But you will not recognize this marriage? It took place when you were too young to understand its import.

CAS. Nay, Luiz, respect my principles and cease to torture me with vain entreaties. Henceforth my life is another's. 435

LUIZ. But stay – the present and the future – *they* are another's; but the past – that at least is ours, and none can take it from us. As we may revel in naught else, let us revel in that!

CAS. I don't think I grasp your meaning. 440

LUIZ. Yet it is logical enough. You say you cease to love me?

CAS. (*demurely*). I say I *may* not love you.

LUIZ. Ah, but you do not say you *did* not love me?

CAS. I loved you with a frenzy that words are powerless to express – and that but ten brief minutes since! 445

LUIZ. Exactly. My own – that is, until ten minutes since, my own – my lately loved, my recently adored – tell me that until, say a quarter of an hour ago, I was all in all to thee! (*Embracing her.*)

CAS. I see your idea. It's ingenious, but don't do that. (*Releasing herself.*) 450

LUIZ. There can be no harm in revelling in the past.

CAS. None whatever, but an embrace cannot be taken to act retrospectively.

LUIZ. Perhaps not! Casilda, you were to me as the sun is to the earth! 455

CAS. And now our love, so full of life, is but a silent, solemn memory!

LUIZ. Must it be so, Casilda?

CAS. Luiz, it must be so!

481–2 *Don Alhambra del Bolero*: One of the great bass-baritone roles in the Savoy Operas, the Grand Inquisitor was first played by W. H. Denny, whose appearance in the part was thought by many to bear a striking resemblance to Lord Granville, Foreign Secretary in Gladstone's first two governments.

Kenneth Sandford, who has played Don Alhambra in three different D'Oyly Carte productions of *The Gondoliers* stretching over twenty-five years, told me that the role has greatly changed in that period:

> In the old days a Grand Inquisitor was a Grand Inquisitor in name, bearing and looks. Now we have humanized the part. You accept the fact that you are a Grand Inquisitor, but the man is as normal as anyone else, and if he's tempted to look down the front of a lady's dress, it doesn't alter the fact that he's a Grand Inquisitor. In the old days that just wouldn't have been done. But now you can put a little light in your eye and enjoy it, as I'm quite sure Gilbert would have liked, because he was quite a boy.

Certainly Kenneth Sandford's lecherous portrayal of the Don was one of the delights of the last days of the D'Oyly Carte Company.

488 *Jimp*: A word of Scandinavian origin meaning slender, slim, graceful or neat.

489 *Offers his hand*: The original stage direction at this point was 'Proceeds to inspect her'. J. M. Gordon, stage director of the D'Oyly Carte Opera Company from 1907 to 1939, altered it in 1914.

DUET – CASILDA *and* LUIZ.

LUIZ.	There was a time –	460
	A time for ever gone – ah, woe is me!	
	It was no crime	
	To love but thee alone – ah, woe is me!	
	One heart, one life, one soul,	
	One aim, one goal –	465
	Each in the other's thrall,	
	Each all in all, ah, woe is me!	
BOTH.	Oh, bury, bury – let the grave close o'er	
	The days that were – that never will be more!	
	Oh, bury, bury love that all condemn,	470
	And let the whirlwind mourn its requiem!	
CAS.	Dead as the last year's leaves –	
	As gathered flowers – ah, woe is me!	
	Dead as the garnered sheaves,	
	That love of ours – ah, woe is me!	475
	Born but to fade and die	
	When hope was high,	
	Dead and as far away	
	As yesterday! – ah, woe is me!	
BOTH.	Oh, bury, bury – let the grave close o'er, etc.	480

(*Re-enter from the Ducal Palace the* DUKE *and* DUCHESS, *followed by* DON ALHAMBRA DEL BOLERO, *the Grand Inquisitor.*)

DUKE. My child, allow me to present to you His Distinction Don Alhambra del Bolero, the Grand Inquisitor of Spain. It was His Distinction who so thoughtfully abstracted your infant husband and brought him to Venice.   485

DON AL. So this is the little lady who is so unexpectedly called upon to assume the functions of Royalty! And a very nice little lady, too!

DUKE. Jimp, isn't she?

DON AL. Distinctly jimp. Allow me! (*Offers his hand. She turns away scornfully.*) Naughty temper!   490

DUKE. You must make some allowance. Her Majesty's head is a little turned by her access of dignity.

DON AL. I could have wished that Her Majesty's access of dignity had turned it in this direction.

DUCH. Unfortunately, if I am not mistaken, there appears to be some   495 little doubt as to His Majesty's whereabouts.

CAS. (*aside*). A doubt as to his whereabouts? Then we may yet be saved!

503–50 *I stole the Prince, and I brought him here*
    Gilbert almost certainly took the idea for this song, and indeed the central theme of *The Gondoliers*, from an experience which had befallen him as a child. At the age of two he was taken by his parents on holiday to Naples. One afternoon he was out for a pram ride with his nurse when two Italians came up and told her that they had been sent by 'the Engleesh papa' to bring back 'dis lofly bambino'. The credulous nurse handed over the baby and a few hours later Gilbert's father received a ransom demand for £25. Happily for posterity, William Gilbert senior considered that his son was worth that amount and so redeemed him from the kidnappers.

507 *timoneer*: From the French word *timonier*, meaning helmsman or steersman.

508 *bratling*: A diminutive form of 'brat', a slightly contemptuous term for a child.

515 *But owing, I'm much disposed to fear*: This verse, and the next one, beginning 'Time sped', were transposed in early editions of the libretto.

530 *bier*: The movable stand on which a corpse is placed before burial and on which it is carried to the grave.

DON AL. A doubt? Oh dear, no – no doubt at all! He is here, in
Venice, plying the modest but picturesque calling of a gondolier. I can give
you his address – I see him every day! In the entire annals of our history   500
there is absolutely no circumstance so entirely free from all manner of doubt
of any kind whatever! Listen, and I'll tell you all about it.

SONG – DON ALHAMBRA (*with* DUKE, DUCHESS,
CASILDA, *and* LUIZ).

I stole the Prince, and I brought him here,
    And left him gaily prattling
With a highly respectable gondolier,   505
Who promised the Royal babe to rear,
And teach him the trade of a timoneer
    With his own beloved bratling.

        Both of the babes were strong and stout,
            And, considering all things, clever.   510
        Of that there is no manner of doubt –
        No probable, possible shadow of doubt –
            No possible doubt whatever.

ALL.   No possible doubt whatever.

But owing, I'm much disposed to fear,   515
    To his terrible taste for tippling,
That highly respectable gondolier
Could never declare with a mind sincere
Which of the two was his offspring dear,
    And which the Royal stripling!   520

        Which was which he could never make out
            Despite his best endeavour.
        Of *that* there is no manner of doubt –
        No probable, possible shadow of doubt –
            No possible doubt whatever.   525

ALL.   No possible doubt whatever.

Time sped, and when at the end of a year
    I sought that infant cherished,
That highly respectable gondolier
Was lying a corpse on his humble bier –   530
I dropped a Grand Inquisitor's tear –
    That gondolier had perished.

533 *combined with gout*: Little did Gilbert realize when he wrote this that he himself was to become crippled with gout within a few years. In a letter to Richard D'Oyly Carte in 1893 he wrote 'I have been laid up with a most violent attack of gout in both feet and in the right hand, so I have not been able to do anything but swear for the last eighteen days.'

559 *a Grand Inquisitor is always up to date*: This line was originally written: 'A Grand Inquisitor is a well informed personage'.

562 *Cordova*: A town on the Guadalquivir river in southern Spain. It is more usually spelt Cordoba.

A taste for drink, combined with gout,
    Had doubled him up for ever.
Of *that* there is no manner of doubt –   535
No probable, possible shadow of doubt –
    No possible doubt whatever.

ALL.   No possible doubt whatever.

The children followed his old career –
    (This statement can't be parried)   540
Of a highly respectable gondolier:
Well, one of the two (who will soon be here) –
But *which* of the two is not quite clear –
    Is the Royal Prince you married!

Search in and out and round about,   545
    And you'll discover never
A tale so free from every doubt –
All probable, possible shadow of doubt –
    All possible doubt whatever!

ALL.   A tale so free from every doubt, etc.   550

CAS. Then do you mean to say that I am married to one of two
gondoliers, but it is impossible to say which?

DON AL. Without any doubt of any kind whatever. But be reassured:
the nurse to whom your husband was entrusted is the mother of the musical
young man who is such a past-master of that delicately modulated   555
instrument (*indicating the drum*). She can, no doubt, establish the King's
identity beyond all question.

LUIZ. Heavens, how did he know that?

DON AL. My young friend, a Grand Inquisitor is always up to date. (*To*
CAS.) His mother is at present the wife of a highly respectable and old-   560
established brigand, who carries on an extensive practice in the mountains
around Cordova. Accompanied by two of my emissaries, he will set off at
once for his mother's address. She will return with them, and if she finds
any difficulty in making up her mind, the persuasive influence of the torture
chamber will jog her memory.   565

RECITATIVE – CASILDA *and* DON ALHAMBRA.

CAS.   But, bless my heart, consider my position!
            I am the wife of one, that's very clear;
          But who can tell, except by intuition,
            Which is the Prince, and which the Gondolier?

572   *Life is one closely complicated tangle*: This line was the cue for a splendid bit of business introduced by Anthony Besch in his 1968 D'Oyly Carte production. Shortly after the entrance of the Duke and Duchess and Don Alhambra at line 481, a steaming bowl of spaghetti was brought on to the stage. This the ducal party proceeded to devour while Don Alhambra sang 'I stole the Prince'. The spaghetti became more and more tangled up, and at the line 'Life is one closely complicated tangle' the Duke lifted the whole glutinous and soggy mess with his fork and spoon.

Peter Riley, successively stage manager, stage director, technical director, company manager and general manager of D'Oyly Carte, told me that he has spent many an anxious time at the stage door waiting for that evening's consignment of spaghetti to arrive. Normally, wherever the company was playing, there was an Italian restaurant nearby. In the wilds of Wilmbledon, however, there was apparently a dearth of such establishments, and during a season there procuring the precious pasta involved a five-mile taxi journey. 'We had to put it in a thermos flask,' Peter Riley recalls, 'and I don't think it tasted very good by the time it reached the stage. One night it didn't arrive at all so I sent a ham sandwich on instead. Dame Bridget D'Oyly Carte suggested that it would be much easier to use false spaghetti made out of white knitting wool but it wouldn't have been as realistic. Eventually we took to heating up tins on a hot plate back-stage.'

598   *goes off in gondola*: At one rehearsal Gilbert, precise and meticulous as ever, told the stage-hands: 'Please get the gondola off as quickly as can reasonably be expected, not as fast as a steam launch, but as quickly as a normally active gondola.'

601–8   *Bridegroom and bride*
       As sung in early performances, this chorus had a second verse and a different ending to the first verse. After the second 'Bridegroom and bride!' (line 605), this original version continued:

> Hail it with merriment;
> It's an experiment
> Frequently tried.
> Bridegroom and bride!
>   Bridegrooms all joyfully,
>   Brides, rather coyfully,

DON AL.   Submit to Fate without unseemly wrangle: 570
           Such complications frequently occur –
           Life is one closely complicated tangle:
           Death is the only true unraveller!

QUINTET – DUKE, DUCHESS, CASILDA, LUIZ,
                and GRAND INQUISITOR.

ALL.   Try we life-long, we can never
           Straighten out life's tangled skein,   575
           Why should we, in vain endeavour,
               Guess and guess and guess again?
LUIZ.   Life's a pudding full of plums,
DUCH.   Care's a canker that benumbs.
ALL.   Life's a pudding full of plums,   580
                  Care's a canker that benumbs.
           Wherefore waste our elocution
           On impossible solution?
           Life's a pleasant institution,
               Let us take it as it comes!   585

           Set aside the dull enigma,
               We shall guess it all too soon;
           Failure brings no kind of stigma –
               Dance we to another tune!
                  String the lyre and fill the cup,   590
                  Lest on sorrow we should sup.
                  String the lyre and fill the cup,
                  Lest on sorrow we should sup.
           Hop and skip to Fancy's fiddle,
           Hands across and down the middle –   595
           Life's perhaps the only riddle
               That we shrink from giving up!

(Exeunt all into Ducal Palace except LUIZ, *who goes off in gondola.)*

(Enter Gondoliers and Contadine, followed by MARCO,
    GIANETTA, GIUSEPPE, *and* TESSA.)   600

CHORUS.

Bridegroom and bride!
    Knot that's insoluble,
    Voices all voluble
Hail it with pride.

> Stand at their side.
> Bridegroom and bride!
> We in sincerity
> Wish you prosperity,
> Bridegroom and bride!

Gilbert was upbraided by the *Globe* for using the word 'coyfully'. He replied:

> Your critic takes exception to it because one cannot be full of 'coy'. That is quite true; but
> is it a conclusive argument against the use of the word? We use the word 'manfully', though
> one cannot be full of 'man'. We use the word 'bashfully', though one cannot – at least I don't
> think one can – be full of 'bash'.

609–40   *When a merry maiden marries*
Several critics detected a strong resemblance between the opening bars of this song and
the chorus 'Just a song at twilight' from the popular Victorian parlour ballad composed
by James Molloy, 'Love's Old Sweet Song'. When this was put to him, Sullivan responded 'I do not happen to have heard the song, but even if I had, you must remember
that Molloy and I had only seven notes on which to work between us'.

Bridegroom and bride! 605
We in sincerity
Wish you prosperity,
Bridegroom and bride!

SONG – TESSA.

TESS.   When a merry maiden marries,
Sorrow goes and pleasure tarries; 610
Every sound becomes a song,
All is right, and nothing's wrong!
From to-day and ever after
Let our tears be tears of laughter.
Every sigh that finds a vent 615
Be a sigh of sweet content!
When you marry, merry maiden,
Then the air with love is laden;
Every flower is a rose,
Every goose becomes a swan, 620
Every kind of trouble goes
Where the last year's snows have gone!

CHORUS.   Sunlight takes the place of shade
When you marry, merry maid!

TESS.   When a merry maiden marries, 625
Sorrow goes and pleasure tarries;
Every sound becomes a song,
All is right, and nothing's wrong.
Gnawing Care and aching Sorrow,
Get ye gone until to-morrow; 630
Jealousies in grim array,
Ye are things of yesterday!
When you marry, merry maiden,
Then the air with joy is laden;
All the corners of the earth 635
Ring with music sweetly played,
Worry is melodious mirth,
Grief is joy in masquerade;

CHORUS.   Sullen night is laughing day –
All the year is merry May! 640

(At the end of the song, DON ALHAMBRA *enters at back. The Gondoliers and
Contadine shrink from him, and gradually go off, much alarmed.)*

643   *And now our lives* . . . : The passage of dialogue which begins here and continues until line 650 was one of several cut in performance by the D'Oyly Carte Opera Company in recent years in an effort to speed up the long First Act of *The Gondoliers*. Other passages generally cut were the cornet-à-piston exchange already mentioned in the note to line 278, and lines 320–22, 330–35, 440–45, 449–50, and 719–23 inclusive.

653   *Ceremony of some sort going on*: Gilbert originally wrote this line as 'Festivities of some sort going on?' It seems to have been altered at an early revival.

663   *Remarkably fine children*: This line was added in 1907.

680   *who led the last revolution*: There were not, as far as I can discover, any revolutions in Venice in the first half of the eighteenth century, although there was one in 1848, when Daniele Manin led a revolt against Austrian rule and proclaimed the re-establishment of the Venetian Republic. It was short-lived, and in 1849 the Austrians regained control of the city.

G I U. And now our lives are going to begin in real earnest! What's a bachelor? A mere nothing – he's a chrysalis. He can't be said to live – he exists.

M A R. What a delightful institution marriage is! Why have we wasted all this time? Why didn't we marry ten years ago? 645

T E S S. Because you couldn't find anybody nice enough.

G I A. Because you were waiting for *us*.

M A R. I suppose that *was* the reason. We were waiting for you without knowing it. (D O N A L H A M B R A *comes forward*.) Hallo! 650

D O N A L. Good morning.

G I U. If this gentleman is an undertaker, it's a bad omen.

D O N A L. Ceremony of some sort going on?

G I U. (*aside*). He *is* an undertaker! (*Aloud*.) No – a little unimportant family gathering. Nothing in *your* line. 655

D O N A L. Somebody's birthday, I suppose?

G I A. Yes, mine!

T E S S. And mine!

M A R. And mine!

G I U. And mine! 660

D O N A L. Curious coincidence! And how old may you all be?

T E S S. It's a rude question – but about ten minutes.

D O N A L. Remarkably fine children! But surely you are jesting?

T E S S. In other words, we were married about ten minutes since.

D O N A L. Married! You don't mean to say you are married? 665

M A R. Oh yes, we are married.

D O N A L. What, both of you?

A L L. All four of us.

D O N A L. (*aside*.) Bless my heart, how extremely awkward!

G I A. You don't mind, I suppose? 670

T E S S. You were not thinking of either of us for yourself, I presume? Oh, Giuseppe, look at him – he was. He's heart-broken!

D O N A L. No, no, I wasn't! I wasn't!

G I U. Now, my man (*slapping him on the back*), we don't want anything in your line to-day, and if your curiosity's satisfied – you can go! 675

D O N A L. You mustn't call me your man. It's a liberty. I don't think you know who I am.

G I U. Not we, indeed! We are jolly gondoliers, the sons of Baptisto Palmieri, who led the last revolution. Republicans, heart and soul, we hold all men to be equal. As we abhor oppression, we abhor kings: as we detest vain-glory, we detest rank: as we despise effeminacy, we despise wealth. We are Venetian gondoliers – your equals in everything except our calling, and in that at once your masters and your servants. 680

D O N A L. Bless my heart, how unfortunate! One of you may be Baptisto's son, for anything I know to the contrary; but the other is no less 685

707   *the Grand Canal*: The widest and most important of Venice's 180 canals, it runs for $2\frac{1}{2}$ miles bisecting the island on which the city is built.

709   *the Rialto*: The bridge across the Grand Canal mid-way between the railway station and the *Dogana*, or customs house, on the edge of the lagoon. Until 1854 the Rialto was the sole connecting link between the east and west quarters of Venice. The present bridge is the sixth on the site and dates from 1592. Each of its ends rests on 6000 wooden piles. With its picturesque arcades of shops it was a favourite meeting place for Venetians, as Shakespeare recognized when he made Shylock ask in Act I of *The Merchant of Venice*: 'What news on the Rialto?'

718   *Oh! they've often been convicted*: This line was officially included in the libretto at the time of the 1907 revival, although it was almost certainly spoken in earlier performances as an ad-lib gag. It was probably originally coined by Rutland Barrington, who created the role of Giuseppe.

722   *Oh, he's a fine fellow*: In the version of the libretto which she apparently prepared for performance in the United States (see the note to line 246), Helen D'Oyly Carte deleted this and the next line and substituted the following:

MAR. I feel more than half convinced already.
GIA. *and* TESS. So do we.

a personage than the only son of the late King of Barataria.

ALL. What!

DON AL. And I trust – I *trust* it was that one who slapped me on the shoulder and called me his man! 690

GIU. One of us a king!

MAR. Not brothers!

TESS. The King of Barataria! } *Together*

GIA. Well, who'd have thought it!

MAR. But which is it? 695

DON AL. What does it matter? As you are both Republicans, and hold kings in detestation, of course you'll abdicate at once. Good morning! (*Going.*)

GIA. *and* TESS. Oh, don't do that! (MARCO *and* GIUSEPPE *stop him.*)

GIU. Well, as to that, of course there are kings and kings. When I say that I detest kings, I mean I detest *bad* kings. 700

DON AL. I see. It's a delicate distinction.

GIU. Quite so. Now I can conceive a kind of king – an ideal king – the creature of my fancy, you know – who would be absolutely unobjectionable. A king, for instance, who would abolish taxes and make everything cheap, except gondolas – 705

MAR. And give a great many free entertainments to the gondoliers —

GIU. And let off fireworks on the Grand Canal, and engage all the gondolas for the occasion —

MAR. And scramble money on the Rialto among the gondoliers.

GIU. Such a king would be a blessing to his people, and if I were a 710 king, that is the sort of king I would be.

MAR. And so would I!

DON AL. Come, I'm glad to find your objections are not insuperable.

MAR. *and* GIU. Oh, they're not insuperable.

GIU. *and* TESS. No, they're not insuperable. 715

GIU. Besides, we are open to conviction.

GIA. Yes; they are open to conviction.

TESS. Oh! they've often been convicted.

GIU. Our views may have been hastily formed on insufficient grounds. They may be crude, ill-digested, erroneous. I've a very poor opinion of the 720 politician who is not open to conviction.

TESS. (*to* GIA.). Oh, he's a fine fellow!

GIA. Yes, that's the sort of politician for *my* money!

DON AL. Then we'll consider it settled. Now, as the country is in a state of insurrection, it is absolutely necessary that you should assume the 725 reins of Government at once; and, until it is ascertained which of you is to be king, I have arranged that you will reign jointly, so that no question can arise hereafter as to the validity of any of your acts.

MAR. As one individual?

DON AL. As one individual. 730

733   *And we may take our friends with us*: In the same American version this passage was altered
      to:

> MAR. And we may take all our relatives and friends with us and give them lucrative
> appointments even if they know nothing of the duties they are to perform?
> DON AL. Undoubtedly. That is the usual course of procedure – in Barataria.
> MAR. I'm utterly convinced.

735   *That's always done*: This phrase did not appear in the original libretto. Its first formal ap-
      pearance was in 1914, but I suspect it had been said unofficially before that.

740–43   *Stop, stop . . .* : The exchange about the admission of ladies to Barataria has been altered
      several times. As performed on the opening night it ran as follows:

> DON AL. Stop, stop – that won't do at all – we can't have any ladies. (*Aside*). What will
> Her Majesty say!
> ALL. What!
> DON AL. Not at present. Afterwards, perhaps. We'll see.

In 1897 Gilbert changed Don Alhambra's second remark (line 742) to 'Not admitted.
We must keep the place respectable at first.' This, in turn, was later changed to 'We
must keep the island respectable' and finally to its present version.

749–84   *Kind sir, you cannot have the heart*
      In a letter sent to Sullivan on 9 November 1889, Gilbert wrote:

> If I remember right, you expressed some doubt as to whether Gianetta's song, 'Kind sir,
> you cannot have the heart,' was not too long for the situation, and said something about
> cutting it down to one verse. This was some time ago, and perhaps you are no longer of that
> opinion. I have come across a song which I wrote for the same situation, and which perhaps
> presents better opportunities for action than the other. Anyhow, I enclose it for your infor-
> mation. If you don't like it, tear it up. Or if you want the original song shortened, could it be
> done by taking the second half of the first verse and the first half of the second verse? Don't
> trouble to answer this.

In the event, Sullivan obviously decided that the song was not too long and it was preserved intact.

The earlier song which Gilbert mentioned in his letter was apparently written
for Tessa rather than Gianetta. It was published in *The Strand Magazine* in 1891 where
it was described as having been intended to be sung 'in the ear of the Grand
Inquisitor, when he commands the two kings of Barataria to leave their lovers and rule
their kingdoms'. A copy of the words was sent to me by Mr Geoffrey Wilson. They run
as follows:

> Good sir, I wish to speak politely –
>   Forgive me if the words are crude –
> I find it hard to put it rightly
>   Without appearing to be rude.
> I mean to say you're old and wrinkled,
>   It's rather blunt, but it's the truth –
> With wintry snow your hair is sprinkled;
>   What can you know of love and youth?
> Indeed I wish to speak politely
>   But, pray forgive me, truth is truth:
> You're old and – pardon me – unsightly.
>   What can you know of love and youth?

GIU. (*linking himself with* MARCO). Like this?

DON AL. Something like that.

MAR. And we may take our friends with us, and give them places about the Court?

DON AL. Undoubtedly. That's always done! 735

MAR. I'm convinced!

GIU. So am I!

TESS. Then the sooner we're off the better.

GIA. We'll just run home and pack up a few things (*going*) —

DON AL. Stop, stop – that won't do at all – ladies are not admitted. 740

ALL. What!

DON AL. Not admitted. Not at present. Afterwards, perhaps. We'll see.

GIU. Why, you don't mean to say you are going to separate us from our wives! 745

DON AL. (*aside*). This is very awkward! (*Aloud.*) Only for a time – a few months. After all, what is a few months?

TESS. But we've only been married half an hour! (*Weeps.*)

FINALE, ACT I.

SONG – GIANETTA.

Kind sir, you cannot have the heart
    Our lives to part
  From those to whom an hour ago 750
    We were united!
Before our flowing hopes you stem,
    Ah, look at them,
  And pause before you deal this blow, 755
    All uninvited!
You men can never understand
    That heart and hand
  Cannot be separated when
    We go a-yearning; 760
You see, you've only women's eyes
    To idolize
  And only women's hearts, poor men,
    To set *you* burning!
Ah me, you men will never understand 765
That woman's heart is one with woman's hand!

Some kind of charm you seem to find
    In womankind –

You are too aged to remember
    That withered bosom's earliest glow,
Dead is the old romantic ember
    That warmed your life-blood years ago.
It is from our sweethearts we are parted
    (Old men know nothing of such pain)
Two maidens will be broken-hearted
    And quite heart-broken, lovers twain!
Now pray, for goodness' sake remember
    I've no desire to be uncouth
But we are June and you're December
    What can you know of love and youth?

800–849   *Then one of us will be a Queen*

This proved to be one of the most popular numbers with the audience during the initial run of *The Gondoliers*. The *Daily News* reported that after its conclusion on the first night 'the excited house encored, the pit emphatically demanding "All of it!", a request laughingly granted by Sir Arthur Sullivan.' The same paper went on to note that it was also whistled from the gallery during the inordinately long interval while the complicated scenery for Act II was being assembled on stage.

    The song also greatly appealed to Queen Victoria. During a Royal Command performance of *The Gondoliers* at Windsor Castle on 6 March 1891 she was observed delightedly beating time to its catchy rhythm.

    This performance was the first entertainment to be given at Windsor Castle since the death of Prince Albert in 1861. Neither Gilbert nor Sullivan was present for the occasion, and the former was somewhat annoyed to discover later that his name had been left off the posters by mistake. Victoria, however, thoroughly enjoyed the piece and made the following entry in her diary, which shows the admiration of a real 'rightdown regular Royal Queen' for the work of two of her most talented subjects:

Some source of unexplained delight
(Unless you're jesting), 770
But what attracts you, I confess,
I cannot guess,
To me a woman's face is quite
Uninteresting!
If from my sister I were torn, 775
It could be borne –
I should, no doubt, be horrified,
But I could bear it; –
But Marco's quite another thing –
He is my King,
He has my heart and none beside 780
Shall ever share it!
Ah me, you men will never understand
That woman's heart is one with woman's hand!

RECITATIVE – DON ALHAMBRA.

Do not give way to this uncalled-for grief, 785
Your separation will be very brief.
To ascertain which is the King
And which the other,
To Barataria's Court I'll bring
His foster-mother; 790
Her former nurseling to declare
She'll be delighted.
That settled, let each happy pair
Be reunited.

MAR., GIU.,   Viva! His argument is strong! 795
GIA., TESS.   Viva! We'll not be parted long!
Viva! It will be settled soon!
Viva! Then comes our honeymoon!
(*Exit* DON ALHAMBRA.)

QUARTET – MARCO, GIUSEPPE, GIANETTA, TESSA.

GIA.   Then one of us will be a Queen, 800
And sit on a golden throne,
With a crown instead
Of a hat on her head,
And diamonds all her own!

At nine we went over to the Waterloo Gallery where all the seats were filled by the Ladies and Gentlemen of the Household. All the Princes and Princesses sat with me in the front row. *The Gondoliers* the last of Sir A. Sullivan's comic operas, was performed by D'Oyly Carte's company of the Savoy Theatre, and lasted about two hours and a half. The music, which I know and am very fond of, is quite charming throughout and was well acted and sung. The opening scene with the contadini singing and binding flowers, with a lovely view of Venice and the deep blue sea and sky, was really extraordinarily pretty. The dancing which often comes in was very graceful and pretty.

The dialogue is written by Gilbert and very amusing. The Grand Inquisitor (Mr Denny) was excellent and most absurd, also Mr Rutland Barrington, who is very fat and one of the gondolieri. Miss Jessie Bond is a clever little actress and sings nicely. The dresses are very gay and smart and the whole ensemble brilliant and well put on the stage. In the last scene there were eighty people on the stage, which for an extemporized one was wonderful. I really enjoyed the performance very much. Afterwards I spoke to Mr D'Oyly Carte and complimented him. We then went to the Drawing-room, into which all the company came, but I only stayed a short while. Everybody was much pleased.

The Gondoliers found favour with the Royal Family in general. The Prince of Wales, later to become King Edward VII, saw the opera at least four times. Would it have been quite so popular in royal circles, I wonder, if Gilbert and Sullivan had kept in a 'Baratarian National Anthem' which was cut out at an early stage of their work? In it the subjects of Barataria told their monarch exactly what to do. The first line was 'As long as you are good as gold', and subsequent lines enjoined the king to:

> Knuckle down with humble mien
> And keep your crown and sceptre clean.

831 *She'll bear away the bell*: To bear away the bell is to carry off the prize. It probably derives from the old custom of presenting a little gold or silver bell as a prize to the winners of horse races.

With a beautiful robe of gold and green,   805
  I've always understood;
    I wonder whether
    She'd wear a feather?
  I rather think she should!

ALL.   Oh, 'tis a glorious thing, I ween,   810
  To be a regular Royal Queen!
No half-and-half affair, I mean,
But a right-down regular Royal Queen!

MAR.   She'll drive about in a carriage and pair,
  With the King on her left-hand side,   815
    And a milk-white horse,
    As a matter of course,
  Whenever she wants to ride!
With beautiful silver shoes to wear
  Upon her dainty feet;   820
    With endless stocks
    Of beautiful frocks
  And as much as she wants to eat!

ALL.   Oh, 'tis a glorious thing, I ween, etc.

TESS.   Whenever she condescends to walk,   825
  Be sure she'll shine at that,
    With her haughty stare
    And her nose in the air,
  Like a well-born aristocrat!
At elegant high society talk   830
  She'll bear away the bell,
    With her 'How de do?'
    And her 'How are you?'
  And 'I trust I see you well!'

ALL.   Oh, 'tis a glorious thing, I ween, etc.   835

GIU.   And noble lords will scrape and bow,
    And double themselves in two,
      And open their eyes
      In blank surprise
    At whatever she likes to do.   840
And everybody will roundly vow
  She's fair as flowers in May,

852 *ebullition*: A sudden outburst or state of agitation.

870 *And all shall equal be*: This line had a particular message for the members of the D'Oyly
Carte Opera Company, as Jessie Bond, who created the role of Tessa, noted many years
later in an article, 'Memories of an Old Savoyard', which is quoted in Leslie Baily's *The
Gilbert and Sullivan Book*. In the summer of 1889, she recalled, she was in the midst of an
argument with Gilbert about her salary and her *prima donna* status:

> Gilbert snapped out that he was tired to death of artists who thought that they were re-
> sponsible for the success of the operas, and that he intended to put a stop to the whole
> thing. 'We'll have an opera,' he exclaimed, rather angrily, 'in which there will be no principal
> parts. No character shall stand out more prominently than another.' Surely enough, when
> *The Gondoliers* was written a little later, we discovered that it contained more than the usual
> number of big parts. In case we missed the significance of that, he gave the two gondoliers
> their duet which told that 'all shall equal be'.

871 *peruke*: A variation of the word periwig, meaning a wig.
875 *Coutts*: One of the most exclusive banking houses in Britain, which numbers the Queen
among its customers. It had its origins in the late seventeenth century in a goldsmith's
and money-lender's business in the Strand, where Coutts now has its modern headquarters. In the eighteenth century the firm was taken over and greatly developed by two
Scottish brothers, Thomas and James Coutts, who gave their name to the business.

And say, 'How clever!'
At whatsoever
She condescends to say! 845

ALL.   Oh, 'tis a glorious thing, I ween,
To be a regular Royal Queen!
No half-and-half affair, I mean,
But a right-down regular Royal Queen!

(*Enter Chorus of Gondoliers and Contadine.*) 850

CHORUS.

Now, pray, what is the cause of this remarkable hilarity?
This sudden ebullition of unmitigated jollity?
Has anybody blessed you with a sample of his charity?
Or have you been adopted by a gentleman of quality?

MAR. *and* GIU.   Replying, we sing 855
As one individual,
As I find I'm a king,
To my kingdom I bid you all.
I'm aware you object
To pavilions and palaces, 860
But you'll find I respect
Your Republican fallacies.

CHORUS.   As they know we object
To pavillions and palaces,
How can they respect 865
Our Republican fallacies?

MARCO *and* GIUSEPPE.

MAR.   For every one who feels inclined,
Some post we undertake to find
Congenial with his frame of mind –
And all shall equal be. 870

GIU.   The Chancellor in his peruke –
The Earl, the Marquis, and the Dook,
The Groom, the Butler, and the Cook –
They all shall equal be.

MAR.   The Aristocrat who banks with Coutts – 875

888   *Sing high, sing low*: In his *Treasury of Gilbert and Sullivan* Martyn Green says that a conundrum traditionally put to new members of the D'Oyly Carte Company was 'Who are the two Chinese characters in *The Gondoliers*?' The answer, of course, is Sing-Hi and Sing-Lo.

907   *Then hail! O King*: In early libretti, this chorus was longer. After the line 'But do not bend the knee' it continued:

> It may be thou –
> > Likewise it may be thee –
> So hail! O King,
> > Whichever you may be.

908   *Come, let's away*: In the licence copy this line is printed: 'Then let's away – our island home awaits me –'.

The Aristocrat who hunts and shoots –
The Aristocrat who cleans our boots –
They all shall equal be!

GIU.   The Noble Lord who rules the State –
The Noble Lord who cleans the plate –   880

MAR.   The Noble Lord who scrubs the grate –
They all shall equal be!

GIU.   The Lord High Bishop orthodox –
The Lord High Coachman on the box –

MAR.   The Lord High Vagabond in the stocks –   885
They all shall equal be!

BOTH.   For every one, etc.

               Sing high, sing low,
               Wherever they go,
                   They all shall equal be!   890

CHORUS.   Sing high, sing low,
               Wherever they go,
                   They all shall equal be!

The Earl, the Marquis, and the Dook,
The Groom, the Butler, and the Cook,   895
The Aristocrat who banks with Coutts,
The Aristocrat who cleans the boots,
The Noble Lord who rules the State,
The Noble Lord who scrubs the grate,
The Lord High Bishop orthodox,
The Lord High Vagabond in the stocks –   900

For every one, etc.

               Then hail! O King,
                   Whichever you may be,
               To you we sing,
                   But do not bend the knee.   905
               Then hail! O King.

MARCO *and* GIUSEPPE (*together*).

Come, let's away – our island crown awaits me –
Conflicting feelings rend my soul apart!

934   *Than forty-five*: Another example of Gilbert's obsession with women in their forties.
      Readers will recall that in *The Pirates of Penzance* Ruth sings that her love has been accu-
      mulating for forty-seven years, and that the same age is given to the lady who figures in
      the Bab Ballad 'Haunted' (see the note to Act I, line 172, page 200). The judge in *Trial by
      Jury* tells us that the rich attorney said of his daughter:

                    She may very well pass for forty-three
                    In the dusk, with a light behind her!

The thought of Royal dignity elates me,   910
   But leaving thee behind me breaks my heart!

      (*Addressing* GIANETTA *and* TESSA.)

    GIANETTA *and* TESSA (*together*).

Farewell, my love; on board you must be getting;
   But while upon the sea you gaily roam,
   Remember that a heart for thee is fretting –   915
   The tender little heart you've left at home!

GIA.
        Now, Marco dear,
        My wishes hear:
          While you're away
        It's understood   920
        You will be good
          And not too gay.
        To every trace
        Of maiden grace
          You will be blind,   925
        And will not glance
        By any chance
          On womankind!

        If you are wise,
        You'll shut your eyes   930
          Till we arrive,
        And not address
        A lady less
          Than forty-five.
        You'll please to frown   935
        On every gown
          That you may see;
        And, O my pet,
        You won't forget
          You've married me!   940

    And O my darling, O my pet,
    Whatever else you may forget,
    In yonder isle beyond the sea,
    Do not forget you've married me.

TESS.
        You'll lay your head   945
        Upon your bed

974 *Xebeque*: A small, three-masted ship used for carrying merchandise in the Mediterranean.

At set of sun.
You will not sing
Of anything
  To any one.   950
You'll sit and mope
All day, I hope,
  And shed a tear
Upon the life
Your little wife   955
  Is passing here.

And if so be
You think of me,
  Please tell the moon!
I'll read it all   960
In rays that fall
  On the lagoon:
You'll be so kind
As tell the wind
  How you may be,   965
And send me words
By little birds
  To comfort me!

And O my darling, O my pet,
Whatever else you may forget,   970
In yonder isle beyond the sea,
Do not forget you've married me.

QUARTET.   O my darling, O my pet, etc.

CHORUS (*during which a 'Xebeque' is hauled
        alongside the quay*).   975

Then away { they / we } go to an island fair
  That lies in a Southern sea:
We know not where, and we don't much care,
  Wherever that isle may be.

THE MEN (*hauling on boat*).   One, two, three,   980
           Haul!
        One, two, three,
           Haul!

993–1000 *Away we go*
Both the licence copy and the first American edition of the libretto give Marco another four lines in this song:

> And the birds all twitter
>> Through the winter weather,
> Like a spinnet and a zither
>> That are played together.

The licence copy then continues:

ALL.   The pull, yeo ho! and again, yeo ho! (*hoisting sail*)
And again yeo ho! with a will!
When the breezes are a-blowing,
Then our ship will be a-going,
When they don't we shall all stand still!
And away we go to the island fair,
That lies in a southern sea,

$$\left. \begin{array}{l} \text{We} \\ \text{They} \end{array} \right\} \text{know not where, and} \left\{ \begin{array}{l} \text{we} \\ \text{they} \end{array} \right. \text{don't much care,}$$

Wherever that isle may be.

END OF ACT I

The above version of the final chorus was also used at the first night and early performances at the Savoy Theatre, where it followed the present shortened version of Marco's solo.

One, two, three,
  Haul!   985
With a will!

ALL.   When the breezes are blowing
        The ship will be going,

       When they don't $\left\{ \begin{array}{c} \text{we shall} \\ \text{they shall} \end{array} \right\}$ all stand still!

    Then away $\left\{ \begin{array}{c} \text{they} \\ \text{we} \end{array} \right\}$ go to an island fair,   990

     We know not where, and we don't much care,
       Wherever that isle may be.

SOLO – MARCO.

Away we go
  To a balmy isle,
Where the roses blow   995
  All the winter while.

ALL (*hoisting sail*).   Then away $\left\{ \begin{array}{c} \text{we} \\ \text{they} \end{array} \right\}$ go to an island fair

      That lies in a Southern sea:

     Then away $\left\{ \begin{array}{c} \text{we} \\ \text{they} \end{array} \right\}$ go to an island fair,

      Then away, then away, then away!   1000

(*The men embark on the 'Xebeque'.* MARCO *and* GIUSEPPE *embracing* GIANETTA *and* TESSA. *The girls wave a farewell to the men as the curtain falls.*)

END OF ACT I

6   *cup and ball*: A game played with a ball which is attached by string to a rod which has a
    cup at one end of it. The object is to toss the ball and catch it in the cup.
    morra: A favourite Italian game in which two people face each other and alternately raise
    their hands quickly. The object is to guess how many fingers are being held up. The win-
    ner is the first player to guess correctly nine times.

15–22   *Two kings, of undue pride bereft*
        This duet is not included in the licence copy sent to the Lord Chamberlain. Instead it
        contains at this point a solo for Pietro, one of the gondoliers brought over by Marco
        and Giuseppe to Barataria, who has been appointed a judge by the island's new rulers.
        The song was adapted before the opening night into the duet now sung by Marco and
        Giuseppe. Here it is:

PIETRO.   Two monarchs free from all ambition,
                           Who do not presume on their condition,
                                But do their very best to please
                                And justify their bread and cheese.
                           A people dignified and polished,
                           Who class distinctions have abolished,
                                And, one and all, with zeal combine
                                To make their monarchs toe the line.
                           When joined in such harmonious tether,
                           Both king and people pull together.
                                No wonder peace and plenty smile
                                Upon this highly-favoured isle.

ALL.   When joined in such harmonious tether, etc.

ACT II

SCENE. – *Pavilion in the Court of Barataria.* MARCO *and* GIUSEPPE, *magnificently dressed, are seated on two thrones, occupied in cleaning the crown and the sceptre. The Gondoliers are discovered, dressed, some as courtiers, officers of rank, etc., and others as private soldiers and servants of various degrees. All are enjoying themselves without reference to social distinctions – some playing cards, others throwing dice, some reading, others playing cup and ball, 'morra', etc.* 5

CHORUS OF MEN *with* MARCO *and* GIUSEPPE.

Of happiness the very pith
　　　　In Barataria you may see:
A monarchy that's tempered with
　　　　Republican Equality. 10
This form of government we find
The beau-ideal of its kind –
A despotism strict, combined
　　　　With absolute equality!

MARCO *and* GIUSEPPE.

Two kings, of undue pride bereft, 15
　　　　Who act in perfect unity,
Whom you can order right and left
　　　　With absolute impunity.
Who put their subjects at their ease
By doing all they can to please! 20
And thus, to earn their bread-and-cheese,
　　　　Seize every opportunity.

CHORUS.　　　Of happiness the very pith, etc.

MAR. Gentlemen, we are much obliged to you for your expressions of satisfaction and good feeling – I say, we are much obliged to you for your 25 expressions of satisfaction and good feeling.

48 *We want our tea*: This was one of several gags introduced by Rutland Barrington into early performances. Gilbert specifically approved it, and the line was included in the libretto for the 1907 revival.

There is an amusing story, recounted in Leslie Baily's *The Gilbert and Sullivan Book*, about Richard D'Oyly Carte's explanation of the gags in *The Gondoliers* to Queen Victoria after the Royal Command performance at Windsor in March 1891. It comes from the magazine *The Era*:

> Her Majesty, who followed her copy of Mr Gilbert's libretto closely, observed that certain additions were made to the text by the leading performers. Mr Carte was summoned to the elbow of Royalty and the Queen graciously inquired of him the meaning of these interpolations which she had noticed.
>
> 'These, your Majesty,' said Mr Carte, 'are what we call gags.'
>
> 'Gags?' replied the Queen, 'I thought gags were things that were put by authority into people's mouths.'
>
> 'These gags, your Majesty,' answered the manager, bowing profoundly, 'are things that people put into their own mouths without authority.'
>
> The Queen smiled benignly and seemed perfectly satisfied with the ready reply.

61–124 *Rising early in the morning*

Giuseppe's famous catalogue of the duties of a working monarch is said to have greatly amused Queen Victoria. Gilbert's original version of the song, contained in the licence edition, is worth quoting in full although on the whole I think the revised version now sung is an improvement. It will be noted that it has a slightly different metre. The first six lines are the same in both cases. The first version then proceeds:

> First we polish off some batches
> Of political despatches,
>   Give the usual assent
>   To some Acts of Parliament.
> If the business isn't heavy
> We may hold a Royal *levée*,
>   Or review the household troops –
>   Shalloo humps! and shalloo hoops!

ALL. We heard you.

MAR. We are delighted, at any time, to fall in with sentiments so charmingly expressed.

ALL. That's all right. 30

GIU. At the same time there is just one little grievance that we should like to ventilate.

ALL (*angrily*). What?

GIU. Don't be alarmed – it's not serious. It is arranged that, until it is decided which of us two is the actual King, we are to act as one person. 35

GIORGIO. Exactly.

GIU. Now, although we act as *one* person, we are, in point of fact, *two* persons.

ANNIBALE. Ah, I don't think we can go into that. It is a legal fiction, and legal fictions are solemn things. Situated as we are, we can't recognize 40 two independent responsibilities.

GIU. No; but you can recognize two independent appetites. It's all very well to say we act as one person, but when you supply us with only one ration between us, I should describe it as a legal fiction carried a little too far.

ANNI. It's rather a nice point. I don't like to express an opinion off- 45 hand. Suppose we reserve it for argument before the full Court?

MAR. Yes, but what are we to do in the meantime?

MAR. *and* GIU. We want our tea.

ANNI. I think we may make an interim order for double rations on their Majesties entering into the usual undertaking to indemnify in the event of an 50 adverse decision?

GIOR. That, I think, will meet the case. But you must work hard – stick to it – nothing like work.

GIU. Oh, certainly. We quite understand that a man who holds the magnificent position of King should do something to justify it. We are called 55 'Your Majesty', we are allowed to buy ourselves magnificent clothes, our subjects frequently nod to us in the streets, the sentries always return our salutes, and we enjoy the inestimable privilege of heading the subscription lists to all the principal charities. In return for these advantages the least we can do is to make ourselves useful about the Palace. 60

SONG – GIUSEPPE *with* CHORUS.

> Rising early in the morning,
>> We proceed to light the fire,
> Then our Majesty adorning
>> In its workaday attire,
>>> We embark without delay 65
>> On the duties of the day.
> First, we polish off some batches

On returning, *inter alia*,
We plate-powder the regalia,
   (With a special rubbing down
   For the sceptre and the crown.)
Then in view of cravings inner,
We go down and order dinner,
Do some labour literary
For our private secretary,
Spend an hour in titivating
All our gentlemen-in-waiting.
Then, if nothing up is cropping,
We may do a little shopping,
Buy some fruit and vegetables,
Or be useful in the stables.
After that we generally
Go and dress our private *valet*,
   Or have a *tête-à-tête*
   With the presentation plate,
Or we run on little errands for the Ministers of State.

After luncheon (making merry
On a bun and glass of sherry)
   If we've nothing in particular to do,
   We create a peer or two –
Make a Royal Proclamation,
Or receive a Deputation –
   Toddle off, in semi-state,
   To a function or a *fête*.
After that, we take our orders
From the keepers and the warders.
   We prepare their tea and toast,
   Take their letters to the post;
Then we go and stand as sentry
At the Palace (private entry),
While the warrior on duty .
Goes in search of beer and beauty.
He relieves us if he's able
Just in time to lay the table,
Hand the beef and the potaters
(We are admirable waiters).
After dinner, in a manner,
We perform on the pianner
(All our little skill invoking),
While the gentlemen are smoking.
   If objection there is none,
   We may go to bed at one,
With the gratifying feeling that our duty has been done!

ALL.   After dinner, in a manner, etc.

103 *the Garter or the Thistle or the Bath*: Three orders of knighthood in Great Britain. The Most
     Noble Order of the Garter is the highest. It was instituted by Edward III in *c*.1348. Le-
     gend has it that it originated when the Countess of Salisbury had accidentally lost her
     garter at a court ball. It was picked up by the king, who, noticing the looks of the specta-
     tors, rebuked them by binding the blue band around his own knee, saying as he did so
     'Honi soit qui mal y pense' ('Evil be to him who evil thinks').
       The Most Ancient Order of the Thistle is the highest Scottish order of knighthood
     and ranks second only to the order of the Garter. It was instituted by King James VII of
     Scotland and II of England in 1687. The Most Honourable Order of the Bath dates from

Of political despatches,
    And foreign politicians circumvent;
Then, if business isn't heavy,   70
We may hold a Royal *levée*,
    Or ratify some Acts of Parliament.
Then we probably review the household troops –
With the usual 'Shalloo humps!' and 'Shalloo hoops!'
Or receive with ceremonial and state   75
An interesting Eastern potentate.
    After that we generally
    Go and dress our private *valet* –
(It's a rather nervous duty – he's a touchy little man) –
    Write some letters literary   80
    For our private secretary –
He is shaky in his spelling, so we help him if we can.
    Then, in view of cravings inner,
    We go down and order dinner;
Then we polish the Regalia and the Coronation Plate –   85
    Spend an hour in titivating
    All our Gentlemen-in-Waiting;
Or we run on little errands for the Ministers of State.

    Oh, philosophers may sing
    Of the troubles of a King;   90
Yet the duties are delightful, and the privileges great;
    But the privilege and pleasure
    That we treasure beyond measure
Is to run on little errands for the Ministers of State.

CHORUS. Oh, philosophers may sing, etc.   95

After luncheon (making merry
On a bun and glass of sherry),
    If we've nothing in particular to do,
We may make a Proclamation,
Or receive a deputation –   100
    Then we possibly create a Peer or two.
Then we help a fellow-creature on his path
With the Garter or the Thistle or the Bath,
Or we dress and toddle off in semi-state
To a festival, a function, or a *fête*.   105
    Then we go and stand as sentry
    At the Palace (private entry),
Marching hither, marching thither, up and down and to and fro,

1399 and derives its name from the ceremony of bathing which was formerly practised at the inauguration of a knight as a symbol of purity.

120 *of worries there are none*: The phrase was originally 'of troubles there are none'. It was changed to 'worries' in the third edition of the libretto.

141–68 *Take a pair of sparkling eyes*
This eternal favourite of amateur tenors has always evoked a mixed response from critics. The *Sunday Times* review of the first night described it as 'one of Sir Arthur Sullivan's inspirations – a strain of the purest melody, exquisitely accompanied by divided strings *pizzicati* in imitation of a guitar'. More recently, however, writing in the foreword to the 1962 Oxford University Press edition of the Savoy Operas, Lord David Cecil complained of its 'insensitiveness of taste' and of 'a genteel vulgarity . . . which is distressing'.

Sullivan composed the tune to the song, which began in Gilbert's first version 'Take a pair of bright blue eyes', at five o'clock in the morning of 9 November 1889. He had been working solidly since 5.15 the previous afternoon after taking a three-and-a-half-hour rehearsal earlier that day. During his marathon session through the night he had also composed 'There lived a King' and had rewritten the opening of Act I and Luiz and Casilda's two duets, 'Ah, well-beloved' and 'There was a time'. It is small wonder that for the last two lines which form the coda of 'Take a pair of sparkling eyes' he borrowed and transposed a theme which he had already used in a ballad entitled 'A Life That Lives for You'.

For a long time it was customary in D'Oyly Carte productions for all other performers to leave the stage when one of the principals was singing a solo aria. This practice was started by Gilbert, who wrote in a letter to Helen D'Oyly Carte in June 1909: 'Giuseppe should leave the stage during the refrain of the first verse of "Take a pair" .'

145 *Having passed the Rubicon*: The Rubicon was a small river which separated ancient Italy from Cisalpine Gaul. When Julius Caesar crossed it in 49 B.C. he passed beyond the limits of his territory and became an invader. The incident has given rise to the expression 'to cross the Rubicon', meaning to take an irrevocable step.

         While the warrior on duty
            Goes in search of beer and beauty   110
      (And it generally happens that he hasn't far to go).
         He relieves us, if he's able,
            Just in time to lay the table,
      Then we dine and serve the coffee, and at half-past twelve or one,
         With a pleasure that's emphatic,   115
            We retire to our attic
      With the gratifying feeling that our duty has been done!

         Oh, philosophers may sing
            Of the troubles of a King,
      But of pleasures there are many and of worries there are none;   120
         And the culminating pleasure
            That we treasure beyond measure
      Is the gratifying feeling that our duty has been done!

CHORUS. Oh, philosophers may sing, etc.
                    (*Exeunt all but* MARCO *and* GIUSEPPE.)   125

   GIU. Yes, it really is a very pleasant existence. They're all so singularly
kind and considerate. You don't find them wanting to do this, or wanting to
do that, or saying 'It's my turn now'. No, they let us have all the fun to
ourselves, and never seem to grudge it.
   MAR. It makes one feel quite selfish. It almost seems like taking   130
advantage of their good nature.
   GIU. How nice they were about the double rations.
   MAR. Most considerate. Ah! there's only one thing wanting to make us
thoroughly comfortable.
   GIU. And that is?   135
   MAR. The dear little wives we left behind us three months ago.
   GIU. Yes, it *is* dull without female society. We can do without
everything else, but we can't do without that.
   MAR. And if we have that in perfection, we have everything. There is
only one recipe for perfect happiness.   140

                    SONG – MARCO.

            Take a pair of sparkling eyes,
               Hidden, ever and anon,
                  In a merciful eclipse –
            Do not heed their mild surprise –
               Having passed the Rubicon,   145
                  Take a pair of rosy lips;

182 *And we wanted variety*: This line was originally sung 'And we long for variety'.

Take a figure trimly planned –
  Such as admiration whets –
    (Be particular in this);
Take a tender little hand,   150
  Fringed with dainty fingerettes,
    Press it – in parenthesis; –
Ah! Take all these, you lucky man –
Take and keep them, if you can!

Take a pretty little cot –   155
  Quite a miniature affair –
    Hung about with trellised vine,
Furnish it upon the spot
  With the treasures rich and rare
    I've endeavoured to define.   160
Live to love and love to live –
  You will ripen at your ease,
    Growing on the sunny side –
Fate has nothing more to give.
  You're a dainty man to please   165
    If you are not satisfied.
Ah! Take my counsel, happy man;
Act upon it, if you can!

(*Enter Chorus of Contadine, running in, led by* FIAMETTA *and* VITTORIA.
  They are met by all the Ex-Gondoliers, who welcome them heartily.)   170

SCENA – CHORUS OF GIRLS, QUARTET, DUET *and* CHORUS.

Here we are, at the risk of our lives,
From ever so far, and we've brought your wives –
And to that end we've crossed the main,
And don't intend to return again!

FIA.   Though obedience is strong,   175
                  Curiosity's stronger –
              We waited for long,
                  Till we couldn't wait longer.

VIT.   It's imprudent, we know,
                  But without your society   180
              Existence was slow,
                  And we wanted variety –

BOTH.   Existence was slow, and we wanted variety.

189–92 *Tessa! Giuseppe . . .:* In the licence copy, Marco, Giuseppe, Tessa and Gianetta are given a brief quartet after their mutual greetings and before the girls embark on their long series of questions. It was struck out before the opening performance although the caption 'Quartet' remains in the vocal score to this day.

> A pleasanter kind of surprise
> We ⎫
> You ⎭ possibly couldn't devise.
> It's a genuine species of joy
> Which hasn't a grain of alloy!
> When husband is parted from wife
> A slice is cut out of his life;
> And when they're united again
> The pleasure makes up for the pain.

ALL.   So here we are, at the risk of our lives,
              And we've brought your wives –   185
              And to that end we've crossed the main,
              And we don't intend to return again!

(*Enter* GIANETTA *and* TESSA. *They rush to the arms of* MARCO *and* GIUSEPPE.)

GIU.   Tessa! ⎫
TESS.   Giuseppe! ⎬ *Embrace.*   190
GIA.   Marco!   ⎥
MAR.   Gianetta! ⎭

TESSA *and* GIANETTA.

TESS.   After sailing to this island –
GIA.   Tossing in a manner frightful,
TESS.   We are all once more on dry land –   195
GIA.   And we find the change delightful,
TESS.   As at home we've been remaining –
                  We've not seen you both for ages,
GIA.   Tell me, are you fond of reigning? –
                  How's the food, and what's the wages?   200
TESS.   Does your new employment please ye? –
GIA.   How does Royalizing strike you?
TESS.   Is it difficult or easy? –
GIA.   Do you think your subjects like you?
TESS.   I am anxious to elicit,   205
                  Is it plain and easy steering?
GIA.   Take it altogether, is it
                  Better fun than gondoliering?
BOTH.   We shall both go on requesting
                  Till you tell us, never doubt it;   210
          Everything is interesting,
                  Tell us, tell us all about it!

CHORUS.   They will both go on requesting, etc.

TESS.   Is the populace exacting?
GIA.   Do they keep you at a distance?   215
TESS.   All unaided are you acting,
GIA.   Or do they provide assistance?
TESS.   When you're busy, have you got to
                  Get up early in the morning?
GIA.   If you do what you ought not to,   220
                  Do they give the usual warning?

244 *I've done*: In the version originally intended by Gilbert, Tessa and Gianetta had not, in
fact, quite done at this point. The licence copy contains the following additional lines:

> GIA. Your employer won't be angry, will he?
> MAR. My employer?
> GIA. The old gentleman in mourning.
> GIU. O lord, I forgot him! But he won't know – he's not here. He's in Spain, hunting after
> Nurse.
> GIA. Then we may stay?
> MAR. Stay? I should think you might! Why, we've been longing for this! (*kisses her*).
> TESS. That accounts for it. And now – which of you is king?
> GIU. That we shan't know, etc.

253 *Dance a cachucha, fandango, bolero*: A tall – not to say exhausting – order. These three Spanish dances all have different rhythms and speeds. The cachucha, which is what is actually
played and danced in *The Gondoliers*, is the fastest. It is danced by couples and includes
the completion of a circle by four quarter-turns and a backward glissade of alternate feet
at the second and fourth sections of the measure.

The fandango is a slowish dance in six-eight time, usually danced by one couple and
accompanied by castanets.

The bolero, which Gilbert has, of course, already used for the surname of the Grand
Inquisitor, is a slow minuet-like dance which was also normally danced by only two peo-
ple at a time. My information tells me that it was invented by one Zerezo in 1780, so the
Baratarians must have been very well ahead of their time to be dancing to it in 1750.

254 *Xeres . . . Manzanilla, Montero*: Xeres is an old Spanish word for the fortified wine which
we call sherry; the name derives from the town of Xeres (now Jerez) in Andalusia, which
is famous for its wine. Manzanilla is a light dry sherry, and Montero is a wine from the
Pyrenees region of Spain (the word literally means mountaineer).

TESS.	With a horse do they equip you?
GIA.	Lots of trumpeting and drumming?
TESS.	Do the Royal tradesmen tip you?
GIA.	Ain't the livery becoming!
TESS.	Does your human being inner
	Feed on everything that nice is?
GIA.	Do they give you wine for dinner;
	Peaches, sugar-plums, and ices?
BOTH.	We shall both go on requesting
	Till you tell us, never doubt it;
	Everything is interesting,
	Tell us, tell us all about it!

CHORUS.   They will both go on requesting, etc.

MAR. This is indeed a most delightful surprise!

TESS. Yes, we thought you'd like it. You see, it was like this. After you left we felt very dull and mopey, and the days crawled by, and you never wrote; so at last I said to Gianetta, 'I can't stand this any longer; those two poor Monarchs haven't got any one to mend their stockings or sew on their buttons or patch their clothes – at least, I hope they haven't – let us all pack up a change and go and see how they're getting on.' And she said, 'Done', and they all said, 'Done'; and we asked old Giacopo to lend us his boat, and *he* said, 'Done'; and we've crossed the sea; and, thank goodness, *that's* done; and here we are, and – and – *I've* done!

GIA. And now – which of you is King?

TESS. And which of us is Queen?

GIU. That we shan't know until Nurse turns up. But never mind that – the question is, how shall we celebrate the commencement of our honeymoon? Gentlemen, will you allow us to offer you a magnificent banquet?

ALL. We will!

GIU. Thanks very much; and, ladies, what do you say to a dance?

TESS. A banquet *and* a dance! Oh, it's too much happiness!

CHORUS *and* DANCE.

Dance a cachucha, fandango, bolero,
Xeres we'll drink – Manzanilla, Montero –
Wine, when it runs in abundance, enhances
The reckless delight of that wildest of dances!
  To the pretty pitter-pitter-patter,
  And the clitter-clitter-clitter-clatter –
    Clitter – clitter – clatter,
    Pitter – pitter – patter,
Patter, patter, patter, patter, we'll dance.

265   *Cachucha*: This wild dance has always given the D'Oyly Carte ladies an opportunity to show their paces, and other things as well. The first-night review in the *Topical Times* commented: 'The attractions of *The Gondoliers* are numerous. To begin with, the chorus wore comparatively short skirts for the first time, and the gratifying fact is revealed to a curious world that the Savoy chorus are a very well-legged lot.'

271   *Sorry you're late*: This was one of Rutland Barrington's gags later incorporated in the libretto.

276   *the servants'-hall*: Helen D'Oyly Carte obviously thought that the classless Americans would not know the meaning of this term. In her version prepared for performance in the United States, this line was changed to 'But surely, surely the kitchen rather than the drawing room is the proper place for these gentry', to which Giuseppe's reply was 'We have appropriated the kitchen and the attic'.

279–80   *accessible only by tickets* . . . : The line about the Lord Chamberlain was almost certainly another of Barrington's gags. Gilbert's original line was simply 'It's the Royal Apartment, and we permit no intruders'. The Lord Chamberlain is the official in overall charge of the Royal Household. He was also, until 1968, the censor of all plays performed in Britain. Like all other dramatists, Gilbert was required to send copies of his new works to the Lord Chamberlain's office for licensing before they could be performed.

294–5   *A plate of macaroni and a rusk*: In Helen D'Oyly Carte's American version this becomes 'pretzels or a Boston cracker?'

298   *Yes – gout*: Not gout, but the equally uncomfortable condition of rheumatism affected one of the D'Oyly Carte's distinguished line of Grand Inquisitors and nearly caused a minor revolution in the way this scene was played.

    When she took over the running of the company in 1948 on the death of her father, Dame Bridget D'Oyly Carte was very surprised to find that shortly after coming on in this scene, Don Alhambra sat down on the royal throne and remained there for his conversation with Marco and Giuseppe and the singing of 'There lived a King'. Even for a monarchy remodelled on Republican principles, this seemed rather presumptuous and disrespectful behaviour on the part of one so proper. She inquired about the origins of this practice and eventually found that it had been introduced ten years or so earlier for the benefit of the then Don Alhambra, Sydney Granville, who was in his mid-sixties and suffered badly from rheumatism. When Granville finally left in 1942 after thirty-five years with the company, his successor, Richard Walker, continued the business of sitting down on the throne, and so what had been intended as a temporary expedient became established as a regular practice. Dame Bridget, however, put a stop to it and ever since, gout or no gout, the Don has respectfully remained standing in the presence of their Majesties the Kings of Barataria.

Old Xeres we'll drink – Manzanilla, Montero;
For wine, when it runs in abundance, enhances
The reckless delight of that wildest of dances!

CACHUCHA.   265

(The dance is interrupted by the unexpected appearance of DON ALHAMBRA, *who looks on with astonishment.* MARCO *and* GIUSEPPE *appear embarrassed. The others run off, except Drummer Boy, who is driven off by* DON ALHAMBRA.*)*

DON AL. Good evening. Fancy ball?   270
GIU. No, not exactly. A little friendly dance. That's all. Sorry you're late.
DON AL. But I saw a groom dancing, and a footman!
MAR. Yes. That's the Lord High Footman.
DON AL. And, dear me, a common little drummer boy!
GIU. Oh no! That's the Lord High Drummer Boy.   275
DON AL. But surely, surely the servants'-hall is the place for these gentry?
GIU. Oh dear no! *We* have appropriated the servants'-hall. It's the Royal Apartment, and accessible only by tickets obtainable at the Lord Chamberlain's office.   280
MAR. We really must have some place that we can call our own.
DON AL. (*puzzled*). I'm afraid I'm not quite equal to the intellectual pressure of the conversation.
GIU. You see, the Monarchy has been re-modelled on Republican principles.   285
DON AL. What!
GIU. All departments rank equally, and everybody is at the head of his department.
DON AL. I see.
MAR. I'm afraid you're annoyed.   290
DON AL. No. I won't say that. It's not quite what I expected.
GIU. I'm awfully sorry.
MAR. So am I.
GIU. By the by, can I offer you anything after your voyage? A plate of macaroni and a rusk?   295
DON AL. (*preoccupied*). No, no – nothing – nothing.
GIU. Obliged to be careful?
DON AL. Yes – gout. You see, in every Court there are distinctions that must be observed.
GIU. (*puzzled*). There are, are there?   300
DON AL. Why, of course. For instance, you wouldn't have a Lord High Chancellor play leapfrog with his own cook.

308 *tuck in his tuppenny*: tuck in his head. The Grand Inquisitor was very advanced to be using this particular colloquialism in 1750. According to the *Oxford English Dictionary* its first recorded use in England was not until 1859.

322 *Rhenish wine*: Wine produced in the Rhine region. It figures prominently in one of Gilbert's *Bab Ballads*, 'The Baron Klopfzetterheim'.

324 *at junket or at jink*: A junket is a feast or banquet, particularly one at public expense. The word jink is more usually found in its plural form, and most commonly in the phrase 'high jinks' meaning pranks, frolics or generally lively and boisterous occasions.

325 *toddy*: A drink made with hot water, whisky, sugar and sometimes also lemon juice, which is said to be particularly efficacious in easing colds and influenza. Making great play with its Scottish associations, Sullivan scored an accompaniment to Marco and Giuseppe's line 'With toddy, must be content with toddy' which suggests the droning of bagpipes at the start of a reel.

336 *shovel hats*: A stiff broad-brimmed hat, turned up at the sides and with a shovel-like curve at the front and the back, which was formerly worn by many ecclesiastics.

MAR. Why not?

DON AL. Why not! Because a Lord High Chancellor is a personage of
great dignity, who should never, under any circumstances, place himself in 305
the position of being told to tuck in his tuppenny, except by noblemen of his
own rank. A Lord High Archbishop, for instance, might tell a Lord High
Chancellor to tuck in his tuppenny, but certainly not a cook, gentlemen,
certainly not a cook.

GIU. Not even a Lord High Cook? 310

DON AL. My good friend, that is a rank that is not recognized at the
Lord Chamberlain's office. No, no, it won't do. I'll give you an instance in
which the experiment was tried.

SONG – DON ALHAMBRA, *with* MARCO *and* GIUSEPPE.

DON AL.	There lived a King, as I've been told,
	In the wonder-working days of old,
	When hearts were twice as good as gold,
	And twenty times as mellow.
	Good-temper triumphed in his face,
	And in his heart he found a place
	For all the erring human race
	And every wretched fellow.
	When he had Rhenish wine to drink
	It made him very sad to think
	That some, at junket or at jink,
	Must be content with toddy.

315

320

325

MAR. *and* GIU.   With toddy, must be content with toddy.

DON AL.   He wished all men as rich as he
            (And he was rich as rich could be),
            So to the top of every tree
               Promoted everybody.

330

MAR. *and* GIU.   Now, that's the kind of King for me.
            He wished all men as rich as he,
            So to the top of every tree
               Promoted everybody!

DON AL.   Lord Chancellors were cheap as sprats,   335
            And Bishops in their shovel hats
            Were plentiful as tabby cats –
               In point of fact, too many.
            Ambassadors cropped up like hay,

344 *Lords-Lieutenant*: The office of Lord-Lieutenant was created in 1549 to take over the military duties of the sheriff. Later the duties became more administrative and involved the recommendation of local magistrates and justices of the peace to the Lord Chancellor. Lords-Lieutenant are still the Queen's representatives in each county, although their functions now are largely ceremonial.

347 *With Admirals all round his wide dominions*: This provides Sullivan with the opportunity for another musical joke. This time he accompanies Marco and Giuseppe's line with a snatch of hornpipe.

367 *shoddy*: Woollen yarn obtained by shredding refuse woollen rags, which, with the addition of some new wool, is made into a kind of cloth. The word has more generally come to mean any worthless material made to look like something of superior quality. Sullivan's original accompaniment to Marco and Giuseppe's refrain 'Of shoddy, up goes the price of shoddy' included a few bars of 'Yankee Doodle Dandy' to show what he thought of the American pirate versions of his operas.

	Prime Ministers and such as they	340
	Grew like asparagus in May,	
	And Dukes were three a penny.	
	On every side Field–Marshals gleamed,	
	Small beer were Lords-Lieutenant deemed,	
	With Admirals the ocean teemed	345
	All round his wide dominions.	

MAR. *and* GIU.   With Admirals all round his wide dominions.

DON AL.   And Party Leaders you might meet
In twos and threes in every street
Maintaining, with no little heat,   350
    Their various opinions.

MAR. *and* GIU.   Now that's a sight you couldn't beat –
Two Party Leaders in each street
Maintaining, with no little heat,
    Their various opinions.   355

DON AL.   That King, although no one denies
His heart was of abnormal size,
Yet he'd have acted otherwise
    If he had been acuter.
The end is easily foretold,   360
When every blessed thing you hold
Is made of silver, or of gold,
    You long for simple pewter.
When you have nothing else to wear
But cloth of gold and satins rare,   365
For cloth of gold you cease to care –
    Up goes the price of shoddy.

MAR. *and* GIU.   Of shoddy, up goes the price of shoddy.

DON AL.   In short, whoever you may be,
To this conclusion you'll agree,   370
When every one is somebodee,
    Then no one's anybody!

MAR. *and* GIU.   Now that's as plain as plain can be,
To this conclusion we agree –

ALL.   When every one is somebodee,   375
    Then no one's anybody!

386   *lucky dog*: This was originally 'lucky fellow'.

401   *what will Her Majesty say*: This line was originally 'What will the Duke say', which was a popular Victorian catch-phrase. It occurs several times in Don Alhambra's dialogue in the first edition of the libretto. I cannot discover when this particular line was changed to its present form, but it would be nice to think that it was for the Command performance before Queen Victoria in 1891.

416   *There's something in that*: A handwritten addition to Helen D'Oyly Carte's corrected copy of the 1907 libretto has Giuseppe saying to Tessa at this point 'Go in the corner'. This was no doubt originally another Barrington gag. It does not appear in the next master copy of the libretto prepared by J. M. Gordon in 1914.

(GIANETTA *and* TESSA *enter unobserved. The two girls, impelled by curiosity, remain listening at the back of the stage.*)

DON AL. And now I have some important news to communicate. His Grace the Duke of Plaza-Toro, Her Grace the Duchess, and their beautiful daughter Casilda – I say their beautiful daughter Casilda — 380
GIU. We heard you.
DON AL. Have arrived at Barataria, and may be here at any moment.
MAR. The Duke and Duchess are nothing to us.
DON AL. But the daughter – the beautiful daughter! Aha! Oh, you're a 385
lucky dog, one of you!
GIU. I think you're a very incomprehensible old gentleman.
DON AL. Not a bit – I'll explain. Many years ago when you (whichever you are) were a baby, you (whichever you are) were married to a little girl who has grown up to be the most beautiful young lady in Spain. That 390
beautiful young lady will be here to claim you (whichever you are) in half an hour, and I congratulate that one (whichever it is) with all my heart.
MAR. Married when a baby!
GIU. But we were married three months ago!
DON AL. One of you – only one. The other (whichever it is) is an 395
unintentional bigamist.
GIA. *and* TESS. (*coming forward*). Well, upon my word!
DON AL. Eh? Who are these young people?
TESS. Who are we? Why, their wives, of course. We've just arrived.
DON AL. Their wives! Oh dear, this is very unfortunate! Oh dear, this 400
complicates matters! Dear, dear, what will Her Majesty say?
GIA. And do you mean to say that one of these Monarchs was already married?
TESS. And that neither of us will be a Queen?
DON AL. That is the idea I intended to convey. (TESSA *and* 405
GIANETTA *begin to cry.*)
GIU. (*to* TESSA). Tessa, my dear, dear child —
TESS. Get away! perhaps it's you!
MAR. (*to* GIA.) My poor, poor little woman!
GIA. Don't! Who knows whose husband you are? 410
TESS. And pray, why didn't you tell us all about it before they left Venice?
DON AL. Because, if I had, no earthly temptation would have induced these gentlemen to leave two such extremely fascinating and utterly irresistible little ladies! 415
TESS. There's something in that.
DON AL. I may mention that you will not be kept long in suspense, as the old lady who nursed the Royal child is at present in the torture chamber, waiting for me to interview her.

437   *O Mount Vesuvius*: Is it too fanciful to speculate whether the fact that Tessa chooses for
her apostrophe the famous volcano on the edge of the Bay of Naples suggests that it
might be visible from Barataria? In that case, the southern sea in which the island stands
is that part of the Mediterranean known as the Tyrrhenian, which is certainly southern
to the Venetians, and Barataria lies somewhere between Sardinia and Sicily.

438   *a vulgar fraction*: A common-or-garden fraction in which the numerator and denomina-
tor are represented by numbers placed the one above and the other below a horizontal
line. For complex, compound, continued, decimal, proper and improper fractions,
consult the modern Major-General in *The Pirates of Penzance*. He is, after all, very well
acquainted with matters mathematical. I'm not.

442–87 *In a contemplative fashion*
This quartet, so splendidly muddled and yet at the same time so tightly controlled, is
perhaps the supreme example of Sullivan's trick of setting several different vocal themes
one against another. He himself wrote in a letter to a friend, quoted in Leslie Baily's *The
Gilbert and Sullivan Book*:

> You get the germ of it in *The Sorcerer* and it is afterwards worked in a greater degree in *The
> Pirates* (the policemen's chorus with the counter theme for the sopranos). In *The Mikado*
> there is amongst others the Trio for the three men in the first act, with all three different
> themes going at the same time. The most ingenious bit of work (certainly the most difficult)
> is the quartet in *The Gondoliers*, 'In a contemplative fashion'.

Certainly both composer and librettist seem to have laboured over this more than any
other number in the opera. Sullivan first asked Gilbert to rewrite his original draft at
the end of August 1889, and on 12 September he received an amended version and the
following letter:

> Will this do? It is dactylic, but it is difficult to get the contrast you want without dactyls.
> Probably it will be impracticable to set the accompanying lines, 'In a contemplative fash-
> ion,' so as to be a running accompaniment to the verses as they now stand. If so, I suppose
> they could be omitted during the verses and introduced at the end to finish with. If the
> verses won't do, send them back and I'll try again.

G I U. Poor old girl. Hadn't you better go and put her out of her suspense? 420
D O N A L. Oh no – there's no hurry – she's all right. She has all the
illustrated papers. However, I'll go and interrogate her, and, in the
meantime, may I suggest the absolute propriety of your regarding yourselves
as single young ladies. Good evening!

(*Exit* D O N A L H A M B R A.) 425

G I A. Well, here's a pleasant state of things!
M A R. Delightful. One of us is married to two young ladies, and nobody
knows which; and the other is married to one young lady whom nobody can
identify!
G I A. And one of us is married to one of you, and the other is married 430
to nobody.
T E S S. But which of you is married to which of us, and what's to
become of the other? (*About to cry.*)
G I U. It's quite simple. Observe. Two husbands have managed to
acquire three wives. Three wives – two husbands. (*Reckoning up.*) That's two-435
thirds of a husband to each wife.
T E S S. O Mount Vesuvius, here we are in arithmetic! My good sir, one
can't marry a vulgar fraction!
G I U. You've no right to call me a vulgar fraction.
M A R. We are getting rather mixed. The situation is entangled. Let's try 440
and comb it out.

QUARTET – M A R C O, G I U S E P P E, G I A N E T T A, T E S S A.

In a contemplative fashion,
And a tranquil frame of mind,
Free from every kind of passion,
Some solution let us find.
Let us grasp the situation, 445
Solve the complicated plot –
Quiet, calm deliberation
Disentangles every knot.

T E S S. I, no doubt, Giuseppe wedded – That's, of course, a slice of luck. He is rather dunder-headed, Still distinctly, he's a duck.	T H E O T H E R S. In a con- templative fashion, etc. 450
G I A. I, a victim, too, of Cupid, Marco married – that is clear. He's particularly stupid, Still distinctly, he's a dear.	T H E O T H E R S. Let us grasp the situation, etc. 455

Sullivan clearly found that the new version was not satisfactory and sent it back to be altered once again, as on 22 September we find Gilbert writing to him:

I have altered 'In a contemplative fashion' as suggested. The only question is whether the two last verses which the two girls sing at each other, and with which the two men have nothing to do, wouldn't be better in the original flowing metre, as lending itself to the volubility of two angry girls. I don't care a pin myself which it is, but I thought you might find the original dactylic metre better for the purpose.

In the event, the dactylic metre (i.e. one long syllable followed by two short ones) was used for the girls' angry utterances at the end and it produces a splendid crescendo of confusion before the controlled calmness of the final ensemble lines, 'Quiet, calm deliberation/Disentangles every knot!'

481 *Messer*: From the old Italian word *Messere*, meaning sir or master.

MAR. To Gianetta I was mated;
　　　　I can prove it in a trice:
　　　Though her charms are overrated,
　　　　Still I own she's rather nice.

THE OTHERS. In a con-
　　　templative fashion, etc.

460

GIU. I to Tessa, willy-nilly,
　　　　All at once a victim fell.
　　　She is what is called a silly,
　　　　Still she answers pretty well.

THE OTHERS. Let us
　　　grasp the situation, etc.

465

MAR. 　　　Now when we were pretty babies
　　　　　Some one married us, that's clear –

GIA. 　　　　　And if I can catch her
　　　　　　I'll pinch her and scratch her
　　　　　And send her away with a flea in her ear.

470

GIU. 　　　He whom that young lady married,
　　　　　To receive her can't refuse.

TESS. 　　　If I overtake her
　　　　　　I'll warrant I'll make her
　　　　To shake in her aristocratical shoes!

475

GIA. (to TESS.). 　　　If she married your Giuseppe
　　　　　You and he will have to part –

TESS. (to GIA.). 　　　If I have to do it
　　　　　　I'll warrant she'll rue it –
　　　　　I'll teach her to marry the man of my heart!

480

TESS. (to GIA.). 　　　If she married Messer Marco
　　　　　You're a spinster, that is plain –

GIA. (to TESS.). 　　　No matter – no matter.
　　　　　　If I can get at her
　　　　　I doubt if her mother will know her again!

485

ALL. 　　　Quiet, calm deliberation
　　　　　Disentangles every knot!

(*Exeunt, pondering.*)

(MARCH. *Enter procession of Retainers, heralding approach of* DUKE,
DUCHESS, *and* CASILDA. *All three are now dressed with the utmost*
magnificence.)

490

509 *She's excelled by none*: In the version originally intended for performance and printed in the licence copy, the solo 'On the day when I was wedded', now sung by the Duchess of Plaza-Toro slightly later in Act II, did not appear. Instead, she and the Duke were given the following song immediately after their duet 'This polite attention touches':

DUCH.	Oh, a mother is a mother,
	Though of ducal state,
	And her love she cannot smother
	Like the low-born mate
	Of a butcher, or a baker –
DUKE.	Or a baker's man –
DUCH.	Or a parish undertaker –
DUKE.	Or a publican –
DUCH.	Or a cowman, or a ploughman –
DUKE.	Or an artisan –
DUCH.	Or a pieman, or a flyman –
DUKE.	With his shandrydan.
DUCH.	Or a soldier, or a sailor,
	Or a tinker, or a tailor,
	Or a jockey, or a jailor –
DUKE.	With his big black van.

527 *Oh! couldn't he, though*: This line was not in the original first-night libretto and was almost certainly an ad-lib which was later authorized.

CHORUS OF MEN, *with* DUKE *and* DUCHESS.

	With ducal pomp and ducal pride	
	(Announce these comers,	
	O ye kettle-drummers!)	
	Comes Barataria's high-born bride.	495
	(Ye sounding cymbals clang!)	
	She comes to claim the Royal hand –	
	(Proclaim their Graces,	
	O ye double basses!)	
	Of the King who rules this goodly land.	500
	(Ye brazen brasses bang!)	
DUKE *and*	This polite attention touches	
DUCH.	Heart of Duke and heart of Duchess	
	Who resign their pet	
	With profound regret.	505
	She of beauty was a model	
	When a tiny tiddle-toddle,	
	And at twenty-one	
	She's excelled by none!	
CHORUS.	With ducal pomp and ducal pride, etc.	510

DUKE (*to his attendants*). Be good enough to inform His Majesty that His Grace the Duke of Plaza-Toro, Limited, has arrived, and begs —

CAS. Desires —

DUCH. Demands —

DUKE. And demands an audience. (*Exeunt attendants.*) And now, my child, prepare to receive the husband to whom you were united under such interesting and romantic circumstances.

CAS. But which is it? There are two of them!

DUKE. It is true that at present His Majesty is a double gentleman; but as soon as the circumstances of his marriage are ascertained, he will, *ipso facto*, boil down to a single gentleman – thus presenting a unique example of an individual who becomes a single man and a married man by the same operation.

DUCH. (*severely*). I have known instances in which the characteristics of both conditions existed concurrently in the same individual.

DUKE. Ah, he couldn't have been a Plaza-Toro.

DUCH. Oh! couldn't he, though!

CAS. Well, whatever happens, I shall, of course, be a dutiful wife, but I can never love my husband.

DUKE. I don't know. It's extraordinary what unprepossessing people one can love if one gives one's mind to it.

538–89 *On the day when I was wedded*
As already pointed out in the note to line 509, this song, although written, was missing from the licence copy and was not originally destined for performance. Gilbert was unhappy that, placed where it now is, it held up the action. He first proposed to Sullivan that it be moved to Act I, since, as he pointed out, the Duchess 'will have plenty to say in Act II and as present arranged she has practically nothing in Act I'. Later he suggested that it be dropped completely. However, it was saved, but whether by the entreaties of Sullivan or of Rosina Brandram, who played the Duchess, I have not been able to establish.

551 *this Tartar*: Originally a native inhabitant of the region of Central Asia extending eastward from the Caspian Sea, 'Tartar' has come to mean one who is savage, irritable and violent.

DUCH. I loved your father.

DUKE. My love – that remark is a little hard, I think? Rather cruel, perhaps? Somewhat uncalled-for, I venture to believe?

DUCH. It was very difficult, my dear; but I said to myself, 'That man is   535
a Duke, and I *will* love him.' Several of my relations bet me I couldn't, but
I did – desperately!

SONG – DUCHESS.

On the day when I was wedded
  To your admirable sire,
I acknowledge that I dreaded   540
  An explosion of his ire.
I was overcome with panic –
For his temper was volcanic,
  And I didn't dare revolt,
  For I feared a thunderbolt!   545
I was always very wary,
  For his fury was ecstatic –
His refined vocabulary
  Most unpleasantly emphatic.
    To the thunder   550
      Of this Tartar
    I knocked under
      Like a martyr;
    When intently
      He was fuming,   555
    I was gently
      Unassuming –
    When reviling
      Me completely,
    I was smiling   560
      Very sweetly:
Giving him the very best, and getting back the very worst –
That is how I tried to tame your great progenitor – at first!

    But I found that a reliance
      On my threatening appearance,   565
    And a resolute defiance
      Of marital interference,
    And a gentle intimation
      Of my firm determination
    To see what I could do   570
      To be wife and husband too

592–6 *Shady*: In the American version prepared by Helen D'Oyly Carte, this passage is altered
to:

> DUKE. Shady? A nobleman shady who is listed upon the Stock Exchange, and is upon
> the point of declaring an extra dividend? A nobleman shady who has never commanded a
> premium of less than ten per cent since he was first floated? A nobleman shady who is regu-
> larly sought for by Savings Banks, Trust Companies, executors, widows and – and –
> DUCH. Sheriffs.
> DUKE. And so forth, as an investment which combines unsurpassed profit with un-
> equalled security! Oh fie!

596 *floated at a premium*: The expression used when the initial sale of shares in a company
commands a price in excess of their nominal value.

598 *he was applied for over and over again*: When a public company is formed it issues a prospectus designed to attract investors. Those who want to invest then apply for shares.

601 *the Limited Liability Act*: Limited liability is a condition under which the loss that an
owner, or shareholder, of a business may incur is limited to the amount of capital invested by him and does not extend to his personal assets. In Britain the Duke of Plaza-
Toro could not legally have formed himself into a limited liability company until the
mid-nineteenth century. However, in Spain, and indeed in Barataria, company legislation may well have been more advanced!

   The idea of individuals forming themselves into limited companies is picked up again
in *Utopia Limited*, where Mr Goldbury, the company promoter, has 'applied the Limited
Liability principle to individuals, and every man, woman and child is now a Company
Limited with liability restricted to the amount of his declared Capital! There is not a
christened baby in Utopia who has not already issued his little Prospectus!'

607 *Recorders*: A magistrate or judge appointed by the Crown to exercise certain criminal and
civil jurisdictions. Recorders were originally people with legal knowledge appointed by
mayors to record the proceedings of their courts and the customs of their cities.

Was the only thing required
    For to make his temper supple,
And you couldn't have desired
    A more reciprocating couple.   575
    Ever willing
        To be wooing,
    We were billing –
        We were cooing;
    When I merely   580
        From him parted,
    We were nearly
        Broken-hearted –
    When in sequel
        Reunited,   585
    We were equal-
        Ly delighted.
So with double-shotted guns and colours nailed unto the mast,
I tamed your insignificant progenitor – at last!

CAS. My only hope is that when my husband sees what a shady family   590
he has married into he will repudiate the contract altogether.

DUKE. Shady? A nobleman shady, who is blazing in the lustre of
unaccustomed pocket-money? A nobleman shady, who can look back upon
ninety-five quarterings? It is not every nobleman who is ninety-five quarters
in arrear – I mean, who can look back upon ninety-five of them! And this,   595
just as I have been floated at a premium! Oh fie!

DUCH. Your Majesty is surely unaware that directly Your Majesty's
father came before the public he was applied for over and over again.

DUKE. My dear, Her Majesty's father was in the habit of being applied
for over and over again – and very urgently applied for, too – long before he   600
was registered under the Limited Liability Act.

RECITATIVE – DUKE.

To help unhappy commoners, and add to their enjoyment,
Affords a man of noble rank congenial employment;
Of our attempts we offer you examples illustrative:
The work is light, and, I may add, it's most remunerative.   605

DUET – DUKE *and* DUCHESS.

DUKE.   Small titles and orders
                 For Mayors and Recorders
                     I get – and they're highly delighted –

610 *baronetted*: Baronets are members of the lowest hereditary titled order, which was instituted by James I in the early seventeenth century. They are styled 'Sir', and the title is
normally shortened to 'Bart.' after their names.

611 *gazetted*: Promotions in the armed forces are published along with many other official
appointments in *The London Gazette*, a Government publication which appears every
Tuesday and Friday.

612 *Aldermen knighted*: Aldermen were important co-opted members of certain local
authorities. With the reorganization of local government they have now largely disappeared.

The first section of the Duke and Duchess's song recalls the second verse of 'Henceforth all the crimes that I find in *The Times*', a song from Act II of *Ruddigore*, now seldom
performed, in which Sir Ruthven Murgatroyd pours scorn on:

> Ye well-to-do squires, who live in the shires,
>   Where petty distinctions are vital,
> Who found Athenaeums and local museums,
>   With views to a baronet's title –
> Ye butchers and bakers and candlestick-makers
>   Who sneer at all things that are tradey –
> Whose middle-class lives are embarrassed by wives
>   Who long to parade as 'My Lady',
> Oh! allow me to offer a word of advice,
> The title's uncommonly dear at the price!

For all Gilbert's jeering at the honours system, he had no hesitation in accepting the
knighthood which was conferred on him in 1907. Indeed, it was for long a matter of
some irritation to him that Sullivan, who was knighted in 1883, had been honoured while
he had not. Perhaps small titles and orders were not to be sneered at too much after all.

DUCH.	They're highly delighted!

DUKE.	M.P.s baronetted,	610
	Sham Colonels gazetted,	
	And second-rate Aldermen knighted –	

DUCH.	Yes, Aldermen knighted.

DUKE.	Foundation-stone laying	
	I find very paying:	615
	It adds a large sum to my makings –	

DUCH.	Large sums to his makings.

DUKE.	At charity dinners	
	The best of speech-spinners,	
	I get ten per cent on the takings –	620

DUCH.	One-tenth of the takings.

DUCH.	I present any lady
	Whose conduct is shady
	Or smacking of doubtful propriety –

DUKE.	Doubtful propriety.	625

DUCH.	When Virtue would quash her,
	I take and whitewash her,
	And launch her in first-rate society –

DUKE.	First-rate society!

DUCH.	I recommend acres	630
	Of clumsy dressmakers –	
	Their fit and their finishing touches –	

DUKE.	Their finishing touches.

DUCH.	A sum in addition	
	They pay for permission	635
	To say that they make for the Duchess –	

DUKE.	They make for the Duchess!

DUKE.	Those pressing prevailers,

648 *Companies bubble*: A bubble is a worthless, unstable, unsound project, usually in the
financial or commercial sphere. The most famous was the South Sea Bubble of 1720,
when the price of shares in the South Sea Company rose out of all proportion to its
earnings as a result of massive over-speculation, with the inevitable aftermath of a disastrous crash and the ruin of thousands. The bursting of the South Sea Bubble led to
tight restrictions on the formation of joint-stock companies in Britain, which were not
eased until 1855, when limited liability companies – the kind formed by the Duke of
Plaza-Toro – were permitted.

655 *écarté*: A French card game which involves discarding cards. The word *écarté* means
discarded.

The ready-made tailors,
   Quote me as their great double-barrel –   640

DUCH.   Their great double-barrel –

DUKE.   I allow them to do so,
     Though Robinson Crusoe
       Would jib at their wearing apparel –

DUCH.   Such wearing apparel!   645

DUKE.   I sit, by selection,
     Upon the direction
       Of several Companies bubble –

DUCH.   All Companies bubble!

DUKE.   As soon as they're floated   650
     I'm freely bank-noted –
       I'm pretty well paid for my trouble –

DUCH.   He's paid for his trouble!

DUCH.   At middle-class party
     I play at *écarté* –   655
       And I'm by no means a beginner –

DUKE (*significantly*).   She's not a beginner.

DUCH.   To one of my station
     The remuneration –
       Five guineas a night and my dinner –   660

DUKE.   And wine with her dinner.

DUCH.   I write letters blatant
     On medicines patent –
       And use any other you mustn't –

DUKE.   Believe me, you mustn't –   665

DUCH.   And vow my complexion
     Derives its perfection
       From somebody's soap – which it doesn't –

690–91 *Allow me to present*: The original libretto printed in the licence copy has some extra lines
         and some extra business at this point, as follows:

> GIU. (*indicating* DUCHESS). The young lady one of us married? Marco, I begin to hope
> it was you.
> DUCH. (*pleased at the mistake*). Pardon me – her mother. This is our daughter (*presenting*
> CARLOTTA) – the Queen, and wife of one of you.
> GIU. Delighted, I'm sure – if it's me.
> MAR. Some time since we met – if it's me.
> GIU. (*aside to* MARCO). Neat little body!
> MAR. But not a patch on Gianetta.
> CAR. (*curtseying*). Gentlemen, I am the most obedient servant, etc.

DUKE (*significantly*).　　It certainly doesn't!

DUKE.　　We're ready as witness　　　　　　　　670
To any one's fitness
　　To fill any place or preferment –

DUCH.　　　　A place or preferment.

DUCH.　　We're often in waiting
At junket or *fêting*,　　　　　　　　675
　　And sometimes attend an interment –

DUKE.　　　　We enjoy an interment.

BOTH.　　In short, if you'd kindle
The spark of a swindle,
　　Lure simpletons into your clutches –　　680
　　　　Yes; into your clutches.
Or hoodwink a debtor,
You cannot do better

DUCH.　　Than trot out a Duke or a Duchess –

DUKE.　　　　A Duke or a Duchess!　　　　685

(*Enter* MARCO *and* GIUSEPPE.)

DUKE. Ah! Their Majesties. Your Majesty! (*Bows with great ceremony.*)
MAR. The Duke of Plaza-Toro, I believe?
DUKE. The same. (MARCO *and* GIUSEPPE *offer to shake hands with him.
The* DUKE *bows ceremoniously. They endeavour to imitate him.*) Allow me to　　690
present —
GIU. The young lady one of us married?

(MARCO *and* GIUSEPPE *offer to shake hands with her.* CASILDA *curtsies
formally. They endeavour to imitate her.*)

CAS. Gentlemen, I am the most obedient servant of one of you. (*Aside.*)　　695
Oh, Luiz!
DUKE. I am now about to address myself to the gentleman whom my
daughter married; the other may allow his attention to wander if he likes, for
what I am about to say does not concern him. Sir, you will find in this young
lady a combination of excellences which you would search for in vain in any　　700

709 *what do I find*: The cue for another of Barrington's gags. After the Duke's 'what do I find?', Giuseppe came in with 'What have I lost?' This was added to the libretto prepared for the 1907 revival but was cut by 1914.

728 *I'll take off anything else in reason*: There was some more ad-libbing at this point. Marco said 'You've done it now', to which Giuseppe replied 'I don't mean what they mean'. Once again, this was included in the libretto prepared for the 1907 revival but was cut again in 1914.

735 *They are very off-hand with us*: Barrington extended this line to 'No, they're a mean lot. They wouldn't stand for anything, besides they are very off-hand with us – very offhand indeed.'

739 *We've got a carriage*: Another Barrington gag, this time approved by Gilbert and allowed to be permanently enshrined in the libretto.

742 *a soupçon of this sort of thing*: Barrington generally interpolated at this point 'What song?' *Soupçon* is, of course, a perfectly respectable French word meaning a suggestion, very small quantity or slight trace. For the 'business' at the end of this phrase, the following words, also devised by Barrington, were introduced for the Duke to show the kind of thing he had in mind: 'Saw you in the Park this morning: Little Heartkiller: anytime you're passing – pass'. Gilbert emphatically did not approve of this last gag. He wrote to Helen D'Oyly Carte in June 1909: 'I never sanctioned "any time you are passing, pass". I don't know what it means: it seems arrant nonsense.'

young lady who had not the good fortune to be my daughter. There is some
little doubt as to which of you is the gentleman I am addressing, and which
is the gentleman who is allowing his attention to wander; but when that
doubt is solved, I shall say (still addressing the attentive gentleman), 'Take
her, and may she make you happier than her mother has made me.'   705

DUCH. Sir!

DUKE. If possible. And now there is a little matter to which I think I am
entitled to take exception. I come here in state with Her Grace the Duchess
and Her Majesty my daughter, and what do I find? Do I find, for instance,
a guard of honour to receive me? No!   710

MAR. *and* GIU. No.

DUKE. The town illuminated? No!

MAR. *and* GIU. No.

DUKE. Refreshment provided? No!

MAR. *and* GIU. No.   715

DUKE. A Royal salute fired? No!

MAR. *and* GIU. No.

DUKE. Triumphal arches erected? No!

MAR. *and* GIU. No.

DUKE. The bells set ringing?   720

MAR. *and* GIU. No.

DUKE. Yes – one – the Visitors', and I rang it myself. It is not enough!
It is not enough!

GIU. Upon my honour, I'm very sorry; but you see, I was brought up
in a gondola, and my ideas of politeness are confined to taking off my cap to   725
my passengers when they tip me.

DUCH. That's all very well in its way, but it is not enough.

GIU. I'll take off anything else in reason.

DUKE. But a Royal Salute to my daughter – it costs so little.

CAS. Papa, I don't want a salute.   730

GIU. My dear sir, as soon as we know which of us is entitled to take
that liberty she shall have as many salutes as she likes.

MAR. As for guards of honour and triumphal arches, you don't know
our people – they wouldn't stand it.

GIU. They are very off-hand with us – very off-hand indeed.   735

DUKE. Oh, but you mustn't allow that – you must keep them in proper
discipline, you must impress your Court with your importance. You want
deportment – carriage —

GIU. We've got a carriage.

DUKE. Manner – dignity. There must be a good deal of this sort of   740
thing – (*business*) – and a little of this sort of thing – (*business*) – and possibly
just a *soupçon* of this sort of thing! – (*business*) – and so on. Oh, it's very
useful, and most effective. Just attend to me. You are a King – I am a subject.
Very good —

745–80 *I am a courtier grave and serious*

This celebrated song in which Marco and Giuseppe are taught courtly manners and graces was originally written for Don Alhambra. It was then transferred to the Duke of Plaza-Toro. It was also changed from a trio to a quintet by bringing in Casilda and the Duchess.

The version of the song printed in the licence edition, part of which is quoted in Leslie Baily's *The Gilbert and Sullivan Book*, is substantially different from that actually performed on the first night and subsequently. Here it is:

SONG – D<small>UKE</small>.

> Now I'm about to kiss your hand –
>> Look haughty, proud and somewhat freezy;
> Yet gracious, affable and bland –
>> It's not particularly easy.
>> *(They endeavour to carry out his instructions.)*
> Humph! Pretty well; it's not supreme –
>> If anything, it's *too* unbending.
>> *(They endeavour to modify their demeanour.)*
> Now that's the opposite extreme –
>> Don't be so deuced condescending!

M<small>AR</small>. *and* G<small>IU</small>. (*depressed*).
> Oh hard to please some people seem!
>> At first our pose was too unbending;
> Then came the opposite extreme –
>> We were too deuced condescending!

D<small>UKE</small>.
> Now try a cold, Imperial air –
>> Half-close your eyes and stick your nose out;
> Assume a blank and vacant stare –
>> Shut up your mouth and turn your toes out.
>> *(They carry out his instructions.)*
> That's very good, that's very fair;
>> That's dignified, yet blandly winning!
> Upon my honour, I declare
>> That's very good for a beginning.

M<small>AR</small>. *and* G<small>IU</small>. (*cheerfully*).
> That comes of taking proper care –
>> We're dignified and blandly winning!
> Upon my honour, I declare
>> That's very good for a beginning.

D<small>UKE</small>.
> Now walk about with stately stride,
>> Your army ready to review it,
> Put on a quantity of side –
>> *(They endeavour to carry out his instruction.)*
> No – not too much – don't overdo it!
>> *(They modify their manner.)*
> That's capital! That's excellent!
>> You've caught the style of thing precisely!
> Both gentlemen I compliment,
>> I think you do it very nicely!

M<small>AR</small>. *and* G<small>IU</small>. (*joyfully*).
> We've got it now! That's what he meant!
>> We've caught the style of thing precisely!

GAVOTTE.

DUKE, DUCHESS, CASILDA, MARCO, GIUSEPPE.

DUKE.   I am a courtier grave and serious   745
             Who is about to kiss your hand:
             Try to combine a pose imperious
             With a demeanour nobly bland.

MAR. *and*   Let us combine a pose imperious
GIU.   With a demeanour nobly bland.   750

(MARCO *and* GIUSEPPE *endeavour to carry out his instructions.*)

DUKE.   That's, if anything, *too* unbending –
             Too aggressively stiff and grand;

             (*They suddenly modify their attitudes.*)

             Now to the other extreme you're tending –   755
             Don't be so deucedly condescending!

DUCH. *and* Now to the other extreme you're tending –
CAS.   Don't be so dreadfully condescending!

MAR. *and*   Oh, hard to please some noblemen seem!
GIU.   At first, if anything, *too* unbending;   760
             Off we go to the other extreme –
                 Too confoundedly condescending!

DUKE.   Now a gavotte perform sedately –
             Offer your hand with conscious pride;
             Take an attitude not too stately,   765
             Still sufficiently dignified.

MAR. *and*   Now for an attitude not too stately,
GIU.   Still sufficiently dignified.

(*They endeavour to carry out his instructions.*)

DUKE (*beating time*).
             Oncely, twicely – oncely, twicely –   770
             Bow impressively ere you glide.

                                     (*They do so.*)

MAR. (*to* GIU.).   That's capital!
GIU. (*to* MAR.).   That's excellent!

ALL.   I think $\left\{ \begin{array}{c} \text{we} \\ \text{you} \end{array} \right\}$ do it very nicely!

781 *Gavotte*: A stately dance, originating from France, which resembles the minuet but is
more lively. The gavotte at the end of 'I am a courtier' was originally designed to be
danced by Giuseppe and the Duke, with Marco accompanying them on his mandolin.
This was because both Rutland Barrington and Frank Wyatt were excellent dancers.
When the song became a quintet, the dance was revised to involve all five principals on
stage.

788 *I'd rather not – you*: Another Barrington gag, as is the phrase in the next line, 'I – we, that
is, several of us'.

797 *Then you are married*: At this point Barrington interpolated 'Yes, here's some of them'.

802–3 *we shall get hopelessly complicated*: The first American edition of the libretto, which was
printed in Cincinnati in 1889, has a different quintet at this point followed by a lengthy
passage of dialogue missing from the English edition. It is cued in as follows:

> MAR. It's a difficult position. It's nobody's fault – let us treat it good-humoredly and
> make the best of it.
> CAS. Oh yes; let's make the best of it by all means.
> TESS. *and* GIU. Certainly, let's make the best of it.
> MAR. Very well. It seems that we two have married you three. Now I have a proposition
> to make which I think will meet the difficulty.

QUINTET.
MARCO, GIUSEPPE, CASILDA, TESSA, GIANETTA.

MAR.   Till time shall choose
                                    To solve the hitch
                              Which wife is whose –
                                  Whose wife is which,
                        Our three young brides must please agree
                        To act as one and not as three.

CAS., TESS., GIA.   Your three young brides hereby agree
                        To act as one, and not as three.
                        Then you must be, till that is done,
                        Two gentlemen rolled into one.

MAR. *and* GIU.   Then we will be, till that is done,
                        Two gentlemen rolled into one.

ALL.   Till time shall choose
                                    To solve the hitch
                              Which wife is whose –
                                  Whose wife is which,
                        The three young brides hereby agree

Capital both, capital both – you've caught it nicely!
That is the style of thing precisely!

DUCH *and*   Capital both, capital both – they've caught it nicely!   775
CAS.   That is the style of thing precisely!

MAR. *and*   Oh, sweet to earn a nobleman's praise!
GIU.   Capital both, capital both – we've caught it nicely!
              Supposing he's right in what he says,
                  This is the style of thing precisely!   780

(GAVOTTE. *At the end exeunt* DUKE *and* DUCHESS, *leaving* CASILDA *with*
                    MARCO *and* GIUSEPPE.)

GIU. (*to* MARCO). The old birds have gone away and left the young
chickens together. That's called tact.

MAR. It's very awkward. We really ought to tell her how we are   785
situated. It's not fair to the girl.

GIU. Then why don't you do it?

MAR. I'd rather not – you.

GIU. I don't know how to begin. (*To* CASILDA.) A – Madam – I – we,
that is, several of us —   790

CAS. Gentlemen, I am bound to listen to you; but it is right to tell you
that, not knowing I was married in infancy, I am over head and ears in love
with somebody else.

GIU. Our case exactly! *We* are over head and ears in love with
somebody else! (*Enter* GIANETTA *and* TESSA.) In point of fact, with our   795
wives!

CAS. Your wives! Then you are married?

TESS. It's not our fault.

GIA. We knew nothing about it.

BOTH. We are sisters in misfortune.   800

CAS. My good girls, I don't blame you. Only before we go any further
we must really arrive at some satisfactory arrangement, or we shall get
hopelessly complicated.

QUINTET AND FINALE.

MARCO, GIUSEPPE, CASILDA, GIANETTA, TESSA.

ALL.   Here is a case unprecedented!
                  Here are a King and Queen ill-starred!   805
              Ever since marriage was first invented
                  Never was known a case so hard!

> To act as one and not as three;
> And both their lords, till that is done,
> Two gentlemen rolled into one!

GIA., TESS. and CAS. (*speaking together*). I think that is a very satisfactory arrangement.

MAR. and GIU. (*speaking together*). Ingenious, isn't it, Jenny?

GIA., TESS. and CAS. (*surprised*). Jenny?

MAR. and GIU. I must call you something, you know.

GIA., TESS. and CAS. Well, if you call me Jenny, I shall call you Thomas.

MAR. and GIU. Oh hang it all – Tommaso!

GIA., TESS. and CAS. No – Thomas.

MAR. and GIU. But it's so British!

GIA., TESS. and CAS. Never mind that. The question is, will you always be true to me?

MAR. and GIU. My dear Jenny, can you doubt it?

GIA., TESS. and CAS. Certainly. How can I trust a husband who married one-third of me when I was a baby and waited twenty years before he married the remainder?

MAR. and GIU. It does sound dilatory. Regard it as an instalment on account.

GIA., TESS. and CAS. And now I come to think of it, you've only married two-thirds of me, after all.

MAR. and GIU. I've married as much as I might.

GIA., TESS. and CAS. But I've married the whole of you!

MAR. and GIU. Pardon me – one-third of you is still single.

GIA., TESS. and CAS. My dear Thomas, what is the use of one-third of me being single when I don't know which third it is?

The above dialogue led straight into the singing of the quintet 'Here is a case unprecedented' (originally 'Here is a fix unprecedented'). Presumably both this dialogue and the song 'Till time shall choose' were performed in the first American production. They were also clearly originally intended to be used in the opening performance in London, as they occur in broadly the same form in the licence copy sent to the Lord Chamberlain. The licence copy has a slightly different version of the dialogue, and particularly of the last speech for Marco and Giuseppe: 'Besides, I'm married all over, whereas one-third of you is single, and can do what it likes'.

A note in Sullivan's diary for 2 December 1889, just five days before the opening night, apparently explains the dropping of this entire passage: 'Gilbert came down after rehearsal at Savoy . . . settled to cut dangerous dialogues at end of the piece'.

The licence copy also contains a second verse for 'Here is a fix unprecedented':

MAR. and GIU.	Here is a King – an extremely rich one –
	Somebody's married him – deuce knows who!
GIA., TESS. and CAS.	A third of myself – but I don't know which one –
	Is married to half of ye or you!
	O moralists all,
	How can you call
	Marriage a state of union true,
	When half of myself ⎱ but I don't know which one
	One third of myself ⎰
	Has married two thirds ⎱ of ye or you!
	Is married to half ⎰

The lines now sung from 'O moralists all' to 'ye or you?' (817–21) were not sung in early performances. They first appear in the third edition of the libretto (*c.* 1912).

826 *She will declare*: At this point the licence copy has the following ensemble to be sung by all:

> O time of eager expectation!
> Moment of uneasy doubt!
> O period of perturbation!
> Truth, at last, is coming out!

MAR. *and* GIU.	I may be said to have been bisected, By a profound catastrophe!

CAS., GIA., TESS.	Through a calamity unexpected I am divisible into three!	810

ALL.	O moralists all, How can you call Marriage a state of unitee, When excellent husbands are bisected, 815 And wives divisible into three? O moralists all, How can you call Marriage a state of union true?

CAS., GIA., TESS.	One-third of myself is married to half of ye or you.	820
MAR. *and* GIU.	When half of myself has married one-third of ye or you?	

(Enter DON ALHAMBRA, *followed by* DUKE, DUCHESS,
and all the CHORUS.)

FINALE.

RECITATIVE – DON ALHAMBRA.

Now let the loyal lieges gather round –
The Prince's foster-mother has been found!   825
She will declare, to silver clarion's sound,
The rightful King – let him forthwith be crowned!

CHORUS.	She will declare, etc.

*(*DON ALHAMBRA *brings forward* INEZ, *the Prince's*
foster-mother.)   830

TESS.	Speak, woman, speak –
DUKE.	We're all attention!
GIA.	The news we seek –
DUCH.	This moment mention.
CAS.	To us they bring – 835
DON AL.	His foster-mother.
MAR.	Is he the King?

840-47 *The Royal Prince was by the King entrusted*

Gilbert had originally written a song for Inez. However, he later changed it to eight lines of recitative for reasons which he explained in a letter to Sullivan: 'firstly, because I thought the audience wouldn't care for a set ballad from a stranger at the end of the piece; and secondly, because the situation became too like the situation at the end of *Pinafore*, where little Buttercup explains she has changed the children at birth'.

Inez, described by Gilbert in an earlier letter to Sullivan as 'a Spanish bandit's wife – a picturesque, fierce, melodramatic, old woman', has, I think, the doubtful distinction of being on stage for a shorter time and having less to sing than any other principal in the Savòy Operas, not counting those with minor walk-on, non-speaking roles like Mr Bunthorne's solicitor in *Patience*. The notary in *The Sorcerer* has the same number of solo lines, but he also has a part in an ensemble and appears on stage on three separate occasions.

GIU.	Or this my brother?

ALL.	Speak, woman, speak, etc.

RECITATIVE – INEZ.

The Royal Prince was by the King entrusted   840
To my fond care, ere I grew old and crusted;
When traitors came to steal his son reputed,
My own small boy I deftly substituted!
The villains fell into the trap completely –
I hid the Prince away – still sleeping sweetly: 845
I called him 'son' with pardonable slyness –
His name, Luiz! Behold his Royal Highness!

(*Sensation.* LUIZ *ascends the throne, crowned
and robed as King.*)

CAS. (*rushing to his arms*). Luiz.   850
LUIZ. Casilda! (*Embrace.*)

ALL.	Is this indeed the King?
	Oh, wondrous revelation!
	Oh, unexpected thing!
	Unlooked-for situation! 855

MAR., GIA.,	This statement we receive
GIU., TESS.	With sentiments conflicting;
	Our hearts rejoice and grieve,
	Each other contradicting;
	To those whom we adore 860
	We can be reunited –
	On one point rather sore,
	But, on the whole, delighted!

LUIZ.	When others claimed thy dainty hand,
	I waited – waited – waited, 865

DUKE.	As prudence (so I understand)
	Dictated – tated – tated.

CAS.	By virtue of our early vow
	Recorded – corded – corded,

875 *A royal crown and a golden throne*: In the licence copy this is the last line of the opera. According to Leslie Baily, Gilbert postponed writing the finale until Sullivan had decided on a rhythm which would bring the opera to an exhilarating climax. The composer eventually decided on a reprise of the cachucha used earlier in Act II. Gilbert at first intended to preface it with a gallop, but this was later deleted. It went:

> With the cymbals clanging,
>   And the trumpets tooting,
> And the tabors banging,
>   And the fluters fluting,
> And the drummers drumming,
>   And the harpers twiddling,
> And the hautboys humming,
>   And the fiddlers fiddling –
> Let us sing, let us shout, let us ring, let us rout,
> Let us drink, let us dance, let us prank, let us prance.

The full version of this gallop is in Gilbert's papers in the British Library. It includes the following delightful lines:

> From the country of the thistle
> Bring the bagpipe's drone,
> And the little penny whistle
> And the loud trombone!

877 *Once more gondolieri*: In early performances the reprise of this song was given to Marco and Giuseppe only, and not, as now, to all.

884 *premé, stalì*: Two genuine gondoliers' cries. *Premé* means push down on your pole, *stalì* means stop.

DUCH.　　Your pure and patient love is now　　　　870
　　　　　　Rewarded – warded – warded.

ALL.　　Then hail, O King of a Golden Land,
　　　　　And the high-born bride who claims his hand!
　　　　　The past is dead, and you gain your own,
　　　　　A royal crown and a golden throne!　　　875

　　　　　(*All kneel:* LUIZ *crowns* CASILDA.)

ALL.　　Once more *gondolieri*,
　　　　　Both skilful and wary,
　　　　　Free from this quandary
　　　　　　　Contented are we. Ah!　　　880
　　　　　From Royalty flying,
　　　　　Our gondolas plying,
　　　　　And merrily crying
　　　　　　　Our '*premé*,' '*stalì!*' Ah!

　　　　　So good-bye, cachucha, fandango, bolero –　　885
　　　　　　We'll dance a farewell to that measure –
　　　　　Old Xeres, adieu – Manzanilla – Montero –
　　　　　We leave you with feelings of pleasure!

CURTAIN

UTOPIA LIMITED

or

The Flowers of Progress

DRAMATIS PERSONÆ

KING PARAMOUNT THE FIRST (*King of Utopia*)

SCAPHIO ⎱ (*Judges of the Utopian Supreme Court*)
PHANTIS ⎰

TARARA (*the Public Exploder*)

CALYNX (*the Utopian Vice-Chamberlain*)

IMPORTED FLOWERS OF PROGRESS

LORD DRAMALEIGH (*a British Lord Chamberlain*)

CAPTAIN FITZBATTLEAXE (*First Life Guards*)

CAPTAIN SIR EDWARD CORCORAN, K. C. B. (*of the Royal Navy*)

MR. GOLDBURY (*a Company Promoter; afterwards Comptroller of the Utopian Household*)

SIR BAILEY BARRE, Q. C., M. P.

MR BLUSHINGTON (*of the County Council*)

THE PRINCESS ZARA (*Eldest Daughter of King Paramount*)

THE PRINCESS NEKAYA ⎱ (*her Younger Sisters*)
THE PRINCESS KALYBA ⎰

THE LADY SOPHY (*their English Gouvernante*)

SALATA ⎫
MELENE ⎬ (*Utopian Maidens*)
PHYLLA ⎭

ACT I. – A Utopian Palm Grove.
ACT II. – Throne Room in King Paramount's Palace.

UTOPIA LIMITED

Although *The Gondoliers* briefly united Gilbert and Sullivan in mutual admiration, it was not long before the two men were at loggerheads again. Shortly after its opening in December 1889, Gilbert went off with his wife on a cruise to India. When he returned home he was appalled to discover that £4,500 of the partners' money had been spent on preliminary expenses for *The Gondoliers*, including a sum of £500 for new carpets for the Savoy Theatre. He exploded at Richard D'Oyly Carte, who responded by saying, 'Very well, then – you write no more for the Savoy Theatre.'

The famous carpet quarrel soured relations between librettist and composer for much of 1890 and 1891. Both men went their separate ways and found new collaborators. Sullivan at last fulfilled his desire to be a composer of grand opera, writing a work based on Sir Walter Scott's novel *Ivanhoe* which opened on 31 January 1891 at the Royal English Opera House (now the Palace Theatre in Cambridge Circus), which Carte had built as the home for what he hoped would be a new English school of grand opera. Sullivan noted in his diary 'a rough and insolent refusal' from Gilbert to attend the first night. The opera achieved 160 performances in its initial run. Carte's other theatre, the Savoy, had to rely on non-Gilbert and Sullivan operettas to fill the bill when *The Gondoliers* finished its run in June 1891. These included *The Nautch Girl, or the Rajah of Chutneypore* by George Dance and Frank Desprez and *The Vicar of Bray* by Sydney Grundy and Edward Solomon.

Gilbert, meanwhile, was changing the direction of his life and exchanging the status of London dramatist for that of country gentleman. In September 1890 he bought Grim's Dyke, a large mansion near Harrow in Middlesex which came complete with 110 acres of farmland and a staff of 20. Here he settled down to play croquet and tennis and swim in the lake. He did not, however, forsake writing altogether and collaborated with Alfred Cellier in a musical play, *The Mountebanks*, which opened at the Lyric Theatre on 4 January 1892. Sullivan also returned to the world of light opera, working with Sydney Grundy on *Haddon Hall*, which was based on the true story of the elopement of Dorothy Vernon from her ancestral Derbyshire home and set in the turbulent period of the English Civil War. It opened at the Savoy Theatre on 24 September 1892 and enjoyed an initial run of 214 performances. It was followed at the Savoy by a comic opera by J. M. Barrie and Arthur Conan Doyle entitled *Jane Annie*.

Neither *The Mountebanks* nor *Haddon Hall* saw Gilbert and Sullivan at their best and there was increasing pressure on them, not least from Richard D'Oyly Carte and his wife, Helen, to come together again and revive the old Savoy magic. Gilbert seems to have taken the initiative, suggesting that their collaboration on another comic opera would not prevent Sullivan's continuing activity in more musically exalted spheres. 'If you can write an oratorio like *The Martyr of Antioch* while you are occupied with pieces like *Patience* and *Iolanthe*,' he asked, 'cannot you write a grand opera without giving up pieces like *The Yeomen*? Are the two things irreconcilable. . . . From me the Press and the public will take nothing but what is in essence humorous.'

Although composer and librettist were effectively reconciled and willing to work with each other by the end of 1891, it was to be another year before they got down to collaborating on a new work. In December 1892, just as Sullivan was preparing to leave London to winter in Monte Carlo, Gilbert visited him and mentioned his idea of an opera set on a south sea island. At the end of April 1893 the two men had a further meeting on the Riviera to go over the outline plot of *Utopia Limited*. Gilbert spent the next few weeks working hard on the songs and dialogue for Act I and Sullivan, now back in England and working from a rented house in Weybridge, Surrey, began writing the music for the new opera in June. He finished setting Act I in a month and was complimented by Gilbert for producing his best ever finale for it. Act II proved more troublesome, not least because of serious disagreements between composer and librettist over the character of Lady Sophy and difficulties over the finale. There was also a further diversion for Sullivan when his pet parrot went missing.

Relations between composer and librettist became somewhat strained again during rehearsals, no doubt partly because of the irritation caused to Gilbert by a bad attack of gout which left him hobbling around on crutches. *Utopia Limited* was the most expensive of all the Savoy Operas to stage, costing a total of £7,200. It also had the longest first act, which in its original uncut version lasted for an hour and three-quarters. It opened on 7 October 1893 and ran for 245 performances.

For *Utopia Limited* Gilbert borrowed considerably from one of his earlier plays, *The Happy Land*, which dated from 1873. Despite the exotic south sea setting, the opera is, of course, just like *The Mikado*, a satire on thoroughly English institutions like the law, local government and party politics. Although it has distinct echoes of earlier Savoy operas, notably *H.M.S. Pinafore* (the character of Captain Corcoran), *Iolanthe* (party politics), and *Princess Ida* (female education), it has its own originality and also has the merit of having a very straightforward plot without any topsy-turvydom or cases of mistaken identity. Nor is a work based around the twin themes of scandal in the Royal Family and the privatization of public institutions without its relevance to Britain in the 1990s.

Rupert D'Oyly Carte considered reviving *Utopia Limited* in the 1920s but was deterred by the cost. On 4 April 1975, as part of its centenary celebrations, the D'Oyly Carte Opera Company gave the opera its first professional performance in Britain since the opening run. Michael Heyland produced and sets and costumes were designed by Peter Rice. This single centenary performance was so over-subscribed that four further performances were given at the Royal Festival Hall. A recording of this production was issued by Decca in 1976 and since 1993 has been available on CD. Since then, apart from the BBC production broadcast on Radio 2 in 1989, there have been, as far as I am aware, no professional British performances of the opera. However, its centenary in 1993 revived interest among amateur companies and maybe we will hear it more often in future. I hope so. Interestingly, in the United States, where its themes would seem to be much less relevant, it has for some time been a much more established part of the Savoy canon. The American Savoyards revived it in 1956 and kept it thereafter in their permanent repertoire. In his *Handbook of Gilbert and Sullivan*, published in 1962, Frank Ledlie Moore commented that *Utopia* 'is now played as frequently as any of the other operas with the exception of *The Mikado*, *The Pirates of Penzance* and *H.M.S. Pinafore*'. I doubt if this is still the case.

1–4 *Scene*: Thanks to the survival in the British Library of the manuscript books in which Gilbert sketched out successive versions of the plot of *Utopia Limited* we are able to see the various stages through which the play went before reaching its final stage.

Gilbert's first idea was to build the story around a group of sea nymphs living on a romantic island. Their life is lazy and happy but incomplete. Feeling that the cause of the world's misery is human love, they have forsworn the company of men (shades of *Princess Ida*). However, all this is changed when a party of sailors lands on the island. The nymphs fall madly in love with them and resolve to accompany them back to civilization.

In a later development of this original idea, the sailors turn out to be Russian. One of them is chosen as king and rules as a despot tempered by dynamite. Another sketch has the sailors introducing parliamentary democracy on to the island and dividing the people into Liberals and Conservatives with the result that there is constant strife. Gilbert's later re-working of the plot, under the title *The Happy Valley*, switched to the theme of a land governed by an autocratic monarch, King Rasselas the Thirtieth, who is dominated by two counsellors and has a daughter being educated in England. In several of his drafts, the kingdom is situated in Abyssinia. Just about all that survives from the original sea nymph idea is the opening chorus of maidens 'lying lazily about the stage'.

17–24 *The song of birds*
In Gilbert's manuscript copy of the libretto now in the British Museum this solo is marked as being 'to harp accompaniment'.

25 *The song of birds*: The Oxford University Press World's Classics Edition of the Savoy Opera libretti erroneously misses out this chorus.

ACT I

SCENE. *A Utopian Palm Grove in the gardens of* KING PARAMOUNT's *Palace, showing a picturesque and luxuriant tropical landscape, with the sea in the distance.* SALATA, MELENE, PHYLLA, *and other Maidens discovered, lying lazily about the stage and thoroughly enjoying themselves in lotus-eating fashion.*

OPENING CHORUS.

In lazy languor – motionless,   5
We lie and dream of nothingness;
   For visions come
   From Poppydom
     Direct at our command:
Or, delicate alternative,   10
In open idleness we live,
   With lyre and lute
   And silver flute,
     The life of Lazyland!
In lazy languor – motionless,   15
We lie and dream of nothingness.

SOLO – PHYLLA *with* CHORUS.

The song of birds
   In ivied towers;
     The rippling play
     Of waterway;   20
The lowing herds;
   The breath of flowers;
     The languid loves
     Of turtle doves.

CHORUS.   The song of birds, etc.   25
These simple joys are all at hand
Upon thy shores, O Lazyland!

29 *Princess Zara*: In his early manuscript sketches of what was to become *Utopia Limited* Gilbert named the King's daughter Princess Soza. Since 1981 the name Zara has featured in the British royal family tree although not with the prefix Princess. Zara Phillips is the daughter of Princess Anne, the Princess Royal, and is the Queen's oldest granddaughter.

31 *a high degree at Girton*: Girton College grew out of a college for women established at Hitchin in Hertfordshire in 1869 by Emily Davies, a pioneer of women's education. Initially, it had just five students. It moved to Cambridge in 1873 when it was re-named Girton College but it was not fully incorporated into the University until 1948.

50 *Enter Tarara*: Gilbert originally gave the character of the public exploder the name Tarara Boomdeay. This was the title of one of the great 'hit songs' of the 1890s, first heard in Britain in the pantomime *Dick Whittington* which opened at the Grand Theatre, Islington, on Boxing Night 1891. 'Ta-ra-ra-boom-de-ay' was based on a tune which a nigger minstrel had heard in a low dive in St Louis seven years earlier. It made little impact when it was first sung in New York but when Lottie Collins belted it out to the accompaniment of high kicks, the London audience went wild and demanded encore after encore. Although Gilbert dropped 'Boomdeay' from the name of his character, the allusion to the song was still clearly there in the truncated 'Tarara'.

51 *Lalabalele talala*: There is, mercifully, only a small amount of Utopian gobbledegook in the final version of the *Utopia* libretto. In one of his earlier drafts, Gilbert had begun the opera with an opening chorus in the language, '*Kala si falada pa callala telay*'. He proposed following this with a short sequence of dialogue in Utopian which was brought to a swift conclusion by Tarara coming in and reminding those speaking it that the language was entirely forbidden at Court.

59–60 *an explosive cracker*: Only one other Savoy Opera features pyrotechnics on stage. In *The Sorcerer* there are flashes when John Wellington Wells pours his magic love potion into the tea-pot (Act I, lines 579–83).

63 *I must accustom myself by degrees*: Shades of *The Mikado*, Act II, line 134 where in order to get accustomed to Nanki-Poo embracing his bride-to-be, Ko-Ko asks him to do it by degrees.

(*Enter* C A L Y N X.)

C A L. Good news! Great news! His Majesty's eldest daughter, Princess Zara, who left our shores five years since to go to England – the greatest, the most   30
powerful, the wisest country in the world – has taken a high degree at Girton, and is on her way home again, having achieved a complete mastery over all the elements that have tended to raise that glorious country to her present pre-eminent position among civilized nations!

S A L. Then in a few months Utopia may hope to be completely Anglicized?   35

C A L. Absolutely and without a doubt.

M E L. (*lazily*). We are very well as we are. Life without a care – every want supplied by a kind and fatherly monarch, who, despot though he be, has no other thought than to make his people happy – what have we to gain by the great change that is in store for us?   40

S A L. What have we to gain? English institutions, English tastes, and oh, English fashions!

C A L. England has made herself what she is because, in that favoured land, every one has to think for himself. Here we have no need to think, because our monarch anticipates all our wants, and our political opinions are formed for us   45
by the journals to which we subscribe. Oh, think how much more brilliant this dialogue would have been, if we had been accustomed to exercise our reflective powers! They say that in England the conversation of the very meanest is a coruscation of impromptu epigram!

(*Enter* T A R A R A *in a great rage.*)   50

T A R. Lalabalele talala! Callabale lalabalica falahle!

C A L. (*horrified*). Stop – stop, I beg! (*All the ladies close their ears.*)

T A R. Callamalala galalate! Caritalla lalabalee kallalale poo!

L A D I E S. Oh, stop him! stop him!

C A L. My Lord, I'm surprised at you. Are you not aware that His Majesty, in   55
his despotic acquiescence with the emphatic wish of his people, has ordered that the Utopian language shall be banished from his court, and that all communications shall henceforward be made in the English tongue?

T A R. Yes, I'm perfectly aware of it, although – (*suddenly presenting an explosive 'cracker'*). Stop – allow me.   60

C A L. (*pulls it*). Now, what's that for?

T A R. Why, I've recently been appointed Public Exploder to His Majesty, and as I'm constitutionally nervous, I must accustom myself by degrees to the startling nature of my duties. Thank you. I was about to say that although, as Public Exploder, I am next in succession to the throne, I nevertheless do my   65
best to fall in with the royal decree. But when I am over-mastered by an indignant sense of overwhelming wrong, as I am now, I slip into my native tongue without knowing it. I am told that in the language of that great and pure nation,

80–1 *a Despotism tempered by Dynamite*: Compare *The Gondoliers*, Act II, lines 9–10, where Barataria is described as 'a monarchy that's tempered with Republican Equality'.

84 *the Palace Peeper*: This has been well described as the '*Private Eye* of the Naughty Nineties'. The title *Palace Peeper* has for many years been used for the journal of the New York Gilbert and Sullivan Society.

90 *Heliogabalian*: Heliogabalus was possibly the most dissolute of all the Roman emperors. He ruled from 218 to 222 A.D. under the name Marcus Aurelius Antonius and was murdered by the pretorian guards. An ability to quote all his crimes in elegiacs features in the remarkable list of Major General Stanley's accomplishments in *The Pirates of Penzance*, Act I, line 469.

92 *They wink at his immoralities*: In Gilbert's manuscript copy of the libretto preserved in the British Library the following lines appear at this point, crossed out apparently in the author's own hand: 'I have reason to know that they recently consulted an eminent oculist for an affection of the eyelids – the direct result of their confirmed habit of winking at the king's immoralities.'

95 *escorting Scaphio and Phantis*: The parts of Scaphio and Phantis were significantly changed by Gilbert during the course of his work on the plot of *Utopia Limited*. Originally he had Scaphio as the proprietor of an opera house who had persuaded the king to write him a comic opera and Phantis as the owner of a scandalous society paper to which the king contributed stories. Scaphio was subsequently changed to being a Stock Exchange speculator and in a later version both men were made proprietors of a society paper with Phantis having responsibility for the political pages and Scaphio for the social pages. The constant theme throughout all the reworkings of the plot is the two men's hold over the king. In one version they agree to ignore his lapses from propriety only on condition that he falls in with their speculations on the stock market, contributes to their radical paper and keeps the theatre constantly supplied with comic operas in which he himself appears. Traces of this theme appear in the final version of the libretto even though Scaphio and Phantis have now been given the rather more staid profession of supreme court judges.

strong expressions do not exist, consequently when I want to let off steam I have
no alternative but to say, 'Lalabalele molola lililah kallalale poo!' 70
CAL. But what is your grievance?
TAR. This – by our Constitution we are governed by a Despot who,
although in theory absolute – is, in practice, nothing of the kind – being
watched day and night by two Wise Men whose duty it is, on his very first lapse
from political or social propriety, to denounce him to me, the Public Exploder, 75
and it then becomes my duty to blow up His Majesty with dynamite – allow me.
(*Presenting a cracker which* CALYNX *pulls.*) Thank you – and, as some compensa-
tion to my wounded feelings, I reign in his stead.
CAL. Yes. After many unhappy experiments in the direction of an ideal
Republic, it was found that what may be described as a Despotism tempered by 80
Dynamite provides, on the whole, the most satisfactory description of ruler –
an autocrat who dares not abuse his autocratic power.
TAR. That's the theory – but in practice, how does it act? Now, do you ever
happen to see the *Palace Peeper*? (*Producing a 'Society' paper.*)
CAL. Never even heard of the journal. 85
TAR. I'm not surprised, because His Majesty's agents always buy up the
whole edition; but I have an aunt in the publishing department, and she has
supplied me with a copy. Well, it actually teems with circumstantially convincing details of the King's abominable immoralities! If this high-class journal
may be believed, His Majesty is one of the most Heliogabalian profligates that 90
ever disgraced an autocratic throne! And *do* these Wise Men denounce him to
me? Not a bit of it! They wink at his immoralities! Under the circumstances I
really think I am justified in exclaiming 'Lalabalele molola lililah kalabalele
poo!' (*All horrified.*) I don't care – the occasion demands it.   (*Exit* TARARA.)

(*March. Enter Guard, escorting* SCAPHIO *and* PHANTIS.) 95

CHORUS.

O make way for the Wise Men!
    They are prizemen –
  Double-first in the world's university!
For though lovely this island, 100
    (Which is *my* land),
  She has no one to match them in *her* city.
They're the pride of Utopia –
    Cornucopia
Is each in his mental fertility. 105
O they never make blunder,
    And no wonder,
  For they're triumphs of infallibility.

So make way, &c.

110 *In every mental lore*: In Gilbert's manuscript copy of the libretto this phrase appears as 'In intellectual lore'.

131 *Explodes in his auriculars*: A posh way of saying ears. The word occurs again in a slightly truncated adjectival form in *The Grand Duke* (Act II, line 524) when the herald informs the assembled company that the Prince of Monte Carlo wishes to let everyone know 'by word of mouth auric'lar'.

134 *Its force all men confess*: In Gilbert's manuscript copy of the libretto this phrase appears as 'This scheme all people bless'.

DUET – SCAPHIO *and* PHANTIS

SCA.	In every mental lore
	(The statement smacks of vanity)
PHAN.	We claim to rank before
	The wisest of humanity.
SCA.	As gifts of head and heart
	We're wasted on 'utility',
PHAN.	We're 'cast' to play a part
	Of great responsibility.

SCA.	Our duty is to spy
	Upon our King's illicities,
	And keep a watchful eye
	On all his eccentricities.
BOTH.	If ever a trick he tries
	That savours of rascality,
	At our decree he dies
	Without the least formality!

SCA.	We fear no rude rebuff,
	Or newspaper publicity;
PHAN.	Our word is quite enough,
	The rest is electricity.
SCA.	A pound of dynamite
	Explodes in his auriculars;
PHAN.	It's not a pleasant sight –
	We'll spare you the particulars.

SCA.	Its force all men confess,
	The King needs no admonishing –
PHAN.	We may say its success
	Is something quite astonishing.
BOTH.	Our despot it imbues
	With virtues quite delectable:
	He minds his P's and Q's,
	And keeps himself respectable.

SCA.	Of a tyrant polite
PHAN.	He's a paragon quite.
SCA.	He's as modest and mild
PHAN.	In his ways as a child;
SCA.	And no one ever met
	With an autocrat, yet,

Line numbers: 110, 115, 120, 125, 130, 135, 140, 145

159 *the accumulated fervour of sixty-six years*: Scaphio makes Ruth in *The Pirates of Penzance* seem positively youthful. Her love has only been accumulating for forty-seven years!

186 *Come, take heart*: In several editions of the libretto, including the 1928 edition of Gilbert's plays and Reginald Allen's *First Night Gilbert and Sullivan*, this sentence and the next one ('I cannot bear to see you sad') are placed at the end of Scaphio's speech (after 'Is he not our very slave?').

PHAN.   So delightfully bland
                To the least in the land!, &c.

CHORUS.   Oh make way for the wise men, &c.   150

(*Exeunt all but* SCAPHIO *and* PHANTIS. PHANTIS *is pensive*.)

SCA. Phantis, you are not in your customary exuberant spirits. What is
wrong?

PHAN. Scaphia, I think you once told me that you have never loved?

SCA. Never! I have often marvelled at the fairy influence which weaves its   155
rosy web about the faculties of the greatest and wisest of our race; but I thank
Heaven I have never been subjected to its singular fascination. For, O Phantis,
there is that within me that tells me that when my time *does* come, the convulsion will be tremendous! When *I* love, it will be with the accumulated fervour
of sixty-six years! But I have an ideal – a semi-transparent Being, filled with an   160
inorganic pink jelly – and I have never yet seen the woman who approaches
within measurable distance of it. All are opaque – opaque – opaque!

PHAN. Keep that ideal firmly before you, and love not until you find her.
Though but fifty-five, I am an old campaigner in the battle-fields of Love; and,
believe me, it is better to be as you are, heart-free and happy, than as I am –   165
eternally racked with doubting agonies! Scaphio, the Princess Zara returns
from England today!

SCA. My poor boy, I see it all.

PHAN. Oh! Scaphio, she is so beautiful. Ah, you smile, for you have never
seen her. She sailed for England three months before you took office.   170

SCA. Now tell me, is your affection requited?

PHAN. I do not know – I am not sure. Sometimes I think it is, and then
come these torturing doubts! I feel sure that she does not regard me with absolute indifference, for she could never look at me without having to go to bed
with a sick headache.   175

SCA. That is surely something.

PHAN. Do you think so?

SCA. Come, take heart, boy; you are young and beautiful. What more could
maiden want?

PHAN. Ah! Scaphio, remember she returns from a land where every youth   180
is as a young Greek god, and where such poor beauty as I can boast is seen at
every turn.

SCA. Be of good cheer! Marry her, boy, if so your fancy wills, and be sure
that love will come.

PHAN. (*overjoyed*). Then you will assist me in this?   185

SCA. Why, surely! Silly one, what have you to fear? Come, take heart. I cannot bear to see you sad. Remember, we have but to say the word, and her father
must consent. Is he not our very slave?

191 *Let all your doubts take wing*: In Gilbert's manuscript version, the opening line of this duet is 'My aid depend upon' and the third line 'If king Phalarion'. As mentioned above, the name of the King in the earliest versions of the story which became *Utopia Limited* was Rasselas. It was later changed to Phalarion, very similar in sound to Hilarion in *Princess Ida*, and only at a very late stage does it seem to have been altered to Paramount.

216 *Of course it does*: In Reginald Allen's *First Night Gilbert and Sullivan* and in the 1928 Chatto edition of Gilbert's plays, the refrain taken up by Scaphio and Phantis is printed as:

And happiness – and happiness –
Of course it does – and happiness

PHAN. Now I may hope, indeed! Scaphio, you have placed me on the very pinnacle of human joy! 190

DUET – SCAPHIO *and* PHANTIS.

SCA.
  Let all your doubts take wing –
   Our influence is great.
  If Paramount our King
   Presume to hesitate,
    Put on the screw, 195
     And caution him
    That he will rue
     Disaster grim
    That must ensue
     To life and limb, 200
   Should he pooh-pooh
   This harmless whim.

  PHANTIS.   SCAPHIO.
This harmless whim – this harmless whim,

BOTH.
It is, as $\left\{ \begin{array}{c} \text{I} \\ \text{you} \end{array} \right\}$ say, a harmless whim.

PHAN. (*dancing*).
  Observe this dance 205
   Which I employ
  When I, by chance,
   Go mad with joy.
  What sentiment
   Does this express? 210
  What sentiment does this express?

(PHANTIS *continues his dance while* SCAPHIO *vainly endeavours to discover its meaning.*)

  Supreme content
   And happiness! 215

BOTH.
  Of course it does! Of course it does!
  Supreme content and happiness!, &c.

PHAN.
  Your friendly aid conferred,
   I need no longer pine.
  I've but to speak the word, 220
   And lo! the maid is mine!
    I do not choose
    To be denied,

243 *Of course it does*: In the two sources mentioned above (note to line 216), this refrain is
     given as:

                        Unselfishness! Unselfishness!
                        Of course it does – unselfishness!

     It is followed there by a repeat of 'This step to use' sung as a duet by both men.

247 *preceded by girls dancing before him*: The stage direction in Gilbert's manuscript copy of the
     libretto now in the British Library indicates that the girls should have garlands and
     wine cups.

253 *Far niente*: An Italian phrase meaning idleness or doing nothing which was particularly
     beloved by Gilbert. He also uses it in *The Gondoliers* (Act I, line 54) and in *Iolanthe* (Act I,
     line 571).

Or wish to lose
　　A lovely bride –　　　　　　　　　　225
If to refuse
　　The King decide,
The Royal shoes
　　Then woe betide!

　　　SCA.　　　　　PHAN.
Then woe betide – then woe betide!　　　230
BOTH.　　The Royal shoes then woe betide!

SCA. (*dancing*).　　This step to use
　　　　　　　　　I condescend
　　　　　　　　Whene'er I choose
　　　　　　　　　To serve a friend.　　235
　　　　　　　　What it implies
　　　　　　　　　Now try to guess;
　　　　　What it implies now try to guess:

(SCAPHIO *continues his dance while* PHANTIS *is vainly endeavouring to
discover its meaning.*)　　　　　　240

　　　　　　　It typifies
　　　　　　　Unselfishness!

BOTH (*dancing*).　　Of course it does! Of course it does!
　　　　　　It typifies unselfishness!, &c.

(*Exeunt* SCAPHIO *and* PHANTIS.)　　245

(*March. Enter* KING PARAMOUNT, *attended by guards and nobles, and
preceded by girls dancing before him.*)

　　　　　CHORUS.

　　　　La, la, &c.
Quaff the nectar – cull the roses –　　　　250
　　Gather fruit and flowers in plenty!
For our King no longer poses –
　　Sing the songs of *far niente*!
　　　　La, la, &c.
Wake the lute that sets us lilting,　　　　255
　　Dance a welcome to each comer;
Day by day our year is wilting –
　　Sing the sunny songs of summer!
　　　　La, la, la, la!

260 *A King of autocratic power we*: Gilbert originally wrote two four-line verses to be sung by
the King before this song. They appear in his manuscript version of the libretto:

> Why should Royalty be stately
>   King and people widely parted?
> Why should I, jocose innately,
>   Seem reserved and strong hearted?
>
> Life is what you please to make it,
>   Happy all who best employ it.
> Sad are they who wisely take it,
>   Let's be foolish and enjoy it!

271 *With our enjoyment much*: There is a second verse to the King's song. It appears in the
current Chappell editions of both the vocal score and the libretto but not in the World's
Classics edition of the Savoy Opera libretti, nor the Chatto edition of Gilbert's plays
and it was not sung in the 1976 D'Oyly Carte recording. For those who do not feel that
the opera is already too long, here it is:

KING.
> Stupendous when we rouse ourselves to strike –
> Resistless when our tyrant thunder peals –
> We often wonder what obstruction's like,
> And how a contradicted monarch feels!
> But as it is our Royal whim
> Our Royal sails to set and trim
> To suit whatever wind may blow,
> What buffets contradiction deals,
> And how a thwarted monarch feels,
> We probably shall never know.

CHORUS.
> No, no – what thwarted monarch feels
> You'll never, never know.

274 *Great Britain*: At this point the orchestra strikes up with the opening bars of 'Rule Britannia'.

275 *Ireland*: Another cue for appropriate music, this time a snatch of an Irish jig.

278 *our two younger daughters*: Gilbert had originally intended that Scaphio, Phantis and the
King would each have a daughter who was being educated in England.

SONG – KING *with* CHORUS.

A King of autocratic power we – 260
  A despot whose tyrannic will is law –
Whose rule is paramount o'er land and sea,
  A Presence of unutterable awe!
But though the awe that I inspire
Must shrivel with imperial fire 265
    All foes whom it may chance to touch,
To judge by what I see and hear,
It does not seem to interfere
  With popular enjoyment, much.

CHORUS.   No, no – it does not interfere 270
      With our enjoyment much.

RECITATIVE – KING.

My subjects all, it is your wish emphatic
That all Utopia shall henceforth be modelled
Upon that glorious country called Great Britain –
To which some add – but others do not – Ireland. 275
ALL.   It is!
KING.   That being so, as you insist upon it,
    We have arranged that our two younger daughters
    Who have been 'finished' by an English Lady –
(Tenderly.) 280
A grave, and good, and gracious English Lady –
Shall daily be exhibited in public,
That all may learn what, from the English standpoint,
Is looked upon as maidenly perfection!
Come hither, daughters! 285

(Enter NEKAYA *and* KALYBA. *They are twins, about fifteen years old; they are very modest and demure in their appearance, dress, and manner. They stand with their hands folded and their eyes cast down.)*

CHORUS.

How fair! how modest! how discreet! 290
  How bashfully demure!
    See how they blush, as they've been taught,
    At this publicity unsought!
  How English and how pure!

295–335 *Although of native maids the cream*
This duet was sung by Carol Lesley-Green and Gaynor Keeble of the D'Oyly Carte Opera Company during a service of Evensong held in Birmingham Cathedral on 18 October 1992 to celebrate the 150th anniversary of the birth of Sir Arthur Sullivan. It seems a
slightly curious choice for inclusion in a church service – the other Sullivan song chosen
was *The Lost Chord* – but was clearly appreciated by those present. A report in the magazine of the Friends of D'Oyly Carte noted that the duet 'was observed to set at least one
eminent ecclesiastical head nodding in time'.

330 *The Kodaks do their best*: The first Kodak camera was introduced by George Eastman in
1888. Its relative simplicity and portability made it extremely popular with amateur
photographers. It was sold with a film sealed inside and the whole apparatus had to be
mailed back to Rochester, New York, for processing and replacement. The simpler Brow-
nie camera was developed in 1900.

DUET – NEKAYA *and* KALYBA.

BOTH.   Although of native maids the cream,   295
We're brought up on the English scheme –
    The best of all
    For great and small
      Who modesty adore.

NEK.   For English girls are good as gold,   300
Extremely modest (so we're told),
Demurely coy – divinely cold –

KAL.   And we are that – and more.
To please papa, who argues thus –
All girls should mould themselves on us   305
    Because we are,
    By furlongs far,
      The best of all the bunch.
We show ourselves to loud applause
From ten to four without a pause –   310

NEK.   Which is an awkward time because
    It cuts into our lunch.

BOTH.   Oh, maids of high and low degree,
Whose social code is rather free,
Please look at us, and you will see   315
What good young ladies ought to be!

NEK.   And as we stand, like clockwork toys,
A lecturer whom papa employs
    Proceeds to praise
    Our modest ways   320
      And guileless character –

KAL.   Our well-known blush – our downcast eyes –
Our famous look of mild surprise

NEK.   (Which competition still defies) –

KAL.   Our celebrated 'Sir!!!'   325

Then all the crowd take down our looks
In pocket memorandum books.
    To diagnose
    Our modest pose
    The Kodaks do their best: 330

NEK.   If evidence you would possess
    Of what is maiden bashfulness,
You only need a button press –

344–415   *Bold-faced ranger*

Musicologists tend to be rather disparaging of Sullivan's setting and accompaniment for this song which they feel rely over-much on tonic pedal point. As a result, they maintain, it is dull and predictable. Gervase Hughes, in his book, *The Music of Arthur Sullivan*, sees it as an example of Sullivan's downright laziness.

The song was, however, much appreciated by the first night audience. The *Sunday Times* critic reported that it was 'deliciously sung by Miss Rosina Brandram in her old-fashioned English Quaker costume'. It was the first song in the opera to receive an encore.

349   *Each a little bit afraid is*: A line that is lifted wholesale from *The Mikado*, Act I, line 323.

367   *Chorus*: Neither Reginald Allen's *First Night Gilbert and Sullivan* nor the Chatto edition of Gilbert's plays give any lines for the chorus but simply print this number as a solo.

KAL.   And *we* do all the rest.

BOTH.   Oh, maids of high and low degree, &c.   335

(*Enter* LADY SOPHY – *an English lady of mature years and extreme gravity of demeanour and dress. She carries a lecturer's wand in her hand. She is led on by the* KING, *who expresses great regard and admiration for her.*)

RECITATIVE – LADY SOPHY.

This morning we propose to illustrate
A course of maiden courtship, from the start   340
To the triumphant matrimonial finish.

(*Through the following song the two Princesses illustrate in gesture the description given by* LADY SOPHY.)

SONG – LADY SOPHY.

  Bold-faced ranger
  (Perfect stranger)   345
Meets two well-behaved young ladies.
  He's attractive,
  Young and active –
Each a little bit afraid is.
  Youth advances,   350
  At his glances
To their danger they awaken;
  They repel him
  As they tell him
He is very much mistaken.   355
Very very much mistaken.
Though they speak to him politely,
Please observe they're sneering slightly,
Just to show he's acting vainly.
This is Virtue saying plainly,   360
  'Go away, young bachelor,
  We are not what you take us for!'
When addressed impertinently,
English ladies answer gently,
  'Go away, young bachelor,   365
  We are not what you take us for!'

CHORUS.   English ladies answer gently, &c.,

As he gazes,
Hat he raises,
Enters into conversation.   370
Makes excuses –
This produces
Interesting agitation.
He, with daring,
Undespairing,   375
Gives his card – his rank discloses.
Little heeding
This proceeding,
They turn up their little noses.
Yes their little, little noses.   380
Pray observe this lesson vital –
When a man of rank and title
His position first discloses,
Always cock your little noses.
When at home, let all the class   385
Try this in the looking-glass.
English girls of well-bred notions
Shun all unrehearsed emotions.
English girls of highest class
Practise them before the glass.   390

CHORUS.   English girls of well-bred notions, &c.

His intentions
Then he mentions.
Something definite to go on –
Makes recitals   395
Of his titles,
Hints at settlements, and so on.
Smiling sweetly,
They, discreetly,
Ask for further evidences: 400
Thus invited,
He, delighted,
Gives the usual references
(Don't forget the references).
This is business. Each is fluttered   405
When the offer's fairly uttered.
'Which of them has his affection?'
He declines to make selection.
Do they quarrel for his dross?

416   *The lecture's ended*: In Gilbert's manuscript edition of the libretto, these two lines of recitative for Lady Sophy are crossed out and the following extra lines for the chorus substituted:

> Thus from these two budding roses
>   Cull we full-blown flowers in plenty –
> If at fifteen thus each poses
>   What will she be when she's twenty

432   *But then it's a quaint world*: Echoes of Dick Deadeye's observation, 'Ah, it's a queer world' in *H.M.S. Pinafore*, Act I, line 120.

438–40   *Junius Junior, Senex Senior, Mercury Major, Mephistopholes Minor*: Just in case any of my readers have forgotten their classical education, here is a quick run-down of the salient facts about the original figures from which these pseudonyms are taken.

Junius earned the nickname Brutus when he feigned insanity to save his life when his father and elder brother were murdered by Tarquin the Proud. He later inspired the Romans to get rid of the Tarquins and became the first consul of Rome in 509. He gets another mention in *The Mikado*, Act I, line 485. Between 1768 and 1772 a series of anonymous letters appeared in the London *Public Advertiser* under the pseudonym Junius. Among the suggested authors are Edmund Burke, Edward Gibbon, Lord Chatham and Lord Shelburne. Senex is simply the Latin word for an old man so Senex Senior must be really old.

Mercury is the Roman counterpart of the Greek god Hermes. He acted as messenger to his father Jupiter and was also the god of science and commerce and the patron of travellers, rogues, vagabonds and thieves. He is generally represented as a young man with a winged hat and winged sandals.

Mephistopholes is a manufactured name (possibly from three Greek words meaning 'not loving the light') for the Devil which first appeared in the Faust legend in the late Middle Ages.

Not a bit of it – they toss!   410
Ah! Please observe this cogent moral –
English ladies never quarrel.
     When a doubt they come across,
     English ladies always toss.

CHORUS.   We'll observe this cogent moral, &c.   415

RECITATIVE – LADY SOPHY.

The lecture's ended. In ten minutes' space
'Twill be repeated in the market-place!
(*Exit* LADY SOPHY, *followed by* NEKAYA *and* KALYBA.)

CHORUS.   Quaff the nectar – cull the roses –
                    Bashful girls will soon be plenty!   420
                 Maid who thus at fifteen poses
                    Ought to be divine at twenty!
                                   (*Exit Chorus. Manet* KING.)

KING. I requested Scaphio and Phantis to be so good as to favour me with
an audience this morning. (*Enter* SCAPHIO *and* PHANTIS.) Oh, here they are!   425
     SCA. Your Majesty wished to speak with us, I believe. You – you needn't
keep your crown on, on our account, you know.
     KING. I beg your pardon (*removes it*). I always forget that! Odd, the notion of
a King not being allowed to wear one of his own crowns in the presence of two
of his own subjects.   430
     PHAN. Yes – bizarre, is it not?
     KING. Most quaint. But then it's a quaint world.
     PHAN. Teems with quiet fun. I often think what a lucky thing it is that you
are blessed with such a keen sense of humour!
     KING. Do you know, I find it invaluable. Do what I will, I *cannot* help look-   435
ing at the humorous side of things – for, properly considered, everything has its
humorous side – even the *Palace Peeper* (*producing it*). See here – 'Another Royal
Scandal', by Junius Junior. 'How long is this to last?' by Senex Senior. 'Ribald
Royalty', by Mercury Major. 'Where is the Public Exploder?' by Mephistopheles Minor. When I reflect that all these outrageous attacks on my morality   440
are written by me, at your command – well, it's one of the funniest things that
have come within the scope of my experience.
     SCA. Besides, apart from that, they have a quiet humour of their own which
is simply irresistible.
     KING (*gratified*). Not bad, I think. Biting, trenchant sarcasm – the rapier,   445
not the bludgeon – that's my line. But then it's so easy – I'm such a good subject

451 *no one can hold a candle to you*: Reginald Allen's *First Night Gilbert and Sullivan* contains the
following extra lines of dialogue at this point:

> KING (*doubtfully*). Ye-yes. You refer, of course, to the literary quality of the paragraphs?
> SCAPHIO. Of course.
> KING. Because the essence of the joke lies in the fact that instead of
> being the abominable profligate they suggest, I'm one of the most
> fastidiously respectable persons in my whole dominions!

454 *Mr. Wilkinson*: The figure of Mr Wilkinson, the English tenor, assumed a much greater
importance in the early drafts of the plot than in the final version. As I have already mentioned, one of Gilbert's early ideas was that Scaphio and Phantis had forced the King to
fall in with their speculations on the Stock Exchange, edit a radical society paper and
produce a constant supply of comic operas in which he himself appeared in the guise of
Mr Wilkinson, an English tenor. The result was that the poor King, his duties of the
day finished, was compelled to make nightly appearances on stage incognito. This explains Scaphio's speech at lines 464–9. A further twist of the plot in one early sketch of
the play involved the daughter of Tarara falling in love with Mr Wilkinson.

474 *what a farce life is, to be sure*: This remark, and the song which follows it, could, I suppose,
be taken to sum up Gilbert's philosophy of life and his sense of its unpredictability and
the need to take it as it comes. Similar sentiments are expressed in the quintet 'Try we
life-long' in *The Gondoliers* (Act I, lines 574–597). The specific theme of 'First you're
born', of course, is the sad slide from youth into middle and old age. It is perhaps worth
remembering that Gilbert was 57 when he wrote it.

486 *de trop*: Unwanted. As the peers (and the fairies) in *Iolanthe* would have delighted in
pointing out, the phrase *de trop* is French, meaning too much or too many.

– a bad King but a good Subject – ha! ha! – a capital heading for next week's leading article! (*Makes a note.*) And then the stinging little paragraphs about our Royal goings-on with our Royal Second Housemaid – delicately sub-acid, are they not? 450

SCA. My dear King, in that kind of thing no one can hold a candle to you.

PHAN. But the crowning joke is the Comic Opera you've written for us – 'King Tuppence, or A Good Deal Less than Half a Sovereign' – in which the celebrated English tenor, Mr. Wilkinson, burlesques your personal appearance and gives grotesque imitations of your Royal peculiarities. It's immense! 455

KING. Ye – es – That's what I wanted to speak to you about. Now I've not the least doubt but that even *that* has its humorous side, too – if one could only see it. As a rule I'm pretty quick at detecting latent humour – but I confess I do *not* quite see where it comes in, in this particular instance. It's so horribly personal! 460

SCA. Personal? Yes, of course it's personal – but consider the antithetical humour of the situation.

KING. Yes. I – I don't think I've quite grasped that.

SCA. No? You surprise me. Why, consider. During the day thousands tremble at your frown, during the night (from 8 to 11) thousands roar at it. During 465 the day your most arbitrary pronouncements are received by your subjects with abject submission – during the night, they shout with joy at your most terrible decrees. It's not every monarch who enjoys the privilege of undoing by night all the despotic absurdities he's committed during the day.

KING. Of course! Now I see it! Thank you very much. I was sure it had its 470 humorous side, and it was very dull of me not to have seen it before. But, as I said just now, it's a quaint world.

PHAN. Teems with quiet fun.

KING. Yes. Properly considered, what a farce life is, to be sure!

SONG – KING.

First you're born – and I'll be bound you 475
Find a dozen strangers round you.
'Hallo,' cries the new-born baby,
'Where's my parents? Which may they be?'
　　Awkward silence – no reply –
　　Puzzled baby wonders why! 480
Father rises, bows politely –
Mother smiles (but not too brightly) –
Doctor mumbles like a dumb thing –
Nurse is busy mixing something. –
　　Every symptom tends to show 485
　　You're decidedly *de trop* –

ALL. 　　　　　　Ho! ho! ho! ho! ho! ho! ho! ho!

528   *Time has had his little joke*: In Reginald Allen's *First Night Gilbert and Sullivan* and in the 1926 Chatto edition of Gilbert's plays this is the last line of the King's solo and the following lines, starting with 'Ho! ho! ho!', are sung by the three men together. In the 1976 D'Oyly Carte recording, the King sings the lines down to 'the joke is over' but then all three come in with a repeat of 'Ho! ho! ho!' etc. The version printed opposite, which has the reprise being taken up with the line 'Daily driven' follows the OUP World's Classics edition and the current Chappell editions of the libretto and vocal score.

Time's teetotum,
  If you spin it,
Gives its quotum 490
  Once a minute.
I'll go bail
You hit the nail,
And if you fail
  The deuce is in it! 495

KING. You grow up, and you discover
What it is to be a lover.
Some young lady is selected –
Poor, perhaps, but well-connected,
  Whom you hail (for Love is blind) 500
  As the Queen of fairy kind.
Though she's plain – perhaps unsightly,
Makes her face up – laces tightly,
In her form your fancy traces
All the gifts of all the graces. 505
  Rivals none the maiden woo,
  So you take her and she takes you!

ALL. Ho! ho! ho! ho! ho! ho! ho! ho!
  Joke beginning,
    Never ceases, 510
  Till your inning
    Time releases,
  On your way
  You blindly stray,
  And day by day 515
    The joke increases!

KING. Ten years later – Time progresses –
Sours your temper – thins your tresses;
Fancy, then, her chain relaxes;
Rates are facts and so are taxes. 520
  Fairy Queen's no longer young –
  Fairy Queen has got a tongue.
Twins have probably intruded –
Quite unbidden – just as you did –
They're a source of care and trouble – 525
Just as you were – only double.
  Comes at last the final stroke –
  Time has had his little joke!

551 *My monarch is soliloquizing*: Shades of Bunthorne's 'Do let a poet soliloquize' in *Patience*,
      Act II, line 239.

563 *elsewhere*: Originally this speech was even longer than it is now. Reginald Allen's *First
      Night Gilbert and Sullivan* includes the following sentence at this point:

      As there is not a civilized king who is sufficiently single to realize my ideal of Abstract Re-
      spectability, I extended my sphere of action to the Islands of the South Pacific – only to dis-
      cover that the monarchs of those favoured climes are at least as lazy in their domestic
      arrangements as the worst of their European brethren.

566 *Respectability enough for Six*: Compare Lord Tolloller's assertion in *Iolanthe*, Act I, lines
      336–7, 'I've grammar and spelling for two and blood and behaviour for twenty'.

Ho! ho! ho! ho! ho! ho! ho! ho!
   Daily driven 530
     (Wife as drover)
   Ill you've thriven –
   Ne'er in clover:
   Lastly, when
   Three-score and ten 535
     (And not till then),
     The joke is over!

ALL.   Daily driven, &c.

       (*Exeunt* S C A P H I O *and* P H A N T I S. *Manet* K I N G.)

K I N G (*putting on his crown again*). It's all very well. I always like to look on the 540
humorous side of things; but I do *not* think I ought to be required to write libels
on my own moral character. Naturally, I see the joke of it – anybody would – but
Zara's coming home today; she's no longer a child, and I confess I should *not* like
her to see my Opera – though it's uncommonly well written; and I should be
sorry if the *Palace Peeper* got into her hands – though it's certainly smart – very 545
smart indeed. It is almost a pity that I have to buy up the whole edition, because
it's really too good to be lost. And Lady Sophy – that blameless type of perfect
womanhood! Great Heavens, what would *she* say if the Second Housemaid
business happened to meet *her* pure blue eye!

              (*Enter* L A D Y S O P H Y.) 550

L A D Y S. My monarch is soliloquizing. I will withdraw.   (*Going.*)
  K I N G. No – pray don't go. Now I'll give you fifty chances, and you won't
guess whom I was thinking of.
  L A D Y S. Alas, sir, I know too well. Ah! King, it's an old, old story, and I'm
wellnigh weary of it! Be warned in time – from my heart I pity you, but I am not 555
for you!   (*Going.*)
  K I N G. But hear what I have to say.
  L A D Y S. It is useless. Listen. In the course of a long and adventurous career
in the principal European Courts, it has been revealed to me that I uncon-
sciously exercise a weird and supernatural fascination over all Crowned Heads. 560
So irresistible is this singular property, that there is not a European Monarch
who has not implored me, with tears in his eyes, to quit his kingdom, and take
my fatal charms elsewhere. As time was getting on it occurred to me that by
descending several pegs in the scale of Respectability I might qualify your
Majesty for my hand. Actuated by this humane motive and happening to possess 565
Respectability enough for Six, I consented to confer Respectability enough for
Four upon your two younger daughters – but although I have, alas, only

577 *the Tivoli Gardens*: Pleasure gardens opened in Copenghagen in 1843. The name was subsequently adopted for similar parks in other places.

596–7 *I am in constant communication with the Mikado of Japan*: This is the only instance that I can think of where a character in one of the Savoy Operas is mentioned in the dialogue of another. Of course Captain Corcoran appears in the flesh in both *H.M.S. Pinafore* and *Utopia Limited* but that is rather different.

Respectability enough for Two left, there is still, as I gather from the public press
of this country (*producing the 'Palace Peeper'*), a considerable balance in my favour.

KING (*aside*). Da—! (*Aloud.*) May I ask how you came by that? 570

LADY S. It was handed to me by the officer who holds the position of Public
Exploder to your Imperial Majesty.

KING. And surely, Lady Sophy, surely you are not so unjust as to place any
faith in the irresponsible gabble of the Society press!

LADY S. (*referring to paper*). I read on the authority of Senex Senior that your 575
Majesty was seen dancing with your Second Housemaid on the Oriental
Platform of the Tivoli Gardens. That is untrue?

KING. Absolutely. Our Second Housemaid has only one leg.

LADY S. (*suspiciously*). How do you know that?

KING. Common report, I give you my honour. 580

LADY S. It may be so. I further read – and the statement is vouched for by
no less an authority than Mephistopheles Minor – that your Majesty indulges
in a bath of hot rum-punch every morning. I trust I do not lay myself open to
the charge of displaying an indelicate curiosity as to the mysteries of the royal
dressing-room when I ask if there is any foundation for this statement? 585

KING. None whatever. When our medical adviser exhibits rum-punch it is
as a draught, not as a fomentation. As to our bath, our valet plays the garden
hose upon us every morning.

LADY S. (*shocked*). Oh, pray – pray spare me these unseemly details. Well,
you are a Despot – have you taken steps to slay this scribbler? 590

KING. Well, no – I have *not* gone so far as that. After all, it's the poor devil's
living, you know.

LADY S. It is the poor devil's living that surprises me. If this man lies, there
is no recognized punishment that is sufficiently terrible for him.

KING. That's precisely it. I – I am waiting until a punishment is discovered 595
that will exactly meet the enormity of the case. I am in constant communication
with the Mikado of Japan, who is a leading authority on such points; and,
moreover, I have the ground plans and sectional elevations of several capital
punishments in my desk at this moment. Oh, Lady Sophy, as you are powerful,
be merciful! 600

DUET – KING *and* LADY SOPHY.

KING.

> Subjected to your heavenly gaze
> (Poetical phrase),
> My brain is turned completely.
> Observe me now,
> No Monarch, I vow, 605
> Was ever so far afflicted!

LADY S.

> I'm pleased with that poetical phrase,
> 'A heavenly gaze',

613   *crush me this contemptible worm*: This sounds like the language of Isaac Watts, the father of English hymnody, who was rather fond of comparing himself to a worm, as in the stanza:

> Alas! and did my Saviour bleed!
> And did my Sovereign die?
> Would he devote that sacred head
> For such a worm as I?

640   *March*: The opening bars of this are very similar to those which usher in the peers in *Iolanthe*.

    Gilbert originally planned a chorus before the entrance of Zara and her escorts. It appears in the manuscript version of the libretto now in the British Library:

> After exile home returning
>   Crammed with first-class English learning
> Our Princess is doubtless yearning
>   To complete our education.
>
> Lamp of wisdom burning brightly,
>   For your coming daily, nightly,
> We've been waiting all politely –
>   So indeed has all the nation.

<pre>
                   But though you put it neatly,
                       Say what you will,   610
                       These paragraphs still
                           Remain uncontradicted.

                   Come, crush me this contemptible worm
                       (A forcible term),
                       If he's assailed you wrongly.   615
                       The rage display,
                       Which, as you say,
                           Has moved your Majesty lately.

KING.   Though I admit that forcible term,
                       'Contemptible worm',   620
                       Appeals to me most strongly,
                       To treat this pest
                       As you suggest
                           Would pain my Majesty greatly!

LADY S.   This writer lies!   625
KING.   Yes, bother his eyes!
LADY S.   He lives, you say?
KING.   In a sort of a way.
LADY S.   Then have him shot.
KING.   Decidedly not.   630
LADY S.   Or crush him flat.
KING.   I cannot do that.
BOTH.   O royal Rex,
</pre>

$$\left.\begin{array}{l}\text{My}\\\text{Her}\end{array}\right\}\text{ blameless sex}$$

Abhors such conduct shady.   635

$$\left.\begin{array}{l}\text{You}\\\text{I}\end{array}\right\}\text{ plead in vain,}$$

$$\left.\begin{array}{l}\text{You}\\\text{I}\end{array}\right\}\text{ never will gain}$$

Respectable English lady!

(*Dance of repudiation by* LADY SOPHY. *Exit, followed by* KING.)

(*March. Enter all the Court, heralding the arrival of the* PRINCESS ZARA, *who*   640
enters, escorted by CAPTAIN FITZBATTLEAXE *and four Troopers, all in the*
full uniform of the First Life Guards.)

664 *First Life Guards*: The oldest cavalry regiment in the British Army and first in order of precedence, the First Life Guards originated as the bodyguard formed for Charles I by a group of Royalists in 1639. At the restoration of the monarchy in 1660 they became known as the Household Cavalry and in 1788 they were divided into the First and Second Life Guards. In 1922 they were amalgamated to form the Life Guards.

CHORUS (GIRLS ONLY).

Oh, maiden, rich
   In Girton lore,   645
That wisdom which
   We prized before,
We do confess
Is nothingness,
And rather less,   650
   Perhaps, than more.
On each of us
   Thy learning shed.
On calculus
   May we be fed.   655
And teach us, please,
To speak with ease
All languages,
   Alive and dead!
On each of us thy learning shed.   660

SOLO – PRINCESS ZARA *and* CHORUS.

ZARA.   Five years have flown since I took wing –
    Time flies, and his footstep ne'er retards –
  I'm the eldest daughter of your king.

FITZ. *and* TROOPERS.
    And we are the escort – First Life Guards!
    On the royal yacht,   665
      When the waves were white,
    In a helmet hot
      And a tunic tight,
    And our great big boots,
      We defied the storm: 670
    For we're not recruits,
      And his uniform
    A well-drilled trooper ne'er discards –
    And we are her escort – First Life Guards!, &c.

ZARA.   These gentlemen I present to you,   675
    The pride and boast of their barrack-yards;
  They've taken, O, such care of me!

FITZ. *and* TROOPERS.
    For we are the escort – First Life Guards!
    When the tempest rose,
      And the ship went *so* –   680

789 *Knightsbridge nursemaids*: Knightsbridge, the fashionable district of West London in which Harrods is situated, makes another appearance in the Savoy Operas when Ko-Ko tells the Mikado that his son, Nanki-Poo, has gone there (*Mikado*, Act II, line 499). Knightsbridge nursemaids would be well known to the Life Guards whose barracks are in the area.

790 *Belgravian airies*: Another posh London residential district, famed as a location for embassies, which also features in *Iolanthe* (Act 1, line 387) when Lord Tolloller reminds Phyllis that 'hearts just as pure and fair may meet in Belgrave Square as in the lowly air of Seven Dials'.

799 *First Life Guards*: In both the 1926 edition of Gilbert's plays and Reginald Allen's *First Night Gilbert and Sullivan* the men's chorus at this point is unaccountably and surely erroneously given as beginning 'When soldier seeks' (the words which Fitzbattleaxe has in lines 859–62).

Do you suppose
  We were ill? No, no!
Though a qualmish lot
  In a tunic tight,
And a helmet hot,   685
  And a breastplate bright
(Which a well-drilled trooper ne'er discards),
We stood as the escort – First Life Guards!, &c.

CHORUS.   Knightsbridge nursemaids – serving fairies –
             Stars of proud Belgravian airies;   790
             At stern duty's call you leave them,
             Though you know how that must grieve them!
ZARA.   Tantantarara-rara-rara!
FITZ.   Trumpet-call of Princess Zara!
CHORUS.   That's trump-call, and they're all trump cards –   795
FITZ. *and* TROOPERS.
             And we are the escort – First Life Guards!

ENSEMBLE.

CHORUS.	PRINCESS ZARA *and* CAPTAIN
LADIES.	FITZBATTLEAXE (*aside*).
They're her escort, &c.	Oh! the hours are gold
	And the joys untold,
MEN.	When $\left\{ \begin{array}{c} \text{your} \\ \text{my} \end{array} \right\}$ eyes behold
First Life Guards, &c.	
	$\left. \begin{array}{c} \text{Your} \\ \text{My} \end{array} \right\}$ beloved Princess; 800

And the years will seem
But a brief day-dream,
In our happiness,
And the years will seem
But a brief day-dream,   805
In the joy extreme
  Of our happiness!

(*Enter* KING, PRINCESSES NEKAYA *and* KALYBA, *and* LADY
SOPHY. *As the* KING *enters the escort present arms*.)

KING. Zara! my beloved daughter! Why, how well you look and how lovely   810
you have grown! (*Embraces her.*)

ZARA. My dear father! (*Embracing him.*) And my two beautiful little sisters!
(*Embracing them.*)

847 *Horse Guards*: The Life Guards can still, of course, be seen standing sentry here, or more often mounted on horses. The Horse Guards building in Whitehall was constructed in the mid-eighteenth century on the site of the old Palace of Whitehall. Built to house the offices of the Commander-in-Chief of the British army, it is now used as an annexe of the Ministry of Defence. The huge open space behind it is the site of the annual ceremony of Trooping the Colour.

NEK. Not beautiful.

KAL. Nice-looking. 815

ZARA. But first let me present to you the English warrior who commands my escort, and who has taken, O! such care of me during the voyage – Captain Fitzbattleaxe!

TROOPERS.   The First Life Guards.

When the tempest rose, 820

And the ship went *so* –

(FITZBATTLEAXE *motions them to be silent. The Troopers place themselves in the four corners of the stage, standing at ease, immovably, as if on sentry. Each is surrounded by an admiring group of young ladies, of whom they take no notice.*)

KING (*to* FITZBATTLEAXE). Sir, you come from a country where every 825 virtue flourishes. We trust that you will not criticize too severely such short-comings as you may detect in our semi-barbarous society.

FITZ. (*looking at* ZARA). Sir, I have eyes for nothing but the blameless and the beautiful.

KING. We thank you – he is really very polite! (LADY SOPHY, *who has been* 830 *greatly scandalized by the attentions paid to the Lifeguardsmen by the young ladies, marches the* PRINCESSES NEKAYA *and* KALYBA *towards an exit.*) Lady Sophy, do not leave us.

LADY S. Sir, your children are young, and, so far, innocent. If they are to remain so, it is necessary that they be at once removed from the contamination 835 of their present disgraceful surroundings. (*She marches them off.*)

KING (*whose attention has thus been called to the proceedings of the young ladies – aside*). Dear, dear! They really shouldn't. (*Aloud.*) Captain Fitzbattleaxe —

FITZ. Sir.

KING. Your Troopers appear to be receiving a troublesome amount of 840 attention from those young ladies. I know how strict you English soldiers are, and I should be extremely distressed if anything occurred to shock their puritanical British sensitiveness.

FITZ. Oh, I don't think there's any chance of that.

KING. You think not? They won't be offended? 845

FITZ. Oh no! They are quite hardened to it. They get a good deal of that sort of thing, standing sentry at the Horse Guards.

KING. It's English, is it?

FITZ. It's particularly English.

KING. Then, of course, it's all right. Pray proceed, ladies, it's particularly 850 English. Come, my daughter, for we have much to say to each other.

ZARA. Farewell, Captain Fitzbattleaxe! I cannot thank you too emphatically for the devoted care with which you have watched over me during our long and eventful voyage.

855–77   *Ah! gallant soldier, brave and true*

This song appears opposite as it was printed in the World's Classics edition of the Savoy Opera libretti and as it was sung in the 1976 D'Oyly Carte recording. The current Chappell edition of the libretto, the vocal score and other sources reflect Gilbert's original intention and print a longer version as follows:

ZARA.

Ah! gallant soldier, brave and true
In tented field and tourney,
I grieve to have occasioned you
So very long a journey.
A British soldier gives up all –
His home and island beauty –
When summoned by the trumpet call
Of Regimental duty.

ENSEMBLE.

FITZBATTLEAXE.	CHORUS.
	WOMEN.
Oh my joy, my pride	Knightsbridge nursemaids –
My delight to hide	Serving fairies, etc.

ZARA & FITZBATTLEAXE.	MEN.
Let us sing, aside,	A British soldier gives up all, etc.
What in truth we feel.	
Let us whisper low	
Of our love's glad glow,	
Lest the truth we show	
We would fain conceal.	

FITZBATTLEAXE.

Such escort duty, as his due,
To young Life-guardsman falling
Completely reconciles him to
His uneventful calling.
When soldier seeks Utopian glades
In charge of Youth and Beauty,
Then pleasure merely masquerades
As Regimental Duty!

877   *Of our happiness:* Gilbert originally intended there to be another song at this point. It appears in his manuscript copy of the libretto but it is not entirely clear whom he intended should sing it:

For England rules from East to West
And when she lifts her warlike crest
(I'm quoting our distinguished guest)
    There'll be the deuce to pay!

Gets set to work without relapse –
Who knows but some fine day, perhaps,
When we our warlike crest display
    There'll also be the deuce to pay!

DUET – ZARA *and* FITZBATTLEAXE.

ZARA.	Ah! gallant soldier, brave and true	855
	In tented field and tourney,	
	I grieve to have occasioned you	
	So very long a journey.	

FITZ.	When soldier seeks Utopian glades	
	In charge of Youth and Beauty,	860
	Then pleasure merely masquerades	
	As Regimental Duty!	

ALL.	Tantantarara-rara-rara!	
	The trumpet-call of Princess Zara!	

CHORUS.	That's the trump-call, &c.	865

FITZ. *and* TROOPERS.

   And we are the escort, &c.

ENSEMBLE.

CHORUS. LADIES.	ZARA *and* FITZBATTLEAXE (*aside*).	
They're her escort, &c.	Oh! the hours are gold	
	And the joys untold	
MEN.	When $\left\{ \begin{matrix} \text{your} \\ \text{my} \end{matrix} \right\}$ eyes behold	
First Life Guards, &c.		
	$\left. \begin{matrix} \text{Your} \\ \text{My} \end{matrix} \right\}$ beloved Princess;	870
	And the years will seem	
	But a brief day-dream,	
	In our happiness,	
	And the years will seem	
	But a brief day-dream,	875
	In the joy extreme	
	Of our happiness!	

(*Exeunt* KING *and* ZARA *in one direction, Lifeguardsmen and crowd in opposite direction. Enter, at back,* SCAPHIO *and* PHANTIS, *who watch* ZARA *as she goes off.* SCAPHIO *is seated, shaking violently, and obviously under the influence of some strong emotion.*)   880

PHAN. There – tell me, Scaphio, is she not beautiful? Can you wonder that I love her so passionately?

890 *enthralling*: Originally Scaphio had a longer speech here. Reginald Allen's *First Night Gilbert and Sullivan* contains the following additional lines:

> Her walk – her smile – her play of feature! What eyes – what lips! Why, it's bewildering – dazzling – intoxicating etc.

895 *My ideal*: Another point at which there was once more dialogue, as follows:

> SCAPHIO. My ideal, did I say?
> PHANTIS (*much disconcerted*). Yes, you said so.
> SCAPHIO. Then I lied, for by all that's dazzling I had no conception that the world contained such transcendent loveliness! Why what's this? etc.

922 *the Tontine principle*: A form of annuity shared by several subscribers in which the shares of those who die are added to the holdings of the survivors until the last one inherits all. It derives its name from Lorenzo Tonti, a Neapolitan banker who introduced the system into France in 1653.

SCA. No. She is extraordinarily – miraculously lovely! Good heavens, what a
singularly beautiful girl!   885
PHAN. I knew you would say so!
SCA. What exquisite charm of manner! What surprising delicacy of
gesture! Why, she's a goddess, a very goddess!
PHAN. (*rather taken aback*). Yes – she's – she's an attractive girl.
SCA. Attractive? Why, you must be blind! – She's entrancing – enthralling!   890
intoxicating! (*Aside.*) God bless my heart, what's the matter with me?
PHAN. (*alarmed*). Yes. You – you promised to help me to get her father's
consent, you know.
SCA. Promised! Yes, but the convulsion has come, my good boy! It is she –
my ideal! Why, what's this? (*Staggering.*) Phantis! Stop me – I'm going mad – mad   895
with the love of her!
PHAN. Scaphio, compose yourself, I beg. The girl is perfectly opaque!
Besides, remember – each of us is helpless without the other. You can't succeed
without my consent, you know.
SCA. And you dare to threaten? Oh, ungrateful! When you came to me,   900
palsied with love for this girl, and implored my assistance, did I not unhesitatingly promise it? And this is the return you make? Out of my sight, ingrate!
(*Aside.*) Dear! dear! what is the matter with me?

(*Enter* FITZBATTLEAXE *and* ZARA.)

ZARA. Dear me. I'm afraid we are interrupting a *tête-à-tête*.   905
SCA. (*breathlessly*). No, no. You come very appropriately. To be brief, we – we
love you – this man and I – madly – passionately!
ZARA. Sir!
SCA. And we don't know how we are to settle which of us is to marry you.
FITZ. Zara, this is very awkward.   910
SCA. (*very much overcome*). I – I am paralysed by the singular radiance of your
extraordinary loveliness. I know I am incoherent. I never was like this before – it
shall not occur again. I – shall be fluent, presently.
ZARA (*aside*). Oh, dear, Captain Fitzbattleaxe, what *is* to be done?
FITZ. (*aside*). Leave it to me – I'll manage it. (*Aloud.*) It's a common situation.   915
Why not settle it in the English fashion?
BOTH. The English fashion? What is that?
FITZ. It's very simple. In England, when two gentlemen are in love with the
same lady, and until it is settled which gentleman is to blow out the brains of the
other, it is provided, by the Rival Admirers' Clauses Consolidation Act, that the   920
lady shall be entrusted to an officer of Household Cavalry as stakeholder, who is
bound to hand her over to the survivor (on the Tontine principle) in a good
condition of substantial and decorative repair.
SCA. Reasonable wear and tear and damages by fire excepted?
FITZ. Exactly.   925

958 *As both will live and neither die*: Here's a state of things! The World's Classics edition of the Savoy Opera libretti, the Chappell edition of the vocal score and the D'Oyly Carte recording agree on the version of Fitzbattleaxe's and Zara's lines printed opposite. However, the Chatto edition of Gilbert's plays, Reginald Allen's *First Night Gilbert and Sullivan* and the Chappell edition of the libretto print different words for the couple:

> As both of us are positive
> That both of them intend to live,
> There's nothing in the case to give
> Us cause for grave reflections.
> As both will live and neither die,
> I see no kind of reason why
> You/I should not if you/I wish it, try
> To gain my/your young affections

PHAN. Well, that seems very reasonable. (*To* SCAPHIO.) What do you say –
Shall we entrust her to this officer of Household Cavalry? It will give us time.

SCA. (*trembling violently*). I – I am not at present in a condition to think it
out coolly – but if he *is* an officer of Household Cavalry, and if the Princess
consents —   930

ZARA. Alas, dear sirs, I have no alternative – under the Rival Admirers'
Clauses Consolidation Act!

FITZ. Good – then that's settled.

QUARTET – FITZBATTLEAXE, ZARA, SCAPHIO, *and* PHANTIS

FITZ.   It's understood, I think, all round
                             That, by the English custom bound,   935
                             I hold the lady safe and sound
                                  In trust for either rival,
                             Until you clearly testify
                             By sword or pistol, by and by,
                             Which gentleman prefers to die,   940
                             And which prefers survival.

ENSEMBLE.

SCAPHIO *and* PHANTIS.	ZARA *and* FITZBATTLEAXE (*aside*).
It's clearly understood, all round,	We stand, I think, on safish ground,
That, by your English custom bound,	Our senses weak it will astound
He holds the lady safe and sound	If either gentleman is found
In trust for either rival,	Prepared to meet his rival.
Until we clearly testify	Their machinations we defy;
By sword or pistol, by and by	We won't be parted, you and I –
Which gentleman prefers to die,	Of bloodshed each is rather shy –
And which prefers survival.	They both prefer survival.

(945 appears at right of "Prepared to meet his rival.")

SCA. (*aside to* FITZ.).   If I should die and he should live,   950
                           To you, without reserve, I give
                           Her heart so young and sensitive,
                           And all her predilections.
PHAN. (*aside to* FITZ.).If he should live and I should die,
                           I see no kind of reason why   955
                           You should not, if you wish it, try
                           To gain her young affections.

ENSEMBLE.

SCAPHIO *and* PHANTIS (*angrily to each other*).	FITZBATTLEAXE *and* ZARA (*aside*).
If I should die and you should live,	As both will live and neither die
To this young officer I give	I ⎱ see no kind of reason why
Her heart so soft and sensitive,	You ⎰

987–9 *Upon your breast, my blushing face I think I'd rest*: Compare Phoebe's line 'Upon thy breast my loving head would rest' in *The Yeomen of the Guard*, Act I, lines 706–7.

993 *Is sorely in the way*: In the libretto text printed in Reginald Allen's *First Night Gilbert and Sullivan* there are two additional lines for Zara at this point:

> That is, supposing it were true
> That I'm engaged to both – and both were you!

And all her predilections.
If you should live and I should die,
I see no kind of reason why
He should not, if he chooses, try
   To win her young affections.

$\left.{I \atop You}\right\}$ should not, if $\left\{{I \atop you}\right.$ wish it, try   960

To gain $\left.{your \atop my}\right\}$ young affections!
As both of us are positive
That both of them intend to live,
There's nothing in the case to give
   Us cause for grave reflections.   965

(*Exeunt* SCAPHIO *and* PHANTIS *together*.)

DUET – ZARA *and* FITZBATTLEAXE.

ENSEMBLE.

Oh admirable art!
   Oh neatly-planned intention!
   Oh happy intervention –
     Oh well-constructed plot!   970
When sages try to part
   Two loving hearts in fusion,
   Their wisdom's a delusion,
     And learning serves them not!

FITZ.   Until quite plain   975
     Is their intent,
These sages twain
     I represent.
Now please infer
     That, nothing loth,   980
You're henceforth, as it were,
     Engaged to marry both –
Then take it that I represent the two –
On that hypothesis, what would you do?

ZARA (*aside*).   What would I do? What would I do?   985
  (*To* FITZ.)   In such a case,
     Upon your breast,
My blushing face
     I think I'd rest –   (*Doing so*)
Then perhaps I might   990
     Demurely say –
'I find this breastplate bright
     Is sorely in the way!'

1004 *Manet Zara*: At this point the first night libretto had Zara remain on stage alone for a soliloquoy and a song as follows:

> ZARA (*looking off, in the direction in which* SCAPHIO *and* PHANTIS *have gone*). Poor, trusting, simple-minded, and affectionate old gentlemen! I'm really sorry for them! How strange it is that when the flower of a man's youth has faded, he seems to lose all charm in a woman's eyes; and how true are the words of my expurgated Juvenal:
>
> 'Festinat decurrere velox Flosculus, angustae,
> miseroeque brevissima vitae Portio!'
>
> Ah, if we could only make up our minds to invest our stock of youth on commercial principles instead of squandering it at the outset, old age would be as extinct as the Dodo!

SONG – ZARA.

Youth is a boon avowed –
A gift of priceless worth
To rich and poor allowed –
  With which all men at birth –
    The lowly and the proud –
  Are equally endowed.
But sorrow comes anon,
  For Man's a prodigal
Who madly lives upon
  His little capital.
    And this, alas, goes on
    Till every penny's gone:
He finds himself, at Life's concluding stage,
With no Youth left to comfort his old age!

Ah, dame improvident,
  If you in very sooth
In infancy had lent
  Your Capital of Youth
    At four or five per cent –
    (As Nature doubtless meant),
Resolved, within your breast,
  To do as others do
Who Capital invest,
  And live a lifetime through,
    With modest comfort blest,
    Upon the interest –
You might be still in girlhood's mid-career
A merry madcap maid of fourscore year!

    The above song seems to have been cut during rehearsals in an attempt to shorten the first act and was not sung at the public dress rehearsal on 6 October 1893. However, it was reinstated for the following evening's first night performance when it was sung to considerable critical acclaim by Miss Nancy McIntosh, an American soprano who was plucked by Gilbert from the world of oratorio to take the leading role in *Utopia Limited*. The critic of *The Globe* went so far as to describe this song as one of Sir Arthur Sullivan's best works. It does not appear to have been sung in subsequent performances and is missing from all published libretti or vocal scores. The only form in which it has survived is in the American copyright copy of the libretto which was deposited on 9 October 1893.

FITZ.   Our mortal race
                      Is never blest –
                   There's no such case   995
                      As perfect rest;
                   Some petty blight
                      Asserts its sway –
                   Some crumpled roseleaf light   1000
                      Is always in the way!

ZARA.   In such a case, &c.

FITZ.   Our mortal race, &c.

                   (*Exit* FITZBATTLEAXE. *Manet* ZARA.)

                   (*Enter* KING.)   1005

KING. My daughter! At last we are alone together.

ZARA. Yes, and I'm glad we are, for I want to speak to you very seriously. Do you know this paper?

KING (*aside*). Da—! (*Aloud.*) Where in the world did you get this from?

ZARA. It was given to me by Lady Sophy – my sisters' governess.   1010

KING (*aside*). Lady Sophy's an angel, but I do sometimes wish she'd mind her own business! (*Aloud.*) It's – ha! ha! – it's rather humorous.

ZARA. I see nothing humorous in it. I only see that you, the despotic King of this country, are made the subject of the most scandalous insinuations. Why do you permit these things?   1115

KING. Well, they appeal to my sense of humour. It's the only really comic paper in Utopia, and I wouldn't be without it for the world.

ZARA. If it had any literary merit I could understand it.

KING. Oh, it *has* literary merit. Oh, distinctly, it has literary merit.

ZARA. My dear father, it's mere ungrammatical twaddle.   1020

KING. Oh, it's not ungrammatical. I can't allow that. Unpleasantly personal, perhaps, but written with an epigrammatical point that is, I flatter myself, very rare nowadays – very rare indeed.

ZARA (*looking at cartoon*). Why do they represent you with such a big nose?

KING (*looking at cartoon*). Eh? Yes, it *is* a big one! Why, the fact is that, in the   1025
cartoons of a comic paper, the size of your nose always varies inversely as the square of your popularity. It's the rule.

ZARA. Then you must be at a tremendous discount, just now! I see a notice of a new piece called 'King Tuppence', in which an English tenor has the audacity to personate you on a public stage. I can only say that I am surprised   1030
that any English tenor should lend himself to such degrading personalities.

KING. Oh, he's not really English. As it happens he's a Utopian, but he calls himself English.

1037–8 *pointless burlesque*: In Gilbert's manuscript copy of the libretto the following dialogue
and song appears here, possibly as a relic from the earlier version of the play when the
King himself appeared nightly in the theatre incognito as the English tenor:

> KING: Oh, it's not pointless, it's very smartly written. If it were pointless I wouldn't
> allow it, but the piece really has very remarkable literary merit. See here. This gets a double
> encore.
>
> (*Sings*)   Oh, I'm a kind of a king –
> A sort of despot bold,
> An utterly insignificant thing
> Who does whatever he's told –
>
> Oh, cruel is my lot
> My fate unkind I call –
> For I'm a Kingly Never Mind What,
> A Royal Nothing at All!
>
> (*Breaks down and sinks sobbing into a chair*)
>
> ZARA. My dear father, there's something wrong here. If you were a free agent, you would
> never permit these outrages.

1047 *I have brought with me six representatives*: Gilbert took some time to settle the six professions which he felt would best represent the triumphs of British civilization. In one of
his earlier versions of the plot he had the Princess Soza, as she then was, bring back
with her a policeman, personifying social and public order, a life guardsman (military
supremacy), a curate (moral blamelessness), an earl (aristocratic supremacy), a flunkey
(domestic order) and a stockbroker (commercial propriety). A later version came slightly
closer to the final selection with a life guardsman, a butler, a policeman, a QC, a physi-
cian and a county councillor.

ZARA. Calls himself English?

KING. Yes. Bless you, they wouldn't listen to any tenor who didn't call 1035
himself English.

ZARA. And you permit this insolent buffoon to caricature you in a pointless
burlesque! My dear father – if you were a free agent, you would never permit
these outrages.

KING (*almost in tears*). Zara – I – I admit I am not altogether a free agent. I – I 1040
am controlled. I try to make the best of it, but sometimes I find it very difficult –
very difficult indeed. Nominally a Despot, I am, between ourselves, the helpless
tool of two unscrupulous Wise Men, who insist on my falling in with all their
wishes and threaten to denounce me for immediate explosion if I remonstrate!
(*Breaks down completely.*) 1045

ZARA. My poor father! Now listen to me. With a view to remodelling the
political and social institutions of Utopia, I have brought with me six
Representatives of the principal causes that have tended to make England the
powerful, happy, and blameless country which the consensus of European
civilization has declared it to be. Place yourself unreservedly in the hands of 1050
these gentlemen, and they will reorganize your country on a footing that will
enable you to defy your persecutors. They are all now washing their hands after
their journey. Shall I introduce them?

KING. My dear Zara, how can I thank you? I will consent to anything that
will release me from the abominable tyranny of these two men. (*Calling.*) What 1055
ho! Without there! (*Enter* CALYNX.) Summon my Court without an instant's
delay!   (*Exit* CALYNX.)

FINALE.

(*Enter everyone, except the Flowers of Progress.*)

CHORUS.

Although your Royal summons to appear 1060
From courtesy was singularly free,
Obedient to that summons we are here –
What would your Majesty?

RECITATIVE – KING.

My worthy people, my beloved daughter
Most thoughtfully has brought with her from England 1065
The types of all the causes that have made
That great and glorious country what it is.

CHORUS.   Oh, joy unbounded!

1071 *Ye South Pacific Island viviparians*: One might well echo Scaphio, Phantis and Tarara and
ask what does this mean? The answer is that viviparous is a zoological term used of animals and means bringing forth young in a live state. The *Oxford English Dictionary*
does not give the term 'viviparian' but I suppose that it could reasonably be used for
those giving birth to live offspring. If it seems a trifle incongruous as applied to the Utopians, we should remember that Gilbert had to come up with something that rhymed
with 'barbarians' after he had altered the name of the Utopian king from Phalarion to
Paramount. The original version of this line contained in his manuscript edition of the
libretto makes much more sense:

> Ye worthy subjects of good King Phalarion's

1075–6 *Yes! Contrasted when with Englishmen*: The version of this chorus given in Reginald Allen's
First Night Gilbert and Sullivan is somewhat different:

> That's true – we South Pacific viviparians,
> Contrasted when
> With Englishmen,
> Are little better than half-clothed barbarians!

Scaphio, Phantis and Tarara's interjection 'What does this mean?' is also missing from
this text.

1084 *In serried ranks assembles*: As, of course, do the warriors of Titipu (*The Mikado*, Act I, line
51).

1089 *Yes-yes-yes*: These lines were originally given to Captain Fitzbattleaxe who continued:

> I represent a military scheme
> In all its proud perfection!

SCA., TAR., *and* PHAN. *(aside).*
    Why, what *does* this mean?

RECITATIVE – ZARA.

    Attend to me, Utopian populace,   1070
        Ye South Pacific Island viviparians;
    All, in the abstract, types of courtly grace,
    Yet, when compared with Britain's glorious race,
    But little better than half-clothed barbarians!

CHORUS.

    Yes! Contrasted when   1075
    With Englishmen,
    We're little better than half-clothed barbarians!

SCA., PHAN., *and* TAR.
    What does this mean?

    (Enter all the Flowers of Progress.)

SOLO – ZARA.

    (Presenting CAPTAIN FITZBATTLEAXE.*)*   1080

    When Britain sounds the trump of war
        (And Europe trembles),
    The army of the conqueror
        In serried ranks assembles;
    'Tis then this warrior's eyes and sabre gleam   1085
        For our protection –
    He represents a military scheme
        In all its proud perfection!

CHORUS.   Yes – yes – yes,
    He represents a military scheme   1090
        In all its proud perfection!
    Ulahlica! Ulahlica! Ulahlica!

SOLO – ZARA.

    (Presenting SIR BAILEY BARRE, Q. C., M. P.*)*

A complicated gentleman allow me to present,
Of all the arts and faculties the terse embodiment,   1095

1113 *What these may be, Utopians all*: Who but Sullivan would have ever thought of setting a song introducing the Lord High Chamberlain in waltz time?

1117 *a Lord High Chamberlain*: Under the Licensing Act of 1737 all new plays had to be sent to the Lord Chamberlain's office for scrutiny by the Examiner of Plays before they could be performed on stage. The Theatres Act of 1968 ended this system of licensing and brought plays within the scope of the common law of libel and obscenity.

1122 *Court reputations*: In Reginald Allen's *First Night Gilbert and Sullivan* this chorus begins 'Yes – yes – yes' and continues with a reprise of the lines beginning 'New plays'. The chorus following Mr Blushington's solo takes a similar course.

1127 *This County Councillor acclaim*: County councillors were still a comparatively recent species when *Utopia Limited* was written. The 1888 Local Government Act created 62 democratically elected county councils in place of the old system whereby the shires were largely administered by justices of the peace at quarter sessions.

He's great Arithmetician who can demonstrate with ease
That two and two are three, or five, or anything you please;
An eminent Logician who can make it clear to you
That black is white – when looked at from the proper point of view;
A marvellous Philologist who'll undertake to show   1100
That 'yes' is but another and a neater form of 'no'.

SIR BAILEY.   Yes – yes – yes –
'Yes' is but another and a neater form of 'no'.
All preconceived ideas on any subject I can scout,
And demonstrate beyond all possibility of doubt,   1105
That whether you're an honest man or whether you're a thief
Depends on whose solicitor has given me my brief.

CHORUS.   Yes – yes – yes –
That whether you're an honest man, &c.
Ulahlica! Ulahlica! Ulahlica!   1110

SOLO – ZARA.

(*Presenting* LORD DRAMALEIGH *and* MR. BLUSHINGTON *of the County Council.*)

What these may be, Utopians all,
Perhaps you'll hardly guess –
They're types of England's physical   1115
And moral cleanliness.
This is a Lord High Chamberlain,
Of purity the gauge –
He'll cleanse our Court from moral stain
And purify our Stage.   1120

LORD D.   Yes – yes – yes –
Court reputations I revise,
And presentations scrutinize,
New plays I read with jealous eyes,
And purify the Stage.   1125

CHORUS.   Court reputations, &c.

ZARA.   This County Councillor acclaim,
Great Britain's latest toy –
On anything you like to name
His talents he'll employ –   1130

1144 *Contango*: In Stock Exchange parlance, the sum paid by the purchaser of stock to the seller for the privilege of deferring the completion of the bargain until some future settling day.
Backwardation: Another technical term used in the Stock Exchange to denote the sum paid by a seller on a bear account (a speculation on a fall in the price of certain shares) in order to postpone the completion of the transaction to the next settling day.

All streets and squares he'll purify
    Within your city walls,
And keep meanwhile a modest eye
    On wicked music halls.

MR. BLUSH.   Yes – yes – yes –   1135
In towns I make improvements great,
Which go to swell the County Rate –
I dwelling-houses sanitate,
    And purify the Halls!

CHORUS.   In towns he makes improvements great, &c.   1140
Ulahlica! Ulahlica! Ulahlica!

SOLO – ZARA.

(*Presenting* MR. GOLDBURY.)

A Company Promoter this, with special education,
Which teaches what Contango means and also Backwardation –
To speculators he supplies a grand financial leaven,   1145
Time was when *two* were company – but now it must be seven.

MR. GOLD.   Yes – yes – yes –
Time was, &c.
Stupendous loans to foreign thrones
    I've largely advocated;   1150
In ginger-pops and peppermint-drops
    I've freely speculated;
Then mines of gold, of wealth untold,
    Successfully I've floated,
And sudden falls in apple-stalls   1155
    Occasionally quoted:
And soon or late I always call
    For Stock Exchange quotation –
No schemes too great and none too small
    For Companification!   1160

CHORUS.   Yes! Yes! Yes! No schemes too great, &c.

SOLO – ZARA.

(*Presenting* CAPTAIN SIR EDWARD CORCORAN, R. N.)

And lastly I present
    Great Britain's proudest boast,

1170 *I'm Captain Corcoran, K.C.B*: If this is a re-appearance of Captain Corcoran of *H.M.S. Pinafore*, there is, of course, a problem. At the end of that opera Corcoran was revealed to be a common sailor. Even if he had managed to attain the rank of captain again, which seems unlikely, he would hardly have climbed so high as to become a Knight Commander of the Bath, putting him on a par with the Admiralty's First Lord, Sir Joseph Porter. Are we perhaps confronted here by Captain Rackstraw, who has changed his name and also deepened his voice from tenor to baritone? If so, he is, in fact, following a precedent set in one of Gilbert's Bab Ballads where Private James changes his name and his rank to that of General John when it is revealed that the two men have been mixed up at birth.

Corcoran's appearance is introduced by a snatch of the sailor's hornpipe (with a bewildering number of flats). It scored a tremendous hit and met with an encore on the opening night. The quotation of the whole 'what never' / Hardly ever' sequence is the only occasion when a whole tune from one opera is quoted in another (apart, of course, from the re-use of 'Climbing over Rocky Mountain' from *Thespis* in *The Pirates of Penzance*). The *Daily News* critic pointed out that Sullivan was in good company, Mozart having done the same when he quoted a tune from *The Marriage of Figaro* in the supper scene of *Don Giovanni*.

The *Daily Graphic*, however, was unhappy about the content of Corcoran's song: 'We are glad to meet with our old friend Captain Corcoran again, and the quotation from *Pinafore* fairly brought down the house. But it is nothing short of a lamentable error in taste which has prompted Mr Gilbert to indulge in sarcastic allusions to the steering and running aground of ships of war within a few months after the loss of H.M.S. *Victoria*'.

H.M.S. *Victoria* was sunk after colliding with another Royal Navy vessel, H.M.S. *Camperdown*, during naval manœuvres off Tripoli on 22 June 1893. If Gilbert did, in fact, have that event in mind when he penned the lines for Corcoran, and there is no evidence that he did, it would represent a unique example of a topical reference to a disaster in his libretti.

1175 *Maxim gun and Nordenfeldt*: The Maxim was the world's first automatic machine-gun. It was devised by the Anglo-American inventor, Sir Hiram Maxim, in 1884 and first used in West Africa three years later. It was issued for general use in the British Army in 1889. The Nordenfeldt was an earlier crank-operated five-barrel machine-gun invented in 1880 by Torsten Nordenfeldt, a Swedish gun designer who is chiefly remembered for constructing a steam-powered submarine driven by twin propellors. The Chappell editions of the libretto and vocal score mis-spell Nordenfeldt as 'Nordenfelt' – hardly a heinous crime but the kind of slip that Gilbert and Sullivan addicts love to discover. Please be gentle on me for mine!

1178 *Unbend your sails and lower your yards*: A sail is 'bent' when it is attached to the mast by ropes. So both these nautical terms mean the same thing: reduce sail.

1179 *Unstep your masts*: Masts are 'stepped' by being set in the correct vertical position. To unstep them is therefore to dismantle them.

1197 *Ye wanderers from a mighty State*: In the 1976 D'Oyly Carte recording the word 'pilgrims' was substituted for 'wanderers'. I have not been able to find this change made in any edition of the libretto or vocal score and can only assume that its purpose was to aid singing rather than to introduce a religious note.

Who from the blows   1165
Of foreign foes
    Protects her sea-girt coast –
And if you ask him in respectful tone,
He'll show you how you may protect your own!

SOLO – Captain Corcoran.

I'm Captain Corcoran, K.C.B.,   1170
I'll teach you how we rule the sea,
    And terrify the simple Gauls;
And how the Saxon and the Celt
Their Europe-shaking blows have dealt
With Maxim gun and Nordenfeldt   1175
    (Or will, when the occasion calls).
If sailor-like you'd play your cards,
Unbend your sails and lower your yards,
    Unstep your masts – you'll never want 'em more.
Though we're no longer hearts of oak,   1180
Yet we can steer and we can stoke,
And, thanks to coal, and thanks to coke,
    We never run a ship ashore!

ALL.   What never?
CAPT. COR.   No, never!   1185
ALL.   What *never*?
CAPT. COR.   Hardly ever!
ALL.   Hardly ever run a ship ashore!
            Then give three cheers, and three cheers more,
            For the tar who never runs his ship ashore;   1190
            Then give three cheers, and three cheers more,
                For he never runs his ship ashore!

            All hail, ye types of England's power –
                Ye heaven-enlightened band!
            We bless the day, and bless the hour   1195
                That brought you to our land.

ENSEMBLE – King, Zara, Lady Sophy, *and* Fitzbattleaxe.

            Ye wanderers from a mighty State,
            Oh teach us how to legislate –
            Your $\Big\}$ lightest word will carry weight
            Our
                In $\left\{ {\text{our} \atop \text{your}} \right\}$ your attentive ears.   1200

1201 *Oh, teach the natives of this land*: In *The First Night Gilbert and Sullivan* these lines are given
to the quartet of the King, Zara, Lady Sophy and Fitzbattleaxe. They sing:

> Oh, teach the natives of this land
> (Who are not quick to understand)
> How to work off their social and political arrears!

1210 *a Company Limited*: The principle of limited liability ensures that the loss that an owner
or shareholder of a business may incur is limited to the amount of capital invested by
him in the business and does not extend to his personal assets. In Britain the Joint-Stock
Companies Act of 1844 made incorporation of limited liability companies possible on
the basis of simple registration. Further important measures extending the principle of
limited liability were the Joint Stock Companies Act of 1862, mentioned in the finale of
this act, and the Directors' Liability Act of 1890.

1218–62 *Some seven men form an Association*
This was the third song in Act I of *Utopia Limited* to receive an encore on the first night. It
is a considerable tribute to Sullivan's skills that he could turn lyrics about the setting up
of a limited company into a hit song. His trick was in finding the delightful 6:8 tune,
redolent of the Palais Glide, and hitting a high F on the words 'pay', 'so' and 'pay' to give
a dramatic effect at the end of each verse.

ALL.	Oh, teach the natives of this land
	Who are not quick to understand
	Ye ⎫
	We ⎭ wanderers, &c.

FITZ.	Increase your army!	
LORD D.	Purify your Court!	1205
CAPT. COR.	Get up your steam and cut your canvas short!	
SIR B. BAR.	To speak on both sides teach your sluggish brains!	
MR. BLUSH.	Widen your thoroughfares, and flush your drains!	
MR. GOLD.	Utopia's much too big for one small head –	
	I'll float it as a Company Limited!	1210

KING.	A Company Limited? What may that be?
	The term, I rather think, is new to me.

CHORUS.	A Company Limited? &c.

SCA., PHAN., *and* TAR. (*aside*).

What does he mean? What does he mean?
 Give us a kind of clue!   1215
What does he mean? What does he mean?
 What is he going to do?

SONG – MR. GOLDBURY.

Some seven men form an Association,
 (If possible, all Peers and Baronets)
They start off with a public declaration   1220
 To what extent they mean to pay their debts.
That's called their Capital: if they are wary
 They will not quote it at a sum immense.
The figure's immaterial – it may vary
 From eighteen million down to eighteenpence.   1225
  I should put it rather low;
  The good sense of doing so
Will be evident at once to any debtor.
  When it's left to you to say
  What amount you mean to pay,   1230
Why, the lower you can put it at, the better.

CHORUS.	When it's left to you to say, &c.

They then proceed to trade with all who'll trust 'em,
 Quite irrespective of their capital

1236 *Panama Canal*: This was still in process of construction at the time *Utopia Limited* was written. Ferdinand de Lesseps, builder of the Suez Canal, had embarked on the project of a waterway linking the Atlantic and Pacific oceans in 1881 but there were numerous problems along the way and the Panama Canal was not finally opened to shipping until 1914.

1254 *You merely file a Winding-Up Petition*: Another highly topical reference. The Companies (Winding Up) Act became law in 1893, the year of *Utopia Limited*'s first performance.

1256 *Though a Rothschild you may be*: The Rothschilds are, of course, one of the most famous of all the European banking families. For further information on them see the note to *Iolanthe* Act II, line 325 which refers to their mention in the Lord Chancellor's nightmare song.

(It's shady, but it's sanctified by custom); 1235
    Bank, Railway, Loan, or Panama Canal.
You can't embark on trading too tremendous –
    It's strictly fair, and based on common sense –
If you succeed, your profits are stupendous –
    And if you fail, pop goes your eighteenpence. 1240
      Make the money-spinner spin!
      For you only stand to win,
    And you'll never with dishonesty be twitted.
      For nobody can know,
      To a million or so, 1245
    To what extent your capital's committed!

CHORUS.   For, nobody can know, &c.

If you come to grief, and creditors are craving,
    (For nothing that is planned by mortal head
Is certain in this Vale of Sorrow – saving 1250
    That one's Liability is Limited), –
Do you suppose that signifies perdition?
    If so you're but a monetary dunce –
You merely file a Winding-Up Petition,
    And start another Company at once! 1255
      Though a Rothschild you may be
      In your own capacity,
    As a Company you've come to utter sorrow –
      But the Liquidators say,
      'Never mind – you needn't pay,' 1260
    So you start another Company tomorrow!

CHORUS.   But the Liquidators say, &c.

RECITATIVE.

KING.   Well, at first sight it strikes us as dishonest,
     But if it's good enough for virtuous England –
     The first commercial country in the world – 1265
     It's good enough for us.
SCA., PHAN., *and* TAR. (*aside* to KING).
      You'd best take care –
     Please recollect *we* have not been consulted.
KING (*not heeding them*).
      And do I understand you that Great Britain
     Upon this Joint Stock principle is governed? 1270
MR. GOLD.   We haven't come to that, exactly – but

1278 *The Joint Stock Company's Act of Sixty Two*: This must count as one of the most amazing lines in the world of light opera – imagine having to set it to music! Believe it or not, it is entirely accurate historically. There was a Companies Act in 1862 which had the effect of greatly encouraging the principle of joint-stock ownership and limited liability in British industry and commerce and led to many firms becoming companies.

1292 *He'll go up*: The current Chappell edition of the vocal score and the World's Classics edition of the Savoy Operas both support the version of this line (and of Scaphio and Phantis' reprise) printed opposite. The Chappell libretto, however, has the longer phrase 'He'll go up to posterity' in both cases.

We're tending rapidly in that direction.
The date's not distant.

KING (*enthusiastically*).

We will be before you!
We'll go down to Posterity renowned   1275
As the First Sovereign in Christendom
Who registered his Crown and Country under
The Joint Stock Company's Act of Sixty-Two.

ALL.   Ulahlica!

SOLO – KING.

Henceforward, of a verity,   1280
   With Fame ourselves we link –
We'll go down to Posterity
   Of sovereigns all the pink!

SCA., PHAN. (*aside to* KING).

If you've the mad temerity
   Our wishes thus to blink,   1285
You'll go down to Posterity
   Much earlier than you think!

TAR. (*correcting them*). He'll go *up* to Posterity,
   If *I* inflict the blow!

SCA. *and* PHAN. (*angrily*).

He'll go *down* to Posterity –   1290
   We think we ought to know!

TAR. (*explaining*). He'll go *up*,
   Blown up with dynamite!

SCA. *and* PHAN. (*apologetically*).

He'll go *up*,
   Of course he will, you're right!   1295

ENSEMBLE.

FITZBATTLEAXE *and* ZARA (*aside*)	SCAPHIO, PHANTIS, *and* TARARA (*aside*)	KING, LADY SOPHY, NEKAYA, KALYBA, CALYNX, *and* CHORUS.
Who love with all sincerity, Their lives may safely link; And as for our Posterity We don't care what they think!	If he has the temerity Our wishes thus to blink, He'll go up to Posterity Much earlier than they think!	Henceforward, of a verity, With fame ourselves we link – And go down to Posterity, Of sovereigns all the pink!

1300

1307 *All hail, astonishing Fact*: What an awful line to have to set to music. 'All hail, Divine Emollient!' is bad enough (*The Pirates of Penzance*, Act I, line 591) but this is even worse.

CHORUS.

Let's seal this mercantile pact –
　　The step we ne'er shall rue –
It gives whatever we lacked –
　　The statement's strictly true.
All hail, astonishing Fact!
　　All hail, Invention new –
The Joint Stock Company's Act –
Of Parliament Sixty-Two! 1310

1305

END OF ACT I

1–2 *Scene*: The night-time setting for Act II gave the designer of the original D'Oyly Carte production, Hawes Craven, ample scope to exploit the opportunities provided by the still relatively recent invention of stage electric lighting. The *Daily News* critic enthusiastically reported, 'The second act takes place in a Moorish Hall, a veritable fairy palace, illuminated by some hundreds of incandescent lamps'. The *Sunday Times* described the palace throne room as 'a magnificent effulgence of the electric light' while the *Daily Graphic* noted that the Act 2 setting 'shows Utopian art to be even more dazzlingly beautiful than Utopian scenery'. Another critic, H. M. Walbrook, described the set as 'a vision of perspective arches, lit with innumerable lights that studded the jewelled walls and hung suspended in the air from what looked like shaking strings of diamonds and with a view through the open doors beyond of the moon and its pale light on the sea'.

4 *my attempted C*: The note which Sullivan provides for the hapless Fitzbattleaxe to land on here is, in fact, an E flat although there is a very high C, right at the top of the tenor range, hovering tantalizingly above it. In the cadenza at the end of the subsequent aria, he has to hit a high A flat three times – poor chap. In *The Pirates of Penzance* Frederic has to reach a high B flat in 'Oh, is there not one maiden breast'.

7 *A tenor, all singers above*: This opera has something of a fixation with tenors. We have already encountered Mr Wilkinson, the English tenor who regularly impersonates the king (and, as we have noted, in earlier versions of the plot was in fact the king in disguise) and now we have a whole song dedicated to the problems that tenors have in singing.

In his book, *The Music of Arthur Sullivan*, Gervase Hughes speculated that Gilbert and Sullivan, in their corporate capacity, did not have much time for tenors: 'Most of the tenor characters have to be content with but one song (in *Ruddigore* a piece of slapstick at that!) and the poor Duke in *Patience* is fobbed off with a short solo in the middle of the first-act finale. In *Utopia Limited* the whole tribe is guyed, and – crowning insult of all – one of the best tenor songs Sullivan ever wrote – 'Would you know the kind of maid' from *Princess Ida* – is allotted not to the leading man but to his stooge.'

ACT II

SCENE. – *Throne Room in the Palace. Night.* FITZBATTLEAXE
discovered, singing to ZARA.

RECITATIVE – FITZBATTLEAXE.

Oh, Zara, my beloved one, bear with me!
Ah, do not laugh at my attempted C!
Repent not, mocking maid, thy girlhood's choice –   5
The fervour of my love affects my voice!

SONG – FITZBATTLEAXE.

A tenor, all singers above
  (This doesn't admit of a question),
    Should keep himself quiet,
    Attend to his diet   10
  And carefully nurse his digestion:
But when he is madly in love
  It's certain to tell on his singing –
    You can't do chromatics
    With proper emphatics   15
  When anguish your bosom is wringing!
When distracted with worries in plenty,
And his pulse is a hundred and twenty,
And his fluttering bosom the slave of mistrust is,
A tenor can't do himself justice.   20
(*Spoken.*)
    Now observe – (*Sings a high note.*) Ah!
You see, I can't do myself justice!
I could sing if my fervour were mock,
  It's easy enough if you're acting –   25
    But when one's emotion
    Is born of devotion

30　*vibrato*: A musical term to indicate much vibration of tone.

33　*agitato*: another musical term used to indicate that a passage should be sung or played in an agitated manner. It crops up again in *The Grand Duke* (Act I, line 312).

You mustn't be over-exacting.
One ought to be firm as a rock
  To venture a shake in *vibrato*,   30
    When fervour's expected
    Keep cool and collected
  Or never attempt *agitato*.
But, of course, when his tongue is of leather,
And his lips appear pasted together,   35
And his sensitive palate as dry as a crust is,
A tenor can't do himself justice.
  (*Spoken*).
    Now observe – (*Sings a cadence*.) Ah!
    It's no use – I can't do myself justice!   40

ZARA. Why, Arthur, what *does* it matter? When the higher qualities of the heart are all that can be desired, the higher notes of the voice are matters of comparative insignificance. Who thinks slightingly of the coco-nut because it is husky? Besides (*demurely*), you are not singing for an engagement (*putting her hand in his*), you have that already!   45

FITZ. How good and wise you are! How unerringly your practised brain winnows the wheat from the chaff – the material from the merely incidental!

ZARA. My Girton training, Arthur. At Girton all is wheat, and idle chaff is never heard within its walls! But tell me, is not all working marvellously well? Have not our Flowers of Progress more than justified their name?   50

FITZ. We have indeed done our best. Captain Corcoran and I have, in concert, thoroughly remodelled the sister-services – and upon so sound a basis that the South Pacific trembles at the name of Utopia!

ZARA. How clever of you!

FITZ. Clever? Not a bit. It's as easy as possible when the Admiralty and   55 Horse Guards are not there to interfere. And so with the others. Freed from the trammels imposed upon them by idle Acts of Parliament, all have given their natural talents full play and introduced reforms which, even in England, were never dreamt of!

ZARA. But perhaps the most beneficent change of all has been effected by   60 Mr. Goldbury, who, discarding the exploded theory that some strange magic lies hidden in the number Seven, has applied the Limited Liability principle to individuals, and every man, woman, and child is now a Company Limited with liability restricted to the amount of his declared Capital! There is not a chris- tened baby in Utopia who has not already issued his little Prospectus!   65

FITZ. Marvellous is the power of a Civilization which can transmute, by a word, a Limited Income into an Income (*Limited*).

ZARA. Reform has not stopped here – it has been applied even to the costume of our people. Discarding their own barbaric dress, the natives of our land have unanimously adopted the tasteful fashions of England in all their rich   70

71 *Scaphio and Phantis*: Gilbert's manuscript copy of the libretto contains the additional line here: 'who are, among other things, Army and civil clothing contractors on a vast scale'.

84–5 *The west wind whispers when he woos the poplars*: Shades of Major General Stanley's song 'Sighing softly to the river' in *The Pirates of Penzance*, Act II, lines 494–523.

89 *Philomel*: Nightingale. From the Greek legend which tells of Philomela, sister of Procne, the wife of Tereus, King of Thrace, being turned into a nightingale by the gods.

90 *Whisper sweetly, whisper slowly*: Gilbert originally intended this song to have a humorous quality but Sullivan insisted that it should not descend into bathos. According to John Wilson in his book *Final Curtain*, the original lines, for which those opposite were substituted at the composer's request, ran as follows:

> 'Tis a truth needs no refutal –
> Always whisper when you woo.
> Sweet and low the ringdoves tootle;
> Sweetly let us tootle too.

94 *Sweet and low*: These are the opening words of a much-loved Victorian parlour ballad with words by Alfred, Lord Tennyson and music by Sir Joseph Barnby, a contemporary and close friend of Sullivan's. It was composed in 1863 and Sullivan can hardly have failed to have had the music of it going round in his head as he set Gilbert's words. He avoids any trace of copying it, however. Barnby sets the words to a series of rising notes, Sullivan to a descending set.

98 *virelay*: One of the fixed forms of French lyric poetry of the fourteenth and fifteenth centuries. The standard *virelai* had three stanzas followed by a refrain. Each stanza had three sections, the first two having the same rhyme scheme and the third having the rhyme scheme of the refrain.

104 *Enter King, dressed as a Field-Marshal*: Gilbert made an uncharacteristic slip when he put Rutland Barrington, who played the part of King Paramount, in a field-marshal's uniform decorated with the Order of the Garter. When the Prince of Wales, later King Edward VII, saw the opera he pointed out that this was a combination which he alone, of all living men, was entitled to wear. Gilbert hurriedly ordered the Garter to be removed to prevent giving any offence.

entirety. Scaphio and Phantis have undertaken a contract to supply the whole of
Utopia with clothing designed upon the most approved English models – and
the first Drawing-Room under the new state of things is to be held here this
evening.

FITZ. But Drawing-Rooms are always held in the afternoon. 75

ZARA. Ah, we've improved upon that. We all look so much better by candle-
light! And when I tell you, dearest, that my Court train has just arrived, you will
understand that I am longing to go and try it on.

FITZ. Then we must part?

ZARA. Necessarily, for a time. 80

FITZ. Just as I wanted to tell you, with all the passionate enthusiasm of my
nature, how deeply, how devotedly I love you!

ZARA. Hush! Are these the accents of a heart that really feels? True love
does not indulge in declamation – its voice is sweet, and soft, and low. The west
wind whispers when he woos the poplars! 85

DUET – ZARA *and* FITZBATTLEAXE.

ZARA.
Words of love too loudly spoken
  Ring their own untimely knell;
Noisy vows are rudely broken,
  Soft the song of Philomel.
Whisper sweetly, whisper slowly, 90
  Hour by hour and day by day;
Sweet and low as accents holy
  Are the notes of lover's lay!

BOTH.
Sweet and low, &c.

FITZ.
Let the conqueror, flushed with glory, 95
  Bid his noisy clarions bray;
Lovers tell their artless story
  In a whispered virelay.
False is he whose vows alluring
  Make the listening echoes ring; 100
Sweet and low when all-enduring
  Are the songs that lovers sing!

BOTH.
Sweet and low, &c.   (*Exit* ZARA).

(*Enter* KING, *dressed as Field-Marshal.*)

KING. To a Monarch who has been accustomed to the uncontrolled use of 105
his limbs, the costume of a British Field-Marshal is, perhaps, at first, a little

121 *like Christy minstrels*: E. P. Christy formed his troupe of five minstrels in 1843 at the
     height of the American cult for singers who had their faces blacked with burnt cork. Un-
     like other American minstrels troupes, the original Christy minstrels never came to
     Britain. Christy himself committed suicide in a fit of depression in 1862. However, sev-
     eral companies took over the name – two, claiming to be the 'original' Christy minstrels,
     competed in advertisements in *The Times* in April 1862. One of these troupes achieved a
     considerable following in Britain, with both W. E. Gladstone and W. M. Thackeray
     among its 'fans'. After appearing before Queen Victoria at Balmoral this company
     earned the right to be known as the Royal Christy Minstrels. The minstrel craze contin-
     ued through the 1890s, when such stars as Eugene Stratton and G. H. Elliott, the
     Chocolate Coloured 'Coon', were at their height.

130–1 *St James's Hall*: Located on the site of the present Piccadilly Hotel in the very heart of
     London's theatreland, St James' Hall was built in 1858 to house popular music concerts.
     It was the venue for the 'classical Monday pops' mentioned in the Mikado's song.

132 *Oh! it seems odd, but never mind*: In Gilbert's manuscript copy of the libretto the following
     material appears at this point:

> *Captain Fitzbattleaxe has his banjo, Mr Blushington takes a set of bones out of his pocket. Mr Gold-*
> *bury finds a tambourine on his chair.*

CHORUS

When the fire-flies dance in the dark,
      And the white moon sails in the sky,
And hushed is the song of the blithe little lark
      (Having warbled his own lullaby)
            To our bowers we steal
            For to ponder awhile
            All our plans for the weal
      Of this lone little isle
Of this lone little, lone little isle!

For at right time, we may remark
That hushed is the song of the lark,
Oh, hushed is the song of the blithe little lark
Having warbled his own lullaby!

MR. BLUSH. I say, Mister King!
KING. Well, Mr Bones?
MR. BLUSH. Do you keep a carriage?
KING. Oh yes, I keep a very nice carriage.
MR. BLUSH. And horses?
KING. Most assuredly. What would be the use of a carriage without horses?
MR. BLUSH. Well it might have been a pre-ambulator.
KING. Very true: that consideration had not occured to me. No, I have, alas! no occasion
for a perambulator.
MR. BLUSH. Well now – what do you call your horses?
KING. What do I call my horses? Oh they have very pretty names. I call one 'Beauty' and
the other 'Prince'.
MR. BLUSH. Ah, I don't think much of those names.
KING (*mildly surprised*). You don't think much of those names, Mr. Bones?
MR. BLUSH. No. Now, I've got a pair of horses.
KING. Indeed, Mr. Bones? You must be prospering in the world.
MR. BLUSH. Oh yes, getting on nicely. Well now, what d'ye think I call them?
KING. Really the question is so wide – it opens out such a vast field of speculation that
really I –
MR. BLUSH. I call one 'Bryant' and the other 'May'.
KING (*mildly surprised*). You call one 'Bryant' and the other 'May'?

cramping. Are you sure that this is all right? It's not a practical joke, is it? No one has a keener sense of humour than I have, but the First Statutory Cabinet Council of Utopia Limited must be conducted with dignity and impressiveness. Now, where are the other five who signed the Articles of Association? 110

FITZ. Sir, they are here.

(*Enter* LORD DRAMALEIGH, CAPTAIN CORCORAN, SIR BAILEY BARRE, MR. BLUSHINGTON, *and* MR. GOLDBURY *from different entrances.*)

KING. Oh! (*Addressing them.*) Gentlemen, our daughter holds her first Drawing-Room in half an hour, and we shall have time to make our half-yearly report 115 in the interval. I am necessarily unfamiliar with the forms of an English Cabinet Council – perhaps the Lord Chamberlain will kindly put us in the way of doing the thing properly, and with due regard to the solemnity of the occasion.

LORD D. Certainly – nothing simpler. Kindly bring your chairs forward – His Majesty will, of course, preside. 120

(*They range their chairs across stage like Christy Minstrels.* KING *sits* C., LORD DRAMALEIGH *on his* L., MR. GOLDBURY *on his* R., CAPTAIN CORCORAN L. *of* LORD DRAMALEIGH, CAPTAIN FITZBATTLEAXE R. *of* MR. GOLDBURY, MR. BLUSHINGTON *extreme* R., SIR BAILEY BARRE *extreme* L.) 125

KING. Like this?

LORD D. Like this.

KING. We take your word for it that this is all right. You are not making fun of us? This is in accordance with the practice at the Court of St. James's?

LORD D. Well, it is in accordance with the practice at the Court of St. 130 James's Hall.

KING. Oh! it seems odd, but never mind.

SONG – KING with CHORUS of SIX FLOWERS of PROGRESS.

KING.	Society has quite forsaken all her wicked courses,
	Which empties our police courts, and abolishes divorces.
CHORUS.	Divorce is nearly obsolete in England.	135
KING.	No tolerance we show to undeserving rank and splendour;
	For the higher his position is, the greater the offender.
CHORUS.	That's a maxim that is prevalent in England.
KING.	No peeress at our Drawing-Room before the Presence passes
	Who wouldn't be accepted by the lower-middle classes.	140
	Each shady dame, whatever be her rank, is bowed out neatly.

MR. BLUSH. Yes, because they're such a good match!
KING. Oh let us kiss him for his mother!

Symphony – banjo, bones and tambourine leads into song (Society has quite forsaken)

Writing to Sullivan on 7 August 1893 from Homburg, where he had gone in an effort to gain relief from his gout, Gilbert indicated that in order to shorten Act II, he would omit the sextet and 'the nigger dialogue'. One has to say that not much is lost by its disappearance.

133–70 *Society has quite forsaken*

This song sung by six distinguished representatives of British civilization in the style of Christy Minstrels was one of the great *coups de theatre* in *Utopia Limited*. It won almost universal acclamation from the first night audience and critics. The *Daily News* commented that 'The Cabinet Council is one of the funniest incidents in the piece. The chairs are arranged in a semi-circle...The various court officials produce banjos and fiddles, tambourines and bones, and a side-splitting burlesque of the Christy Minstrels starts, Mr Rutland Barrington dancing a breakdown and singing alto in the approved style. A double encore rewarded this skit.' The *Sunday Times* noted that 'This irresistible skit might have been encored half-a-dozen times.'

The only note of criticism was struck by the *Punch* critic who accused Gilbert and Sullivan of plagiarizing the idea of the minstrel scene from an earlier burlesque, *Black-Eye'd Susan*, which had played at the Royalty Theatre in 1866 and 1867 and featured a minstrel-show court martial scene. The author of *Black-Eye'd Susan* was Frank Burnand, managing editor of *Punch*, who had been Sullivan's main librettist before Gilbert, working with him on 'Cox and Box' and 'The Contrabandista'.

For the introduction to the song Sullivan used the tune of a negro plantation song, 'Johnny get your gun', which is very similar to the Northumbrian folk tune 'The Keel Row'. The song as a whole won high praise from George Bernard Shaw who recommended 'those who go into solemn academic raptures over themes "in diminution" to go and hear how prettily the chorus of the Christy Minstrel song is used, very much in diminution, to make an exquisite mock-banjo accompaniment. In these examples we are on the plane, not of the bones and tambourine, but of Mozart's accompaniments to "*Soave sia il vento*" in *Cosi fan tutte* and the entry of the gardener in *Le Nozze di Figaro*.'

163 *The Brewers and the Cotton Lords*: The granting of peerages to brewers was a feature of the Conservative Governments of the 1870s and 1880s and reflected the strong alliance between the Conservatives and the drink trade. So influential did this particular interest become, at least in the eyes of the strong temperance lobby within the Liberal Party, that it earned the nickname of 'the beerage'. Not all brewers who were ennobled were Conservatives, however. One of the best-known, Michael Bass, the great Burton-on-Trent brewer, who became Baron Burton in 1886, was a Liberal. The 'worthy members of the brewing interest to the peerage elevated' get another mention in *The Grand Duke*, Act II, lines 568–9.

167 *Earl of Thackeray and Duke of Dickens*: This is not the only time that the two leading novelists of Victorian England are bracketed together in song in the Savoy Operas. Among the ingredients of a heavy dragoon rattled off by Colonel Calverley in *Patience* (Act I, line 143) are 'the narrative powers of Dickens and Thackeray'.

168 *Lord Fildes and Viscount Millais*: Sir Luke Fildes (1844–1927) was particularly known for his portraits which included several members of the Royal Family. Sir John Everett Millais (1829–1896) was a leading member of the Pre-Raphaelite Brotherhood and a president of the Royal Academy.

CHORUS. In short, this happy country has been Anglicized completely!
　　　　　It really is surprising
　　　　　What a thorough Anglicizing
　　　　　We have brought about – Utopia's quite another land;　　　145
　　　　　In her enterprising movements,
　　　　　She is England – with improvements,
　　　　　Which we dutifully offer to our mother-land!

KING.　　Our city we have beautified – we've done it willy-nilly –
　　　　　And all that isn't Belgrave Square is Strand and Piccadilly.　　150
CHORUS. We haven't any slummeries in England!
KING.　　We have solved the labour question with discrimination polished,
　　　　　So poverty is obsolete and hunger is abolished –
CHORUS. We are going to abolish it in England.
KING.　　The Chamberlain our native stage has purged, beyond a question,　155
　　　　　Of 'risky' situation and indelicate suggestion;
　　　　　No piece is tolerated if it's costumed indiscreetly –
CHORUS. In short, this happy country has been Anglicized completely!
　　　　　It really is surprising, &c.

KING.　　Our Peerage we've remodelled on an intellectual basis,　　　160
　　　　　Which certainly is rough on our hereditary races –
CHORUS. We are going to remodel it in England.
KING.　　The Brewers and the Cotton Lords no longer seek admission,
　　　　　And Literary Merit meets with proper recognition –
CHORUS. As Literary Merit does in England.　　　165
KING.　　Who knows but we may count among our intellectual chickens,
　　　　　Like you, an Earl of Thackeray and p'r'aps a Duke of Dickens –
　　Lord Fildes and Viscount Millais (when they come) we'll welcome sweetly –
CHORUS. In short, this happy country has been Anglicized completely!
　　　　　It really is surprising, &c.　　　170

(At the end all rise and replace their chairs.)

178   *the master of the Buck-hounds*: This particular court official also makes an appearance in
      The Mikado, Act I, line 155, as one of the many identities assumed by Poo-Bah.

181   *the Gold and Silver stick*: These two Court appointments date from Tudor times when
      two officers were placed close to the sovereign to ensure his or her protection. They de-
      rive their titles from the staffs of office which they carry. The office of Gold stick in wait-
      ing is the senior appointment and is traditionally held by the Colonel of the Life
      Guards – nowadays it is shared by the Colonels of the Life Guards and the Blues and
      Royals. The office of Silver Stick is held by the Lieutenant Colonel commanding the
      Household Cavalry. The Gold and Silver Sticks in waiting attend the sovereign on state
      occasions such as the Coronation and the state opening of Parliament.

197   *Enter the ladies attending the Drawing-Room*: The Drawing Room scene was the other great
      hit of the first night. Clearly modelled on Queen Victoria's receptions, it was played ab-
      solutely straight and not turned into a parody – much to the surprise of some of the
      first-night critics. The *Daily News* reported: 'Contrary to expectation, no sort of parody
      is attempted. The Royal household and the various Court officials, correct to a button,
      occupy their proper places, and amid the strains of a stately gavotte, a procession of
      ladies in such wondrous Court costumes that no mere male would be bold enough to
      describe them, pass across the stage, every detail of the presentation being carried out
      practically as at Buckingham Palace. The scene is a very handsome one, but the exact
      purpose of its introduction into comic opera is not quite apparent.' The *Pall Mall
      Gazette* also questioned the wisdom of introducing the scene, describing it as 'dull as it
      would be possible for a real Court ceremonial to be'. The *Sunday Times*, however, was
      unqualified in its praise: 'The Drawing-Room scene, superbly managed, brought down
      a hearty round of applause...The handsome throne-room with its dazzling glitter of
      incandescent lamps and the glorious army of rich uniforms and gowns, produced an
      impression quite unprecedented in the annals of Savoy comic opera.'

      Gilbert took enormous trouble to ensure that the correct principles of court etiquette
      were followed on stage. A lady professor of deportment attended rehearsals to teach the
      company how to bow properly. The drawing room scene was also very expensive to stage.
      More than £5,000 of the £7,200 which the original production cost went on costumes,
      accessories and hand props, many of them required just for this one scene. Sullivan
      tried to persuade Gilbert to make the setting rather less elaborate and costly but a letter
      from the librettist dated 30 August 1893 indicates that he was reluctant to make too
      many economies:

           I confess I should be sorry to lose the gentlemen-at-arms, who always stand two at the
           entrance and two at the exit of the Presence Chamber, and I am afraid that without them
           the ladies will have the appearance of loafing on to the stage without any 'circumstance'. Be-
           sides, you must remember that these four people must be dressed somehow. They can't go
           naked (unless you insist upon it), and if they put on good uniforms they will cost at least
           fifty pounds a piece. . . . I am as much for retrenchment as you are. The only question is,
           where can it be best affected with least injury to the piece? I agree with you that the ladies'
           bouquets and diamonds might well be curtailed. The merest paste mixed with glass emer-
           alds and rubies will do for the jewellery.

KING. Now then, for our first Drawing-Room. Where are the Princesses? What an extraordinary thing it is that since European looking-glasses have been supplied to the Royal bedrooms my daughters are invariably late!

LORD D. Sir, their Royal Highnesses await your pleasure in the Ante-room. 175

KING. Oh. Then request them to do us the favour to enter at once.

(*March. Enter all the Royal Household, including (besides the Lord Chamberlain) the Vice-Chamberlain, the Master of the Horse, the Master of the Buck-hounds, the Lord High Treasurer, the Lord Steward, the Comptroller of the Household, the Lord-in-Waiting, the Groom-in-Waiting, the Field Officer in Brigade Waiting, the Gold and Silver Stick, and the Gentlemen Ushers. Then enter the three Princesses (their trains carried by Pages of Honour)*, LADY SOPHY, *and the Ladies-in-Waiting.*) 180

KING. My daughters, we are about to attempt a very solemn ceremonial, so no giggling, if you please. Now, my Lord Chamberlain, we are ready. 185

LORD D. Then, ladies and gentlemen, places, if you please. His Majesty will take his place in front of the throne, and will be so obliging as to embrace all the *débutantes.*

(LADY SOPHY *much shocked.*)

KING. What – must I really?

LORD D. Absolutely indispensable. 190

KING. More jam for the *Palace Peeper!*

(*The* KING *takes his place in front of the throne, the* PRINCESS ZARA *on his left, the two younger Princesses on the left of* ZARA.)

KING. Now, is every one in his place?

LORD D. Every one is in his place. 195

KING. Then let the revels commence.

(*Enter the ladies attending the Drawing-Room. They give their cards to the Groom-in-Waiting, who passes them to the Lord-in-Waiting, who passes them to the Vice-Chamberlain, who passes them to the Lord Chamberlain, who reads the names to the* KING *as each lady approaches. The ladies curtsey in succession to the* KING *and the three Princesses, and pass out. When all the presentations have been accomplished, the* KING, *Princesses, and* LADY SOPHY *come forward, and all the ladies re-enter.*) 200

RECITATIVE – KING.

This ceremonial our wish displays
To copy all Great Britain's courtly ways. 205

208–17 *Eagle high in cloudland soaring*
This is one of two unaccompanied choruses in the Savoy Operas, the other being 'Hail
Poetry!' in *The Pirates of Penzance*. The style of both seems to belong much more to the
world of sacred oratorio than that of light opera. Indeed, 'Eagle high' in particular is
highly reminiscent of several of the numbers from *The Golden Legend*, the oratorio which
Sullivan composed for the Leeds Festival in 1886. It was sung with tremendous power
and feeling by members of the chorus of the English National Opera at the service held
in the Queen's Chapel of the Savoy on 13 May 1992 to mark the 150th anniversary of Sullivan's birth.

220–45 *With fury deep we burn*
Gilbert was prepared to give this song up in the interests of shortening Act II. He indicated as much to Sullivan in the letter from Homburg (see note to line 132). Otherwise,
he indicated, everything should stay.

230 *We think it is our turn*: This whole verse, down to 'He shall' (line 240) is missing both from
Reginald Allen's *First Night Gilbert and Sullivan* and from the Chatto edition of Gilbert's
plays.

Though lofty aims catastrophe entail,
We'll gloriously succeed or nobly fail!

UNACCOMPANIED CHORUS.

Eagle high in cloudland soaring –
  Sparrow twittering on a reed –
Tiger in the jungle roaring –   210
  Frightened fawn in grassy mead –
Let the eagle, not the sparrow,
Be the object of your arrow –
  Fix the tiger with your eye –
  Pass the fawn in pity by.   215
  Glory then will crown the day –
  Glory, glory, anyway!, &c., &c.   (*Then exeunt all.*)

(*Enter* SCAPHIO *and* PHANTIS, *now dressed as judges in red and ermine robes
and undress wigs. They come down stage melodramatically – walking together.*)

DUET–SCAPHIO *and* PHANTIS.

SCA.   With fury deep we burn –   220
PHAN.   We do –
SCA.   We fume with smothered rage –
PHAN.   We do –
SCA.   These Englishmen who rule supreme,
            Their undertaking they redeem   225
            By stifling every harmless scheme
              In which we both engage –
PHAN.   They do –
SCA.   In which we both engage.
PHAN.   We think it is our turn –   230
SCA.   We do –
PHAN.   We think our turn has come –
SCA.   We do.
PHAN.   These Englishmen, they must prepare
            To seek at once their native air.   235
            The King as heretofore, we swear,
            Shall be beneath our thumb –
SCA.   He shall –
PHAN.   Shall be beneath our thumb –
SCA.   He shall.   240
BOTH (*with great energy*).
            For this mustn't be, and this won't do,
            If you'll back me, then I'll back you,

254–5 *our Army Clothing contracts are paralysed*: This line really only makes sense if the earlier reference to army clothing contracts which was cut (see note to line 71) is reinstated.

266 *the Lord Chamberlain*: See note to Act I, line 1117.

270 *four-foot wall to be built up*: Stringent fire regulations covering theatres in Britain were introduced in 1878 but they did not prevent some serious fires taking place after this date. The worst were at the Theatre Royal, Exeter, which was burned down in 1885, rebuilt and then destroyed again by fire in 1887 with the loss of 186 lives.

277 *Winding-up Act*: A highly topical reference – there was a Companies (Winding Up) Act in 1893 – see note to Act I, line 1254.

283 *Are we to understand that we are defied*: With the exception of the closing dialogue (lines 644–67) this is the only piece of dialogue heard on the 1976 D'Oyly Carte record of *Utopia Limited*.

284 *That is the idea I intended to convey*: Yet another line lifted wholesale from an earlier opera, in this case from *H.M.S. Pinafore*, Act II, line 472.

No, this won't do,
No, this mustn't be.
No, this mustn't be, and this won't do.   245

(*Enter the* KING.)

KING. No, this won't do! (*Sung*.)
KING. Gentlemen, gentlemen – really! This unseemly display of energy
within the Royal Precincts is altogether unpardonable. Pray, what do you
complain of?   250
SCA. (*furiously*). What do we complain of? Why, through the innovations
introduced by the Flowers of Progress all our harmless schemes for making a
provision for our old age are ruined. Our Matrimonial Agency is at a standstill,
our Cheap Sherry business is in bankruptcy, our Army Clothing contracts are
paralysed, and even our Society paper, the *Palace Peeper*, is practically defunct!   255
KING. Defunct? Is that so? Dear, dear, I am truly sorry.
SCA. Are you aware that Sir Bailey Barre has introduced a law of libel by
which all editors of scurrilous newspapers are publicly flogged – as in England?
And six of our editors have resigned in succession! Now, the editor of a
scurrilous paper can stand a good deal – he takes a private thrashing as a matter   260
of course – it's considered in his salary – but no gentleman likes to be publicly
flogged.
KING. Naturally. I shouldn't like it myself.
PHAN. Then our BurlesqueTheatre is absolutely ruined!
KING. Dear me. Well, theatrical property is not what is was.   265
PHAN. Are you aware that the Lord Chamberlain, who has his own views as
to the best means of elevating the national drama, has declined to license any
play that is not in blank verse and three hundred years old – as in England?
SCA. And as if that wasn't enough, the County Councillor has ordered a
four-foot wall to be built up right across the proscenium, in case of fire – as in   270
England.
PHAN. It's so hard on the company – who are liable to be roasted alive – and
this has to be met by enormously increased salaries – as in England.
SCA. You probably know that we've contracted to supply the entire nation
with a complete English outfit. But perhaps you do *not* know that, when we send   275
in our bills, our customers plead liability limited to a declared capital of
eighteenpence, and apply to be dealt with under the Winding-up Act – as in
England?
KING. Really, gentlemen, this is very irregular. If you will be so good as to
formulate a detailed list of your grievances in writing, addressed to the Secre-   280
tary of Utopia Limited, they will be laid before the Board, in due course, at their
next monthly meeting.
SCA. Are we to understand that we are defied?
KING. That is the idea I intended to convey.

312 *pas de trois*: This step is not mentioned in any of my daughter's ballet books but if you can have a *pas-de-deux* where a male and female partner each other, I suppose you can have a *pas-de-trois* where three people dance together.

PHAN. Defied! We are defied!   285
SCA. (*furiously*). Take care – you know our powers. Trifle with us, and you die!

TRIO – SCAPHIO, PHANTIS, *and* KING.

SCA.   If you think that when banded in unity,
              We may both be defied with impunity,
                  You are sadly misled of a verity!   290
PHAN.   If you value repose and tranquillity,
              You'll revert to a state of docility,
                  Or prepare to regret your temerity!
KING.   If my speech is unduly refractory
              You will find it a course satisfactory   295
                  At an early Board meeting to show it up.
              Though if proper excuse you can trump any,
              You may *wind* up a Limited Company,
                  You cannot conveniently *blow* it up!
                      (SCAPHIO *and* PHANTIS *thoroughly baffled.*)   300

KING (*dancing quietly.*)
                  Whene'er I chance to baffle you
                  I, also, dance a step or two –
                  Of this now guess the hidden sense:

(SCAPHIO *and* PHANTIS *consider the question as* KING *continues*
              dancing quietly – then give it up.)   305

                  It means – complete indifference.
SCA. *and* PHAN.
                  Of course it does –
                  It means complete indifference –
KING.   Indifference, indifference, indifference!

(KING *dancing quietly.* SCAPHIO *and* PHANTIS *dancing furiously.*)   310

SCA. *and* PHAN.
                  As we've a dance for every mood
                  With *pas de trois* we will conclude.
                  What this may mean you all may guess –
                  It typifies remorselessness!

KING.   It means unruffled cheerfulness!   315

336–89 *With wily brain, upon the spot*
    In its rhythm and melody this song bears striking resemblances to the trio 'They say that Medieval art alone retains its zest' in *Patience*. The business of whispering in the middle of a song is, however, not found anywhere else that I can think of in the Savoy Operas.

(KING *dances off placidly as* SCAPHIO *and* PHANTIS *dance furiously.*)

PHAN. (*breathless*). He's right – we are helpless! He's no longer a human being – he's a Corporation, and so long as he confines himself to his Articles of Association we can't touch him! What are we to do?

SCA. Do? Raise a Revolution, repeal the Act of Sixty-Two, reconvert him 320 into an individual, and insist on his immediate explosion! (TARARA *enters.*) Tarara, come here; you're the very man we want.

TAR. Certainly, allow me. (*Offers a cracker to each; they snatch them away impatiently.*) That's rude.

SCA. We have no time for idle forms. You wish to succeed to the throne? 325

TAR. Naturally.

SCA. Then you won't unless you join us. The King has defied us, and, as matters stand, we are helpless. So are you. We must devise some plot at once to bring the people about his ears.

TAR. A plot? 330

PHAN. Yes, a plot of superhuman subtlety. Have you such a thing about you?

TAR. (*feeling*). No, I think not. No. There's one on my dressing-table.

SCA. We can't wait – we must concoct one at once, and put it into execution without delay. There is not a moment to spare! 335

TRIO – SCAPHIO, PHANTIS, *and* TARARA.

ALL THREE.	With wily brain upon the spot
	A private plot we'll plan,
	The most ingenious private plot
	Since private plots began.
	That's understood. So far we've got 340
	And, striking while the iron's hot,
	We'll now determine like a shot
	The details of this private plot.

SCA.	I think we ought –	(*Whispers*)
PHAN. *and* TAR.	Such bosh I never heard!	345
PHAN.	Ah! happy thought! –	(*Whispers*)
SCA. *and* TAR.	How utterly dashed absurd!	
TAR.	*I'll* tell you how –	(*Whispers*)
SCA. *and* PHAN.	Why, what put that in your head?	
SCA.	I've got it now –	(*Whispers*) 350
PHAN. *and* TAR.	Oh, take him away to bed!	
PHAN.	Oh, put him to bed!	
TAR.	Oh, put him to bed!	
SCA.	What! put *me* to bed?	

367 *Tapis*: Carpet.
390 *Business*: Gilbert's manuscript copy of the libretto contains a good deal of material at
     this point which was clearly cut before the first night. It begins with a conversation be-
     tween Scaphio and Phantis about which one of them should have Zara. They finally de-
     cide to entrust her to Fitzbattleaxe as a shareholder. Zara and Fitzbattleaxe now enter
     and sing a quartet with Scaphio and Phantis. In it Fitzbattleaxe presents his report on
     Zara, making out that she is a tartar, impetuous and out of control. This leads the two
     judges to feel that they do not want her after all and they let Fitzbattleaxe keep her. They
     depart leaving Fitzbattleaxe and Zara on the stage to discuss the new situation. At this
     point Gilbert's manuscript contains what seems to be an early version of the solo for
     Zara that was later moved to Act I and sung on the first night but subsequently dropped
     (see note to line 1004). This original Act II version runs as follows:

> Youth is a gift of worth
>   To one and all allowed
> With which all men, at birth,
>   Are equally endowed.
> But Man's a prodigal
>   Who neatly lives upon
> His little capital
>   Till every penny's gone –
> And finds himself, at Life's concluding stage,
> With no youth left to comfort his old age.
>
> Ah dame, all wrinklefaced,
>   If you, in very sooth
> In infancy had placed
>   Your capital of youth
> At four or five per cent
>   Prepared, within your breast,
> To rub along content
>   Upon the interest –
> You might be still in girlhood's mid-career,
> A merry mad-cap maid of four-score year!

PHAN. *and* TAR.   Yes, certainly put him to bed!   355
SCA.   But, bless me, don't you see –
PHAN.   Do listen to me, I pray –
TAR.   It certainly seems to me –
SCA.   Bah – this is the only way!
PHAN.   It's rubbish absurd you growl!   360
TAR.   You talk ridiculous stuff!
SCA.   You're a drivelling barndoor owl!
PHAN.   You're a vapid and vain old muff!

ALL THREE (*coming down to audience*).
            So far we haven't quite solved the plot –
            They're not a very ingenious lot –   365
                But don't be unhappy,
                It's still on the *tapis*,
            We'll presently hit on a capital plot!
SCA.   Suppose we all –   (*Whispers*)
PHAN.   Now *there* I think you're right.   370
            Then we might all –   (*Whispers*)
TAR.   That's true – we certainly might.
            I'll tell you what –   (*Whispers*)
SCA.   We will if we possibly can.
            Then on the spot –   (*Whispers*)   375
PHAN. *and* TAR.   Bravo! a capital plan!
SCA.   That's exceedingly neat and new!
PHAN.   Exceedingly new and neat.
TAR.   I fancy that that will do.
SCA.   It's certainly very complete.   380
PHAN.   Well done, you sly old sap!
TAR.   Bravo, you cunning old mole!
SCA.   You very ingenious chap!
PHAN.   You intellectual, intellectual soul!

ALL THREE (*coming down and addressing audience*).
            At last a capital plan we've got;   385
            We won't say how and we won't say what:
                It's safe in my noddle –
                Now off we will toddle,
            And slyly develop this capital plot!

            (*Business. Exeunt* SCAPHIO *and* PHANTIS *in one direction, and*   390
                                      TARARA *in the other.*)

(*Enter* LORD DRAMALEIGH *and* MR. GOLDBURY.)

398–9 *The cup of tea and the plate of mixed biscuits were a cheap and effective inspiration*: According to Thomas Dunhill, this line actually prompted a change in the practices of the Court of Queen Victoria. Previously, it had not been the custom to provide refreshments of any kind at Royal 'Drawing-Rooms' but after the Prince of Wales had seen *Utopia Limited*, this omission was remedied and tea and biscuits were forthwith provided.

LORD D. Well, what do you think of our first South Pacific Drawing-Room?
Allowing for a slight difficulty with the trains, and a little want of familiarity
with the use of the rouge-pot, it was, on the whole, a meritorious affair?   395
MR. GOLD. My dear Dramaleigh, it redounds infinitely to your credit.
LORD D. One or two judicious innovations, I think?
MR. GOLD. Admirable. The cup of tea and the plate of mixed biscuits were
a cheap and effective inspiration.
LORD D. Yes – my idea entirely. Never been done before.   400
MR. GOLD. Pretty little maids, the King's youngest daughters, but timid.
LORD D. That'll wear off. Young.
MR. GOLD. *That'll* wear off. Ha! here they come, by George! And without
the Dragon! What can they have done with her?

(*Enter* NEKAYA *and* KALYBA, *timidly.*)   405

NEK. Oh, if you please, Lady Sophy has sent us in here, because Zara and
Captain Fitzbattleaxe are going on, in the garden, in a manner which no well-
conducted young ladies ought to witness.
LORD D. Indeed, we are very much obliged to her Ladyship.
KAL. Are you? I wonder why.   410
NEK. Don't tell us if it's rude.
LORD D. Rude? Not at all. We are obliged to Lady Sophy because she has
afforded us the pleasure of seeing you.
NEK. I don't think you ought to talk to us like that.
KAL. It's calculated to turn our heads.   415
NEK. Attractive girls cannot be too particular.
KAL. Oh, pray, pray do not take advantage of our unprotected innocence.
MR. GOLD. Pray be reassured – you are in no danger whatever.
LORD D. But may I ask – is this extreme delicacy – this shrinking sensitive-
ness – a general characteristic of Utopian young ladies?   420
NEK. Oh no; we are crack specimens.
KAL. We are the pick of the basket. *Would* you mind not coming quite so
near? Thank you.
NEK. And please don't look at us like that; it unsettles us.
KAL. And we don't like it. At least, we *do* like it; but it's wrong.   425
NEK. *We* have enjoyed the inestimable privilege of being educated by a
most refined and easily shocked English lady, on the very strictest English
principles.
MR. GOLD. But, my dear young ladies —
KAL. Oh, don't! You mustn't. It's too affectionate.   430
NEK. It really does unsettle us.
MR. GOLD. Are you really under the impression that English girls are so
ridiculously demure? Why, an English girl of the highest type is the best, the
most beautiful, the bravest, and the brightest creature that Heaven has con-

440–81 *A wonderful joy our eyes to bless*
This song shows Gilbert in his most Betjemanesque mood. It anticipates those poems in which the Poet Laureate serenaded the wholesome qualities of muscular young English ladies like Miss Joan Hunter Dunn.

448 *At cricket, her kin will lose or win*: This is the only reference that I can think of in the Savoy Operas to the game of cricket. Gilbert doesn't seem to have had a particular fondness for it, unlike a subsequent librettist, Donald Hughes, who managed to construct an entire operetta around the theme of a cricket game. 'The Batsman's Bride', with music by Percy Haywood, is a delightful work which was once a staple of the prep-school repertoire – I made my stage debut in it as a member of the chorus of village batsmen at the age of eleven – but I fear like the works of G & S it has now given way to the likes of 'Grease', 'Guys and Dolls' and 'Jesus Christ Superstar'.

457 *She golfs, she punts, she rows, she swims*: Like Betjeman, Gilbert seems to have had a liking for girls who excelled at sports. Swimming was his own great love and it was how he came to meet his death. His house at Grim's Dyke, near Harrow, to which he moved in 1890, had a lake 170 yards long and 50 yards wide in which he bathed several times a day when the weather was warm. On 29 May 1911 he had arranged to bathe with two local young ladies, no doubt bright and beautiful English girls. Unlike the object of Mr Goldbury's affections, however, neither was a strong swimmer and one, Ruby Preece, got out of her depth and cried out for help. Gilbert plunged in and swam towards her. 'Put your hands on my shoulders and don't struggle', he said as he reached her. They were the last words he uttered. He sank under her weight. Ruby went under the water for a moment but found on coming up that she could stand in the water. When she got to the bank there was no sign of Gilbert, who had died of heart-failure from the sudden exertion to rescue her.

460 *At ball or drum*: The word 'drum' was applied to afternoon tea parties, apparently through a rather tortuous piece of word association: tea → kettle → kettle-drum → drum.

464 *Lawn-tennis*: Tennis was another game that Gilbert enjoyed along with many of his contemporaries. The all-England lawn tennis champions at Wimbledon had started in 1877. Assiduous readers of this volume blessed with an encyclopaedic memory (of a kind that seems to go with devotion to the Savoy Operas) will recall the character of the Reverend Lawn Tennison, the vicar idolized by the village ladies, who was to have been

ferred upon this world of ours. She is frank, open-hearted, and fearless, and   435
never shows in so favourable a light as when she gives her own blameless im-
pulses full play!

NEK. *and* KAL. Oh, you shocking story!

MR. GOLD. Not at all. I'm speaking the strict truth. I'll tell you all about her.

SONG – MR. GOLDBURY.

A wonderful joy our eyes to bless,   440
In her magnificent comeliness,
Is an English girl of eleven stone two,
And five foot ten in her dancing shoe!
   She follows the hounds, and on she pounds –
      The 'field' tails off and the muffs diminish –   445
   Over the hedges and brooks she bounds
      Straight as a crow, from find to finish.
   At cricket, her kin will lose or win –
      She and her maids, on grass and clover,
   Eleven maids out – eleven maids in –   450
      And perhaps an occasional 'maiden over!'

Oh! Go search the world and search the sea,
Then come you home and sing with me
There's no such gold and no such pearl
As a bright and beautiful English girl!   455

With a ten-mile spin she stretches her limbs,
She golfs, she punts, she rows, she swims –
She plays, she sings, she dances, too,
From ten or eleven till all is blue!
   At ball or drum, till small hours come   460
      (Chaperon's fan conceals her yawning)
   She'll waltz away like a teetotum,
      And never go home till daylight's dawning.
   Lawn-tennis may share her favours fair –
      Her eyes a-dance and her cheeks a-glowing –   465
   Down comes her hair, but what does she care?
      It's all her own and it's worth the showing!
      Ah! Go search the world, &c.

Her soul is sweet as the ocean air,
For prudery knows no haven there;   470
To find mock-modesty, please apply
To the conscious blush and the downcast eye.
   Rich in the things contentment brings,

one of the stars of the original clerical version of *Patience* before it was secularized and his part turned into that of the fleshly poet, Reginald Bunthorne.

    In every pure enjoyment wealthy,
    Blithe as a beautiful bird she sings,   475
       For body and mind are hale and healthy.
    Her eyes they thrill with right goodwill –
       Her heart is light as a floating feather –
    As pure and bright as the mountain rill
       That leaps and laughs in the Highland heather!   480
       Ah! Go search the world, &c.

QUARTET – NEKAYA, KALYBA, LORD DRAMALEIGH *and*
       MR GOLDBURY.

NEK.	Then I may sing and play?
LORD D.	You may!
KAL.	And I may laugh and shout?
MR. GOLD.	No doubt!

485

NEK.	These maxims you endorse?
LORD D.	Of course!
KAL.	You won't exclaim 'Oh fie!'
MR. GOLD.	Not I!

NEK. *and* KAL.   Then I may sing and play,   490
       And I may laugh and shout,
       You won't exclaim 'Oh fie!'

MR. GOLD. *and* LORD. D.
       Ha, ha, ha, &c.

MR. GOLD.   Whatever you are – be that:
       Whatever you say – be true: 495
         Straightforwardly act –
         Be honest – in fact
       Be nobody else but *you.*

LORD. D.   Give every answer pat –
       Your character true unfurl;   500
         And when it is ripe,
         You'll then be a type
       Of a capital English girl.

ALL.   Oh, sweet surprise – oh, dear delight,
       To find it undisputed quite,   505
       All musty, fusty rules despite,
       That Art is wrong and Nature right!, &c.

NEK.   When happy I,
       With laughter glad
         I'll wake the echoes fairly,   510

521 *It needn't be a hymn one*: No, although if Kalyba was possessed of a desire to hum a hymn
tune, there were several from Sullivan's pen as jaunty and vigorous as anything he wrote
for his comic operas. In all, he wrote more than fifty hymn tunes, including such stirring
and upbeat ones as *Courage, brother* (for Norman Macleod's hymn of the same name),
Lux Eoi (now most commonly used for 'Alleluia, Alleluia, hearts to heaven and voices
raise' but also highly suitable for 'Glorious things of thee are spoken') and, of course,
the immortal *St Gertrude* for 'Onward, Christian soldiers'. Those who want to pursue
this somewhat neglected aspect of the composer's work are directed to my attempt to
rehabilitate it in the October 1992 number of the Bulletin of the Hymn Society for Great
Britain and Ireland.

526 *Enter Lady Sophy*: Sullivan was profoundly unhappy about Gilbert's proposed portrayal
of Lady Sophy in Act II and sent him a letter on the subject on 1 July 1893:

> The part of Lady Sophy, as it is to be treated in the second act, is in my opinion a blot on
> an otherwise brilliant picture, and to me personally unsympathetic and distasteful. If there
> is to be an old or middle-aged woman in the piece at all, is it necessary that she should be
> very old, ugly, raddled and perhaps grotesque, and still more is it necessary that she should
> be seething with love and passion (requited or unrequited) and other feelings not usually
> associated with old age? I thought that 'Katisha' was to be the last example of that type – (a
> type which however carefully drawn can never be popular with the public, as experience
> has taught me) – because the same point was raised then, and you even modified a good
> many of the lines at my request. A dignified, stately, well made-up and dressed elderly lady
> is a charming feature in a piece, and can be of real service to the composer because the mu-
> sic he writes for her is so well contrasted with the youthful bustle of the other elements. On
> the other hand, the elderly spinster, unattractive and grotesque, either bemoaning her faded
> charms, or calling attention to what is still left of them, and unable to conceal her passionate
> longing for love, is a character which appeals to me vainly, and I cannot do anything with it.

Gilbert replied two days later to try and allay his partner's fears:

> Most assuredly it is not necessary that she should be 'very old, ugly, raddled or grotesque'
> – she may be and *should* be a dignified lady of 45 or thereabouts, and no more ugly than
> God Almighty has made the lady who is to play the part. Nor do I propose that she should
> be seething with love and passion. She is in love with the King (as a lady of 45 may very well
> be with a man of 50) – but her frenzy is not of the gross or animal type at all, as you seem to
> imagine. Her position is this. Being compelled, by her duties as governess to the young
> princesses, to impose upon herself a restraint and an appearance of prudishness which is
> foreign to her nature, she takes the opportunity of being alone to express her natural dislike
> of conventional shackles. This she does in a strong quasi-dramatic scene (or by some other

And only sigh
When I am sad –
And that will be but rarely!

KAL. I'll row and fish,
  And gallop, soon –   515
   No longer be a prim one –
 And when I wish
  To hum a tune,
   It needn't be a hymn one?

MR. GOLD. *and* LORD D.
  No, no! No, no!   520
ALL. It needn't be a hymn one!

Oh, sweet surprise. Oh, dear delight (*dancing*)
To find it undisputed quite –
All musty, fusty rules despite –
That Art is wrong and Nature right!, &c. (*Dance and off.*) 525

(*Enter* LADY SOPHY.)

RECITATIVE – LADY SOPHY.

Oh, would some demon power the gift impart
To quell my over-conscientious heart –
Unspeak the oaths that never had been spoken,
And break the vows that never shall be broken!   530

SONG – LADY SOPHY.

When but a maid of fifteen year,
 Unsought – unplighted –
Short-petticoated – and, I fear,
 Still shorter-sighted –
I made a vow, one early spring,   535
That only to some spotless King
Who proof of blameless life could bring
 I'd be united.
For I had read, not long before,
Of blameless Kings in fairy lore,   540
And thought the race still flourished here –
 I was a maid of fifteen year!
 Well, well, I was a maid of fifteen year!

form of musical expression) with enough of suggested humour in it to keep it in harmony with the humorous and satirical character of the piece – and in this she declares her impatience of the Quakerish restraint which her position as the governess of the Princesses imposes upon her and her regret that, having regard to the scandalous conduct which is attributed to the King in the *Palace Peeper*, she cannot accept attentions which, but for these considerations, she would gladly do. The King overhears this with infinite pleasure and explains that the pars were all written by him. Embarrassed at the turn affairs have taken she is nevertheless bound to admit, now that his character is cleared, that the King is not wholly indifferent to her. She and the King, having thus come to an understanding, indulge in a joyous duet leading to a dance, which is witnessed and joined in by the two princesses and their lovers.

580 *Boil him on the spot*: There are several variations in the ending of this piece of recitative. The current Chappell editions of the libretto and the vocal score contain the version printed opposite, as does the World's Classics Edition of the Savoy Opera libretti. Reginald Allen's *First Night Gilbert and Sullivan* has Lady Sophy's last line 'I couldn't think why etc.' being followed by a final comment from the King: 'But I know why I didn't boil the author on the spot.' It also omits the final shared line 'Boil him on the spot'. The D'Oyly Carte recording has this final line but precedes it with the King singing 'I knew very well why I didn't.'

(*The* KING *enters and overhears this verse.*)

Each morning I pursued my game   545
  (An early riser);
For spotless monarchs I became
  An advertiser:
But all in vain I searched each land,
So, kingless, to my native strand   550
Returned, a little older, and
  A good deal wiser!
I learnt that spotless King and Prince
Have disappeared some ages since –
Even Paramount's angelic grace –   555
  Is but a mask on Nature's face!
    Ah, me! Ah, me! Is but a mask on Nature's face!

(KING *comes forward.*)

RECITATIVE.

KING.   Ah, Lady Sophy – then you love me!
             For so you sing –   560
LADY S. (*indignant and surprised; producing 'Palace Peeper'*).
             No, no, by the stars that shine above me,
               Degraded King!
           For while these rumours, through the city bruited,
           Remain uncontradicted, unrefuted,
           The object thou of my aversion rooted,   565
               Repulsive thing!

KING.   Be just – the time is now at hand
             When truth may published be.
           These paragraphs were written and
             Contributed by me!   570
LADY S. By you? No, no!
KING.   Yes, yes, I swear, by me!
           I, caught in Scaphio's ruthless toil,
             Contributed the lot!
LADY S. And *that* is why you did not boil   575
             The author on the spot!
KING.   And *that* is why I did not boil
             The author on the spot!
LADY S. I *couldn't* think why you did not boil the author on the spot!
BOTH.   Boil him on the spot!   580

593 *asinorum pons*: The *Pons Asinorum* is the fifth proposition in Euclid's *Elements of Geometry*. It is the first difficult theorem in geometry and is really anything but a bridge but rather a *pedica asinorum* or stumbling-block for asses.

605 *a wild Tarantella*: A very quick Neapolitan dance for one couple said to have been based on the gyrations of those poisoned by the tarantula.

exeunt severally: On the first night Tarara made an entrance at this point before the arrival of the chorus:

(*Enter excitedly* TARARA, *meeting* SCAPHIO *and* PHANTIS.)

SCAPHIO. Well – how works the plot? Have you done our bidding? Have you explained to the happy and contented populace the nature of their wrongs, and the desperate consequences that must ensue if they are not rectified?

TARARA. I have explained nothing. I have done better – I have made an affidavit that what they supposed to be happiness was really unspeakable misery – and they are furious! You know you can't help believing an affidavit.

SCAPHIO. Of course – an admirable thought! Ha! they come!

(*Enter all the male chorus, etc.*)

DUET – LADY SOPHY *and* KING.

LADY S. Oh, the rapture unrestrained
    Of a candid retractation!
For my sovereign has deigned
    A convincing explanation –
And the clouds that gathered o'er,   585
    All have vanished in the distance,
And of Kings of fairy lore
    One, at least, is in existence!, &c.

KING. Oh, the skies are blue above,
    And the earth is red and rosal,   590
Now the lady of my love
    Has accepted my proposal!
For that *asinorum pons*
    I have crossed without assistance,
And of prudish paragons   595
    One, at least, is in existence!

BOTH. Oh, the clouds, &c.

(KING *and* LADY SOPHY *dance gracefully. While this is going on* LORD DRAMALEIGH *enters unobserved with* NEKAYA *and* MR. GOLDBURY *with* KALYBA. *Then enter* ZARA *and* FITZBATTLEAXE. *The two girls*   600 *direct* ZARA's *attention to the* KING *and* LADY SOPHY, *who are still dancing affectionately together. At this point the* KING *kisses* LADY SOPHY, *which causes the Princesses to make an exclamation. The* KING *and* LADY SOPHY *are at first much confused at being detected, but eventually throw off all reserve, and the four couples break into a wild Tarantella, and at the end exeunt severally.*   605 *Enter all the male Chorus, in great excitement, from various entrances, led by* SCAPHIO, PHANTIS, *and* TARARA, *and followed by the female Chorus.*)

CHORUS. Upon our sea-girt land
At our enforced command
Reform has laid her hand   610
    Like some remorseless ogress –
And made us darkly rue
The deeds she dared to do –
And all is owing to
    Those hated Flowers of Progress!   615
    So down with them!
    So down with them!

646   *I don't know*: The first night libretto contains the following additional dialogue at this
      point:

> ZARA. I don't know – there's something wrong. I don't understand it.
> KING. Is everything at a standstill in England? Is there no litigation there? no bank-
> ruptcy? no poverty? no squalor? no sickness? no crime?
> ZARA. Plenty; it's the most prosperous country in the world! We must have omitted
> something.

653   *Government by Party*: Zara's lines about party government echo an old Gilbertian obses-
      sion. The subject forms a major theme in the plot of *Iolanthe*. Some of the first-night
      critics felt her speech as originally delivered went too far. The *Daily Graphic* reported
      that this speech was 'about the bitterest thing Mr Gilbert has ever penned'. It may well
      be that it was in response to these criticisms that Gilbert toned down the content of the
      speech, cutting the following passage which originally came after the words 'all the other
      party has done' (line 656):

> Inexperienced civilians will govern your Army and your Navy; no social reforms will be at-
> tempted, because out of vice, squalor, and drunkenness no political capital is to be made.

The tone of this deleted passage is very similar to that of the song 'Fold your flapping
wings' which was cut from *Iolanthe* (see note to *Iolanthe*, Act II, line 399).

Reform's a hated ogress.
So down with them!
So down with them!   620
Down with the Flowers of Progress!

(*Flourish. Enter* KING, *his three daughters,* LADY SOPHY, *and the*
FLOWERS OF PROGRESS.)

KING.   What means this most unmannerly irruption?
            Is this your gratitude for boons conferred?   625
SCA.   Boons? Bah! A fico for such boons, say we!
            These boons have brought Utopia to a standstill!
            Our pride and boast – the Army and the Navy –
            Have both been reconstructed and remodelled
            Upon so irresistible a basis   630
            That all the neighbouring nations have disarmed –
            And War's impossible! Your County Councillor
            Has passed such drastic Sanitary laws
            That all the doctors dwindle, starve, and die!
            The laws, remodelled by Sir Bailey Barre,   635
            Have quite extinguished crime and litigation:
            The lawyers starve, and all the jails are let
            As model lodgings for the working-classes!
            In short –
            Utopia, swamped by dull Prosperity,   640
            Demands that these detested Flowers of Progress
            Be sent about their business, and affairs
            Restored to their original complexion!

KING (*to* ZARA). My daughter, this is a very unpleasant state of things. What
is to be done?   645
    ZARA. I don't know – I don't understand it. We must have omitted some-
thing.
    KING. Omitted something? Yes, that's all very well, but —

(SIR BAILEY BARRE *whispers to* ZARA.)

ZARA (*suddenly*). Of course! Now I remember! Why, I had forgotten the most   650
essential element of all!
    KING. And that is? –
    ZARA. Government by Party! Introduce that great and glorious element –
at once the bulwark and foundation of England's greatness – and all will be well!
No political measures will endure, because one Party will assuredly undo all   655
that the other Party has done; and while grouse is to be shot, and foxes worried

663–4   *away with them and let them wait my will*: At this point in Gilbert's manuscript copy of the libretto the King has the following lines addressed to Tarara:

> KING: Tarara, you deserve some compensation in exchange for the privilege of blowing us up and succeeding to the throne, so we appoint you Perpetual Chief Inspector of Explosives, under 38 and 39 Vic., Cap. 17, s. 62. (*Tarara immediately pulls out a cracker, and putting on his spectacles, proceeds to inspect it*).

668–90   *Finale*

The finale to *Utopia Limited* caused both Gilbert and Sullivan considerable difficulty. Sullivan at first found it impossible to set Gilbert's words 'There's a little group of isles beyond the waves' and it was suggested that he should compose a tune with which he was happy to which the librettist would then write words. This is one of the very few recorded occasions in the long partnership between Gilbert and Sullivan when the music was written first and the words fitted to it. Sullivan composed his music for the finale at Weybridge and sent it to Gilbert at Grim's Dyke.

On 26 September, just eleven days before the opening of the opera, Gilbert wrote to Sullivan: 'I got up at seven this morning and polished off the new finale before breakfast. It is mere doggerel, but words written to an existing tune are nearly sure to be that. I am sorry to lose the other finale, but I quite see your difficulty and that can't be helped. You can chop this about as you please – a verse to Zara and a verse to the King, or the first half of each to Zara and the last half to the King, or the first half of the first verse to Zara and the first half of the second verse to Fitzbattleaxe, giving the King the end of each verse, which perhaps is the arrangement that will suit you best.'

I have not been able to trace the words of this second attempt at the finale although Arthur Jacobs in his biography of Sullivan quotes its opening line as 'There's an isle beyond the wave, held by a blameless race'. It clearly proved unsatisfactory in rehearsal and the *Westminster Gazette* reported that there was no finale in the public dress rehearsal on 6 October, the cast having been told that a new one was being written and would not be ready for rehearsal until a few hours before the first performance.

The first night audience heard the following hastily written third version of the finale:

KING.   When monarch of barbaric land,
                                 For self-improvement burning,
                        Foregathers with a glorious band
                                   Of sweetness, light and learning –
                        A group incalculably wise –
                                   Unequalled in their beauty –
                        Their customs to acclimatize
                        Becomes a moral duty.

ZARA (*to* FITZBATTLEAXE).   Oh gallant soldier, brave and true
                                   In tented field and tourney,
                        I'll trust you'll ne'er regret that you
                                   Embarked upon this journey.

FTZBATTLEAXE.   To warriors all may it befall
                                   To gain so pure a beauty,
                        When they obey the trumpet call
                                 Of Regimental Duty!

This version of the finale, which contains no part for chorus, was felt by the critics to be unsatisfactory. The *Daily Graphic* spoke for many in finding it 'insignificant'. Sullivan returned to Gilbert's original words and at last hit on a tune that fits them extremely well. This final version of the finale was first performed on Friday 13 October. The one feature which all the various versions seem to have had is an introduction consisting of a few bars of 'Rule Britannia'.

to death, the legislative action of the country will be at a standstill. Then there will be sickness in plenty, endless lawsuits, crowded jails, interminable confusion in the Army and Navy, and, in short, general and unexampled prosperity!

ALL. Ulahlica! Ulahlica! 660

PHAN. (*aside*). Baffled!

SCA. But an hour *will* come!

KING. Your hour has come already – away with them, and let them wait my will! (SCAPHIO *and* PHANTIS *are led off in custody.*) From this moment Government by Party is adopted, with all its attendant blessings, and hencefor- 665 ward Utopia will no longer be a Monarchy (Limited), but, what is a great deal better, a Limited Monarchy!

FINALE.

ZARA. There's a little group of isles beyond the wave –
　　　　So tiny, you might almost wonder where it is –
　　　That nation is the bravest of the brave, 670
　　　　And cowards are the rarest of all rarities.
　　　The proudest nations kneel at her command;
　　　　She terrifies all foreign-born rapscallions;
　　　And holds the peace of Europe in her hand
　　　　With half a score invincible battalions! 675

ALL. Such, at least, is the tale
　　　Which is borne on the gale,
　　　　From the island which dwells in the sea.
　　　Let us hope, for her sake,
　　　That she makes no mistake – 680
　　　　That she's all she professes to be!

KING. Oh, may we copy all her maxims wise,
　　　　And imitate her virtues and her charities;
　　　And may we, by degrees, acclimatize
　　　　Her Parliamentary peculiarities! 685
　　　By doing so, we shall, in course of time,
　　　　Regenerate completely our entire land –
　　　Great Britain is that monarchy sublime,
　　　　To which some add (but others do not) Ireland.

ALL. Such, at least, is the tale, &c. 690

CURTAIN

THE GRAND DUKE

or

The Statutory Duel

DRAMATIS PERSONÆ

RUDOLPH (*Grand Duke of Pfennig Halbpfennig*)
ERNEST DUMMKOPF (*a Theatrical Manager*)
LUDWIG (*his Leading Comedian*)
DR. TANNHÄUSER (*a Notary*)
THE PRINCE OF MONTE CARLO
VISCOUNT MENTONE
BEN HASHBAZ (*a Costumier*)
HERALD
THE PRINCESS OF MONTE CARLO (*betrothed to* RUDOLPH)
THE BARONESS VON KRAKENFELDT (*betrothed to* RUDOLPH)
JULIA JELLICOE (*an English Comédienne*)
LISA (*a Soubrette*)
OLGA
GRETCHEN
BERTHA } (*Members of Ernest Dummkopf's Company*)
ELSA
MARTHA

Chamberlains, Nobles, Actors, Actresses, &c.

Act I. – Scene. Public Square of Speisesaal.
Act II. – Scene. Hall in the Grand Ducal Palace.

Time—1750.

THE GRAND DUKE

Despite hopes that the relative success of *Utopia Limited* would keep Gilbert and Sullivan together and lead to a string of new collaborations, the two drifted apart again. When it closed at the Savoy Theatre in the summer of 1894, there was no new Gilbert and Sullivan opera to succeed it and Richard D'Oyly Carte had to fall back on a piece by Messager entitled *Mirette*.

Gilbert now teamed up with composer Dr Osmond Carr to write *His Excellency*, which opened at the Lyric Theatre on 27 October 1894 with a strong cast headed by three Savoy favourites, George Grossmith, Rutland Barrington and Jessie Bond. Sullivan, meanwhile, collaborated with F. C. Burnand in a revision of their 1867 operetta, *The Contrabandista*. This now became *The Chieftain* and opened at the Savoy in October 1894. It ran for only 96 performances and was replaced with a hugely successful revival of *The Mikado*.

Eventually, in the summer of 1895, Gilbert approached Sullivan, who was recently back from trips to Monte Carlo and Paris and staying in a rented house in Walton-on-Thames, with the outline of a new libretto which he had entitled *The Grand Duke*. For the plot, he had reverted to the idea of a touring theatrical company which he had given up in favour of *The Gondoliers* in deference to the composer's wishes six years earlier. Sullivan completed the music by the end of February 1896 and the new opera received its first performance at the Savoy Theatre on 7 March. 'Parts of it dragged a little, dialogue too redundant', noted Sullivan in his diary, 'but success great and genuine I think. Thank God opera is finished and out.' After conducting the first performance he took off once again for Monte Carlo from where he wrote to F. C. Burnand: 'I arrived here dead beat. Another week's rehearsal with W.S.G. and I should have gone raving mad. I had already ordered some straw for my hair.'

Although the critics were generally enthusiastic about the new work, Gilbert was less certain about its merits, describing *The Grand Duke* to Mrs Bram Stoker as 'an ugly misshapen little brat'. The public seem to have agreed: the opera closed after a run of just 123 performances, four fewer than for the *Mikado* revival that had preceded it. Richard D'Oyly Carte replaced *Utopia Limited* with *The Mikado* at the Savoy and the old Japanese warhorse proved its worth yet again, clocking up its 1,000th performance towards the end of 1896.

The failure of *The Grand Duke* finally ended Gilbert and Sullivan's increasingly fragile partnership. Gilbert devoted himself to the pursuits of a country gentleman. Sullivan went on composing, producing a ballet, *Victoria and Merrie*

England, a musical drama, *The Beauty Stone*, and two more comic operas, *The Rose of Persia* and *The Emerald Isle*. The two men did not speak to one another again. When *The Sorcerer* was put on at the Savoy Theatre towards the end of 1898 composer and librettist came on stage and bowed to the audience without exchanging a word. When *Patience* was revived in November 1900, Gilbert wrote to Sullivan expressing the hope that they might bury the hatchet and take a curtain call together. Sullivan, however, was too ill to appear. He died on 22 November 1900. Gilbert, who was in Egypt, where he was trying to recover from rheumatic fever, wrote to the composer's nephew to express his sympathy. He added: 'It is a satisfaction to me to feel that I was impelled, shortly before his death, to write to him to propose shaking hands over our recent differences, and even a greater satisfaction to learn, through you, that my offer of reconciliation was cordially accepted.'

It is a strange coincidence that the plot of Gilbert and Sullivan's last work together should so closely echo that of their first nearly twenty-five years earlier. Like *Thespis*, *The Grand Duke* tells the story of the members of a theatrical troupe who find themselves acting out the roles of those to whom they are supposed to be performing (in this case the court of Pfennig Halbpfennig rather than the gods of Mount Olympus). In a sense the underlying theme of the opera is that of role playing – everyone is playing a part, the real characters no less than the actors. The action hinges around ritualized games – the statutory duel and the cutting of a pack of cards – and there is a good deal about the extent to which the theatre mirrors real life. In an interesting paper presented to an International Conference on Gilbert and Sullivan at the University of Kansas in May 1970 Max Sutton argued that the theme of *The Grand Duke* is the way in which social roles can obscure a person's real sense of identity.

Other scholars have seen *The Grand Duke* as epitomizing the decadent *fin de siècle* atmosphere of the late 1890s. Its characters are certainly full of physical and moral flaws – not least the profoundly unattractive Grand Duke Rudolph. It is not the happiest of Gilbert's libretti in any sense, having a particularly convoluted plot and far too much rather tedious dialogue, but Sullivan shines where he is able and several of the songs, particularly in Act II, have a real vivacity and sparkle.

The old D'Oyly Carte Opera Company only once revived *The Grand Duke* after its first run and that was for a single concert performance on 5 April 1975, the last night of its centenary season. Richard Baker was the narrator. A recording of the opera was made by the company and issued by Decca in 1976 and the BBC included its own production in the 1989 Radio 2 season of Savoy Operas. The centenary of the first performance was marked by a number of fine amateur productions, notably by the City of Durham Light Opera Group, and a professional performance in Oxford Town Hall on 29 June as part of the 1996 Sullivan Society Festival. Let us hope this revival of interest will inspire more amateur companies to include it in their repertoire. For all its faults *The Grand Duke* deserves to be seen and heard more often.

1–5 *Scene*: An early draft of the plot for *The Grand Duke* in a notebook among the Gilbert papers in the British Library indicates the opera's main theme and also shows how different the author's original conception was from the final version. This is what Gilbert wrote in November 1894:

> The Grand Duchy of Hesse Halbpfennig is governed by the Grand Duke Wilhelm. This Grand Duchy is only 10 acres in extent and it has one small town – Speisesaal. The Grand Duke is not at all popular – he is practically penniless and imposes dreadful taxes which cripple his fifty subjects.
>
> In babyhood he was betrothed to Casilda, daughter of the Prince and Princess of Monaco. They have never met because the Prince of Monaco cannot afford to travel to Hesse Halbpfennig and the Grand Duke cannot afford to travel to Monaco.
>
> After winning a large sum at roulette, however, the Prince can at last afford to travel. His daughter has come of age and they announce their intention of coming to Hesse Halbpfennig in order that her marriage to the Grand Duke may be accomplished. But meanwhile he has fallen in love with Bertha, a beautiful villager.
>
> The Grand Duke's Court consists of a Chamberlain, a Chaplain, a Treasurer, a Lady Housekeeper, a Minister of Police and a Commander in Chief. There are, besides, some domestic servants, including three housemaids, and there is a garrison of six soldiers. There is great discontent among these people for none of them have received any pay for several months.
>
> The piece may open with a meeting of these people called by the Commander in Chief who suggests to them that the approaching visit of the Prince and Princess of Monaco and their daughter will afford an excellent opportunity for them to demand payment in full and arrears. If this is denied, they will strike and leave the Grand Duke to receive his visitors alone.

This early draft goes on to mention a secret society engaged in a conspiracy to dethrone the Grand Duke in which the figures of Ernest Dummkopf and Ludwig are leading members. The idea of making them members of a theatrical company came later and represented a return in the last of the Savoy Operas to a theme found in the first work on which Gilbert and Sullivan had collaborated. *Thespis*, written in 1871, tells the story of a group of actors who come to Mount Olympus and find themselves taking on the roles of the gods. Gilbert had tried several times to revive the idea of a theatrical troupe in his opera plots but Sullivan had strongly resisted it, most recently and emphatically in 1889 when he steered the librettist towards *The Gondoliers* instead.

22 *If upon her train she stumbled*: Both the first night libretto and the 1928 Chatto edition of Gilbert's plays have the following lines for Olga and Gretchen's solos:

OLGA.	If her wreath is all lop-sided,
	That's a thing one's always dreading.
GRETCHEN.	If her hair is all untidied,
	Still, it is a pretty wedding

26 *Such a pretty, pretty wedding*: The *Grand Duke* is the only Savoy Opera to begin with a wedding, or at least the promise of a wedding. *The Sorcerer* begins with a betrothal and *Ruddigore* opens with a chorus of bridesmaids but sadly no bride or bridegroom for them to hail. *Trial by Jury* is all about a promised wedding that never takes place.

ACT I

S C E N E. *Market-place of Speisesaal, in the Grand Duchy of Pfennig Halbpfennig. A well, with decorated ironwork, up* L.C. G R E T C H E N, B E R T H A, O L G A, M A R T H A, E L S A, *and other members of* E R N E S T D U M M K O P F 's *theatrical company are discovered, seated at several small tables, enjoying a repast in honour of the nuptials of* L U D W I G, *his leading comedian, and* L I S A, *his soubrette.*

C H O R U S.

Won't it be a pretty wedding?
 Will not Lisa look delightful?
Smiles and tears in plenty shedding –
 Which in brides of course is rightful.
 One could say, if one were spiteful,
Contradiction little dreading,
 Her bouquet is simply frightful –
Still, 'twill be a pretty wedding!
Oh, it is a pretty wedding!
 Such a pretty, pretty wedding!
 Such a charming wedding!

ELSA.   If her dress *is* badly fitting,
    Theirs the fault who made her *trousseau.*

BERTHA. If her gloves *are* always splitting,
    Cheap kid gloves, we know, will do so.

OLGA.   If upon her train she stumbled,
    On one's train one's always treading.

GRET.   If her hair *is* rather tumbled,
    Still, 'twill be a pretty wedding!

FOUR GIRLS. Such a pretty, pretty wedding!

37 *sposo*: Italian for bridegroom.

39 *Perhaps you think I'm only so-so*: In the 1976 D'Oyly Carte recording Kenneth Sandford as
    Ludwig sang 'Perhaps you think me only so-so'.

CHORUS.

Such a very pretty wedding, &c.

Here they come, the couple plighted –
   On life's journey gaily start them.
Man and maid for aye united, 30
   Till divorce or death shall part them.

(LUDWIG *and* LISA *come forward.*)

DUET – LUDWIG *and* LISA.

LUD.	Pretty Lisa, fair and tasty,
	Tell me now, and tell me truly,
	Haven't you been rather hasty? 35
	Haven't you been rash unduly?
	Am I quite the dashing *sposo*
	That your fancy could depict you?
	Perhaps you think I'm only so-so? *(She expresses admiration)*
	Well, I will not contradict you! 40

CHORUS.	No, he will not contradict you!

LISA.	Who am I to raise objection?
	I'm a child, untaught and homely –
	When you tell me you're perfection,
	Tender, truthful, true, and comely – 45
	That in quarrel no one's bolder,
	Though dissensions always grieve you –
	Why, my love, you're so much older
	That, of course, I must believe you!

CHORUS.	Yes, of course, she must believe you! 50

CHORUS.

If he ever acts unkindly,
Shut your eyes and love him blindly –
Should he call you names uncomely,
Shut your mouth and love him dumbly –
Should he rate you, rightly – leftly – 55
Shut your ears and love him deafly.
   Ha! ha! ha! ha! ha! ha! ha!
     Thus and thus and thus alone
     Ludwig's wife may hold her own!

60 *NotaryTannhauser*: *Tannhauser* was Richard Wagner's third opera, staged in 1845.

77–8 *his approaching marriage with the enormously wealthy Baroness von Krakenfeldt*: Initially, as we
have seen, Gilbert had the Grand Duke fall in love with Bertha, a beautiful villager. In a
subsequent re-working of the plot she became a wealthy Countess with the Grand
Duke falling for her because of her wealth rather than her beauty. Finally, Countess
Bertha was replaced by the Baroness von Krakenfeldt.

80–1 *Troilus and Cressida*: This is not the only Shakespeare play to be mentioned in the Savoy
Operas. Among the ingredients of a Heavy Dragoon rattled off by Colonel Calverley in
Patience (Act I, line 164) is 'the flavour of Hamlet'. *Romeo and Juliet* crops up a little later
in *The Grand Duke* (lines 175–6).

87 *Hush, rash girl*: The first night libretto has additional material at this point, which was
included in the 1989 BBC recording of the opera:

> LUDWIG. Hush, rash girl! You know not what you say.
> OLGA. Don't be absurd! We're all in it – we're all tiled here.
> LUDWIG. That has nothing to do with it. Know ye not, etc.

94 *You must eat a sausage roll*: This was the first song in *The Grand Duke* to be encored on the
opening night. The *Daily Chronicle* noted that it was 'capitally sung by Mr. Rutland Barrington' and 'started a series of requests for repetition which Sir Arthur Sullivan frequently had difficulty in repressing'.

Gilbert's use of the sausage roll device, reminiscent of his earlier flirtation with the
idea of a magic lozenge, was felt by some critics to be rather overdone. The *Musical
Standard* commented: 'The idea is not really funny, and it is enlarged upon to weari-
someness' while the *City* reviewer remarked: 'The humour of the "kipper" has for a
long time held an honoured place in music hall patter; now we have the humour of the
sausage roll at the Savoy. I do not greatly prefer the latter form of wit myself.'

Other songs have been written about sausages. There was that spirited duet from the
early 1960s sung by Pearl Carr and Teddy Johnson, 'Give us a bash of the bangers and
mash my mother used to make' and there is, of course, the reference in Lionel Bart's
'Food, glorious food' from the musical *Oliver* to 'Hot sausage and mustard'. I very much
doubt, however, if anyone but Gilbert has ever written a song about a sausage roll.

(*Enter* NOTARY TANNHÄUSER.)   60

NOT. Hallo! Surely I'm not late?
                                        (*All chatter unintelligibly in reply.*)
NOT. But, dear me, you're all at breakfast! Has the wedding taken place?
                                        (*All chatter unintelligibly in reply.*)
NOT. My good girls, one at a time, I beg. Let me understand the situation.
As solicitor to the conspiracy to dethrone the Grand Duke – a conspiracy in   65
which the members of this company are deeply involved – I am invited to the
marriage of two of its members. I present myself in due course, and I find, not
only that the ceremony has taken place – which is not of the least consequence –
but the wedding breakfast is half eaten – which is a consideration of the most
serious importance.   70
                        (LUDWIG *and* LISA *come to table and sit.*)

LUD. But the ceremony has *not* taken place. We can't get a parson!
NOT. Can't get a parson! Why, how's that? They're three a penny!
LUD. Oh, it's the old story – the Grand Duke!
ALL. Ugh!   75
LUD. It seems that the little imp has selected this, our wedding day, for a
convocation of all the clergy in the town to settle the details of his approaching
marriage with the enormously wealthy Baroness von Krakenfeldt, and there
won't be a parson to be had for love or money until six o'clock this evening!
LISA. And as we produce our magnificent classical revival of *Troilus and*   80
Cressida tonight at seven, we have no alternative but to eat our wedding break-
fast before we've earned it. So sit down, and make the best of it.
GRET. Oh, I should like to pull his Grand Ducal ears for him, that I should!
He's the meanest, the cruellest, the most spiteful little ape in Christendom!
BERTHA. Well, we shall soon be freed from his tyranny. Tomorrow the   85
Despot is to be dethroned!
LUD. Hush, rash girl. Know ye not that in alluding to our conspiracy
without having first given and received the secret sign, you are violating a
fundamental principle of our Association?

SONG – LUDWIG.

By the mystic regulation   90
Of our dark Association,
Ere you open conversation
        With another kindred soul,
You must eat a sausage-roll!   (*Producing one*)

ALL.   You must eat a sausage-roll!   95

114 *Oh, bother the secret sign*: In the first night libretto (and the BBC recording) this line was
given to Martha, one of the other members of Ernest Dummkopf's theatrical company,
and the subsequent dialogue expanded as follows:

> MARTHA. Oh, bother the secret sign! I've eaten it until I'm quite uncomfortable! I've
> given it six times already today – and (*whimpering*) I can't eat any breakfast.
> BERTHA. And it's so unwholesome. Why, we should all be as yellow as frogs if it wasn't
> for the make-up!
> LUDWIG. All this is rank treason to the cause. I suffer as much as any of you., etc.

127–8 *King Agamemnon, in a Louis Quartorze wig*: In Greek mythology, Agamemnon was the son
of Atreus, brother of Menelaus and husband of Clytemnestra. He was king of Mycenae
and leader of the Greek forces in the Trojan War. Louis XIV, also known as the Sun
King, ruled France from 1643 to 1715. Rutland Barrington's appearance in this costume
caused considerable amusement to the first night audience and critics. The *Man of the
World* commented: 'Fancy Barrington in Greek costume; Barrington as Agamemnon, in
a breastplate and nothing else to speak of but a big Louis Quartorze wig. He is figuratively and literally immense.'

130 *for our marriage*: Following the first night libretto, the 1989 BBC recording contained the
following additional material at this point:

> LUDWIG. Think of the effect of a real Athenian wedding procession cavorting through
> the streets of Speisesaal! Torches burning – cymbals banging – flutes tootling – citharae
> twanging – and a throng of fifty lovely Spartan virgins capering before us, all down the
> High Street, singing 'Eloia! Eloia! Opoponax, Eloia!' It would have been tremendous.

In the BBC recording at the point where Ludwig talks about the Spartan virgins singing, the female chorus launched into an elaborate rendering of 'Opoponax, opoponax,
opoponax, Eloia!' which is not in the vocal score.

LUD.	If, in turn, he eats another,
	That's a sign that he's a brother –
	Each may fully trust the other.
	It is quaint and it is droll,
	But it's bilious on the whole. 100
ALL.	Very bilious on the whole.
LUD.	It's a greasy kind of pasty,
	Which, perhaps, a judgement hasty
	Might consider rather tasty:
	Once (to speak without disguise) 105
	It found favour in our eyes.
ALL.	It found favour in our eyes.
LUD.	But when you've been six months feeding
	(As we have) on this exceeding
	Bilious food, it's no ill-breeding 110
	If at these repulsive pies
	Our offended gorges rise!
ALL.	Yes, at these repulsive pies, &c.

ELSA. Oh, bother the secret sign! I've eaten it until I'm quite uncomfortable!   115

BERTHA. And it's so unwholesome. Why, we should all be as yellow as frogs if it wasn't for the make-up!

LUD. I suffer as much as any of you. I loathe the repulsive thing – I can't contemplate it without a shudder – but I'm a conscientious conspirator, and if you won't give the sign I will. (*Eats a sausage-roll with an effort.*)   120

LISA. Poor martyr! He's always at it, and it's a wonder where he puts it!

NOT. Well now, about *Troilus and Cressida*. What do *you* play?

LUD. (*struggling with his feelings*). If you'll be so obliging as to wait until I've got rid of this feeling of warm oil at the bottom of my throat, I'll tell you all about it. (LISA *gives him some brandy.*) Thank you, my love; it's gone. Well, the   125 piece will be produced upon a scale of unexampled magnificence. It is confidently predicted that my appearance as King Agamemnon, in a Louis Quatorze wig, will mark an epoch in the theatrical annals of Pfennig Halbpfennig. I endeavoured to persuade Ernest Dummkopf, our manager, to lend us the classical dresses for our marriage. It would have been tremendous!   130

NOT. And he declined?

LUD. He did, on the prosaic ground that it might rain, and the ancient Greeks didn't carry umbrellas! If, as is confidently expected, Ernest Dumm-

138 *according to professional precedence*: The first night libretto has a substantial piece of extra dialogue here which was subsequently cut:

> MARTHA. I'm sure he'll make a lovely Grand Duke. How he will stage-manage the processional.
>
> GRETCHEN. And won't it make Julia Jellicoe jealous! That English woman has always rejected his advances, hitherto – but now I fancy the tables will be turned and he'll reject hers. The pretentious little London cockney – there's nobody good enough for her!
>
> LUDWIG. Bah! – Ernest's a stick – a very stick! And what a part it is! What a chance for an actor who is really a master of stage resource! Why, a Grand Duke of Pfennig Halbpfennig might have a different make-up for every day in the week! Monday, touch-and-go light comedy in lavender trousers and a flaxen wig. Tuesday, irritable old uncle from India. Wednesday, heavy philanthropist with benevolent 'bald'. Thursday, incisive baronet with diamond ring and cigarette to show it off. Friday, slimy solicitor with club foot and spectacles. Saturday, escaped convict with one eye and a gulp! It's one of those parts that really give a man a chance!
>
> (*He strolls up and off with* LISA, *as* ERNEST *enters in great excitement.*)

167 *early and late*: The first night libretto, 1928 Chatto edition of Gilbert's plays and 1989 BBC recording all render this phrase as 'little and great'.

kopf is elected to succeed the dethroned one, mark my words, he will make a
mess of it.   (*Exit* LUDWIG *with* LISA.)   135
    OLGA. He's sure to be elected. His entire company has promised to plump
for him on the understanding that all the places about the Court are filled by
members of his troupe, according to professional precedence.
                        (ERNEST *enters in great excitement.*)

BERTHA (*looking off*). Here comes Ernest Dummkopf. Now we shall know   140
all about it!
    LADIES. Well – what's the news?
    GENTLEMEN. How is the election going?
    ERN. Oh, it's a certainty – a practical certainty! Two of the candidates have
been arrested for debt, and the third is a baby in arms – so, if you keep your   145
promises, and vote solid, I'm cocksure of election!
    OLGA. Trust to us. But you remember the conditions?
    ERN. Yes – all of you shall be provided for, for life. Every man shall be en-
nobled – every lady shall have unlimited credit at the Court Milliner's, and all
salaries shall be paid weekly in advance!   150
    GRET. Oh, it's quite clear he knows how to rule a Grand Duchy!
    ERN. Rule a Grand Duchy? Why, my good girl, for ten years past I've ruled a
theatrical company! A man who can do that can rule anything!

SONG – ERNEST.

Were I a king in very truth,
And had a son – a guileless youth –   155
    In probable succession;
To teach him patience, teach him tact,
How promptly in a fix to act,
He should adopt, in point of fact,
    A manager's profession.   160
To that condition he should stoop
    (Despite a too fond mother),
With eight or ten 'stars' in his troupe,
    All jealous of each other!
Oh, the man who can rule a theatrical crew,   165
Each member a genius (and some of them two),
And manage to humour them, early and late,
    Can govern this tuppenny State!

CHORUS.   Oh, the man, &c.

ERN.   Both A and B rehearsal slight –   170
           They say they'll be 'all right at night'
               (They've both to go to school yet);

177   *hoydens*: Rude, ill-bred girls who are boisterous and noisy.

185   *with Ireland thrown in*: A hark-back to King Paramount's 'To which some add, but others do, not, Ireland' (*Utopia Limited*, Act II, line 689)

189   *Troilus of Troy*: In Greek mythology, the younger son of King Priam of Troy and Hecuba.

196   *her feelings towards me*: At this point in the BBC recording Ernest added 'If so . . . Ah, she is here', presumably simply as a device to let the radio audience know that Julia had appeared.

199   *Beautiful English maiden*: Shades of *Utopia Limited* again and 'a wonderful joy our eyes to bless' (Act II, lines 440–81)

C in each act *must* change her dress,
D *will* attempt to 'square the press';
E won't play Romeo unless   175
  His grandmother plays Juliet;
F claims all hoydens as her rights
  (She's played them thirty seasons);
And G must show herself in tights
  For two convincing reasons –   180
  Two very well-shaped reasons!
Oh, the man who can drive a theatrical team,
With wheelers and leaders in order supreme,
Can govern and rule, with a wave of his fin,
  All Europe – with Ireland thrown in!   185

CHORUS. Oh, the man, &c.   (*Exeunt all but* ERNEST.)

ERN. Elected by my fellow conspirators to be Grand Duke of Pfennig Halbpfennig as soon as the contemptible little occupant of the historical throne is deposed – here is promotion indeed! Why, instead of playing Troilus of Troy for a month, I shall play Grand Duke of Pfennig Halbpfennig for a lifetime! Yet,   190 am I happy? No – far from happy! The lovely English *comédienne* – the beautiful Julia, whose dramatic ability is so overwhelming that our audiences forgive even her strong English accent – that rare and radiant being treats my respectful advances with disdain unutterable! And yet, who knows? She is haughty and ambitious, and it may be that the splendid change in my fortunes may work a   195 corresponding change in her feelings towards me!

(*Enter* JULIA JELLICOE.)

JULIA. Herr Dummkopf, a word with you, if you please.
ERN. Beautiful English maiden —
JULIA. No compliments, I beg. I desire to speak with you on a purely   200 professional matter, so we will, if you please, dispense with allusions to my personal appearance, which can only tend to widen the breach which already exists between us.
ERN. (*aside*). My only hope shattered! The haughty Londoner still despises me! (*Aloud.*) It shall be as you will.   205
JULIA. I understand that the conspiracy in which we are all concerned is to develop tomorrow, and that the company is likely to elect you to the throne on the understanding that the posts about the Court are to be filled by members of your theatrical troupe, according to their professional importance.
ERN. That is so.   210
JULIA. Then all I can say is that it places me in an extremely awkward position.

224 *Oh, certainly*: This line was missing from both the first night libretto and the 1928 Chatto edition of Gilbert's plays.

234 *we're used to these long runs in England*: Not, sadly, for the *Grand Duke* which managed to clock up only 123 performances, the shortest run for any of the Savoy Operas. Gilbert and Sullivan's longest opening run was for *The Mikado* – 672 performances.

237 *Gerolstein*: A climatic health resort in the German Rhineland with a romantic ruined castle dating from 1115. Offenbach put it on the map with his operetta *The Grand Duchess of Gerolstein*, first performed in Paris in 1867.

ERN. (*very depressed*). I don't see how it concerns you.

JULIA. Why, bless my heart, don't you see that, as your leading lady, I am bound under a serious penalty to play the leading part in all your productions? 215

ERN. Well?

JULIA. Why, of course, the leading part in this production will be the Grand Duchess!

ERN. My wife?

JULIA. That is another way of expressing the same idea. 220

ERN. (*aside – delighted.*) I scarcely dared even to hope for this!

JULIA. Of course, as your leading lady, you'll be mean enough to hold me to the terms of my agreement.

ERN. Oh, certainly!

JULIA. Oh, that's so like a man! Well, I suppose there's no help for it – I shall 225 have to do it!

ERN. (*aside*). She's mine! (*Aloud.*) But – do you really think you would care to play that part?

JULIA. Care to play it? Certainly not – but what am I to do? Business is business, and I am bound by the terms of my agreement. 230

ERN. It's for a long run, mind – a run that may last many, many years – no understudy – and once embarked upon there's no throwing it up. (*Takes her hand.*)

JULIA. (*withdrawing hand*). Oh, we're used to these long runs in England: they are the curse of the stage – but, you see, I've no option. 235

ERN. You think the part of Grand Duchess will be good enough for you?

JULIA. Oh, I think so. It's a very good part in Gerolstein, and oughtn't to be a bad one in Pfennig Halbpfennig. Why, what did you suppose I was going to play?

ERN. (*keeping up a show of reluctance*). But, considering your strong personal 240 dislike to me and your persistent rejection of my repeated offers, won't you find it difficult to throw yourself into the part with all the impassioned enthusiasm that the character seems to demand? Remember, it's a strongly emotional part, involving long and repeated scenes of rapture, tenderness, adoration, devotion – all in luxuriant excess, and all of the most demonstrative description. 245

JULIA. My good sir, throughout my career I have made it a rule never to allow private feeling to interfere with my professional duties. You may be quite sure that (however distasteful the part may be) if I undertake it, I shall consider myself professionally bound to throw myself into it with all the ardour at my command. 250

ERN. (*aside – with effusion*). I'm the happiest fellow alive! (*Aloud.*) Now – would you have any objection – to – to give me some idea – if it's only a mere sketch – as to how you would play it? It would be really interesting – to me – to know your conception of – of – the part of my wife.

JULIA. How would I play it? Now, let me see – let me see. (*Considering.*) Ah, I 255 have it!

257–96 *How would I play this part*

The idea of this song is very similar to that of Phoebe's 'Were I thy bride' in *The Yeomen of the Guard* (Act I, lines 701–42). In both cases women pretend to be in love with men who are totally besotted with them but make clear in the end that they are only play-acting.

In an interesting paper presented at an international conference on Gilbert and Sullivan held at the University of Kansas in May 1970 Max Sutton suggested that the whole theme of *The Grand Duke* is really the playing of parts, or more specifically the extent to which social roles can obscure a person's real sense of identity. He points out that in the opera everyone is playing a part, not just the actors. It dramatizes the close similiarity between the theatre and politics. As the plot develops, it is the real rulers who behave most like actors while the actors show themselves to be shrewd politicians, not least Ludwig.

Sutton suggests that Julia Jellicoe is the most compulsive role player of all. Her rule is never to allow private feelings to interfere with professional duties and she is prepared to deny her human individuality for the sake of achieving higher social status. But all the characters, he suggests, are basically playing games with each other.

277 *I'd pinch the forward jade*: Another echo from *The Yeomen of the Guard*, this time from Wilfred Shadbolt's lost song, 'When jealous torments wrack my soul', where he sings of the agony of loving 'a heartless jade'.

BALLAD – JULIA.

How would I play this part –
    The Grand Duke's Bride?
All rancour in my heart
    I'd duly hide –   260
    I'd drive it from my recollection
    And 'whelm you with a mock affection,
    Well calculated to defy detection –
That's how I'd play this part –
    The Grand Duke's Bride.   265

With many a winsome smile
    I'd witch and woo;
With gay and girlish guile
    I'd frenzy you –
    I'd madden you with my caressing,   270
    Like turtle, her first love confessing –
    That it was 'mock', no mortal would be guessing,
With so much winsome wile
    I'd witch and woo!

Did any other maid   275
    With you succeed,
I'd pinch the forward jade –
    I would indeed!
    With jealous frenzy agitated
    (Which would, of course, be simulated),   280
    I'd make her wish she'd never been created –
Did any other maid
    With you succeed!

And should there come to me,
    Some summers hence,   285
In all the childish glee
    Of innocence,
    Fair babes, aglow with beauty vernal,
    My heart would bound with joy diurnal!
    This sweet display of sympathy maternal,   290
Well, that would also be
    A mere pretence!
My histrionic art
    Though you deride,
That's how I'd play that part –   295
    The Grand Duke's Bride!

312 *What means this agitato*: Shades of *Iolanthe* and the Lord Chancellor's 'What means this mirth unseemly' (*Iolanthe*, Act I, line 565).

ENSEMBLE.

ERNEST.	JULIA.
Oh joy! when two glowing young hearts,	My boy, when two glowing young hearts,
From the rise of the curtain,	From the rise of the curtain,
Thus throw themselves into their parts,	Thus throw themselves into their parts,
Success is most certain!	Success is most certain!
If the role you're prepared to endow	The role I'm prepared to endow
With such delicate touches,	With most delicate touches,
By the heaven above us, I vow	By the heaven above us, I vow
You shall be my Grand Duchess!	I will be your Grand Duchess!

300

(Dance.)   305

(Enter all the Chorus with LUDWIG, NOTARY, *and* LISA –
all greatly agitated.)

EXCITED CHORUS.

GIRLS.
    My goodness me! what shall I do? Why, what a dreadful situation!
MEN *(to* LUD.*)*.
    It's all your fault, you booby you – you lump of indiscrimination!
GIRLS *and* MEN.
    I'm sure I don't know where to go – it's put me into such a tetter –   310
    But this at all events I know – the sooner we are off, the better!

ERN.   What means this *agitato*? What d'ye seek?
        As your Grand Duke elect I bid you speak!

SONG – LUDWIG.

Ten minutes since I met a chap
    Who bowed an easy salutation –   315
Thinks I, 'This gentleman, mayhap,
    Belongs to our Association.'
        But, on the whole,
        Uncertain yet,
        A sausage-roll   320
        I took and eat –
That chap replied (I don't embellish)
By eating *three* with obvious relish.

CHORUS *(angrily)*.   Why, gracious powers,
                No chum of ours   325
      Could eat three sausage-rolls with relish!

327 *Quite reassured*: These words appear in the first night libretto and the World's Classics edition of the Savoy Operas. Both the current Chappell libretto and vocal score, however, have: ''Then reassured'.

335 *the more I muckled*: Is there such a verb as muckle? I don't think so. The *Oxford English Dictionary* simply allows its use as an adjective, noun or adverb. That dictionary gives the meaning of muckle as a large quantity or amount of something and suggests that it is interchangeable with the word mickle. Hence my note about the phrase ' 'Tis but mickle sister reaps' in *The Yeomen of the Guard*, Act 2, line 567. I have quite reasonably been taken to task for this by Thomas Potts of St Cyprien in France who points to the old Scottish saying 'Many a mickle makes a muckle' as suggesting that mickle should properly mean a little and muckle a lot. That is certainly how I have always understood it and how Gilbert clearly did too – but who are we to disagree with the Oxford lexicographers? Such dilemmas are certainly muckle (or should it be mickle?) for one foolish enough to attempt the task of annotating G & S!

349 *Grand Duke Rudolph's own detective*: This is the first time in the opera that the Grand Duke is mentioned by name. As has already been pointed out, Gilbert initially called him Grand Duke Wilhelm and the land over which he presided Hesse Halbpfennig. There was, in fact, a real-life Grand Duchy of Hesse in the 1890s. Made up of a number of smaller territories, including Hesse-Cassel and Hesse-Damstadt, it had since 1866 formed part of the German Empire. There had also, within comparatively recent memory, been Grand Dukes in Hesse by the name of Friedrich Wilhelm. One of them, who was George III's grandson, and who had presided over Hesse-Cassel had even, according to some sources, been nicknamed 'Halbpfennig' on account of his greedy financial practices.

At one stage Gilbert contemplated changing the Grand Duke's name to Max but it appeared as Wilhelm in the libretto used for rehearsal. It is unclear whether the late change to Rudolph, and the switch from Hesse Halbpfennig to Pfennig Halbpfennig, was made in order not to give offence to the Germans. Arthur Jacobs points out in his biography of Sullivan that as the date neared for the opening of *The Grand Duke* Anglo-German hostility was rising. The defeat of the Jameson Raid, in which the British made a foray into Boer territory, prompted the German emperor (who was also called Wilhelm and was Queen Victoria's grandson) to send a telegram of congratulation to Kruger, the Boer president. It would not have been surprising in these circumstances if Gilbert had made the tone of his new work more anti-German and it is something of a mystery why he removed all references which could possibly offend the Germans (see also note to lines 549–56) unless it was for the sake of the Queen.

The Grand Duke's detective who is mentioned here was at one stage in Gilbert's plans to have been a significant character in the play. Indeed, the manuscript notebook now in the British Library indicates that he was going to be given at least one song, making him, perhaps, the prototype for Dennis Potter's singing detective who made such an impact on British television in the early 1980s.

LUD.	Quite reassured, I let him know	
	Our plot – each incident explaining;	
	That stranger chuckled much, as though	
	He thought me highly entertaining.	330
	I told him all,	
	Both bad and good;	
	I bade him call –	
	He said he would:	
	I added much – the more I muckled,	335
	The more that chuckling chummy chuckled!	

ALL (*angrily*).	A bat could see	
	He couldn't be	
	A chum of ours if he chuckled!	

LUD.	Well, as I bowed to his applause,	340
	Down dropped he with hysteric bellow –	
	And *that* seemed right enough, because	
	I *am* a devilish funny fellow.	
	Then suddenly,	
	As still he squealed,	
	It flashed on me	345
	That I'd revealed	
	Our plot, with all details effective,	
	To Grand Duke Rudolph's own detective!	

ALL.	What folly fell,	350
	To go and tell	
	Our plot to any one's detective!	

CHORUS.

(*Attacking* LUDWIG.)

You booby dense –
You oaf immense,   355
With no pretence
To common sense!
A stupid muff
Who's made of stuff
Not worth a puff   360
Of candle-snuff!

Pack up at once and off we go, unless we're anxious to exhibit
Our fairy forms all in a row, strung up upon the Castle gibbet!

371   *who presents himself*: At this point in the first night libretto Ludwig has the following lines
      (which were heard on the BBC recording):

> LUDWIG. Yes – I should never do that. If I were chairman of this gang, I should hesitate
> to enrol any baboon who couldn't produce satisfactory credentials from his last Zoological
> Gardens.

376   *English remarks*: The BBC recording followed the first night libretto in including at this
      point the words 'that would shrivel your trusting nature into raisins'.

385   *It's not the game*: Yet another piece of dialogue now cut but included in the first night
      libretto and the BBC recording follows here:

> LUDWIG. When one of the Human Family proposes to eat a sausage-roll, it is his duty
> to ask himself, 'Am I a conspirator?' And if, on examination, he finds that he is not a con-
> spirator, he is bound in honour to select some other form of refreshment.
> LISA. Of course he is. One should always play the game, etc.

394–5   *a Statutory Duel*: Duelling was banned in the British Army in 1844 and the last fatal duel
        in Great Britain took place in 1852. The practice lingered on longer on the Continent.

397   *A Stat-tat-tatutory Duel*: At this point in both the first night libretto and the BBC re-
      cording Julia follows her attempt to get round the words 'Statutory Duel' by remarking
      'Ach! what a crack-jaw language this German is.'

400   *the laws of Pfennig Halbpfennig*: The first night libretto adds the useful information here
      that the laws of Pfennig Halbpfennig are 'framed upon those of Solon, the Athenian
      law-giver'. It also points out that their natural death after a hundred years is again
      modelled on the laws of Solon.

(*Exeunt Chorus. Manet* LUDWIG, LISA, ERNEST, JULIA, *and* NOTARY.)

JULIA. Well, a nice mess you've got us into! There's an end of our precious   365
plot! All up – pop – fizzle – bang – done for!

LUD. Yes, but – ha! ha! – fancy my choosing the Grand Duke's private
detective, of all men, to make a confidant of! When you come to think of it, it's
really devilish funny!

ERN. (*angrily*). When you come to think of it, it's extremely injudicious to   370
admit into a conspiracy every pudding-headed baboon who presents himself!

LISA. Ludwig is far from being a baboon. Poor boy, he could not help giving
us away – it's his trusting nature – he was deceived.

JULIA (*furiously*). His trusting nature! (*To* LUDWIG.) Oh, I should like to
talk to you in my own language for five minutes – only five minutes! I know some   375
good, strong, energetic English remarks – only you wouldn't understand them!

LUD. Here we perceive one of the disadvantages of a neglected education!

ERN. (*to* JULIA). And I suppose you'll never be my Grand Duchess now!

JULIA. Grand Duchess? My good friend, if you don't produce the piece
how can I play the part?   380

ERN. True. (*To* LUDWIG.) You see what you've done.

LUD. But, my dear sir, you don't seem to understand that the man ate three
sausage-rolls. Keep that fact steadily before you. Three large sausage-rolls.

JULIA. Bah! – Lots of people eat sausage-rolls who are not conspirators.

LUD. Then they shouldn't. It's bad form. It's not the game.   385

LISA. Of course. One should always play the game. (*To* NOTARY, *who has
been smiling placidly through this.*) What are you grinning at, you greedy old man?

NOT. Nothing – don't mind me. It is always amusing to the legal mind to see
a parcel of laymen bothering themselves about a matter which to a trained
lawyer presents no difficulty whatever.   390

ALL. No difficulty!

NOT. None whatever! The way out of it is quite simple.

ALL. Simple?

NOT. Certainly! Now attend. In the first place, you two men fight a
Statutory Duel.   395

ERN. A Statutory Duel?

JULIA. A Stat-tat-tatutory Duel!

LUD. Never heard of such a thing.

NOT. It is true that the practice has fallen into abeyance through disuse.
But all the laws of Pfennig Halbpfennig run for a hundred years, when they die   400
a natural death, unless, in the meantime, they have been revived for another
century. The Act that institutes the Statutory Duel was passed a hundred years
ago, and as it has never been revived, it expires tomorrow. So you're just in time.

JULIA. But what is the use of talking to us about Statutory Duels when we
none of us know what a Statutory Duel is?   405

NOT. Don't you? Then I'll explain.

426   *With falchions bright*: A falchion is a curved broad sword with the edge on the convex
side. It makes another appearance in song in that great student parody of Longfellow's
poem *Excelsior*, 'The Shades of night were falling fast' (otherwise known as 'Upidee'),
the second verse of which begins:

> His brow was sad, his eye beneath
> Flashed like a falchion from its sheath

434   *Orthography*: Correct spelling. There are not, in fact that many occasions in the Savoy
Operas where orthography forgoes her spells because of the exigence of rhyme. Duke
appears as 'dook' in *The Gondoliers* (Act I, line 872) to rhyme with 'peruke' and Russia is
somewhat needlessly changed to 'Russher' in *Trial by Jury* (line 383) to rhyme with usher.
Doubtless there are other examples as well – please don't send them to me on a postcard
– but on the whole Gilbert manages to avoid mis-spelling words for the sake of making
them rhyme.

435   *And 'ghost' is written 'ghoest'*: In a cutting review, the critic of the *Musical Standard* took this
line as symptomatic of a malaise running through the entire opera: 'In Mr Gilbert's
libretto one of the characters, for the sake of a rhyme, pronounces ghost as "ghoest". We
may be pardoned if we call *The Grand Duke* a "ghoest" of Gilbert and Sullivan opera.'

SONG – NOTARY.

About a century since,
   The code of the duello
     To sudden death
     For want of breath   410
   Sent many a strapping fellow.
The then presiding Prince
   (Who useless bloodshed hated),
     He passed an Act,
     Short and compact,   415
   Which may be briefly stated.
Unlike the complicated laws
A Parliamentary draftsman draws,
   It may be briefly stated.

ALL.

We know the complicated laws,   420
A Parliamentary draftsman draws,
   Cannot be briefly stated.

NOT.

By this ingenious law,
   If any two shall quarrel,
     They may not fight   425
     With falchions bright
   (Which seemed to him immoral);
But each a card shall draw,
   And he who draws the lowest
     Shall (so 'twas said)   430
     Be thenceforth dead –
In fact, a legal 'ghoest'
(When exigence of rhyme compels,
Orthography forgoes her spells,
   And 'ghost' is written 'ghoest').   435

ALL. (*aside*).

With what an emphasis he dwells
Upon 'orthography' and 'spells'!
   That kind of fun's the lowest.

NOT.

When off the loser's popped
   (By pleasing legal fiction),   440
     And friend and foe
     Have wept their woe
   In counterfeit affliction,
The winner must adopt
   The loser's poor relations –   445

457   *the Revising Barrister*: From 1843 the list of people eligible to vote in Parliamentary and local government elections was revised each autumn in courts held up and down the country by revising barristers. From 1888 they also revised parish burgess lists but in 1915 their revising duties were taken over by town and county clerks.

465   *King's evidence*: An accused person who gives evidence against other persons associated with him in an alleged crime and who is, in consideration thereof, not put on trial.

471–2   *it is a beautiful maxim of our glorious Constitution*: Shades of Sir Joseph Porter's 'It is one of the happiest characteristics of this glorious country' (*H.M.S. Pinafore*, Act II, line 232).

481   *Ludwig doesn't know what fear is*: There is an extra bit here in the first night libretto. Heard on the BBC recording, it runs as follows:

    LUDWIG. Oh, I don't mind this sort of duel.
    ERNEST. It's not like a duel with swords. I hate a duel with swords. It's not the blade I mind – it's the blood.
    LUDWIG. And I hate a duel with pistols. It's not the ball I mind – it's the bang.
    NOTARY. Altogether it is a great improvement on the old method of giving satisfaction.

> Discharge his debts,
> Pay all his bets,
> And take his obligations.
> In short, to briefly sum the case,
> The winner takes the loser's place,   450
> With all its obligations.

ALL.   How neatly lawyers state a case!
    The winner takes the loser's place,
    With all its obligations!

LUD. I see. The man who draws the lowest card —   455

NOT. Dies, *ipso facto*, a social death. He loses all his civil rights – his identity disappears – the Revising Barrister expunges his name from the list of voters, and the winner takes his place, whatever it may be, discharges all his functions, and adopts all his responsibilities.

ERN. This is all very well, as far as it goes, but it only protects one of us.   460
What's to become of the survivor?

LUD. Yes, that's an interesting point, because *I* might be the survivor.

NOT. The survivor goes at once to the Grand Duke, and, in a burst of remorse, denounces the dead man as the moving spirit of the plot. He is accepted as King's evidence, and, as a matter of course, receives a free pardon.   465
Tomorrow, when the law expires, the dead man will, *ipso facto*, come to life again – the Revising Barrister will restore his name to the list of voters, and he will resume all his obligations as though nothing unusual had happened.

JULIA. When he will be at once arrested, tried, and executed on the evidence of the informer! Candidly, my friend, I don't think much of your plot!   470

NOT. Dear, dear, dear, the ignorance of the laity! My good young lady, it is a beautiful maxim of our glorious Constitution that a man can only die once. Death expunges crime, and when he comes to life again, it will be with a clean slate.

ERN. It's really very ingenious.   475

LUD. (*to* NOTARY). My dear sir, we owe you our lives!

LISA (*aside to* LUDWIG). May I kiss him?

LUD. Certainly not: you're a big girl now. (*To* ERNEST.) Well, miscreant, are you prepared to meet me on the field of honour?

ERN. At once. By Jove, what a couple of fire-eaters we are!   480

LISA. Ludwig doesn't know what fear is.

NOT. Altogether it is a great improvement on the old method of giving satisfaction.

QUINTET – LUDWIG, LISA, NOTARY, ERNEST, *and* JULIA.

> Strange the views some people hold!
> Two young fellows quarrel –   485

495 *Ding dong! Ding dong*: These vocal imitations of the ringing of church bells closely recall the lines in the quartet 'Strange adventure' in *The Yeomen of the Guard*:

> While the funeral bell is tolling,
> Tolling, tolling, Bim-a-boom!

510 *If society were poll'd*: The first night libretto, followed in the Chatto edition of Gilbert's plays and the BBC recording, renders this and the next line rather differently:

> Some prefer the churchyard mould!
> Strange the views some people hold!

Then they fight, for both are bold –
Rage of both is uncontrolled –
Both are stretched out, stark and cold!
　　Prithee, where's the moral?
　　　Ding dong! Ding dong!　　　　　　490
There's an end to further action,
And this barbarous transaction
Is described as 'satisfaction'!
　　Ha! ha! ha! ha! satisfaction!
　　　Ding dong! Ding dong!　　　　　　495
Each is laid in churchyard mould –
Strange the views some people hold!

Better than the method old,
　　Which was coarse and cruel,
Is the plan that we've extolled.　　　　500
Sing thy virtues manifold
(Better than refinèd gold),
　　Statutory Duel!
　　　Sing song! Sing song!
Sword or pistol neither uses –　　　　　505
Playing card he lightly chooses,
And the loser simply loses!
　　Ha! ha! ha! ha! simply loses.
　　　Sing song! Sing song!
If society were poll'd!　　　　　　　　510
Who'd suppose the method old!
Strange the views some people hold.

NOT. (*offering a card to* ERNEST).
　　Now take a card and gaily sing
　　How little you care for Fortune's rubs –

ERN. (*drawing a card*).
　　Hurrah, hurrah! – I've drawn a King!　　515

ALL.　　　　　A King!
　　　　　He's drawn a King!
　　Sing Hearts and Diamonds, Spades and Clubs!

ALL (*dancing*).　　How strange a thing!
　　　　　He's drawn a King!　　　　　　520
　　An excellent card – his chance it aids –
　　Sing Diamonds and Hearts, Spades and Clubs –
　　Sing Diamonds, Hearts and Clubs and Spades!

546 *Dance and exeunt Ludwig etc.*: Michael Jefferson, an experienced Savoyard who has twice produced *The Grand Duke* and worked as the D'Oyly Carte Opera Company's Education Administrator, advises splitting the opera into three acts to avoid a very long first act of around 95 minutes. He recommends bringing the curtain down on Act I at this point and beginning a new Act II with the march and entrance of Grand Duke Rudolph.

547 *March*. This march begins with a drum roll very similar to that at the start of *H.M.S. Pinafore*.

548–55 *The good Grand Duke of Pfennig Halbpfennig*
This must surely go down as one of the worst choruses Gilbert ever wrote and one of the most difficult to set to music. Sullivan manages it somehow.

The text of this song printed for rehearsal purposes included descriptions of the Grand Duke as being 'of German royalty a sprig' and 'a miserable pig'. These were changed for the first night, presumably as part of the same desire not to offend German feeling which led to the substitution of 'Rudolph' for 'Wilhelm' (see note to line 349 above).

NOT. (*to* LUDWIG).
        Now take a card with heart of grace –
        (Whatever our fate, let's play our parts).   525

LUD. (*drawing card*).
        Hurrah, hurrah! – I've drawn an Ace!

ALL.   An Ace!
        He's drawn an Ace!
    Sing Clubs and Diamonds, Spades and Hearts!

ALL (*dancing*).   He's drawn an Ace!   530
        Observe his face –
    Such rare good fortune falls to few –
    Sing Clubs and Diamonds, Spades and Hearts –
    Sing Clubs, Spades, Hearts and Diamonds too!

NOT.   That both these maids may keep their troth,   535
        And never misfortune them befall,
    I'll hold 'em as trustee for both –
ALL.   He'll hold 'em both!
        Yes, he'll hold 'em both!
    Sing Hearts, Clubs, Diamonds, Spades and all!   540

ALL (*dancing*).   By joint decree

$$\text{As} \left\{ \begin{array}{l} \text{our} \\ \text{their} \end{array} \right\} \text{trustee}$$

$$\text{This Notary} \left\{ \begin{array}{l} \text{we} \\ \text{they} \end{array} \right\} \text{will now install} -$$

$$\text{In custody let him keep} \left\{ \begin{array}{l} \text{their} \\ \text{our} \end{array} \right\} \text{hearts,}$$

$$\text{By joint decree as} \left\{ \begin{array}{l} \text{our} \\ \text{your} \end{array} \right\} \text{trustee! \&c.} \qquad 545$$

(*Dance and exeunt* LUDWIG, ERNEST, *and* NOTARY *with the two Girls.*)

(*March. Enter the seven Chamberlains of the* GRAND DUKE RUDOLPH.)

CHORUS OF CHAMBERLAINS.

The good Grand Duke of Pfennig Halbpfennig,
Though, in his own opinion, very very big,
In point of fact he's nothing but a miserable prig   550
Is the good Grand Duke of Pfennig Halbpfennig!

567 *Observe. My Snuff box*: The BBC recording conveyed the idea of the snuff box being passed around by having a series of voices repeating the words 'snuff box' (and later 'handkerchief') with varying degrees of incredulity and impatience.

573 *my orders are emphatical*: Not another case of orthography forgoing her spells because of the exigence of rhyme (see note to line 435 above), as I at first supposed. There is a word 'emphatical' and what else, after all, can you find to rhyme with mathematical – unless, of course, you are Major-General Stanley and understand equations both simple and quadratical.

583 *It's stately and impressive*: The first night libretto, followed in the BBC recording but not on the 1976 D'Oyly Carte record, renders this line:

It's sometimes inconvenient, but it's always very cheap!

584 *My Lord Chamberlain*: This must surely count as the longest single speech in the Savoy Operas. When so many other bits of dialogue were pruned from the first night libretto, it is somewhat surprising that it escaped unscathed. It can hardly be described as riveting.

Though quite contemptible, as everyone agrees,
We must dissemble if we want our bread and cheese,
So hail him in a chorus, with enthusiasm big,
The good Grand Duke of Pfennig Halbpfennig!   555

(*Enter the* GRAND DUKE RUDOLPH. *He is meanly and miserably dressed in old and patched clothes, but blazes with a profusion of orders and decorations. He is very weak and ill, from low living.*)

SONG – RUDOLPH.

A pattern to professors of monarchical autonomy,
I don't indulge in levity or compromising *bonhomie*,   560
But dignified formality, consistent with economy,
    Above all other virtues I particularly prize.
I never join in merriment – I don't see joke or jape any –
I never tolerate familiarity in shape any –
This, joined with an extravagant respect for tuppence-ha'penny,   565
    A keynote to my character sufficiently supplies.

(*Speaking.*) Observe. (*To Chamberlains.*) My snuff-box!

(*The snuff-box is passed with much ceremony from the Junior Chamberlain, through all the others, until it is presented by the Senior Chamberlain to* RUDOLPH, *who uses it.*)

    570

That incident a keynote to my character supplies.

RUD. I weigh out tea and sugar with precision mathematical –
    Instead of beer, a penny each – my orders are emphatical –
    (Extravagance unpardonable, any more than that I call),
       But, on the other hand, my Ducal dignity to keep –   575
All Courtly ceremonial – to put it comprehensively –
I rigidly insist upon (but not, I hope, offensively)
Whenever ceremonial can be practised inexpensively –
    And, when you come to think of it, it's really very cheap!

(*Speaking.*) Observe. (*To Chamberlains.*) My handkerchief!   580

(*Handkerchief is handed by Junior Chamberlain to the next in order, and so on until it reaches* RUDOLPH, *who is much inconvenienced by the delay.*)

It's stately and impressive, and it's really very cheap!

RUD. My Lord Chamberlain, as you are aware, my marriage with the wealthy Baroness von Krakenfeldt will take place tomorrow, and you will be   585

593 *Speisesaal*: As all German scholars and most package-holiday enthusiasts will know, this word means dining room, though it can also be used of a banqueting hall, refectory or officers' mess.

594–5 *At night, everybody will illuminate*: I cannot resist pointing out the similarity of this line to the memorable phrase delivered by Lieutenant Commander Thomas Woodroofe in the first live outside broadcast on BBC television on the occasion of the Coronation naval review at Spithead in May 1937: 'The fleet is all lit up'.

620 *jujube*: The *Oxford English Dictionary* informs us that a jujube is an edible berry-like drupe, the fruit of various species of the Zizyphus plant. It goes on to say that the Zizyphus is found in different forms in the Mediterranean, China and North Africa. The word 'jujube' can also be used of a lozenge made of gelatin flavoured with or in imitation of this fruit – I rather suspect that it is this latter kind of jujube that the Baroness offers Rudolph for his breakfast – the real thing would be much too expensive and extravagant.

good enough to see that the rejoicings are on a scale of unusual liberality. Pass
that on. (*Chamberlain whispers to Vice-Chamberlain, who whispers to the next, and so
on.*) The sports will begin with a Wedding Breakfast Bee. The leading pastry-
cooks of the town will be invited to compete, and the winner will not only enjoy
the satisfaction of seeing his breakfast devoured by the Grand Ducal pair, but 590
he will also be entitled to have the Arms of Pfennig Halbpfennig tattoo'd between his shoulder-blades. The Vice-Chamberlain will see to this. All the public
fountains of Speisesaal will run with Gingerbierheim and Currantweinmilch at
the public expense. The Assistant Vice-Chamberlain will see to this. At night,
everybody will illuminate; and as I have no desire to tax the public funds un- 595
duly, this will be done at the inhabitants' private expense. The Deputy Assistant
Vice-Chamberlain will see to this. All my Grand Ducal subjects will wear new
clothes, and the Sub-Deputy Assistant Vice-Chamberlain will collect the usual
commission on all sales. Wedding presents (which, on this occasion, should be
on a scale of extraordinary magnificence) will be received at the Palace at any 600
hour of the twenty-four, and the Temporary Sub-Deputy Assistant Vice-
Chamberlain will sit up all night for this purpose. The entire population will be
commanded to enjoy themselves, and with this view the Acting Temporary
Sub-Deputy Assistant Vice-Chamberlain will sing comic songs in the Market-
place from noon to nightfall. Finally, we have composed a Wedding Anthem, 605
with which the entire population are required to provide themselves. It can be
obtained from our Grand Ducal publishers at the usual discount price, and all
the Chamberlains will be expected to push the sale. (*Chamberlains bow and exeunt.*) I don't feel at all comfortable. I hope I'm not doing a foolish thing in getting married. After all, it's a poor heart that never rejoices, and this wedding of 610
mine is the first little treat I've allowed myself since my christening. Besides,
Caroline's income is very considerable, and as her ideas of economy are quite on
a par with mine, it ought to turn out well. Bless her tough old heart, she's a
mean little darling! Oh, here she is, punctual to her appointment!

        (*Enter* BARONESS VON KRAKENFELDT.) 615

BAR. Rudolph! Why, what's the matter?
RUD. Why, I'm not quite myself, my pet. I'm a little worried and upset. I
want a tonic. It's the low diet, I think. I am afraid, after all, I shall have to take the
bull by the horns and have an egg with my breakfast.
    BAR. I shouldn't do anything rash, dear. Begin with a jujube. (*Gives him one.*) 620
    RUD. (*about to eat it, but changes his mind*). I'll keep it for supper. (*He sits by her
and tries to put his arm round her waist.*)
    BAR. Rudolph, don't! What in the world are you thinking of?
    RUD. I was thinking of embracing you, my sugar-plum. Just as a little cheap
treat. 625
    BAR. What, here? In public? Really, you appear to have no sense of delicacy.
    RUD. No sense of delicacy, Bon-bon!

636 *the reign of Charlemagne*: Now this all depends on which reign you mean – take your pick
between his time as King of Franks (768–814), King of the Lombards (774–814) or Holy
Roman Emperor (800–814). Whichever way, they are pretty old drains.

663–4 *you were betrothed in infancy to the Princess of Monte Carlo*: Gilbert reverts here to a theme
which he had already made much of in an earlier opera. Central to the plot of *The Gondoliers* is the marriage by proxy of the six-month-old daughter of the Duke of Plaza-
Toro to the infant son of the King of Barataria.
     Interestingly, Gilbert originally gave the same name to the object of the Grand Duke's
infant betrothal as he had to the Duke of Plaza-Toro's daughter. The earliest draft of the
plot of *The Grand Duke* contained in his notebook now in the British Library has the
Grand Duke Wilhelm, as he then was, betrothed to Casilda, daughter of the King and
Queen of Castile. Subsequently, her parents were changed to being the Prince and Princess of Monaco and she was re-named Carlotta before eventually she became simply the
Princess of Monte Carlo with no name specified in the list of *dramatis personae* or in the
course of the opera.
     Why Gilbert changed the home of the princess from Castile to Monaco and then
again to Monte Carlo is not clear, unless it was to gain more syllables to facilitate rhyming. Conceivably, it was Sullivan who suggested or prompted the final choice – Monte
Carlo was a favourite retreat of the composer. He was there in 1888, twice in 1892 and
again in 1895.

BAR. No. I can't make you out. When you courted me, all your courting was done publicly in the Market-place. When you proposed to me, you proposed in the Market-place. And now that we're engaged you seem to desire that our first 630 *tête-à-tête* shall occur in the Market-place! Surely you've a room in your Palace – with blinds – that would do?

RUD. But, my own, I can't help myself. I'm bound by my own decree.

BAR. Your own decree?

RUD. Yes. You see, all the houses that give on the Market-place belong to 635 me, but the drains (which date back to the reign of Charlemagne) want attending to, and the houses wouldn't let – so, with a view to increasing the value of the property, I decreed that all love-episodes between affectionate couples should take place, in public, on this spot, every Monday, Wednesday, and Friday, when the band doesn't play. 640

BAR. Bless me, what a happy idea! So moral too! And have you found it answer?

RUD. Answer? The rents have gone up fifty per cent., and the sale of opera-glasses (which is a Grand Ducal monopoly) has received an extraordinary stimulus! So, under the circumstances, *would* you allow me to put my arm 645 round your waist? As a source of income. Just once!

BAR. But it's so very embarrassing. Think of the opera-glasses!

RUD. My good girl, that's just what I *am* thinking of. Hang it all, we must give them *something* for their money! What's that?

BAR. (*unfolding paper, which contains a large letter, which she hands to him*). It's a 650 letter which your detective asked me to hand to you. I wrapped it up in yesterday's paper to keep it clean.

RUD. Oh, it's only his report! That'll keep. But, I say, you've never been and bought a newspaper?

BAR. My dear Rudolph, do you think I'm mad? It came wrapped round my 655 breakfast.

RUD. (*relieved*). I thought you were not the sort of girl to go and buy a newspaper! Well, as we've got it, we may as well read it. What does it say?

BAR. Why – dear me – here's your biography! 'Our Detested Despot!'

RUD. Yes – I fancy that refers to me. 660

BAR. And it says – Oh, it can't be!

RUD. What can't be?

BAR. Why, it says that although you're going to marry me tomorrow, you were betrothed in infancy to the Princess of Monte Carlo!

RUD. Oh yes – that's quite right. Didn't I mention it? 665

BAR. Mention it! You never said a word about it!

RUD. It's so like me! Well, it doesn't matter, because, you see, it's practically off.

BAR. Practically off?

RUD. Yes. By the terms of the contract the betrothal is void unless the Prin- 670 cess marries before she is of age. Now, her father, the Prince, is stony-broke, and

701 *No doubt it is expensive*: We come here to the first of five significant cuts which were made
in *The Grand Duke* during the course of the twentieth century. It is a little difficult to be
precise about exactly when they were made, not least because of the absence of any professional performances of the opera between 1896 and 1975, but they certainly had the
authorization of Dame Bridget D'Oyly Carte. It is possible that they were made in an-
ticipation of a projected revival of the opera in the 1940s. Two involve substantial parts
of songs (this one and Julia's song 'Ah, pity me, my comrades true') while the others
involve the deletion of whole numbers ('Come bumpers aye ever so many', 'Take my
advice when deep in debt' and 'Well, you're a pretty kind of fellow').

The Oxford University Press World's Classics edition of the Savoy Operas, published
in 1963, reflects these cuts. So does the official production text for the 1975 revival of the
opera. However, much of the material that was cut found its way back into the 1976
D'Oyly Carte record of *The Grand Duke* and it is virtually all included in the current
Chappell editions of the vocal score and libretto. As a result, it is often used in amateur
productions and I have therefore felt it right to include it in the text of this book, indicating in the notes where cuts have been made.

In this particular instance, the material cut in the World's Classics edition of the
Savoy Operas is also missing from the 1926 Chatto edition of Gilbert's plays. It is also
absent from the 1976 D'Oyly Carte recording. In all these sources, the line 'no doubt it
is expensive' leads straight on to 'Oh, he who has an income clear' (line 733).

hasn't left his house for years for fear of arrest. Over and over again he has implored me to come to him to be married – but in vain. Over and over again he
has implored me to advance him the money to enable the Princess to come to
me – but in vain. I am very young, but not as young as that; and as the Princess   675
comes of age at two tomorrow, why, at two tomorrow I'm a free man, so I
appointed that hour for our wedding, as I shall like to have as much marriage as
I can get for my money.

BAR. I see. Of course, if the married state is a happy state, it's a pity to waste
any of it.   680

RUD. Why, every hour we delayed I should lose a lot of you and you'd lose a
lot of me!

BAR. My thoughtful darling! Oh, Rudolph, we ought to be very happy!

RUD. If I'm not, it'll be my first bad investment. Still, there *is* such a thing as
a slump even in Matrimonials.   685

BAR. I often picture us in the long, cold, dark December evenings, sitting
close to each other and singing impassioned duets to keep us warm, and thinking of all the lovely things we could afford to buy if we chose, and, at the same
time, planning out our lives in a spirit of the most rigid and exacting economy!

RUD. It's a most beautiful and touching picture of connubial bliss in its   690
highest and most rarefied development!

DUET – BARONESS *and* RUDOLPH.

BAR.

> As o'er our penny roll we sing,
>   It is not reprehensive
> To think what joys our wealth would bring
> Were we disposed to do the thing   695
>   Upon a scale extensive.
> There's rich mock-turtle – thick and clear –

RUD. (*confidentially*).

> Perhaps we'll have it once a year!

BAR. (*delighted*).   You *are* an open-handed dear!

RUD.   Though, mind you, it's expensive.   700

BAR.   No doubt it *is* expensive.

BOTH.

> How fleeting are the glutton's joys!
> With fish and fowl he lightly toys,

RUD.

> And pays for such expensive tricks
> Sometimes as much as two-and-six!   705

BAR. (*surprised*).   As two-and-six?

RUD.   As two-and-six!

BOTH.   Sometimes as much as two-and-six!
                 It gives him no advantage, mind –
                 For you and he have only dined.   710

BAR.   And you remain, when once it's down,
                 A better man by half-a-crown!

RUD. (*doubtfully*).   By half a crown?
BAR. (*decisively*).   By half a crown!
BOTH.   Yes, two-and-six is half a crown.   715
   (*Dancing.*) Then let us be modestly merry,
                 And rejoice with a derry down derry,
                     For to laugh and to sing
                     No extravagance bring –
                 It's a joy economical, very!   720

BAR.   Although, as you're of course aware
                 (I never tried to hide it),
                 I moisten my insipid fare
                 With water – which I can't abear –

RUD.   Nor I – I can't abide it.   725
BAR.   This pleasing fact our souls will cheer
                 With fifty thousand pounds a year
                 We *could* indulge in table beer!

RUD. (*incredulously*).   Get out!
BAR.   We could – I've tried it!   730
RUD.   God bless my soul, she's tried it!

BOTH.   Oh, he who has an income clear
                 Of fifty thousand pounds a year –
BAR.   Can purchase all his fancy loves,
                 Conspicuous hats –   735
RUD.   Two-shilling gloves –
BAR. (*doubtfully*).   Two-shilling gloves?
RUD. (*positively*).   Two-shilling gloves –
BOTH.   Yes, think of that, two-shilling gloves!
BAR.   Cheap shoes and ties of gaudy hue,   740
                 And Waterbury watches, too –
                 And think that he could buy the lot
                 Were he a donkey –
RUD.   Which he's *not*!
BAR.   Oh no, he's *not*!   745

757-8 *For the future I'll employ none but Scotchmen*: Gilbert generally steers clear of jokes at the expense of the Scots, Welsh or Irish. I suppose this remark could, indeed, be construed as a compliment to the Scots, suggesting as it does that they are serious-minded and not diverted from their task by humour. One would certainly expect Gilbert to be pro-Scottish. His mother was the daughter of a Scottish doctor (of whom little is known beyond the fact that he had the rather Welsh-sounding name of Thomas Morris) and he himself was a captain in the Royal Aberdeenshire Highlanders militia.

One of Sullivan's other librettists had no such qualms about jokes at the expense of the Scots. For *Haddon Hall* (1892) Sydney Grundy created the character of McCrankie, a grotesque mixture of dour Calvinism and over-indulgence with the whisky bottle.

762-800 *When you find you're a broken-down critter*

This patter song, which has obvious affinities with the Lord Chancellor's nightmare song in *Iolanthe*, had its origin in a number which Gilbert had written for *The Mountebanks*, an operetta on which he collaborated with the composer Alfred Cellier and which was first performed at the Lyric Theatre in January 1892. Cellier died before he was able to set this particular song and it did not appear in the English libretto of *The Mountebanks*. However, it was included in the American libretto and apparently sung when the work was put on in New York. It was written for the character of Pietro, the proprietor of a troupe of mountebanks who is dying by slow poisoning, and went as follows:

When your clothes, from your hat to your socks,
   Have tickled and scrubbed you all day;
When your brain is a musical box
   With a barrel that turns the wrong way;
When you find you're too big for your coat,
   And a great deal too small for your vest,
With a pint of warm oil in your throat,
   And a pound of tin-tacks in your chest;
When you've got a beehive in your head,
   And a sewing-machine in each ear;
And you feel that you've eaten your bed,
   And you've got a bad headache down here;
When your lips are like underdone paste,
   And you're highly gamboge in the gill;
And your mouth has a coppery taste,
   As if you'd just eaten a pill;
     And whatever you tread,
      From a yawning abyss
       You recoil with a yell, –
     You are better in bed,
      For, depend upon this,
       You are not at all well.

When everything spins like a top
   And your stock of endurance gives out;
If some miscreant proposes a chop
   (Mutton-chop, with potatoes and stout),
When your mouth is of flannel – like mine –
   And your teeth not on terms with their stumps,
And spiders crawl over your spine,
   And when your muscles have all got the mumps;
When you're bad with the creeps and the crawls,
   And the shivers, and shudders, and shakes,
And the pattern that covers the walls
   Is alive with black-beetles and snakes;
When you doubt if your head is your own,
   And you jump when an open door slams,

RUD.	Oh no, he's *not*!
BOTH (*dancing*).	That kind of donkey he is *not*!

Then let us be modestly merry,
And rejoice with a derry down derry,
    For to laugh and to sing   750
    Is a rational thing –
It's a joy economical, very!   (*Exit* BARONESS.)

RUD. Oh, now for my detective's report. (*Opens letter.*) What's this! Another
conspiracy! A conspiracy to depose *me*! And my private detective was so
convulsed with laughter at the notion of a conspirator selecting him for a   755
confidant that he was physically unable to arrest the malefactor! Why, it'll come
off! This comes of engaging a detective with a keen sense of the ridiculous!
For the future I'll employ none but Scotchmen. And the plot is to explode
tomorrow! My wedding day! Oh, Caroline, Caroline! (*Weeps.*) This is perfectly
frightful! What's to be done? I don't know! And I'm going to be ill! I know I am!   760
I've been living too low, and I'm going to be very ill indeed!

SONG – RUDOLPH.

When you find you're a broken-down critter,
Who is all of a trimmle and twitter,
With your palate unpleasantly bitter,
    As if you'd just bitten a pill –   765
When your legs are as thin as dividers,
And you're plagued with unruly 'insiders',
And your spine is all creepy with spiders,
    And you're highly gamboge in the gill –
        Creepy! Creepy!   770
When you've got a beehive in your head,
    And a sewing machine in each ear,
And you feel that you've eaten your bed,
    And you've got a bad headache *down here* –
      When such facts are about,   775
      And those symptoms you find
        In your body or crown –
      It's a shady look out,
      You may make up your mind
        You had better lie down!   780
        Go at once, go at once, and lie down!

When your lips are all smeary – like tallow,
And your tongue is decidedly yallow,
With a pint of warm oil in your swallow,
    And a pound of tin-tacks in your chest –   785

And you've got to the state which is known
To the medical world as 'jim-jams', –
If such medical symptoms you find
In your body or head
They're not easy to quell
You may make up your mind
That you're better in bed,
For you're not at all well!

787 *Morris wallpapers*: A reference to the designs of William Morris (1834–96), the Pre-Raphaelite artist who was also a prominent poet and early Socialist. He gets another mention in *Ruddigore* (Act I, line 402).

Like the mention of Waterbury watches (line 742 above) this is, of course, a highly anachronistic reference. How on earth could people living in Pfennig-Halbpfennig in 1750, which is when *The Grand Duke* was set, possibly know of English wallpapers produced more than a century later? At least, I suppose, their ability to see into the future was not quite as spectacular as it would have been had Gilbert stuck to his earlier intention, revealed in his manuscript notebooks, to set the action in the 1580s (13 September 1584 to be exact according to one note and for those who are really into the minutiae).

805–6 *What are you doing there? Get up, sir*: This line is not in the first night libretto.

808–9 *my Acting Temporary Sub-Deputy Assistant Vice-Chamberlain*: Who, according to extra dialogue in the first night libretto, 'will fling himself at the feet of his immediate superior, and so on, with successive foot-flingings through the various grades.'

When you're down in the mouth with the vapours,
And all over your Morris wall-papers
Black-beetles are cutting their capers,
    And crawly things never at rest –
          Crawly things! Crawly things!   790
When you doubt if your head is your own,
    And you jump when an open door slams –
Then you've got to a state which is known
    To the medical world as 'jim-jams'.
      If such symptoms you find   795
        In your body or head,
          They're not easy to quell –
    You may make up your mind
      You are better in bed,
        For you're not at all well!   800

(Sinks exhausted and weeping at foot of well.)

(Enter LUDWIG.*)*

LUD. Now for my confession and full pardon. They told me the Grand
Duke was dancing duets in the Market-place, but I don't see him. *(Sees*
RUDOLPH.*)* Hallo! Who's this? *(Aside.)* Why, it *is* the Grand Duke! What are   805
you doing there? Get up, sir!

RUD. *(sobbing).* Who are you, sir, who presume to address me in person? If
you've anything to communicate, you must fling yourself at the feet of my Acting Temporary Sub-Deputy Assistant Vice-Chamberlain – your communication will, in course of time, come to my august knowledge.   810

LUD. But when I inform your Highness that in me you see the most unhappy, the most unfortunate, the most completely miserable man in your whole
dominion —

RUD. *(still sobbing). You* the most miserable man in my whole dominion? How
can you have the face to stand there and say such a thing? Why, look at me! Look   815
at me!   *(Bursts into tears.)*

LUD. Well, I wouldn't be a cry-baby.

RUD. A cry-baby? If you had just been told that you were going to be deposed tomorrow, and perhaps blown up with dynamite for all I know, wouldn't
you be a cry-baby? I do declare if I could only hit upon some cheap and painless   820
method of putting an end to an existence which has become insupportable, I
would unhesitatingly adopt it!

LUD. You would? *(Aside.)* I see a magnificent way out of this! By Jupiter, I'll
try it! *(Aloud.)* Are you, by any chance, in earnest?

843   *But suppose I were to lose*: This looks like a very rare example of Gilbert making a mistake. In line 831 Ludwig tells Rudolph: 'You fight-you lose-you are dead for a day.' He subsequently makes sure that Rudoph will lose the duel by putting an Ace up his own sleeve and a King up Rudolph's. Surely, therefore, this line should be 'But suppose I were to win?'. I am grateful to John Holt, producer of the superb centenary production of *The Grand Duke* by the City of Durham (New College) Light Opera Group performed on 7 March 1996, for pointing out this uncharacteristic Gilbertian gaffe.

859   *Oh, a devil of a quarrel*: At this point the first night libretto has the following interpolation by Rudolph:

No half-measures. Big words – strong language – rude remarks. Oh, a devil of a quarrel!

RUD. In earnest? Why, look at me! 825

LUD. If you are really in earnest – if you really desire to escape scot-free from this impending – this unspeakably horrible catastrophe – without trouble, danger, pain, or expense – why not resort to a Statutory Duel?

RUD. A Statutory Duel?

LUD. Yes. The Act is still in force, but it will expire tomorrow afternoon. 830
You fight – you lose – you are dead for a day. Tomorrow, when the Act expires, you will come to life again and resume your Grand Duchy as though nothing had happened. In the meantime, the explosion will have taken place and the survivor will have had to bear the brunt of it.

RUD. Yes, that's all very well, but who'll be fool enough to *be* the survivor? 835

LUD. (*kneeling*). Actuated by an overwhelming sense of attachment to your Grand Ducal person, I unhesitatingly offer myself as the victim of your subjects' fury.

RUD. You do? Well, really that's very handsome. I daresay being blown up is not nearly as unpleasant as one would think. 840

LUD. Oh, yes it is. It mixes one up, awfully!

RUD. But suppose I were to lose?

LUD. Oh, that's easily arranged. (*Producing cards.*) I'll put an Ace up my sleeve – you'll put a King up yours. When the drawing takes place, I shall seem to draw the higher card and you the lower. And there you are! 845

RUD. Oh, but that's cheating.

LUD. So it is. I never thought of that. (*Going.*)

RUD. (*hastily*). Not that I mind. But I say – you won't take an unfair advantage of your day of office? You won't go tipping people, or squandering my little savings in fireworks, or any nonsense of that sort? 850

LUD. I am hurt – really hurt – by the suggestion.

RUD. You – you wouldn't like to put down a deposit, perhaps?

LUD. No. I don't think I should like to put down a deposit.

RUD. Or give a guarantee?

LUD. A guarantee would be equally open to objection. 855

RUD. It would be more regular. Very well, I suppose you must have your own way.

LUD. Good. I say – we must have a devil of a quarrel!

RUD. Oh, a devil of a quarrel!

LUD. Just to give colour to the thing. Shall I give you a sound thrashing 860
before all the people? Say the word – it's no trouble.

RUD. No, no, I think not, though it would be very convincing and it's extremely good and thoughtful of you to suggest it. Still, a devil of a quarrel!

LUD. Oh, a devil of a quarrel! Now the question is, how shall we summon the people? 865

RUD. Oh, there's no difficulty about that. Bless your heart, they've been staring at us through those windows for the last half-hour!

868–78 *Come hither, all you people*
The first night libretto distributes these lines as follows:

RUDOLPH.   Come hither, all you people –
                                       When you hear the fearful news,
                            All the pretty women weep'll,
                                       Men will shiver in their shoes.

LUDWIG.   And they'll all cry 'Lord, defend us!'
                            When they learn the fact tremendous
                                       That to give this man his gruel
                                       In a Statutory Duel –

BOTH.   This plebeian man of shoddy –
                            This contemptible nobody –
                                       Your Grand Duke does not refuse.

893 *Now you begin*: The current Chappell editions of the libretto and vocal score have 'No, you begin' here. This is also what John Reed sings on the 1976 D'Oyly Carte record. The Oxford World's Classics edition, prepared under the supervision of Dame Bridget D'Oyly Carte, however, has 'now' as opposite.

FINALE.

RUD.	Come hither, all you people –
	When you hear the fearful news,
LUD.	All the pretty women weep'll, 870
	Men will shiver in their shoes.

BOTH.	And they'll all cry 'Lord, defend us!'
	When they learn the fact tremendous
RUD.	That to give this man his gruel
LUD.	In a Statutory Duel – 875

RUD.	This plebeian man of shoddy –
LUD.	This contemptible nobody –
BOTH.	Your Grand Duke does not refuse!

(During this, Chorus of men and women have entered, all trembling with apprehension under the impression that they are to be arrested for their complicity in   880 the conspiracy.)

CHORUS.	With faltering feet,
	And our muscles in a quiver,
	Our fate we meet
	With our feelings all unstrung! 885
	If our plot complete
	He has managed to diskiver,
	There is no retreat –
	We shall certainly be hung!

RUD. (*aside to* LUDWIG).
    Now *you* begin and pitch it strong – walk into me abusively –   890
LUD. (*aside to* RUDOLPH).
    I've several epithets that I've reserved for you exclusively.
    A choice selection I have here when you are ready *to* begin.
RUD.
    Now *you* begin —
LUD.   No, *you* begin —
RUD.   No, *you* begin —   895
LUD.   No, *you* begin!
CHORUS (*trembling*).
    Has it happed as we expected?
    Is our little plot detected?

DUET – RUDOLPH *and* LUDWIG.

RUD. (*furiously*).	Big bombs, small bombs, great guns and little ones!
	Put him in a pillory! 900
	Rack him with artillery!

913 *When two doughty heroes thunder*: The current Chappell editions of the libretto and vocal
score follow the first night libretto in including material here which was cut in the
World's Classics edition and in the D'Oyly Carte recording:

CHORUS.   When two doughty heroes thunder,
                     All the world is lost in wonder;
                     When such men their tempers lose,
                     Awful are the words they use!
LUDWIG.   Tall snobs, small snobs, rich snobs and needy ones!
RUDOLPH (*jostling him*). Whom are you alluding to?
LUDWIG (*jostling him*).   Where are you intruding to?
RUDOLPH.   Fat snobs, thin snobs, swell snobs and seedy ones!
LUDWIG.   I rather think you err.
                     To whom do you refer?
RUDOLPH.   To you, sir!
LUDWIG.   To me, sir?
RUDOLPH.   I do, sir!
LUDWIG.   We'll see, sir!
RUDOLPH.   I jeer, sir!
(*Makes a face at* LUDWIG.) Grimace, sir!
LUDWIG.   Look here, sir!
(*Makes a face at* RUDOLPH.) A face, sir!
CHORUS (*appalled*). When two heroes, once pacific,
                     Quarrel, the effect's terrific!
                     What a horrible grimace!
                     What a paralysing face!
ALL.   Big bombs, small bombs, etc.
LUDWIG & RUDOLPH (*recit.*). He has insulted me, etc.

LUD. (*furiously*). Long swords, short swords, tough swords and brittle ones!
      Fright him into fits!
      Blow him into bits!
RUD.   You muff, sir!   905
LUD.   You lout, sir!
RUD.   Enough, sir!
LUD.   Get out, sir!   (*Pushes him*)
RUD.   A hit, sir?
LUD.   Take that, sir!   (*Slaps him*)   910
RUD.   It's tit, sir,
LUD.   For tat, sir!
CHORUS (*appalled*). When two doughty heroes thunder,
      All the world is lost in wonder;
      When two heroes, once pacific,   915
      Quarrel, the effect's terrific!
LUD. *and* RUD. (*recitative*). He has insulted me, and, in a breath,
      This day we fight a duel to the death!
NOT. (*checking them*). You mean, of course, by duel (*verbum sat.*),
      A Statutory Duel.   920
ALL.   What is that?
NOT.   According to established legal uses,
      A card apiece each bold disputant chooses –
      Dead as a doornail is the dog who loses –
      The winner steps into the dead man's shoeses!   925
ALL.   Dead as a doornail, &c.
RUD. *and* LUD.   Agreed! Agreed!
RUD.   Come, come – the pack!
LUD. (*producing one*). Behold it here!   (*Hands pack to* NOTARY.)
RUD.   I'm on the rack!   930
LUD.   I quake with fear!

         (NOTARY *offers card to* LUDWIG.)
LUD.   First draw to you!
RUD.   If that's the case,
      Behold the King!   (*Drawing card from his sleeve.*)   935
LUD. (*same business*). Behold the Ace!
CHORUS.   Hurrah, hurrah! Our Ludwig's won,
      And wicked Rudolph's course is run –
      So Ludwig will as Grand Duke reign
      Till Rudolph comes to life again –   940
RUD.   Which will occur tomorrow!
      Yes, Yes, I'll come to life tomorrow!
GRET. (*with mocking curtsey*). My Lord Grand Duke, farewell!

958 *Rapscallions, in penitential fires*: There are echoes of two other operas in these lines. Rapscallions, and foreign-born ones at that, make an appearance in the finale of Act II of *Utopia Limited*. Penitential fires might, with a fairly amazing stretch of the imagination, make you think of Captain Shaw, the leader of the London Fire Brigade whose skill with the fire hose is hymned by the Fairy Queen in Act II of *Iolanthe*. Sir Eyre Massey Shaw, to give him his full name and title, was one of the many important personages present in the Savoy Theatre for the opening performance of The Grand Duke. According to the *Sunday Times*, 'the audience was, if possible, more brilliant than at any previous Savoy premiere, and celebrities were to be seen on every hand'. It also reported that 'the new opera was received with the utmost enthusiasm by a crowded house'.

979–93 *Oh, a monarch who boasts intellectual graces*
A patter song which comes pretty high up the tongue-twisting and breath-defying stakes, perhaps just a little behind 'I am the very model of a modern major-general' and the nightmare song from *Iolanthe*. Certainly, the great Keith Sandford sounds a shade breathless in the D'Oyly Carte recording.

A pleasant journey, very,
To your convenient cell   945
In yonder cemetery!

LISA (*curtseying*).   Though malcontents abuse you,
We're much distressed to lose you!
You were, when you were living,
So liberal, so forgiving!   950

BERTHA.   So merciful, so gentle!
So highly ornamental!

OLGA.   And now that you've departed,
You leave us broken-hearted!

ALL (*pretending to weep*).   Yes, truly, truly, truly, truly –   955
Truly broken-hearted!
Ha! ha! ha! ha! ha! ha!   (*Mocking him.*)

RUD. (*furious*).   Rapscallions, in penitential fires,
You'll rue the ribaldry that from you falls!
Tomorrow afternoon the law expires,   960
And then – look out for squalls!

(*Exit* RUDOLPH, *amid general ridicule.*)

CHORUS.   Give thanks, give thanks to wayward fate –
By mystic fortune's sway,
Our Ludwig guides the helm of State   965
For one delightful day!

(*To* LUDWIG.)

We hail you, sir!
   We greet you, sir!
Regale you, sir!   970
   We treat you, sir!
Our ruler be
By fate's decree
For one delightful day!

NOT.   You've done it neatly! Pity that your powers   975
Are limited to four-and-twenty hours!

LUD.   No matter, though the time will quickly run,
In hours twenty-four much may be done!

SONG – LUDWIG *with* CHORUS.

Oh, a Monarch who boasts intellectual graces
Can do, if he likes, a good deal in a day –   980
He can put all his friends in conspicuous places,
With plenty to eat and with nothing to pay!

1002 *by Jingo*: I cannot recall another occasion in the Savoy Operas when this expression is
      used. *Brewer's Dictionary of Phrase and Fable* surmises that it comes from the patter of se-
      venteenth century conjurors. In the late 1870s, during the Russo-Turkish War, its use in
      a music hall song 'We don't want to fight, but by Jingo if we do', gave the word 'Jingoism'
      to the English language.

You'll tell me, no doubt, with unpleasant grimaces,
Tomorrow, deprived of your ribbons and laces,
You'll get your dismissal – with very long faces –   985
    But wait! on that topic I've something to say!
(Dancing)   I've something to say – I've something to say –

CHORUS.   He's something, &c.

Oh, our rule shall be merry – I'm not an ascetic –
    And while the sun shines we will get up our hay –   990
By a pushing young Monarch, of turn energetic,
    A very great deal may be done in a day!

CHORUS.   Oh, his rule will be merry, &c.

(During this, LUDWIG *whispers to* NOTARY, *who writes.)*

For instance, this measure (his ancestor drew it),   995
                                (Alluding to NOTARY*)*
    This law against duels – tomorrow will die –
The Duke will revive, and you'll certainly rue it –
    He'll give you 'what for' and he'll let you know why!
But in twenty-four hours there's time to renew it –   1000
With a century's life I've the right to imbue it –
It's easy to do – and, by Jingo, I'll do it!
                            (Signing paper, which NOTARY *presents)*
    It's done! Till I perish your Monarch am I!
Your Monarch am I – your Monarch am I!   1005

CHORUS.   Our Monarch, &c.

Though I do not pretend to be very prophetic,
    I fancy I know what you're going to say –
By a pushing young Monarch, of turn energetic,
    A very great deal may be done in a day!   1010

CHORUS *(astonished)*.
    Oh, it's simply uncanny, his power prophetic –
        It's perfectly right – we *were* going to say,
    By a pushing, &c.

1027–64 *Ah, pity me, my comrades true*
This song appears in full, as it is printed opposite, in the current editions of the libretto and vocal score. However, it is one of the numbers that was severely cut (see note to line 702 above) and the 1963 Oxford World's Classics edition offers this much truncated version which was used with some variations in both the 1976 record and the 1989 BBC recording:

SONG – JULIA (LISA *clinging to her*).

JULIA.	Ah, pity me, my comrades true,
	Who love, as well I know you do,
	This gentle child,
	To me so fondly dear!
ALL.	Why, what's the matter?
JULIA.	Each sympathetic tear will bruise
	When you have heard the frightful news
	Her love for him is all in all!
	Ah, cursed fate! that it should fall
	Unto *my* lot
	To break my darling's heart!
ALL.	Why, what's the matter?
JULIA.	Our duty, if we're wise, we never shun.
	This Spartan rule applies to every one.
	In theatres, as in life,
	Each has her line –
	This part – the Grand Duke's wife
	(Oh agony!) is mine!
ALL.	A maxim new I do not start –
	The canons of dramatic art
	Decree that this repulsive part
	(The Grand Duke's wife)
	Is mine!
	Oh, *that's* the matter!

LISA (*appalled, to* LUDWIG). Can this be so?

(*Enter* JULIA, *at back*.)

LUD. (*recitative*).	This very afternoon – at two (about) –	1015
	The Court appointments will be given out.	
	To each and all (for that was the condition)	
	According to professional position!	
ALL.	Hurrah! Hurrah!	
JULIA.	Oh heaven!	1020
CHORUS.	What's the matter?	
JULIA (*coming forward*).	According to professional position?	
LUD.	According to professional position!	
JULIA.	Then, horror!	
ALL.	Why, what's the matter? What's the matter?	1025
	What's the matter?	

SONG – JULIA (LISA *clinging to her*).

JULIA.   Ah, pity me, my comrades true,
           Who love, as well I know you do,
           This gentle child,
           To me so fondly dear!   1030

ALL.   Why, what's the matter?

JULIA.   Our sister-love so true and deep
           From many an eye unused to weep
           Hath oft beguiled
           The coy, reluctant tear!   1035

ALL.   Why, what's the matter?

JULIA.   Each sympathetic tear will bruise
           When you have heard the frightful news
           (O will it not?)
           That I must now impart!   1040

ALL.   Why, what's the matter?

JULIA.   Her love for him is all in all!
           Ah, cursed fate! that it should fall
           Unto my lot
           To break my darling's heart!   1045

ALL.   Well, what's the matter?

LUD.   What means our Julia by those fateful looks?

LUD.	I do not know – But time will show If this be so.
ALL.	Time will show if this be so.
LISA.	Be merciful!

The final 'Be merciful' in that truncated version of the song also appears in the first night libretto where it is marked as recitative.

In *The Music of Arthur Sullivan* Gervase Hughes hazards a guess that the tune for this song may have been lifted from *Thespis*, so insecurely are the voice parts based on the natural melodic outline.

JULIA.	Ah, cursed fate!

LUD.   Please do not keep us all on tenter-hooks! 1050
    Now, what's the matter?

ALL.   What's the matter?

JULIA.   Our duty, if we're wise, we never shun.
This Spartan rule applies to every one.
In theatres, as in life,
Each has her line – 1055
This part – the Grand Duke's wife

ALL.   Well, what's the matter?

JULIA.   Oh agony! Is Mine!

ALL.   Oh that's the matter, that's the matter, is it?

JULIA.   A maxim new I do not start – 1060
The canons of dramatic art
Decree that this repulsive part
(The Grand Duke's wife)
Is mine!

LISA (*appalled, to* LUDWIG.)   Can this be so? 1065

LUD.   I do not know –
But time will show
If this be so.

ALL.   Time will show if this be so.

DUET – LISA *and* JULIA.

LISA.   Oh, listen to me, dear – 1070
I love him only, darling!
Remember, oh, my pet,
On him my heart is set!
This kindness do me, dear –
Nor leave me lonely, darling! 1075
Be merciful, my pet,
On him my love is set!

JULIA.   Now don't be foolish, dear –
You couldn't play it, darling!

1081 *soubrette*: An actress or singer taking the part of a lady's maid in a play or opera.

1104–5 *My light has fled, my hope is dead*: There is an interesting and comparatively rare discrepancy here between the current vocal score and libretto. The former has 'my hope has fled, my life is dead' which is what is sung on the D'Oyly Carte record. The latter, in common with the first-night libretto and the World's Classics edition, has 'My light has fled, my hope is dead'.

It's 'leading business', pet, 1080
And you're but a soubrette.
So don't be mulish, dear –
Although I say it, darling,
It's not your line, my pet –
I play that part, you bet! 1085
I play that part –
I play that part, you bet!

(LISA *overwhelmed with grief.*)

NOT.   The lady's right. Though Julia's engagement
                         Was for the stage meant – 1090
It certainly frees Ludwig from his
                         Connubial promise.
Though marriage contracts – or whate'er you call 'em –
                         Are very solemn,
Dramatic contracts (which you all adore so) 1095
                         Are even more so!

ALL.   That's very true!
Though marriage contracts, &c.

SONG – LISA *with* CHORUS.

The die is cast,
    My hopes have perished! 1100
Farewell, O Past,
Too bright to last,
Yet fondly cherished!
My light has fled,
My hope is dead, 1105
Its doom is spoken –
My day is night,
My wrong is right
In all men's sight –
Ah me! My heart is broken!   (*Exit* LISA, *weeping.*) 1110

LUD. (*recitative*).   Poor child, where will she go? What will she do?
JULIA.   *That* isn't in your part, you know.
LUD. (*sighing*).   Quite true!
    (*With an effort.*) Depressing topics we'll not touch upon –
                        Let us begin as we are going on! 1115

1118 *as merry as a grig*: A grig is a small eel, a cricket or a grasshopper but according to *Brewer's Dictionary of Phrase and Fable* the expression 'merry as a grig' may be a corruption of 'merry as a Greek'. Both phrases were apparently in use in the sixteenth century. Given the strongly Greek strain running through the dialogue of *The Grand Duke*, I think we had better settle for the latter explanation.

1122 *Tollolish*: An adjective derived from Lord Tolloller of *Iolanthe*, perhaps?

1134 *Now let us guess*: This chorus is missing from the first night libretto.

1142 *Shall live in song and story*: Compare the last line of Sergeant Meryll's song 'A laughing boy but yesterday' from *The Yeomen of the Guard*:

The theme of song and story.

SONG – LUDWIG and CHORUS.

For this will be a jolly Court, for little and for big!

ALL. Sing hey, the jolly jinks of Pfennig Halbpfennig!

LUD. From morn to night our lives shall be as merry as a grig!

ALL. Sing hey, the jolly jinks of Pfennig Halbpfennig!

LUD. All state and ceremony we'll eternally abolish –   1120
We don't mean to insist upon unnecessary polish –
And, on the whole, I rather think you'll find our rule tollolish!

ALL. Sing hey, the jolly jinks of Pfennig Halbpfennig!

JULIA.   But stay – your new-made Court
                    Without a courtly coat is –   1125
                        We shall require
                        Some Court attire,
                    And at a moment's notice.
                In clothes of common sort
                    Your courtiers must not grovel –   1130
                        Your new *noblesse*
                        Must have a dress
                    Original and novel!

ALL.   Now let us guess what kind of dress
                    Would be both neat and novel.   1135

LUD.   Old Athens we'll exhume!
                    The necessary dresses,
                        Correct and true
                        And all brand-new,
                    The company possesses: 1140
                Henceforth our Court costume
                    Shall live in song and story,
                        For we'll upraise
                        The dead old days
                    Of Athens in her glory!   1145

ALL.   Yes, let's upraise
                    The dead old days
                    Of Athens in her glory!
                Hurrah! Hurrah! Hurrah! Hurrah!

ALL.   Agreed! Agreed! Agreed!

LUD.   For this will be a jolly Court for little and for big!, &c.

ALL.   Sing hey, &c.

(*They carry* LUDWIG *round stage and deposit him on the ironwork of well.* JULIA *stands by him, and the rest group round them.*)

END OF ACT I

3 *Citharae*: The cithara was an ancient instrument of triangular shape resembling a lyre with between seven and eleven strings.

7–26 *As before you we defile*

This chorus received more approbation from critics than any other musical number in *The Grand Duke*. 'No number last night was more warmly applauded on its merits', The *Sunday Times* noted, 'than the superb processional chorus sung as the curtain rises on the lovely picture of the Grand Ducal Hall. This massive and impressive piece – worthy in every respect of the pen that wrote the choruses in *The Martyr of Antioch* – was splendidly given by the Savoy choristers.' The *Times* critic was equally enthusiastic: 'It is a good many years since the composer has given us anything so fine as the opening chorus of the second act, with a sham-Greek refrain, a melody so spontaneous, dignified and original that it hardly seems suited to its surroundings, or to the taste of most of the audience.'

This chorus was used in the Canadian premiere of *Thespis*, performed by the St Patrick's Players of Toronto in January 1993, for the entrance of the Thespians in Act II.

19 *Lesbian wine*: Presumably a drink made from grapes grown on Lesbos, the island which lies off the western coast of Turkey but belongs to Greece.

24 *Diergeticon*: Despite extensive research I cannot locate this word, or any like it, even in the great Liddell and Scott Greek Dictionary. I will keep on searching. I cannot believe that Gilbert made it up.

ACT II

(THE NEXT MORNING)

SCENE. – *Entrance Hall of the Grand Ducal Palace.*

(*Enter a procession of the members of the theatrical company* (*now dressed in the costumes of* Troilus and Cressida), *carrying garlands, playing on pipes, citharae, and cymbals, and heralding the return of* LUDWIG *and* JULIA *from the marriage ceremony, which has just taken place.*)   5

CHORUS.

As before you we defile,
　　Eloia! Eloia!
Pray you, gentles, do not smile
If we shout, in classic style,   10
　　Eloia!
Ludwig and his Julia true
Wedded are each other to –
So we sing, till all is blue,
　　Eloia! Eloia!   15
　　Opoponax! Eloia!

Wreaths of bay and ivy twine,
　　Eloia! Eloia!
Fill the bowl with Lesbian wine,
And to revelry incline –   20
　　Eloia!
For as gaily we pass on
Probably we shall, anon,
Sing a Diergeticon –
　　Eloia! Eloia!   25
　　Opoponax! Eloia!

27 *Your loyalty our Ducal heartstrings touches*: Shades of the Duke of Plaza-Toro's 'This polite attention touches heart of Duke and heart of Duchess' (*The Gondoliers*, Act II, lines 502–3).

31–96 *At the outset I may mention*
This was another of the most well-received songs on the opening night, with the audience calling for a double encore. It is a patter song of unusual style and variety, bearing out the judgement of the *Sunday Times* critic that 'perhaps the most taking solos are the patter-songs which are not only more numerous than usual, but simply astonishing in their variety'.

35 *hyporchematic*: Pertaining to a form of Greek choral lyric in which dance and mime were prominent. Very few fragments of *hyporchema* survive.

36 *choreutae*: Choral dancers.

37 *criticaster*: A petty critic. The first recorded use of the word in the *Oxford English Dictionary* is in 1684: 'I perceived that note to be added by some Jewish Criticaster.'

38 *choregus*: In ancient Athens choruses competed for prizes at festivals. The *choregus*, or chorus master, was responsible for choosing members of a chorus and paid for their costumes, training and rehearsal rooms.

41 *oboloi and drachmae*: The *obolos* was a small silver coin used by the Ancient Greeks from the sixth century BC. It was worth one sixth of a *drachma*. The word *drachma* originally meant a handful.

42 *Kalends*: The ancient Greek calendar was extremely complex – indeed there were two different calendars in operation in Athens, but basically the year began in July and was divided into twelve months. In the Roman calendar the Kalends are the first day of each month but they are not found in the Greek calendar so this seems to be a subtle way of saying that they will never get paid.

48 *Periphrastic*: Talking about something in an indirect or circuitous way and using more words than are really necessary. No prizes for pointing out examples of periphrastic dialogue in the Savoy Operas.

53 *Socratic*: The time of Socrates, the Greek philosopher, who lived from 469 to 399 BC.

55 ἄριστον: morning meal or breakfast – a little difficult to satisfy one's *thirst* on – but never mind. It is pronounced 'ariston'.

57 τρέπεσθαι πρὸς τὸν πότον: my somewhat shaky Greek (which is of the New Testament rather than the classical variety) renders this as 'They'd be turning to the drink'. The verb τρεπω means to change or turn, the preposition προς means towards and the noun ποτον is used for drink and specifically for wine. The phrase is pronounced 'Trepesthai pros ton poton'.

RECITATIVE – Ludwig.

Your loyalty our Ducal heartstrings touches:
Allow me to present your new Grand Duchess.
Should she offend, you'll graciously excuse her –
And kindly recollect *I* didn't choose her! 30

SONG – Ludwig.

At the outset I may mention it's my sovereign intention
    To revive the classic memories of Athens at its best,
For the company possesses all the necessary dresses
    And a course of quiet cramming will supply us with the rest.
We've a choir hyporchematic (that is, ballet-operatic) 35
    Who respond to the *choreutae* of that cultivated age,
And our clever chorus-master, all but captious criticaster
    Would accept as the *choregus* of the early Attic stage.
This return to classic ages is considered in their wages,
    Which are always calculated by the day or by the week – 40
And I'll pay 'em (if they'll back me) all in *oboloi* and *drachmae*,
    Which they'll get (if they prefer it) at the Kalends that are Greek!

(Confidentially to audience.)

    At this juncture I may mention
      That this erudition sham 45
    Is but classical pretension,
      The result of steady 'cram.':
    Periphrastic methods spurning,
    To this audience discerning
    I admit this show of learning 50
      Is the fruit of steady 'cram.'!

Chorus.   Periphrastic methods, &c.

In the period Socratic every dining-room was Attic
    (Which suggests an architecture of a topsy-turvy kind),
There they'd satisfy their thirst on a *recherché* cold ἄριστον, 55
    Which is what they called their lunch – and so may you, if you're inclined.
As they gradually got on, they'd τρέπεσθαι πρὸς τὸν πότον
    (Which is Attic for a steady and a conscientious drink).
But they mixed their wine with water – which I'm sure they didn't oughter –
    And we modern Saxons know a trick worth two of that, I think! 60
Then came rather risky dances (under certain circumstances)
    Which would shock that worthy gentleman, the Licenser of Plays,

63 *Corybantian*: *Corybantes* were male priests who took part in orgiastic cults and rituals as-
    sociated with various gods. They especially followed the Asiatic goddess Cybele whom
    they worshipped with wild dances and music.
    Dionysiac and Bacchic: A somewhat tautologous coupling since Dionysus and Bacchus
    were one and the same god. Bacchus was the Roman name for the god of wine, Dionysus
    the Greek. He was celebrated in two great Greek festivals, or *Dionysia*, in December and
    March.

64 *Dithyrambic*: The *dithyramb* was a chorus sung to the god Dionysus and performed by a
    choir who sang and danced in a circle. There were contests for the best Dithyrambic
    chorus at festivals in honour of Dionysus.

78 *Mrs. Grundy*: The personification of strait-laced puritanism and moral outrage. The
    original Mrs Grundy was a character in a novel by Tom Morton called *Speed the Plough*
    which was first published in 1798. Those tempted to transgress the codes of respectabil-
    ity and strict moral propriety are taunted with the question 'What will Mrs Grundy
    say?' I suppose the modern equivalent would be Mrs Whitehouse.

84 *Coan silk*: A fine silk with a transparent texture made an the Greek island of Cos.

96 *Yet his classic lore*: In the current editions of both the libretto and vocal score (although
    not in the first night libretto or World's Classics edition) the chorus's reprise of the last
    four lines of Ludwig's song leads straight into a further reprise, in slightly abbreviated
    form, of 'Wreaths of bay and ivy twine'.

Corybantian mani*ac* kick – Dionysiac or Bacchic –
And the Dithyrambic revels of those undecorous days.

(*Confidentially to audience.*) 65
And perhaps I'd better mention,
Lest alarming you I am,
That it isn't our intention
To perform a Dithyramb –
It displays a lot of stocking,
Which is always very shocking, 70
And of course I'm only mocking
At the prevalence of 'cram.'!

CHORUS.   It displays a lot, &c.

Yes, on reconsideration, there are customs of that nation 75
Which are not in strict accordance with the habits of our day,
And when I come to codify, their rules I mean to modify,
Or Mrs. Grundy, p'r'aps, may have a word or two to say.
For they hadn't macintoshes or umbrellas or goloshes –
And a shower with their dresses must have played the very deuce, 80
And it must have been unpleasing when they caught a fit of sneezing,
For, it seems, of pocket-handkerchiefs they didn't know the use.
They wore little underclothing – scarcely anything – or no-thing –
And their dress of Coan silk was quite transparent in design –
Well, in fact, in summer weather, something like the 'altogether'. 85
And it's *there*, I rather fancy, I shall have to draw the line!

(*Confidentially to audience.*)
And again I wish to mention
That this erudition sham
Is but classical pretension,
The result of steady 'cram.' 90
Yet my classic lore aggressive
(If you'll pardon the possessive)
Is exceedingly impressive
When you're passing an exam. 95

CHORUS.   Yet his classic lore, &c.

(*Exeunt Chorus. Manent* LUDWIG, JULIA, *and* LISA.)

104–31 *Take care of him – he's much too good to live*

Another fine song by Gilbert, much above the level of some of the doggerel that disfigures Act I. The critic of the *Musical Standard* observed that 'Mr Gilbert is decidedly at his best in the first half of the second act, when we have left the tiresome Statutory Duel and Sausage Rolls far behind us.'

The tune of this aria was used, with suitable adaptation, for Lady Sangazure's long-lost ballad 'In days gone by, these eyes were bright' (see notes to *The Sorcerer*, Act I, lines 217–20) in a performance of *The Sorcerer* by the Valley Light Opera of Amherst, Massachusetts, in November 1988.

120 *hardbake*: A clear dark toffee containing pieces of almond.

Lud. (*recitative*).   Yes, Ludwig and his Julia are mated!
         For when an obscure comedian, whom the law backs,
            To sovereign rank is promptly elevated,   100
         He takes it with its incidental drawbacks!
            So Julia and I are duly mated!

(Lisa, *through this, has expressed intense distress at having to surrender* Ludwig.)

SONG – Lisa.

     Take care of him – he's much too good to live,
        With him you must be very gentle: 105
     Poor fellow, he's so highly sensitive,
        And O, so sentimental!
     Be sure you never let him sit up late
        In chilly open air conversing –
     Poor darling, he's extremely delicate,   110
        And wants a deal of nursing!

Lud.   I want a deal of nursing!

Lisa.   And O, remember this –
        When he is cross with pain,
     A flower and a kiss –   115
     A simple flower – a tender kiss
        Will bring him round again!

     His moods you must assiduously watch:
        When he succumbs to sorrow tragic,
     Some hardbake or a bit of butter-scotch   120
        Will work on him like magic.
     To contradict a character so rich
        In trusting love were simple blindness –
     He's one of those exalted natures which
        Will only yield to kindness!   125

Lud.   I only yield to kindness!

Lisa.   And O, the bygone bliss!
        And O, the present pain!
     That flower and that kiss –
     That simple flower – that tender kiss   130
        I ne'er shall give again!   (*Exits, weeping.*)

143 *hoity-toity*: *Brewer's Dictionary of Phrase and Fable* suggests that this 'reduplicated word',
     meaning stuck up, haughty or petulant, probably derives from the obsolete verb, hoit,
     which means to romp about noisily. It figures prominently in the refrain of the duet for
     Melissa and Lady Blanche in *Princess Ida* (Act II, lines 561–90).
     virago: Generally used to describe a man-like or heroic woman, particularly a female
     warrior or amazon.

167 *up centre and off left*: The first night libretto ends Ludwig's speech here and omits the two
     'splendids' that somehow crept into subsequent additions. It is rare to find words added
     to the libretto of *The Grand Duke*. Generally, Gilbert seems to have heeded the plea of
     the *Sunday Times* critic: 'If the opera could only be compressed, for it becomes very
     wearisome in places.'

JULIA. And now that everybody has gone, and we're happily and comfortably married, I want to have a few words with my new-born husband.

LUD. (*aside*). Yes, I expect you'll often have a few words with your new-born husband! (*Aloud.*) Well, what is it? (*Sits.*) 135

JULIA. Why, I've been thinking that as you and I have to play our parts for life, it is most essential that we should come to a definite understanding as to how they shall be rendered. Now, I've been considering how I can make the most of the Grand Duchess.

LUD. Have you? Well, if you'll take my advice, you'll make a very fine part 140 of it.

JULIA. Why, that's quite *my* idea.

LUD. I shouldn't make it one of your hoity-toity vixenish viragoes.

JULIA. You think not?

LUD. Oh, I'm quite clear about that. I should make her a tender, gentle, 145 submissive, affectionate (but not too affectionate) child-wife – timidly anxious to coil herself into her husband's heart, but kept in check by an awestruck reverence for his exalted intellectual qualities and his majestic personal appearance.

JULIA. Oh, that is your idea of a good part?

LUD. Yes – a wife who regards her husband's slightest wish as an inflexible 150 law, and who ventures but rarely into his august presence, unless (which would happen seldom) he should summon her to appear before him. A crushed, despairing violet, whose blighted existence would culminate (all too soon) in a lonely and pathetic death-scene! A fine part, my dear.

JULIA. Yes. There's a good deal to be said for your view of it. Now there are 155 some actresses whom it would fit like a glove.

LUD. (*aside*). I wish I'd married one of 'em!

JULIA. But, you see, I *must* consider my temperament. For instance, my temperament would demand some strong scenes of justifiable jealousy.

LUD. Oh, there's no difficulty about that. You shall have *them*. 160

JULIA. With a lovely but detested rival —

LUD. Oh, *I'll* provide the rival.

JULIA. Whom I should stab – stab – stab!

LUD. Oh, I wouldn't stab her. It's been done to death. I should treat her with a silent and contemptuous disdain, and delicately withdraw from a position 165 which, to one of your sensitive nature, would be absolutely untenable. Dear me, I can see you delicately withdrawing, up centre and off left! Splendid! Splendid!

JULIA. *Can* you?

LUD. Yes. It's a fine situation – and in your hands, full of quiet pathos!

DUET – LUDWIG *and* JULIA.

LUD. Now, Julia, come, 170
Consider it from
This dainty point of view –

181 *Innocent ingenoo*: Another example of orthography forgoing her spells because of the exigence of rhyme (see note to Act I, line 435). The correct spelling of the word Ludwig has in mind here is *ingénue*. It is French, the feminine of *ingénu*, and means an artless innocent girl, especially, according to the *Oxford English Dictionary*, of the type represented on the stage.

185 *Miminy-piminy*: Shades of Reginald Bunthorne's 'Francesca di Rimini, miminy, piminy, Je-ne-sais-quoi young man' (*Patience*, Act II, lines 498–9).

187 *I'm much obliged to you*: The first night libretto has these lines sung by Julia in an ensemble with Ludwig as follows:

LUDWIG.	JULIA.
The part you're suited to –	I'm much obliged to you,
(To give the deuce her due)	I don't think that would do –
A sweet (O, jiminy!)	To play (O, jiminy!)
Miminy-piminy	Miminy-piminy
Innocent inge*noo*!	Innocent inge*noo*!

202 *I have a rival*: This number represents a genre that was very familiar in Victorian entertainment but very seldom found in the Savoy Operas, the dramatic monologue delivered to a musical accompaniment. There is really nothing else like it in the canon – I suppose the nearest thing is the Fairy Queen's 'Every bill and every measure' (*Iolanthe*, Act I, lines 796–816) but it is much less dramatic.

A timid tender
Feminine gender,
   Prompt to coyly coo – 175
Yet silence seeking,
Seldom speaking
   Till she's spoken to –
A comfy, cosy,
Rosy-posy 180
   Innocent *ingenoo*!
    The part you're suited to –
    (To give the deuce her due)
   A sweet (O, jiminy!)
   Miminy-piminy, 185
    Innocent inge*noo*!

JULIA.   I'm much obliged to you,
    I don't think that would do.

ENSEMBLE.

LUDWIG.	JULIA.	
O sweet (O, jiminy!)	To play (O, jiminy!)	
Miminy-piminy,	Miminy-piminy,	190
Innocent inge*noo*!	Innocent inge*noo*!	

JULIA.   You forget my special magic
      (In a high dramatic sense)
    Lies in situations tragic –
      Undeniably intense. 195
    As I've justified promotion
      In the histrionic art,
    I'll submit to you my notion
      Of a first-rate part.

LUD.   Well, let us see your notion 200
      Of a first-rate part.

JULIA (*dramatically*).   I have a rival! Frenzy-thrilled,
    I find you both together!
    My heart stands still – with horror chilled –
      Hard as the millstone nether! 205
    Then softly, slyly, snaily, snaky –
    Crawly, creepy, quaily, quaky –
      I track her on her homeward way,
      As panther tracks her fated prey!

217 *Remorse! Remorse!*: These words are in the first night libretto, the Chatto edition of Gilbert's plays and the BBC recording but are missing from the World's Classics edition
and currently available versions of the libretto or vocal score.

237 *And satisfies my notion of a first-rate part*: The current edition of the vocal score (though
not the libretto) has this line repeated by Julia with Ludwig joining here to sing 'And
satisfies her notion of a first-rate part!'.

(*Furiously.*)   I fly at her soft white throat –   210
                The lily-white laughing leman!
On her agonized gaze I gloat
                With the glee of a dancing demon!
My rival she – I have no doubt of her –
So I hold on – till the breath is out of her!   215
              – till the breath is out of her!
And then – Remorse! Remorse!
O cold unpleasant corse,
          Avaunt! Avaunt!
        That lifeless form   220
          I gaze upon –
        That face, still warm
          But weirdly wan –
        Those eyes of glass
          I contemplate –   225
And then, alas,
          Too late – too late!
I find she is – your Aunt!

(*Shuddering.*)   Then, mad – mad – mad!
          With fancies wild – chimerical –   230
Now sorrowful – silent – sad –
          Now hullaballoo hysterical!
            Ha! ha! ha! ha!
But whether I'm sad or whether I'm glad,
          Mad! mad! mad! mad!   235

This calls for the resources of a high-class art,
And satisfies my notion of a first-rate part!   (*Exit* JULIA.)

(*Enter all the Chorus, hurriedly, and in great excitement.*)

CHORUS.

Your Highness, there's a party at the door –
      Your Highness, at the door there is a party –   240
          She says that we expect her,
          But we do not recollect her,
For we never saw her countenance before!

With rage and indignation she is rife,
      Because our welcome wasn't very hearty –   245
          She's as sulky as a super,

247 *swearing like a trooper*: The earliest recorded use of this particular phrase in the *Oxford Book of Proverbs* is in 1821 but there are much earlier versions which employ the formula 'swearing like a soldier'. One of the first is in a play by Beaumont and Fletcher published in 1608: 'This would make a saint swear like a soldier'.

250 *With fury indescribable I burn*: This looks at first sight like a throwback to the last G & S collaboration and the song 'With fury deep we burn' (*Utopia Limited*, Act II, line 220).

281 *matrimonially matrimonified*: A tautology if ever there was one. At least the pirates of Penzance had the rather more linguistically correct desire to be 'conjugally matrimonified' (*Pirates of Penzance*, Act I, line 431), but sadly 'conjugally' doesn't provide quite as many syllables as 'matrimonially' and it was syllables more than anything else that Gilbert was after at this point.

And she's swearing like a trooper,
O, you never heard such language in your life!

(*Enter* BARONESS VON KRAKENFELDT, *in a fury.*)

BAR. With fury indescribable I burn!   250
 With rage I'm nearly ready to explode!
There'll be grief and tribulation when I learn
 To whom this slight unbearable is owed!
  For whatever may be due I'll pay it double –
 There'll be terror indescribable and trouble! 255
 With a hurly-burly and a hubble-bubble
I'll pay you for this pretty episode!

ALL. Oh, whatever may be due she'll pay it double! –
It's very good of her to take the trouble –
But we don't know what she means by 'hubble-bubble' – 260
No doubt it's an expression *à la mode.*

BAR. (*to* LUDWIG). Do you know who I am?
LUD. (*examining her*).   I don't;
 Your countenance I can't fix, my dear.
BAR. This proves I'm not a sham. (*Showing pocket-handkerchief.*) 265
LUD. (*examining it*). It won't;
 It only says 'Krakenfeldt, Six,' my dear.
BAR. Express your grief profound!
LUD.   I shan't!
 This tone I never allow, my love.   270
BAR. Rudolph at once produce!
LUD.   I can't;
 He isn't at home just now, my love.
BAR. (*astonished*). He isn't at home just now!
ALL. He isn't at home just now, (*Dancing derisively.*) 275
 He has an appointment particular, very –
You'll find him, I think, in the town cemetery;
 And that's how we come to be making so merry,
  For he isn't at home just now!
BAR. But bless my heart and soul alive, it's impudence personified! 280
I've come here to be matrimonially matrimonified!
LUD. For any disappointment I am sorry unaffectedly,
But yesterday that nobleman expired quite unexpectedly –
ALL (*sobbing*). Tol the riddle lol!
 Tol the riddle lol!   285
 Tol the riddle, lol the riddle, lol lol lay!
(*Then laughing wildly.*) Tol the riddle, lol the riddle, lol lol lay!

314 *For another hundred years*: The first night libretto contained a small piece of further dialogue here which was later cut:

> BARONESS: For another hundred years! Am I to understand that you, having taken
> upon yourself all Rudolph's responsibilities, will occupy the Grand Ducal throne for the en-
> suing century?
> LUDWIG. If I should live so long.
> BARONESS. Set the merry joy-bells ringing etc.

315 *festive epithalamia*: In both Greek and Latin poetry, the *epithalamium* was a marriage song
sung by young men and girls outside the bedroom of the bridal couple on their wedding
night. The most famous *epithalamia* are those by Catullus.

316 *The exhilirating Marsala*: A white wine resembling a light sherry which takes its name
from the small town on the west coast of Sicily from where it is exported.

BAR. Is this Court Mourning or a Fancy Ball?

LUD. Well, it's a delicate combination of both effects. It is intended to express inconsolable grief for the decease of the late Duke and ebullient joy at the accession of his successor. *I* am his successor. Permit me to present you to my Grand Duchess. (*Indicating* JULIA.) 290

BAR. Your Grand Duchess? Oh, your Highness! (*Curtseying profoundly.*)

JULIA (*sneering at her*). Old frump!

BAR. Humph! A recent creation, probably? 295

LUD. We were married only half an hour ago.

BAR. Exactly. I thought she seemed new to the position.

JULIA. Ma'am, I don't know who you are, but I flatter myself I can do justice to *any* part on the very shortest notice.

BAR. My dear, under the circumstances you are doing admirably – and you'll improve with practice. It's so difficult to be a lady when one isn't born to it. 300

JULIA (*in a rage, to* LUDWIG). Am I to stand this? Am I not to be allowed to pull her to pieces?

LUD. (*aside to* JULIA). No, no – it isn't Greek. Be a violet, I beg. 305

BAR. And now tell me all about this distressing circumstance. How did the Grand Duke die?

LUD. He perished nobly – in a Statutory Duel.

BAR. In a Statutory Duel? But that's only a civil death! – and the Act expires tonight, and then he will come to life again! 310

LUD. Well, no. Anxious to inaugurate my reign by conferring some inestimable boon on my people, I signalized this occasion by reviving the law for another hundred years.

BAR. For another hundred years? Then set the merry joy-bells ringing! Let festive epithalamia resound through these ancient halls! Cut the satisfying sandwich – broach the exhilarating Marsala – and let us rejoice today, if we never rejoice again! 315

LUD. But I don't think I quite understand. We have already rejoiced a good deal.

BAR. Happy man, you little reck of the extent of the good things you are in for. When you killed Rudolph you adopted all his overwhelming responsibilities. Know then that I, Caroline von Krakenfeldt, am the most overwhelming of them all! 320

LUD. But stop, stop – I've just been married to somebody else!

JULIA. Yes, ma'am, to somebody else, ma'am! Do you understand, ma'am? To somebody else! 325

BAR. Do keep this young woman quiet: she fidgets me!

JULIA. Fidgets you!

LUD. (*aside to* JULIA). Be a violet – a crushed, despairing violet.

JULIA. Do you suppose I intend to give up a magnificent part without a struggle? 330

336 *So then summon the charioteers*: The first night libretto, the Chatto edition of Gilbert's plays and the World's Classics Edition of the Savoy Operas all have 'So summon the charioteers', producing a line of just eight syllables instead of the nine found in the Chappell libretto and vocal score.

340 *In the form of impetuous tears*: In the first night libretto, the Chatto edition of Gilbert's plays and the World's Classics edition, this line is given as 'for the rest of her maidenly years'.

349 *All is darksome – all is dreary*: In the first night libretto the order of the first two lines in this song is reversed so that it begins 'Broken every promise plighted'. The list of songs on the sleeve of the 1976 D'Oyly Carte record also gives the song this title although on the actual recording it begins, as here and in all modern editions of the libretto and vocal score, 'All is darksome – all is dreary'. The first-night libretto also reverses the order of the third and fourth lines of the song.

355 *living, living*: In both the first night libretto and the World's Classics edition of the Savoy Operas, the second 'living' is left out.

357 *No, no*: These words are the cue for one of the greatest cadenza-like runs in the whole of the Savoy canon – a dazzling coloratura display reminiscent of Italian grand opera. First night critics were in some doubt as to whether this represented Sullivan at his most serious or at his most mischievous. The *Times* reviewer felt that the whole song 'was written in evident imitation and derision of the conventional operatic aria of the last generation'.

358 *For no good*: The World's Classics edition omits 'for' and has this line as 'no good ever came of repining'.

LUD. My good girl, she has the law on her side. Let us both bear this calamity with resignation. If you must struggle, go away and struggle in the seclusion of your chamber.

SONG – BARONESS *and* CHORUS.

Now away to the wedding we go,   335
 So then summon the charioteers –
No kind of reluctance we show
 To embark on our married careers.

Though Julia's emotion may flow
 In the form of impetuous tears,   340
To our wedding we eagerly go,
 So summon the charioteers!

CHORUS.   To the wedding we'll eagerly go, &c.

(All dance off to wedding except JULIA.*)*

RECITATIVE – JULIA.

So ends my dream – so fades my vision fair!   345
Of hope no gleam – distraction and despair!
My cherished dream, the Ducal throne to share,
That aim supreme has vanished into air!

SONG – JULIA.

All is darksome – all is dreary.
 Broken every promise plighted –   350
Sad and sorry – weak and weary!
 Every new-born hope is blighted!
Death the Friend or Death the Foe,
Shall I call upon thee? No!
I will go on living, living, though   355
 Sad and sorry – weak and weary!

No, no! Let the bygone go by!
 For no good ever came of repining:
If today there are clouds o'er the sky,
 Tomorrow the sun may be shining!   360
  Tomorrow, be kind,
  Tomorrow, to me!
  With loyalty blind
  I curtsey to thee!

Today is a day of illusion and sorrow, 365
So *viva* Tomorrow!
  God save you, Tomorrow!
  Your servant, Tomorrow!
God save you, Tomorrow! (*Exit* JULIA.)

(*Enter* ERNEST.) 370

ERN. It's of no use – I can't wait any longer. At any risk I must gratify my
urgent desire to know what is going on. (*Looking off.*) Why, what's that? Surely
I see a wedding procession winding down the hill, dressed in my *Troilus and
Cressida* costumes! That's Ludwig's doing! I see how it is – he found the time
hang heavy on his hands, and is amusing himself by getting married to Lisa. No 375
– it can't be to Lisa, for here she is!

(*Enter* LISA.)

LISA (*not seeing him*). I really cannot stand seeing my Ludwig married twice
in one day to somebody else!
ERN. Lisa! 380

(LISA *sees him, and stands as if transfixed with horror.*)

ERN. Come here – don't be a little fool – I want you.

(LISA *suddenly turns and bolts off.*)

ERN. Why, what's the matter with the little donkey? One would think
she saw a ghost! But if he's not marrying Lisa, whom *is* he marrying? (*Suddenly.*) 385
Julia! (*Much overcome.*) I see it all! The scoundrel! He had to adopt all my
responsibilities, and he's shabbily taken advantage of the situation to marry the
girl I'm engaged to! But no, it can't be Julia, for here *she* is!

(*Enter* JULIA.)

JULIA (*not seeing him*). I've made up my mind. I won't stand it! I'll send in my 390
notice at once!
ERN. Julia! Oh, what a relief!

(JULIA *gazes at him as if transfixed.*)

ERN. Then you've not married Ludwig? You are still true to me?

(JULIA *turns and bolts in grotesque horror.* ERNEST *follows and stops her.*) 395

407 *My love, I've heard nothing*: In the first night libretto Ernest adds here: 'How could I? There are no daily papers where I come from.'

418–19 *I'll play broken-English in London as you play broken-German here*: The part of Julia Jellicoe, the English *comedienne* who finds herself in a German theatrical troupe and has to wrestle with the difficulties of the Teutonic language, was not in Gilbert's original plans for *The Grand Duke*. It is quite possible that it was specially created for the Hungarian soprano, Ilka von Palmay, who won considerable acclaim when she appeared at Drury Lane Theatre in a Saxe-Coburg operatic company's production of Zeller's operetta *Der Vogelhändler* (The Bird-Seller).

Ilka Palmay, as she was also known, had already appeared in German productions of *The Mikado*. Indeed, she had taken the roles of both Yum-Yum and Nanki-Poo until Sullivan had intervened to stop this transvestite casting. Both Gilbert and Sullivan were much impressed with her voice and it may well be that the part of Julia was created for her. Perhaps her broken English accent provided the inspiration for the character of the English actress with her broken German. She was engaged by Richard D'Oyly Carte for the opening run of the *Grand Duke* and was much admired by the critics. The *Musical Standard* critic detected 'a pleasing voice of rare freshness' and reported that 'her acting quite lifted the piece when she was on stage'.

In his book *The Final Curtain* John Wolfson suggests that Ilka von Palmay's 'heavily accented English' resembled the speech of Queen Victoria and that Gilbert intended this comparison to be drawn when he cast her as Julia Jellicoe. However, as Arthur Jacobs points out in his biography of Sullivan, there is in fact no evidence at all that the Queen spoke with a German accent.

434 *I own that that utterance*: The second 'that' is missing from the Oxford World's Classics edition of the Savoy Operas.

ERN. Don't run away! Listen to me. Are you all crazy?

JULIA (*in affected terror*). What would you with me, spectre? Oh, ain't his eyes sepulchral! And ain't his voice hollow! What are you doing out of your tomb at this time of day – apparition?

ERN. I do wish I could make you girls understand that I'm only technically　400
dead, and that physically I'm as much alive as ever I was in my life!

JULIA. Oh, but it's an awful thing to be haunted by a technical bogy!

ERN. You won't be haunted much longer. The law must be on its last legs, and in a few hours I shall come to life again – resume all my social and civil functions, and claim my darling as my blushing bride!　405

JULIA. Oh – then you haven't heard?

ERN. My love, I've heard nothing.

JULIA. Why, Ludwig challenged Rudolph and won, and now *he's* Grand Duke, and he's revived the law for another century!

ERN. What! But you're not serious – you're only joking!　410

JULIA. My good sir, I'm a light-hearted girl, but I don't chaff bogies.

ERN. Well, that's the meanest dodge I ever heard of!

JULIA. Shabby trick, *I* call it.

ERN. But you don't mean to say that you're going to cry off!

JULIA. I really can't afford to wait until your time is up. You know, I've　415
always set my face against long engagements.

ERN. Then defy the law and marry me now. We will fly to your native country, and I'll play broken-English in London as you play broken-German here!

JULIA. No. These legal technicalities cannot be defied. Situated as you are,　420
you have no power to make me your wife. At best you could only make me your widow.

ERN. Then be my widow – my little, dainty, winning, winsome widow!

JULIA. Now what would be the good of that? Why, you goose, I should marry again within a month!　425

DUET – ERNEST *and* JULIA.

ERN.　　　　If the light of love's lingering ember
　　　　　　Has faded in gloom,
　　　　You cannot neglect, O remember,
　　　　　　A voice from the tomb!
　　　　That stern supernatural diction　　　　430
　　　　Should act as a solemn restriction,
　　　　Although by a mere legal fiction
　　　　　　A voice from the tomb!

JULIA (*in affected terror*).
　　　　I own that that utterance chills me –
　　　　　　It withers my bloom!　　　　435

442 *Thou voice from the tomb*: This line is missing from the first night libretto and the World's Classics edition.

469 *Brindisi*: A drinking song derived from the Italian word 'brindisi' which means a toast. I suppose the most famous brindisi in Italian opera is 'Libiamo' in Act I of Verdi's *La Traviata* (1853). It became an almost obligatory feature of late nineteenth-century operetta after Johann Strauss introduced his toast to the joys of champagne in *Die Fledermaus* (1874). Early twentieth-century musical comedies continued to include drinking songs, one of the finest being 'Drink, drink, drink' in Sigmund Romberg's *The Student Prince* (1924).

During the era of prohibition in the 1920s the United States Congress tried to outlaw the practice of including a brindisi in musicals but the American composer John Philip Sousa successfully resisted the proposal, arguing that it would go against the whole tradition of musical theatre.

469–500 *Come, bumpers*

This song does not appear in the 1963 World's Classics edition of the Savoy Opera libretti, prepared on the authorization of Dame Bridget D'Oyly Carte. It is also missing from a 1975 official production text of *The Grand Duke* mentioned by Reginald Allen in his *First Night Gilbert and Sullivan*.

For their production of *The Sorcerer* in November 1988 (see note above to lines 104–31), the Valley Light Opera Company used the tune of 'Come, bumpers' for the duet sung by Aline and Lady Sangazure (see note to *The Sorcerer*, Act I, lines 217–20).

With awful emotion it thrills me –
   That voice from the tomb!
Oh, spectre, won't anything lay thee?
Though pained to deny or gainsay thee,
In this case I cannot obey thee,   440
   Thou voice from the tomb!

BOTH.   Thou voice from the tomb!

JULIA (*dancing*).   So, spectre appalling,
   I bid you good-day –
Perhaps you'll be calling   445
   When passing this way.
Your bogydom scorning,
And all your love-lorning,
I bid you good-morning,
   I bid you good-day.   450

ERN. (*furious*).   My offer recalling,
   Your words I obey –
Your fate is appalling,
   And full of dismay.
To pay for this scorning   455
I give you fair warning
I'll haunt you each morning,
   Each night, and each day!

(*Repeat Ensemble, and exeunt in opposite directions.*)

(*Re-enter the Wedding Procession of* LUDWIG *and* BARONESS, *dancing.*)   460

CHORUS.

Now bridegroom and bride let us toast
   In a magnum of merry champagne –
Let us make of this moment the most,
   We may not be so lucky again.
So drink to our sovereign host   465
   And his highly intelligent reign –
His health and his bride's let us toast
   In a magnum of merry champagne!

BRINDISI – BARONESS.

Come, bumpers – aye, ever-so-many –
And then, if you will, many more!   470

472 *Pommery, Seventy-four*: The firm of Pommery and Greno, based in Reims, is one of the great champagne houses. 1874 was an excellent year for champagnes, rivalled only by the 1889 and 1904 vintages in the whole period between 1870 and 1920.

This wine doesn't cost us a penny,
   Though it's Pommćry, Seventy-four!
Old wine is a true panacea
   For every conceivable ill,
When you cherish the soothing idea   475
   That somebody else pays the bill!
Old wine is a pleasure that's hollow
   When at your own table you sit,
For you're thinking each mouthful you swallow
   Has cost you a threepenny bit!   480

CHORUS.   So bumpers – aye, ever-so-many –
   And then, if you will, many more!
This wine doesn't cost us a penny,
   Though it's Pommćry, Seventy-four!

I once gave an evening party   485
   (A sandwich and cut-orange ball)
But my guests had such appetites hearty,
   That I couldn't enjoy it at all!
I made a heroic endeavour
   To look unconcerned, but in vain,   490
And I vowed that I never – oh never –
   Would ask anybody again!
But there's a distinction decided –
   A difference truly immense –
When the wine that you drink is provided   495
   At somebody else's expense.

CHORUS.   So bumpers – aye, ever-so-many –
   The cost we may safely ignore!
For the wine doesn't cost us a penny,
   Though it's Pommćry, Seventy-four!   500

(*Exit* BARONESS. *March heard.*)

LUD. (*recit.*)   Why, who is this approaching,
   Upon our joy encroaching?
   Some rascal come a-poaching
   Who's heard that wine we're broaching?   505

ALL.   Who may this be?
       Who may this be?
    Who is he? Who is he? Who is he?

510–38   *The Prince of Monte Carlo*
This song, performed on the opening night by Mr Jones Hewson, delighted both audience and critics. *The Times* found it 'one of the most taking things in the opera' and noted
that 'it was deservedly encored'.

524   *word of mouth auric'lar*:   Compare *Utopia Limited*, Act I, line 131.

533   *his Principality*:   Strictly speaking, Monte Carlo is not a principality at all, nor does it
have a prince. It is one of the four *quartiers* of the principality of Monaco, the tiny sovereign state of just 0.73 square miles which is situated on the Cote d'Azure nine miles east
of Nice and five miles west of the French–Italian border. Monaco, which is ruled by a
hereditary royal family, has a population of 29,300 and derives most of its income from
tourism, gambling and the sale of postage stamps.
    In 1856 Prince Charles III of Monaco granted a charter allowing a joint stock company
to build a casino in the principality. It opened in 1861 and the surrounding district became known as Monte Carlo. The gaming tables of Monte Carlo attracted gamblers
from around the world, among them Arthur Sullivan who was there in 1888, twice in
1892 and again in 1895.

(*Enter* HERALD.)

HER.	The Prince of Monte Car*lo*,
	From Mediterranean water,
	Has come here to bestow
	On you his beautiful daughter.
	They've paid off all they owe,
	As every statesman oughter –
	That Prince of Monte Car*lo*
	And his be-eautiful daughter!

510

515

CHORUS. The Prince of Monte Car*lo*, &c.

HER.	The Prince of Monte Car*lo*,
	Who is so very partickler,
	Has heard that you're also
	For ceremony a stickler –
	Therefore he lets you know
	By word of mouth auric'lar –
	(That Prince of Monte Car*lo*
	Who is so very particklar) –

520

525

CHORUS. The Prince of Monte Carlo, &c.

HER.	The Prince of Monte Car*lo*,
	He lets you know,
	He's here to bestow
	His be-eautiful daughter!

530

LUD. (*recit.*).	His Highness we know not – nor the locality
	In which is situate his Principality;
	But, as he guesses by some odd fatality,
	This *is* the shop for cut and dried formality!
	Let him appear –
	He'll find that we're
	Remarkable for cut and dried formality.

535

(*Reprise of March. Exit* HERALD. LUDWIG *beckons his Court.*)

LUD.	I have a plan – I'll tell you all the plot of it –
	He wants formality – he shall have a lot of it!

540

(*Whispers to them, through symphony.*)

566   *their shortcomings manifest*: The current editions of the libretto and vocal score have 'these shortcomings'.

568   *wealthy members of the brewing interest*: Another highly topical reference to the beerage (see note to *Utopia Limited*, Act II, line 163).

Conceal yourselves, and when I give the cue,
Spring out on him – you all know what to do!

(All conceal themselves behind the draperies that enclose the stage. Pompous March. 545
Enter the PRINCE *and* PRINCESS OF MONTE CARLO, *attended by six*
theatrical-looking nobles and the Court Costumier.)

DUET – PRINCE *and* PRINCESS.

PRINCE.   We're rigged out in magnificent array
                 (Our own clothes are much gloomier)
               In costumes which we've hired by the day   550
                 From a very well-known costumier.
COST. (*bowing*). *I* am the very well-known costumier.
PRINCESS. With a brilliant staff a Prince should make a show
                 (It's a rule that never varies),
               So we've engaged from the Theatre Monaco   555
                 Six supernumeraries.
NOBLES.   We're the supernumeraries.
ALL.   At a salary immense,
                   Quite regardless of expense,
                 Six supernumeraries!   560
PRINCE.   They do not speak, for they break our grammar's laws,
                 And their language is lamentable –
               And they never take off their gloves, because
                 Their nails are not presentable.
NOBLES.   Our nails are not presentable!   565

PRINCESS. To account for their shortcomings manifest
                 We explain, in a whisper bated,
               They are wealthy members of the brewing interest
                 To the Peerage elevated.

NOBLES.   To the Peerage elevated.   570

ALL.   They're $\Big\}$ very, very rich,
                 We're
                 And accordingly, as sich,
                 To the Peerage elevated.

PRINCE. Well, my dear, here we are at last – just in time to compel Duke
Rudolph to fulfil the terms of his marriage contract. Another hour and we   575
should have been too late.

584 *Roulette*: The game of roulette derives its name from the French word for a little wheel. It involves players betting on which red or black numbered compartment of a revolving wheel a small ball, spun in the opposite direction, will come to rest in. The seventeenth-century French philosopher and mathematician, Blaise Pascal, an unknown French monk and the Chinese have variously been credited with inventing the game which took off in late eighteenth-century Europe as a favourite attraction for gamblers and the idle rich. It is especially associated with Monte Carlo.

594 *my goot friend*: The costumier is the only G & S character I can think of who is given a foreign accent.

596 *Oh, he's a swell*: Shades of Ko-Ko's description of Pooh-Bah: 'That is a tremendous swell' (*The Mikado*, Act I, line 403). The *Oxford English Dictionary* defines 'swell' in its colloquial sense as 'a fashionably or stylishly dressed person; hence, a person of good social position, a highly distinguished person'. The cult of the swell was at its height in Britain in the 1890s.

596 *Duke of Riviera*: Monte Carlo is, of course, on the French Riviera but there is, as far as I am aware, no such title as this.

599 *That's better*: The first night libretto has further dialogue here as follows:

> PRINCE. Now (*passing to another*) here's a nobleman's coat all in holes!
> COSTUMIER (*to Noble*). Vhat a careless chap you are! Vhy don't you take care of the clo's? These cost money, these do! D'ye think I stole 'em?
> PRINCE. It's not the poor devil's fault – it's yours. I don't wish you to end our House of Peers, but you might at least mend them. (*Passing to another.*) Now, who's this with his moustache coming off?

601 *Viscount Mentone*: Mentone is the Italian name for the town of Menton which lies six miles north east of Monte Carlo just inside the French border with Italy. It was purchased by France from Monaco in 1860 and for all I know may well have a viscounty attached to it.

606 *Adjusts his moustache*: A further piece of business and dialogue follows here in the first night libretto:

> (*Adjusts his moustache and hat – a handkerchief falls out.*)
>
> PRINCE. And may we be permitted to hit to the Noble Viscount, in the most delicate manner imaginable, that it is not the practice among the higher nobility to carry their handkerchiefs in their hats.
> NOBLE. I ain't got no pockets.
> PRINCE. Then stick it in here. (*Sticks it in his breast.*) Now, once for all, you Peers, etc.

612–13 *There is positively no one here to receive us*: The lack of a welcome party to receive the Prince of Monte Carlo and his daughter recalls the non-appearance of the entourage which the Duke of Plaza-Toro had hoped would accompany him for his arrival in Venice. The difference, of course, is that here it is the hosts who are at fault in not providing a proper welcome whereas in the Duke's case it is his lack of money which prevents him as a visitor appearing with the pomp and ceremony that he would like.

The first night libretto has the following additional dialogue at this point:

> PRINCE. Well, my love, you must remember that we have taken Duke Rudolph somewhat by surprise. These small German potentates are famous for their scrupulous adherence to ceremonial observances, and it may be that the etiquette of this Court demands that we should be received with a certain elaboration of processional pomp – which Rudolph may, at this moment, be preparing.
> PRINCESS. I can't help feeling that he wants to get out of it. First of all you implored him to come to Monte Carlo and marry me there, and he refused on account of the expense. Then you implored him to advance us the money to enable us to go to him – and again he refused, on account of the expense. He's a miserly little wretch – that's what he is.

PRINCESS. Yes, papa, and if you hadn't fortunately discovered a means of making an income by honest industry, we should never have got here at all.

PRINCE. Very true. Confined for the last two years within the precincts of my palace by an obdurate bootmaker who held a warrant for my arrest, I devoted my enforced leisure to a study of the doctrine of chances – mainly with the view of ascertaining whether there was the remotest chance of my ever going out for a walk again – and this led to the discovery of a singularly fascinating little round game which I have called Roulette, and by which, in one sitting, I won no less than five thousand francs! My first act was to pay my bootmaker – my second, to engage a good useful working set of second-hand nobles – and my third, to hurry you off to Pfennig Halbpfennig as fast as a *train de luxe* could carry us!

PRINCESS. Yes, and a pretty job-lot of second-hand nobles you've scraped together!

PRINCE (*doubtfully*). Pretty, you think? Humph! I don't know. I should say tol-lol, my love – only tol-lol. They are not wholly satisfactory. There is a certain air of unreality about them – they are not convincing.

COST. But, my goot friend, vhat can you expect for eighteen-pence a day!

PRINCE. Now take this Peer, for instance. What the deuce do you call *him*?

COST. Him? Oh, he's a swell – he's the Duke of Riviera.

PRINCE. Oh, he's a Duke, is he? Well, that's no reason why he should look so confoundedly haughty. (*To Noble.*) Be affable, sir! (*Noble takes attitude of affability.*) That's better. (*Passing to another.*) Now, who's this with his moustache coming off?

COST. Vhy, you're Viscount Mentone, ain't you?

NOBLE. Blest if I know. (*Turning up sword-belt.*) It's wrote here – yes, Viscount Mentone.

COST. Then vhy don't you say so? 'Old yerself up – you ain't carryin' sandwich boards now. (*Adjusts his moustache.*)

PRINCE. Now, once for all, you Peers – when His Highness arrives, don't stand like sticks, but appear to take an intelligent and sympathetic interest in what is going on. You needn't say anything, but let your gestures be in accordance with the spirit of the conversation. Now take the word from me. Affability! (*attitude*). Submission! (*attitude*). Surprise! (*attitude*). Shame! (*attitude*). Grief! (*attitude*). Joy! (*attitude*). That's better! You can do it if you like!

PRINCESS. But, papa, where in the world is the Court? There is positively no one here to receive us! I can't help feeling that Rudolph wants to get out of it because I'm poor. He's a miserly little wretch – that's what he is.

PRINCE. Well, I shouldn't go so far as to say that. I should rather describe him as an enthusiastic collector of coins – of the realm – it's a pretty hobby: I've often thought I should like to collect some coins myself.

PRINCESS. Papa, I'm sure there's some one behind that curtain. I saw it move!

PRINCE. Then no doubt they are coming. Now mind, you Peers – haughty

PRINCE. Well, I shouldn't go so far as to say that. I should rather describe him as an enthusiastic collector of coins – of the realm – and we must not be too hard upon a numismatist if he feels a certain disinclination to part with some of his really very valuable specimens. It's a pretty hobby, etc.

623   *Gong*: In one of his early drafts Gilbert sketched out an elaborate scene at this point. The prince's arrival would be greeted by a gathering of Court officials assembled by Ludwig and consisting of a Lord Chamberlain cutting a sausage with a pocket knife, a Treasurer smoking a large German pipe, a Minister of Police carrying a pair of handcuffs, a Master of Horse dressed as a circus ring-master and also possibly a clown. When the prince and princess first appeared, there would be no one in evidence except the Chamberlain who would greet them with a dumb show. Then he would sound a gong and suddenly the whole Court would appear and dance wildly round the visitors. All that remained of this idea in the final version were the gong and the wild dance. The first night libretto contains the additional stage direction: 'At the end all fall down exhausted'.

654   *I've paid my debts*: In the current Chappell vocal score and in the Oxford World's Classics edition everything from this point until 'Why, you forward little hussy, how dare you?' (line 741) is missing.

affability combined with a sense of what is due to your exalted ranks, or I'll fine you half a franc each – upon my soul I will!

(*Gong. The curtains fly back and the Court are discovered. They give a wild yell and rush on to the stage dancing wildly, with* PRINCE, PRINCESS, *and Nobles, who are taken by surprise at first, but eventually join in a reckless dance.*)   625

LUD. There, what do you think of that? That's our official ceremonial for the reception of visitors of the very highest distinction.

PRINCE (*puzzled*). It's very quaint – very curious indeed. Prettily footed, too. Prettily footed.

LUD. Would you like to see how we say 'good-bye' to visitors of distinction?   630
That ceremony is also performed with the foot.

PRINCE. Really, this tone – ah, but perhaps you have not completely grasped the situation?

LUD. Not altogether.

PRINCE. Ah, then I'll give you a lead over. (*Significantly.*) I am the father of   635
the Princess of Monte Carlo. Doesn't that convey any idea to the Grand Ducal mind?

LUD. (*stolidly*). Nothing definite.

PRINCE (*aside*). H'm – very odd! Never mind – try again! (*Aloud.*) This is the daughter of the Prince of Monte Carlo. Do you take?   640

LUD. (*still puzzled*). No – not yet. Go on – don't give it up – I daresay it will come presently.

PRINCE. Very odd – never mind – try again. (*With sly significance.*) Twenty years ago! Little doddle doddle! *Two* little doddle doddles! Happy father – hers and yours. Proud mother – yours and hers! Hah! *Now* you take? I see you do! I   645
see you do!

LUD. Nothing is more annoying than to feel that you're not equal to the intellectual pressure of the conversation. I wish he'd say something intelligible.

PRINCE. You didn't expect me?

LUD. (*jumping at it*). No, no. I grasp that – thank you very much. (*Shaking*   650
hands with him.) No, I did *not* expect you!

PRINCE. I thought not. But ha! ha! at last I have escaped from my enforced restraint. (*General movement of alarm.*) (*To crowd who are stealing off.*) No, no – you misunderstand me. I mean I've paid my debts! And how d'you think I did it? Through the medium of Roulette!   655

ALL. Roulette?

LUDWIG. Now you're getting obscure again. The lucid interval has expired.

PRINCE. I'll explain. It's an invention of my own – the simplest thing in the world – and what is most remarkable, it comes just in time to supply a distinct   660
and long-felt want! I'll tell you all about it.

663–733   *Take my advice – when deep in debt*: This song is in the current Chappell edition of the vocal score of *The Grand Duke* but missing from the libretto which simply has a box saying 'SONG (Prince of Monte Carlo) with Chorus is no longer used'. It is not found in either the Chatto edition of Gilbert's plays or the 1963 World's Classics edition of the Savoy Operas and was excised from the 1975 official production text mentioned by Reginald Allen in his *First Night Gilbert and Sullivan*.

The roulette song was, however, included in both the 1976 D'Oyly Carte record and the 1989 BBC recording and is almost always sung in amateur productions. So it should be for it is one of the undoubted gems in the show. Sullivan told the critic Vernon Blackburn that he had purposely tried to hit the French *Café Chantant* style. It has an infectious bounce and vitality. It was a favourite party piece of John Ayldon, the last soloist to play the bass-baritone parts in the old D'Oyly Carte Opera Company and he sang it on the company's last night at the Adelphi Theatre, London, on 27 February 1982.

674   *Vos louis d'or*: The *louis d'or* was a gold coin circulated in pre-Revolutionary France. The value of the two existing silver coins, the franc and the livre, had sunk so low that the French kings had gold coins struck and called after their name. After the Revolution Napoleon continued to keep them in circulation and they became known as 'Napoleons'. The value of the *louis d'or* was 20 francs.

675   *roues d'charette*: *Roue de charrette* is the French for a cartwheel. Why the Prince of Monte Carlo was calling on punters to do cartwheels at his roulette table, and why he mis-spelt his native language, I think we had better leave to the whims of his librettist and the exigence of rhyme.

691   *Whom six-and-thirty suitors sue*: The roulette wheel has 36 numbered compartments, alternately coloured red and black. Bets can be made on a ball landing on a particular number, a particular colour or on a number within a particular group.

(Nobles bring forward a double Roulette table, which they unfold.)

SONG – PRINCE.

Take my advice – when deep in debt,
Set up a bank and play Roulette!
At once distrust you surely lull, 665
And rook the pigeon and the gull.
The bird will stake his every franc
In wild attempt to break the bank –
But you may stake your life and limb
The bank will end by breaking him! 670

(All crowd round and eagerly stake gold on the board.)

Allons, encore –
Garçons, fillettes –
Vos louis d'or
Vos roues d'charette! 675
Holà! holà!
Mais faites vos jeux –
Allons, la classe –
Le temps se passe –
La banque se casse – 680
Rien n'va plus!
Le dix-sept noir, impair et manque!
Holà! holà! vive la banque!
For every time the board you spin,
The bank is bound to win! 685

CHORUS.   For every time, &c.

(During Chorus, PRINCESS *and* COSTUMIER *rake in all the stakes.)*

PRINCE.   A cosmic game is this Roulette!
The little ball's a true coquette –
A maiden coy whom 'numbers' woo – 690
Whom six-and-thirty suitors sue!
Of all complexions, too, good lack!
For some are red and some are black,
And some must be extremely green,
For half of them are not nineteen! 695
                    (All stake again.)

709 *The bank is bound to win*: The first night libretto has 'Be sure the bank is bound to win' here (and in lines 685 & 732). In roulette, all bets are placed against the bank (i.e. the proprietor of the casino). The bank wins when the ball lands on the number 'zero' (the thirty-seventh compartment). It has been calculated that in games using a European-style wheel the bank will win 2.7% of all bets. Where an American-style wheel is used, there is both a zero and a double zero compartment and the bank's winnings go up to 5.26% of all bets placed.

729 *le double zéro*: Somewhat surprisingly, but greatly to his profit, the Prince obviously employs the American style of roulette wheel with the additional double zero compartment rather than the more usual European type where there is just one single zero compartment.

> *Allons, encore –*
>> *Garçons, fillettes –*
> *Vos louis d'or*
>> *Vos roues d'charette!*
>>> *Holà! holà!* 700
> *Mais faites vos jeux –*
>> *Allons, la foule!*
>> *Ça roule – ça roule*
>> *Le temps s'écoule –*
> *Rien n'va plus!* 705
> *Le trente-cinq rouge – impair et passe!*
> *Très bien, étudiants de la classe –*
> The moral's safe – when you begin
> The bank is bound to win!

CHORUS.   The moral's safe, &c.   (PRINCE *rakes in all the stakes.*) 710

PRINCE.   The little ball's a flirt inbred –
She flirts with black – she flirts with red;
From this to that she hops about
Then back to this as if in doubt.
To call her thoughtless were unkind – 715
The child is making up her mind,
For all the world like all the rest,
Which *prétendant* will pay the best!

> *Allons, encore –*
>> *Garçons, fillettes –* 720
> *Vos louis d'or –*
>> *Vos roues d'charette!*
>>> *Holà! holà!*
>> *Mais faites vos jeux –*
>>> *Qui perte fit* 725
>>> *Au temps jadis*
>>> *Gagne aujourd'hui!*
>> *Rien n'va plus!*
> *Tra, la, la, la! le double zéro!*
> *Vous perdez tout, mes nobles héros –* 730
> Where'er at last the ball pops in,
> The bank is bound to win!

CHORUS.   Where'er at last, &c.

(PRINCE *gathers in the stakes. Nobles fold up table and take it away.*)

745 *I've got three Grand Duchesses*: The first night libretto has the following much expanded dialogue at this point:

> PRINCESS. Three Grand Duchesses! But let us understand each other. Am I not addressing the Grand Duke Rudolph?
>
> LUDWIG. Not at all. You're addressing another–guess sort of Grand Duke altogether.
>
> PRINCESS. This comes of not asking the way. We've mistaken the turning and got into the wrong Grand Duchy.
>
> PRINCE. But – let us know where we are. Who the deuce is this gentleman?
>
> LISA. He's the gentleman I married yesterday –
>
> JULIA. He's the gentlemen I married this morning.
>
> BARONESS. He's the gentlemen I married this afternoon.
>
> PRINCESS. Well, I'm sure! Papa, let's go away – this is not a respectable Court.
>
> PRINCE. All these Grand Dukes have their little fancies, my love. This Potentate appears to be collecting wives. It's a pretty hobby – I should like to collect a few myself. This (*admiring* BARONESS) is a charming specimen – an antique, I should say – of the early Merovingian period, if I'm not mistaken; and here's another – a Scotch lady, I think (*alluding to* JULIA), and (*alluding to* LISA) a little one thrown in. Two half-quarters and a make-weight! (*To* LUDWIG.) Have you such a thing as a catalogue of the Museum?
>
> PRINCESS. But this is getting serious. If this is not Rudolph, the question is, where in the world is he?
>
> LUDWIG. No – the question is, where *out* of the world is he? And *that's* a very curious question, too!
>
> PRINCE and PRINCESS. What do you mean?
>
> LUDWIG (*pretending to weep*). The Grand Duke Rudolph – died yesterday!
>
> PRINCE and PRINCESS. What!

LUDWIG. Capital game. – Haven't a penny left! 735
PRINCE. Pretty toy, isn't it? Have another turn?
LUDWIG. Thanks, no. I should only be robbing you.
PRINCESS (*affectionately*). Do, dearest – it's such fun!
BARONESS. Why, you forward little hussy, how dare you? (*Takes her away from* LUDWIG.) 740
BAR. Why, you forward little hussy, how dare you? (*Takes* LUDWIG *away.*)
LUD. You mustn't do that, my dear – never in the presence of the Grand Duchess, I beg!
PRINCESS (*weeping*). Oh, papa, he's got a Grand Duchess!
LUD. *A* Grand Duchess! My good girl, I've got three Grand Duchesses! 745
PRINCESS. Well, I'm sure! Papa, let's go away – this is not a respectable Court.
PRINCE. All these Grand Dukes have their little fancies, my love. (*To* LUDWIG.) Have you such a thing as a catalogue of the Museum?
PRINCESS. But I cannot permit Rudolph to keep a museum – 750
LUD. Rudolph? Get along with you, I'm not Rudolph! Rudolph died yesterday!
PRINCE *and* PRINCESS. What!
LUD. Quite suddenly – of – of – a cardiac affection.
PRINCE *and* PRINCESS. Of a cardiac affection? 755
LUD. Yes, a pack-of-cardiac affection. He fought a Statutory Duel with me and lost, and I took over all his engagements – including this imperfectly preserved old lady, to whom he has been engaged for the last three weeks.
PRINCESS. Three weeks! But I've been engaged to him for the last twenty years! 760
BAR., LISA, *and* JULIA. Twenty years!
PRINCE (*aside*). It's all right, my love – they can't get over that. (*Aloud*). He's yours – take him, and hold him as tight as you can!
PRINCESS. My own! (*Embracing* LUDWIG.)
LUD. Here's another! – the fourth in four-and-twenty hours! Would 765
anybody else like to marry me? You, ma'am – or you – anybody! I'm getting used to it!
BAR. But let me tell you, ma'am —
JULIA. Why, you impudent little hussy —
LISA. Oh, here's another – here's another! (*Weeping.*) 770
PRINCESS. Poor ladies, I'm very sorry for you all; but, you see, I've a prior claim. Come, away we go – there's not a moment to be lost!

CHORUS. (*as they dance towards exit*).

Hurrah! Hurrah! Hurrah!
Now away to the wedding we'll go
So summon the charioteers, 775

776 *No kind of reluctance we show*: Both the first night libretto and the World's Classics edition
have different lines here:

> Though her rival's emotion may flow
> In the form of impetuous tears.

787–817 *Well, you're a pretty kind of fellow*
This song is missing from the current edition of the libretto which prints a note saying
that it is no longer used. It is also missing from the World's Classics edition and the
1975 official production text mentioned by Reginald Allen. It is, however, found in full
in the vocal score and was included in both the BBC and D'Oyly Carte recordings.
    The first night libretto prints only three verses of the song. The first is a hybrid of the
later first and second verses which runs as follows:

> Well, you're a pretty kind of fellow, thus my life to shatter, O!
> My dainty bride, my bride elect, you wheedle and you flatter, O!
> You fascinate her tough old heart with vain and vulgar patter, O!
> And eat my food and drink my wine – especially the latter, O!

No kind of reluctance we show
To embark on our married careers.

(At this moment RUDOLPH, ERNEST, *and* NOTARY *appear.*
All kneel in astonishment.)

RECITATIVE.

RUD., ERN., *and* NOT.   Forbear! Forbear! Forbear!   780
                        This may not be!
                           Frustrated are your plans!
                        With paramount decree
                           The Law forbids the banns!   785

CHORUS.   The Law forbids the banns!

SONG–RUDOLPH.

(Furiously). Well, you're a pretty kind of fellow, thus my life to shatter, O!
   My little store of gold and silver recklessly you shatter, O!
   You guzzle and you gourmandize all day with cup and platter, O!
   And eat my food and drink my wine – especially the latter, O!   790

ALL.   The latter, O!
                 The latter, O!
           Especially the latter, O!

RUD.   But when compared with other crimes, for which your head I'll batter, O!
   This flibberty gibberty kind of a liberty scarcely seems to matter, O!   795

ALL.   But when compared &c.

RUD.   My dainty bride – my bride elect – you wheedle and you flatter, O!
   With coarse and clumsy compliment her senses you bespatter, O!
   You fascinate her tough old heart with vain and vulgar patter, O!
   Although – the deuce confound you – you're unworthy to look at her, O!   800

ALL.   Look at her, O!
              Look at her, O!
        Unworthy to look at her, O!

RUD.   But even this, compared with deeds that drive me mad as hatter, O!
   This flibberty gibberty kind of a liberty scarcely seems to matter, O!   805

839   *Very well*: The first night libretto has the following additional dialogue here:

> JULIA. Very well. But will you promise to give me some strong scenes of justifiable jealousy?
> ERNEST. Justifiable jealousy! My love, I couldn't do it!
> JULIA. Then I won't play.
> ERNEST. Well, well, I'll do my best! (*They retire up together.*)
> LUDWIG. And am I to understand that, all this time, I've been a dead man without knowing it?
> BARONESS. And that I married a dead man without knowing it?
> PRINCESS. And that I was on the point of marrying a dead man, etc.

ALL. But even this, &c.

RUD. For O, you vulgar vagabond, you fount of idle chatter, O!
　　　You've done a deed on which I vow you won't get any fatter, O!
　　　You fancy you've revived the law – mere empty brag and clatter, O!
　　　You can't – you shan't – you don't – you won't – you thing of rag and 　　810
　　　　tatter, O!

ALL.　　　　　　　　　Of tatter, O!
　　　　　　　　　　　Of tatter, O!
　　　　　　　You thing of rag and tatter, O!

RUD. For this you'll suffer agonies like rat in clutch of ratter, O! 　　　　815
　　　This flibberty gibberty kind of a liberty's quite another matter, O!

ALL. For this, &c.

(RUDOLPH *sinks exhausted into* NOTARY'S *arms*)

LUD. My good sir, it's no use your saying that I can't revive the Law, in face
of the fact that I *have* revived it.　　　　　　　　　　　　　　　　　820
　　RUD. You didn't revive it! You couldn't revive it! You – you are an impostor,
sir – a tuppenny rogue, sir! You – you never were, and in all human probability
never will be – Grand Duke of Pfennig Anything!
　　ALL. What!!!
　　RUD. Never – never, never! (*Aside.*) Oh, my internal economy! 　　　825
　　LUD. That's absurd, you know. I fought the Grand Duke. He drew a King,
and I drew an Ace. He perished in inconceivable agonies on the spot. Now, as
that's settled, we'll go on with the wedding.
　　RUD. It – it isn't settled. You – you can't. I – I – (*to* NOTARY). Oh, tell him –
tell him! I can't! 　　　　　　　　　　　　　　　　　　　　　　830
　　NOT. Well, the fact is, there's been a little mistake here. On reference to the
Act that regulates Statutory Duels, I find it is expressly laid down that the Ace
shall count invariably as lowest!
　　ALL. As lowest!
　　RUD. (*breathlessly*). As lowest – lowest – lowest! So *you're* the ghoest – ghoest – 　835
ghoest! (*Aside.*) Oh, what *is* the matter with me inside here!
　　ERN. Well, Julia, as it seems that the law hasn't been revived – and as, con-
sequently, I shall come to life in about three minutes – (*consulting his watch*) —
　　JULIA. My objection falls to the ground. (*Resignedly.*) Very well!
　　PRINCESS. And am I to understand that I was on the point of marrying a 　840
dead man without knowing it? (*To* RUDOLPH, *who revives.*) Oh, my love, what a
narrow escape I've had!
　　RUD. Oh – you are the Princess of Monte Carlo, and you've turned up just

844   *You're as poor as a rat*: The first night libretto (yet again) has the following additional material here:

> PRINCE: Pardon me – there you mistake. Accept her dowry – with a father's blessing!
> (*Gives him a small Roulette board, then flirts with* BARONESS.)
> RULDOLPH. Why, what do you call this?
> PRINCESS. It's my little wheel of fortune. I'll tell you all about it. (*They retire up, conversing.*)
> LISA. That's all very well, etc.

851–60   *Happy couples, lightly treading*

Although the words are different, the tune of this finale is the same as that for the Act I opening chorus. *The Grand Duke* is the only one of the Savoy operas to begin and end with the same tune.

in time! Well, you're an attractive little girl, you know, but you're as poor as a rat!
(*They retire up together.*)   845
    LISA. That's all very well, but what is to become of me? (*To* LUDWIG.) If
you're a dead man — (*Clock strikes three.*)
    LUD. But I'm not. Time's up – the Act has expired – I've come to life – the
parson is still in attendance, and we'll all be married directly.
    ALL. Hurrah!   850

FINALE.

CHORUS.   Happy couples, lightly treading,
                Castle chapel will be quite full!
           Each shall have a pretty wedding,
                As, of course, is only rightful,
                Though the brides be fair or frightful.   855
           Contradiction little dreading,
                This will be a day delightful –
           Such a pretty, pretty wedding!
              Such a pretty wedding!
                Such a charming wedding!   860

       (*All dance off to get married as the curtain falls.*)

CURTAIN